P9-CRH-978

Small Business Management

16e

LAUNCHING & GROWING ENTREPRENEURIAL VENTURES

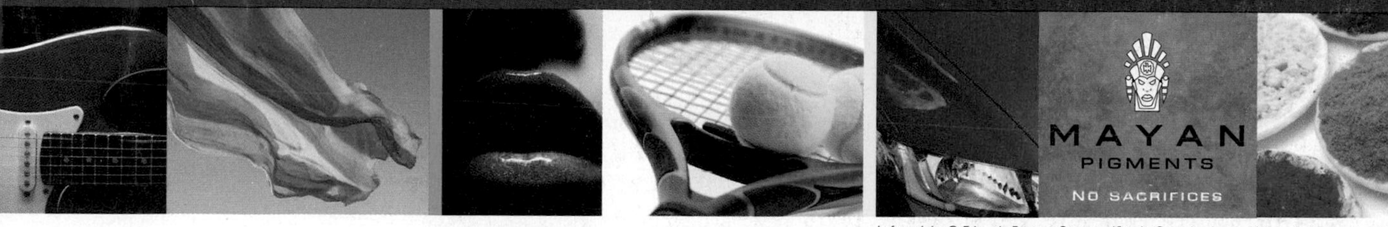

Left to right: © Eduardo Fuentes Guevara, iStock; © ac_bnphotos, iStock; © jack carlton, iStock; © Brian A. Jackson, Shutterstock; Burwell and Burwell Photography, iStock; © Mayan Pigments; © Youssouf Cader, iStock

Justin G. Longenecker
Baylor University

J. William Petty
Baylor University

Leslie E. Palich
Baylor University

Francis Hoy
Worcester Polytechnic Institute

Australia • Brazil • Japan • Korea • Mexico • Singapore • Spain • United Kingdom • United States

Small Business Management: Launching & Growing Entrepreneurial Ventures, Sixteenth Edition
Justin G. Longenecker, Leslie E. Palich, J. William Petty, and Frank Hoy

VP/Editorial Director: Jack W. Calhoun
Publisher: Erin Joyner
Senior Acquisitions Editor: Michele Rhoades
Senior Developmental Editor: Susanna C. Smart
Senior Editorial Assistant: Ruth Belanger
Senior Marketing Communications Manager: Jim Overly
Marketing Manager: Jonathan Monahan
Content Project Manager: Jacquelyn K. Featherly
Media Editor: Rob Ellington
Manufacturing Planner: Ronald Montgomery
Production House/Compositor: Cenveo Publisher Services
Director Rights Acquisition: Audrey Pettengill
Rights Acquisition Specialist: Deanna Ettinger
Senior Art Director: Tippy McIntosh
Internal Designer: Beckmeyer Design
Cover Designer: Beckmeyer Design
Cover Images:
© Adam Radosavlijevic, © Katrin Solansky, © Duncan Walker, © jennifer willis, iStock

Library of Congress Control Number: 2011925838
Student Edition ISBN 13: 978-1-111-53287-1
Student Edition ISBN 10: 1-111-53287-7

South-Western Cengage Learning
5191 Natorp Boulevard
Mason, OH 45040
USA

Cengage Learning products are represented in Canada by Nelson Education, Ltd.

For your course and learning solutions, visit **www.cengage.com**
Purchase any of our products at your local college store or at our preferred online store **www.ichapters.com**

Printed in the United States of America
1 2 3 4 5 6 7 15 14 13 12 11

BC BRIEF CONTENTS

CONTENTS

Part 1

©Tomas Bercic, iStock

©weareadventurers, iStock

©Tomas Bercic, iStock

©weareadventurers, iStock

PREFACE

> Life is a journey, not a destination. But that does not mean that life should be an aimless journey. The most successful and fulfilled entrepreneurs are always advancing toward a vision that gives meaning to their lives.
>
> **Jeff Sandefer**
> ***Stars & Steppingstones***

Welcome to the 16th edition of *Small Business Management: Launching and Growing Entrepreneurial Ventures* by Longenecker, *et al.*! Textbooks rarely survive in the marketplace for more than five or six editions—much less 16—but *Small Business Management* has proven to be one of those outliers. This edition of the book represents more than four decades of writing about small business.

Furthermore, it is a book that students frequently choose to hold on to rather than selling it back to a bookstore at the end of a semester. As one student explained, "It is one of the few books from my college days that I have kept for future reference."

Why has Longenecker's *Small Business Management* not only survived, but been a market leader for so long? We believe there are two reasons: *passion* and *commitment*—which are key success factors for any entrepreneurial venture. Our teaching, research, and consulting as related to small businesses are not something we do as an afterthought. Neither is it merely an academic exercise. It is our passion! We believe that what we are doing makes a difference in others' lives. As a consequence, we have always been committed to giving you our very best. Over all these years, there has been one absolute constant—we have measured our success by the effectiveness of our presentation to you, the reader. Toward this end, we are thrilled to announce the addition of Dr. Frank Hoy to the author team. Dr. Hoy is an internationally recognized expert in the field of small business. Many know him for his leadership in the field of small business and entrepreneurship. He has truly made a difference in the education of untold thousands of individuals who want to be entrepreneurs. His academic and practical experience bring a fresh perspective to this edition. With Dr. Hoy's involvement, you can be assured that *Small Business Management* will only become better with each new edition.

In writing *Small Business Management*, we celebrate the values and initiative of small business owners everywhere. For most of them, it is about more than the money; they want to make a difference. There is no group that is more giving. When they are successful, their strong tendency is to share with others. They are our heroes! And one of them is Mayan Pigments, featured on our cover.

The cover art for the 16th edition comes from the website of Mayan Pigments (www.mayanpigments.com). This company is almost a stereotype of a university spin-off venture. You will read their story in the Spotlight that opens Chapter 7. A professor of chemistry and one of his students attending an academic conference visited some Mayan ruins in Mexico. They were fascinated by how vivid the paints on the walls of the ancient buildings were, despite being exposed to the elements for centuries. Countless others had seen these colors, marveling at them, then proceeding to other sights and scenes. But these two entrepreneurial thinkers viewed them in a different way. They visualized a change in the way pigments are now formulated that could have commercial potential.

The professor and student returned to their laboratory and began experimenting with various materials and colors. After developing the first pigment, which they labeled "Maya Blue," they put together a team including other faculty and students, found investors, and made their vision real. In addition to obtaining funding from financial institutions and wealthy individuals, they received a grant from the Texas Emerging Technologies Fund, something they felt represented a strong endorsement of their patents as being feasible for the market.

Mayan Pigments is a great example of the spark that can occur at universities. This story shows how your courses, research, and teamwork can lead to the creation of small businesses.

Our getting to be a small part of a number of entrepreneurial dreams and endeavors, either directly or indirectly, has added so much to our lives. For this reason, writing *Small Business Management* continues to be a blessing for us. We hope reading it helps move you toward your entrepreneurial aspirations.

Follow Your Dreams

As an entrepreneur, we would encourage you not to dream small, but rather to dream *big*—to see opportunities where others only see chaos. Did you know that Benjamin Franklin was admonished to stop experimenting with electricity? It's true! Trying to improve on the reliable and perfectly functional oil lamp was considered an absurd waste of time! And even Thomas Edison, a shrewd entrepreneur in his own right, tried to discourage his friend Henry Ford from working on his daring idea of building a motorcar. Convinced the idea was worthless, Edison advised Ford to give up his wild fancy and work for him instead. Ford, however, remained steadfast and tirelessly pursued his dream. Progress was slow. Although his first attempt produced a vehicle without a reverse gear, Ford knew he could make it happen—and, of course, he did. People like Franklin and Ford dreamed big dreams and dared to do great things, and now we all benefit from their achievements. Can you imagine a world without electric lights and automobiles? Obviously, the entrepreneurial legacy of men such as Ford and Edison is not the end of the story. In our own times, we quickly recognize the names of entrepreneurs who have changed the way we live and interact with one another. Just to name a few:

Mary Kay Ash (Mary Kay Cosmetics)
Jeff Bezos (Amazon)
Michael Dell (Dell Computer)
Walt Disney (Disney Corporation)
Debbi Fields (Mrs. Fields Cookies)
Steve Jobs (Apple)
Herb Kelleher (Southwest Airlines)
Bill Gates (Microsoft)
Ray Kroc (McDonald's)
Pierre Omidyar (eBay)
David Packard (Hewlett-Packard)
Howard Schultz (Starbucks)
Fred Smith (Federal Express)
Sam Walton (Walmart)

No doubt, you could add the names of others who come to mind. But even more importantly, we all know entrepreneurs and small business owners who will not be the next Bill Gates, but will build small businesses that create value and make a difference in the community. These small companies are the heart and soul of any economy.

Small Business Management lays out, in a step-by-step fashion, the knowledge and insights needed to lead and manage a small business. At the same time, it focuses on a much broader concern—the pursuit of entrepreneurial dreams. Entrepreneurs build businesses to fulfill dreams—for themselves, for their families, for their employees, and for their communities. When we write about small companies, therefore, we are writing about individuals whose business lives have had an impact on a wide range of people.

The aim of the 16th edition of *Small Business Management* is to provide instruction and guidance that will greatly improve your odds for success as you take your own entrepreneurial journey. It is our hope that what we present in this book—and in the tools and ancillaries that accompany it—will support the varied goals of those seeking independent business careers, either directly or indirectly, through the wise counsel of the instructor who has selected this book.

There has never been a more exciting time to be an entrepreneur. If for no other reason, the cost of starting a business is less than it has ever been, in part thanks to the falling cost of technology. Even when we were revising the text in 2010–2011 and the U.S. economy was still struggling to recover from the recent recession, opportunities abounded. The truth is that many vibrant, high-potential new ventures are launched during and following recessions, and there is no reason that yours cannot be one of them! We are seeing tremendous change these days, to be sure, but change opens the door to opportunity for those with the courage to pursue it. If you are committed strongly enough to your dream, in one creative way or another, you can overcome obstacles that lie ahead. New ventures can create tremendous personal value both for entrepreneurs and the investors who back them with time and money. New ventures can also protect and improve quality of life by creating jobs and providing new products and services to those who value them. On all of these fronts, you can make a difference.

Our best wishes to you for a challenging and successful learning experience!

To be successful even as an employee in today's global economy, you will need the kind of drive, creativity, and innovative spirit more commonly found among entrepreneurs.

What's New?

As with previous editions, the primary purpose of this revision of *Small Business Management* is to present current, relevant content in unique and interesting ways, drawing on an abundance of real-world examples to keep the reader totally engaged. Thus, the 16th edition of *Small Business Management* offers plenty that's new, including the following:

- In the last edition, we made significant revisions in presenting the material on financial statements and how a small business owner can effectively prepare financial forecasts (Chapters 10 and 11). The presentation became much more intuitive for the reader, recognizing that many students struggle with grasping accounting information. In this edition, we have built on this intuitive approach to make the material even more understandable, while not wanting to overwhelm a student with too much information. We believe we have found a good balance between the amount of information presented and making certain to address what every entrepreneur needs to know about the financial performance of the business. In this way, we have created a level playing field for the "non-accounting" student. As a further commitment, Bill Petty, the co-author who wrote these chapters, invites any instructor using the text to feel free to contact him for any suggestions or assistance in teaching these chapters. Just call him directly (254-710-2260) or e-mail him (bill_petty@baylor.edu).
- One question that all entrepreneurs need to ask themselves is "What is the firm's *business model*?" This issue deserves serious attention, especially when trying to raise capital for the business. The key issue here is how will the business generate profits and cash flows? We have added a section in Chapter 6 when describing the business plan that explains the concept and then applies the concept in Chapter 11 when discussing financial forecasting.
- We have also worked to give students a solid understanding of multi-level marketing, e-business, and legal and global issues affecting entrepreneurs in tough economic times.

- Much of the change we see in the world today is being driven by the use of social media tools, and business is no exception. From finding potential business partners to promoting new products to streamlining operations, the advent of social media is more than upon us. Given this trend, we have added more coverage of social media and its applicability to small business to several chapters in this current edition.
- The Internet has been a game-changer in the world of small business, turning many business models upside down and dramatically transforming the way business is done in many startups and entrepreneurial companies. With that in mind, we increased the already-substantial attention given to the Internet in the book, pointing out even more ways in which online ventures and other concerns have been using cyberspace to expand their businesses.
- Benjamin Franklin said that there is nothing certain in life other than birth, death, and paying taxes. He apparently was not thinking of small businesses; otherwise, he would have added "having problems" to the list! Every small business owner runs into and has to deal with problems, so it is good to have some working examples of how entrepreneurs have overcome various challenges. We have added a number of such examples to the chapters this time around. In fact, you will notice that many of the Living the Dream features are focused on problems encountered by one small business or another. This should help you to anticipate scenarios that you are likely to encounter in business and to sort out in advance how you might respond to these. To be forewarned is to be forearmed.
- We are absolutely convinced that the integrity of the entrepreneur is the foundation for great success in business, so we dedicate an entire chapter to this important topic and place it very early in the order of chapters. However, we have rebalanced the information in the chapter, tightening up sections that deal with mainstream ethical issues and expanding our coverage of "the greening of business" to include more depth on this growing emphasis and to offer an introduction of the concept of "sustainable small business." We think this is timely and important, given recent trends and the heightened market interest in concern for the natural environment.
- Technically speaking, the recession ended in June 2009, but the U.S. economy continues to stumble along with lackluster and inconsistent growth and stubborn unemployment. In other words, these are still very difficult times for many small businesses. In recognition of that fact, the 16th edition of the book features frequent references to the effects of the recent recession and the slow and uncertain recovery on small businesses. It is our hope that this new emphasis will help small business owners to negotiate the obstacles and challenges of the current economic climate and to know better how to make the most of business opportunities during difficult economic times.
- New START-UP features throughout provide direction/guidance on entrepreneurial Skills, Tools, Action, Resources, and ways to Transform (go to the next level).
- Numerous updated Living the Dream features in each chapter capture entrepreneurs in action as they face the challenges of small business and entrepreneurship. To add depth to these features and ensure accuracy, the authors had personal conversations or correspondence with a number of the entrepreneurs profiled.
- Several new text cases update the case selection at the end of the text, including TWO MEN AND A TRUCK, *ReadyMade* Magazine, PortionPac Chemicals, River Pools & Spas, Numi Tea, and many others. This edition's up-to-date cases provide opportunities for students

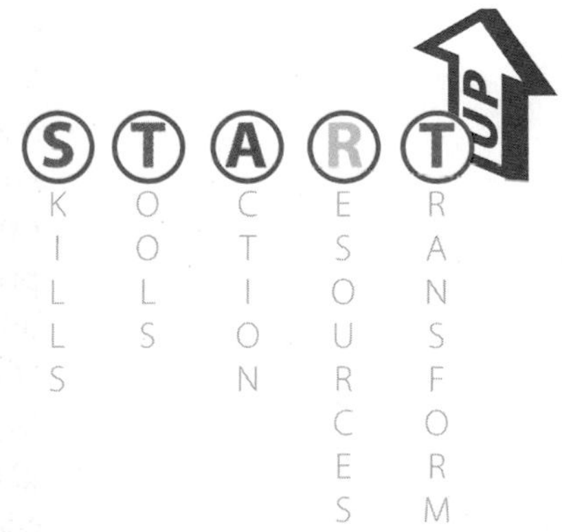

to apply chapter concepts to realistic entrepreneurial situations. Some cases that appeared in the 15th edition are still included in this edition so that the "favorite" cases are not lost. In addition to the cases appearing in the book, there are more cases, old and new, that are available on the Longenecker website (www.cengagebrain.com).

- New to this edition, CourseMate provides students with an array of learning tools to enrich their course experience. Access to the invaluable CourseMate student website is available with every new text. Students gain immediate access to a robust library of Small Business School videos, all new video cases, useful business plan templates, exercises to accompany the optional Small Business and Entrepreneurship Resource Center (SBERC) as well as helpful interactive quizzes and e-lectures. Student exercises for the SBERC in CourseMate are included at the end of each chapter. These exercises direct students to articles and company information on various entrepreneurial ventures, and ask them to discuss how the chapter topics apply to each situation. Companies covered include Dyson, Bear Naked Granola, Blue Nile, iSoldIt, LLC, and many others.
- A business plan for Benjapon's Thai restaurant illustrates what a thorough business plan contains. Of course, there is no *one right plan*, but it does let us visualize what a good plan looks like.
- A link on the Longenecker website (www.cengagebrain.com) where instructors can share course syllabi. It is always good to draw on each other's work. Excellent ideas deserve such a forum.

Achieving Your Best

Small Business Management is organized to help students and future entrepreneurs achieve success in whatever field they choose. The wide spectrum of content, applications, cases, graphics, stories, and other details offered in *Small Business Management* has assisted many small business entrepreneurs in making their dreams come true. With a focus on learning, our features emphasize hands-on activities that capture student interest and guarantee practical knowledge, including the following:

- **Unique Spotlight Features.** The chapter-opening "In the Spotlight" features profile an amazing collection of business owners, whose unique insights into how to start, run, and grow a business will help readers identify and explore the full range of issues facing today's business owners. More than half of the spotlights are video enriched, because nothing helps students master the lessons of small business and entrepreneurship as much as seeing them put into practice.
- **Unique Support for Building a Business Plan.** The material in Part 3, "Developing the New Venture Business Plan," is integral to learning how to develop workable plans. Closely aligned with the approaches to planning that we present in the textbook, additional business plan templates can be found in *Small Business Management Online* (www.cengagebrain.com) by registering the access code that accompanies this text.
- **Integrated Learning System.** Our integrated learning system uses each chapter's learning objectives to give structure and coherence to the text content, study aids, and instructor's ancillaries, all of which are keyed to these objectives. The numbered objectives are introduced in the "Looking Ahead" section, and each is concisely addressed in the "Looking Back" section at the end of each chapter. The integrated learning system also simplifies lecture and test preparation. The lecture notes in the ***Instructor's Manual*** are grouped by learning objective and identify the PowerPoint slides that relate to each objective. Questions in the ***Test Bank*** are grouped by objective as well. A correlation table at the

beginning of each *Test Bank* chapter permits selection of questions that cover all objectives or that emphasize objectives considered most important.

- **You Make the Call.** "You Make the Call" incidents at the end of each chapter are very popular with both students and instructors because they present realistic business situations that require examining key operating decisions. By having students take on the role of a small business owner, these exercises give them a leg up in addressing the concerns of small businesses.
- **Living the Dream.** Practical examples from the world of small business and entrepreneurship carry both instructional and inspirational value. "Living the Dream" boxes appear at critical junctures throughout the chapters, refueling and refreshing chapter concepts with documented experiences of practicing entrepreneurs.
- **Start-Ups.** "Start-Up" features highlight useful entrepreneurial Skills, Tools, Action, Resources for new businesses, and ways to Transform the ventures. These features are interspersed throughout the chapters in appropriate settings.
- **Video Cases.** The video-enriched cases available with the 16th edition of *Small Business Management* are nearly all new for this edition. The cases are created from actual interviews with small business owners and entrepreneurs to bring together these high-interest video segments and in-text case material. Case instruction augmented by video filmed on location in diverse businesses such as TWO MEN AND A TRUCK, PortionPac, Cookies-N-Cream, *ReadyMade* Magazine, and other entrepreneurial success stories makes studying effective small business management all the more interesting.

Updated and Enhanced Supplements

All resources and ancillaries that accompany *Small Business Management*, 16th edition, have been created to support a variety of teaching methods, learning styles, and classroom situations.

- **Instructor's Manual.** Lecture notes in the ***Instructor's Manual*** are grouped by learning objective and tied to PowerPoint slides that relate to each objective. The manual also contains sources of audio/video and other instructional materials, answers to the "Discussion Questions," comments on "You Make the Call" situations, and teaching notes for the cases. This edition's *Instructor's Manual* has been revised by Patricia Worsham of Cal Poly Pomona. It is available on the text website at www.cengagebrain.com and on the Instructor's Resource CD-ROM (IRCD).
- **Test Bank.** The ***Test Bank*** has also been revised, by Julia Truitt Poynter of Transylvania University. Questions in the *Test Bank* are grouped by learning objectives and include true/false, multiple-choice, and discussion questions. A correlation table at the beginning of each *Test Bank* chapter helps instructors select questions that cover all objectives or that emphasize objectives most important to the instructor's specific course. The *Test Bank* in Word is available on the text website at www.cengagebrain.com and on the Instructor's IRCD.
- **ExamView® Testing Software.** ExamView contains all of the questions in the printed *Test Bank*. This program is an easy-to-use test creation software compatible with Microsoft Windows. Instructors can add or edit questions, instructions, and answers. Questions may be selected by previewing them on screen, selecting them randomly, or selecting them by number. Instructors can also create quizzes online whether over the Internet, a local area network (LAN), or a wide area network (WAN).
- **PowerPoint® for Instructors.** A complete PowerPoint package is available to aid in lecture presentation. Computer-driven projection makes it easy to use these colorful images to add emphasis and interest to lectures. The PowerPoint slides, revised by

Charlie Cook of the University of West Alabama, are available on both the IRCD and on the password protected instructor's website.

- **Instructor's Resource CD-ROM.** Instructors can get quick access to all of these ancillaries from the easy-to-use ***Instructor's Resource CD-ROM (IRCD)*** that lets the user electronically review, edit, and copy what's needed. The *IRCD* contains the *Instructor's Manual, Test Bank* in Microsoft Word and in *ExamView, PowerPoint* slides, and business plan templates.
- **New "Startup Stories" Videos.** Available in DVD format and online through the CourseMate site, 17 new videos created for this edition let you in on some very big ideas at work in a variety of innovative small businesses. Some of the small businesses covered include *ReadyMade* Magazine, TWO MEN AND A TRUCK, River Pools & Spas, and Graeter's Ice Cream, among many others. Use these videos to bring the real world into your classroom and let your students learn from the experts.
- **Small Business and Entrepreneurship Resource Center.** The Small Business and Entrepreneurship Resource Center (SBERC) from Gale, a part of Cengage Learning and a leader in e-research for libraries and schools, can be accessed through CourseMate and directs students to 900,000 published full text articles directly related to small business management that are easily searchable by business topic, business type, and commonly asked how-to questions. This powerful resource also includes access to hundreds of sample business plans and legal forms necessary to start a new venture in every state. Powered by InfoTrac, the how-to section provides direct access to the most popular topics and questions students have about starting and running a small business.
- **WebTutor™ on Blackboard or WebCT.** This dynamic technology tool complements *Small Business Management* by providing interactive reinforcement that helps you fully grasp key concepts. WebTutor's online teaching and learning environment brings together content management, assessment, communication and collaboration capabilities including quizzes, tutorials, and other opportunities for interactive instruction that makes the world of small business come alive.

Optional Course Add-Ons

BizPlan Builder® Express: A Guide to Creating a Business Plan with BizPlan Builder
By JIAN and KAPRON

Now you can learn how to use the award-winning, best-selling professional software BizPlan Builder 8.1 to create your business plan.

This workbook/CD-ROM package provides all the essentials to create winning business plans, from the latest BizPlanBuilder software to step-by-step instructions for preparing each section of a plan. Ready-to-customize samples, advice, a detailed marketing analysis with links to demographic and marketing tools, and helpful financial tools make it easy to create a solid plan. Hands-on exercises and activities throughout the workbook ensure you fully understand how to maximize BizPlanBuilder's dynamic tools.

Bundle your text with *BizPlanBuilder® Express* for a package that places you well ahead on your path to business success.

Contact your South-Western Cengage representative or visit http://www.cengage.com/management/JIAN for more information.

Special Thanks and Acknowledgments

There are numerous individuals to whom we owe a debt of gratitude for their assistance in making this project a reality. In particular, we thank our friends—and we mean *good friends*—at South-Western Cengage; we really counted on them! We are especially indebted to Michele

Rhoades, Susan Smart, Jacquelyn K Featherly, Anne Talvacchio, and word master Jeanne Yost. Without them, this book would only exist in our heads! They are masters of coordination and motivation, keeping us on track and moving forward. Besides that, they let us have a little fun along the way. They are just fun people, but who also take seriously their role in making certain that *Small Business Management* continues in its tradition of excellence.

We thank, too, others who worked on various aspects of the package: our designer, Tippy McIntosh; our marketing group consisting of Jon Monahan and Jim Overly; and media editor Rob Ellington. We also offer our thanks to Mary Abrahams and Alyssa Pendley for their careful review of selected chapters, which means a lot fewer errors for readers to encounter.

We also want to offer words of appreciation and acknowledgment to Wes Bailey who was a contributing author for the risk management chapter. Mr. Bailey is president of Bailey Insurance and Risk Management, Inc. (Waco, Texas) and is well recognized as a leader in the industry. His serving as the author for this chapter insures readers that they are receiving timely and relevant information for managing risk in a small business. And we thank Bradley Norris, a colleague and lecturer at Baylor University, for his suggestions regarding the operations chapter. Finally, we thank Charles Goldwait at Baylor University in assisting us with our research and for his contribution to the writing of some of the cases.

A talented team of writers contributed an outstanding set of ancillary materials. Special thanks go to Julia Truitt Poynter of Transylvania University for her revision of the Test Bank, and to Patricia Worsham of Cal Poly Pomona for preparation of the Instructor's Manual. We offer our thanks as well to Charlie Cook, of the University of West Alabama, who created the PowerPoint slides.

Finally we offer a special word of appreciation for the understanding and patient support of our wives—Donna, Dianna, and Patricia—during this process.

For their helpful suggestions and thoughtful comments, which helped to shape this edition, we are grateful to the following reviewers:

J. David Allen
Baylor University
Dr. Jeffrey Alstete
Iona College
David Ambrosini
Cabrillo College
Chandler Atkins
Adirondack Community College
Lee Baldwin
University of Mary Hardin-Baylor
Francis B. Ballard
Florida Community College
Andrea Balsamo
Consumnes River College
Hilton Barrett
Elizabeth City State University
Bill Bauer
Carroll College–Waukesha Wisconsin
Verona K. Beguin
Black Hills State University
Narendra C. Bhandari
Pace University, New York
Greg Bier
Stephens College
Karen Bishop
University of Louisville
Ross Blankenship
State Fair Community College
John Boos
Ohio Wesleyan University
Marvin Borgelt
University of Mary Hardin-Baylor
Steven Bradley
Austin Community College
Don B. Bradley III
University of Central Arkansas
Margaret Britt
Eastern Nazarene College
Mark Brosthoff
Indiana University
Penelope Stohn Brouwer
Mount Ida College
Rochelle R. Brunson
Alvin Community College
Kevin Chen
County College of Morris
Felipe Chia
Harrisburg Area Community College
Mike Cicero
Highline Community College
Edward G. Cole
St. Mary's University
Michael D. Cook
Hocking College
Roy A. Cook
Fort Lewis College
George R. Corbett
St. Thomas Aquinas College
Brad Cox
Midlands Technical College
Karen Cranford
Catawba College
George W. Crawford
Clayton College & State University
Bruce Davis
Weber State University
Helen Davis
Jefferson Community College

Terri Davis
Howard College
Bill Demory
Central Arizona College
Michael Deneen
Baker College
Sharon Dexler
Southeast Community College
Warren Dorau
Nicolet College
Max E. Douglas
Indiana State University
Bonnie Ann Dowd
Palomar College
Michael Drafke
College of Dupage
Franklin J. Elliot
Dine College
Franceen Fallett
Ventura College
R. Brian Fink
Danville Area Community College
Dennette Foy
Edison College
David W. Frantz
Purdue University
Janice S. Gates
Western Illinois University
Armand Gilinsky, Jr.
Sonoma State University
Darryl Goodman
Trident Technical College
William Grace
Missouri Valley College
William W. Graff
Maharishi University of Management
Mark Hagenbuch
University of North Carolina, Greensboro
Carol Harvey
Assumption College
James R. Hindman
Northeastern University
Betty Hoge
Limestone College
Eddie Hufft
Alcorn State University
Sherrie Human
Xavier University
Ralph Jagodka
Mt. San Antonio College
Larry K. Johansen
Park University
Michael Judge
Hudson Valley Community College
Mary Beth Klinger
College of Southern Maryland
Charles W. Kulmann
Columbia College of Missouri
Rosemary Lafragola
University of Texas at El Paso
William Laing
Anderson College
Ann Langlois
Palm Beach Atlantic University
Rob K. Larson
Mayville State University
David E. Laurel
South Texas Community College
Les Ledger
Central Texas College
Michael G. Levas
Carroll College
Richard M. Lewis
Lansing Community College
Thomas W. Lloyd
Westmoreland County Community College
Elaine Madden
Anne Arundel Community College
Kristina Mazurak
Albertson College
James J. Mazza
Middlesex Community College
Lisa McConnell
Oklahoma State University
Angela Mitchell
Wilmington College
Frank Mitchell
Limestone College
Douglas Moesel
University of Missouri–Columbia
Michael K. Mulford
Des Moines Area Community College
Bernice M. Murphy
University of Maine at Machias
Eugene Muscat
University of San Francisco
John J. Nader
Grand Valley State University
Marc Newman
Hocking College
Charles "Randy" Nichols
Sullivan University
Robert D. Nixon
University of Louisville
Marcella M. Norwood
University of Houston
Mark Nygren
BYU–Idaho
Donalus A. Okhomina, Sr.
Jackson State University
Rosa L. Okpara
Albany State University
Timothy O'Leary
Mount Wachusett Community College
Pamela Onedeck
University of Pittsburgh at Greensburg
Claire Phillips
North Harris College
Dean Pielstick
Northern Arizona University
Mark S. Poulos
St. Edward's University
Julia Truitt Poynter
Transylvania University
Fred Pragasam
University of North Florida
Thomas Pressly
Penn State–Shenango
Mary Ellen Rosetti
Hudson Valley Community College
June N. Roux
Delaware Technical and Community College
Jaclyn Rundle
Central College
John K. Sands
Western Washington University
Craig Sarine
Lee University
Duane Schecter
Muskegon Community College
Joseph A. Schubert
Delaware Technical and Community College
Matthew Semadeni
Texas A&M University
Marjorie Shapiro
Myers University
Sherry L. Shuler
American River College

Cindy Simerly
Lakeland Community College
James Sisk
Gaston College
Victoria L. Sitter
Milligan College
Bernard Skown
Stevens Institute of Technology
Kristin L. H. Slyter
Valley City State University
William E. Smith
Ferris State University
Bill Snider
Cuesta College
Roger Stanford
Chippewa Valley Technical College
George Starbuck
McMurry University
Phil Stetz
Stephen F. Austin State University
Peter L. Stone
Spartanburg Technical College
John Streibich
Monroe Community College
Ram Subramanian
Montclair State University
James Swenson
Minnesota State University Moorhead
Ruth Tarver
West Hills Community College
Paul B. Thacker
Macomb Community College
Darrell Thompson
Mountain View College
Melodie M. Toby
Kean University
Charles N. Toftoy
George Washington University
Charles Torti
Schreiner University
Gerald R. Turner
Limestone College
Barry L. Van Hook
Arizona State University
Brian Wahl
North Shore Community College
Mike Wakefield
University of Southern California
Charles F. Warren
Salem State College
Bill Waxman
Edison Community College
Janet Wayne
Baker College
Charles Wellens
Fitchburg State College
Nat B. White, Jr.
South Piedmont Community College
Jim Whitlock
Brenau University
Ira Wilsker
Lamar Institute of Technology
Patricia A. Worsham
Cal Poly Pomona

To the Instructor

As a final word of appreciation, we express our sincere thanks to the many instructors who use our text in both academic and professional settings. Based on years of teaching and listening to other teachers and students, *Small Business Management* has been designed to meet the needs of its readers. And we continue to listen and make changes in the text. Please write or call us to offer suggestions to help us make the book even better for future readers. Our contact information is Bill Petty (254-710-2260, bill_petty@baylor.edu), Les Palich (254-710-6194, les_palich@baylor.edu), or Frank Hoy (508-831-4998, fhoy@wpi.edu). We would love to hear from you.

ABOUT THE AUTHORS

JUSTIN G. LONGENECKER Justin G. Longenecker's authorship of *Small Business Management* began with the first edition of this book. He authored a number of books and numerous articles in such journals as *Journal of Small Business Management, Academy of Management Review, Business Horizons*, and *Journal of Business Ethics*. He was active in several professional organizations and served as president of the International Council for Small Business. Dr. Longenecker grew up in a family business. After attending Central Christian College of Kansas for two years, he went on to earn his B.A. in political science from Seattle Pacific University, his M.B.A. from Ohio State University, and his Ph.D. from the University of Washington. He taught at Baylor University, where he was Emeritus Chavanne Professor of Christian Ethics in Business until his death in 2005.

J. WILLIAM PETTY J. William "Bill" Petty is Professor of Finance and the W. W. Caruth Chairholder in Entrepreneurship at Baylor University and the first Executive Director of the Baylor Angel Network. He holds a Ph.D. and an M.B.A. from the University of Texas at Austin and a B.S. from Abilene Christian University. He has taught at Virginia Tech University and Texas Tech University and served as dean of the business school at Abilene Christian University. He has taught entrepreneurship and small business courses in China, the Ukraine, Kazakhstan, Indonesia, Thailand, and Russia. He has been designated a Master Teacher at Baylor and was named the National Entrepreneurship Teacher of the Year in 2008 by the Acton Foundation for Excellence in Entrepreneurship. His research interests include acquisitions of privately held companies, shareholder value-based management, the financing of small and entrepreneurial firms, angel financing, and exit strategies for privately held firms. He has served as co-editor for the *Journal of Financial Research* and as editor of the *Journal of Entrepreneurial Finance*. He has published articles in a number of finance journals and is the co-author of a leading corporate finance textbook, *Foundations of Finance*. He is a co-author of *Value-Based Management in an Era of Corporate Social Responsibility* (Oxford University Press, 2010). Dr. Petty has worked as a consultant for oil and gas firms and consumer product companies. He also served as a subject matter expert on a best-practices study by the American Productivity and Quality Center on the topic of shareholder value-based management. He was a member of a research team sponsored by the Australian Department of Industry to study the feasibility of establishing a public equity market for small- and medium-sized enterprises in Australia. Finally, he serves as the audit chair for a publicly traded energy firm.

LESLIE E. PALICH Leslie E. Palich is Associate Professor of Management and Entrepreneurship and the Ben H. Williams Professor of Entrepreneurship at Baylor University, where he teaches courses in small business management, international entrepreneurship, strategic management, and international management to undergraduate and graduate students in the Hankamer School of Business. He is also Associate Director of the Entrepreneurship Studies program at Baylor. He holds a Ph.D. and an M.B.A. from Arizona State University and a B.A. from Manhattan Christian College. His research has been published in the *Academy of Management Review, Strategic Management Journal, Entrepreneurship Theory & Practice, Journal of Business Venturing, Journal of International*

Business Studies, Journal of Management, Journal of Organizational Behavior, Journal of Small Business Management, and several other periodicals. He has taught entrepreneurship and strategic management in a large host of overseas settings, including Austria, Costa Rica, Czech Republic, Germany, Italy, Switzerland, Cuba, France, the Netherlands, the United Kingdom, and the Dominican Republic. His interest in entrepreneurial opportunity and small business management dates back to his grade school years, when he set up a produce sales business to experiment with small business ownership. That early experience became a springboard for a number of other enterprises. Since that time, he has owned and operated domestic ventures in agribusiness, automobile sales, real estate development, and educational services, as well as an international import business.

FRANK HOY Frank Hoy is the Paul R. Beswick Professor of Innovation and Entrepreneurship in the School of Business at Worcester Polytechnic Institute. Dr. Hoy, who was most recently director of the Centers for Entrepreneurial Development, Advancement, Research and Support at the University of Texas at El Paso (UTEP), also serves as director of the Collaborative for Entrepreneurship & Innovation (CEI), WPI's nationally ranked entrepreneurship center. Dr. Hoy joined the WPI faculty in August 2009. He holds a bachelor's degree in business administration from the University of Texas at El Paso, an M.B.A. from the University of North Texas, and a Ph.D. in management from Texas A&M University. He spent 10 years as a faculty member in the Department of Management at the University of Georgia, where he founded and directed the Center for Business and Economic Studies, coordinated the entrepreneurship curriculum, and served as director of the Georgia Small Business Development Center. In 1991 he returned to El Paso, Texas, to join UTEP as a professor of management and entrepreneurship and dean of the College of Business Administration. Dr. Hoy is a past president of the United States Association for Small Business and Entrepreneurship and past chair of the Entrepreneurship Division of the Academy of Management. His research has appeared in the *Academy of Management Journal, Academy of Management Review, Journal of Business Venturing*, and *Family Business Review*, and he is a past editor of *Entrepreneurship Theory and Practice.*

ENTREPRENEURSHIP: A WORLD OF OPPORTUNITY

PART 1

© mangostock/Shutterstock.com

CHAPTERS

The Entrepreneurial Life

In the SPOTLIGHT
Table Occasions

A booming business. A community's respect. A success story. It all began as a whim for Chia Stewart and her lifelong friend Claudia Narvaez. In 2006, the dynamic duo pooled their talents and put their determination to the test by entering an ambitious local table-decorating competition, El Paso Pro Musica Tablescapes, to benefit the nonprofit music organization. The friends decided that if their table was recognized, they would launch a related business; and if not, at least they would have exercised their creativity and had fun. Their inspired entry, "An Enchanted Garden Baby Shower," won first place and marked the dawning of a new business, Table Occasions.

Table Occasions is represented by a simple table transformed into a celebration through creativity, dedication, and collaboration.

©Tony Florez

Stewart maintains that the most basic element of planning a table setting is the selection of linens, which are made in the region—an added economic benefit to their border community. "The fabrics are like works of art that provide the inspiration and passion for our designs as well as for our collaborators' contributions, whether flowers, food, or music."

For Narvaez, it's about bringing it all together—from the perfect chair to the right wine goblet to the ideal vase filled with flowers that complement the design perfectly. "We are passionate about the creative aspects of our business, along with our desire to please our customers. We experience the greatest fulfillment when we see the joy in the eyes of our customers when their dream 'table occasion' comes to life," Narvaez exclaims.

When Table Occasions opened its doors, its founders were averaging only one event a weekend—certainly not enough business to survive.

After studying this chapter, you should be able to . . .

1. Define the terms *entrepreneur* and *small business owner*, and explain how the terms are related.
2. Explain the basic characteristics of entrepreneurial opportunities, and give examples of individuals who successfully started their own businesses.
3. Describe some motivators or rewards for owning your own business.
4. Identify some of the basic types of entrepreneurs and entrepreneurial ventures.
5. Describe five potential competitive advantages of small entrepreneurial companies compared to large firms.
6. Discuss factors related to readiness for entrepreneurship and getting started in an entrepreneurial career.
7. Explain the concept of an entrepreneurial legacy and the challenges involved in crafting a meaningful legacy.

LOOKING AHEAD

© iStockphoto.com/Dan Bachman

Today, they plan and coordinate more than 10 events each week, from intimate dinner parties to lavish events with hundreds of guests. They work with brides, event planners, wedding consultants, floral designers, caterers and others to come up with the perfect colors and schemes for any occasion. "The most rewarding part of this business," Stewart observes, "is the opportunity to work one on one with clients and guide them to find their perfect visions." The business has established a new decorating standard for events in its hometown community of El Paso, Texas, taking parties to the next level of creativity and elegance.

Stewart and Narvaez have now begun to give back to their community. In Stewart's words,

> *We believe it is important for any business, no matter how large or small, to support the community that supports it. We facilitate nonprofits by taking their events to the next level of attractiveness and warmth, thereby increasing the awareness of their cause and in turn enhancing their support. At the same time, it gives us a renewed sense of purpose. As a result, Table Occasions is now sought out by many nonprofit organizations in the community, including the El Paso Children's Rehabilitation Center, the El Paso Symphony Orchestra, the El Paso Chapter of the American Heart Association, and El Paso Pro Musica.*

Stewart and Narvaez remain humbled by their success and are grateful for the support that comes from their families. When they are in "creative mode," patient husbands and grandmothers help them work around family obligations. "We had a dream and worked hard to make it come to life with the help of our support network," Stewart says. "We hope our story inspires others to dedicate their skills to spending every day doing what they love."

Source: Personal conversation with Chia Stewart, December 2, 2010.

The purpose of this chapter is to provide an overview of small business and entrepreneurship, along with stories and examples of entrepreneurs who started and grew businesses. The chapter will give you a better understanding of what it takes to be an owner of a small business. It is our hope for anyone contemplating owning a business that this chapter will "light the fire" of your creativity and encourage you to act on your intentions. Subsequent chapters will build on this chapter by providing increasing details about how to start and grow a small business.

If you have a serious interest in starting and operating your own business—whether now or in the future—you are not alone. A major theme of the past 60 years in business is the large number of persons, in the United States and around the globe, who want to own their own business. Within the United States, it is estimated that 12 million people are involved in some form of entrepreneurial venture, and that as many as half of all adults will be engaged in self-employment at some point during their working careers.[1] The Small Business Administration reports that small firms[2]

- Represent 99.7 percent of all firms with employees.
- Employ more than 50 percent of all employees working in the private sector.
- Account for 45 percent of private payrolls.
- Generated 60 to 80 percent of all new jobs (net) over the past decade.

- Create more than half of the country's gross domestic product.
- Hire 40 percent of high-tech employees, such as scientists, engineers, and programmers.
- Represent 97.3 percent of all exporters.

In a study sponsored by the Kauffman Foundation Research Series, Tim Kane talks about the role of startups in job creation:

> *The oft-quoted American sports slogan "Winning isn't everything. It's the only thing" could well be attributed to the economic importance of firm formation in creating jobs. . . . A relatively new data set from the U.S. government called Business Dynamics Statistics validates that U.S. startups classified as "less than one year old" create an average of 3 million new jobs annually. All other ages of firms, including . . . firms established two centuries ago, are net job destroyers, losing 1 million jobs net per year.*[3]

Paul Reynolds, a leading researcher in the field, says that entrepreneurship is "on the scale of a lot of other major social phenomena."[4] Henrik Fisker, formerly the head designer for BMW and Ford and founder of Fisker Automotive, based in Irvine, California, concurs with Reynolds. Fisker Automotive's first product, the Fisker Karma, is the world's first luxury plug-in hybrid electric vehicle. When considering how to compete with the major auto manufacturers, Fisker contends,

> *We don't have to do things the same way. We can take the economy in hand and drive our own destinies. And a movement that has been slowly building in the business world is finally taking hold: We're seeing the beginnings of the entrepreneurial economy, a system built on nimble, low-overhead, oftentimes small companies with fluid workforces, rather than the massive conglomerates that have upheld the economy for decades.*[5]

An entrepreneurial fever is also sweeping the nation's community colleges, universities, and career schools, as students take classes to learn how to launch, finance, and run their own companies. Universities across the United States are adding entire programs on entrepreneurship, and many more schools offer at least one or two classes—and still cannot handle the student demand for information.

Twenty years ago, taking a course on starting a business was of little interest to students who wanted to be consultants and Wall Streeters. Today, entrepreneurship education is widely available. More than two-thirds of U.S. colleges and universities—well over 2,000—are teaching the subject, up from 200 in the 1970s.[6] There is also a network of over 200 university entrepreneurship centers, comprising the Global Consortium of Entrepreneurship Centers, that meet each year and share what they are doing. John Fernandes, president and CEO of the Association to Advance Collegiate Schools of Business International (the organization that accredits business schools around the world), puts it this way: “Entrepreneurship will continue to grow and mature into a distinct management discipline. Elements of entrepreneurship will emerge as essential to any business education.”[7] In other words, in today’s world your business courses, whatever your particular specialty or major, should include the study of entrepreneurship. Business students, along with engineers, teachers, artists, pharmacists, lawyers, nurses, and many others, are heeding the call to own their own businesses.

© mangostock/Shutterstock.com

You are about to embark on a course of study that will prove invaluable if you aspire at some point to own your own business. Doing so can provide an exciting life and offer substantial personal rewards, while also contributing to the welfare of society. As a general rule, when small business owners talk about what they are doing and what their plans are for the future, you can feel their excitement and anticipation—mixed at times with a bit of fear and trepidation. But as one entrepreneur told us, “Owning my own business keeps me from being lazy. You must constantly be learning, or you will not survive.”

Taking a small business or entrepreneurship class is not likely to turn a student who lacks basic business intuition into an opportunity-spotting, money-making prodigy. Yet there is considerable evidence suggesting that such classes can facilitate the learning curve for those who have the “right stuff.” These classes teach many of the basic skills required for success, such as determining if a business idea is a good opportunity, acquiring needed resources, writing a business plan, marketing a product or service, and learning how to impose structure and deadlines on your dreams.

Having worked for over three decades with both entrepreneurs and students who aspire to own businesses, we have designed this book to prepare you for the entrepreneurial journey. In addition, we will be drawing on the extensive experience of entrepreneurs who offer their advice and counsel on important issues. So, buckle up, you are in for an exciting adventure!

Entrepreneurship and Small Business

Thus far, we have used the terms *entrepreneurship* and *small business* in a very general way. Let’s take a more detailed look at these two terms to gain a better understanding of what they represent. Both are at the heart of all that you will study in this book.

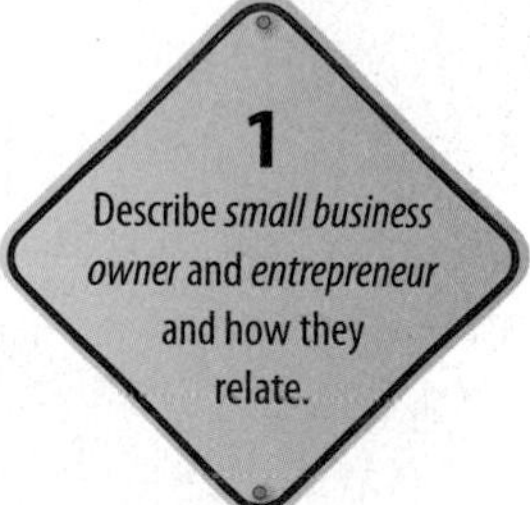

WHO ARE THE ENTREPRENEURS?

Entrepreneurs are frequently thought to be individuals who discover market needs and launch new firms to meet those needs. They are risk takers who provide an impetus for change, innovation, and progress in economic life. (In contrast, salaried employees receive a specified compensation and do not assume ownership risks.)

For our purposes, we will not limit the term *entrepreneur* only to business founders; instead, we will include second-generation firm owners, franchisees, and owner-managers who have bought existing firms. While we will most often focus on owners of businesses in this book, our thinking also includes individuals in not-for-profit organizations who

entrepreneur
A person who is relentlessly focused on an opportunity, in either a new or an existing business, to create value while assuming both the risk and the reward for his or her effort.

bootstrapping
Doing more with less in terms of resources invested in a business, and, where possible, controlling the resources without owning them.

small business
A business that is small compared to large companies in an industry, has geographically localized operations, is financed by only a few individuals, and has a small management team.

think and act entrepreneurially. So for us, an **entrepreneur** is a person who relentlessly pursues an opportunity, in either a new or an existing enterprise, to create value while assuming both the risk and the reward for his or her efforts. Furthermore, entrepreneurs think differently about resources than do employee-managers. While managers in large corporations so often think like administrators or bureaucrats—wanting larger budgets or more employees in their departments—entrepreneurs work to do more with less. They even try to find ways to use other people's resources, or what is called **bootstrapping**. So for the entrepreneur, it is all about identifying a value-creating opportunity and, *equally important,* executing the opportunity. Many people see opportunities, but don't follow through. Execution is what separates entrepreneurs from the rest of the world.

WHAT IS A SMALL BUSINESS?

What does it mean to talk about "small business"? A neighborhood restaurant or bakery is clearly a small business, and Toyota is obviously not. But among small businesses, there is great diversity in size.

Many efforts have been made to define the term **small business**, using such criteria as number of employees, sales volume, and value of assets. But there is no generally accepted or universally agreed-on definition. Size standards are basically arbitrary, adopted to serve a particular purpose. For example, legislators sometimes exclude firms with fewer than 10 or 15 employees from certain regulations, so as to avoid imposing a financial burden on the owner of a very small business. However, for our purposes, primary attention will be given to businesses that meet the following criteria:

1. Compared to the biggest firms in the industry, the business is small; in most instances, the number of employees in the business is fewer than 100.
2. Except for its marketing function, the business's operations are geographically localized.
3. Financing for the business is provided by no more than a few individuals.
4. The business may begin with a single individual, but it has the potential to become more than a "one-person show."

Obviously, some small firms fail to meet all of these standards. For example, a small executive search firm—a firm that helps corporate clients recruit high-level managers—may operate in many sections of the country and thereby fail to meet the second criterion. Nevertheless, the discussion of management concepts in this book is aimed primarily at the type of firm that fits the general pattern outlined by these criteria.

Thus, small businesses include tiny one-person firms—the kind you may decide to start—and small firms that have up to 100 employees. In most cases, however, they are drastically different in their structure and operations from the huge corporations that are generally featured in the business media.

YOU CAN BE BOTH AN ENTREPRENEUR AND A SMALL BUSINESS OWNER

While certainly not all entrepreneurial endeavors are geared toward owning a small business, having an entrepreneurial mindset is critical to the success of any venture, regardless of size. That mindset focuses small business owners on seeking new opportunities that can prove extremely beneficial to the success of the venture. It can also make the trip along the way more rewarding and provide for more growth of the business, as well as challenging the owner to grow personally. In this book, we'll focus on small business owners who are unrelenting in their search for opportunities that create value for customers and owners alike.

You may start small, but you should still dream big. Ewing Marion Kauffman, the founder of Marion Labs, offers this encouragement to entrepreneurs and small business owners:

> *You should not choose to be a common company. It is your right to build an uncommon company if you can—to seek the opportunity to compete, to desire to take the calculated risks, to dream, to build—yes, even to fail or succeed.*[8]

Entrepreneurial Opportunities

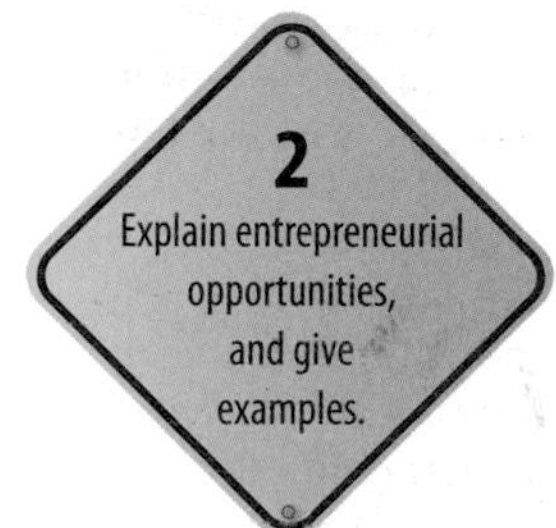

As an entrepreneur, you must be able to identify attractive entrepreneurial opportunities. Such opportunities make the enterprise economically attractive for the owners while offering customers a product or service that is so appealing that they are willing to pay their hard-earned money for it. In other words, an entrepreneur must find a way to create value for customers. An **entrepreneurial opportunity**, then, is an *economically attractive* and *timely* opportunity that creates value for both prospective customers and the firm's owners. It involves much more than merely having a good idea.

entrepreneurial opportunity An economically attractive and timely opportunity that creates value for interested buyers or end users.

Let's look at three ventures started by some present-day entrepreneurs who have successfully created value for customers and themselves alike.

THREE SUCCESS STORIES

Ace Hotels (Seattle, WA)[9]

The Ace Hotel brand is so cool, it even has its own special-edition Converse high tops. Alex Calderwood, co-founder and creative mastermind behind the industry's hippest hotel properties, is showing off a pair to his business partners, Wade Weigel and Doug Herrick, in the airy, stripped-down lobby of the Seattle Ace. . . .

Ace Hotels reflect Calderwood's individualistic spirit. Seattle's Ace—the chain's first—is like nowhere you've stayed before. Located in a bustling downtown bar district, the hotel has unobtrusive double glass doors that open onto a flight of stairs leading up to the front desk and narrow hallways that resemble a modern art installation. The building's 28 uniquely decorated rooms (some share bathrooms and one boasts a revolving door and private deck) have been transformed into bright, understated spaces, with Vizio flatscreen TVs, platform beds and exposed bricks and pipes. The shower curtain is a red recycled welding curtain, a copy of the Kama Sutra sits next to a Bible with a camouflage-style cover and the vending machine sells hangover pills, playing cards, and Botan Japanese rice candies.

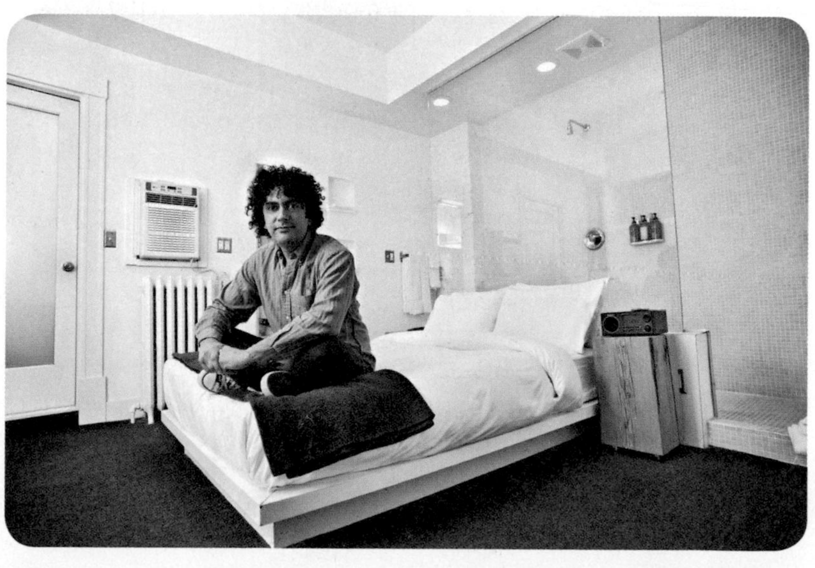
© Rick Dahms

The most unusual part? Rates start below $100, so weekends are regularly booked a month in advance. And, in fact, Calderwood and his partners planned for only one hotel, but following the immediate success of the 1999 opening—Ace Seattle was cash flow positive before the first year was up, with an occupancy rate on par with established hotels' during its second—they decided to open larger locations in Portland in 2002, Palm Springs, California, in 2009 and Manhattan earlier this year. "We've actually exceeded our own projections," Calderwood says. And most likely everyone else's, given the continuing economic gloom.

"It's the most successful hotel model in New York right now," says Chris Mohney, senior vice president of content at BlackBook Media, a New York publisher of city guides, a magazine and website devoted to hotels, restaurants, and nightlife. He says the recession killed the big, expensive hotel model and Calderwood has filled a niche

It's a personality-driven hotel, so creating that kind of success is more alchemy than science," he says, noting that one of the biggest innovations is the creation of a "lobby scene" that encourages people to linger, coffeehouse style. "It's a madhouse around lunch."

Calderwood didn't break the bank creating it, either. He financed the first hotel for less than $2 million, through an equal mix of debt and investor and personal money.

Four hit hotels later, it's clear Calderwood has discovered a way to engineer the vibe of a lifestyle brand, complete with product collaborations, agreements with local vendors and partnerships with independent artists. Most recently, he collaborated with three independent film directors associated with the social media website Massify, providing the New York Ace as a location for three short films—a genius marketing ploy that cost next to nothing.

Now that the dust has settled in Palm Springs and Manhattan, Calderwood took a moment out of his crazy travel schedule to chat with *Entrepreneur* about what's next–and all he knows (or is willing to reveal) about the art of creating a cool business.

Late Model Restoration Supply (Waco, TX)

At the early age of 6 years, Shannon Guderian fell in love with his uncle's Ford Mustang. Then when he turned 15, his mother bought him a 1965 Ford Mustang. Sneaking out at night to hear the V8 engine before he acquired his driver's license sparked his love for Mustangs. To Guderian, Mustangs were a lifestyle; the car represented image and freedom.

Guderian began his career in the automotive world by working for a Mustang parts company. At age 26, Guderian saw the need for parts for late model cars. So he quit his job and pursued his dream. With only $7,000 in his pocket from selling his car, and without any business experience, he started calling on everyone he knew in the industry, asking for their advice. He explains, "My goal was to create credibility within the industry."

The business was originally located in a 650-square-foot "hole in the wall." Guderian started with 17 part numbers from one vendor and a $20,000 bank loan to help finance his small inventory. Today, the business is in a 27,000-square-foot building, with a showroom where he displays Mustangs. His annual sales have now reached over $17 million.

Guderian is proud of his accomplishments, but he is not patting himself on the back. "This is not something I could have created on my own," he says, crediting God and friends for his success. He continues, "Twenty-three of the 35 people who work for the business now own Mustangs. A lot of these people I knew before they had driver's licenses." They are an important part of my foundation."

When asked what he wished he had known at the beginning, he replies, "I wish I had known the importance of leveraging my assets to acquire financing. If I had worked my business off a cash-only basis over the years, I would not be number one today."

Guderian is characterized by passion for his work and passion for people, explaining "People do business with people, not companies, so I view employees and vendors as gold, and I treat them as such."[10]

Today, Guderian has essentially turned the day-to-day operations of the business over to his management team so that he has the time to pursue other opportunities, including advising other entrepreneurs who need help in their businesses. He also now gets to spend time in activities that he missed out on when he was younger, such as hunting for Indian arrowheads. [11]

Five Guys Burgers and Fries (Lorton, VA)

The website for Five Guys Burgers and Fries states, "You might be a Five Guys Fanatic if: You know all of the 15 free toppings by heart; Your heart skips a beat when you see a grease-stained brown paper bag; The sight of foil causes you to salivate…." Five Guys opened their first hamburger joint in Arlington, Virginia, in 1986. The "Five Guys" were Jerry Murrell's five sons. The décor is simple "military canteen and '50s diner." The tiles are red and white, and the food is fresh and great!

RICHARD B. LEVINE/Newscom

Jerry Murrell ran a fraternity house's kitchen while earning a business degree at the University of Michigan. He let the cook do the ordering, "because she knew what she was doing," he says. When the kitchen started making money, he knew he'd made the right decision. After graduation, he moved to northern Virginia to sell stocks and bonds. But he decided that a good hamburger-and-fry place could make it, so he and his sons started with a takeout shop in Arlington, Virginia.

After more than 20 years, the menu hasn't changed much. But Five Guys' food prices fluctuate, because they are based solely on profit margins—the company's prices reflect whatever its food costs are. If the price of potatoes increases, the price of fries is adjusted accordingly. Still, customers line up, eating free peanuts while they wait.

Murrell believes that the best blend of fresh sirloin and chuck and the fresh-cut Idaho fries fried in peanut oil are the best advertising for his chain. Five Guys toasts its buns on a grill instead of a bun toaster, the burgers are made to order, and the customer can choose from 15 toppings, but they can't have a shake. They don't do drive-throughs and they don't deliver, not even to the Pentagon.

When they opened their first store in Arlington, not far from the Pentagon, someone at the Pentagon called and said, "We want 15 hamburgers; what time can you deliver?" Murrell responded, "What time can you pick them up? We don't deliver." He was told that "Everyone delivers food to the Pentagon." Murrell and a son made a 22-foot-long banner that said ABSOLUTELY NO DELIVERY and hung it in front of their store. Surprisingly enough, their business from the Pentagon picked up.

In California, Five Guys patrons are generally 25 to 50 years old, with an income of more than $100,000. They are a little more expensive across the country than the standard fast-food burger places, but it has an almost cult-like following. And Zagat's 2010 Fast Food Survey ranked Five Guys as the best fast food burger place. Five Guys has been

ZAGAT survey rated every year since 2001 and has been voted the *Washingtonian Magazine*'s "Readers' Choice" #1 Burger every year since 1999! Since expanding outside of the Washington, D.C. metro area, Five Guys has continued to garner awards and praise in nearly every market they enter.

Five Guys once turned down an offer from a private equity firm, saying they preferred to keep control to keep it what it is. And it is a successful franchising business. In 2011 Five Guys had 770 stores across the United States and Canada. Their website provides information on franchising, saying "Five Guys is rapidly expanding across the nation and we want to find the best location for new Five Guys restaurants" and to contact their Franchise Development department. With consistent growth, the Murrells prove that flipping burgers doesn't have to be a dead-end job.[12]

So You Want to Be an Entrepreneur

Don't let anyone deceive you: Being an entrepreneur is extremely challenging. As one entrepreneur said, "You get sand kicked in your face all the time, and worse. It takes undying love and passion to keep going. If your mind is wandering to something else you'd rather do, go do that." There will be times when you will be discouraged, maybe even terrified. Some days you will wish you had opted for the "security" of a regular job in an established company, or at least the perception of security. So why do people choose an entrepreneurial career?

For one thing, owning a business can run in a family, even for those who may not continue working in their parent's company. Someone in your childhood—a parent or older sibling or close family friend—may have served as an inspirational role model. Researchers at Case Western Reserve University's Weatherhead School of Management have found a strong connection between entrepreneurship and genetics. Also, the U.S. Census Bureau reports that half of all small business owners who were raised in a small business family worked in the family business before founding their own ventures.[13] In other words, it may just be in your DNA.

What other factors might cause you to consider running your own business? Clearly, different individuals have varied reasons and motivations for wanting to be a small business owner. But we suggest a primary reason for becoming an entrepreneur and owning your own business: *to make the world a better place*. John Doerr, one of the most famous venture capitalists of all time, inspired the phrase *make meaning*, suggesting that the most impactful and sustainable businesses are built on such a foundation.[14] Your first goal should be to create a product or service that makes the world a better place. Your company should be about something more significant than yourself. Then, when the days get long or you become discouraged, you will have a sense that what you are trying to do is significant and well worth the effort.

While we believe one of the most important reasons for becoming an entrepreneur is to make meaning, a number of other reasons also make becoming an entrepreneur tremendously attractive. Any attempt to identify all of the various rewards would at best be incomplete, but Exhibit 1-1 summarizes some of the reasons frequently cited for becoming an entrepreneur. We will discuss each in turn.

ENJOY SATISFYING WORK

Entrepreneurs frequently speak of the satisfaction they experience from running their own businesses; some even refer to their work as fun. Rick Davis, founder and CEO of Davaco, a Dallas-based company, says, "There is nothing else I would rather do. I love the

entrepreneurial experiences

Teaching Kids How to Cook

© Monkey Business Images/Dreamstime.com

© iStockphoto.com/Angelika Schwarz

What started as a simple idea in Waco, Texas, has grown into an international business.

If your children's culinary interest begins with a Happy Meal and ends at the McNuggets, then two Waco moms have an idea for you. In the right environment, with the right teaching, kids enjoy cooking and eating different kinds of foods.

"The kids come in and have a blast," says Suzy Nettles, of Young Chef's Academy. "And the parents are blown away because the kids are learning and preparing food."

Suzy and her business partner, Julie Burleson, started Young Chef's Academy (YCA) in 2003 to teach kids ages 3 to 18 the finer points of kitchen creativity. YCA began when Julie, preparing food for a catering job, kept hearing her then 4-year-old son offering to help. Julie phoned her catering partner. "I said, 'Oh my gosh—I've got it: teaching cooking to kids. It's the perfect business.'"

Two years later, they sold their original YCA location and watched it spin off into 85 franchises spreading into 25 states, Canada, and—coming soon—South Africa. These days, Julie, an entrepreneur, and Suzy, a former elementary school teacher, design curriculum, train franchisees, and oversee a growing YCA empire.

"It starts with fun, definitely," Suzy says. "Then we go into that whole culinary thing—all the different things you do with food that will really keep them interested in coming back. It could be background material on history, geography, ancient food techniques. It covers a little bit of everything in every class, birthday party, field trip, whatever they come to."

Parents are surprised, and more than a little pleased, to see that YCA instructors teach so much math and science, [and] some schools contract with them to provide enrichment activities.

"The entire time we're doing a birthday party, we're teaching," says Suzy. "They find out that yeast is a one-celled organism, they find out that the reason they have to knead dough is to create gluten, and we explain what gluten is. And that's all in the middle of a birthday party."

Source: Nick Patterson, "Teaching Kids How to Cook," *Southern Living*, November 2009, pp. 14–15. Reprinted with permission by *Southern Living*.

challenges, working with others to see our dreams come true, and making a difference in the community. It is fun."[15]

Most small business owners report satisfaction in their careers. In a Gallup Poll of over 100,000 working adults, researchers examined the relationship between work and happiness for different occupational groups. The researchers developed an overall index of contentment based on six criteria: emotional health, physical health, job satisfaction, healthy behaviors, access to basic needs, and self-reports on overall life quality. Business owners were found to outrank all other occupational groups in terms of overall well-being. The results "reflect the importance of being free to choose the work you do and how you do it, the way you manage your time, and the way you respond to adversity."[16] John Howard, director of the National Institute for Occupational Safety and Health, says the survey "reaffirms my view that the more control you have over your work, the happier you are."[17]

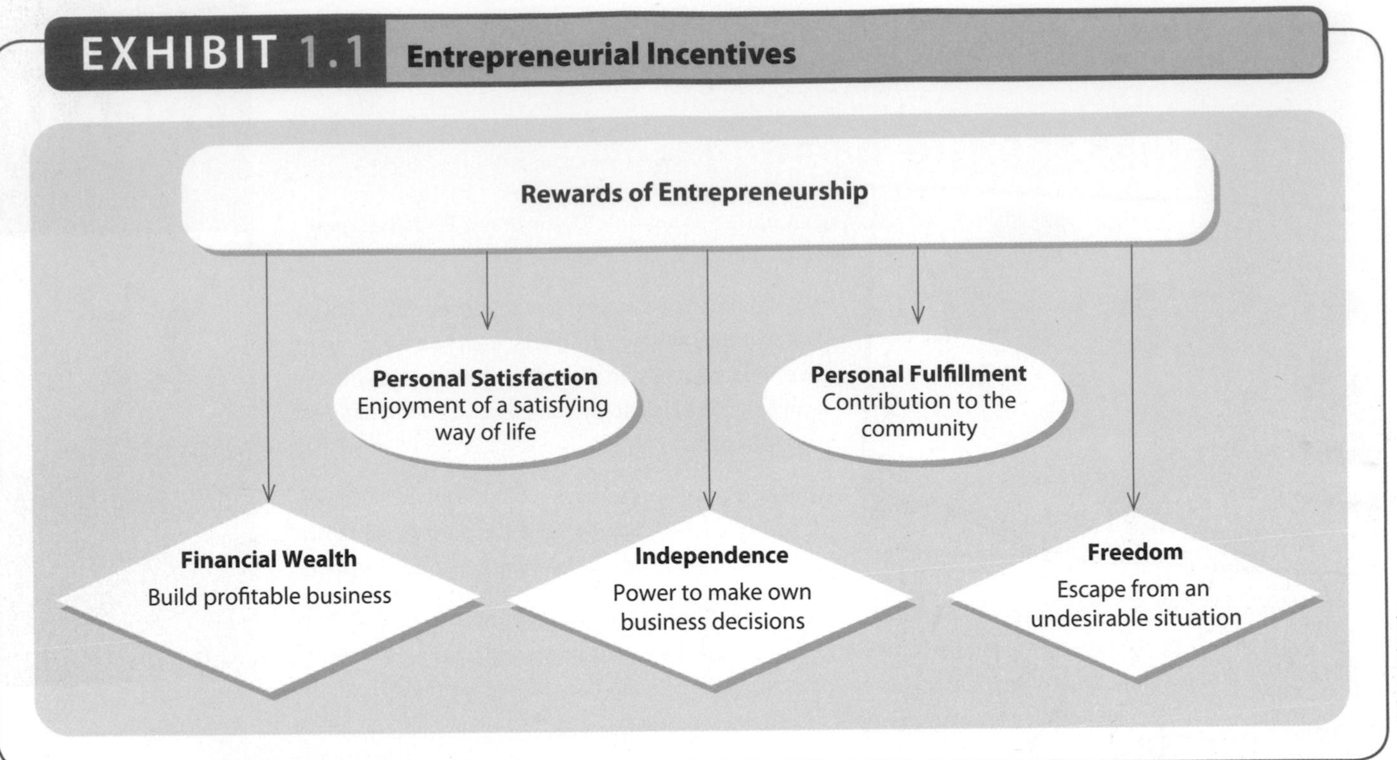

Roper Peugeot agrees. As the owner of the 14-employee Overland Park, Kansas, plumbing company that bears his name, Peugeot's business experienced really tough times during the 2007–2009 recession. During that period, he took comfort in the fact that his fate remained in his own hands and not someone else's. Even when things get tough, I am in control," he says.[18]

We also know that entrepreneurs are rewarded through the work they do with a particular product or service, enjoyable associations, and respect from their community. For many entrepreneurs, the personal satisfaction they receive from their businesses is even more important than the money.

FINDING FULFILLMENT

Some people are drawn to entrepreneurship as a way to make a positive contribution to their community. They want not only personal satisfaction, but also fulfillment by making a difference in their employees' lives and in their communities. Take, for example, Nick Sarillo. When Sarillo started his pizza business, his goal was to create a corporate culture unlike any he had seen. One part of his plan was to develop a strong relationship with the communities where he had restaurants. He wanted to "feel the community's pain, share its joy." In recognition of the difficult times many in the community were facing, Sarillo offered half prices on Mondays for anyone dining in the restaurants and half price for takeouts on Tuesdays. On one evening, Sarillo charged nothing for the meals he served, at a cost of $20,000 to the business. The company also hosts fundraisers every week and contributes 15 percent of its gross profits to charitable causes. And it sponsors benefits one or two times a year for families who are experiencing large medical bills. Christopher Adams, Sarillo's partner, believes that giving back to the community has an ancillary benefit for the business: "It reminds our team members how incredibly different we are from any other place they know."[19]

entrepreneurship + integrity

© iStockphoto.com/Angelika Schwarz

One for One

Blake Mycoskie's first venture was a door-to-door laundry business serving students, EZ Laundry, which he started while on a partial tennis scholarship at Southern Methodist University in Dallas. After expanding EZ Laundry to four colleges, Mycoskie sold his interest in the business and moved to Nashville to start an outdoor media company. Clear Channel bought his company three years later.

a27/ZUMA Press/Newscom

In 2002, Mycoskie and his sister teamed up to compete on the CBS reality show "The Amazing Race." They didn't win, but he ended up back in Argentina. "On my visit, I saw lots of kids with no shoes who were suffering from injuries to their feet." Wanting to help, he created TOMS Shoes, a company that would match every pair of shoes purchased with a pair of new shoes given to a child in need, Mycoskie returned to Argentina with a group of family, friends, and staff later that year with 10,000 pairs of shoes made possible by TOMS customers.

Mycoskie explains "A leading cause of disease in developing countries is soil-transmitted diseases, which can penetrate the skin through bare feet. Wearing shoes can help prevent these diseases, and the long-term physical and cognitive harm they cause."

The TOMS mission of giving shoes has attracted other brands, resulting in unique and successful collaborations. Ralph Lauren sold co-branded Polo Rugby TOMS, giving a matched pair with every pair sold. Element Skateboards has issued limited edition TOMS + Element shoes as well as a One for One skateboard. With every skateboard purchased, one will be given to a child at the Indigo Skate Camp in Durban, South Africa. Mycoskie explains, "It is TOMS' hope that as our One for One movement continues to grow, more and more companies will look to incorporate giving into what they do."

TOMS can be found online and in stores like Whole Foods and Nordstrom. As of September 2010, TOMS has given over one million pairs of new shoes to children in need around the world through Giving Partners.

Source: Adapted from Jessica Shambora, "Blake Mycoskie, Founder of TOMS Shoes," *Fortune*, Vol. 161, No. 4 (March 22, 2010), p. 72; http://www.youtube.com/user/tomsshoes; and http://www.toms.com/our-movement.

In most cases, the desire to give back is one element in a mix of motivations. In some endeavors, however, it is a particularly strong force that drives the thinking of the entrepreneur. A survey by the National Federation of Independent Business found that[20]

- Ninety-one percent of small business owners contributed to their community through volunteering, in-kind contributions, and/or direct cash donations. About 41 percent contributed in all three ways. The estimated average value of contributions is $6,600 per small employer, for a total of roughly $40 billion.
- The most important reason for giving tended to be associated with personal satisfaction and fulfillment. The least important reason was direct business benefits. Owners of larger small firms were more likely to see a direct business benefit in

contributing to the community, but they, too, were much more likely to attribute their behavior to personal reasons.

- Creating a better business climate and making the community a better place to live were also important reasons to contribute, though typically not as important as personal satisfaction and fulfillment.

If you are at a university, notice the names on the buildings. In most cases, the names are those of entrepreneurs who have given back to their alma mater. One university president commented to one of the authors, "It is entrepreneurs who endow universities." It was Winston Churchill who once said, "We make a living by what we get, but we make a life by what we give." It is the authors' experience that entrepreneurs are one of the most giving groups we know.

Small business owners don't—and shouldn't—expect anything in return for their community stewardship. But, as Gary Deaton points out, "To say there's not a benefit would be naive. Everything you do in life has a positive or a negative effect. So the more things you do for the right reasons, the more positive results you'll see."[21]

DEVELOP FINANCIAL WEALTH

Contrary to what some people believe, there is nothing wrong with making money. As a general rule, when businesses are profitable, everyone benefits. Jobs are created, taxes are paid, and charities receive donations. Furthermore, like any other job or career, starting a business is a way to earn money and make ends meet. Of course, some entrepreneurs earn *lots* of money. In *The Millionaire Next Door*, Stanley and Danko note that self-employed people are four times more likely to be millionaires than are those who work for others.[22]

How much money should an entrepreneur expect to get in return for starting and running a business? Making a profit is certainly necessary for a firm's survival. Many entrepreneurs work night and day (literally, in some cases) just to generate enough profits to survive; others receive a modest income for their time and investment. From an economic perspective, however, the financial return of a business should compensate its owner not only for his or her investment of personal time (in the form of a salary equivalent), but also for any personal money invested in the business (in the form of cash distributed to the owner and the increased value of the business) and for the risk he or she is taking. That is, entrepreneurs should seek a financial return that will compensate them for the time and money they invest and also reward them for the risks and initiative they take in starting and operating their own businesses.

A significant number of entrepreneurs are, no doubt, highly motivated by the prospect of making money. They have heard the stories about people who launched dot-com companies and quickly became multimillionaires. While some entrepreneurs do become rich quickly, the majority do not. Therefore, a more reasonable goal would be to "get rich slowly." Wealth will most likely come, provided the business is economically viable and the owner has the patience and determination to make it happen.

BE YOUR OWN BOSS

Many people have a strong desire to make their own decisions, take risks, and reap the rewards. Being one's own boss can be an attractive ideal. For these individuals, freedom to operate independently is important. When we ask entrepreneurs about their main reason for leaving their jobs at other companies, about 40 percent say that they wanted to be their own boss.

The smallest businesses (i.e., part-time businesses and one-person firms), of which there are millions in the United States, probably offer the greatest flexibility to entrepreneurs.

Some of these businesses can even hang a "Gone Fishing" (or the equivalent) sign on the door when the entrepreneur feels the urge to engage in nonbusiness activities. Even the owner of a larger firm may have a lot of discretion in how he or she spends time. In general, there is a good deal of independence inherent in the work. Entrepreneurs can do things their own way, reap their own profits, and set their own schedules.

Of course, independence does not guarantee an easy life. Most entrepreneurs work very hard and for long hours. They must remember that the customer is, ultimately, the boss. But they do have the satisfaction of making their own decisions within the constraints required to build a successful business.

ESCAPE A BAD SITUATION

People sometimes use entrepreneurship as an escape hatch, to free themselves from an undesirable situation. Some may wish to leave an unpleasant job situation, while others may seek change out of necessity. Other individuals become entrepreneurs after being laid off by an employer. Unemployed personnel with experience in professional, managerial, technical, and even relatively unskilled positions often contemplate the possibility of venturing out on their own. Those who started or acquired small businesses as a result of financial hardship or other severely negative conditions have appropriately been called **reluctant entrepreneurs**.

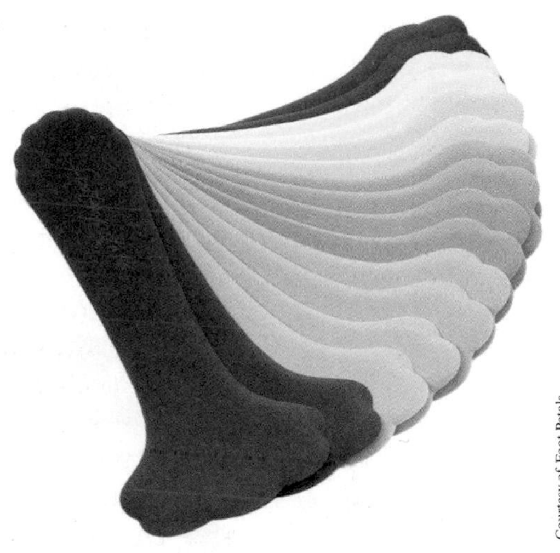

Courtesy of Foot Petals

In 2001, Tina Aldatz faced her now-or-never moment when she was laid off from her job at an Internet startup. Deciding to test her entrepreneurial skills, she set a deadline of six months to see what she could do before trying to get a new job. Aldatz had burned her feet as a child, so high heels were terribly painful to wear. She had been thinking about creating a designer insole that looked good and felt better than those in other shoes. In no time, she had a working prototype of a new insole for high heels, and by six months, she was shipping out her first product, in spite of some early obstacles. Nine years later, her firm, Foot Petals, had sales of over $10 million.[23]

reluctant entrepreneur
A person who becomes an entrepreneur as a result of some severe hardship.

Individuals may also flee the bureaucratic environment of a corporation that seems stifling or oppressive to them. In a survey of 721 office workers, 42 percent had considered quitting their jobs over bureaucratic hassles.[24] Entrepreneurship often provides an attractive alternative for individuals fleeing from such undesirable situations (sometimes called **refugees**).

refugee
A person who becomes an entrepreneur to escape an undesirable situation.

Karyn Couvillion, co-founder of Reeboot Strategy in Austin, Texas, is an example of a corporate refugee, someone who decided to leave a bad situation.

> *Three hundred and fifty e-mails a day in my inbox. BlackBerry, cell phone, and laptop constantly in tow. Check my Outlook calendar and see that I'm double- or triple-booked in meetings every hour, plus a 7 a.m. global conference call. Being told by management that we cannot hire additional head count because of a hiring freeze, despite the hefty increase in responsibilities for my team. That was me a year ago. The red tape, politics, ridiculous expectations, and meager resources made it nearly impossible to do my job as an advertising and brand manager for a large tech company.*
>
> *So I quit. So did my husband, who worked in a top advertising agency. We decided that life was too short and we had had enough. What was our worst-case scenario if we quit? Having to sell our home and look for jobs elsewhere? Better than losing our marriage and our sanity.*
>
> *My husband started consulting immediately. I wanted to spend some time with my ill father. The marketing consulting business my husband started took off, and because of our similar backgrounds and experience, it was a natural fit for us to work together.*

Ten months after quitting, we have more business than we can handle. My husband named the business Reeboot Strategy because in explaining our rationale for quitting our big corporate jobs, he would say: "We needed to hit Control + Alt + Delete on our lives and start over."

When my father died, I was there by his side.[25]

Only you can know why owning your own business is appealing to you. It could be a combination of some or all of the reasons just discussed, or even one that was not mentioned. Whatever the reason, it is wise to identify what motivates you to be an entrepreneur. It will help you understand what is important to you and give you guidance when making decisions. The old adage "Know thyself" is particularly relevant here. The following questions will help you determine whether owning a small business is a good fit for you:

1. Am I passionate about my product or service?
2. What is my tolerance for risk?
3. Am I effective in making decisions?
4. Am I willing to take on numerous responsibilities?
5. Will I be able to avoid burnout?

The Many Varieties of Entrepreneurship

4 Identify some of the basic types of entrepreneurs and entrepreneurial ventures.

Entrepreneurship is marked by diversity—that is, there is great variety both in the people and in the firms that are *entrepreneurial*. As a potential entrepreneur, you can be encouraged by this diversity; you do not need to fit some narrow stereotype. Let's consider some of the variety we observe in the entrepreneurial world.

FOUNDER ENTREPRENEURS VERSUS OTHER BUSINESS OWNERS AND FRANCHISEES

founder An entrepreneur who brings a new firm into existence.

"Pure" entrepreneurs are **founders** who initiate businesses that bring new or improved products or services to market. They may also be artisans who develop skills upon which they can start their own firms. Or they may be enterprising individuals, often with marketing backgrounds, who draw on the ideas of others to launch new ventures. Whether acting as individuals or as part of a group, founders bring companies into existence by surveying the market, raising funds, and assembling the necessary resources. The process of starting an entirely new business is discussed in detail in Chapter 3.

At some point after a new firm is established, it may be purchased or taken over by a second-generation family member or another entrepreneur who was managing the company. These "second-stage" entrepreneurs do not necessarily differ greatly from founding entrepreneurs in the way they manage their businesses. Sometimes, these well-established small firms grow rapidly, and their orientation will be more akin to that of a founder than to that of a manager. Nevertheless, it is helpful to distinguish between entrepreneurs who start or substantially change companies and those who direct the continuing operations of established businesses.

franchisee An entrepreneur whose power is limited by a contractual relationship with a franchising organization.

Franchisees comprise yet another category of entrepreneurs. **Franchisees** differ from other business owners in the degree of their independence. Because of the guidance and constraints provided by contractual arrangements with franchising organizations, franchisees function as limited entrepreneurs. Chapter 4 presents more information about franchisees.

entrepreneurial experiences

Work Less (It's Good for Business)

© iStockphoto.com/Angelika Schwarz

Brett Schklar was a fast-rising, burn-the-candle-at-both-ends kind of executive. So naturally, he was on a business trip the day of his 31st birthday.

His career as a vice president at a promising tech company was flourishing, and if that came at the expense of time with his family, time spent taking care of himself, time to even pause to celebrate his birthday, well, he was willing to make that sacrifice.

But something happened that day to make him question all that: He had a heart attack.

John Johnston Photography

"Doctors told me I have a condition that needs monitoring, and that stress is a particularly important factor," he recalls. "I needed to work less and reprioritize. I had to change my lifestyle—diet, exercise, everything."

Suddenly he had no choice: He eased off the accelerator both personally and professionally, focused more on his family and young son, and cut back on the 80-hour work weeks, the constant travel, and the late-night, bedside text messaging.

And he started his own business.

"I realized the reason I had a lot of stress in the corporate environment was because I didn't fit in that environment," Schklar says. "I came to understand that my real passion is getting things done in ways that probably aren't always acceptable in a corporate setting, like saying what's on your mind, actually telling people when you think they're going about something the wrong way, and trying to help them find a better way to do it.

Just four months after he was rushed from his Seattle hotel room to a nearby hospital, he launched the Market Creation Group, a Denver-based business-to-business technology marketing firm, and he did it while working less. Today the business is thriving and growing, and Schklar is living proof that what the work/life experts tell us and what we never quite believe that paying more attention to our lives outside of work makes us better workers–is actually true....

Brett Schklar built Market Creation Group into Denver's fastest-growing private company by working fewer hours and relying on shrewd planning and execution. Some of the keys:

- **Make sure somebody needs what you are offering**. Identify a niche–a void your company is uniquely positioned to fill–and exploit it.
- **Define the types of clients you want**. And avoid the ones you don't. They're not worth the trouble.
- **Tap your network**. Known quantities offer fewer unpleasant surprises.
- **Hire people to bolster your weaknesses**. The goal is to build a balanced, highly capable staff.
- **Plan, plan and plan some more**. "It's about having a big, awesome long-term vision, plus a staged approach to growth," Schklar says.
- **Make team members privy to your company strategy**. "That gives everybody a compass," he explains, "and leaves less room for error."
- **Deliver superior work**. Satisfied clients are sticky clients. In 2008, Schklar notes, Market Creation Group doubled its revenue without adding a single new client.

Source: David Port, "Work Less (It's Good for Business)," *Entrepreneur*, December 2009, pp. 83–89. Reprinted with permission of Entrepreneur Media, Inc. © 2009 by Entrepreneur Media. Inc. All rights reserved. **http://www.demandmcg.com**

HIGH-POTENTIAL VENTURES VERSUS ATTRACTIVE SMALL FIRMS AND MICROBUSINESSES

high-potential venture (gazelle)
A small firm that has great prospects for growth.

attractive small firm
A small firm that provides substantial profits to its owner.

Small businesses differ drastically in their growth potential. The few businesses that have phenomenal prospects for growth are called **high-potential ventures, or gazelles**. Even within this group, there is variation in styles of operation and approaches to growth. Some are high-tech startups—the kind that made Silicon Valley in California famous. These success stories often feature a technology wizard with a bright idea, backed by venture capitalists eager to finance the next Microsoft. When such companies prosper, they usually grow at blinding speed and make their founders and investors wealthy by being sold or by issuing shares of stock to public investors.

In contrast to such high-potential ventures, **attractive small firms** offer substantial financial rewards for their owners. Income from these entrepreneurial ventures may easily be in the millions or even tens of millions. They represent a major segment of small businesses—solid, healthy firms that can provide rewarding careers. Many of these are owned by women, who are starting new businesses at twice the rate of men. And an increasing number of them are starting firms in previously male-dominated industries—some of the fastest-growing companies in construction, manufacturing, and computer services are now owned by women.

Despite their progress in the business arena, women-owned companies are significantly smaller than men-owned firms. One reason for this, suggested by Sharon Hadary, the former director and founder of the Center for Women's Business Research, is that women have lower expectations for their businesses than do men. In her opinion,

> *Men tend to start businesses to be the "boss," and their aim is for their businesses to grow as big as possible. Women start businesses to be personally challenged and to integrate work and family and they want to stay at a size where they personally can oversee all aspects of the business.*[26]

microbusiness
A small firm that provides minimal profits to its owner.

lifestyle business
A microbusiness that permits the owner to follow a desired pattern of living.

The least profitable types of businesses—including many service companies, such as dry cleaners, beauty shops, and appliance repair shops—provide modest returns to their owners. These are called **microbusinesses**, and their distinguishing feature is their limited ability to generate significant profits. Entrepreneurs who devote personal effort to such ventures receive a profit that does little more than compensate them for their time. Many companies of this type are also called **lifestyle businesses** because they permit an owner to follow a desired lifestyle, even though they provide only modest financial returns. They employ fewer than 10 employees and make up the largest sector of the U.S. economy. Such enterprises usually do not attract investors and are financed through microfinancing, where loans as small as 25 cents will help fund a small business in some part of the world. Microbusinesses are seen not only in developing countries in Asia, South America, and Africa, but also in the United States.

ARTISAN VERSUS OPPORTUNISTIC ENTREPRENEURS

artisan entrepreneur
A person with primarily technical skills and little business knowledge who starts a business.

Because of their varied backgrounds, entrepreneurs display differences in the degrees of professionalism and the styles of management they bring to their businesses. The ways in which they analyze problems and approach decision making may differ radically.

In this regard, there are two basic types of entrepreneurs: artisan (or craftsman) entrepreneurs and opportunistic entrepreneurs. **Artisan entrepreneurs** normally have technical job experience, but may lack good communication skills and managerial training.

An artisan entrepreneur's approach to business decision making is often characterized by the following features:

- They are paternalistic—they guide their businesses much as they might guide their own families.
- They are reluctant to delegate authority.
- They use few (usually only one or two) capital sources to create their firms.
- They define marketing strategy in terms of the traditional components of price, quality, and company reputation.
- Their sales efforts are primarily personal.
- Their time orientation is short, with little planning for future growth or change.

A mechanic who starts an independent garage, a beautician who operates a beauty shop, or a painter who opens a studio are examples of artisan entrepreneurs.

In contrast to the artisan entrepreneur, an **opportunistic entrepreneur** is one who has supplemented his or her technical education with the study of such nontechnical subjects as economics, law, or history. Opportunistic entrepreneurs generally avoid paternalism, delegate authority as necessary for growth, employ various marketing strategies and types of sales efforts, obtain original financing from more than two sources, and plan for future growth. An example of an opportunistic entrepreneur is a small building contractor and developer who adopts a relatively sophisticated approach to management, including detailed accounting and budgeting, precise bidding, and systematic marketing research.

opportunistic entrepreneur
A person with both sophisticated managerial skills and technical knowledge who starts a business.

You should understand that our descriptions of these two entrepreneurial styles represent extremes: At one end is a craftsperson, and at the other end is a knowledgeable and experienced manager. The former frequently "flies by the seat of the pants," and the latter uses systematic management procedures and something resembling a "scientific" approach. In practice, of course, entrepreneurial styles are far less polarized, with entrepreneurs scattered along a continuum of managerial sophistication. This book is intended to help you move toward the opportunistic end of the continuum and away from the artisan end.

ENTREPRENEURIAL TEAMS

Our discussion thus far has focused on entrepreneurs who function as individuals, each with his or her own firm. And this is frequently the case. However, entrepreneurial teams are becoming increasingly common, particularly in ventures of any substantial size. An **entrepreneurial team** consists of two or more individuals who combine their efforts to function in the capacity of entrepreneurs. In this way, the talents, skills, and resources of two or more entrepreneurs can be concentrated on one endeavor. This very important form of entrepreneurship is discussed at greater length in Chapter 8.

entrepreneurial team
Two or more people who work together as entrepreneurs on one endeavor.

When to Quit—and When to Stick

As you contemplate owning or growing your own business, take a little time to read *The Dip: A Little Book That Teaches You When to Quit (and When to Stick)*, by Seth Godin.

The Competitive Edge of Entrepreneurs

To maintain their position as a robust part of the total economy, small entrepreneurial companies must compete effectively with firms of all sizes, including large publicly owned companies.

How is it that small and entrepreneurial firms can hold their own and often gain an edge over successful, more powerful businesses? The answer lies in the ability of new and smaller firms to exploit opportunities. If a business can make its product or service "cheaper, faster, and better," then it can be competitive. Small companies—if well managed—are just as able as larger firms to develop strategies that offer a competitive advantage.

In this section, we will take a look at some ways in which new firms can gain a competitive advantage. In Chapter 3, we'll elaborate on strategies for exploiting these potential advantages and capturing the business opportunities they make possible.

CUSTOMER FOCUS

Business opportunities exist for those who can produce products and services desired by customers. Small companies are particularly adept at competing when they commit to a strong customer focus. Good customer service can be provided by a business of any size; however, in many instances, small businesses have a greater potential than larger firms to achieve this goal. If properly managed, small entrepreneurial companies have the advantage of being able to serve customers directly and effectively, without struggling through layers of bureaucracy or breaking corporate policies that tend to stifle employee initiative. In many cases, customers are personally acquainted with the entrepreneur and other key people in the small business.

Not all small enterprises manage to excel in customer service, but many realize their potential for doing so. Having a smaller number of customers and a close relationship with them makes customer service a powerful tool for entrepreneurial businesses. For further discussion of this subject, see Chapter 14.

QUALITY PERFORMANCE

There is no reason that a small business needs to take a back seat to larger firms when it comes to achieving quality in operations. We frequently talk to owners of small businesses whose operations not only equal the quality performance of larger firms, but in fact surpass the performance of the giants.

No finer examples of quality performance can be found than MFI International in El Paso, Texas, owned by Cecilia Levine, and J&S Construction in Cookeville, Tennessee, owned by Jack and Johnny Stites. A visitor to these companies—a manufacturer and a general contractor, respectively—can feel their commitment to quality. It is a part of their DNA. In fact, these small business owners can insist on high levels of quality without experiencing the frustration of a large-company CEO who may have to push a quality philosophy through many layers of bureaucracy.

In short, quality is mostly independent of firm size, but if there is an advantage, it most often goes to the smaller business—which is a surprise to most people. As a small business owner, you do not and should not have to accept anything less than the highest-quality performance. An uncompromising commitment to quality will move you a long way down the road to having a competitive advantage relative to other firms in your industry.

INTEGRITY AND RESPONSIBILITY

In order to maintain a strong competitive advantage, it is essential that you add to good customer service and excellent product quality a solid reputation for honesty and dependability. In fact, the quickest way to lose a competitive advantage is to act without regard for others, or worse, to act dishonestly. We all respond positively to evidence of integrity because we all have, at times, been taken advantage of when buying a product or service.

Jeffry Timmons and Stephen Spinelli, nationally recognized entrepreneurship researchers at Babson College, conducted a study of 128 presidents/founders who were attending a management program at Harvard Business School. The participants were asked to identify the most critical concepts, skills, and know-how for success at their companies. It is not surprising that 72 percent of the respondents stated that the single most important factor in long-term success was high ethical standards.[27]

Consistently operating with integrity can set a small business apart as being trustworthy at a time when stories of corporate greed and corruption abound. Above all else, the core values of the entrepreneur, as reflected in what she or he says and how she or he acts, determine the culture within a business. After all, others will do business with a company only when they feel that they can trust that company. Trust is the foundation of all relationships, including business relationships. Chapter 2 discusses the critical importance of integrity and its role in entrepreneurship.

INNOVATION AND GLOBALIZATION

How the world is changing! When Bill Clinton was elected president in 1992, hardly anyone—with the exception of a small number of people in the government and academia—had e-mail. In his book *The World Is Flat*, Thomas Friedman describes the convergence of 10 forces that have "flattened" the world.[28] Friedman's contention that the world is flat means that anything can now be done from anywhere in the world. Individuals, not governments or large corporations, are driving the globalization that we are experiencing all around us, Friedman says. Innovation, both in products or services and in competitive strategies, is within the reach of the small business in ways that were not thought possible a few years ago.

New product innovation often comes from small businesses. Most of the radical inventions of the last century, such as the computer and the pacemaker, came from small companies, not large ones. And this will not change.

Research departments of big businesses tend to focus on improving existing products. Creative ideas may be sidetracked because they are not related to existing product lines or because they are unusual. But preoccupation with an existing product can obscure the value of a new idea. In his book, *The Innovator's Dilemma,* Clayton Christensen documents how large established companies have missed major transformations in a number of industries—computers (mainframes to PCs), telephones (landline to mobile), photography (film to digital), stock markets (floor trading to online trading), and many others.[29]

When discussing the role of entrepreneurs in innovation, Amar Bhide, a noted business researcher at Columbia University, describes how entrepreneurs are good at developing others' ideas. Bhide advises us not to equate innovation with technological breakthroughs and scientists in white coats, because few small businesses can afford the luxury of spending large amounts of money on R&D. Instead, he contends that entrepreneurs are better able to take inventions or innovations developed elsewhere and put them into use, which requires marketing, sales, and organization.[30] In Bhide's opinion, these latter activities are just as much innovation as creating something in a science lab. The mere fact that a small business is not "high tech" should not mean that it is not innovative; it may be just the opposite.

As an example of using existing technology to innovate, consider the current trend among many small businesses to take advantage of "location-based social networking." Restaurants, retailers, and other types of small businesses are signing up for services provided by such companies as Facebook, Foursquare, and Gowalla, Inc., that allow consumers equipped with smartphones to "check-in" and broadcast their current store location to their entire social network. This type of viral marketing is an inexpensive and easy way for small businesses to get their names out in the marketplace and engage other consumers who might be perusing their social networks. While these small businesses did not create this innovative technology, they are clearly being innovative in using the technology.

Access to technology has also helped smaller firms compete. Mike Whaling, president of 30 Lines, a social media marketing company, explains, "It starts to level the playing field. It gives small businesses the opportunity to put themselves out there and really compete with larger companies."[31] Sophisticated computer software, once accessible only to large businesses, is now available at prices small companies can afford. In fact, the Web is full of free tools to help entrepreneurs start, run, and grow their businesses. Offshoring is another phenomenon of recent years that has allowed small companies to be competitive. In a *Bloomberg Businessweek* cover story on outsourcing, Pete Engardio, Michael Arndt, and Dean Foust observe, "Creative new companies can exploit the possibilities of offshoring even faster than established players." They use Crimson Consulting Group as a good example. This firm, with only 14 full-time employees, provides global market research on everything from routers to software. It farms out the research to 5,000 independent consultants all around the world. Crimson's CEO, Gleen Gow, comments, "This allows a small firm like us to compete with [giant consulting firms like] McKinsey and Bain on a very global basis with very low costs."[32]

SPECIAL NICHE

niche market
A specific group of customers with an identifiable but narrow range of product or service interests.

Almost all small businesses try to shield themselves from competition by targeting a specific group of customers who have an identifiable but very narrow range of product or service interests and comprise what is called a **niche market**. The niche might consist of a uniquely specialized product or service, or it might be a focus on serving a particular geographical area.

A *Wall Street Journal* article highlighted the re-emergence of small, niche specialty shops in the United States by writing somewhat humorously about Tom Hanks and Meg Ryan as stars in a sequel to the 1998 hit movie "You've Got Mail." Tom's mega-bookstore chain Fox & Sons has to file for bankruptcy because the Internet has taken away much of his large-volume discount business. At the same time, an opportunity develops for the re-emergence of a local store to better serve those consumers who prefer not to spend their time searching for books online. Tom and Meg find themselves investing their savings to re-open Meg's old neighborhood bookstore to take advantage of this niche market.[33] This entertaining example is only one of many reasons why the future looks

RESOURCES

Websites for Every Entrepreneur

Every entrepreneur should take advantage of the following three websites:

- U.S. Small Business Administration: http://www.sba.gov.
- Entrepreneurship website, sponsored by the Kauffman Foundation and the U.S. Commerce Department to promote entrepreneurial activity globally: http://www.entrepreneurship.org.
- SCORE, a network of more than 360 offices nationwide where veteran small business executives offer free confidential advice and mentoring: http://www.score.org.

bright for those who are willing to put in the necessary work to follow their dream. In reality, numerous small businesses are uniquely positioned to capture niche markets.

Successful entrepreneurs are not overly concerned about their ability to compete with their larger counterparts. With few exceptions, large corporations are bureaucracies, with bureaucrats as managers. As already pointed out, their R&D methods focus on the status quo. In addition, large companies have difficulty in creating effective incentives for employees so that they will think entrepreneurially. There is considerable evidence that most workers in today's huge corporations are simply not engaged in their work. Many, like Jim Halpert from the popular TV show "The Office," would declare, "This is just a job. . . . If this were my career, I'd have to throw myself in front of a train."[34]

The bottom line is that small companies with an entrepreneurial culture can compete and compete well.

NBC/LUBIN, JUSTIN/Album/Newscom

Getting Started

Starting any type of business career is exciting. Launching one's own business, however, can be far more demanding because of the risk and great potential of such a venture. Let's think for a moment about some special concerns of individuals who are ready to get their feet wet in the exciting waters of entrepreneurship.

6 Discuss factors related to starting an entrepreneurial career.

AGE AND ENTREPRENEURIAL OPPORTUNITY

One practical question is, "What is the right age to become an entrepreneur?" As you might guess, there is no "correct" answer to this question. The driving factor is not so much age as it is a matter of knowledge and experience. You will need to know and understand the industry you plan to enter, as well as the finances and operations of the business you hope to launch.

Most prospective entrepreneurs must also accumulate at least some of the financial resources needed to launch a business. Some have the impression that startups are financed with bank loans and money provided by venture capitalists. As you will learn, nothing could be further from the truth. New ventures are financed mostly with a founder's personal savings. This initial investment may then be followed by money from friends and family, based largely on personal relationships and not on the merits of the venture. So, having enough time to accumulate startup money is an important factor in determining when you will be able to launch a new business.

Although the timing will vary according to individual circumstances, conventional wisdom suggests that the ideal age to start a business is somewhere between the late 20s and the early 40s, when a balance exists between preparatory experiences and family obligations. Research conducted by Paul Reynolds shows that the highest percentage of new ventures are launched by entrepreneurs in the 25- to 35-year age group.[35] As Tyler Self, co-founder of Vision Research Organization, observes, "It's about the trade-off between confidence usually characterized by youth and wisdom based on experience."[36]

Given both the conventional wisdom and the research findings, members of the demographic group called Generation X currently would be in their prime for starting and growing new businesses. And according to Tamera Erikson, in an article appearing in *Bloomberg Businessweek*, they are doing just that:

> *Xers want jobs that offer a variety of career paths and allow them to gain fresh, marketable skills, build a strong network of contacts, and put money in the bank. . . . Xers aspire to run their own entrepreneurial ventures.*[37]

But conventional wisdom goes only so far. Many people, younger and older, aspire just as strongly to own their own businesses. In fact, a record number of Millennials, otherwise known as Generation Y, who are entering business schools are not interested in traditional careers. Instead, many are writing business plans with the intention of entering the large number of business plan competitions. "It's a sea of change," says Thomas Kinnear, director of Michigan's Zell Lurie Institute of Entrepreneurial Studies.[38]

Almost 80 million strong, Millennials make up the largest, the most educated, and the most diverse generation in American history. As entrepreneurs, they have been described as follows:[39]

- They have no fear regarding technology. Many of them cannot even recall life before the Internet.
- They are idealistic and optimistic, and this, in turn, influences their perceptions about business. Their heroes include Steve Jobs and Mark Zuckerberg.
- They are far more collaborative than their predecessors. The idea of being a solo entrepreneur holds little attraction for them. Instead, they start businesses with partners, if not entire teams.
- They frequently build elements of community into their businesses. Matt Mullenweg's wildly successful software company, Automattic, began as an open-source project to create better blogging software. At the time, Mullenweg was a teenager with no experience in software development. He recruited volunteer coders who built, tested, and refined what has become WordPress—one of the most popular blogging platforms—all for no pay.
- They are impatient. Rather than spending large amounts of time on business plans, they throw out something rough, then tweak and experiment.
- They are committed to making the world a better place. For instance, Meraki, a business backed by Google, builds mesh Wi-Fi networks that provide free or low-cost Internet service to poor communities.
- They may start companies in dorm rooms while simultaneously studying entrepreneurship in the classroom. A number of colleges and universities have created funds to provide money to students so that they can develop their ideas.

"One thing that differentiates the young founders is whom they can connect with early on," says David Cohen, executive director of TechStars, a Boulder, Colorado, incubator that works with Millennial company founders. "People are starting companies at young ages. They fail fast, learn a lot, and keep going."[40]

At the other end of the age spectrum, an increasing number of 50- and 60-year-olds are walking away from successful careers in big businesses when they become excited by the prospects of entrepreneurship and doing something on their own. According to the Ewing Marion Kauffman Foundation, for more than a decade, individuals between the ages of 55 and 64 have experienced higher rates of entrepreneurial activity than even their younger counterparts. Like the younger generations, many older entrepreneurs are seeing opportunities to offer products or services for their peers because they feel no one else understands or is interested in the needs of older persons.[41] More than the money, their new businesses offer them a chance to work on something they really want and love to do.

So what is the ideal age to get into the game? It's whenever your passion, experience, and determination collide with an entrepreneurial opportunity.

CHARACTERISTICS OF SUCCESSFUL ENTREPRENEURS

What kinds of people become successful entrepreneurs? Clearly, no well-defined entrepreneurial profile exists; individual entrepreneurs differ greatly from each other. Knowing this should encourage you if you wish to start your own business: You do not have to fit some prescribed stereotype.

Some qualities, however, are common among entrepreneurs and probably contribute to their success. One of these characteristics is a strong commitment to or passion for the business. It is an attitude that results in tenacity in the face of difficulty and a willingness to work hard. Entrepreneurs do not give up easily. In fact, on most days they are confident of their ability to meet the challenges confronting them. They believe that success depends on their own efforts, as opposed to luck or fate determining their success. That is not to say that they do not have down days when they cannot clearly see how they will survive.

Entrepreneurs are also portrayed as risk takers. Certainly, they do assume risk. By investing their own money, they assume financial risk. If they leave secure jobs, they risk their careers. Starting and running a business can place stress on the entrepreneur's family. After all, when someone with a family starts and runs a business, the whole family is affected, and this must be considered. Even though entrepreneurs assume risk, they are usually what we might term moderate risk takers—accepting risks over which they have some control. Some entrepreneurs are so focused on the opportunity that they do not even think they are taking a risk.

Doug Hall, founder and CEO of Eureka! Ranch, believes that entrepreneurs must first and foremost have the courage and inspiration to embark on any new business venture. He calls it a "Maverick Mindset," which for him is the willingness to take the "riskier, rockier, less-traveled path because you know it's right. It takes this courage to turn a dream into reality. An entrepreneur's dream can't begin to happen until he/she finds the courage to take the first step, even if it is a small step." His advice: "Stop saving yourself for tomorrow. Start living now. Get up, get out, get going!"[42]

Timmons and Spinelli have summarized research on entrepreneurial characteristics. The entrepreneurs they describe as having and exhibiting "desirable and acquirable attitudes and behaviors" fall under the following six descriptors:[43]

1. *Commitment and determination*—tenacious, decisive, and persistent in problem solving
2. *Leadership*—self-starters and team builders who focus on honesty in their business relationships
3. *Opportunity obsession*—aware of market and customer needs
4. *Tolerance of risk, ambiguity, and uncertainty*—risk takers, risk minimizers, and uncertainty tolerators
5. *Creativity, self-reliance, and adaptability*—open-minded, flexible, uncomfortable with the status quo, and quick learners
6. *Motivation to excel*—goal-oriented and aware of personal strengths and weaknesses

On the other side of the coin, there are some attitudes and behaviors that should be avoided at all cost. An almost certain way to fail as an entrepreneur, and there are many who have done just that, is to do the following:

1. Overestimate what you can do.
2. Lack an understanding of the market.
3. Hire mediocre people.
4. Fail to be a team player, which is usually the result of taking oneself too seriously.
5. Be a domineering manager.
6. Not share ownership in the business in an equitable way.

For the most part, this list describes a leader without humility. Contrary to popular belief, humility is a quality that serves leaders well. Scott Cook is the founder and CEO of Intuit, a computer software company that helps millions of consumers and businesses manage their financing, with products such as Quicken, QuickBooks, TurboTax, QuickBase, and Payroll. Cook believes that humility is an essential trait for any entrepreneur:

> *The future belongs to humble leaders. Humble to let your people lead and be led by them. Humble to make the customer your boss. Humble to listen and listen intently. Humble to know that almost all of the best ideas come from others. Humble to admit you were wrong, and tell your team.*[44]

THE IMPORTANCE OF MENTORS

Although there are many different types of entrepreneurs, most have one thing in common— they have found mentors along the way.

mentor
A knowledgeable person who can offer guidance based on experience in a given field.

As you begin and continue on the entrepreneurial journey, you can make no better decision than to find mentors who can show you the way. **Mentors** are individuals to whom you can go for advice and counsel—people who are pulling for you, wanting you to succeed, and supporting your efforts. They are people who can teach you what to do and

© iStockphoto.com/Angelika Schwarz

entrepreneurial experiences

Rick Davis on Mentoring

Rick Davis, founder and CEO of Davaco, Inc., explains how influential and important a mentor's guidance, help, and encouragement can be.

> *My number one mentor and the person who had the biggest influence on my professional career was my father, Charles "Skip" Davis. While both my father and my mother served as role models in many areas throughout my life, it was my father who nurtured my entrepreneurial spirit. He led by example through his own professional accomplishments and supported me—financially, emotionally, and spiritually.*
>
> *Like my father, I served as a fireman, and, like him, I chose to take advantage of my "off-days" to venture into other business opportunities. He delved into plumbing and eventually started his own insurance company, while my interests were in real estate and construction.*
>
> *Like many young men with an entrepreneurial spirit, I had a vision, but I didn't have the capital to make it all happen. Without my dad to co-sign my first $4,500 loan, I could not have financed my first HUD renovation project. In effect, his signature launched my career. Later, as I set my sights on multi-family apartment complexes, my dad was there to co-sign for me again. Obviously, this was a significant investment that could have resulted in financial ruin. Fortunately, that particular project turned a profit for both of us. His ongoing guidance and leadership throughout that project, as well as his support, demonstrated incredible faith in my abilities. This blend of risk taking, hard work, and trust ultimately gave me the confidence I needed to be successful.*
>
> *My dad taught me values and skills that make for both an entrepreneur and a great person. Do what you say you are going to do, never settle for anything less than the best, and learn from your mistakes and your triumphs.*

© Rick Davis

Source: Interview with Rick Davis, October 11, 2010. **http://www.davacoinc.com**

how to do it and, most importantly, encourage you on those days when you want to throw in the towel. These "coaches" can show you how to avoid mistakes and be there to give you the benefit of their years of experience.

Success in Business and Success in Life

7

Explain the concept of an entrepreneurial legacy and its challenges.

So far, we have discussed entrepreneurship and small business from a number of angles. As you contemplate taking such a direction yourself, we urge you to broaden your perspective. As aptly expressed by author and very seasoned entrepreneur Norm Brodsky,

> *Building a successful business is not an end in itself. It is a means to an end. It is a way to create a better life for you and those whom you love, however you—and they—may define it. You need to do the life plan first and then keep revisiting it, to make sure it's up to date and your business plan is helping you achieve it. That habit, I can assure you, will prove to be the most important of them all.*[45]

LOOKING BACK AT AN ENTREPRENEURIAL LIFE

When an entrepreneur makes that final exit from the entrepreneurial stage, his or her business achievements become history. Reflecting on their lives and businesses at that point in their journeys, many entrepreneurs have come face to face with questions such as these: Was it a good trip? What kind of meaning does it hold for me now? Can I feel good about it? What are my disappointments? How did I make a difference? Such questions lead entrepreneurs to reassess their values, priorities, and commitments. By anticipating these questions well in advance, an entrepreneur can identify his or her most basic concerns early in the journey. Without reflection, the entrepreneurial journey and its ending are much more likely to prove disappointing in the end.

Assessment of entrepreneurial performance requires establishing criteria. Obviously, no single standard can be applied. For example, a person who measures everything by the dollar sign would determine the degree of an entrepreneur's success by the size of his or her bank account. However, we believe that most entrepreneurs will eventually think about achievements in terms of personal values and goals, rather than textbook criteria, popular culture, or financial rules of thumb. In all likelihood, a number of basic considerations will be relevant to the entrepreneur's sense of satisfaction.

In anticipating this time of looking back, an entrepreneur should think in terms of a legacy. A legacy consists of those things passed on or left behind. In a narrow sense, it describes material possessions bequeathed to one's heirs. In a broader sense, it refers to everything that one leaves behind—material items, good or bad family relationships, and a record of integrity or greed, of contribution or exploitation. An **entrepreneurial legacy** includes both tangible items and intangible qualities passed on not only to heirs but also to the broader society. You can appreciate, then, the seriousness with which the entrepreneur needs to consider the kind of legacy he or she is building.

entrepreneurial legacy
Material assets and intangible qualities passed on to both heirs and society.

WINNING THE WRONG GAME

It is easy for entrepreneurs to get caught up in an activity trap, working harder and harder to keep up with the busy pace of life. Ultimately, such entrepreneurs may find their business accomplishments overshadowed by the neglect or sacrifice of something more important to them. It's possible to score points in the wrong game or win battles in the wrong war.

Ed Bonneau revolutionized the distribution of sunglasses in the United States and eventually dominated that market with his highly successful business. While growing the firm, Bonneau purchased Pennsylvania Optical (with its patents and contracts with Walmart and Kmart) and industry giant Foster Grant (with its patents and manufacturing divisions). Then, Bonneau sold the business and walked away from it all. From a business standpoint, his was a huge entrepreneurial success story. However, in a comment on how he'd like to be remembered, Bonneau downplayed his financial wealth:

> *I would hope that they knew something else besides that I once ran the biggest sunglass company in the world. That's not the number one thing that I'd want to be known for. It's okay, but I'd much rather have that final assessment made by my kids and have them say, "He was a terrific dad." I never wanted to sacrifice my family or my church for my business.*[46]

And Bonneau's advice to younger entrepreneurs follows a similar theme:

> *Take God and your family with you when you go into business, and keep that balance in your life. Because when you get to be 60 years old and you look back over your life, if all you have is the biggest sunglass company in the world and a pot full of money in the bank . . . it won't be enough. Your life is going to be hollow, and you can't go back and redo it.*[47]

Entrepreneurs typically work very long hours, especially in the beginning. Sometimes, however, their obsession with work and the business becomes too extreme. Based on interviews with repeat entrepreneurs, Ilan Mochari summarized their reports of early mistakes: "If they had it to do all over again, most of the group would have spent more time away from their first companies, hanging with the family, schmoozing up other CEOs, and pondering the long-term picture."[48]

An excessive focus on money or work, then, can twist the entrepreneurial process. The outcome appears less satisfying and somehow less rewarding when the time for exit arrives.

CRAFTING A WORTHY LEGACY

In entrepreneurial terms, what constitutes a worthy legacy? One issue is the nature of the endeavor itself. A business that operates within the law, provides jobs, and serves the public provides a good foundation for a satisfying entrepreneurial experience. Although a business that peddles pornography on the Internet might make a lot of money for its owner, most of us would dismiss it as an unworthy enterprise because of its harmful, destructive effects.

Within many individuals is a streak of nobility that gives them a genuine concern for the well-being of others. Their positive attitudes propel them toward endeavors of practical service to society.

Bernard Rapaport, a highly successful, principled, and generous entrepreneur, has stressed the importance of the means a person takes to achieve a given end. "Whatever it is you want to achieve," he said, "*how* you achieve it is more important than if you achieve it." At 93 years of age, reflecting on life and legacy, he said, "What do I want to do? I want to save the world."[49]

Such idealism can guide an entrepreneur into many endeavors that are useful to our economic system. In fact, some entrepreneurial ventures are specifically designed to meet the particular needs of society. J. O. Stewart, a successful entrepreneur, has in his later years launched a firm whose primary objective is to provide good, low-cost housing to families

entrepreneurship + integrity

© iStockphoto.com/Angelika Schwarz

Leaving a Legacy as Seen Through a Son's Eyes

This feature is based on an interview by Ty Findley, an MBA student at the time, of his father, Steven Findley, founder and CEO of Titan Dynamics Systems, Inc., along with Ty's own perception of his father's legacy.

> *After having sold his battle effects simulations (BES) company, Titan Dynamics Systems Inc., my dad, Steve Findley, has had the time to look back and reflect on the entrepreneurial legacy he worked to create. Founding Titan Dynamics in 1992, Dad was awarded the largest BES contract in the history of the United States, valued at $500 million, and orchestrated the growth of his company from zero to $11.5 million in revenues in 2006. But when I asked about the legacy he hopes to leave behind with his business, those numbers were not what came to his mind. In my dad's words, "My business revolved around designing and producing quality military training equipment that increased the chances of American soldiers returning safely back home because of the training they received through our product."*

In other words, Steve Findley was driven primarily by his desire to make the world a safer place for his country's soldiers.

Ty says that his dad's legacy was not limited to what he did as an entrepreneur who was building a company. Ty explains, "My dad also wanted to make a difference through his family and community involvement. Dad managed to balance operating Titan Dynamics with raising and supporting a family of eight children." Steve says, "It means a lot to know that my children have always felt loved by their father, and that they are growing into individuals who will hopefully have a positive impact on the world."

Giving back to society is also something that Steve wants to be remembered for. For example, he volunteered his time to serve as a political representative for his local county congressional district. As he commented, "I believe that everyone should try to leave the world in a little better shape than they found it for the next generation."

These qualities have helped guide Steve's life and have crafted a legacy that his family and friends admire and respect. His actions have had a far-reaching positive impact and can serve as an example of how choosing to leave a meaningful and significant legacy should be something that everyone strives for.

While an entrepreneurial legacy may seem a distant objective for many budding entrepreneurs, it is something that should not be ignored. As Ty says, "Someday it will be my turn to look back on my life journey and on what I will be able to say about the legacy I left."

Source: Based on Ty Findley's interview of his dad, Steve Findley, October 15, 2010.

who cannot otherwise afford it. His motivation for this venture is personal concern for the needs of low-income families.

For most entrepreneurs looking back on their careers, *fulfillment* requires that their businesses have been constructive or positive in their impact—at the least, their effect should have been benign, causing no harm to the social order. In most cases, entrepreneurial businesses make positive contributions by providing jobs and services. A few businesses make an additional contribution in addressing special needs in society, as is the case for TOMS Shoes, described earlier in the chapter.

RESOURCES

Begin with the End in Mind

As an aspiring or new owner of your own business, begin with the end in mind. Visualize what you want the journey to be like and what you will have when it is completed. Be clear in your own mind as to what would be a "home run" for you.

Steven Covey's *Seven Habits of Highly Effective People* has helped a lot of entrepreneurs and business leaders, especially when it comes to the important relationships in life. After all, if you don't take your friends and family with you, you will be disappointed, no matter how much money you have.

BEGINNING WITH THE END IN MIND

The criteria by which one evaluates entrepreneurship must be personal. Stephen R. Covey, in *The Seven Habits of Highly Successful People,* suggests that the most effective way "to begin with the end in mind" is to develop a personal mission statement or philosophy or creed.[50] Though individuals will have different mission statements because their goals and values will vary, widely shared values will underlie many of their judgments.

An entrepreneur builds a business, a life, and a legacy day by day, starting with the initial launch and proceeding through the months and years of operations that follow. A person exiting an entrepreneurial venture has completed the business part of his or her legacy—it must be constructed during the life of the enterprise itself. Therefore, an entrepreneur needs to keep the end in mind while making innumerable operating decisions. By selecting the proper values and wisely balancing their application, an entrepreneur can make a satisfying exit, leaving a positive and substantial legacy to heirs, employees, the community, and the broader society.

It is the authors' deepest hope that your journey in owning your own business and being an entrepreneur—if you choose to do so—will be a richly rewarding experience, not only financially but also, more importantly, in the things that matter most in life. Above all, we hope that your legacy will bring both satisfaction *and* fulfillment for you and the important people in your life.

WHERE TO FROM HERE

An airplane pilot not only controls the plane during takeoff but also flies it and lands it. Similarly, entrepreneurs not only launch firms but also "fly" them; that is, they manage their firm's subsequent operation. In this book, you will find a discussion of the entire entrepreneurial process. It begins in the remainder of Part 1 (Chapter 2) with an examination of the fundamental values of the entrepreneur. Parts 2 and 3 look at a firm's basic strategy, the various types of entrepreneurial ventures, and the initial planning that is required for business startups. Parts 4 through 6 deal with the marketing and management of a growing business, including its human resources, operations, and finances.

1. Define the terms *entrepreneur* and *small business owner*, and explain how the terms are related.

- An entrepreneur is a person who relentlessly pursues an opportunity, in either a new or an existing enterprise, to create value, while assuming both the risk and the reward for his or her efforts.
- An entrepreneur thinks differently about how to use resources than do employee-managers.
- Owner-managers who buy out founders of existing firms, franchisees, and second-generation operators of family firms may also be considered entrepreneurs.
- Definitions of small business are arbitrary, but we focus on firms that are small compared to the biggest firms in the industry, that have mostly localized operations, are financed by a small number of individuals, and have growth potential.
- Our focus is on small business owners who are unrelenting in their search for opportunities that create value for customers and owners alike.

2. Explain the basic characteristics of entrepreneurial opportunities, and give examples of individuals who successfully started their own businesses.

- An entrepreneurial opportunity is an *economically attractive* and *timely* opportunity that creates value for prospective customers and the firm's owners alike, which involves much more than merely having a good idea.
- Entrepreneurial opportunities make the enterprise economically attractive for the owners while offering customers a product or service that is so appealing that they are willing to pay their hard-earned money for it.
- Ace Hotels, Late Model Restoration Supply, and Five Guys Burgers and Fries are examples of highly successful startups in different industries and different types of owners.

3. Describe some motivators or rewards for owning your own business.

- One of the primary reasons for becoming an entrepreneur is to make the world a better place (make meaning).
- Important secondary attractions to entrepreneurship are personal satisfaction, personal fulfillment (contributing to one's community), profit, independence, and freedom (escaping from a bad situation).

4. Identify some of the basic types of entrepreneurs and entrepreneurial ventures.

- Founders of firms are "pure" entrepreneurs, but those who acquire established businesses and franchisees may also be considered entrepreneurs.
- A few entrepreneurs start high-potential ventures (gazelles); other entrepreneurs operate attractive small firms and microbusinesses (lifestyle businesses).
- Women entrepreneurs are starting new businesses at twice the rate of men, and they are entering many nontraditional fields previously dominated by men.
- Based on their backgrounds and management styles, entrepreneurs may be characterized as artisan entrepreneurs or opportunistic entrepreneurs.
- Entrepreneurial teams consist of two or more individuals who combine their efforts to function as entrepreneurs.

5. Describe five potential competitive advantages of small entrepreneurial firms compared to large companies.

- *Customer focus*: Small business owners have an opportunity to know their customers well and to focus on meeting their needs.
- *Quality performance*: By emphasizing quality in products and services, small firms can build a competitive advantage.
- *Integrity and responsibility*: Independent business owners can build an internal culture based on integrity and responsibility that is reflected in relationships both inside and outside the firm. Such a culture helps strengthen the firm's position in a competitive environment.
- *Innovation and globalization*: Many small firms and individual operators have demonstrated a superior talent for finding innovative products and developing better ways of doing business. Offshoring has also given some small companies a competitive edge.
- *Special niche*: Small firms that find a special niche of some type can gain an advantage in the marketplace.

6. Discuss factors related to readiness for entrepreneurship and getting started in an entrepreneurial career.

- The ideal age to start a business appears to be between the late 20s and early 40s, when a person's education (knowledge), work experience, family situation, and financial resources are most likely to enable him or her to become an entrepreneur.
- Many of the Millennials, or Generation Y, are proving to be effective entrepreneurs, in spite of their young age.
- Persons in their 50s and 60s are becoming entrepreneurs at a faster rate than those at any other age.
- There is no well-defined entrepreneurial profile, but many entrepreneurs have such characteristics as a passion for their business, self-confidence, and a willingness to assume moderate risks.
- Successful entrepreneurs are also thought to possess leadership skills, a strong focus on opportunities, creativity and adaptability, and motivation to excel.
- Entrepreneurs can make no better decision than to develop relationships with mentors who can provide advice and counsel.

7. Explain the concept of an entrepreneurial legacy and the challenges involved in crafting a meaningful legacy.

- An entrepreneur's legacy includes not only money and material possessions but also such nonmaterial things as personal relationships and values.
- Part of the legacy is the contribution of the business to the community.
- A worthy legacy includes a good balance of values and principles important to the entrepreneur.
- Building a legacy is an ongoing process that begins with the launch of the firm and continues throughout its operating life.

Key Terms

entrepreneur p. 6
bootstrapping p. 6
small business p. 6
entrepreneurial opportunity p. 7
reluctant entrepreneur p. 15
refugee p. 15
founder p. 16
franchisee p. 16
high-potential venture (gazelle) p. 18
attractive small firm p. 18
microbusiness p. 18
lifestyle business p. 18
artisan entrepreneur p. 18
opportunistic entrepreneur p. 19
entrepreneurial team p. 19
niche market p. 22
mentor p. 26
entrepreneurial legacy p. 27

Discussion Questions

1. The three stories discussed at the beginning of the chapter are to some extent exceptions to the rule in the amount of success the entrepreneurs experienced. What, then, is their significance in illustrating entrepreneurial opportunity? Are these stories misleading?
2. What is meant by the term *entrepreneur*?
3. Consider an entrepreneur you know personally. What was the most significant reason for his or her deciding to follow an independent business career? If you don't already know the reason, discuss it with that person.
4. The motivators/rewards of profit, independence, and personal satisfaction are three reasons individuals enter entrepreneurial careers. What problems might be anticipated if an entrepreneur were to become obsessed with one of these rewards—for example, if she or he had an excessive desire to accumulate wealth, operate independently, or achieve a particular lifestyle?
5. Distinguish between an artisan entrepreneur and an opportunistic entrepreneur.
6. What is the advantage of using an entrepreneurial team?
7. Explain how customer focus and innovation can be special strengths of small businesses.
8. Why is the period from the late 20s to the early 40s considered to be the best time in life to become an entrepreneur?
9. Explain the concept of an entrepreneurial legacy.
10. Explain the following statement: "One can climb the ladder to success only to discover it is leaning against the wrong wall."

You Make the Call

SITUATION 1

In the following statement, a business owner attempts to explain and justify his preference for slow growth in his business.

> *I limit my growth pace and make every effort to service my present customers in the manner they deserve. I have some peer pressure to do otherwise by following the advice of experts—that is, to take on partners and debt to facilitate rapid growth in sales and market share. When tempted by such thoughts, I think about what I might gain. Perhaps I could make more money, but I would also expect a lot more problems. Also, I think it might interfere somewhat with my family relationships, which are very important to me.*

Question 1 Should this venture be regarded as entrepreneurial? Is the owner a true entrepreneur?
Question 2 Do you agree with the philosophy expressed here? Is the owner really doing what is best for his family?
Question 3 What kinds of problems is this owner trying to avoid?

SITUATION 2

Bear Bills, Inc., was started in 2008 by three Baylor University alumni in their early 20s as a solution to a problem every college student faces—paying utilities! The company's name originated from the university's mascot, the Baylor Bears. The business helps students pay their utility bills without all the hassles of having to collect from each roommate and getting a check to the utility company. Bear Bills pays the bills each month and splits the amount based on each student's pro-rated portion. The utility companies like the arrangement and are willing to give Bear Bills a commission for increasing their market share. The apartment houses where the students live like the deal because the utilities remain in the renters' names and the management receives a referral fee from Bear Bills. Of course, the students sign up because they do not have to bug a roommate to pay their share of the bill. And Bear Bills makes money.

The first year, Bear Bills signed up over 2,000 college students at the university. The second year, it incorporated as Simple Bills, Inc., and went to other college campuses, doubling its customers to over 4,000.

At this point, the concept is proven, but the owners have a decision to make. They can raise money from investors and grow the company faster to capture market share, but that will mean they will have to give up some of their ownership in the company. Alternatively, they can continue to bootstrap the business to conserve ownership percentage but cannot grow as rapidly. In other words, they would limit the growth of the business to what can be financed from the cash flows currently being generated from operations

Question 1 What do you like and not like about the Simple Bills concept?
Question 2 Would you recommend raising funds from outside investors and growing faster or continuing to bootstrap the operations to conserve ownership? Why?
Question 3 What strategy would you suggest for growing the business, assuming new investors are brought in?
Question 4 If you choose to raise funds, whom might you seek as investors?

SITUATION 3

Dover Sporting Goods Store occupies an unimpressive retail location in a small city in northern Illinois. Started in 1935, it is now operated by Duane Dover—a third-generation member of the founding family. He works long hours trying to earn a reasonable profit in the old downtown area.

Dover's immediate concern is an announcement that Walmart is considering opening a store at the southern edge of town. As Dover reacts to this announcement, he is overwhelmed by a sense of injustice. Why should a family business that has served the community honestly and well for 60 years have to fend off a large corporation that would take big profits out of the community and give very little in return? Surely, he reasons, the law must offer some kind of protection against big business predators of this kind. Dover also wonders whether small stores such as his have ever been successful in competing against business giants like Walmart.

Question 1 Is Dover's feeling of unfairness justified? Is his business entitled to some type of legal protection against moves of this type?
Question 2 How should Dover plan to compete against Walmart, if and when this becomes necessary?

Experiential Exercises

1. Analyze your own education and experience as qualifications for entrepreneurship. Identify your greatest strengths and weaknesses.
2. Explain your own interest in each type of entrepreneurial reward. Identify which type of incentive is most significant for you personally and explain why.
3. Interview someone who has started a business, being sure to ask for information regarding the entrepreneur's background and age at the time the business was started. In your report of the interview, indicate whether the entrepreneur was in any sense a refugee, and show how the timing of her or his startup relates to the ideal time for starting a business, as explained in this chapter.

Small Business & Entrepreneurship Resource Center

The Small Business & Entrepreneurship Resource Center offers complete small business management resources through a comprehensive database that covers all major areas of starting, operating, and maintaining a business, including financing, management, marketing, accounting, taxes, and more. Use the access code that came with your new book to access the site and perform the exercises in each chapter.

1. Sherwood T. "Woody" Phifer, who builds handcrafted guitars, exemplifies the artisan entrepreneur. His business success rests on his extraordinary skill in building outstanding electric and acoustic guitars. As a child, if he wanted a toy that he could not afford or find, he would simply make his own. His childhood helped to prepare him for his career. Describe how his ability to create, along with his fascination in taking things apart and rebuilding them, have helped him to differentiate his business from large guitar competitors, such as Fender and Gibson.

   Source: Sonia Alleyne, "Guitar Man: His Instruments Have Resounding Curves," *Black Enterprise,* Vol. 33, No. 9 (April 2003), p. 64.

2. Entrepreneurial opportunities exist for those who can produce enough products or services desired by customers to make the enterprise economically attractive. Describe how Sara Blakely discovered "the need" for footless pantyhose, and how the product was initially perceived by manufacturers and retailers.

   Source: P. Kelly Smith, "The Kindest Cut: Sure, Oprah Cut the Feet Off Her Pantyhose, but She's Not the One Making Money Off 'Em," *Entrepreneur,* Vol. 29, No. 11 (November 2001), p. 134.

Case 1

NAU (P. 693)

Several business associates in the clothing industry start a new clothing company, knowing that the world did not need just another clothing business. Thus, they develop a business model that is unique, combining profits and social responsibility.

ALTERNATIVE CASE FOR CHAPTER 1

Video Case 1, KlipTech, website only

CHAPTER 2

Integrity and Ethics: Foundations for Success in Small Business

In the SPOTLIGHT
PortionPac Chemical
http://www.portionpaccorp.com

PortionPac Chemical stands alone in its class. After nearly half a century in existence, the Chicago-based company remains a small business (especially when compared to the industry giants against which it competes), but it is doing just fine with 84 employees and increasing sales. And because of the way PortionPac puts people first, Winning Workplaces (a national nonprofit organization) and *Inc.* magazine named it a "2010 Top Small Company Workplace." The recognition was clearly deserved.

PortionPac specializes in what the company calls Sustainable Solutions®, providing a complete system of safe, effective, and environmentally friendly cleaning products—but that is only a small part of its business formula. When it comes to working with its employees and customers, the company is clearly exemplary. Who would have guessed that a chemical company would get the "people side" of its business so right?

© PortionPac Chemical Corporation

The company's culture emphasizes three things—trust, satisfaction, and good relationships—and this shows up in the satisfaction and loyalty of its employees. (In 2009, the company's turnover was a mere 2 percent, with average employee tenure of 13 years.) Out of respect for family life, PortionPac never runs a third

LOOKING AHEAD

After studying this chapter, you should be able to ...

1. Define *integrity*, and understand its importance to small businesses.
2. Explain how integrity applies to various stakeholder groups, including owners, customers, employees, the community, and the government.
3. Identify challenges to integrity that arise in small businesses, and explain the benefits of integrity to small firms.
4. Describe the impact of the Internet and globalization on the integrity of small businesses.
5. Suggest practical approaches for building a business with integrity.
6. Define *sustainable small business*, and describe the influence this trend is having on the management of small companies and startup opportunities.

© iStockphoto.com/Dan Bachman

shift, and it has been known to change work schedules so that employees could spend more time with their kids. The factory floor is more like an atrium than a place to mix chemicals, with natural light pouring in through skylights to bathe a thriving assortment of plants. To help with the long hours the employees spend working together, the machines on the floor were designed to produce less noise, which encourages conversation. Warren Weisberg, co-owner and vice president of the company, spends a lot of time in the factory, learning from the employees and soliciting opinions about their work. When employees request personal time, it is usually granted, and their special needs are always given serious consideration. It figures that the company's workers feel they are very well cared for.

But PortionPac's concern for people does not end with its employees—the company also takes care of its customers, with a special focus on janitors, who are the ultimate users of the company's products. To make their work more manageable, the firm has narrowed the range of products it sells from the dozens that typically clutter supply closets to a few color-coded basics that come in portion-controlled packages. Beyond this, PortionPac offers innovative safety and effective cleaning classes for janitors, and was the first in the industry to hire a national education director to address their needs. These actions reinforce the message that custodians are part of a modern-day, chemical-wielding nobility—an honorable occupation that is more of a calling than a ho-hum job.

Marvin Klein, the company's chairman and co-founder, actually thinks beyond the custodial staff when he points out that a clean building can lead to improved student performance and increased office productivity. But the firm's concerns are even more far-ranging—PortionPac is very concerned about the impact of harmful chemicals on the environment. To help with this, the company's products come in premeasured packages to reduce waste. And because they are sold as concentrates that take up only one-tenth the volume of products in their final mix, packaging and shipping require far less energy. Janitors are also encouraged to ease the burden on landfills by reusing the spray bottles and mixing containers for products. Taken together, these features of PortionPac's strategy underscore the firm's uncommon respect for other people and its robust commitment to the well-being of the planet—all without hindering its financial performance. Despite the slow economy, the company's revenue increased by 8 percent in 2009, with annual sales approaching $20 million.

So, what should be the focus of a well-managed firm? People or profits? PortionPac proves that a company may not have to choose between the two, and that's good news for everyone involved.

Sources: Leigh Buchanan, "The Un-Factory," *Inc.* Vol. 32, No. 5 (June 2010), pp. 63–67; "PortionPac," http://www.portionpaccorp.com, accessed October 14, 2010; and "RedOrbit," http://www.redorbit.com/modules/news/tools.php?tool=print&id=1877240, accessed October 14, 2010.

Even a casual scan of this chapter's opening Spotlight reveals that the company profiled, PortionPac Chemical, is a unique small business. Its leadership is intensely interested in financial performance, but they also pay very careful attention to the crucial relationships (especially those involving employees and customers) that make the business tick.

Some would say that it is precisely because of this emphasis on the people part of the puzzle that PortionPac performs so well. This may very well be the case. Others will claim that the company's emphasis on the environment is also important and plays a key role in generating positive results. This may also be true. The most important point, however, is that the leadership of PortionPac has the freedom to emphasize important relationships as they see fit. And consistent with the values of the company's founders, they have chosen to give serious consideration to the needs and interests of those who impact or are impacted by the firm's operations. They see this as a matter of integrity—of being true to the character of the enterprise and those who run it—and the emphasis seems to be paying off in many ways.

But what is integrity, anyway? That's a very important question. And in this chapter, we define and discuss this fundamental concept, recognizing that it is the foundation for ethical behavior in small businesses. We also provide frameworks to guide you toward the principled management of such enterprises.

What Is Integrity?

1 Define *integrity*, and understand its importance to small businesses.

integrity An uncompromising adherence to the lofty values, beliefs, and principles that an individual claims to hold.

The seeds of business misdeeds are sown when individuals compromise their personal **integrity**—that is, they do not behave in a way that is consistent with the noble values, beliefs, and principles they claim to hold. According to Karl Eller—the highly successful entrepreneur who turned the business of outdoor advertising into the revenue powerhouse that it is today—a person has integrity if his or her character remains whole, despite the pressure and circumstances of the worst of situations. In his words,

> *[A person of integrity] doesn't fold in a crunch; doesn't lie, cheat, flatter; doesn't fake credentials or keep two sets of books. He doesn't blame others for his mistakes or steal credit for their work. She never goes back on a deal: her handshake matches the tightest contract drawn up by the fanciest law firm in town.*[1]

In other words, integrity refers to a general sense of honesty and reliability that is expressed in a strong commitment to doing the right thing, regardless of the circumstances. Some acts, such as cheating on taxes, clearly violate this standard, while others are less obvious but just as inappropriate. For example, one entrepreneur who owned a flooring sales business often sold sheets of linoleum at first-quality prices, even though they were graded as "seconds" by the factory. To hide his deception, he developed an ink roller that changed the factory stamp from "SECONDS" to read "SECONDS TO NONE!" Those who caught the inaccuracy probably figured it was a typo and gave it no more thought, but unsuspecting customers were paying for first-quality flooring, only to receive imperfect goods. By any measure, this shady business practice reveals a lack of integrity on the part of the entrepreneur.

TOOLS

Perceiving Integrity

The integrity of a small business is determined mostly by the nature and quality of its relationships. However, *perceptions* of integrity also make a difference. As strange as it sounds, researchers Niels van Quaquebeke and Steffen Giessner found that people associate symmetrical company logos with more ethical, socially responsible behavior.

As discussed in Chapter 1, a successful entrepreneur seeks financially rewarding opportunities while creating value, first and foremost, for prospective customers and the firm's owners. This perspective makes clear that relationships are critical and integrity is essential to success. Financial gain is important, but it cannot be the only goal of interest. In fact, "doing anything for money" can quickly lead to distortions in business behavior. There are numerous motivations for misconduct in companies, but inappropriate acts such as price fixing, overcharging customers, using pirated software in the business, and a host of others are driven primarily by financial motives. To act with integrity, however, requires an individual to think differently by considering the welfare of others.

Fortunately, many small business owners strive to achieve the highest standards of honesty, fairness, and respect in their business relationships. Although unethical practices receive extensive attention in the news, most entrepreneurs and other business leaders are people of principle whose integrity regulates their quest for profits.

Integrity and the Interests of Major Stakeholders

It is probably evident by now that the notion of integrity is closely tied to **ethical issues**, which involve questions of right and wrong.[2] Such questions go far beyond what is legal or illegal; entrepreneurs often must make decisions regarding what is honest, fair, and respectful.

In order to pinpoint the types of ethical issues that are most troublesome for small companies, a group of researchers from Baylor University asked small business owners nationwide the following question: "What is the most difficult ethical issue that you have faced in your work?" As might be expected, the question yielded a wide variety of responses, which have been grouped into the categories shown in Exhibit 2.1.

ethical issues Issues that involve questions of right and wrong.

These responses provide a general idea of the issues that challenge the integrity of small business owners. As you can see in the exhibit, the issues mentioned most often are related to customers and competitors, such as failing to disclose conflicts of interest when representing clients in the same field, selling defective products, or misrepresenting unfavorable test results. However, the second most common category is concerned with the way a company treats its employees, including decisions about layoffs, workplace discrimination, and fairness in promotions. That this set of issues received almost as many responses as the first should not be surprising, given the challenges of the current business

EXHIBIT 2.1 The Most Challenging Ethical Issues for Small Businesses

environment. In fact, this category was near the bottom of the list when entrepreneurs responded to the same survey six years earlier.[3] Times are definitely changing.

The third category is related to the obligations of employees to their employers, focusing on the actions of personnel that may not align with the best interests of their companies—for example, accepting kickbacks, taking supplies for personal use, or loafing on the job. Fourth on the list are management processes and relationships, which can be put at risk when an employee must report to an unethical supervisor, cover for a superior's lies, or face other such uncomfortable situations. Management relationship issues can be especially disturbing because they reflect the moral fiber or culture of the firm, including weaknesses in managerial actions and commitments. Other issues—legal compliance and reporting, supplier relationships, and social and environmental responsibilities—received less attention in the survey than the other categories.

The results of this survey reveal that entrepreneurs must consider the interests of a number of groups when making decisions—owners (or stockholders), customers, employees, the community, and the government. The individuals in these groups are sometimes referred to as stakeholders, indicating that they have a "stake" in the operation of the business. Though definitions vary, **stakeholders** are typically described as those individuals or groups who either can affect the performance of the company or are affected by it.

stakeholders
Individuals or groups who either can affect or are affected by the performance of the company.

Because the interests of various stakeholder groups are different, they sometimes conflict; thus, decisions can be very difficult to make. And because there may not be one completely right or wrong position to take, managing the process can be extremely complicated.[4]

One executive observed that running a business is sometimes like juggling (see Exhibit 2.2). In his words, "I am given four balls to balance: the customers', the employees', the community's, and the stockholders', by which I mean profit. It's never made clear to me how I am to keep them all going, but I know for certain that there is one that I'd better not drop, and that's profit."[5]

As if the job were not already difficult enough, we must add one more ball to the mix—government.[6] Wandering beyond the limits of the law can quickly land a company in hot water, and there is no more certain way to compromise its integrity and its reputation.

EXHIBIT 2.2 Juggling the Interests of Stakeholder Groups and the Government

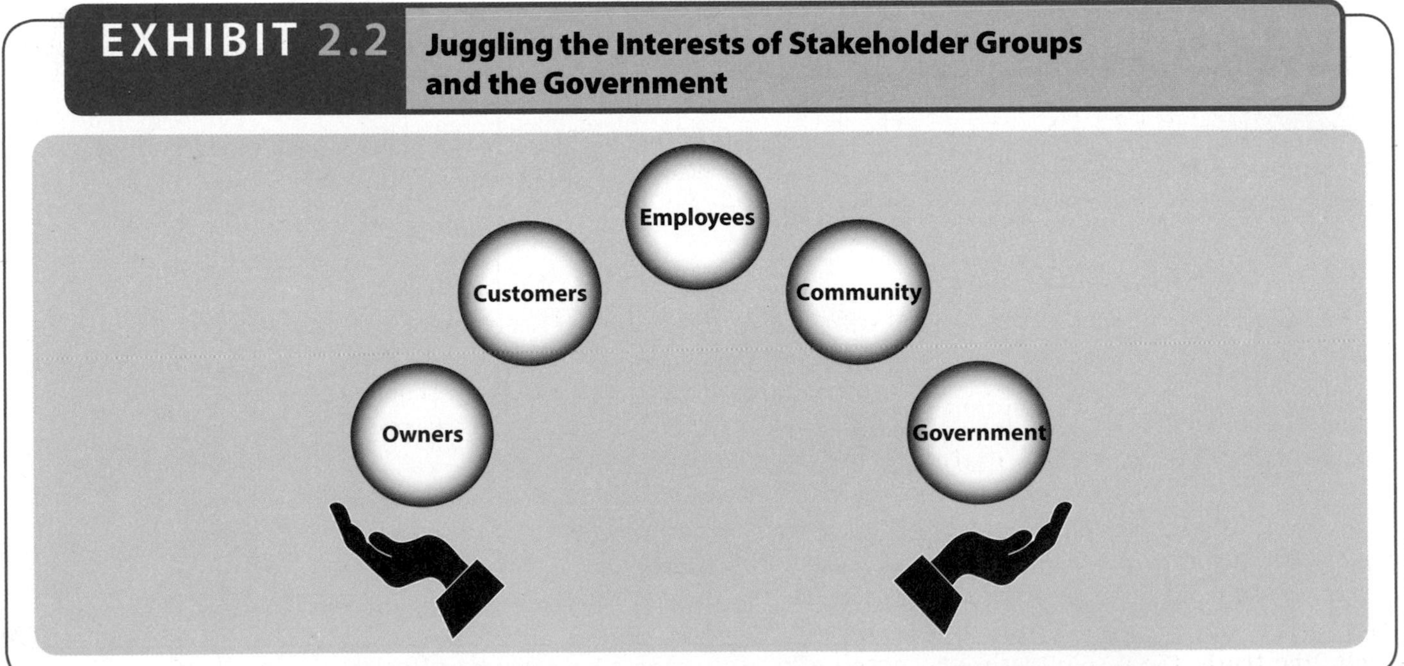

However, the concerns of all of these groups are fundamental to the management of the business. If neglected, any one group can use its influence to negatively affect the performance of the company.

PROMOTING THE OWNERS' INTERESTS

Nobel Prize–winning economist Milton Friedman outlined the responsibilities of businesses to society in very focused terms: "There is only one social responsibility of business—to use its resources and engage in activities designed to increase its profits so long as it stays within the rules of the game, which is to say, engages in open and free competition without deception or fraud."[7]

Friedman argued that businesses should be expected simply to earn profits honestly; any other use of the firm's resources is justified only if it enhances the firm's value. Though we believe there is adequate room for entrepreneurs to adopt a broader view of their social responsibilities, it is undeniable that owners have a clear and legitimate right to benefit from the financial performance of the company.

Many businesses, even small ones, have more than one owner. When this is the case, high standards of integrity require an honest attempt to promote the interests of all the owners, which include a commitment to financial performance and protection of the firm's reputation. But this does not always happen, which Jeff Dennis learned the hard way. In 1989, he and three co-founders started a financial investment company called Ashton-Royce Capital Corporation. When the venture started to take off, two of the partners decided to "check out" and spend a good part of their time in California in semiretirement. This left the two remaining co-founders with more of the day-to-day work of the business and a growing resentment about the unfairness of the situation. In time, the conflict led to the dissolution of what had been a very profitable business.[8] Though entrepreneurs should be able to make their own decisions about personal matters, they have an obligation to make choices that protect the financial investment that others have in the company.

In many small businesses, a number of people own a small part of the enterprise but have no direct involvement in its operation. When this is the case, questions concerning proper conduct can show up in a number of areas. For example, entrepreneurs sometimes face ethical issues when reporting financial information. They must decide the extent to which they will be honest and candid. Because a firm has considerable discretion in reporting performance results, financial reports can sometimes be misleading without technically being illegal. But providing misleading financial information could easily persuade owners to make poor decisions regarding their investment in the company. The same could also be said for some who do not have ownership, outsiders such as bankers and suppliers who depend on a firm's financial reports to be accurate. It is always best to err on the side of honest disclosures that do not tend to mislead; doing so protects critical relationships and the reputation of the firm.

CARING ABOUT CUSTOMERS

What do you call a business without customers? *Bankrupt!* Customers are obviously one of the most important stakeholder groups that a company must please. The fact that they are central to the purpose of any business has implications for integrity. Entrepreneurs who take customers seriously and care about them as individuals are apt to have more of them. And those they have are likely to return often because of that attitude.

It is easy to fall into the habit of seeing every client as merely a dollar sign, but this narrow and self-serving view can lead to a wide range of questionable practices. For example, entrepreneurs are often tempted to take advantage of customers by being less than honest with them. And marketing decisions can be particularly complicated when it comes to ethical issues. Advertising content must sell the product or service but also tell "the truth, the whole truth, and nothing but the truth." Salespeople often must

Photo courtesy of Steelcase, Inc.

walk a fine line between persuasion and deception. In some businesses, a sales representative might obtain contracts more easily by offering improper incentives to buyers or by joining with competitors to rig bids. This is clearly illegal and eventually may result in damage to the company's reputation, which will affect relationships with existing and potential customers.

Caring for customers is always important, but in some cases it can lead to life-or-death consequences. Steelcase, Inc., an office furnishings maker, is explicit about its commitment to integrity and customer care, but this was tested when the company started selling panels that could be used for waist-high office cubicles or be stacked to form floor-to-ceiling walls. Building managers loved them because they offered great flexibility, but there was a problem: The fire standards for full-length walls were more demanding than those for cubicle panels. Many wanted to ignore the oversight—including some very satisfied customers—but Steelcase's CEO, Jim Hackett, recognized that the company's commitment to integrity would require him to recall the defective panels from dealers and replace them with an improved, more fire-retardant product. This was very costly, and Hackett and his executive team lost their bonuses that year. But following the terrorist attacks that destroyed a part of the Pentagon building on 9/11, authorities found that some of the walls installed in that part of the complex were from Steelcase—and fortunately they were made of panels with the added fire-retardant materials. It was determined that these reduced the spread of burning jet fuel, saving many lives and no telling how much pain and suffering.[9] It also allowed Steelcase to avoid some very expensive lawsuits. The company has grown tremendously since it was a small office furnishings startup, but its high standards of integrity and deep concern for customers, as illustrated here, helped to fuel this growth. Though this situation is clearly unique, it shows that a firm's guiding principles sometimes can have a very serious impact on a business and its customers.

Companies with integrity recognize the importance of treating their customers with care, but it should be clear by now that this also just makes good sense. At its core, the formula for business success is actually quite simple: When a company delivers an excellent product with excellent service, customer satisfaction and healthy sales are almost certain to follow. Mike Jacobs, owner of two Wetzel's Pretzels franchises in California, believes his success in the marketplace has come from building employee teams that make things happen. With virtually no turnover since launching his businesses, Jacobs has communicated to his employees how important they are and how their performance impacts the business. In fact, their service orientation generates well over $1.1 million in annual sales.[10] The returns from high-quality customer care are apparent.

VALUING EMPLOYEES

A firm's level of integrity is also expressed by the value it places on employees. Through management decisions, an owner affects employees' personal and family lives. Issues of fairness, honesty, and impartiality are inherent in decisions and practices regarding hiring, promotions, salary increases, dismissals, layoffs, and work assignments. Employees are also concerned about privacy, safety, and health issues, and these should not be ignored.

In communicating with employees, an owner may be truthful and fair, vague and misleading, or totally dishonest. Some entrepreneurs treat outsiders with great courtesy but display demeaning behavior or attitudes toward subordinates, whom they regard as mere pawns in the game of business. Showing proper appreciation for subordinates as human beings and as valuable members of the team is an essential ingredient of managerial integrity. It is also wise, since employees are a firm's most important resource.

Many entrepreneurs recognize the great importance of looking after the needs of their employees, creating a positive work environment and rewarding them generously for their contribution. Tom Rath, a researcher with The Gallup Organization and co-author of the book, *Wellbeing: The Five Essential Elements*, found that workers in well-managed workplaces actually *want* to spend time with their bosses, if those bosses truly care about the individuals they lead and are interested in what's going on in their lives. And when employees feel socially connected at work, they tend to be highly engaged and much more productive.[11] To complete the picture, employees who are loyal to the business naturally want to pour themselves into their work, which leads to high-quality service, very loyal customers, and ultimately, repeat business.[12] Once again, managing with integrity is the right thing to do, but it can also be very good for business.

Tony Hsieh recognized the virtuous cycle involved, a guiding concept that helped him lead online shoe store Zappos from a struggling startup in 1999 to a colossal category superstar worth $1.2 billion just a decade later. In his words,

> *We'd bet that by being good to our employees—for instance by paying for 100 percent of health care premiums, spending heavily on personal development, and giving customer service reps more freedom than at a typical call center—we would be able to offer better service than our competitors. Better service would translate to lots of repeat customers, which would mean lower marketing expenses, long-term profits, and fast growth.*[13]

Hsieh is so committed to supporting his people and protecting interactions with customers that he actually established a policy of paying employees $2,000 to quit if they were unhappy with their jobs. In his mind, forming strong personal and emotional bonds with customers is the surest way to provide unbeatable service, and from there, sales results will naturally follow. Zappos certainly generated plenty of sales, which is why Amazon.com decided to acquire the company on November 1, 2009. Signaling the importance of Hsieh's employee-centered philosophy to the company's success, Amazon asked him to stay on as CEO of the enterprise.[14]

To be sure, small businesses do not always show the level of concern for employees that Zappos expresses—not even within the limits of their resources—and we do not intend to imply that Hsieh's way of taking care of employees is right for every company. But there are many ways that companies can stray from the integrity track. For example, some small business owners give little thought to the standards of conduct that guide everyday behavior, thinking that a shortcut here and there won't hurt anything. But lapses in integrity can easily be passed down from superiors to subordinates, replicating like a life-threatening virus that spreads throughout the organization. As this influence expands, employees of small firms are likely to face pressure from various sources to act in ways that conflict with their own sense of what is right and wrong. For example, a salesperson may be pushed to compromise personal ethical standards in order to make a sale. Or an office employee may feel forced by her or his boss to act unethically, perhaps by destroying documents or misrepresenting production data. Such situations are guaranteed to spawn an organizational culture that erodes integrity.

Ronda Churchill/Bloomberg via Getty Images

LIVING THE DREAM

entrepreneurship + integrity

© iStockphoto.com/Angelika Schwarz

This, That, or the Other

What stakeholder priority should drive the business? Some say companies must follow the Golden Rule—that is, those that hold the gold (owners) make the rules! Others lean on the philosophy that the customer is always right. Or, how many times have you heard someone say that a company's people are its most important resource? There are different answers to the original question.

When it comes to stakeholders, the "Big 3" (owners, customers, and employees) are all supremely important, and balancing their interests can be very challenging. As resources are shifted from one stakeholder group to another, someone is bound to feel slighted. At one time, the hierarchy was very well established, with owners' interests trumping all others. It was understood that the primary purpose of the business was simply to maximize shareholder wealth—period! But many younger companies are adopting a different way of looking at this.

In 1999, Matt Blumberg and Jack Sinclair co-founded Return Path, an e-mail certification company. Their enterprise turned conventional wisdom on its head. Blumberg says that many an investor's eyebrow would raise when he announced, "Our No. 1 stakeholder is our employee base, No. 2 is the customer, and No. 3 is the shareholder." What heresy! But Return Path is far from alone in its philosophy. Companies like Google, Starbucks, Marriott, and Southwest Airlines (which earned first place in four categories in the 2010 Zagat Airline survey) have all taken the same position, and they've become household names. Why stray from a formula that has served business so well for so long? Herb Kelleher, co-founder of Southwest, explains why: "Employees come first, and if you treat them well, they treat customers well. That makes customers keep coming back, and that makes shareholders happy." So, the owners' interests are well taken care of, and everyone is happy in the end. This really is no mystery—it all works beautifully when you see how the pieces fit together.

© Lim Yong Hian/Shutterstock.com

But does this new model work for startups and small businesses as well? It did for these companies, even when they were just getting off the ground. And though small companies may not have deep pockets to support employees like their size-advantaged cousins, keep in mind that the intimacy and close personal relationships that are common in most small-firm workplaces give most workers what they want most—the security of knowing that someone cares about them. In such settings, integrity can truly shine!

Sources: Jason Del Rey, "Prove It," *Inc.*, Vol. 32, No. 5 (June 2010), pp. 72–75; Knowledge@Wharton, "What Makes Southwest Airlines Fly," http://www.wharton.universia.net/index.cfm?fa=viewArticle&id=585& language=english, accessed August 27, 2010; "Employees First: Strategies for Service," Knowledge@W.P.Carey, http://knowledge.wpcarey.asu.edu/article.cfm?articleid=1620, accessed August 27, 2010; and "ReturnNet—Improving the Email Business," http://www.returnpath.net/about, accessed August 27, 2010.

Fortunately, most employees of small firms do not face such expectations, as was discovered by a research team at Baylor University.[15] In a nationwide survey of individuals holding managerial and professional positions in small firms, nearly three-fourths of the respondents (72.3 percent) reported an absence of pressure to compromise personal standards. This is encouraging, but the study also revealed that more than one-fourth of the respondents experienced either slight (24.1 percent) or extreme pressure (3.6 percent) to give in, which leaves room for improvement. The ideal is to develop a business environment in which the best ethical practices are consistently and uniformly encouraged, where employees feel completely free to do what they know is right.

Sometimes, employees may engage in unethical behavior at their employer's expense. They may fail in their ethical obligation to do "an honest day's work." Loafing on the job, working too slowly, and taking unjustified sick leave are all examples of such failure. Some employees even feign injury and draw fraudulent workers' compensation checks, thereby inflating the company's insurance costs.

According to FBI statistics, employees who steal supplies, merchandise, tools, or equipment from work cost employers as much as $150 billion dollars each year,[16] a figure that does not even include losses from embezzlement (that is, when an employee steals money from the firm). These problems are serious, with some experts estimating that one-third of all new businesses fail because of employee theft of one kind or another.[17]

SOCIAL RESPONSIBILITY AND SMALL BUSINESS

To most people, an ethical business is one that not only treats customers and employees honestly but also acts as a good citizen in its community. These broader obligations of citizenship are called **social responsibilities**.

social responsibilities
A company's ethical obligations to the community.

Some regard social responsibility as a price of freedom to operate independently in a free economy. They believe that the public has certain social expectations regarding business behavior, not all of which are required by law. Accordingly, they regard some expenditures on social responsibilities as proper, even when they are costly.

To varying degrees, companies have increasingly accepted responsibility to the communities where they do business. Their contribution starts with creating jobs and adding to local tax revenues, but many entrepreneurs feel a duty to give back even more to the community in return for the local support they enjoy—and they usually benefit from increased goodwill as a result. It is important to recognize that opinions differ as to the extent to which businesses are obligated to engage in socially desirable activities, and the response of small businesses to those obligations also varies. Some emphasize environmentalism, minority contracting, or regional economic development, while others focus their attention on volunteerism, philanthropy, or day care for employees' dependents. Still others give only minimal attention to peripheral social issues.

Examples of Citizenship in the Community

Contributions to the community can take many different forms. Ryan Allis and Aaron Houghton met when they were still students at the University of North Carolina. With combined experience in Web marketing, Web design, and software development, they soon joined forces and started a new company to sell an innovative Web-based e-mail list management tool that Houghton had developed. They called their new venture iContact Corp., and the market loved their product. Because the venture was profitable from its second year in business, Allis and Houghton chose to support charitable enterprises very early on. They established a social responsibility policy called the "4-1s" program. Under the program, iContact gives away 1 percent of its employee time, 1 percent of its payroll, 1 percent of its product, and 1 percent of its equity to worthy nonprofit organizations. In raw numbers, for 2009 alone iContact gave away 475 days of employee time to 63 organizations, contributed $109,000 in cash donations, and allowed 700 nonprofits to use its product free of charge. And with projections for continued growth, these numbers are very likely to increase in the years ahead.

In 1998, David Shapiro and Andrew Sherman started Fluid, an original music, sound design, and visual effects studio located in New York City. Today, the company has more than 20 employees, a growing list of very high-profile clients, and more than $6 million in annual revenues, but the company also does a great deal of pro bono work—that is, free service to the community. Many small businesses encourage their employees to make a difference in the community by donating their time to worthwhile causes, but companies like Fluid want more than just good PR from employee contributions of time and talent—they want maximum impact, which happens best when specific job skills are put to use.[18]

This trend toward "skills-based volunteering" is growing rapidly; in fact, recent research shows that around 40 percent of volunteers look for opportunities to put their specific skill sets to use. The bottom line for Fluid: Nonprofit organizations receive services for free that they would otherwise not be able to afford, and the company's employees give back to their community by doing what they love to do. Now they are all making beautiful music together.[19]

Entrepreneurs should think carefully about their community commitments, because building a business on the foundation of "doing good" may add to a small company's financial burden. However, this is often more than offset by increased loyalty among customers and employees who buy into the mission, which leads to improved productivity and morale. It can also help to set a company apart from competitors that offer similar products or services but make no charitable contributions. Perhaps most important, this commitment is often rewarded by customers in two ways—repeat sales and a willingness to pay a little more for what they get. These are strong incentives for a company to give serious consideration to its dedication to the community.[20]

Differing Views on Social Responsibility

How do small business owners compare with big-business CEOs in their view of social responsibility? The evidence is limited, but research suggests that entrepreneurs who head small, growth-oriented companies may be more narrowly focused on profits and therefore less socially sensitive than CEOs of large corporations. Because simple survival may be the most pressing priority, many small, growing firms see social responsibility as a luxury they simply cannot afford. And in defense of small firm owners, we note that they usually spend their own money rather than corporate funds—it is much easier to be generous when someone else is footing the bill. Small business philanthropy often takes place anyway, but in the form of personal contributions by business owners.

Entrepreneurs must reconcile their social obligations with the need to earn profits. Earning a profit is absolutely essential. Without profits, a firm will not be in a position to recognize its social responsibilities for very long. But meeting the expectations of society can be expensive. For example, small firms must sometimes make expensive changes to conserve energy or emphasize recycling, and auto repair shops incur additional costs when they dispose of hazardous waste responsibly. It is evident that acting in the public interest often requires spending money, which reduces profits. There are limits to what particular businesses can afford.

Fortunately, many types of socially responsible actions can be consistent with a firm's long-term profit objective.[21] Some degree of goodwill is earned by such behavior. A firm that consistently fulfills its social obligations makes itself a desirable member of the community and may attract customers because of that image. Conversely, a firm that refuses its social responsibilities may find itself the target of restrictive legislation or local protests and discover that its customers and employees lack loyalty to the business.

Research conducted by Cone, Inc., a Boston-based strategic marketing firm, revealed that eight out of ten Americans claim corporate support of causes earns their trust in that firm. Eighty-six percent of respondents said they would be very or somewhat likely to switch brands based on corporate citizenship commitments. Carol Cone, CEO of the research firm, concludes, "It's clear from our research that the public wants to know . . . what a company is doing in the community—good and bad."[22] Small businesses seem to be responding to this message. A National Federation of Independent Business study found that 91 percent of small businesses made contributions to their communities through volunteering, in-kind assistance, and/or direct cash donations. The same study reported 74 percent of all small business owners volunteered for community and charitable activities, and the average commitment was just over 12 hours per month (which translates to 18 working days per year).[23] Overall, the evidence on performance impact is far from certain, but it suggests that commitment to the community may very well be good for business.

GOVERNMENTAL LAWS AND REGULATIONS

Government at all levels serves a purpose, though there is room to debate whether it has too much power or too little. It intervenes directly in the economy when it establishes laws to ensure healthy competition. But its reach extends into other business matters as well—workplace safety, equal employment opportunities, fair pay, clean air, and safe products, to name a few. Entrepreneurs must comply with governmental laws and regulations if they are to maintain integrity, and avoid spending time behind bars.

One glaring example of unethical behavior by small firm management is fraudulent reporting of income and expenses for income tax purposes. This conduct includes *skimming*—that is, concealing some income—as well as improperly claiming personal expenses as business expenses. We do not mean to imply that all or even most small companies engage in such practices. However, tax evasion does occur within some of these firms, and the practice is common enough to be recognized as a general problem.

Tax avoidance can be flagrant and very intentional, but entrepreneurs often come up short on their tax commitments because of casual accounting systems, single-minded focus on their product or service, or both. One student entrepreneur confesses that he had a close brush with the law because he and his friends were creating clothing in his dorm room and selling it on his campus, but the company did not legally exist and he was not keeping track of sales and expenses because he didn't take seriously the obligations and advantages of keeping good records. But after a close encounter with Internal Revenue Service (IRS) agents, this young entrepreneur learned that accurate recordkeeping and legal formalities are necessary to ethical practice and, just as important, to peace of mind.[24]

When the topic of tax avoidance comes up, most people think of income taxes, but employee payroll tax—local, state, and federal obligations such as Social Security, Medicare, and unemployment—and other taxes must also be withheld. These often present the biggest tax burden on small businesses because they are owed regardless of whether the company makes a profit or not. And because tax authorities like the IRS do not always push hard enough to collect these taxes, small businesses can easily fall behind.[25]

This is what got Gus Rancatore into trouble. As co-owner of Toscanini's, a popular ice cream shop in Cambridge, Massachusetts, he sometimes struggled just to stay one step ahead of the business. As Rancatore puts it,

> *The bottom line is that, in the day-to-day craziness of running a business that was in danger of going off the rails, I missed tax payments—both employment taxes and my state meals tax. When it came to paying the state on time or making payroll and paying the milkman, I felt I had to worry about taxes second.*[26]

© Mikki Ansin

Getting Assistance from the SBA

If all this talk of laws and regulation and compliance seems daunting, take heart! The Small Business Administration can help (go to http://www.sba.gov and choose the "Starting and Managing a Business" option). The information provided there can help small businesses understand their legal requirements and lead them to helpful government services from federal, state, and local agencies.

This financial neglect went on for some time—but it could not go on forever. Eventually, Rancatore owed the government a crippling $177,000, and there was no way he could come up with that kind of cash on demand. So, on the morning of January 17, 2008, state authorities showed up at the shop, padlocked the door, and put a bright orange "seized" sticker on the window. It was only with the support of friends and loyal customers that Rancatore was able to convince officials to allow him to reopen, and it was a long and painful road back from the financial abyss into which the business had descended.[27] And the damage to Rancatore's reputation is irreversible. Regardless of the circumstances, entrepreneurs must meet *all* tax obligations to preserve their integrity—or even to stay in business.

The Challenges and Benefits of Acting with Integrity

3 Identify challenges and benefits to integrity that arise in small businesses.

Small companies sometimes face unique challenges to maintaining integrity, but the benefits of integrity are real and can offer small businesses a distinct advantage in the marketplace. However, small companies are often vulnerable because of their size and their desire to succeed. We'll discuss how the payoff from managing with integrity can make a small business, and how lack of it can break one.

SMALL COMPANIES AND THE LEGITIMACY LIE

Walking the straight and narrow may be more difficult and costly on Main Street than it is on Wall Street. That is, small, privately held firms that are not part of the corporate world epitomized by Wall Street may face greater pressures than large businesses do to act unethically. Indeed, because small firms usually do not have the deep pockets and superior resources of their larger competitors, entrepreneurs may find it easier to rationalize, say, inappropriate gift giving or bribery as a way of offsetting what seem to be unfair limitations in order to establish a level playing field. And at times it may seem that a "little white lie" is justified when the life and future of the company are at risk. It's easy to cave in to the pressure when your back is against the wall.

Because startups do not have a history and a reputation to lean on when trying to sell customers on their new product or service or to impress other important stakeholders, entrepreneurs often are uniquely tempted to resort to telling what some researchers call "legitimacy lies."[28] That is, they sometimes misrepresent the facts to mislead others intentionally and earn their confidence. How do you feel about the following situations (which actually took place)?

- An entrepreneur launched his own fundraising business in South Carolina with only a few local projects to work on. Profits were slim, but that didn't stop him from telling everyone that business was great. Consistent with this false storyline, he set up an 800 number and launched a website to create an image of greater scale.[29]

- A small business owner who had just started a trucking company in Michigan sometimes used the phone in "creative ways" to shade customer impressions about the business. For example, "she pretended to transfer customers to different lines and used phony voices to make the company seem bigger."[30]

© Waynerd/Dreamstime.com

- Partners in an auto sales startup rented a large lot for their business but could afford only four cars for inventory—a turn-off for would-be buyers. To adapt, the partners offered free parking in their lot to any employee of the big firm next door who would allow them to put a false price tag on their car during the day as if it were for sale. Many accepted, and soon the lot was full every morning and mostly empty by late afternoon. Passersby figured the company must be doing a booming business, and predictably, actual sales soon followed.[31]

When small business owners create false impressions to make their companies look good, are they being dishonest or simply resourceful? While there is nothing wrong with setting up an 800 number or establishing a Web presence to gain scale advantages to compete better against larger competitors, pretending to be something he or she is not is less than forthright and can lead a small business owner into what is, at best, a gray area. The drive and ingenuity of these entrepreneurs is certainly impressive, but their behavior raises questions about ethical standards. Such moves may save companies, but how would customers feel if they knew they were being manipulated in this way?

Telling legitimacy lies threatens the reputation of the business. If (when) the truth is revealed, the news could spread like wildfire and future sales or support could very well be compromised. It would be better—and much more honest—to understand the levers that move customers to confidence in a purchase and provide honest information that backs up your appeal. Research has shown that customers are less likely to decide to purchase if they have significant questions about three features of a new venture—the product or service that it offers, those who represent and/or run the business, and the organization itself.[32] (We call these features PRO factors—standing for *P*roducts, *R*epresentatives, and the *O*rganization—to emphasize that they can promote firm performance when customers are satisfied with them.) Prospective customers may have many different doubts and concerns about these factors, including the following:

- Will the *product* (or *service*) serve my needs better than alternatives, and will it be a hassle to change over from the brand I currently buy? (Research indicates that product/service knowledge is the most important of the three factors when customers make purchase decisions.[33])

- Do the company's *representatives* know what they are talking about, and will they (can they) live up to their assurances?

- Will the *organization* still be around to stand behind its product or service if I have a problem with it six months from now?

Considered in light of your own purchasing decisions, it should be clear that these are all reasonable concerns, and it is important that the new venture find a way to address them. For example, advertising can help to get product or service information out to prospective customers, but this can be expensive, so many new ventures choose to lean on a well-crafted publicity program, social media tools, or other promotional strategies instead (more on these in Chapter 17).

Often a small firm's legitimacy is staked on the reputation of its owner, but it is important to highlight and honestly bolster the credibility of anyone who represents the venture. It is best to make the credentials (educational background, expertise, industry experience, etc.) of key employees known, as well as to encourage the participation of those employees in trade, business, and community organizations where they can build important relationships and associations. The business itself can establish legitimacy by setting up a high-quality website, insisting on professional behavior from all customer-contact employees, forming strategic alliances with well-respected partner firms, and taking other, similar measures. The point is that a new venture or small company may be at a legitimacy disadvantage when compared to established competitors, but there are ways to close the gap. And while the research and our discussion above is concerned specifically with the reactions of customers, many of these principles clearly apply to relationships with investors, suppliers, and other important stakeholders as well.

THE INTEGRITY EDGE

The price of integrity is high, but the potential payoff is incalculable. For example, it is impossible to compute the value of a clear conscience. The entrepreneur who makes honorable decisions, even when it comes to the smallest of details, can take satisfaction in knowing that she or he did what was right, even if things do not turn out as planned.

But integrity yields other important benefits as well. In his book *Integrity Is All You've Got,* Karl Eller observes that through his long career as a successful entrepreneur, he has seen one constant: the crucial role of integrity to achievement in business. As he puts it, "Those who have [integrity] usually succeed; those who don't have it usually fail."[34] Eller suggests that integrity lubricates the important traits of an entrepreneur so that they work harmoniously together, which can give a company an enormous advantage over competitors. Entrepreneurs with integrity are aware of the importance of the bottom line, but this is not their singular focus; nonetheless, extraordinary financial performance often follows their efforts.

A growing body of research supports the notion that ethical business practices are good for business, pure and simple. Citing specific studies, the advocacy group Business for Social Responsibility contends that there are numerous long-term benefits to adopting ethical and responsible business practices. These benefits include the following:[35]

- Improved financial performance
- Enhanced brand image and reputation
- Increased sales and customer loyalty
- Improved productivity and quality
- Better recruitment and reduced employee turnover
- Fewer regulatory inspections and less paperwork
- Improved access to capital

This is consistent with research conducted by the Institute of Business Ethics, which found that firms operating according to a "clear commitment to ethical conduct" consistently outperform those companies that do not. These findings prompted Philippa Foster Black, director of the institute, to declare, "Not only is ethical behavior in the business world the right and principled thing to do, but it has been proven that ethical behavior pays off in financial returns."[36]

Perhaps the greatest benefit of integrity in business is the *trust* it generates. Trust results only when the stated values of a company and its behavior in the marketplace match. When a small business owner looks to the needs of others and follows through on her or his promises, stakeholders notice. Customers buy more of what a firm sells when they realize that the company is doing its best to make sure that its products are of high quality and its customer service is excellent. Employees are much more likely to "go the extra mile" for a small company when it is clear that they are more than simply replaceable parts in an impersonal machine.

And members of the community also respond positively to business integrity. When they are convinced that a firm is living up to its commitments to protect the environment and pay its fair share of taxes, their support can keep the company going even if it falls on hard times. It all comes down to trust. If they conclude that the business is simply taking advantage of them, then all bets are off. There is no substitute for trust, and there is little hope for trust without integrity.

Integrity and the New Economy

4
Describe the impact of the Internet and globalization on the integrity of small businesses.

For the entrepreneur with integrity, decisions are often complicated by developments in the world economy. Businesses that operate across national boundaries must consider the ethical standards that exist in other cultures, which often differ from those of their own country. And firms using the Internet face a host of ethical issues that have arisen in the online marketplace. As small firms move toward international commerce and harness the power of the Internet to launch and sustain their enterprises, these issues become all the more important.

INTEGRITY AND THE ONLINE WORLD

It is not surprising that issues of honesty, deception, and fraud have affected Internet-based businesses, just as they have traditional commerce. It simply follows from the fact that those who buy and sell on the Internet are the same people who participate in all other arenas of the marketplace. One quickly encounters questions of right and wrong in business relationships in every venue.

An issue of great concern to Internet users is personal privacy. Businesses and consumers often disagree about how private the identity of visitors to websites should be. For example, businesses can use cookies (digital "ID tags" that track online activity) to collect data on patterns of usage related to a particular Internet address. In this way, a business may create a detailed profile of customers, which it may then sell to other parties for profit. Internet businesses—and even many of their customers—see the collection of personal information as helpful. A bookseller might, for example, welcome a customer back by name and tell him or her about a special book similar to those the customer ordered previously. To address customer concerns, a number of firms have developed privacy policies—they either will not share personal data or will not share it if the customer requests privacy.

The extent to which an employer may monitor an employee's Internet activity is also hotly debated. Many workers believe it is inappropriate for employers to monitor their e-mail, a practice they consider to be an invasion of privacy. Employers, on the other hand, are concerned that employees may be wasting company time dealing with personal e-mail, shopping online, and surfing the Internet. And it appears there is reason for concern. Business journalist David Freedman reviewed research indicating that accessing the Internet at work for personal reasons is escalating rapidly. In an *Inc.* article, he states,

> *American workers spent the equivalent of 2.3 million years' worth of 40-hour work-weeks reading nonwork-related blogs while at work, according to a study by* Advertising Age *magazine. And that's just blogs. Millions more work years were spent shopping online, checking eBay listings, cruising social networks, looking for vacation deals, Googling old flames, and, of course, ogling porn. [This research indicates that] employers spend nearly $760 billion a year paying employees to goof off on the Web.*[37]

Freedman concluded that this Internet activity is not all bad (for example, everyone needs a break now and then,[38] and an employee who spends time on the Internet can spot emerging trends and bring that insight to his or her work). But many employers are convinced such activity hinders workplace productivity and thus are taking steps to do something about it.[39]

An increasing number of small businesses are installing software to monitor Internet use, and one study found that 38 percent of firms go so far as hiring staff to read or otherwise analyze employees' e-mail.[40] Beyond productivity concerns, companies are very worried these days about deliberate or accidental leaks of sensitive information, employee access to inappropriate content, and system exposure to risky viruses and malware. But these must be balanced against respect for employee privacy. In the past, the courts tended to give firms great freedom to monitor personal e-mail accounts accessed from company networks, but that is quickly changing. In a number of cases, the courts have ruled that a firm does not have a legal right to monitor personal e-mail at work unless it has explicitly informed employees that it may do so.[41] Most small companies choose not to monitor workers' Internet use, but those that do should be sure to develop a carefully worded and legally sound policy first, and then ensure that all employees are aware of it.[42] Taking such measures is very practical—it helps head off costly legal challenges—and it also communicates that the firm respects its employees and signals sound commitment to high standards of integrity.

intellectual property Original intellectual creations, including inventions, literary creations, and works of art, that are protected by patents or copyrights.

Widespread use of the Internet has also focused attention on the issue of protecting **intellectual property**. Traditionally, protection has been granted to original intellectual creations—whether inventions, literary works, or artistic products such as music—in the form of patents, copyrights, trademarks, design rights, and trade secrets. The law allows originators of such intellectual property to require compensation for its use. However, the Internet has made it easy for millions of users to copy intellectual property free of charge.

Protection of intellectual property is a political as well as an ethical issue. Recent congressional hearings, lawsuits, and proposed legislation suggest that additions or changes to current laws are likely, and international enforcement continues to be a major problem. As Internet use continues to grow and practices such as online selling and file sharing are made increasingly easier, it is safe to assume that property rights will become more difficult to protect. Therefore, content providers and other intellectual property owners will have to take stronger measures to guard what is legally theirs.

The problem of intellectual property rights violations was highlighted recently when accusations were leveled against eBay Inc., claiming that the online auction powerhouse was materially responsible for the rise in the sale of counterfeit goods (that is, unauthorized

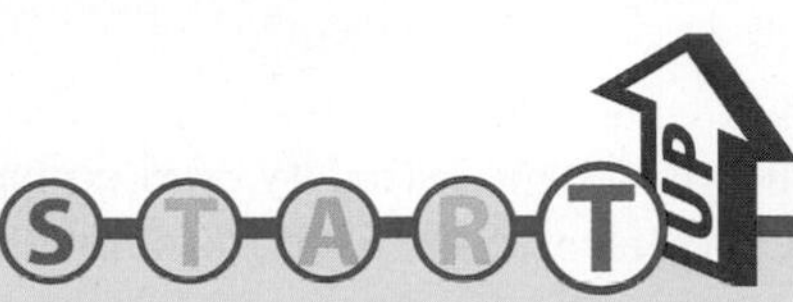

Managing Your Online Reputation

Contrary to the old saying, what you don't know *can* hurt you! With the rising popularity of social media, the chances are good that someone is trashing your company's reputation online. And if they are, it's important that you know about it so you can deal with the potential fallout. Many firms are using tools like Google Alerts, Yext Rep, Viralheat, and Trackur to keep tabs on competitors and scan online customer comments about their business. You can, too, and for some of these tools there is no charge. For more on managing your online reputation, see April Joyner, "Who's Talking about You?" *Inc.*, Vol. 32, No. 7 (September 2010), pp. 63–64.

copies of a legitimate product). *The Economist* provides an idea of how widespread the problem has become:

> *A few years ago sellers on eBay were mostly private individuals flogging second-hand goods. But now eBay is increasingly used by professional retailers selling new items. Many of them sell fakes. [The French company] LVMH claims that out of 300,000 products [labeled] Dior and 150,000 Louis Vuitton handbags offered on eBay in the second quarter of 2006, fully 90% were fake.*[43]

Despite its aggressive fight against counterfeiting, the problem continues to dog the Internet icon. In fact, eBay has already lost lawsuits in Europe to luxury goods makers, though the online company's legal efforts have been more successful in the United States.[44] Regardless of eBay's legal liabilities, it is clear that the sale of counterfeit goods, though increasing, is a violation of the law and a breach of integrity. The practice cannot be defended.

INTERNATIONAL BUSINESS AND INTEGRITY

Every country faces questionable business behavior within its borders, but some must deal with very serious forms of illegal business activity. For example, Italian police raided a Chinese-owned counterfeiting factory in the Tuscan town of Prato and confiscated more than 650,000 fake Gucci and Louis Vuitton handbags and accessories. Many such factories are setting up shop in Tuscany to be close to European consumers and to be able to add a "Made in Italy" label to their goods.[45] Other rogue businesses—some located in the United States—routinely exploit the weak and vulnerable in ways that stray far from ethical practice. For example, some companies exploit labor in countries with weak labor laws in order to procure products at low costs. Though practices of this kind may be tolerated (even encouraged) by local governments, labor activists and human rights organizations have condemned them, and they are increasingly targeted by law enforcement authorities.

In operating abroad, U.S. businesspeople often encounter ethical issues that are clouded by cultural differences. So what are entrepreneurs to do? Frequently, they simply apply U.S. standards to the situation. In some cases, however, this approach has been criticized for resulting in **ethical imperialism**, an arrogant attempt to impose American perspectives on other societies. Some guidance is provided by restrictions specified in the Foreign Corrupt Practices Act, which makes it illegal for U.S. businesses to use bribery in their dealings anywhere in the world. Regardless of local practices, American firms must comply with these laws, even though "gray areas" exist in which there are no definite answers.

ethical imperialism
The belief that the ethical standards of one's own country can be applied universally.

Another viewpoint is embodied in the saying "When in Rome, do as the Romans do." This philosophy, sometimes called **ethical relativism**, is troublesome, because it implies that anything goes if the local culture accepts it. To define its ethical landscape and work out its position on difficult issues, a small business must consider the nuances of its particular international environment. Training is also needed to ensure that each

ethical relativism
The belief that ethical standards are subject to local interpretation.

employee understands the firm's commitment to integrity, and consulting an attorney in the United States with appropriate expertise is highly recommended.

Also, bear in mind that one-time practices may set a pattern for future behavior. Some business owners have observed that offering a bribe to make a business deal possible often creates expectations for more of the same in the future. Owners who refuse to pay these "fees" say that they may have to deal with frustrating inconveniences in the short term (for example, shipped products being held up by customs), but it is likely to discourage such demands in the future. This is one of the ways in which integrity in business may offer unanticipated rewards.

Building a Business with Integrity

5 Suggest practical approaches for building a business with integrity.

The goal of an entrepreneur with integrity is to have a business that operates honorably in all areas, which sets the entrepreneur on the path toward crafting a worthy legacy, as discussed in Chapter 1. This goal is not reached automatically, however. To build a business with integrity, management must provide the leadership, culture, and instruction that support ethical perspectives and appropriate behavior.

THE FOUNDATIONS OF INTEGRITY

underlying values Unarticulated ethical beliefs that provide a foundation for ethical behavior in a firm.

The business practices that a firm's leaders or employees view as right or wrong reflect their **underlying values**. An individual's beliefs affect what that person does on the job and how she or he acts toward customers and others. Talk is cheap (that is, *anyone* can *sound* ethical), but actual behavior provides the best clues to a person's true underlying system of basic values. Business behavior generally reflects the level of a person's commitment to honesty, respect, truthfulness, and so forth—in other words, to integrity in all of its dimensions. Such values are often organized into the business enterprise's mission statement.

Values that serve as a foundation for integrity in business are based on personal views of the role of humankind in the universe and, naturally, are part of basic philosophical and/or religious convictions.[46] In the United States, Judeo-Christian ideals have traditionally served as the general body of beliefs underlying business behavior, although there are plenty of examples of honorable behavior based on principles derived from other religions. Since religious and/or philosophical principles are reflected in the business practices of firms of all sizes, a leader's personal commitment to certain basic values is an important determinant of a small firm's commitment to business integrity.

Entrepreneurs who are deeply committed to underlying standards of integrity operate their businesses in ways that reflect their personal values and ideals. One business that places the entrepreneur's personal values above dollars is Ukrop's Super Markets, a Richmond, Virginia–based grocery chain that does not sell alcohol, closes every Sunday, and donates 10 percent of its profits to charity. Several times, *Fortune* magazine has named Ukrop's in its list of the 100 best companies to work for. And customers are happy with the company's policies, such as having staff carry and load groceries and refusing to take tips for this service.[47]

Steadfast devotion to integrity can lead to many other positive outcomes, as well. For example, a long-time observer of high-tech startups commented on the significance of an entrepreneur's personal standards to investment decisions:

> *I can tell you, even with the smallest high-technology companies, the product had to be good, the market had to be good, the people had to be good. But the one thing that was checked out most extensively by venture capitalists was the integrity of the management*

team. And if integrity wasn't there, it didn't matter how good the product was, how good the market was—they weren't funded.[48]

It seems apparent that a deep commitment to basic values affects behavior in the marketplace and gives rise to business practices that are widely appreciated and admired. Without a strong commitment to integrity on the part of small business leadership, ethical standards can easily be compromised.

LEADING WITH INTEGRITY

In a small organization, the influence of a leader is more pronounced than it is in a large corporation, where leadership can become diffused. This fact is recognized by J. C. Huizenga, the founder and CEO of a public school management company called Heritage Academies, which was ranked as one of the fastest-growing U.S. companies by *Inc.* magazine:

> *The executive of a small company must often face moral challenges more directly, because he or she has more direct contact with customers, suppliers, and employees than an executive in a large corporation who may have a management team to deliberate with. The consequences of his or her choices often affect the business more significantly because of the size of the issue relative to the size of the company.*[49]

The opportunity for establishing high standards of integrity is more apparent in small firms than in large ones. For example, an entrepreneur who believes strongly in honesty and truthfulness can insist that those principles be followed throughout the organization. In effect, the founder or head of a small business can say, "My personal integrity is on the line, and I want you to do it this way." Such statements are easily understood. And a leader becomes even more effective when he or she backs up such statements with appropriate behavior. In fact, a leader's behavior has much greater influence on employees than his or her stated philosophy does. Everyone watches how the leader behaves, and this conduct establishes the culture of the company, underscoring what is allowed or encouraged and what is prohibited.

In summary, the personal integrity of the founder or owner is the key to a firm's ethical performance. The dominant role of this one person (or the leadership team) gives him or her (or the team) a powerful voice in shaping the ethical performance of the small company, for good or for ill. Think about it: Employees owe their position to the founder or owner, so that person wields profound influence deriving from his or her unique position in the organization.

AN ETHICAL ORGANIZATIONAL CULTURE

Integrity in a business requires a supportive organizational culture. Ideally, every manager and employee should instinctively resolve every ethical issue by simply doing what is right. An ethical culture requires an environment in which employees at every level are confident that the firm is fully committed to honorable conduct. To a considerable degree, strong leadership helps build this understanding. As a small business grows, however, personal interactions between the owner and employees occur less often, creating the need to articulate and reinforce principles of integrity in ways that supplement the personal example of the entrepreneur. A good place to start is to establish an ethics policy for the company.

In their highly influential book *The Power of Ethical Management,* Kenneth Blanchard and Norman Vincent Peale offer insights to guide the development of an ethics policy. They suggest that the policy be based on the following five fundamental principles:[50]

- **Purpose.** The vision for the company and your core values will guide business conduct.

- **Pride.** When employees take pride in their work and their company, they are much more likely to be ethical in their dealings.
- **Patience.** If you push too hard for short-term results, sooner or later acting unethically will seem to be the only way to achieve the outcomes you seek.
- **Persistence.** Stand by your word, which is the foundation of trust. If you are not committed to an ethical framework, your integrity is at risk, as is the reputation of the company.
- **Perspective.** Stopping from time to time to reflect on where your business is going, why it is going that way, and how you plan to get there will allow you to be more confident that you are on the right track now and will continue to be in the future.

code of ethics Official standards of employee behavior formulated by a business owner.

To define ethical behavior in the company more specifically, the owner-manager of a small firm should formulate a **code of ethics** similar to that of most large corporations. A survey of MBA students employed by small- and medium-size companies revealed that codes of ethics shape and improve conduct in their organizations in a number of ways: by defining behavioral expectations, by communicating that those expectations apply to employees at all levels in the business, by helping employees convey the company's standards of conduct to suppliers and customers, by serving as a tool for handling peer pressure, and by providing a formal channel for communicating with superiors without fear of reprisal.[51] In other words, a code of ethics identifies conduct that is ethical and appropriate, but it is also a practical tool that can encourage and protect ethical behavior.

A well-written code expresses the principles to be followed by employees of the firm and gives examples of these principles in action. A code of ethics might, for example, prohibit acceptance of gifts or favors from suppliers but point out standard business courtesies, such as a lunch or a couple of movie tickets, that might be accepted without violating the policy.[52] If a code of ethics is to be effective, employees must be aware of its nature and convinced of its importance. At the very least, each employee should read and sign it. As a company grows larger, employees will need training to ensure that the code is well understood and taken seriously.

Entrepreneurs further reinforce ethical culture in the business when they hire and promote ethical people, recognize and correct behavior that is unethical, and lead by example in business dealings, while encouraging all employees to do the same. With training and consistent management, a firm can develop the level of understanding that employees need to act in the spirit of the code in situations not covered by specific rules. However, a code of ethics will be effective only to the degree that the entrepreneur's behavior is consistent with her or his own stated principles. Some business owners are surprised by how readily employees spot hypocrisy, and these double standards quickly dull the ethical sensibilities of the organization.

ACTION

Drafting an Ethical Code

Many small businesses have drafted ethical codes to guide employee behavior. If you are searching for a code on which to model your own, take a look at the "Code of Values" created by the Dwyer Group, a holding company for various service-based franchises. It can be found at http://www.dwyergroup.com/code_of_values.aspx.

BETTER BUSINESS BUREAUS

Sometimes the business conduct of small companies is shaped by external forces. Because unethical operations reflect adversely on honest members of the business community, privately owned companies in many cities have joined together to form Better Business Bureaus (BBBs). The purpose of such organizations is to promote ethical conduct on the part of all businesses in a region, and they do so in the following ways:

- By providing consumers with free information to help them make informed decisions when dealing with a company
- By creating an incentive for businesses to adhere to proper business practices and earnestly address customer complaints
- By resolving questions or disputes concerning purchases through mediation or arbitration

As a result, unethical business practices often decline in a community served by a Better Business Bureau.

Though BBBs report relevant information to law enforcement agencies, they are not government entities, and they cannot collect money or impose penalties on companies that engage in unethical business practices. However, a BBB can provide information on a company's operating track record, which will affect the firm's reputation and, in turn, its success in the marketplace. This creates an incentive for companies to adopt fair and proper business practices and address customer complaints appropriately in order to avoid losing business.

THE ETHICAL DECISION-MAKING PROCESS

Ethical decision making often is not a very clear-cut process. In fact, even after much thought and soul searching, the appropriate course of action still may not be apparent in some business situations. The Ethics Resource Center in Washington, DC, offers a decision-making process that may help with challenging dilemmas. We have adapted this simple six-step decision-making process here to help small business owners see the issues more clearly and make better, ethical decisions.[53]

Step 1: Define the problem

How you define the problem is important because this will guide where you look for solutions. For example, in the case of a student who is consistently late for class, is the problem that he is not managing his time well, he is coming from a classroom that is on the other side of a very large campus, or the professor in the prior class consistently lets him out late? If the student is careless with his time, a penalty for tardiness may correct the problem; however, penalizing the student will not solve the problem if his tardiness is actually the result of one of the other two causes. Looking for the root of the problem is the best place to start in your search for a solution to a challenging ethical problem, whether it is a customer who is slow to settle his accounts or an overseas client who wants to give you a "tip" to overlook a questionable practice.

Step 2: Identify alternative solutions to the problem

It's tempting to go with an "obvious" solution or one that has been used in the past, but often this is not the best answer—even if it is ethical. Be open-minded and consider creative alternatives. Often an innovative solution is available that is consistent with your personal ethics, protects the interests of other affected parties, and offers superior outcomes. Seeking advice from trusted friends and advisors who have faced similar situations can spur your thinking and lead to options that you might otherwise overlook.

Step 3: Evaluate the identified alternatives

Rotary Club International, a worldwide organization of business and professional leaders, has set a high standard for business conduct. It calls on its members to ask the following four questions when they prepare to make a decision about the things they think, say, or do:[54]

1. Is it the **Truth?**
2. Is it **Fair** to all concerned?
3. Will it build **Goodwill** and **Better Friendships?**
4. Will it be **Beneficial** to all concerned?

Taking a similar approach, you might ask yourself, "How would I feel if my decision were reported in the daily newspaper?" Or, the question can be even more personal: "How well could I explain this decision to my mother or children?" The answer could help to steer you away from unethical behavior.

Perhaps the most widely recommended principle for ethical behavior is simply to follow the Golden Rule: "Treat others as you would want to be treated." This simple rule is embraced, in one form or another, by most of the world's religions and philosophies,[55] and its influence is very far reaching. For example, the philosopher Immanuel Kant introduced the so-called categorical imperative, a sophisticated way of asking, "How would it be if everyone decided to do what you intend to do?"[56] Raising questions like these can be a very practical way for an entrepreneur to evaluate ethical decisions and guard her or his integrity.

No matter what approach you take, evaluating alternatives requires time and patience. And to make the exercise even more challenging, personal perceptions and biases are likely to cloud the way you see solutions. Therefore, it is important to separate what you *think* is the case from what you *know* to be true. It often helps to write down your thoughts about alternatives so that you can keep track of your concerns as well as important facts and details. You might list the ethical pros and cons of each alternative or identify the impact of each option on every person or company that will be affected. Another possibility is to rank all potential options based on their overall merits and then narrow the list to the two or three best solutions so that you can consider these further. This will allow you to organize your thoughts and make a better selection.

Step 4: Make the decision

The next step is to choose the "best" ethical response, based on your evaluation of all possible alternatives. On the surface, this sounds easy enough, but unfortunately no single option will completely solve the problem in most cases; in fact, you may not even be able to identify an obvious winner. No matter how you go about making the decision, keep your vision and core values firmly in mind—this is essential to making solid decisions that do not compromise your ethical standards.

Step 5: Implement the decision

This may seem like a "no-brainer," but entrepreneurs sometimes put off responding to ethical challenges because the solution is not apparent or because any response will be bad news for someone involved. But putting off the decision may allow a small problem to grow into a major crisis. Even if the decision is not pressing, delaying your response will cause you to spend more time thinking about the dilemma when other important matters deserve your attention.

Step 6: Evaluate the decision

The goal of making a decision is to resolve an ethical dilemma. So, how has your response panned out? Has the situation improved, gotten worse, or stayed about the same? Has the solution created ethical issues of its own? Has information come to light indicating that your decision was not the most ethical course of action? Everyone makes mistakes. You may very well need to reopen the matter to make things right. But remember, if your decision was based on the best of intentions and information available at the time, you can wade back into the waters of ethical turmoil with a clear conscience, and there is no substitute for that.

Small Business and the Natural Environment

At one time there was little concern for the impact business had on the environment, but that is rapidly changing. For instance, releasing industrial waste into streams, contaminants into the air, and noise into neighborhoods is no longer acceptable. In fact, escalating concern for the environment has spawned a shift toward **sustainable small business**. This movement recognizes that a company must be profitable to stay in business, but it also promotes the use of eco-friendly practices (careful use of resources, energy conservation, recycling, etc.) through all facets of a company's operations. In short, a sustainable enterprise must respond to customer needs while showing reasonable concern for the environment. This is consistent with the concept of integrity outlined in this chapter.

sustainable small business
A profitable company that responds to customers' needs while showing reasonable concern for the environment.

SUSTAINABILITY MATTERS

The interests of small business owners and environmentalists are not necessarily—or uniformly—in conflict. Some business leaders, including many in small companies, have consistently worked and acted for the cause of **environmentalism**, and in many cases this emphasis makes sound financial sense. For example, companies can actually save money by buying or leasing LEED-certified buildings. (This designation stands for "Leadership in Energy and Environmental Design" and is a stamp of approval granted only to those facilities that have been built to strict standards established by the U.S. Green Building Council to promote energy and water conservation, reduce CO_2 emissions, and improve indoor air quality.) Though more expensive to construct, such buildings can decrease energy costs from operations by as much as 20 percent, and healthier workplace environments improve employee productivity, reduce illness and absences, improve recruitment, and raise retention—all of which can create a net savings to the company. One analyst estimates that a 2 percent initial investment in eco-friendly design can generate a 10-fold savings in operating costs.[57] Though actual results may vary, evidence indicates that it "pays green" (money, that is) to "go green," which is obviously good for business.

environmentalism
The effort to protect and preserve the environment.

We need to emphasize, however, that the sustainability news for small business is not all good. For example, some firms are adversely affected by new laws passed to protect the environment. Businesses such as fast lube and oil change centers, medical waste disposal operations, self-service car washes, and asbestos removal services have been especially hard hit by expanding environmental regulations. The costs can be punishing. In fact, many companies in these industries and others have closed because of the financial burden of environmental controls. Small companies that enjoy favorable market conditions can often pass higher environmental costs on to their customers, but these can easily sink a small, struggling firm with older equipment and limited resources to upgrade.

Regardless of the financial impact, it is critical to follow the environmental regulations that apply to your business; to ignore this responsibility is to violate the law. The authors of *Greening Your Business: A Primer for Smaller Companies* caution businesses to comply with regulations at all levels—federal, state, and local—but their overall message is actually very upbeat: "There are dozens of ways companies of all sizes can reduce their environmental footprints, save money, earn consumer trust and stakeholder confidence, comply with government regulations, be ready to snag new market opportunities, and boost efficiency and productivity."[58]

Win-win solutions are possible. For example, firms whose products leave minimal environmental impact are generally preferred by customers over competitors whose products pollute. And some small companies are able to build their business on planet-saving products and services, such as repair shops that service pollution-control equipment on automobiles. Furthermore, compliance with environmental regulations may actually lead to unexpected benefits, such as a reduction in paperwork for companies that can show they are in line with regulations. In any case, assistance is available to help with all of this. The Small Business Administration is prepared to lead you through the sometimes choppy waters of environmental law, and the U.S. Environmental Protection Agency (EPA) offers the Small Business Gateway, an Internet portal that will connect you to information, technical assistance, and solutions to challenges related to the environment. Also, the EPA provides online access to a guide called *Managing Your Hazardous Waste: A Guide for Small Businesses,* which makes compliance much easier to manage.[59] Taking advantage of such resources can help you avoid the potentially disastrous consequences of noncompliance.

GREEN OPPORTUNITIES FOR SMALL BUSINESS

Although they add to the cost of doing business for some small companies, environmental concerns open up great opportunities for others. In fact, many startups have come to life precisely because of "the greening of business" and the potential opportunities that this has created.

The flow of investment dollars into ventures based on technologies that are labeled "green," "clean," "sustainable," or "environmental" has been rapidly increasing in recent years, and this trend has led to the launching of many new and innovative eco-focused startups.[60] Some of these businesses are based on sophisticated technologies that run well beyond the reach of the typical small business. However, many opportunities in this category are very accessible to small companies and startups. Here are a few recent green startup stories to inspire you to think about new venture possibilities that could be right for you.

Boo Bicycle

Over 18 months of research and development at Princeton University resulted in high-performance, expertly engineered bamboo bicycles. Every frame is handmade and requires 50 hours of labor.

- Bamboo is one of the world's fastest-growing plants, and a number of new ventures have sprouted up to make bicycles out of the sturdy stuff. Nick Frey is one of the many entrepreneurs who hope to cash in on the trend. As owner of Boo Bicycles, Frey builds and sells high-performance bikes with bamboo frames, and business is good. His prices range from $3,000 for a basic frame to $10,000 for a tricked-out racer—he even sold a frame recently as art to a Spanish gallery![61] But beyond aesthetics, the company's website points out that "The ride quality of bamboo is unmatched . . . stiff and light, but the smoothest riding material on the market."[62] The product definitely turns heads—and opens wallets, too.

- Joey Santley and Steve Cox launched a company in 2009 called Green Foam Blanks in San Clemente, California, with the goal of overturning half a century of surfboard-making tradition. They developed an innovative process that allowed them to be the first to produce and sell a recycled polyurethane blank (the foam core inside a surfboard) that lacks the cancer-causing materials that all other makers use. Recent demand has been so strong that the business is struggling to keep up with it.[63]
- When Warren Paul Anderson learned that few tools are available to track water use accurately in a world where 1.1 billion people lack sufficient access to clean drinking water, he started a new business to do something about it. His company, Hydrolosophy, creates software that allows firms to monitor and reduce their water usage by spotting inefficiencies.[64] Firms of all sizes like the product and are signing up to cut their utility costs and conserve natural resources at the same time.

Interest in the sustainability trend varies. For a growing number of small business owners, the ultimate goal is to save the planet; others recognize that sustainable business practices can hold down costs, attract customers, and generate value for shareholders. According to Stuart L. Hart, a professor of strategy at the University of North Carolina, the movement will provide huge opportunities for companies with "moxie" and creativity, as long as they can execute the plan.[65] This sounds like prime territory for small entrepreneurial companies, given their flexibility and innovative thinking. Entrepreneurs may be able to do well *and* do good—guarding the environment and their integrity at the same time.

1. Define *integrity*, and understand its importance to small businesses.

- Integrity is an uncompromising adherence to the lofty values, beliefs, and principles that an individual claims to hold.
- "Doing anything for money" can quickly lead to distortions in business behavior.
- Many small business owners strive to achieve the highest standards of honesty, fairness, and respect in their business relationships.

2. Explain how integrity applies to various stakeholder groups, including owners, customers, employees, the community, and the government.

- Closely tied to integrity are ethical issues, which go beyond what is legal or illegal to include more general questions of right and wrong.
- The most troublesome ethical issues for small businesses involve relationships with customers and competitors, human resource decisions, employee obligations, and relationships with management.
- When they make business decisions, entrepreneurs must consider the interests of all stakeholder groups, in particular those of owners, customers, employees, the community, and the government.
- A company's owners have a clear and legitimate right to benefit from the financial performance of the business.
- Those companies who take customers seriously and serve them well are likely to have more of them.
- Showing proper appreciation for employees as human beings and as valuable members of the team is an essential ingredient of managerial integrity. Research shows that about one-fourth of the employees in small businesses experience some degree of pressure to act unethically in their jobs.
- Most people consider an ethical small business to be one that acts as a good citizen in its community.
- Entrepreneurs must obey governmental laws and follow applicable regulations if they want to maintain their integrity and avoid jail time.

3. **Identify challenges to integrity that arise in small businesses, and explain the benefits of integrity to small firms.**
   - The limited resources of small firms make them especially vulnerable to allowing or engaging in unethical practices.
   - Startups and small companies sometimes resort to telling "legitimacy lies," but they can win customers and attract other important stakeholders by paying especially close attention to the PRO factors (those related to the firm's products, its representatives, and the organization itself).
   - Research suggests that most entrepreneurs exercise great integrity, but some are likely to cut ethical corners when it comes to issues that directly affect profits.
   - Exhibiting integrity in business can boost a firm's performance along a number of dimensions.
   - Perhaps the greatest benefit of integrity is the trust it generates.

4. **Describe the impact of the Internet and globalization on the integrity of small businesses.**
   - Use of the Internet has highlighted ethical issues such as invasion of privacy and threats to intellectual property rights.
   - Cultural differences complicate decision making for small firms operating in the global marketplace.
   - The concept of ethical relativism is troublesome because it implies that anything goes if the local culture accepts it.

5. **Suggest practical approaches for building a business with integrity.**
   - The underlying values of business leaders and the behavioral examples of those leaders are powerful forces that affect ethical performance.
   - An organizational culture that supports integrity is key to achieving appropriate behavior among a firm's employees.
   - Small firms should develop codes of ethics to provide guidance for their employees.
   - Many small companies join Better Business Bureaus to promote ethical conduct throughout the business community.
   - Following an ethical decision-making process can help entrepreneurs protect their integrity and that of their business.

6. **Define *sustainable small business*, and describe the influence this trend is having on the management of small companies and startup opportunities.**
   - A sustainable small business is a profitable company that responds to customer needs while showing reasonable concern for the natural environment.
   - Some small firms, such as fast lube and oil change centers, are adversely affected by costly environmental regulations.
   - Win-win outcomes are possible in many cases—the cost of eco-friendly business practices can often be more than offset by operational savings, increased customer interest, reduced paperwork, etc.
   - The SBA, EPA, and other public and private resources stand ready to help small businesses comply with environmental regulations.
   - Small companies are sometimes launched precisely to take advantage of opportunities created by environmental concerns.Creating environmentally friendly products and services requires creativity and flexibility, areas in which small businesses tend to excel.

Key Terms

integrity p. 38
ethical issues p. 39
stakeholders p. 40
social responsibilities p. 45
intellectual property p. 52
ethical imperialism p. 53
ethical relativism p. 53
underlying values p. 54
code of ethics p. 56
sustainable small business p. 59
environmentalism p. 59

Discussion Questions

1. The owner of a small business felt an obligation to pay $15,000 to a subcontractor, even though, because of an oversight, the subcontractor had never submitted a bill. Can willingness to pay under these circumstances be reconciled with the profit goal of a business in a free enterprise system?
2. Give an example of an unethical business practice that you have personally encountered.
3. Based on your experience as an employee, customer, or observer of a particular small business, how would you rate its ethical performance? On what evidence or clues do you base your opinion?

4. Give some examples of the practical application of a firm's basic commitment to supporting the family life of its employees.
5. What is skimming? How do you think owners of small firms might attempt to rationalize such a practice?
6. What are some of the advantages of conducting business with integrity? Some people say they have no responsibility beyond maximizing the value of the firm in financial terms. Can this position be defended? If so, how?
7. Explain the connection between underlying values and integrity in business behavior.
8. Why might small business CEOs focus more attention on profit and less on social goals than large business CEOs do?
9. Give some examples of expenditures required on the part of small business firms to protect the environment.
10. Should all firms use biodegradable packaging? Would your answer be the same if you knew that using such packaging added 15 percent to the company's cost of producing a product?

You Make the Call

SITUATION 1

Sally started her consulting business a year ago and has been doing very well. About a month ago, she decided she needed to hire someone to help her since she was getting busier and busier. After interviewing several candidates, she decided to hire the best one of the group, Mary. She called Mary on Monday to tell her she had gotten the job. They both agreed that Mary would start the following Monday and that she could come in and fill out all the hiring paperwork at that time.

On Tuesday of the same week, a friend of Sally's called her to say that she had found the perfect person for Sally. Sally explained that she had already hired someone, but the friend insisted. "Just meet this girl. Who knows, maybe you might want to hire her in the future!"

Rather reluctantly, Sally consented. "Alright, if she can come in tomorrow, I'll meet with her, but that's all."

"Oh, I'm so glad. I just know you're going to like her!" Sally's friend exclaimed.

And Sally did like her. She liked her a lot. Sally had met with Julie on Wednesday morning. She was everything that Sally had been looking for and more. In terms of experience, Julie far surpassed any of the candidates Sally had previously interviewed, including Mary. On top of that, she was willing to bring in clients of her own which would only increase business. All in all, Sally knew this was a win-win situation. But what about Mary? She had already given her word to Mary that she could start work on Monday.

Source: http://www.sba.gov/smallbusinessplanner/manage/lead/SERV_BETHICS.html, accessed September 30, 2010.

Question 1 What decision on Sally's part would contribute most to the success of her business?
Question 2 What ethical reasoning would support hiring Mary?
Question 3 What ethical reasoning would support hiring Julie?

SITUATION 2

Darryl Wilson owns Darryl's Deals on Wheels, a small used car dealership in Humble, Texas. Wilson started the company three years ago, but he is still struggling to get a solid footing in the industry. The down economy isn't helping—no one seems to have money to buy cars right now—and there is plenty of competition. The business provides the main source of income for his family, which includes his wife and two teenage daughters, whose needs seem to grow by the day. Wilson has to make this business work to keep food on the table and to pay the typical expenses involved in raising a family.

Finding customers is essential to success in the car sales business, but so is holding down costs. This means Wilson has to find "rolling stock" that is in demand and inexpensive, but that is not easy to do because all the other dealers in his area are in the same boat. They, too, are trying to snap up the best deals, and this is driving up the cost of inventory. So, controlling costs means looking at other features of the business, and Wilson thinks he has found something that just may help. The state of Texas requires dealers to report the purchase of all vehicles they acquire for resale, which means the dealer will have to pay a 2.5 percent inventory tax (based on the purchase price) when it sells the car later. But when Wilson buys a car from a private seller, he can usually convince him or her to sign over the title without designating a specific buyer. This allows Wilson to fill in that part of the title and the transfer form with the name of the person who buys the car from him, when that time comes. In the end, the state has no evidence of Wilson's involvement in the transaction, which allows him to avoid paying administrative fees and the inventory tax—a savings of about $250 on a typical sale. As he puts it, "It's like finding money on the sidewalk!" The state doesn't catch on, and his customers never seem to notice because they have to pay administrative fees and sales tax anyway when they buy the car and transfer the title into their own names.

So far Wilson has not run into any problems with this practice. In his mind, this is nothing more than "heads-up business." Furthermore, his profits are so slim right now that playing by the book would probably mean that he would have to go out of business. How would that help anyone? Even the state would lose money then, because a company that is out of business pays no income taxes and Wilson would have to start collecting unemployment.

Question 1 What are the advantages and possible drawbacks to Wilson's title-transfer scheme?
Question 2 Which stakeholders are affected by this approach, either positively or negatively? How great are their gains/losses?
Question 3 Wilson finds it hard to identify a downside to his approach, and so far it is working like a charm. What risks might he be overlooking?
Question 4 What would you do if you were in Wilson's shoes? If his competitors are following the same practice (and some of them surely are), would that make any difference to you?

SITUATION 3

WizeGuyz Media, a small marketing firm, ordered key chains for a client named Bob Whitaker. The key chains were imprinted with three initials related to the theme of an advertising campaign created specifically for Whitaker's automobile sales business. The client approved the artwork but then, upon delivery, noticed there was no period after the last letter. Whitaker asked for a price adjustment and the owner of WizeGuyz responded by asking what he considered to be a reasonable discount. Whitaker still wanted the key chains but proposed that WizeGuyz pay $3,000 of the bill, which was 65 percent of the total cost.

Question 1 Is this a customer relations problem or an ethics problem?
Question 2 Is Whitaker's request reasonable?
Question 3 Should WizeGuyz accept the proposed settlement?

Experiential Exercises

1. Examine a recent business periodical online, and report briefly on some lapse in integrity that is in the news. Could this type of problem occur in a small business? Explain.
2. Employees sometimes take sick leave when they are merely tired, and students sometimes miss class for the same reason. Separate into groups of four or five, and prepare a statement on the nature of the ethical issue (if any) in these practices.
3. With a current or previous employer in mind, write a simple code of ethics that would show due regard for the interests of all of the company's primary stakeholders (most notably the owners, customers, employees, the community, and the government). How difficult was it to protect and balance the concerns of these groups in the code that you came up with? Report briefly on your findings.
4. Search for "top environmental concerns" on the Internet and select five concerns that seem to be most relevant to small business. Analyze these to determine how they will shape business practice in small firms over the next decade. Then, identify five to ten new venture opportunities that could be created based on the concerns you select. Explain your findings and recommendations.

Small Business & Entrepreneurship Resource Center

The Small Business and Entrepreneurship Resource Center offers complete small business management resources through a comprehensive database that covers all major areas of starting, operating, and maintaining a business from financing, management, marketing, accounting, taxes, and more. Use the access code that came with your new book to access the site and perform the exercises in each chapter.

1. Craig Hall, the author of *The Responsible Entrepreneur*, encourages small business owners to practice what he calls "responsible entrepreneurship." His company donates 5 percent of its income to charity, and

any employee can take off up to 40 hours per year to work with charitable organizations. He believes that being responsible is vital to business success. Describe what is meant by the term "responsible entrepreneur" and the ways in which you feel that entrepreneurs can "make a difference."

2. An executive once observed that running a business is sometimes like juggling. In his words, "I am given four balls to balance: the customer's, the employees', the community's, and the stockholders', by which I mean profit. It's never made clear to me how I am to keep them all going, but I know for certain that there is one that I'd better not drop, and that's profit."

   Hall Office Park has been built by Hall Financial Group in an effort to redefine the typical office environment and promote corporate responsibility toward employees. After reading these two articles, describe what Hall Office Park offers, and how you feel it contributes to social responsibility.

Sources: Entrepreneurs make a difference. (Interview). (Craig Hall)(Interview). *Journal of Property Management* 67.3 (May 2002): p72(2).

Redefining the office. (The Buzz). (Hall Office Park amenities)(Brief Article). *Buildings* 96.1 (Jan 2002): p6(1).

Video Case 2

PORTIONPAC CHEMICALS (P. 696)

PortionPac® manufactures highly concentrated, premeasured cleaning products that reduce the resources used throughout the life cycle of its products and provide sustainable, cost-effective, and environmentally friendly solutions. This case discusses PortionPac's progressive leadership, user-centric educational services, and innovative products and packaging—that all result in integrity and ethical behavior toward various stakeholder groups, including customers, employees, and the community.

ALTERNATIVE CASES FOR CHAPTER 2

Case 1, Nau, p. 693

Case 20, Salary Envy, p. 732

STARTING FROM SCRATCH OR JOINING AN EXISTING BUSINESS

PART 2

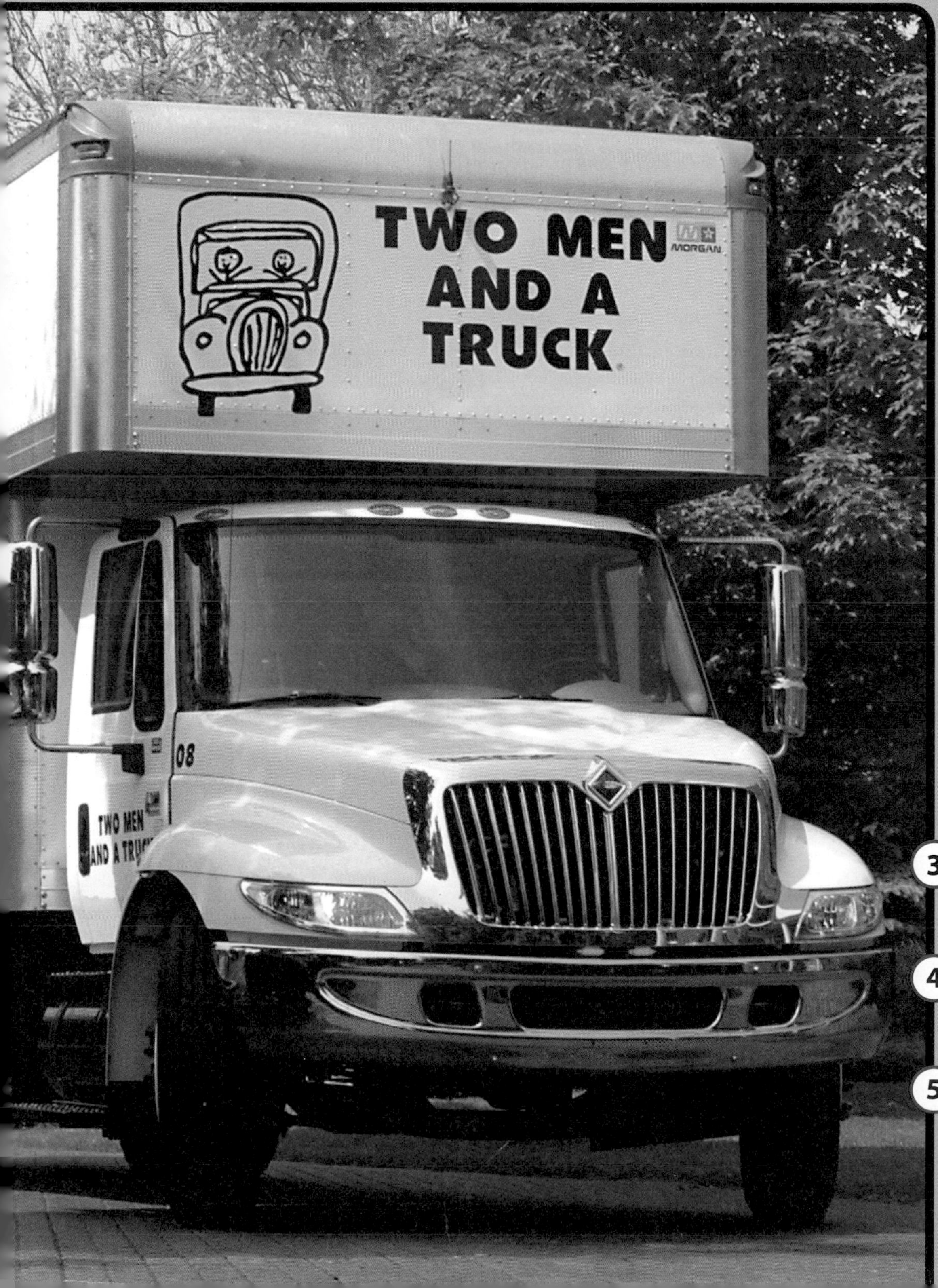

Two Men and a Truck

CHAPTERS

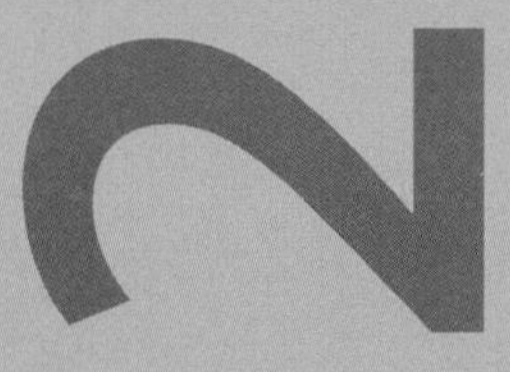

Starting a Small Business

In the SPOTLIGHT
Shorts International
http://www.shortsinternational.com

Every great business begins with a high-potential business idea. Carter Pilcher was pursuing a career in investment banking when he stumbled upon what he considers to be an amazing "video playground" in short films. "I just felt like I'd discovered a part of the world of content that didn't take a lot of money to create but was really riveting," says Pilcher, an American who was working in London at the time. "In 10 minutes, you're in tears, or you're shocked, or [you're laughing] really hard."

These short works don't take a lot of money to make, but at the same time they are notorious for not making any money. This segment of the industry is filled with wannabe filmmakers who can survive on fame without fortune (since profits are hard to come by).

Creatas Images/Jupiter Images

Pilcher, however, came up with an idea for a startup that would tweak that formula, if even just a bit. His new business, Shorts International, would buy the rights for these brief works of video art from their creators and make money by showing or distributing them through various channels. This would give aspiring filmmakers access to a much larger market, while making it possible to generate enough profits for Pilcher's company to grow. Based on this simple business model, Pilcher launched his new enterprise.

By the company's formula—which pays only a few hundred dollars over several years for each short movie—no content creator is going to get rich, but some return on investment in such a project is better than none. And the real value is in the exposure Shorts International provides. No one walks off the street into a Hollywood studio and gets a big-time director's gig; it takes a track record to get started, and Shorts International makes it

After studying this chapter, you should be able to . . .

1. Distinguish among the different types and sources of startup ideas, and identify the most common sources of startup ideas.
2. Use innovative thinking to generate ideas for high-potential startups.
3. Describe external and internal analyses that might shape the selection of venture opportunities.
4. Explain broad-based strategy options and focus strategies.
5. Assess the feasibility of a startup idea before writing a business plan.

LOOKING AHEAD

© iStockphoto.com/Dan Bachman

possible to get that footing. Newbies in the industry may still feel slighted when they see how small their royalty checks are ("Ridiculous!" was how one director put it), but they are still signing up with the company because of the increased visibility they get from the service.

So far, this experiment in the media industry seems to be working well. Already, Shorts International holds the rights to more than 3,000 short movies that it can distribute across various platforms. For example, the company offers ShortsHD™ (a high-definition TV channel offered on Dish Network in the United States), ShortsTV™ (a pay TV channel available in the United Kingdom, France, Turkey, and elsewhere), and Shorts™, which provides a movie-on-demand service through iTunes Stores in a number of countries. And when it comes to the creation of innovative content, the company stands ready to help with production through its Shorts Studio™ service. But how is this new enterprise panning out? We have no numbers to go by, but with offices in London, Paris, New York, and Los Angeles, it appears that Shorts International is off to a very impressive start.

Sources: "Shorts International—About," http://www.shortsinternational.com, accessed October 15, 2010; and Ryan Nakashima, "Entrepreneur Finds Audience for Short Filmmakers," September 6, 2010, http://abcnews.go.com/Technology/wireStory?id=11568333, accessed October 15, 2010.

An undeniable fact of life is that entrepreneurs keep coming up with innovative ways of doing things, and the new businesses they create often change the way we live. But to get the ball rolling in the right direction, an entrepreneur must be able to recognize high-potential startup ideas that others have overlooked. This is precisely what Carter Pilcher was able to do when he came up with the concept for Shorts International, which is profiled in the opening Spotlight feature. We should emphasize that identifying imaginative new products or services that may lead to promising business ventures is so central to the entrepreneurial process that it has its own name: **opportunity recognition**.

opportunity recognition Identification of potential new products or services that may lead to promising businesses.

Business opportunities are like air—they are always around, even though you may not realize it. What sets entrepreneurs apart from everyone else is their ability to see the potential that others overlook and then take the bold steps necessary to get businesses up and running. How do they do it? Most entrepreneurs have uncommon observational skills and the motivation to act on what they see. In some cases, the identification of a new business opportunity may be the result of an active search for possibilities or insights derived from personal experiences or work background. In other cases, the search for opportunities may be a less deliberate and more automatic process.[1] Economist Israel Kirzner proposed that entrepreneurs have a unique capability, which he called **entrepreneurial alertness**. According to this view, entrepreneurs are not actually the source of innovative ideas; rather, they are simply "alert to the opportunities that exist *already* and are waiting to be noticed."[2] When these opportunities are aligned with an entrepreneur's knowledge, experience, and aspirations, they are even more likely to be spotted.

entrepreneurial alertness Readiness to act on existing, but unnoticed, business opportunities.

A discussion of the finer points of entrepreneurial alertness is beyond the scope of this book, but it is important to understand that thinking about the world around you and being aware of conditions that might lead to new business opportunities can really pay off.[3] Try it for yourself and see if new possibilities for a business become apparent. Over the next week or so, take note of trends, changes, or situations that might support a new business. Jot them down, and then tally them up. You will probably be surprised at how many potential opportunities you can identify. If you continue this rather deliberate search, over time you may find that it becomes a habit.[4]

TOOLS

Mindfulness and Opportunity Recognition

Going beyond Kirzner's concept of alertness, Andrew C. Corbett and Jeffery S. McMullen introduce the practice of "mindfulness" to the opportunity recognition discussion. Unlike alertness, mindfulness can be learned, and they provide some tools to help you pick it up. For more on this concept and to see a questionnaire that can help you measure your levels of mindfulness in everyday experiences, see their chapter called "Perceiving and Shaping New Venture Opportunities Through Mindful Practice," in Andrew Zacharakis and Stephen Spinelli, Jr. (eds.), *Entrepreneurship: The Engine of Growth* (Westport, CT: Praeger Perspectives, 2007), pp. 43–64.

Perhaps you already have a business idea in mind that you would like to pursue. With good planning and the right strategy, you may soon be on your way to success as an entrepreneur. On the other hand, you may have a passionate desire to start your own company but are not sure that you have locked onto the right business idea to get you there. Or maybe you have an *idea* in mind but are not sure if it is a good *business opportunity*. No matter which group you fall into, this chapter will help to get you started on the right foot, with the right idea and the right strategy.

In Part 1 of this book (Chapters 1 and 2), we discussed the mindset and lifestyle of the entrepreneur and the importance of integrity in any business. Now, in Part 2, we focus on topics that can help individuals decide what kind of venture would be best for them.

startups New business ventures created "from scratch."

In this chapter, we focus mostly on opportunity recognition and strategy options as these apply to **startups**—that is, businesses that did not exist before entrepreneurs created them. However, the chapters that follow will go beyond a discussion of new ventures "started from scratch" and consider business opportunities that already exist, such as purchasing a franchise or buying an existing business (Chapter 4) or joining a family business (Chapter 5). These can all be high-potential options. As you read this chapter, keep in mind that many of the insights and strategies described here also apply to ongoing small businesses, not just to startups.

Coming Up with Startup Ideas

As outlined in Chapter 1, you may choose to become an entrepreneur for any of a number of different reasons. But several motivations may lead you to consider starting an enterprise from scratch rather than pursuing other alternatives. For example, you may have a personal desire to develop the commercial market for a recently invented or newly developed product or service, or you may be hoping to tap into high-potential resources that are uniquely available to you—an ideal location, new equipment technologies, a powerful network of connections, and so forth. Some entrepreneurs get "startup fever" because they want the challenge of succeeding (or failing) on their own, or they hope to avoid undesirable features of existing companies, such as unpleasant work cultures or smothering legal commitments. There are almost as many reasons as there are aspiring entrepreneurs!

So how do you get started? It all begins with a promising business idea. But new venture concepts are not all equal, and they can come from many different sources. By recognizing the nature and origin of startup ideas, an entrepreneur can broaden the range of new ideas available for his or her consideration.

TYPES OF STARTUP IDEAS

Exhibit 3.1 shows the three basic types of ideas from which most startups are launched: ideas to enter new markets, ideas based on new technologies, and ideas that offer new benefits. Each of these has its own unique features.

Numerous startups develop from what we will call **Type A ideas**—those concerned with providing customers with a product or service that does not exist in a particular market but that exists somewhere else. Randall Rothenberg, an author and the director of intellectual capital at the consulting firm Booz Allen Hamilton, says that this type of startup idea may have the greatest potential: "There's ample evidence that some of the biggest businesses are built by taking existing ideas and applying them in a new context."[5]

Type A ideas
Startup ideas centered around providing customers with an existing product or service not available in their market.

Many small businesses are built on this platform. Filmmaker Christian D'Andrea was making a documentary on Special Operations forces when he saw a soldier chomping down a U.S. military–issued energy bar that was developed specifically to provide the extra boost that those in uniform need on the battlefield. D'Andrea recognized an opportunity to take the product, which civilians couldn't buy, to a whole new market. He and his brother, Mark, signed a deal giving them license to tap the science behind the product, and they used it to create the "Hooah! Bar" (since renamed "Soldier Fuel," so that civilians would understand the name). Today, this pick-me-up snack sells in thousands of stores and online outlets. Business is good, and growing; in fact, their Los Angeles–based startup, D'Andrea Brothers, LLC, recently expanded its product line to include an energy drink based on the same formulation. With sales continuing to climb, it's clear that tapping "military intelligence" to take an existing product to the civilian market can yield impressive results.[6]

Type B ideas
Startup ideas involving new or relatively new technology, centered around providing customers with a new product.

Courtesy of Christian D'Andrea

Some startups are based on **Type B ideas**, which involve new or relatively new technology. This type of business can be high risk because there is usually no model of success to follow, but it can also have tremendous potential. Rick Alden

EXHIBIT 3.1 Types of Ideas That Develop into Startups

Type A Ideas	Type B Ideas	Type C Ideas
New Market	New Technology	New Benefit
Example: Targeting the "New Age" beverage market by selling soft drinks with nutritional value	Example: Using high-tech computers to develop a simulated helicopter ride	Example: Developing a personal misting device to keep workers cool

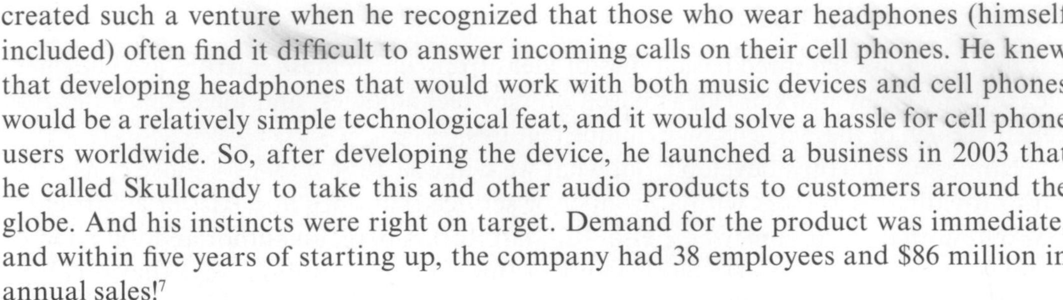

created such a venture when he recognized that those who wear headphones (himself included) often find it difficult to answer incoming calls on their cell phones. He knew that developing headphones that would work with both music devices and cell phones would be a relatively simple technological feat, and it would solve a hassle for cell phone users worldwide. So, after developing the device, he launched a business in 2003 that he called Skullcandy to take this and other audio products to customers around the globe. And his instincts were right on target. Demand for the product was immediate, and within five years of starting up, the company had 38 employees and $86 million in annual sales![7]

Type C ideas
Startup ideas centered around providing customers with new or improved products or services.

Type C ideas—those based on offering customers benefits from new and improved products or ways of performing old functions—account for a large number of startups. Many new ventures, especially in the service industry, are founded on "me, too" strategies, but they usually set themselves apart through features such as superior service or lower prices. Laurie Johnson's effort to redefine the common crutch fits into the Type C category. As founder of LemonAid Crutches, Johnson found a way to take some of the sting out of having to be on crutches after an injury. Her designer props were born from experience. While Johnson was recovering from a broken leg sustained in a small-plane crash that took the lives of her husband and two-year-old son, her sister tried to brighten her day by spray painting her crutches and trimming the handles in fabric. Her response? "I sat there thinking, 'Oh my gosh, this is so silly, but they make me feel better!'" Determined to turn life's lemons into lemonade (hence, the name of the company), Johnson decided to run with the concept and help other crutch users feel better, too. In mid-2005, she launched her venture to sell a variety of fashionably functional crutches, and sales have been so good that Johnson's startup is now on a solid footing.

COMMON SOURCES OF STARTUP IDEAS

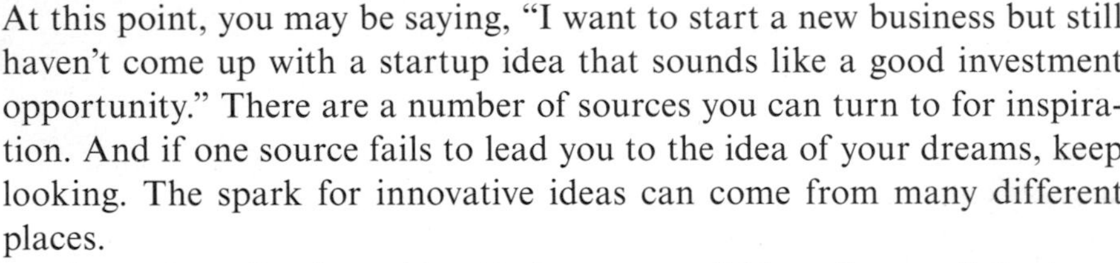

At this point, you may be saying, "I want to start a new business but still haven't come up with a startup idea that sounds like a good investment opportunity." There are a number of sources you can turn to for inspiration. And if one source fails to lead you to the idea of your dreams, keep looking. The spark for innovative ideas can come from many different places.

Several studies have identified sources of ideas for small business startups. Exhibit 3.2 shows the results of one such study by the National Federation of Independent Business (NFIB), which found that prior work experience accounted for 45 percent of new ideas. This finding is consistent with another national study of entrepreneurs, the Panel Study of Entrepreneurial Dynamics (PSED). The PSED data also show that entrepreneurs most often consider work experience in a particular industry or market to be the source of their startup ideas.[8] However, there are other important sources. As confirmed in the exhibit, the NFIB study found that personal interests and hobbies represented 16 percent of the total, and chance happenings accounted for 11 percent.

Ideas for a startup can come from anywhere, but for now we will focus on four possible sources: personal experience, hobbies, accidental discovery, and change-based sources.

Personal Experience

One of the primary sources of startup ideas is personal experience. Often, knowledge gleaned from a present or former job allows a person to see possibilities for modifying an existing product, improving a service, becoming a supplier that meets an employer's needs better than current vendors, or duplicating a business concept in a different

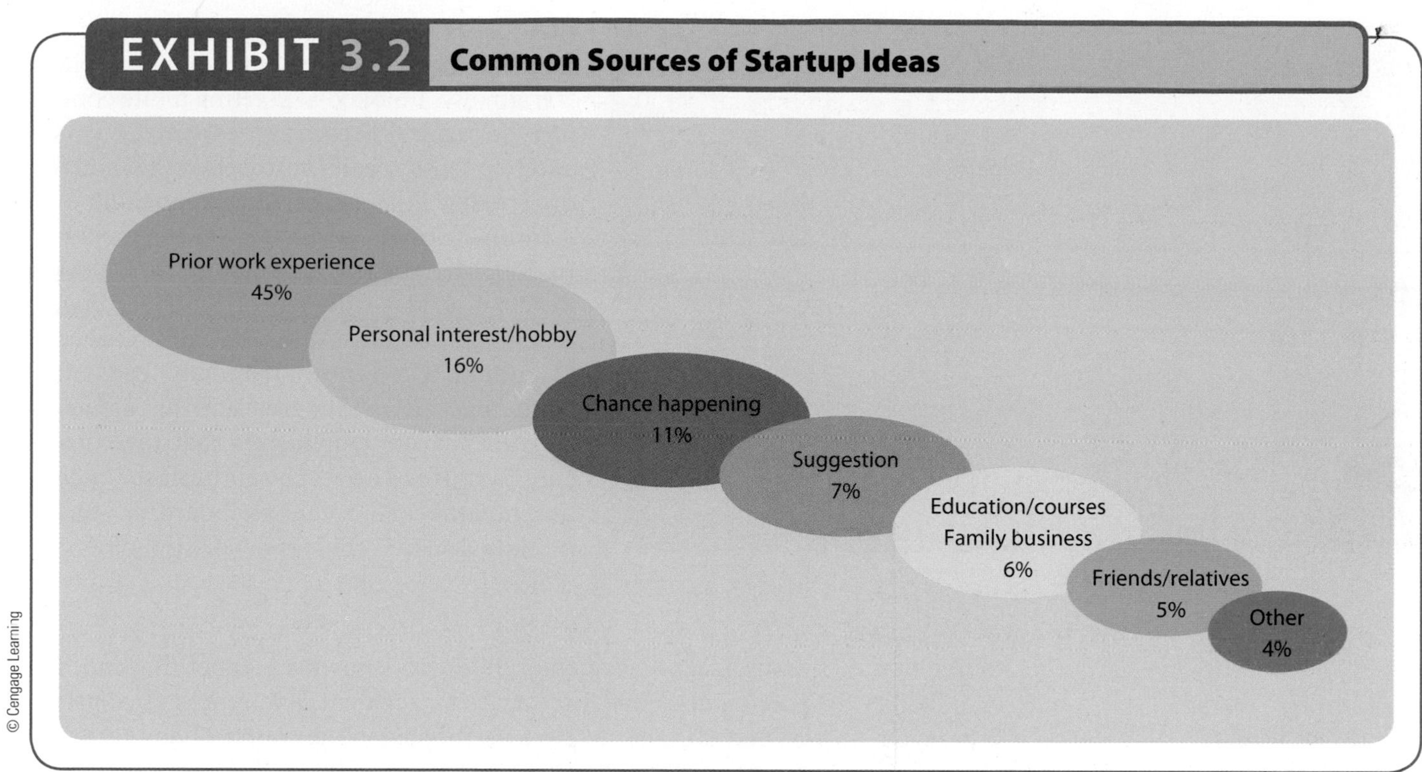

location. Or personal contacts (your network) may open up conversations with suppliers who are interested in working with you or customers who have needs that are not currently being met. Startup concepts may even come to mind as a result of trying personal circumstances or misfortunes, especially when the entrepreneur is able to use work experience or technical skills to address the challenge at hand. Regardless of the situation, these insights may lead you to an opportunity with tremendous potential.[9]

How much does a typical, lightweight cotton T-shirt cut down the sun's rays before they reach your skin? Melissa Marks Papock found that the answer to that question is, *not much*. She was diagnosed with skin cancer at age 26, which led her to conclude that her clothing was not protecting her skin from sun damage. After overcoming cancer, she decided to focus her skills as a fashion industry veteran on helping others beat the disease, too. In 2005, Papock started a company called Cabana Life to offer a line of sun-protective clothing that uses a patented technology to block 98 percent of the sun's UV rays. The concept seems to be catching on, with sales reaching the $700,000 mark only a few years after launch. Reflecting on her progress, Papock concludes that facing challenges in life can actually help prime the pump of entrepreneurial success. "Using your own experience can make you more passionate about your business and help you convey more sincerity to customers," she says. "You discover the need when you're faced with a situation."[10]

Hobbies and Personal Interests

Sometimes, hobbies grow beyond being leisure activities to become businesses. For instance, people who love skiing might start a ski equipment rental operation as a way to make income from an activity that they enjoy, and those who love books might explore concepts that lead to new bookstores. Hobbies and personal interests can add surprising energy to the startup process, which was certainly the case for 39-year-old Alex Shogren. The number of extreme sports has grown exponentially over the past decade, and Shogren is bound and determined to ride that wave. His sport of choice is kiteboarding—which uses a large kite to propel a person across land, snow, or water on a board (similar to a

Jody MacDonald http://offshoreodysseys.com. Courtesy of www.bestkiteboarding.com

surfboard) or other platform—and he has found a way to make it pay handsomely. "Originally, I looked at starting a kite company to write off my travel expenses," says Shogren. "But when I researched the industry, I realized there was a huge opportunity." And his instincts were right on the money. In 2003, he started a company in Delray Beach, Florida, called Best Kiteboarding, and in less than five years, its sales reached $1 million. The venture definitely feeds off of the passion of Shogren and his associates. Its website emphasizes that the company is staffed and run by enthusiasts "who live, breathe, and dream kiteboarding" and proudly declare, "This is my dream job."[11]

Accidental Discovery

serendipity
A facility for making desirable discoveries by accident.

Another source of new startup ideas—accidental discovery—involves something called **serendipity**, a facility for making desirable discoveries by accident. Awareness obviously plays a role here, but anyone may stumble across a useful idea in the course of day-to-day living. That is exactly what happened to a 26-year-old struggling artist, Simone Gonzales, as she was wandering through the garment district in Los Angeles one day. When she came across some thick, stretchy fabric that looked interesting, she decided to see what she could do with it. Here is what happened next: "She hauled her find to a friend's studio nearby and after playing with the thick, mummy-like elastic bands and shaping them into a simple tube skirt—no zipper, hem, or serious tailoring required—Gonzales realized she may be onto something."[12] So she went back to the garment district in serious shopping mode and bought all the elastic stock she could find, adding to the rainbow of colors as she went along. Gathering this novel material was like pouring gas on the fire of her new skirt-making passion.

Gonzales sold the very first skirt she put up for sale at a friend's boutique. That small start (along with a $10,000 loan from her mother) led Gonzales to launch a new clothing company, which she calls Pleasure Doing Business. In 2010, with 16 full-time employees and the help of a few friends and family members, the company grossed more than $2 million in sales.[13] Gonzales may not have set out to become an elastic skirt mogul, but it seems that may be her destiny. Her experience shows that promising business ideas sometimes just happen—even when you're not really looking for them.

Keeping an Eye on Change

Change is one of the most important sources of ideas for entrepreneurs. Whereas large firms often prefer the status quo—why fix it if it's not broken?—entrepreneurs are much more likely to recognize change as an opportunity and to have the creativity and flexibility to adjust to it. Business guru Peter Drucker believed entrepreneurs should consider seven sources of opportunity as they prepare to launch or grow their enterprises.[14] These change-based sources of opportunity are outlined in Exhibit 3.3.

According to Drucker, "Innovation is the specific instrument of entrepreneurship." He further described it as "the act that endows resources with a new capacity to create wealth."[15] In other words, entrepreneurship harnesses the power of creativity to provide innovative products and services. Since change inspires innovation, recognizing

EXHIBIT 3.3 Change-Based Sources of Entrepreneurial Opportunities

Change Factor	Definition	Illustration
Industry or Enterprise Factors		
The unexpected	Unanticipated events lead to either enterprise success or enterprise failure.	Pet pharmaceuticals have been very successful, with more than 30% of dogs and cats now taking medication.
The incongruous	What is expected is out of line with what will work.	Low-fat ice cream was developed for those trying to lose weight.
Process needs	Current technology is insufficient to address an emerging challenge.	General Motors creates an electric car called the Volt to deal with rising energy costs.
Structural change	Changes in technologies, markets, etc., alter industry dynamics.	The use of digital cinema technology has led to the widespread showing of 3-D movies.
External Factors		
Demographics	Shifts in population size, age structure, ethnicity, and income distribution impact product demand.	The rapid growth of the Hispanic market in the United States has spawned a flood of Spanish-language newspapers.
Changes in perception	Perceptual variations determine product demand.	Perceived security threats have led to the development of gated communities.
New knowledge	Learning opens the door to new product opportunities with commercial potential.	Breakthroughs in solar power technologies have fueled the growth of "green" residential developments.

shifts in the factors described in Exhibit 3.3 can expand the range of entrepreneurial opportunities.

Other Idea Leads

If the sources of startup ideas just discussed do not reveal the specific entrepreneurial opportunity that is right for you, other sources of leads are available. The following have been useful to many entrepreneurs:

- Tapping personal contacts with potential customers and suppliers, professors, patent attorneys, former or current employees or co-workers, venture capitalists, and chambers of commerce
- Visiting trade shows, production facilities, universities, and research institutes
- Observing trends related to material limitations and energy shortages, emerging technologies, recreation, fads, pollution problems, personal security, and social movements
- Reading trade publications, bankruptcy announcements, Commerce Department publications, and business classifieds
- Reading articles on the creativity of entrepreneurs and various business opportunities in *Inc., Entrepreneur, MyBusiness,* and similar periodicals
- Visiting the library and even looking through the Yellow Pages in other cities
- Traveling to other states to visit entrepreneurs in your field of interest

- Searching the Internet, where you can find an unlimited supply of information regarding the startup process and even specific opportunities. For example, *Entrepreneur* magazine (http://www.entrepreneur.com) offers online tools, such as the Business Idea Center, which profiles around 1,000 business ideas that can be browsed by category, interest, profession, startup costs, and other criteria.

LIVING THE DREAM

© iStockphoto.com/Angelika Schwarz

using technology

Necessity Is the Mother of (a Mother's) Invention

The story goes something like this: A loving mother needs a babysitter to provide care for her young child. She considers her son's preschool teacher, who seems to be the perfect candidate. Exercising caution, the mother decides to run a background check. The teacher turns out to have a very sketchy past and is not hired. The mother finds that it can be very difficult (and risky) to locate a suitable and safe babysitter. The story, in some variation, repeats every time the mother and her husband need to be away. In response to this recurrent dilemma, the couple launches a new business.

That's exactly how it happened for Adrienne Kallweit, who knew the drill on background checks from her work as a private investigator. And from this experience—which reflects a very real need for so many young couples who want access to safe and reliable child care—Kallweit and her husband, David, decided to launch SeekingSitters. Started in 2004, the company offers "an on-demand babysitter referral service," and it has been expanding rapidly in recent years through franchising.

Anyone who wants to be referred by SeekingSitters must pass a very rigorous screening process, which involves identity verification, criminal and sexual predator checks, and validation of work and education histories. They must also be inclined toward child care (sitters tend to be college students studying education, childhood development, or nursing) and have CPR and general first aid certifications. Beyond that, every adult who lives with the applicant (including parents, spouses, and roommates) must also be screened, and professionalism is absolutely a requirement. "I had one great candidate—good references, her background check was clear—but on Twitter she was bashing the families she cared for," reports one franchisee. "Needless to say, that ruled her out."

You may be wondering how the company generates its revenue. Clients (who are also screened, by the way, to ensure the safety of the sitter) pay a one-time, up-front membership fee of $39.99. Then, sitting fees run from $11.50 to $20.00 an hour, depending on the number of children being watched. Sitters receive a portion of these fees, the company gets the rest, and the clients (usually parents) gain the peace of mind that comes from knowing that all is well at home. As families continue to scatter across the country in search of work opportunities and settle far from relatives and familiar settings, the need and demand for the referral service are sure to increase. Thus, it appears that necessity will continue to be the mother of this (sustained) invention.

SeekingSitters Franchise System Inc.

Sources: Melissa Preddy, "Market for Trustworthy Baby-Sitters Growing," *The Detroit News*, October 14, 2010, http://detnews.com/article/20101014/BIZ/10140350, accessed October 27, 2010; "SeekingSitters' Business Model," *Inc.*, August 25, 2010, http://www.inc.com/inc5000/profile/seekingsitters, accessed October 27, 2010; and Kevin Manahan, "Baby-Sitter Referral Service Born of Necessity, *Entrepreneur*, Vol. 37, No. 5 (May 2009), p. 90. **https://www.seekingsitters.com**

Using Innovative Thinking to Generate Business Ideas

If you haven't come up with a startup idea from the common sources identified above, you may need to dig deeper. A creative person can find useful ideas in many different places. But it will be important for you to commit to a lifestyle of creative thinking so that everyday thoughts can work in your favor to generate opportunities.[16] Although the following suggestions are designed to help guide your search for that one great idea for a startup, they can also help keep an existing business fresh, alive, and moving forward.

1. *When it comes to ideas, borrow heavily from existing products and services or other industries.* "Good artists borrow; great artists steal," said Pablo Picasso or T.S. Eliot or Salvador Dali—no one seems to know for sure. This principle launched Apple Computer on the road to greatness when one of its co-founders, Steve Jobs, identified technologies that Xerox had developed but was not using. It can work for you, too, within the limits of the law and ethical conduct. Explore ideas and practices that you come across, and think deeply about how you might put them to work in launching a startup or accelerating the growth of an existing business. Research shows that this is a powerful starting place for innovation.

2. *Combine two businesses into one to create a market opening.* Aimie's Dinner and Movie is just what you might guess: a restaurant and movie theater in one. This revolutionary concept is exceptionally practical for patrons. How many times have you rushed through dinner to get to the theater, only to find that the movie you wanted to see was already sold out? That won't happen at this Glens Falls, New York, startup. After a leisurely dinner, when the lights begin to dim, you need only to sit back in cushioned comfort and enjoy the show.[17] The restaurant business is often ruthless, and the theater industry is even more competitive, but bringing the two together puts Aimie's in a unique position.

   At some point, it may make sense to start (or buy) more than one business without merging their operations, a strategy known as *diversification.* To see how this can work to your advantage, consider C and D Landscape Company, a business that Isaac Kearns helps to run. The Dayton, Oregon–based enterprise is owned by his parents, and it does very well most of the year, but demand dries up in September, October, and November. So what could he do to keep the cash flow going during the dead months of fall and avoid having to lay off faithful employees during this slow period? It was Christmas in 2005 when Kearns finally saw the light—literally! After wrestling with his holiday decorations and nearly creating what he calls "the biggest disaster I've ever seen," he decided to buy a Christmas Décor franchise with his brother, Josh, and father, Calvin, as partners. It was a natural fit with their landscaping customers, who are willing to pay for services they would rather not do themselves, and it leads to plenty of Christmas season business. This cross-selling opportunity helps even out cash flows, and it eliminates the need for layoffs. Becoming too diversified can sometimes cause an entrepreneur to lose focus, and the performance edge that goes with it, but Kearns will tell you that spreading out sensibly can be very helpful.[18]

3. *Begin with a problem in mind, or think of a "pain" that you can relieve.* High-potential business ideas often address problems that people have or a "pain" that a new venture idea could relieve. Think about a significant problem or hassle that people have to deal with, dissect it, chart it out on a sheet of paper, roll it over and over in your mind, and consider possible solutions. Amazing business ideas are likely to come to mind.

the.

Sherwood Forlee and Mihoko Ouchi are young graphic and product designers who have started their own small company, called the. (Yes, you read that right: "the" is all there is to the venture's moniker, which is meant to reflect the founders' short attention spans and "their inability to get past the definite article of a company name.") On their website, the owners sell an interesting line of "lighthearted and mirthful products," including Anti-Theft Lunch Bags. Having a problem with a sticky-fingered co-worker or a schoolyard bully who is stealing your sack lunch? Then this will surely solve it. Essentially, the simple product consists of clear zippered bags with appetite-killing, mold-green splotches printed on both sides, making any sandwich look spoiled and absolutely nauseating.[19] And even if it fails to bring an end to your theft problem, it will certainly offer plenty of entertainment value, precisely because it is so disgusting. To have a look at some of the products that the company offers, go to http://www.thinkofthe.com.

4. *Recognize a hot trend and ride the wave. Fads* can lead to serious, though sometimes short-lived, money-making opportunities (for example, google the Pet Rocks, Big Mouth Billy Bass, or Garbage Pail Kids phenomena), but *trends* provide a much stronger foundation for businesses because they are connected to a larger change in society. Even more powerful is the product or service that builds on three or four trends as they come together. For example, consider Apple's iPad. Its outrageous success is the result of multiple merging trends: consumer desires for increased mobility, instant gratification, and no hassles (including those that come in the form of invading malware or programs that can steal your private data or trash your battery), all melded together with the natural pull toward fashion.[20]

But what if the wave has already crashed on the shore? Look for countertrends—every trend has one. For example, even as wireless technologies extend the reach of communication, people pay more to travel to destinations beyond the reach of their BlackBerries. Interesting, isn't it? To identify a countertrend, you should make it a habit to ask those who resist a trend (such as the coffee drinker who refuses to go to Starbucks) what products or services would appeal to them and then see what possibilities come to mind. Try to set aside your preconceived notions of what "ought to be" and get into the minds of those who resist the flow. If you use the trend as your starting point, you will

RESOURCES

Spotting Trends

If you want to stay ahead of a wave, it helps to see it coming. The same is true for trends. But how should a small business owner go about spotting trends to make the most of them in his or her company? Listening to customers, staying in tune with industry changes, and using marketing tools like online or in-person focus groups, social media groups, and chat rooms can certainly help. Many businesses are turning to the vast power of the Internet to get out in front of "the next big thing." Websites like trendhunter.com and jwtintelligence.com can help you spot emerging developments, but you need to surf beyond those waters to get a complete picture. Try not to limit your selections; cast a wide net online, and look for meaningful patterns.

know better where to look for the countertrend, and that's where you can get ahead of the game.

5. *Study an existing product or service and explore ways to improve its function.* It seems that everyone uses text messaging these days. But while Derek Johnson was having lunch with a friend (the communications director of a sorority at the University of Houston), he learned that some people would like to use texting to reach many people with the same message. From conversations with others and some online research, Johnson learned that mass text messaging was not available to average consumers. So he decided to launch a website to sell group text messaging, and it is really catching on. His new company, called Tatango, and its five employees peddle services that start at just $19 a month. And with 2,500 subscribers and sales closing in on $500,000, he may be onto something really big.[21] Looking back, though, the secret to his success is clear: Johnson studied a popular service that was working well but found a way to make it perform even better.

6. *Think of possibilities that would streamline a customer's activities.* Many people are busy, so they look to firms that can bear some of the burdens of life for them. That's what keeps businesses like dry cleaners and grocery-delivery services going. Take some time to ponder the day-to-day experiences of people in the market segment you would like to serve. What activities would they gladly off-load onto a startup that could make life more manageable for them?

7. *Consider ways to adapt a product or service to meet customer needs in a different way.* Darren Hitz realized that bachelor parties could be about more than just serious drinking and exotic dancers. That's when he came up with the idea to launch Adventure Bachelor Party, a company that brings thrills to bachelor parties by taking guys on packaged experiences, such as whitewater rafting trips. The startup has been around since 2004, and Hitz now offers a wide variety of options, from cattle herding in Texas to fishing off the California coast to bungee jumping over the Columbia River. He also provides trips for bachelorette parties, weekend adventures, and corporate events. Business is good and the company continues to expand, but just as important, Hitz is having a good time doing what he does: "I enjoy being able to provide a service where everyone has a great time and is happy."[22]

8. *Imagine how the market for a product or service could be expanded.* Sell boxes of tea-bag-like packets filled with dried cow manure? Yep, that's right. It's the brainchild of Annie Haven, and she has found more interested buyers than you might imagine. Since 2005, sales for her all natural soil-conditioning tea have been growing 30 percent a year. Her family's ranch had been providing fertilizer to local farmers in the San Juan Capistrano area in California, but that market was losing ground (literally) as farms were being displaced by new housing developments. So Haven decided to package the growth-stimulating stuff in three-inch by five-inch pouches and sell it to gardening enthusiasts. Customers simply steep each bag in one to five gallons of water and use that "tea" to water their plants. At $21.95 for a box of nine bags, Authentic Haven Brand is turning a tidy profit, and its customers are happy with the concoction, which works wonders on plants and is free of antibiotics, growth hormones, and pesticides. Haven has

Courtesy of Authentic Haven Brand

definitely found a way to expand the market for her product, riding the rising tide of enthusiasm for gardening.[23]

9. *Study a product or service to see if you can make it "green."* In recent years, a great surge of effort and investment has been flowing toward businesses that focus on protecting the environment. Just pick up an issue of any business publication and see for yourself! To tap into this trend, Jon Grobe, David Morgan, and Ken Scheer launched Calsaway Pool Services, Inc. This Tempe, Arizona, startup offers an innovative filtration device that strips trouble-making minerals and other substances from pool water, allowing owners to reuse the same water for up to 12 years. Demand is strong: The company filters more than seven million gallons of water a year, and annual sales are approaching $350,000.[24] Fifteen years ago, this business would not have gotten off the ground, but rising environmental concerns have changed all that, and demand in the future is certain to increase. These days, it can pay to think "green."

10. *Keep an eye on new technologies.* New technologies often open up potential opportunities for startups, but only those who take note of the possibilities can reap the rewards. Read widely, talk to industry experts, consult government offices that promote new technologies, or go to a nearby research university and drop by its technology transfer office or visit with faculty who work at the cutting edge of their fields—there are so many sources of insight! But regardless of where you look, be sure to research innovations that have commercial value, particularly for new ventures.

    That's what Chris Savarese did. He found a way to use new tracking technology (the kind used in the security tags that stores attach to apparel items) to locate golf balls hacked into the rough and high brush. The radio frequency identification (RFID) technology can detect golf balls from as far away as 100 feet. Savarese's San Ramon, California–based company, Radar Corporation, now packages a dozen radio-tagged balls with a locator to find them for $199.99, and the market really likes his innovation. His business has been growing as much as 30 percent a year.[25] New technology was clearly the key that got the ball rolling for Savarese.

These options represent only a few of the many possibilities, but if you follow some of the suggestions provided here, you just might hit pay dirt with your own new venture. We encourage you to seek and size up new venture ideas in whatever circumstances you find yourself. Then, by considering a number of internal and external factors, you should be able to fit together the pieces of the opportunity puzzle.

Using Internal and External Analyses to Assess Business Ideas

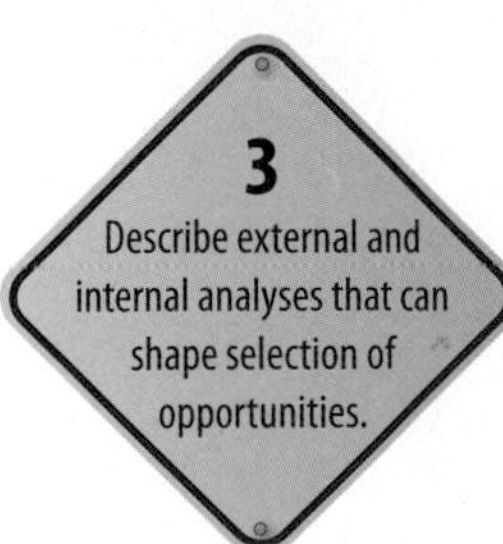

From his experience as a serial software entrepreneur, Leon Presser knows a thing or two about spotting promising startup opportunities. And in his book *What It Takes to Be an Entrepreneur,* he points out that there are two general approaches that can help to identify business ideas, which we describe as inside-out and outside-in.[26] In other words, entrepreneurs can evaluate their own capabilities and then consider new products or services they might be able to offer to the market (inside-out), or they can first look for needs in the marketplace and then determine how to use their own resources and capabilities to pursue those opportunities (outside-in).[27] It is important to understand the finer points of the two methods because they can reveal business ideas that may otherwise be overlooked.

OUTSIDE-IN ANALYSIS

According to research, entrepreneurs are more successful when they study a business context in order to identify potential startup opportunities and determine which are most likely to lead to success.[28] This outside-in analysis should consider the general environment, or big picture, and the industry setting in which the venture might do business. It should also factor in the competitive environment that is likely to have an impact. The **general environment** is made up of very broad factors that influence most businesses in a society. In comparison, the **industry environment** is defined more narrowly as the context for factors that directly impact a given firm and all of its competitors. Even more specifically, the **competitive environment** focuses on the strength, position, and likely moves and countermoves of competitors in an industry.

general environment The broad environment, encompassing factors that influence most businesses in a society.

industry environment The environment that includes factors that directly impact a given firm and its competitors.

competitive environment The environment that focuses on the strength, position, and likely moves and countermoves of competitors in an industry.

The General Environment

The general environment profiles a number of important trends, as shown in Exhibit 3.4. *Economic trends* include changes in the rate of inflation, interest rates, and even currency exchange rates, all of which promote or discourage business growth. *Sociocultural trends* refer to societal currents that may affect consumer demand, opening up new markets and forcing others into decline. *Political/legal trends* that are of interest here include changes in tax law and government regulation (perhaps safety rules) that may pose a threat to existing companies or devastate an inventive business concept. *Global trends* reflect international developments that create new opportunities to expand markets, outsource, and invest abroad. As people and markets around the world become increasingly connected, the impact of the global segment on small business opportunities will increase.

Technological trends are very important to small businesses, since developments that grow out of these spawn—or wipe out—many new ventures. For example, one new technology that is making life interesting for many entrepreneurs is satellite-based cameras and the aerial imaging services they provide. At one time considered the stuff of military intelligence gathering and James Bond–like spy thrillers, the ready and free availability of this technology through services like Google Earth and Microsoft's Bing Maps is changing the opportunity landscape for anyone with the vision to use it. For example, Jay Saber, founder of RoofAds in Woodside, California, noticed a surge of interest in his rooftop advertising business when companies realized that a logo or message painted on the top of their buildings could be seen by anyone with a computer and an Internet connection, not just the occasional helicopter passenger.[29]

EXHIBIT 3.4 Trends in the General Environment

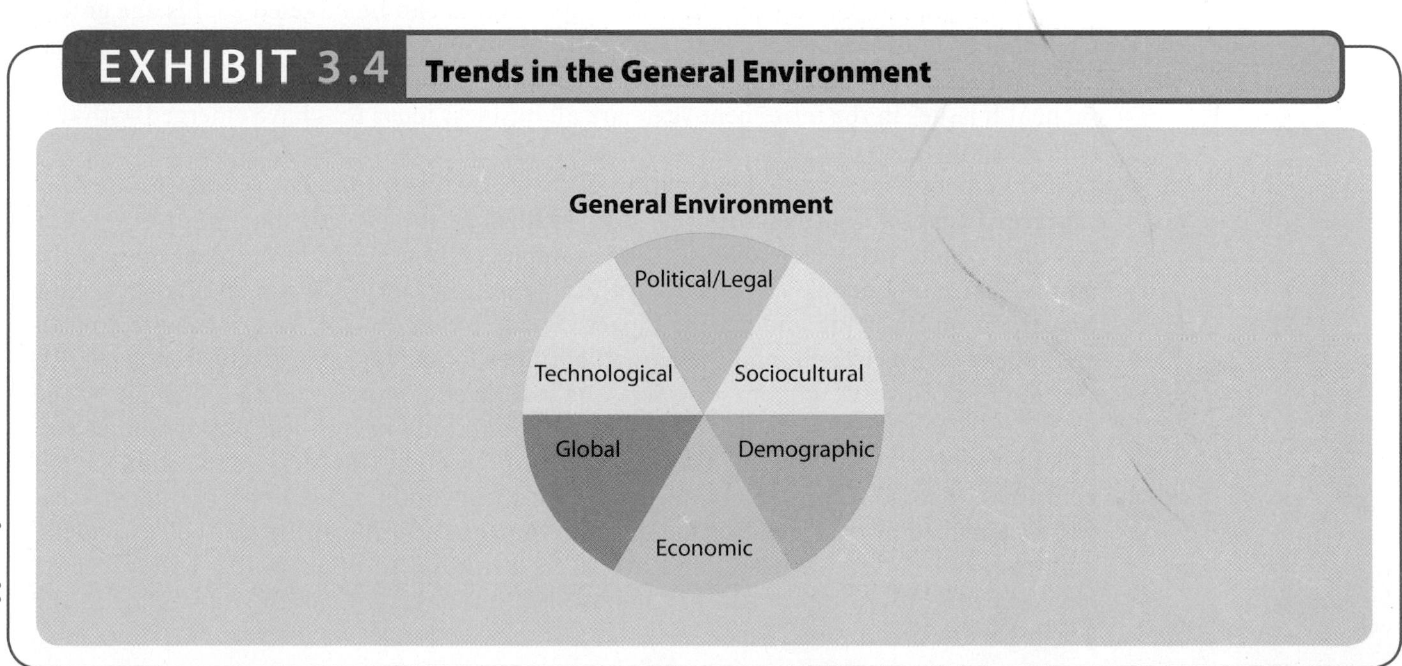

RESOURCES

Reading Economic Trends

When it comes to reading economic trends in the general environment, it's good to know what other business leaders are seeing. "Visa Small Business Insights" can come pretty close to telling you just that by providing a window on the economy with very up-to-date information and analyses. This free report routinely monitors the economic confidence of U.S. small business owners by analyzing both Visa spending data and responses to a quarterly survey. Small companies and those who work with them can use the trends and insights generated from Visa's proprietary research to help them make business decisions with hard data and careful analyses as background. You can go to http://www.visabusinessnetwork.com/spendinsights to look up current and archived versions of the newsletter.

But it's not just advertising that notices the impact—this technology is revolutionizing a host of other industries as well. For example, real estate marketing has been changed forever by companies like Zillow.com, which offers a website that allows a user to type in a home address and pull up a satellite photo of it, along with its price and a host of other details related to that house and its neighborhood.[30] And Keith Harper of Chattanooga, Tennessee, has used Google Earth to locate homes with large lawns that his landscaping business could mow, or those with large concrete patios that might be interested in his pressure-washing services. Pool maintenance firms are using it to identify homes with pools whose owners may need help with upkeep.[31] And this is just the beginning. As the technology develops further, the business landscape will again be reshaped and the rules will change.

Demographic trends also play an important role in shaping opportunities for startups; they include population size, age structure, ethnic mix, and wage distribution. Many entrepreneurs, for example, are looking at aging baby boomers (the 78 million Americans born between 1946 and 1964) and seeing dollar signs. Given their $2 trillion in annual spending power and willing self-indulgence, the focus on this segment may really pay off. And there is no limit to the products and services that can be targeted to this age group. Cell phones with larger keys that can easily be seen in dim lighting, health clubs that cater to those with more gray hair and less revealing apparel, and magazines that focus on health issues in the retirement years are all business ideas that have emerged with this demographic trend in mind.

Some people believe that evaluation of the general environment is appropriate only for large firms that have a corporate staff to manage the process, but small businesses can also benefit from such analysis. For example, entrepreneurs have taken note of the reality that many people struggle with their weight; in fact, government statistics show that the problem is big and getting bigger. Today, 68 percent of Americans are considered obese or overweight, and the figure continues to increase. If current trends persist, the number of overweight/obese Americans will reach a worrisome 86.3 percent by the year 2030.[32] Entrepreneurs have realized that a multitude of business opportunities can be launched based on the rising tide of obesity, from weight-loss services to products that help obese people live more comfortably with their condition. Among the many businesses launched by those reading the trend are startups offering airline seatbelt extenders, high-capacity bathroom scales, and oversized furniture. In other words, entrepreneurs have already proven that it can pay handsomely to look very carefully at trends in the general environment.

Finding Success with Baby Boomers

Few demographic trends hold more promise for new businesses than the aging of baby boomers. Companies like Jitterbug (easy-to-use cell phones), Senior Helpers (in-home care of the elderly), the FloH Club (tech support for seniors only), and thousands of others are already capitalizing on this segment. If you are thinking of joining them, here are some tips that should boost your odds for success:

- *Aim inward.* Boomers are interested in life-enriching experiences.
- *Be positive.* Older adults tend to ignore negative images, concepts, and ideas.
- *Focus on life stage.* Avoid age-based marketing and focus more on stage of life (for example, grandparents tend to be grandparents, no matter their age).
- *Use traditional media.* Boomers are loyal to radio, newspapers, and TV.
- *Follow the moving target.* If you lose touch with your customers, they'll take their money elsewhere.

To learn more about success with boomer-focused businesses, see Matt Thornhill, "Age Against the Machine," *Entrepreneur*, Vol. 37, No. 5 (May 2009), pp. 47–48.

The Industry Environment

An entrepreneur will be even more directly affected by the startup's industry than by the general environment. In his classic book *Competitive Advantage,* Michael Porter lists five factors that determine the nature and degree of competition in an industry:[33]

- **New competitors.** How easy is it for new competitors to enter the industry?
- **Substitute products/services.** Can customers turn to other products or services to replace those that the industry offers?
- **Rivalry.** How intense is the rivalry among existing competitors in the industry?
- **Suppliers.** Are industry suppliers so powerful that they will demand high prices for inputs, thereby increasing the company's costs and reducing its profits?
- **Buyers.** Are industry customers so powerful that they will force companies to charge low prices, thereby reducing profits?

Exhibit 3.5 shows these five factors as weights that offset the potential attractiveness and profitability of a target industry. It illustrates how profits in an industry tend to be inversely related to the strength of these factors—that is, strong factors yield weak profits, whereas weak factors yield strong profits.

Entrepreneurs who understand industry influences can better identify high-potential startup opportunities—situations where, say, rivalry is weak and neither buyers nor suppliers have enough power to drive hard bargains on price. But these insights can also help entrepreneurs to anticipate threats they are likely to encounter and to begin thinking about ways to defend their startups from any downside risk. If entrepreneurs recognize and understand these forces, they can position their ventures in a way that makes the most of what the industry offers. In other words, analyzing Porter's five industry factors will provide a good overview of the broad sweep of the industry environment.

EXHIBIT 3.5 **Major Factors Offsetting Market Attractiveness**

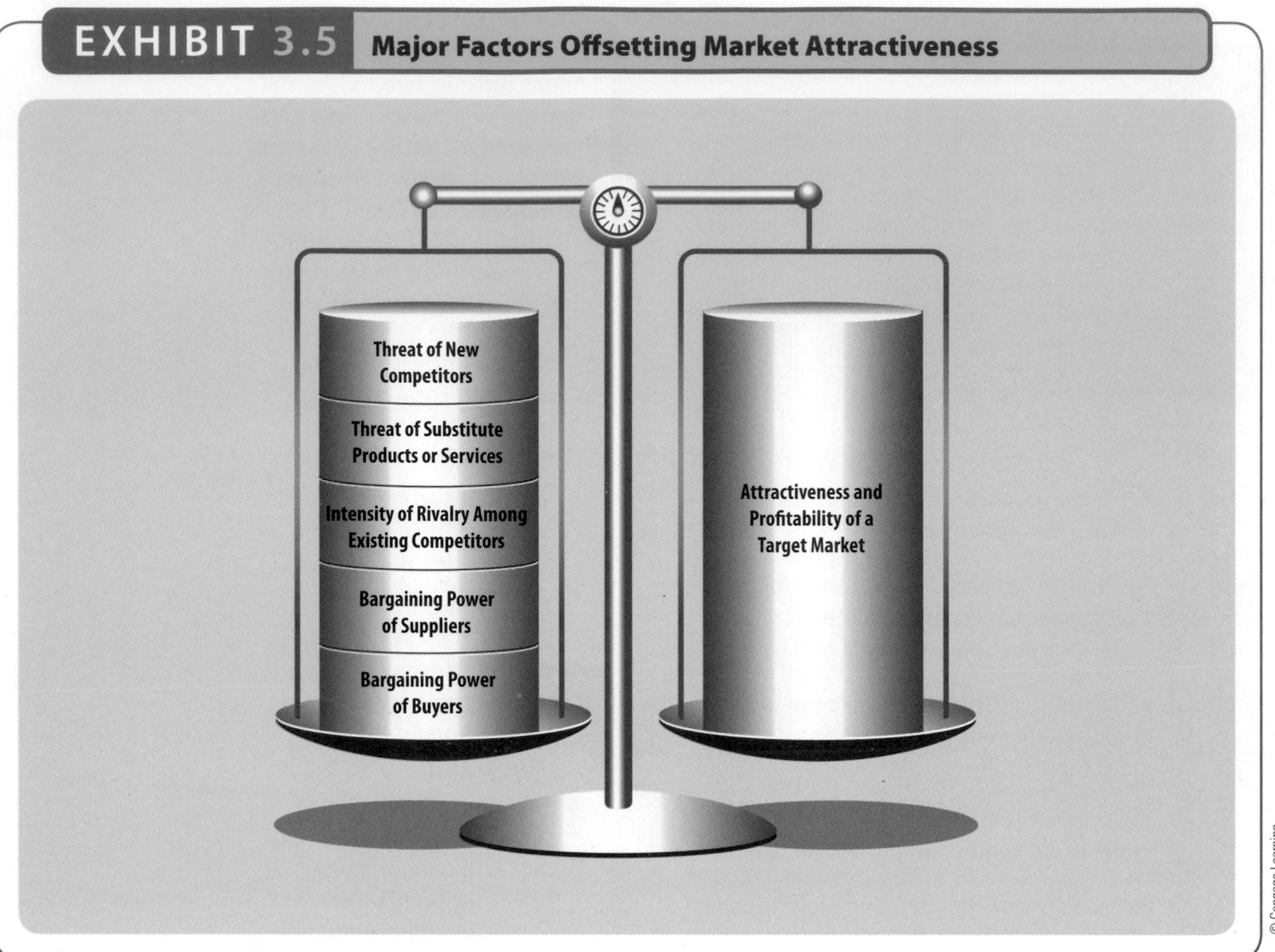

The Competitive Environment

Within any given industry, it is important to determine the strength, position, and likely responses of rival businesses to newcomers. In fact, experts insist such analyses are a critical input for the assessment of any business idea. William A. Sahlman of Harvard University contends that every aspiring entrepreneur should answer several questions about the competitors he or she is likely to encounter in the marketplace:[34]

- Who would be the new venture's current competitors?
- What unique resources do they control?
- What are their strengths and weaknesses?
- How will they respond to the new venture's decision to enter the industry?
- How can the new venture respond?
- Who else might see and exploit the same opportunity?
- Are there ways to co-opt potential or actual competitors by forming alliances?

This analysis helps an entrepreneur to evaluate the nature and extent of existing competition and to fine-tune future plans. It can also help to identify high-potential business opportunities based on the competitive situation.

Awareness of the competition has paid off in a big way for three German brothers in their 30s—Alexander, Oliver, and Mark Samwer. They have been accused of copying great ideas, and that is a fair assessment, but their fast-follower tactics have worked time and again. In January of 1999, at a time when eBay was still focused mostly on the U.S. market, the Samwer brothers started a clone of the company (Alando.de) in Germany. Five months later, eBay came calling and bought the knockoff venture for $50 million. Then came StudVZ, a two-year-old European Facebook-like venture that was sold to a publishing company in 2007 for $100 million. So, what is the secret to the Samwers' success? Know your competitors, stay one step ahead of them, and create unique value by adapting a business idea to local culture and practices.[35] With a little luck and excellent timing, amazing results may just follow.

Entrepreneurs should take one more step when analyzing the competition: They should identify the thinking that shapes their rivals' moves. As a highly regarded thinker, writer, and consultant on Internet technologies and the new media, Clay Shirky observes that he has sometimes assumed that businesses must operate in a certain way because they always have. For example, he thought he knew that teenagers buy music CDs from stores, that customers have to try on pants before they buy them, that people read newspapers to catch up on the latest in the world of politics, and that tourists arrange their trips by visiting a travel agent. But then he points out the folly of this mental habit: "In the last 15 years or so, I have had to unlearn every one of [these] things and a million others."[36] To put it another way, entrepreneurs keep coming up with innovative ways of doing things and often overtake established rivals by using their commitment to time-honored approaches against them. That's how the success of Netflix in video rentals put Blockbuster on the ropes. Its old way of doing business left Blockbuster vulnerable to a startup that challenged conventional wisdom and adopted an inventive set of "rules for the game" (offering videos online or through the mail) to which Blockbuster could not seem to adapt. The rest, as they say, is history—and so, it seems, is Blockbuster, which filed for bankruptcy in 2010.

INSIDE-OUT ANALYSIS

Identifying opportunities in the external environment is definitely worth the effort, but business concepts make sense only if they fit well with the potentials that an entrepreneur can bring to the world of business. Furthermore, the search for a startup opportunity can actually *begin* with an inside-out analysis, one that catalogues the resources and capabilities available to the startup (or those that can reasonably be obtained or created) as well as its core competencies. These can provide a platform from which the fruit of new business opportunities can be reached and harvested.

Resources and Capabilities

In order to assess the internal potentials of a business, it helps if the entrepreneur understands the difference between resources and capabilities. **Resources** refers to those available inputs that an entrepreneur can use to start a business and can include factors such as cash for investment, knowledge of important technologies, access to equipment, and capable business partners. Companies have both tangible and intangible resources. **Tangible resources** are visible and easy to measure. An office building, computer equipment, and cash reserves are all tangible resources. These are very different from **intangible resources**, which are invisible and difficult to assess. Intangible assets include intellectual property rights such as patents and copyrights, an established brand, a firm's reputation, and an entrepreneur's personal network of contacts and relationships.

Though the terms are often used interchangeably, *resources* technically are not the same as *capabilities*. That is, whereas resources are singular in nature, **capabilities** are best viewed as the integration of various resources in a way that boosts a firm's **competitive advantage**, which enables the firm to provide products or services that its target market prefers to those offered by competitors. Like a keyboard, which is of no practical value until it is integrated into a computer system, resources are unlikely to provide a platform for competitive advantage until they are bundled into some useful configuration.

resources
The basic inputs that a firm uses to conduct its business.

tangible resources
Those organizational resources that are visible and easy to measure.

intangible resources
Those organizational resources that are invisible and difficult to assess.

capabilities
The integration of various organizational resources that are deployed together to the firm's advantage.

competitive advantage
A benefit that exists when a firm has a product or service that is seen by its target market as better than those of competitors.

Core Competencies

core competencies Those capabilities that provide a firm with a competitive edge and reflect its personality.

Once entrepreneurs have an accurate view of their resources and capabilities, they may be able to identify core competencies that can be created. **Core competencies** are those capabilities that distinguish a company competitively and reflect its personality. To illustrate how this works, consider Starbucks, which is known for its wide selection of gourmet coffees. But that is not its only edge in the marketplace. In fact, many of its competitors—large and small—also provide high-quality coffee products. So why has the company been so successful? Most observers believe that it is the premium product, combined with the special "Starbucks experience," that has allowed the coffee icon to grow from a single store in the mid-1980s to more than 16,000 retail locations in over 50 countries today.[37]

Though the success of Starbucks is undeniable, the franchise has not eliminated its competition. So how do small firms compete in a Starbucks-saturated market? By focusing on the unique core competencies they have. Many small shops thrive in this environment by providing free refills, paying meticulous attention to product quality, emphasizing connections with the local community, or taking other steps to showcase their own unique character and individuality (something a large chain like Starbucks cannot afford to do). In other words, they establish core competencies by using resources and capabilities in unique ways that reflect the "personality" of their own enterprises. Though the words are different, the tune is still the same: Entrepreneurs who can identify core competencies and apply them effectively are in the best position to launch ventures that will achieve a competitive advantage and superior performance.

INTEGRATING INTERNAL AND EXTERNAL ANALYSES

SWOT analysis An assessment that provides a concise overview of a firm's strategic situation.

A solid foundation for competitive advantage requires a reasonable match between the strengths and weaknesses of a business and the opportunities and threats present in its relevant environments. This integration is best revealed through a **SWOT analysis** (standing for *S*trengths, *W*eaknesses, *O*pportunities, *T*hreats), which provides a simple overview of a venture's strategic situation. Exhibit 3.6 lists a number of factors that can be classified by this framework; however, these are merely representative of the countless possibilities that may exist.

In practice, a SWOT analysis provides a snapshot view of current conditions. Outside-in and inside-out approaches come together in the SWOT analysis to help identify potential business opportunities that match the entrepreneur and his or her planned venture. However, because a SWOT analysis focuses on the present rather than considering future opportunities, at this point the entrepreneur should ask a few additional questions:

- Will the targeted opportunity lead to other opportunities in the future?
- Will the opportunity help to build skills that can open the door to new opportunities in the future?
- Will pursuit of the opportunity be likely to lead to competitive response by potential rivals?

Obviously, the most promising opportunities are those that lead to others (which may offer value and profitability over the long run), promote the development of additional skills that equip the venture to pursue new prospects, and yet do not provoke competitors to strike back.

While still a student at Northeastern University, Neil Wadhawan met Raj Raheja, and in 2002 they partnered to launch Heartwood Studios, a company that produces 3-D images and animations for architects and designers. "We knew our [product] was a necessary tool," says Wadhawan. "Being able to visualize something before it's built is powerful." It wasn't long, however, before the co-founders recognized that their 3-D animations could be important to more than just architects, so they began to investigate other industries where their technologies and skills could be adapted for use. They soon found clients in the defense and aerospace industries. And, more recently, they have been moving into the sports world by providing stadium

EXHIBIT 3.6 Examples of SWOT Factors

	POSITIVE FACTORS	NEGATIVE FACTORS
Inside the Company	***Strengths*** • Important core competencies • Financial strengths • Innovative capacity • Skilled or experienced management • Well-planned strategy • Effective entry wedge • A strong network of personal contacts • Positive reputation in the marketplace • Proprietary technology	***Weaknesses*** • Inadequate financial resources • Poorly planned strategy • Lack of management skills or experience • Inadequate innovation capacity • Negative reputation in the marketplace • Inadequate facilities • Distribution problems • Limited marketing skills • Production inefficiencies
Outside the Company	***Opportunities*** • An untapped market potential • New product or geographic market • Favorable shift in industry dynamics • High potential for market growth • Emerging technologies • Changes allowing overseas expansion • Favorable government deregulation • Increasing market fragmentation	***Threats*** • New competitors • Rising demands of buyers or suppliers • Sales shifting to substitute products • Increased government regulation • Adverse shifts in the business cycle • Slowed market growth • Changing customer preferences • Adverse demographic shifts

animations for teams like the Dallas Cowboys and New Jersey Nets. Wadhawan and Raheja will tell you that branching out requires careful study and modification, but Heartwood Studios has profited nicely from its expansion, with annual sales exceeding $2 million. And the future looks even brighter! "There's a need in every [industry] for 3-D," says Wadhawan. "Our biggest challenge . . . will be deciding what *not* to do."[38]

Like most successful entrepreneurs, Wadhawan and Raheja discovered areas of business opportunity that were flowing out of emerging potentials in the environment, but they moved in the direction of those that matched their personal capabilities and the strengths of their current businesses. As shown in Exhibit 3.7, this is what we call the entrepreneur's "opportunity sweet spot."

EXHIBIT 3.7 The Entrepreneur's Opportunity "Sweet Spot"

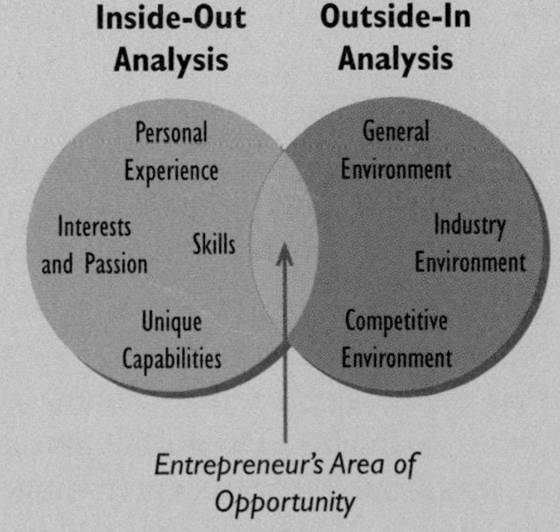

EXHIBIT 3.8 Setting a Direction for the Startup

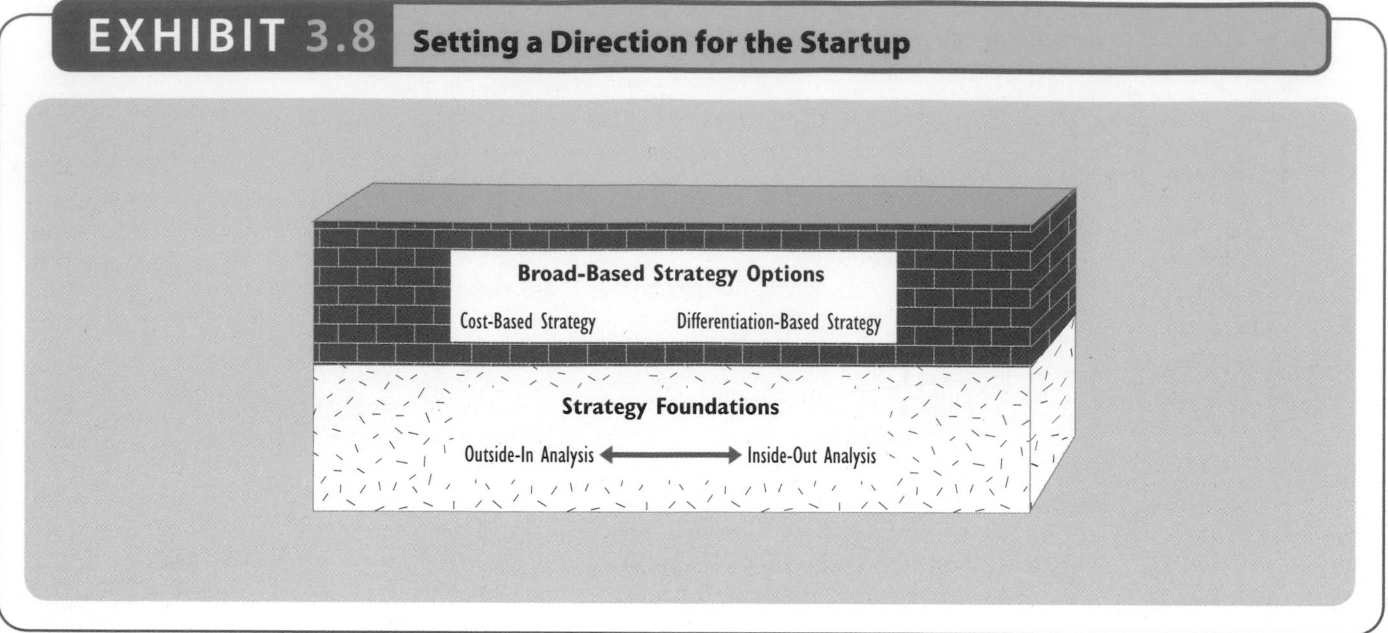

When potentials in the external environment (revealed through analysis of the general, industry, and competitive environments) fit with the unique capabilities and core competencies of the entrepreneur (highlighted by internal assessment) and threats outside the startup or weaknesses within it are manageable, the odds of success are greatly improved. Therefore, we encourage you to be observant and systematic in your search for opportunities and to think carefully about how these opportunities fit your background and skills, as well as your interests and passions. If you do so, you are much more likely to enjoy the adventure. Not a bad payoff!

Clearly, conducting outside-in and inside-out analyses and integrating the results can help to build a solid foundation for competitive advantage. With that foundation, an entrepreneur can begin to create a strategy for achieving superior financial performance (see Exhibit 3.8), and it is to that subject that we turn next.

Selecting Strategies That Capture Opportunities

4 Explain broad-based strategy options and focus strategies.

A **strategy** is, in essence, a set of actions that coordinate the resources and commitments of a business to boost its performance. Strategy selections should be guided by the firm's situation, rather than by past choices, the latest industry fad, or whatever "feels" right at the moment. Choosing a strategy that makes sense for a particular entrepreneur and his or her startup is a critical early step toward superior performance. But keeping an eye on strategy options—both broad-based and focus strategies—can also guide established companies toward success.

strategy A plan of action that coordinates the resources and commitments of an organization to achieve superior performance.

BROAD-BASED STRATEGY OPTIONS

Firms competing in the same industry can adopt very different strategies. Broadly speaking, companies can choose to build their strategies around an emphasis on either low cost or differentiation as they consider how to position themselves relative to their competitors.

Cost-Based Strategy

To follow a **cost-based strategy**, a firm must hold down its costs so that it can compete by charging lower prices for its products or services and still make a profit. The sources of cost advantages are varied, ranging from low-cost labor to efficiency in operations. Many people assume that cost-based strategies will not work for small companies, and often this is true.[39] However, cost-advantage factors are so numerous and diverse that, in some cases, small businesses may be able to use them with great success, especially if they do not spark a price war with established competitors who have deeper pockets and a great dislike for any company that steals their customers. Of course, the great downside of this strategy is that it attracts customers who always search for the best deal. In other words, it can be a challenge to develop customer loyalty with this strategy.

cost-based strategy
A plan of action that requires a firm to hold down its costs so that it can compete by charging lower prices and still make a profit.

© Route66/Shutterstock.com

Spirit Airlines provides an example of an entrepreneurial company that has relentlessly followed a cost-based strategy from its founding. In fact, it is now billed as an "ultra-low-cost carrier." The venture operates 32 Airbus planes (the youngest fleet in the Americas) and serves mostly eastern and midwestern cities in the United States, with flights to many Caribbean and Latin American destinations—but this is no ordinary airline. Cost is always front and center in the firm's strategy deliberations. The company describes the heart and soul of its approach on its website.

> *[Spirit Airlines] liberates customers from being forced into paying for services they do not desire or use. When customers are seeking the best value in travel, they can choose a low fare at spiritair.com and select the services and options appropriate for their travel needs. Spirit's ultra-low-cost model, driven from numerous efficiencies, new aircraft, advanced technology, and dedicated staff, allows the airline to take this approach, offering savings to millions of customers. . . .*[40]

Achieving its ambitious goals has required some bold moves. For example, Spirit charges passengers extra to check luggage, change reservations, and even to use pillows and blankets. To make the bargain-basement fare model work (charging as little as $8 each way for some flights), the company has had to be innovative in its search for alternative revenues, which has included placing ads in airplane cabins and on flight attendants' uniforms. While the company's revenue-stretching methods don't always fly well with some passengers, Spirit Airlines certainly presents an interesting example of the use of a creative, cost-based strategy.[41]

Differentiation-Based Strategy

The second general option for building a competitive advantage is creating a **differentiation-based strategy**, an approach that emphasizes the uniqueness of a firm's product or service (in terms of some feature other than cost). A firm that can create and sustain an attractive differentiation strategy is likely to be a successful performer in the marketplace. For the strategy to be effective, the consumer must be convinced of the uniqueness and value of the product or service, whether real or perceived. A wide variety of operational and marketing tactics, ranging from design to promotion, can lead to product or service differentiation.

differentiation-based strategy
A plan of action designed to provide a product or service with unique attributes that are valued by consumers.

After spending many years in the music industry, Brian Landau and Pete Rosenblum were bothered that hit songs didn't always generate the music sales they deserved.

So, in 2003, they launched New York City–based Radio Tag, a full-service marketing agency. Right from the start, differentiation was the foundation of their strategy, and at the core of that strategy was a rich promotional concept that has become the signature feature of the company. You see, most radio stations let the DJs do all the talking, but Radio Tag has changed all of that by allowing artists to introduce their own work via

LIVING THE DREAM

entrepreneurial experiences

A Differentiation Strategy That Has People Going GaGa

No matter what you may think of her work, Lady Gaga has taken the music industry by storm. In 2009 alone, four songs from her debut album soared to number 1, she sold 15.3 million digital tracks, and her spacey Euro vibe (think dance hits like "Poker Face" and "Paparazzi") has shaded the sounds of artists from rock to rap. But she is just getting started. Who can overlook her outrageous hairdos and sci-fi-like outfits and more-than-over-the-top accessories—which is exactly the point, right? Some might say these are huge distractions and nothing more, but in truth they are all part of a carefully crafted image that stands at the center of Gaga's (admittedly extreme) differentiation strategy, one that launched her from relative obscurity to international celebrity in just a few years. And by the way, we should add that many of those who should know also contend that she actually brings great talent to the mix. But with all the buzz and distraction, it's easy to overlook her musical depth.

Born Stefani Germanotta, on March 28, 1986, Lady Gaga is a New York native who studied music at New York University's Tisch School of the Arts. Her movement to the top started in 2007 when she began to get musical traction on the downtown Manhattan club scene with a performance art show known as Lady Gaga and the Starlight Review. Since then, there has been little time to look back.

But it's not just about the music—there are important business lessons to be learned from this story. Lady Gaga's rapid rise to success in the music world is actually the product of a carefully orchestrated and highly effective business strategy. As one observer put it, "Underneath Gaga's haystack wigs is a case study of what it takes to succeed in the music business today." In addition to signing with a major label, she also makes shrewd use of new distribution platforms. And her recording contract is nearly as innovative as the artist herself, going beyond record sales alone to include a piece of the action from touring, merchandise—even a make-up deal. She writes her own music, but she is just as focused on the visual theatrics and unforgettable fashion that shape her global image. However, Gaga's phenomenal startup success and meteoric rise to international stardom may have as much to do with digital savvy as any other feature of her business strategy. She spurs market interest by giving music away for free online (her "Bad Romance" video has had more views on YouTube than any other, *ever*—180 million and counting!), and she maintains close interaction with her nearly 5 million Twitter fans via regular "tweets" that keep the surge of affection flowing. Because the reach of social media is global, Gaga deliberately writes her songs in simple language so that fans in every country will be able to sing along. She makes it look fun, of course, but her strategy is a serious work of business art, and entrepreneurs everywhere can learn much from her approach and phenomenally successful new venture.

Sources: Jason Birchmeier, "MTV—Lady Gaga," http://www.mtv.com/music/artist/lady_gaga/artist.jhtml, accessed November 1, 2010; Kelly Crow, "The Lessons of Lady Gaga," *Wall Street Journal*, January 29, 2010, pp. W1, W12; and Salma Jafri, "Lady Gaga's Social Media Success and Strategy," http://www.suite101.com/content/lady-gagas-social-media-success-and-strategy-a257336, accessed November 1, 2010.

recording. With this approach, for example, Beyoncé can describe her emotional connection to a song, or members of the alternative metal band Breaking Benjamin can explain how their latest album came together. "That was really the whole point," says Rosenblum. "Put an artist on the radio and let people become more familiar with who the artist is, what the song is, and how they can buy it." It is clearly a different approach, and a successful one. Radio stations benefit from the free promotional content, artists are able to promote their creative works using their own voices, and the company has profited nicely, reaching nearly $5 million in sales within five years of startup—just the kind of outcome you would expect for a business with a well-designed and competently executed differentiation strategy. It has certainly set Radio Tag apart from its competitors.[42]

FOCUS STRATEGIES

If one firm controlled the only known water supply in the world, its sales volume would be huge. Such a business would not be concerned about differences in personal preferences regarding taste, appearance, or temperature. It would consider its customers to be one market. As long as the water product was wet, it would satisfy everyone. However, if someone else discovered a second water supply, the first company's view of the market would change. The first business might discover that sales were drying up and take measures to modify its strategy. In any case, the level of rivalry would likely rise as competitors struggled for position in the same industry space.

If the potential for water sales were enormous, small businesses would eventually become interested in entering the market. However, given their limited resources and lack of experience, these companies would be more likely to succeed if they avoided head-to-head competition with industry giants and sought a protected market segment instead. In other words, they could be competitive if they implemented a **focus strategy** by adapting their efforts to concentrate on the needs of a very limited portion of the market. To get started, these businesses might focus their resources on a narrow slice of the market that was small enough to escape the interest of major players (for example, filtered water delivered to individual homes) or perhaps take a completely new approach to permit entry without immediate competitive response (perhaps by filling market gaps resulting from supply shortages).

focus strategy
A plan of action that isolates an enterprise from competitors and other market forces by targeting a restricted market segment.

Focus strategies represent a strategic approach in which entrepreneurs try to shield themselves from market forces by targeting a specific group of customers who have an identifiable but very narrow range of product or service interests (often called a *market niche*). By focusing on a specialized market, some small businesses develop unique expertise that leads to higher levels of value and service for customers, which is great for business. In fact, this advantage prompted marketing guru Philip Kotler to declare, "There are riches in niches."[43]

The two broad options discussed earlier—a cost-based strategy and a differentiation-based strategy—can also be used when focusing on a niche market. Although few entrepreneurs adopt a cost-based focus strategy, it does happen. For example, outlets with names like The Watermarket Store, Drinking Water Depot, and H2O To Go have opened over the years, most using an efficient purification system to offer high-quality, good-tasting drinking water to price-sensitive customers at a fraction of the price charged by competitors. These small businesses are following a cost-based focus strategy.

Contrast this approach with the differentiation-based focus strategy that Mark Sikes adopted for his small business, Personalized Bottle Water. Sikes may be in the business of selling bottled water, but his startup grew out of his knowledge of what goes on the outside of a bottle rather than what goes in it. He was traveling around the country selling stick-on labels to manufacturers for his successful label-brokering company when it dawned on him that he could go in a completely different direction with his enterprise. Why not sell bottled water featuring custom labels for corporate clients and anyone who wants to celebrate a special occasion? Sikes explains the thrust of his business on the company's website:

> *I decided to enter the market . . . with one simple goal in mind, to offer great tasting bottled water to small businesses and schools with their own personalized label. From that single thought, our business has grown into several areas, and we now supply businesses, both big and small, as well as [provide] a single case of water for an individual or a special event.*[44]

Sikes launched Personalized Bottle Water in 1997, operating out of a warehouse in Little Rock, Arkansas. This friendly and energetic man in his 30s hustled his product around the state and soon found interested customers—schools (especially during football season), funeral homes, hotels, and brides and grooms. By 2005, the company was very profitable, with around $350,000 in annual sales, but Sikes has even higher hopes for the future of the business.[45] The focus, however, remains the same: *personalization*. Without this emphasis, his enterprise would be dead in the water, so to speak. There is no way that Sikes would be able to compete head to head with the likes of bottling giants Coca-Cola Company (Dasani), Dr Pepper Snapple Group (Deja Blue), and PepsiCo (Aquafina), but flexibility and customization—foundations for differentiation—give Personalized Bottle Water a fighting chance.

Entrepreneurs can usually select and implement a focus strategy that will allow them to target a niche market within a sizeable industry, thereby avoiding direct competition with larger competitors. This can be accomplished in a number of ways, as discussed in the next section.

Focus Strategy Selection and Implementation

By selecting a particular focus strategy, an entrepreneur decides on the basic direction of the business. Such a choice affects the very nature of the business and is thus referred to as a **strategic decision**. A firm's overall strategy is formulated, therefore, as its leader decides how the firm will relate to its environment—particularly to the customers and competitors in that environment. This can require the entrepreneur to manage a delicate balancing act, one that keeps the venture out of the crosshairs of industry heavyweights and yet offers enough market promise to provide the startup with a reasonable shot at getting off the ground.

strategic decision A decision regarding the direction a firm will take in relating to its customers and competitors.

Selection of a very specialized market is, of course, not the only possible strategy for a small firm. But focus strategies are very popular because they allow a small firm to operate in the gap that exists between larger competitors. If a small firm chooses to compete head to head with other companies, particularly large corporations, it must be prepared to distinguish itself in some way—for example, by attention to detail, highly personalized service, or speed of service—in order to make itself a viable competitor.

Focus strategies can be implemented in any of the following ways:

- Restricting focus to a single subset of customers
- Emphasizing a single product or service
- Limiting the market to a single geographical region
- Concentrating on the superiority of the product or service

To illustrate these strategies, consider how the following entrepreneurs—Dale Fox, Leslie Vander Baan, and Trey Cobb—each implemented a different focus strategy related to the automobile industry.

Dale Fox's company, Spin Automotive Group, is a car rental business, but his Venice, California, venture is anything but average. His "rolling stock" consists of classic, one-of-a-kind automobiles in museum-quality condition—a blue Space Age–looking 1962 Cadillac Eldorado convertible, a stylish 1961 Alpha Romeo Giulietta sports car with a flashy and flawless red exterior, a 1962 V8-powered Ford Cobra finished in blue with white racing stripes that is "loud, fast, and unapologetically rugged." A one-day rental of any of the company's cars will set you back $499, but renters can also choose to purchase the cars if they wish (with posted prices running from $28,000 to $69,000).[46] There was no way Spin could have gone head to head with mainstream car rental agencies, but Fox has his carefully considered niche pretty much all to himself, which is extremely good for business. The company generated $5 million in revenue in its first full year of operation.[47]

Leslie Vander Baan's start in the car business was inspired by her personal experience while trying to sell a car on her own. With all of the hassles and uncertainties involved, she realized that there had to be a better way for buyer and seller to complete such transactions—and she was right. The solution was a unique used-car dealership called Auto Consignment, a business that Vander Baan and her husband started in 2003 to help people sell their cars with less hassle and for more than the trade-in value. The company's "nearly a dozen" employees handle test drives, complete necessary paperwork, offer financing, and deal with other auto-sales frustrations. The business now sells cars off its $1.5 million property on auto row in Charlotte, North Carolina, and generates around $5 million a year in consignment sales.[48]

Trey Cobb's fascination with the automobile industry doesn't involve car rentals or sales—he is all about parts. As a huge fan of Subarus, he found that he could not get the high-performance parts he wanted to modify his Impreza 2.5RS, so he decided to make his own. That humble start in 1999 expanded into a sizeable business that today offers 40 to 50 aftermarket parts for cars built by five Asian automakers (including Subaru, of course). With only $10,000 in startup capital, Cobb launched his venture, COBB Tuning, out of his father's tire shop in Texas, but he moved the business to Salt Lake City, Utah, in 2002 to take advantage of weather that is ideal for product testing.[49] Today, the company's 35 employees keep sales revved up to an impressive $6 million per year, driven largely by the 33-year-old founder's resolute focus on a well-defined market niche: "tech-savvy enthusiasts with strong brand allegiances."[50]

But Cobb's niche concept is only one of many possibilities. Together, Spin Automotive Group, Auto Consignment, and COBB Tuning prove that very different focus strategies can be implemented within the same industry and that all of these strategies can be profitable. However, overspecialization and competition can threaten to erode the profits of such strategies.

Drawbacks of Focus Strategies

One small business analyst expresses a word of caution about selecting a niche market:

> *Warning! A firm can be so specialized that it may not have enough customers to be viable. Do not plan to open a pen repair shop, a shoelace boutique, or a restaurant based on the concept of toast (although one based on breakfast cereal has apparently been founded).*[51]

In addition to the dangers of becoming too specialized, firms that adopt a focus strategy tread a narrow path between maintaining a protected market and attracting competition. If their ventures are profitable, entrepreneurs must be prepared to face new competitors.

Strategy guru Michael Porter cautions that a segmented market can erode under any of the following four conditions:[52]

- The focus strategy is imitated.
- The target segment becomes structurally unattractive because the structure erodes or because demand simply disappears.
- The target segment's differences from other segments narrow.
- New firms subsegment the industry.

The experience of Minnetonka, a small firm widely recognized as the first to introduce liquid hand soap, provides an example of how a focus strategy can be imitated. The huge success of its brand, Softsoap, quickly attracted the attention of several giants in the industry, including Procter & Gamble. Minnetonka's competitive advantage was soon washed away. Some analysts believe this happened because the company focused too much on the advantages of liquid soap in general and not enough on the particular benefits of Softsoap. It should be clear that focus strategies do not guarantee a sustainable advantage. Small firms can boost their success, however, by developing and extending their competitive strengths. Good strategic planning can help point the way through these challenging situations, as well as determine the feasibility of success.

Is Your Startup Idea Feasible?

5
Assess the feasibility of a startup idea before writing a business plan.

Coming up with a business idea that you are excited about is the first step toward an adventure in entrepreneurship. Next, performing an outside-in analysis will show you the big picture, providing an overview of the general environment, the industry, and the competition. And an inside-out analysis will help you match your personal strengths and capabilities to the external environment. If a SWOT analysis reveals a fit between the strengths and weaknesses of your planned venture and the opportunities and threats in its external environment, your business idea deserves an even closer look. Finally, you can use the framework provided in this chapter to consider a strategic direction for the venture—low cost or differentiation—and to learn how to identify and maintain a market niche, as well as a focus strategy, that might work for your startup.

These are all important steps on the road to launching your own business, but you can't stop there. We will show you in later chapters how to create a business plan that will spell out the details of your planned enterprise and its startup considerations. But it is very important that you take an intermediate step first, one that tells you how *feasible* your business idea may be. A **feasibility analysis** is a preliminary assessment of a business idea that gauges whether or not the venture envisioned is likely to succeed. Of course, it may also indicate that the concept has merit, but only if it is adapted in some important way.

feasibility analysis
A preliminary assessment of a business idea that gauges whether or not the venture envisioned is likely to succeed.

But you really want to get started, right? If so, you may be tempted to skip directly to the business plan. This can be a serious mistake. Many entrepreneurs have ideas about new products or services that seem like winners, but those who become infatuated with an idea sometimes underestimate the challenging factors they may face—such as trying to tap a target market that is hard to access or overestimating its size. Aspiring small business owners may also misjudge the power of competitors to close out new rivals or to imitate an innovative approach and make it their own. In other cases, an entrepreneur may not be able to build the organization required to capture the business opportunity he or she has in mind. Such mistakes are the cause of the majority of startup failures.

Developing a solid feasibility analysis before jumping ahead to the business plan can help ensure that the planned venture will not be doomed by a **fatal flaw**—that is, a circumstance or development that, in and of itself, could render a new business unsuccessful. John Osher, serial innovator and entrepreneur, estimates that nine out of ten entrepreneurs fail because their business concept is deficient. In his words, "They want to be in business so much that they often don't do the work they need to do ahead of time, so everything they do is doomed. They can be very talented, do everything else right, and fail because they have ideas that are flawed."[53] It is important to look deeply and honestly for potential weaknesses in your own startup ideas. No matter how remarkable the business concept may seem to be, moving forward is pointless if it uses a manufacturing process that is patent protected, requires startup capital that cannot be raised, ignores market limitations, or is unsound in some other way.

fatal flaw
A circumstance or development that alone could render a new business unsuccessful.

John W. Mullins is a serial entrepreneur and a professor at the prestigious London Business School. He is also author of *The New Business Road Test*, a book that underscores the importance of identifying the fatal flaws of a business idea before it is too late:

> *If [entrepreneurs] can find the fatal flaw before they write their business plan or before it engulfs their new business, they can deal with it in many ways. They can modify their ideas—shaping the opportunity to better fit the hotly competitive world in which it seeks to bear fruit. If the flaw they find appears to be a fatal one, they can even abandon the idea before it's too late—before launch, in some cases, or soon enough thereafter to avoid wasting months or years in pursuit of a dream that simply won't fly.*
>
> *Better yet, if, after [questioning] and probing, testing and especially experimenting for answers, the signs remain positive, they embrace their opportunity with renewed passion and conviction, armed with a new-found confidence that the* evidence*—not just their intuition—confirms their [insight]. Their idea really is an opportunity worth pursuing. Business plan, here we come!*[54]

Deciding to complete a feasibility analysis before proceeding to the business plan stage can save a lot of time, money, and heartache. Or, as Mullins points out, it may reaffirm the power of a business idea and strengthen your resolve to move forward, providing a reserve of energy and commitment that will come in handy when the going gets tough—and it definitely *will* get tough as the venture unfolds.

Keep in mind that success in entrepreneurship is generally the result of three elements that come together in such a way that the new enterprise gets the thrust it needs to launch and the sustained power to keep it going. These three elements are a market with potential, an attractive industry, and a capable individual or team with the skills and capabilities to pull it all together (see Exhibit 3.9). We will discuss each of these in the following sections.

MARKET POTENTIAL

It is important to make clear the distinction between a market and an industry, as the two are very different. A market consists of *buyers*, current or potential customers who are interested in purchasing a particular class of products or services to satisfy wants or needs—and they must also have the ability to pay for them. An industry, on the other hand, is composed of *sellers* who compete with one another by offering identical or similar products or services for sale to the same general group of buyers.

When assessing the pool of potential buyers that a business might serve, it is important to think of that market on two levels—the broad macro-market and the fragments or niches (micro-markets) that can be identified within the broader market. Entrepreneurs with limited business aspirations may find attractive niche opportunities acceptable. However, Mullins points out that "it is also important to know which way the tides are flowing."[55] That is, a desirable niche today is likely to lose its luster over time if the broad

EXHIBIT 3.9 A Feasibility Analysis Framework

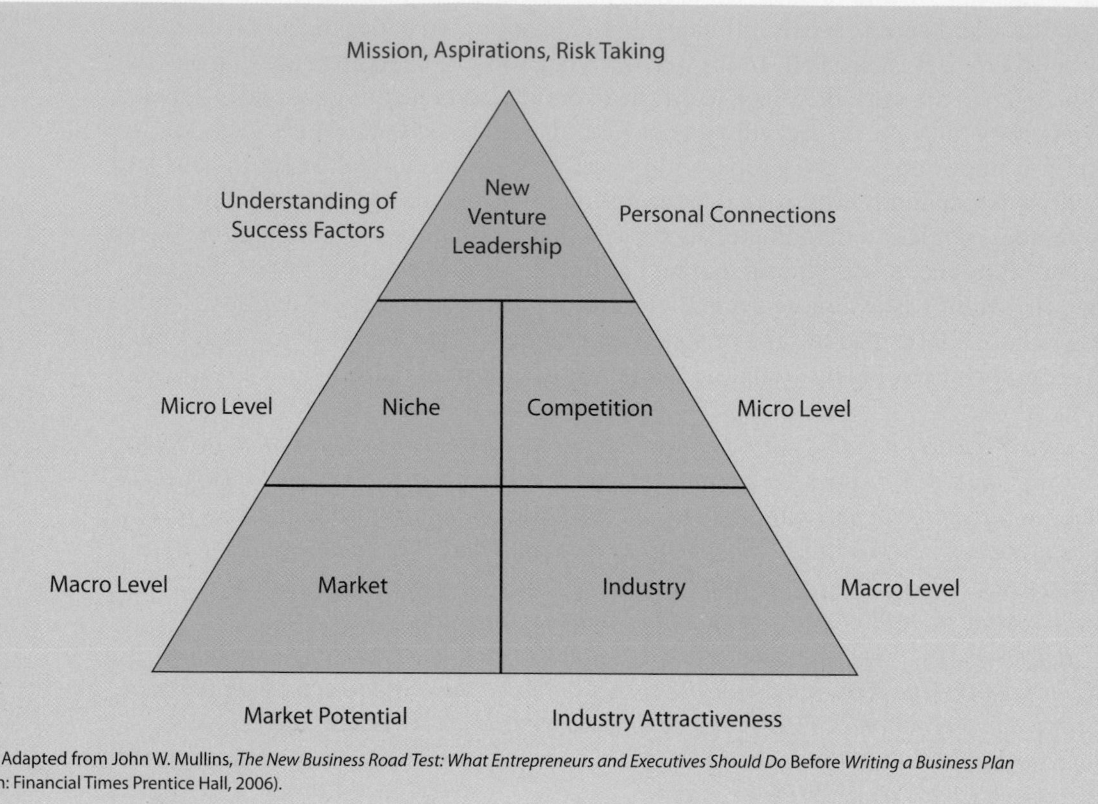

Source: Adapted from John W. Mullins, *The New Business Road Test: What Entrepreneurs and Executives Should Do* Before *Writing a Business Plan* (London: Financial Times Prentice Hall, 2006).

market from which it is derived is trending toward the negative. In most cases, the health of the macro-market can be a very useful predictor of the future potential of the micro-markets located within it.

An entrepreneur with lofty ambitions and visions of "mogul status" down the road may be satisfied with an attractive niche, but only if it can serve as a point of entry into a macro-market with prospects for fast growth and ample long-term potential. The attractiveness of that niche is limited if the fundamental features of the macro-market that support it are not promising. In any case, assessments of the market should be completed on both levels, and each level will be driven by a very different set of questions (see the appendix to this chapter on pp. 102–103).

As part of a feasibility analysis, an evaluation of the general environment (described on pp. 81–82) will help to identify a potential-laden trend that can support promising startup ideas, one of which you will likely select for more thorough consideration. This will set the frame for a macro-market analysis, establishing the boundaries for the research you will need to conduct regarding the number of customers targeted and their overall purchasing power and habits.

The micro-market assessment, however, goes in a very different direction. A startup idea will most likely be tied to a market niche that seems to offer acceptable prospects for growth and, perhaps more important, a path to market entry that is more protected from existing competition. (These dynamics are explained in some detail in the Focus Strategies section on pp. 91–94.) Your evaluation of the micro-market should clarify the unique value the startup idea would offer customers, but it should also provide estimates of the size of the niche, its rate of growth, and its long-run prospects.

INDUSTRY ATTRACTIVENESS

As is the case with markets, industries should be considered from both a "big-picture" and a more focused point of view. A macro-level analysis assesses the overall attractiveness of the industry in which the startup will be established, perhaps summarized best by Michael Porter's model of industry forces (see p. 83). This general view of the industry will be further shaped by answers to the associated questions presented in the appendix to this chapter. Ultimately, these insights will tell you whether the industry provides conditions that would be favorable for the startup you hope to pursue. The more favorable the forces, the more attractive the industry—but keep in mind that a single unfavorable force can be enough to tip the balance toward unattractiveness, so it is important to consider these forces with great care. Knowing about adverse conditions in advance can certainly show the entrepreneur how to make adjustments to compensate, or it may suggest that it is time to pull the plug on that particular enterprise concept. Either way, the feasibility analysis will have served its purpose by highlighting problems in that particular industry setting.

A micro-level industry assessment is focused less on whether industry conditions overall are suitable to launching a new business and more on the probability of a startup's success over the long run. This requires the aspiring entrepreneur to think carefully about the proposed venture to determine whether the advantage it has going for it can be protected from competitive pressures once rivals realize that they have a new challenger. This will be determined mostly by the startup's potential to generate sales and the strength of protective barriers that will shield it from competitors' efforts to replicate its strengths, which would erode the advantages that made the startup possible in the first place. The appendix to this chapter lists a number of questions that can guide this part of the feasibility analysis.

NEW VENTURE LEADERSHIP

Finally, a new business will only be as strong as its leader, so it is important to assess whether the entrepreneur, or entrepreneurial team, is up to the task. Mullins suggests that three dimensions of capability are important here: (1) the fit of the venture with its leader's mission, aspirations, and level of comfort with the risk involved, (2) the leader's grasp of factors that are critical to the success of the enterprise and his or her ability to execute on these, and (3) the leader's connection to suppliers, customers, investors, and others who will be essential to making the venture work.[56] The questions in the appendix to this chapter will direct this part of the assessment.

Completing a feasibility analysis takes a lot of time and effort, but it serves the very important purpose of identifying flaws in a business concept that may be fatal to the proposed startup. As Yogi Berra, the former major leaguer and king of malapropisms (confused sayings), once said, "When you come to a fork in the road, take it." Berra's adage offers little insight to baseball or the startup decision. Feasibility analysis, on the other hand, will indicate when your proposed new venture has come to a fork in the road because it is faced with a serious weakness of one kind or another—and it can also give you some idea of where to go from there. If well executed, a feasibility analysis *will* reveal flaws—every business concept has them. But many of these flaws can be corrected, in which case a course adjustment may take care of the problem. On the other hand, the analysis might expose major flaws that cannot be addressed or corrected. If it does, you would be wise to abandon the concept and shift your energies to a more attractive alternative. Regardless of the final outcome, completing a feasibility analysis will let you know what needs to be done before you commit time, money, and energy to complete a full-scale business plan.

Looking Forward

This chapter has been all about launching new ventures. But you may not be interested in starting a business from scratch. This may leave you asking, "Is there room left in the entrepreneurial game for me?" Absolutely! Chapters 4 and 5 will provide a closer look at franchise and buyout opportunities and help you figure out whether you might want to join a family-owned business. These are all forms of entrepreneurship.

If, on the other hand, you really want to try a startup, and the feasibility analysis suggests that "all systems are go," then it is time to start thinking about a business plan. Chapters 6 through 13 will show you how to flesh out the specifics of your business concept, from start to finish. After communicating the importance of the business plan and providing a model to get you started (Chapter 6), the rest of Part 3 will help you plan for marketing (Chapter 7), organizing (Chapter 8), locating (Chapter 9), and financing (Chapters 10, 11, and 12) your new venture. Looking down the road a bit, Chapter 13 even shows you how to plan for your eventual exit from that venture. It's time to continue the journey!

1. **Distinguish among the different types and sources of startup ideas, and identify the most common sources of startup ideas.**
   - Entrepreneurs decide to start businesses from scratch for many different reasons.
   - Type A startup ideas are concerned with products or services that exist but are not present in all markets.
   - Type B ideas involve new or relatively new technology.
   - Type C ideas are based on new and improved ways of performing old functions.
   - Research shows that entrepreneurs claim prior work experience is the leading source of inspiration for startup ideas.
   - Personal experience leads many aspiring entrepreneurs to the startup decision.
   - Some entrepreneurs start their new ventures based on their hobbies and personal interests, which can add passion and energy to the enterprise.
   - Accidental discoveries may also spur startup efforts.
   - Change often inspires innovation, which can expand the range of possible entrepreneurial opportunities.

2. **Use innovative thinking to generate ideas for high-potential startups.**
   - A commitment to creative thinking can generate many ideas for new businesses.
   - Business ideas can also be spurred by borrowing ideas from existing products and services or other industries, combining businesses to create a market opening, focusing on a problem, and responding to a trend.
   - Other ideas for new businesses can come from improving an existing product or service, making customers' lives easier, meeting customer needs in a new way, expanding the market for a product or service, making a product or service "green," and tapping into new technologies.

3. **Describe external and internal analyses that might shape the selection of venture opportunities.**
   - Outside-in analysis considers the external environment, including the general, industry, and competitive environments.
   - Major trends in the general environment are economic, sociocultural, political/legal, global, technological, and demographic in nature.
   - The major forces that determine the potential attractiveness and profitability of a target industry include the threat of new competitors, the threat of substitute products or services, the intensity of rivalry among existing competitors, the bargaining power of suppliers, and the bargaining power of buyers.

- Opportunities arise for small businesses that are alert to changes or openings in the general, industry, and competitive environments.
- Inside-out analysis helps the entrepreneur to understand the internal potentials of the business.
- Tangible resources are visible and easy to measure, whereas intangible resources are invisible and difficult to quantify.
- Capabilities represent the integration of several resources in a way that boosts the firm's competitive advantage.
- Core competencies are those resources and capabilities that can be leveraged to enable a firm to do something that its competitors cannot do.
- A SWOT analysis provides an overview of a firm's strengths and weaknesses, as well as opportunities for and threats to the organization.
- The entrepreneur's "opportunity sweet spot" is found at the point of overlap of emerging potentials in the external environment and the unique strengths and capabilities of the entrepreneur and his or her venture.

4. Explain broad-based strategy options and focus strategies.

- A competitive advantage can be created using broad-based strategy options—cost-based or differentiation-based strategies.
- A cost-based strategy requires the firm to become a low-cost producer within the market.
- Product or service differentiation is frequently used as a means of achieving superior performance.
- Focusing on a specific market niche is a strategy that small firms often use successfully.
- A focus strategy may involve restricting focus to a single subset of customers, emphasizing a single product or service, limiting the market to a single geographical region, or concentrating on product/service superiority.
- Entrepreneurs can exploit very different market niches that derive from the same general industry.
- The basic direction of the business is chosen when the entrepreneur makes a strategic decision and selects a particular focus strategy.
- The benefits of a focus strategy can diminish when the firm becomes too specialized, the strategy is imitated, the target segment becomes unattractive or demand dwindles, the segment loses its uniqueness, or new firms subsegment the industry.

5. Assess the feasibility of a startup idea before writing a business plan.

- A feasibility analysis should be conducted before moving on to the business plan to identify potentially fatal flaws prior to making the decision to invest the substantial time, energy, and other resources required to put together a full-scale plan.
- A market consists of all buyers of a product or service; an industry is made up of all sellers who compete for the same market.
- A feasibility analysis should assess the potential of a market on two levels—the broad macro-market and the micro-market—because the long-run potential of a market niche is determined largely by the outlook for the overall market.
- The industry should be assessed for its overall attractiveness (potential for profits) and the specific context of direct competition that can greatly impact a startup's prospects for success.
- Entrepreneurs are likely to be successful in a startup situation to the degree that the planned venture fits with their mission, aspirations, and risk tolerance.
- Successful entrepreneurs understand and are able to manage the factors that are critical to the operation of the enterprise, and they are able to connect to suppliers, customers, investors, and others whose involvement is crucial to the future performance of the planned venture.

Key Terms

opportunity recognition p. 69
entrepreneurial alertness p. 69
startups p. 70
Type A ideas p. 71
Type B ideas p. 71
Type C ideas p. 72
serendipity p. 74
general environment p. 81
industry environment p. 81
competitive environment p. 81
resources p. 85
tangible resources p. 85
intangible resources p. 85
capabilities p. 85
competitive advantage p. 85
core competencies p. 86
SWOT analysis p. 86
strategy p. 88
cost-based strategy p. 89
differentiation-based strategy p. 89
focus strategy p. 91
strategic decision p. 92
feasibility analysis p. 94
fatal flaw p. 95

Discussion Questions

1. Why might an entrepreneur prefer to launch an entirely new venture rather than buy an existing firm?
2. What are the three basic types of startup ideas? What are the most common sources of inspiration for startup ideas?
3. List the six most important trends of the general environment. Give a hypothetical example of a way in which each trend might affect a small business.
4. What are the primary factors shaping competition in an industry, according to Porter's model? In your opinion, which of these factors will have the greatest impact on industry prices and profits?
5. How are capabilities related to tangible and intangible resources? How are capabilities related to core competencies?
6. What is a SWOT analysis? How can a SWOT analysis help the entrepreneur match opportunities in the external environment with organizational capabilities?
7. What are the two basic strategy options for creating a competitive advantage?
8. Explain what is meant by the term *focus strategy.*
9. What are the advantages and disadvantages of a focus strategy? What must an entrepreneur know and do to maintain the potential of a focus strategy?
10. Name and describe the major features of a feasibility analysis. Why is feasibility analysis important?

You Make the Call

SITUATION 1

Jonathan Lugar, 17, had just finished helping his mom with a garage sale when it occurred to him that he might create a business to do for others what he had done for her and make a little money that he could save for college. The idea was to offer a service that could take all of the headaches out of running a garage sale. Lugar would handle all advertising and sale setup, and his experience with other garage sales in the area would allow him to coach sellers on pricing so that items would actually be purchased. Lugar figured he could charge $200 per job for sales that bring in $400 or less, but he and the seller would split sales above $400 on a 50-50 basis. Lugar believes the greatest value added from his services would be from his pricing insights, since most people rarely have a garage sale and thus have little idea about how much to ask for items. Pricing wisely should make his customers happy since they could maximize their sales and minimize the risk that they would be left with the very items they were trying to get rid of. In fact, Lugar planned to keep track of how much things sold for to fine-tune his pricing advice. He estimates that his startup costs would be minimal and would come mostly in the form of the use of a truck (which he already owned) and some fuel.

Question 1 How would you classify Lugar's startup idea? Is it a Type A, Type B, or Type C idea?
Question 2 What was the source of Lugar's startup idea?
Question 3 Would you recommend that he give this startup concept a try? Explain your reasoning.

SITUATION 2

Nick Anglada is *really* into motorcycles. But his attention is not invested in just any motorized transport that happens to run on two wheels—he likes bikes that are fast, fun, and true works of art. And that is the focus of his startup, Nick Anglada Originals, a company name so good that it immediately gives away the essence of the business. Since the launch of his company in February 2009, Anglada has ridden his new venture to $2 million worth of business by selling bikes (at $25,000 to $100,000 a pop) that are "tricked out" to the specific tastes of celebrities like Blink-182's Travis Barker, and his "rolling art" has graced the covers of dozens of motorcycle magazines.

Uniqueness is key to the company's strategy, but it goes further than that. Anglada elaborates the firm's emphasis as follows:

> *Customization is a work of art, but ultimately it must be in harmony with the customer's revelation. I like Picasso. Picasso is viewed as a great artist. But not everyone wants a Picasso hanging on [his] wall. When you tell people you build bikes, they instantly envision some big, sweaty mean guy covered in tattoos and coveralls. I despise that vision. I am first and foremost an artist; my canvas just happens to be a large, fast machine."*

So Anglada uses stunning paint work, creative pinstriping, and lots and lots of chrome to create breath-taking, one-of-a-kind motorcycles that are guaranteed to turn heads—but designed in each case to the precise tastes of the individual who orders them. "Balancing high performance, functionality, and ground breaking aesthetics, a Nick Anglada Original is the epitome of modern motorcycle design," declares the company's website. There is little question that the product allows purchasers to "transcend the average and become something more," and that is exactly what Anglada has in mind.

Sources: Susan Carpenter, "Switching Gears," *Entrepreneur*, Vol. 38, No. 3 (March 2010), p. 74; and "Nick Anglada Originals," http://www.nickangladaoriginals.com, accessed November 1, 2010.

Question 1 Based on the frameworks introduced in this chapter, what kind of strategy is Anglada following in his new venture?
Question 2 Identify the strengths upon which this business is built. Do you see any weaknesses that may be of concern to the company?
Question 3 Are there any particular threats that will put Nick Anglada Originals at risk as time goes on? Can you see any opportunities that may allow the company to expand in the future?
Question 4 What resources and capabilities form the foundation for the business? Do you think these will be sufficient to create a *sustainable* competitive advantage for the company? Why or why not?

SITUATION 3

One day, after picking up a cup of coffee, Jay Sorenson promptly dropped it in his lap because the paper cup was simply too hot to hold. From that unpleasant experience, he concluded that there had to be a better way to serve a steaming "cup of joe." He was right. His lap-scorching encounter inspired him to create a product called the Java Jacket, which is a patented insulating sleeve that slides over a paper cup to make any hot beverage comfortable to hold. But coming up with the product was the easy part; getting started in business was a bit more challenging because startup resources were meager. In fact, the company had to use the Sorenson house as its headquarters in the early days. But sales began to pour in after Jay and his wife, Colleen, attended a coffee trade show in Seattle, and the business has grown impressively since then. In fact, the family-run business has already sold more than one billion sleeves to a wide range of customers, from small independent espresso stands to some of the biggest coffee chains in the world. You could say that business is really . . . well . . . percolating.

Source: "About Java Jacket," http://www.javajacket.com/about-java-jacket, accessed November 1, 2010.

Question 1 Will the market for Sorenson's product continue to grow in the years ahead?
Question 2 Given the company's success, what sources of competition should he expect?
Question 3 What steps would you recommend that Sorenson take to protect his company from the onslaught of competition that is likely to come?

Experiential Exercises

1. The U.S. Census Bureau provides massive amounts of data that can be used to shape business ideas so that they are compelling and more likely to succeed. It is helpful to dig deeply into the data the bureau provides, but you can also check out its brief, "snapshot" profiles through the QuickFacts feature to get a feel for how useful these data can be (go to http://quickfacts.census.gov/qfd/index.html to learn more).

   Visit the QuickFacts website, choose a specific city from the drop-down menus, review the data provided, and propose three businesses that would be supported by the demographics of your selected city. Prepare a brief report on your findings, outlining the proposed businesses and rank-ordering them according to your assessment of their potential based on the data. Be prepared to justify each proposed business and your ordering of them.
2. Select a product that is manufactured by a small business and try to determine which features of the general and/or industry environments are the foundation for its creation and success (if it is, in fact, successful).
3. Visit the website of a business publication, such as *Fortune Small Business*, *Inc.*, or the *Wall Street Journal*, and describe the type of target market strategy you believe the newspaper or magazine uses.
4. The next time you visit a local small retailer, ask the manager to describe the firm's customer service policies. Do you think these policies are consistent with what you know about the company's primary strategy? Be prepared to present a case defending your conclusions.
5. Working in small groups, write a brief but specific description of the best target market for a new product that is familiar to most of the class. Designate a member of each group to read the group's market profile to the class.

6. Go to the website of a small business and identify the external factors (such as those in the general, industry, and/or competitive environments) as well as the internal factors around which the business has been created. Does the firm seem to be more sensitive to internal or external dynamics? Given your knowledge of the business, is that good or bad?

7. NYCeWheels sells electrically powered bicycles, like the high performance line of eZee bikes. Take a look at the information found at the company's website (http://store.nycewheels.com). Using the terminology introduced in this chapter, identify the specific type of strategy NYCeWheels is using to expand its business.

Small Business and Entrepreneurship Resource Center

1. Type C ideas, those based on offering customers benefits from new and improved ways of performing old functions, probably account for the largest number of startups. Also, the number one source for startup ideas is personal experience, either at work or at home. Insights gained can lead to opportunities with tremendous potential. Ken and Jennifer Miller started their outdoor clothing company based on Ken's personal experience as a lifeguard. Describe the process of how Ken and Jennifer moved forward based on this experience as the source of their startup idea. Describe also how they combined their experience with a Type C idea as the type of startup idea for their business.

2. Entrepreneurial ideas can come at what may be considered the most inopportune time—when you are dreaming. Focus on that last word—*dreaming*—because that was literally the source of the idea for Monster.com. It's been more than a decade now, but when company founder Jeff Taylor awoke at 4:30 a.m. one morning after an interesting dream, he had a feeling he was on to something. Getting the idea is one thing, but pursuing it is another. Describe how Monster.com founder Jeff Taylor put his dream into action. Also describe his attitude toward entrepreneurship and new ideas.

Sources: Ken & Jennifer Miller: 43, 40, co-founders of Thousand Mile, in Vista, California. (Snapshot)(Brief Article). April Y. Pennington. *Entrepreneur* 31.9 (Sept 2003): p. 23(1).

Monster mash: monster.com's founder moves on to his next big startup. (FORWARD)(Brief Article)(Interview). Amanda C. Kooser. *Entrepreneur* 33.11 (Nov 2005): p. 32(1).

In your dreams: need a business idea? Take a cue from these entrepreneurs, and try sleeping on it. (FORWARD). Geoff Williams. *Entrepreneur* 33.6 (June 2005): p. 36(1).

Case 3

FIREWIRE SURFBOARDS (P. 698)

This case describes the experiences of entrepreneurs who started an innovative surfboard manufacturing business and are shifting its strategy to extend the company's competitive reach.

ALTERNATIVE CASES FOR CHAPTER 3

Case 1, Nau, p. 693
Case 6, Benjapon's, p. 704
Case 8, D'Artagnan, p. 707
Case 11, Missouri Solvents, p. 714

APPENDIX: Questions for Feasibility Analysis

MACRO-MARKET

- Define your entrepreneurial aspirations. Do you want to start a business with the potential to become a huge corporation or a small "lifestyle" enterprise that will never expand beyond a narrow niche market? (It is important to answer this first question to determine the importance of the questions that follow to your particular startup.)
- How large is the broad market you hope to serve? How have you measured its size?
- How fast has it grown over the past one to five years?
- How quickly do you expect it to grow over the next five to ten years?
- What economic, demographic, sociocultural, technological, political/legal, or global trends can you identify that will shape your market? What effect—positive or negative—will these trends have on your business?

MICRO-MARKET

- What specific customer need or benefit will your proposed product or service address?
- Define precisely the customer group you plan to serve. Do you have detailed, accurate, and current information about who the customers are, where they live or do business, and how they live their lives?
- What benefits will customers get from your product or service that they cannot get from those offered by competitors?
- What evidence do you have that customers will buy what you hope to sell?
- What evidence suggests that the market niche you have targeted is likely to grow, and at a reasonable rate?
- What other market niches or segments could also benefit from the product or service that you propose to sell, or one that is similar to it?

MACRO-INDUSTRY

- What industry do you plan to compete in? Provide a specific definition of it.
- Is it difficult or easy for new businesses to enter that industry?
- Do suppliers to that industry have the bargaining power to set terms and conditions, or do buyers have the bargaining power?
- How difficult will it be for substitute products or services to take away your market?
- Is rivalry in the industry best described as intense or contained?
- Considering all of Porter's five forces, is the industry attractive or unattractive?
- If profitability in the industry overall is low, is there good reason to conclude that your startup will outperform this standard? (If not, it's time to move on.)

MICRO-INDUSTRY

- Is your intellectual property—patents, trade secrets, copyrights—protected so that other companies will not be able to duplicate or imitate your business?
- Will the startup face significant legal liability? If so, is adequate and affordable insurance available to cover that liability?
- Can your venture develop and employ extraordinary organizational resources or capabilities that others would find difficult to duplicate or imitate? What evidence do you have to support your conclusion?
- Can you show that your startup will not run out of cash quickly? Your conclusion should be based on your answers to the following questions:
  - Will your sales revenue be adequate relative to the projected financial investment and profit margins (after figuring in all relevant costs)?
  - How much will it cost to acquire and retain customers?
  - How long will it take to attract customers?
  - How much cash must be tied up in working capital (in inventory, for example), and for how long?
  - How long will it take customers to pay?
  - How long can payments to others (such as suppliers) be delayed?

NEW VENTURE LEADERSHIP

Mission, Aspirations, and Risk Propensity

- What is your entrepreneurial mission? To serve a particular market niche? To change a particular industry? To market a particular product or service?
- What is the essence of your entrepreneurial vision? To work for yourself? To start a substantive business that will always be limited in size, with very few employees? To build something really big? To change the world in some important way?
- What kinds of risks are you willing, or unwilling, to take? Will you risk a secure salary and the lifestyle that goes along with your current job? (If so, for how long?) Will you put your own money at risk? (If so, how much?) Will you risk your home or time with your family or loved ones? (Do those you love accept the risks you intend to take?)

Managing Success Factors

- Identify two to five factors that are critical to success in your selected industry.
- How do you know that you have identified these factors correctly?
- Can you demonstrate that you, or your team, can execute on each and every one of the critical factors you have identified?
- Have you identified critical factors that you, or your team, cannot manage? If so, what can you do to address these shortcomings?

Personal Connections

- Whom do you (or your team) know in the companies that are likely to be suppliers to your proposed business, to competitors in your industry, and to companies in other industries that offer products or services that may be substitutes for yours? Write down names, titles, and contact information.
- Whom do you (or your team) know in the companies that are likely to be distributors of and target customers for your product or service, immediately and in the future? Write down names, titles, and contact information.
- Whom do you (or your team) know in the companies that are likely to be competitors or to offer substitute products or services? Write down names, titles, and contact information.

Source: Adapted from John W. Mullins, *The New Business Road Test: What Entrepreneurs and Executives Should Do* Before *Writing a Business Plan* (London: Financial Times Prentice Hall, 2010), pp. 49, 75, 101, 128, 145, 170, 187.

CHAPTER 4

Franchises and Buyouts

In the SPOTLIGHT
Veteran Franchise Centers: Growing America—with America's Best!
http://recruitmilitary.com/franchises

Sometimes you can look back at an event and realize that it changed your life. For Lonnie Helgerson, that day occurred in the late 1980s when he took a photograph of Ron Rivett, co-founder of Super 8 Motels, standing in front of an airplane hangar in Aberdeen, South Dakota.

After his tour of active duty in the United States Army, Helgerson used the GI Bill for higher education and then began a career with companies growing through franchising. He started with Computerland in the mid-1980s, moved to MicroAge Computer Centers, and joined Super 8 Motels in 1987. He describes his years with Super 8 as the most fun of his career.

When Helgerson took Rivett's picture in front of his Learjet, it occurred to him that by creating his own company and growing

Veteran Franchise Centers

through franchising, he could achieve his own personal career and life goals. And his experience at Super 8 gave him his first venture idea.

Helgerson saw the growing need for personal computer use and expertise at Super 8. With experience in the computer business from his days at MicroAge and Computerland, in 1993 he launched Computer Doctor, the first computer service–based franchise concept that created an entirely new franchising sector. This was followed by two other franchise startups as well as opportunities to cash out, leading him to serve as a consultant to others in franchising. Through consulting, Helgerson was presented with the opportunity to become CEO of the largest child safety franchise in the United States: Ident-A-Kid Services of America, which he ran successfully until the end of 2009. To this day, the picture of Ron Rivett with his Learjet still

After studying this chapter, you should be able to . . .

1. Define *franchising,* and become familiar with franchise terminology.
2. Understand the pros and cons of franchising and the structure of the industry.
3. Describe the process for evaluating a franchise opportunity.
4. List four reasons for buying an existing business, and describe the process of evaluating a business.

LOOKING AHEAD

© iStockphoto.com/Dan Bachman

hangs in his office, reminding Helgerson every day that he still has goals that need to be achieved.

In 2010, Helgerson found himself presented with a new venture concept. During his years as a franchisor, he had become active in the International Franchise Association, serving in several volunteer capacities. His favorite project was the VetFran Committee, dedicated to encouraging franchisors to actively seek and provide financial incentives to veterans, enabling them to become franchisees. Through his work on this committee, Helgerson met Drew Myers, a Marine veteran who had founded RecruitMilitary, an employment firm specializing in helping veterans transition into civilian careers. Together, they launched Veteran Franchise Centers (VFC).

VFC was created as a resource center for veterans. The company motto, "Growing America—with America's Best!" makes the statement that veterans are valuable assets and can contribute to the nation's future. VFC assists them in acquiring franchised businesses from companies that have shown themselves to be military-friendly. Helgerson and Myers designed VFC to act as a strategic partner not just with franchisors, but also with financial institutions and suppliers to ease the entrance of veterans into business ownership and success. In October of 2010, VFC began its own growth strategy by soliciting its first franchisees.

Sources: http://www.veteranfranchising.com, accessed October 17, 2010; http://www2.recruitmilitary.com, accessed October 17, 2010; and personal interviews with Lonnie Helgerson, October 14 and 20, 2010.

Avenues for entrepreneurship involve options beyond just starting a new business. Chapter 3 examined how entrepreneurs identify opportunities and pursue their entrepreneurial dreams by starting a business from scratch. But entrepreneurs also buy existing businesses. Many times, they see opportunities that the seller overlooked and take the acquired company to new heights. In other cases, they decide the best way to start is with a partner, a franchisor who has experienced the trials and errors of starting a business and can now make life easier for the franchisee. This chapter considers franchises and buyouts—strategies for ownership involving existing businesses.

What Is Franchising?

The franchise model has been around for a long time in various forms. Some say the model for modern franchising was the Roman Catholic Church, when the pope authorized parish priests to collect tithes and remit a portion to the Vatican while retaining the remainder for parish maintenance.[1] Others trace the beginning of franchising to the United Kingdom in the Middle Ages, when a feudal lord would grant certain rights to laymen in return for a fee and their obedience in carrying out certain community activities, such as operating ferries and drawing water from wells.[2]

The Singer Sewing Machine company is credited with being the first franchisor in the United States.[3] In 1850, the company began contracting with local retailers to give them exclusive rights to sell Singer sewing machines. There are some historians, however, who contend that Benjamin Franklin was actually the first U.S. franchisor.[4] They cite the arrangement he made with a printer in South Carolina to reproduce the *Poor Richard's Almanac* columns that Franklin was producing in Philadelphia. (An interesting side note is that the widow of the South Carolina printer eventually took over her late husband's business, making her the first female franchisee in North America.)

franchising
A business relationship in which an entrepreneur can reduce risk and benefit from the business experience of all members of the franchise system.

The word **franchising** labels a type of business relationship that offers entrepreneurs the possibility of reducing the overall risk associated with buying an independent business or starting a company from scratch. The franchise arrangement allows new business owners to benefit from the accumulated business experience of all members of the franchise system.

What defines this method of doing business? According to the International Franchise Association, franchising is a method of distributing products or services. At least two parties are involved in the franchise system:

LIVING THE DREAM

entrepreneurship + integrity

© iStockphoto.com/Angelika Schwarz

1-800-GOT-MOLD?

Jason Earle had serious respiratory problems as a child—asthma compounded by chronic pneumonia combined with allergies to grass, wheat, corn, eggs, milk, cotton, animals, pollen, and just about everything else. The symptoms disappeared after his family moved to a new house. Earle was later told by his father that their previous house had been infested with mold.

After a nine-year career as a stockbroker, Earle felt drawn to an opportunity that he felt was directly related to his childhood health problems. He heard about a hotel's closing due to a mold problem in the ventilation system (a $55-million problem!). Earle decided that reducing and eliminating mold offered a new career path, and he took a job in New Jersey with a mold-remediation firm. A year later, wanting to help others avoid the problems he had suffered as a child, he bought Oreo, a dog trained to detect mold, and set up his own research company, Lab Result LLC, which evolved into 1-800-GOT-MOLD? The company specialized in the integration of traditional testing, detection, and investigative methods with mold-detection dogs. Earle saw that the mold-detection industry was growing fast, so he decided in 2010 on franchising as the means to take his business nationwide.

© iStockphoto.com/Ekspansio

On the company's website, prospective franchisees are asked the following questions:

Do you want to . . .

- make a huge difference in people's lives?
- create an extraordinary life for you and your family?
- work from home with your dog every day?
- have more freedom to do the things you love?
- make the world a healthier place—one family at a time?

Those interested are invited to ask themselves other questions—about their desire for personal freedom, their wish to help their communities, their interest in new technologies, their desire to have an experienced business partner, and, not the least, their passion for owning and working with a trained dog that has been rescued from the prospect of euthanasia.

Earle's efforts to grow through franchising reflect his intent to have franchisees who share his value system.

Sources: http://www.1800gotmold.com, accessed October 24, 2010; and Jason Daley, "The Mold Breaker," http://www.entrepreneur.com/article/217456, accessed October 24, 2010. **http://www.1800gotmold.com**

1. The **franchisor**, who lends the trademark or trade name and a business system, and
2. The **franchisee**, who pays a royalty and often an initial fee for the right to do business under the franchisor's name and system. Technically, the contract binding the two parties is the "franchise," but that term is often used to mean the actual business that the franchisee operates.[5]

FRANCHISING TERMINOLOGY

If you are considering entering into a legal agreement with a franchisor, you will want to learn all you can about that firm and its leaders. Why did the owners decide on the franchise model? What is their business philosophy? Do you want them as your business partners?

The potential value of any franchising arrangement is defined by the rights contained in a legal agreement known as the **franchise contract**; the rights it conveys are called the **franchise**. The extent and importance of these rights may be quite varied. There are two major types of franchising. When the main benefit the franchisee receives is the privilege of using a widely recognized product name, the arrangement between the franchisor (supplier) and the franchisee (buyer) is called **product and trade name franchising**. Chevrolet automobile dealers, Coca-Cola soft drink bottlers, and ExxonMobil service stations are examples of companies engaged in this type of franchising.

Alternatively, entrepreneurs who receive an entire marketing and management system are participating in a broader type of arrangement referred to as **business format franchising**. Fast-food outlets (such as SONIC), hotels and motels (such as Hilton), and business services (such as Veteran Franchise Centers) typically engage in this type of franchising. Although most people's stereotype of business format franchising is the fast-food restaurant, companies in over 75 industries make use of this structure.

Franchisors do not grow their organizations by sitting back and waiting for franchisees to come to the door. They establish organizational structures and designate employees or partners to expand the number of franchised outlets and to monitor their performance. The most frequent means for carrying out the growth strategies are through use of the following:

- **Master licensee**, a firm or individual having a continuing contractual relationship with a franchisor to sell its franchises. This independent company or businessperson is a type of middleman or sales agent responsible for finding new franchisees within a specified territory. Master franchisees may provide support services such as training and warehousing, which are more traditionally provided by the franchisor. Franchisors often expand internationally through agreements with master franchisees.
- **Multiple-unit ownership**, in which a single franchisee owns more than one unit of the franchised business.
- **Area developers**, individuals or firms that obtain the legal right to open several outlets in a given area.

Although franchised outlets are often thought of as stand-alone, brick-and-mortar enterprises, companies use the following variations to expand their market coverage:

- **Piggyback franchising** refers to the operation of a retail franchise within the physical facilities of a host store. An example of piggyback franchising occurs when Subway operates a restaurant within a truck stop.
- **Multi-brand franchising** involves operating several franchise organizations within a single corporate structure. The Dwyer Group is a pioneer in this form of franchising with six brands: Rainbow International, Mr. Appliance Corp., Mr. Rooter, Aire Serv, Mr. Electric, and Glass Doctor.

franchisor
The party in a franchise contract that specifies the methods to be followed and the terms to be met by the other party.

franchisee
An entrepreneur whose power is limited by a contractual relationship with a franchising organization.

franchise contract
The legal agreement between franchisor and franchisee.

franchise
The privileges conveyed in a franchise contract.

product and trade name franchising
A franchise agreement granting the right to use a widely recognized product or name.

business format franchising
A franchise arrangement whereby the franchisee obtains an entire marketing and management system geared to entrepreneurs.

master licensee
An independent firm or individual acting as a middleman or sales agent with the responsibility of finding new franchisees within a specified territory.

multiple-unit ownership
Ownership by a single franchisee of more than one franchise from the same company.

area developers
Individuals or firms that obtain the legal right to open several franchised outlets in a given area.

piggyback franchising
The operation of a retail franchise within the physical facilities of a host store.

multi-brand franchising The operation of several franchise organizations within a single corporate structure.

co-branding Bringing two franchise brands together under one roof.

- **Co-branding** involves bringing two franchise brands together under one roof. A&W and KFC found that co-locating their brands worked so well in one outlet that they agreed to combine the brands in over 300 locations.

THE IMPACT OF FRANCHISING

Periodically, the International Franchise Association (IFA) sponsors studies of the impact of franchising on the American economy. The mission of the IFA is to protect, enhance, and promote franchising.[6] Founded in 1960, the IFA has more than 1,000 franchisors, 7,000 franchisees, and 350 suppliers as members.[7] The impact studies report economic activity in franchised businesses—in terms of number of establishments, jobs, payroll, and output—and from the purchasing of goods and services by franchise businesses and the expenditures of franchise owners and employees in their communities.

According to the IFA's *2010 Franchise Business Economic Outlook,* there were 901,093 establishments in franchise systems, employing 9,558,000 people, and producing an output of $868.3 billion (see Exhibit 4.1). The report showed that franchised businesses actually provided more jobs than entire industries, including durable goods manufacturing, financial services, construction, nondurable goods manufacturing, and information (software and print publishing, motion pictures and videos, radio and television broadcasting, and telecommunications carriers and resellers). Use of the franchise model of business formation and growth is expected to increase. Not only are United States–based companies expanding internationally, but also franchisors headquartered in other countries are seeking to enter the U.S. market by contracting with franchisees. One more reason growth in franchising may occur is the fact that so many people entering the workforce get their first jobs in franchises. Because of the detailed operations manuals used in franchising, businesses are able to hire people who lack prior work experience. With their initial exposure to the workplace coming from franchise organizations, more and more of these entrants will see franchising as a viable business ownership option for their career goals.

EXHIBIT 4.1 Economic Impact of Franchising

Economic Activity in Franchised Businesses

There were estimated to be 901,093 establishments in franchise systems in the United States in 2010. These businesses *directly* provided

- 9.558 million jobs
- output worth $868.3 billion.

These businesses accounted for approximately 3 percent of all U.S. business establishments. During the economic turmoil in the United States from 2007 to 2010, employment in eight of ten lines of franchise business activity increased. The two exceptions were Commercial and Residential Services and Lodging.

Economic Activity Because of Franchised Businesses

According to the most recent economic impact study by PriceWaterhouseCoopers, the economic significance of franchising is greater than indicated by the activity in franchised businesses alone, for it stimulates still more activity and causes growth in many nonfranchised businesses. Counting economic results both inside and outside of franchising, franchised businesses in the United States were the cause of

- 21 million jobs, or 15.3 percent of private-sector jobs
- $660.9 billion of payroll, or 12.5 percent of private-sector payrolls
- $2.31 trillion of output, or 11.4 percent of private-sector output.

Sources: PriceWaterhouseCoopers, *2010 Franchise Business Economic Outlook* (Washington, DC: International Franchise Association, 2010); and PriceWaterhouse Coopers, *The Economic Impact of Franchised Businesses, Volume II* (Washington, DC: International Franchise Association, 2008).

The Pros and Cons of Franchising

2
Understand the pros and cons of franchising and the structure of the industry.

In a way, we are all "experts" in franchising. You have been making purchases in franchise outlets since you were a child. If you have work experience, your first job may have been with a franchised business. Because the franchise model is so well defined, franchisees are more likely than other employers to hire individuals who lack prior work experience.

We see advertisements for franchise businesses everywhere. Yet how much do we really know about an opportunity until we have studied it? "Look before you leap" is an old adage that should be heeded by entrepreneurs who are considering franchising. Weighing the purchase of a franchise against alternative paths to starting a business is an important task and deserves careful consideration. Exhibit 4.2 lists some of the major advantages you can gain through franchising.

THE PROS

Buying a franchise can be attractive for a variety of reasons. The greatest advantage is the probability of success. Franchisors offer a business model with a proven track record. A reputable franchisor has been through the trials and errors that an entrepreneur might face when starting a business from scratch. One explanation for the low failure rate of franchises is how selective many franchisors are when granting franchises; even potential franchisees who qualify financially can still be rejected.

There are other reasons why a franchise opportunity is appealing. Attractive franchises have names that are well known to prospective

RESOURCES

Getting the Basics

Many franchisors and franchisees find the International Franchise Association (IFA) to be a valuable source of information for understanding how the franchise model works. Start with an *Introduction to Franchising*, published by the IFA's Educational Foundation. You can find this 45-page document at http://www.franchise.org/uploadedFiles/_Home/Rotator/introtofranchising_final.pdf.

EXHIBIT 4.2 Advantages of the Franchise Model

- Reduced risk of failure
- Going into business for yourself, but not by yourself
- Use of a valuable trade name and trademark
- Access to a proven business system
- Management training provided by the franchisor
- Immediate economies of scale
- A way for an existing business to diversify

customers. They provide detailed operations manuals for franchisees to follow, so the hard work of blazing the trail has already been done. And they also support their franchisees by providing training, reducing purchasing costs, designing promotional campaigns, and assisting in obtaining capital. Naturally, different franchises vary in the depth of support they provide for each of these forms of assistance.

Trade Names and Trade Marks

When you open your own business, it can take a long time and a lot of money to get your name established and customers in your door or to your website. When you become a franchisee, however, you expect the franchisor to have laid the groundwork. An entrepreneur who enters into a franchising agreement acquires the right to use the franchisor's nationally advertised trademark or brand name, and this serves to identify the local enterprise with a widely recognized product or service. If customers have been satisfied with the products and services they have received from one unit in a franchise chain, they are likely to do business with another store that carries that company's name. Doctor's Associates Inc., the company that owns Subway Restaurants, reports that over half of their new franchisees purchase their stores from retiring owners, demonstrating the value they attach to the brand.[8]

Success for many businesses results from their intellectual property. Patents usually come to mind when we think about intellectual property, but a trademarked name can be just as valuable if it has become part of common public use. A trademark protects "words, names, symbols, sounds, or colors that distinguish goods and services from those manufactured or sold by others and to indicate the source of the goods. Trademarks, unlike patents, can be renewed forever as long as they are being used in commerce."[9] Think McDonald's Golden Arches, "Oh Thank Heaven for 7-Eleven®," "Trust the Midas Touch®," the graphic image of Colonel Sanders of KFC, and many others. Doctor's Associates Inc. has registered 15 different trademarks.[10] Trademarks and trade names make a business instantly identifiable to prospective customers and clients and can bring them right through the door.

Operations Manual

In addition to a proven line of business and readily identifiable products or services, franchisors offer well-developed and thoroughly tested methods of marketing and management. The manuals and procedures supplied to franchisees enable them to function more efficiently from the start. Reputable firms that grow through franchising begin with company-owned stores in which they develop their fundamental business model, leading to a tried-and-true method of operating the business. They document the procedures that work, compile them in an operations manual, and provide the manual to franchisees. Guidelines in the manual explain to franchisees and managers the specific steps required to operate the enterprise profitably.

An operations manual may be the single most valuable tool provided to a franchisee. Following the path laid out in the manual helps the owner to avoid mistakes that often occur with a startup business, such as employing unqualified personnel, investing in the wrong equipment or inventory, or failing to control costs. The franchisee should use the manual to channel his or her energy toward the most productive activities leading to survival and profitability. And the franchisee should expect to be held accountable for following the manual. One of the most critical aspects of franchising is that customers find the same products, services, and methods of conducting business from one outlet to another. If one franchise is allowed to operate at a substandard level, it could easily destroy customers' confidence in the entire chain.

Training Support

The training received from franchisors is invaluable to many small entrepreneurs because it compensates for weaknesses in their managerial skills. Training by the franchisor often begins with an initial period of a few days or a few weeks at a central training school or another established location and then continues at a franchise site. McDonald's is widely recognized for its off-site franchisee training at Hamburger University. More and more franchisors are providing their training programs online.

© McDonald's Corporation

The nature of both the product and the business affect the amount and type of training needed by the franchisee. In most cases, training constitutes an important advantage of the franchising system, as it permits individuals who have had little training or education in the industry to start and succeed in businesses of their own.

Economies of Scale

Joining a franchise network makes the entrepreneur part of a larger organization, which provides significant economies of scale. One critical benefit of these economies is efficiency in the purchasing function. A franchise network can buy in larger quantities than an individual business can, lowering per-unit costs for franchisees. Additionally, centralized purchasing activities reduce operating expenses for the various outlets.

Franchisees are often required to contribute to marketing expenses above and beyond the royalties they pay on sales. These expenses are pooled for the benefit of the entire network. The franchisor is then able to invest in more sophisticated marketing research, higher-quality advertising campaigns, and more extensive media outlets than franchisees could invest in independently. This ability leads to wider and deeper acceptance of the brands and trade names and benefits each franchisee.

Financial Support

Some franchisors provide financial support to prospective and existing franchisees, assistance that can come in many forms. Companies such as GNC and Wingstop have formed alliances with banks to create preferred lending programs for franchisees. The International Franchise Association (IFA) encourages franchisors to recruit minorities and veterans as franchisees by offering financial incentives. In order for a franchisor to be listed in the IFA's VetFran Directory, the company must agree to provide initial fee discounts, special financing terms, or other incentives. Nearly 400 companies are now listed in the directory. They range alphabetically from A (AAMCO Transmissions) to Z (Ziebart Car Care).[11] Support for franchisees includes such examples as programs by Burger King and Yum! Brands (KFC, Taco Bell, Pizza Hut, etc.) to assist in restructuring financing.[12]

Many prospective franchisees find that they can work with banks to obtain loans guaranteed by the U.S. Small Business Administration (SBA) in order to finance the franchise fee and startup costs. The SBA maintains a Franchise Registry (http://www.franchiseregistry.com), which speeds up loan processing for small business franchisees. The Registry attests that "the SBA has already reviewed the franchise agreement and has determined that there are no unacceptable control provisions by the franchisor over its franchisees."[13] This determination provides an assurance that the franchisor will not become dictatorial in the business relationship. More importantly, the Registry designation enables lenders for registered franchises to review and process loan applications more quickly.

Although many franchising systems have developed excellent support programs, understand that this is by no means universal. There are many pros to the franchise system, but, as in any negotiation, the buyer must be aware of the cons.

THE CONS

The founders of the International Franchise Association were disturbed by dishonest and unethical acts of some companies that were growing through franchising and damaging the reputation of the entire industry; they also sought to preempt government regulation of franchising. Firms joining the IFA are required to adhere to a code of ethics, the foundational values of which are "trust, truth, and honesty"[14] The code requires IFA members to practice mutual respect and open and frequent communication. The IFA also demands adherence to laws and offers a conflict resolution service for franchisors and franchisees. To this day, however, some companies engage in practices that trouble regulators, legislators, and the business community at large. Some concerns that government officials have regarding franchising are listed in Exhibit 4.3.

Financial Issues

Major concerns have arisen regarding the true costs of becoming and remaining a franchisee. New franchisees of some franchise organizations have felt misled about their earnings opportunities. They report being told that they could expect high returns on their investments, only to discover that few, if any, franchisees achieved those results. Current and former franchisees of Quiznos, for example, sued the firm in Illinois, Pennsylvania, and Wisconsin for luring "franchisees into the system by misrepresenting contract terms and financial projections."[15] A settlement was reached for $207 million in 2010. The settlement included credits for purchasing supplies and equipment, and payment amounts were authorized to plaintiffs who chose not to proceed with Quiznos' franchises.[16]

Other criticisms of franchisors that have come to the attention of government agencies include refusing to permit franchisees to sell their businesses in order to invest their money elsewhere and forcing franchisees to purchase products and services from subsidiaries or business associates, resulting in higher-than-market costs. There have also been complaints of **churning**, which refers to actions by franchisors to void the contracts of franchisees in order to sell the franchise to someone else and collect an additional fee.

churning
Actions by franchisors to void the contracts of franchisees in order to sell the franchise to someone else and collect an additional fee.

Franchisor Competition

Franchisors have actually competed directly against their franchisees on occasion. This can occur when the franchisor opens a corporate-owned store near the franchisee's

EXHIBIT 4.3 Government Concerns About Franchising

1. Misleading or exaggerated earnings claims by franchisors
2. Opportunity behavior by which the franchisor becomes a competitive threat to franchisees
3. Restrictions on franchisees who desire to liquidate their holdings in favor of alternative investment opportunities
4. Conflicts of interest, such as when a franchisor forces franchisees to be captive outlets for other suppliers owned by the franchisor
5. Churning: terminating a successful franchise operation in order to resell it and gain additional franchise fees
6. Encroachment: locating a new outlet or point of distribution too close to an existing franchisee, causing a material loss of sales
7. Imposing noncompete clauses on franchisees
8. One-sided contracts devised by franchisors
9. The imposition of new restrictions as a requirement of contract renewal
10. Franchisor intimidation of franchisees who attempt to form franchisee associations, seek alternative sources for products, or make other efforts to create a more level playing field

location or sells products via mail or over the Internet. A variation on this complaint is referred to as **encroachment**. A franchisor is said to encroach on a franchisee's territory when the franchisor sells another franchise location within the market area of an existing franchisee. Such actions can be virtual in the electronic age. For example, Edible Arrangements was sued by a group of their franchisees contending that DippedFruit.com, a subsidiary of Edible Arrangements, competed unfairly with the franchisees by offering identical products online.[17]

encroachment The franchisor's selling of another franchise location within the market area of an existing franchisee.

Another complaint stems from special clauses inserted into some franchise agreements. A number of franchisors impose noncompete clauses on their franchisees. From the franchisors' perspective, this makes perfect sense—after training and sharing secrets and strategies with a franchisee, they do not want the franchisee to sever the relationship and become a competitor. From the franchisees' perspective, this constitutes restraint of trade, especially if they find the franchisor to be nonresponsive to their needs or if they project that they can make more money on their own. It is only natural to think that the next business you start would evolve from your current experience. Yet the franchisor may keep you from applying those experiential skills by claiming that your new enterprise competes with the franchisor's business.

Management Issues

The final set of issues focuses on the freedom of the franchisee to run his or her own business. As a franchisee, you are not a truly independent business owner. You have a contractual arrangement with the franchisor that stipulates various conditions, and that contract may specify the products you carry, the services you offer, your hours of operation, and other aspects of how you run your company. The contract was drafted by, and most likely favors, the franchisor. Many prospective franchisees fail to recognize that many franchisors are willing to negotiate some portions of the contract. In any case, you should always have an attorney review the contract before you sign it. Some of the most common restrictions that these contracts impose on franchisees fall into the following categories:

- Limiting sales territories
- Requiring site approval for the retail outlet, and imposing requirements regarding outlet appearance
- Limiting goods and services offered for sale
- Limiting advertising and hours of operation

A frequently heard complaint from franchisees is that when their contract expires, they are required to accept new and often costly provisions. Franchisees suspect this is an effort to extract more revenues and/or concessions from them, to force them out in order to sell the franchise to someone else, or to take it over as a company store. Of course, the franchisor may have another explanation. During the years the contract was in force, the franchisor should have gained experience in working with multiple franchisees and may have discovered ways to improve the system that were incorporated into more recent franchise contracts. Additionally, franchisors may find that some long-time franchisees have not maintained their facilities or have failed to adapt to new marketing and operating procedures. From the franchisor's point of view, these franchisees need to improve their businesses so that they will not harm the entire network.

THE COSTS OF BEING A FRANCHISEE

If you choose to become a franchisee, you pay for the privilege. You are buying a proven model, and the franchisor will charge you for the benefits being offered. Generally speaking, higher costs characterize the better known and more successful franchises. Franchise costs have several components, all of which need to be recognized and considered.

© Jeff Greenberg / Alamy

1. *Initial franchise fee.* The total cost of a franchise begins with an initial franchise fee, which may range from several hundred to many thousands of dollars. Veteran Franchise Centers, mentioned in the Spotlight at the start of this chapter, estimates a $75,000 startup cost, with the total investment ranging from $47,550 to $95,800, but it offers qualified veterans a $10,000 discount on the initial fee.[18]
2. *Investment costs.* Significant costs may be involved in renting or building an outlet and stocking it with inventory and equipment. Certain insurance premiums, legal fees, and other startup expenses must also be paid, and it is often recommended that funds be available to cover personal expenses and emergencies for at least six months. On its website, Oreck Clean Home Center (known best for the Oreck vacuum cleaner) presents estimated startup costs, but it also indicates the benefits that a franchisee can expect to receive[19] (see Exhibit 4.4).
3. *Royalty payments.* A royalty is a fee charged to the franchisee by the franchisor. It is calculated as a percentage of the gross income that the franchisee receives from customers for selling the franchised products and services. Two Men and a Truck, a moving services company described in more detail in Chapter 5, charges a 6 percent royalty. For America's largest drive-in restaurant business, SONIC Corporation, the royalty fee ranges from 4 to 5 percent.[20]
4. *Advertising costs.* Many franchisors require that franchisees contribute to an advertising fund to promote the franchise. These fees are generally 1 to 2 percent of sales, sometimes even more. Franchisees pay these fees to support the franchisor in establishing the name and reputation of the business in the minds of targeted customers. Successful, well-managed franchise organizations will promote the company and its products and services more cost-efficiently than individual stores could do on their own.

EXHIBIT 4.4 An Estimate of Investment Costs and Benefits by Oreck Clean Home Center

Business Established:	1963
Franchising Since:	2006
Franchised Units:	330
Company Owned Units:	98
Start-up Cost:	$30,000
Total Investment:	$84,600 to $221,000

Offering Financial Assistance

The initial investment is different for each situation, but it is approximately $84,600 to $221,000. The estimate includes the Franchise Fee which is $30,000. Oreck offers third party financing through our partner, GE Capital.

Special Incentives

VetFran Participant

Franchise Resale Opportunity

VetFran Incentive

Oreck will provide $10,000 of product inventory to qualified veterans who purchase an Oreck Clean Home Center Franchise.

Source: Copied with permission International Franchise Association, http://franchise.org/Oreck_Franchise_Services_LLC_franchise.aspx.

If entrepreneurs could generate the same level of sales by setting up an independent business, they would save the franchise fee and some of the other costs. However, if the franchisor provides the benefits previously described, the money that franchisees pay to start and maintain their relationship with the franchisor may well prove to be a very good investment.

Evaluating Franchise Opportunities

3 Describe the process for evaluating a franchise opportunity.

After making a decision to pursue a franchising opportunity, the prospective franchisee must identify a franchising company and investigate it completely. As we discuss the investigation process, we will use an example, The Glass Doctor, a company offering residential, commercial, and auto glass services.

SELECTING A FRANCHISE

With the growth of franchising over the years, the task of selecting an appropriate franchise has become easier. Personal observation frequently sparks interest, or awareness may begin with exposure to an advertisement in a newspaper or magazine or on the Internet. The headlines of these advertisements usually highlight the financial and personal rewards sought by the entrepreneur. *Inc.*, *Entrepreneur*, and the *Wall Street Journal* are only three examples of the many publications that not only print stories about franchising, but also include the advertisements of franchisors.

INVESTIGATING THE POTENTIAL FRANCHISE

The nature of the commitment required in franchising justifies careful investigation of the situation. The investment is substantial, and the business relationship generally continues over many years.

The evaluation process is a two-way effort. The franchisor wishes to investigate the franchisee, and the franchisee obviously wishes to evaluate the franchisor and the type of opportunity being offered. Time is required for this kind of analysis. You should be skeptical of a franchisor who pressures you to sign a contract without time for proper investigation. Some of the factors to consider in assessing different franchise opportunities are listed in Exhibit 4.5. The first factor on the list warns against entering into an agreement with a company that primarily distributes its goods and services through corporate-owned stores. If the primary distribution system does not consist of franchised stores, will the franchisor give as much attention to franchisees as to their own outlets? You should ask yourself whether this company will provide as much attention and the same support services to its franchisees as it does to the outlets that it owns. You also want to be associated with an organization that is well established and has enjoyed success in the marketplace.

ACTION

Consumers' Guide for Buying a Franchise

Don't even think about becoming a franchisee until you've read this FTC document: *Buying a Franchise: A Consumer Guide*. The Federal Trade Commission (FTC), the nation's consumer protection agency, has prepared this booklet to explain how to shop for a franchise opportunity, the obligations of a franchise owner, and questions to ask before you invest. You can download the booklet at http://business.ftc.gov/documents/inv05-buying-franchise-consumer-guide.

EXHIBIT 4.5 Evaluating Franchise Opportunities

1. Is the franchisor dedicated to a franchise system as its primary mechanism of product and service distribution?
2. Does the franchisor produce and market quality goods and services for which there is an established market demand?
3. Does the franchisor enjoy a favorable reputation and broad acceptance in the industry?
4. Will the franchisor offer an established, well-designed marketing and business plan and provide substantial and complete training to franchisees?
5. Does the franchisor have good relations with its franchisees, and do the franchisees have a strong franchisee organization that has negotiating leverage with the franchisor?
6. Does the franchisor have a history of attractive earnings by its franchisees?

And you need to speak with current and past franchisees. What was their working relationship with the franchisor? Would they do it all over again?

There are many sources of information about franchisors to help you in your evaluation, including state and federal agencies. Since many states require registration of franchises, a prospective franchisee should not overlook state offices as a source of assistance. The Federal Trade Commission has produced various helpful reports and documents regarding franchising, including *Buying a Franchise: A Consumer Guide*. (These are available at http://business.ftc.gov/documents/inv05-buying-franchise-consumer-guide.)

Also, a comprehensive listing of franchisors can be found on the website of the International Franchise Association (http://franchise.org). Exhibit 4.6 displays the listing for Glass Doctor from the IFA's website, http://franchise.org/Glass_Doctor_franchise.aspx. In assessing published information about franchises, Mark Liston, vice president of operations for the Glass Doctor, cautions,

> *As you choose a franchisor remember—this is a marriage . . . usually for at least 10 years. This is why it is extremely important to understand the culture of the franchisor to determine if this truly will be a partnership with the franchisor and the franchisee interdependent with each other. The best way to validate this is by talking to several of the franchisor's franchisees. Ask about the culture. Ask about the leadership of the franchisor. See what kind of support the franchisor provides.*[21]

When considering which franchisor to choose, there is often a trade-off between the size of the organization and the fee to become a franchisee. The better-known, more successful franchisors are likely to offer a greater chance of long-term survival and prosperity, but they are also in a position to charge premium prices for becoming part of their network. *Entrepreneur* magazine's website contains a profile of the top-10 fastest-growing franchises in 2010 (see Exhibit 4.7). Most franchisors will have cost estimates for prospective franchisees available on their websites. The rankings are based on the number of franchise units added in the United States and Canada from 2008 to 2009.

In recent years, franchise consultants have appeared in the marketplace to assist individuals seeking franchise opportunities. Some consulting firms, such as Francorp, conduct seminars on choosing the right franchise. Of course, the prospective franchisee needs to be careful to select a reputable consultant. And since franchise consultants are not necessarily attorneys, an experienced franchise attorney should evaluate all legal documents.

EXHIBIT 4.6 Profile from International Franchise Association (2010)

Glass Doctor

> Company Details	**Business Established:**	1962
> Contact Info	**Franchising Since:**	1981
> Traning	**Franchised Units:**	195
> Qualifications	**Company Owned Units:**	0
> Request More Info	**Start-up Cost**	$20,000 to $125,000
	Total Investment:	$107,000 to $260,000

Offering Financial Assistance

Partial financing available to those who qualify.

Special Incentives

VetFran Participant
International Opportunity Franchise Resale Opportunity

VetFran Incentive

Discount franchise fee by $6,000

COMPANY DETAILS

Description

Glass Doctor is the largest chain of full-service glass franchises in the nation, serving the residential, automotive, and commercial markets. From windows to windshields and storefronts, Glass Doctor can handle any glass need. Glass Doctor also offers custom glass services, such as tub/shower enclosures, entry door glass, mirrors, tabletops, and commercial door hardware. The Glass Doctor national accounts program has agreements with facility maintenance providers for major retailers, restaurant chains, and hotels. Other local commercial accounts include insurance agents, apartment communities, remodelers, auto dealers, rental fleets, and government entities.

Training

Upon becoming a Glass Doctor franchisee, you will attend a proprietary training course where our knowledgeable corporate team assists you in putting financial, marketing, management, and customer service strategies to work for you. Two weeks of initial training are required, including seminars at the world headquarters, classroom sessions at the Glass Doctor University training center, hands-on workshops at the Glass Doctor University shop (the only one of its kind in the industry), and job shadowing at a fully operational Glass Doctor shop.

Qualifications

Strong Work Ethic, Financially Qualified, High Achievement Drive, Honesty & Integrity, Strong Image/Self-Esteem, Team Player, Willingness To Learn & Apply Proven Successful Business Systems.

Source: Copied with permission International Franchise Association, http://franchise.org/Glass_Doctor_franchise.aspx.

The Franchisor as a Source of Information

Obviously, the franchisor being evaluated is a primary source of information. However, information provided by a franchisor must be viewed in light of its purpose—to promote the franchise. Mark Liston from the Glass Doctor adds,

> *[You] must remember that you won't get glowing remarks from everyone. That is good. Although successful franchise organizations have an interdependency, there will be times*

EXHIBIT 4.7 Top 10 Fastest Growing Franchises for 2010

Name/Rank	Startup Costs (2009)
1. Jan-Pro Franchising Int'l. Inc. Commercial cleaning	$3,145–50,405
2. Subway Submarine sandwiches and salads	$84,300–258,300
3. Stratus Building Solutions Commercial cleaning	$3,450–57,750
4. Dunkin' Donuts Coffee, doughnuts, baked goods	$358,200–1,980,300
5. Anago Cleaning Systems Commercial cleaning	$8,543–65,406
6. McDonald's Hamburgers, chicken, salads	$1,057,200–1,885,000
7. CleanNet USA Inc. Commercial cleaning	$6,655–92,950
8. Bonus Building Care Commercial cleaning	$9,020–41,919
9. Liberty Tax Service Individual and online tax preparation	$56,800–69,900
10. Vanguard Cleaning Systems Commercial cleaning	$8,200–38,100

Source: Entrepreneur's 2010 Fastest-Growing Franchises Rankings (Top 10) with Start-Up Cost Ranges in 2009 from http://www.entrepreneur.com, accessed October 29, 2010. Reprinted with permission of Entrepreneur Media, Inc.

when they simply disagree. The franchisor has to make decisions that is good for the entire network. Those decisions may not make some individual franchisees happy.[22]

One way to obtain information about franchisors is to review their websites. For most franchisors, the website will be directed toward customers, presenting information about products, services, store locations, and so on. The websites should also direct you to information for prospective franchisees. If you enter your contact information, you can expect to receive brochures and marketing materials that contain such information as startup costs and franchisees' testimonials. Your search may also lead you to websites or blogs of disgruntled franchisees, customers, or others.

If you express further interest in a franchise by completing the application form and the franchisor has tentatively qualified you as a potential franchisee, a meeting is usually arranged to discuss the disclosure document. A **Franchise Disclosure Document (FDD)** is a detailed statement of such information as the franchisor's finances, experience, size, and involvement in litigation. The document must inform potential franchisees of any restrictions, costs, and provisions for renewal or cancellation of the franchise. Important considerations related to this document are examined more fully later in this chapter.

Franchise Disclosure Document (FDD)
A document that provides the accepted format for satisfying the franchise disclosure requirements of the FTC.

Existing and Previous Franchises as Sources of Information

There may be no better source of franchise facts than existing franchisees. Sometimes, however, the distant location of other franchisees precludes a visit to their place of

© iStockphoto.com/Angelika Schwarz

entrepreneurship + integrity

Growing Your Business the Right Way!

Franchising is such a distinct way of doing business that an entire industry has sprung up to guide and assist prospective and existing franchisors and franchisees. Craig Slavin was an early entrant in this industry and has been in the franchise consulting arena for over 30 years. He is the chairman and founder of Franchise Architects, a consulting firm with a client list that reads like a who's who of worldwide companies: AT&T, Apple Computers, Hewlett-Packard, Intel, Bally Total Fitness, Shell Oil, Circle K Corporation, Sears Roebuck & Co., Ryder/PIE, TCBY, Mrs. Fields' Cookies, The Walt Disney Company, and more.

Slavin trained to be an architect at the University of Arizona. Eventually, he found it necessary to leave school just short of earning his degree. He answered an ad in a newspaper from a company offering someone a chance to make money and have fun. Slavin found himself with a firm that was seeking to expand, and it was immediately obvious to him that you cannot grow a company without a structure to support that growth. Over time, he found himself drawn to franchise organizations because the franchise model provides the structure many business owners need.

Beginning in 1979, Slavin became a franchisor on five occasions, and he discovered that other franchisors were soliciting his advice and expertise. This led to the creation of Franchise Architects, which specializes in advising franchisors on growing their networks, focusing on identifying, selecting, and collaborating with franchisees. Early on, Slavin led a research team to analyze the characteristics of successful franchisees and to determine the best matches of prospective franchisees with different models of franchise organizations. From the results of the studies, Slavin and his team learned a company might have the best business model in the world, but if it sells franchises to individuals who cannot execute the model, the franchisees will not be as effective as they could or should be.

As Slavin sees it, too many ventures are built top down, based on the vision of the founding entrepreneur. Instead, they must be built from the bottom up. He uses the analogy of an eight-cylinder engine: If one cylinder goes down, they all go down. Slavin learned early on that he is more interested in making rules than in following them. He helps franchisors and franchisees wrap rules around their cylinders to make them stronger.

Sources: Personal interview with Craig Slavin, October 28, 2010; http://franchisearchitects.com/index.html, accessed October 27, 2010; http://franmarket.ning.com/profile/CraigSlavin, accessed October 27, 2010; and http://www.sn.franchisecentral.com/home.php, accessed October 28, 2010. **http://franchisearchitects.com**

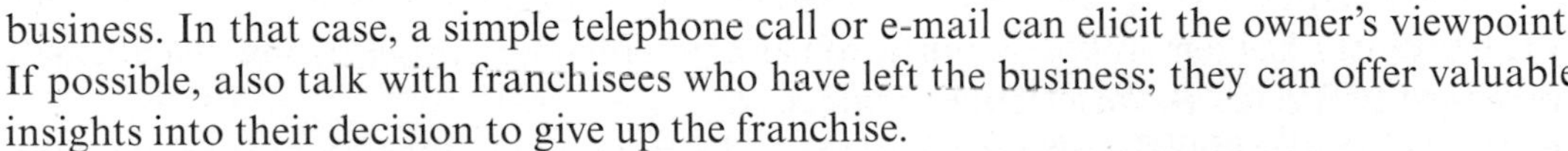

business. In that case, a simple telephone call or e-mail can elicit the owner's viewpoint. If possible, also talk with franchisees who have left the business; they can offer valuable insights into their decision to give up the franchise.

BECOMING A FRANCHISOR

We do not want to end the discussion of franchising without considering how you might choose this method to grow your independent business, just as Lonnie Helgerson of Veteran Franchise Centers did. After a few years of running your own business, you may conclude that you want to expand and that franchising is a reasonable option for you. It is not unusual for the owners of successful businesses to be approached by individuals who ask to become franchisees. Before entering into an agreement with a potential franchisee, consider the questions discussed in the following subsections.

A Reproducible Model

Is your business replicable? In other words, do you have a model of doing business that someone else could adopt and use successfully in another location? A franchisee purchases an operating system as well as a product or service and a brand name. Is your system efficient, and can it be clearly explained so that others can apply it?

In the case of Veteran Franchise Centers, Lonnie Helgerson and his partner, Drew Myers, began soliciting prospective franchisees within their first year of operation. They were able to do so based on their many years of experience with multiple franchise networks, combined with Drew's existing RecruitMilitary enterprise. They were able to design and refine their replicable model for VFC in a short period of time.

Financial Considerations

How will you finance the growth of the company? Many entrepreneurs think that franchising is a novel mechanism for financing their growing enterprises. They come up with a concept, collect franchise fees, and use those revenues to expand their operations. But franchising is not cost-free for the franchisor. There are legal documents to prepare, an operations manual to write, personnel to hire, and other tasks to be completed. Who will recruit and select franchisees? Who will orient and train them and their managers? Who will monitor their performance to ensure that they conform to contract requirements? Responsible franchisors often find that establishing a franchise costs more than the fee covers and that they only become profitable as a result of the royalties they eventually collect from successful franchisees.

Required Assistance

What expert assistance will you need to become a franchisor? Successful entrepreneurs learn quickly that they must choose the right experts, individuals who are qualified to provide the necessary help. If you decide to franchise your business, you should have an attorney with knowledge of and experience with the franchise method. As mentioned previously, there are many consultants, such as Franchise Architects, who specialize in franchising and can assist with drafting operations manuals, preparing disclosure documents, assisting with franchisee selection, and many other aspects of the process. A good starting place for any prospective franchisor is joining the International Franchise Association and gathering information about reputable consultants.

Operations Manual

Earlier in this chapter, we looked at the operations manual from the franchisee's point of view. For the franchisor, this is an essential element in the value the business model offers to franchisees. What will go into your operations manual? Many companies that have grown successfully through franchising brought in consultants who specialize in making the business operating model more efficient and easier to replicate prior to writing the manual. You should be able to present an operations manual to your franchisees that spells out what steps to take in daily activities to ensure customer satisfaction while controlling expenses. The operations manual should offer detailed instructions that help franchisees avoid pitfalls and increase sales. It needs to be written from the perspective of the franchisee, who will not know the business as well as the franchisor. It is usually wise to hire a professional technical writer to put the manual together so that it communicates the process effectively. Many new franchisors have found that experts who assist in writing operations manuals also help the businesses improve the efficiencies of their operations, making startup and management easier and lower cost for franchisees.

SKILLS

Opportunities in Diversity

With the growing diversity of franchisees, franchising's embrace of inclusion is paying off in dramatic, measurable ways. About a dozen companies on the DiversityInc Top 50 list are franchise operations. Success for franchisors, franchisees, and other small business owners often depends on their ability to serve and to reflect their changing customer base. And franchisors are also looking for diversity officers to employ within their organizations.

Government Regulations

Are you willing to satisfy the government's disclosure requirements? The Federal Trade Commission issued an amended **Franchise Rule** in May 2008. This rule prescribes that the franchisor must disclose certain information to prospective franchisees. Some business owners may decide that they would rather not disclose information that they consider confidential such as prior bankruptcies, the business experience of the principals, or litigation in which the firm is involved. In such cases, franchising may not be the appropriate method to use for growth.

Franchise Rule
A rule that prescribes that the franchisor must disclose certain information to prospective franchisees.

Long-Term Value

Can you add value for your franchisees year after year? There are many good and successful business models. Those models may provide the right steps for another entrepreneur to follow in order to avoid trials and errors in the startup process. But does the originating business offer value to prospective franchisees year in and year out? A franchise agreement is in effect for a long time, typically between 10 and 15 years. What benefits will the franchisees derive from the franchisor each year? Will new products or services be introduced? Will improved marketing strategies be implemented? Will additional, updated training be offered to franchisees and their managers? Why will franchisees want to continue to make royalty payments once they have been up and running and have learned the operating procedures? If the business model does not add value for franchisees each year, franchising is not the right method for growing your company.

LEGAL ISSUES IN FRANCHISING

The agreement between franchisors and franchisees results from the parties signing legal documents. For the business alliance to be successful for both parties, trust is important. But a contract is essential to avoid or resolve problems that may arise.

The Franchise Contract

The basic features of the relationship between the franchisor and the franchisee are embodied in the franchise contract. This contract is typically a complex document, running to many pages. Because of its importance as the legal basis for the franchised business, the franchise contract should never be signed by the franchisee without legal counsel. In fact, reputable franchisors insist that the franchisee have legal counsel before signing the agreement. An attorney may anticipate trouble spots and note any objectionable features of the contract.

In addition to consulting an attorney, a prospective franchisee should use as many other sources of help as would be practical. In particular, she or he should discuss the franchise contract with a banker, going over it in as much detail as possible. The prospective franchisee should also obtain the services of a professional accounting firm to examine the franchisor's statements of projected sales, operating expenses, and net income. An accountant can help evaluate the quality of these estimates and identify projections that may be overstated.

One of the most important features of the franchise contract is the provision relating to termination and transfer of the franchise. Some franchisors have been accused of devising agreements that permit arbitrary cancellation of the franchise relationship. Of course, it is reasonable for the franchisor to have legal protection in the event that a franchisee fails to obtain an appropriate level of operation or does not maintain satisfactory quality standards. However, the prospective franchisee should be wary of contract provisions that contain overly strict or vague cancellation policies. Similarly, the rights of the franchisee to sell the business to a third party should be clearly spelled out. A franchisor who can restrict the sale of the business to a third party could potentially take back ownership of the business at an unfair price. The right of a franchisee to renew the contract after the business has been built up to a successful operating level should also be clearly stated in the contract.

Franchise Disclosure Statements

The offer and sale of a franchise are regulated by both state and federal laws. At the federal level, the minimum disclosure standards are specified by Rule 436 of the Federal Trade Commission (FTC). The original rule, formally entitled Disclosure Requirements and Prohibitions Concerning Franchising and Business Opportunity Ventures, went into effect in October of 1979. A guide to the rule can be found on the Federal Trade Commission's website at http://www.ftc.gov/bcp/edu/pubs/business/franchise/bus70.pdf. Addresses of the state offices that enforce franchise disclosure laws can be found at http://www.ftc.gov/bcp/franchise/netdiscl.htm.

The Franchise Disclosure Document (FDD) provides the accepted format for satisfying the requirements of the FTC. In May 2008, the FDD replaced the Uniform Franchise Offering Circular (UFOC) as the legal document satisfying the FTC Franchise Rule. The UFOC had been created by the North American Securities Administrators Association (NASAA) to meet both state and federal government requirements.

The FDD must include information on a variety of items, including investment requirements and conditions that would affect renewal, termination, or sale of the franchise. Most franchise experts recommend that a franchisee's attorney and accountant review the document.

To this point in the chapter, we have been focusing on franchising opportunities. Another option for making your dream a reality is buying an existing business. You can be just as entrepreneurial buying an existing enterprise as creating one from scratch. As you look at companies available for purchase, you may discover an opportunity to turn around a company in trouble. Or perhaps you have the skills needed to make an already good business excellent. The existing firm may be the perfect platform on which to build your dream. In the next section, we discuss some of the issues facing the individual who chooses this alternative.

Buying an Existing Business

We think of franchisees as people who buy business concepts and the right to use names and sell products. But many franchisees buy stores that are up and running from the current business owners. When Landrie Peterman learned that an Anytime Fitness outlet was about to close, she acted fast. She had helped her brother set up two Anytime Fitness franchises in Oregon and was convinced that if you followed the franchisor's guide book, you would succeed. In less than a week, she had changed the franchise rights, renegotiated the lease, and purchased the business. Within six months, she had grown the membership from about 300 to over 1,000 clients.[23]

The decision to purchase an existing business should not be made lightly. It involves serious investment of funds, so you must give careful consideration to the advantages and disadvantages of this option. In this section of the chapter, we examine buying a business as an ownership option and explain the steps that a prospective buyer should take.

© Anytime Fitness

REASONS FOR BUYING AN EXISTING BUSINESS

The reasons for buying an existing business can be condensed into the following four general categories:

- To reduce some of the uncertainties and unknowns that must be faced in starting a business from the ground up
- To acquire a business with ongoing operations and established relationships with customers and suppliers
- To obtain an established business at a price below what it would cost to start a new business or to buy a franchise
- To get into business more quickly than by starting from scratch

Let's examine each of these reasons in more detail.

Reduction of Uncertainties

A successful business has already demonstrated its ability to attract customers, manage costs, and make a profit. Although future operations may be different, the firm's past record shows what it can do under actual market conditions. For example, just the fact that the location must be satisfactory eliminates one major uncertainty. Although traffic counts are useful in assessing the value of a potential location, the acid test comes when a business opens its doors at that location. This test has already been met in the case of an existing firm. The results are available in the form of sales and profit data. Noncompete agreements are needed, however, to discourage the seller from starting a new company that will compete directly with the one he or she is selling.

Acquisition of Ongoing Operations and Relationships

The buyer of an existing business typically acquires its personnel, inventories, physical facilities, established banking connections, and ongoing relationships with trade suppliers and customers. You are also acquiring the goodwill that the prior owner created. Extensive time and effort would be required to build these elements from scratch. Of course, the advantage derived from buying an established firm's assets depends on the nature of the assets. For example, a firm's skilled, experienced employees constitute a valuable asset only if they will continue to work for the new owner.

TRANSFORM

Buying and Converting

Just because you own an independent business or are considering buying one doesn't mean franchising isn't for you. Some business owners looking to grow decide to contract with a franchisor and convert their companies into units of the larger chain. In this way, they continue to own their businesses but have the advantage of the resources and expertise of a large corporation.

The physical facilities must not be obsolete, and the firm's relationships with banks, suppliers, and customers must be healthy. In any case, new agreements will probably have to be negotiated with current vendors and leaseholders.

A Bargain Price

If the seller is more eager to sell than the buyer is to buy, an existing business may be available at what seems to be a low price. Whether it is actually a good buy, however, must be determined by the prospective new owner. Several factors could make a "bargain price" anything but a bargain. For example, the business may be losing money, the neighborhood location may be deteriorating, or the seller may intend to open a competing business nearby. On the other hand, if research indicates that the business indeed is a bargain, purchasing it is likely to turn out to be a wise investment.

A Quick Start

Most entrepreneurs are eager to get going in their new business and may not be comfortable waiting the months and years sometimes required to launch a business from scratch. Buying an existing business may be an excellent way to begin operations much more quickly.

FINDING A BUSINESS TO BUY

matchmakers
Specialized brokers that bring together buyers and sellers of businesses.

Sources of leads about businesses available for purchase include suppliers, distributors, trade associations, and even bankers. Realtors—particularly those who specialize in the sale of business firms and business properties—can also provide leads. In addition, there are specialized brokers, called **matchmakers**, who handle all the arrangements for closing a buyout. Entrepreneurs need to be wary of potential conflicts of interest with matchmakers, however. For example, if matchmakers are paid only if a buy–sell transaction occurs, they may be tempted to do whatever it takes to close the deal, even if doing so is detrimental to the buyer.

Inc. magazine offers its readers the following guidance on finding a business to buy:[24]

1. *Determine your commitment.* Are you a window shopper or serious player?
2. *Establish what you can afford.* Think about the down payment you need to make, your credit rating, your collateral, and whether you have other sources of income.
3. *Figure out what skills you have.* What business sector matches your skills, what are you comfortable selling, is a license or special qualifications required, and do you want to manage people or be on your own?
4. *Consider lifestyle impact.* How many hours are you willing to work, will you relocate, and how does your family feel about this?

TOOLS

Advocates for Entrepreneurs

In this textbook, we encourage you to attend meetings and conferences, to get out and meet people, to join organizations—in other words, to network. Your network contacts may help you discover businesses that may be for sale, see opportunities, find financing, obtain customers, and put together a venture team. One such organization is the Young Entrepreneur Council (http://www.nevergetarealjob.com). Its "mission is to teach young people how to build successful businesses and fight the devastating epidemics of youth underemployment and unemployment."

INVESTIGATING AND EVALUATING AVAILABLE BUSINESSES

Regardless of the source of the lead, a business opportunity requires careful evaluation—what some call **due diligence**. As a preliminary step, the buyer needs to acquire background information about the business, some of which can be obtained through personal observation or discussion with the seller. Talking with other informed parties, such as suppliers, bankers, employees, and customers of the business, is also important.

due diligence The exercise of reasonable care in the evaluation of a business opportunity.

The website for the U.S. Small Business Administration provides an extensive amount of information for performing due diligence in the purchase of a business (see Exhibit 4.8). This list may appear extensive and intimidating, but the purchase of a business is a serious investment and should be investigated thoroughly. If a seller cannot supply the documents on this list, you may want to back away. Some items will not exist, of course, for every business. For example, not every company will require government certifications. Nevertheless, you should be exhaustive in your efforts to uncover relevant information that could influence the selling price or whether you should even enter into the sale. If you do not conduct a thorough investigation, you may find yourself "on the hook" for unanticipated expenses that show up later.

Relying on Professionals

Although some aspects of due diligence require personal checking, a buyer can also seek the help of outside experts. The two most valuable sources of outside assistance are accountants and lawyers. It is also wise to seek out others who have acquired a business, in order

EXHIBIT 4.8 Due Diligence for Purchasing a Business

Once you've found a business that you would like to buy, it's important to conduct a thorough, objective investigation. Look into every aspect of the business, verifying whether the owner's stated reasons for selling are legitimate and double-check every detail for accuracy. The following list includes important information you want to include when researching the business you want to buy.

1. Contracts and lease agreements
2. Financial statements
3. Tax returns
4. Real and personal property documents
5. Bank accounts
6. Customer lists
7. Sales records
8. Supplier/purchaser list
9. Contracts
10. Advertisement materials
11. Inventory receipts/lists
12. Organization charts
13. Payroll, benefits, and employee pension/profit sharing info
14. Employee roster
15. Certification by federal, state or local agencies
16. List of owners

Source: U.S. Small Business Administration, http://www.sba.gov/content/researching-business-purchase, accessed April 18, 2011.

to learn from their experience. Their perspective will be different from that of a consultant, and it will bring some balance to the counsel received. The time and money spent on securing professional help in investigating a business can pay big dividends, especially when the buyer is inexperienced. Prospective buyers should seek advice and counsel, but they must make the final decision themselves, as it is too important to entrust to someone else.

Finding Out Why the Business Is for Sale

The seller's *real* reasons for selling may or may not be the *stated* ones. When a business is for sale, always question the owner's reasons for selling. There is a real possibility

LIVING THE DREAM

© iStockphoto.com/Angelika Schwarz

entrepreneurial experiences

Buying Out Dad

After earning his college degree, Brian Schraff joined his father's small advertising company in 1982. The business had been successful since its founding in 1976. Brian's father kept it intentionally small, feeling that he could keep costs down and operations efficient if he limited the size of the business to seven employees. Over time, Schraff began to see opportunities that he felt the company was missing. He wanted to add new services, offering more value and attracting more revenue from each client.

By 1996, Schraff and a co-worker, Rick Roelofs, felt the time had come to move forward. They approached Schraff's father with a proposal to buy the business. But this was not a business that the father wanted to sell. He had built it from nothing and was proud of what it had become. He was not ready to let go.

Eventually, Schraff presented his father with an ultimatum: either he would purchase the company, or his father could buy back stock that Schraff held and Schraff would leave. Neither of these options was attractive, and the negotiation process became unpleasant. A key problem was establishing a value for the company that everyone could agree upon. Schraff later described the year of working out a buy/sell agreement as the worst relationship he and his father ever had. A two-year transition period followed, with Schraff and Roelofs gaining ownership and Schraff's father moving into the role of chief financial officer. By controlling the money, he kept a close eye on the changes Brian and Rick made. Over time, this led to his developing confidence in their changes, and he eventually withdrew from active management.

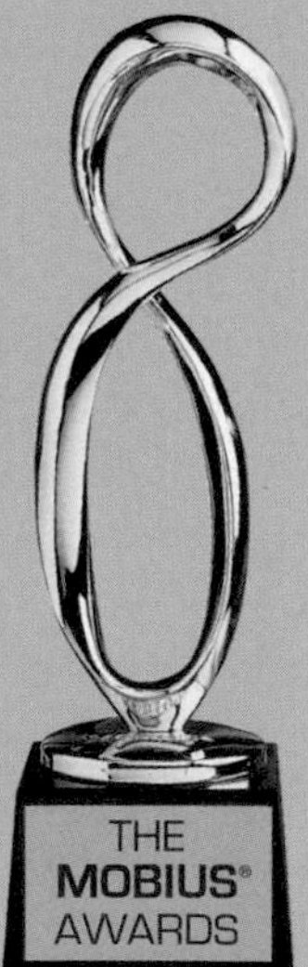

Mobius Awards, Ltd.

Today, the Schraff Group Communications, Inc., is an award-winning company (gaining ICON, Summit, and Mobius awards). The company operates at a multi-million dollar level, providing clients with a balanced, single-resource approach to enhancing their Web presence through Web design, SEO (search engine optimization), Web development, brand strategy, publicity, and advertising.

Schraff's conclusions from his experience in buying out his father include the recognition that negotiating a value for a small firm can be the most difficult step and that he should have used a third party to mediate the negotiations. Multiple subjective factors surface in setting a mutually agreeable price for a business. An objective investment banker could have reduced some of the conflict.

Sources: Brian Schraff, http://www.inc.com/magazine/20010601/22700.html, accessed December 12, 2010; and The Schraff Group, http://www.schraff.com/, accessed March 11, 2011. **http://www.schraff.com**

that the firm is not doing well or that underlying problems exist that will affect its future performance. The buyer must be wary, therefore, of taking the seller's explanations at face value. Here are some of the most common reasons why owners offer their businesses for sale:

- Old age or illness
- Desire to relocate to a different part of the country
- Decision to accept a position with another company
- Unprofitability of the business
- Loss of an exclusive sales franchise
- Maturing of the industry and lack of growth potential

A prospective buyer cannot be certain that the seller-owner will be honest in presenting all the facts about the business, especially concerning financial matters. Background checks on key personnel are essential when conducting due diligence.

Examining the Financial Data

The first stage in evaluating the financial health of a firm is to review the financial statements and tax returns for the past five years or for as many years as they are available. (*If these statements are not available, think twice before buying the business.*) This first stage helps to determine whether the buyer and the seller are in the same ballpark. If so, the parties can move on to valuing the firm. You will find details on compiling and interpreting financial statements in Chapter 10.

To determine the history of the business and the direction in which it is moving, the buyer must examine financial data pertaining to the company's operation. If financial statements are available for the past five years, the buyer can use these to get some idea of trends for the business. As both a legal and an ethical matter, the prospective buyer may expect to sign a **nondisclosure agreement**. Under the restrictions of such an agreement, the buyer promises the seller that he or she will not reveal confidential information or violate the trust that the seller has offered in providing the information. Buyers are typically allowed to share such information with others, such as a potential lender or legal advisor, on a need-to-know basis.

nondisclosure agreement
An agreement in which the buyer promises the seller that he or she will not reveal confidential information or violate the seller's trust.

The buyer should recognize that financial statements can be misleading and may require normalizing to yield a realistic picture of the business. For example, business owners sometimes understate business income in an effort to minimize their taxes. On the other hand, expenses for such entries as employee training and advertising may be reduced to abnormally low levels in an effort to make the income look good in the hope of selling the business.

Other financial entries that may need adjustment include personal expenses and wage or salary payments. For example, costs related to the personal use of business vehicles frequently appear as a business expense, and family members may receive excessive compensation or none at all. All entries must be examined to ensure that they relate to the business and are appropriate.

The buyer should also compare the seller's balance sheet to actual assets and liabilities. Property may appreciate in value after it is recorded on the books, but physical facilities, inventory, and receivables may decline in value, so their actual worth may be less than their accounting book value.

QUANTITATIVE FACTORS IN VALUING THE BUSINESS

fair market value
The price at which the property would change hands between a willing buyer and willing seller, both parties having reasonable knowledge of relevant facts.

Once the initial investigation and evaluation have been completed, the buyer must arrive at a fair value for the firm. **Fair market value** is defined by the United States Internal Revenue Service in Revenue Ruling 59-60 as "the price at which the property would change hands between a willing buyer and willing seller when the former is not under any compulsion to buy and the latter is not under any compulsion to sell, both parties having reasonable knowledge of relevant facts."[25] In valuing firms, the buyer will have to rely on federal tax returns and state sales tax statements. It may also be helpful to scrutinize supplier invoices and customer receipts, as well as the company's bank statements.

Although numerous techniques are used for valuing a company, they are typically derivations of three basic approaches: (1) asset-based valuation, (2) market-comparable valuation, and (3) cash flow–based valuation. These techniques are examined in detail in Appendix B.

NONQUANTITATIVE FACTORS IN VALUING A BUSINESS

When applying the quantitative techniques discussed in Appendix B, you should also consider a number of nonquantitative factors in evaluating an existing business. In particular, is it likely that the firm you are considering buying might be subject to change regarding any of the following?

- **Market.** The ability of the market to support all competing business units, including the one to be purchased, should be determined. This requires marketing research, study of census data, and personal, on-the-spot observation at each competitor's place of business.
- **Competition.** The prospective buyer should look into the extent, intensity, and location of competing businesses. In particular, the buyer should check to see whether the business in question is gaining or losing in its race with rivals. Additionally, new competitors in the local marketplace (e.g., Walmart) may dramatically change an existing firm's likelihood of success. Past performance is no guarantee of future performance.
- **Future community development.** Examples of future developments in the community that could have an indirect impact on a business include a change in zoning ordinances already enacted but not yet in effect, a change from a two-way traffic flow to a one-way traffic flow, and the widening of a road or construction of an overpass.
- **Legal commitments.** Legal commitments may include contingent liabilities, unsettled lawsuits, delinquent tax payments, missed payrolls, overdue rent or installment payments, and mortgages of record on any of the real property acquired.
- **Union contracts.** The prospective buyer should determine what type of labor agreement, if any, is in force, as well as the quality of the firm's employee relations. Private conversations with key employees and rank-and-file workers can be helpful in determining their job satisfaction and the company's likelihood of success.
- **Buildings.** The quality of the buildings housing the business should be checked, with particular attention paid to any fire hazards. In addition, the buyer should determine whether there are any restrictions on access to the buildings.
- **Product prices.** The prospective owner should compare the prices of the seller's products with those listed in manufacturers' or wholesalers' catalogs and also

with the prices of competing products in the locality. This is necessary to ensure full and fair pricing of goods whose sales are reported on the seller's financial statements.

NEGOTIATING AND CLOSING THE DEAL

The purchase price of a business is determined by negotiation between buyer and seller. Although the calculated value may not be the price eventually paid for the business, it gives the buyer an estimated value to use when negotiating price. Typically, the buyer tries to purchase the firm for something less than the full estimated value; of course, the seller tries to get more than that value.

In some cases, the buyer may have the option of purchasing the assets only, rather than the business as a whole. When a business is purchased as a total entity, the buyer takes control of the assets but also assumes any outstanding debt, including any hidden or unknown liabilities. Even if the financial records are audited, such debts may not surface. If the buyer instead purchases only the assets, then the seller is responsible for settling any outstanding debts previously incurred. When buying the business as a whole, an indemnification clause in the sales contract may serve a similar function, protecting the buyer from liability for unreported debt.

An important part of the negotiation process is the terms of purchase. In many cases, the buyer is unable to pay the full price in cash and must seek extended terms. At this point, a lender may enter the picture and alter the purchase price. If a bank is providing a loan for buying the business, the bank may require the assets of the company to serve as collateral for the loan. Any lender must perform its own due diligence and estimate a value for the assets, and that value may be at a different level than the buyer and seller have agreed upon. Remember, bankers represent their depositors and cannot just accept a number because the buyer and seller are happy with it.

At the same time, the seller may be concerned about taxes on the profit from the sale. Terms may become more attractive to the buyer and the seller as the amount of the down payment is reduced and/or the length of the repayment period is extended. Like a purchase of real estate, the purchase of a business is closed at a specific time, and a title company or an attorney usually handles the closing. Preferably, the closing will occur under the direction of an independent third party. If the seller's attorney is the closing agent, the buyer should exercise great caution—*a buyer should never go through a closing without the aid of an experienced attorney who represents only the buyer.*

A number of important documents are completed during the closing. These include a bill of sale, certifications as to taxing and other government regulations, and agreements pertaining to future payments and related guarantees to the seller. The buyer should apply for new federal and state tax identification numbers to avoid being held responsible for past obligations associated with the old numbers. If you want a happy ending from the purchase and a clear path to your future, do not take short cuts at this stage. Meeting all legal and regulatory requirements secures your investment and your ability to successfully manage the business.

Starting a business, becoming a franchisee, or buying an existing business are all paths to your entrepreneurial dream. Although franchising and buying a business are usually considered to be strategies for reducing the risks associated with starting a venture, each path still requires careful research and planning. Whatever your particular circumstances are, it is important to keep in mind that business owners must invest themselves as well as their money, if they want their companies to succeed. As is so often the case in life, it is up to you to devote your time, effort, and resources to achieve your goals.

1. Define *franchising,* and become familiar with franchise terminology.

- *Franchising* is a business relationship in which an entrepreneur can reduce risk and benefit from the business experience of all members of the franchise system.
- According to the International Franchising Association, franchising is a method of distributing products or services involving two primary parties, a franchisor and a franchisee.
- The potential value of any franchising arrangement is determined by the rights contained in the franchise contract.
- In product and trade name franchising, the main benefit the franchisee receives is the privilege of using a widely recognized product name.
- In business format franchising, entrepreneurs receive an entire marketing and management system.
- A master licensee is a firm or individual having a continuing contractual relationship with a franchisor to sell its franchises.
- Multiple-unit ownership, in which a single franchisee owns more than one unit of a franchised business, is becoming widely used.
- Some single franchisees are area developers—individuals or firms that obtain the legal right to open several outlets in a given area.
- Piggyback franchising is the operation of a retail franchise within the physical facilities of a host store.
- Multi-brand franchising involves operating several franchise organizations within a single corporate structure.
- Co-branding brings two or more franchise brands together within a single enterprise.
- Franchising has a significant impact on the economies of the United States and other nations, as measured by employment and output.

2. Understand the pros and cons of franchising and the structure of the industry.

- The primary advantage of franchising is its high rate of success.
- Other advantages of franchising include the value of trade names and trademarks, the franchisor's operations manual, training support, economies of scale, and financial support.
- Disadvantages of franchising include financial issues, franchisor competition, and management issues.
- Costs associated with franchises go beyond just fees and royalties.

3. Describe the process for evaluating a franchise opportunity.

- The substantial investment required by most franchisors justifies careful investigation by a potential franchisee.
- Independent third parties such as state and federal government agencies, the International Franchise Association, and business publications can be valuable sources of franchise information.
- The most logical source of the greatest amount of information about a franchise is the franchisor.
- Existing and previous franchisees are also good sources of information for evaluating a franchise.
- Before becoming a franchisor, consider the efficiency of your business model, how you will finance the growth, what expert assistance you will need, what will go into your operations manual, government disclosure requirements, and your ability to add long-term value for franchisees.
- A franchise contract is a complex document and should be evaluated by a franchise attorney.
- An important feature of the franchise contract is the provision relating to termination and transfer of the franchise.
- Franchise disclosure requirements are specified by FTC Rule 436.
- The Franchise Disclosure Document (FDD) provides the accepted format for satisfying the franchise disclosure requirements of the FTC.

4. List four reasons for buying an existing business, and describe the process of evaluating a business.

- Buying an existing firm can reduce uncertainties.
- In acquiring an existing firm, the entrepreneur can take advantage of the firm's ongoing operations and established relationships.
- An existing business may be available at a bargain price.
- Another reason for buying an existing business is that an entrepreneur may be in a hurry to start an enterprise.
- Investigating a business requires due diligence.
- A buyer should seek the help of outside experts, the two most valuable sources of outside assistance being accountants and lawyers.
- The buyer needs to investigate why the seller is offering the business for sale.
- The financial data related to the business should always be examined.
- Nonquantitative information about the business for sale should also be used in determining its value.

Key Terms

franchising p. 106
franchisor p. 107
franchisee p. 107
franchise contract p. 107
franchise p. 107
product and trade name franchising p. 107
business format franchising p. 107
master licensee p. 107
multiple-unit ownership p. 107
area developers p. 107
piggyback franchising p. 107
multi-brand franchising p. 108
co-branding p. 108
churning p. 112
encroachment p. 113
Franchise Disclosure Document (FDD) p. 118
Franchise Rule p. 121
matchmakers p. 124
due diligence p. 125
nondisclosure agreement p. 127
fair market value p. 128

Discussion Questions

1. What makes franchising different from other forms of business? Be specific.
2. What is the difference between product and trade name franchising and business format franchising?
3. Identify and describe at least four of the key terms in franchising.
4. Discuss the pros and cons of franchising from the viewpoints of both the potential franchisee and the potential franchisor.
5. Should franchise information provided by a franchisor be discounted? Why or why not?
6. Do you believe that the Franchise Disclosure Document is useful for franchise evaluation? Defend your position.
7. Evaluate loss of control as a disadvantage of franchising from the franchisor's perspective.
8. What are possible reasons for buying an existing company as opposed to starting a new business from scratch?
9. What are some common reasons that owners offer their businesses for sale? Which of these reasons might a buyer consider to be negative?
10. What are some of the nonquantitative factors in valuing a business?

You Make the Call

SITUATION 1

Danny Bone understands due diligence. He spent months investigating franchise options, before focusing specifically on Elevation Burger. Elevation Burger uses the slogan "Ingredients Matter," emphasizing its "organically raised, grass-fed, free-range cows and fresh-cut french fries cooked in heart-healthy olive oil." The company had been in business three years when it started franchising in 2008. Danny's brother Dennis brought franchising experience to the company from his days of managing their parents' Dunkin' Donuts franchise. Danny and Dennis began their franchise agreement with Elevation Burger in the spring of 2008, intending to open their Austin, Texas, location by the end of that year.

What Danny hadn't counted on was the recession. Financing suddenly tightened, and forecasts for restaurant sales were especially negative. Nevertheless, Danny and Dennis remained confident and were convinced that they understood how to run a cost-efficient operation. The brothers were committed to opening three Elevation Burger restaurants in the Austin area.

Sources: "Optimistic Franchisees Undeterred by Downer Economy," *Franchise Times*, Vol. 15, No. 1 (January 2009), p. 15; http://elevationburger.com, accessed December 11, 2010; and http://www.franchisewire.com, accessed December 11, 2010.

Question 1 Should the Bone brothers have anticipated an economic downturn as part of their due diligence investigation?
Question 2 What steps would you take to attract customers to your franchised restaurant when they are trying to save money?
Question 3 What can the Elevation Burger franchisor do to help franchisees during a recession?

SITUATION 2

Siler Chapman worked in a Pizza Works franchise while he was a student at the University of North Carolina at Charlotte. When he saw people losing jobs in an economic downturn, he decided he'd rather be his own boss than find himself fired by someone else. So he opened (what else?) a pizza place.

While building his business, he also found that he had a talent for tossing pizzas and became part of a U.S. team that won the Pizza Olympics in Italy four years in a row.

Tossing pizzas was fun, and Chapman found it to be a good marketing tool, but he also found the day-to-day management demands of growing a business to be hard. As he expressed it, "I was running around with my head cut off." When Chapman was approached by Donato's Pizzeria, he decided to convert his three stores to Donato's franchises. Within two years, his three stores had expanded to fifteen. And Chapman is planning two hundred more!

Sources: Jason Daley, "Acrobat of Pizza," *Entrepreneur*, Vol. 38, No. 11 (November 2010), p. 140; and http://www.donatos.com/about_donatos/index.asp, accessed October 30, 2010.

Question 1 If Siler Chapman had so much trouble running three restaurants as an independent owner, why do you think he was able to manage so many more as a franchisee?
Question 2 From a franchisor's perspective, why might you choose to convert an existing chain of stores to your model instead of having franchisees who start from scratch?

SITUATION 3

Dave Garrett of Evansville, Indiana, wants to buy a business. He sold his minority interest in the construction company where he worked and left his job. He and a partner are concentrating full time on finding a company to buy. They are targeting manufacturing concerns with sales of $1 million to $8 million, businesses with strong cash flow and with management teams that want to remain with the company. They are working through business brokers and searching online, and they have offered a $10,000 finder's fee to anyone who gives them a lead that results in a purchase. So far, they have bid on two companies, but did not buy either one.

Question 1 Do you think Garrett's experience is normal for someone looking for a business to buy? Can you think of other sources of information about companies that might be for sale that would fit his criteria?
Question 2 For what reasons might someone bid on a business but not be successful in buying it?

Experiential Exercises

1. Interview a local owner-manager of a franchise. What was the process by which the owner obtained the franchise? Would she or he do it all over again?
2. Find an advertisement for the sale of a franchise in a magazine or newspaper. Research the franchise, and report back to the class on how the advertisement describes the franchise.
3. Is there a franchise operating on your campus? Interview the official who is responsible for that contract. Why did the school decide to have the outlet on campus? Who is the franchisee?
4. Consult the Yellow Pages of your local telephone directory for the name of a business broker. Interview the broker, and report to the class on how she or he values businesses.

The Small Business & Entrepreneurship Resource Center

1. McDonald's is well-known for its hamburgers worldwide, and is a popular choice for potential franchisees that do not want to fail in business. Of course, McDonald's likes reducing its odds of failure, too. The most successful quick-service restaurant chain in the world doesn't let just anybody buy a McDonald's restaurant and open for business. Their secret weapon to success isn't the Big Mac's secret sauce. It lies in the training that the company provides to every single franchise owner. McDonald's is McDonald's because of Hamburger University. Describe how Hamburger University works and why you feel it is such an effective training source.

Source: Geoff Williams, "Behind the Arches: Our Writer Takes a Sneak Peek into the Training Grounds of McDonald's Franchisees: Hamburger University," *Entrepreneur*, Vol. 34, No. 1 (January 2006), pp. 104–109.

2. Financing is often a major concern for those wanting to start a business, and with a franchise, there is no exception. The SBA has created the Franchise registry to help potential franchisees gain quick access to financing. Describe how the program works and the potential benefits to potential franchisees.

Source: The Franchise Registry, Small Business & Entrepreneurship Resource Center, Cengage Learning Gale, Cengage Learning Higher Ed., August 23, 2007, http://www.franchiseregistry.com, accessed March 11, 2011.

Video Case 4

TWO MEN AND A TRUCK® (P. 700)

Two Men and a Truck® started in the early 1980s as a way for two brothers to make extra money while they were in high school. Now, over 20 years later, the company has grown to more than 200 locations worldwide, and is the nation's largest franchised local moving company.

ALTERNATIVE CASES FOR CHAPTER 4

Case 1, Nau, p. 693
Case 6, Benjapon's, p. 704
Case 13, Greenwood Dairies, p. 719

CHAPTER 5

The Family Business

In the SPOTLIGHT
Two Men and a Truck
http://www.twomen.com

It was a wonderful retreat and meeting in Puerto Vallarta, but Melanie Bergeron was glad to be home. The annual Leaders in Excellence trip with the firm's headquarters staff and franchisees had left everyone feeling good about how Two Men and a Truck (TMT) had survived the housing crisis and economic downturn and was back on a growth path. At the same time, Bergeron shook her head in wonder at how far this company had come since her brothers started it as teenagers in 1981.

Brig and Jon Sorber were just 17 and 15 years old, respectively, when they began hauling junk for customers in a 1967 pickup truck. After their first ad in a local paper, they started getting calls from people who wanted their households moved. This work gave them some spending money, but they left the company in their mother's hands when they started college.

Two Men and a Truck

Mary Ellen Sheets had invested $350 in Two Men and a Truck when she bought her sons an old used bread delivery truck. When the boys went off to school, she hired a couple of workers to keep the business going. At the end of her first year, she found herself with $1,000 profit and wrote 10 checks for $100 each to 10 charities. Thanks to word-of-mouth advertising, customers kept calling.

When an acquaintance suggested that she might grow the company by franchising, Sheets made a series of calls to Bergeron, who was a pharmaceutical representative in Atlanta, Georgia, at the time, asking her to join the business. Bergeron gave in to her mother's persistence and launched her own moving company. Eventually, she moved back to Michigan, started another TMT franchise, then got recruited

After studying this chapter, you should be able to . . .

1. Define the terms *family* and *family business.*
2. Explain the forces that can keep a family business moving forward.
3. Describe the complex roles and relationships involved in a family business.
4. Identify management practices that enable a family business to function effectively.
5. Describe the process of managerial succession in a family business.

LOOKING AHEAD

© iStockphoto.com/Dan Bachman

by Sheets to take over running the corporate headquarters so that Sheets could turn her attention to other interests (although she did remain a franchisee).

In 1994, Bergeron took the title of company president at no salary and with a copy machine as her desk. At that time, the firm was doing about $6 million in revenue. In addition to being president, Bergeron had her own Two Men franchise, as did her mother. Her brothers reunited as franchisees, becoming part of the organization while holding down full-time jobs. Bergeron proved to be a good student, learning from mentors in the franchising industry and from an advisor in a major accounting and consulting firm. Two Men and a Truck overcame obstacles, grew, and prospered.

One day, Bergeron looked up to see her husband and two sons in her office and decided she wanted to see more of them and less of the 50+ hour workweeks she was putting into the job. She called her brother Brig in, asked if he was ready to be president, and then handed him the baton. Today, Brig Sorber continues to serve as president and CEO. Jon Sorber is executive vice president, Bergeron chairs the Board of Directors, and Sheets carries the title of founder.

Reflecting on the Leaders in Excellence retreat, Bergeron felt good about Two Men's double-digit growth over the previous nine months. She also felt good about the attendees celebrating the company's nearly 30 years of success at that leadership retreat, a solid group of professionals that included her mother and her two brothers.

***Sources:* http://www.twomen.com, accessed October 31, 2010; personal interview with Melanie Bergeron, October 18, 2010; and personal correspondence with Melanie Bergeron, October 20, 2010.**

When you are in trouble, whom do you call for help? When you achieve success, whom do you want to tell? For most of us, the answer is family. The car goes into a ditch, and we need dad or mom. If we receive an award at school or work, it is all the more special when our parents or children see it happen. So when we start our own business, whom do we count on to encourage and support us? Family.

It is well documented that a majority of businesses in most free-market economies fit some definition of family ownership and control. Even when examining large corporations, we find a sizeable percentage to be controlled by a single family. The list of the largest family businesses includes such publicly traded companies as Walmart Stores, Ford Motor Co., News Corp., Comcast Corp., and General Dynamics Corp.[1] Although the stereotypical entrepreneur may not intentionally start a family enterprise, he or she often relies on family members to obtain the resources necessary for the startup and to pitch in when a problem arises. Family members are often the first people to lend you money or make an investment in your company, or to step in if you get sick or if an essential employee suddenly quits. Many times, it is that family member who knows and accepts your strengths and weaknesses and who is willing to work long hours, often at no pay, who helps to start the new venture.

But family members are not always cordial, cooperative, and compatible. Family members know which buttons to push to make you mad, to make you feel guilty, to embarrass you. Such actions have caused the downfall of many a family enterprise, large and small. In this chapter, we investigate how family and business interact, what makes them strong, and what can destroy them. From extensive research into family firms, we introduce strategies that have helped family businesses succeed.

What Is a Family Business?

family
A group of people bound by a shared history and a commitment to share a future together, while supporting the development and well-being of individual members.

owner-managed business
A venture operated by a founding entrepreneur.

sibling partnership
A business in which children of the founder become owners and managers.

cousin consortium
A business in third and subsequent generations when children of the siblings take ownership and management positions.

The family firm predates recorded history. Relatives, often in extended family tribal groups, hunted together, farmed together, governed together, and engaged in other, similar activities to sustain and improve their lives. As economies and governments started to take shape, families created enterprises that passed knowledge and skills from one generation to another. Entrepreneurs generated and conserved wealth that led to the establishment of dynasties that survived wars and famines. Family enterprises in many countries have survived for centuries.

But what exactly is a family? Definitions of *family* vary in different parts of the world. They include the classic "nuclear" family, restricted to parents and children, and an "extended" family, that comprises an entire community of extended relatives.

In this book, the word **family** refers to a group of people bound by a shared history and a commitment to share a future together, while supporting the development and well-being of individual members.[2] This definition acknowledges that there can be considerable differences in the compositions of families. Among other things, they can vary according to blood relationships, generational representation, and legal status.

Experts on family businesses try to sort through family relationships and apply labels to firms as they evolve from one generation to another. The **owner-managed business** is a venture that is operated by a founding entrepreneur. If the children of the founder become the owners and managers of the business, that second generation is referred to as a **sibling partnership**. Two Men and a Truck falls into that category, with the brothers and sister running the company, although their mother, the founder, still has her say in how the business should work. A **cousin consortium** describes a business in the third and subsequent generations when children of the siblings take ownership and management positions. But whichever generation is leading the company, the influence of other generations is felt. Beyond her personal relationships with her mother and brothers, Bergeron finds that she continues to feel the presence of her grandmother, who allowed her mother to use her farm as a place to park trucks, who helped with business paperwork, and who held onto the cash the drivers collected.

WHY SHOULD ANYONE CARE ABOUT FAMILIES IN BUSINESS?

Family-owned and controlled firms are among the world's largest and oldest enterprises. Houshi Onsen, a spa and inn located a few hours from Tokyo that was founded in 718, took the title of oldest family business in 2006. This followed the demise of Osaka temple-builder Kongo Gumi Company, founded in 578, after struggling for more than a decade to deal with overextension and recession in its primary business.[3]

Family businesses are both common and important. They are estimated to represent 80 to 98 percent of all enterprises in the world's free enterprise economies and to account for 75 percent of total employment. In the United States, family businesses generate 49 percent of the gross domestic product. Over 35 percent of Fortune 500 firms have been identified as family businesses.[4]

RESOURCES

Old and Large

You may be surprised at how old and large some family-owned companies are. *Family Business* magazine (http://www.familybusinessmagazine.com) periodically publishes lists of the oldest and largest family enterprises, both in the United States and in the world.

So, you should care about families in business. If you start your own venture, family members are likely to be involved. Perhaps you will join a firm owned by one or more of your relatives. Even if it is not your family's company, you may be employed in a business that is family-owned and controlled.

FAMILY AND BUSINESS OVERLAP

Any family business is composed of both a family and a business. Although the family and the business are separate institutions—each with its own members, goals, and values—they overlap in the family firm. For many people, these two overlapping institutions represent the most important areas of their lives.

Families and businesses exist for fundamentally different reasons. The family's primary function is the care and nurturing of family members, while the business is concerned with the production and distribution of goods and/or services. The family's goals include the personal development of each member (sometimes with scant concern for limitations in abilities) and the creation of equal opportunities and rewards for each member; the business's goal is to create value for the customer and wealth for the firm's owners.

Individuals involved, directly or indirectly, in a family business have interests and perspectives that differ according to their particular situations. The model in Exhibit 5.1

EXHIBIT 5.1 The Three-Circle Model of Family Firms

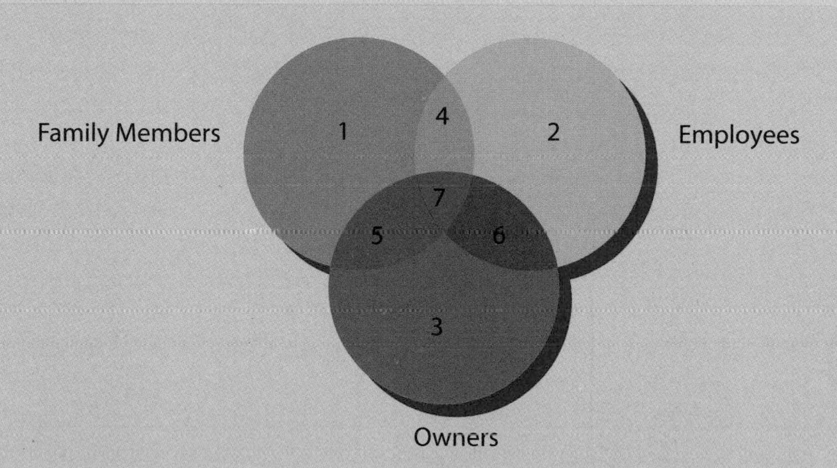

Legend:

1. Family members (not involved in business)
2. Nonfamily employees
3. Nonfamily owners (not involved in operations of the business)
4. A family member employee (not an owner)
5. A family member owner (not involved in operations of the business)
6. An employee owner (not a member of the family)
7. A family member owner and employee

FAMILY MEMBERS = Individuals in areas 1 + 4 + 5 + 7
EMPLOYEES = Individuals in areas 2 + 4 + 6 + 7
OWNERS = Individuals in areas 3 + 5 + 6 + 7

Sources: Frank Hoy and Pramodita Sharma, *Entrepreneurial Family Firms* (Boston: Prentice Hall, 2010); and James J. Chrisman, Franz W. Kellermanns, Kam C. Chan, and Kartono Liano, "Intellectual Foundations of Current Research in Family Business: An Identification and Review of 25 Influential Articles," *Family Business Review*, Vol. 23 (2010), pp. 9–26.

(a Venn diagram) shows the ways in which individuals may be involved—as members of the family, employees of the business, individuals with a vested interest in the business, and various combinations of these. In addition, the configuration of roles can affect the way these individuals think about the enterprise. For example, a family member who works in the firm but has no personal or ownership interest (segment 4) might favor more generous employment and advancement opportunities for family members than, say, a family member who owns part of the business but works elsewhere (segment 5) or an employee with neither family nor ownership interest (segment 2).

family business
An organization in which *either* the individuals who established or acquired the firm *or* their descendants significantly influence the strategic decisions and life course of the firm.

With Exhibit 5.1 in mind, we can define a **family business** as an organization in which *either* the individuals who established or acquired the firm *or* their descendants significantly influence the strategic decisions and life course of the firm.[5] The family influence might be exerted through management and/or ownership of the firm.[6]

Competing interests can complicate the management process, creating tension and sometimes leading to conflict. Relationships among family members in a business are more sensitive than relationships among unrelated employees. For example, disciplining an employee who consistently arrives late is much more problematic if he or she is also a family member. Or, consider a performance review session between a parent-boss and a child-subordinate. Even with nonfamily employees, performance reviews are potential minefields. The existence of a family relationship adds emotional overtones that vastly complicate the review process.

ADVANTAGES OF A FAMILY BUSINESS

Problems with family firms can easily blind people to the unique advantages that come with participating in a family business. The benefits associated with family involvement should be recognized and discussed when recruiting both relatives and nonfamily members to work in the family firm.

One primary benefit derives from the strength of family relationships. Family members have a unique motivation because the firm is a family firm. Business success is also family success. Studies of family firms have examined how the cohesiveness of the family, their unity of feeling and purpose, may enable members to work in harmony toward the common goal of a successful enterprise.[7] Family members are often drawn to the business because of family ties, and they tend to stick with the business through thick and thin. A downturn in business fortunes might cause nonfamily employees to seek greener employment pastures elsewhere, but a son or daughter may be reluctant to leave. The family name, its welfare, and possibly its fortune are at stake. In addition, a person's reputation in the family and in the business community may hinge on whether she or he can continue the business that Mom or Grandfather built.

Businesses that are family owned often highlight this feature in their promotional materials to set themselves apart from competitors. On the SC Johnson Company website, for example, you will find the firm name consistently represented as "SC Johnson: A Family Company."[8]

And such messages are not only for customers. Family businesses can convey a sense of tradition and achievement to relatives who are considering joining the firm and to nonfamily employees who have become part of an epic saga. After all, any company that has achieved generational succession has undoubtedly overcome countless challenges and threats. True heroism emerges as firms are launched, survive, and prosper. Everyone who accepts a position with the business should learn the heritage and accomplishments of those who created and grew the company. They should be proud to be accepted into the extended family. For Melanie Bergeron and Two Men and a Truck, it means adhering to what the family has labeled the Gramma Rule: "Treat everyone with dignity, respect, and patience."[9]

In his book *Family Business: The Essentials*, Peter Leach summarizes what he sees as the strengths that family enterprises possess (see also Exhibit 5.2):

1. *Family business culture and values*, providing guidance toward accomplishing shared goals
2. *Commitment*, the passion that grows out of a family's sense of responsibility
3. *Knowledge*, applied as a competitive advantage by family members who have learned through intimate involvement
4. *Long-range thinking*, looking toward the next generation, not just the next quarter
5. *A stable culture*, typically found in durable, low-profile, profitable niche enterprises
6. *Speedy decisions*, a function of trust among family members
7. *Reliability and pride*, recognized by customers, suppliers, creditors, and other outsiders

DISADVANTAGES OF A FAMILY BUSINESS

Even before a venture is created, conflict may arise among family members. The spouse, parents, in-laws, or others may accuse a budding entrepreneur of putting the family at risk in launching the business. When this happens between married couples, the eventual result is often the failure of either the business or the marriage. From the perspective of the opposing family members, their position may appear quite reasonable. The entrepreneur may be gambling with retirement savings, the children's college funds, or the home mortgage. Consequences can be severe.

As the business grows, inherent differences in family and business values and commitments emerge:

- A family is a unit that balances relationships; a business must deal with differences in competence and merit.

EXHIBIT 5.2 Advantages of a Family Business

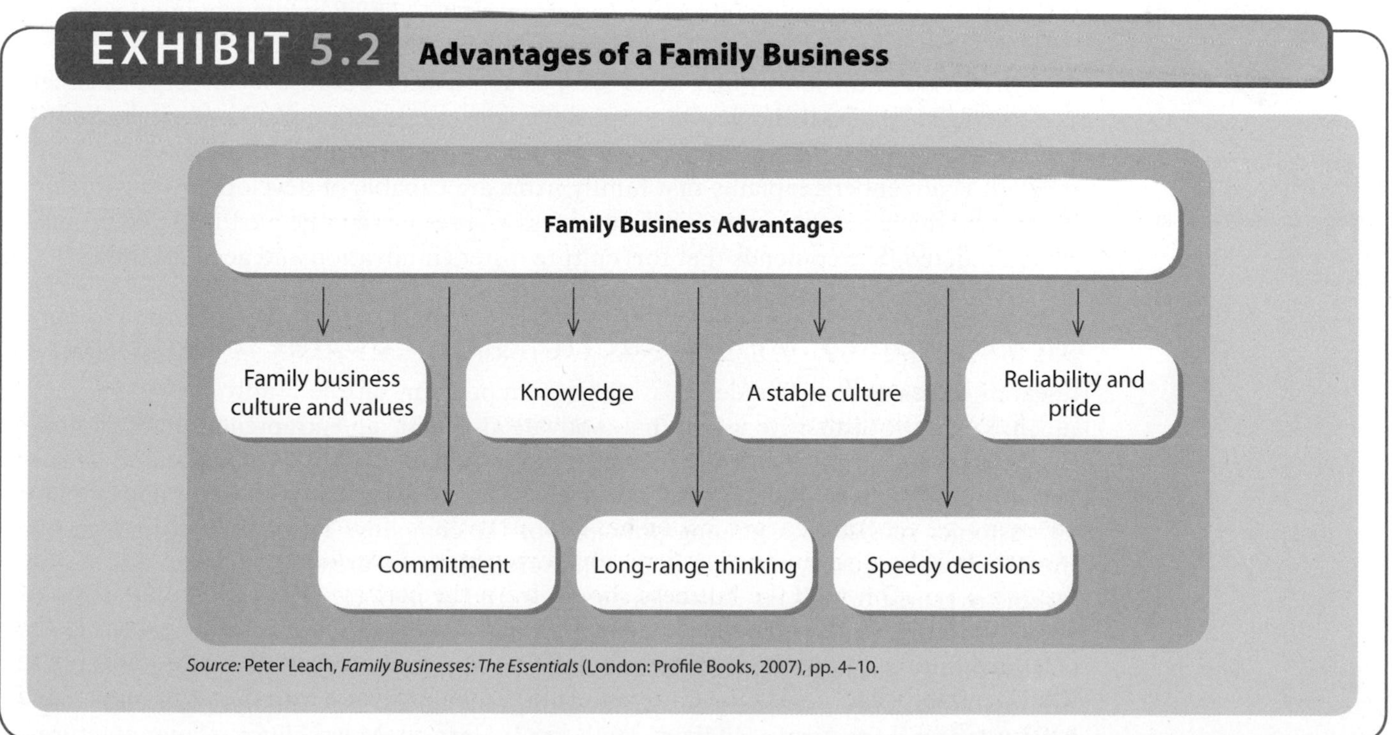

Source: Peter Leach, *Family Businesses: The Essentials* (London: Profile Books, 2007), pp. 4–10.

- The family seeks to perpetuate traditions, while the business must innovate to prosper.
- A family is characterized by unity and cooperation, but a business grows through diversity and competition.
- Families tend to be stable, while businesses, especially those competing in the global economy, often face instability.
- For families, loyalty usually trumps opportunity, but businesses are regularly challenged by opportunities that arise for both the company and its employees.

nepotism
The practice of employing relatives in the family firm.

Many companies have policies against hiring of family members. The assumption is that employees and executives may show favoritism toward their relatives, regardless of competence or performance. **Nepotism** is the practice of employing relatives in the family firm. Unfortunately, many businesses do, in fact, provide employment to relatives regardless of their qualifications and may keep them on the payroll even after their poor performance has become obvious to everyone. Not only is the effectiveness of the company diminished, but these practices also demoralize competent employees.

Peter Leach also discusses the dilemmas and challenges of family businesses: resistance to change because of family influences, which in turn may contribute to problems in leadership transition; and the options for raising capital being limited because of family ownership.[10] The fact that so many family firms are able to survive generational transitions, however, demonstrates that the disadvantages can be overcome.

Family Business Momentum

organizational culture
Patterns of behaviors and beliefs that characterize a particular firm.

Like other organizations, family businesses develop particular ways of doing things and certain priorities that are unique to each firm. These special patterns of behaviors and beliefs comprise the firm's **organizational culture** (we introduced you to this term in Chapter 2, p. 44). As new employees and family members enter the business, they pick up these unique viewpoints and ways of operating, which create staying power for the company.

The culture of the family firm deserves special attention because it can serve as either an advantage or a disadvantage. On the positive side, organizational culture can be a strategic resource that promotes learning, risk taking, and innovation. Family business advisor Ellen Frankenberg explains that family firms are capable of developing stewardship cultures in which members care for the business as a resource to be nurtured and grown, not squandered. She contends that this culture fosters innovation and accountability.[11]

THE FOUNDER'S IMPRINT ON THE FAMILY BUSINESS CULTURE

Research indicates that founders leave a deep impression on the family businesses they launch.[12] And the distinctive values that motivate and guide an entrepreneur in the founding of a company may help to create a competitive advantage for the new business. Business founders are often innovators who may cater to customer needs in a special way and emphasize customer service as a guiding principle for the company. The new firm may go far beyond normal industry practices in making sure customers are satisfied, even if it means working overtime or making deliveries on a weekend or at odd hours. Those who work in such an enterprise quickly learn that customers must always be handled with special care.

In a family business, the founder's core values may become part of both the business culture and the family code—that is, "the things we believe as a family." America's oldest family firm,[13] the Avedis Zildjian Company of Norwell, Massachusetts, manufacturer of cymbals and associated products, proudly traces the firm's origin to the year 1623 and provides bios on its website of those who led the company through the centuries.[14] This is a "high-touch" message, one that resonates with customers who don't want to be treated as "just another number." The Zildjian Company wants to be seen as emphasizing family character and traditions that involve staying close to working musicians.

© Lee Martin / Alamy

Of course, there is always a darker possibility—that of a founder's *negative* imprint on the organizational culture. Successful business founders may have an unhealthy narcissism, or exaggerated sense of self-importance. Such individuals occasionally develop a craving for attention, a fixation with success and public recognition, and a lack of empathy for others. Unfortunately, these attitudes can harm the business by creating a general feeling of superiority and a sense of complacency. While contributions of founders deserve proper acknowledgment, any negative legacy must be avoided.

THE COMMITMENT OF FAMILY MEMBERS

All organizations develop a culture, intentionally or otherwise. The culture of a particular firm includes numerous distinctive beliefs and behaviors that should help to keep the business moving forward. For startups and enterprises where the founder is still present, the culture is shaped by the vision of the entrepreneur. In family firms, when the founder turns over the reins of leadership (most often, to a new generation), the continuity of the business depends, in large part, on those next-generation family members and their level of commitment to the business. Recent research suggests that family members coming into a business do so for a variety of reasons, and these reasons shape the strength and nature of their commitment to the company.[15]

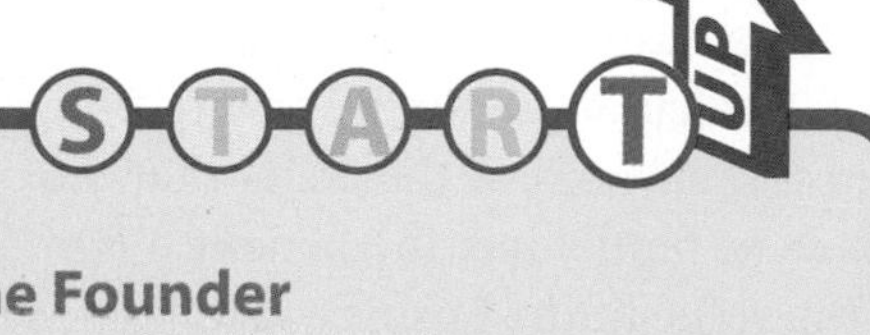

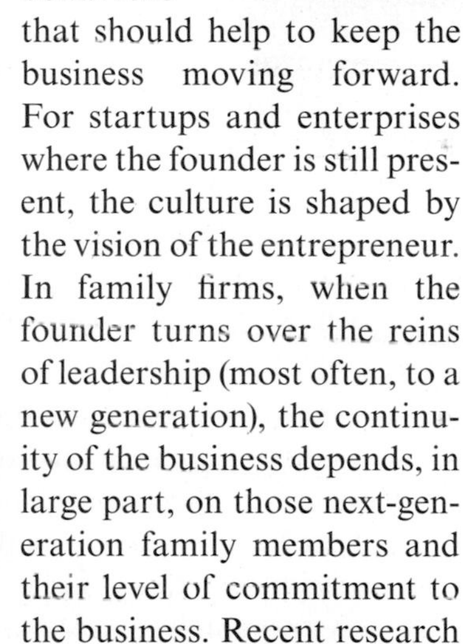

TRANSFORM

The Spirit of the Founder

Read a biography of a founder who put his or her name on a company. If you read about Walt Disney, for example, you will learn that, even though the Disney family no longer owns the corporation, the legacy of "Uncle Walt" continues, with all new "cast members" expected to carry on his legacy.

The model pictured earlier in Exhibit 5.1 on p. 137 is often used to summarize the complexities of dealing with the family firm's interactive components: the business, the family, and the individual. This model can help founders recognize that they have to balance their obvious interest in the business, their personal aspirations, and the needs of the family. Next-generation family members who choose to pursue a career in the business must also deal with these challenges, and their commitment to the company will likely determine the value of their contributions, the financial benefits they bring to the family, and their personal satisfaction with work-related roles.

To explore the connection between commitment and family business involvement, two family business experts from Canada studied the research on family enterprises. They found the following four bases of commitment among successors in family businesses: emotional attachment, a sense of obligation, cost considerations, and personal need.[16] In all cases, the outcome was the same—members of the family were persuaded to join the business—but the reasons for joining were very different.

desire-based commitment Commitment based on a belief in the purpose of a business and a desire to contribute to it.

obligation-based commitment Commitment that results from a sense of duty or expectation.

cost-based commitment Commitment based on the belief that the opportunity for gain is too great to pass up.

need-based commitment Commitment based on an individual's self-doubt and belief that he or she lacks career options outside the current business.

- **Desire-based commitment.** When family members join a firm based on a deep-seated, gut-level attraction to the business, it is usually because they believe in and accept the purpose of the enterprise. This is referred to as **desire-based commitment**, a belief in the purpose of a business and a desire to contribute to it. Typically, the personal identity of family members is closely tied to the business, and they believe they have the ability to make a significant contribution to it. In short, these individuals join the company because they genuinely *want to.*
- **Obligation-based commitment. Obligation-based commitment** is what drives individuals who feel that they really *ought to* pursue a career in the family business. Often, the goal is to do what the parent-founder wants, even if that career path is not what the family member had in mind. In many cases, parental pressure can be the primary motivator, as was the case with Melanie Bergeron, who played no role in the business when her teenage brothers started Two Men and a Truck. When her brothers went off to college and left the business in the hands of their mother, Mary Ellen Sheets, Bergeron was busy with her own career as a pharmaceutical sales representative. When Sheets talked Bergeron into starting her own Two Men operation, Bergeron treated it as a hobby. Then Sheets decided to run for state senate. At that point the pressure was on, and Bergeron agreed to step in as president of the company, a job that paid no salary at the start. Would anyone but a family member have taken such a chance?
- **Cost-based commitment.** If a family member concludes that there is too much to lose by turning away from a career opportunity within the family business, then his or her decision to join is based on a calculation, not a sense of obligation or emotional identification. This **cost-based commitment** is the belief that the opportunity for gain is too great to pass up. In this case, family members make a *have to* response, motivated by the perception that the value of the business will fall if somebody doesn't step in to take care of it. In other words, joining the business may be the best way to benefit from what the family firm has to offer or to protect the investment value of what is likely to be inherited in the future.
- **Need-based commitment.** When family members join the business because of self-doubt or a concern that they might not be able to reach significant career success on their own, their commitment to the family enterprise is based on perceived necessity. That is, they *need to* join the business because they lack options for career success outside of it. **Need-based commitment** is common among young heirs who leapfrog over nonfamily employees into coveted positions, the demands of which exceed their knowledge and experience. They often feel guilty for their privileged status and are left to wonder if they have what it takes to succeed on their own. Exhibit 5.3 illustrates the four forms of commitment and their implications for family businesses.

The Fear of Commitment

Greg McCann, founding director of the Family Business Center at Stetson University, learned from his students and from the family firms that he coached that commitment is not automatic. Members of the succeeding generation in family firms may have emotional resistance to joining the firm. Typical fears include the following:[17]

1. **Fear of failure.** *If I really take ownership of my life, I might fail.* Realize that if emotional resistance prevents your progress, you are destined to fail.
2. **Fear of success.** *If I succeed, then others will expect more of me in the future.* It's true that successful people have to deal with the pressure of high expectations. But isn't this pressure preferable to others having no expectations of you? Or worse yet, having no expectations of yourself?

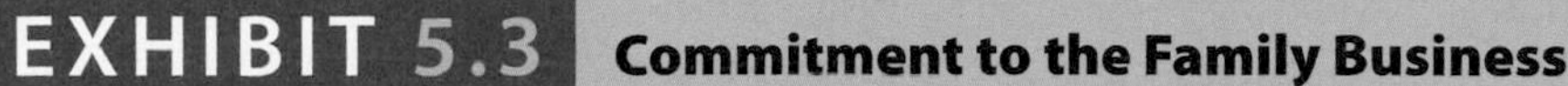
EXHIBIT 5.3 Commitment to the Family Business

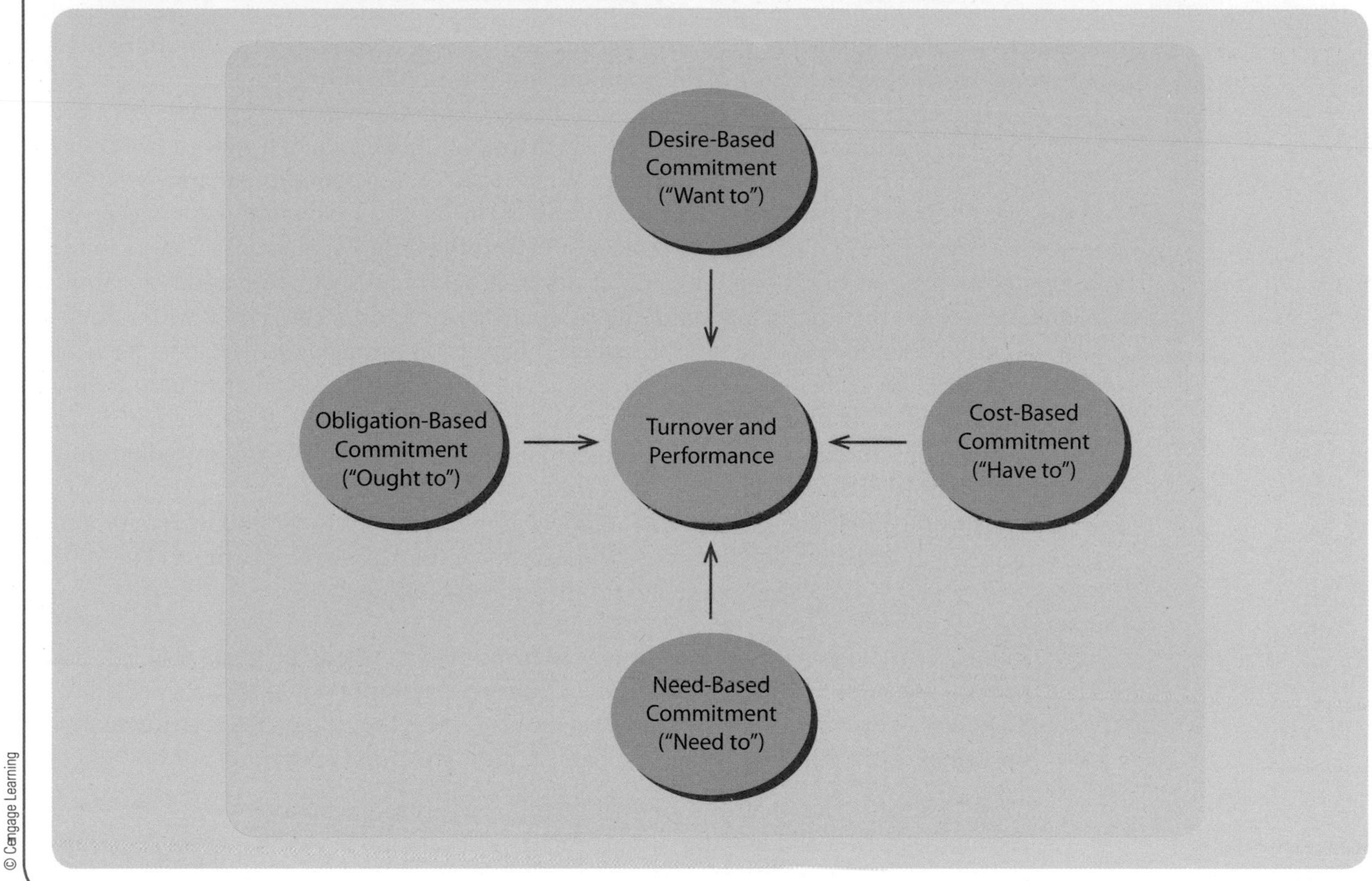

3. **Fear of commitment.** *If I never really try, then I will never really fail.* Avoiding a decision may feel safe, but many people don't understand that not deciding *is* a decision, and it is a poor one.
4. **Fear of disappointing your parents.** *It would break my dad's heart if I worked for another company instead of the family business.* Your parents want you to be happy, and if you are working to achieve that, almost all parents will be happy with your decision. Beyond that, you have to decide whether being authentic is important to you. If it is, you will have to confront this fear.
5. **Fear of disappointing others.** *If I don't go with all my friends to an internship in Chicago, I might lose their friendship.* This fear is similar to the last one, but it plays out with friends, mentors, colleagues, and bosses. It is a real and understandable fear, but you need to look at it more deeply to determine what pleasing others costs you and to question the assumption that you know what they want. Remember that you are responsible for your own happiness.

McCann's final advice is that each individual should make her or his own decisions and not let emotional resistance influence those decisions. How each person handles fears such as those just described is often influenced by the sense of unity within her or his family.

COMMITMENT THROUGH UNITY

family unity
Oneness of mind, feeling, and action among family members.

Family unity has been thoroughly documented as an important characteristic of successful and long-lived families in business.[18] Unity can be seen as oneness of mind, feeling, and action, as among a number of persons. The various bases for commitment shown in Exhibit 5.3 should be reflected in a sense of unity among family members. For instance, family members with higher levels of desire- and obligation-based commitments to the business are more likely to support efforts to promote change, which are common in small businesses and very important to their performance and survival. While desire-based commitment may motivate family members to pursue careers within the family firm, cost-based commitment may result in going "beyond the call of duty" to protect or extend the family's financial interests in the company. Obligation-based commitment, however, provides no such motivation, as family members may see their participation in the company as a requirement. Those with a deep-seated sense of identity with the enterprise (desire-based commitment) are the most likely to work hard, because of their passion for the business. Family members who are committed to the business mostly out of personal need, however, are often in a perpetual state of self-doubt and lack the confidence to excel; this problem is compounded if they are promoted only because of their last name and honestly lack the capabilities to do the job.

MassMutual Financial Group, in conjunction with Kennesaw State University and the Family Firm Institute, conducts periodic surveys of family business owners. The 2007 survey summarized responses related to family unity as follows:[19]

- Family unity and cohesion were found to be critical to family business success, especially when family members identified unity as an important goal. In particular, 87 percent of respondents said family members share the same values. Agreement on values, attitudes, and beliefs indicates family unity and cohesion.
- Considering business matters such as strategy, ownership, and management, 82.9 percent of the owners said that they were completely or very unified as an ownership group.
- Unity of the ownership group is significantly associated with family commitment to the business in each generation, predictions of sales growth, and demonstrations of past growth. It is important to note that the greater the family unity, the more the firms had grown in the previous three years and the more they expected to grow in the future.
- Family unity affects other stakeholders as well. Unified families reported they were more likely to share their values with customers and employees, with 85 percent sharing to a large extent with both groups.

In summary, the researchers concluded that the overlap between individual and organizational values may result in increased levels of employee loyalty, commitment, and organizational citizenship behavior.

Family Roles and Relationships

3 Describe the complex roles and relationships involved in a family business.

The overlapping of two institutions—a family and a business—adds complexity to management. According to columnist Meg Cadoux Hirshberg, "People start companies to do their own things, while marriage is about doing things together. . . . [T]here is no tension a business can't make worse."[20] Hirshberg provides this as a warning to couples thinking about going into business together. This dim view of the family enterprise is not shared by everyone; however, significant conflicts

RESOURCES

Roles—Yesterday and Today

If you want to see how roles and attitudes have changed in society, read one of the early contributions about operating a family firm: *Beyond Survival* (Cleveland, OH: The Center for Family Business, 1975) by Léon Danco. First published in the mid-1970s, this book will introduce you to viewpoints held about men and women in family businesses a generation ago.

can result when family roles and business interests collide. Anticipating these challenges and planning for them can really pay off. This section examines a few of the many possible family roles and relationships that can contribute to the managerial complexity in a family business.

CO-PRENEURS

Some family businesses are owned and managed by couples teams. Such couples are popularly known as **co-preneurs**. Their roles vary depending on their backgrounds and expertise. Whatever the arrangement, both individuals are integral parts of the business.

co-preneurs
Couples teams who own and manage businesses.

One potential advantage of the couples team is the opportunity to work with someone you really trust and to share more of your lives together. For some couples, however, the benefits can be overshadowed by problems related to the business. Differences of opinion about business matters can carry over into family life. And the energy of both parties may be so spent by working long hours in a struggling company that little zest remains for a strong family life. There is a recent trend of couples starting Web-based businesses, often from home. In some of these cases, the co-preneurs have found that there can be too much togetherness, in which case they must establish rules for time apart.[21]

Many couples have had to set boundaries and develop routines to cope with the demands of everyday life (like raising children) and still have sufficient time for the business. For example, the objective of former NFL linebacker Nate Wayne and his wife, Tamiko, was to open a business that would be both lucrative and family friendly so that their three children, ages 4, 8, and 13, would enjoy spending time with mom and dad at work. Tamiko convinced Nate that they should invest in a Cold Stone Creamery ice cream franchise. The Waynes set rules from the beginning, separating their business and personal accounts. To stay on track, they meet regularly with a business attorney, certified public accountant, and financial advisor. The Waynes are careful to give both their children and their marriage attention. Tamiko goes into Cold Stone early, while Nate sends their children off to school, after which he manages a trucking business they launched. They reserve weekends and most evenings for family time.[22]

Courtesy of Kahala

MOM OR DAD, THE FOUNDER

A common figure in family businesses is the founding entrepreneur who plans to pass it on to a son or a daughter. The business and the family have typically both grown since the company was organized. Entrepreneurs with children think naturally in terms of passing the business on to the next generation. Parental concerns associated with this process include the following:

- Does my child possess the temperament and ability necessary for business leadership?
- How can I, the founder, motivate my child to take an interest in the business?
- What type of education and experience will be most helpful in preparing my child for leadership?
- What timetable should I follow in employing and promoting my child?
- How can I avoid favoritism in managing and developing my child for a leadership role?
- Is sibling rivalry likely to be a problem, and can it be avoided?
- How can I prevent the business relationship from damaging or destroying the parent–child relationship?

Of all the relationships in a family business, the parent–child relationship has been recognized for generations as the most troublesome. In recent years, the problems inherent in this relationship have been addressed by counselors, seminars, and books too numerous to count. In spite of all this attention, however, the parent–child relationship continues to perplex many families involved in family businesses.

SONS AND DAUGHTERS

Should sons and daughters be groomed for the family business, or should they pursue careers of their own choosing? In the entrepreneurial family, the natural tendency is to think in terms of a family business career and to push a child, either openly or subtly, in that direction. Little thought may be given to the underlying issues, including the child's talent, aptitude, and temperament. The child may be "a chip off the old block" in many ways but may also be an individual with unique abilities and aspirations. He or she may prefer music or medicine to the world of business and may fit the business mold very poorly. It is also possible that the abilities of the son or daughter may simply be insufficient for a leadership role. Or, a child's talents may be underestimated by parents merely because there has been little opportunity for the child to develop or demonstrate those talents.

Another issue is personal freedom. Today's society values the right of the individual to choose his or her own career and way of life. If this value is embraced by a son or daughter, that child must be granted the freedom to select a career of his or her own choosing. Still, a strong argument can be made for an early introduction to the family firm, perhaps an entry-level part-time or summer job that exposes a teenaged child to what the parents face every day. Owners must remember, however, that their children are still children and may not have the maturity to cope with the responsibilities of employment. And nonfamily managers in the company should not be placed in the awkward position of reprimanding the boss's daughter or son, who refuses to follow procedures.[23]

A son or daughter may feel a need to go outside the family business, for a time at least, to prove that he or she can make it without help from the family. To build self-esteem, he or she may wish to operate independently of the family. Entering the family business immediately after graduation from high school or college may seem stifling, as the child continues to "feel like a little kid with Dad telling me what to do."

In other cases, it is the parents who lay down the rules. Brothers Dan and Bubba Cathy established a policy that required members of the third generation to gain at least two years of experience outside of Chick-fil-A before they could apply for employment in the family firm.[24] Most consultants to family businesses agree with this practice. Obtaining external work experience has two key benefits. First, it builds confidence for the family member that he or she can succeed without the family safety net. Second, nonfamily employees of the company will have more respect for a junior family member who has proven herself or himself in another setting.

SIBLING COOPERATION, SIBLING RIVALRY

In families with a number of children, two or more may become involved in the family business. This depends, of course, on the interests of the individual children. In some cases, parents feel fortunate if even one child elects to stay with the family firm. Nevertheless, it is not unusual for siblings to take positions within the company. Even those who do not work in the business may be more than casual observers on the sidelines because of their stake as heirs or partial owners.

At best, siblings work as a smoothly functioning team, each contributing services according to his or her respective abilities. Just as families can experience excellent cooperation and unity in their relationships with one another, some family businesses benefit from effective collaboration among brothers and sisters.

However, just as there are sometimes squabbles within a family, there can also be sibling rivalry within a family business. Business issues tend to generate competition, and

entrepreneurial experiences

LIVING THE DREAM

© iStockphoto.com/Angel ka Schwarz

The Cautious Successors

Fred Lackland was doing fine as a builder in New Jersey. But a new idea caught his attention when he was on vacation in California in the 1970s. He'd heard about something new called "self-storage," and he made a point of visiting one of these storage facilities while he was on the West Coast. He immediately saw it as a chance to offer more services and expand his business.

Lackland Self Storage

Lackland Self Storage is now one of the largest operations of its kind in New Jersey, and Fred Lackland is considered a pioneer in the industry. By the late 1990s, though, he had turned over daily management of the business to his sons, Michael and Bruce, while he concentrated on construction of new properties. The brothers admired what their father had accomplished and enjoyed working with him. This led to an unexpected problem: Mike and Bruce were hesitant to make major decisions whenever their father was absent and neglected to push for change.

In 2002, the Lackland management team brought in an outside consultant to deal with some frustrations the team was experiencing in moving the company forward. The consultant quickly saw the love and admiration among the family members. What was lacking was a full-time leader. Even though Mike carried the title of president, he did not want to give the appearance of pushing his dad aside. As the meetings progressed, everyone began to recognize that Fred, for all practical purposes, had moved on to other interests and was more than willing to let Mike and Bruce set the direction for the company. The consultant helped the family to set some ground rules for examining and reexamining their work relationships and the goals of the business. In the case of the Lackland family, guidelines were needed for open communication, with the understanding that each generation must incorporate change for the business to survive and prosper.

Today, Lackland Self Storage is firmly in the hands of the second generation. Mike is president and CEO and a public speaker on growth strategies. Bruce is vice president and director of quality assurance, and Fred continues to oversee building construction. Lackland Self Storage has 23 locations in New Jersey and 2 locations in Pennsylvania.

Sources: Lackland Self Storage, http://www.lacklandselfstorage.com/Home.aspx, accessed December 18, 2010; and Aldonna R. Ambler, "When the Successors Don't Take Charge," http://www.familybusinessmagazine.com, accessed December 18, 2010. **http://www.lacklandselfstorage.com**

this affects family, as well as nonfamily, members. Siblings, for example, may disagree about business policy or about their respective roles in the business. And, in some cases, the conflicts can spiral seriously out of control.[25]

Family Business publishes a column entitled "Ask the Experts." In the magazine's Autumn 2007 issue, a fourth-generation business owner wrote in with the following request:

> *Since our father's death, my brother's ego has gone through the roof. He also has a problem keeping employees. I am treated as his employee, and he demands an explanation from me for every move I make, even though I am the president of the holding company. . . . Can you give me some advice?*[26]

The advice of the experts included using a facilitator or a board of directors, improving the strategy and structure of the firm, and increasing communication. Imagine how much better this situation might have been if the writer's father had had the foresight to engage in these activities before his death.

Another sibling dilemma has been labeled the *predator/parasite conflict*. Family members working in the firm are sometimes seen by relatives who work outside the company as predators—extracting money from the business that the outsiders believe is rightfully theirs. From the inside, family members external to the firm are seen, in turn, to be parasites. That is, they have ownership rights, receive dividends, or make other claims on the business without contributing to its success.

After working for years for large companies in the packaging industry, Jeff and Alice[27] decided to strike out on their own. Their business prospered as their family grew. Their oldest daughter became an attorney, and their oldest son chose a career as a financial adviser. The three younger children eventually joined the company. Jeff and Alice saw their industry maturing with limited growth opportunities. They knew there would not be room at the top for all three children. Because of the success their firm enjoyed, the parents had the financial resources to invest in an expanding national franchise. Although the new venture was in a completely different industry, the management skill sets required were similar, and the franchise presented additional leadership positions. Today, each child has emerged as a senior executive in the diversified company. The family plan accommodated the needs and interests of the children, avoiding potential conflict in the ownership transition.

Later in the chapter, you will learn that many enterprises have sought to preempt conflicts by formalizing structures. Some have implemented written guidelines by way of constitutions, while others have formed structures such as family business councils.

IN-LAWS IN AND OUT OF THE BUSINESS

Marriage can bring significant actors into the family business drama. In-laws can and will become directly or indirectly involved in the firms. They may have been employed in the company and married a family member. They may have sought or been induced to accept a position in the company following their marriage. At a minimum, they will have opinions about the family business and their spouses' relatives that they will express.

When an in-law joins a company, effective collaboration may be achieved by assigning family members to different branches or roles within the company. But competition for leadership positions may eventually force decisions that distinguish among the children and in-laws employed in the business. Being fair and maintaining family loyalty become more difficult as the number of family employees increases.

In-laws who are on the sidelines are also participants with an important stake in the business, and their influence on the business and the family can be considerable. They are keenly interested in family business issues that impact their spouses. But their perspective is typically distorted because they often hear only half of the story when it comes to work-related situations.

When family frustrations come up at work, spouses tend to hear all about it at home, often just before the couple goes to bed. The family member vents, then feels better, and goes to sleep. The spouse, on the other hand, is just hearing about the situation and spends the rest of the night worried, angry, or both. Then, when the two siblings sort everything out at the office the next morning and get back to the challenging, satisfying work at hand, neither even thinks about phoning the spouse to let him or her know that the problem was just a silly little matter and that everything is fine. Spouses tend to hear only one side of the story—the bad side—and it shades their view of the business. So, the criticism they receive for having a bad attitude about the family and its enterprise is often undeserved.[28]

When in-laws are employed in the family business, a variety of dynamics can emerge. In the case of one independent financial services firm, when the founding CEO died, he was succeeded by his son-in-law. Years later, that CEO passed away unexpectedly. He, in turn, was succeeded by his son-in-law. Today, that son-in-law continues to run the firm. His two children are both male. Will a daughter-in-law come forward to run the company?

THE ENTREPRENEUR'S SPOUSE

One of the most critical roles in the family business is that of the entrepreneur's spouse. Traditionally, this role has been fulfilled by the male entrepreneur's wife and the mother of his children. However, many husbands have now assumed the role of entrepreneur's spouse, as did Melanie Bergeron's husband, Noel, who married Melanie after she had become president of Two Men and a Truck. Noel did not join the company, but supported Melanie through all the hours that the business demanded of her.

In order for the spouse to play a supporting role in the entrepreneur's career, there must be effective communication between the spouse and the entrepreneur. The spouse needs to hear what's going on in the business; otherwise, she or he may begin to feel detached and respond by competing with the business for attention. Columnist Meg Cadoux Hirshberg also reports that family sacrifices and support go beyond the time spent in the business. She describes her husband's need for tennis and skiing that take him away from the family. As the spouse, she can resent that additional loss of time together, or she can recognize the value it has in relieving stress or generating creative ideas.[29] The spouse can offer understanding and act as a sounding board for the entrepreneur only if the couple communicates on matters of obvious importance to them, both as individuals and as a family.

As a parent, the spouse helps prepare the children for possible careers in the family business. Researchers have found that one of the most frequent and stressful roles performed by the spouse is to serve as a mediator in business relationships between the entrepreneur and the children. A strategy taken by some parents is to involve their children directly in the business at young ages:

> *Packing boxes after school or counting inventory on weekends is often a terrific first job. Laboring alongside a parent, children feel proud of the family business—this is ours! We are making this! And they watch their parents acting as leaders, taking responsibility for both their own lives and the lives of others.*[30]

Ideally, the entrepreneur and his or her spouse form a team committed to the success of both the family and the family business. Such teamwork does not occur automatically—it requires a collaborative effort by both parties to the marriage.

The Need for Good Governance in the Family Firm

Family businesses sometimes face the stereotype of not being professionally managed. Yet several research studies have shown that publicly traded family firms perform as well as or better than nonfamily corporations.[31] As with all companies facing global competition and rapidly changing markets, family businesses have to look carefully at family members who want a leadership position in the enterprise and determine whether they are up to the task. The complex relationships in family firms require the oversight of competent and professional management, whether from inside or from outside the family. Significant deviations, for family reasons, from what would be considered good management practices only serve to weaken the firm. Compromising in this way runs counter to the interests of both the firm and the family.

Family business experts and practitioners have proposed a number of "best practices" for family enterprises. Each family and each family business is different, so what is actually "best" will depend on the individual situation. Nonetheless, the best practices listed in Exhibit 5.4 have helped many family businesses design effective management systems.

The family firm is a business—a competitive business. Observing these and other practices of good management will help the business thrive and permit the family to function as a family. Disregarding them will pose a threat to the business and strain family relationships.

NONFAMILY EMPLOYEES IN A FAMILY FIRM

Those employees who are not family members are still affected by family considerations. In some cases, their opportunities for promotion are lessened by the presence of family members who may have the inside track. Few parents will promote an outsider over a competent daughter or son who is being groomed for future leadership, and this is understandable. But this limits the potential for advancement of nonfamily employees, which may lead them to become frustrated, to feel cheated, or to leave the firm.

Consider the case of a young business executive who worked for a family business that operated a chain of restaurants. When hired, he negotiated a contract that gave him a specified percentage of the business based on performance. Under this arrangement, he was doing extremely well financially—until the owner called on him to say, "I am here to buy you out." When the young man asked why, the owner replied, "You are doing too well, and your last name is not the same as mine!"

RESOURCES

Nonfamily CEOs

There are actually many family-owned businesses that have appointed nonfamily members as CEOs. You can find examples of these businesses and guidelines to follow if you choose this path in many newsletters and blogs that target family business consultants. (See, for example, Northeastern University's *Family BusinessBriefs* at www.fambiz.neu.edu.)

EXHIBIT 5.4 Best Practices for Family Businesses

- Promote learning to stimulate new thinking and fresh strategic insights.
- Solicit ample input from outsiders to keep things in perspective.
- Establish channels for constructive communication and use them often.
- Build a culture that accepts continuous change.
- Promote family members only according to their skill levels.
- Attract and retain excellent nonfamily managers.
- Ensure fair compensation for all employees, including those outside the family.
- Establish a solid leadership succession plan.
- Exploit the unique advantages of family ownership.

Those outside the family may also be caught in the crossfire between family members who are competing with each other. It is difficult for outsiders to maintain strict neutrality in family feuds. If a nonfamily executive is perceived as siding with one of those involved in the feud, she or he may lose the support of other family members. Hardworking employees often feel that they deserve hazard pay for working in a firm plagued by family conflict.

The extent of limitations on nonfamily employees depends on the number of family members active in the business and the number of managerial or professional positions in the business to which nonfamily employees might aspire. It also depends on the extent to which the owner demands competence in management and maintains an atmosphere of fairness in supervision. To avoid future problems, the owner should make clear, when hiring nonfamily employees, the extent of opportunities available to them and identify the positions, if any, that are reserved for family members.

Reasons why the leader of a family-owned enterprise might decide to bring in a nonfamily member as an executive with the firm include the following:

- To bridge the gap between generations
- To set new directions for the firm
- To deal with change
- To provide new skills and expertise

In such cases, the owner should look for certain traits, including maturity, facilitation skills, mentoring skills, emotional sensitivity, trustworthiness, and the ability to understand and share the values of the family.

Family business owners need to plan carefully when bringing in an executive from outside. They should ensure that the position's responsibilities are commensurate with the nonfamily member's experience and have mechanisms for open communication. The nonfamily executive must also be involved in strategic planning and decision making.[32]

FAMILY RETREATS

Although consultants to family businesses recommend establishing mechanisms and protocols early in the life of a company to address the relationship between the family and the firm, such actions usually take place after the business matures and has created wealth. One of the first steps in formalizing processes for building a healthy family-to-business relationship is to hold a retreat. A **family retreat** is a meeting of family members (often including in-laws), usually held away from company premises, to discuss family business matters. In most cases, the atmosphere is informal to encourage family members to communicate freely and discuss their concerns about the business in an environment that does not feel adversarial. The retreat is not so much an *event* as it is the *beginning of a process* of connecting family members. It presents an opportunity to celebrate the founders and their sacrifices, as well as highlight the legacy they wanted to pass down to future generations of the family.

family retreat
A gathering of family members, usually at a remote location, to discuss family business matters.

The prospect of sitting down together to discuss family business matters may seem threatening to some family members. As a result, some families avoid extensive communication, fearing it will stir up trouble. They assume that making decisions quietly or secretly will preserve harmony. Unfortunately, this approach often glosses over serious differences that become increasingly troublesome. Family retreats are designed to open lines of communication and to bring about understanding and agreement on family business issues.

© Monkey Business Images/Shutterstock.com

Initiating discussion can be difficult, so it is standard for family leaders to invite an outside expert or facilitator to coordinate early sessions. The facilitator can help develop an agenda and establish ground rules for discussion. While chairing early sessions, the moderator can establish a positive tone that emphasizes family achievements and encourages rational consideration of sensitive issues. If family members can develop an atmosphere of neutrality, however, they may be able to chair the sessions without using an outsider.

To ensure the success of a family business retreat, David Lansky, CEO of a family business consulting firm, suggests that these guidelines be followed:[33]

1. *Be clear about the purpose of the retreat.* The "Miracle Question" is: "If the meeting accomplished everything you could possibly hope for, what would that look like?"
2. *Set small, attainable goals.* Don't look at the retreat as having to accomplish all possible goals.
3. *Use an agenda and stick to it.* Schedule the meeting for a fixed period of time, and appoint someone to take notes.
4. *Give everyone a chance to participate.* This is a critical step in establishing trust among the participants. People need to feel that they have been heard.
5. *Know the difference between consensus and agreement.* Participants don't have to see things the same way (agreement) in order to concur on a course of action (consensus).

But the talk at family retreats is not always about business. After a retreat, families often speak of the joy of sharing family values and stories of past family experiences. Thus, retreats can strengthen the family as well as the company.

FAMILY COUNCILS

family council
An organized group of family members who gather periodically to discuss family-related business issues.

A family retreat could pave the way for creation of a **family council**, in which family members meet to discuss values, policies, and direction for the future. A family council functions as the organizational and strategic planning arm of a family. It provides a forum for the ongoing process of listening to the ideas of all members and discovering what they believe in and want from the business. A family council formalizes the participation of the family in the business to a greater extent than does the family retreat. It can also be a focal point for planning the future of individual family members, the family as a whole, and the business, as well as how each relates to the others.

A council should be a formal organization that provides governance for family members in their relationship with the business. Council members are normally elected by the extended adult family members. The representatives hold regular meetings, keep minutes, and make suggestions to the firm's board of directors. During the first several meetings, an acceptable mission statement is usually generated, as well as a family creed.

Family businesses that have such councils find them useful for developing family harmony. The meetings are often fun and informative and may include speakers who discuss items of interest. Time is often set aside for sharing achievements, milestones, and family history. The younger generation is encouraged to participate because much of the process is designed to increase their understanding of family traditions and business interests and to prepare them for working effectively in the business.

FAMILY BUSINESS CONSTITUTIONS

Family councils also may be charged with the responsibility of writing a **family business constitution**, which is a statement of principles intended to guide a family firm through times of crisis and change, including the succession process. While this is not a legally binding document, it nonetheless helps to preserve the intentions of the founder and ensure that the business survives periods of change largely intact. When a transfer between generations occurs and there is no guiding document, issues such as ownership, performance, and compensation can become flash points for conflict.[34]

family business constitution
A statement of principles intended to guide a family firm through times of crisis and change.

When Randall Clifford's father died in 1994, the ownership and control of Ventura Transfer Company, the oldest trucking company in California, were suddenly called into question. Clifford's stepmother sued him and his three brothers for an interest in the business. Then, to make matters worse, the four Clifford brothers began to struggle among themselves for control of the company. After a drawn-out legal battle, the sons decided to enlist the help of a consultant to draft a family business constitution. The resulting document helped the family sort out many of the issues that had plagued the transition process.

A family business constitution, sometimes labeled a *family creed*, provides the framework for a family's system of governance of the firm and may include the following topics:[35]

- The core values that all family members should follow
- A process for decision making
- The benefits that family members may receive from the business
- A mechanism for introducing younger members to the family business and its governance structures
- A dispute resolution procedure
- The philanthropic ambitions of the family

At the end of her first year as owner of Two Men and a Truck, Mary Ellen Sheets found that she had accumulated a $1,000 profit. She immediately wrote 10 checks to various charities. Not realizing what her business was destined to become, Sheets did not draft a creed at that point, but she set the precedent. Today, giving back to the community is a core value of the company.[36]

A family business constitution cannot foresee every eventuality, but like any such document it can be amended as needed. The important point is that this document can smooth any transitions, including a change in leadership, which is the subject of the next section.

The Process of Leadership Succession

The task of preparing family members for careers and, ultimately, leadership within the business is difficult and sometimes frustrating. Professional and managerial requirements tend to become intertwined with family feelings and interests, and making the process work right can take years.

In a 2008 survey of business owners by PNC Wealth Management, part of PNC Financial Services Group, 77 percent of business owners said they have a will, but only 33 percent have a succession plan.[37] A more recent survey of family business executives in 35 countries reported that only 50 percent of those companies with succession plans have actually decided who will take over leadership.[38]

Because everyone is so uncomfortable with the subject, plans for succession often are not well developed or at least are poorly communicated. It is not unusual to hear family business owners begin to discuss eventualities with the phrase "If I die, . . ." It is not a question of "if," but of "when." Yet it is hard for the entrepreneurial owner to think of not being around and in charge. And the succeeding generation finds it difficult to confront mom and dad with the prospect of death. The successor may feel that she or he is appearing to be mercenary. Certainly, even grown children do not want to contemplate the death of a parent.

According to Barbara Spector, editor of *Family Business* magazine,

> *In a family business, poor succession planning can have implications for the future of the family as well as the company. Optimally, succession is a process, not a one-time event. Next-generation members are taught to develop a sense of stewardship so they understand that the needs of the business, not their personal desires, take top priority.*[39]

The process begins with the determination of whether appropriate talent exists within the family.

SKILLS

Making Succession Work

With regard to family businesses, nothing has been studied or written about more than succession. Lots of mistakes have been made when changing hands in both ownership and management. A good place to learn about practices that work is the journal of the Family Firm Institute, *Family Business Review*.

AVAILABLE FAMILY TALENT

A stream can rise no higher than its source, and the family firm can be no more brilliant than its leader. The business is dependent, therefore, on the quality of existing leadership talent. If the available talent is not sufficient, the owner must bring in outside leadership or supplement family talent to avoid a decline in the business under the leadership of second- or third-generation family members.

The question of competency is both a critical and a delicate issue. With experience, individuals can improve their abilities; younger family members should not be judged too harshly early on. Furthermore, potential successors may be held back by the reluctance of a parent-owner to delegate responsibility to them. When Richard A. Lumpkin asked his father to authorize him to create a holding company that would allow their firm to break into other businesses, his dad answered, "Son, I wouldn't be for that even if I thought it was a good idea." Lumpkin found the board of directors to be more receptive, and they convinced his father to allow the change. Twenty-five years later, Lumpkin's company, Consolidated Communications, Inc., was the 14th largest telephone company in the United States.[40]

Photo courtesy of C. F. Martin & Co., Inc.

In some cases, a younger family member's skills may actually help to rescue the company, especially when the business becomes mired in the past and fails to keep up with changing technology and emerging markets. In 1986, Chris Martin stepped in as the sixth-generation CEO of C. F. Martin & Co., Inc., a guitar maker. Interviewed in 2008, he recalled that when he joined the firm, it "was barely breaking even." The company had overexpanded through ill-advised acquisitions and was making and selling only 3,000 guitars a year, down from 20,000 in the late 1970s. Concentrating on the core business and on employee empowerment and teamwork, Martin increased production to 85,000 guitars in 2007. He proudly reported paying out $15 million to employees in profit sharing during his tenure as CEO.[41]

Question 1

In any case, a family firm need not accept the existing level of family talent as an unchangeable given. Instead, the business may offer various types of development programs to teach younger family members and thereby improve their skills. It is not unusual for firms to specify programs and other requirements in formal documents such as a family constitution. Some businesses include mentoring as a part of such programs. **Mentoring** is the process by which a more experienced person guides and supports the work, progress, and professional relationships of a new or less-experienced employee. In the family business, a mentor and protégé have the opportunity to navigate and explore family as well as business-related roles and responsibilities.[42]

mentoring
The process by which a more-experienced person guides and supports the professional progress of a new or less-experienced employee.

Perhaps the fairest and most practical approach is to recognize the right of family members to prove themselves. A period of development and testing may occur either in the family business or, preferably, in another organization. If children show themselves to be capable, they earn the right to increased leadership responsibility. If potential successors are found, through a process of fair assessment, to have inadequate leadership abilities, preservation of the family business and the welfare of family members demand that they be passed over for promotion. The appointment of competent outsiders to these jobs, if necessary, increases the value of the firm for all family members who have an ownership interest in it.

PREPARING FOR SUCCESSION

Sons or daughters do not typically assume leadership of a family firm at a particular moment in time. Instead, a long, drawn-out process is involved. This process can be intentionally designed and implemented, or it can simply occur as all parties age. In the latter case, no one should be surprised if the next generation is not prepared at the time a transition is necessary. Successful management and ownership transitions require thoughtful action by both the current and the future leadership teams. Family business educator Greg McCann proposed actions for both generations, as discussed in the following subsections.[43]

Responsibilities of the Senior Generation

As we saw with the Lackland family in the *Living the Dream* feature on p. 147, parents should not automatically expect their children to take on senior management responsibilities without being told that they actually have authority. Listed below are some topics that the senior generation should consider and some steps it should take:

1. *Communication*. Parents need to listen and ask questions. Communication can be used to build trust and to convey values. Providing support and feedback are important, but not just in a one-way direction.
2. *Planning*. Not only should the company's vision be articulated, but also the family's values and even the plan for settling the estate of the senior generation. Planning should encompass the three areas—family members, employees, and owners—that were introduced in Exhibit 5.1, on p. 137.
3. *Accountability*. The senior generation engages in roles as both parent and business owner. In each case, there should be investments in and support for the development of the succeeding generation. That means holding the next generation accountable for their actions, especially those that relate to credibility and integrity.
4. *Owner development*. To prepare the next generation to participate in the governance of the firm, the senior generation should be specific about the job structure of an active owner-manager or board member.
5. *Long-term planning*. When asking the next generation to develop long-term plans that prepare them for leadership, the current generation of leaders must simultaneously prepare their own plans. Such plans should take into account future business development, boards of directors and advisors, family councils, and other structures.

Responsibilities of the Junior Generation

If prospective future leaders of the family enterprise expect to advance to executive positions, they must proactively share in their preparation by doing the following:

1. *Be open to communication.* The succeeding generation should understand the values that led to the creation and growth of the family enterprise and to its current mission. If they believe change is necessary, their actions should result from conscious decisions. They should seek to be fully informed about the history and direction of the company.
2. *Develop a personal action plan.* At this stage, prospective successors should seriously assess whether they have addressed such questions as: Who am I? What are my core values? What are the most important areas of my personal and professional life that I should work on?
3. *Implement the personal action plan.* This involves pursuing relevant education, training, and experience. Actions should lead to the establishment of personal credibility and marketability. The junior generation should not be joining the family business because they lack alternatives.
4. *Prepare for ownership.* Future leaders need to develop basic management skills, such as the ability to comprehend financial statements and to effectively supervise employees. They must grasp the role of a board of directors in terms of its relationship to the management team of the firm. And they need to understand the relationship between the business and the family.
5. *Design life plans.* Life plans are for both the individual and the business. What should the résumé of the family company CEO look like in five or ten years?

TRANSFER OF OWNERSHIP

transfer of ownership Passing ownership of a family business to the next generation.

A final and often complex step in the traditional succession process in the family firm is the **transfer of ownership**. Questions of inheritance affect not only the leadership successor but also other family members who have no involvement in the business. In distributing their estate, parent-owners typically wish to treat all their children fairly, both those involved in the business and those on the outside.

One of the most difficult decisions is determining the future ownership of the business. If there are several children, should they all receive equal shares? On the surface, this seems to be the fairest approach. However, such an arrangement may play havoc with the future functioning of the business. Family business specialist Richard Salomon advises, "Don't worry about 'fairness' and treading on toes: Put a definitive governance mechanism in place."[44] Salomon contends that family members may believe that consensus can be achieved, but he has observed too many cases where deadlocks have paralyzed the ability of businesses to function.

One step taken by some parents to avoid such deadlocks involves changing the ownership structure of the firm. Those children active in the firm's management, for example, might be given common (voting) stock and others given preferred (nonvoting) stock.

Tax considerations are relevant, and they tend to favor gradual transfer of ownership to all heirs. As noted, however, transfer of equal ownership shares to all heirs may be inconsistent with the future successful operation of the business. Tax advantages should not be allowed to blind one to possible adverse effects on management.

Ideally, the founder has been able to arrange his or her personal holdings to create wealth outside the business as well as within it. This is an area where outside experts who grasp financial and estate planning, as well as tax law and accounting, can be invaluable. Planning and discussing the transfer of ownership is not easy, but it is strongly recommended.

Over a period of time, the owner must reflect seriously on family talents and interests as they relate to the future of the firm. The plan for transfer of ownership can then be firmed up and modified as necessary when it is discussed with the children or other potential heirs. In discussing exit strategies in Chapter 13, we explain a variety of possible financial arrangements for the transfer of ownership.

In this chapter, we have tried to make one message very clear to prospective family business owners—families and businesses are interrelated. Trying to separate them would be like trying to unscramble eggs. The better you understand that going in, the more successful you can be in both areas of your life. Despite what many people believe, family members can work together not just successfully, but also happily. Planning in advance can avoid a lot of problems.

1. Define the terms *family* and *family business*.

- The word *family* refers to a group of people bound by a shared history and a commitment to share a future together while supporting the development and well-being of individual members.
- Most businesses in the United States and other countries with free enterprise economies are family-owned and controlled.
- A family business comprises the individual, the family, and the organization, yet each maintains its independent identity.
- A *family business* is an organizational entity in which either the individuals who established or acquired the firm or their descendants significantly influence the strategic decisions and life course of the firm.
- The advantages of a family business include the guidance provided by the family business culture and values, the strong commitment of family members to the success of the firm, the competitive advantage derived from firm-specific knowledge, a focus on long-term goals, a stable culture, the ability to make speedy decisions based on trust, and reliability and pride in the firm's reputation.
- Disadvantages of a family business include resistance to change because of family influences and limited options for raising capital.

2. Explain the forces that can keep a family business moving forward.

- The organizational culture of a family business is composed of the patterns of behaviors and beliefs that emerge from the interaction of family and business.
- The founder often leaves a deep imprint on the culture of a family firm.
- The long-term survival of the business is dependent on the commitment of family members. They may be committed to the family business for different reasons (emotional attachment, sense of obligation, calculated costs, and personal needs), and these reasons will likely determine the nature and strength of that commitment.
- Because commitments among individuals can vary, family unity becomes an important factor in moving the business forward.

3. Describe the complex roles and relationships involved in a family business.

- Couples known as co-preneurs join in business together, which can strengthen or weaken their relationship.
- A primary and sensitive relationship is that between founder and son or daughter.
- Siblings and other relatives may similarly strengthen or weaken their working and personal relationships through a family business.
- In-laws play a crucial role in the family business, either as direct participants or as sideline observers.
- The role of the founder's spouse is especially important, as he or she often serves as a mediator in family disputes and helps prepare the children for possible careers in the family business.

4. Identify management practices that enable a family business to function effectively.

- Good management practices are as important as good family relationships in the successful functioning of a family business.
- Following best practices can help family firms design effective management systems.
- Motivation of nonfamily employees can be enhanced by open communication and fairness.
- Family retreats bring all family members together to discuss business and family matters.
- Family councils provide a formal framework for the family's ongoing discussion of family and business issues.
- Family business constitutions can guide a company through times of crisis or change.

5. Describe the process of managerial succession in a family business.

- Discussing and planning the transfer of leadership is sometimes difficult.
- The quality of leadership talent available in the family determines the extent to which outside managers are needed.
- Succession is a long-term process starting early in the successor's life.
- The succession process requires actions and effective communication on the part of both the senior generation and the succeeding generation.
- Transfer of ownership involves issues of fairness, taxes, and managerial control.

Key Terms

family p. 136
owner-managed business p. 136
sibling partnership p. 136
cousin consortium p.136
family business p. 138
nepotism p. 140
organizational culture p. 140
desire-based commitment p. 142
obligation-based commitment p. 142
cost-based commitment p. 142
need-based commitment p. 142
family unity p. 144
co-preneurs p. 145
family retreat p. 151
family council p. 152
family business constitution p. 153
mentoring, p. 155
transfer of ownership p. 156

Discussion Questions

1. Explain what makes a business a family business. What is the difference between a family business and any other type of business?
2. Suppose that you, as the founder of a business, have a sales manager position open. You realize that sales may suffer somewhat if you promote your son from sales representative to sales manager. However, you would like to see your son make some progress and earn a higher salary to support his wife and young daughter. How would you go about making this decision? Would you promote your son?
3. What advantages result from family involvement in a business? What are some disadvantages?
4. What are the bases of commitment to the family firm? What is the difference between commitment and family unity?
5. With a college-level business degree in hand, you are headed for a job in the family business. As a result of your education, you have become aware of some outdated business practices in the family firm. In spite of them, the business is showing a good return on investment. Should you "rock the boat"? How should you proceed in updating what you see as obsolete approaches?
6. Describe a founder–son or founder–daughter relationship in a family business with which you are familiar. What strengths or weaknesses are evident in that business relationship?
7. Should a son or daughter feel an obligation to carry on a family business? What might happen if that prospective successor chooses not to join the firm?
8. Assume that you are an ambitious, nonfamily manager in a family firm and that one of your peers is the son or daughter of the founder. What, if anything, would keep you interested in pursuing a career with this company?
9. In making decisions about transferring ownership of a family business from one generation to another, how much emphasis should be placed on estate tax laws and other concerns that go beyond the family? Why?

You Make the Call

SITUATION 1

As a single mother of three teenagers, Jessica began her career as an interior designer. She put in long hours, but never ignored her children. As they came of age and left home for college and careers, a new man came into Jessica's life. Charley was a sales executive with a large electronics firm and had children from his prior marriage. Jessica and Charley married, and Charley joined her company, eventually becoming co-owner. By that time, Jessica had built a solid presence for her firm in her hometown. Coming out of a large corporation, Charley had bigger ideas for the business. They made a great team, with Jessica concentrating on design and Charley on sales and expansion.

At various times, other family members joined, and then left, the business. Jessica's sister worked in the family business for awhile, as did Charley's daughter. The one family member who joined and stayed was Jessica's second son, Lou. Lou was the classic computer nerd. He held the title of operations manager for the company, overseeing the work orders and delivery. He spent most of his time, however, working on the company's website and eventually started accepting contracts to do websites for other firms.

Lou's freelancing increasingly distracted him from his responsibilities to his mother's business. Orders were mishandled, deliveries were late, customers were irate. Behind the scenes, Jessica and Charley's other employees were grumbling. They wanted to know why Lou was drawing the salary of an executive, when all his time was spent on his own projects. And they wondered if this was the person who would eventually own the business.

Jessica and Charley did not have their eyes closed. They knew what Lou was doing and had spoken directly with him regarding their concerns. Lou's response was always that he was doing his job and did not see any reason for them to complain. He acknowledged his outside contracts, but said that he worked on those in his spare time. On one occasion, after a particularly heated conversation, Charley went to the restroom to wash up. He recognized Lou's sandals on the person sitting in a stall and could hear that person tapping away on a laptop.

Question 1 What do you think the employees of this family business will do if Lou's behavior continues as it has been?

Question 2 What advice would you offer to Jessica and Charley for handling Lou?

SITUATION 2

Morris was turning 80 and feeling great. Forty years earlier, he had founded a trucking and storage company and grown it into one of the industry's largest in his region. And he was proud that his two sons had chosen to make their careers with the family business. Tony, Morris's son from his first marriage, served as marketing manager, and Steven, his son with his current wife, was chief operating officer. Morris held the titles of CEO and Chairman of the Board.

Morris was especially happy at how well the boys got along. There had never been a sign of jealousy between them. Both had carved out their specialties in the business and cooperated beautifully. They made important contributions to the growth of the firm. They also showed respect to Morris and his wife, Irma, in the business and at home. It was not unusual for Tony and Steven to bring their respective families to their parents' house for Sunday dinner.

It was dawning on Morris that he was not going to live forever and that he had to make some disposition of his ownership of the business. Irma had been pressuring him for some time to back away and consider retirement. Although Morris had confidence in both boys, he faced a dilemma in management and ownership succession. He had applauded the accomplishments of his sons, but had come to the conclusion that Steven was the best one to take charge of the firm. But how could he make such a decision when his older son was a solid and competent executive in the company?

One night, Morris sat down with Irma and told her his decision. He was going to remain permanently in the CEO position. When he died, his sons would learn in the will that Steven was to be designated his successor. Irma gasped in response, stood up, and walked out of the room.

Question 1 If you learned your father's wishes for your position and ownership share in the family business at the reading of the will, how do you think you would react?

Question 2 Does Irma have a role to play in this? What would you recommend that she do at this point?

SITUATION 3

Brothers Sebastian and Alfonso grew up competing for their parents' attention. Everyone was surprised when they decided to go into business with each other. Alfonso was the reserved one. An engineer, he had developed the product that was the basis of their venture. Sebastian was outgoing, a born salesman. He was CEO of the company, while Alfonso worked in the laboratory, overseeing research and development. The business took off, but building it into a national competitor required that all profits be invested in product development and market expansion. After a few years, Sebastian wanted to know where his share of the profits were. He knew sales were growing exponentially. What was his brother doing with his money? One day, the brothers' dad called and offered to come in and run the business. He would make sure that everyone got their fair share.

Question 1 What would you recommend to Sebastian at this point?

Question 2 What would you recommend to Alfonso at this point?

Experiential Exercises

1. Interview someone in your community who has grown up in a family business about the ways she or he has been trained or educated, both formally and informally, for entry into the business. Prepare a brief report, identifying whether or not they carried out the five responsibilities of the junior generation.
2. Interview a college student who has grown up in a family business about parental attitudes toward his or her possible entry into the business. Submit a one-page report describing the extent of pressure on the student to enter the family business and the direct or indirect ways in which family expectations have been communicated.
3. Identify a family business and prepare a brief report on its history, including its founding, family involvement, and any leadership changes that have occurred.
4. Read and report on a biography or autobiography about a family in business or on a nonfictional book about a family business.

Small Business & Entrepreneurship Resource Center

1. The text states that it is a well-known fact that founders leave a deep impression on the family businesses they launch. Such is the case with Chick-fil-A, founded by Truett Cathy. This founder is raising eyebrows, not because of corporate missteps, but for adhering to old-fashioned values and principles. In his book, *Eat Mor Chikin: Inspire More People*, Cathy tells of the secrets of his success. Describe the recipe for Chick-fil-A success.

   Source: "New on the Shelf—Franchisor's Vision Serves Up Recipe for Success: Put People Ahead of Profits," *Franchising World*, Vol. 34, No. 8 (November–December 2002), p. 48.

2. Jay Oxenhorn cofounded Hot Headz of America, Inc., a Philadelphia-based manufacturer and distributor of herbal products for health and wellness. Hot Headz has 10 employees, one of whom is Oxenhorn's mother. Describe his reasons for hiring her, along with some of the pros and cons.

   Source: Mark Henricks, "Parent Trap? Keeping Mom or Dad Busy in Their Retirement Years May Be a Noble Reason to Hire Them, but Be Sure You Know What You're Getting into First," *Entrepreneur*, Vol. 33, No. 3 (March 2005), p. 96–97.

Case 5

W.S. DARLEY & CO. (P. 702)

On the firm's website, the leaders of W.S. Darley & Co. proudly declare, "We remain a family-owned and operated business committed to customer service and our employees." The current CEO, Bill Darley, was seven years old when his father, company founder W. S. Darley, died. Bill's mother might have sold the business then; instead, she selected a nonfamily member to manage the company until Bill was ready to take charge. In 1960, the year he turned 31, Bill Darley accepted responsibility for the family business.

W.S. Darley & Co. provides products and services for fire fighting and emergency services. The company was founded in 1908 and sold its first fire truck in the 1920s for $690. Today, the company offers thousands of products on a global basis. In recent years, it has sold systems, pumps, and truck bodies and engaged in design services for customers in Australia, Brazil, Indonesia, Saudi Arabia, New Zealand, and many other countries. Most recently, it began investing heavily in the development of water purification and conservation products.

ALTERNATIVE CASES FOR CHAPTER 5

Video Case 4, Two Men and a Truck, p. 700
Case 8, D'Artagnan, p. 707
Case 13, Greenwood Dairies, p. 719
Case 22, Pearson Air Conditioning & Service, p. 736

PART 3

DEVELOPING THE NEW VENTURE BUSINESS PLAN

CHAPTERS

Radius Images/ Jupiter Images

CHAPTER 6

The Business Plan: Visualizing the Dream

In the SPOTLIGHT
CitiSlips
http://www.citislips.com

PUTTING SCHOOL TO WORK

Long walks in high heels inspired two women to create something easier on the feet—with a little help from their university.

Wouldn't it be nice if your college helped your business make money? Susie Levitt and Katie Shea thought so, and during the course of their senior year at New York University, they enlisted the school's faculty, staff and even the PR department to help them launch a fashion company based on solving a single problem: Their feet hurt when they walked in high heels.

The two were working as summer interns on Wall Street and bonded over their complaints about covering the long blocks to and from work in heels.

Courtesy of Laura Boyd Studio

"They were killing our feet, but we didn't want to give them up because we aren't the tallest people out there," says Levitt, 22. "So we came up with the idea of emergency footwear."

Back at NYU for their senior year, Levitt and Shea designed a stylish, foldable black ballet flat with a carrying case that could be tucked in a handbag and pulled out when their dogs started to howl. They gave the shoes a catchy name, CitiSoles, and a reasonable price, $24.99

Levitt and Shea figured they had a potentially lucrative idea in hand, but they knew senior year was going to be busy. So in an act of self-preservation, Shea enrolled in a business-plan writing course.

LOOKING AHEAD

After studying this chapter, you should be able to...

1. Explain the purpose and objectives of business plans.
2. Give the rationale for writing (or not writing) a business plan when starting a new venture.
3. Describe the preferred content and format for a business plan.
4. Offer practical advice on writing a business plan.
5. Explain the concept and process for developing a firm's business model.
6. Identify available sources of assistance in preparing a business plan.
7. Maintain the proper perspective when writing a business plan.

© iStockphoto.com/Dan Bachman

"We were both involved in extracurricular activities," says Shea, 22. "The class really helped us stay on track."

The class also encouraged them to enter the Stern Business Plan Competition, which gave them even more access to advice from professors and advisors.

After completing the class and competition, Levitt and Shea had a solid business plan. But before they could begin selling, they needed to secure intellectual property rights. This time, they enrolled in a class about the patent process and worked with their professor to file an application.

"Schools often have lawyers who will come in and work with students pro bono," Levitt says. "We got free advice from lawyers who would have typically charged $500 to $700 an hour, all because we took the time to send an e-mail and ask."

Their company, FUNK-tional Enterprises LLC, was born June 1, when the first 1,000 pairs of CitiSoles arrived. Today, they sell two versions of the foldable flats: CitySlips (the original but in a variety of colors, $24.99) and AfterSoles (a simpler version of CitySlips, $14.95). The shoes are available in boutiques around the country, and on their website, CitiSoles.com.

With the help of NYU's marketing department, there was soon a story about CitiSoles in the New York Daily News, which led to more stories, including one in the *New York Times*. And Levitt and Shea were off and running.

Source: Joel Holland, "Putting School to Work," *Entrepreneur*, December 2009, p. 78.

You're excited about an idea for a new business. But when you mention it to a friend who's also a business owner, she says, "You'll need to prepare a business plan." While the business idea sounds great, sitting down and writing some cold, formal document is not exactly your idea of fun, and you wonder if it is really necessary. After all, you know an entrepreneur who started and successfully grew a company based on an idea developed on the back of a napkin over dinner at a local restaurant. And isn't it true that the founders of such notable companies as Microsoft, Dell Computers, *Rolling Stone* magazine, and Calvin Klein all started their businesses without business plans?

An Overview of the Business Plan

To answer the question of whether or not you should write a business plan, you'll need to first understand its purpose and objectives. We'll help you examine the reasons for writing (or not writing) a business plan for your venture. Then we'll look at the two basic forms a plan might take.

THE PURPOSE OF A BUSINESS PLAN

There is no one correct formula for a business plan. After all, no single plan will work in all situations. But, in general, a **business plan** is a document that outlines the basic concept underlying a business and describes how that concept will be realized—specifically, what problem will be solved. A business plan is an entrepreneur's game plan; it crystallizes the dreams and hopes that motivate an entrepreneur to take the startup plunge. The business plan should lay out your basic idea for the venture and include descriptions of where you are now, where you want to go, and how you intend to get there. John Mullins, the author of *The New Business Road Test*, offers three key elements that should be in every business plan:

business plan
A document that outlines the basic concept underlying a business and describes how that concept will be realized.

- A logical statement of a problem and its solution
- A significant amount of cold, hard evidence
- Candor about the risks, gaps, and other assumptions that might be proved wrong.

No better words of advice could be given.

David Gumpert, who for years headed up the MIT Enterprise Forum,[1] offers a concise and practical definition of a business plan, focusing on how it should lead to action: "It's a document that convincingly demonstrates that your business can sell enough of its product or service to make a satisfactory profit and to be attractive to potential backers."[2] For Gumpert, the business plan is essentially a selling document used to convince key individuals, both inside and outside the firm, that the venture has real potential.

Equally important, writing a business plan is an opportunity to convince yourself, the entrepreneur, that what appears to be a good idea is also a good investment opportunity, both financially and in terms of your personal goals. The issue of your personal aspirations deserves careful thought: *If the business does not align with your personal goals, you are not likely to succeed and you certainly will not enjoy the journey.* So be sure to think about where you want to go in life and the personal costs of starting a business before becoming immersed in that special business opportunity.

For the entrepreneur starting a new venture, a business plan has three basic objectives:

1. To identify the nature and the context of the business opportunity—that is, why does such an opportunity exist?
2. To outline the approach the entrepreneur plans to use to exploit the opportunity
3. To recognize factors that will determine whether the venture will be successful

EXHIBIT 6.1 Users of Business Plans

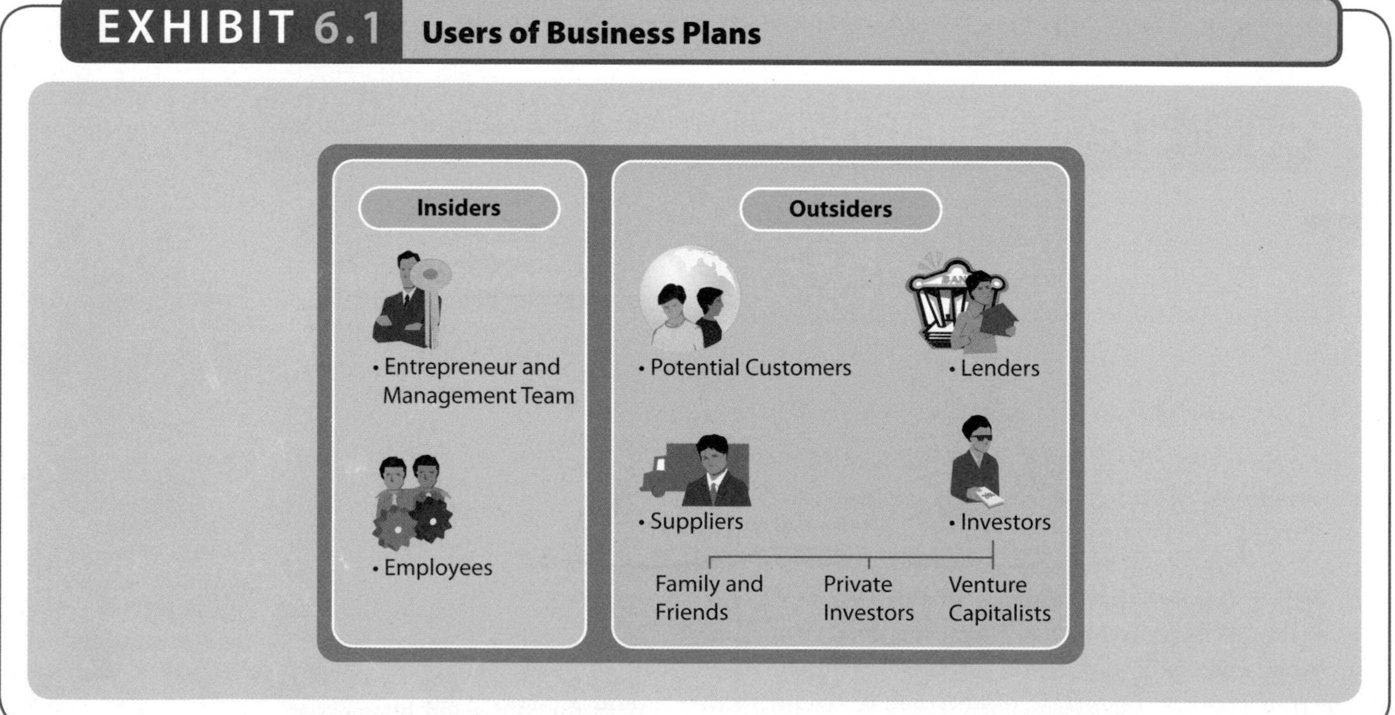

Stated differently, a business plan is used to provide a statement of goals and strategies to be used by company *insiders* and to aid in the development of relationships with *outsiders* (investors and others) who could help the company achieve its goals. Exhibit 6.1 provides an overview of those who might have an interest in a business plan for a proposed venture. The first group consists of the internal users of the plan: the entrepreneur and the new firm's management and employees. The second group consists of outsiders who are critical to the firm's success: its prospective customers, suppliers, lenders, and investors.

DO YOU REALLY NEED A BUSINESS PLAN?

2 Give the rationale for writing (or not writing) a business plan.

The justification often used for *not* writing a business plan goes something like this: "Companies that start up based on business plans are no more successful than those that do not." It is true that studies attempting to measure the success of entrepreneurs with business plans against the success of those without them have produced mixed results. Some findings suggest a relationship; others find none.

Given what we know about Apple, Calvin Klein, and other businesses started without business plans, having such a plan is clearly not an absolute prerequisite for success. *This simply tells us that the business plan is not the business.* It may well be that some entrepreneurs spend hours writing a 60-page business plan with another 50 pages of appendixes but are not effective at executing the plan. In such cases, we can say confidently that writing the plan was a waste of time. What matters is not writing a plan, but implementing it. If the plan is not going to lead to action, don't bother to write it. Only if you *execute* the business plan does it have a reasonable chance of making a difference. Thomas Stemberg, the founder of Staples, who later became a venture capitalist, says it well:

> *In my experience, entrepreneurs often confuse envisioning what a business will be with laying the foundation for what it could be. So they dream big dreams and construct detailed business plans, which is fine. But it's nowhere near as important as putting in place as early as humanly possible the people and systems that will carry them through their journey, no matter what unexpected directions changing markets or technology force them to take.*
>
> *To me, business plans are interesting chiefly as indications of how an entrepreneur thinks. Here at Highland Capital Partners, the venture capital firm I'm part of now, we spend most of our time talking about what really matters: management and markets. If you have the right management team and an exciting market, the rest will take care of itself.*[3]

Thus, an entrepreneur must find the right balance between planning and becoming operational. No matter how well your plan has been thought out, unexpected events will happen. One of the key attributes of a successful entrepreneur is adaptability, regardless of what the business plan says to do. So, if you have to choose between planning and action, go for action—but it's even better if you can do both.

Vinay Gupta of Ann Arbor, Michigan, spent six months attending conferences, meeting with consultants, and writing a 60-page business plan before launching an outsourcing consulting firm for mid-sized businesses.

TOOLS

Answer This Question

Debating about whether or not to write a business plan? Before you decide not to write a plan, give some thought to this question: If a lender or other investor demands to see a business plan before investing, why wouldn't you require the same before investing your personal savings, or even worse, your family's savings? Think about it.

But soon after he started the business, it became clear that far fewer mid-sized firms actually sought outsourcing help than his research had suggested. So he scrapped his original idea and developed outsourcing-management software geared toward companies with annual revenues of more than $1 million. While the planning helped Gupta learn about the industry, it hadn't pointed out the fundamental flaw in his original idea—there were not enough customers willing to buy his services.[4]

The benefits of a business plan also depend on the individual circumstances surrounding the startup. Consider the following possibilities:

- For some startups, the environment is too turbulent for extensive planning to be beneficial. Entrepreneurs in new fields may find that there is not enough information to allow them to write a comprehensive plan. In this instance, an entrepreneur's ability to adapt may be more important than a careful plan for the future.

- Planning may also pose a problem when the timing of the opportunity is a critical factor. In some cases, becoming operational as quickly as possible may have to take priority over in-depth planning, but be careful not to use timing as an easy excuse not to write a business plan.

- A business may also be so constrained by a shortage of capital that planning is not an option. In a study of firms identified by *Inc.* magazine as the fastest-growing firms in the United States, Amar Bhide concluded that a lack of planning may make sense for some companies: "Capital-constrained entrepreneurs cannot afford to do much prior analysis and research. The limited profit potential and high uncertainty of the opportunity they usually pursue also make the benefits low compared to the costs."[5]

Writing a detailed business plan is not a guarantee of success, but most entrepreneurs need the discipline that comes with the process. The path of an enterprise started without adequate preparation tends to be haphazard. In the words of Thomas Carlyle, the Scottish mathematician and writer, "Nothing is more terrible than activity without insight." This is particularly true for a complex process like initiating a new business.

Although planning is a mental process, it should go beyond the realm of speculation. Thinking about a proposed new business must be more thorough for rough ideas to come together. A written plan *based on good research* helps to ensure the necessary systematic and complete coverage of factors important in starting a new business. Frank Moyes, a successful entrepreneur who for many years has taught courses on business planning at the University of Colorado, offers the following observation:

> *Perhaps the most important reason to write a business plan is that it requires you to engage in a rigorous, thoughtful and often painful process that is essential before you start a venture. It requires you to answer hard questions about your venture. Why is there a need for your product/service? Who is your target market? How is your product/service different than your competitor's? What is your competitive advantage? How profitable is the business and what are the cash flows? How should you fund the business?*[6]

So the business plan becomes a model that helps the entrepreneur and the management team focus on important issues and activities for the new venture. Furthermore, it helps the entrepreneur communicate his or her vision to current and prospective employees of the firm. After all, entrepreneurs who are building good companies seldom, if ever, work alone.

The business plan also matters to outsiders. Although typically thought to be the primary risk takers in a startup, the entrepreneur and the management team are by no means the only risk takers. To make the company successful, the entrepreneur must convince outsiders—prospective customers, suppliers, lenders, and investors—to become linked with the firm. Why should they do business with your startup, rather than with an established firm? They need evidence that you will be around in the future. As Amar Bhide explains, "Some entrepreneurs may have an innate capability to outperform their rivals, acquire managerial skills, and thus build a flourishing business. But it is difficult for customers (and others) to identify founders with these innate capabilities."[7]

By enhancing the venture's credibility, the business plan serves as an effective selling tool with prospective customers and suppliers, as well as investors. For example, a well-prepared business plan can be helpful in gaining a supplier's trust and securing favorable credit terms. Likewise, a plan can improve sales prospects by convincing prospective customers that the new firm is likely to be around for a long time to service a product or to continue as a source of supply.

Finally, the entrepreneur may face the task of raising money to supplement personal savings. This requires an effective presentation to bankers, individual investors, or, in some cases, venture capitalists. Approach almost any investor for money today and the first thing she or he will ask is, "Where is your business plan?"

As already noted, a business plan is not an absolute prerequisite for entrepreneurial success. A plan may not be needed in certain situations, especially if you want only to build a very small company and have no plans for significant growth. But we encourage you to dream and hope for more. Ewing Marion Kauffman, who founded Marion Labs with $5,000 and later sold it for $6 billion, once said, "You should not choose to build a common company. It's your right to be uncommon if you can."[8] And Peter Drucker wrote, "Even if you are starting your business on a kitchen table, you must have a vision of becoming a world leader in your field, or you will probably never be successful."[9] Granted, you may have no interest in building a company that is a world leader in its field, but neither should you dream too small.

HOW MUCH PLANNING?

For most entrepreneurs, the issue is not *whether* to prepare a business plan but *how* to engage in effective planning, given the situation. As already observed, different situations lead to different needs and, thus, to different levels of planning.

The issue, then, goes beyond answering the question "Do I plan?" It is more about deciding how much to plan. In starting a business, an entrepreneur has to make some tradeoffs, as preparing a plan requires time and money, two resources that are always in short supply. At the extremes, an entrepreneur has two basic choices when it comes to writing a business plan: the dehydrated plan or the comprehensive plan.

The Dehydrated Plan

As noted earlier, extensive planning may be of limited value when there is a great amount of uncertainty in the environment or when timing is a critical factor in capturing an opportunity. A **dehydrated plan** is a short form of a business plan, presenting only the most important issues and projections for the business. Focusing heavily on market issues, such as pricing, competition, and distribution channels, the dehydrated plan provides little in the way of supporting information.

dehydrated plan A short form of a business plan that presents only the most important issues and projections for the business.

This type of plan will often be adequate for seeking outside financing from banks, especially if it includes past and projected financial results. In fact, it is so rare for an entrepreneur to provide any form of a plan when requesting a loan that a dehydrated plan will probably make a favorable impression on a banker. Furthermore, a dehydrated plan may be helpful in trying to gauge investor interest and to determine whether writing a full-length plan would be worth the time and effort.

The Comprehensive Plan

When entrepreneurs and investors speak of a business plan, they are usually referring to a **comprehensive plan**, a full business plan that provides an in-depth analysis of the critical factors that will determine a firm's success or failure, along with all the underlying

comprehensive plan A full business plan that provides an in-depth analysis of the critical factors that will determine a firm's success or failure, along with all the underlying assumptions.

assumptions. Such a plan is beneficial when you are describing a new opportunity (startup), facing significant change in the business or the external environment (changing demographics, new legislation, developing industry trends), or explaining a complex business situation. In the remainder of this chapter and in those that follow, we will be discussing the comprehensive business plan.

Preparing a Business Plan

So you have decided to write a business plan. Like writing a term paper or report, getting started is usually the hardest part. Recall that in Chapter 3, we emphasized the importance of first conducting a feasibility analysis and only then writing a business plan if your idea "passes muster," to use military speak. Three elements must be evident from the feasibility analysis before you move on to the business plan: strong market potential, an attractive industry, and the right individual or team to execute the plan. Often, entrepreneurs rush past these issues, wanting to "get going." Being oriented to action is a positive trait for an entrepreneur, but not at the expense of doing the basic homework. Never forget the need for balance. One entrepreneur told us, "It's not that hard. To meet the basic requirements, you have to have a large and growing market, an unfair competitive advantage, and a team of people who can capture the advantage."[10] So before you write a business plan, begin with a feasibility analysis to see if the basics are present.

Once the feasibility analysis is completed, it's time to begin the process of writing a business plan. For this, two issues are of primary concern: the content and format of the plan and the effectiveness of the written presentation.

THE CONTENT AND FORMAT OF A BUSINESS PLAN

When considering the content of a business plan, continue to think first and foremost about the opportunity, as identified by your feasibility analysis. Strategies and financial plans will follow naturally if the opportunity is a good one. The business plan should give thorough consideration to the following basic factors (presented graphically in Exhibit 6.2):

1. The *opportunity* should reflect the potential and the attractiveness of the market and industry.
2. *Critical resources* include not just money, but also human assets (suppliers, accountants, lawyers, investors, etc.) and hard assets (accounts receivable, inventories, etc.). An entrepreneur should think of ways to minimize the resources necessary for startup.
3. The *entrepreneurial team* must possess integrity and breadth and depth of experience.
4. The *financing structure*—how a firm is financed (debt versus equity) and how the ownership percentage is shared by the founders and investors—will have a significant impact on an entrepreneur's incentive to work hard. The goal is to find a win-win deal.
5. The *context* (or external factors) of an opportunity includes the regulatory environment, interest rates, demographic trends, inflation, and other factors that inevitably change but cannot be controlled by the entrepreneur.

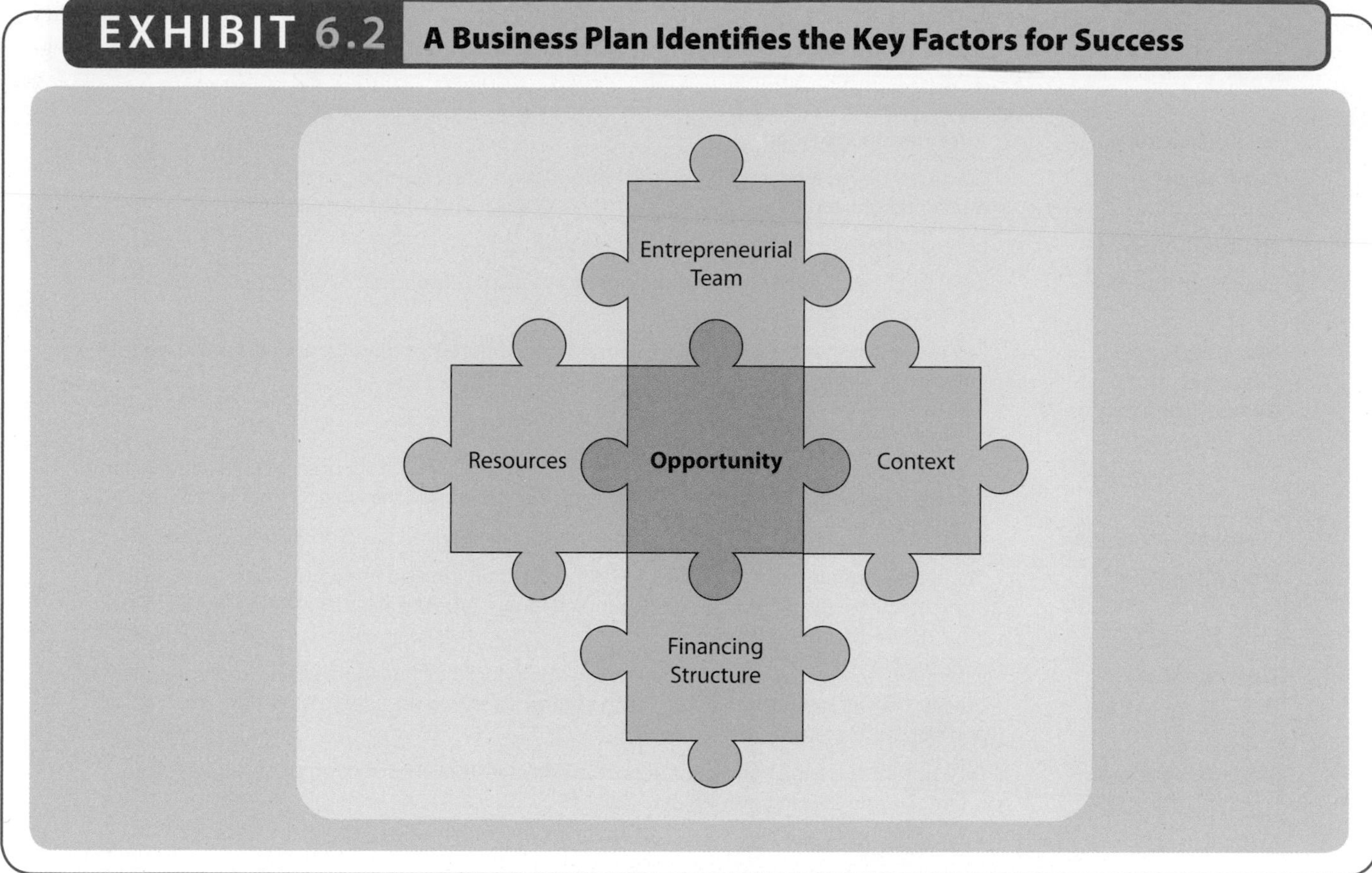

EXHIBIT 6.2 **A Business Plan Identifies the Key Factors for Success**

Thus, the business plan will need to demonstrate that the entrepreneur has pulled together the right opportunity, the right resources, the right people, and the right financing structure, all within the right context. Admittedly, there will always be uncertainties and ambiguities; the unanticipated is bound to happen. But by making decisions about these key factors, you can be sure that you are dealing with the important issues, and this will help you in determining the appropriate content to include in the plan.

There is no single format to be followed in writing a business plan. A plan for a retail store, restaurant, or wholesaling business will, by necessity, be somewhat different in terms of topics, order of presentation, and what is emphasized. However, investors want to see a format that is familiar to them. So you do not want to write a business plan that is fundamentally different from what they are accustomed to seeing. Deviating significantly from this format would be a mistake.

Exhibit 6.3 summarizes the major sections common to most business plans, providing a bird's-eye view of what's usually included. A brief overview of each of these sections follows;[11] Chapters 7 through 13 take an in-depth look at each section of the business plan.

Cover Page

The cover page should contain the following information:

- Company name, address, phone number, fax number, and website
- Tagline and company logo
- Name of contact person (preferably the president) with mailing address, phone number, fax number, and e-mail address

EXHIBIT 6.3 Abbreviated Business Plan Outline

Section Heading	Information Provided
Cover Page	Company name, logo, tagline, contact information, copy number, date prepared, and disclaimer (if needed)
Table of Contents	Listing of the key sections of the business plan
Executive Summary	One- to three-page overview of the significant points, intended to motivate the reader to continue reading
Industry, Target Customer, and Competitor Analysis	Key characteristics of the industry, including the different segments, and the niche where you plan to compete
Company Description	Company objectives, the nature of the business, its primary product or service, its current status (startup, buyout, or expansion) and history (if applicable), and the legal form of organization
Product/Service Plan	Justification for why people will buy the product or service, based on its unique features
Marketing Plan	Marketing strategy, including the methods of identifying and attracting customers, selling approach, type of sales force, distribution channels, types of sales promotions and advertising, and credit and pricing policies
Operations and Development Plan	Operating or manufacturing methods, operating facilities (location, space, and equipment), quality-control methods, procedures to control inventory and operations, sources of supply, and purchasing procedures
Management Team	Description of the management team, outside investors and/or directors, and plans for recruiting and training employees
Critical Risks	Any known inherent risks in the venture
Offering	How much capital the entrepreneur needs and how the money will be used (section used to attract investors)
Exit Strategy	Ways an investor—and the entrepreneur—may be able to harvest their business investment
Financial Plan	Contemplated sources of financing; any historical financial statements, if available; pro forma financial statements for three to five years, including income statements, balance sheets, cash flow statements, and cash budgets
Appendix of Supporting Documents	Various supplementary materials and attachments to expand the reader's understanding of the plan

- Date on which the business plan was prepared
- If the plan is being given to investors, a disclaimer that the plan is being provided on a confidential basis to qualified investors only and is not to be reproduced without permission
- Number of the copy (to help keep track of how many copies have been given out)

Table of Contents

The table of contents provides a sequential listing of the sections of the plan, with page numbers. This allows the reader to spot-read the plan (a common practice) rather than reading it from front to back. Exhibit 6.4 presents the table of contents for the business plan for Benjapon's, a Thai restaurant. (While the table of contents for Benjapon's business plan does not follow exactly the format presented in Exhibit 6.3, note that it has much of the same content and follows a similar order.)

EXHIBIT 6.4 Table of Contents for Business Plan of Benjapon's

I	EXECUTIVE SUMMARY
II	THE INDUSTRY, TARGET CUSTOMERS, AND COMPETITORS
III	THE COMPANY
IV	THE MARKETING PLAN
V	THE OPERATIONS PLAN
VI	THE DEVELOPMENT PLAN
VII	THE GROWTH PLAN
VIII	THE TEAM
IX	THE FINANCIAL PLAN
X	APPENDICES

To see the complete table of contents for Benjapon's business plan, go to Appendix A.

Source: Used by permission of Benjapon's.

Executive Summary

The **executive summary** is often thought to be the most important section of the business plan. If you don't catch the readers' attention in the executive summary, most likely they will not continue reading. At the very outset, it must convey a clear and concise picture of the proposed venture and, at the same time, create a sense of excitement regarding its prospects. This means that it must be written—and, if necessary, rewritten—to achieve clarity and create interest. Even though the executive summary comes at the beginning of the business plan, it provides an overview of the whole plan and should be written last. In no more than three (preferably two) pages, the executive summary should include the following subsections:

executive summary A section of the business plan that conveys a clear and concise overall picture of the proposed venture.

- A description of the opportunity
- An explanation of the business concept
- An industry overview
- The target market
- The competitive advantage you hope to achieve in the market
- The economics of the opportunity
- The management team
- The amount and purpose of the money being requested (the "offering") if you are seeking financing

Depending on the situation and the preference of the entrepreneur, the executive summary may be in the form of a synopsis or a narrative.

SYNOPSIS The synopsis is the more straightforward of the two summary formats. A synopsis briefly covers all aspects of the business plan, giving each topic relatively equal treatment. It relates, in abbreviated fashion, the conclusions of each section of the completed business plan. Although it is easy to prepare, the synopsis can be rather dry reading for the prospective investor.

NARRATIVE Because the narrative tells a story, it can convey greater excitement than the synopsis. However, composing an effective narrative requires a gifted writer who can communicate the necessary information and generate enthusiasm without crossing the line into hyperbole. A narrative is more appropriate for businesses that are breaking new ground with a new product, a new market, or new operational techniques. It is also a better format for ventures that have one dominant advantage, such as holding an important patent or being run by a well-known entrepreneur. Finally, the narrative works well for companies with interesting or impressive backgrounds or histories.

Benjapon's again provides us with an example, as Exhibit 6.5 shows the executive summary for the business.

Industry, Target Customer, and Competitor Analysis

The primary purpose of this section is to present the opportunity and demonstrate why there is a significant market to be served. You should describe the broader industry in which you will be competing, including industry size, growth rate, fundamental trends, and major players. You should next identify the different segments of the industry and finally describe in detail the niche in which you plan to participate. It is tempting to begin describing your own company at this point. Instead, you should provide the context of the opportunity and demonstrate that a market segment is being underserved. There will be an opportunity later to introduce your product and/or service.

Next, describe your target customers in terms of demographics and psychological variables, such as their values, their attitudes, and even their fears. The more clearly you can identify your customer, the more likely it is that you will provide a product or service that is actually in demand. Finally, knowing what the customer looks like and wants serves as the basis for understanding who your competitors are. Analyze competitors in terms of product or service attributes that they are or are not providing.

Company Description

This section gives a brief description of the firm. If the business is already in existence, its history is included. The company description informs the reader of the type of business being proposed, the firm's objectives, where the firm is located, and whether it will serve a local or international market. In many cases, legal issues—especially those concerning the firm's form of organization—are addressed in this section of the plan. (Legal issues regarding the form of organization are discussed at length in Chapter 8.) In writing this section, the entrepreneur should answer the following questions:

- When and where is the business to be started?
- What is the history of the company?
- What are the firm's objectives?
- What changes have been made in structure and/or ownership?
- In what stage of development is the firm—for example, seed stage or full product line?
- What has been achieved to date?
- What is the firm's distinctive competence?
- What are the basic nature and activity of the business?

(Continued p. 176)

EXHIBIT 6.5 Executive Summary for Business Plan of Benjapon's

1.1 The Opportunity

1. Thai food is one of the fastest growing food trends in the U.S. and is rapidly moving into the mainstream[1].
2. Americans are leading a busier lifestyle and thus rely more on meals outside the home. Restaurants account for 46% of total food dollars spent[2], up from 44.6% in 1990 and 26.3% in 1960[3]. By 2010, 53% of food dollars will be spent on away-from-home sources[4].
3. Americans are demanding better quality food and are willing to pay for that quality. As a result, fast food establishments have recently added premium items to their menu. For example, Arby's has a line of "Market Fresh" items[5]; Carl's Jr. offers "The Six Dollar Burger."[6]

The fast casual segment emerged to meet the demands for better-quality foods at a slightly higher price than that of fast food. Despite the immense popularity of Asian food, and Thai food in particular, the fast casual segment is dominated by cafes/bakeries (Panera Bread, Au Bon Pain) and Mexican (Chipotle Grill, Baja Fresh, Qdoba). In recent years, however, Asian fast casual players have begun to emerge in various regions in the U.S. Such players include Mama Fu's, Nothing but Noodles, and Pei Wei Asian Diner, but are still considered regional players.

Therefore, customers are limited in choices:

- Thai food patrons are currently limited to full-service restaurant options, requiring more time and money than fast food or fast casual options.
- Busy consumers are currently limited to hamburgers, sandwiches, pizzas, and Mexican, when it comes to fast-served options.

1.2 The Company

- Benjapon's is a fast-casual restaurant serving fresh Thai food, fast, at affordable prices, in a fun and friendly atmosphere. We will open two company locations, with future plans to grow through franchising.
- The restaurant will be counter-order and table-service with an average ticket price of $8.50. Store hours are from 11 am-10 pm, seven days a week. We expect 40% of our business to come from take-out orders.
- The company will offer Thai culture and food "information fun facts" on the menu, on the packaging, and as part of the restaurant décor to enhance the overall experience.
- Our target customers are urban, 18–35-year-old college students and young working professionals.
- The size of the restaurant will be approximately 1,500 square feet with 50 seats. The first location will be selected from one of the bustling neighborhood squares in the cities of Somerville or Cambridge, Massachusetts, due to proximity to the target market.

1.3 The Growth Plan

Our plan is to grow via franchising after opening two company-owned stores. We plan to first saturate the Greater Boston Area, and move towards national expansion via Area Development Agreements. According to our calculations, the city of Boston can support three to five stores, while the Greater Boston Area can support twenty stores.

1.4 The Team

Management Team

Benjapon Jivasantikarn, Founder and Owner—Six years of experience in finance and business incentives at KPMG, a Big Four professional services firm. MBA, Magna Cum Laude, from Babson College. Douglass Foundation Graduate Business Plan Competition Finalist. Sorensen Award for Entrepreneurial and Academic Excellence.

[1] Packaged Facts, Marketresearch.com, 2003.
[2] "Restaurant Industry Report," The Freedonia Group, Inc. 2003.
[3] "Restaurant Industry Report," Standard and Poor's, 2003.
[4] National Restaurant Association
[5] Arby's website: www.arbys.com
[6] Carl's Jr. website: www.carlsjr.com

(Continued)

EXHIBIT 6.5 Executive Summary for Business Plan of Benjapon's (Continued)

Zack Noonprasith, General Manager—Six years experience in financial services. Five years experience in restaurant management.

Supranee Siriaphanot, Chef—Over 15 years experience as Thai restaurant owner and chef in the U.S.

Board of Advisors:

Rick Hagelstein—Lifelong successful entrepreneur. Founder and CEO of The Minor Group, a marketing, manufacturing, food, property, and hotel development company in Thailand and Asia Pacific. The Minor Food Group is the Thai franchisee of Burger King, Swensen's, Dairy Queen, and Sizzler, and a franchisor of The Pizza Company, which owns 75% of the pizza market in Thailand.

Steve Sabre—Co-founder of Jiffy Lube International and expert in entrepreneurship and franchising.

Hull Martin—Former venture capitalist in the restaurant industry and current advisor to start-up ventures.

1.5 The Financials

We estimate an initial required investment of $550,000. The following are our summary financials for a five-year forecast period.

Summary Financials ($)	Year 1	Year 2	Year 3	Year 4	Year 5
# Company-Owned Stores	1	1	2	2	2
# Franchises Sold	—	—	—	3	13
# Franchises in Operations	—	—	—	—	3
Revenue	691,200	881,280	1,977,592	2,293,859	2,874,559
Gross Profit	451,080	601,749	1,380,195	1,623,578	2,122,505
EBIT	(110,145)	74,104	129,202	363,687	525,670
EBITDA	(72,526)	111,723	204,440	430,592	592,575
Net Earnings	(138,145)	48,904	81,602	196,068	296,922
Cash	109,784	168,277	561,526	751,112	989,152
Total Equity	(28,179)	20,725	302,327	498,395	795,317
Total Debt	350,000	315,000	595,000	525,000	385,000
Profitability					
Gross Profit %	65.3%	68.3%	69.8%	70.8%	73.8%
EBIT %	−15.9%	8.4%	6.5%	15.9%	18.3%
EBITDA %	−10.5%	12.7%	10.3%	18.8%	20.6%
Net Earnings %	−20.0%	5.5%	4.1%	8.5%	10.3%
Returns					
Return on Assets	−37.1%	12.2%	8.0%	16.8%	21.8%
Return on Equity	490.2%	236.0%	27.0%	39.3%	37.3%
Return on Capital (LT Debt + Equity)	−42.9%	14.6%	9.1%	19.2%	25.2%

Source: Used by permission of Benjapon's.

- What is its primary product or service?
- What customers will be served?
- What is the firm's form of organization—sole proprietorship, partnership, limited liability company, corporation, or some other form?

- What are the current and projected economic states of the industry?
- Does the firm intend to sell to another company or an investment group, does it plan to be a publicly traded company, or do the owners want to transfer ownership to the next generation of the family?

Product/Service Plan

The **product/service plan** describes the products and/or services to be offered to the firm's customers. Now is the time to make a convincing presentation of your company's competitive advantage. Based on your earlier description of the industry and its major players, explain how your product or service fills a gap in the market or how your product or service is "better, cheaper, and/or faster" than what is currently available. In the case of a physical product, try to provide a working model or prototype. Investors will naturally show the greatest interest in products that have been developed, tested, and found to be functional. Any innovative features should be identified and any patent protections explained. (Chapter 15 discusses this topic more fully.) Also, your growth strategy for the product or service should be explained in this section, as growth is a primary determinant of a firm's value. If relevant, describe secondary target markets the firm will pursue.

product/service plan
A section of the business plan that describes the products and/or services to be provided and explains its merits.

Marketing Plan

The **marketing plan** describes how the firm will reach and service customers within a given market. In other words, how will you entice customers to make the change to your product or service and to continue using it? This section should present the marketing strategy, including the methods of identifying and attracting customers; pricing strategies, selling approach, type of sales force, and distribution channels; types of sales promotions and advertising; and credit and pricing policies. Sales forecasts will need to be developed, based on this information. Finally, in terms of servicing the customer, this section should describe any warranties, as well as planned product updates. (Chapter 7 provides in-depth coverage of the marketing plan.)

marketing plan
A section of the business plan that describes the user benefits of the product or service and the type of market that exists.

The Art of Beginning

Naeem Zafer, a successful entrepreneur, provides practical advice for starting a business at his website www.startup-advisor.com. He also offers excellent insights in "The Art of Writing a Business Plan" at http://www.slideshare.net/naeemz/the-art-of-writing-a-business-plan-zafar?from=share_email.

Operations and Development Plan

The **operations and development plan** offers information on how the product will be produced or the service provided. Here, you will explain how the operations will contribute to the firm's competitive advantage—that is, how operations will create value for the customer. This section discusses such items as location and facilities, including how much space the business will need and what type of equipment it will require. In today's age, it is important to describe the choice between in-house production and outsourcing in order to minimize costs. Remember, however, that you should never plan to outsource a part of operations that contributes to your competitive advantage. (These aspects of the plan are discussed at length in Chapters 9 and 21.) The operations and development plan should also explain the firm's proposed approach to assuring quality, controlling inventory, and using subcontractors for obtaining raw materials. (See Chapter 21 for further discussion of these issues.)

operations and development plan
A section of the business plan that offers information on how a product will be produced or a service provided, including descriptions of the new firm's facilities, labor, raw materials, and processing requirements.

Management Team

Prospective investors look for well-managed companies. Of all the factors they consider, the quality of the management team is paramount. Some investors say that they would rather have an "A" management team and a "B" product or service than a "B" team and an "A" product. But it can also be said that the right management in the wrong market is likely headed for failure. For success, you must have a good team working in an exciting market.

management team
A section of the business plan that describes a new firm's organizational structure and the backgrounds of its key players.

The **management team** section should detail the proposed firm's organizational structure and the backgrounds of those who will fill its key positions. Ideally, a well-balanced management team—one that includes financial and marketing expertise as well as production experience and innovative talent—will already be in place. Managerial experience in related enterprises and in other startup situations is particularly valuable. (The factors involved in preparing the management team section are discussed in greater detail in Chapter 8.)

Critical Risks

critical risks
A section of the business plan that identifies the potential risks that may be encountered by an investor.

The business plan is intended to tell a story of success, but there are always risks associated with starting a new venture. Thus, the plan would be incomplete if it did not identify the risks inherent in the venture. The **critical risks** section identifies the potential pitfalls that may be encountered by an investor. Common risks include a lack of market acceptance (customers don't buy the product as anticipated), competitor retaliation, longer time and higher expenses than expected to start and grow the business, inadequate financing, and government regulations.

Offering

offering
A section of the business plan that indicates to an investor how much money is needed, and when and how the money will be used.

If the entrepreneur is seeking capital from investors, an **offering** should be included in the plan to indicate clearly how much money is needed and when. It is helpful to convey this information in a *sources and uses table* that indicates the type of financing being requested (debt or equity) and how the funds will be used. For example, for a firm needing $500,000, including any money borrowed and the founder's investment, the sources and uses table for the first year might appear as follows:

Sources:	
Bank debt	$100,000
Equity:	
New investors	300,000
Founders	100,000
Total sources	$500,000

Uses:	
Product development	$125,000
Personnel costs	75,000
Working capital:	
Cash	20,000
Accounts receivable	100,000
Inventory	80,000
Machinery	100,000
Total uses	$500,000

If equity is being requested, the entrepreneur will need to decide how much ownership of the business she or he is willing to give up—not an easy task in most cases. Typically, the amount of money being raised should carry the firm for 12 to 18 months—enough time to reach some milestones. Then, if all goes well, it will be easier and less costly to raise more money later. (These issues will be discussed in greater detail in Chapters 11 and 12.)

Exit Strategy

exit strategy
A section of the business plan that focuses on options for cashing out of the investment.

If a firm is using the business plan to raise equity financing, investors will want to know the possible options for cashing out of their investment, or what is called the **exit strategy**.

Most equity investors absolutely will not invest in a startup or early-stage business if they are not somewhat confident that at some time in the future there will be an opportunity to recover their principal investment, plus a nice return on the investment. The issue of crafting an exit strategy, or what we like to call the *harvest*, will be discussed in Chapter 13.

Financial Plan

The **financial plan** presents financial forecasts in the form of pro forma statements. In the words of Paul Gompers, a Harvard professor,

> *One of the major benefits of creating a business plan is that it forces entrepreneurs to confront their company's finances squarely. That's because a business plan isn't complete until entrepreneurs can demonstrate that all the wonderful plans concerning strategy, markets, products, and sales will actually come together to create a business that will be self-sustaining over the short term and profitable over the long term.*[12]

financial plan
A section of the business plan that projects the company's financial position based on well-substantiated assumptions and explains how the figures have been determined.

And as Rudy Garza, a venture capitalist in Austin, Texas, explains, "The financial plan helps me understand the entrepreneur's thought process about the opportunity."[13]

Pro forma statements, which are projections of the company's financial statements, are presented for at least three years and preferably up to five years. The forecasts ideally include balance sheets, income statements, and statements of cash flows on an annual basis for three to five years, as well as cash budgets on a monthly basis for the first year and on a quarterly basis for the second and third years. It is vital that the financial projections be supported by well-substantiated assumptions and explanations of how the figures have been determined. (More will be said about this issue later in this chapter when we discuss the *business model.*)

pro forma statements
Projections of a company's financial statements for up to five years, including balance sheets, income statements, and statements of cash flows, as well as cash budgets.

While all the financial statements are important, the statement of cash flows deserves special attention, because a business can be profitable but fail if it does not produce positive cash flows. A well-prepared statement of cash flows identifies the sources of cash—how much will be generated from operations and how much will be raised from investors. It also shows how much money will be devoted to investments in such areas as inventories and equipment. The statement of cash flows should clearly indicate how much cash is needed from lenders and prospective investors and for what purpose. (The preparation of pro forma statements and the process of raising needed capital are discussed in Chapters 11 and 12.)

Appendix of Supporting Documents

The appendix should contain various supplementary materials and attachments to expand the reader's understanding of the plan. These supporting documents include any items referenced in the text of the business plan, such as the résumés of the key investors and owners/managers; photographs of products, facilities, and buildings; professional references; marketing research studies; pertinent published research; and signed contracts of sale.

The fact that it appears at the end of the plan does not mean that the appendix is of secondary importance. First, the reader needs to understand the assumptions underlying the premises set forth in the plan. Also, nothing is more important to a prospective investor than the qualifications of the management team. Thus, the presentation of the management team's résumés is no small matter, so each one should be carefully prepared.

Each chapter in this section (Part 3) of the book, with the exception of Chapter 10, ends with a special set of exercises to walk you through the process of writing a business plan. These exercise sets consist of questions to be thoughtfully considered and answered. They are entitled "The Business Plan: Laying the Foundation," because they deal with issues that are important to starting a new venture and provide guidelines for preparing the different sections of a business plan.

4
Offer practical advice on writing a business plan.

ADVICE FOR WRITING A BUSINESS PLAN

When it comes to making an effective written presentation, we should emphasize again that the quality of a business plan ultimately depends on the quality of the underlying business opportunity. We repeat, *the plan is not the business.* A poorly conceived new venture idea cannot be rescued by a good presentation. But, on the other hand, a good concept may be destroyed by a presentation that fails to communicate effectively. Below are recommendations that will help you avoid some of the common mistakes.

Analyze the Market Thoroughly

In analyzing the market for your product or service, you must answer some basic questions. Investors and lenders require answers to these questions, and so should you. If you try to proceed without the answers, you are significantly increasing your chances of failure. You should be able to answer such questions as

- What is your target market?
- How large is the target market?
- What problems concern the target market?
- Are any of these problems greater than the one you're addressing?
- How does your product or service fix the problem?
- Who will buy your product or service?
- How much are they willing to pay for it?
- Why do they need it?
- Why would they buy from you?
- Who are your competitors?
- What are their strengths and weaknesses?

As we have already said, your presentation should be the result of evidence-based statements. Nowhere in the business plan is it more important to provide hard evidence to support your claims than when presenting your analysis of the market. Gathering secondary data about the market is important, but if you are not out talking to prospective customers, then your analysis has no credibility. It requires hard work, but it is far better to realize that customers are not going to buy your product or service at this point than after you have invested your personal savings.

Finally, when it comes to competition, understand that everyone has competitors. Saying "We have no competition" is almost certain to make readers skeptical. You must show in your plan where your business will fit in the market and what your competitors' strengths and weaknesses are. If possible, include estimates of their market shares and profit levels.

Provide Solid Evidence for Any Claims

Too often, entrepreneurs make broad statements without solid data to support them. Factual support must be supplied for any claims or assurances made. When promising to provide superior service or explaining the attractiveness of the market, for example, include strong supporting evidence. In short, the plan must be believable.

On frequent occasions, the authors have had the opportunity to watch entrepreneurs present business plans to prospective investors. More than once, an entrepreneur has presented financial projections that were extremely optimistic, being beyond believable. The opportunity might still have been attractive with more conservative projections. But instead of adjusting the forecasts to make them more credible to the investors, the entrepreneur continued to argue that the numbers were already "conservative." It's no surprise that investors declined to invest in these deals.

Page after page of detailed computer-generated financial projections suggest—intentionally or unintentionally—that the entrepreneur can predict with great accuracy what will happen. Experienced investors know this isn't the case. They want to know what is behind the numbers; this allows them to see how the entrepreneur thinks and if he or she understands the key factors that will drive success or failure. To determine this information, investors often ask a common question: "What is your business model?" This key question will be discussed later in the chapter.

ACTION

Tell Your Story with Facts

Most business plans present no compelling story and thus fail to make much of an impression on the readers, whoever they may be. Only a small number of business plans are even read in full. If you want investors to pay attention to your business plan, then show—not just tell—your story by using solid evidence that your business idea is a good one.

Think Like an Investor

Many small firms do not seek outside capital, except in the form of small loans. But whether or not you are preparing a business plan in order to seek outside financing, you would benefit from understanding the world as an investor sees it—that is, you should think as an investor thinks. As Jeffrey Bussgang, who has been both an entrepreneur and a venture capitalist, advises, "You should think like [an investor] and act like an entrepreneur."[14] In this way, you bring to the analysis both the energy of the entrepreneur and the discipline of an investor.

At the most basic level, prospective investors have a single goal: to maximize potential return on an investment through cash flows that will be received, while minimizing the risk they are taking. Even investors in startups who are thought to be risk takers want to minimize their exposure to risk. For one thing, they look for ways to shift risk to others, usually to the entrepreneur. Given the fundamentally different perspectives of the investor and the entrepreneur, the important question becomes "How do I write a business plan that will satisfy what a prospective investor wants to know?" There is no easy answer, but two facts are relevant: Investors have a short attention span, and certain features attract investors while others repel them.

Because most investors receive so many business plans, they cannot possibly read them all in any detailed fashion. To illustrate, one of the authors delivered an entrepreneur's business plan to a prospective investor with whom he had a personal relationship. The plan was well written, clearly identifying a need. While the investor was courteous and listened carefully, he made a decision not to consider the opportunity in a matter of five minutes. A quick read of the executive summary did not spark his interest, and the discussion quickly changed to other matters.

Furthermore, investors are more *market-oriented* than *product-oriented,* realizing that most patented inventions never earn a dime for the inventors. The essence of the

EXHIBIT 6.6 A Glossary of Business Plan Terms

What They Say . . .	*. . . and What They Really Mean*
We conservatively project . . .	We read a book that said we had to be a $50 million company in five years, and we reverse-engineered the numbers.
We took our best guess and divided by 2.	We accidentally divided by 0.5.
We project a 10% margin.	We did not modify any of the assumptions in the business plan template that we downloaded from the Internet.
The project is 98% complete.	To complete the remaining 2% will take as long as it took to create the initial 98% but will cost twice as much.
Our business model is proven . . .	If you take the evidence from the past week for the best of our 50 locations and extrapolate it for all the others.
We have a six-month lead.	We tried not to find out how many other people have a six-month lead.
We only need a 10% market share.	So do the other 50 entrants getting funded.
Customers are clamoring for our product.	We have not yet asked them to pay for it. Also, all of our current customers are relatives,
We are the low-cost producer.	We have not produced anything yet, but we are confident that we will be able to.
We have no competition.	Only IBM, Microsoft, Netscape, and Sun have announced plans to enter the business.
Our management team has a great deal of experience . . .	Consuming the product or service.
A select group of investors is considering the plan.	We mailed a copy of the plan to everyone in Pratt's Guide.
We seek a value-added investor.	We are looking for a passive, dumb-as-rocks investor.
If you invest on our terms, you will earn a 68% rate of return.	If everything that could ever conceivably go right does go right, you might get your money back.

Source: Reprinted by permission of *Harvard Business Review*. "How to Write a Great Business Plan" by William A. Sahlman, July/August 1997, p. 106.

entrepreneurial process is to identify new products or services that meet an identifiable customer need. Thus, it is essential for the entrepreneur to appreciate investors' concerns about target customers' responses to a new product or service and to reach out to prospective customers.

Bill Sahlman at the Harvard Business School has seen a lot of business plans in his time and has heard most of the "lines" used by entrepreneurs when presenting to investors. With tongue only a little in cheek, Sahlman tells how investors interpret an entrepreneur's language in his "Glossary of Business Plan Terms" (see Exhibit 6.6). When writing and then presenting a business plan, keep in mind how skeptical your audience is likely to be.

Don't Hide Weaknesses—Identify Potential Fatal Flaws

One difficult aspect of writing a business plan is effectively dealing with problems or weaknesses—and every business has them. An entrepreneur, wanting to make a good impression, may become so infatuated with an opportunity that he or she cannot see potential fatal flaws.

For instance, an entrepreneur might fail to ask, "What is the possible impact of new technology, e-commerce, or changes in consumer demand on the proposed venture?" And ignoring or glossing over a negative issue when trying to raise financing for the venture can prove damaging, even fatal. If there are weaknesses in the plan, the investors will find them. At that point, an investor's question will be "What else haven't you told me?" The best way to properly handle weaknesses is to thoroughly consider all potential issues, to be open and straightforward about those issues, and to have an action plan that effectively addresses any problems. To put it another way, *integrity matters.*

Maintain Confidentiality

When presenting your business plan to outsiders (especially prospective investors), prominently indicate that all information in the plan is proprietary and confidential. Number every copy of the plan, and account for each outstanding copy by requiring all recipients of the plan to acknowledge receipt in writing.

When a startup is based on proprietary technology, be cautious about divulging certain information—for example, the details of a technological design or the highly sensitive specifics of a marketing strategy— even to a prospective investor.

While you should be cautious about releasing proprietary information, entrepreneurs at times become overly anxious about someone stealing their idea and using it. Certainly, it does happen on rare occasions and you want to protect yourself, *but do not become fixated on the notion that someone may take your idea and beat you to the market with it.* Remember, the plan is not the key to your success; your execution is what matters! If someone can "out-execute" you, then you may not be the right person to start the business. Besides, being paranoid about someone stealing your idea is usually a turnoff for investors and can discourage you from moving forward with your enterprise.

Remember That the Little Things Are the Big Things

You should pay attention to the details, which may seem small to you but likely are not to others who read the plan to decide whether to be associated with the firm. The following suggestions will help you attend to the "little things":

1. *Use good grammar.* Nothing turns off a reader faster than a poorly written business plan. Find a good editor, and then review and revise, revise, revise.
2. *Limit the presentation to a reasonable length.* The goal is not to write a *long* business plan, but to write a *good* business plan. People who read business plans appreciate brevity and view it as an indication of your ability to identify and describe in an organized way the important factors that will determine the success of your business. In all sections of your plan, especially the executive summary, get to the point quickly.
3. *Go for an attractive, professional appearance.* To add interest and aid readers' comprehension, make liberal but effective use of visual aids, such as graphs, exhibits, and tabular summaries. The plan should be in a three-ring loose-leaf binder to facilitate future revisions, as opposed to being bound like a book and printed on shiny paper with flashy images and graphs.
4. *Describe your product or service in lay terms.* Entrepreneurs with a technical background are so often inclined to become infatuated with their new invention and think it is all about the product. They also tend to use technical or industry jargon that is not easily understood by individuals who are unfamiliar with the industry. That is a big mistake! Present your product and/or service in simple, understandable terms, and avoid the temptation to use too much industry jargon.

The foregoing advice is intended to help you know how to think about preparing a business plan. If you ignore these recommendations, the plan will detract from the opportunity itself, and you may lose the chance to capture a good opportunity. We recommend that you have experienced entrepreneurs critique the business concept and

© iStockphoto.com/Angelika Schwarz

entrepreneurial experiences

What Can Go Wrong, and Still Be Right

Many universities around the country are holding competitions to attract attention, generate ideas, and launch startups. The big question is, what happens afterward? For entrepreneurs Will Anderson, Rory McDonald, and Jared Archibald of Stanford University, it was a rocky road after a golden finish in the business plan contest of the Business Association of Stanford Engineering Students. Their winning idea was to adapt a speech- and noise-separating filter technology (that was being developed in Stanford's electrical engineering school) to dramatically improve hearing aids.

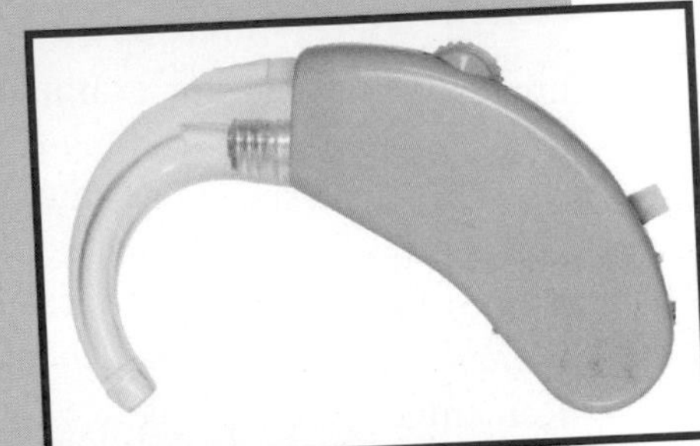
© andras_csontos/Shutterstock.com

The team won the grand prize of $25,000. With the help of their faculty advisor, they built a company around the idea, called Adaptive Hearing Solutions, and received $500,000 in venture capital. However, after several clinical trials, the technology showed few improvements over the existing technology. The team made the decision to end the business to pursue other interests instead of running a small business that was unlikely to capture value in the process.

Even though the business "failed," the team learned a good lesson in entrepreneurship: Failure can be a profitable experience. The members of the team are using the connections and reputations that they made through the contest to either develop new businesses or further specialize in their fields through higher education.

Still the question remains: Is it worth the effort to participate in business competitions? Regardless of the outcome, the overall experiences of the participants are generally positive. One huge reason is the prize money awarded to the winners. Many startups have been able to get established with the prize money and have not had to seek additional outside money.

However, even if the winning company eventually fails, as it did for the Stanford team, the benefits of a business plan contest victory are lasting. Connections with other professionals and aspiring entrepreneurs are priceless. And the experience forces teams to articulate what their business means and learn how to turn a concept into a feasible plan.

Sources: Adapted from Jeffrey Gangemi, "The Afterlife of Business Plan Contest Winners," *Bloomberg Businessweek*, http://www.businessweek.com/print/smallbiz/content/dec2006/sb20061212_410722.htm, accessed January 8, 2011.

the effectiveness of the business plan presentation; they know the minefields to avoid. And, as we have said on more than one occasion, *talk to your customers*.

UNDERSTANDING THE BUSINESS MODEL[15]

business model
An analysis of how a firm plans to create profits and cash flows given its revenue sources, its cost structures, and the required size of investment.

As mentioned earlier, the term *business model* has become a popular phrase in business, especially among entrepreneurs and their investors. While it is widely discussed in business circles, it is little understood by most businesspeople in small and large firms alike. Basically, a **business model** explains in a systematic and clear way how a business will generate profits and cash flows, given its revenue sources, its cost structures, and the required size of investment. It is the "nuts and bolts" of how a business will make money. As such, it measures the anticipated results of the core business decisions and all the trade-offs that determine a company's profits and cash flows.

Some business models are easy to understand: A firm produces a product and/or service and sells it to customers; if sales exceed expenses, the company makes a profit.

Other models are less straightforward. For instance, television broadcasting is part of a complex network of distributors, content creators, advertisers, and viewers. How the eventual profits and cash flows are created and shared depends on a number of competing factors, which are not always clear at the outset. Furthermore, e-commerce is giving rise to new business models. Consider auctions, one of the oldest ways for setting prices for such things as agricultural commodities, art, and antiques. Today, the Internet has popularized the auction model and broadened its use to a wide array of goods and services.

Understanding the business model is especially important in a startup, where there is so much uncertainty. Specifically, a business model for a startup forces the entrepreneur to be more disciplined and avoid wishful thinking about financial projections. When it comes time to create a business plan, the entrepreneur needs to know the drivers that will determine the firm's future profits and cash flows. Thus, a business model is intended to provide the best evidence on whether a business concept can be translated into a viable, profitable business and how large of an investment will be required to make it happen. Exhibit 6.7 provides a basic overview of the process for building a business model for a company with three sources of revenues.

An entrepreneur should begin by developing the venture's mission statement, its strategic goals, and the principles that are to guide its operations (see Exhibit 6.7). Three key elements then make up the business model:

EXHIBIT 6.7 Basic Business Model Framework

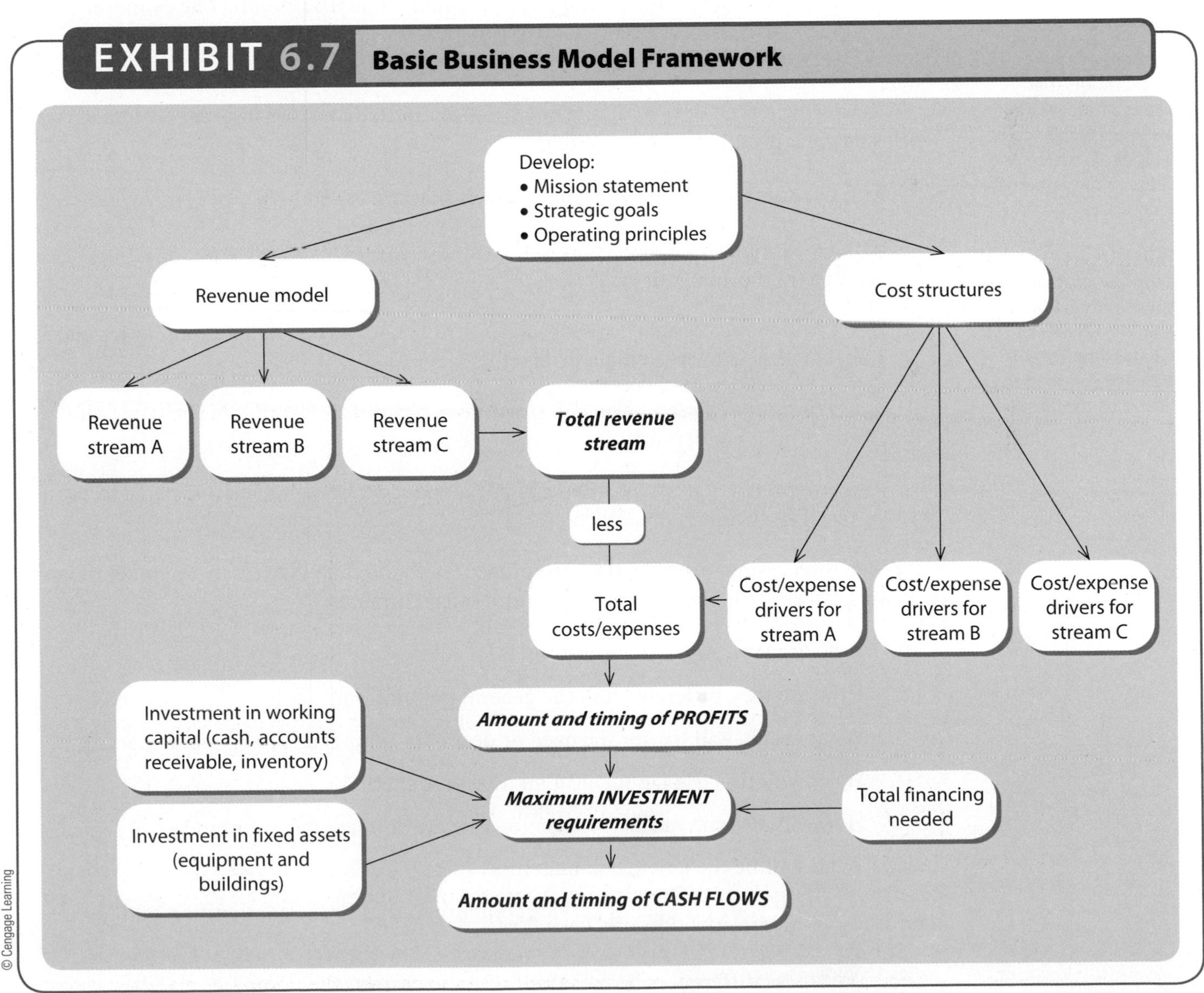

revenue model
A component of the business model that identifies the different types of revenue streams a firm expects to receive.

1. The **revenue model**, which defines the nature and types of a company's sources of revenues
2. The **cost structures** that drive the company's costs and expenses
3. The **maximum investment** that will be required to make the business profitable and cash flows positive.

Let's briefly consider each element.

"After closer investigation, it's become clear that we need to enter more than one value."

Mark Anderson, Andertoons.com
www.andertoons.com

Revenue Model

It is essential to first understand whether the business model is based on a single or a hybrid revenue stream. Examples of the types of revenue streams typically experienced include

- *Single stream.* A firm's revenues come from a single product or service.
- *Multiple streams.* A business realizes revenues from a combination of multiple products and services.
- *Interdependent streams.* A company's revenues come from selling one or more products and/or services as a way to generate revenues from other products and/or services, such as printers and printer cartridges.
- *Loss leader.* One or several revenue streams are sold at a loss in order to create sales in a profitable revenue stream.

cost structures
A component of the business model that provides a framework for estimating the nature and types of costs and expenses a firm may incur.

The more common types of revenue models that are found in business include

- *Volume or unit-based revenue model.* Customers pay a fixed price per unit in exchange for a product or service.
- *Subscription/membership revenue model.* Customers pay a fixed amount at regular intervals, prior to receiving a product or service.
- *Advertising-based revenue model.* Customers pay only a fraction of the true value of the product or service.
- *Licensing revenue model.* Customers pay a one-time licensing fee to be able to use or resell the product or service.

maximum investment
A component of the business model that provides estimates of the types and amounts of investment required to achieve positive profits and cash flows.

When forecasting revenues, the entrepreneur will find that answers to a number of key questions can provide the rationale for future sales estimates:

1. Who are your most likely customers?
2. How are they different from the general population?
3. What events will trigger the need or desire for your type of product or service?
4. When will this trigger occur? Can it be predicted?
5. How will customers make decisions on whether or not to buy your product or service?
6. What will be the key decision factors?
7. How will your product or service compare to that of the competition on these key factors?
8. Will these differences be meaningful to the customer?

9. Are these differences known to the customer?
10. How can your product or service be exposed to your most likely potential customers?

Additional questions could and should be developed depending on the product or service, the industry, and the customers being served. The more you understand the answers to such questions, the more likely it is that your financial projections will be believable and achievable. But even if the questions don't provide the answers you were hoping for, you will better understand why your financial projections may not be realized and what needs to be done to improve the forecasts.

Cost Structures

Cost structures consist of the drivers that affect a firm's costs and expenses. These expenses can vary with either time or volume of sales. Common types of cost drivers include unit cost of goods sold, payroll, marketing activities, administrative costs, and

entrepreneurial experiences

LIVING THE DREAM

College Students Write Business Plans, Too

© iStockphoto.com/Angelika Schwarz

A large number of colleges are now offering business plan competitions to prepare young aspiring entrepreneurs for starting businesses and to provide some seed capital to get them started. Here are the stories of three students who competed in these events:

> *Alex Farkas and Greg Rosborough, both 24 years old, and Stephen Tanenbaum, 25, won $20,000 in a business plan competition, combined with an additional $80,000 contributed from friends and family. The money helped them launch their business plan idea, Ugallery.com. The University of Arizona graduates attended three competitions during their senior year, including one in Canada. "I think we succeeded in the business plan competitions because our business model was very realistic," says Tanenbaum.*
>
> *The business plan developed by 26-year-old Dee Murthy and 27-year old Andres Izquieta also won an award. But [along with] thousands of dollars in prize money from the University of Southern California, which hosted the competition, Five Four Clothing had something else working in its favor: the right place and the right timing. Los Angeles proved to be the ideal location for the business partners to launch their hip urban men's line of apparel. Murthy says his friends started wearing Five Four to local clubs, and soon they were in talks with hot boutiques like Fred Segal.*
>
> *For 28-year-old entrepreneur Rodrigo Veloso, winning the Latin American division of the Moot Corp Competition while a graduate student in Sao Paulo, Brazil, provided him with the contacts he needed to introduce Brazilian coconut water to the United States. As the first-place winner, Veloso was invited to attend the global competition at the University of Texas at Austin. Though he didn't win, Veloso gained valuable business contacts and met his now-wife, Emilie Fritz. . . . Veloso relied on his new-found connections when he moved to Los Angeles to turn his plan into a business. Upon his arrival, Veloso met with investors who introduced him to other investors. He combined the seed money from one investor and contributions from friends and family with his own savings to create O.N.E. World Enterprises.*

Sources: Adapted from Kristin Edelhauser, "College Business Plans That Made the Grade," *Entrepreneur*, http://www.entrepreneur.com/startingabusiness/ businessplans/article182608.html, accessed March 2011.

marketing expenses. Expenses and costs that are useful in making projections are frequently classified as follows:

- *Fixed costs.* Costs that do not vary at all with volume, such as rent expenses.
- *Variable costs.* Expenses that vary directly and proportionately with changes in volume, for example, sales commissions.
- *Semi-variable costs.* Expenses that include both variable costs and fixed costs. These costs vary in the direction of, but not proportionately with, changes in the volume of sales, such as certain types of payrolls that change as a firm becomes larger but do not change proportionally with sales changes.

The core business decisions and trade-offs of a company's business model can be better understood if the entrepreneur knows the key cost drivers, in both type and importance, as well as whether any of the cost drivers provide a strategic cost advantage.

Maximum Investment

The final key component of a business model is the amount of investment required for a company to achieve positive cash flows and profits. It not only includes the amount of investment in hard assets, such as equipment and buildings but, equally important, the amount of working capital in the form of operating cash, accounts receivable, and inventory.

Once a business model has been developed and used to provide pro forma financial statements, it is worthwhile for an entrepreneur to perform a sensitivity analysis to identify the factors that are critical to the company's success. Only by doing so will the business model yield its greatest value in determining if the venture has a reasonable chance of success. (This explanation of a business model will be illustrated further in Chapter 11, when we look at projecting a firm's financial requirements.)

Resources for Business Plan Preparation

When writing a business plan, it is important to know what works and what does not work. There are many books, websites, and computer software packages that offer extensive guidance on preparing a business plan, even step-by-step instruction. (A listing of some of these materials appears at the end of this chapter.) Such resources can be invaluable. In general, however, you should resist the temptation to adapt an existing business plan for your own use. Changing the numbers and some of the verbiage of another firm's business plan is simply a waste of time.

COMPUTER-AIDED BUSINESS PLANNING

The use of a computer greatly facilitates preparation of a business plan. Its word-processing capabilities, for example, can speed up the writing of the narrative sections of the report. Computer spreadsheets are likewise helpful for preparing the financial statements needed in the plan.

A number of business plan software packages have been designed to help an entrepreneur think through the important issues in starting a new company and organize her or his thoughts to create an effective presentation. However, these software packages are not capable of producing a unique plan and thus may limit an entrepreneur's creativity and flexibility. Just plain old common sense is also required when using business plan

The SBA as a Resource

You can find many websites, workshops, and software packages online to help you write a business plan. Begin at the Small Business Administration's website at http://www.sba.gov. The SBA provides extensive information on planning for a new business, including writing a business plan.

software. One of the authors recently received a business plan that was almost 80 pages in length. When questioned about the excessive length, the entrepreneur responded, "By the time I answered all the questions in the software package, that's the length that resulted."

Remember, there is no simple procedure for writing a business plan—no "formula for success"—despite what software advertisements may claim. If you recognize their limitations, however, you can use business plan software packages to facilitate the process.

PROFESSIONAL ASSISTANCE IN BUSINESS PLANNING

As previously discussed, company founders are most notably doers—and evidence suggests that they had better be, if the venture is to be successful. But some small business owners lack the breadth of experience and know-how, as well as the inclination, needed for planning.

A small business owner who is not able to answer tough questions about the business may need a business planning advisor—someone accustomed to working with small companies, startups, and owners who lack financial management experience. Such advisors include accountants, marketing specialists, attorneys (preferably with an entrepreneurial mindset), incubator organizations, small business development corporations (SBDCs), and regional and local economic development offices.

An investment banker or financial intermediary can draw up a business plan as part of a firm's overall fundraising efforts. Also, a well-chosen advisor will have contacts you lack and may even help you reformulate your business plan entirely. However, using a business planning advisor will cost you; consultants frequently charge an hourly fee as well as a contingency percentage based on the amount raised.

The Small Business Administration (SBA) and the Service Corps of Retired Executives (SCORE) can also be helpful. Both organizations have programs to introduce business owners to volunteer experts who will advise them. SCORE, in particular, is a source for all types of business advice, such as how to write a business plan, investigate market potential, and manage cash flows. SCORE counselors work out of local chapters throughout the United States and can be found by contacting the national office.

Another source of assistance is the FastTrac Entrepreneurial Training Program sponsored by the Kauffman Center for Entrepreneurial Leadership in Kansas City, Missouri. Located in universities, chambers of commerce, and SBDCs across the country, the FastTrac program teaches the basics of product development, concept recognition, financing strategies, and marketing research, while helping entrepreneurs create a written business plan in small, well-organized increments.

Fuse/Jupiter Images

You definitely have options when it comes to getting business plan assistance. However, if you choose to hire a consultant, the following suggestions may help you avoid some costly mistakes:[16]

- *Get referrals.* Ask colleagues, acquaintances, and professionals such as bankers, accountants, and lawyers for the names of business plan consultants they recommend. A good referral goes a long way to easing any concerns you may have. Few consultants advertise anyway, so referrals may be your only option.
- *Look for a fit.* Find a consultant who is an expert in helping businesses like yours. Ideally, the consultant should have lots of experience with companies of similar size and age in related industries. Avoid general business experts or those who lack experience in your particular field.
- *Check references.* Get the names of at least three clients the consultant has helped to write business plans. Call the former clients and ask about the consultant's performance. Was the consultant's final fee in line with the original estimate? Was the plan completed on time? Did it serve the intended purpose?
- *Get it in writing.* Have a legal contract outlining the consultant's services. It should state in detail the fee, when it will be paid, and under what circumstances. And make sure you get a detailed written description of what the consultant must do to earn the fee. Whether it's an hourly rate or a flat fee isn't as important as each party knowing exactly what's expected of them.

Keep in mind that securing help in business plan preparation does not relieve the entrepreneur of the responsibility of being the primary planner. Her or his ideas remain essential to producing a plan that is realistic and believable.

Keeping the Right Perspective

To summarize, we contend that the business plan has an important place in starting and growing a business. As suggested in the chapter, writing an effective plan is important both for internal purposes and for telling the firm's story to outsiders who can contribute to the firm's success. But good judgment should be used in deciding if and how much to plan, given your unique circumstances. No single answer can be applied to all situations. Furthermore, it is important to avoid the misconception, held by far too many aspiring entrepreneurs, that a good plan will ensure success. The business plan, no matter how beneficial, is not the business. A good business plan leads to a successful company only when it is effectively executed by the entrepreneur and the management team.

Writing a business plan should be thought of as an ongoing process and not as the means to an end. In fact, when it comes to writing a plan, the process is just as important as the final outcome. Some entrepreneurs have difficulty accepting this, given their orientation to "bottom-line" results. But this point deserves to be repeated: *Writing a business plan is primarily an ongoing process and only secondarily the means to an outcome. The process is just as important as—if not more so than—the finished product.*

While your plan will represent your vision and goals for the firm, it will rarely reflect what actually happens. With a startup, too many unexpected events can affect the final outcome. Thus, a business plan is in large part an opportunity for an entrepreneur and management team to think about the potential key drivers of a venture's success or failure. Anticipating different scenarios and the ensuing consequences can significantly enhance an entrepreneur's adaptability—an essential quality, when so much is uncertain.

Now that you are aware of the role of the business plan in a new venture, you are ready to move on to Chapters 7 through 13, which will closely examine each of the plan's components.

1. Explain the purpose and objectives of business plans.

- A business plan is a document that sets out the basic idea underlying a business and describes related startup considerations. It should describe where the entrepreneur is presently, indicate where she or he wants to go, and outline how she or he proposes to get there.
- A business plan has three basic objectives: (1) to identify the nature and the context of a business opportunity, (2) to present the approach the entrepreneur plans to take to exploit the opportunity, and (3) to recognize factors that will determine whether the venture will be successful.

2. Give the rationale for writing (or not writing) a business plan when starting a new venture.

- Studies attempting to test whether entrepreneurs who have business plans do better than those who don't have produced mixed results. Some findings suggest a relationship; others do not.
- What ultimately matters is not writing a plan, but implementing it. The goal is to execute the plan.
- An entrepreneur must find the right balance between planning and becoming operational.
- The benefits of a business plan depend on the individual circumstances surrounding a startup.
- Most entrepreneurs need the discipline that comes with writing a business plan. A written plan helps to ensure systematic, complete coverage of the important factors to be considered in starting a new business.
- A business plan helps an entrepreneur communicate his or her vision to current and prospective employees of the firm.
- By enhancing the firm's credibility, a business plan serves as an effective selling tool with prospective customers and suppliers, as well as investors.
- A dehydrated plan is a short form of a business plan that presents only the most important issues and projections for the business.
- A comprehensive plan is a full business plan that provides an in-depth analysis of the critical factors that will determine a firm's success or failure, along with the underlying assumptions.

3. Describe the preferred content and format for a business plan.

- The opportunity, the critical resources, the entrepreneurial team, the financing structure, and the context of an opportunity are all interdependent factors that should be given consideration when thinking about the content of a business plan.
- Key sections of a business plan are the (1) cover page, (2) table of contents, (3) executive summary, (4) industry, target customer, and competitor analysis, (5) company description, (6) product/service plan, (7) marketing plan, (8) operations and development plan, (9) management team, (10) critical risks, (11) offering, (12) exit strategy, (13) financial plan, and (14) appendix of supporting documents.

4. Offer practical advice on writing a business plan.

- Analyze the market thoroughly.
- Provide solid evidence for any claims.
- When preparing a business plan to present to investors, understand how they think about investing in a business.
- Don't hide weaknesses; try to identify potential fatal flaws.
- Maintain confidentiality, when appropriate.
- Pay attention to the details.

5. Explain the concept and process for developing a firm's business model.

- The term *business model* has become a popular phrase in business, especially among entrepreneurs and their investors.
- A business model explains in a systematic and clear way how a business will generate profits and cash flows, given its revenue sources, its cost structures, and the required size of investment.
- The business model measures the anticipated results of the core business decisions and all the trade-offs that determine a company's profits and cash flows.
- Understanding the business model is especially important in a startup, where there is so much uncertainty.
- Three key elements make up a business model: the revenue model, the cost structures, and the investments needed to achieve positive profits and cash flows.

6. **Identify available sources of assistance in preparing a business plan.**
   - A variety of books, websites, and computer software packages are available to assist in the preparation of a business plan.
   - Professionals with planning expertise, such as attorneys, accountants, and marketing specialists, can provide useful suggestions and assistance in the preparation of a business plan.
   - The Small Business Administration (SBA), the Service Corps of Retired Executives (SCORE), and the FastTrac Entrepreneurial Training Program can also be helpful.

7. **Maintain the proper perspective when writing a business plan.**
   - Despite the potential benefits of a well-drafted plan, good judgment should be used in deciding how much to plan in view of the specific circumstances.
   - The business plan, no matter how beneficial, is not the business. A good business plan leads to a successful company only when it is effectively executed by the entrepreneur and the management team.
   - A business plan can be viewed as an opportunity for the entrepreneur and the management team to think about the potential key drivers of a venture's success or failure.

Key Terms

business plan p. 165
dehydrated plan p. 169
comprehensive plan p. 169
executive summary p. 173
product/service plan p. 177
marketing plan p. 177
operations and development plan p. 177
management team p. 178
critical risks p. 178
offering p. 178
exit strategy p. 178
financial plan p. 179
pro forma statements p. 179
business model p. 184
revenue model p. 186
cost structures p. 186
maximum investment p. 186

Discussion Questions

1. Describe what entrepreneurs mean when they talk about a business plan.
2. When should you write a business plan? When might it not be necessary or even advisable to write a plan?
3. Explain the two types of business plans. In what situation(s) would you use each type of plan?
4. Why is the executive summary so important?
5. How might an entrepreneur's perspective differ from that of an investor in terms of the business plan?
6. Describe the major sections to be included in a business plan.
7. If the income statement of a financial plan shows that the business will be profitable, why is there a need for a statement of cash flows?
8. Describe common mistakes that entrepreneurs make in writing a business plan.
9. Investors are said to be more market-oriented than product-oriented. What does this mean? What is the logic behind this orientation?
10. What is a business model, and why is it important?

You Make the Call

SITUATION 1

You want to start an online clothing store and need information about the size of the market for the marketing section of your business plan. From a Google search, you found that Americans spent $18.3 billion online for apparel, accessories, and footwear last year and that the forecast for their spending on these items in the coming year is $22.1 billion. You have also researched publicly traded apparel companies, like Gap, to discover trends in online sales for these firms.

Question 1 Why is your research thus far inadequate for what you need to know?
Question 2 Do you think it will be difficult to find all the information you need?

Question 3 What else might you do to find the information you need?

SITUATION 2

You recently visited with a friend who knew you had taken a small business course when you attended college. During your visit, she made the comment, "I plan to open a business this summer. I won't be applying for a bank loan to fund this company, so I don't have a business plan. Do I need one?"

Question 1 What would you need to know in order to answer her question?
Question 2 If she decides to write a business plan, what advice would you give her?

SITUATION 3

John Martin and John Rose decided to start a new business to manufacture noncarbonated soft drinks. They believed that their location, close to high-quality water, would give them a competitive edge. Although Martin and Rose had never worked together, Martin had 17 years of experience in the soft drink industry. Rose had recently sold his firm and had funds to help finance the venture; however, the partners needed to raise additional money from outside investors. Both men were excited about the opportunity and spent almost 18 months developing their business plan. The first paragraph of their executive summary reflected their excitement:

> *The "New Age" beverage market is the result of a spectacular boom in demand for drinks with nutritional value from environmentally safe ingredients and waters that come from deep, clear springs free of chemicals and pollutants. Argon Beverage Corporation will produce and market a full line of sparkling fruit drinks, flavored waters, and sports drinks that are of the highest quality and purity. These drinks have the same delicious taste appeal as soft drinks while using the most healthful fruit juices, natural sugars, and the purest spring water, the hallmark of the "New Age" drink market.*

With the help of a well-developed plan, the two men were successful in raising the necessary capital to begin their business. They leased facilities and started production. However, after almost two years, the plan's goals were not being met. There were cost overruns, and profits were not nearly up to expectations.

Question 1 What problems might have contributed to the firm's poor performance?
Question 2 Although several problems were encountered in implementing the business plan, the primary reason for the low profits turned out to be embezzlement. Martin was diverting company resources for personal use, even using some of the construction materials purchased by the company to build his own house. What could Rose have done to avoid this situation? What are his options after the fact?

Experiential Exercises

1. Appendix A provides the complete business plan for Benjapon's. Based on your reading of this chapter, write a one-page report on what you like about the plan and what you do not like.
2. A former chef wants to start a business to supply temporary kitchen help (such as chefs, sauce cooks, bakers, and meat cutters) to restaurants in need of staff during busy periods. Prepare a one-page report explaining which section or sections of the business plan would be most crucial to this new business and why.
3. Suppose that you wish to start a tutoring service for college students in elementary accounting courses. List the benefits you would realize from preparing a written business plan.
4. Interview a person who has started a business within the past five years. Prepare a report describing the extent to which the entrepreneur engaged in preliminary planning and his or her views about the value of business plans.

Small Business & Entrepreneurship Resource Center

1. Matt Ferris and Bruce Black registered for the business plan competition course that was part of their MBA program at the University of Georgia in Athens. They took the class and wrote a business plan, not expecting it to result in any real-life activities. Describe what happened with their ideas and how they started their business. Also describe some of the benefits derived from preparing a business plan.

   Source: Sara Wilson, "Trial by Fire," *Entrepreneur*, Vol. 33, No. 10 (October 2005), pp. 112–113.

2. The Small Business Development Center (SBDC) is a federally and locally funded small business assistance program that offers advisory services at no charge. Its staff can offer business planning assistance as the firm is developing and growing. A recent study has found that entrepreneurs who used SBDC services and then later started their businesses had higher than average rates of survival. Discuss the types of services that are offered by the SBDC, and how its counseling services are different than consulting services.

   Source: James J. Chrisman and W. Ed McMullan, "A Preliminary Assessment of Outsider Assistance as a Knowledge Resource: The Longer-Term Impact of New Venture Counseling," *Entrepreneurship: Theory and Practice*, Vol. 24, No. 3 (Spring 2000), p. 37.

Case 6

BENJAPON'S, P. 704

Benjapon Jivasantikarn is planning to start Benjapon's, a Thai restaurant, after graduating from Babson College. In recent years, Asian fast casual restaurant players have begun to emerge in various regions in the United States. This is Jivasantikarn's story of joining this emerging market. To do so, she'll need to raise the needed capital and prepare a business plan.

ALTERNATIVE CASES FOR CHAPTER 6

Case 3, Firewire Surfboards, p. 698
Video Case 6, KindSnacks, website only

Business Plan Laying the Foundation

Part 3 (Chapters 6 through 13) deals with issues that are important in starting a new venture. This chapter presented an overview of the business plan and its preparation. Chapters 7 through 13 focus on major segments of the business plan, such as the marketing plan, the organizational plan, the location plan, the financial plan, and the exit plan, or what we call the harvest. After you have carefully studied these chapters, you will have the knowledge you need to prepare a business plan.

Since applying what you study facilitates learning, we have included, at the end of each chapter in Part 3 (except Chapter 10), a list of important questions that need to be addressed in preparing a particular segment of a business plan. In this chapter, we have also included lists of books, websites, and software packages useful in preparing business plans.

Company Description Questions

Now that you have learned the main concepts of business plan preparation, you can begin the process of creating a business plan by writing a general company description. In thinking about the key issues in starting a new business, respond to the following questions:

1. When and where is the business to start?
2. What is the history of the company?
3. What are the company's objectives?

4. What changes have been made in structure and/or ownership?
5. In what stage of development is the company?
6. What has been achieved to date?
7. What is the company's distinctive competence?
8. What are the basic nature and activity of the business?
9. What is its primary product or service?
10. What customers will be served?
11. What is the company's form of organization?
12. What are the current and projected economic states of the industry?
13. Does the company intend to become a publicly traded company or an acquisition candidate, or do the owners want to transfer ownership to the next generation of the family?

Books on Preparing Business Plans

Abrams, Rhonda, *The Successful Business Plan,* 4th ed. (Palo Alto, CA: The Planning Shop, 2010).

Bangs, David H., *The Business Planning Guide: Creating a Winning Plan for Success,* 9th ed. (New York: Kaplan Professional Company, 2002).

Bangs, David H., *Business Plans Made Easy,* 3rd ed. (Irvine, CA: Entrepreneur Press, 2005).

Barringer, Bruce R., *Preparing Effective Business Plans* (Upper Saddle River, NJ: Prentice Hall, 2009).

Burke, Franklin, Jill E. Kapron, and JIAN Tools for Sale, Inc., *BizPlan*Builder *Express: A Guide to Creating a Business Plan with BizPlan*Builder, 2nd ed. (Mason, OH: South-Western, 2007).

Bygrave, William D., and Andrew Zacharakis (eds.), *The Portable MBA in Entrepreneurship,* 3rd ed. (Hoboken, NJ: John Wiley & Sons, 2003).

Deloitte & Touche, LLP, *Writing an Effective Business Plan* (New York: Author, 2003).

Ford, Brian R., Jay M. Bernstein, and Patrick T. Pruitt, *The Ernst & Young Business Plan Guide,* 3rd ed. (Hoboken, NJ: John Wiley & Sons, 2002).

Gumpert, David E., *Burn Your Business Plan* (Needham, MA: Lauson Publishing, 2002).

Gumpert, David E., *How to Really Create a Successful Business Plan,* 4th ed. (Needham, MA: Lauson Publishing, 2003).

Kauffman Center for Entrepreneurial Leadership, *Planning and Growing a Business Venture*: *FastTrac,* 2007.

Kawasaki, Guy, *The Art of the Start: The Time-Tested, Battle-Hardened Guide for Anyone Starting Anything* (New York: Portfolio, 2004).

King, Jan B., *Business Plans to Game Plans: A Practical System for Turning Strategies into Action,* rev. ed. (Hoboken, NJ: John Wiley & Sons, 2004).

Mancuso, Joseph R., *How to Write a Winning Business Plan* (New York: Simon & Schuster, 2006).

McKeever, Mike, *How to Write a Great Business Plan,* 9th ed. (Berkeley, CA: Nolo, 2008).

Mullins, John, and Randy Komisar, *Getting to Plan B.* (Boston: Harvard Business Press, 2009).

Osterwalder, Alexander, and Yves Pigneur, *Business Model Generation* (Hoboken, NJ: John Wiley & Sons, 2010).

Osteryoung, Jerome S., and Diane L. Denslow, *So You Need to Write a Business Plan* (Mason, OH: South-Western, 2003).

Patsula, Peter J., and William Nowik (eds.), *Successful Business Planning in 30 Days: A Step-by-Step Guide for Writing a Business Plan and Starting Your Own Business,* 2nd ed. (Singapore: Patsula Media, 2002).

Peterson, Steven D., and Peter E. Jaret, *Business Plans Kit for Dummies* (Indianapolis, IN: For Dummies, 2005).

Pinson, Linda, *Anatomy of a Business Plan: A Step-by-Step Guide to Building a Business and Securing Your Company's Future* (Chicago: Enterprise/Dearborn, 2004).

Rich, Stanley R., and David E. Gumpert, *Business Plans That Win $$$: Lessons from the MIT Enterprise Forum* (New York: HarperCollins, 1987).

Rogoff, Edward, *Bankable Business Plans* (Mason, OH: South-Western, 2003).

Ryan, J. D., and Gail P. Hiduke, *Small Business, An Entrepreneur's Business Plan,* 8th ed. (Mason, OH: South-Western Cengage Learning, 2009).

Sahlman, William A., *Harvard Business Press Classics, How to Write a Great Business Plan* (Boston: Harvard Business Press, 2008).

Sutton, Garrett, and Robert T. Kiyosaki, *The ABC's of Writing Winning Business Plans: How to Prepare a Business Plan That Others Will Want to Read—and Invest In* (New York: Rich Dad's Advisors, 2005).

Tiffany, Paul, and Steven Peterson, *Business Plans for Dummies,* 2nd ed. (Indianapolis, IN: For Dummies, 2004).

Timmons, Jeffrey A., Andrew Zacharakis, and Stephen Spinelli, *Business Plans That Work* (New York: McGraw-Hill, 2004).

Tooch, David, *Building a Business Plan,* 2nd ed. (Upper Saddle River, NJ: Prentice Hall, 2004).

Articles on Preparing Business Plans

Adams, Rob, "Taking the Trouble to Research Your Market," *Bloomberg Businessweek*, http://www.businessweek.com/smallbiz/content/oct2004/sb20041020_9945.htm.

Bygrave, W. D., J. E. Lange, and T. Evans, "Do Business Plan Competitions Produce Winning Businesses?" *Frontiers of Entrepreneurship Research*, 2004, p. 275.

Chrisman, J. J., E. McMullan, and J. Hall, "The Influence of Guided Preparation on Long-Term Performance of New Ventures," *Journal of Business Venturing*, Vol. 20 (2005), pp. 769–791.

Delmar, Frederic, and Scott Shane, "Does Business Planning Facilitate the Development of New Ventures?" *Strategic Management Journal,* Vol. 24, No. 12 (2003), pp. 1165–1185.

Gartner, W. B., and J. Liao, "Cents and Sensemaking in Pre-Venture Business Planning: Evidence from the Panel Study of Entrepreneurial Dynamics," *Frontiers of Entrepreneurship Research*, 2005, p. 298.

Guber, M., "Uncovering the Value of Planning in New Venture Creation: A Process and Contingency Perspective," *Journal of Business Venturing*, Vol. 22 (2007), pp. 782–807.

Honig, B., and T. Karlsson, "Institutional Forces and the Written Business Plan," *Journal of Management*, Vol. 30, No. 1 (2004), pp. 29–48.

Hormozi, Amir M., et al., "Business Plans for New or Small Businesses: Paving the Way to Success," *Management Decision,* Vol. 40, Nos. 7 and 8 (2002), pp. 755–763.

Karlsson, Thomas, Benson Honig, and Wilfrid Laurrier, "Business Planning Practices in New Ventures: An Institutional Perspective," paper presented at the Babson Conference, April 2007.

Lange, Julian E., et al., "Pre-Startup Formal Business Plans and Post-Startup Performance: A Study of 116 Ventures," *Venture Capital Journal*, Vol. 9, No. 4 (2007), pp. 237–256.

Liao, J., and W. B. Gartner, "The Effects of Pre-Venture Plan Timing and Perceived Environmental Uncertainty on the Persistence of Emerging Firms," *Small Business Economics*, Vol. 27 (2006), pp. 23–40.

Mason, C., and M. Stark, "What Do Investors Look for in a Business Plan?: A Comparison of the Investment Criteria of Bankers, Venture Capitalists, and Business Angels," *International Small Business Journal*, Vol. 22, No. 3 (2004), pp. 227–248.

Melloan, J., "*Inc.*'s 5000 Fastest Growing Privately Owned Companies," *Inc.*, August 2007.

Mullins, John W. "Why Business Plans Don't Deliver," *Wall Street Journal,* June 22, 2009, http://online.wsj.com/article_email/SB10001424052970204830304574133501980701202-lMyQjAxMTAwMDIwNzEyNDcyWj.html#printMode.

Perry, Stephen C., "The Relationship Between Written Business Plans and the Failure of Small Business in the U.S.," *Journal of Small Business Management,* Vol. 39, No. 2 (2001), pp. 201–208.

Rich, Stanley R., and David E. Gumpert, "How to Write a Winning Business Plan," *Harvard Business Review,* Vol. 63, No. 3 (May–June 1985), pp. 156–166.

Sahlman, William A., "How to Write a Great Business Plan," *Harvard Business Review,* Vol. 75, No. 4 (July-August 1997), pp. 114–121.

Shane, Scott, and Frederick Delmar, "Planning for the Market: Business Planning Before Marketing and the Continuation of Organizing Efforts," *Journal of Business Venturing,* Vol. 19 (2004), pp. 767–785.

Online Resources for Preparing Business Plans

Bank websites can be a source for business planning tools and advice. For example, Bank of America has a downloadable outline and business planning guide at http://www.bankofamerica.com/smallbusiness/resourcecenter/index.cfm?template=rc_startingyourbusiness&context=rc_businessplan.

BPlans.com, Inc., *BPlans.com: The Business Planning Experts,* http://www.bplans.com. Designed for self-preparers by PaloAlto Software; provides advice, sample plans, and links to many consultants.

Business Confidant, Inc., *Business Confidant: Your Business Planning Specialist,* http://businessconfidant.com. Provides strategic thinking, technical writing, and financial analytical skills needed to produce professional, investor-ready business plans.

Business PlanWare, *Business Plan Software,* http://www.planware.org. Features financial projection and cash flow forecasting software, business plan freeware, white papers, and other tools and resources.

Business Tools and Advice, *Bloomberg Businessweek,* http://www.businessweek.com/. Provides guidelines and examples for writing business plans.

Dow Jones & Company, *Startup Journal: The Wall Street Journal Center for Entrepreneurs,* http://www.startupjournal.com. Features a mini-plan business assumptions test, sample business plans, and calculators for startup costs and cash flow, as well as articles on starting a business.

Entrepreneur.com, *Entrepreneur.com: Solutions for Growing Businesses,* http://www.entrepreneur.com. Offers a site search feature through which you can find articles and tips by entering keywords such as *business plan writing*.

Good-to-Go Business Plans, Inc., *Good-to-Go Business Plans: Plans for Every Business,* http://www.goodtogobusinessplans.com. Provides a range of services, including business-specific templates in pre-drafted language and other tools and forms.

One Economy Corporation, *Entrepreneur's Center,* http://www.thebeehive.org. Serves as a clearinghouse for Web links to business planning articles.

Small Business Administration, *Small Business Administration: Your Small Business Resource,* http://www.sba.gov. The federal government's online business planning and finance resource center classroom and library. The Small Business Administration also funds programs designed to help entrepreneurs. One of these programs, the Service Corps of Retired Executives (SCORE), has a gallery of detailed downloadable templates for business plans and financial statements on its website (http://www.score.org), under "business toolbox."

SmartOnline, http://smallbusiness.smartonline.com. Builds a business plan around simple questions posed to the user one by one, with explanations and examples; uses a wizard-driven approach; also integrates forms for incorporation and loan applications from the Small Business Administration.

Software for Preparing Business Plans

JIAN, Inc., *BizPlan*Builder *2007,* http://www.jian.com. A suite of business planning software and other business tools.

PaloAlto Software, *Business Plan Pro 2011,* http://www.paloalto.com. Business plan–creating software featuring over 400 sample business plans.

CHAPTER 7

The Marketing Plan

In the SPOTLIGHT
Mayan Pigments
http://mayanpigments.com

"When you create colors that survive centuries of blistering sunshine and still remain brilliant, you're probably onto something. Which is why we wanted to discover how the ancient Mayans pulled it off. After much rigorous research and scientific analysis, we unlocked their secret."

The opening sentences from the Mayan Pigments home page capture your attention immediately. When you click on the video icon, music and visuals carry you to a locale and time unfamiliar and exotic. The visionaries at Mayan Pigments want you to get excited not only about their products, but also about their products' almost mystical origins.

Thoughts of marketing strategies were not running through the minds of Lori Polette-Niewold and Russell Chianelli when they visited the Mayan ruins in Mexico. As research chemists specializing in materials science, they were fascinated by the chemical compositions that were able to survive all that nature could throw at them. In the 1990s, when Lori was a doctoral student and Russ was her advisor, they attended an academic conference in Mexico and took time for a tour of Mayan archeological sites. The vivid colors triggered their scientific curiosity. They returned to their laboratory and eventually emerged with what they labeled Maya Blue, a pigment that was not heavy metal–based, yet exhibited high-performance properties, including chemical resistance, temperature stability, and light stability. And it was earth-friendly and nontoxic.

After studying this chapter, you should be able to . . .

1. Describe small business marketing.
2. Identify the components of a formal marketing plan.
3. Discuss the nature of the marketing research process.
4. Define *market segmentation*, and discuss its related strategies.
5. Explain the different methods of forecasting sales.

LOOKING AHEAD

Continuing their research, Polette-Niewold and Chianelli developed a full spectrum of pigments and began thinking of commercial applications. That led to the formation of Mayan Pigments, Inc., an investor-backed company that sought to commercialize the products. The initial marketing strategy was to target industrial manufacturers of inks, paints, coatings, plastics, and other applications such as paper, cement, and glass. Not surprisingly, the fledgling venture found itself up against entrenched and fierce competitors. The obvious customers were large corporations that, for the most part, had long and deep relationships with those existing competitors.

In time, company leaders devised a niche marketing plan. One course of action was to become a supplier to another recent startup, Clementine Art. This Boulder, Colorado, firm specializes in paint, glue, modeling dough, crayons, and other children's products that are creative, natural, and green. As Clementine Art expanded, Mayan Pigments found that they were being introduced internationally.

Polette-Niewold is the chief technology officer for Mayan Pigments. In that role, she is continually on the lookout for further applications in additional niches. She and her team discovered that they could not hit the big market as a large corporation might do. Instead, they focus on segments that recognize the special features that Mayan Pigments offers that are valued as benefits by consumers.

Sources: http://mayanpigments.com, accessed October 19, 2010; http://www.clementineart.com, accessed October 19, 2010; and personal interview with Russell Chianelli, October 18, 2010.

Business owners tend to be doers, not planners. And they are often passionate about their product or service. They can talk about its features all day—it's the biggest; it weighs less; it's made of the best materials. They sometimes ignore the fact that customers buy a product or service because they get a benefit from it. Customers ask, "How does this item solve my problem? Make me a better person? Keep me safe?" Business owners need to put themselves in the shoes of their customers and figure out why customers buy what they do. In other words, they need a marketing plan.

The founders of Mayan Pigments did not have business degrees. They were scientists. They were excited about the discoveries they made in their laboratory and wanted other people to be excited, too. But excitement alone does not make a company. There must be a market, and you must know why that market will buy from you. Lori Polette-Niewold and Russell Chianelli and the rest of their team quickly learned that they had to prepare and implement a plan to sell their pigments.

In this chapter, we look at the nature of marketing and the marketing plan. Although our presentation does not cover the specific elements of all plans, the features that we discuss here are important components of any well-written plan.

It is appropriate first to answer a few basic questions about marketing:

- How can marketing be defined for a small business?
- What are the components of an effective marketing philosophy?
- What does having a consumer orientation imply about a business?

What Is Small Business Marketing?

Marketing means different things to different people. Some owners view marketing as simply selling a product or service. For others, it is the same as advertising. Still others see marketing as those activities directing the flow of goods and services from producer to consumer or user. In reality, small business marketing has a much broader scope. It consists of many activities, some of which occur even before a product is produced and made ready for distribution and sale. People who are thinking about starting businesses should do their homework to make sure a market exists for what they plan to sell before they ever launch their companies.

small business marketing
Business activities that direct the creation, development, and delivery of a bundle of satisfaction from the creator to the targeted user.

core product/service
The fundamental benefit or solution sought by customers.

actual product/service
The basic physical product and/or service that delivers those benefits.

augmented product/service
The basic product and/or service plus any extra or unsolicited benefits to the consumer that may prompt a purchase.

Small business marketing consists of those business activities that direct the creation, development, and delivery of a bundle of satisfaction from the creator to the targeted user. This definition emphasizes the benefits customers will gain from the core product and/or service. It may be helpful to view a product and/or service as having three levels: core product/service, actual product/service, and augmented product/service (see Exhibit 7.1). The **core product/service** is the fundamental benefit or solution sought by customers. The **actual product/service** is the basic physical product and/or service that delivers those benefits. The **augmented product/service** is the basic product and/or service plus any extra or unsolicited benefits to the consumer that may prompt a purchase. In the case of shoes, for example, the core product is basic protection for the feet; the actual product is the shoe itself. The augmented product might be increased running speed, greater comfort, or less wear and tear on feet and legs. Augmentation could also be reflected in how the customer feels. Do the shoes give a sense of style, of prestige, of social identity?

For Mayan Pigments, the first step in choosing a market for their product was to look at industrial users. The technology-focused startup team was familiar with the pigment industry, but less so with ultimate consumers of the products that would contain the pigments. The experience of this company is representative of the limitations small businesses face in taking their products to markets. Smaller firms generally cannot afford the talented marketing experts that large corporations employ. As a result, they conduct many trials and endure numerous problems. A marketing plan will not enable you to avoid all missteps, but it can

EXHIBIT 7.1 The Three Levels of a Product and/or Service

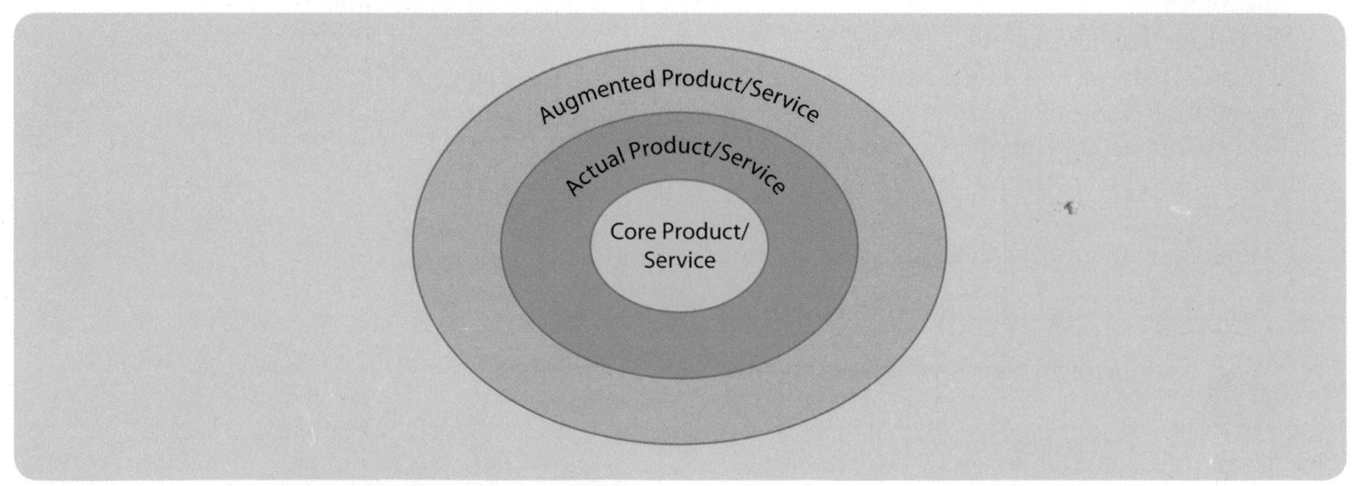

Startup Advice

When your company is in the startup stage, planning for marketing is different from when your business has been running for a few years. Startup Professionals, Inc., is one of a number of companies that specializes in advising ventures that are just getting underway. At its website, http://startupprofessionals.com/, you can find articles about how to plan under conditions of uncertainty, such as "Five Elements of a Credible Startup Marketing Plan."

drastically reduce the number of errors by forcing you to think through available options, given the resources you have.

Ultimately, a business provides a bundle of satisfaction to its customers, not merely the tangible product or intangible service that is the focus of the exchange. Consider the case of ModCloth. According to co-founder Susan Gregg Koger, "We can get our customers involved, helping decide what we sell."[1] ModCloth is an online clothing, accessories, and decor retailer. The business is based on the founders' love of vintage and retro clothing. But the owners—Koger and her husband, Eric—do not let their personal preferences stand in the way of what their customers want. Using social network sites such as Twitter and Facebook, they ask their customers to help them decide what items to carry. Accessing the company's website, customers are invited to click on "Be the Buyer" and vote on the designs they would like to see created.[2] The Kogers saw an immediate jump in traffic to ModCloth.com when they began offering this option.

MARKETING PHILOSOPHIES MAKE A DIFFERENCE

Just as an individual's personal philosophy influences the strategies he or she uses to achieve personal goals, a firm's marketing philosophy determines how its marketing activities are developed, reflected in the marketing plan, and used to achieve business goals. Three different marketing perspectives that guide most small businesses are the production-oriented, sales-oriented, and consumer-oriented philosophies. We see the first two philosophies used most often, as they are associated with the experience and aptitudes of entrepreneurs who may have a manufacturing or technology-based background or who may have had a career in sales.

A *production-oriented philosophy* emphasizes the product as the single most important part of the business. The firm concentrates resources on developing the product or service in the most efficient manner, even if promotion, distribution, and other marketing activities are slighted. On the other hand, a *sales-oriented philosophy* deemphasizes production efficiencies and customer preferences in favor of a focus on "pushing product." Achieving sales goals becomes the firm's highest priority. In contrast, a firm adopting a *consumer-oriented philosophy* believes that everything, including production and sales, centers on the consumer and his or her needs. The result: All marketing efforts begin and end with the consumer.

A CONSUMER ORIENTATION—THE RIGHT CHOICE

Over the years, both large and small businesses have gradually shifted their marketing emphasis from production to sales and, more recently, to consumers. Adhering to this approach is essential to marketing success. The marketing concept is a two-stage process that underlies all marketing efforts: identifying customer needs and satisfying those needs. This simple formula is easy to understand but difficult to implement, given the competitive nature of most markets. Still, for a company to be successful, it is essential that a product or service meet a real need in the marketplace. *We strongly recommend that all new businesses begin with a consumer orientation, as this philosophy is most consistent with long-term success.* Remember, customer satisfaction is not a means to achieving a goal—it *is* the goal!

Why have some small firms failed to adopt a consumer orientation when the benefits seem so obvious? The answer lies in three key factors. First, the state of competition always affects a firm's marketing orientation. If there is little or no competition and if demand exceeds supply, a firm is tempted to emphasize production. This is usually a short-term situation, however, and concentrating on production to the exclusion of marketing can lead to disaster in due time.

Second, as mentioned before, an entrepreneur may have a strong background in production or in selling but be weak other areas. It is natural for an owner to play to his or her strength.

Third, some small business owners are simply too focused on the present. Recall the discussion in Chapter 4 about choosing a franchise. Prospective franchisees often ask, "What is the hot franchise this year?" They overlook the fact that they are about to enter a multi-year contract, of perhaps 10 years or more. What is hot today may not be hot five years from now. The better course of action is to identify a franchise organization that knows how to please consumers in the long term. Of course, this principle of thinking long term applies to all small businesses.

Both production- and sales-oriented philosophies may generate short-run success. However, a consumer orientation not only recognizes production efficiency goals and professional selling but also adds concern for customer satisfaction. In effect, a firm that adopts a consumer orientation incorporates the best of each marketing philosophy.

market analysis The process of locating and describing potential customers.

marketing mix The combination of product, pricing, promotion, and distribution activities.

Once a small firm makes a commitment to a customer orientation, it is ready to develop a marketing strategy to support this goal. Marketing activities include taking the steps necessary to locate and describe potential customers—a process called **market analysis**. Marketing activities also encompass product and/or service, pricing, promotion, and distribution, which combine to form the **marketing mix**.

Exhibit 7.2 depicts the major components of the marketing plan—market analysis, the competition, and marketing strategy—and the marketing activities required to generate

EXHIBIT 7.2 The Marketing Plan and Supporting Marketing Activities

the information needed for the plan—marketing research, market segmentation, and sales forecasting. In the remainder of the chapter, we will take a more in-depth look at these plan components and marketing activities.

The Formal Marketing Plan

2 Identify the components of a formal marketing plan.

After the entrepreneur completes a feasibility study (discussed in Chapter 3) and determines the venture idea to be a viable opportunity, he or she is ready to prepare the formal marketing plan. Each business venture is different; therefore, each marketing plan is unique. An entrepreneur should avoid developing a cloned version of a plan created by someone else, even one suggested by the authors of this textbook. But certain subjects—market analysis, the competition, and marketing strategy—must be covered.

This chapter contains excerpts from actual marketing plans as examples of what might be included. The following discussion is not intended to be complete or comprehensive. In fact, more detailed treatment of marketing activities and strategies for both new and established small businesses is provided in Part 4, in Chapters 14 through 18. Much of this later material will also be helpful for writing the actual marketing plan.

Blogs Offer Marketing Advice

At the blog site http://www.ipmarketingadvisor.com, you can find information directed toward commercializing innovations. Even though this site is focused on technology transfer by universities, government agencies, and corporations, it provides solid marketing advice for small business owners. An entry on November 30, 2010, entitled "TTO Finds Many Marketing Uses for 'Lowly' Excel," explains how one university developed its marketing strategy for commercializing technologies using Excel spreadsheets. Check it out!

MARKET ANALYSIS

In the market analysis section of the marketing plan, the entrepreneur describes the target market. This description of potential customers is commonly called a **customer profile**. The profile contains the key demographic and psychological characteristics that describe the customers you consider most likely to be qualified purchasers of your products and services. Marketing research information, compiled from both secondary and primary data, can be used to construct this profile. A detailed discussion of the major benefits to customers provided by the new product or service should also be included in this section of the plan. Obviously, these benefits must be reasonable and consistent with statements in the product and/or service section of the plan.

customer profile A description of potential customers in a target market.

Spira™ Footwear, Inc., produces running and walking shoes that contain a patented WaveSpring® technology. It is easy for Spira's management team to get excited about the unique technology their shoes offer to wearers. They can talk at length about the product's lateral stability, height and size, weight and appearance.[3] But they also understand that customers buy their shoes more for the benefits they receive than for the features that the designers love. Excerpts from the company's marketing plan concentrate on those benefits:[4]

> **Comfort**
> Management believes that shoes incorporating the WaveSpring® technology are extremely comfortable, perhaps the most comfortable ever produced. Consumers

Spira Footwear

report that WaveSpring® feels like walking on a cushion of air or a moving sidewalk in an airport. Superior cushioning combined with a significant energy return generated by the WaveSpring® technology creates this remarkable sensation.

Universal Application
The WaveSpring® technology has applications in almost any type of footwear. To date, the Company has produced and distributed running shoes, walking shoes, and casual shoes.

Heel and Forefoot Applications
The WaveSpring® technology can be placed both in heel and forefoot of the shoe. The WaveSpring® allows for tremendous cushioning while still providing the necessary energy return for use as a propulsive force in both heel and forefoot.

Injury Protection
The Company contends that the WaveSpring® reduces fatigue and stress on muscles and joints, which in turn reduces the potential for injury. Users report that their legs feel fresher after activity with Spira than any other shoe.

Performance Enhancement
Management believes that one is able to participate in physical activities for longer periods of time at higher exertion levels as a result of the WaveSpring® technology. World class athletes and everyday users report tremendous benefits from the shoe and technology.

If a business owner envisions several target markets, each segment must have a corresponding customer profile. Likewise, different target markets may call for a corresponding number of related marketing strategies. Typically, however, a new venture will initially concentrate on a select few target markets—or even just one. Think for a moment just how expensive it would be to try to market to all possible customers: You might be spending money in geographic areas where none of your customers live or work, trying to reach people with a broad range of reading, listening, and viewing habits, instead of on the television shows, websites, radio stations, and magazines that most of your customers access. Attempting to reach all potential customers would be way too costly for a small business.

Another major component of market analysis is the actual sales forecast. It is usually desirable to include three sales forecasts covering the "most likely," "best-case," and "worst-case" scenarios. These alternatives provide investors and the entrepreneur with different numbers on which to base their decisions.

It is always difficult to forecast. For companies that have been around a few years, you might expect to extend the trends from the past. But anyone who has followed global business cycles knows that it is not possible to predict all the variables that will affect how a company sells its product or service. Forecasting sales for a new venture is even more difficult. While it will be necessary to make assumptions during forecasting, these should be minimized. The forecasting method should be fully described and backed up by data whenever feasible.

THE COMPETITION

Frequently, entrepreneurs ignore the reality of competition for their new ventures, believing that the marketplace contains no close substitutes or that their success will not attract other entrepreneurs. This is simply not realistic.

Existing competitors should be studied carefully, and their key management personnel profiled. A brief discussion of competitors' overall strengths and weaknesses should be a part of the competition section of the plan. Also, related products currently being marketed or tested by competitors should be noted. The entrepreneur should also assess the likelihood that any of these firms will enter the targeted market. Performing a SWOT analysis at this point is always a good idea. (As we discussed in Chapter 3, SWOT stands for *S*trengths, *W*eaknesses, *O*pportunities, and *T*hreats.) It is important that your company have a clear understanding of what it does well (strengths), what it doesn't do so well (weaknesses), available market opportunities, and threats from competitors as well as from changes in the company's operating environment (social, technological, economic, political, and other environmental variables).

JavaNet Internet Cafe defines itself as "a unique forum for communication and entertainment through the medium of the Internet." This startup cybercafe sees both coffee retailers and online service providers as competitors. Its plan describes the competitive environment as follows:

> *The main competitors in the retail coffee segment are Cafe Paradisio, Full City, Coffee Corner and Allann Bros. These businesses are located in or near the downtown area, and target a similar segment to JavaNet's (i.e., educated, upwardly mobile students and business people).*
>
> *Competition from online service providers comes from locally owned businesses as well as national firms. There are approximately eight local, online service providers in Eugene. This number is expected to grow with the increasing demand for Internet access. Larger online service providers, such as AOL and CompuServe, are also a competitive threat to JavaNet. Due to the nature of the Internet, there are no geographical boundaries restricting competition.*
>
> *There are approximately 16 coffee wholesalers in Lane County. These wholesalers distribute coffee and espresso beans to over 20 retailers in the Eugene area. Competition in both channels creates an even amount of bargaining power between buyers and suppliers resulting in extremely competitive pricing. Some of these major players in the industry (i.e., Allann Brothers Coffee Co., Inc. and Coffee Corner Ltd.) distribute and retail coffee products.*
>
> *The number of online service providers in Eugene is approximately eight and counting. These small, regional service providers use a number of different pricing strategies. Some charge a monthly fee, while others charge hourly and/or phone fees. Regardless of the pricing method used, obtaining Internet access through one of these firms can be expensive. Larger Internet servers such as America Online (AOL), Prodigy, and CompuServe are also fighting for market share in this rapidly growing industry. These service providers are also rather costly for the average consumer. Consumers who are not convinced they would frequently and consistently travel the Internet, will not be willing to pay these prices.*[5]

If you were the owner of JavaNet Internet Cafe, would these descriptions give you information about your strengths and weaknesses relative to those of competitors? Would you know how to compete with two different kinds of businesses?

Many competitors can be monitored by visiting their websites. Todd Stoner, owner of Waco, Texas–based Disciplined Investors, an investment advisement firm, uses several search engines to keep tabs on his competition. "I am always curious to see what other investment firms in and around Waco are up to," Stoner says. "I can see which firms are growing and what types of products and services they offer."[6]

MARKETING STRATEGY

A well-prepared market analysis and a discussion of the competition are important to the formal marketing plan. But the information on marketing strategy forms the most detailed

Papa Murphy's International

section of the marketing plan and, in many respects, is subject to the closest scrutiny from potential investors. Such a strategy plots the course of the marketing actions that will make or break the owner's vision. It's one thing to know that a large target market exists for a product or service. It's another to be able to explain why customers will buy that product or service from you!

Papa Murphy's International, Inc., is a franchise chain that specializes in making pizzas that customers take home and bake for themselves. Unlike other major quick-serve restaurant franchisors, Papa Murphy's relies on its franchisees to develop local marketing strategies. You will recall from Chapter 4 that franchisees are business owners who enter into a contractual relationship with franchisors to sell products and services based on the franchisor's model. In Papa Murphy's case, corporate headquarters provides the franchisees with a library of promotional concepts/materials and training so that the local owners can create promotional partnerships with local, noncompetitive businesses. This strategy takes advantage of the intimate knowledge the franchises have of their communities and customers. Knowing how their customers made buying decisions proved especially effective during the recessionary period that began in 2008, when people began showing a preference for preparing meals at home. By offering convenient, yet fresh and reasonably priced, meal solutions, Papa Murphy's enjoyed 7 percent growth while that of competitive chains was down 6 to 7 percent.[7]

The marketing mix of the "4 Ps" highlights the areas that a company's marketing strategy should address: (1) product decisions that will transform the basic product or service idea into a bundle of satisfaction, (2) place, also called distribution, activities regarding the delivery of the product to customers, (3) pricing decisions that will set an acceptable exchange value on the total product or service, and (4) promotional activities that will communicate the necessary information to target markets.

Obviously, the limited resources of small businesses have a direct bearing on the emphasis given to each of these areas. Additionally, a service business will not have the same distribution problems as a product business, and the promotional challenges facing a retail store will be quite different from those faced by a manufacturer. Despite these differences, we can offer a generalized format for presenting marketing strategies in a plan for those who will carry out those strategies.

The Product and/or Service Section

The product and/or service section of the marketing plan includes the name of the product and/or service and the name of the business and why they were selected. Any legal protection that has been obtained for the names should be described. It is also important to explain the logic behind the name selection. An entrepreneur's family name, if used for certain products or services, can sometimes make a positive contribution to sales. Think about how cleverly the J.M. Smucker Company has used the slogan "With a name like Smucker's, it has to be good."® We can cite many examples of the successful use of family names—Howard Johnson or jcpenny, for example. But you may lose an opportunity to attract customers if your company name has no connection with the product you are selling or if it confuses people about the type of business you are running. And negative publicity related to a name may damage a company's image. Look up the stock price for Martha Stewart Living Omnimedia, Inc., before and after her indictment and prison sentence.[8] A good name is simple, memorable, and descriptive of the benefit provided by the product or service. (We will look at this in more depth in Chapters 14 and 15.) Whatever the logic behind the choice of names, the selection should be defended and the names registered with the appropriate agencies so that they are protected.

Courtesy of jcpenney

Sometimes names selected for a business or a product or service may be challenged, even many years later, particularly if they haven't been registered. In fact, this happened to Apple Computer, a company that can afford all the legal advice anyone could ask for. The iPad trademark in Europe is owned by STMicroelectronics, a Swiss semiconductor corporation that uses it as an acronym for "integrated passive and active devices."[9] A small business that changes its name or the name of a key product or service may find that advertising, packaging, and other materials become prohibitively expensive.

In the marketing plan, other components of the total product, such as the packaging, should be presented via drawings. It may be desirable to use professional packaging consultants to develop these drawings in some cases. Customer service plans such as warranties and repair policies also need to be discussed in this section. All of these elements of the marketing strategy should be tied directly to customer satisfaction. (Chapter 14 further examines the importance of creating and maintaining good customer relationships.)

Another legal issue many small business owners face relates to unique features of their products or services. These special features may not merely be why people buy from you; they may also justify why someone might invest in your company or lend you money. For this reason, Mayan Pigments obtained patents on its pigments and processes; the company wanted to differentiate its products from those of other manufacturers and to prevent rivals from stealing that competitive advantage.

Rather than patenting their products or technologies, some enterprises prefer to maintain trade secrets. We all have heard the stories of the secret Coca-Cola formula and of KFC's mysterious 11 herbs and spices. These features fall under the term **intellectual property**. Many companies build their marketing strategies around their intellectual property, promoting the idea that only they offer a particular benefit to customers.

intellectual property
Original intellectual creations, including inventions, literary creations, and works of art, that are protected by patents or copyrights.

The Distribution Section

Quite often, new ventures will use established intermediaries to handle the distribution of their product. This strategy reduces the investment necessary for launch and helps the new company get its products to customers faster. How those intermediaries will be persuaded to carry the new product should be explained in the distribution section of the marketing plan. Any intention the new business may have of licensing its product or service should also be covered in this section.

Some retail ventures require fixed locations; others need mobile stores. For many, the Internet is their location, but they may rely on others in a distribution chain to transport and/or warehouse merchandise. Layouts and configurations of retail outlets should be described in this section of the marketing plan. Many questions should be addressed—for example, will the customer get the product by regular mail or by express delivery? Will the service be provided from home or the office or from the location of a licensed representative? How long will it take between order placement and actual delivery?

LIVING THE DREAM

using technology

Social Media Marketing

© iStockphoto.com/Angelika Schwarz

Adam Kidron is among a new generation of entrepreneurs who are using social media to reinvent traditional marketing strategies. If you visit the website for 4food, a New York City restaurant becoming known for its burgers, you will see an animated video explaining how Kidron got the idea for his health-conscious enterprise.

Kidron took a consumer approach to his business. He first wanted to create a product that could be customized to customers' tastes. He designed a burger with a pop-out center, replaced by a variety of "scoops" of the customer's choosing. According to Kidron,

> *Once we'd gone down that path, all the social media aspects came in. If a consumer creates a new product, it has to be saved in a database. It has to have a new name. Then we have to figure out how to sell it to other consumers. Really, social media is part of the fundamentals of the product.*

© iStockphoto.com/Martin Turzak

The customer-designed-and-named burgers can be posted to Twitter or Facebook. Customers can even put together YouTube videos that 4food will display on a video wall in the store. And the burger creator gets a 25¢ credit on their 4food account anytime another customer orders their burger.

Social media, Kidron says, "[i]s how we communicate." He believes that any business wanting to succeed today needs to have social media in its marketing plan.

Sources: http://4food.com, accessed March 30, 2011; and Jason Daley, "Tearing Down the Walls," *Entrepreneur*, Vol. 38, No. 12 (December 2010), pp. 56–60.
http://4food.com

When a new firm's method of product delivery is exporting, the distribution section must discuss the relevant laws and regulations governing that activity. Knowledge of exchange rates between currencies and distribution options must be reflected in the material discussed in this section. (Distribution concepts are explained in greater detail in Chapter 15, and exporting is discussed in Chapter 18.)

The Pricing Section

At a minimum, the price of a product or service must cover the cost of bringing it to customers. Therefore, the pricing section must include a schedule of both production and marketing costs. Break-even computations should be included for alternative prices. (Naturally, forecasting methods used for analysis in this section should be consistent with those used in preparing the market analysis section.) However, setting a price based exclusively on break-even analysis is not advisable, as it ignores other aspects of pricing. If the entrepreneur has found a truly unique niche, he or she may be able to charge a premium price—at least in the short run.

Competitors should be studied to learn what they are charging. To break into a market, an entrepreneur will usually have to price a new product or service within a reasonable range of that of the competition. Many new business owners think their best strategy is to underprice the competition in order to gain market acceptance and boost sales. It is important to keep in mind, however, that existing competitors probably have more resources than you do. If they consider your business to be a threat and engage you in a price war, they can probably outlast you. In addition, do you really want your customers to come to you only because you sell a cheaper product or service? That's no way to build loyalty; you will lose those customers to the next company that prices lower than you do. (Chapter 16 examines break-even analysis and pricing strategy in more depth.)

The Promotion Section

The promotion section of the marketing plan should describe the entrepreneur's approach to creating customer awareness of the product or service and explain why customers will be motivated to buy. Among the many promotional options available to the entrepreneur are personal selling (that is, direct person-to-person selling) and advertising. The management team at Mayan Pigments found that their website could be an effective promotional sales tool, encouraging visitors to follow up with contacts.

If personal selling is appropriate, the section should outline how many salespeople will be employed and how they will be compensated. The proposed system for training the sales force should also be mentioned. If advertising is to be used, a list of the specific media to be employed should be included and advertising themes should be described. Often, it is advisable to seek the services of a small advertising agency when developing a marketing strategy. In this case, the name and credentials of the agency should be provided. A brief mention of successful campaigns supervised by the agency can add to the appeal of this section of the marketing plan. (Personal selling and advertising are discussed more extensively in Chapter 17.)

Marketing Research for the Small Business

For many small business owners, a marketing plan may be based on intuition or on their personal, limited experiences and observations. If you are serious about meeting the needs of your customers, it is advisable to write the marketing plan only after collecting and evaluating marketing research data. A marketing plan based on research will be stronger than a plan without such a foundation.

THE NATURE OF MARKETING RESEARCH

marketing research The gathering, processing, interpreting, and reporting of market information.

Marketing research may be defined as the gathering, processing, interpreting, and reporting of market information. It is all about finding out what you want to know. A small business typically conducts less marketing research than does a big business, partly because of the expense involved but also because the entrepreneur often does not understand the basic research process. Therefore, our discussion of marketing research focuses on the more widely used and practical techniques that entrepreneurs can employ as they analyze potential target markets and make preparations to develop their marketing plans.

Low- and No-Cost Marketing Strategies

In a *Wall Street Journal* online article, Emily Maltby described low- and no-cost marketing strategies for small business owners (see "On a Tight Budget? How to Land a Client," http://online.wsj.com/article/SB10001424052748704554104575435430531588968.html?mod=dist_smartbrief, August 18, 2010). Her advice on finding clients offers several inexpensive ways to gather information about your market niche.

Although a small business can conduct marketing research

without the assistance of an expert, the cost of hiring such help is often money well spent, as the expert's advice may help increase revenues or cut costs. Marketing researchers are trained, experienced professionals, and prices for their research services typically reflect this. For example, focus groups run from $3,000 to $10,000 each, and a telephone survey may range anywhere from $5,000 to $25,000 or more, depending on the number of interviews and the length of the questionnaire. However, companies such as SurveyMonkey (http://www.surveymonkey.com) are now reducing overall research costs by taking advantage of the Internet to offer Web-based

© iStockphoto.com/Angelika Schwarz

entrepreneurial experiences

Research and Rewards

The winners of *Entrepreneur* magazine's Entrepreneur of 2010 Awards relied on market research to lead their companies to success. While many entrepreneurs, like one of the winners, may believe that great products do the marketing for you, these winners all found ways of gathering information that helped them get started and moving in the right direction.

Daniel Lubetzky, who received the Entrepreneur of 2010 award, describes the venture that he founded in 1994, PeaceWorks Holdings LLC, as a not-only-for-profit company. PeaceWorks is a food company that promotes trade between Israelis and Palestinians with the motto of "Cooperation Never Tasted So Good™." The business did not show much growth until 2003 when it introduced a snack bar that Lubetzky labeled KIND. According to Lubetzky, "It took us years to find the right formula, and we hit every challenge you could imagine trying to scale and get into stores." Scaling up, or growing the business rapidly, often proves to be harder than entrepreneurs expect. Lubetzky discovered that consumers not only liked the product, but also became "obsessed" with the company's philosophy.

The 2010 Emerging Entrepreneur of the Year is Derek Zobrist, founder of the Enovative Group. Under the name Enovative Kontrol Systems, Zobrist offers a line of energy-efficient technologies that reduce the waste of precious resources through intelligent automation and strategic design. As a junior at Pepperdine University, Zobrist acquired access to a new demand-controlled water pump system that could sharply reduce water-heating costs. He began his company by donating units to customers on the condition that they allow him to collect data to improve product engineering. By conducting these case studies, he learned how to satisfy customer needs and to build evidence demonstrating the benefits the product supplied. By the end of 2010, Enovative had made $1 million and had contracts with several of the largest multi-family building owners in the country.

The third award given by *Entrepreneur* magazine was for the College Entrepreneur of 2010. The winner, Allen Kim, is the co-founder (along with Luis Calderon) of Bebarang, described by Kim as a "Netflix for baby clothes." Kim had an "aha!" moment when he heard a relative complain about how expensive baby clothes are and how quickly babies outgrow their clothes. He spent hours interviewing more than 100 mothers, getting a sense of their frustrations and ideas for solving the problem. This led to a clothing rental business. Kim and Calderon had raised approximately $500,000 by the end of 2010 to be used in launching their website, building inventory, and developing a distribution system.

Courtesy of Bebarang Inc.

These entrepreneurs report that much of what they learned was through trial and error. But by examining their mistakes, they acquired information that they used to achieve their success.

Sources: Jennifer Wang, "The Envelope, Please . . .," *Entrepreneur*, Vol. 39, No. 1 (January 2011), pp. 47–50; http://www.peaceworks.com/, accessed March 30, 2011; http://www.enovativegroup.com/, accessed March 30, 2011; and http://bebarang.com/, accessed March 30, 2011. **http://www.peaceworks.com**

surveys and online focus groups. In this chapter, we provide you with some basic principles of marketing research, but do not be misled in thinking that you will be as well prepared as someone with years of training and practice in conducting research studies.

Before committing to research, an entrepreneur should always estimate the projected costs of marketing research and compare them with the benefits expected. Such analysis is never exact, but it will help the entrepreneur to decide how much and what kind of research should be conducted.

STEPS IN THE MARKETING RESEARCH PROCESS

The typical steps in the marketing research process are (1) identifying the informational need, (2) searching for secondary data, (3) collecting primary data, and (4) interpreting the data gathered.

Step One: Identifying the Informational Need

The first step in marketing research is to identify and define the informational need. Although this step seems almost too obvious to mention, the fact is that small business owners sometimes commission surveys without pinpointing the specific information they need. Broad statements such as "Our need is to know if the venture will be successful" will do little to guide the research process, but even a more specific goal can easily miss the mark. For example, an entrepreneur thinking about a location for a restaurant may decide to conduct a survey to ascertain customers' menu preferences and reasons for eating out when, in fact, what he or she needs to know most is how often residents of the target area eat out and how far they are willing to drive to eat in a restaurant.

Once a venture's informational needs have been defined correctly, research can be designed to concentrate on those specific needs. Later in this chapter, we provide a survey questionnaire that was developed for the owner of a therapeutic spa who wanted to assess customer satisfaction and identify growth opportunities for her business (see Exhibit 7.3).

Step Two: Searching for Secondary Data

Information that has already been compiled is known as **secondary data**. Generally, collecting secondary data is much less expensive than gathering new, or primary, data. Therefore, after defining their informational needs, entrepreneurs should exhaust available sources of secondary data before going further into the research process. It may be possible to base much of the marketing plan for the new venture solely on secondary data. A massive amount of information is available in libraries throughout the United States and on the Internet. The libraries of higher education institutions can be especially valuable. Not only do they have access to numerous databases containing business-related information, but they also have librarians with the skills necessary to guide you through those databases.

secondary data
Market information that has been previously compiled.

As you already know, the Internet is a rich source of secondary data. Information that once took days and even weeks to obtain is now often only a mouse click away. Software programs and hundreds of websites (many offering free information) can help an entrepreneur research customers for her or his product or service. Don't make the mistake, however, of thinking that the Internet is the only source of secondary data or even the most reliable source. Like all repositories of information, it is most helpful when used in tandem with other sources. Be very careful to verify the accuracy of all secondary data gathered from the Internet and other sources.

A particularly helpful source of secondary data for the small firm is the Small Business Administration, or SBA (http://www.sba.gov). This agency publishes extensive bibliographies on many topics, including marketing research.

Unfortunately, the use of secondary data has several drawbacks. One is that the data may be outdated. Another is that the units of measure in the secondary data may not fit the current problem. For example, a firm's market might consist of individuals with incomes between $20,000 and $25,000, while secondary data may report only the number of individuals with incomes between $15,000 and $50,000.

Finally, the question of credibility is always present. Some sources of secondary data are less trustworthy than others. Mere publication of data does not in itself make the data valid and reliable. It is advisable to compare several different sources to see whether they are reporting similar data. Professional research specialists can also help assess the credibility of secondary sources.

Step Three: Collecting Primary Data

primary data
New market information that is gathered by the firm conducting the research.

If the secondary data are insufficient, a search for new information, or **primary data**, is the next step. Observational methods and questioning methods are two techniques used in accumulating primary data. Observational methods avoid interpersonal contact between respondents and the researcher, while questioning methods involve some type of interaction with respondents.

OBSERVATIONAL METHODS Observation is probably the oldest form of research in existence; indeed, learning by observing is quite common. It is hardly surprising that observation can provide useful information for small businesses. A simple but effective form of observational research is mystery shopping. Mystery shoppers gather observational data by going into a store (yours or a competitor's) and looking at how items are displayed, checking out in-store advertising, and assessing other features of the store. Mystery shopping can also be used to test employee product knowledge, sales techniques, and more. The results of such activities are used to make important changes in store design and merchandising as well as to reward good employees.[10]

Lisa Barone is co-founder and chief branding officer at Outspoken Media, Inc., an Internet marketing company. She advocates social media as offering effective ways for gathering information about people, products, companies, and many other topics. Although a researcher can ask questions of individuals and groups through these media, he or she can also learn a lot by tracking conversations. Barone finds Twitter chats to be especially useful for gaining valuable insights that can help small businesses. Twitter chats are guided conversations on specific subjects. Each chat has a hashtag so that you can identify it and participate in the discussion. Many business owners use these chats as mechanisms to expand their networks, but they can also simply monitor conversations to get real-time information that may offer ideas about marketing strategies. Barone suggests using a Twitter tool to help you monitor the Twitter chat hashtag that you're following. This will help you isolate the conversation so that your "regular" Twitter stream isn't polluting it with outside information. Some tools you may want to use include the following:

- *Twitter Search* (http://search.twitter.com/) lets you choose a topic and begin a search.
- *Tweetchat* (http://tweetchat.com/) connects you with others who are chatting about a particular subject.
- *Tweetdeck* (http://www.tweetdeck.com/) provides applications that allow users to exceed the Twitter limit of 140 characters.
- *Monitter* (http://monitter.com/)[11] enables users to narrow searches based on keywords, such as a geographic location.

QUESTIONING METHODS Surveys and experimentation are questioning methods that involve contact with respondents. Surveys can be conducted by mail, telephone, the Web, or personal interview. Mail surveys are often used when target respondents are widely dispersed. However, they usually yield low response rates—only a small percentage of the surveys sent out are typically returned. Telephone surveys and personal interview surveys achieve higher response rates. But personal interviews are very expensive, and individuals are often reluctant to grant such interviews if they think a sales pitch is coming. Some marketing researchers, such as iThink, offer firms a new way to survey customers—through an online questionnaire. Although some websites claim that online surveys have better response rates than do paper surveys, Internet surveying is still relatively new, and data on response rates are questionable.

A questionnaire is the basic instrument guiding the researcher who is administering the survey and the respondent who is taking it. A questionnaire should be developed carefully and pretested before it is used in the market. Here are several considerations to keep in mind when designing and testing a questionnaire:

- Ask questions that relate to the issue under consideration. An interesting question may not be relevant. A good test of relevance is to assume an answer to each question and then ask yourself how you would use that information.
- Select the form of question, such as open-ended and multiple-choice, that is most appropriate for the subject and the conditions of the survey.
- Carefully consider the order of the questions. Asking questions in the wrong sequence can produce biased answers to later questions.
- Ask the more sensitive questions near the end of the questionnaire. Age and income, for example, are usually sensitive topics.
- Carefully select the words in each question. They should be as simple, clear, and objective as possible.
- Pretest the questionnaire by administering it to a small sample of respondents who are representative of the group to be surveyed.

Exhibit 7.3 shows a questionnaire developed for Changes Therapeutic Practices, an alternative medicine spa in El Paso, Texas. This survey illustrates how the considerations

EXHIBIT 7.3 Small Business Survey Questionnaire

Changes Therapeutic Practices of El Paso

Customer satisfaction survey

Gender:						
O	O					
M	F					
Age range:						
O	O	O	O	O	O	
4–15	16–25	26–35	36–45	46–55	56–over	
Annual Income range:						
O	O	O	O	O		
Less than $20,000	$20,001–$25,000	$25,001–$35,000	$35,0001–$45,000	More than $45,000		

(Continued)

EXHIBIT 7.3 Small Business Survey Questionnaire (Continued)

In what part of the city do you live?						
○	○	○	○			
West	East	North East	Central			
For how long have you been using Changes' services?						
○	○	○	○			
Days	Weeks	Months	Years			
How often do you visit Changes Therapeutic of El Paso?						
○	○	○	○			
Daily	Weekly	Monthly	Annually			
What services of Changes Therapeutic of El Paso do you normally use?						
○	○	○	○	○	○	○
Massage	Facials	Synergie cellulite treatments	Reiki	Waxing	Paraffin Treatments	Aromatherapy
Which of the following services would you like to see in Changes?						
○	○	○	○	○		
Yoga	Karate	Acupuncture	Self-care workshops	None		
How did you hear about Changes Therapeutic of El Paso?						
○	○	○	○	○		
Friend	Yellow Pages	Internet	Doctor	Other		

What is your knowledge of the following?	None	Little	Fair	Very Much
1) Massage therapy:	○	○	○	○
2) Yoga:	○	○	○	○
3) Acupuncture:	○	○	○	○
4) Facial:	○	○	○	○
5) Synergie (massage helps to reduce cellulite):	○	○	○	○

How often do you :	Not at all	Once a week	Once a month	Twice a month	Other
1) Receive a massage service?	○	○	○	○	○
2) Practice yoga?	○	○	○	○	○
3) Get acupuncture services?	○	○	○	○	○
4) Get facial services?	○	○	○	○	○
5) Get Synergie services?	○	○	○	○	○

If you have tried any of the services mentioned above, where did you receive those services? (Specify business name, home, etc. . . .)

____

____

EXHIBIT 7.3 Small Business Survey Questionnaire (Continued)

Would you like to attend a workshop where you can learn more about these services?						
O	O					
No	Yes (if time permits)	If no, why?____________				
In which of the services are you most interested? (please select one or more)						
O	O	O	O	O	O	
Therapeutic Massage	Yoga	Acupuncture	Facials	Synergie	None	
Would you prefer a spa that offers all of these services?						
O	O	O				
No	Yes	Maybe				
How far are you willing to travel to such a spa?						
O	O	O	O	O		
0–10 miles	11–20 miles	21–30 miles	31–40 miles	41–50 miles		

Source: Used by permission of Changes Therapeutic Practices of El Paso.

just described can be incorporated into a questionnaire. Note the use of both multiple-choice and open-ended questions. As it turned out, the answers to the open-ended questions were particularly useful to this firm.

Poorly designed questionnaires may lead to results that cause you to make bad decisions. Again, we encourage drawing on the expertise of research specialists when gathering primary data. Some guidelines for improving how you interpret the data you collect are presented in the next step.

Step Four: Interpreting the Data Gathered

After the necessary data have been gathered, they must be transformed into usable information. Without interpretation, large quantities of data are only isolated facts. Methods of summarizing and simplifying information for users include tables, charts, and other graphics. Descriptive statistics (for example, the average response) are most helpful during this step in the research procedure. Inexpensive personal computer software, such as Excel, is now available to perform statistical calculations and generate report-quality graphics.

It is important to remember that formal marketing research is not always necessary. The business owner's first decision should be whether to conduct primary research at all. It may be best not to conduct formal research in the following situations:[12]

- Your company doesn't have the resources to conduct the research properly or to implement any findings generated from the proposed research.
- The opportunity for a new business or product introduction has passed. If you've been beaten to the punch, it may be wise to wait and see how the early entrant to the market fares.
- A decision to move forward has already been made. There's no need to spend good money on a decision that has already been made.

- You can't decide what information is needed. If you don't know where you are going, any road will take you there.
- The needed information already exists (that is, secondary information is available).
- The cost of conducting the research outweighs the potential benefits.

Bloomberg Businessweek journalist John Tozzi suggests several ways entrepreneurs can do their own research with very little money.

1. Conduct your research in the same way that you sell your product or service. If your salespeople make personal calls, they can gather information while they are out. If sales are over the phone, survey over the phone. If you market primarily online, conduct Web surveys.
2. Mine public sources. Use government sites, such as that of the U.S. Census Bureau. After all, you've paid for this information through your taxes.
3. Enlist students from local colleges to help stretch your limited research budget. In addition, their professors may prove to be good sources of research interpretation expertise.[13]

As important as marketing research is, it should never be allowed to suppress entrepreneurial enthusiasm or be used as a substitute for a hands-on feel for the target market. It should be viewed as a supplement to, not a replacement for, good judgment and cautious experimentation in launching new products and services. Ultimately, the marketing plan should reflect the entrepreneur's belief about the best marketing strategy for her or his firm.

Understanding Potential Target Markets

4 Define *market segmentation*, and discuss its related strategies.

To prepare the market analysis section of the marketing plan, an entrepreneur needs a proper understanding of the term *market*, which means different things to different people. It may refer to a physical location where buying and selling take place ("They went to the market"), or it may be used to describe selling efforts ("We must market this product aggressively"). Still another meaning is the one we emphasize in this chapter: A **market** is a group of customers or potential customers who have purchasing power and unsatisfied needs. Note carefully the three ingredients in this definition of a market:

market
A group of customers or potential customers who have purchasing power and unsatisfied needs.

1. A market must have buying units, or *customers*. These units may be individuals or business entities. Thus, a market is more than a geographic area; it must contain potential customers.
2. Customers in a market must have *purchasing power*. Those who lack money and/or credit do not constitute a viable market because they have nothing to offer in exchange for a product or service. In such a situation, no transactions can occur.
3. A market must contain buying units with *unsatisfied needs*. Consumers, for instance, will not buy unless they are motivated to do so—and motivation can occur only when a customer recognizes his or her unsatisfied needs. It would be extremely difficult, for example, to sell luxury urban apartments to desert nomads!

RESOURCES

Connecting with Your Market

In their book *Get Connected: The Social Networking Toolkit for Business* (Entrepreneur Press, 2009), Starr Hall and Chadd Rosenberg offer guidelines for getting your company's name known. They offer tactics that can help you target your messages for specific customer groups.

In light of our definition of a market, determining market potential is the process of locating and investigating buying units that have both purchasing power and needs that can be satisfied with the product or service that is being offered.

MARKET SEGMENTATION AND ITS VARIABLES

In Chapter 3, cost- and differentiation-based strategies were described as they apply to marketplaces that are relatively homogeneous, or uniform, in nature. As discussed, these strategies can also be used to focus on a market niche within an industry. In his book *Competitive Advantage*, Michael Porter refers to this type of competitive strategy—in which cost- and differentiation-based advantages are achieved within narrow market segments—as a *focus strategy*.[14]

A focus strategy depends on market segmentation and becomes a consideration in competitive markets. Formally defined, **market segmentation** is the process of dividing the total market for a product or service into smaller groups with similar needs, such that each group is likely to respond favorably to a specific marketing strategy. Think about what used to be called "sneakers." They were comfortable canvas and rubber shoes worn primarily by students and athletes, distinguished only by whether they were low-top or high-top styles. Consider how many market segments for this type of shoe exist today: running, walking, basketball, tennis, hiking and outdoor, and many others, all of which have their own subcategories.

market segmentation
The division of a market into several smaller groups with similar needs.

In order to divide the total market into appropriate segments, an entrepreneur must consider **segmentation variables**, which are parameters that identify the particular dimensions that distinguish one form of market behavior from another. Two broad sets of segmentation variables that represent major dimensions of a market are benefit variables and demographic variables.

segmentation variables
The parameters used to distinguish one form of market behavior from another.

Benefit Variables

The definition of a market highlights the unsatisfied needs of customers. **Benefit variables** are related to customer needs since they are used to identify segments of a market based on the benefits sought by customers. For example, senior citizens might patronize a health club to get cardiovascular exercise. The draw for young men might be bodybuilding, while young girls may attend gymnastics classes there. A single health club may offer services that are used for different reasons and in different ways by different market segments.

benefit variables
Specific characteristics that distinguish market segments according to the benefits sought by customers.

Demographic Variables

Benefit variables alone are insufficient for market analysis; it is impossible to implement forecasting and marketing strategy without defining the market further. Therefore, small businesses commonly use **demographic variables** as part of market segmentation. Recall the definition of a market: customers with purchasing power and unsatisfied needs. Demographic variables refer to certain characteristics that describe customers, their purchasing power, their consumption patterns, and other factors. Typical demographic variables are age, marital status, gender, occupation, and income.

demographic variables
Specific characteristics that describe customers and their purchasing power.

MARKETING STRATEGIES BASED ON SEGMENTATION CONSIDERATIONS

There are several types of strategies based on market segmentation efforts. The three types discussed here are the unsegmented approach, the multi-segment approach, and the single-segment approach. Few companies engage in all three approaches simultaneously. These strategies can best be understood by using an example, so we'll return to Changes Therapeutic Practices.

The Unsegmented Strategy

unsegmented strategy (mass marketing)
A strategy that defines the total market as the target market.

When a business defines the total market as its target, it is following an **unsegmented strategy** (also known as **mass marketing**). This strategy can sometimes be successful, but it assumes that all customers desire the same basic benefit from the product or service. This may hold true for water but certainly does not hold true for shoes, which satisfy numerous needs through a wide range of styles, prices, colors, and sizes. With an unsegmented strategy, a firm develops a single marketing mix—one combination of product, price, promotion, and distribution. Its competitive advantage must be derived from either a cost- or a differentiation-based advantage. The unsegmented strategy of the Changes Therapeutic spa is shown in Exhibit 7.4. The company's initial service was therapeutic massages. Tanya Finney, founder of Changes Therapeutic, discovered that virtually anyone was a prospect for a therapeutic massage—her customers ranged in age from 8 to 90 years. One promotional tactic that worked in reaching this broad customer base was sponsoring races for charitable causes, including breast cancer, heart disease, arthritis, and many others.

EXHIBIT 7.4 An Unsegmented Market Strategy

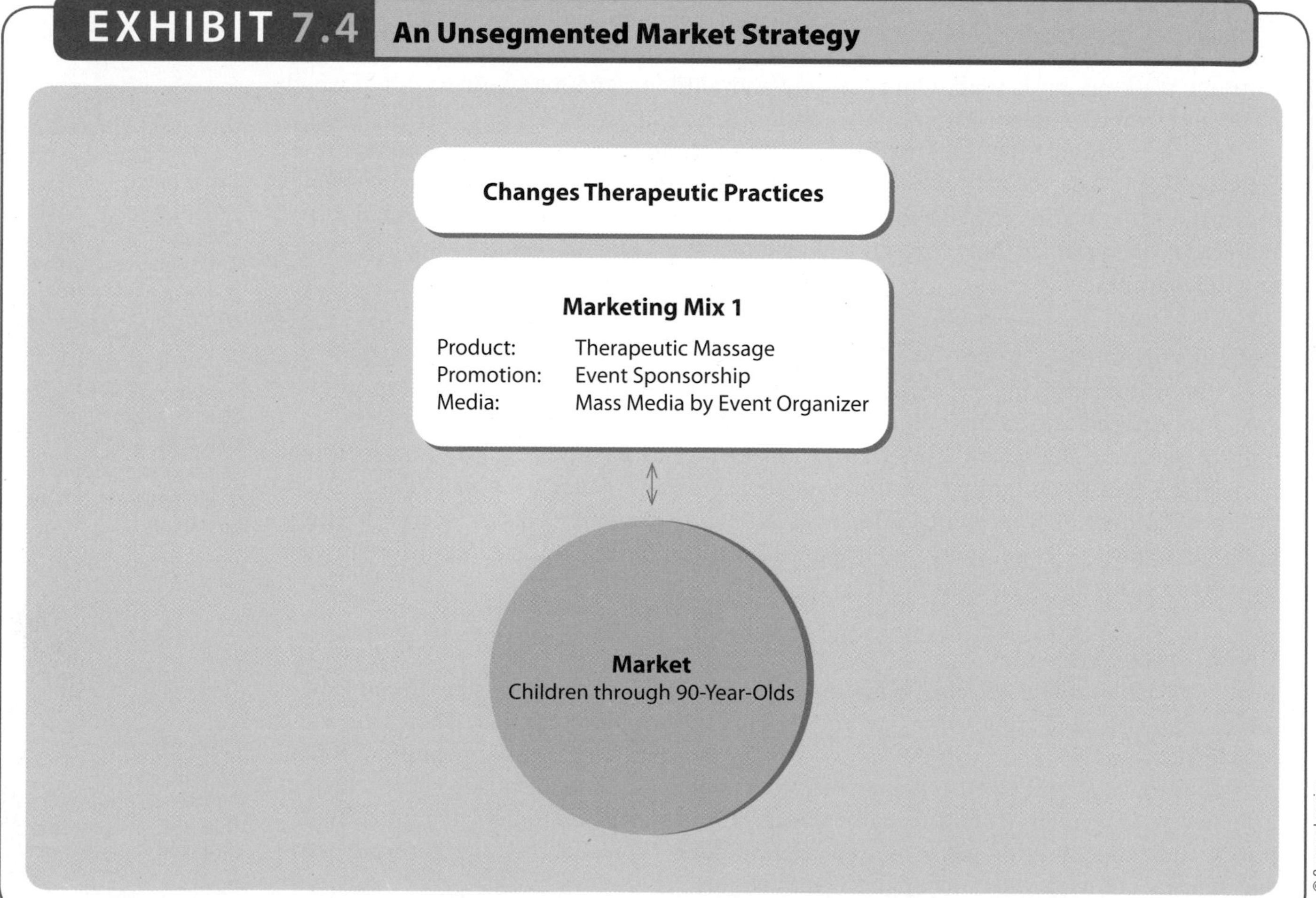

The Multi-Segment Strategy

With a view of the market that recognizes individual segments with different preferences, a firm is in a better position to tailor marketing mixes to various segments. If a firm determines that two or more market segments have the potential to be profitable and then develops a unique marketing mix for each segment, it is following a **multi-segment strategy**.

multi-segment strategy
A strategy that recognizes different preferences of individual market segments and develops a unique marketing mix for each.

Although Tanya Finney initially chose to adopt an unsegmented approach for Changes Therapeutic, over time she discovered that she did indeed have multiple market segments: athletes, autistic children, executives, people with arthritis, women ages 35 to 55, and more. Following the multi-segment approach, the company developed competitive advantages with multiple marketing mixes, based on differences in pricing, promotion, distribution, or the product itself, as shown in Exhibit 7.5. For stressed executives and office workers, Finney designed a chair massage offered in offices and schools at $1 per minute. She reached these customers through health fairs and advertisements in school administration offices. For autistic children, Finney developed scented menthol and lavender creams that are especially appealing to children diagnosed as autistic. Other oils were found to be attractive to other market segments. A third market segment is composed of people who spend much of their workday on their feet—military personnel, law enforcement officers, retail workers,

EXHIBIT 7.5 A Multi-Segment Market Strategy

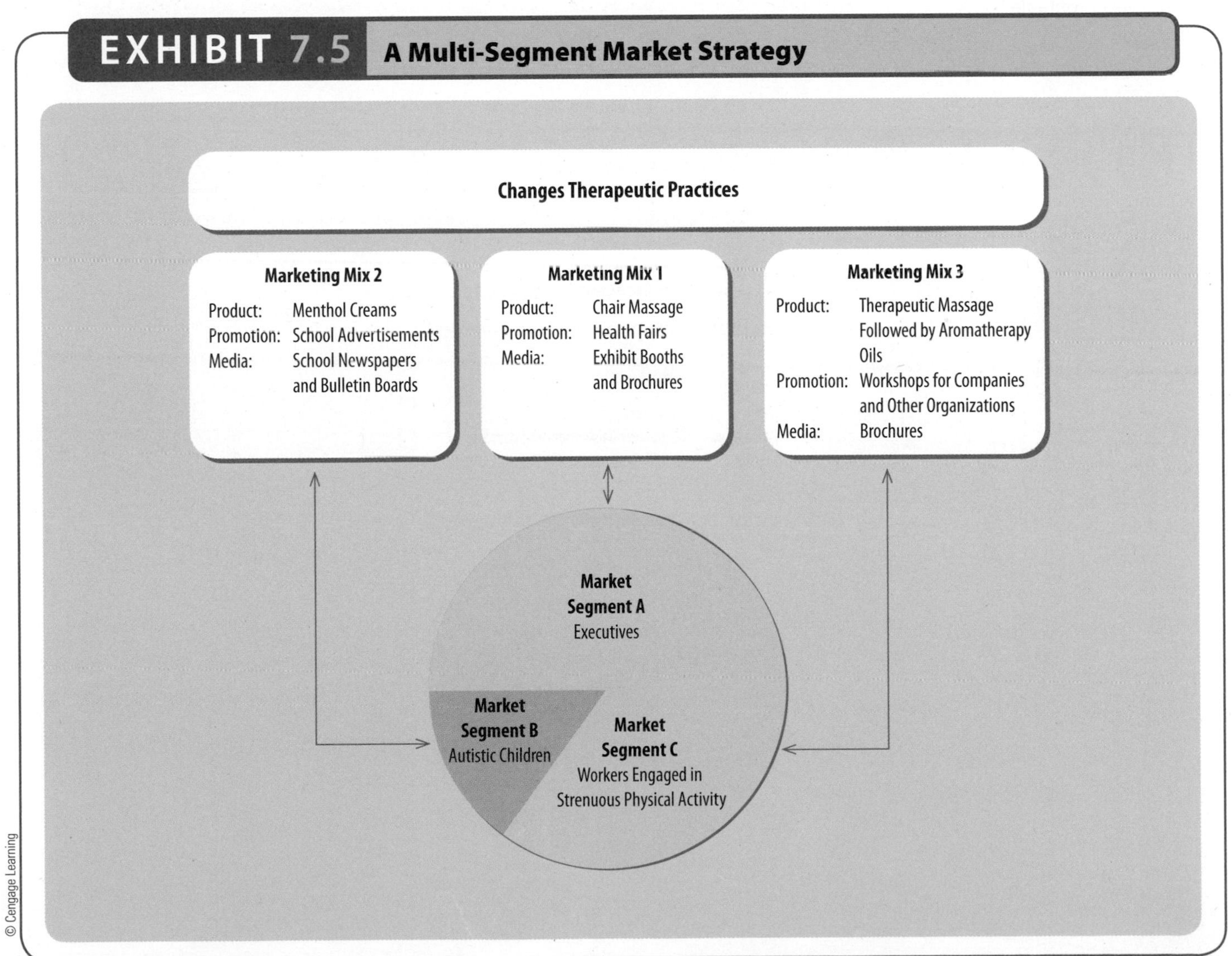

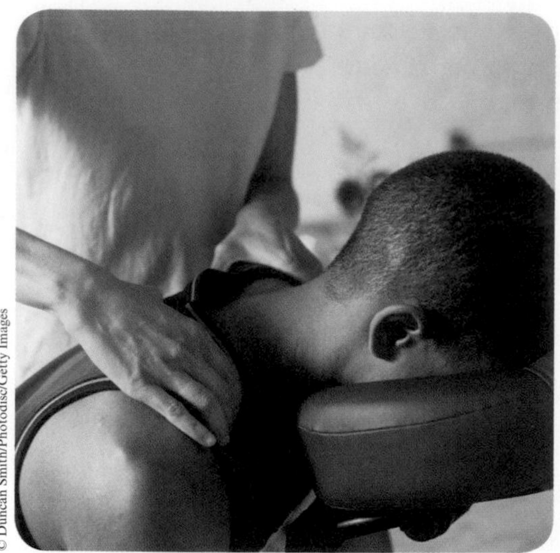
© Duncan Smith/Photodisc/Getty Images

etc. Finney found that this segment often has to be educated about the nature of therapeutic massages. She typically begins with chair massages, attending to neck and shoulder. In this way, the client becomes acclimated to the service and discovers the benefits of the massage for health and stress reduction. This experience leads them to purchase other products and services. Many small businesses in their early stages are resistant to using the multi-segment strategy because of the risk of spreading their limited resources too thinly among several marketing efforts.

The Single-Segment Strategy

When a firm recognizes that several distinct market segments exist but chooses to concentrate on reaching only one segment, it is following a **single-segment strategy**. The segment selected is the one that promises to offer the greatest profitability. Once again, a competitive advantage is achieved through a cost- or differentiation-based strategy. Changes Therapeutic decided to pursue a single-segment approach and selected the teenager market segment (see Exhibit 7.6). In this case, the firm specifically targeted young people with acne problems. Its products and services have been introduced to that market segment by way of school and health fairs.

single-segment strategy
A strategy that recognizes the existence of several distinct market segments but focuses on only the most profitable segment.

EXHIBIT 7.6 A Single-Segment Market Strategy

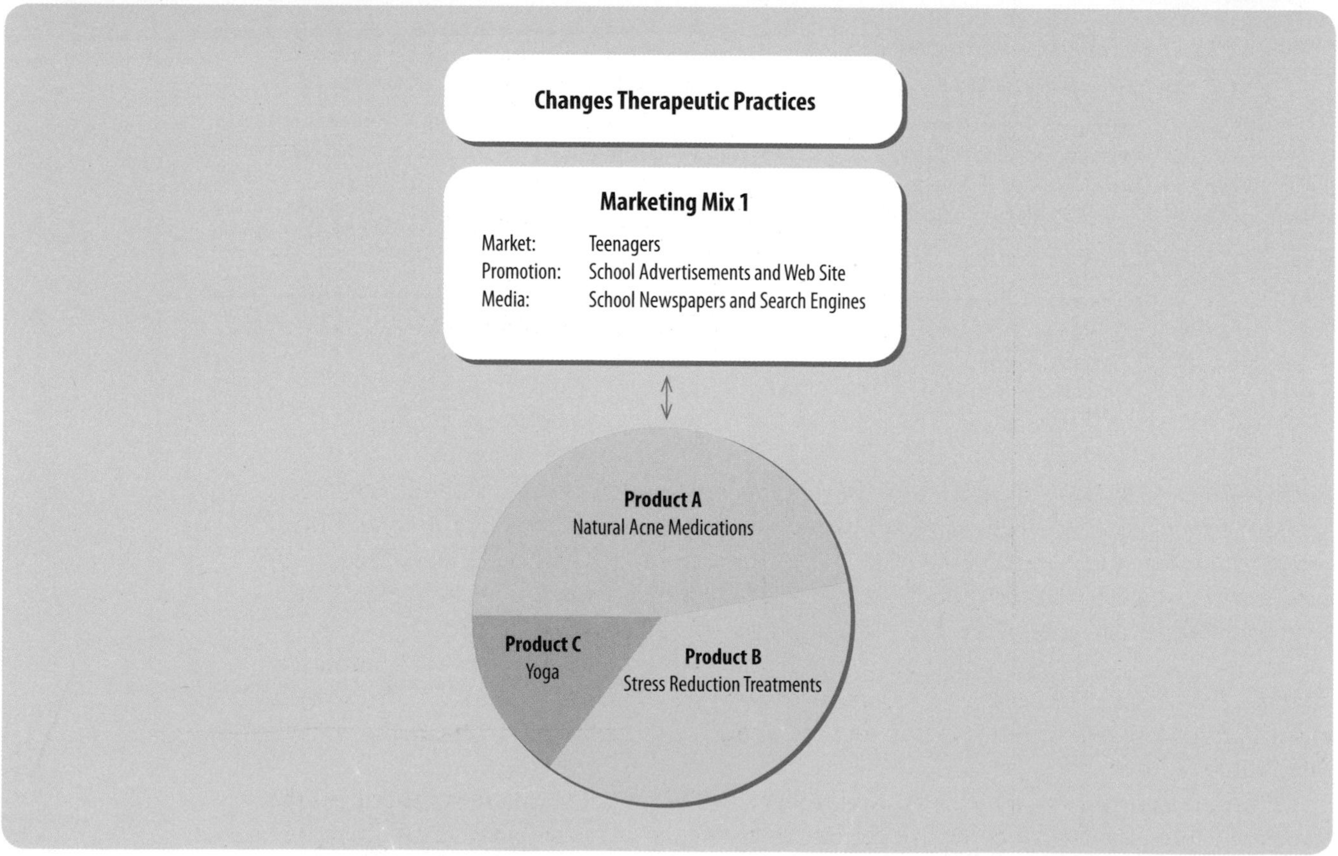

Changes Therapeutic Practices

Marketing Mix 1

Market:	Teenagers
Promotion:	School Advertisements and Web Site
Media:	School Newspapers and Search Engines

Product A Natural Acne Medications

Product B Stress Reduction Treatments

Product C Yoga

The single-segment approach is probably the wisest strategy for small businesses to use during initial marketing efforts. It allows a small firm to specialize and make better use of its limited resources. Then, once its reputation has been established, the firm will find it easier to enter new markets.

Estimating Market Potential

A small business can be successful only if sufficient market demand exists for its product or service. A sales forecast is the typical indicator of market adequacy, so it is particularly important to complete this assessment prior to writing the marketing plan. An entrepreneur who enters the marketplace without a forecast is much like an enthusiastic swimmer who leaves the diving board without checking the depth of the water—and the results can be nearly as painful! Many types of information from numerous sources are required to gauge market potential. This section discusses these information needs as it examines the forecasting process.

THE SALES FORECAST

Formally defined, a **sales forecast** is an estimate of how much of a product or service can be sold within a given market in a defined time period. The forecast can be stated in terms of dollars and/or units.

sales forecast
A prediction of how much of a product or service will be purchased within a given market during a specified time period.

Because a sales forecast revolves around a specific target market, that market should be defined as precisely as possible. The market description forms the forecasting boundary. If the market for desks is described as "all offices," the sales forecast will be extremely large. A more precise definition, such as "government agencies seeking solid wood desks priced between $800 and $1200," will result in a much smaller but possibly more useful forecast.

One sales forecast may cover a period of time that is a year or less, while another may extend over several years. Both short-term and long-term forecasts are needed for a well-constructed business plan.

A sales forecast is an essential component of the business plan because it is critical to assessing the feasibility of a new venture. If the market is insufficient, the business is destined for failure. A sales forecast is also useful in other areas of business planning. Production schedules, inventory policies, and personnel decisions all start with a sales forecast. Obviously, a forecast can never be perfect, and entrepreneurs should remember that a forecast can be wrong in either direction—either underestimating potential sales or overestimating potential sales.

LIMITATIONS TO FORECASTING

For a number of practical reasons, forecasting is used less frequently by small firms than by large firms. First, for any new business, forecasting circumstances are unique. Entrepreneurial inexperience, coupled with a new idea, represents the most difficult forecasting situation, as illustrated in Exhibit 7.7. An ongoing business that requires only an updated forecast for its existing product is in the most favorable forecasting position.

Second, a small business manager may be unfamiliar with methods of quantitative analysis. Not all forecasting must be quantitatively oriented—qualitative forecasting is often helpful and may be sufficient—but quantitative methods have repeatedly proven their value in forecasting.

Third, the typical small business entrepreneur and his or her team know little about the forecasting process. To overcome this deficiency, the owners of some small firms attempt to keep in touch with industry trends through contacts with appropriate trade associations.

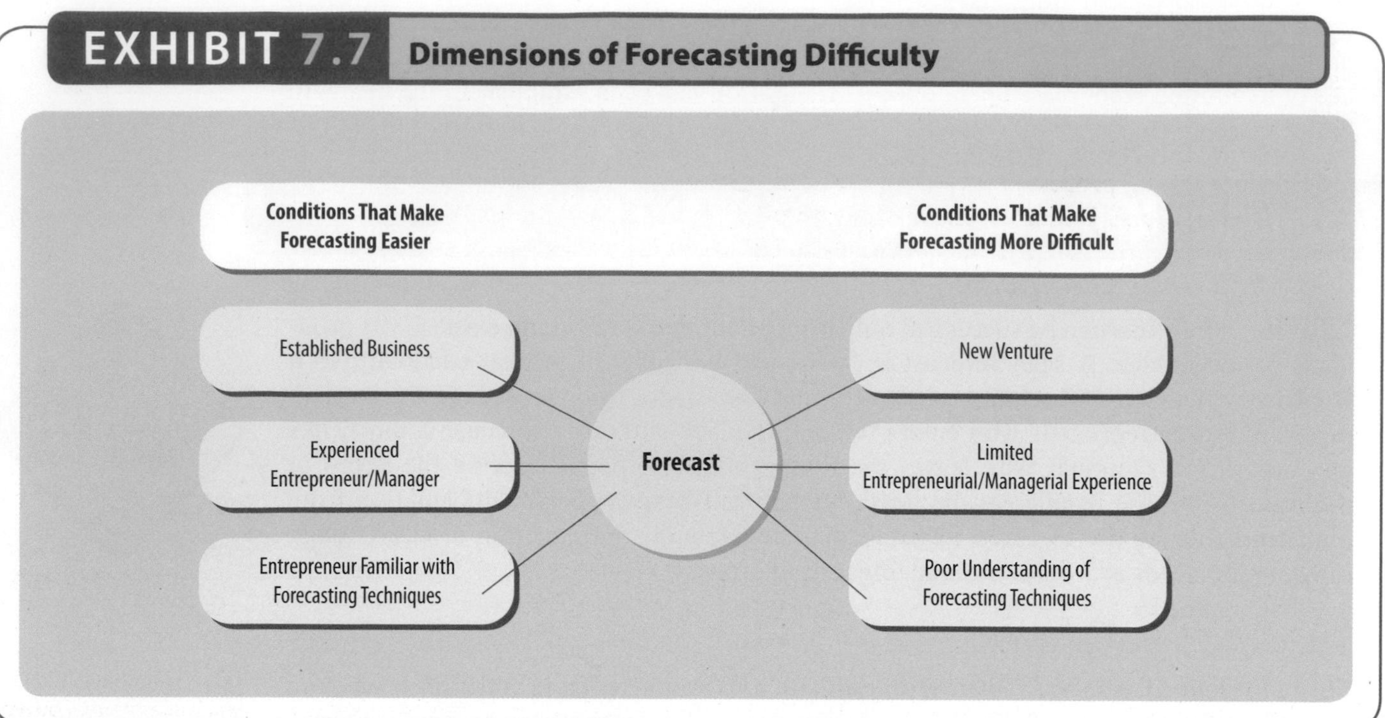

The professional members of a trade association are frequently better qualified to engage in sales forecasting. Most libraries have a copy of *National Trade and Professional Associations of the United States*, which lists these groups. Entrepreneurs can also obtain current information about business trends by regularly reading trade publications and magazines focused on small business ownership, such as *Entrepreneur* and *Inc.* Government publications, such as the *Federal Reserve Bulletin*, *Survey of Current Business*, and *Monthly Labor Review*, may also be of general interest. Subscribing to professional forecasting services is another way to obtain forecasts of general business conditions or specific forecasts for given industries.

Despite the difficulties, a small business entrepreneur should not neglect the forecasting task. Instead, she or he should remember how important the sales outlook in the business plan is to obtaining financing. The statement "We can sell as many as we can produce" does not satisfy the information requirements of potential investors.

TRANSFORM

Improving Forecasts Through Personal Networking

One of the mistakes many business owners make is failing to follow up on their forecasts and assess what went right and what went wrong. In an article entitled "Face-to-Face Marketing: Why It Matters More Now Than Ever!" for Skyline Trade Show Tips (http://www.skylinetradeshowtips.com, February 23, 2010), John Backstrom emphasizes that even in today's online world, nothing substitutes for face-to-face contact and that personal networking can help you determine how your plans can be improved.

THE FORECASTING PROCESS

Estimating market demand with a sales forecast is a multi-step process. Typically, the sales forecast is a composite of several individual forecasts, so the process involves merging these individual forecasts properly.

The forecasting process can be characterized by two important dimensions: the point at which the process is started and the nature of the predicting variable. Depending on the starting point, the process may be designated as a *breakdown process* or a *buildup process*. The nature of the predicting variable determines whether the forecasting is direct or indirect.

The Starting Point

In the **breakdown process**, sometimes called the **chain-ratio method**, the forecaster begins with a variable that has a very large scope and systematically works down to the sales forecast. This method is frequently used for consumer products forecasting. The initial variable might be a population figure for the target market. Through the use of percentages, an appropriate link is built to generate the sales forecast. For example, in an early marketing plan, the founders of Mayan Pigments identified market segments, including printing inks, paints and coatings, plastics, textiles and leathers, and paper and paperboard. Relying on secondary data from industry sources, they forecast global and domestic market demands for the various segments both in dollars and by product weight. They identified direct competitors and estimated their percentage shares of the market. Working from their startup size and target market, they then forecast the share they felt they could acquire in their first years.

breakdown process (chain-ratio method)
A forecasting method that begins with a large-scope variable and works down to the sales forecast.

buildup process
A forecasting method in which all potential buyers in a target market's submarkets are identified and then the estimated demand is added up.

direct forecasting
A forecasting method in which sales is the estimated variable.

One source of data is the U.S. Census Bureau, which compiles statistics on various population segments by, for example, gender, age, geographic location, and household income. Additional data on customer segments may be obtained through state and local government agencies, chambers of commerce, trade associations, and private enterprise sources, such as *Sales & Marketing Management* magazine's "Survey of Buying Power."

In contrast to the breakdown process, the **buildup process** calls for identifying all potential buyers in a target market's submarkets and then adding up the estimated demand. For example, a local dry-cleaning firm that is forecasting demand for cleaning high school letter jackets might estimate its market share within each area school as 20 percent. Then, by determining the number of high school students obtaining a letter jacket at each school—perhaps from school yearbooks—an analyst could estimate the total demand.

The buildup process is especially helpful for industrial goods forecasting. To estimate potential, forecasters often use data from the Census of Manufacturers by the U.S. Department of Commerce. The information can be broken down according to the North American Industry Classification System (NAICS), which classifies businesses by type of industry. Once the code for a group of potential industrial customers has been identified, the forecaster can obtain information on the number of establishments and their geographic location, number of employees, and annual sales. A sales forecast can be constructed by summing this information for several relevant codes.

Mayan Pigments

The Predicting Variable

In **direct forecasting**, which is the simplest form of forecasting, sales is the forecasted variable. Many times, however, sales cannot be predicted directly

indirect forecasting A forecasting method in which variables related to sales are used to project future sales.

and other variables must be used. **Indirect forecasting** takes place when surrogate variables are used to project the sales forecast. For example, if a firm lacks information about industry sales of baby cribs but has data on births, the strong correlation between the two variables allows planners to use the figures for births to help forecast industry sales for baby cribs.

For a new business, there are few things as important as identifying your market—nothing happens until someone buys something from your company. And if you plan to grow your business, understanding your market is essential. In this chapter, we introduced you to the steps necessary for putting together a marketing plan. The plan will be a living document for you as you manage your business. Every day, you will learn more about your market and how you can meet customer needs. And the marketing plan has an impact on many other areas of your business. In later chapters, you will see that your marketing strategy affects how many people you employ and what skills they need, the volume and selection of your inventory, the production processes you use, and many other business functions.

1. **Describe small business marketing.**
   - Small business marketing consists of business activities that direct the creation, development, and delivery of a bundle of satisfaction from the creator to the targeted user.
   - The product and/or service as a bundle of satisfaction has three levels: (1) core product/service, (2) actual product/service, and (3) augmented product/service.
   - Three distinct marketing philosophies are the production-, sales-, and consumer-oriented philosophies.
   - A small business should adopt a consumer orientation to marketing, as that philosophy is most consistent with long-term success.
   - Small business marketing activities include market analysis and determining the marketing mix.

2. **Identify the components of a formal marketing plan.**
   - The formal marketing plan should include sections on market analysis, the competition, and marketing strategy.
   - The market analysis should include a customer profile.
   - A SWOT analysis is helpful in assessing the competition.
   - The "4 Ps" of marketing strategy that should be discussed in the marketing plan are (1) product decisions affecting the total product and/or service, (2) place (distribution) activities, (3) pricing decisions, and (4) promotional activities.

3. **Discuss the nature of the marketing research process.**
   - Marketing research involves the gathering, processing, interpreting, and reporting of marketing information.
   - The cost of marketing research should be evaluated against its benefits.
   - The steps in the marketing research process are identifying the informational need, searching for secondary data, collecting primary data, and interpreting the data gathered.

4. **Define *market segmentation*, and discuss its related strategies.**
   - A focus strategy relies on market segmentation, which is the process of dividing the total market for a product and/or service into smaller groups with similar needs, such that each group is likely to respond favorably to a specific marketing strategy.
   - Broad segmentation variables that represent major dimensions of a market are benefit variables and demographic variables.
   - Three types of market segmentation strategies are (1) the unsegmented approach, (2) the multi-segment approach, and (3) the single-segment approach.
   - The unsegmented strategy—when a business defines the total market as its target—is also known as mass marketing.
   - A firm that determines that two or more market segments have the potential to be profitable and then develops a unique marketing mix for each segment is following a multi-segment strategy.

- A firm that follows a single-segment strategy recognizes that several distinct market segments exist but chooses to concentrate on reaching only one segment, which promises the greatest profitability.

5. Explain the different methods of forecasting sales.

- A sales forecast is an estimate of how much of a product or service will be purchased within a given market during a defined time period.
- Business owners frequently lack experience or skills in making forecasts and should be cautious about the accuracy of their predictions.
- The forecasting process may be either a breakdown or a buildup process and may be either direct or indirect, depending on the predicting variable.

Key Terms

small business marketing p. 200
core product/service p. 200
actual product/service p. 200
augmented product/service p. 200
market analysis p. 202
marketing mix p. 202
customer profile p. 203
intellectual property p. 207
marketing research p. 209
secondary data p. 211
primary data p. 212
market p. 216
market segmentation p. 217
segmentation variables p. 217
benefit variables p. 217
demographic variables p. 217
unsegmented strategy (mass marketing) p. 218
multi-segment strategy p. 219
single-segment strategy p. 220
sales forecast p. 221
breakdown process (chain-ratio method) p. 223
buildup process p. 223
direct forecasting p. 223
indirect forecasting p. 224

Discussion Questions

1. What is the scope of small business marketing? What do you think the differences in marketing might be if you were a manager in a large corporation?
2. How do the three marketing philosophies differ? Select a product and discuss marketing tactics that could be used to implement each philosophy.
3. What are the obstacles to adopting a consumer orientation in a small firm?
4. Briefly describe each of the components of a formal marketing plan.
5. What are the steps in the marketing research process? Which step do you feel would be the hardest for you to take? Why?
6. What are the major considerations in designing a questionnaire?
7. Briefly explain the three components of the definition of a market, as presented in this chapter.
8. What types of variables are used for market segmentation? Would a small firm use the same variables as a large business? Why or why not?
9. Explain the difference between a multi-segment strategy and a single-segment strategy. Which one is more likely to be appealing to a small firm? Why?
10. Explain why forecasting is used more widely by large firms than by small ones.

You Make the Call

SITUATION 1

Tina and George Showalter opened the Blonde Bear Bed & Breakfast in Kenai, Alaska, in 2005. According to Tina, "Our first summer, we did great with word-of-mouth advertising, and then we got involved in the Internet, and it has pretty much exploded from there." In this town with a population of under 10,000, 50 businesses signed up with MerchantCircle.com, a local business listing service. The site provides business descriptions, reviews, blogs, coupons, maps, and links among the companies. The cross-promotional and networking benefits have proven valuable to the businesses on the site.

Sources: Amanda C. Kooser, "Go Local," *Entrepreneur*, March 2007, pp. 72–75; and http://www.merchantcircle.com, accessed March 14, 2009.

Question 1 What businesses do you think would benefit most from being on a local website in your hometown?
Question 2 How do businesses that provide such local Web services differ from newspapers and Yellow Pages?

SITUATION 2

Should infomercials be part of your marketing plan? The Sharper Image began marketing with infomercials in 2000, when they ran a two-minute spot for the Razor Scooter 10 to 50 times per day. According to company founder Richard Thalheimer, The Sharper Image sold just enough scooters over the phone to break even on the ads. What made it worthwhile was the effect on in-store sales. Those jumped tenfold.

Thalheimer developed some guidelines for infomercials:

- Margins for products advertised should be at least 50 percent.
- You have to cover the costs of airtime.
- Longer infomercials are more costly, but the costs are worth it for complex products.
- If you are breaking even or better, expand to more channels and time slots.
- When sales flatten, stop.

Flattening sales at The Sharper Image eventually led to Thalheimer's departure. His newest company, RichardSolo.com, relies on Internet sales rather than infomercials.

Sources: Richard Thalheimer, "Ask Richard Thalheimer," *Inc.*, March 2007; and http://richardsolo.com, accessed March 14, 2009.

Question 1 Do you think that infomercials might work better for certain market segments than others? If so, describe those segments.
Question 2 Do you watch infomercials? If so, did you ever purchase a product as a result? If not, why not?

SITUATION 3

Ricardo De La Blanca Brigati is CEO of the DLB Group, a full-service marketing company with about $10 million in revenues operating throughout the Americas and in Spain. He encourages his clients to focus on African American, Hispanic, Asian American, and Native American consumers. He sees the buying power of these segments, but few small businesses are making adjustments to serve them. De La Blanca Brigati reports that instead of developing a focused marketing plan aimed at these groups, companies might hire a minority salesperson or conduct a condescending advertising campaign in which they represent minorities as poor people in sad situations. DLB's website, on the other hand, gives examples of how the company helps clients, both in the United States and abroad, develop comprehensive marketing strategies that set them apart by adapting to (and respecting) other cultures.

Sources: http://www.dlbgroup.com/, accessed January 23, 2011; and Karen E. Klein, "What Companies Get Wrong When Marketing to Minorities," http://www.businessweek.com/smallbiz/content/dec2010/sb20101213_643259.htm, accessed January 23, 2011.

Question 1 Identify a minority group to which you do not belong. What steps could you take to learn about that market segment in order to sell the consumers a product or service?
Question 2 Suppose your small business were contacted by a company in another country that wanted to sell your products in its market. What would you want to know about that market before going into it? Choose any country besides the United States and determine what changes you would have to make to your marketing plan to adjust to the different culture.

Experiential Exercises

1. View the website of a local small business. Interview the owner of that business about how the website fits into his or her overall marketing plan.
2. Assume you are planning to market a new breath mint. What social media do you think would be the best to get the word out about your product? Describe the strategy you would use.
3. Interview someone from a small business assistance organization (e.g., Small Business Development Center, Service Corps of Retired Executives, chamber of commerce, etc.). Does she or he help clients or members with marketing research or with sales forecasting? What does she or he consider to be the best sources of market information?

Small Business & Entrepreneurship Resource Center

1. A business must supply satisfaction to its customers if it is to thrive in today's markets. Mark Vadon started a company called Blue Nile, which sells diamonds and jewelry online. Describe why Vadon started his firm, and how it is differentiated from other diamond sellers.

   Source: Amanda C. Kooser, April Y. Pennington, Karen E. Spaeder, and Nichole L. Torres, "Beyond Their Years: These Entrepreneurs Have It All: Brains, Business Savvy and Millions of Dollars," *Entrepreneur*, Vol. 31, No. 11 (November 2003), pp. 74–83.

2. To forecast sales using the buildup process, forecasters often use data from the U.S. Census and U.S. Department of Commerce. The information is broken down according to the North American Industry Classification System (NAICS), which categorizes businesses by type of industry. Describe the NAICS system and how it has been accepted (or not) as an alternative to the older Standard Industrial Classification (SIC).

   Source: "NAICS Not Yet a Common Language," *Catalog Age*, Vol. 21, No. 11 (October 1, 2004).

Video Case 7

READYMADE MAGAZINE (P. 706)

ReadyMade markets itself as a magazine catering to GenNest, the group of consumers ages 25 to 35 who are just settling down after college. But *ReadyMade* appeals to a wide variety of readers, with subscribers in all age groups. This diversity offers a unique challenge to *ReadyMade* as it tries to promote itself to advertisers who need to know what sort of people will be reached through advertisements in the publication.

ALTERNATIVE CASE FOR CHAPTER 7

Case 18, Smarter.com, p. 728

Business Plan Laying the Foundation

As part of laying the foundation for your own business plan, respond to the following questions regarding the marketing plan, marketing research, market segmentation, and sales forecasting.

Marketing Plan Questions

1. Who is your competition?
2. Have you conducted a SWOT analysis?
3. What is the customer profile for your product and/or service?
4. How will you identify prospective customers?
5. What geographic area will you serve?
6. What are the distinguishing characteristics of your product and/or service?
7. What steps have already been taken to develop your product and/or service?
8. What do you plan to name your product and/or service?
9. Will there be a warranty?
10. How will you set the price for your product and/or service?
11. What type of distribution plan will you use?
12. Will you export to other countries?

13. What type of selling effort will you use?
14. What special selling skills will be required?
15. What types of advertising and sales promotion will you use?
16. Can you use the Internet to promote your company and product/service?

Marketing Research Questions

1. What types of research should be conducted to collect the information you need?
2. How much will this research cost?
3. What sources of secondary data will address your informational needs?
4. What sources of relevant data are available in your local library?
5. What sources of outside professional assistance would you consider using to help with marketing research?
6. Is there information available on the Internet that might be helpful?
7. What research questions do you need answers to?

Market Segmentation Questions

1. Will you focus on a limited market within the industry?
2. What segmentation variables will you use to define your target market?
3. If you determine that several distinct market segments exist, will you concentrate on just one segment?

Forecasting Questions

1. How do you plan to forecast sales for your product and/or service?
2. What sources of forecasting assistance have you consulted?
3. What sales forecasting techniques are most appropriate to your needs?
4. What is the sales forecast for your product and/or service?
5. How reliable is your sales forecast?

CHAPTER 8

The Organizational Plan: Teams, Legal Structures, Alliances, and Directors

In the SPOTLIGHT
Company X

In the fairytale of entrepreneurship, your partners work as hard and as diligently as you. They watch your back as you build armies of skilled employees, take strategic market positions, and share the triumphs of vanquished competition and exceeded milestones.

Yuri Arcurs/Getty Images

During the early years of my partnership, I imagined my partner sharing important family moments—whether that meant beaming at each other's children at graduation or leaning on each other in times of personal loss and need. It hardly mattered. My belief was I had formed a team to tackle the coming journey.

As a seasoned entrepreneur of fifteen years who had never had a business partner, I imagined the new venture as more of a brotherhood. We would combine our Rolodexes, our life experiences, and be twice as prepared for any eventuality. We had different styles, of course, and very different strengths, which would bring differing and invaluable perspectives to each new business problem. We were roughly the same age and both had new families with young children.

Although I didn't know him well, his family was well-known and respected, and his educational credentials were solid. Our fledgling company was growing in triple digits and cash was pouring in. By all appearances, we were well-positioned for a happy ending to the story.

Like any good "B" movie, after the build up just detailed, you know the train wreck is eminent. Yet as a participant, I never saw it coming. There was one moment a year into the venture when I took a cryptic e-mail, which had

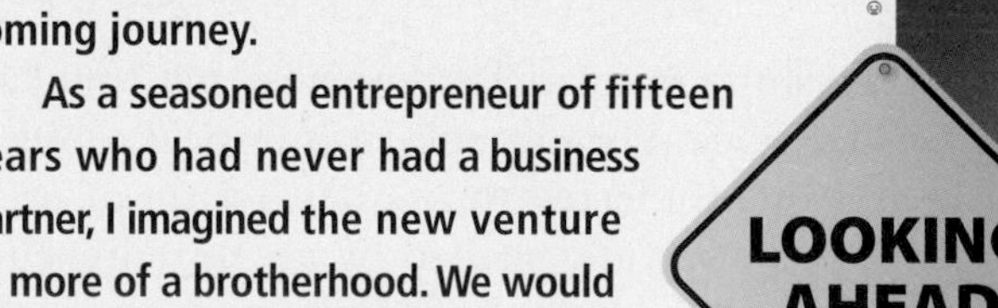

LOOKING AHEAD

© iStockphoto.com/Dan Bachman

After studying this chapter, you should be able to...

1. Describe the characteristics and value of a strong management team.
2. Explain the common legal forms of organization used by small businesses.
3. Identify factors to consider in choosing among the primary legal forms of organization.
4. Discuss the unique features and restrictions of five specialized organizational forms.
5. Understand the nature of strategic alliances and their uses in small businesses.
6. Describe the effective use of boards of directors and advisory councils.

raised my suspicion, to my lawyer. Together we puzzled over it until, with great feigned wisdom, he responded, "If you can't trust your partners, who can you trust?" Who indeed? The opportunity to discover a big problem was missed and we pressed ahead.

When the problem was finally discovered, two and a half years after our founding, I was completely unprepared. The headlines of this story are gory and embarrassing; more than $1 million lost from the company, balance sheet inventory securing bank debt revealed to lack title (it had never been paid for), one-third of the company employees (mostly located overseas) involved in some way in this, as well as two of our three joint-venture factories.

We had outstanding contracts for personal residences of household names in the entertainment industry and suddenly had neither the cash, staff, nor production facilities to fulfill them. To make matters worse, consistent with our industry, we had taken 50 percent deposits on these multi-million dollar contracts and had spent the money to procure materials; the money was now gone.

Meanwhile, my now ex-partner had liquidated all his U.S. assets and moved them overseas, and he contacted my customers and offered to finish their contracts for lower prices. With no sizeable assets to recover, huge legal bills burning limited capital and a disinterested judiciary, it became painfully obvious that I was unlikely to find satisfaction.

***Source:* Excerpted from Richard Rhodes, "Partnership Problems and Loss," http://www.entrepreneurship.org/en/resource-center/partnership-problems-and-loss.aspx, accessed November 3, 2010. © 2007 Richard Rhodes. Used with permission.**

Popular notions aside, most successful entrepreneurs do not operate as "Lone Rangers" in the business world. In fact, research suggests enterprises that thrive are usually led by talented and effective *teams* of entrepreneurs, especially those who have had prior new venture experience.[1] Entrepreneurship experts Jeffrey Timmons and Stephen Spinelli emphasize this point: "Owning and running the whole show effectively puts a ceiling on growth. . . . It is extremely difficult to grow a higher-potential venture by working single-handedly. Higher-potential entrepreneurs build a team, an organization, and a company."[2]

Unfortunately, team leadership in a small enterprise all too often presents its share of heartaches, as was the case for Richard Rhodes and his unnamed startup (see In the Spotlight). The high hopes of partnership and camaraderie in business can easily be dashed on the rocks of real life. People are imperfect, after all, so working closely with others is bound to lead to a certain amount of disappointment. But in all but the simplest of businesses, the entrepreneur's personal talents often need to be supplemented with the experience and abilities of other individuals. Therefore, a venture's prospects typically are most promising when its leadership is composed of competent, resourceful, and tenacious individuals who are committed to doing their best.[3] With that in mind, it is important for an entrepreneur to identify and attract a strong management team. A business plan that provides for effective leadership is appealing to both potential investors and prospective managerial personnel.

Beyond assembling a well-balanced leadership group, an entrepreneur must make a number of other important organizational decisions. For example, it is critical to select an appropriate ownership structure, which is often referred to as a legal form of organization. The direction of the business will be powerfully shaped by an entrepreneur's decision to organize as a sole proprietorship, a partnership, a corporation, or one of the other available forms. The organizational form should match the needs of the business, but getting it right can be a challenge.

This chapter also explains the use of strategic alliances, which are becoming increasingly popular among small businesses and can be strategically important to their performance. And, finally, we describe the role of boards of directors or advisory councils for small businesses and provide insights on how to make the most of them. All of these elements of a small business should be carefully considered in the organizational plan. The quality of an entrepreneur's decisions on these issues can greatly enhance the performance of the company—or doom it to failure. But in the sections that follow, we will show you how to navigate the potentially dangerous waters of planning for these facets of the business and guide you toward improved odds for success.

Building a Management Team

management team Managers and other key persons who give a company its general direction.

If a firm is extremely small, the founder will probably be the key manager and perhaps the only manager. In most firms, however, others share leadership roles with the owner(s), which creates opportunities to leverage their combined networks and resources for the good of the company. In general, the **management team** consists of individuals with supervisory responsibilities, as well as nonsupervisory personnel who play key roles in the business.[4] For example, members of a management team might include a financial manager who supervises a small office staff and another person who directs the marketing effort.

If you should find that you don't have your "dream team" in place when you are just getting started (after all, most talented people are well rewarded where they are and are likely to resist the idea of joining a high-risk venture), understand that the team arrangement does not have to be permanent. Though it can be difficult to do, sometimes you have to respectfully and appropriately let individuals go when they cannot or will not effectively support the business; new members can be added to the team as the need arises.[5]

Strong management can make the best of a good business idea by securing the resources needed to make it work. Of course, even a highly competent management team cannot rescue a firm that is based on a weak business concept or that lacks adequate resources. But the importance of strong management to startups is evident in the attitudes of prospective investors, who consider the quality of a new venture's management to be one of the most important factors in decisions to invest or to take a pass. In other words, investors know that enterprises typically perform poorly if they are guided by weak or incapable managers.

As indicated earlier, a management team often can bring greater strength to a venture than an individual entrepreneur can. One reason for this is that a team can provide a diversity of talent to meet various managerial needs, which can be especially helpful to startups built on new technologies that must manage a broad range of factors. In addition, a team can provide greater assurance of continuity, since the departure of one member of a team is less devastating to a business than the departure of a sole entrepreneur.

The competence required in a management team depends on the type of business and the nature of its operations.[6] For example, a software development firm and a restaurant call for very different types of business experience. Whatever the business, a small firm needs managers with an appropriate combination of educational background and experience. In evaluating the qualifications of an applicant for a key position, an entrepreneur needs to know whether the individual has experience in a related type of business, as a manager or as an entrepreneur.

In many cases, startup owners stack the management team with family and friends, rather than seeking balanced expertise. This has a definite upside. The owner knows these people well and trusts them, they often work for less compensation (despite the elevated risk of joining a new venture), and they are more likely to make personal sacrifices to keep the business alive. The downside is that the team can quickly become very homogeneous, lack overall competence, lean toward feelings of entitlement, and carry the baggage of family dysfunction into the enterprise. All of these factors—the negative and the positive—should be taken into consideration when hiring family and friends.

ACHIEVING BALANCE

Not all members of a management team need competence in all areas—the key is balance. If one member has expertise in finance, another should have an adequate marketing background. And the venture will need someone who can supervise employees effectively.[7] This diversity in perspectives and work styles is what enables the completion of complex tasks, but it can also lead to serious conflict, which can squeeze all the energy and enthusiasm out of a venture.[8]

Even when entrepreneurs recognize the need for team members with varying expertise, they frequently seek to replicate their own personalities and management styles. Interpersonal compatibility and cooperation among team members are necessary for effective collaboration, and cohesive teams tend to perform better.[9] However, experience suggests that a functionally diverse and balanced team will be more likely to cover all the business bases, giving the company a competitive edge.

To ensure balance, a management team should comprise both competent insiders and outside specialists. For example, a small firm will benefit greatly by developing working relationships with a commercial bank, a law firm, and an accounting firm. (A number of outside sources of managerial assistance are identified and discussed in Chapter 19.) In

LIVING THE DREAM

entrepreneurial experiences

© iStockphoto.com/Angelika Schwarz

Can't Afford a CFO? Why Not Rent One?

As businesses struggle to keep their financial heads above water, they may not be able to add the personnel they need to their management teams. It's just too expensive! The economic downturn in recent years has only compounded the problem. During these challenging times, many small businesses could use some help in balancing their books or establishing a strategy that will pull them out of the "financial black hole" in which they may find themselves. What they need is the leadership of a CFO (a chief financial officer), but that would easily run up annual salary costs by $100,000 or more—*twice* as much, in some cases. That's far more than many small firms can afford, so what's an entrepreneur to do?

© Yuri Arcurs/Shutterstock.com

Jerry L. Mills is sure he has an answer. Mills launched B2B CFO Partners LLC in 1987 to address this very problem. Rather than expanding the executive team and bearing the related costs, businesses are encouraged to *rent* a CFO from his company instead. What Mills has in mind is not exactly renting, though—it's more like a long-term outsourcing relationship, where the CFO stays with the company indefinitely and knowledge gained remains with the firm. With services starting at $300 to $400 per month, many small companies are very interested, and B2B CFO Partners is growing (650 clients and counting). For the price, client firms get the services of a seasoned professional (25 years of CFO experience, on average), along with access to financial software and established banking and lending relationships.

Far beyond establishing proper bookkeeping systems, these CFOs can help business owners understand the big picture of their financial situation, while guiding them through strategic and day-to-day decisions and charting a sensible path for long-term growth. And, being outsiders, they can also provide a money- and time-saving reality check. "[Bringing in a part-time CFO] has really given us a level of confidence that we did not have in decision making," observes one small business manager. That alone can make it all worthwhile.

Sources: Raymund Flandez, "For Rent: Chief Financial Officer," *Wall Street Journal*, September 22, 2009, p. B7; and "About B2B CFO," http://www.b2bcfo.com/part-time-cfo/about-b2b-cfo, accessed November 9, 2010. **http://www.b2bcfo.com**

addition to providing counsel and guidance to the management team, an active board of directors or advisory council (discussed later in this chapter) can also help connect the venture with external sources of expertise and assistance through the members' networks of business relationships. The value of a good board, in this regard, cannot be overstated.

EXPANDING SOCIAL NETWORKS

Sometimes it's not *what* you know but *who* you know that matters. Not only can the management team help the venture obtain investment and technology resources, but it can also (perhaps most importantly) connect the enterprise with a social network that provides access to a wide range of resources beyond the reach of individual team members. A **social network** is the web of relationships that a person has with other people, including roommates or other acquaintances from college, former employees and business associates, contacts through community organizations like the Rotary Club, and friends from church or synagogue. But it doesn't end there. A friend from college may not have what you need, but she may know someone who does. It is often said that business is all about relationships, a principle that is certainly not lost on successful entrepreneurs. And the power of social networks is expanded tremendously as well-connected people are added to the management team.

social network An interconnected system of relationships with other people.

What does an entrepreneur need from his or her network? That all depends on the situation. Howard Aldrich and Nancy Carter, two highly regarded experts on building management teams and social networks, have found that nearly half of those who are starting businesses use their networks to access information or get advice. About one-fourth use their networks to gain introductions to other people, while a much smaller percentage use connections to obtain money, business services, physical facilities and equipment, help with personal needs, and other forms of assistance.[10] Clearly, a healthy system of personal relationships can help a small business access the resources it needs to get established and grow.

Beyond providing access to resources, social networks can be especially helpful in communicating legitimacy and jump-starting sales. New ventures and small businesses often find it difficult to "get the business ball rolling" because potential customers simply don't know them well enough. Reputable firms may hesitate to do business with a company that doesn't have a demonstrated track record for reliable delivery or quality products or services. But acquiring one or more high-profile customers may persuade others to give a relatively unknown company a shot at their business, too. For an entrepreneur, having a healthy social network and a management team with helpful connections can be critical in establishing a solid reputation.

Some small business owners are tapping into the expanding universe of social-networking tools to attract customers, connect with peers, and share advice about common problems. In fact, a recent study found that the rate of adoption of social media tools by small companies has doubled in the last year, which greatly expands the reach of their network-building efforts.[11] Here are a few of the more popular choices:

- **LinkedIn.com:** Allows users to record contact details of people they know and trust in business; excellent for recruiting professionals or for connecting with groups of individuals who share common interests
- **Twitter.com:** Enables people to send brief updates, or micro-blogs, to those signed up to receive them via computer or cell phone; powerful tool for sending out information and doing publicity and mobile marketing
- **Yelp.com:** Permits users to rate and comment on local businesses; good for getting feedback from customers; cheaper than surveys
- **Facebook.com:** Lets users join networks organized by city, workplace, school, or region; superb for connecting with business contacts users seldom see and for observing how people interact in social networks

Network Development

Research shows that we can only maintain 150 close connections at any one time, so we need to make them count! Branch out and consider diversifying by location and industry to add breadth to your network. Remember that relationships work both ways, so share useful information, knowledge, and compassion if you want to see your investment pay off. To learn more, see Chris Brogan, "The Network Is Everything," *Entrepreneur*, Vol. 38, No. 11 (October 2010); and Michael Port, "Keep Your Cards to Yourself," *Entrepreneur*, Vol. 37, No. 12, p. 34 (December 2009).

The number of social-networking tools continues to expand rapidly, and keeping up with all of them is a challenge. However, these alternatives can help you make connections easier, faster, and more conveniently—but only if you use them.

Regardless of how you pull it together, an active and robust network is necessary for building **social capital**, which we refer to as the advantage created by an individual's connections within a network of social relationships. But this advantage doesn't develop overnight or by accident. It takes years to build social capital, and the building blocks are well known—being reliable as a friend, being fair in your dealings, being true to your word.

social capital
The advantage created by an individual's connections in a social network.

The principle of reciprocation can be extremely helpful in adding to whatever social capital you already have. In his popular book on influence, Robert Cialdini defines **reciprocation** as a subtle but powerful sense of obligation, deeply embedded in every society, to repay in kind what another person has done for us or provided to us.[12] In general, people naturally feel that they should return favors. You can easily prime the pump of social capital by being the first to lend a hand and then watch those you assist come to your rescue when you run up against a challenge and ask for help. You don't have to fake it; just slow down a bit and take a genuine interest in the needs of your friends and acquaintances. And helping others doesn't have to be costly; in today's information economy, passing along an important bit of news or insight is easy and free—but it can be as good as gold! So think ahead, and reach out to help where you can. Your social capital is sure to increase, binding friends and contacts to you and providing a solid foundation for building a business.

reciprocation
A powerful social rule based on an obligation to repay in kind what another has done for or provided to us.

Choosing a Legal Form of Organization

Social networks are fundamental to success in business, but these focus on external relationships. When launching a new business, an entrepreneur must also choose a legal form of organization, which will determine who the actual owners of the business are. The most basic options are the sole proprietorship, partnership, and C corporation. More specialized forms of organization exist, but many small businesses find one of these common forms suitable for their needs. After outlining the primary options, we look first at some criteria for choosing among them and then introduce a number of specialized forms (see Exhibit 8.1) that offer their own unique features and advantages.

THE SOLE PROPRIETORSHIP OPTION

sole proprietorship
A business owned by one person, who bears unlimited liability for the enterprise.

A **sole proprietorship**, the most basic business form, is a company owned by one person. An individual proprietor has title to all business assets and is subject to the claims of creditors. He or she receives all of the firm's profits but must also assume all losses, bear

EXHIBIT 8.1 Forms of Legal Organization for Small Businesses

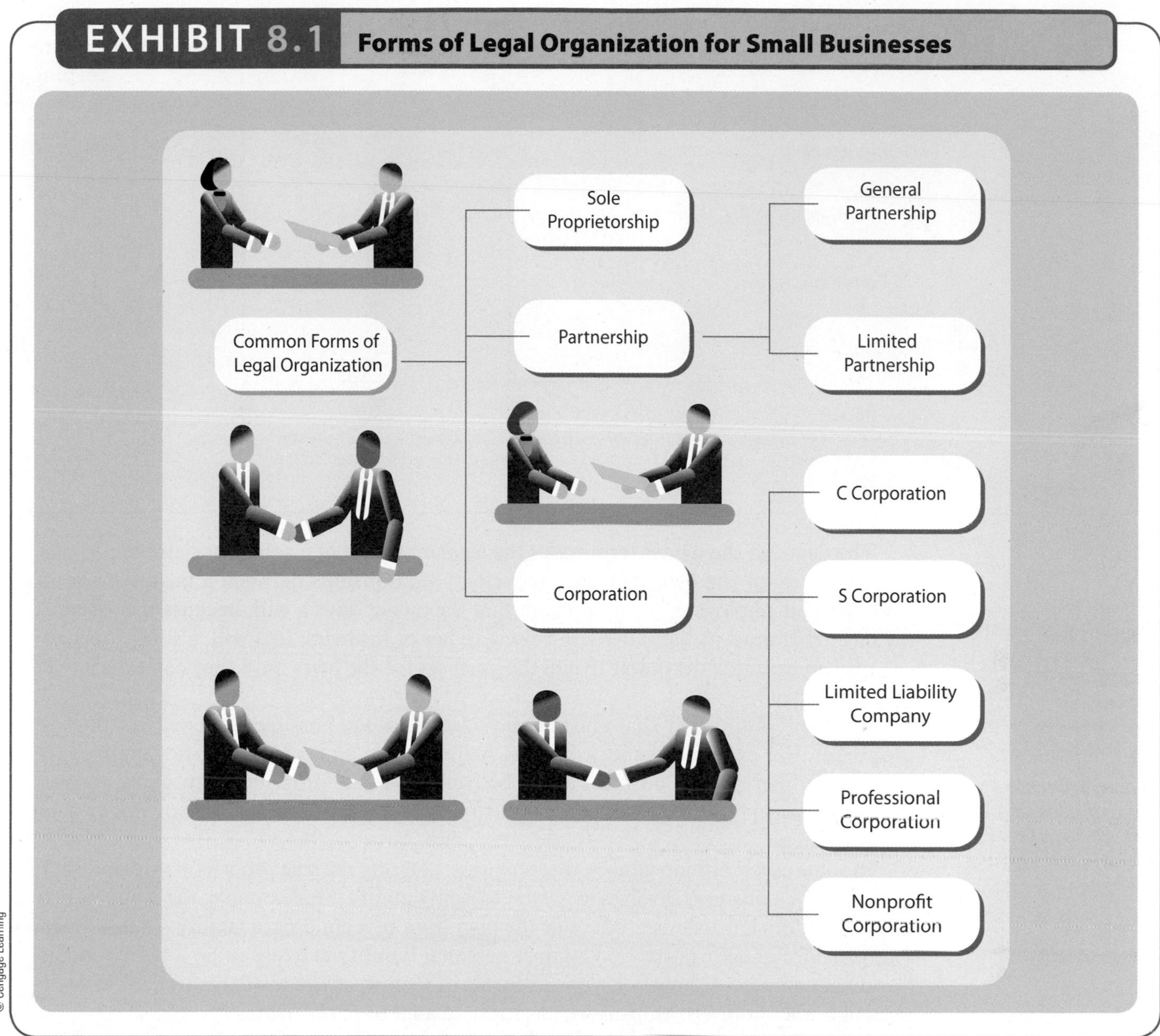

all risks, and pay all debts. Although this form certainly is not right for everyone, forming a sole proprietorship is nonetheless the simplest and cheapest way to start operation. Most states do not even require such companies to have a business license. Because of the ease of startup, the vast majority of small businesses (68.5 percent)[13] adopt this legal structure (see Exhibit 8.2).

In a sole proprietorship, an owner is free from interference by partners, shareholders, and directors. However, a sole proprietorship lacks some of the advantages of other legal forms. For example, there are no limits on the owner's personal liability—that is, the owner of the business has **unlimited liability**, and thus his or her personal assets can be taken by business creditors if the enterprise fails. For this reason, the sole proprietorship form is usually the practical choice only for very small businesses. In addition, sole proprietors are not employees of the business and cannot benefit from the advantage of many tax-free fringe benefits, such as insurance and hospitalization plans, which are often provided by corporations for their employees.

unlimited liability
Liability on the part of an owner that extends beyond the owner's investment in the business.

EXHIBIT 8.2 Percentage of Small Businesses by Legal Form of Organization[14]

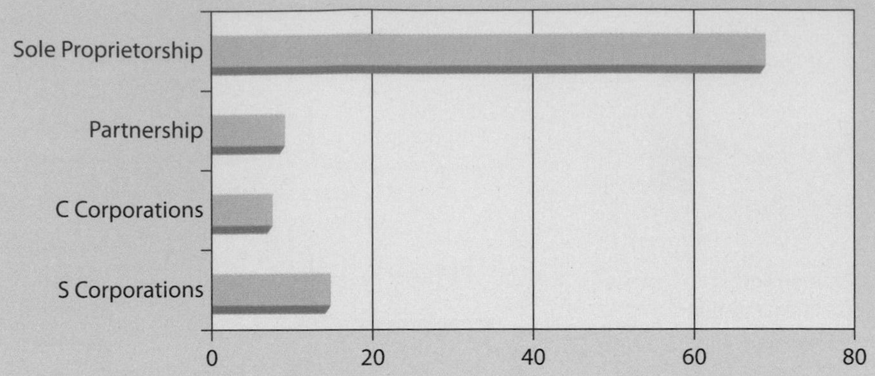

Source: Table 1A, Internal Revenue Service, http://www.irs.gov/pub/irs-soi/d6187.pdf, accessed November 11, 2010; and Table 1, Internal Revenue Service, http://www.irs.gov/pub/irs-soi/d6292.pdf, accessed November 11, 2010.

The death of the owner terminates the legal existence of a sole proprietorship. Thus, the possibility of the owner's death may cloud relationships between a business and its creditors and employees. It is important that the owner have a will, because the assets of the business minus its liabilities will belong to her or his heirs. In a will, a sole proprietor can give an executor the power to run the business for the heirs until they can take it over or it can be sold.

Another contingency that must be provided for is the possible incapacity of the sole proprietor. For example, if she or he were badly hurt in an accident and hospitalized for an extended period, the business could be ruined. A sole proprietor can guard against this contingency by giving a competent person legal power of attorney to carry on in such circumstances.

In some cases, circumstances argue against selecting the sole proprietorship option. If the nature of a business involves exposure to legal liability—for example, the manufacture of a potentially hazardous product or the operation of a child-care facility—a legal form that provides greater protection against personal liability is likely to be a better choice. For most companies, however, various forms of insurance are available to deal with the risks of a sole proprietorship, as well as those related to partnerships.[14]

THE PARTNERSHIP OPTION

partnership
A legal entity formed by two or more co-owners to operate a business for profit.

A **partnership** is a legal entity formed by two or more co-owners to operate a business for profit. Because of a partnership's voluntary nature, owners can set it up quickly, avoiding many of the legal requirements involved in creating a corporation. A partnership pools the managerial talents and capital of those joining together as business partners. As in a sole proprietorship, however, the owners share unlimited liability.

Qualifications of Partners

Any person capable of contracting may legally become a business partner. Individuals may become partners without contributing capital or having a claim to assets at the time of dissolution; such persons are partners only in regard to management and profits. The formation of a partnership involves consideration not only of legal issues but also of personal and managerial factors. A strong partnership requires partners who are honest, healthy, capable, and compatible.

Operating a business as a partnership has benefits, but it is also fraught with potential problems. Most experts discourage the use of partnerships as a way to run a business,

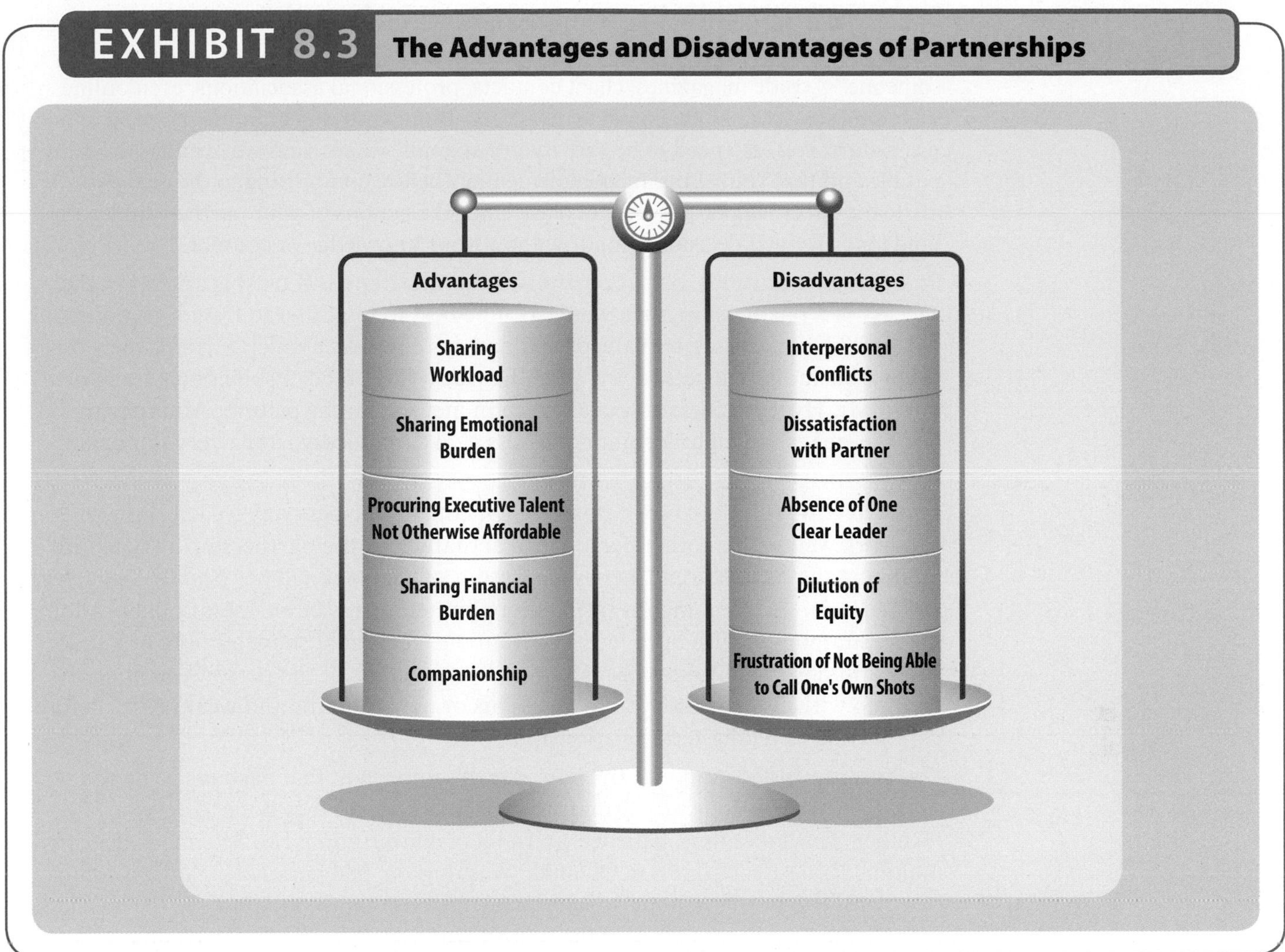

even though there are good and bad qualities associated with this form of organization (see Exhibit 8.3). The benefits of partnerships include the ability to share the workload as well as the emotional and financial burdens of the enterprise and to buy management talent that might otherwise break the budget. And it should not be overlooked that partners can add companionship to life in a small business.

However, many believe that the personal conflicts common in partnerships more than offset the benefits, and partners often fall short of one another's expectations—sometimes *far* short of what was anticipated, as was the case for Richard Rhodes's failed partnership (see In the Spotlight at the beginning of this chapter). Of course, decision making is more complicated in partnerships because leadership is shared, and owners must also share their equity position in the business, which naturally dilutes the control of each partner. While some of the difficulties of partnerships are financial in nature, most are relational—for example, coping with a partner's dishonesty or dealing with differing priorities. Partnerships clearly have both disturbing and redeeming qualities, so the issue is not black and white. The important point is that *a partnership should be formed only if it appears to be the best option when all features of the enterprise are taken into consideration.*

Many entrepreneurs have learned about partnerships the hard way—from "the school of hard knocks." Based on the experiences of those who have seen firsthand the extraordinary ups and debilitating downs of partnerships, the following suggestions may help entrepreneurs make the most of this form of organization:

- **Choose your partner carefully.** Partnerships are like marriages—they work best when you pick the right partner. Many sources are available to help you find that "perfect someone"—trade magazines, client contacts, professional associations, even online matching services like BusinessPartners.com. But identifying a promising partner is just a start; you also need to be sure that your goals, values, and work habits are compatible and that your skills are complementary before committing to the deal. Above all, team up with a person you can trust, since the actions of your partner can legally bind you, even if a decision is made without your knowledge or consent.[15]
- **Be open, but cautious, about partnerships with friends.** If trust is critical to the success of a partnership, then wouldn't it be best to look first to friends as potential partners? Not necessarily. Valued relationships can take a quick turn for the worse when a business deal gets rocky, and a Dr. Jeckyll friend can sometimes transform into a Mr. Hyde business associate when money enters the picture. And remember, the stakes are high: A minor business deal can quickly ruin a very important friendship.
- **Test-drive the relationship, if possible.** Of course, the best way to determine if you can work well with another person is to actually give the partnership a try before finalizing the deal. Karen Cheney, co-author of the book *How to Start a Successful Home Business,* recommends trying more limited forms of business collaboration before jumping in with both feet. For example, you could share a booth at a trade show and observe the behavior, style, and work habits of the person you hope to team up with. This allows you to assess his or her strengths and weaknesses before committing to a long-term relationship.[16]
- **Create a combined vision for the business.** It's important that partners be on the same page when it comes to forming the business concept they hope to develop together. This takes time, patience, and a lot of conversation. Hal Scogin, owner of a multimedia design business in Olympia, Washington, had hopes of creating a company with two partners, but it soon became obvious that they did not see the business in the same way. Scogin thought the venture was a multimedia design company, but his partners considered it to be a technology company. Needless to say, the partnership did not last long.[17] Some of the specific matters you should discuss before joining forces include the expectations of all partners (contributions of time, money, expertise, etc.), planned division of work, anticipated vacation time, and the sharing of profits and losses.
- **Prepare for the worst.** Keep in mind that more than half of all partnerships fail. That is why most experts recommend having an exit strategy for the partnership from the beginning. What looks like a good business arrangement at the outset can quickly fall apart when market conditions shift, a partner becomes involved in another business venture, or personal circumstances change. For example, the birth of a child, a sudden divorce, or the unexpected death of a spouse can alter everything. If it becomes necessary, exiting a partnership is far more difficult when plans for such an unfortunate outcome were not considered early on.

Failure to take suggestions like these seriously can derail efforts to build an effective working relationship or doom an otherwise workable partnership to an unnecessary or painful demise.

Rights and Duties of Partners

partnership agreement
A document that states explicitly the rights and duties of partners.

An oral partnership agreement is legal and binding, but memory is always less than perfect. In his book *Legal Guide for Starting and Running a Small Business,* author and practicing business attorney Fred Steingold strongly recommends that partners sign a written **partnership agreement** to avoid problems later on.[18] This document, which explicitly spells out the partners' rights and duties, should be drawn up before the venture is launched. Though the partners may choose to have an attorney draft the agreement in order to ensure that all important features are included, many other sources of assistance (such as online resources) also are available to guide you through this process. For example, a Google search on "partnership agreements" will pull up more resources than you could use in a lifetime. Many of these are very helpful.

© indianstockimages/Shutterstock.com

Unless the articles of the partnership agreement specify otherwise, a partner is generally recognized as having certain implicit rights. For example, partners share profits or losses equally, unless they have agreed to a different ratio. But these rights are also balanced against serious liabilities. In a general partnership, each party bears **joint and several liability**, which means that a business decision by one partner binds all other partners, even if they were not consulted in advance, didn't approve the agreement or contract in question, or didn't even know about it![19] And as with a sole proprietorship, the unlimited personal liability of the partners can be terrifying. The assets of the business are at risk, of course, but so are the personal assets of the partners, including their homes, cars, and bank accounts. Good faith, together with reasonable care in the exercise of managerial duties, is required of all partners in the business.

joint and several liability
The liability of each partner resulting from any one partner's ability to legally bind the other partners.

Unfortunately, complications can arise even if partners have been careful to match their expectations at the start of the partnership and the arrangement has been formalized through a partnership agreement. When problems emerge and trust begins to break down, partners should move quickly to try to resolve the underlying issues. If they cannot do so, they should consider hiring a business mediator. Working with a business mediator can be expensive, but the dissolution of the partnership is likely to be far more costly.

Termination of a Partnership

Death, incapacity, or withdrawal of a partner ends a partnership and requires liquidation or reorganization of the business. Liquidation often results in substantial losses to all partners, but it may be legally necessary, because a partnership represents a close personal relationship of the parties that cannot be maintained against the desire of any one of them.

When one partner dies, loss due to liquidation may be avoided if the partnership agreement stipulates that surviving partners can continue the business after buying the decedent's interest. This option can be facilitated by having each partner carry life insurance that names the other partners as beneficiaries.

Partnerships sometimes have immediate concerns to address when a partner decides to leave the business, especially if the departure was unexpected. Aaron Keller, Brian Aducci, and a third partner started a marketing and design firm in Minneapolis called Capsule. Eighteen months later, when their partner decided to leave the business and start a competing company (taking several employees and clients with him), Keller and Aducci knew they would have to move quickly to avoid serious losses. Lea A. Strickland, small business expert and author of *Out of the Cubicle and Into Business,* analyzed their situation and offered the following emergency prescription: First, cut off the departing partner's access to bank accounts, physical facilities, and company assets to avoid loss or damage to equipment critical to the business. Then quickly assess that partner's role in the enterprise and take steps to fill his shoes, to get the business back to normal as soon as possible. Once these very pressing matters are under control, sort out any legal issues that remain, such as abiding by any exit agreements that may have been signed. With time, and a lot of hard work, Keller and Aducci were able to regain their footing, but the experience helped them to understand just how fragile a partnership can be—and how important it is to have a rapid response plan when things go wrong.[20]

THE C CORPORATION OPTION

corporation
A business organization that exists as a legal entity and provides limited liability to its owners.

legal entity
A business organization that is recognized by the law as having a separate legal existence.

C corporation
An ordinary corporation, taxed by the federal government as a separate legal entity.

In 1819, Chief Justice John Marshall of the United States Supreme Court defined a **corporation** as "an artificial being, invisible, intangible, and existing only in contemplation of the law." With these words, the Supreme Court recognized the corporation as a **legal entity**, meaning that it can file suit and be sued, hold and sell property, and engage in business operations that are stipulated in the corporate charter. In other words, a corporation is a separate entity from the individuals who own it, which means that the corporation, *not* its owners, is liable for the debts of the business. The implications of this arrangement for risk taking and business formation are profound and far-reaching, prompting one highly influential business executive to declare the creation of the modern corporation to have been the single greatest innovation over the last several hundred years, at least where wealth creation is concerned.[21] The ordinary corporation—often called a **C corporation** to distinguish it from more specialized forms—is discussed in this section.

The Corporate Charter

corporate charter
A document that establishes a corporation's existence.

To form a corporation, one or more persons must apply to the secretary of state (at the state level) for permission to incorporate. After completing preliminary steps, including payment of an incorporation fee, the written application (which should be prepared by an attorney) is approved by the secretary of state and becomes the **corporate charter**. This document—sometimes called *articles of incorporation* or *certificate of incorporation*—shows that the corporation exists.

A corporation's charter should be brief, in accord with state law, and broad in its statement of the firm's powers. Details should be left to the *corporate bylaws,* which outline the basic rules for ongoing formalities and decisions of corporate life, including the size of the board of directors, the duties and responsibilities of directors and officers, the scheduling of regular meetings of the directors and shareholders, the means of calling for a special meeting of these groups, procedures for exercising voting rights, and restrictions on the transfer of corporate stock.

Rights and Status of Stockholders

stock certificate
A document specifying the number of shares owned by a stockholder.

pre-emptive right
The right of stockholders to buy new shares of stock before they are offered to the public.

Ownership in a corporation is evidenced by **stock certificates**, each of which stipulates the number of shares owned by a stockholder. An ownership interest does not confer a legal right to act for the firm or to share in its management. It does, however, provide the stockholder with the right to receive dividends in proportion to stockholdings, but only when the dividends are properly declared by the firm. Ownership of stock typically carries a **pre-emptive right**, or the right to buy new shares, in proportion to the number of shares already owned, before new stock is offered for public sale.

The legal status of stockholders is fundamental, of course, but it may be overemphasized. In many small corporations, the owners typically serve both as directors and as managing officers. The person who owns most or all of the stock can control a business as effectively as if it were a sole proprietorship. Thus, this form of organization can work well for individual- and family-owned businesses, where maintaining control of the firm is important.

Limited Liability of Stockholders

For most stockholders, their limited liability is a major advantage of the corporate form of organization. Their financial liability is restricted to the amount of money they invest in the business. Creditors cannot require them to sell personal assets to pay the corporation's debts. However, the owners of small companies are frequently asked to sign a second document in addition to the note that they will personally guarantee the note. As a result, a bank that makes a loan to a small firm may insist that the owners assume personal liability for the firm's debts. If the corporation is unable to repay the loan, the banker can then look to the owners' personal assets to recover the amount of the loan. In this case, the corporate advantage of limited liability is lost.

Why would owners agree to personally guarantee a firm's debt? Simply put, they may have no choice if they want the money. Most bankers are unwilling to loan money to an entrepreneur who is not prepared to put his or her own personal assets at risk.

Death or Withdrawal of Stockholders

Unlike a partnership interest, ownership in a corporation is readily transferable. Exchange of shares of stock is sufficient to transfer an ownership interest to a different individual.

Stock of large corporations is exchanged continually without noticeable effect on the operation of the business. For a small firm, however, a change of owners, though legally similar, can involve numerous complications. For example, finding a buyer for the stock of a small company may prove difficult. Also, a minority stockholder in a small firm is vulnerable. If two of three equal shareholders in a small business sold their stock to an outsider, the remaining shareholder would then be at the mercy of that outsider.

The death of a majority stockholder can have unfortunate repercussions in a small firm. An heir, the executor, or a purchaser of the stock might well insist on direct control, with possible adverse effects for other stockholders. To prevent problems of this nature, legal arrangements should be made at the outset to provide for management continuity by surviving stockholders and fair treatment of a stockholder's heirs. As in the case of a partnership, taking out life insurance ahead of time can ensure the ability to buy out a deceased stockholder's interest.

Maintaining Corporate Status

Establishing a corporation is one thing; keeping that status is another. Certain steps must be taken if the corporation is to retain its standing as a separate entity. For example, the corporation must hold annual meetings of both the shareholders and the board of directors, keep minutes to document the major decisions of shareholders and directors, maintain bank accounts that are separate from owners' bank accounts, and file a separate income tax return for the business.

Criteria for Choosing an Organizational Form

Choosing a legal form for a new business deserves careful attention because of the various, sometimes conflicting features of each organizational option. Depending on the particular circumstances of a specific business, the tax advantages of one form, for example, may offset the limited-liability advantages of another form. Some trade-offs may be necessary. Ideally, an experienced attorney or knowledgeable accountant should be consulted for guidance in selecting the most appropriate form of organization.

Some entrepreneurship experts insist that the two most basic forms of business—sole proprietorship and partnership—should *never* be adopted. While these forms clearly have drawbacks, they are workable. As illustrated in Exhibit 8.2, the IRS projected that 68.5 percent of all new businesses in 2011 would be formed as sole proprietorships, 9.6 percent would be set up as partnerships, 6.4 percent would be established as C corporations, and 15.5 percent would be formed as S corporations.[22] (The S corporation represented in Exhibit 8.2 is a special form of organization that will be described later in the chapter.)

Exhibit 8.4 summarizes the main considerations in selecting one of the three primary forms of ownership. A brief description of each factor follows.

EXHIBIT 8.4 **Comparison of Basic Legal Forms of Organization**

Form of Organization	Initial Organizational Requirements and Costs	Liability of Owners	Continuity of Business
Sole proprietorship	Minimum requirements; generally no registration or filing fee	Unlimited liability	Dissolved upon proprie-tor's death
General partnership	Minimum requirements; generally no registration or filing fee; written partnership agreement not legally required but strongly suggested	Unlimited liability	Unless partnership agreement specifies differently, dissolved upon withdrawal or death of partner
C corporation	Most expensive and greatest requirements; filing fees; compliance with state regulations for corporations	Liability limited to investment in company	Continuity of business unaffected by shareholder withdrawal or death
Form of organization preferred	Proprietorship or partnership	C corporation	C corporation

(Continued)

Initial Organizational Requirements and Costs

Organizational requirements and costs rise as the formality of the organization increases. That is, a sole proprietorship is typically less complex and less expensive to form than a partnership, and a partnership is less complex and less expensive to form than a corporation. In view of the relatively modest costs, however, this consideration is of minimal importance in the long run.

Liability of Owners

As discussed earlier, a sole proprietorship and a partnership have the built-in disadvantage of unlimited liability for the owners. With these forms of organization, there is no distinction between the firm's assets and the owners' personal assets. In contrast, setting up a corporation limits the owners' liability to their investment in the business. Liability risks are among the most important factors to consider when selecting an organizational form.

Choosing a form of organization merely for the sake of simplicity can sometimes cost an entrepreneur dearly—and more than just money! Against the advice of his attorney, Max Baer decided to operate his production studio in Memphis, Tennessee, as a sole proprietorship, to make startup easier. Things were going well until he was sued by a former employee. That's when the folly of Baer's decision became evident. The litigation went on for nearly a year. During that agonizing period, Baer was tormented by the possibility of losing all of his personal assets, including his house, his boat, and his savings account. Fortunately, the suit was settled for a modest sum, but Baer learned his lesson. He decided to convert his business to a corporation and enjoy the peace of mind that comes with limited liability.[23]

Two final cautions are in order regarding liability and organizational forms. First, incorporation will not protect a firm's owners from liability if it is used to perpetuate a fraud, skirt a law, or commit some wrongful act. In such cases, the courts may decide that

EXHIBIT 8.4 Comparison of Basic Legal Forms of Organization (Continued)

Transferability of Ownership	Management Control	Attractiveness for Raising Capital	Income Taxes
May transfer ownership of company name and assets	Absolute management freedom	Limited to proprietor's personal capital	Income from the business is taxed as personal income to the proprietor
Requires the consent of all partners	Majority vote of partners required for control	Limited to partners' ability and desire to contribute capital	Income from the business is taxed as personal income to the partners
Is easily transferred by transferring shares of stock	Shareholders have final control, but usually board of directors controls company policies	Usually the most attractive form for raising capital	The C corporation is taxed on its income and the stockholder is taxed if and when dividends are received
Depends on the circumstances	Depends on the circumstances	C corporation	Depends on the circumstances

there is no legal separation between the owners and the corporate entity, a concept known as **piercing the corporate veil**. Protection from financial liability may be jeopardized if, for example, the company is bankrupt but its owners knowingly take on debt, the board of directors does not meet as required by law or observe other corporate formalities, or business and personal accounts are not kept separate and company funds are used to pay an owner's personal expenses. Legal action is taken most often against smaller, privately held business entities and "sham corporations" that are set up with the specific goal of deceiving others.[24] In any case, some forms of organization, such as the sole proprietorship, offer no shield against liability in the first place, which is one of the reasons that choosing a form carefully is so important.

piercing the corporate veil
A situation in which the courts conclude that incorporation has been used to perpetuate a fraud, skirt a law, or commit some wrongful act and thus remove liability protection from the corporate entity.

Second, no form of organization can protect entrepreneurs from *all* forms of liability. For example, if an owner causes a traffic accident and is taken to court and declared personally liable for damages or injuries, he or she will have to pay the judgment, even if it means selling personal assets to satisfy the ruling. If, on the other hand, an employee caused the accident while on company business, the assets of the business will be at risk, but the personal assets of the owner(s) will be shielded from liability—*but only if the business is organized as a corporation or limited liability company* (which will be discussed later in the chapter). This protection does not extend to the owners of a sole proprietorship or a partnership, whose personal assets would also be at risk.

As previously discussed, most banks and many suppliers will require small business owners to sign a personal guarantee before loaning money or extending credit to them, regardless of the form of organization. The entrepreneurs will have to pay off these obligations if their businesses are unable to, even if doing so requires the use of personal assets. This is the lender's way of trying to ensure that debts are repaid, but it illustrates one of the practical limitations of selection of an organizational form when it comes to liability protection.[25]

Continuity of Business

A sole proprietorship is immediately dissolved on the owner's death. Likewise, a partnership is terminated on the death or withdrawal of a partner, unless the partnership agreement states otherwise. A corporation, on the other hand, offers continuity. The status of an individual investor does not affect the corporation's existence.

Transferability of Ownership

Ownership is transferred most easily in the corporation. The ability to transfer ownership, however, is not necessarily good or bad—it all depends on the owners' preferences. In some businesses, owners may want the option of evaluating any prospective new investors; under other circumstances, unrestricted transferability may be preferred.

Management Control

A sole proprietor has absolute control of the firm. Control within a partnership is normally based on the majority vote, so it follows that an increase in the number of partners reduces each partner's voice in management. Within a corporation, control has two dimensions: (1) the formal control vested in the stockholders who own the majority of the voting common shares and (2) the functional control exercised by the corporate officers in conducting daily operations. In a small corporation, these two forms of control usually rest with the same individuals.

Attractiveness for Raising Capital

A corporation has a distinct advantage when raising new equity capital, due to the ease of transferring ownership through the sale of common shares and the flexibility in distributing the shares. In contrast, the unlimited liability of a sole proprietorship and a partnership discourages new investors.

Income Taxes

Income taxes frequently have a major effect on an owner's selection of a form of organization. To understand the federal income tax system, you must consider this twofold question: Who is responsible for paying taxes, and how is tax liability determined? The three major forms of organization are taxed in different ways:

- **Sole proprietorship.** Self-employed individuals who operate a business as a sole proprietorship report income from the business on their individual federal income tax returns. They are then taxed on that income at the rates set by law for individuals.
- **Partnership.** A partnership reports the income it earns to the Internal Revenue Service, but the partnership itself does not pay any taxes. The income is allocated to the partners according to their agreement. The partners each report their own shares of the partnership's income on their personal tax returns and pay any taxes owed.
- **C corporation.** The C corporation, as a separate legal entity, reports its income and pays any taxes related to these profits. The owners (stockholders) of the corporation must report on their personal tax returns any amounts paid to them by the corporation in the form of dividends. (They must also report capital gains or losses, but only at the time they sell their stock in the company.) Keep in mind that dividends are, in essence, taxed twice—first as part of a corporation's earnings and then as part of the owners' personal income.

To learn more about the specifics of tax matters relevant to the various forms of organization outlined in this chapter, visit the IRS's small business website at http://www.irs.gov/businesses/small/index.html. It's easy to navigate and provides hundreds of pages of useful information with just a few clicks of a mouse. You'll find links to tax information on the different organizational forms, insights related to important small business topics, and answers to industry-specific questions, as well as forms and publications that will help with tax planning and preparation.

Specialized Forms of Organization

The majority of new and small businesses use one of the three major ownership structures just described—the sole proprietorship, partnership, or C corporation. However, other specialized forms of organization are also used by small firms. Five of these alternatives merit further consideration: the limited partnership, the S corporation, the limited liability company, the professional corporation, and the nonprofit corporation.

The Limited Partnership

The **limited partnership** is a special form of partnership involving at least one general partner and one or more limited partners. The **general partner** remains personally liable for the debts of the business, but **limited partners** have limited personal liability as long as they do not take an active role in the management of the partnership. In other words, limited partners risk only the capital they invest in the business. An individual with substantial personal wealth can, therefore, invest money in a limited partnership without exposing his or her personal assets to liability claims that might arise through activities of the business. If a limited partner becomes active in management, however, his or her limited liability is lost. To form a limited partnership, partners must file a certificate of limited partnership with the proper state office, as state law governs this form of organization.

limited partnership
A partnership with at least one general partner and one or more limited partners.

general partner
A partner in a limited partnership who has unlimited personal liability.

limited partner
A partner in a limited partnership who is not active in its management and has limited personal liability.

The S Corporation

The designation **S corporation**, or **Subchapter S corporation**, is derived from Subchapter S of the Internal Revenue Code, which permits a business to retain the limited liability feature of a C corporation while being taxed as a partnership. To obtain S corporation status, a corporation must meet certain requirements, including the following:

S corporation (Subchapter S corporation)
A type of corporation that offers limited liability to its owners but is taxed by the federal government as a partnership.

- No more than 100 stockholders are allowed.[26]
- All stockholders must be individuals or certain qualifying estates and trusts.[27]
- Only one class of stock can be outstanding.
- Fiscally, the corporation must operate on a calendar-year basis.
- Shareholders may not include nonresident aliens.[28]

A restriction preventing S corporations from owning other corporations, including C corporations, has recently been removed, resulting in tax advantages for some small firms. Whereas in the past different businesses had to be legally separate, individual subsidiaries now may consolidate under one S corporation and submit one tax return.[29] However, combining two businesses under one legal entity can create problems. For example, liability is shared, so if one business gets sued or is bogged down in debt, the other will be exposed to that legal or financial risk. And combined businesses are more difficult to market and sell because potential buyers find it hard to distinguish between the two and determine their individual values.[30]

An S corporation does not pay corporate income taxes and instead passes taxable income or losses on to the stockholders. This allows stockholders to receive dividends from the corporation without double taxation on the firm's profit (once through a corporate tax and again through a personal tax on received dividends). A competent tax attorney should be consulted before selecting S corporation status, as tax law changes have considerable effect on this arrangement. A partial tax return form for an S corporation is shown in Exhibit 8.5.

The Limited Liability Company

limited liability company
form of organization in which owners have limited liability but pay personal income taxes on business profits.

The **limited liability company** is a relatively new form of organization. It has grown in popularity because it offers the simplicity of a sole proprietorship and the liability protection of a corporation. A limited liability company can have an unlimited number of owners (even a single owner), and these may include non-U.S. citizens. This form differs from the C corporation in that it avoids double taxation. Limited liability companies are not taxed on corporate income but simply pass that income on to their owners, who pay taxes on it as part of their personal income.

The major advantage of the limited liability company over the partnership form is the liability protection it affords. While general partners are exposed to personal liability, owners in a limited liability company are, as the name implies, protected with respect to their personal assets.

According to many attorneys, the limited liability company is usually the best choice for new businesses. It has the same ability as the S corporation to pass taxable income on to shareholders, and compared to an S corporation, the limited liability company is easier

EXHIBIT 8.5 Income Tax Return Form for an S Corporation

Form **1120S** — Department of the Treasury, Internal Revenue Service

U.S. Income Tax Return for an S Corporation

▶ Do not file this form unless the corporation has filed or is attaching Form 2553 to elect to be an S corporation.
▶ See separate instructions.

OMB No. 1545-0130 — **2010**

For calendar year 2010 or tax year beginning , 2010, ending , 20

A S election effective date | Name | D Employer identification number

B Business activity code number *(see instructions)* | TYPE OR PRINT | Number, street, and room or suite no. If a P.O. box, see instructions. | E Date incorporated

City or town, state, and ZIP code | F Total assets *(see instructions)* $

C Check if Sch. M-3 attached ☐

G Is the corporation electing to be an S corporation beginning with this tax year? ☐ Yes ☐ No If "Yes," attach Form 2553 if not already filed

H Check if: (1) ☐ Final return (2) ☐ Name change (3) ☐ Address change
(4) ☐ Amended return (5) ☐ S election termination or revocation

I Enter the number of shareholders who were shareholders during any part of the tax year . . . . ▶

Caution. *Include **only** trade or business income and expenses on lines 1a through 21. See the instructions for more information.*

Income	1a	Gross receipts or sales ___ b Less returns and allowances ___ c Bal ▶	1c	
	2	Cost of goods sold (Schedule A, line 8)	2	
	3	Gross profit. Subtract line 2 from line 1c	3	
	4	Net gain (loss) from Form 4797, Part II, line 17 *(attach Form 4797)*	4	
	5	Other income (loss) *(see instructions—attach statement)*	5	
	6	**Total income (loss).** Add lines 3 through 5 ▶	6	
nstructions for limitations)	7	Compensation of officers	7	
	8	Salaries and wages (less employment credits)	8	
	9	Repairs and maintenance	9	
	10	Bad debts	10	
	11	Rents	11	
	12	Taxes and licenses	12	
	13	Interest	13	
	14	Depreciation not claimed on Schedule A or elsewhere on return *(attach Form 4562)*	14	

to set up, is more flexible, and offers some significant tax advantages.[31] But a limited liability company isn't always the best way to go. For example, under the following conditions, it would be better to use a C corporation:

- **You want to provide extensive fringe benefits to owners or employees.** The C corporation can deduct these benefits, and they are not treated as taxable income to the employees.
- **You want to offer stock options to employees.** Since limited liability companies do not have stock, they cannot offer such incentives.
- **You hope to go public or sell the business at some time in the future.** A C corporation can go public or be sold to another corporation in a tax-free, stock-for-stock exchange.
- **You plan to convert to a C corporation eventually.** You cannot change from a pass-through entity like a limited liability company without paying additional taxes.

professional corporation
A form of corporation that shields owners from liability and is set up for individuals in certain professional practices.

nonprofit corporation
A form of corporation for enterprises established to serve civic, educational, charitable, or religious purposes but not for generation of profits.

organizational test
Verification of whether a nonprofit organization is staying true to its stated purpose.

The Professional Corporation

Have you noticed the initials PC or PA as part of the corporate name on the letterhead or signage of your doctor, dentist, or attorney? These letters indicate that the practice is set up as a **professional corporation** in order to offer professional services. Though its meaning varies from state to state, the term *professional* usually applies to those individuals whose professions require that they obtain a license before they can practice, so this would include doctors, chiropractors, lawyers, accountants, engineers, architects, and other highly trained individuals. But unlike other liability-shielding organizational forms, the professional corporation does not protect a practitioner from her or his own negligence or malpractice; rather, it shields one owner from the liability of other owners in the practice. In some states, a different business structure called a limited liability partnership can serve the same purpose and may have additional advantages. Obviously, the professional corporation applies to a fairly narrow range of enterprises, but it is usually the best option for businesses that fall into that category. In fact, many state laws require this form of organization before a practice can operate.

The Nonprofit Corporation

For some ventures, the most practical form of organization is the **nonprofit corporation**. Most elect to become 501(c)(3) organizations, which are created to serve civic, educational, charitable, or religious purposes. To qualify for 501(c)(3) status, the money-raising concern, fund, or foundation must be a corporation; the IRS will not grant this option to an individual or partnership. In the application process, the officers need to submit articles of organization that spell out and limit the range of activities of the enterprise—for a tax exemption to be granted, the organization must pass the **organizational test** ("IRS-speak" for verification that the organization is staying true to the articles filed). A nonprofit corporation must establish a board of directors or trustees to oversee its operations, and if it should dissolve, it is required to transfer its assets to another nonprofit corporation.

© westock Images / Alamy

Though social entrepreneurs certainly do not have to charter their enterprises as nonprofit corporations, they often choose this option. Matthew Gutschick and Ben Whiting, both 2006 graduates of Wake Forest University, started a social enterprise called MagicMouth Theatre, to teach theater and magic to young people and offer opportunities for them to perform. As Gutschick recalls, when they selected a business structure, the two entrepreneurs "decided to go nonprofit because it gave us a larger measure of credibility and authenticity."[32] In other words, choosing to structure an organization as a nonprofit corporation can be a way to reinforce the message and work of the organization.

Forming Strategic Alliances

5 Understand the uses of strategic alliances in small businesses.

strategic alliance An organizational relationship that links two or more independent business entities in a common endeavor.

A **strategic alliance** is an organizational relationship that links two or more independent business entities in some common endeavor. Without affecting the independent legal status of the participating business partners, it provides a way for companies to improve their individual effectiveness by sharing certain resources. And these alliances can take many forms, from informal information exchanges to formal equity- or contract-based relationships and everything in between. According to a study by the National Federation of Independent Business, some types of alliances that are most popular with small businesses include licensing contracts, working with long-term outside contractors, entering production agreements, and distribution-focused deals (see Exhibit 8.6).[33]

Strategic alliances are more important to small businesses today than ever before, and an increasing number of entrepreneurs are finding creative ways to use these cooperative strategies to their advantage. In fact, statistics show that nearly two-thirds of small businesses use alliances, and three-fourths of these companies report having positive experiences with them.[34] Given the escalating pace of competition and the rising costs of developing essential capabilities, alliances provide a way for small companies to access another firm's first-rate resources so that they can be more competitive. Since a competitive advantage often goes to the entrepreneur who is quick to exploit it, many small business owners see strategic alliances as an essential part of their plan for growth. These cooperative strategies represent one way to keep up with the accelerating pace of change in today's business environment. (See Chapter 18 for a discussion of strategic alliances as these apply to global enterprises.)

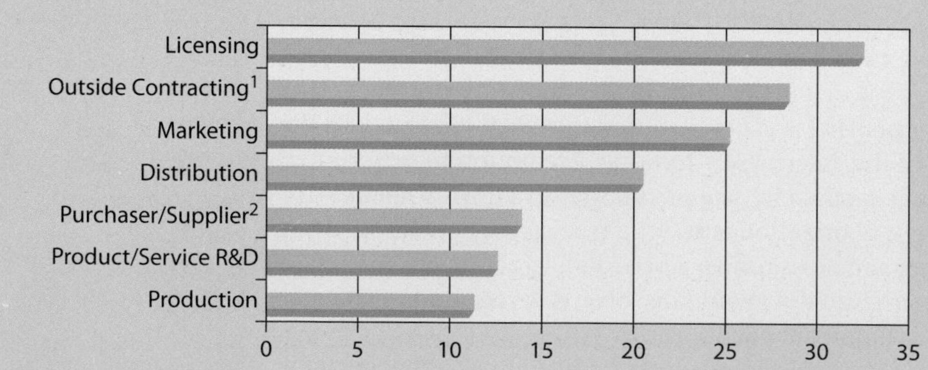

[1]These alliances include only relationships that are long-term in nature.

[2]These alliances include agreements relating to programs, such as just-in-time supply or total quality management that are relatively long-term in nature.

Source: William J. Dennis, Jr. (ed.), "Strategic Alliances," *National Small Business Poll*, Vol. 4, No. 4 (Washington, DC: NFIB Research Foundation, 2004), pp. 1–8.

Building Business Alliances

A strategic alliance could help your business enter a new market, increase its sales, or improve its image. Regardless of your reasons for building a business alliance, there are some basic rules to remember. For example, it is crucial that you select a long-term partner who won't hurt your reputation and will help you increase your current profit margins. Also, be sure to set the tone for the relationship at the beginning, and choose a partner who is passionate about the deal. For more information, see *Inc.* Staff, "How to Build Business Alliances," *Inc. Guidebook*, Vol. 2 No. 3, pp. 49-52 (June 2010).

STRATEGIC ALLIANCES WITH LARGE COMPANIES

Large corporations create strategic alliances not only with other large corporations but also with small businesses. Typically, these alliances are formed to join the complementary skills and expertise of the partnered firms, in order to promote the competitive edge of both (or all) parties. For example, large manufacturers sometimes team up with innovative small manufacturers in product development efforts, and giant retailers form alliances with smaller suppliers to work hand in hand to achieve specific quality requirements and meet demanding delivery schedules.

Combining the speed, flexibility, and creative energy of a small business with the industry experience, production capabilities, and market reach of a large corporation can be a winning strategy. In 1998, Katherine Kent started The Solar Store in Tucson, Arizona, to retrofit existing homes with solar power systems. The focus of her business changed six years later, however, when she struck a deal with residential construction heavyweight Pulte Homes. Pulte was scheduled to start a new subdivision that would eventually have 1,500 new homes with solar heating and electricity, but it needed a supplier to demonstrate how to install and operate the energy-saving equipment. Enter The Solar Store. Kent's company "gave Pulte's people a crash course in solar power," and "Pulte showed The Solar Store how to outfit entire subdivisions from the ground up and how to save time in the assembly process." Furthermore, the arrangement gave The Solar Store tremendous purchasing power and allowed it to start buying directly from manufacturers, which shaved the tiny partner's materials costs by a very helpful 7 percent in the first year alone.[35]

Alliances with large firms can give a tremendous boost to performance, but some small businesses discover that bigger isn't always better. The advantages created by joining forces with large firms must be weighed against the risk of being squeezed financially or of running into smothering bureaucratic complications. One small company, for example, jumped at the chance to form an alliance with a major multinational firm in the same industry. Everything seemed to be running smoothly until the small enterprise learned that a simple invoice discrepancy was holding up a $1.2 million payment that it desperately needed to meet future expansion commitments. Part of the problem may have been that the money seemed like small change to the multinational—it didn't see the urgency of the matter, and it certainly wasn't going to pay on a disputed invoice. But the cash was critical to its small partner. The two companies reached a stalemate, the alliance failed, and the small business was never able to recover $300,000 of the money that it was owed.

This true story reveals how small venture alliances with prestigious partners can be a double-edged sword. Such affiliations may offer a substantial boost to status and market access, but the parties' strategic priorities may not mesh and a major corporation can wield enormous power over a small, struggling enterprise. Some large firms have a track

© iStockphoto.com/Angelika Schwarz

entrepreneurial experiences

A Strategic Alliance That Made a Ton of Cash—Literally!

In many ways, the two companies could not have been more different. Crane & Co., based in Dalton, Massachusetts, can trace its start back to 1770—when British troops still occupied the American colonies! It has been making highly specialized paper products for the U.S. government since 1879. Today, the company has considerable size, as well, with annual revenues exceeding $200 million. Nanoventions, Inc., on the other hand, was founded in 2000, as the new millennium was just dawning. Nanoventions' stock-in-trade involves "optical and non-optical microstructure [technologies that] are used in document and product security and authentication . . . to prevent counterfeiting of currency, driver's licenses, event and transit services, and pharmaceuticals," among other related technology-focused offerings. As you might guess, the company is small, highly entrepreneurial, and not nearly as established as Crane & Co.

© Photolinc/Shutterstock.com

So what brought these two companies together? Their alliance was the product of matchmaking efforts by the U.S. Bureau of Engraving and Printing to try to work Nanoventions' innovative anti-counterfeiting technology (which uses tiny lenses in micro-printed images that move in opposite directions when tilted) into the new counterfeit-resistant $100 bill that the government wanted Crane to produce. But bringing these two very different companies together created a steady stream of conflict and frustration. For starters, Nanoventions executives were concerned that they would lose control of the technology, and tempers flared when Crane prevented its small partner from building a larger machine to get up to speed on production demand for security strips because the Alpharetta, Georgia–based startup had no guards or fencing around its facility to secure the new equipment. "Neither company knew if the other company was going to be a friend or a foe," said Brian Martin, Nanoventions president and CEO. And there were lots and lots of production bugs to be worked out—many related to trying out new adhesives, some of which required paper so thick that it jammed presses or stock so thin that it wouldn't allow the moving images to stay focused.

Needless to say, frustrations between the partners ran high. Though first initiated in 2004, the strategic alliance was still struggling to bear expected fruit some four years later. Eventually, federal officials threatened to pull the plug on the dysfunction-riddled project, which motivated Crane to offer to acquire Nanoventions' security-technology unit to get the control it needed to complete its bill-printing mission. But even that did not go well. In fact, Nanoventions executives threatened several times to walk away from a deal for which they had already signed a letter of intent. Crane eventually prevailed, retained all 20 Nanoventions employees, and got the job done, but it was no walk in the park. And that's the way it sometimes works when small companies form strategic alliances with large firms. There are many potential potholes on the road to cooperation, and some of them are large enough to do some serious damage. And that's what happened in this case. Nanoventions could have been rolling in the dough—but it was not to be.

Sources: "Crane & Co.—What Do Paul Revere, Eleanor Roosevelt and the Queen Mum Have in Common?" http://www.crane.com/about-us/crane-company?RPL, accessed November 10, 2010; *Bloomberg Businessweek*, "Nanoventions Holdings, LLC," http://investing.businessweek.com/research/stocks/private/snapshot.asp?privcapId=616306, accessed November 10, 2010; and Joann S. Lublin, "Bringing a New Business into the Fold," *Wall Street Journal*, April 20, 2009, p. B4. **http://www.crane.com**

record of misbehavior as partners, and you need to know this *before* entering an alliance with them. The guidelines provided in Chapter 4 for the evaluation of a franchisor (see pages 115–119) can be helpful when deciding whether to take on a particular venture partner. For example, it would be wise to investigate whether the corporation has been a good, ethical partner for other small companies. Knowing this in advance will help you to make an informed and profitable decision.

STRATEGIC ALLIANCES WITH SMALL COMPANIES

Small businesses can also form strategic alliances with other firms that are similar in size, in ways that enhance mutual competitive strength. Recent statistics suggest that about half of all small businesses maintain one or more strategic alliances with companies that are smaller or equal in size, with most of these involving outside contractors, licensing partners, import/export operations, marketing agreements, and shared manufacturing.[36] When *Inc.* researchers asked dozens of entrepreneurs which alliance partners had performed best for them, they were surprised to learn that the most enthusiastic anecdotes were about other small companies.[38] These partnerships were more flexible, dedicated, creative, and understanding of the specific needs of small businesses. Apparently, it takes one to know one!

The Center for Systems Management (CSM), a small Vienna, Virginia–based consulting and training company, found that it was in over its head when it accepted a contract from NASA to develop coursework that would help with problems in the space shuttle program. CSM had been given just 45 days to produce a slick video for an internal marketing campaign. This was a huge opportunity, one that could boost the small company's image and generate business in a whole new category of work, but a botched job would probably damage its relationship with NASA for good. Rather than attempting to go it alone, CSM contracted the job out to Technovative Marketing, a seven-person business in Peapack, New Jersey. Within a few days, Harriet Donnelly, Technovative's president, was on the job, and she personally worked on the video and stayed with the project, even attending all meetings with NASA as if she were the chief marketing officer of CSM. As far as Donnelly was concerned, she was part of the CSM team. In the end, the video project was a huge success. CSM was hired to do more internal marketing campaign work for NASA as a result and, of course, Donnelly was asked to help.[39]

Strategic alliances hold great promise for small entrepreneurial businesses. By combining resources with carefully selected partners, small firms can increase their competitive strength and reach goals that would otherwise be too costly or too difficult for them to accomplish on their own.

SETTING UP AND MAINTAINING SUCCESSFUL STRATEGIC ALLIANCES

An alliance strategy can be powerful for growing companies—it spreads the risk of entering new markets and helps small players with unattractive balance sheets appear stable to the end buyer. It can also provide a fast track to reaching the critical mass required for pre-sale and post-sale support. To make alliances work for everyone involved, entrepreneurs should select partners with a "division of labor" mentality that allows all parties to focus their efforts on what they do best. This can be very powerful. For example, identifying intersections between product lines and expertise opens up the potential for cross-selling that creates growth opportunities for everyone involved.[40]

Working closely with other companies has its upside, but it can also introduce significant hazards. Because alliance partners are in a unique position to learn about your strategy and customer base, they can become competitors overnight. Therefore, it is crucial to select partners with care and to structure contracts to ensure growth, including an "easy out" clause if the alliance does not work out for some reason.[41]

While strategic alliances often are not easy to set up, they can be even more difficult to maintain. Many small businesses report that they are happy with the results of their strategic alliances,[42] but a number of alliances run into trouble and, in time, fail. Fortunately, when setting up alliances, entrepreneurs can take the following steps to improve their chances for success:

- **Establish a healthy network of contacts.** These people can lead you to still other contacts, and eventually to the one you need. Industry analysts, executive recruiters, public relations agencies, business reporters, and even the government can provide important leads.
- **Identify and contact individuals within a firm who are likely to return your call.** "Dialing high" (calling contacts at the vice-presidential level or higher) works in small or medium-size firms, but in large firms you may need to call managers or other mid-level employees to get a response.
- **Do your homework, and you will win points just for being prepared.** You should be able to clearly outline the partner's potential financial benefits from the alliance. If possible, show that your firm can deliver value to the alliance across several fronts.
- **Learn to speak and understand the "language" of your partner.** You will not pick up on subtle messages in conversations with partners unless you know how they communicate, and this can eventually make or break the alliance.
- **Make sure any alliance offer is clearly a win–win opportunity.** It's easy to push for terms that are good for your own business and forget that only those agreements that benefit all participating parties will endure.
- **Continue to monitor the progress of the alliance to ensure that goals and expectations are being met, and make changes as they become necessary.** And you can be sure that adjustments will be needed, sooner or later.

The goal is to form strategic alliances that are beneficial to all partners and to manage these alliances effectively. In their book *Everyone Is a Customer,* Jeffrey Shuman, Janice Twombly, and David Rottenberg point out that a key to successful strategic alliances is understanding the true nature of the relationship: "Relationships are advertised as being between companies, whereas in reality relationships are built between people. And that's a very important distinction."[43] Cultivating relationships is essential to business success in general, and these can be promoted through an effective board of directors or advisory council.

Making the Most of a Board of Directors

board of directors
The governing body of a corporation, elected by the stockholders

In entrepreneurial firms, the **board of directors** tends to be small (usually five or fewer members[44]) and serves as the governing body for corporate activity. In concept, the stockholders elect the board, which in turn chooses the firm's officers, who manage the enterprise. The directors also set or approve management policies, consider reports on operating results from the officers, and declare any dividends.

All too often, the majority stockholder in a small corporation (usually the entrepreneur) appoints a board of directors only to fulfill a legal requirement (since corporations are required by law to have a board of directors) or as mere window dressing for investors. Such owners make little or no use of directors in managing their companies. In fact, the entrepreneur may actively resist the efforts of these directors to provide managerial assistance. When appointing a board of directors, such an entrepreneur often will select personal friends, relatives, or businesspersons who are too busy to analyze the firm's circumstances and are not inclined to argue. Entrepreneurs who take a more constructive approach find an active board to be both practical and beneficial, especially when the members are informed, skeptical, and independent.

Making use of boards of directors is becoming increasingly attractive for a number of reasons. The growing complexity of small businesses, arising in part from globalization and technological developments, makes the expertise of well-chosen directors especially valuable. In a family business, outsiders can play a unique role in helping evaluate family talent and mediate differences among family members.

CONTRIBUTIONS OF DIRECTORS

A small business stands to gain significantly from a strong board of directors, especially when its members help the entrepreneur look beyond the next few months to make important, long-term strategic decisions. In other words, good directors will be able to help entrepreneurs keep their eyes on the big picture, to step back and see the forest for the trees.

A well-selected board of directors can also bring supplementary knowledge and broad experience to enterprise management. By virtue of their backgrounds, directors can fill gaps in the expertise of a management team and monitor its actions. The board should meet regularly to provide maximum assistance to the chief executive. In board meetings, ideas should be debated, strategies determined, and the pros and cons of policies explored. In this way, the chief executive is informed by the unique perspectives of all the board members. Their combined knowledge makes possible more intelligent decisions on issues crucial to the firm.

By utilizing the experience of a board of directors, the chief executive of a small corporation is in no way giving up active control of its operations. Instead, by consulting with and seeking the advice of the board's members, he or she is simply drawing on a larger pool of business knowledge. A group will typically make better decisions than will a single individual working in isolation.

An active board of directors serves management in several important ways: by reviewing major policy decisions, by advising on external business conditions and on proper reaction to the business cycle, by providing informal advice from time to time on specific problems that arise, and by offering access to important personal contacts. With a strong board, a small firm may gain greater credibility with the public, as well as with business and financial communities.

SELECTION OF DIRECTORS

Many resources are available to an entrepreneur who is attempting to assemble a cooperative and experienced group of directors. The firm's attorney, banker, accountant, local management consultants, and other business executives might all be considered as potential directors, but such individuals usually lack the independence needed to critically review an entrepreneur's plans. Also, the owner is already paying for their expertise. For this reason, the owner needs to consider the value of an outside board, one with members whose income does not depend on the firm. Many small company boards have independent

Radius Images/Jupiter Images

outside directors, and this number is rising—which is good, because small companies tend to have far fewer independent directors than large, publicly traded firms and therefore miss out on the benefits they bring to the oversight process.

Objectivity is a particularly valuable contribution of outside directors. They can look at issues more dispassionately than can insiders who are involved in daily decision making. Outside directors, for example, are freer to evaluate and to question a firm's ethical standards. Some operating executives, without the scrutiny of outside directors, may rationalize unethical or illegal behavior as being in the best interest of the company.

In a family business, an outside board can help mediate and resolve issues related to leadership succession, in addition to providing more general direction. As outsiders, they bring to the business a measure of detachment from potentially explosive emotional differences.

Working with outside board members is not always easy, but an entrepreneur who is advised by the board to make tough decisions may find that those decisions provide the subtle (or not-so-gentle) pressure required to move the business forward. For example, they may keep bringing the conversation back to issues that are easy to avoid, such as the need to build long-term relationships with important individuals in the banking community or the value of converting intentions for the company's future into a formal business plan that can be studied, debated, perfected, and used as a tool to attract crucial resources to the enterprise. Entrepreneurs often spend as much as 20 percent of their time on board-related activities, but the time commitment is worth the cost if the directors are doing their jobs well.

The nature and needs of a business will help determine the qualifications required in its directors. For example, a firm that faces a marketing problem may benefit greatly from the counsel of a board member with a marketing background. Business prominence in the community is not essential, although it may help to give the company credibility and enable it to attract other well-qualified directors. Having a "fat Rolodex" can only be beneficial, as directors with influential business contacts can contribute greatly to the company's performance.

After deciding on the qualifications to look for, a business owner must seek suitable candidates as board members. Effective directors are honest and accountable, offer valuable insights based on business experience, and enhance the company's credibility with its stakeholders (especially customers and suppliers). Suggestions for such candidates may be obtained from the firm's accountant, attorney, banker, and other associates in the business community. Owners or managers of other, noncompeting small companies, as well as second- and third-level executives in large companies, are often willing to accept such positions. Before offering candidates positions on the board, however, a business owner would be wise to do some discreet background checking.

COMPENSATION OF DIRECTORS

The compensation paid to board members varies greatly, and some small firms pay no fees at all. If compensation is provided, it is usually offered in the form of an annual retainer, board meeting fees, and pay for committee work. (Directors may serve on committees that evaluate executive compensation, nominate new board members, and oversee the work of the company's auditors.) Annual retainers for board work at small businesses typically range from $5,000 to $10,000, and board meeting fees can run from $500 to $2,000 per meeting. These costs to the firm are usually in addition to reimbursements for travel expenses related to board meetings and the financial burden of providing Directors and Officers Liability Insurance, which protects board members if they should be sued in the course of carrying out their duties as directors.[45] Sometimes board members are also given a small percentage of the company's profits for their participation, and some cash-strapped businesses may grant them stock (often 1 percent, but this could go as high as 2 percent or more to lure top talent) in lieu of compensation.[46] But keep in mind that some directors may serve for free because of their interest in seeing a new or small business prosper. This is not uncommon.

The relatively modest compensation offered for the services of well-qualified directors suggests that financial reward is not their primary motivation for serving on a board. Reasonable compensation is appropriate, however, if directors are making important contributions to the firm's operations. In any case, it is good to keep in mind that you usually get what you pay for.

AN ALTERNATIVE: AN ADVISORY COUNCIL

In recent years, increased attention has been directed to the legal responsibilities of directors. Because outside directors may be held responsible for illegal company actions, even though they are not directly involved in wrongdoing, some individuals are reluctant to accept directorships. Thus, some small companies use an **advisory council** as an alternative to a board of directors. Qualified outsiders are asked to serve on a council as advisors to the company. This group then functions in much the same way as a board of directors does, except that its actions are only advisory in nature.

advisory council
A group that serves as an alternative to a board of directors, acting only in an advisory capacity.

The legal liability of members of an advisory council is not completely clear. However, limiting their compensation and power is thought to lighten, if not eliminate, the personal liability of members. Since its role is advisory in nature, the council also may pose less of a threat to the owner and possibly work more cooperatively than a conventional board.

Without a doubt, a well-selected board of directors or advisory council can do a great deal for a small company, but bear in mind that this is only one part of an effective organizational plan. The success of any business depends on the quality of its people, who must also be well organized and skillfully led. That's why having a balanced management team, selecting an organizational form that makes sense for the enterprise and its circumstances, and joining advantageous strategic alliances are all so important. This chapter has touched on each of these topics to help you think through key factors involved in developing a solid organizational plan that will give your business a good running start and help to ensure its long-term success.

1. Describe the characteristics and value of a strong management team.

- A strong management team nurtures a good business idea and helps provide the necessary resources to make it succeed.
- The skills of management team members should complement each other, forming an optimal combination of education and experience.
- A small firm can enhance its management by drawing on the expertise of competent insiders and outside specialists.
- Social media tools can be very helpful in attracting customers, connecting with peers, and sharing advice about common problems.
- Building social capital through networking and goodwill is extremely helpful in developing a small business.

2. Explain the common legal forms of organization used by small businesses.

- The most basic legal forms of organization used by small businesses are the sole proprietorship, partnership, and C corporation.
- In a sole proprietorship, the owner receives all profits and bears all losses. The principal disadvantage of this form is the owner's unlimited liability.
- In a partnership, which should be established on the basis of a written partnership agreement, success

depends on the partners' ability to build and maintain an effective working relationship.

- C corporations are particularly attractive because of their limited liability feature. The fact that ownership is easily transferable makes them well suited for combining the capital of numerous owners.

3. Identify factors to consider in choosing among the primary legal forms of organization.

- Currently, 68.5 percent of all new businesses are organized as sole proprietorships, 9.6 percent are set up as partnerships, and 6.4 percent are established as C corporations.
- The key factors in the choice among different legal forms of organization are initial organizational requirements and costs, liability of the owners, continuity of the business, transferability of ownership, management control, attractiveness for raising capital, and income tax considerations.
- Self-employed individuals who operate businesses as sole proprietorships report income from the businesses on their individual tax returns.
- A partnership reports the income it earns to the Internal Revenue Service, but the partnership itself does not pay income taxes. The income is allocated to the owners according to their partnership agreement.
- A C corporation reports its income and pays any taxes due on this corporate income. Individual stockholders must also pay personal income taxes on dividends paid to them by a corporation.

4. Discuss the unique features and restrictions of five specialized organizational forms.

- In a limited partnership, general partners have unlimited liability, while limited partners have only limited liability as long as they are not active in the firm's management.
- S corporations, also called Subchapter S corporations, enjoy a special tax status that permits them to avoid the corporate tax but requires individual stockholders to pay personal taxes on their proportionate shares of the business profits.
- In limited liability companies, individual owners have the advantage of limited liability but pay only personal income taxes on the firm's earnings.
- Professional corporations are set up for those who offer professional services (usually those that require a license), to protect them from the liability of other owners in the practice.
- Some enterprises (especially those with a social focus) benefit from greater credibility and authenticity when they organize as a nonprofit corporation, such as a 501(c)(3) organization.

5. Understand the nature of strategic alliances and their uses in small businesses.

- Strategic alliances allow business firms to combine their resources without compromising their independent legal status.
- Strategic alliances may be formed by two or more independent businesses to achieve some common purpose. For example, a large corporation and a small business or two or more small businesses may collaborate on a joint project.
- Entrepreneurs can improve their chances of creating and maintaining a successful alliance by establishing productive connections, identifying the best person to contact, being prepared to confirm the long-term benefits of the alliance, learning to speak the partner's "language," ensuring a win-win arrangement, and monitoring the progress of the alliance.

6. Describe the effective use of boards of directors and advisory councils.

- Boards of directors can assist small corporations by offering counsel and assistance to their chief executives.
- To be most effective, a board of directors should include properly qualified, independent outsiders.
- One alternative to an active board of directors is an advisory council, whose members are not personally liable for the company's actions.

Key Terms

management team p. 231
social network p. 233
social capital p. 234
reciprocation p. 234
sole proprietorship p. 234
unlimited liability p. 235
partnership p. 236
partnership agreement p. 238
joint and several liability p. 239
corporation p. 240
legal entity p. 240
C corporation p. 240
corporate charter p. 240
stock certificate p. 240
pre-emptive right p. 240
piercing the corporate veil p. 243
limited partnership p. 245
general partner p. 245
limited partner p. 245
S corporation (Subchapter S corporation) p. 245
limited liability company p. 246
professional corporation p. 247
nonprofit corporation p. 247
organizational test p. 247
strategic alliance p. 248
board of directors p. 252
advisory council p. 255

Discussion Questions

1. Why would investors tend to favor a new business led by a management team over one headed by a lone entrepreneur? Is this preference justified?
2. Discuss the merits of the three most basic legal forms of organization.
3. Does the concept of limited liability apply to a sole proprietorship? Why or why not?
4. Suppose a partnership is set up and operated without a formal partnership agreement. What problems might arise? Explain.
5. Evaluate the three most basic forms of organization in terms of management control by the owner and sharing of the firm's profits.
6. What is an S corporation, and what are its principal advantages?
7. Why are strategic alliances helpful to many small businesses? What steps can an entrepreneur take to create strategic alliances and to prevent their failure?
8. How might a board of directors be of value to management in a small corporation? What qualifications are essential for a director? Is ownership of stock in the firm a prerequisite for being a director?
9. What may account for the failure of most small companies to use boards of directors as more than "rubber stamps"? What impact is this likely to have on the business?
10. How do advisory councils differ from boards of directors? Which would you recommend to a small company owner? Why?

You Make the Call

SITUATION 1

Ted Green and Mark Stroder became close friends as 16-year-olds when both worked part-time for Green's dad in his automotive parts store. After high school, Green went to college, while Stroder joined the National Guard Reserve and devoted his weekends to auto racing. Green continued his association with the automotive parts store by buying and managing two of his father's stores.

In 2009, Green conceived the idea of starting a new business that would rebuild automobile starters, and he asked Stroder to be his partner in the venture. Originally, Stroder was somewhat concerned about working with Green because their personalities are so different. Green has been described as outgoing and enthusiastic, while Stroder is reserved and skeptical. However, Stroder is now out of work, and so he has agreed to the offer. They will set up a small shop behind one of Green's automotive parts stores. Stroder will do all the work; Green will supply the cash. The company will be called Startover Automotive Services, which seems appropriate, given the nature of the business.

Question 1 How relevant are the individual personalities to the success of this entrepreneurial team? Do you think Green and Stroder have a chance to survive their "partnership"? Why or why not?
Question 2 Do you consider it an advantage or a disadvantage that the members of this team are the same age?
Question 3 On balance, is it good or bad that the company will be started by two men who are very close friends? What are the potential benefits and drawbacks of mixing business and friendship in this case?

SITUATION 2

Matthew Freeman started a business in 2005 to provide corporate training in project management. He initially organized his business as a sole proprietorship. Until 2011, he did most of his work on a contract basis for Corporation Education Services (CES). Under the terms of his contract, Freeman was responsible for teaching 3- to 5-day courses to corporate clients—primarily *Fortune* 1000 companies. He was compensated according to a negotiated daily rate, and expenses incurred during a course (hotels, meals, transportation, etc.) were reimbursed by CES. Although some expenses were not reimbursed by CES (such as those for computers and office supplies), Freeman's costs usually amounted to less than 1 percent of his revenues.

In 2011, Freeman increasingly found himself working directly with corporate clients rather than contracting with CES. Over the years, he had considered incorporating but had assumed the costs and inconveniences of this option would outweigh the benefits. However, some of his new clients said that they would prefer to contract with a corporation rather than with an individual. And Freeman sometimes wondered about potential liability problems. On the one hand, he didn't have the same liability issues as some other businesses—he worked out of his home, clients never visited his home office, all courses were conducted in hotels or corporate facilities, and his business involved only services. But he wasn't sure what would happen if a client ended up being dissatisfied with the content and outcomes of his instruction. Finally, he wondered whether there would be tax advantages to incorporating.

Question 1 What are the advantages and disadvantages of running the business as a sole proprietorship? As a corporation?

Question 2 If Freeman decided to incorporate his business, which types of corporations could he form? Which type would you recommend? Why?

SITUATION 3

Julie Patton is co-founder and president of PM Meals, a food-services business that prepares and sells boxed meals and convenience snacks to hotels, convention operators, corporate clients, and community event planners. Patton makes most of the business decisions related to the company and is in charge of generating new accounts; the firm's other co-founder, Angela Marks, has culinary training and oversees the meal-preparation side of the operation. The food they offer represents relatively simple fare, but it is flavorful and attractively presented, exceeding by far what most clients would expect from a boxed-meal provider.

The company has entered a growth phase, which has attracted the attention of a high-potential investor. PM Meals could certainly use the money to support its growing business, but the investment would come with major strings attached. For example, even though the company has been performing nicely without a board of directors, the investor insists that it form one and that he be given a seat on the new board. In his words, "If I am going to put up money for the business, I want to be able to influence how my money is being used."

Patton and Marks are concerned that forming a board and including at least one outside investor (the one who insists on having a seat) will undermine their control and paralyze the business. As they weigh alternatives, they are leaning toward forming a three-person board and accepting the new investment—but they are far from certain as to what they should do.

Question 1 Would you accept the investment and the conditions that go along with it, or refuse it and go a different direction?

Question 2 Can one outside member on a board of three make any real difference in the way the board operates?

Question 3 If you were the owners, whom would you include on the board?

Question 4 If Patton and Marks decide to form a board of directors, what will determine its usefulness or effectiveness? Do you predict that it will be helpful? Why or why not?

Experiential Exercises

1. Prepare a one-page résumé of your personal qualifications to launch a software instruction business at your college or university. Then write a critique that might be prepared by an investor, evaluating your strengths and weaknesses, as shown on the résumé. Identify in the critique any gaps or weaknesses you have that could be covered by forming a management team to start the business.
2. Interview an attorney whose clients include small businesses. Inquire about the legal considerations involved in choosing the form of organization for a new business. Report your findings to the class.
3. Interview the partners of a local business. Inquire about the factors they considered when drawing up their partnership agreement. Report your findings to the class.
4. Discuss with a corporate director, attorney, banker, or business owner the contributions of directors to small firms. Prepare a brief report on your findings. If you discover a particularly well-informed individual, suggest that person to your instructor as a possible guest speaker.

Small Business & Entrepreneurship Resource Center

1. Small businesses often think that they must invent new innovative products or services in order to start successfully. Large companies often partner with entrepreneurs to make such products and services available. A good example is Microsoft, which has an Intellectual Property (IP) Ventures division. Describe how large corporations benefit by making intellectual property available for licensing. Also describe how entrepreneurs benefit as well.

   Source: Mark Henricks, "License to Thrive: How You Can Profit from Big Companies' Tech Ideas," *Entrepreneur*, Vol. 33, No. 10 (October 2005): pp. 22–23.

2. One of the stated advantages of the corporate business form is the concept of limited liability. Limited liability refers to the fact that stockholders personal assets can not be taken by business creditors if

the business fails. Describe the concept of limited liability for corporate business owners. Also discuss if and how the limited liability aspect can be overcome when trying to collect debts from a corporate debtor.

Source: Jane Bahls Easter, "Behind the Mask: When the Corporation Doesn't Protect Its Owner," *Entrepreneur*, Vol. 34, No. 3 (March 2006): p. 80.

Case 8

D'ARTAGNAN (P. 707)

This case highlights some of the common problems that surface when entrepreneurs work together to start and manage a small business.

ALTERNATIVE CASE FOR CHAPTER 8

Case 5, W.S. Darley & Co., p. 702

Business Plan Laying the Foundation

As part of laying the foundation to prepare your own business plan, respond to the following questions regarding your management team, legal form of organization, strategic alliances, and board of directors.

1. Who are the members of your management team? What skills, education, and experience do they bring to the team?
2. What other key managers do you plan to recruit?
3. Do you plan to use consultants? If so, describe their qualifications.
4. What are your plans for future employee recruitment?
5. What will be the compensation and benefit plans for managers and other employees?
6. What style of management will be used? What will be the decision-making process in the company? What mechanisms are in place for effective communication between managers and employees? If possible, present a simple organization chart.
7. How will personnel be motivated? How will creativity be encouraged? How will commitment and loyalty be developed?
8. What employee retention and training programs will be adopted? Who will be responsible for job descriptions and employee evaluations?
9. Who will have an ownership interest in the business?
10. Will the business function as a sole proprietorship, partnership, or corporation? If a corporation, will it be a C corporation, an S corporation, a limited liability company, a professional corporation, or a nonprofit corporation?
11. What are the liability implications of this form of organization?
12. What are the tax advantages and disadvantages of this form of organization?
13. If a corporation, where will the corporation be chartered and when will it be incorporated?
14. What attorney or legal firm has been selected to represent the firm? What type of relationship exists with the company's attorney or law firm?
15. What legal issues are presently or potentially significant?
16. What licenses and/or permits may be required?
17. What strategic alliances are already in place, and what others do you plan to establish in the future? Describe the forms and nature of these alliances. What are the responsibilities of and benefits to the parties involved? What are the exit strategies should an alliance fail?
18. Who are the directors of the company? What are their qualifications? How will they be compensated?

The Location Plan

In the SPOTLIGHT
Use My Accent
www.UseMyAccent.com

Actors face great challenges as they ply their trade, especially when they play characters with foreign accents. Want some proof? Just Google "worst movie accents" and see what you find. Some dialect disasters voted the worst of the worst include Kevin Costner in *Robin Hood: Prince of Thieves* (British, occasionally . . . conceivably), Tom Cruise in *Far and Away* (Irish or leprechaunish?), and Angelina Jolie in *Alexander* (what was that!?!). It's difficult enough to get into character, so managing the character's accent may be asking too much—or so it would seem.

Actors can hire a dialect coach to help them get their lines just right, but that can be very expensive. They can also listen to dialect tapes or CDs, but those won't match up with the lines they have to read. There was no perfect solution—until Odile Rault came up with an idea for a new service. Rault, an actor who lives in Gloucester, England, was practicing lines for a part when she came up against an accent challenge: "I wanted to use an Irish accent for one of the scenes, but I wasn't sure of the pronunciation of a few words like *bodies*." She remembers wishing that she could find a native speaker to read the script so that she could listen to it and get it right and realizing that she would be willing to pay someone for such a service. At that moment, it struck her: "Other actors might be prepared to pay for it, too." So, late in 2009, Rault launched UseMyAccent.com, an online company that brings together

© Kachalkina Veronika/Shutterstock.com

After studying this chapter, you should be able to...

1. Describe the five key factors in locating a brick-and-mortar startup.
2. Discuss the challenges of designing and equipping a physical facility.
3. Recognize both the attraction and the challenges of creating a home-based startup.
4. Understand the potential benefits of locating a startup on the Internet.

LOOKING AHEAD

© iStockphoto.com/Dan Bachman

native "readers" who agree to record a script that will allow an actor to speak a part with perfect authenticity. Readers receive a modest fee for services rendered (less than $10, in some cases), and actors get the assistance they need to improve their auditions and increase their odds of being selected for a part. Readers must be at least 16 years of age to sign up and may register only one accent—their natural, native one. Actors can leave feedback on a reader's profile to encourage good service.

By locating her business on the Internet, Rault's venture brings together buyers (mostly actors) and sellers (readers) from anywhere in the world—in other words, she is using technology to close the distance gap. Readers from many different countries have already registered with the site and uploaded voice samples, and users like what they hear in the MP3 files they are receiving. For example, Jonathan Taylor, a South African performer, hoped to add an Australian accent to his repertoire and found just what he wanted from a young singer/actress in Perth. He got the basic accent in the words he needed "without any imposed interpretation," and he was thrilled with the results. Rault herself used the website to get a handle on an East Coast accent that she needed to audition for a corporate gig. When asked about the quality of the reading she received, she reports, "It was absolutely fabulous!" It must have been. She got the job.

Sources: UseMyAccent.com, http://www.usemyaccent.com/about_usemyaccent.html, accessed November 19, 2010; Patricia Chui, "Worst Movie Accents: 15 Manglings of the Foreign (and Southern) Tongue," http://blog.moviefone.com/2009/08/26/worst-movie-accents, accessed November 22, 2010; and Joanne Kaufman, "Talk Like an Egyptian," *Wall Street Journal*, January 13, 2010, p. A1.

As a practical matter, a new venture idea begins to take shape materially as an entrepreneur works through all of the basic parts of the business plan. And that idea becomes even more real as resources are committed to the implementation of the plan, including the selection of a business location and any facilities and equipment that may be required. For a growing number of small enterprises, this can be nothing more than a briefcase, a cell phone, a little desk space at home, and a website on the Internet. That's the way it was for Odile Rault when she started UseMyAccent.com (see In the Spotlight). As it did for Rault's company, locating on the Internet has changed everything for many startups. It offers global market reach at minimal cost, which provides a tremendous boost to budding ventures that desperately need customers but are lean on funding. The rise of the Internet-based venture has been a game-changing phenomenon.

RESOURCES

Beginning on a Budget

When searching for a location to lease for your business, be sure to use a broker who understands your business, knows what you can afford, and is on your side. Couple the broker with an attorney who can make sure that you understand the lease implications and your team is ready to go!

Remember, you don't need the flashiest equipment and the best of furnishings to get started, just stuff that works. With deals on sites like Craigslist and Freecycle, you could save a bundle! For more information and important specifics on leasing, see Julie Bennett, "How to Negotiate a Lease," *Entrepreneur*, Vol. 38, No. 5 (May 2010), pp. 75–83.

Entrepreneurs at the other end of the location continuum, however, might need a new building and/or a fully stocked warehouse facility and perhaps even forklifts and other equipment to get their planned operations off the ground. You see, it all depends on the nature of the business. But, regardless of the specific resources involved, every location decision should be based on certain fundamental principles that can guide the process and minimize mistakes.

While entrepreneurs who purchase an existing business or a franchise usually receive considerable location guidance from members of the acquired firm or the franchisor, those who choose to start a venture from scratch will quickly find that the location decision can be very time consuming. To help make the task more manageable, this chapter addresses some of the major factors that should be considered when choosing a location and setting up physical facilities. And because starting a home-based business and launching on the Internet have become such popular options, these alternatives are also covered in some detail.

Regardless of how the selection is made, a discussion of key location factors and how they support the location decision should be included in the business plan. This chapter will guide you through that process. But keep in mind that the depth of this discussion will vary from plan to plan, depending on the nature and form of the new venture.

Locating the Brick-and-Mortar Startup

1
Describe the five key factors in locating a brick-and-mortar startup.

The choice of a location is often a one-time decision, but a small business owner may later relocate a venture to reduce operating costs or tap other advantages. A recent survey found that 42 percent of entrepreneurs in the United States believe their current location is best for their business, but nearly half of those polled said they would consider a move if it would help their companies.[1] That flexibility has drawn many entrepreneurs to places like Las Vegas, Nevada, where commercial real estate costs tanked in the wake of the mortgage meltdown. But costs are not the only factor. One small business owner says she likes Las Vegas because it feels "like a giant small town."[2] But location needs and motivations change over time. As a business grows, for example, it is sometimes desirable to expand operations to other locations in order to be closer to customers.[3]

In this chapter, we focus on three primary location options—a traditional physical building, the entrepreneur's home, and a website on the Internet. Although we recognize that the Internet can be an integral part of operations for both a traditional and a home-based business, we treat e-commerce ventures in a separate category because of the Internet's significance as a sole sales outlet for these small businesses. Exhibit 9.1 highlights the three options.

brick-and-mortar store
The traditional physical store from which businesses have historically operated.

THE IMPORTANCE OF THE LOCATION DECISION

The importance of the initial decision as to where to locate a traditional physical building—a **brick-and-mortar store**—is underscored by both the high cost of such a store and the hassle of pulling up stakes and moving an established business. Also, if the site is particularly poor, the business may never become successful, even with adequate

EXHIBIT 9.1 Location Options for the Startup

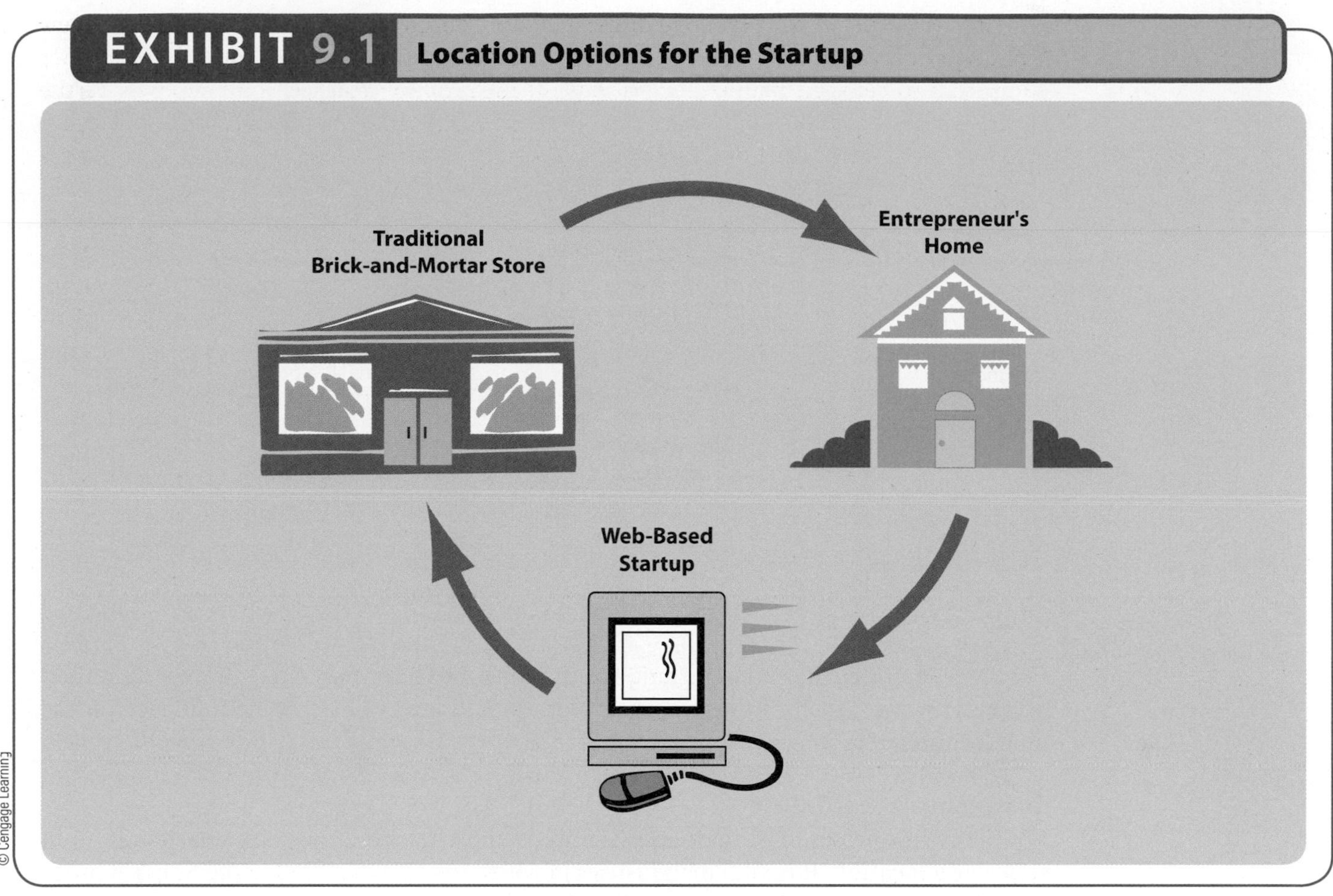

financing and superior managerial ability. The importance of location is so clearly recognized by national chains that they spend hundreds of thousands of dollars investigating sites before establishing new stores.

The choice of a good location is much more vital to some businesses than to others. For example, the site chosen for a clothing store can make or break the business because it must be convenient for customers. The physical location of a painting contractor's office, on the other hand, is of less importance, since customers do not need frequent access to the facility. But even painting contractors may suffer if their business site is poorly chosen. For example, some communities are more willing or able than others to invest resources to keep property in good condition, thereby providing greater opportunities for painting jobs.

KEY FACTORS IN SELECTING A GOOD LOCATION

Five key factors, shown in Exhibit 9.2, guide the location selection process: customer accessibility, business environment conditions, availability of resources, the entrepreneur's personal preference, and site availability and costs. Other factors relevant to the location decision include the following:[4]

- **Neighbor mix:** Who's next door?
- **Security and safety:** How safe is the neighborhood?
- **Services:** Does the city provide trash pickup, for example?
- **Past tenants' fate:** What happened to previous businesses in that location?
- **Location's lifecycle stage:** Is the area developing, stagnant, or in decline?

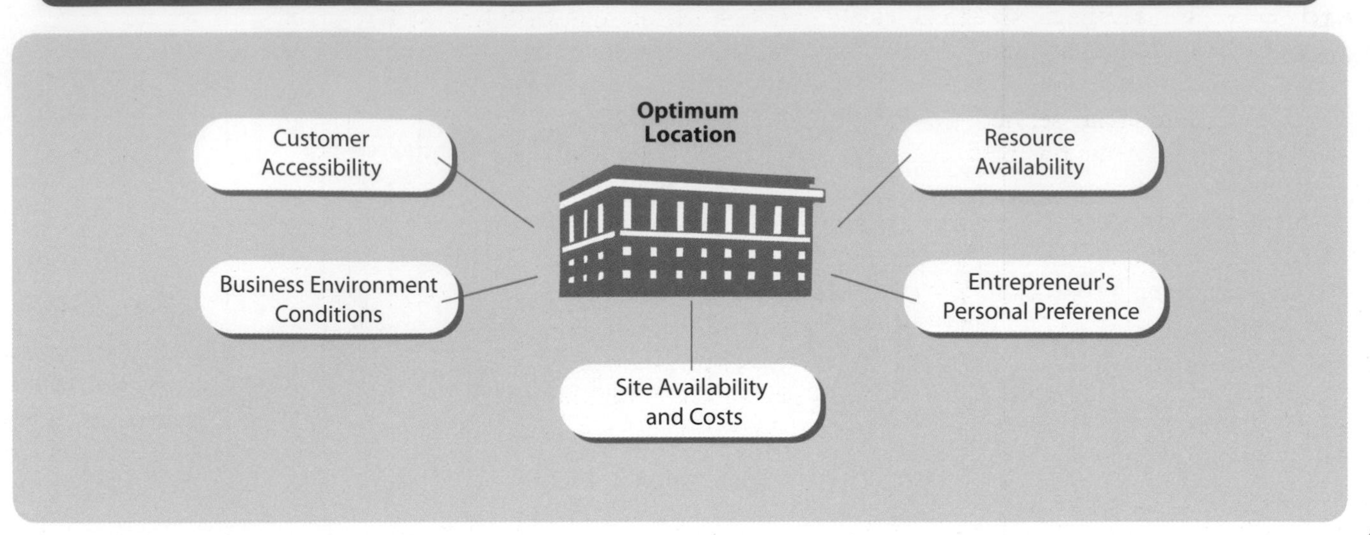

EXHIBIT 9.2 Five Key Factors in Determining a Good Business Location

© Cengage Learning

For a particular business and its unique situation, one factor may carry more weight than others. However, each of the five key factors should always have some influence on the final location decision.

Customer Accessibility

For many businesses, customer accessibility is an extremely important consideration in selecting a location. It is vital in industries in which the cost of shipping the finished product is high relative to the product's value. Products such as packaged ice and soft drinks, for example, must be produced near consuming markets because of the excessive transportation costs involved.

© Transtock Inc. / Alamy

Retail outlets and service firms are typical examples of businesses that must be located so as to make access convenient for target customers. For example, stores offering convenience goods, such as snack foods and gasoline, require a retail location close to target customers; otherwise, consumers will substitute competitive brands when a need arises. Services such as tire repair and hair styling also require a location readily accessible to customers.

Rarely will customers be willing to travel long distances on a repeat basis just to shop. That's why Glenn Campbell and Scott Molander decided to sell hats in high-traffic areas through their startup Hat World, Inc. (selling mostly under the Lids retail brand). Each store, located in a shopping mall or airport, offers a vast assortment of officially licensed baseball-style hats. And this positioning works. From its start in 1995, and after some consolidation moves, the total operation has grown to more than 850 stores nationwide.[5]

Choosing the best location for a retail store used to be a hit-or-miss proposition. The recent emergence of site-selection software has removed much of the guesswork from finding a good place to set up shop, and the popularity of these packages among small business owners has taken off as the software has become more sophisticated and user-friendly. Site-selection programs can give users access to demographic information such as age, income, and race for specific neighborhoods, as well as details about other businesses located nearby, climate conditions, traffic flow, and much more. Just keep in mind that these software packages also have their limitations. For example, many emphasize traffic counts and geographic distance, which can easily overlook factors like rush-hour driving patterns, the potential of railroads or interstates to divide buying clusters, and other, similar issues.

Many commercial service providers (such as ESRI, Inc.) can help you identify an excellent site for your business, but their services are typically far too expensive for a startup or small company. If you want to go it alone but still capture the power of detailed data to make your decision, it may be helpful to visit the official website of the United States Census Bureau (www.census.gov). Users are often overwhelmed when they first see all of the options presented on this site, but don't let this discourage you. If you are patient and work your way through some of the links, you will be amazed by the depth of helpful information you can uncover. We also suggest that you visit the website of *Site Selection* magazine (www.siteselection.com), which offers online tools for researching locations and demographics, including a link to "Fast, Free Location Assistance" (found under "Directories & Tools"). This website also offers a wealth of practical information to those with a little patience and the willingness to sift through it.

Convenient access for customers is one reason many small businesses have successfully established a strong presence on the Internet. With a suitable computer connection, customers can access a small company's home page from anywhere in the world. (Locating a startup on the Internet is discussed later in this chapter.)

Business Environment Conditions

A startup business is affected in a number of ways by the environment in which it operates. Weather is one important environmental feature that influences the location decision, as well as the demand for many products such as air conditioners and outdoor swimming pools. Such factors are particularly important to entrepreneurs like Trey Cobb, the owner of COBB Tuning, the high-performance car parts maker you learned about in Chapter 3. In 2002, Cobb took the bold step of moving his entire small company from Texas to a custom-built facility in Utah. This particular move was all about climate—in this case, improving product-testing conditions. Cobb recognized the advantages of locating the company in an area that provided access to the varied geographic and weather conditions that would be necessary to fully test the car parts that his company manufactures. According to his analysis, Salt Lake City was just the place for that.[6]

Competition, legal requirements, and tax structure are a few of the other critical environmental factors. Entrepreneurs need profits to sustain their businesses; therefore, all factors affecting the financial picture are of great concern. State and local governments can help or hinder a new business by forgiving or levying taxes. State corporate income tax rates vary considerably across the United States, with only a few states having no such tax. One of those with a very generous tax policy is Wyoming,[7] whose website proudly declares, "The state of Wyoming does not levy a personal or corporate income tax. . . . Further, there is no legislative plan to implement any of these types of taxes."[8] This is certainly an attractive feature to consider.

Tax relief for the business is important, but don't forget to factor in the impact of a state's personal income tax rates, which will affect the pay your employees ultimately receive for their labor. These taxes will determine how far wage dollars will go and, in turn, the benefit and satisfaction your workers receive from the business.[9] And there are other important elements in the equation, such as the overall cost of living, which is driven by the price of residential real estate, food, energy, and other necessities of life. A lower *cost of living* can mean a higher *standard of living* for employees. It's possible to do cost-of-living research yourself: Consult websites like http://money.cnn.com and http://salary.com, or contact local economic development agencies and request data on this and other factors, which they will provide free of charge.[10]

© iStockphoto.com/Angelika Schwarz

entrepreneurial experiences

We're from the Government, and We're Here to Help You

You would think that governments, at all levels, would do everything they could to help new businesses get started and flourish—and some do—but this is not always the case. Consider the following "wrinkles in the law" from cities around the United States that have caused setbacks in entrepreneurs' business aspirations.

© Noam Armonn/Shutterstock.com

- Esmeralda Rodriguez was in the process of opening a play center in Chicago and had to pay rent on her facility while she waited for the permits required to open her business. After a year of delays, and with her savings running out, she decided to give up on her dream.
- Window signs may be a vital and affordable form of advertising for small businesses, but don't expect Houston officials to think of them that way. The city strictly limits all such promotion in the name of aesthetics.
- James Tia, a former lawyer, sold meatless burritos in Washington, D.C.—that is, until the city shut the operation down "because his rice was not on the list of approved foods." After a year and a half of lobbying and with favorable test results from a food-safety expert in hand, he was finally able to get the business back on track. "I couldn't have done it without the help of an attorney," says Tia. "And I was the attorney."
- Want to operate a home-based business in Los Angeles? Then be sure to read the fine print. The city's regulations could keep you from using your home to advertise, manufacture, or sell any products—among many other limitations.
- In Miami, jitney van services were allowed to flourish briefly because of an accidental loophole in the law. The county responded swiftly, however, banning jitneys and closing the gap in the law by requiring startups first to prove that they would not be cutting into the business of existing competitors. Does this sound like a level playing field?
- Philadelphia required small business owner Ramesh Naropanth to install new gates on his convenience store before the city would permit him to sell sandwiches. The unnecessary improvement set him back $8,000.

So what's a small business owner to do? Before getting discouraged, understand that these situations are by no means universal, and entrepreneurs manage to start more than half a million new businesses in the United States *every month*! Also, it helps to know that many cities are taking steps to make it easier and cheaper for businesses to comply with their rules and regulations. For example, New York just announced that it is implementing 14 new measures that will moderate the challenges and encourage startups and business expansion. You can make your new venture dreams come true; however, you should definitely brace yourself for at least a few regulatory bumps and bruises along the way.

Sources: Robert Frommer, "D.C. Entrepreneurs Wrapped in Red Tape," *Washington Times*, October 25, 2010, http://www.washingtontimes.com/news/2010/oct/25/dc-entrepreneurs-wrapped-in-red-tape/, accessed November 24, 2010; Frank Lombardi, "City Revamps Regulations to Give Small Owners a Break," *New York Daily News*, April 28, 2010, http://www.nydailynews.com/ny_local/2010/04/28/2010-04-28_city_revamps_regulations_to_give_small_business_owners_a_break.html, accessed November 24, 2010; Chip Mellor and Dana Berliner, "Small Businesses Losing Out to Red Tape," *USA Today*, October 25, 2010, http://www.usatoday.com/news/opinion/forum/2010-10-21-mellor26_st_N.htm, accessed November 24, 2010; and Laura Petrecca, "Recession, Layoffs Fuel Many to Start Small Businesses," *USA Today*, September 18, 2009, http://www.usatoday.com/money/smallbusiness/startup/week1-exploring-small-business-options.htm, accessed November 24, 2010.

Many states offer location incentives. One popular strategy is to establish **enterprise zones**, which are created to attract jobs to economically deprived areas. Sponsored by local city and county governments, these zones lure businesses by offering regulatory and tax relief. In exchange for locating or expanding in these areas, eligible business firms receive total exemption, for three to five years, from the property taxes normally assessed on a new plant and equipment. To give you an idea of how widespread enterprise zones are becoming, Oregon had 59 such zones as of November 2010.[11]

enterprise zones State-designated areas that are established to bring jobs to economically deprived regions through regulatory and tax incentives.

Enterprise zones are not a cure-all. Locating a business or facility in one of these areas will not solve problems such as those created by poor management, and it certainly will not make up for an ill-conceived business idea. However, enterprise zones can be used as a catalyst to help jump-start a small firm.

While most efforts of state and city governments are designed to support startups, many cities have regulations that restrict new business operations under certain circumstances. For example, some cities have zoning ordinances that may limit the operations of home-based businesses. These ordinances often apply to factors related to traffic and parking, signage, nonrelated employees working in a home, the use of a home more as a business than as a residence, the sale of retail goods to the public, and the storage of hazardous materials and work-related equipment.[12]

Availability of Resources

The availability of resources needed to operate a business should also be considered when selecting a location. Raw materials, labor supply, and transportation are some of the factors that have a bearing on location. The proximity of important sources of raw materials and a suitable labor supply are particularly critical considerations in the location of most manufacturing businesses.

If raw materials required by a company's operations are not readily available in all areas, then regions in which these materials abound will offer significant location advantages. This is especially true for businesses that are dependent on bulky or heavy raw materials that lose much of their size or weight in the manufacturing process. A sawmill is an example of a business that must stay close to its raw materials in order to operate economically.

The suitability of the labor supply for a manufacturer depends on the nature of its production process. Labor-intensive operations need to be located near workers with appropriate skills and reasonable wage requirements. A history of acceptable levels of labor productivity and peaceful relations with employers are also important factors. Companies that depend on semiskilled or unskilled workers usually locate in an area with surplus labor, while other firms may need to be close to a pool of highly skilled labor. If the required talent is unavailable, relocation may be necessary, even it if means moving to another state. This is certainly true for small businesses that are in high-technology manufacturing. According to Tim Nitti, a location expert with a major site-selection firm, "Probably the single biggest emerging reason why anyone is moving companies . . . is access to talent."[13]

Access to good transportation is important to many companies. For example, good highways and bus systems provide customers with convenient access to retail stores, which encourages sales. For small manufacturers, quality transportation is especially vital. They must carefully evaluate all trucking routes, considering the costs of both transporting supplies to the manufacturing location and shipping the finished product to customers. It is critical that they know whether these costs will allow their product to be competitively priced.

Personal Preference of the Entrepreneur

As a practical matter, many entrepreneurs tend to focus primarily on their personal preference and convenience when locating a business. Statistics hint at this, showing that nearly half of all entrepreneurs (47 percent) live no more than a five-minute drive from their venture's location.[14] And, despite a world of alternatives, small business owners often choose to stay in their home community; in fact, the thought of locating elsewhere never even enters their minds. Just because an individual has always lived in a particular town, however, does not automatically make the town a satisfactory business location.

On the other hand, locating a business in one's home community sometimes makes perfect sense. In fact, doing so may offer certain unique advantages that cannot be found elsewhere. From a personal point of view, the entrepreneur generally appreciates and feels comfortable with the atmosphere of the home community, whether it is a small town or a large city. As a practical business matter, the entrepreneur may find it easier to establish credit; hometown bankers who know an entrepreneur's personal background and reputation can be more confident in their support of a startup. And having personal connections in the local business community can lead to invaluable business advice. If local residents are potential customers, the prospective entrepreneur probably has a better idea of their tastes and preferences than would an outsider. And friends and relatives may be the entrepreneur's first customers and gladly spread positive reports about the products or services they buy. Though such decisions are usually based on emotion, there are clearly some potential upside benefits of locating a startup close to home.

The personal preferences that drive the location decision are as varied as the entrepreneurs who make it. Sometimes entrepreneurs choose a location offering unique lifestyle advantages. Artist Lolly Shera set up her studio in a 156-square-foot treehouse behind her home in Fall City, Washington. "When it's blowing hard, this structure moves, and it feels like a boat that's moored," says Shera of her leafy workplace. "It groans and creaks. It's like being in a live animal. There's a soul in it that, if you're open to it, you can feel."[15] It's easy to see how an artist would draw inspiration from such an unusual "high-rise" location, but it does have its limitations—convenient parking and customer access, for example.

Personal preference is important, but it would be unwise to allow this to take priority over obvious location weaknesses that are almost certain to limit or even doom the success of the enterprise. The location decision must take all relevant factors into consideration.

Site Availability and Costs

Once an entrepreneur has settled on a certain area of the country, a specific site must still be chosen. The availability of potential sites and the costs associated with obtaining them must be investigated.

After evaluating a site for his new business, one entrepreneur is said to have exclaimed, "It must be a good site—I know of four businesses that have been there in the last two years!" Fortunately, such a misguided approach to site evaluation is not typical of entrepreneurs, many of whom recognize the value of seeking professional assistance in determining site availability and appropriateness, based on the needs of the business. As just one example, local realtors can serve as a good source of insight.

business incubator
A facility that provides shared space, services, and management assistance to new businesses.

If an entrepreneur's top choices are unavailable, other options must be considered. One alternative is to share facilities with other enterprises. In recent years, business incubators have sprung up in all areas of the country. A **business incubator** is a facility that rents space to new businesses or to people wishing to start businesses. Incubators are often located in repurposed buildings, such as abandoned warehouses or schools. They serve fledgling businesses by making space available, offering management advice, and providing other forms of assistance (including clerical support), all of which help lower operating costs. An incubator tenant can be fully operational the day after moving in, without buying phones, renting a copier, or hiring office employees.

Most incubators can accommodate different kinds of early-stage ventures, but some are beginning to focus on a specific business niche, such as fashion, food, or design. And though these may be aimed at emerging fields or specializations that require expensive equipment or other resources in order to get a start, they are not all technology-focused. Many provide access to industry-specific resources. Hot Bread Kitchen Incubates, for example, provides food startups with access to "seven kitchens complete with industrial trial-size convection ovens, deep fryers, blenders, kettles, grills and a host of other devices."[16]

Client businesses also receive recipe scale-up assistance, training in kitchen-use efficiency, supervised production time, general business training, and solid partnership opportunities with other startups in the incubator.[17] To avoid renting space to new ventures that are apt to compete directly with one another, most specialty incubators accept no more than

© iStockphoto.com/Angelika Schwarz

entrepreneurial experiences

Here Today, Gone Tomorrow—or at Least Pretty Soon

Incubators are designed to provide temporary facilities to a budding business, but we tend to think of most small business location selections as permanent decisions. However, if you keep your eyes open, you may notice a lot more "pop-up stores" opening up these days. These may look like regular stores, but they are open for only a few months by design. Small business owners use this strategy for a number of reasons, such as to spread the word on a brand, to unload excess or old inventory, or to test a new business idea or a new market. Jonah Staw, CEO and co-founder of Little Miss Matched—which sells pairs of unmatched but coordinated socks for young girls—opened two pop-up stores in New York City to "get tons of eyeballs and tons of shoppers." He found the slow economy and raft of store closings gave him cheap access to expensive shopping areas, and he figured that a presence there—although temporary—would give the company some exposure that would pay off down the road. What he didn't count on was the rich learning the experience provided. "We learned how customers flowed through the stores, what sold and what didn't," reports Staw. "This gave us real intelligence on product success and failure." And with hopes of just breaking even on these short-term gigs, the fact that the stores actually generated a profit was a very pleasant and unexpected bonus.

© First Light / Alamy

Some small businesses have permanent facilities, but they use them only for part of every year. Think seasonal businesses like haunted houses in October and fireworks stands around New Year's and the Fourth of July.

But what if your location is *always* changing—like, every day? That's the way it is for Cookies-N-Cream, a company started by three entrepreneurs who deal in t-shirts and collectible toys, sold to pulsating hip-hop rhythms, from a window cut into the side of a converted DHL delivery truck. But with a shop on wheels, how will customers know where to find it? Ganiu Ladejobi, the startup's creative director, expresses little concern about that. In his mind, they do have a location, of sorts. As he puts it, "We're at the intersection of cool and cooler." And he must be justified in his relaxed attitude, because sales are impressive. On a good day, they can bring in $1,000; but even on a slow day, it's still an adequate $300. That doesn't seem like a lot of revenue until you consider the startup's low overhead, which is the key to their location strategy. It cost just $10,433 to buy and equip the truck, which is an amazing bargain compared to the $53,000 *a month* rent for shops near where the trio parks to wheel and deal! Going mobile as a vendor can have its wrinkles (for example, New York City gives out only 853 general merchandise vending licenses a year, and New Orleans permits only food to be sold from a truck), but Cookies-N-Cream has shown that the formula works. And like Jonah Staw's Little Miss Matched, they prove that being here today and gone tomorrow might not be such a bad thing.

Sources: Jason Del Rey, "Shop Now, Before It All Disappears," *Inc.*, Vol. 32, No. 6 (July/August 2010), pp. 126–127; Sarah E. Needleman, "Farm House to Haunted House: Making Hay with Horror," *Wall Street Journal* (October 19, 2010), pp. A1, A16; and Regina Schrambling, "Four Wheels & Style to Burn," *Entrepreneur*, Vol. 38, No. 11 (November 2010), pp. 102–111. **http://www.littlemissmatched.com; http://www.claytonfearfarm.com; http:www.bakedinny.com (for Cookies-N-Cream)** two startups that target the same market. Nonetheless, this arrangement can still lead to its share of complications—for example, similar businesses sometimes try to tie up crucial pieces of equipment for their own use and advantage. But despite the drawbacks, locating in a niche incubator must be worth the trouble—spaces are reportedly in short supply.[18]

The purpose of business incubators is to see new businesses hatch, grow, and leave the incubator, so the situation is temporary *by design*. But it appears that many businesses are looking for a permanent shared-office arrangement. As an indication of the demand, Regus Group PLC, a leading provider of shared office space, finds that its business is booming. The firm currently operates more than 1,100 business centers in 500 cities spread over 85 countries.[19]

But perhaps you are more of a free spirit. One variation on the shared-office-space theme is the "co-working" movement, which involves shared working spaces (sometimes an office) that allow mostly freelancers, consultants, artists, and other independent workers "to work and connect under the same roof." Office Nomads is one such place. Owned by Jacob Sayles and Susan Evans, this Seattle-based facility "combines the best of a home office, an Internet café and a traditional office" to give its tenants prospects for greater interaction, a sense of camaraderie, and networking opportunities—all without toxic office politics (for the most part) and mind-numbing commutes. And if you are on the road, you can drop in and work, at little or no cost, at reciprocating co-working establishments in 17 states and 13 countries. With typical rates running from $25 a day to around $500 a month, co-working facilities can be a real bargain.[20] They're not for everyone, but they are a good working alternative for some entrepreneurs.

When it comes to site selection—whether permanent or more flexible—the process should factor in all relevant costs. Unfortunately, an entrepreneur is frequently unable to afford the "best" site. The costs involved in building on a new site may be prohibitive, or the purchase price of an existing structure may exceed the entrepreneur's budget.

Assuming that suitable building space is available, the entrepreneur must decide whether to lease or buy. Although more small business owners choose to purchase their buildings,[21] the advantages of leasing often outweigh the benefits of owning. Leasing certainly offers two important advantages:

- A large cash outlay is avoided. This is important for a new small firm, which typically lacks adequate financial resources.
- Risk is reduced by minimizing investment and by postponing commitments for space until the success of the business is assured and the nature of building requirements is better known.

When entering into a lease agreement, the entrepreneur should check the landlord's insurance policies to be sure there is proper coverage for various types of risks. If not, the lessee should seek coverage under his or her own policy. And it is important to have the terms of the lease agreement reviewed by an attorney. Sometimes, an attorney can arrange for special clauses to be added to a lease, such as an escape clause that allows the lessee to exit the agreement under certain conditions. And an attorney can also ensure that an entrepreneur will not be unduly exposed to liability for damages caused by the gross negligence of others. Consider the experience of one firm that wished to rent

300 square feet of storage space in a large complex of offices and shops. On the sixth page of the landlord's standard lease, the firm's lawyer found language that could have made the firm responsible for the entire 30,000-square-foot complex if it burned down, regardless of blame! Competent legal counsel may not be cheap, but the services that it provides can certainly save an entrepreneur a lot of money and heartache.

Designing and Equipping the Physical Facilities

2
Discuss the challenges of designing and equipping a physical facility.

A well-written location plan should describe the physical space in which the business will be housed and include an explanation of any equipment needs. The plan may call for a new building or an existing structure, but ordinarily a new business occupies an existing building, with minor or major remodeling.

CHALLENGES IN DESIGNING THE PHYSICAL FACILITIES

When specifying building requirements, the entrepreneur must avoid committing to a space that is too large or too luxurious for the company's needs. At the same time, the space should not be so small or limiting that operations are hindered or become inefficient. Buildings do not produce profits directly; they merely house the operations and personnel that do so. Therefore, the ideal building will be practical, not extravagant.

The general suitability of a building for a given type of business operation depends on the functional requirements of the enterprise. For example, a restaurant should ideally be on one level; a manufacturer's production processes that are interlinked should be in the same building and located near one another. Other important factors to consider include the age and condition of the building, potential fire hazards, the quality of heating and air conditioning systems, the adequacy of lighting and restroom facilities, and appropriate entrances and exits. Obviously, these factors are weighted differently for a factory operation than for a wholesale or retail operation. But in every case, the comfort, convenience, and safety of the business's employees and customers should be taken into consideration.

CHALLENGES IN EQUIPPING THE PHYSICAL FACILITIES

The final step in arranging for physical facilities is the purchase or lease of equipment and tools. The *Wall Street Journal* reported that, overwhelmingly, owners of small businesses would rather own their equipment than lease it (see Exhibit 9.3). The majority believe that, in the long run, it is cheaper to buy than to lease. Having the flexibility to use the equipment as they wish and to keep it until it is no longer needed are also important reasons why small business owners prefer to own rather than lease. Still, the leasing option has advocates as well. So what should a small business owner do? To make an informed decision on this, use an equipment lease-versus-buy calculator. (A number of these can be found online with a simple Internet search.) It's also a good idea to check with an accountant to be sure that any tax consequences of your decision to lease or buy are considered.

The types of equipment and tools required vary greatly, depending on the nature of the business. This is obvious in the three areas discussed in the following subsections—manufacturing, retailing, and office equipment.

Manufacturing Equipment

Machines used in factories can include either general-purpose or special-purpose equipment. **General-purpose equipment** requires minimal investment and is easily adapted to various operations. Small machine shops and cabinet shops, for example, use this type of equipment, which can be set up to handle two or more shop operations using the same piece of machinery. This offers flexibility, which is most important to industries in which

general-purpose equipment
Machines that serve many functions in the production process.

EXHIBIT 9.3 Small Business Owners Choose Buying over Leasing

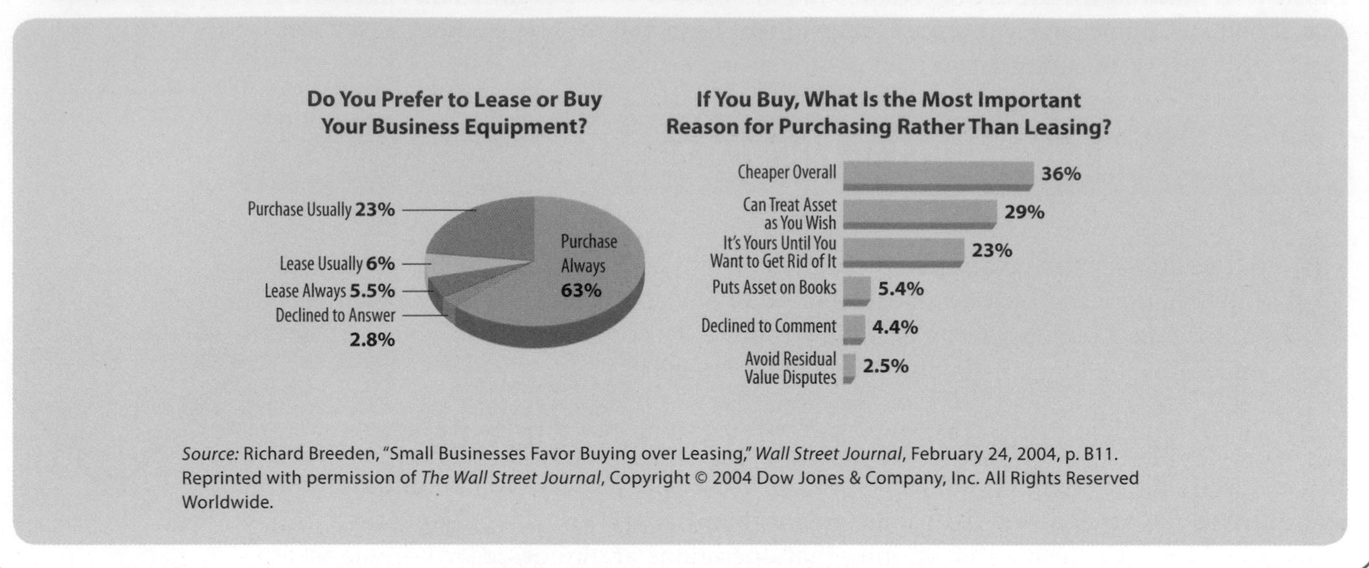

Source: Richard Breeden, "Small Businesses Favor Buying over Leasing," *Wall Street Journal*, February 24, 2004, p. B11. Reprinted with permission of *The Wall Street Journal*, Copyright © 2004 Dow Jones & Company, Inc. All Rights Reserved Worldwide.

special-purpose equipment Machines designed to serve specialized functions in the production process.

products are so new that the technology is not yet well developed or there are frequent design changes. **Special-purpose equipment**, such as bottling machines and manufacturing robots used in factories, offers a more narrow range of possible applications and is more expensive to buy or lease. And a small firm can use special-purpose equipment economically only if it makes a standardized product on a fairly large scale. Upgrades via special tooling can lead to greater output per machine-hour of operation and reduce the labor cost per unit of product even further. On the downside, though, it is important to remember that this equipment has little or no resale value due to its narrow range of possible applications.

Retailing Equipment

Small retailers need merchandise display racks or counters, storage racks, shelving, mirrors, seats for customers, customer pushcarts, cash registers, and other items to facilitate selling. Such equipment may be costly, but it is usually less expensive than that necessary for a factory operation. And enterprising entrepreneurs often find ways to reduce startup or expansion costs by purchasing used equipment, making their own, or finding other ways to improvise.

© Jeffrey Liao/Shutterstock.com

If a store is intended to serve a high-income market, its fixtures should signal this by displaying the elegance and style expected by such customers. For example, polished mahogany showcases with bronze fittings can help to create an upscale setting. Indirect lighting, thick rugs, and oversized easy chairs also communicate luxury to clients. In contrast, a store that caters to lower-income customers should concentrate on simplicity. Luxurious fixtures and plush seating would suggest an atmosphere that is inconsistent with low prices and only add to the cost of the operation, making it more difficult to keep prices low.

Office Equipment

Every business office—even a home office—needs furniture, storage cabinets, and other such items. Major manufacturers of office furniture, such as Steelcase, Herman Miller, and Haworth, can certainly provide the necessary desks, chairs, and cabinetry, but so can scores of smaller vendors. Check out local sources of used office furniture, which may have items for sale that are still very presentable but a lot less expensive. And always make your decisions with the future in mind. If you select furnishings that are simple, free-standing, and detachable, then, when your business takes off, you can easily move them all to a larger facility.

Perhaps an even more challenging task is selecting office equipment—computers, fax machines, copiers, printers, and telephone systems—that reflect the latest technological advances applicable to a particular business. Careful selection of these items can help a business operate efficiently.

The location plan should list the major pieces of equipment needed to outfit a business office. By identifying major equipment needs in this part of the business plan, the small business owner can ensure that the financial section of the plan will include funds for their purchase.

BUSINESS IMAGE

All new ventures, whether they are retailers, wholesalers, manufacturers, or service businesses, should be concerned with projecting the most appropriate image to customers and the public at large. The look and "feel" of the workplace should create an impression that says something about the quality of a firm's product or service and about the way the business is operated in general. For a small firm, and especially a startup, it is important to use the physical facilities to convey the image of a stable, professional company. Potential customers are likely to avoid doing business with a company that has every appearance of a fly-by-night operation.

Factors as basic as color and interior design should be considered. Even before the first customer shows up, companies sometimes find that their financial backers are unwilling to hand over investment dollars until an office or retail store is perceived as attractive and inviting. It is not unusual for a small company to go through a process similar to that of a California-based chain of sandwich shops, which had to choose between suggested color/design options: First, came a palette inspired by images of a sun-drenched picnic at the beach or one that played on farmers' markets, with warm yellow light and baskets full of colorful vegetables.[22]

The farmers' market theme was eventually chosen because "it evokes intimacy, freshness, and quality in a casual environment."[23] This design choice may have been obvious, but only to the trained eye. And that is exactly the point. If the image aspect of the facilities equation is beyond your expertise and insight, consult with someone who can help you to make decisions that work.

Image is the engine of sales, so carefully consider how to mold your space to create a distinct and appropriate impression, yet still provide plenty of space, allow easy traffic flow, pass building inspections, and more—all in keeping with your budget and business goals. The way your facilities, customers, and employees come together will be critical to the success of your new business.

Locating the Startup in the Entrepreneur's Home

Rather than lease or buy a commercial site, many entrepreneurs choose instead to use their basement, garage, or spare room for their operations, creating a **home-based business**. In the past, a home location for a business was almost always considered second-rate. But times have changed. Despite the limitations and potential for image problems, home-based entrepreneurs no longer feel embarrassed about their location. In fact, recent research has shown that home-based businesses may actually enjoy an advantage

home-based business
A business that maintains its primary facility in the residence of its owner.

over other companies when it comes to certain dimensions of financial performance (for example, achieving a first sale).[24] The home office, once viewed as a passing phase on the path to growth for many businesses, has become a viable permanent option for some. According to recent reports, more than 18.4 million Americans work from home,[25] and many of them have no plans ever to change their location.

THE ATTRACTION OF HOME-BASED BUSINESSES

Why do many entrepreneurs find operating a business at home so appealing? Motivations vary (see Exhibit 9.4), but the main attractions of a home-based business relate to financial and family lifestyle considerations such as these.

- Get a business up and running quickly and cheaply
- Have something interesting to do, and get paid for doing it
- Be your own boss, and reap the rewards from your efforts
- Spend more time with family and friends
- Save time and money wasted on daily commutes

Financial Considerations

Like most business ventures, a home-based business has an important goal—earning money—and locating at home helps increase profits by reducing costs. For example, a freelance writer of magazine articles may need only a computer, a few office supplies, and an Internet connection to launch a business from home. Nearly all writers own a computer, so the true startup costs for such a business may be only a few hundred dollars.

EXHIBIT 9.4 Some Common Reasons for Starting a Home-Based Business

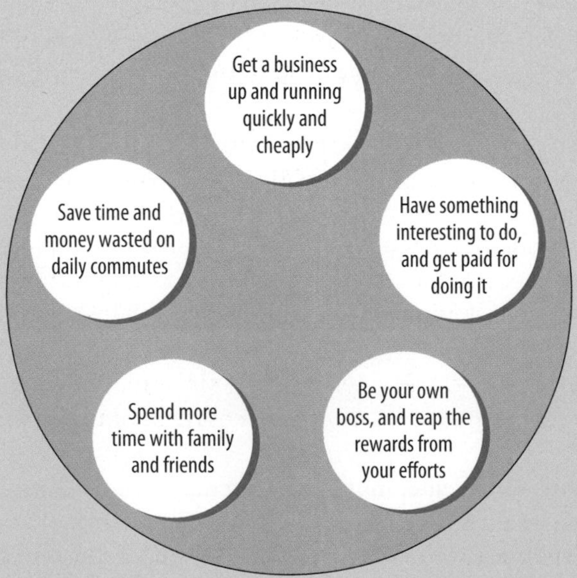

Source: Ken Harthun, "Top 5 Reasons for Starting a Home-Based Business," April 14, 2010, http://www.examiner.com/home-based-business-in-cincinnati/top-5-reasons-for-starting-a-home-based-business, accessed January 31, 2011.

With the ups and downs of the advertising industry, Donavan Andrews and Stephen Smyk thought it would be best to start their fledgling agency, called Performance Bridge Advertising, in their home. "[We] built the business slowly and were conservative until we got to the point where we had excess capital," says Andrews. This conservative approach worked well; Andrews and Smyk moved into office space in a professional building only four months after they started the business.[26]

Family Lifestyle Considerations

Many young entrepreneurs remain in a family business because of close ties to relatives. Similarly, entrepreneurs who locate business operations in the home are frequently motivated by the desire to spend more time with family members.

Marissa Shipman, owner of Shipman Associates, Inc., the manufacturer of The Balm line of cosmetics, launched her business from her home in 2001. "I love working from home," says Shipman. Her home, however, has had to change several times to accommodate her growing business. Shipman Associates is a true family affair; despite being spread across the country, her family helps run the business. Her dad, who lives in Greenwich, Connecticut, and a sister in Philadelphia both work out of their homes to help grow the business. Shipman thinks that a home is a great place to start a business: "If you have something you think could work, do it on a small scale and see."[27]

THE CHALLENGES OF HOME-BASED BUSINESSES

Just as most businesses located at commercial sites have their problems, home-based businesses face special challenges because of their location. We briefly examine two of these—business image and legal considerations. A third challenge—family and business conflicts—was discussed in Chapter 5.

Professional Image

Maintaining a professional image when working at home is a major challenge for many home-based entrepreneurs. Allowing young children to answer the telephone, for example, may undermine a company's image. Likewise, a baby crying or a dog barking in the background during a phone call can be distracting to a client and discourage sales.

If clients or salespeople visit the home-based business, it is critical that a professional office area be maintained. Space limitations sometimes make this difficult. For example, when you own a home-based business, house guests can create a real problem. Unless you want Aunt Zerelda wandering into a client meeting in her bathrobe or your nephew Jimmie playing his electric guitar during a work call, ground rules need to be set for house guests. Otherwise, major disruptions to the business are bound to occur.

But establishing appropriate boundaries between home and business is easier said than done. Consider one successful work-at-home small business owner's take on this:

> *The moment you create a business, you step into a twilight zone where the barrier between what is work and what is not starts to break down. The deterioration accelerates for entrepreneurs who work out of their homes. You may start off with a home-based business but soon find yourself with a business where you and your family also happen to live.*[28]

So, it's not just a matter of preventing family members from spoiling business opportunities; family life is paramount and should be shielded, in reasonable ways, from the creeping reach of the company's operations. The groan of extra car traffic, the presence of strangers (customers and employees) wandering through the house, inconvenient stacks of inventory and packing materials cluttering common areas, brusquely rejected invitations to break the focus on work to join one's spouse for lunch—these and many other hassles and inconveniences are everyday fare for the family of a home-based entrepreneur. And they call for patience and an extra dose of understanding from everyone involved.

Legal Considerations

zoning ordinances Local laws regulating land use.

Local laws can sometimes pose serious problems for home-based businesses. **Zoning ordinances**, for example, regulate the types of enterprises permitted to operate within certain areas, and some cities outlaw any type of home-based business within city limits.

Many zoning laws, dating as far back as the 1930s, have never been updated. The intent of such laws is to protect a neighborhood's residential quality by forbidding commercial signs and preventing parking problems. The neighborhood you live in may have a homeowners' association that can limit your ability to run a home-based business. Some entrepreneurs first become aware of these zoning laws when neighbors initiate zoning enforcement actions. Consider "good neighbor" Lauren Januz of Libertyville Township, Illinois.

> *One of Januz's neighbors was running a landscaping and tree-service business out of his home. He erected a large fence to obscure the view of his heavy equipment which was fine with the subdivision's other residents, but he had 10 to 15 workers parking their cars on the street every day. "This is an area of $300,000 homes, and a lot of the cars were really wrecks," explains Januz. Although several neighbors approached the offending property owner, he made no attempt to correct the problem, and a complaint was finally filed with the Lake County Building and Zoning Department. He ended up selling the property and relocating the business.*[29]

There are also tax issues related to a home-based business. For example, a separate space must be clearly devoted to the activities of the business if an entrepreneur is to claim a tax deduction for this. A knowledgeable accountant can help explain these tax regulations.

And don't forget the insurance considerations that may affect a home-based business. A homeowner's policy is not likely to cover an entrepreneur's business activities, liabilities, and equipment. Therefore, he or she should always consult a trustworthy insurance agent about policy limitations to avoid unpleasant surprises down the road.

The bad news for home-based businesses is that they often face significant hassles and limitations, such as those outlined above. The good news is that these ventures now have access to powerful business-application technologies that can help them compete against rivals, even those with a commercial site. Tools like the Internet make it possible to operate many types of businesses from almost any location—in fact, virtually every product sold in traditional retail outlets is now also available online. In the next section, we examine the potential of the Internet as a place to host a new business.

Locating the Startup on the Internet

We live in an ever-changing digital economy that is fueled by the tremendous growth of the Web. Access to the Internet continues to transform the way we live and the way business is conducted. It is important for aspiring entrepreneurs to learn as much as they can about cyberspace because online business opportunities continue to expand.

How does the Internet support e-commerce? What benefits does e-commerce offer a startup? What business models reflect an e-commerce strategy? These are the primary questions we address in this section of the chapter. We hope that our discussion will help you understand both the opportunities and the limitations associated with today's digital economy. Additional topics on this subject are discussed in other chapters.

WHAT IS E-COMMERCE?

What does the term *e-commerce* really describe? **E-commerce** refers to electronic commerce, or the buying or selling of products or services over the Internet. It is an alternative means of conducting business transactions that traditionally have been carried out by telephone, by mail, or face to face in a brick-and-mortar store. Following the crash of Web-based enterprises about a decade ago, Internet businesses are now growing in new ways and faster than ever. And with good reason! Locating on the Web can fundamentally reshape the way small firms conduct business. Far more than a simple alternative to the brick-and-mortar store, the Internet can significantly boost a small company's financial performance.[30]

e-commerce
Electronic commerce, or the buying and selling of products or services over the Internet.

ACTION

Online Companies

If you want to establish an online presence, be sure that you have a quality product to offer or you will never gain and hold your customers' trust. And if you want your website to generate a lot of hits, it must be easy to navigate and skillfully targeted to your audience. So, get some help from professional website developers and continually ask for customer feedback so that you can fine-tune what you are doing. And if you are planning to adapt content to your site, be sure to run everything by your lawyer—the last thing a new business needs is a copyright lawsuit!

BENEFITS OF E-COMMERCE TO STARTUPS

Electronic commerce can benefit a startup in many ways. It certainly allows a new venture to compete with bigger businesses on a more level playing field. Because of their limited resources, small firms often cannot reach beyond local markets. So those small firms confined to the brick-and-mortar world typically can serve only a restricted region. But the Internet blurs geographic boundaries and expands a small company's reach. In fact, e-commerce allows any business access to customers almost anywhere.

The experience of a company called Beauty Encounter shows how the Internet is proving to be a great equalizer, giving small firms a presence comparable to that of marketplace giants. In a large field of perfume and beauty products heavyweights, this young Southern California-based player is taking on all challengers—and thriving. The business is an extension of three physical stores that were started by a Vietnamese couple who immigrated to the United States in 1980. Their daughter, Jacquelyn Tran, recognized the limitations of such operations and decided to carve out her own space in the global marketplace by establishing an online presence in 1999. Since then, the company has done nothing but grow, proving that the Internet allows small companies to play in the big leagues. In fact, the company recently had to expand into a larger warehouse facility with a retail showroom just to keep up with the pace of growth.[31] Beauty Encounter's experience shows that going online can be the key that unlocks the door of opportunity for small companies, regardless of the industry.

It should also be pointed out that an e-commerce operation can help the startup with early cash flow problems by compressing the sales cycle—that is, reducing the time between receiving an order and converting the sale to cash. E-commerce systems can be designed to generate an order, authorize a credit card purchase, and contact a supplier and shipper in a matter of a few minutes, all without human assistance. The shorter cycle translates into quicker payments from customers and improved cash flows to the business.

Beyond the advantages outlined above, e-commerce enables small firms to build on one of their greatest strengths—customer relationships. The Internet has brought new life and technology to bear on the old-fashioned notion of customer service. **Electronic Customer Relationship Marketing (eCRM)** is an electronically based system that helps a company handle its customer relationships more effectively. At the heart of eCRM is a customer-centric data warehouse. A typical eCRM system allows an e-commerce firm to integrate data from websites, call centers, sales force reports, and other customer contact points, with the goal of building customer loyalty. (You will learn more about customer relationship management in Chapter 14, which focuses on this very important topic.)

Electronic Customer Relationship Marketing (eCRM) An electronically based system that emphasizes customer relationships.

Most often, an entrepreneur who chooses not to engage in e-commerce has concluded that this option is not important to his or her business,[32] but there are also a number of specific deterrents. For example, e-commerce has significant limitations that should be considered when deciding whether or not to locate a business online and how to operate it. These limitations fall into two categories: technical limitations and nontechnical limitations. *Technical limitations* include the cost and hassle of developing and maintaining a website, insufficient telecommunications bandwidth, constantly changing software, and the need to integrate digital and nondigital sales and production information. The small business owner should also take into account customer access limitations with regard to cable, wireless, and other connectivity options, as well as the fact that some potential customers still do not have convenient access to the Internet. *Nontechnical limitations* include factors such as customers' concerns about their privacy, the security of your company's Internet operations, customers' inability to touch or try on products, and the challenges of dealing with differences in cultures, languages, and legal systems around the world.[33]

E-COMMERCE BUSINESS MODELS

One of the fundamental features of an online operation is the business model upon which it is built. As discussed in Chapter 6, a business model is an approach to doing business by which an enterprise can create value, make money, and sustain itself. Online companies differ in their decisions concerning which customers to serve, how best to become profitable, and what to include on their websites. Exhibit 9.5 shows some possible alternatives for business models. None of these models can currently be considered dominant, and some of the more complex Internet operations cannot be described by any single form. In reality, the world of e-commerce contains endless combinations of business models. As you consider a direction for your small business and its online aspirations, keep in mind that a poorly devised business model is often the primary cause of an online company's failure.

Type of Customers Served

Marketing frameworks classify traditional brick-and-mortar firms as manufacturers, wholesalers, or retailers, depending on the customers they serve. In a similar way, e-commerce businesses also are commonly distinguished according to customer focus. There are three major categories of e-commerce business models: business-to-business (B2B), business-to-consumer (B2C), and consumer-to-consumer (C2C). In this section, we examine some strategies used by e-commerce firms within these three categories.

business-to-business (B2B) model A business model based on selling to business customers electronically.

BUSINESS-TO-BUSINESS MODELS The dollar amounts generated by firms using a **business-to-business (B2B) model** (selling to business customers) are significantly greater than those for firms with a business-to-consumer (B2C) model (selling to final consumers). Because B2B success stories generally receive less publicity than B2C ventures do, the

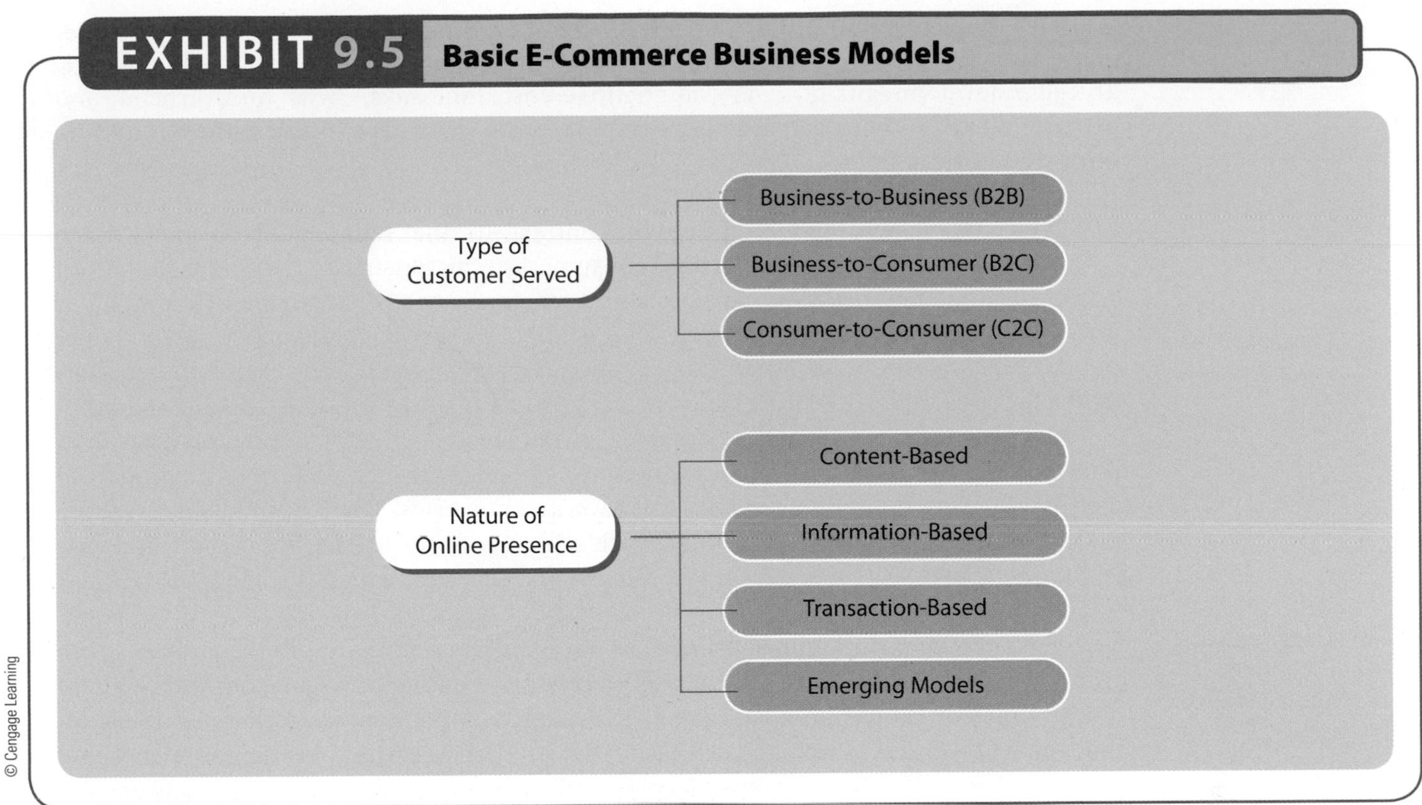

potential of B2B opportunities is often overlooked. Aspiring entrepreneurs should be sure to consider the B2B model.

B2B operations "come in all shapes and sizes," but the most popular form of this strategy emphasizes sales transactions. By using online capabilities, a B2B firm can achieve greater efficiency in its buying and selling activities. International Business Machines (IBM) is a good example of this. By dealing directly with its business clients online, it is able to build its computer systems and related products to meet the specific needs of its customers. IBM relies heavily on the Internet to deliver its business solutions, but it also has an extensive sales force and consulting services to deliver value to its many customers worldwide.

A unique form of B2B trade involves work outsourcing, which helps connect freelancers and other specialists with companies that need their services. One market research firm estimates that close to 100 online marketplaces for work outsourcing already exist, and the market continues to grow rapidly, with sales increasing around 20 percent each year.[34] Some of the better known sites include Elance.com, vWorker.com, oDesk.com, Guru.com, and Sologig.com, which allow you to "hire, manage, and pay remote contractors as if they were in your office."[35] Now, the market for global talent is as close as your computer keyboard. While work-outsourcing marketplaces help freelancers to reach the customers they need to build their businesses, they can also help entrepreneurs locate the support services necessary to improve their own operations. Danielle Godefroy, co-founder of Princeton, New Jersey–based Lingolook Publishing, first used Elance.com to connect with a software developer in Colorado, who contracted to make the language-pronunciation flashcards that the company now offers to travelers for use on their iPhones. Godefroy had to pay the iPhone applications developer $5,000 for his services, but now the company has a product that sells on iTunes and is competitive with offerings from much larger companies. Elance.com has helped Godefroy with a dozen other projects, and she has learned many valuable lessons along the way—that it pays to be specific about project details and to keep the lines of communication open, for example. But the benefits have been considerable. "We have been able to [out]source all these developments at a very competitive cost," she says, "with no overhead, and extremely fast."[36] These advantages can very easily translate to sales growth and an improved bottom line.

business-to-consumer (B2C) model
A business model based on selling to final consumers electronically.

BUSINESS-TO-CONSUMER MODELS In contrast to the B2B option, a **business-to-consumer (B2C) model** focuses on final consumers as customers. In the traditional retail setting, customers typically go to a brick-and-mortar store with the intent of shopping or making a purchase. Alternatively, customers might purchase goods or services via telephone or by mail order, using a printed catalog. The B2C model introduces another alternative for consumers, one with which you are probably quite familiar—buying online.

Amazon.com represents the classic B2C firm, which is directly focused on individual final consumers. B2C ventures sell a wide variety of products, with offerings ranging from clothing to pet items, computer software, toys, and groceries. The B2C model offers three main advantages over brick-and-mortar retailing: convenient use, immediate transactions, and round-the-clock access to products and services, which is sometimes referred to as **24/7 e-tailing**.

24/7 e-tailing
Electronic retailing providing round-the-clock access to products and services.

And opening up an online business has never been easier, thanks to the online "storefront" option and support services offered by online giants like Amazon, Yahoo!, and eBay. Some companies do business only through such a storefront; others establish an independent website as well and sell through both. Benson Altman is the founder, CEO, and president of Kosher.com, an enterprise that sells food items "adher[ing] to the strictest rabbinical supervision guidelines" and nonfood products that appeal to Jewish customers. The focus is on helping buyers find what they need at good prices, with quality service that keeps them coming back for more. However, the company also offers its goods through Amazon.com, which makes it possible for Altman to sell nearly 20,000 kosher products, from canned fish to cosmetics, from all over the world. Customers can readily find what they are looking for through Amazon's search feature, which allows the niche retailer's products to be located and purchased with ease. Kosher.com handles the shipment of products to customers, but Amazon takes care of everything else, including customer support and billing.[37]

There is also a downside to all of this, unfortunately. It cost Altman about $25,000 to integrate operations with Amazon, and the expansion required him to hire four additional employees just to keep up with the increase in orders. Beyond that, Kosher.com has to pay Amazon a commission on each sale, which can add up quickly. Then there are also inventory worries. Still, Altman views the alliance as a platform to boost his sales, since it presents an opportunity to reach a much broader market.[38]

B2C e-commerce businesses certainly face unique challenges (payment security risks, customers who refuse to purchase a product without first seeing it or trying it on, etc.), but they also enjoy the advantages of flexibility. For example, they are able to change merchandise mixes and prices quickly, and they can easily modify the appearance of their online store. Traditional merchants located in brick-and-mortar stores would find such changes to be very costly and time-consuming, making it nearly impossible for them to keep up with fast-moving markets.

Gilt Groupe definitely exploits the flexibility edge that online businesses can have. Started in 2007, and one of a handful of popular "flash sale websites," this online fashion retailer makes e-commerce fun and exciting by offering "invitation-only access to highly coveted products and experiences at insider prices."[39] Gilt's website provides its members with a unique selection of apparel, accessories, and lifestyle items that change every day—and that is the secret to the company's success. Susan Lyne, now chairman of the company, explains what sets Gilt Groupe apart from the competition:

> *Most online shopping mirrors brick-and-mortar stores. They're not taking advantage of what's uniquely possible online, the heightened sense of entertainment and competition. A big part of the Gilt brand promise is discovery: you come every day and it's new every day.*[40]

All indications are that the formula is working like a charm: Gilt's sales grew sixfold in 2009 alone![41] By changing its product offerings daily, customers are drawn to the website often to see what's new, and the pages can be changed to keep up with shifts in consumer demand and product availability. This capacity for flexibility provides a substantial edge over brick-and-mortar operations—at least to those online businesses that position themselves to take advantage of it.

In some cases, market conditions or opportunities persuade wholesalers to bypass the retailer and take their product or service directly to the final consumer through online operations, which is sometimes referred to as **disintermediation**. Eli Mechlovitz and his family had been selling glass and tile as a wholesaler in New York for more than two decades, but slowing sales forced Mechlovitz to reconsider the company's strategy. In September of 2007, he decided to launch GlassTileStore.com to sell custom tiles and mosaics directly to consumers who were looking for deals on the Internet. Through this channel, the company can sell products at much lower prices (sometimes as much as 50 percent below their cost in retail stores), and website sales now exceed those typical during the best of months before online operations began.[42] That's the power of the online option—it offers market reach and flexibility that would not otherwise be available.

disintermediation
A situation where a wholesaler in a B2B operation chooses to bypass the "middleman" and sell its product or service directly to the final consumer.

As B2C e-commerce models continue to develop and evolve, new alternatives will emerge, which is bound to catch some competitors off guard. Even some very large competitors find it difficult to keep up with the online game. For example, Google's creative service offerings have forced Microsoft to reconsider how it prices its software, and full-service travel agencies are still trying to figure out how to adjust their approaches to deal with relatively recent startups like Kayak.com and CheapOAir.com. Major moves in the marketplace are sure to come, but an alert entrepreneur will monitor these changes to be able to respond quickly to potential risks and identify emerging opportunities.

CONSUMER-TO-CONSUMER MODELS A growing number of entrepreneurs who sell their wares over the Internet do so without creating either a website or a storefront. Instead, they use auction sites, which fall under what is sometimes called the **consumer-to-consumer (C2C) model**. This model is usually set up around Internet **auction sites** that allow individuals and companies to list products available for sale to potential bidders. Revenues to the auction site are most often derived from listing fees and commissions on sales.

consumer-to-consumer (C2C) model
A business model usually set up around Internet auction sites that allow individuals and companies to list items available for sale to potential bidders.

auction sites
Web-based businesses offering participants the ability to list products for consumer bidding.

Online auctions have become one of the most celebrated success stories on the Internet. And, as you might have guessed, eBay, founded in 1995 by computer programmer Pierre Omidyar, is the 900-pound gorilla of auction sites. "I got it on eBay" is quickly becoming part of our collective vocabulary. You can buy or sell nearly anything on eBay—and it's incredibly easy. Auction-site consultants abound; for a fee, they will coach you on how to be a successful seller. Or you can attend eBay University, in person or via online tutorials, to learn the ins and outs of operating an eBay business. To show you how easy it is to get started, Exhibit 9.6 provides a simple six-step procedure for selling items on eBay.

As easy as it is to sell a few items on eBay, it is a very different matter to actually make money as an ongoing business on the site. As in the more conventional forms of retailing, a well-thought-out business plan is helpful in turning your business idea (or hobby) into a money-making proposition. Here are a few statistics about eBay that will show you what an amazing phenomenon it has become:[43]

- eBay has nearly 92 million active users around the world.
- Approximately $1,890 in goods are sold on eBay *every second.*
- $14.7 billion in goods was sold on eBay in a single three-month period.
- The most expensive item sold to date on eBay was a private business jet (for $4.9 million).

EXHIBIT 9.6 Selling Your Item on eBay

Step 1: Create an eBay seller's account, which is free of charge.

Step 2: Set up the Q&A feature to communicate with buyers.

Step 3: Research your item and the rules of selling; eBay provides information for both.

Step 4: Create a listing for the item to be offered for sale.

Step 5: Check your listing to see how the bidding is going.

Step 6: Wrap up your sale with the buyer.

Source: Adapted from "Getting Started on eBay," http://pages.ebay.com/help/sell/sell-getstarted.html, accessed December 8, 2010.

As mentioned earlier, auction sites like eBay generate most of their revenue through listing fees and commissions. To continue its rapid growth, eBay is expanding its services and entering additional markets across the globe through new sites, acquisitions, and co-ventures. Overall, eBay does business in 39 countries (including the United States),[44] and PayPal, eBay's global payments platform, has 230 million total accounts.[45] No longer the only show in town, however, eBay faces competition from the likes of Amazon and smaller competitors such as Overstock.com. Exhibit 9.7 provides a list of the top 10 auction sites. How many of these have you visited?

While eBay will most likely maintain the auction format that made it so popular, the company is also taking steps to expand the eBay Stores side of its business, which gives sellers access to millions of shoppers worldwide. Setting up an eBay Store is very easy to

EXHIBIT 9.7 Top 10 Online Auction Sites

1. eBay.com
2. uBid.com
3. Bidz.com
4. Overstock.com
5. Amazon.com
6. OnlineAuction.com
7. WeBidz Auctions
8. Auction-Warehouse
9. ePier.com
10. It's Gotta Go

Source: http://www.auctions.nettop20.com, accessed December 8, 2010.

do (see the firm's website for details), and many eBay merchants find that taking this step can dramatically increase sales. This option makes sellers successful by providing powerful tools to help them build, manage, promote, and track their eBay presence. Plus, eBay Stores sellers can create a listing, with full search exposure, for as little as \$0.03.[46]

Nature of Online Presence

A second broad way of categorizing e-commerce models relates to the firm's intended level of online presence. The role of a website can range from merely offering content and information to enabling complex business transactions.

CONTENT-BASED MODEL In a **content-based model** of e-commerce, a website provides access to information but not the ability to buy or sell products and services. During the early days of e-commerce, the content-based model was the option of choice. Companies like America Online (AOL) got their start using this approach. Originally, revenue for AOL came from fees paid by users for the privilege of connecting and gaining access to its content. Today, content models still operate, but these are found mostly in countries where Internet use by small firms is less advanced.

content-based model
A business model in which the website charges a fee for access to information but does not offer the ability to buy and sell products and services.

INFORMATION-BASED MODEL The **information-based model** is a variation of the content-based alternative. A website built on this model contains information about the business, its products, and other related matters but doesn't charge for its use. It is typically just a complement to an existing brick-and-mortar store. Many small businesses use this model for their online operations. Your dentist or plumber may have a website that simply describes the services offered but probably will require a phone call to set up an appointment. These sites often feature a "Contact Us" link that will take the user to a separate Web page displaying the company's address and phone number and sometimes offer "click-through" access that allows the user to get in touch with the business via e-mail.

information-based model
A business model in which the website provides information about a business, its products, and other related matters but doesn't charge for its use.

TRANSACTION-BASED MODEL In a **transaction-based model** of e-commerce, a website is set up to provide a mechanism for buying or selling products or services. The transaction-based model could be considered the center of the e-commerce universe. This model calls for websites to provide online stores where visitors go to shop, click, and buy.

transaction-based model
A business model in which the website provides a mechanism for buying or selling products or services.

Many Internet ventures sell a single product or service. For example, Huber and Jane Wilkinson market their reading comprehension program, IdeaChain, through their MindPrime, Inc., website (www.mindprime.com). Similarly, Phil and Stephanie Rockell sell hillbilly teeth pacifiers only online. (For a good laugh, see the product for yourself at www.billybobteeth.com.) Other ventures are direct extensions of a brick-and-mortar store, creating what is sometimes called a bricks-and-clicks or a clicks-and-mortar strategy. For example, if you were interested in purchasing a new computer printer, you might research options on Office Depot's website and then choose either to buy your selection online or to drive to the neighborhood Office Depot store and pick up the printer there. Although Office Depot is a large corporation with millions of customers, small businesses can follow the same general model with excellent results.

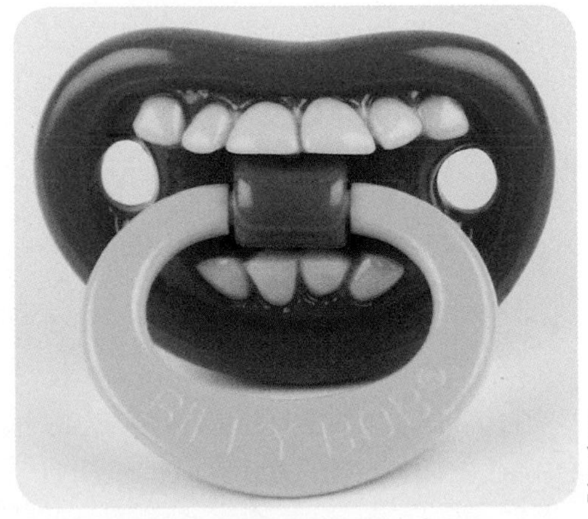

Faketeeth.com

EMERGING MODELS The Internet world is known for how fast it moves, and entrepreneurial minds are constantly finding new ways to cash in on its potential. For example, blogs (short for "Web logs") are set up to create an online venue to chronicle users' thoughts, but these can also be managed as a money-making venture.

Bloggers produce online journals to trade comments with friends and other readers. Small firms have found blogs easy to use and thus an attractive platform from which to promote a sale on an overstocked item or to give an employee special recognition. But drawing Web traffic to a blog can also generate substantial income from advertising, and a growing array of services and tools are making it easier than ever for bloggers to add this feature to their site.

The vast majority of bloggers earn only $10 to $20 a month through advertising, but the amount earned is dependent on such factors as how much traffic the site generates, the trustworthiness of the content offered, and how relevant the ads are to those who visit. A popular blog can bring in more income than you might imagine. Rhett Butler started an environmental conservation blog because of his intense interest in the subject, but he quit his job as a production manager in 2003 when he realized just how much money could be generated through blogging. "The rainforest has always been my passion," says Butler, "but I never expected to make a living off of it." Butler recently reported that he makes between $15,000 and $18,000 a month in ad revenue from the 1.3 million unique visitors drawn to his website each month.[47] And as the number of visitors rises, the number of dollars generated naturally will increase.

INTERNET-BASED BUSINESSES AND THE PART-TIME STARTUP ADVANTAGE

When an entrepreneur launches a new company, many times she or he has to wrestle with the question of whether to give up an existing job and jump full-time into the startup or hold on to the job while getting a part-time business going on the side. There are advantages and drawbacks to each approach, of course, but research shows most entrepreneurs prefer to launch a part-time enterprise and keep the income flowing until they can afford to make a complete transition to the new business. It's also less risky; if the new venture fails, the aspiring entrepreneur's income will not be interrupted. Though many kinds of businesses can be started on a part-time basis, a growing number of small business owners are finding that the flexibility and low cost of launching an online business make this a very attractive option.

Brian Eddy and Chad Ronnebaum chose the part-time startup path back in 1999. In their mid-20s at the time, these long-time friends decided to keep their successful careers *and* launch Q3 Innovations, a product design, development, and distribution company that creates personal safety and monitoring devices. In line with their niche strategy, they came up with some unique and very interesting products to sell. Their AlcoHAWK® Series is a line of handheld breath alcohol screeners for personal or professional use. The pen-sized thermometers of the ThermoHAWK™ Series feature technology that allows a user to determine the surface temperature of almost any object without actually touching it. And the company also offers a product called the UV HAWK™, which measures the intensity of ultraviolet light, making it easier to know when your skin has had enough exposure to the sun. Taken together, these offerings represent an interesting stable of products.[48]

"You hear the news? We've gone from startup to upstart!"

As with most startups, launching Q3 Innovations was a very satisfying, but grueling, experience. Eddy figures that he and Ronnebaum were booking 90- to 100-hour work weeks during the company's six-year startup phase (only about half of those hours were spent at their regular jobs), so the part-time business wasn't always so part-time. They always knew what they were doing for the weekend, and the task took up most of their evenings, too. However, Q3 Innovations grew so much that Eddy decided to leave his legal practice to become the company's full-time CEO, and Ronnebaum made the transition from his career as a pharmacist to become the full-time president of the startup a few years later.[49]

The part-time strategy followed by Q3's founders took much of the risk out of making the transition to life as entrepreneurs. And the decision to use the Internet as a business platform played a significant part in making their Q3 Innovations dream a reality.[50] (The company was acquired by Quest Products, Inc., in 2010, but the enterprise remains intact and the venture's line of products is still being sold on the Q3 Innovations website.[51])

Clearly, the location decision is complicated, but it is extremely important to get it right. If your business needs a physical facility, can you find a location that is convenient to customers, offers a supportive business climate, and provides access to necessary resources? As the owner of the business, would you be happy to show up to work at that location, day after day and year after year? When you think of the costs involved, does the location make sense?

Perhaps you are short on startup funding, which is leading you to think about starting your business at home. A home-based business is certainly cheaper to launch, but it can be challenging to operate. Some entrepreneurs have a difficult time keeping their involvement in the business separate from their life as a parent or spouse, and it can be difficult to operate a business out of your house and still abide by the zoning and legal requirements of your community or to maintain an image for your enterprise that attracts customers. These considerations can make the location decision much more complicated.

Perhaps you've decided to locate your business on the Internet to avoid the image risks and the high costs of starting up in a physical facility. Many other small business owners are making the same decision, but there are still a number of questions that have to be answered—for example, what type of customer will you serve, what sort of business model will you adopt, and what will you need to get started? Are you going to keep your present job and try to start your new venture on the side, or do you plan to jump into the startup with both feet?

There are many questions to be answered, but there are also many sources of information to help you decide what will work best for your planned venture. Don't get impatient—just take your time, do your research, and make a wise choice. A world of endless business opportunities awaits you. So what's holding you back?

1. Describe the five key factors in locating a brick-and-mortar startup.

- Customer accessibility is a key factor in the location decision of retail and service businesses.
- Climate, competition, legal requirements, and the tax structure are types of environmental factors affecting the location decision.
- Availability of resources such as raw materials, a suitable labor supply, and transportation can be important to location decisions.
- Though it can interfere with sound decision making, the entrepreneur's personal preference is a practical consideration in selecting a location.
- An appropriate site must be available and priced within the entrepreneur's budget.

2. Discuss the challenges of designing and equipping a physical facility.

- The general suitability of a building depends on the functional requirements of the business; it should be neither too large and extravagant nor too small and restrictive.
- The comfort, convenience, and safety of the business's employees and customers must not be overlooked.

- Deciding whether to purchase or lease equipment is an important choice many entrepreneurs face.
- Most small manufacturing firms must use general-purpose equipment, but some can use special-purpose equipment for specialized operations.
- Small retailers must have merchandise display racks and counters, storage racks, shelving, mirrors, customer push-carts, cash registers, and other equipment that facilitates selling.
- Display counters and other retailing equipment should create an atmosphere appropriate for customers in the retailer's target market.
- Entrepreneurs should select office equipment that reflects the latest advances in technology applicable to a particular business.
- All new ventures, regardless of their function, should project an image that is appropriate to and supportive of the business and its intentions.

3. Recognize both the attraction and the challenges of creating a home-based startup.

- Home-based businesses are started both to make money and to accommodate family lifestyle considerations.
- Operating a business at home can pose challenges beyond family and business conflict, particularly in the areas of business image and legal considerations.
- Technology, especially the Web, has made it possible to operate many types of businesses from almost any location.

4. Understand the potential benefits of locating a startup on the Internet.

- E-commerce offers small firms the opportunity to compete with bigger companies on a more level playing field.
- Internet operations can help small firms with cash flow problems by compressing the sales cycle.
- E-commerce enables small firms to build stronger customer relationships.
- Business-to-business (B2B) companies generate far more sales than ventures following alternative models.
- The three main advantages of online business-to-consumer (B2C) firms are convenient use, immediate transactions, and continuous access to products and services, often referred to as 24/7 e-tailing.
- Internet auction sites, like eBay, are based on the consumer-to-consumer (C2C) model and can help even the smallest of businesses access a worldwide market with great convenience.
- The role of a website can range from merely offering content and information to permitting the buying and selling of products and services online.
- Emerging models of e-commerce include blogging, which can be used to generate significant amounts of advertising revenue for the entrepreneur-blogger.
- Internet-based businesses can be started on a part-time basis, which reduces the personal risk of the entrepreneur if the venture should fail.

Key Terms

brick-and-mortar store p. 262
enterprise zones p. 267
business incubator p. 268
general-purpose equipment p. 271
special-purpose equipment p. 272
home-based business p. 274
zoning ordinances p. 276
e-commerce p. 277
Electronic Customer Relationship Marketing (eCRM) p. 278
business-to-business (B2B) model p. 278
business-to-consumer (B2C) model p. 280
24/7 e-tailing p. 280
disintermediation p. 281
consumer-to-consumer (C2C) model p. 281
auction sites p. 281
content-based model p. 283
information-based model p. 283
transaction-based model p. 283

Discussion Questions

1. What are the key attributes of a good business location? Which of these would probably be most important for a retail location? Why?
2. What is the special appeal of an enterprise zone to an entrepreneur seeking the best site for his or her business?
3. Which resource factors might be most vital to a new manufacturing venture that produces residential home furniture? Why?
4. Is the hometown of the business owner likely to be a good location? Is it logical for an owner to allow personal preferences to influence a decision about business location? Explain your answers.

5. What is the difference between general-purpose equipment and special-purpose equipment? What are the advantages and disadvantages of each?
6. Under what conditions would it be most appropriate for a new firm to buy rather than lease a building for the business?
7. What factors should an entrepreneur evaluate when considering a home-based business? Be specific.
8. Discuss how zoning and tax laws might impact the decision to start a home-based business.
9. Discuss the two different ways of categorizing business models used for e-commerce.
10. Contrast B2B and B2C businesses. Identify some of the reasons final consumers give for *not* shopping online.

You Make the Call

SITUATION 1

Entrepreneurs Joe Stengard and his wife, Jackie Piel, had a decision to make. Located just outside of Saint Louis, their five-year-old company, S&P Crafts, was growing rapidly. But with only 4,000 square feet of production area, they were in desperate need of more space to make their custom-ordered craft kits.

A move always involves a certain measure of risk, so the couple was hesitant to transfer the company's operations. However, an economic development organization in Warren County, Missouri, offered attractive incentives in the form of tax breaks and financial assistance if they would move to a new facility in the rural town of Hopewell. Initial research indicated that a local workforce was readily available and had skills appropriate to the operation, so Stengard and Piel decided to move.

Since the change of address, company sales have tripled. And the new facility has grown from 10,000 square feet to 40,000 square feet in just two short years.

Question 1 How important was the location decision for these two entrepreneurs? Why?
Question 2 What types of permits and zoning ordinances did Stengard and Piel need to consider before deciding to relocate?
Question 3 How could Stengard and Piel use the Internet to expand the business of S&P Crafts?

SITUATION 2

Entrepreneur Karen Moore wants to start a catering and decorating business to bring in money to help support her two young children. Moore is a single parent; she works in the banking industry but has always had the desire to start a business. She enjoys decorating for friends' parties and is frequently told, "You should do this professionally. You have such good taste, and you are so nice to people."

Moore has decided to take this advice but is unsure whether she should locate in a commercial site or in her home, which is in rural central Texas. She is leaning toward locating at home because she wants more time with her children. However, she is concerned that the home-based location is too far from the city, where most of her potential customers live.

Initially, her services would include planning wedding receptions and other special events, designing flower arrangements, decorating the sites, and even cooking and serving meals.

Question 1 What do you see as potential problems with locating Moore's new business at home?
Question 2 What do you see as the major benefits for Moore of a home-based business?
Question 3 How could Moore use technology to help her operate a home-based business?

SITUATION 3

The SUBWAY® restaurant chain now has more than 32,000 locations in 90 countries, so it knows a thing or two about deciding where to set up shop. But in 2009, the company elected to take its location expertise to new heights. *SUBWAY Restaurant News* reports it this way:

> *Richard Schragger is a multi-unit SUBWAY franchisee in the New York City area. For the next two years, his newest store will be located on top of the world! Richard's newest SUBWAY restaurant will be on a crane, rising alongside the construction of One World Trade Center—also known as the Freedom Tower—providing meals for construction workers as the structure rises 108 stories. At 1,776 feet, it will be the tallest building in the United States and one of the tallest buildings in the world.*

The location of this restaurant will allow the 200 iron workers and 1,500 to 1,800 tradesmen who will be working on the structure to enjoy meals aloft and avoid the 45-minute elevator ride required to reach the ground. DCM Erectors, the construction company that will be overseeing work on the tower, welded together 36 shipping containers to create the new restaurant. That metal shell, along with the food SUBWAY will be serving and the equipment needed to serve it, will be hoisted by crane, level by level, so it will always be positioned near the workers as they rivet, weld, and fabricate the new structure. Then, when mealtime rolls around (which will be breakfast, lunch, and dinner for this unique shop), employees will not have far to go to grab a bite. No matter how you slice it, this is going to be an unusual location for a restaurant chain. And just imagine the view!

Question 1 What are the major advantages that Schragger will enjoy as the result of having this most unique site?

Question 2 What major disadvantages and special challenges will the company likely run into as a result of this towering location?

Question 3 Do you think it was a good idea for Schragger to locate a SUBWAY franchise in this way? What other uncommon locations can you think of that small businesses have used or are using to their advantage?

Sources: Jason Daley, "A Tall Order," *Entrepreneur*, Vol. 38, No. 4 (April 2010), p. 124; and *SUBWAY Restaurant News*, http://www.subway.com/subwayroot/newsItems/newsItem1.aspx, accessed December 13, 2010.

Experiential Exercises

1. Search for articles online that provide rankings of states or cities as business locations. What definite trends do you notice? Report on your findings.
2. Identify and evaluate a local site that is now vacant because of a business closure. Point out the strengths and weaknesses of that location for the former business, and comment on the part location may have played in the closure.
3. Interview a small business owner concerning the strengths and weaknesses of his or her business's location. Prepare a brief report summarizing your findings.
4. Think of a local small business that you believe might benefit from adding e-commerce as a supporting feature of its strategy. Prepare a report on the reasons this particular business is not involved in e-commerce and recommend an e-commerce strategy that would help to boost its performance.
5. Do some research online to determine what e-commerce assistance is available to small firms. Report on your findings.

Small Business & Entrepreneurship Resource Center

1. Entrepreneurs are increasingly using the Internet as one of their location choices when starting their businesses. This chapter introduced eBay as a viable option for a small firm to establish a Web presence. Most entrepreneurs think of eBay as an Internet auction site that is best used to sell second-hand items from around the house or other relatively low-priced goods. What about selling automobiles on eBay? Describe the challenges in selling automobiles on the Internet and how eBay has successfully met them. If you were to sell new automobiles over the Internet, what could you do to help improve your reputation and sales?

   Source: "Will They Buy Vehicles Online?" *Ward's Dealer Business*, Vol. 41, No. 6 (June 1, 2007), p. 8.

2. James Dyson started his vacuum cleaner manufacturing business in his hometown. While enjoying business growth, he hit obstacles as globalization became a reality. After moving his factory to Malaysia, Dyson was able to cut manufacturing costs by two-thirds. Discuss how this location decision (in this era of globalization) impacted his hometown, both positively and negatively.

   Source: "Suck It and See," *The Economist*, Feb 3, 2007, p. 8.

Video Case 9

COOKIES-N-CREAM (P. 710)

This case highlights the importance of the location decision to the success of a small business, illustrating specifically how nontraditional location options, like the use of mobile vending trucks, can open up opportunities for a startup.

ALTERNATIVE CASE FOR CHAPTER 9

Case 18, Smarter.com, p. 728

Business Plan Laying the Foundation

As part of laying the foundation for preparing your own business plan, respond to the following questions regarding location.

Brick-and-Mortar Startup Location Questions

1. How important are your personal reasons for choosing a location?
2. What business environment factors will influence your location decision?
3. What resources are most critical to your location decision?
4. How important is customer accessibility to your location decision?
5. How will the formal site evaluation be conducted?
6. What laws and tax policies of state and local governments need to be considered?
7. What is the cost of the proposed site?
8. Is an enterprise zone available in the area where you want to locate?

Physical Facility Questions

1. What are the major considerations in choosing between a new and an existing building?
2. What is the possibility of leasing a building or equipment?
3. How feasible is it to locate in a business incubator?
4. What is the major objective of your building design?
5. What types of equipment do you need for your business?

Home-Based Startup Location Questions

1. Will a home-based business be a possibility for you?
2. For the venture you are planning, what would be the advantages and disadvantages of locating the business in your home?
3. Have you given consideration to family lifestyle issues?
4. Will your home project the appropriate image for the business?
5. What zoning ordinances, if any, regulate the type of home-based business you want to start?

Internet Startup Questions

1. What type of customers will be served by the Internet startup?
2. What technical limitations (such as the cost of developing a website or constantly changing software needs) might hinder the company you plan to launch?
3. How will you deal with nontechnical issues (privacy concerns, website security, dealing with global languages and cultures, etc.) that may limit the success of your online business?
4. Do you plan to open a storefront hosted by Amazon, eBay, or one of the other online giants, or would an independent website be better suited to the needs of your business?
5. What will be the nature of the online presence you hope to establish—content-based, information-based, transaction-based, or some other form?
6. Will you start the business on a part-time basis, or do you plan to be involved full-time?

CHAPTER 10

Understanding a Firm's Financial Statements

Johnny Stites is CEO of J&S Construction Company, Inc., in Cookeville, Tennessee. After graduating from college, Johnny served in the U.S. Navy for three years and then returned home to work in the family business. Several years later, his younger brother, Jack, joined him in the business. Not long afterward, their father asked if they thought they could run the business without him. Being young and confident, the brothers did not hesitate to say, "Sure. No problem, Dad." Their father walked out and never came back! Jack and Johnny have grown the business into one of the most successful construction firms in the Southeast, if not the United States. A visitor to their business is immediately struck by the passion and detailed attention they give to who they want to be and how they choose to operate their company. When asked how they use financial information to run the business, Johnny made the following observations:

> *When you start and run your own business, it no longer matters whether you were a marketing, management, finance, or any other specific major. As an entrepreneur, you have to know how a business operates, which requires more than having knowledge in a specific academic field.*

Jesse Kaufman/MMA Creative

In the SPOTLIGHT
J&S Construction Company
http://www.jsconstruction.com

© iStockphoto.com/Dan Bachman

LOOKING AHEAD

After studying this chapter, you should be able to . . .

1. Describe the purpose and content of an income statement.
2. Explain the purpose and content of a balance sheet.
3. Explain how viewing the income statement and balance sheets together gives a more complete picture of a firm's financial position.
4. Use the income statement and balance sheets to compute a company's cash flows.
5. Analyze the financial statements using ratios to see more clearly how decisions affect a firm's financial performance.

So whatever your major, you had best know the basics of accounting and finance. You do not need to be an accountant, but you had better be able to read and understand financial statements. Sure, you can hire an accountant, but if you do not understand what the numbers are telling you, you are in big trouble. The construction industry is one of the riskiest industries you can enter, second only to the restaurant industry. For years, we would bid a job based on our best understanding of the costs that would be incurred. Then we would have to wait to the completion of the job to see if we made or lost money—not exactly an ideal situation to be in. Today, we have the ability to know how we are doing in terms of profits and costs on a daily basis. Not having accurate and timely accounting information would be deadly. We simply could not exist in such a competitive industry, and certainly not profitably, without understanding where we are financially.

Does accounting and finance matter to an entrepreneur? Only if you want to have a good understanding of your business.

***Source*: Personal interview with Johnny Stites, February 2011.**

RESOURCES

A Note from the Authors

Accounting requires a different skill set than the topics covered in other chapters and has to do more with experience than ability. This chapter is presented as simply as possible, without sacrificing the content that a small business owner needs. In addition, you will find the following on the website for this text:

1. A spreadsheet that provides all the numerical tables within the chapter, along with computations.
2. Additional examples that are requested by instructors and students to further understanding of a given topic. In addition, we will be available on Facebook, to both instructors and students, for further help and support.

Entrepreneurs do not start companies so that they can learn accounting—that's for certain. In fact, for many students and aspiring entrepreneurs, accounting is not their favorite subject. But, if you have or plan to start a business, you had better learn some accounting, sooner rather than later. Norm Brodsky, a serial entrepreneur and noted columnist for *Inc*., puts it plainly:

When I started out, I thought that CEOs ran businesses with the help of their top executives. What I didn't realize is that a business is a living entity with needs of its own, and unless the leaders pay attention to those needs, the business will fail. So how do you know what those needs are? There's only one way: by looking at the numbers and understanding the relationships between them. They will tell you how good your sales are, whether you can afford to hire a new salesperson or office manager, how much cash you will need to deal with new business coming in, how your market is changing, and on and on. You can't afford to wait until your accountant tells you these things. Nor do you have to become an accountant. You do have to know enough accounting, however, to figure out which numbers are most important in your particular business, and then you should develop the habit of watching them like a hawk.[1]

In other words, some things about a business can be known only by understanding the numbers. And most of us cannot learn accounting by simply reading about accounting; we have to engage with it. We are reminded of the ancient saying by the Chinese philosopher Confucius: "I hear and I forget. I see and I remember. I do and I understand."

In this chapter, you will learn how to construct an *income statement*, a *balance sheet,* and a *cash flow statement.* Equally important, you will learn some basics of interpreting what these **financial statements**, or **accounting statements**, tell you about your business. Then, in Chapter 11, you will learn how to forecast a company's financial requirements, a key part of a business plan.

financial statements (accounting statements) Reports of a firm's financial performance and resources, including an income statement, a balance sheet, and a cash flow statement.

Before we begin a systematic study of financial statements, we will lay a foundation by telling a story about two young children who started their own small business, a lemonade stand.

The Lemonade Kids

Mackenzie and John Dalton, ages 12 and 10, wanted to buy a Wii game system, one game, and an extra remote, which they estimated would cost $360. Their parents said they would pay most of the cost, but that the two children would need to contribute $100 to the purchase price.

To earn money, the children decided to operate a lemonade stand for two Saturdays in a nearby park frequented by walkers and runners. To start the business, they each invested $5 from their savings. Their mom, Kate, liked the children's idea and said she would loan them any additional money they would need with two conditions: (1) The children would have to repay her in two weeks, and (2) she would keep the books for their business and expect them to learn what the numbers meant. Kate thought this would provide the children a valuable opportunity to learn about business.

SETTING UP THE BUSINESS

A balance sheet, Kate explained to the children, is a table that shows on a specific date (1) the dollar amount of the assets owned by the business, and (2) the sources of the money used to pay for the assets. She continued to say that there are two sources

© Sheer Photo, Inc/Digital Vision/Getty Images

of money to pay for assets. The children could either borrow money or, as the owners of the business, they could put their own money into the business. The first means of paying for assets is called *debt* and the second is called *ownership equity* or frequently just called *owner's equity.* A company's total assets will always equal the total debt and equity of the business; that is,

$$\text{Total assets} = \text{Money borrowed from others} + \text{Money invested by the owners}$$

or

$$\text{Total assets} = \text{Debt} + \text{Ownership equity}$$

For instance, the children's beginning $10 in cash represented their only asset and, since it was their own money, it was also their equity in the business. Kate then wrote out a simple balance sheet:

Assets		**Loans (debt) and ownership equity**	
Cash	$10	Mackenzie and John's equity	$10
Total assets	$10	Total loans and equity	$10

After thinking about what they would need in supplies to operate the lemonade stand, the children requested a $40 loan from their mother. After the loan was made, the new balance sheet appeared as follows:

Assets		**Loans (debt) and ownership equity**	
Cash	$50	Loan from Mom	$40
Total assets	$50	Mackenzie and John's equity	10
		Total loans and equity	$50

$40 increase in cash from loan

In preparing for their opening day, the children bought $40 of "premium pink lemonade mix" and paper cups. Kate explained that the lemonade mix and cups constituted their *inventory* of supplies. After the children paid for the inventory, the resulting balance sheet was as follows, where cash decreased and inventory increased by $40:

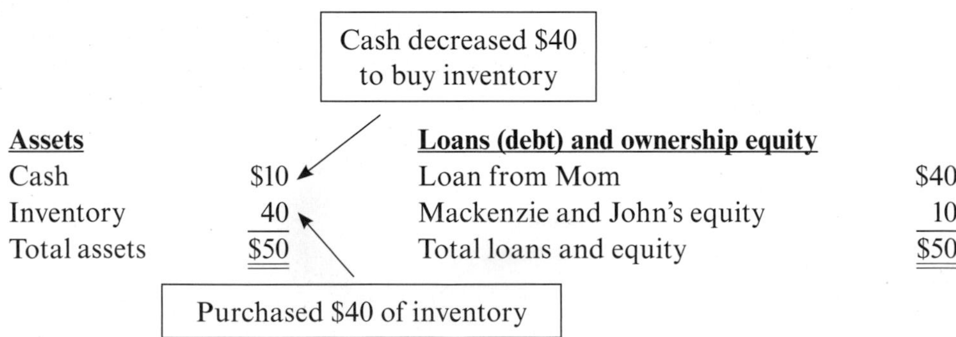

Assets		**Loans (debt) and ownership equity**	
Cash	$10	Loan from Mom	$40
Inventory	40	Mackenzie and John's equity	10
Total assets	$50	Total loans and equity	$50

OPENING DAY

Being astute young entrepreneurs, Mackenzie and John were aware that not all passerby carried cash. So they created a sign-up sheet where customers could record their contact information for payment later in the week. They then chose a prime location for their lemonade stand and prepared to serve some very fine ice-cold pink lemonade. By the end of the day, they had sold 60 cups at $1 each—30 cups that were bought on "credit" and 30 with cash. Since the lemonade only cost the children 25 cents a cup, they made 75 cents per cup in profits, for a total of $45 in profit [$45 = ($1 sales price per cup − $0.25 cost per cup) × 60 cups]. Kate told the children that an income statement reports the results of a firm's operations over a period of time—in this case, for a day. So the income statement for their first Saturday of selling looked like this:

Sales (60 cups × $1 per cup sales price)	$60
Cost of lemonade sold (60 cups × $0.25 cost per cup)	(15)
Profits	$45

Their balance sheet at the end of the day was as follows:

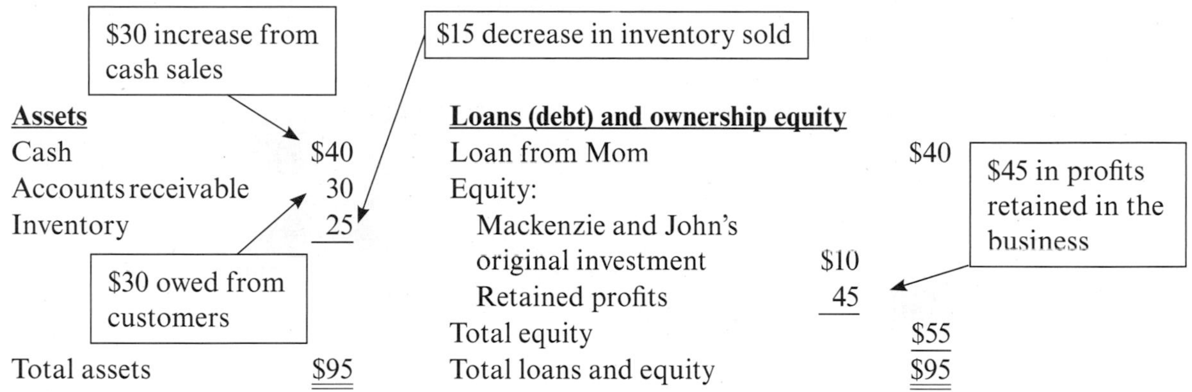

Assets		**Loans (debt) and ownership equity**		
Cash	$40	Loan from Mom		$40
Accounts receivable	30	Equity:		
Inventory	25	Mackenzie and John's original investment	$10	
		Retained profits	45	
		Total equity		$55
Total assets	$95	Total loans and equity		$95

This time, cash increased from $10 to $40, as a result of the cash sales of $30—even though they had sold $60 of lemonade. The remaining $30 was still owed by their credit customers; the children hoped to collect this money during the coming week. These assets, they learned, were called "accounts receivable" in business jargon. Also, there was a $15 decline in inventory, the result of the lemonade sold. Finally, the children's equity increased by $45, the amount of the day's profits.

When John looked at the income statement and balance sheet, he questioned why cash had only increased $30, even though profits were $45 for the day. Why were they not the same? Kate told him he was about to learn an important lesson: *Computing a company's cash flows will require you to look both at the income statement and at the changes in the balance sheet.* For one thing, they did not collect $30 of their sales, which resulted in $30 of accounts receivable, instead of cash. Second, the $15 cost of goods sold was not a cash outflow, since the inventory that was sold had been purchased previously. In other words, they "sold" $15 of inventory and received the cash. Thus, reconciling their profits with the change in cash requires the following calculation:

Profits		$ 45
Increase in accounts receivable	($30)	
Decrease in inventory	15	
Net increase in assets		$(15)
Change in cash		$ 30

COLLECTING ACCOUNTS RECEIVABLE

Not wanting to let their accounts receivable go uncollected too long, the children hired their little sister, Erin, for $5 to make calls during the week on their credit customers. To their delight, by Friday night Erin (accompanied by a few of her friends) had collected all the money owed. With the money collected, cash increased $30 with a corresponding $30 decrease in accounts receivable. As a result, the balance sheet appeared as follows:

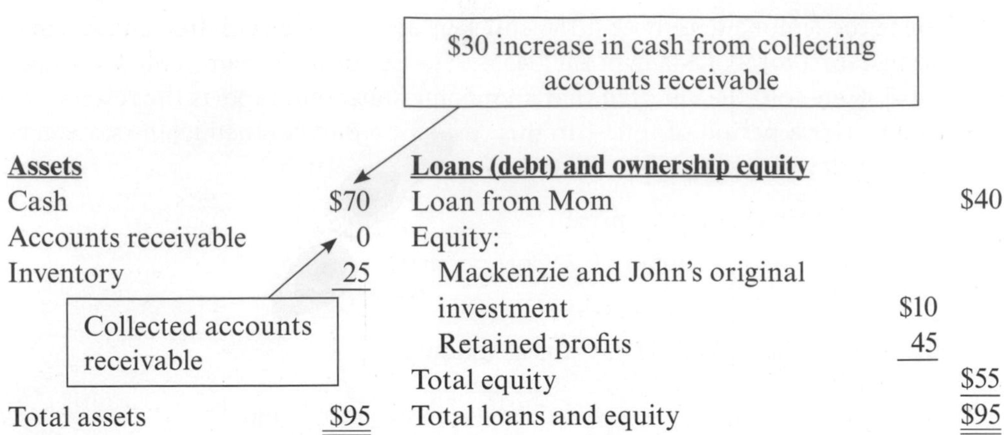

Assets		Loans (debt) and ownership equity		
Cash	$70	Loan from Mom		$40
Accounts receivable	0	Equity:		
Inventory	25	Mackenzie and John's original investment	$10	
		Retained profits	45	
		Total equity		$55
Total assets	$95	Total loans and equity		$95

STRATEGIC PLANNING FOR THE FOLLOWING SATURDAY

Anticipating the next weekend, Mackenzie and John decided to relocate their operation to Two Rivers Park, an area in their city with a high volume of joggers and walkers. In addition, the children decided to hire two friends, agreeing to pay each $10 a day, which allowed them to expand their business operations to three stands. However, since Two Rivers Park is not in their local neighborhood, they would not sell on credit, choosing instead to do business on a cash-only basis.

THE SECOND SATURDAY OF BUSINESS

Mackenzie and John arrived at Two Rivers Park with their two friends early Saturday morning and soon found themselves surrounded by customers. By mid-afternoon, they had sold 100 cups of lemonade, depleting their entire inventory! After paying their two friends $10 dollars each and Erin $5 for her collection work, the children were delighted to see that they had made $50 in profits—their income statement for the second day looked like this:

Sales ($1 sales price per cup × 100 cups)	$100
Cost of lemonade ($0.25 cost per cup × 100 cups)	(25)
Salaries (2 friends × $10 + $5 paid to Erin)	(25)
Profits	$ 50

The balance sheet at the end of the day appeared as follows:

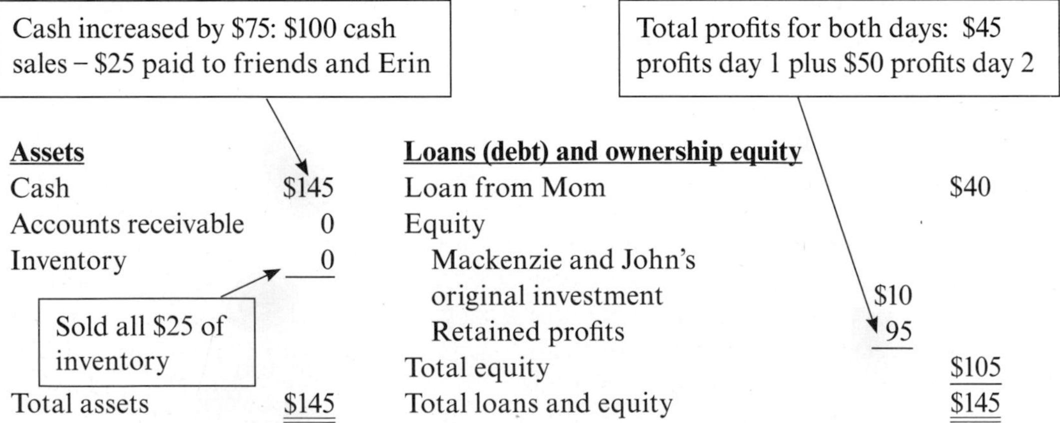

Assets		Loans (debt) and ownership equity		
Cash	$145	Loan from Mom		$40
Accounts receivable	0	Equity		
Inventory	0	Mackenzie and John's original investment	$10	
		Retained profits	95	
		Total equity		$105
Total assets	$145	Total loans and equity		$145

Cash assets had now increased to $145, a $75 increase as a result of the $100 in cash sales less the $25 paid to Erin and the children's two friends. Inventory was now zero, and the children's equity once again increased by the day's profits, in this case, $50.

Avoiding Failure

Why might your business fail? Research convincingly shows that insufficient capital is one of the main reasons for small business failure, along with lack of experience, poor location, poor inventory management, and overinvestment in fixed assets.

Three of the five primary reasons for failure are financial. Should you know your financial capacities? You bet, if you want the odds in your favor!

The children had accomplished their goal! They had enough to pay for their portion of the Wii, repay the $40 loan to their mom, and still had $5 to split. When they went to bed that night, they discussed the possibility of starting a summer business. The entrepreneurial flame had been lit, and they had big dreams for their next venture.

The hypothetical story of Mackenzie and John and their lemonade stand provides a simplified and uncomplicated way of thinking about accounting statements. If you understand—really understand—the Lemonade Kids' financial results, you are ready to move on to the next step. This will not make you an accountant, but it will give you the skill needed to manage a small business by the numbers. Our starting point is the income statement.

income statement (profit and loss statement) A financial report showing the amount of profits or losses from a firm's operations over a given period of time.

cost of goods sold The cost of producing or acquiring goods or services to be sold by a firm.

gross profit Sales less the cost of goods sold.

operating expenses Costs related to marketing and selling a firm's product or service, general and administrative expenses, and depreciation.

The Income Statement

1 Describe the purpose and content of an income statement.

An **income statement**, or **profit and loss statement**, indicates the amount of profits or losses generated by a firm *over a given time period*, usually monthly, quarterly, or yearly. In its most basic form, the income statement may be represented by the following equation:

$$\text{Sales (revenue)} - \text{Expenses} = \text{Profits (income)}$$

(In this text, we generally use the term *profits*, instead of *earnings* or *income*, but all three terms can be used interchangeably. For example, *profits before tax* is the same thing as *earnings before tax*.)

A more complete overview of an income statement is presented in Exhibit 10.1. As shown in the exhibit, you begin with sales (for example, the number of lemonade drinks sold times the sales price per cup). You then subtract the **cost of goods sold** (e.g., the cost per cup of lemonade times the number of cups sold) from sales to compute the firm's **gross profit**. Next, **operating expenses**, consisting of marketing and selling expenses, general and administrative expenses, and depreciation expense (e.g., the amount that Mackenzie and John paid their friends and Erin to work for them), are deducted from gross profits to determine **operating profits**. As shown in the exhibit, operating profits reflect only the decisions the owner has made relating to sales, cost of goods sold, and operating expenses. How the firm is financed, debt versus equity, has no effect on operating profits.

From the firm's operating profits, we deduct any **interest expense** incurred from borrowing money (debt) to find **profits before taxes**, or **taxable profits**—a company's taxable income. A firm's income taxes are calculated by multiplying profits before taxes by the applicable tax rate. For instance, if a firm has profits before taxes of $100,000 and its tax rate is 28 percent, then it will owe $28,000 in taxes (0.28 × $100,000 = $28,000).

The number that results when taxes are subtracted from profits before taxes represents **net profits**, or profits that may be reinvested in the firm or distributed to the owners—provided, of course, the cash is available to do so. As you will come to understand, *positive net profits in an income statement does not necessarily mean that a firm has generated positive cash flows.*

operating profits Earnings after operating expenses but before interest and taxes are paid.

interest expense The cost of borrowed money.

profits before taxes (taxable profits) Earnings after operating expenses and interest expenses but before taxes.

net profits Earnings that may be distributed to the owners or reinvested in the company.

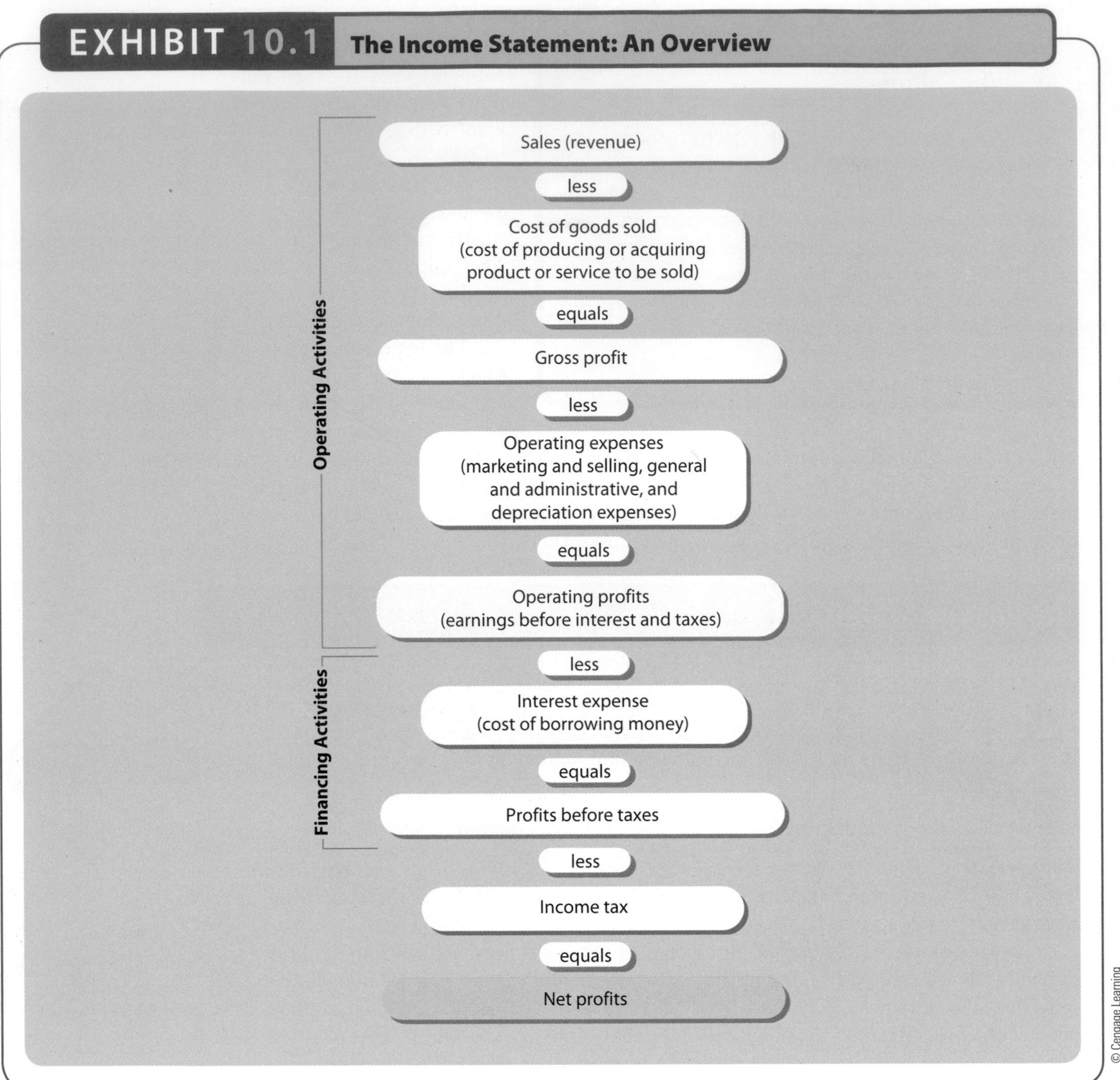

EXHIBIT 10.1 The Income Statement: An Overview

depreciation expense The cost of a firm's building and equipment, allocated over their useful life.

Exhibit 10.2 shows the 2011 income statement for Pendley & Associates, Inc., an equipment leasing company owned by three sisters, Alyssa, Shae, and Micalea Pendley. The company had sales of $850,000 for the 12-month period ending December 31, 2011. The cost of goods sold was $550,000, resulting in a gross profit of $300,000. The company had $200,000 in operating expenses, which included marketing expenses, general and administrative expenses, and depreciation expense. **Depreciation expense** is the cost of a firm's equipment and building, allocated over their useful life. For example, if a business paid $10,000 for a piece of equipment with a four-year life expectancy, the depreciation expense each year would be $2,500 ($10,000 ÷ 4 years = $2,500). So after total operating expenses were subtracted, the company's operating profits would amount to $100,000. To this point, we have calculated profits based *only* on expenses related to the firm's operations—and not those affected by how the firm finances its assets.

© iStockphoto.com/Don Wilkie

Pendley & Associates' interest expense of $20,000 (the expense it incurred from borrowing money) is deducted from operating profits to arrive at the company's profits before taxes of $80,000. Given a 25 percent tax rate, the company paid $20,000 in income taxes ($80,000 operating income × 0.25 tax rate = $20,000), leaving net profits of $60,000.

The net profits of $60,000 are the profits that the business earned for its owners after paying all expenses—cost of goods sold, operating expenses, interest expense, and income taxes. Now the owners have to decide what to do with these profits. They either can pay themselves a dividend or retain the earnings in the business to help finance the firm's growth, or some combination of the two.

EXHIBIT 10.2 Income Statement for Pendley & Associates, Inc., for the Year Ending December 31, 2011

Sales		$850,000
Cost of goods sold		(550,000)
Gross profits		$300,000
Operating expenses:		
Marketing expenses	$90,000	
General and administrative expenses	80,000	
Depreciation	30,000	
Total operating expenses		$200,000
Operating profits		$100,000
Interest expense		(20,000)
profits before tax		$ 80,000
Income tax (25%)		(20,000)
Net profits		$ 60,000
Net profits		$ 60,000
Dividends paid		(15,000)
Addition to retained earnings		$ 45,000

So what did the Pendley & Associates' stockholders do with their profits? As shown at the bottom of Exhibit 10.2, $15,000 in dividends was paid to the three Pendley sisters; the remaining $45,000 ($60,000 net profits less $15,000 in dividends) was retained by the firm—an amount you will see later in the balance sheet. *Dividends paid to a firm's owners, unlike interest expense, are not considered an expense in the income statement.* Instead, they are viewed as a return of principal to the owners.

In summary, the income statement answers the question "How profitable is the business?" In providing the answer, the income statement reports financial information related to five broad areas of business activity:

1. Sales (revenue)
2. Cost of producing or acquiring the goods or services sold by the company
3. Operating expenses, such as marketing expenses, rent, managers' salaries, and depreciation expense
4. Interest expense
5. Tax payments

A small business owner should pay close attention to the income statement to determine trends and to make comparisons against competitors and against other firms that are considered to provide examples of "best practices"—companies we all can learn from. Moreover, profits as a percentage of sales, or what is called **profit margins**, should be watched carefully. Large expenses should also be monitored to ensure that they are being controlled.

profit margins
Profits as a percentage of sales.

Being able to measure profits, as explained above, isn't enough; you must also consider how your decisions affect your company's profits. Philip Campbell, a CPA, a consultant, and the author of *Never Run Out of Cash: The 10 Cash Flow Rules You Can't Afford to Ignore,* offers this advice:

> *If you ask a business owner whether he runs his company to make money, the answer will always be "Yes." The reality is, he doesn't. . . . More often than not, you hear words like "brand," "market share," or "shelf space." When you hear those words, you can be sure that you've just found an opportunity to make some money.*
>
> *Why? Because those words always are used to justify unprofitable decisions. They are big red flags that you are not making decisions based on a common-sense approach to profitability. When you hear those words, ask yourself this simple question, "Are we making this decision based on profitability or for some other (possibly hidden) reason?"*[2]

Let's Check for Understanding

Understanding the Income Statement

Take a few minutes to see if you can answer the following two questions.

1. What is the difference between gross profits, operating profits, profits before taxes, and net profits?
2. Construct an income statement, using the following information. What are the firm's gross profits, operating profits, and net profits? Which expense is a *noncash* expense?

Interest expense	$ 10,000
Cost of goods sold	160,000
Marketing expenses	70,000
Administrative expenses	50,000
Sales	400,000
Stock dividends	5,000
Income tax	20,000
Depreciation expense	20,000

(Answers to these questions are provided on page 305.)

The Balance Sheet

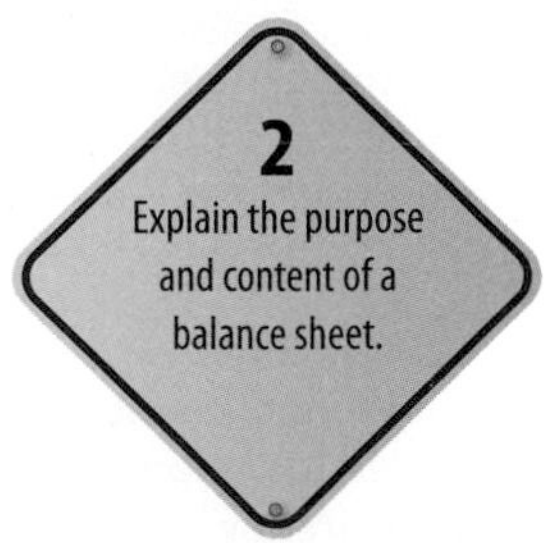

While an income statement reports the results of business operations over a period of time, a **balance sheet** provides a snapshot of a business's financial position at a *specific point in time.* Thus, a balance sheet captures the cumulative effects of all earlier financial decisions up to a specific date. At a given point in time, the balance sheet shows the assets a firm owns, the liabilities (or debt) outstanding or owed, and the amount the owners have invested in the business (ownership equity). In its simplest form, a balance sheet follows this formula:

$$\text{Total assets} = \text{Debt} + \text{Ownership equity}$$

In other words, for every dollar of assets, there must be a dollar of financing in the form of debt or ownership equity (owner's equity).

Exhibit 10.3 illustrates the elements in the balance sheet of a typical firm. Each of the three main components of the balance sheet—assets, debt, and ownership equity—is discussed in the following sections.

2 Explain the purpose and content of a balance sheet.

balance sheet A financial report showing a firm's assets, liabilities, and ownership equity at a specific point in time.

EXHIBIT 10.3 The Balance Sheet: An Overview

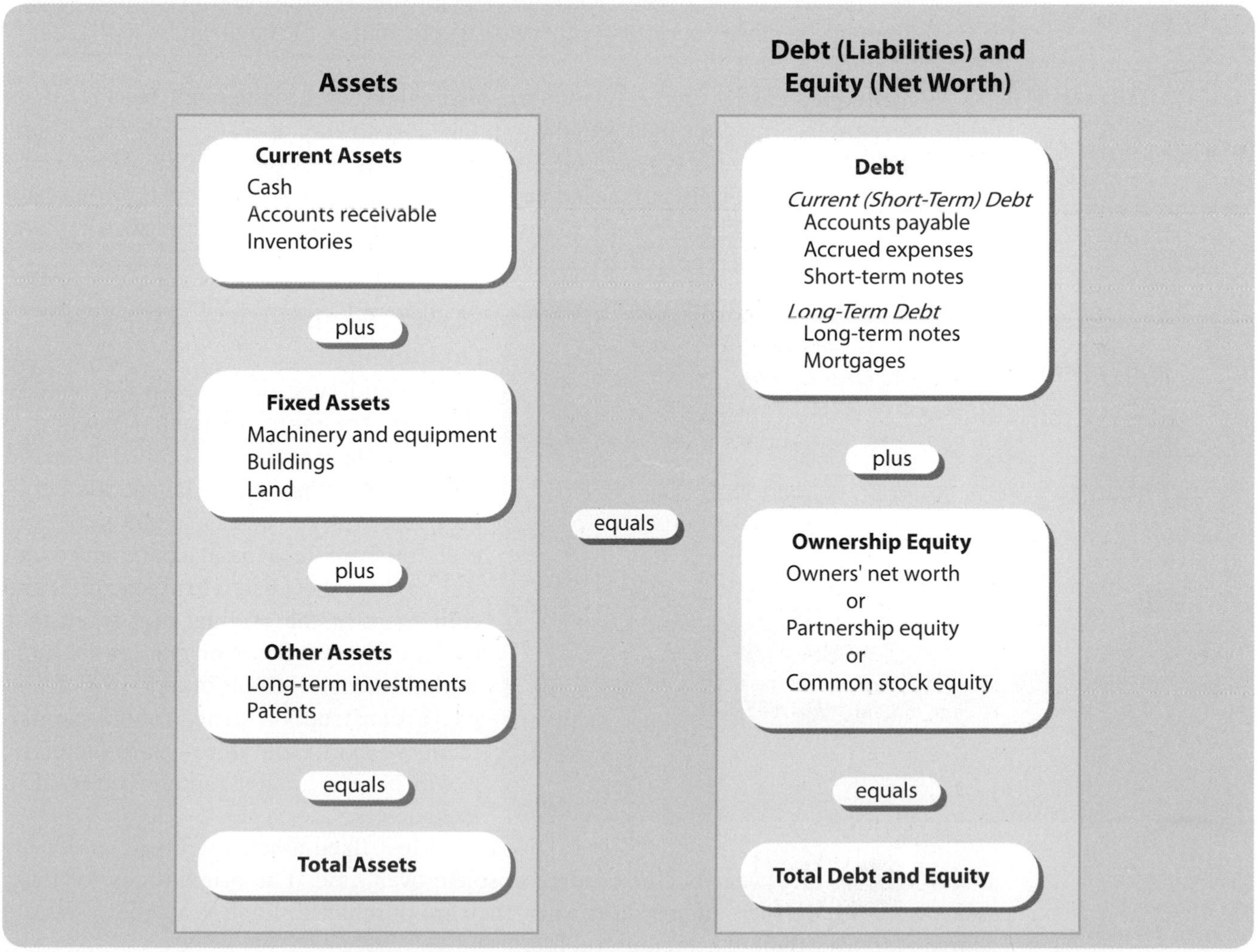

Assets
Current Assets
Cash
Accounts receivable
Inventories
plus
Fixed Assets
Machinery and equipment
Buildings
Land
plus
Other Assets
Long-term investments
Patents
equals
Total Assets
equals
Debt (Liabilities) and Equity (Net Worth)
Debt
Current (Short-Term) Debt
Accounts payable
Accrued expenses
Short-term notes
Long-Term Debt
Long-term notes
Mortgages
plus
Ownership Equity
Owners' net worth
or
Partnership equity
or
Common stock equity
equals
Total Debt and Equity

ASSETS

Assets, shown on the left side of Exhibit 10.3, are what the company owns that has a monetary value. They are always grouped into three categories: (1) current assets, (2) fixed assets, and (3) other assets.

current assets (working capital) Assets that can be converted into cash relatively quickly.

Current Assets

Current assets (working capital), which are always listed first in a balance sheet, include those assets that are relatively liquid—that is, assets that can be converted into cash relatively quickly. Current assets primarily include cash, accounts receivable, and inventory.

accounts receivable The amount of credit extended to customers that is currently outstanding.

1. *Cash* is money in the bank and, possibly, some type of marketable security, such as a short-term government security, that can be sold very quickly. Every firm must have cash for current business operations.
2. **Accounts re ceivable** are like a loan to customers. When a firm sells its products or services, customers may pay in cash or be given credit terms (a loan), such as being allowed 30 days to pay for purchases. Accounts receivable need to be monitored carefully, since they have a lot to do with the cash that will (or will not) come into the business. Creditors are likely to be watching it as well.
3. **Inventory** comprises the raw materials and the products being held by a firm for sale in the ordinary course of business. Service companies typically have little or no inventory, but nearly every other company—manufacturers, wholesalers, retailers—does. As with accounts receivable, the business owner had better manage inventory carefully; otherwise, performance of the business will suffer.

inventory A firm's raw materials and products held in anticipation of eventual sale.

working capital cycle The process of converting inventory to cash.

fixed assets (property, plant and equipment [PPE]) Physical assets that will be used in the business for more than one year, such as equipment, buildings, and land.

As mentioned earlier, current assets are also called working capital, because these assets are vital in providing the needed capital for day-to-day operations. *A firm cannot survive without adequate working capital.* Exhibit 10.4 illustrates the **working capital cycle**, a process where inventory is purchased or produced, and then sold for cash or on credit (accounts receivable). The accounts receivable are later converted into cash when collected. The cycle is then repeated, over and over.

Fixed Assets (Property, Plant, and Equipment)

The second type of assets in the balance sheet are the more permanent assets in a business. **Fixed assets**, also called **property, plant, and equipment (PPE)**, include buildings, machinery, trucks, computers, and every other physical asset a company owns. The balance sheet lists a firm's facilities and equipment at the original cost when they were purchased. Some businesses are more capital-intensive than others—for example, a construction firm is more capital-intensive than a gift store—and, therefore, it will have a greater amount invested in fixed assets.

Most fixed assets are also **depreciable assets**; that is, they wear out or become obsolete over time. The original cost of these assets is shown on the balance sheet when they are purchased. Each year, the assets are depreciated over their expected useful life.

depreciable assets Assets whose value declines, or depreciates, over time.

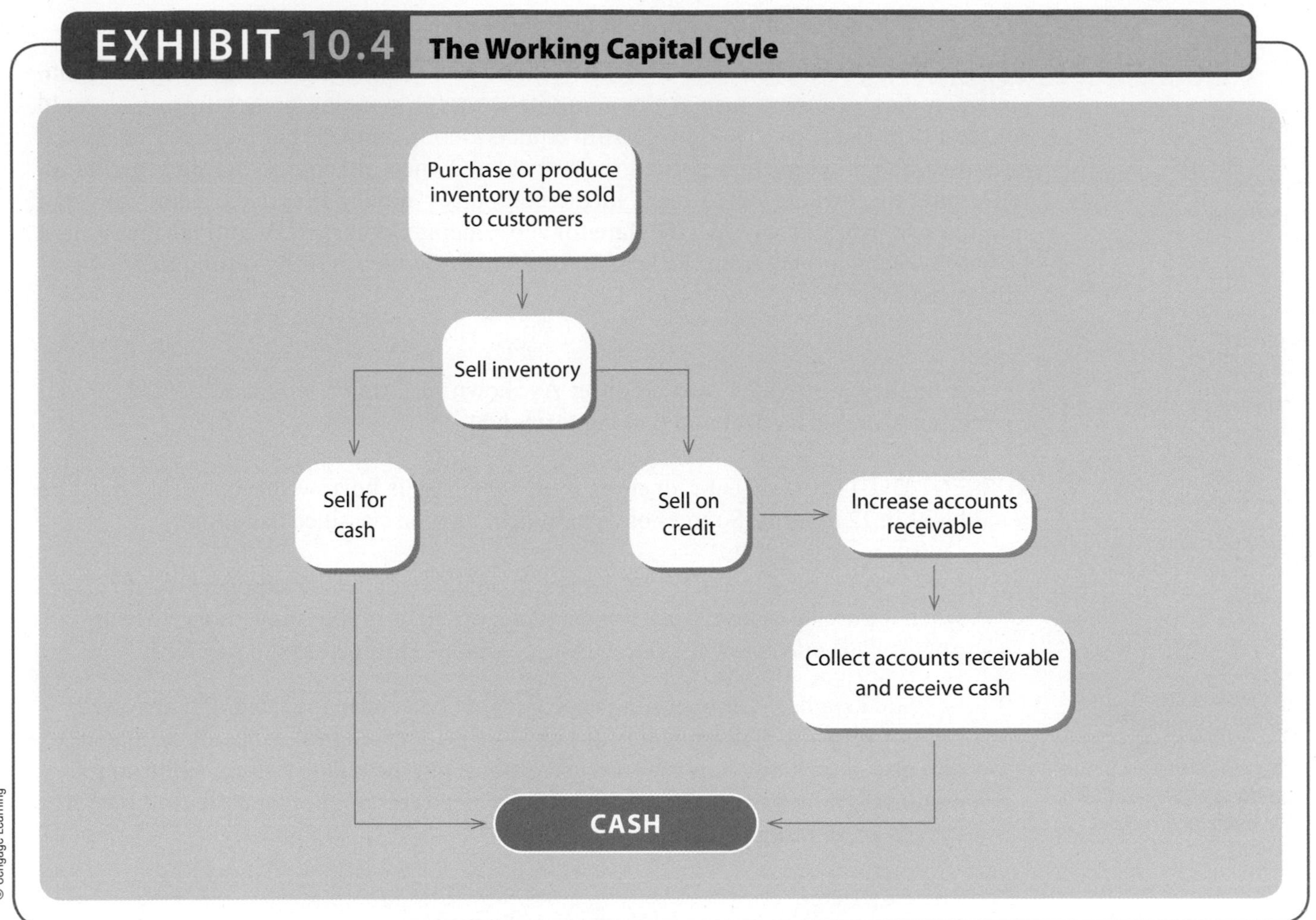

Numerical Example

Assume that a business purchased a truck for $20,000 with an expected useful life of four years. When the firm buys the truck, the original cost of $20,000 is shown on the balance sheet as a **gross fixed asset**. We would then depreciate the cost of the truck over its useful life of four years. A depreciation expense of $5,000 would be shown annually in the income statement ($20,000 ÷ 4 years = $5,000). Each year, the cumulative depreciation expense, or what is called **accumulated depreciation**, is subtracted from the original cost of the fixed asset to yield the **net fixed asset**. In this instance, the balance sheet at the end of each year would appear as follows:

	Year 1	Year 2	Year 3	Year 4
Gross fixed asset	$20,000	$20,000	$20,000	$20,000
Accumulated depreciation	(5,000)	(10,000)	(15,000)	(20,000)
Net fixed asset	$15,000	$10,000	$ 5,000	$ 0

gross fixed assets Depreciable assets at their original cost, before any depreciation expense has been taken.

accumulated depreciation Total (cumulative) depreciation expense taken over an asset's life.

net fixed assets Gross fixed assets less accumulated depreciation.

OTHER ASSETS

The third category of assets, **other assets**, includes patents, copyrights, and goodwill. For a startup company, organizational costs—costs incurred in organizing and promoting the business—may also be included in this category.

other assets A firm's raw materials and products held in anticipation of eventual sale.

DEBT AND EQUITY

The right side of the balance sheet in Exhibit 10.3 (on page 301), showing debt and equity, indicates how a firm is financing its assets. Financing comes from two main sources: debt (liabilities) and ownership equity. Debt is money that has been borrowed and must be repaid at some predetermined date. Ownership equity, on the other hand, represents the owners' investment in the company—money they have personally put into the firm without any specific date for repayment. Owners recover their investment by withdrawing money from the firm in the form of dividends or by selling their ownership in the firm.

Debt

debt
Financing provided by creditors.

Debt is financing provided by a creditor. As shown in Exhibit 10.3, it is divided into (1) current, or short-term, debt and (2) long-term debt.

current debt (short-term liabilities)
Borrowed money that must be repaid within 12 months.

accounts payable (trade credit)
Outstanding credit payable to suppliers.

accrued expenses
Operating expenses that have been incurred but not paid.

CURRENT DEBT **Current debt**, or **short-term liabilities**, is borrowed money that must be repaid within 12 months. Sources of current debt may be classified as follows:

- **Accounts payable (trade credit)** represent credit extended by suppliers to a firm when it purchases inventory. For example, when a firm buys inventory, the supplier (seller) may allow the purchasing company 30 or 60 days to pay for it.
- **Accrued expenses** are operating expenses that have been incurred and are owed but not yet paid. The amount of the expense is included in the income statement and also shown as a liability (accrued expense) in the balance sheet. For example, employees may have performed work for which they will not be paid until the following accounting period.

Numerical Example

As an illustration of accrued expenses, consider an employee who is to receive a salary of $4,000 for work performed in April. However, the company will not be paying the employee until May 1. In this case, the firm would record the salary owed as an expense in the income statement for April. But since no payment is made in April, the company would show it as a liability (accrued wages) in the balance sheet on April 30. When the employee is paid on May 1, the accrued expenses are decreased by $4,000, along with a $4,000 decrease in cash.

short-term notes
Agreements to repay cash amounts borrowed from banks or other lending sources within 12 months or less.

- **Short-term notes** represent cash amounts borrowed from a bank or other lending source for 12 months or less. Short-term notes are a primary source of financing for most small businesses.

Numerical Example

Assume you borrow $50,000 from a bank for 90 days (one-quarter of a year) to purchase inventory during a peak season of business. Further assume that the interest rate on the loan is 8 percent. In this case, you will incur $1,000 in interest ($1,000 = $50,000 principal owed × 0.08 interest rate × ¼ year). The interest paid on the loan would be shown as interest expense in the income statement and the principal amount borrowed as a liability in the balance sheet.

How Did You Do?

Understanding the Income Statement

On page 300, you were asked two questions. Your answers should be similar to those provided below.

1. What is the difference between gross profits, operating profits, profits before taxes, and net profits?

To understand a firm's profits, think about the process. For instance, a retailer buys merchandise from a wholesaler. The merchandise is then placed on display shelves in the store, where sales personnel, a bookkeeper, and a maintenance person work. The retailer sells the merchandise, hopefully for a profit. The difference between what the retailer receives from customers (sales) and the cost of the merchandise is the gross profits. The expenses of operating the store represent the business's operating expenses. So deducting the operating expenses from gross profits gives the operating profits. If the retailer borrowed money from a bank, he or she would have to pay interest. Subtracting any interest expense from operating profits gives profits before taxes. The retailer then pays income taxes on those taxable profits. The remaining earnings are the company's net profits, which are the profits that are left for the owners. (See Exhibit 10.1 for a graphical representation of the process.)

2. Construct an income statement, using the following information. What are the firm's gross profits, operating profits, and net profits? Which expense is a noncash expense?

Sales		$ 400,000
Cost of goods sold		(160,000)
Gross profits		**$ 240,000**
Operating expenses:		
Marketing expenses	$ 70,000	
Administrative expenses	50,000	
Depreciation expense	20,000 ← Noncash expense	
Total operating expenses		$(140,000)
Operating profits		**$ 100,000**
Interest expense		(10,000)
Profits before taxes		$ 90,000
Income tax		(20,000)
Net profits		**$ 70,000**

Note: The $5,000 in dividends is not shown as an expense in the income statement but is considered to be a return of the owner's capital. Thus, the net profits of $70,000 less the $5,000 in dividends, or $65,000, will be added to the firm's retained earnings in the balance sheet.

LONG TERM DEBT Loans granted for longer than 12 months from banks or other financial institutions comprise **long-term debt**. When a firm borrows money for five years to buy equipment, it signs an agreement—a **long-term note**—promising to repay the loan plus interest over five years. As with short-term notes, the interest is an expense shown in the income statement and the amount of the principal is a liability reported on the balance sheet.

When a firm borrows money, say, for 30 years to purchase a warehouse or office building, the real estate usually

A hard lesson was learned by many entrepreneurs during the economic downturn that began in 2008: Do not spend cash in a way that does not move the company forward—not during a recession, not at any time.

long-term debt
Loans from banks or other sources with repayment terms of more than 12 months.

long-term notes
Agreements to repay cash amounts borrowed from banks or other lending sources for periods longer than 12 months.

mortgage
A long-term loan from a creditor for which real estate is pledged as collateral.

ownership equity
Owners' investments in a company plus cumulative net profits retained in the firm.

retained earnings
Profits less dividends paid over the life of a business.

serves as collateral for the long-term loan, which is called a **mortgage**. If the borrower is unable to repay the loan, the lender can take the real estate in settlement.

Ownership Equity

Ownership equity, or owner's equity, is money that the owners invest in a business. The amount of ownership equity in a business is equal to

1. The total amount of the owners' investments in the business, which for sole proprietorships and partnerships is the amount of the money invested and for corporations the amount the owner pays for stock,

   plus

2. The cumulative amount of *net profits* that have been retained and reinvested in the business over the entire life of the company—that is, profits not paid out as dividends, or **retained earnings**. Thus, the basic formula for ownership equity is as follows:

$$\text{Ownership equity} = \text{Owners' investment} + \underbrace{\text{Cumulative profits} - \text{Cumulative dividends paid to owners}}_{\text{Earnings retained within the business}}$$

Exhibit 10.5 presents balance sheets for Pendley & Associates for December 31, 2010, and December 31, 2011, along with dollar changes in the balance sheets for the same time periods. By referring to the columns representing the two balance sheets, you can see the financial position of the firm at the beginning *and* at the end of 2011.

EXHIBIT 10.5 Balance Sheets for Pendley & Associates, Inc., for December 31, 2010 and 2011

	2010	2011	Changes
Assets			
Current assets:			
Cash	$ 45,000	$ 50,000	$ 5,000
Accounts receivable	75,000	80,000	5,000
Inventory	180,000	220,000	40,000
Total current assets	$300,000	$350,000	$ 50,000
Fixed assets:			
Gross fixed assets	$860,000	$960,000	$100,000
Accumulated depreciation	(360,000)	(390,000)	(30,000)
Net fixed assets	$500,000	$570,000	$ 70,000
TOTAL ASSETS	$800,000	$920,000	$120,000
Debt (Liabilities) and Equity			
Current liabilities:			
Accounts payable	$ 15,000	$ 20,000	$ 5,000
Short-term notes	60,000	80,000	20,000
Total current liabilities (debt)	$ 75,000	$100,000	$ 25,000
Long-term debt	150,000	200,000	50,000
Total debt	$225,000	$300,000	$ 75,000
Ownership equity			
Common stock	$300,000	$300,000	$ 0
Retained earnings	275,000	320,000	45,000
Total ownership equity	$575,000	$620,000	$ 45,000
TOTAL DEBT AND EQUITY	$800,000	$920,000	$120,000

Let's Check for Understanding

Understanding the Balance Sheet

Take a few minutes to see if you can answer the questions below.

1. Give an example of accounts receivable.
2. What relationship would you expect between inventory and accounts payable?
3. What is the difference between common stock and retained earnings?
4. Construct a balance sheet, using the following information. What are the firm's current assets, net fixed assets, total assets, current liabilities, long-term debt, total ownership equity, and total debt and equity?

Gross fixed assets	$ 75,000
Cash	10,000
Other assets	15,000
Accounts payable	40,000
Retained earnings	15,000
Accumulated depreciation	20,000
Accounts receivable	50,000
Long-term note	5,000
Mortgage	20,000
Common stock	100,000
Inventory	70,000
Short-term notes	20,000

(The answers to the above questions are provided on page 311.)

The 2010 and 2011 year-end balance sheets for Pendley & Associates show that the firm began 2011 (ended 2010) with $800,000 in total assets and ended 2011 with total assets of $920,000. We see how much has been invested in current assets (cash, accounts receivable, and inventory) and in fixed assets. We also observe how much debt and equity were used to finance the assets. Note that about half of the equity came from investments made by the owners (common stock), and the other half came from reinvesting profits in the business (retained earnings). Referring back to the income statement in Exhibit 10.2, note that the $45,000 increase in retained earnings, shown in the Changes column in Exhibit 10.5, is the firm's net profits for the year ($60,000) less the dividends paid to the owners ($15,000).

Finally, a balance sheet helps the small business owner know the financial strength and capabilities of the business—something that cannot be known in any other way. It helps answer such key questions as

- Is the business in a position to expand?
- Can the firm easily handle the ebbs and flows of sales and expenses?
- Is the firm collecting its accounts receivable as planned and efficiently managing inventory?
- Can accounts payable be paid more slowly to forestall an inevitable cash shortage—without hurting the entrepreneur's credit reputation?

The entrepreneur is not the only one who needs to be well versed about the balance sheet; lenders such as bankers, investors, and suppliers, who are considering how much credit to grant rely heavily on a firm's balance sheet in their decision making.

LIVING THE DREAM

entrepreneurial experiences

Advice from a Veteran Entrepreneur

© iStockphoto.com/Angelika Schwarz

I'm often amused by the reactions of people who come to me for help. I usually start by interviewing them in my office. They explain the problem they're having. I ask them a few questions. They answer as best they can. I then tell them something about their business that they can't believe I could know.

Consider Andrew Blitstein, who took charge of his family's cleaning service a few months ago, after his father passed away. Up to then, Andrew had been handling sales for the company and had little or no experience in other areas of the business. He came to see me at the insistence of his mother, who'd worked with her late husband, and his uncle, who was an old friend of mine.

I started, as I usually do, by asking Andrew general questions about himself and his company. It was a more or less typical commercial janitorial service. In addition to cleaning offices on a regular basis, the company did special jobs, like shampooing the rugs and washing the windows. As for problems, he said he was having a tough time with cash flow. "I see," I said. "Are you having trouble collecting your receivables?" No, receivables weren't a problem, he said. "How about bad debt?" No, bad debt wasn't a problem, either. "Then do you have a big office with lots of people?"

"Oh, no, no," he said. "We run pretty lean." So excessive overhead apparently wasn't a problem, either.

Now, cash-flow problems are common in business, and people often have a hard time figuring out what's behind them, but there are actually just a few potential causes. You could have too much cash tied up in receivables or—if you have a product-based business—in inventory. Or you could have too many deadbeat customers. Or you could be spending too much on overhead. But if receivables, inventory, bad debt, and overhead are all under control—as they appeared to be in Andrew's case—there really is only one other likely culprit: weak gross margins [sales − cost of goods sold = gross profits], which could mean prices are too low, direct costs are too high, or some combination of the two.

I asked Andrew how much he was paying his employees. He said they earned about $20 an hour. "No," I said. "I mean, what's the hourly cost fully loaded with all the taxes, benefits, and so on?" He didn't know, which is not unusual. "So you don't know what your costs are," I said. "It's hard to make a sale—at least a good sale—if you don't know your costs. How do you price a job?"

"Well, when we do the carpet cleaning or the window cleaning, I figure out approximately how much it's going to cost us, and then I try to double it."

"OK," I said, "that's good. But how do you price the regular cleaning service?"

"We just try to be competitive," he said. "We have a lot of competitors, and we want to get the long-term contracts. We make our money on the extras."

So he didn't know how much the regular cleaning service was costing or what a good price for it would be. "Let's take your two biggest clients," I said. "How much business do they do?" He said he had one contract that paid about $350,000 a year and another that paid $300,000. "How much money do you make on those contracts?"

"I don't know," Andrew said. "Not much. But they also use us for the extras."

"And how much do they pay for the extras per year?"

"About $20,000 or $25,000," he said.

"So, given how you price the extras, they contribute $10,000 or $12,500 to covering your overhead," I said. "That's not a lot for accounts of that size. My guess is that you're losing money on them."

I could read his thoughts as he left: But four days later, Andrew contacted me and said he wanted to get together again.

"You were right," Andrew said as he sat down in my office. "We're losing money on those accounts. I figure that, fully loaded, I'm paying $31 an hour."

"OK, well, let's see what fully loaded is," I said. We started to go through his numbers on one of the accounts, and it quickly became apparent that he had underestimated the costs. By the time we finished, we could see he was losing from $50,000 to $60,000 annually on the account. "Think of it this way," I said. "If you stopped doing business with this customer today, you'd make an extra $50,000."

"I don't know . . .," Andrew said.

"I'm not telling you to get rid of the client," I said. "There may be reasons to keep the account. But do you really think any of your competitors would take this account away from you and lose $50,000 a year on it?"

© iStockphoto.com/Eliza Snow

He smiled at the absurdity of the idea. "But I'd have to increase my price something like 20 percent just to break even on the account," he said. "I can't do that."

"Maybe not," I said. "I realize that it's hard to increase prices in a recession. But the client has to recognize that it will never find a company willing to do the work at the rate it's paying you. You just can't go on losing $50,000 a year on the account."

Andrew said he would think about it. I'm sure he will come around eventually. Meanwhile, he has made significant changes in the way he sells. He told me about one prospect who wanted to use him but felt that his bid was a little high. Rather than reduce the price, Andrew stood his ground. "You're talking about saving 10 cents an hour, but look what you get for those 10 cents," he said. "Our service is far superior."

He got the account. More to the point, he got the concept. And he realizes that you don't need to be a genius to deal with cash-flow problems. You just have to know how business works.

Source: Excerpts from Norm Brodsky, "How to Fix Cash Flow Problems," *Inc.* Magazine, May 2009, http://www.inc.com/magazine/20090501/street-smarts-how-to-fix-cash-flow-problems.html, accessed March 2, 2011. *Inc.*: the magazine for growing companies.

Viewing the Income Statement and Balance Sheet Together

3 How do financial statements show a firm's financial position?

Thus far, we have discussed the income statement and the balance sheet as separate reports. But they actually complement each other to give an overall picture of the firm's financial situation. Because the balance sheet is a snapshot of a firm's financial condition at a specific point in time, such as on the exact day of December 31, and the income statement reports results over a given period, such as the period from January 1 through December 31, both are required to determine a firm's financial position.

Exhibit 10.6 shows how the income statement and the balance sheet fit together. To understand how a firm performed during 2011, you must know the firm's financial position at the beginning of 2011 (balance sheet on December 31, 2010), its financial performance during the year (income statement for 2011), and its financial position at the end of the year (balance sheet on December 31, 2011).

EXHIBIT 10.6 The Fit of the Income Statement and Balance Sheet

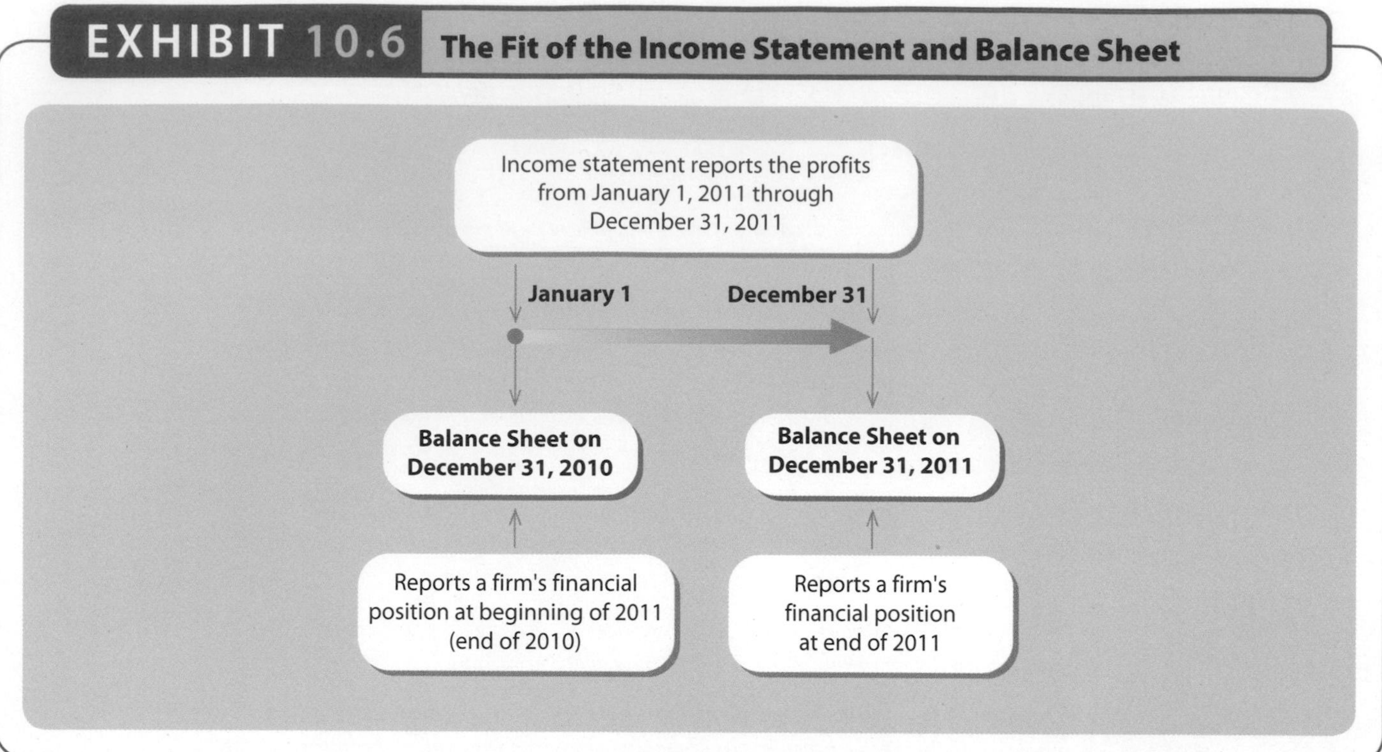

Numerical Example

To illustrate the relationship between the balance sheets and income statement, consider the two balance sheets and income statement shown below for the Maness Corporation. The first balance sheet was prepared on December 31, 2010, which can also be thought of as the beginning of 2011. (Whatever a firm ends with in 2010, it starts with in 2011.) From the combined financial statements, we can see the Maness Corporation's financial position as it started 2011 (the balance sheet as of December 31, 2010), how the firm did in its operations throughout 2011 (presented in the income statement), and the firm's financial position at the end of 2011 (the balance sheet as of December 31, 2011).

Balance Sheets as of December 31, 2010, and December 31, 2011

	2010	2011	Changes
Assets			
Cash	$ 150,000	$ 125,000	$ (25,000)
Accounts receivable	350,000	375,000	25,000
Inventory	475,000	550,000	75,000
Total current assets	$ 975,000	$ 1,050,000	$ 75,000
Gross fixed assets	$ 2,425,000	$ 2,750,000	$ 325,000
Accumulated depreciation	(10,000,000)	(1,200,000)	(200,000)
Net fixed assets	$ 1,425,000	$ 1,550,000	$ 125,000
TOTAL ASSETS	$24,000,000	$ 2,600,000	$ 200,000
Debt (Liabilities) and Equity			
Accounts payable	$ 200,000	$ 150,000	$ (50,000)
Short-term notes	0	150,000	150,000
Total current liabilities	$ 200,000	$ 300,000	$ 100,000
Long-term debt	600,000	600,000	0
Total debt	$ 800,000	$ 900,000	$ 100,000

Ownership equity			
Common stock	$ 900,000	$ 900,000	$ 0
Retained earnings	700,000	800,000	100,000
Total ownership equity	$1,600,000	$1,700,000	$100,000
TOTAL DEBT AND EQUITY	$2,400,000	$2,600,000	$200,000

Income Statement for the Year Ending December 31, 2011

Sales	$1,450,000
Cost of goods sold	(850,000)
Gross profits	$ 600,000
Operating expenses	(240,000)
Operating profits	$ 360,000
Interest expense	(64,000)
Profits before taxes	$ 296,000
Taxes	(118,000)
Net profits	$ 178,000
Net profits	$ 178,000
Dividends paid	(78,000)
Addition to retained earnings	$ 100,000

(Also equals the change in retained earnings in the balance sheets)

How Did You Do?

Understanding the Balance Sheet

On page 307, you were asked four questions. Your answers should be similar to those provided below.

1. Give an example of accounts receivable.

   Accounts receivable represent money owed by a customer to a company for goods or services that have already been received by the customer but not yet paid for. For example, an auto repair shop may purchase parts for $200 from a parts supplier and be given 30 days to pay for the parts. At the time of the transaction, the supplier records the $200 sale and the same amount in accounts receivable. When the repair shop pays the $200, the accounts receivable are decreased and cash increases by $200.

2. What relationship would you expect between inventory and accounts payable?

   Accounts payable are the amounts owed a supplier for inventory that was purchased on credit. When a business purchases inventory on credit, inventory increases along with a corresponding increase in accounts payable.

3. What is the difference between common stock and retained earnings?

   Both common stock and retained earnings represent an owner's equity in a firm. Common stock is cash that has been invested in a firm by its owners. Retained earnings are the amount of profits that have been reinvested in a business, as opposed to distributing the profits in the form of dividends.

4. Based on the financial data provided on page 307, your balance sheet should read as follows:

Assets	
Cash	$ 10,000
Accounts receivable	50,000
Inventory	70,000
Total current assets	$130,000

(Continued)

Gross fixed assets	$ 75,000
Accumulated depreciation	(20,000)
Net fixed assets	$ 55,000
Other assets	15,000
TOTAL ASSETS	$200,000
Debt (Liabilities) and Equity	
Accounts payable	$ 40,000
Short-term notes	20,000
Total current debt	$ 60,000
Long-term note	5,000
Mortgage	20,000
Total long-term debt	$ 25,000
Total debt	$ 85,000
Common stock	$100,000
Retained earnings	15,000
Total ownership equity	$115,000
TOTAL DEBT AND EQUITY	$200,000

The Cash Flow Statement

4 Use the income statement and balance sheets to compute a company's cash flows.

An entrepreneur once told us how intimidated she felt when her accountant presented the firm's monthly financial reports and she had difficulty understanding cash flows. Our advice was to get a new accountant—one who would explain the statements carefully—and also to spend the time necessary to gain a solid understanding of the financial statements and the firm's cash flows.

Effectively managing cash flows is critical—and we do mean *critical*—for small business owners. In the words of Philip Campbell, a CPA and former chief financial officer in several companies, "Despite the fact that cash is the lifeblood of a business—the fuel that keeps the engine running—most business owners don't truly have a handle on their cash flow. Poor cash-flow management is causing more business failures today than ever before."[3]

cash flow statement A financial report showing a firm's sources of cash as well as its uses of cash.

For this reason, the small firm owner must understand the sources and uses of the firm's cash. A **cash flow statement** is a financial report that shows the sources of a firm's cash and its uses of the cash. In other words, it answers the questions "Where did the cash come from?" and "Where did the cash go?"

PROFITS VERSUS CASH FLOWS

Entrepreneurs need to be aware that *the profits shown on a company's income statement are not the same as its cash flows!* Do you remember when John (one of the Lemonade Kids) noticed that their profits were not the same as the increase in cash? That plays out every day in the lives of entrepreneurs. In the words of author Jan Norman, "Even profitable companies can go broke. That's a difficult truth for some business owners to swallow. But the sooner you learn that when you're out of cash, you're out of business, the better your chances for survival will be."[4] Many a business that shows a profit on its income statement has to file bankruptcy because the amount of cash coming in did not compare with the amount of cash going out. Without adequate cash flows, little problems become major problems!

An income statement is not a measure of cash flows because it is calculated on an *accrual* basis rather than a *cash* basis. This is an important point to understand. In

accrual-basis accounting
An accounting method of recording profits when earned and expenses when incurred, whether or not the profit has been received or the expense paid.

cash-basis accounting
An accounting method of recording profits when cash is received and recording expenses when they are paid.

accrual-basis accounting, profits are recorded when earned—whether or not the profits have been received in cash—and expenses are recorded when they are incurred—even if money has not actually been paid out. In cash-basis accounting, profits are reported when cash is received and expenses are recorded when they are paid. For a number of reasons, including the following, profits based on an accrual accounting system will differ from the firm's cash flows.

1. Sales reported in an income statement include both *cash* sales and *credit* sales. Thus, total sales do not correspond to the actual cash collected. A company may have had sales of $1 million for the year, but not collected on all of them. If accounts receivable increased $80,000 from the beginning of the year to the end of the year, then we would know that only $920,000 of the sales had been collected ($920,000 = $1,000,000 sales − $80,000 increase in accounts receivable).
2. Cash spent for inventory doesn't represent all inventory purchases since some inventory is financed by credit. Consider a business that purchased $500,000 in inventory during the year, but the supplier extended $100,000 in credit for the purchases. The actual cash paid for inventory would be only $400,000 ($400,000 = $500,000 total inventory purchases − $100,000 credit granted by the supplier).
3. The depreciation expense shown in the income statement is a noncash expense. It reflects the costs associated with using an asset that benefits the firm's operations over a period of several years, such as a piece of equipment used over five years. Thus, if a business had profits of $250,000 that included depreciation expenses of $40,000, then the cash flows would be $290,000 ($290,000 = $250,000 profits + $40,000 depreciation expense).

So the question—and its answer—that every small business owner should ask and understand is "How do I compute my firm's cash flows?"

ACTION

Cash Is King

Applying for a loan? A banker wants to look at your financial statements to see if the historical cash flows will adequately service the proposed loan. Revenue growth and profits are fine, but only historical cash flows can demonstrate the ability to collect accounts receivable and properly manage inventory and accounts payable. Cash is not only king, but during the last recession, it was said to be the emperor of the universe![5]

MEASURING A FIRM'S CASH FLOWS

It's time to return to our young entrepreneurs, Mackenzie and John, and their lemonade stand. To develop a report that explained the cash flows from their lemonade business, you could simply list all the cash inflows and outflows and see what happened to their cash balance. Here is what it would look like:

Mackenzie and John's initial investment	$ 10
Loan from their mom	40
Purchased inventory	(40)
Cash collected from the first Saturday's sales	30
Collection of accounts receivable	30
Cash collected from the second Saturday's sales	100
Salaries expense	(25)
Ending cash	$145

So they began with a $10 investment in the business and ended with $145 in cash, before repaying their mom the $40 she loaned them and contributing $100 toward the Wii purchase. This works quite well in the world of lemonade stands. But the report would become overwhelming in a business of any significant size, where thousands of transactions are recorded in the financial statements each year. Also, there's a better approach to learning what activities contribute to a firm's cash flows. We can explain the cash inflows and outflows of a business by looking at three **cash flow activities**:

cash flow activities Operating, investing, and financing activities that result in cash inflows or outflows.

1. *Generating cash flows from day-to-day business operations.* It is informative to know how much cash is being generated in the normal course of operating a business on a daily basis, beginning with purchasing inventory on credit, selling on credit, paying for the inventory, and finally collecting on the sales made on credit.
2. *Buying or selling fixed assets.* When a company buys (or sells) fixed assets, such as equipment and buildings, cash outflows (or inflows) result. These cash flows are not part of the regular day-to-day operations and, consequently, are not included in the income statement. They appear only as changes from one balance sheet to the next.
3. *Financing the business.* Cash inflows and outflows occur when the company borrows or repays debt; when it distributes money to the owners, such as when dividends are paid; or when the owners put money into the business in the form of additional equity.

If we know the cash flows from the activities listed above, we can explain a firm's total cash flows. To illustrate how this is done, we use Pendley & Associates' income statement (Exhibit 10.2) and balance sheets (Exhibit 10.5).

Activity 1: Cash Flows from Day-to-Day Business Operations

Here we want to convert the company's income statement from an *accrual* basis to a *cash* basis. This conversion can be accomplished in two steps:

1. By adding back depreciation to net profits, since depreciation is not a cash expense.
2. Subtracting any uncollected sales (increase in accounts receivable) and payments for inventory (increases in inventory less increases in accounts payable).

The reason we add back depreciation should be clear. The changes in accounts receivable, inventory, and accounts payable may be less intuitive. Two comments might be helpful for your understanding:

1. A firm's sales are either cash sales or credit sales. If accounts receivable increase, that means customers did not pay for everything they purchased. Thus, any increase in accounts receivable needs to be subtracted from total sales to determine the cash that has been collected from customers. Remember the Lemonade Kids: On their first day, they sold $60 in lemonade, but they only collected $30; the remainder was accounted for by an increase in accounts receivable.

2. The other activity occurring in the daily course of business is purchasing inventory. An increase in inventory shows that inventory was purchased, but if accounts payable (credit extended by a supplier) increase, then we may conclude that the firm did not pay for the entire inventory purchased. The net payment for inventory is equal to the increase in inventory less what has not yet been paid for (increase in accounts payable).

Referring back to Pendley & Associates' income statement (Exhibit 10.2) and balance sheets (Exhibit 10.5), we can perform the conversion from accrual basis to cash basis as follows:

Net profits	$60,000	
Add back depreciation	30,000	
Profits before depreciation		$90,000
Less increase in accounts receivable (uncollected sales)		($ 5,000)
Less payments for inventory consisting of:		
Increase in inventory	($40,000)	
Less increase in accounts payable (inventory purchased on credit)	5,000	
Cash payments for inventory		($35,000)
Cash flows from operations		$50,000

ACTION

Monitor Your Cash Flows

To improve cash flows, take a close look at your most recent financial statements. Look carefully for the following:[6]

- *Money tied up in excess inventory.* It could be used to grow your business.
- *Overly expensive office space.* Don't spend for a prime location if you don't need it.
- *Unpaid invoices. Collect payments promptly.*
- *Too much inventory. Consolidate purchases to receive the best price, but don't overorder. Ask suppliers to extend credit terms. They might give you an extra 15 or even 30 days* before you have to pay for purchases.

Finding ways to monitor your cash flows may help you to avoid borrowing money and certainly will help you to have more money to grow your business.

Activity 2: Investing in Fixed Assets

The second cash flow activity occurs when a company purchases or sells fixed assets, such as equipment or buildings. These activities are shown as an increase in *gross* fixed assets (not *net* fixed assets) in the balance sheet. An increase means the company spent cash buying fixed assets, while a decrease means it received cash from selling fixed assets. For instance, Pendley & Associates spent $100,000 on new plant and equipment in 2011, based on the change in gross fixed assets from $860,000 to $960,000, as shown in its balance sheets (Exhibit 10.5).

Activity 3: Financing the Business

The cash flows associated with financing a business are as follows:

1. A cash inflow when a company borrows more money (increases short-term and/or long-term debt
2. A cash outflow when a firm repays debt (a decrease in short-term and/or long-term debt

3. A cash inflow when the owners invest in the business to increase their equity
4. A cash outflow when the owners withdraw money from the business. In sole proprietorships and partnerships, the owner(s) would simply write a check on the firm's bank account to take the money out. In a corporation, the company would either pay a dividend to the owners or repurchase the owners' stock.

Note that when we talk about borrowing or repaying debt above, accounts payable and accrued expenses are not included. These sources of financing were included in cash flow activity 1, when we computed cash flows from operations. Here, in activity 3, only debt from such sources as banks in the form of short-term notes and long-term debt is included.

The income statement of Pendley & Associates (Exhibit 10.2) showed that $15,000 in dividends were paid to the owners. From its balance sheets (Exhibit 10.5), we see that short-term debt increased $20,000 and long-term debt increased $50,000, both sources of cash flow. Thus, in net, Pendley & Associates raised $55,000 in financing cash flows:

Cash inflows from borrowing money	
Increase in short-term notes	$ 20,000
Increase in long-term debt	50,000
Less dividends paid to owners	(15,000)
Financing cash flows	$ 55,000

To summarize, Pendley & Associates generated $50,000 in cash flows from operations, invested $100,000 in gross fixed assets (gross property, plant, and equipment), and received a net $55,000 from financing activities, for a net increase in cash of $5,000. This change in cash can be verified from the balance sheets (see Exhibit 10.5), which show that the firm's cash increased by $5,000 during 2011 (from $45,000 to $50,000). Stated somewhat differently, Pendley & Associates had positive cash flows from (1) their day-to-day business operations (cash flow from operations) and (2) borrowing money from a bank. These cash inflows were used to pay for fixed assets and to increase the firm's cash. The complete statement of cash flows for Pendley & Associates is presented in Exhibit 10.7.

Tips for Computing Cash Flows

- Don't look at the cash flow statement as a whole; it can be intimidating. Just work on the three parts of the statement individually, then put it all together. That helps you focus on what needs to be done without being overwhelmed.
- Depreciation expense and net profits are the only two numbers you need from the income statement.
- Be certain to use every change in the company's balance sheet, with two exceptions: (1) Ignore accumulated depreciation and net fixed assets since they involve the noncash item of depreciation. Use only the change in *gross* fixed assets. (2) Ignore the change in retained earnings since it equals net profits and dividends paid, two items that are captured elsewhere.

Let's Check for Understanding

Understanding Cash Flows

Take a few minutes to answer the three questions below.

Earlier in the chapter, we used the Maness Corporation's financial data to illustrate the connections between a company's income statement and its balance sheets. The company's financial statements are shown again below, along with the changes in the balance sheets between 2010 and 2011 (numbers you will need). Use this data again to prepare a cash flow statement and then answer the following questions:

1. How much are the Maness Corporation's cash flows for each of the three cash flow activities: operating activities, investment activities, and financing activities?
2. What was the change in cash between December 31, 2010, and December 31, 2011?
3. Look at your answers for the three cash flow activities and the net change in the firm's cash for the year and describe what you learned about the company's cash flows.

	2010	2011	Changes
Assets			
Cash	$ 150,000	$ 125,000	$ (25,000)
Accounts receivable	350,000	375,000	25,000
Inventory	475,000	550,000	75,000
Total current assets	$ 975,000	$1,050,000	$ 75,000
Gross fixed assets	$2,425,000	$2,750,000	$325,000
Accumulated depreciation	(1,000,000)	(1,200,000)	(200,000)
Net fixed assets	$1,425,000	$1,550,000	$125,000
TOTAL ASSETS	$2,400,000	$2,600,000	$200,000
Debt (Liabilities) and Equity			
Accounts payable	$ 200,000	$ 150,000	$ (50,000)
Short-term notes	0	150,000	150,000
Total current liabilities	$ 200,000	$ 300,000	$ 100,000
Long-term debt	600,000	600,000	0
Total debt	$ 800,000	$ 900,000	$ 100,000
Ownership equity			
Common stock	$ 900,000	$ 900,000	$ 0
Retained earnings	700,000	800,000	100,000
Total ownership equity	$1,600,000	$1,700,000	$ 100,000
TOTAL LIABILITIES AND OWNERSHIP EQUITY	$2,400,000	$2,600,000	$ 200,000

Income Statement January 1 – December 2011	
Sales	$1,450,000
Cost of goods sold	(850,000)
Gross profits	$ 600,000
Operating expenses	(240,000)
Operating profits	$ 360,000
Interest expense	(64,000)
Profits before taxes	$ 296,000
Taxes	(118,000)
Net profits	$ 178,000
Net profits	$ 178,000
Dividends paid	(78,000)
Increase in retained earnings	$ 100,000

(Answers to the questions above are provided on page 322.)

EXHIBIT 10.7 Cash Flow Statement for Pendley & Associates, Inc., for the Year Ending December 31, 2011

Operating activities:		
Net profits	$60,000	
Add back depreciation	30,000	
Profits before depreciation		$ 90,000
Less increase in accounts receivable (uncollected sales)		($ 5,000)
Less payments for inventory consisting of:		
Increase in inventory	(40,000)	
Less increase in accounts payable (inventory purchased on credit)	5,000	
Payments for inventory		($ 35,000)
Cash flows from operations		$ 50,000
Investment activities:		
Less increase in gross fixed assets		($100,000)
Financing activities:		
Increase in short-term notes	20,000	
Increase in long-term debt	50,000	
Less dividends paid to owners	(15,000)	
Financing cash flows		$ 55,000
Increase in cash		$ 5,000

Evaluating a Firm's Financial Performance

Once a firm's owner understands the content of the accounting statements, she or he wants to know how management decisions impact the financial situation of a business. An entrepreneur's decisions play out primarily in four ways when it comes to finances:

1. *The firm's ability to pay its debt as it comes due.* In other words, does the company have the capacity to meet its short-term (one year or less) debt commitments?
2. *The company's profitability from assets.* Is the business providing a good rate of return on its assets? There is no more important question when it comes to determining if a business is strong economically.
3. *The amount of debt the business is using.* Using debt increases a firm's risk, but may also increase the expected rate of return on the owners' equity investment.
4. *The rate of return earned by the owners on their equity investment.* All decisions ultimately affect the rate of return earned by the owners on their equity investment in the business.

entrepreneurial experiences

Collect Early and Pay Later

Judy DeLello, founder of Informed Systems, Inc., launched her company in 1995 without having to borrow to do so. How did she do it? Following the lead of the magazine industry, where customers pay for their subscriptions in advance, the Bluebell, Pennsylvania, technology firm decided to offer its customers a chance to buy consulting hours in advance of service. The savings for the customer can be as much as 20 percent off Informed's rate of $175 for a purchase of 100 hours.

But customers like prepaying for Informed's guidance on installing and using Microsoft's management software, Dynamic GP, for other reasons, too. "If Informed's rates go up, I've already locked in a lower price," says Marie Gunning, a controller for PSC Info Group, which manages collection letters and claim forms for hospitals. Informed's monthly statement, which shows services used over the past three to nine months, also is a useful tool for analyses of spending and future consulting needs.

Asking for payment before performing the work has also supported expansion of the firm. It now has about $1.5 million in revenue and eight employees. To encourage more customers to prepay, DeLello has eliminated travel charges on bulk purchases and offers discounts on other products the company sells.

Bounce/UpperCut Images/Getty Images

© iStockphoto.com/Angelika Schwarz

Source: Ellyn Spragins, "Pay It Forward," *Fortune Small Business*, February 2006, pp. 51–52. **http://www.isisupport.com**

Exhibit 10.8 provides a list of financial ratios as they relate to the four issues listed above. The name of each ratio is given, along with how it is computed. We illustrate the ratios by using the 2011 financial data for Pendley & Associates, as presented in Exhibit 10.2 (income statement) and Exhibit 10.5 (balance sheets). Finally, the last column shows an industry average for each ratio, which comes from financial publications, such as Robert Morris & Associates. Let's look at the ratios as they apply to Pendley & Associates.

PENDLEY & ASSOCIATES' LIQUIDITY (ABILITY TO PAY ITS DEBT)

A business—or a person, for that matter—that has enough money to pay off any debt owed is described as being *liquid*. The **liquidity** of a business depends on the availability of cash to meet maturing debt obligations. The **current ratio** is traditionally used to measure a company's liquidity. This ratio compares a firm's *current assets* to its *current liabilities*, as follows:

liquidity The degree to which a firm has working capital available to meet maturing debt obligations.

current ratio A measure of a company's relative liquidity, determined by dividing current assets by current liabilities.

$$\text{Current ratio} = \frac{\text{Current assets}}{\text{Current liabilities}}$$

As you can see in Exhibit 10.8, for Pendley & Associates the current ratio is 3.50, compared to an industry norm of 2.70. In other words, the firm has $3.50 in current assets for every $1 of short-term debt, compared to an industry average of $2.70 of current assets for every $1 in short-term debt. Thus, based on the current ratio, Pendley & Associates is more liquid than the average firm in the industry.

EXHIBIT 10.8 Financial Ratio Analysis for Pendley & Associates, Inc.

Financial Ratios	Pendley & Associates	Industry Norm
1. Ability to pay debt as it comes due		
Current ratio $= \frac{\text{Current assets}}{\text{Current liabilities}}$	$\frac{\$350{,}000}{\$100{,}000} = 3.50$	2.7
2. Company's profitability on its assets		
Return on assets $= \frac{\text{Operating profits}}{\text{Total assets}}$	$\frac{\$100{,}000}{\$920{,}000} = 10.87\%$	13.2%
Operating profit margin $= \frac{\text{Operating profits}}{\text{Sales}}$	$\frac{\$100{,}000}{\$850{,}000} = 11.76\%$	11.0%
Total asset turnover $= \frac{\text{Sales}}{\text{Total assets}}$	$\frac{\$850{,}000}{\$920{,}000} = 0.92$	1.2
3. The amount of debt the company uses		
Debt ratio $= \frac{\text{Total debt}}{\text{Total assets}}$	$\frac{\$300{,}000}{\$920{,}000} = 32.60\%$	40.0%
4. Rate of return earned by the owners on their equity investment		
Return on equity $= \frac{\text{Net profits}}{\text{Ownership equity}}$	$\frac{\$60{,}000}{\$620{,}000} = 9.68\%$	12.5%

PENDLEY & ASSOCIATES' PROFITABILITY ON ITS ASSETS

A vitally important question to a firm's owners is whether a company's operating profits are sufficient relative to the total amount of assets invested in the company.

Exhibit 10.9 provides a graphical representation of the drivers of a firm's return on assets. As shown in the exhibit, a firm's assets are invested for the express purpose of producing operating profits. A comparison of operating profits to total assets reveals the rate of return that is being earned on the entire firm's capital. We compute the **return on assets** as follows:

return on assets
A measure of a firm's profitability relative to the amount of its assets, determined by dividing operating profits by total assets.

$$\text{Return on assets} = \frac{\text{Operating profits}}{\text{Total assets}}$$

As shown in Exhibit 10.8, Pendley & Associates' return on assets of 10.87 percent is less than the industry norm of 13.2 percent, indicating that Pendley & Associates is generating less operating income on each dollar of assets than its competitors. That is not good!

To gain more understanding about why Pendley & Associates is not doing as well in generating profits on the firm's assets, you can separate the return on assets into two components: (1) the operating profit margin and (2) the total asset turnover. The equation for the return on assets can be restated as follows:

$$\text{Return on assets} = \frac{\text{Operating profits}}{\text{Total assets}} = \underbrace{\frac{\text{Operating profits}}{\text{Sales}}}_{\textbf{Operating Profit Margin}} \times \underbrace{\frac{\text{Sales}}{\text{Total assets}}}_{\textbf{Total Asset Turnover}}$$

operating profit margin
A measure of how well a firm is controlling its cost of goods sold and operating expenses relative to sales, determined by dividing operating profits by sales.

The first component of the expanded equation, the **operating profit margin** (operating profits ÷ sales), shows how well a firm is controlling its cost of goods sold and operating

EXHIBIT 10.9 Return on Assets: An Overview

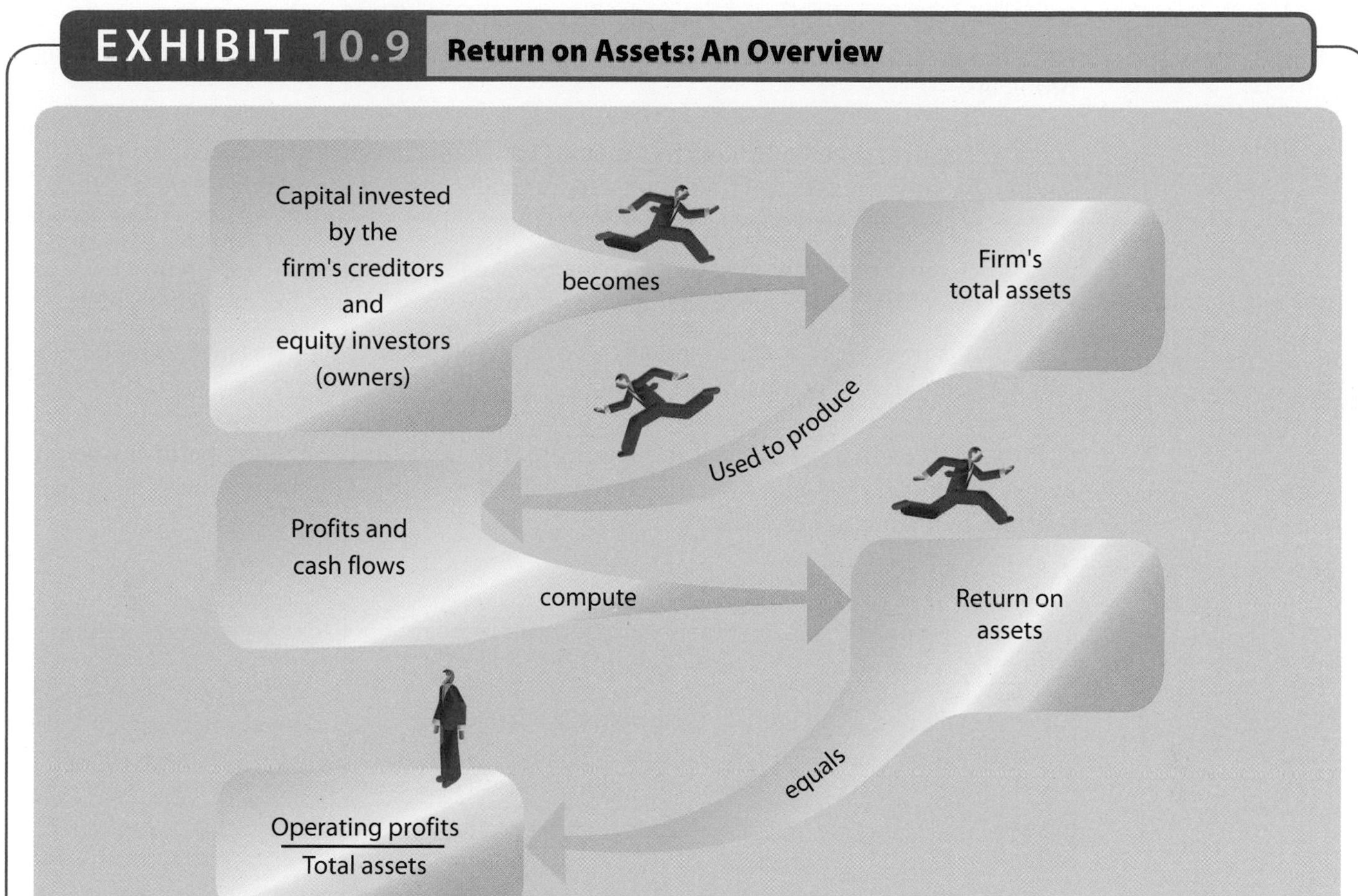

expenses relative to a dollar of sales. The second component of a firm's return on assets, the **total asset turnover** (sales ÷ total assets), indicates how efficiently management is using the firm's assets to generate sales.

total asset turnover A measure of how efficiently a firm is using its assets to generate sales, calculated by dividing sales by total assets.

The operating profit margin and total asset turnover for Pendley & Associates, along with industry averages, are presented in Exhibit 10-8 and shown again below. You can also see how they relate to Pendley & Associates' return on assets, as well as to the industry:

		Operating Profit Margin	×	Total Asset Turnover	=	Return on Assets
Return on $\text{assets}_{\text{Pendley}}$	=	11.76%	×	0.92	=	10.87%
Return on $\text{assets}_{\text{Industry}}$	=	11.00%	×	1.20	=	13.20%

Based on the operating profit margin, Pendley & Associates is competitive when it comes to managing its income statement—that is, in keeping costs and expenses low relative to sales. However, Pendley & Associates' total asset turnover shows why the firm is not earning a good return on its assets. The firm is not using its assets efficiently. The company's problem is that it generates $0.92 in sales per dollar of assets, while the competition produces $1.20 in sales from every dollar in assets. Management needs to assess what is causing the problem, looking carefully at how they are managing the different types of assets, namely, the accounts receivable, inventory, and fixed assets.

The low total asset turnover, showing that Pendley & Associates is using more assets per sales dollar than its competitors, possibly indicates one or more of the following problems:

1. The firm is not collecting its accounts receivable as quickly as the competition. By collecting its receivables on a more timely basis, it would release money that is currently tied up.
2. Given the amount of sales, the owners have too much money tied up in inventory, which suggests that some inventory is slow moving or even obsolete.
3. It is possible that the company has overinvested in fixed assets (such as facilities) compared to competition.

Clearly, the Pendley sisters need to investigate why their firm is not competitive when it comes to managing assets. After all, entrepreneurship is about doing more with less when it comes to managing resources.

How Did You Do?

Understanding Cash Flows

On page 317, you were asked three questions: (1) compute the firms cash flows, (2) determine the change in cash flows, and (3) interpret your findings. Your answers should be similar to those provided below.

1. and 2. The three types of cash flow activities and the company's change in cash for the year are as follows:

Cash flows from operations	$228,000
Cash flows from investing in fixed assets	(325,000)
Cash flows from financing	72,000
Change in cash balance	$ (25,000)

Cash flows from operations:		
Net profits		$ 178,000
Add back depreciation		200,000
Profits before depreciation		$ 378,000
Less increase in accounts receivable (uncollected sales)		$ (25,000)
Less payments for inventory consisting of:		
Increase in inventory	$ (75,000)	
Decrease in accounts payable (reduced accounts payable)	(50,000)	
Cash payments for inventory		$(125,000)
Cash flows from operations		$ 228,000
Cash flows from investing:		
Purchase of fixed assets	(325,000)	
Cash flows from investing		$(325,000)
Cash flows from financing:		
Money borrowed (increase in short-term notes)	$ 150,000	
Dividends paid	(78,000)	
Cash flows from financing		$ 72,000
Change in the company's cash balance		$ (25,000)

3. The Maness Corporation primarily received cash flows from day-to-day operations and to a lesser extent from borrowing on a short-term note (probably from the bank). It also used some of its cash in the bank (decreased cash). All cash flows were used to buy fixed assets and inventory and pay dividends to the owners.

PENDLEY & ASSOCIATES' DEBT

How much debt, relative to the total assets, is used to finance a business is extremely important. For one thing, the more debt a business uses, the more risk it is taking because the debt has to be repaid no matter how much profit the firm earns; it is a fixed cost.

The **debt ratio** tells us what percentage of the firm's assets is financed by debt and is computed as follows:

debt ratio
A measure of what percentage of a firm's assets is financed by debt, determined by dividing total debt by total assets.

$$\text{Debt ratio} = \frac{\text{Total debt}}{\text{Total assets}}$$

Refer again to Exhibit 10.8, which shows Pendley & Associates' debt ratio as 32.6 percent, compared to an industry norm of 40.0 percent. Since Pendley & Associates uses less debt than the average firm in the industry, it has less risk. After all, borrowed money must be repaid regardless of how much money the business makes. All is well if the company prospers and repays the loan. But if not, *watch out*!

PENDLEY & ASSOCIATES' RETURN ON EQUITY

The last financial ratio considered here is the rate of return the owners are receiving on their equity investment, or the **return on equity**. The return on equity is the net profits divided by the total ownership equity shown in the balance sheet.

return on equity
A measure of the rate of return that owners receive on their equity investment, calculated by dividing net profits by ownership equity.

As you can see in Exhibit 10.8, the return on equity for the Pendley sisters is 9.68 percent, while the industry average for return on equity is 12.5 percent. Thus, it appears that the Pendley sisters are not receiving a return on their investment equivalent to that of owners of comparable businesses. Why not? To answer this question, you have to understand the following:

1. A firm with a high (low) return on *assets* will have a high (low) return on *equity*. It simply is not possible to have a good return on equity if you are not earning a good return on your assets.
2. As the amount of a firm's debt increases, its return on equity will increase *provided that* the return on assets is higher than the interest rate paid on any debt.

In the case of Pendley & Associates, the firm has a lower return on *equity* in part because it has a lower return on *assets*. It also uses less debt than the average firm in the industry, causing its return on equity to be lower than that of other firms. However, using less debt does reduce the firm's risk.

Numerical Example

If a business earns a 15 percent return on *assets* but only has to pay 6 percent on its bank debt, the owners will receive 15 percent on the amount of their equity investment plus the 9 percent difference between the return on assets and what they pay the bank (15% − 6% = 9%). The more debt and the less equity they use, the more the owners' return on equity will be; it's called **financial leverage**.

financial leverage
The impact (positive or negative) of financing with debt rather than with equity.

But it is very important to understand that the return on equity will be lower if the return on assets falls below the interest rate on the loan (e.g., if the return on assets is 8 percent, but the interest rate on debt is 10 percent). That is called negative financial leverage. These relationships will be explained further in Chapter 12 when we discuss sources of financing.

Our analysis of financial statements is now complete. Hopefully, you are now better prepared to know what financial statements can tell you about a business—knowledge that can be found in no other way than by interpreting the numbers.

In this chapter, we focused on understanding financial statements related to a firm's historical financial performance. We were essentially looking back to see how a business performed in a previous time period. In the next chapter, we will continue to work with financial statements, but this time we will be looking forward. In writing a business plan, you need to show convincingly how your plans will play out in terms of the firm's financial future; you are now ready to prepare the financial plan.

Let's Check for Understanding

Understanding How to Evaluate a Firm's Financial Performance

Take a few minutes to see if you can answer the four questions below.

Let's return once again to the Maness Corporation's financial data to illustrate how to use financial ratios to evaluate a firm's performance. Using the data for 2011, which are shown below, and the industry norms, compute the financial ratios that were discussed in this chapter and interpret your findings.

Once you have computed the ratios, answer the following questions:

1. Is the Maness Corporation more or less liquid than the average company in the industry?
2. Is the company doing a good job at earning a return on its assets? Explain.
3. How does the owner finance the business in terms of debt and equity?
4. Is Maness receiving a good return on equity? Explain.

Balance Sheet as of December 31, 2011

	2011
Assets	
Cash	$ 125,000
Accounts receivable	$ 375,000
Inventory	550,000
Total current assets	$ 1,050,000
Gross fixed assets	2,750,000
Accumulated depreciation	(1,200,000)
Net fixed assets	$ 1,550,000
TOTAL ASSETS	$ 2,600,000
Debt (Liabilities) and Equity	
Accounts payable	$ 150,000
Short-term notes	150,000
Total current liabilities	$ 300,000
Long-term debt	600,000
Total debt	$ 900,000
Common stock	$ 900,000
Retained earnings	800,000
Total ownership equity	$ 1,700,000
TOTAL LIABILITIES AND OWNERSHIP EQUITY	$ 2,600,000
Income Statement for the Year Ending December 31, 2011	
Sales	$ 1,450,000
Cost of goods sold	(850,000)
Gross profits	$ 600,000
Operating expenses	(240,000)
Operating profits	$ 360,000
Interest expense	(64,000)
Profits before taxes	$ 296,000
Taxes	(118,000)
Net profits	$ 178,000
Industry norms	
Current ratio	3.25
Return on assets	15.0%
Operating profit margin	20.0%
Total asset turnover	0.75
Debt ratio	0.20
Return on equity	9.0%

How Did You Do?

Understanding How to Evaluate a Firm's Financial Performance

On page 324, you were asked four questions about Maness Corporation's financial performance. Your answers should be similar to those provided below.

	Maness	Industry
Current ratio	3.50	3.25
Return on assets	13.8%	15.0%
Operating profit margin	24.8%	20.0%
Total asset turnover	0.56	0.75
Debt ratio	0.35	0.20
Return on equity	10.5%	9.0%

1. Is Maness Corporation more or less liquid than the average company in the industry?

   Based on the current ratio, Maness has $3.50 in liquid assets (current assets) for every $1 in current liabilities, compared to $3.25 for the industry, which suggests that Maness is slightly more liquid.

2. Is the company doing a good job at earning a return on its assets? Explain.

   For every $100 in assets, Maness generates $13.80 in operating profits (based on return on assets of 13.8 percent), compared to $15 in profits for the competition. Thus, Maness is not competitive on its return on assets. Looking at the operating profit margin, we see that Maness actually does quite well in generating profits on sales (operating profit margin)—24 percent compared to 20 percent for the industry. Clearly, Maness is effective at controlling costs and expenses in the income statement. The problem lies with the total asset turnover, which measures how well the firm's assets are being managed. Maness only produces $0.56 in sales for every one dollar of assets, which is less than the $0.75 for the industry. Its management team needs to further evaluate their asset management policies and procedures.

3. How does the owner finance the business in terms of debt and equity?

   Maness uses more debt relative to total assets than does the industry: 35 percent compared to 20 percent. Thus, the firm will encounter more financial risk than the average company in the industry.

4. Is Maness receiving a good return on equity? Explain.

   Maness's return on equity is higher than that of owners in other companies, earning 10.5 percent relative to 9 percent for the industry. But there is good news and bad news. The higher return on equity is not the result of being better at generating profits on the company's total assets—always a good thing to do if you do not have to assume more risk. The lower return on assets described in the answer to question 2 will result in a lower return on equity. Maness's higher return on equity is the consequence of using more debt, which is fine as long as the company does well. But things could get tough if a significant downturn in the economy occurs, such as happened in 2008. Maness would be at a greater risk of not being able to meet his debt commitments.

1. Describe the purpose and content of an income statement.

- An income statement is, in its most basic form, represented by the equation:
- Sales (revenue) − Expenses = Profits (income)
- An income statement answers the question "How profitable is the business?" by looking at five broad areas of business activity: (1) sales, (2) cost of producing or acquiring goods or services, (3) operating expenses, (4) interest expense, and (5) tax payments.

2. Explain the purpose and content of a balance sheet.

- A balance sheet provides a snapshot of a firm's financial position at a specific point in time.

- It shows the amount of assets the firm owns, the amount of outstanding debt, and the amount of ownership equity.
- In its most simple form, the balance sheet is represented by the formula:
- Total assets = Debt + Ownership equity
- Total assets include current, fixed, and other assets.
- Debt includes the money provided by creditors.
- Ownership equity is the owners' investment in the business, both in terms of actual cash invested and earnings that have been retained in the business.

3. Explain how viewing the income statement and balance sheets together gives a more complete picture of a firm's financial position.

- Because the balance sheet offers a snapshot of a firm's financial condition at a point in time and the income statement reports a firm's performance over a period of time, both are needed to fully evaluate a firm's financial position.
- Three financial reports are needed to evaluate a firm's performance over a given time period: a balance sheet showing a firm's performance at the beginning of a year, a balance sheet for the end of the year, and an income statement spanning the time period between the two balance sheets.

4. Use the income statement and balance sheets to compute a company's cash flows.

- A cash flow statement shows the sources of a firm's cash as well as its uses of cash.
- A cash flow statement is comprised of three sections (1) cash flows from daily operations (operating activities), (2) cash flows related to the investment in fixed assets (investing activities), and (3) cash flows related to financing the firm (financing activities)
- Cash flows from operations are calculated by adding back the depreciation expense to the net profits and then subtracting any uncollected sales and payments for inventory.
- Investments in fixed assets are recorded in the statement of cash flows as a change in gross fixed assets.
- Financing a business involves borrowing money, repaying debts, investing by owners, and paying dividends or selling/repurchasing stock.

5. Analyze the financial statements using ratios to see more clearly how decisions are affecting a firm's financial performance.

- Financial ratios help examine a firm's (1) ability to pay debt as it comes due, (2) profitability from assets, (3) use of debt, and (4) rate of return to owners.
- A firm's ability to pay debt as it comes due is most often evaluated by looking at a firm's current ratio (current assets divided by current liabilities).
- A company's profitability on assets is measured by calculating a company's return on assets as affected by its operating profit margin and the total asset turnover.
- The debt ratio, total debt divided by total assets, is used to evaluate the total amount of debt used by the company to finance its assets.
- The return on equity, which is the rate of return earned by the owners on their equity investment, is equal to net profits divided by ownership equity and is driven by a firm's return on assets and its debt ratio.

Key Terms

financial statements (accounting statements) p. 293
income statement (profit and loss statement) p. 297
cost of goods sold p. 297
gross profit p. 297
operating expenses p. 297
operating profits p. 297
interest expense p. 297
profits before taxes (taxable profits) p. 297
net profits p. 297
depreciation expense p. 298
profit margins p. 300
balance sheet p. 301
current assets (working capital) p. 302
accounts receivable p. 302
inventory p. 302
working capital cycle p. 302
fixed assets (property, plant and equipment [PPE]) p. 302
depreciable assets p. 302
gross fixed assets p. 303
accumulated depreciation p. 303
net fixed assets p. 303
other assets p. 303
debt p. 304
current debt (short-term liabilities) p. 304
accounts payable (trade credit) p. 304
accrued expenses p. 304
short-term notes p. 304
long-term debt p. 305
long-term notes p. 305
mortgage p. 306
ownership equity p. 306
retained earnings p. 306
cash flow statement p. 312
accrual-basis accounting p. 313
cash-basis accounting p. 313
cash flow activities p. 314
liquidity p. 319
current ratio p. 319
return on assets p. 320
operating profit margin p. 320
total asset turnover p. 321
debt ratio p. 323
return on equity p. 323
financial leverage p. 323

Discussion Questions

1. Explain the purposes of the income statement and balance sheets.
2. What determines a company's profitability?
3. Distinguish among (a) gross profits, (b) operating profits, and (c) net profits.
4. The balance sheet reports information on a firm's (1) assets, (2) debt, and (3) equity. What is included in each of these reported categories?
5. How are ownership equity and debt different?
6. Distinguish between common stock and retained earnings.
7. What is the relationship between an income statement and a balance sheet?
8. Why aren't a firm's cash flows equal to its profits?
9. Describe the three major components of a cash flow statement.
10. What questions do financial ratios help answer about a firm's financial performance?

You Make the Call

SITUATION 1

The Donahoo Western Furnishings Company was formed on December 31, 2010, with $1,000,000 in equity plus $500,000 in long-term debt. On January 1, 2011, all of the firm's capital was held in cash. The following transactions occurred during January 2011.

- January 2: Donahoo purchased $1,000,000 worth of furniture for resale. It paid $500,000 in cash and financed the balance using trade credit that required payment in 60 days.
- January 3: Donahoo sold $250,000 worth of furniture that it had paid $200,000 to acquire. The entire sale was on credit terms of net 90 days.
- January 15: Donahoo purchased more furniture for $200,000. This time, it used trade credit for the entire amount of the purchase, with credit terms of net 60 days.
- January 31: Donahoo sold $500,000 worth of furniture, for which it had paid $400,000. The furniture was sold for 10 percent cash down, with the remainder payable in 90 days. In addition, the firm paid a cash dividend of $100,000 to its stockholders and paid off $250,000 of its long-term debt.

Question 1 What did Donahoo's balance sheet look like at the outset of the firm's life?

Question 2 What did the firm's balance sheet look like after each transaction?

Question 3 Ignoring taxes, determine how much income Donahoo earned during January. Prepare an income statement for the month. Recognize an interest expense of 1 percent for the month (12 percent annually) on the $500,000 long-term debt, which has not been paid but is owed.

Question 4 What was Donahoo's cash flow for the month of January?

SITUATION 2

At the beginning of 2011, Mary Abrahams purchased a small business, the Maitz Company, whose income statement and balance sheets are shown below.

Income Statement for the Maitz Company for 2011

Sales		$175,000
Cost of goods sold		(105,000)
Gross profits		$ 70,000
Operating expenses:		
Depreciation	$ 5,000	
Administrative expenses	20,000	
Selling expenses	26,000	
Total operating expenses		$ (51,000)
Operating profits		$ 19,000
Interest expense		(3,000)
Profits before taxes		$ 16,000
Taxes		(8,000)
Net profits		$ 8,000

Balance Sheets for the Maitz Company for 2010 and 2011

Assets	**2010**	**2011**
Current assets:		
Cash	$ 8,000	$ 10,000
Accounts receivable	15,000	20,000
Inventory	22,000	25,000
Total current assets	$45,000	$ 55,000
Fixed assets:		
Gross fixed assets	$50,000	$ 55,000
Accumulated depreciation	(15,000)	(20,000)
Net fixed assets	$35,000	$ 35,000
Other assets	12,000	10,000
TOTAL ASSETS	$92,000	$100,000

Debt (Liabilities) and Equity		
Current debt:		
Accounts payable	$10,000	$ 12,000
Accruals	7,000	8,000
Short-term notes	5,000	5,000
Total current debt	$22,000	$ 25,000
Long-term debt	15,000	15,000
Total debt	$37,000	$ 40,000
Equity	$55,000	$ 60,000
TOTAL DEBT AND EQUITY	$92,000	$100,000

The firm has been profitable, but Abrahams has been disappointed by the lack of cash flows. She had hoped to have about $10,000 a year available for personal living expenses. However, there never seems to be much cash available for purposes other than business needs. Abrahams has asked you to examine the financial statements and explain why, although they show profits, she does not have any discretionary cash for personal needs. She observed, "I thought that I could take the profits and add back depreciation to find out how much cash I was generating. However, that doesn't seem to be the case. What's happening?"

Question 1 Given the information provided by the financial statements, what would you tell Abrahams? (As part of your answer, calculate the firm's cash flows.)
Question 2 How would you describe the cash flow pattern for the Maitz Company?

SITUATION 3

Jordan Mettauer, the owner of Wholesome Foods, has hired you to evaluate his firm's financial performance. The firm's financial data is provided below, along with an average for the financial ratios that Mettauer collected on several competing peer firms.

Question 1 Compute the financial ratios discussed in the chapter for Wholesome Foods for 2010 and 2011.
Question 2 Prepare a cash flow statement for the firm for 2010 and 2011.
Question 3 Interpret your findings, both for the firm's financial ratios compared to those of the peer group and for the cash flow statement.

Assets	**2009**	**2010**	**2011**
Cash	$ 21,000	$ 20,200	25,000
Accounts receivable	42,000	33,000	46,000
Inventory	51,000	84,000	96,000
Prepaid rent	1,200	1,100	2,000
Total current assets	$ 115,200	$ 138,300	$ 169,000
Gross property, plant, and equipment	650,000	664,000	740,000
Accumulated depreciation	(364,000)	(394,000)	(434,000)
Net property, plant, and equipment	$ 286,000	$ 270,000	$ 306,000
TOTAL ASSETS	$ 401,200	$ 408,300	$ 475,000

Debt (Liabilities) and Equity	**2009**	**2010**	**2011**
Accounts payable	$ 48,000	$ 57,000	$ 52,400
Accrued expenses	9,500	9,000	12,000
Short-term notes	11,500	9,000	20,000
Total current liabilities	$ 69,000	$ 75,000	$ 84,400
Long-term debt	160,000	150,000	185,000
Common stock	$ 22,200	$ 22,200	$ 34,500
Retained earnings	150,000	161,100	171,100
Total ownership equity	$172,200	$183,300	$205,600
TOTAL DEBT AND EQUITY	$401,200	$408,300	$475,000

Income Statement	**2010**	**2011**
Sales	$600,000	$650,000
Cost of goods sold	(460,000)	(487,500)
Gross profits	$140,000	$162,500
Operating expenses:		
General and administrative expenses	$ 30,000	$ 37,500
Depreciation expense	30,000	40,000
Total operating expenses	$ 60,000	$ 77,500
Operating profits	$ 80,000	$ 85,000
Interest expense	(10,000)	(12,000)
Profits before taxes	$ 70,000	$ 73,000
Taxes	(27,100)	(30,000)
Net profits	$ 42,900	$ 43,000
Net profits	$ 42,900	$ 43,000
Dividends paid	(31,800)	(33,000)
Addition to retained earnings	$ 11,100	$ 10,000

Financial Ratios (Averages)	**Peer Companies**
Current ratio	1.80
Return on assets	16.8%
Operating profit margin	14.0%
Total asset turnover	1.20
Debt ratio	0.50
Return on equity	18.0%

Experiential Exercises

1. Interview an owner of a small firm about the financial statements she or he uses. Ask the owner how important financial data are to her or his decision making.
2. Acquire a small firm's financial statements. Review the statements and describe the firm's financial position. Find out if the owner agrees with your conclusions.
3. Dun & Bradstreet and Robert Morris Associates compile financial information about many companies. They provide, among other information, income statements and balance sheets for an average firm in an industry.

Go to a library and look up, or search online for, financial information on two industries of your choice, and compute the following data for each industry:

a. The percentages of assets in (1) current assets and (2) fixed assets (property, plant, and equipment)
b. The percentages of financing from debt financing and ownership equity
c. The gross profits and the operating profits as percentages of sales

Small Business & Entrepreneurship Resource Center

In the text Johnny Stites, CEO of J&S Construction, says, "We simply could not exist in such a competitive industry, and certainly not profitably, without understanding where we are financially." The article "Looking Beyond the Bottom Line" talks about the multi-step income statement, which provides much more understanding about a business. Describe the multi-step income statement and the trended P&L. How can these be used to help a business become more aware of trends and issues?

Source: Leslie Shiner, "Looking Beyond the Bottom Line," *Journal of Light Construction*, Vol. 23, No. 9 (June 2005), p. 43.

Case 10

DIETRICH & MERCER, INC. (P. 711)

Dietrich & Mercer designs, manufactures, and distributes furniture. Their products are in the medium- to low-price range and are constructed of aluminum, light steel, and plastic. This case allows students to perform financial analysis.

ALTERNATIVE CASES FOR CHAPTER 10

Case 11, Missouri Solvents, p. 714
Case 22, Pearson Air Conditioning & Service , p. 736
Video Case 10, B2B CFO, website only

CHAPTER 11

Forecasting Financial Requirements

In the SPOTLIGHT
Planning for Growth
http://www.builtny.com

Managing rapid growth can become an entrepreneur's worst nightmare. Unhappy customers and employees, a lack of cash, and the inability to fill orders can overwhelm a small business owner.

Entrepreneurs rarely prepare for the challenges that growth brings. "They're too busy working in the business to work on the business," observes Jeff DeGraff, professor at the Ross School of Business at the University of Michigan. But taking the time to plan for growth, especially when it's unexpected, can keep your business on track.

In 2003, Carter Weiss, Aaron Lown, and John Roscoe Swartz started BuiltNY, a supplier of innovative wine totes and other accessories. In the first six months, the company had sales of $600,000 and even turned a profit, which is rare for most startups. By 2006, sales were $13 million; in 2007, the company expected $20 million in sales. Managing this kind of growth is extremely difficult and can be a downfall for many companies.

© Built

Weiss says that they followed three rules: "Go sell it, make it, and figure out how to pay for it." Sounds simple, but Weiss warns that it is not: "You have to match expectations with sufficient financing, so we decided not to maximize sales, nor to focus solely on long-term profits. Instead, we traded some of both to have some short-term profits, too, which allowed us to attract bank financing. As a profitable firm with bank financing, we could then approach venture capitalists for expansion financing on better terms."

Planning for growth, which may be part of the original business plan or done at a later date, is essential if you want to keep your entrepreneurial dream alive, and BuiltNY has done just that. As Weiss says, "You have to

After studying this chapter, you should be able to . . .

1. Describe the purpose and need for financial forecasting.
2. Develop a pro forma income statement to forecast a new venture's profitability.
3. Determine a company's asset and financing requirements based on a pro forma balance sheet.
4. Forecast a firm's cash flows.
5. Provide some suggestions for effective financial forecasting.

LOOKING AHEAD

© iStockphoto.com/Dan Bachman

decide what you want from the business and then know what it will take financially to make it happen. And above all, make sure you never run out of cash."

BuiltNY, while still entrepreneurial as a business, now has an established customer base and no longer has to "build it and figure out how to pay for it." The company's website conveys a sense of a mature business:

> *BUILT designs fashionable and functional totes, bags, and cases that make life on the go more enjoyable. Our roots in the tradition of American industrial design guide us in the belief that form is as important as function, and color is the glue that binds them together. Drawing inspiration from the city that never sleeps, we apply color and pattern to laptop sleeves, iPad cases, camera bags, lunch totes, and more. Whenever you're on the go, BUILT keeps you covered in style.*

Sources: Lena Basha, "Growth Gone Wild," *MyBusiness*, February–March 2007, pp. 36–41; personal interview with Carter Weiss, July 11, 2007; and http://www.builtny.com/story.html, accessed March 8, 2011.

A good idea may or may not be a good investment opportunity. As we discussed in Chapter 3, a good investment opportunity requires a product or service that meets a definite customer need and creates a sustainable competitive advantage. To be attractive, an opportunity must generate strong profits relative to the required amount of investment. Therefore, projections of a venture's profits, its asset and financing requirements, and its cash flows are essential in determining whether a venture is economically viable.

The Purpose and Need for Financial Forecasting

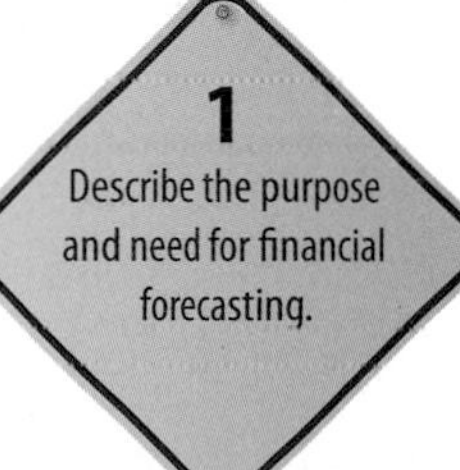

In Chapter 10, we followed the Lemonade Kids to see the accounting implications of what was happening in their venture. In that very simple world, there was really no need to plan for the future. Everything just worked out okay. But that is not the case when starting and operating a business with any complexity. In the real world, you need to forecast, as best you can, the financial outcomes that could result from your decisions. You also may have to make financial forecasts if you need financing from lenders and investors who want to know how they will be paid back. In other words, you need to prepare *pro forma financial statements.*

The necessity of financial forecasting is described quite aptly by small business consultant Paul A. Broni:

> *It doesn't matter whether you're applying for your first bank loan or your fifth, or whether you're seeking venture capital or debt financing. Sooner or later, you'll have to prepare a set of financial projections. Lenders will look for a strong likelihood of repayment; investors will calculate what they think is the value of your company.*[1]

The purpose of **pro forma financial statements** is to answer three questions:

pro forma financial statements
Statements that project a firm's financial performance and condition.

1. How profitable can you expect the firm to be, given the projected sales levels and the expected sales–expense relationships?

2. How much and what type of financing (debt or equity) will be needed to finance a firm's assets?
3. Will the firm have adequate cash flows? If so, how will they be used? If not, where will the additional cash come from?

Preparing historical financial statements, such as income statements, balance sheets, and cash flow statements, is not a difficult task; however, *projecting* the financials for a business presents a real challenge, especially for a startup, where things seldom go as planned. But it can be done, as explained by Rhonda Abrams, a business plan consultant:

> *One of the biggest challenges for a new company doing a business plan is figuring out the financial statements. If you have an existing business, you have a pretty good sense of how much things will cost, how much staff you'll need, and the sales you're likely to make. But when you're just starting out, these things seem a complete mystery.*
>
> *They're not. At least not entirely. Every decision you make when planning your business has a number attached: If you choose to exhibit at a trade show, there's a cost associated with that; if you choose to locate your business in one town versus another, there's a cost associated with that.*
>
> *How do you do this homework? The best place to start is by speaking with others in your industry, attending trade shows, and contacting your industry association. Another excellent source is the RMA [Risk Management Association] Annual Statement Studies, which look at actual financial statements of companies in certain industries.*[2]

A small business owner should always be asking, "What could go wrong, and if it does happen, what will I do?" For instance, you want to plan how to respond if sales are significantly lower or higher than projected. A firm can get into trouble not only when sales are inadequate, but also when the firm is experiencing high growth in sales. James Wong, co-founder and CEO of Avidian Technologies, vigilantly watches cash flows and bottom-line profits. His firm grew at 400 percent a year in both 2004 and 2005. "I've learned that profitability takes conscious effort," he says. "If you just keep growing for growth's sake, you won't be nearly as profitable." Wong never ships a product until payment is received and never lets net profits fall below 15 percent of sales. Consequently, the firm has grown with no significant debt and no outside investors—a feat seldom accomplished by entrepreneurs whose firms are growing rapidly.[3]

When seeking financing, an entrepreneur must be able to give informed answers about the firm's needs. It is vital that she or he be able to answer questions regarding the amount of money needed, the purposes for which it will be used, and when and how the lender or creditor will be paid back. Only careful financial planning can provide answers to these questions.

Let's take a look at the process for projecting a firm's profitability, asset and financing requirements, and cash flows. We suggest that this process be based on a carefully developed *business model*, which was explained in Chapter 6, on pages 164–190.

Forecasting Profitability

Profits reward an owner for investing in a company and constitute a primary source of financing for future growth. Therefore, it is critical for an entrepreneur to understand the factors that drive profits (see also Exhibit 10.1, on page 298):

1. *Amount of sales.* The dollar amount of sales equals the price of the product or service times the number of units sold or the amount of service rendered.

2. *Cost of goods sold.* Cost of goods sold is the cost of producing or purchasing the firm's products or services. These costs can be either *fixed* (those that do not vary with a change in sales volume) or *variable* (those that change proportionally with sales).
3. *Operating expenses.* These expenses relate to marketing and distributing the product, general and administrative expenses, and depreciation expenses. Like cost of goods sold, operating expenses can be fixed or variable in nature.
4. *Interest expense.* An entrepreneur who borrows money agrees to pay interest on the loan principal. For example, a loan of $25,000 for a full year at a 12 percent interest rate results in an interest expense of $3,000 for the year (0.12 × $25,000).
5. *Taxes.* A firm's income taxes are figured as a percentage of profits before taxes, or what is also called taxable profits.

© Harry Hu/Shutterstock.com

A hypothetical example demonstrates how to estimate a new venture's profits.[4] David Allen is planning to start a new business called D&R Products, Inc., which will do wood trim work for luxury homes. In thinking about how to build a company that is economically viable in terms of profits and cash flows, Allen envisions a *revenue model* based on two complementary revenue streams:

1. *Product design.* For customers who want to be engaged in the creation of their own wood trim for new homes or renovations, D&R would provide user-friendly design software. In addition, the firm has developed alliances with professional interior designers who would work with the customer to create a design that is not only aesthetically pleasing but also architecturally sound. Finally, an open platform will allow customers to interface with other customers designing their own wood trim. D&R would receive 10 percent of the interior designers' revenue stream resulting from working with D&R contacts. While Allen does not see this revenue stream as a major source of sales, he does expect it to lead to increased product sales and installations.
2. *Product sales and installations.* The primary source of revenues for D&R will be the actual sale and installation of product in new and renovated homes, with plans to eventually expand to larger commercial projects.

In terms of the company's *cost structure,* Allen has carefully identified expected fixed and variable costs of goods sold and operating expenses. The firm will have a cost advantage in the form of a newly developed lathe that will allow it to adapt to varying design specifications in a very economical manner. Finally, Allen has determined the asset investments that would be required in order to gain positive cash flows.

After extensive interviews with prospective customers, building contractors, and suppliers, along with industry research, Allen has made the following estimates for the first two years of operations:

1. *Amount of sales.*
   a. *Year 1*: Allen already has contracts for 10 jobs and expects to acquire another 10, or 20 jobs in total, by the end of the first year at an average price of $12,500 per job. Thus, revenue from product sales and installations is projected to be $250,000 in the first year ($250,000 = 20 jobs × $12,500 average price per job). Allen further estimates that revenue from product design will amount to only $10,000, thereby resulting in total firm sales for the first year of $260,000 ($260,000 = $250,000 in product and installation sales + $10,000 in revenue from product design).
   b. *Year 2:* Allen forecasts 30 jobs in the second year, again believing that the average revenue per job will be $12,500. He also expects $25,000 in product design sales, for total revenues of $400,000 ($400,000 = 30 jobs × $12,500 average price per job + $25,000 product design sales).
2. *Cost of goods sold.* For product and installation sales, the fixed cost of goods sold (including production costs and employee salaries) is expected to amount to $100,000 per year, while the variable costs of production will be around 20 percent of product and installation sales. In addition, there will be fixed costs of $10,000 related to product design.
3. *Operating expenses.* The firm's fixed operating expenses (marketing expenses, general and administrative expenses) are estimated to be $46,000 per year. In addition, depreciation will be $4,000 annually. The variable operating expenses will be approximately 30 percent of product and installation sales. There will be no operating costs for product designs.
4. *Interest expense.* Based on the anticipated amount of money to be borrowed and the corresponding interest rate, Allen expects interest expense to be $8,000 in the first year, increasing to $12,000 in the second year.
5. *Taxes.* Income taxes will be 25 percent of profits before taxes (taxable profits).

Given the above estimates, we can forecast D&R Products' profits, as shown in the pro forma income statement in Exhibit 11.1. We first enter our assumptions in a spreadsheet (rows 3–18). Then, in rows 20–44, we see the two years of pro forma income statements (columns B and C) and the equations used to compute the numbers (columns D and E), where

- Rows 22 and 23 show the projected revenues for product sales and installations (row 22) and for product design activities (row 23).
- Row 24 shows total sales.
- Rows 28–30 provide the cost of goods sold for product sales and installations.
- Row 31 gives us the expected costs of $10,000 for product design.
- Row 32 then sums the costs of goods sold for both product sales and installations and product design to arrive at the total cost of goods sold.
- Row 33 gives us gross profits, which equals total sales less total cost of goods sold.
- Rows 36–39 present the anticipated operating expenses associated with product sales and installations; there are no operating expenses related to product design.
- Row 40, operating profits, equals gross profits less total operating expenses.
- Row 41 shows the interest expense for borrowing money.
- Row 42 is profits before taxes (operating profits less interest expense).
- Row 43 equals the tax expense. Since D&R Products is expected to have a loss in the first year, the taxes will be zero. The taxes in the second year are calculated as the tax rate (25 percent) multiplied by the profits before taxes. (In reality, the firm

EXHIBIT 11.1 Pro Forma Income Statements for D&R Products, Inc.

	A	B	C	D	E
3	INCOME STATEMENT ASSUMPTIONS:				
4		**Year 1**	**Year 2**		
5	Product sales and installations:				
6	Number of projected jobs	20	30		
7	Average selling price per job	$ 12,500	$ 12,500		
8	Fixed cost of goods sold	$100,000	$100,000		
9	Fixed operating expenses	$ 46,000	$ 46,000		
10	Depreciation expense	$ 4,000	$ 4,000		
11	Interest expense	$ 8,000	$ 12,000		
12	Variable cost of goods sold	20%	20%		
13	Variable operating expenses	30%	30%	**Equations based on assumptions**	
14	Product design:				
15	Projected design revenues	$ 10,000	$ 25,000		
16	Fixed design costs	$ 10,000	$ 10,000		
17					
18	Income tax rate	25%	25%		
19				*Equations for:*	
20				***Year 1***	***Year 2***
21	Sales:				
22	Product sales and installations	$250,000	$375,000	=B6*B7	=C6*C7
23	Product design	10,000	25,000	=B15	=C15
24	Total sales	$260,000	$400,000	=SUM(B22:B23)	=SUM(C22:C23)
25					
26	Cost of goods sold:				
27	Cost of goods sold: product sales and installations				
28	Fixed cost of goods sold	$100,000	$100,000	=B8	=C8
29	Variable cost of goods sold (20% of product sales)	50,000	75,000	=B22*B12	=C22*C12
30	Total cost of goods sold: product sales and installations	$150,000	$175,000	=SUM(B28:B29)	=SUM(C28:C29)
31	Total cost of goods sold: product design	10,000	10,000	=B16	=C16
32	Total cost of goods sold	$160,000	$185,000	=SUM(B30:B31)	=SUM(C30:C31)
33	Gross profits	$100,000	$215,000	=B24-B32	=C24-C32
34					
35	Operating expenses: product sales and installations				
36	Fixed operating expenses	$ 46,000	$ 46,000	=B9	=C9
37	Variable operating expenses (30% of product sales)	75,000	112,500	=B13*B22	=C13*C22
38	Depreciation expense	4,000	4,000	=B10	=C10
39	Total operating expenses: product sales and installations	$125,000	$162,500	=SUM(B36:B38)	=SUM(C36:C38)
40	Operating profits	$ (25,000)	$ 52,500	=B33-B39	=C33-C39
41	Interest expense (interest rate 12%)	8,000	12,000	=B11	=C11
42	Profits before taxes	$ (33,000)	$ 40,500	=B40-B41	=C40-C41
43	Taxes (25% of profits before tax)	0	10,125	0	=C42*C18
44	Net profits	$ (33,000)	$ 30,375	=B42-B43	=C42-C43

would not expect to pay taxes in the second year either, since tax laws allow a firm to carry losses in one year forward into future years. However, we are ignoring this reality in order to provide a simple example.)

- Row 44 shows the firm's projected net profits—profits before taxes minus income taxes.

"What If" Scenarios

When it comes to financial forecasting and budgeting, you should always prepare at least three scenarios: one with an aggressive forecast for sales increases, another using more conservative assumptions, and a third with worst-case scenarios. In an environment where future demand is unclear, as in the recent economic downturn, it's particularly important. Remember that a spreadsheet is a great tool to evaluate "what if" scenarios when forecasting profits and cash flows.

The above computations indicate that D&R Products is expected to have a $33,000 net loss in its first year, followed by a positive net profit of $30,375 in its second year. A startup typically experiences losses for a period of time, frequently as long as two or three years.[5] In a real-world situation, an entrepreneur should project the profits of a new company at least three years into the future (or five years into the future, if it can be done with some degree of confidence).

Let's now shift our attention from forecasting profits to estimating asset and financing requirements.

Forecasting Asset and Financing Requirements

The amount and types of assets required for a new venture will vary, depending on the nature of the business. High-technology businesses—such as computer manufacturers, designers of semiconductor chips, and pharmaceutical companies—often require millions of dollars in investment. Most service businesses, on the other hand, require minimal initial capital. For example, IRM Corporation, a Dallas, Texas–based information technology firm serving the food and beverage industry, has little in the way of assets. The firm leases its office space and has no inventory. Its only asset of any significance is accounts receivable.

Most firms of any size need both working capital (cash, accounts receivable, inventory, etc.) and fixed assets (property, plant, and equipment). For instance, a food store requires operating cash, inventory, and possibly limited accounts receivable. In addition, the owner will have to acquire cash registers, shopping carts, shelving, office equipment, and a building. The need to invest in assets results in a corresponding need for financing.

Working capital is a another term used in the business world for current assets—namely, cash, accounts receivable, and inventory that are required in the day-to-day operations of the business. *It has nothing to do with property, plant, and equipment.* Also, the term is sometimes used loosely to mean current assets less current liabilities, which is really **net working capital**. Net working capital is a measure of a company's liquidity—that is, the greater a firm's net working capital, the greater its ability to pay on any debt commitment as it comes due.[6]

net working capital
Current assets less current liabilities.

Too frequently, small business owners tend to underestimate the amount of capital the business requires. Consequently, the financing they get may be inadequate. Without the money to invest in assets, they try to do without anything that is not absolutely essential and to spend less money on essential items. When Dan Cassidy started Baha's Fajita Bar, a restaurant aimed at serving college students, his goal was to raise $100,000 in capital; however, he opened the restaurant when he had raised only $70,000. As it turned out, Cassidy did not have enough money to operate the business successfully. In six months, he ran out of cash and had to close the restaurant. The problem became critical when students went home for spring break and were slow to eat at restaurants in the week following their return to school. Cassidy's unfortunate experience shows just how risky it can be for a small business to ignore the potential for unexpected challenges and underestimate its capital needs.

While being undercapitalized is rarely, if ever, a good decision, the goal of the entrepreneur should be to minimize and control, rather than maximize and own, resources. To the greatest extent possible, the entrepreneur should use other people's resources—for instance, leasing equipment rather than buying, negotiating with suppliers to provide inventory "just in time" to minimize tied-up inventory, and arranging to collect money owed the firm before having to pay its bills. As discussed in Chapter 1, this is called *bootstrapping*, and it's one of the most common ways entrepreneurs accomplish more with less.[7] When Cecilia Levine, the owner of MFI International, a manufacturing firm, had the opportunity to get a contract to make clothing for a *Fortune* 500 company, she became a master of bootstrapping.

. . . and no cash.

> *I never expected the fast growth and demand that my services would have. To finance the growth, debt financing would have been helpful, but it was not an option. The definition of credit in the dictionary reads, "The ability of a customer to obtain goods or services before payment, based on the trust that payment is going to be made in the future." What it does not say is that for a banker, trust means having collateral, and without collateral you don't get credit. But I still had children to feed and the desire to succeed so I looked for another form of financing—bootstrapping.*
>
> *I had a major customer who believed in me, and who had the equipment I needed. He sold me the equipment and then would reduce his weekly payment of my invoices by an amount to cover the cost of the equipment. Also, the customer paid me each Friday for what we produced and shipped that week. Everyone who worked for me understood that if we didn't perform and finish the needed production for the week, we didn't get paid by our customer. When I received the payment from the customer, I was then able to pay my employees. We were a team, and we understood the meaning of cash flow. Therefore, we performed.*[8]

Working with a limited amount of working capital makes forecasting all the more important because you have less room for error. Moreover, the uncertainties surrounding an entirely new venture make estimating asset and financing requirements difficult. Even for an established business, forecasts are never perfect. There are always surprises—you can count on it.

In gathering needed information for financial forecasting, an entrepreneur should search for relevant information from a variety of sources. Robert Morris Associates, Dun & Bradstreet, banks, trade associations, and similar organizations compile financial information for a variety of industries.

Along with public data, common sense and educated guesswork should also be used. Continually ask yourself: "Does this make economic sense?" and "What could go wrong?" However, no source of information can compare with talking to prospective customers. Sitting in a room with your computer, without ever getting out and talking to potential customers, is a certain way to miss the obvious.

The determination of how much financing will be needed should also take into consideration the owner's personal financial situation, especially if no other income is available to make ends meet. Whether or not the owner's personal living expenses during the initial period of operation are part of the business's capitalization, they must be considered in

LIVING THE DREAM

entrepreneurial experiences

Surviving a Financial Crisis

The financial crisis that mushroomed in 2008 brought with it tremendous uncertainty for large and small firms alike. In a 2009 survey, Inc.com asked its readers, mostly entrepreneurs, "What is the hardest part of owning a business right now?" As shown in the graph below, the leading problem cited was difficulty in forecasting accurately. In summarizing the findings, the author of the study, Kasey Wehrum, commented, "They would settle for just a clearer sense of what lies ahead. Planning a budget, managing inventory, and knowing when to hire and fire employees are never easy, but a dysfunctional economy has now made forecasting all but impossible."

Wehrum also interviewed several entrepreneurs, who provided their own perspectives on planning in a period of tremendous uncertainty. Rick Israel, co-founder of Complete Office, a Seattle supplier of office products, had this to say:

No one knows how bad the economy is going to get. We just knew it would be harder than in prior years. We budgeted for slight growth but factored in the probability that our business would go backward 10 to 12 percent. The idea is to gear up our sales force and go out there and take more market share.

No one said it would be easy

Inc.com recently asked readers: What is the hardest part of owning a business right now? Here's how you responded:

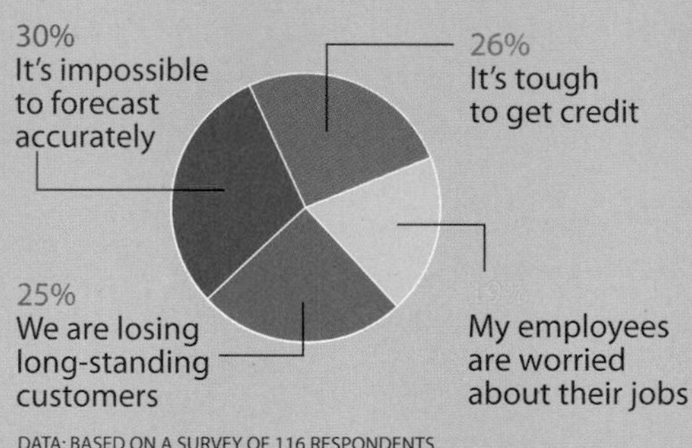

DATA: BASED ON A SURVEY OF 116 RESPONDENTS, JANUARY 14, 2009-FEBRUARY 24, 2009

According to Bryan Zaslow, CEO of JBCStyle, a New York City firm that provides staffing for the fashion and retail industries,

My accounting team and I are sitting here dumbfounded trying to properly budget. Typically, we prepare our budget in the beginning of the year based on last year's numbers. Maybe we'd revisit it halfway through the year. But 2009 is really about revisiting our budget monthly.

Planning for the worst is the most logical course of action. However, I think that negativity has to stay within the executive team. Too much of it puts everyone in a funk. So, my partner and I try to push the positives, like our strong beginning-of-the-year numbers. We try to keep the sleepless nights to ourselves.

Dennis Brown, CEO of Logistic Dynamics, an Amherst, New York, logistics coordinator, said,

In the past, business may have been good or bad, but it was much easier to project what your sales, your revenue, your margins, your overhead were going to be. We could predict the business we would do, because our customers normally have a good feel for their projections. But now, they've got clients pushing back orders and canceling contracts, so they don't know what to expect. That trickles down to us. The more vague our customers are with their projections, the more difficult it is for us to make our projections.

We've tightened our credit terms to our customers. We know this year, somebody significant is going to file bankruptcy on us. Statistically, it's going to happen. Therefore, our forecasts have to be more conservative, because we need to be able to subsidize that kick in the pants we know we are going to get. It may be only $30,000, but it may be $300,000. That would hurt bad. We're hoping it's $30,000.

Based on these observations from entrepreneurs, we know the economic downturn that started in 2008—and remained a problem for some small businesses as late as 2011—created great uncertainty for small business owners. Knowing what to expect was extremely difficult. But it was also a time where anticipating possible shocks and different scenarios were all the more important. An entrepreneur should never stop thinking about what can go wrong—and what can go right—and how to respond to possible changes.

Source: Kasey Wehrum, "Business Forecasting in a Crazy, Mixed-up World," *Inc.* Magazine, April 2009, p. 19–20. *Inc.*: the magazine for growing companies. Copyright 2009 Mansueto Ventures LLC. Reproduced with permission of Mansueto Ventures LLC in the format Textbook via Copyright Clearance Center.

the financial plan. Inadequate provision for personal expenses will inevitably lead to a diversion of business assets and a departure from the plan. Therefore, failing to incorporate these expenses into the financial plan as a cash outflow raises a red flag to any prospective investor.

In fact, a real danger exists that a small business owner will neglect personal finances later as well. As a firm grows, an increasing percentage of the owner's net worth is tied up in the firm. For many entrepreneurs, well over half of their net wealth is invested in their businesses. Even more do not plan adequately for their long-term personal financial health. Former SBA director Hector Barreto explains it well:

> *Small-business people don't know what they don't know when it comes to financial planning. They're busy building the business, and they don't start asking questions until a need or problem comes up. Entrepreneurs are doing a disservice to their businesses when they ignore even the most basic financial planning. The process isn't as time-consuming or as expensive as you might think.*[9]

The key to effectively forecasting financing requirements is first to understand the relationship between a firm's projected sales and its assets. A firm's sales are the primary force driving future asset needs. Exhibit 11.2 depicts this relationship, which can be expressed simply as follows: *The greater a firm's sales, the greater the asset requirements will be and, in turn, the greater the need for financing.*

EXHIBIT 11.2 Assets-to-Sales Financing Relationships

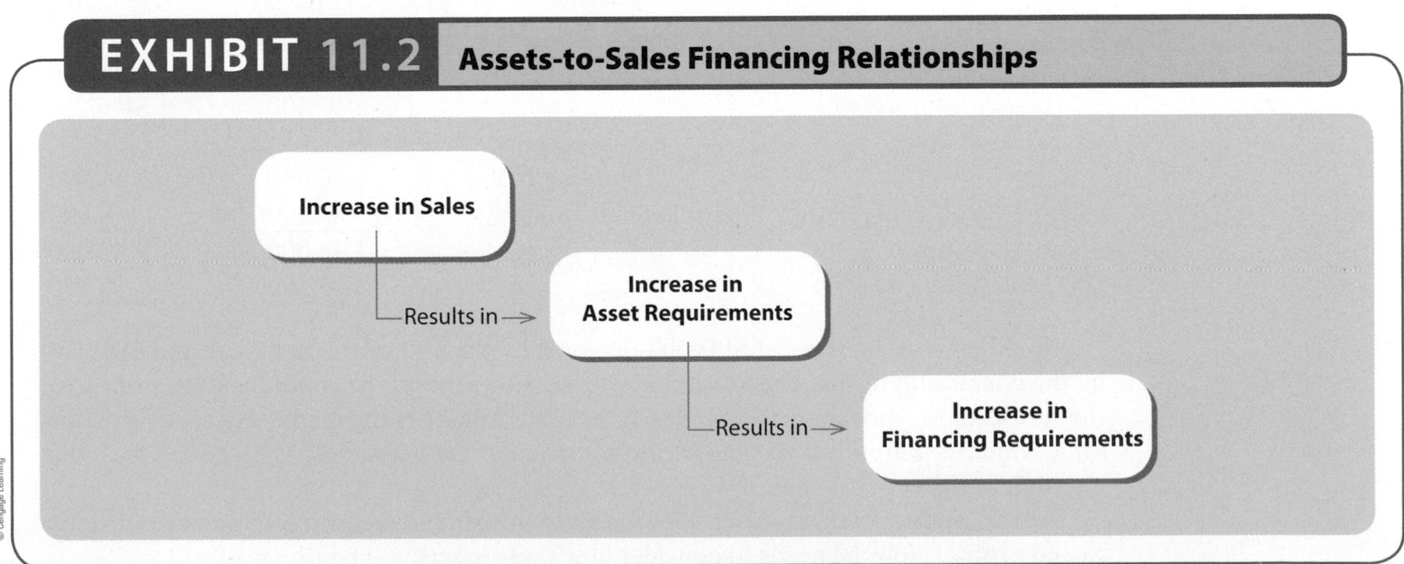

DETERMINING ASSET REQUIREMENTS

Since asset needs increase as sales increase, a firm's asset requirements are often estimated as a percentage of sales. Therefore, if future sales have been projected, a ratio of assets to sales can be used to estimate asset requirements. Suppose, for example, that a firm's sales are expected to be $1 million. If assets in the firm's particular industry tend to run about 50 percent of sales, the firm's asset requirements would be estimated to be 0.50 x $1,000,000, or $500,000.

Although the assets-to-sales relationship varies over time and with individual businesses, it tends to be relatively constant within an industry. For example, assets as a percentage of sales average 20 percent for grocery stores, compared with 65 percent for oil and gas companies. This method of estimating asset requirements is called the **percentage-of-sales technique**. It can also be used to project figures for individual assets, such as accounts receivable and inventory.

percentage-of-sales technique
A method of forecasting asset and financing requirements.

To illustrate the percentage-of-sales technique, let's return to D&R Products, Inc., where we will estimate the firm's asset requirements for the first two years, given the company's sales projections. In Exhibit 11.1, the firm's pro forma income statements, product and installation sales (not including the $10,000 of design revenues) were forecasted to be $250,000 and $375,000 in years 1 and 2, respectively. After considerable investigation of the opportunity, Allen estimated the firm's current asset requirements (cash, accounts receivable, and inventory) as a percentage of product and installation sales:

Assets	Percentage of Sales
Cash	4%
Accounts receivable	10%
Inventory	25%

Allen will need equipment, at a cost of $10,000. Also, he has found a building suitable for a manufacturing facility for $40,000. Combined, these two items total $50,000 and will be reflected in a balance sheet as *gross fixed assets.*

Net fixed assets is equal to gross fixed assets minus accumulated depreciation. Since the depreciation expense reported in the income statement (Exhibit 11.1) is $4,000 per year, then the accumulated depreciation will be $4,000 in year 1, increasing (accumulating) to $8,000 the next year. Given the anticipated sales and the assets-to-sales relationships, Allen is able to forecast the asset requirements for his venture as follows: If product and installation sales are $250,000 in year 1 and $375,000 in year 2, then Allen estimates that

Assets	Assumptions	Year 1	Year 2
Cash	4% of sales	$ 10,000	$ 15,000
Accounts receivable	10% of sales	25,000	37,500
Inventory	25% of sales	62,500	93,750
Total current assets		$ 97,500	$146,250
Gross fixed assets	Equipment and building costs	$ 50,000	$ 50,000
Accumulated depreciation	$4,000 annually	(4,000)	(8,000)
Net fixed assets		$ 46,000	$ 42,000
TOTAL ASSETS		$143,500	$188,250

So Allen expects to need $143,500 in assets by the end of the first year and $188,250 by the conclusion of the second year. However, at this point, he should test how sensitive the results of the model are to changes in the assumptions being made. He needs to determine which assumptions have the greatest impact on the outcomes. Then he can focus his research on what matters most.

At this point, Allen has a sense of the asset investments required to achieve the forecasted profits. Now, he needs to consider how these assets will be financed.

DETERMINING FINANCING REQUIREMENTS

There must be a corresponding dollar of financing for every dollar of assets. Stated another way, debt plus equity must equal total assets. To forecast a company's financing needs effectively, an entrepreneur must understand certain basic principles that govern the financing of firms, which can be stated as follows:

1. The more assets a business needs, the greater its financing requirements. Thus, a firm that is experiencing rapid sales growth requires more assets and, consequently, faces greater pressure to find financing—and that pressure can be unbearable if not managed carefully.
2. A company should finance its growth in such a way as to maintain adequate liquidity. (*Liquidity* measures the degree to which a firm has current assets available to meet maturing short-term debt.) The need for adequate liquidity in small firms deserves special emphasis. As already mentioned, a common weakness in small business financing is the tendency to maintain a disproportionately small investment in liquid assets, or what was defined earlier as *net working capital*. Even more specifically, in Chapter 10 we used the *current ratio* as a measure of liquidity that compares a firm's current assets to its current liabilities on a relative basis. To ensure payment of short-term debts as they come due, small business owners should, as a general rule, maintain a current ratio of at least 2—that is, have current assets of at least two times the amount of current liabilities—or have a good reason for not doing so.
3. The amount of money a firm can borrow is dependent in part on the amount of money the owners put into the business in the form of ownership equity. A bank would never provide *all* of the necessary financing for a firm; for instance, a bank might specify that at least half of the firm's financing must come from ownership equity, while the rest can come from debt. In other words, the owners would have to limit the firm's *debt ratio*, which expresses debt as a percentage of total assets, to 50 percent.
4. Some types of short-term debt—specifically, *accounts payable* and *accrued expenses*—maintain a relatively constant relationship with sales. For example, as sales increase, more inventory will be required. If the inventory is purchased on credit, accounts payable will increase as well. As a result, accounts payable can be used to track increases in sales. If sales increase by $1, accounts payable might increase by $0.15, or 15 percent of sales. So, if you expect a $1,000 increase in sales, you can also expect accounts payable to increase by $150—15 percent of the increase in sales. The same holds true for accrued expenses—more business means more expenses, some of which will be accrued as liabilities, rather than being paid immediately. Given the "spontaneous" relationship of these types of liabilities with sales, they are sometimes called **spontaneous debt financing**. While not the more formal type of debt, such as bank loans, these accrued liabilities can be a significantly large source of financing for many small companies. The rest of debt financing must come from loans by banks and other lending sources.

spontaneous debt financing
Short-term debts, such as accounts payable, that automatically increase in proportion to a firm's sales.

5. Ownership equity in a business comes from two sources: (1) investments the owners make in the business, and (2) profits that are retained within the company rather than being distributed to the owners, or what was discussed in Chapter 10 as *retained earnings*. For the typical small firm, retained earnings are the primary source of equity capital for financing growth. (Be careful not to think of retained earnings as a cash resource. As already noted, a firm may have significant profits but no cash to reinvest.)

The essence of the foregoing principles can be captured in the following equation:

$$\text{Total asset requirements} = \text{Total sources of financing} = \text{Spontaneous debt financing} + \text{Loans from banks, etc.} + \text{Owner's investment} + \text{Retained earnings}$$

Small business owners who thoroughly understand these five principles and their relationships with each other will be effective in forecasting their firm's financial requirements—and they will be effective in acquiring needed financing.

Recall that Allen projected asset requirements of $143,500 and $188,250 for years 1 and 2, respectively. He then made estimates of the financing requirements, based on the following facts and assumptions:

1. Allen negotiated with a supplier to receive 30 days' credit on inventory purchases, which results in accounts payable running about 8 percent of sales.
2. Allen also estimates that accrued expenses that will be shown as short-term liabilities in the balance sheet will amount to about 4 percent of sales.
3. Allen plans to invest $110,000 of his personal savings to provide the needed startup equity for the business. He will receive common stock in return for his investment.
4. A bank has agreed to provide a short-term line of credit of $25,000 to D&R Products. A **line of credit** is simply a short-term loan to help with temporary needs, such as seasonal increases in inventory. It works like a credit card—the company has the option to borrow up to the limit (in this case, $25,000) as needed and then pay it down when it is no longer needed.
5. The bank has also agreed to help finance the purchase of a building for manufacturing and warehousing the firm's products. Of the $40,000 needed to purchase the building, the bank will lend the firm $30,000, with the building serving as collateral for the loan. The loan will be repaid over 10 years in equal principal payments of $3,000 plus interest on the remaining note balance each year.
6. As part of the loan agreement, the bank has imposed two restrictions: (1) The firm's current ratio must remain at 2.0 or above, and (2) no more than 50 percent of the firm's financing may come from debt, both short-term or long-term (that is, total debt should be no more than 50 percent of total assets). Failure to comply with either of these conditions will cause the bank loan to come due immediately.

line of credit
A short-term loan.

With this information, Allen can now estimate the sources of financing for D&R Products. If sales resulting from product and installations are $250,000 in year 1 and $375,000 in year 2, then Allen estimates that

Sources of Financing	**Assumptions**	**Year 1**	**Year 2**
Accounts payable	8% of sales	$ 20,000	$ 30,000
Accrued expenses	4% of sales	$ 10,000	$ 15,000
Mortgage	$30,000 – $3,000 annual payments	$ 27,000	$ 24,000
Common stock	Founder's investment	$110,000	$110,000

EXHIBIT 11.3 Pro Forma Balance Sheets for D&R Products, Inc.

	A	B	C	D	E
3	*BALANCE SHEET ASSUMPTIONS*	**Year 1**	**Year 2**		
4	Projected revenues: product sales and installations	$250,000	$375,000		
5	Cash/sales	4%	4%		
6	Accounts receivable/sales	10%	10%		
7	Inventory/sales	25%	25%		
8	Gross fixed assets	$ 50,000	$ 50,000	**Equations based on assumptions**	
9	Accounts payable/sales	8%	8%		
10	Accrued expenses/sales	4%	4%		
11	Cost of equipment	$ 10,000	$ 10,000		
12	Building cost	$ 40,000	$ 40,000		
13				*Equations for:*	
14	**Assets**			***Year 1***	***Year 2***
15	Cash	$ 10,000	$ 15,000	=B4*B5	=C4*C5
16	Accounts receivable	25,000	37,500	=B4*B6	=C4*C6
17	Inventory	62,500	93,750	=B4*B7	=C4*C7
18	Total current assets	$ 97,500	$146,250	=SUM(B15:B17)	=SUM(C15:C17)
19	Gross fixed assets	$ 50,000	$ 50,000	=B8	=C8
20	Accumulated depreciation	(4,000)	(8,000)	Depreciation expense for year 1	Accumulated depreciation expense for years 1 and 2
21	Net fixed assets	$ 46,000	$ 42,000	=B19+B20	=C19+C20
22	TOTAL ASSETS	$143,500	$188,250	=B18+B21	=C18+C21
23					
24	**Debt (Liabilities) and Equity**				
25	Accounts payable	$ 20,000	$ 30,000	=B4*B9	=C4*C9
26	Accrued expenses	10,000	15,000	=B4*B10	=C4*C10
27	Short-term line of credit	9,500	11,875	Required financing	Required financing
28	Total current liabilities	$ 39,500	$ 56,875	=SUM(B25:B27)	=SUM(C25:C27)
29	Mortgage	27,000	24,000	Original loan of $30,000 – annual payment of $3,000	Year 1 balance of $27,000 – annual payment of $3,000
30	Total debt	$ 66,500	$ 80,875	=SUM(B28:B29)	=SUM(C28:C29)
31	Ownership equity				
32	Common stock	$110,000	$110,000	Given	Given
33	Retained earnings	(33,000)	(2,625)	Year 1 loss	Year 1 loss + year 2 profit
34	Total ownership equity	$ 77,000	$107,375	=SUM(B32:B33)	=SUM(C32:C33)
35	TOTAL DEBT AND EQUITY	$143,500	$188,250	=SUM(B30:B33)	=SUM(C30:C33)
36					
37	Current ratio	$ 2.47	$ 2.57	=B18/B28	=C18/C28
38	Debt ratio	46%	43%	=B30/B35	=C30/C35

Any remaining financing, up to $25,000, can come from the bank line of credit. If the line of credit is inadequate to meet the firm's needs, Allen will have to put more equity into the business.

Based on the information above, Allen can now develop pro forma balance sheets for D&R Products. Exhibit 11.3 shows the assumptions made, the equations underlying the numbers, and the actual balance sheets, as developed in a spreadsheet.

Several points about the projected balance sheets presented in Exhibit 11.3 need to be clarified:

1. Total assets and total sources of financing (debt and equity) must always balance. Note that D&R Products' asset requirements of $143,500 for the first year and $188,250 for the second year are the same as the firm's debt and equity totals.
2. To bring sources of financing into balance with total assets, D&R Products will need to borrow on the company's $25,000 line of credit. By the end of the first year, $9,500 of the line of credit is needed to bring the total debt and equity to $143,500. In the second year, line-of-credit borrowing will increase to $11,875 to gain the $188,250 in total financing needed.
3. Based on Allen's projections, the firm should be able to satisfy the bank's loan restrictions, maintaining both a current ratio of 2.0 or more and a debt ratio of less than 50 percent. The computations are as follows:

Ratio	**Computation**	**Year 1**	**Year 2**
Current ratio	$= \frac{\text{Current assets}}{\text{Current liabilities}}$	$= \frac{\$97{,}500}{\$39{,}500} = 2.47$	$\frac{\$146{,}250}{\$56{,}875} = 2.57$
Debt ratio	$= \frac{\text{Total debt}}{\text{Total assets}}$	$= \frac{\$66{,}500}{\$143{,}500} = 0.46 = 46\%$	$\frac{\$80{,}375}{\$188{,}250} = 0.43 = 43\%$

We have now completed the process for forecasting a company's profitability and its asset and financing needs, as reflected in the income statement and balance sheet, respectively. We will now consider the third and final key financing issue: projecting cash flows.

Forecasting Cash Flows

As we have mentioned numerous times, profits and cash flows are not the same thing. A business can have positive profits and be running out of cash—or it can incur losses, as shown in the income statement, and have positive cash flows. The income statement simply does not give the small business owner the information he or she needs to know about the firm's cash flows. Forecasting cash flows is *critical* for the small business owner: If the business runs out of money, the consequences can be devastating.

Projecting a company's cash flows can be accomplished in one of two ways. First, we can use the information from the pro forma income statement and balance sheets to develop a pro forma statement of cash flows, similar to what we did in Chapter 10 to gain an historical view. Second, we can prepare a cash budget, which is simply a listing of expected cash inflows and outflows.

In forecasting cash flows, an owner must consider the time period used for projections. In a statement of cash flows that covers an entire year, everything may look great on paper, but the firm could very well run out of cash during certain months in that year.

This scenario is particularly true for a business whose sales are seasonal. For instance, a wholesale sunglass company orders inventory in the spring, but most of its sales occur in the summer. Furthermore, the company will extend credit to its customers and not be paid until the end of the summer. If we look at the company's cash flows on an annual basis, all may be well. But during the spring and early summer, there will be large investments in accounts receivable and inventory, putting extreme pressure on the firm's cash flows. In this instance, the owner would want to forecast cash flows on a monthly basis—maybe even on a weekly basis.

In the next two sections, we use D&R Products, Inc., to illustrate how to forecast cash flows. We first prepare pro forma statements of annual cash flows. Then we illustrate how to prepare a monthly cash budget.

entrepreneurial experiences

The Problem with Unplanned Growth

This is a true story, although the names and places have been changed. Everything ended up OK, but the entrepreneur had to endure a lot of unnecessary stress—all of which could easily have been prevented by just a minimum of planning.

The story takes place in a midsize university town on the West Coast. The main players are Leslie and Terry, co-owners of a consulting business offering computer and network services mostly to local businesses.

At the beginning of this story, Leslie and Terry had a small but comfortable office a few blocks off Main Street, near the university, and a comfortable business, averaging about $20,000 in sales per month with a few steady clients and few seasonal variations in sales. Then came the big, wonderful new opportunity—a contract with a large and fast-growing company to install new Internet facilities in offices on its corporate campus, only 10 miles up the freeway. This was a $200,000 contract that had to be acted on quickly, and it opened up an important new relationship with a potential business-changing client. It was also cause for great celebration. Leslie and Terry and their spouses marked the occasion with a fancy dinner at the best restaurant in the area.

© iStockphoto.com/Shane Shaw

Both partners quickly got started fulfilling the contract, delivering the network, connecting the systems, and making good on their promises. To be sure the new relationship would turn into a permanent increase in business, they took on five contractor consultants to deal with the needs of installation, training, and the general increase in business demands.

Within two months, it seemed clear to both partners that they had made the leap. Systems were being installed, the clients were happy, and they were on the road to doubling their business volume in a very short period of time. Leslie and Terry decided they could celebrate more, so they both went to a local car dealership and leased new Mercedes sedans.

But then things started going downhill. Though sales and profits were way up, jobs were done and invoicing was underway, Leslie and Terry had no cash. Their contractors—good people whom Leslie and Terry wanted to keep—needed to be paid, but there was no money. They rushed to their local bank, waving reports of increased sales and profits, but banks need time. The business suffered the classic problems of unplanned growth. Just as the accounting reports looked brightest, the coffers were empty. People were barely done celebrating, but suddenly they were looking at the disaster of unpaid bills and, much worse, unpaid people.

What happened? The company experienced unplanned cash flow problems. The new, larger client had a slow process for paying bills, so the jump in sales didn't mean an immediate jump in cash in the bank. Leslie and Terry were more concerned about delivering good service than delivering necessary paperwork, so their own invoicing process was slow. They were owed about $85,000, but they couldn't go straight to their new clients to get the money—they had already authorized payment and sent the requests to the company's finance department for processing. The people in the finance department were slow to respond and not particularly concerned about paying vendors quickly; their job was to pay slowly, just not so slowly as to get a bad credit rating.

Leslie and Terry had a bad case of "receivables starvation." The money that was owed to them was already showing as sales and profits, but it was not in the bank.

In this case, fortunately, the two partners had enough home equity to get a quick loan and pay their contractors. The business was saved and grew, but not without a great deal of stress and strain, and even second mortgages. The story's ending might have been much different if the owners did not have access to cash from personal assets. This could easily have doomed the company.

The worst moment is worth remembering. One of the partners' spouses was particularly eloquent about the irony of taking on a new mortgage while driving that "[profanity omitted] Mercedes."

The moral of the story: Always have a good cash flow plan. Think ahead about the impact of a sudden rush of new business. Go to the bank early, as soon as you know about new business, and start processing a credit line on receivables. And never lease a Mercedes until you're sure you won't have to take out a new mortgage a few weeks later.

Source: Tim Berry, "The Problem with Unplanned Growth," http://www.entrepreneur.com/startingabusiness/businessplans/businessplancoachtimberry/article172648.html, accessed November 17, 2010.

PRO FORMA STATEMENT OF CASH FLOWS

Earlier, we prepared a pro forma income statement and balance sheets for D&R Products, Inc. We can now use that information to prepare a pro forma statement of cash flows. However, instead of dealing with historical numbers, as we did in Chapter 10, we are now working with projections.

The pro forma cash flow statements for D&R Products are presented in Exhibit 11.4.[10] There are three key numbers that you should pay particular attention to in the exhibit: cash flows from operating activities, cash flows from investing activities, and cash flows from financing activities (these numbers are shown in boxes in Exhibit 11.4). Looking at these numbers, we see that

1. In the first year, the business is expected to have negative cash flows from operations of $86,500 and will be investing $50,000 in the building and equipment. To cover these negative cash flows, Allen expects to raise $146,500 in financing from his personal investment of $110,000, $9,500 on the line of credit from the bank, and $27,000 from the mortgage on the building after making the annual $3,000 payment on the principal. The firm would then end the year with $10,000 in cash. (Note that the change in the pro forma balance sheet for year 1 is the same as the year-end balance shown in the balance sheet, since the business did not exist in the prior year; thus, the balance at the beginning of year 1 would have been zero.)
2. In the second year, the firm's cash flow operations are expected to be $5,625. (Notice that while the business is expected to have $5,625 in cash flows from

EXHIBIT 11.4 Pro Forma Cash Flow Statements for D&R Products, Inc.

		Year 1		Year 2	Sources of Information
Operating activities:					
Net profits		($ 33,000)		$ 30,375	*Pro forma income statement*
Depreciation		4,000		4,000	
Increase in accounts receivable (cash outflow)		($ 25,000)		($ 12,500)	
Increase in inventory (cash outflow)	($62,500)		($31,250)		*Changes in projected balance sheets from founding of business to year 1 and from year 1 to year 2*
Increase in accounts payable)	20,000		10,000		
Cash payments for inventory		($ 42,500)		($ 21,250)	
Increase in accrued expenses		10,000		5,000	
Cash flows from operations		**($ 86,500)**		**$ 5,625**	
Investing activities:					
Increase in gross fixed assets (cash outflow)		($ 50,000)		$ 0	
Cash flows from investing		**($ 50,000)**		**$ 0**	
Financing activities:					
Increase in short-term line of credit		$ 9,500		$ 2,375	
Increase (decrease) in mortgage		27,000		(3,000)	
Increase in stock		110,000		0	
Cash flows from financing		**$146,500**		**$ 625**	
Increase (decrease) in cash		$ 10,000		$ 5,000	
Beginning cash		$ 0		$ 10,000	
Ending cash (as shown in the balance sheets)		**$ 10,000**		**$15,000**	

operations, Allen anticipates having profits of $30,375. Remember, *cash flows and profits are not the same thing.*) Moreover, there are no plans to invest in fixed assets in the second year. Thus, given his underlying assumptions, Allen would need to increase the line of credit (short-term debt) from the bank from $9,500 in year 1 to $11,875 in year 2, for an increase of $2,375, and pay $3,000 on the mortgage. The balance result of all the cash flows would be a $5,000 increase in cash, for an ending cash balance of $15,000.

Allen now has a good estimate of the cash flows for the year as a whole and an idea of what contributes to the cash inflows and outflows. But there is also a need to track the firm's cash flows for a shorter time period, usually on a monthly basis.

THE CASH BUDGET

The **cash budget** is one of the primary tools that a small business owner can use to manage cash flows. The budget is concerned specifically with dollars both received and paid out. *No single planning document is more important in the life of a small company, either for avoiding cash flow problems when cash runs short or for anticipating short-term investment opportunities if excess cash becomes available.*

cash budget
A listing of cash receipts and cash disbursements, usually for a relatively short time period, such as a week or a month.

To help you understand the process of preparing a cash budget, let's continue with the example of D&R Products, Inc. In the previous section, we prepared a pro forma statement of cash flows for the year. But Allen realizes that he also needs to have a sense of the timing of the cash flows throughout the year, so he has decided to prepare a monthly cash budget for the first year of operations. We will look at only the first three months

of the cash budget to understand how it was prepared. While Allen predicts that the firm will have $250,000 in annual sales in the first year, his sales projections for the first three months are as follows:

January	$ 4,000
February	6,000
March	9,000

In addition, the following assumptions will be made:

1. Of the firm's sales dollars, 40 percent are collected the month of the sale, 30 percent one month after the sale, and the remaining 30 percent two months after the sale.
2. Inventory will be purchased one month in advance of the expected sale and will be paid for in the month in which it is sold.
3. Inventory purchases will equal 60 percent of projected sales for the next month's sales.
4. The firm will spend $3,000 each month for advertising.
5. Salaries and utilities for the first three months are estimated as follows:

	Salaries	**Utilities**
January	$5,000	$150
February	6,000	$200
March	6,000	$200

6. Allen will be investing $110,000 in the business from his personal savings.
7. The firm will be investing $10,000 for needed equipment and $40,000 for the purchase of a building, for a total investment of $50,000. However, the bank has agreed to finance $30,000 of the building purchase price in the form of a mortgage.

Based on this information, Allen has prepared a monthly cash budget for the three-month period ending March 31. Exhibit 11.5 shows the results of his computations, which involve the following steps:

Step 1. Determine the amount of collections each month, based on the projected collection patterns given above.

Step 2. Estimate the amount and timing of the following cash disbursements:

a. Inventory purchases and payments. The amount of the purchases is shown in the boxed area at the top of the table. However, the actual payment for inventory will not be made until one month later.

b. Advertising, wages and salaries, and utilities.

Step 3. Calculate the *cash flows from operating activities*, which equals the cash receipts (collections from sales) less cash disbursements.

EXHIBIT 11.5 Three-Month Cash Budget for D&R Product, Inc., for January–March

Assumptions:
Anticipated sales collections:

In the month of sale	*40%*
1 month later	*30%*
2 months later	*30%*

	December	January	February	March
Monthly sales	$ 0	$4,000	$6,000	$9,000
Inventory purchases on credit	$2,400	$3,600	$5,400	$7,800

		December	January	February	March
	Monthly sales	$0	*$ 4,000	$ 6,000	$ 9,000
	Cash receipts				
Step 1:	Collection of sales				
	In month of sale		$ 1,600	$ 2,400	$ 3,600
	1 month later			1,200	1,800
	2 months later				1,200
	Total cash receipts		$ 1,600	$ 3,600	$ 6,600
Step 2:	**Cash disbursements**				
Step 2a:	Payments on inventory purchases		$ 2,400	$ 3,600	$ 5,400
	Advertising		3,000	3,000	3,000
Step 2b:	Wages and salaries		5,000	6,000	6,000
	Utilities		150	200	200
	Total cash disbursements		$10,550	$12,800	$14,600
Step 3:	Cash flows from operations		($8,950)	($9,200)	($8,000)
Step 4:	Allen's personal investment		110,000		
Step 5:	Purchase of equipment and building		(50,000)		
Step 6:	Mortgage (loan from the bank to buy the building)		30,000		
Step 7:	Beginning cash balance		0	81,050	71,850
Step 8:	Ending cash balance		$81,050	$71,850	$63,850

*For example, January sales of $4,000 are collected as follows: (40%) $1,600 in January, (30%) $1,200 in February, (30%) $1,200 in March.

Step 4. Recognize the $110,000 investment in the business by Allen.
Step 5. Note the $50,000 investment in the building and equipment.
Step 6. Show the $30,000 loan from the bank to help pay for the building.
Step 7. Determine the beginning-of-month cash balance (ending cash balance from the prior month).
Step 8. Compute the end-of-month cash balance.

Based on the cash budget, Allen now has a sense of what to expect for the first three months of operations, which could not be seen from the annual pro forma statement of cash flows presented in Exhibit 11.4. He knows now that he will be "burning" somewhere between $8,000 and $9,200 of cash per month for the first three months of operations. Given that he will have almost $64,000 in cash remaining at the end of March, he will run out of cash in about seven or eight months if the cash flows from operations continue to be negative $8,000 or $9,000 each month. At that time, he will have to start borrowing on the bank line of credit.

ACTION

Evaluate Your Suppliers

Budgeting season is the perfect time to scrutinize vendor relationships. Your suppliers are in all likelihood mapping out their expectations for the year, and you can help them do so by providing your outlook. As a best practice, you should share your budget and the variety of scenarios you might face with your suppliers to see whether they can handle each level of demand. If they can't accommodate your needs, you are dealing with the wrong suppliers.

One final thought about the cash budget. Once it has been prepared, an entrepreneur has to decide how to use it. Entrepreneurship is about seeking opportunities, and there is a real danger that a cash budget may lead to inflexibility. A strict cost-containment strategy in order to "make the budget" can discourage managers from being creative and shifting their approach when it makes sense to do so. An inflexible budget can lead to a "use it or lose it" mentality, where managers spend remaining budgeted money at year's end so that allocations will not be cut the following year. Such a mindset negatively impacts the entrepreneurial process. Jeremy Hope, a former venture capitalist, describes the risk of becoming too focused on a budget: "I'm not opposed to a budget as a finance statement, but to the way it's used as an almost fixed performance contract on which employees have to deliver. The pressure to deliver on budgets drives a lot of irrational, stupid, and crazy behavior you see within businesses."[11]

Allowing the management team and employees to become focused on the budget instead of opportunities is counterproductive and should be avoided.

Use Good Judgment When Forecasting

The forecasting process requires an entrepreneur to exercise good judgment in planning, particularly when the planning is providing the basis for raising capital. The overall approach to forecasting is straightforward—entrepreneurs make assumptions and, based on these assumptions, determine financing requirements. But entrepreneurs may be tempted to overstate their expectations in order to acquire much needed financing. So how do you get it right? Here are some practical suggestions about making financial forecasts:[12]

1. *Develop realistic sales projections.* Entrepreneurs often think they can accomplish more than they actually are able to, especially when it comes to forecasting future sales. When graphed, their sales projections for a new venture often resemble a hockey stick—the sales numbers are flat or rise slightly at first (like the blade of a hockey stick) and then soar upward like a hockey stick's handle. Such projections are always suspect—only the most astonishing changes in a business or market can justify such a sudden, rocket-like performance.

2. *Build projections from clear assumptions about marketing and pricing plans.* Don't be vague, and don't guess. Spell out the kinds of marketing you plan to do—for example, state specifically how many customers you expect to attract. Paul A. Broni offers this advice:

    > *When putting together your income statement, revenues should show more than just the projected sales figure for each year. You should also show how many units you plan to sell, as well as the mix of revenue (assuming that you have*

more than one product or service). If you have a service business, you may also want to show how many customers or clients you will have each year. Investors will look at that number to determine whether it's realistic for you to sell to that many customers. For example, if your plan is to go from 12 customers in the first year to 36 customers in the second, can the sales team you've built accomplish that goal? What about marketing and advertising? Does your budget account for the money you'll need to spend to support such an effort?

3. *Do not use unrealistic profit margins.* Projections are immediately suspect if profit margins (profits ÷ sales) or expenses are significantly higher or lower than the average figures reported by firms in the industry with similar revenues and numbers of employees. In general, a new business should not expect to exceed the industry average in profit margins. Entrepreneurs frequently assume that as their company grows it will achieve economies of scale, and gross and operating profit margins will improve. In fact, as the business grows and increases its fixed costs, its operating profit margins are likely to suffer in the short run. If you insist in your projections that the economies can be achieved quickly, you will need to explain your position.
4. *Don't limit your projections to an income statement.* Entrepreneurs frequently resist providing a projected balance sheet and cash flow statement. They feel comfortable projecting sales and profits but do not like having to commit to assumptions about the sources and uses of capital needed to grow the business. Investors, however, want to see those assumptions in print, and they are particularly interested in the firm's cash flows—and you should be as well.
5. *Provide monthly data for the upcoming year and annual data for succeeding years.* Many entrepreneurs prepare projections using only monthly data or annual data for an entire three- or five-year period. Given the difficulty in forecasting accurately beyond a year, monthly data for the later years are not particularly believable. From year 2 on, annual projections are adequate.
6. *Avoid providing too much financial information.* Computer spreadsheets are extremely valuable in making projections and showing how different assumptions affect the firm's financials. But do not be tempted to overuse this tool. Instead, limit your projections to two scenarios: the most likely scenario (base case) and the break-even scenario. The base case should show what you realistically expect the business to do; the break-even case should show what level of sales is required to break even.
7. *Be certain that the numbers reconcile—and not by simply plugging in a figure.* All too often, entrepreneurs plug a figure into equity to make things work out. While everyone makes mistakes, that's one you want to avoid because it can result in a loss of credibility.
8. *Follow the plan.* After you have prepared the pro forma financial statements, check them against actual results at least once a month, and modify your projections as needed.

These suggestions, if followed, will help you avoid the old problem of overpromising and underdelivering. Given the nature of starting a business, entrepreneurs at times simply have to have faith that they will be able to deliver on what they promise, even though it may not be clear exactly how this will be accomplished. Risk is part of the equation, and often things will not go as planned. But integrity requires you to honor your commitments, and that cannot be done if you have made unrealistic projections about what you can accomplish.

The information on financial planning provided in this chapter and in Chapter 10 will serve as a foundation for the examination of an entrepreneur's search for specific sources of financing in Chapter 12.

1. Describe the purpose and need for financial forecasting.

- The purpose of pro forma financial statements is to determine (1) future profitability based on projected sales levels and expected sales–expense relationships, (2) how much and what type of financing will be needed, and (3) whether the firm will have adequate cash flows.
- Accurate financial forecasting is important not only for ensuring that a firm has the resources it needs to grow, but also for managing growth.

2. Develop a pro forma income statement to forecast a new venture's profitability.

- It is important for an entrepreneur to understand the drivers of a firm's profits, not only in a general sense but in the specific ways each factor applies to a unique firm.
- A firm's net profit is dependent on (1) amount of sales, (2) cost of goods sold, (3) operating expenses, (4) interest expense, and (5) taxes.
- In a real-world situation, an entrepreneur should project the profits of a company for at least three years into the future.

3. Determine a company's asset and financing requirements based on a pro forma balance sheet.

- The amount and type of assets required for a venture will vary according to the nature of the business; however, all firms need to understand how much working capital and fixed assets will be required.
- An entrepreneur should try to bootstrap as many resources as possible in order to minimize a firm's investment while simultaneously ensuring adequate resources.
- Funding for a new venture should cover its asset requirements and also the personal living expenses of the owner.
- A direct relationship exists between sales growth and asset needs: as sales increase, more assets are required. For every dollar of assets needed, there must be a corresponding dollar of financing.
- A firm's financing is determined by considering its (1) asset requirements, (2) need to maintain adequate liquidity, (3) debt ratio, (4) sources of spontaneous debt financing, and (5) ownership equity.

Total asset requirements = Total sources of financing = Owner's investment + Spontaneous debt financing + Loans from banks, etc. + Retained earnings

4. Forecast a firm's cash flows.

- Forecasting cash flows can be accomplished in one of two ways; (1) prepare a pro forma statement of cash flows, or (2) develop a cash budget. Ideally, an entrepreneur would do both.
- A firm's cash flows involve three activities: operations, investments, and financing.
- A cash budget is concerned specifically with dollars both received and paid out.
- A cash budget should provide boundaries but should not limit creativity and flexibility; entrepreneurship is all about seizing opportunity.

5. Provide some suggestions for effective financial forecasting.

- Develop realistic sales projections and build projections from clear assumptions about marketing and pricing plans.
- Do not use unrealistic profit margins; in general, new businesses do not exceed industry average profit margins in their first years.
- Do not limit your projections to an income statement; go a step further and provide a balance sheet and cash flow statement.
- Provide monthly data for the upcoming year and annual data for succeeding years.
- Avoid providing too much financial information by limiting projections to two scenarios: the most-likely scenario (base case) and the break-even scenario.
- Be certain that the numbers reconcile.
- Follow the plan, and measure how actual performance compares with forecasted performance so that modifications to future forecasts may be more accurate.

Key Terms

pro forma financial statements p. 331
net working capital p. 336
percentage-of-sales technique p. 340
spontaneous debt financing p. 341
line of credit p. 342
cash budget p. 347

Discussion Questions

1. What determines a company's profitability?
2. Discuss how asset and financing requirements might differ among a retail business, a service company, and an information system–based venture.
3. Why is it important to consider an entrepreneur's personal finances when conducting the short- and long-term financial forecasts of a firm?
4. Describe the process for estimating the amount of assets required for a new venture.
5. What are some of the basic principles that govern the financing of a firm? Why are they important?
6. How are a startup's financing requirements estimated?
7. Describe two ways for projecting a venture's cash flows, and discuss when each is appropriate to use.
8. When forecasting cash flows, why is it important to consider the time period covered by the forecast? What issues should the entrepreneur consider when doing financial forecasts?
9. Why is it important for an entrepreneur not only to create a cash budget, but also to decide how it will be used within the firm?
10. Choose three of the practical suggestions for making financial forecasts. Discuss their importance as well as the potential consequences of ignoring these suggestions.

You Make the Call

SITUATION 1

D&R Products, Inc., used as an example in this chapter, is an actual firm (although some of the facts were changed to maintain confidentiality). David Allen bought the firm from its founding owners and moved its operations to his hometown. Although he has estimated the firm's asset needs and financing requirements, he cannot be certain that these projections will be realized. The figures merely represent the most-likely case. Allen also made some projections that he considers to be the worst-case and best-case sales and profit figures. If things do not go well, the firm might have sales of only $200,000 in its first year. However, if the potential of the business is realized, Allen believes that sales could be as high as $325,000. If he needs any additional financing beyond the existing line of credit, he could conceivably borrow another $5,000 in short-term debt from the bank by pledging some personal investments. Any additional financing would need to come from Allen himself, thereby increasing his equity stake in the business.

Source: Personal conversation with David Allen. (The entrepreneur's name and financial numbers are hypothetical.)

Question If all of D&R Products' other relationships hold, how will Allen's worst-case and best-case projections affect the income statement and balance sheet in the first year? (To help you in your analysis, the D&R Product's pro forma statements as presented in Exhibits 11.1, 11.3, and 11.4 are available at www.cengagebrain.com.

SITUATION 2

Adrian Fudge of the Fudge Corporation wants you to forecast the firm's financing needs over the fourth quarter (October through December). He has made the following observations relative to planned cash receipts and disbursements:

- Interest on a $75,000 bank note (principal due next March) at an 8 percent annual rate is payable in December for the three-month period just ended.
- The firm follows a policy of paying no cash dividends.
- Actual historical and future predicted sales are as follows:

Historical Sales		**Predicted Sales**	
August	$150,000	October	$200,000
September	175,000	November	220,000
		December	180,000
		January	200,000

- The firm has a monthly rental expense of $5,000.
- Wages and salaries for the coming months are estimated at $25,000 per month.
- Of the firm's sales, 25 percent is collected in the month of the sale, 35 percent one month after the sale, and the remaining 40 percent two months after the sale.
- Merchandise is purchased one month before the sales month and is paid for in the month it is sold. Purchases equal 75 percent of sales.
- Tax prepayments are made quarterly, with a prepayment of $10,000 in October based on earnings for the quarter ended September 30.
- Utility costs for the firm average 3 percent of sales and are paid in the month they are incurred.
- Depreciation expense is $20,000 annually.

Question 1 Prepare a monthly cash budget for the three-month period ending in December.

Question 2 If the firm's beginning cash balance for the budget period is $7,000, and this is its desired minimum balance, determine when and how much the firm will need to borrow during the budget period. The firm has a $50,000 line of credit with its bank, with interest (10 percent annual rate) paid monthly. For example, interest on a loan taken out at the end of September would be paid at the end of October and every month thereafter as long as the loan was outstanding.

SITUATION 3

New York City–based Plum Organics was two weeks away from a production run of its organic kids' meals when the phone rang. On the other line was the company's organic cheese supplier.

"They said, 'We're out of organic parmesan cheese because there's a shortage of organic milk,'" recalls Plum Organics' founder, Gigi Lee Chang. The supplier said it expected a shipment of organic milk to arrive soon and that it could probably meet three-year-old Plum Organics' production deadline. Chang was skeptical. She called another supplier, but because its organic parmesan wasn't fully aged, Chang, 41, feared it would change the taste of the product.

Chang weighed her options: She could either rely on her primary supplier to come through, or use the parmesan the secondary supplier had to offer.

Source: Chris Penttila, "Risky Business," *Entrepreneur*, November 2008, http://www.entrepreneur.com/magazine/entrepreneur/2008/november/197996.html, accessed August 10, 2010.

Question 1 What would you do, if you were Chang? Support your decision.

Question 2 Is there anything Chang should do in the future to avoid, or at least anticipate, such a situation?

Question 3 What lesson should Chang learn from this situation?

Experiential Exercises

1. Dun & Bradstreet and Robert Morris Associates compile financial information about many companies. They provide, among other information, the income statement and balance sheets for an average firm in an industry. Go to a library and look up, or search online for, financial information on firms in two industries of your choice. Compute the following data for each industry:
   a. The percentages of assets in (1) current assets and (2) fixed assets (property, plant, and equipment)
   b. The percentages of financing from (1) spontaneous debt financing and (2) retained earnings
   c. The cost of goods sold and the operating expenses as percentages of sales
   d. The total assets as a percentage of sales

   Given your findings, how would you summarize the differences between the two industries?
2. Obtain the business plan of a firm that is three to five years old. Compare the techniques used in the plan to forecast the firm's profits and financing requirements with those presented in this chapter. If actual data are available, compare the financial forecasts with the eventual outcome. What accounts for the differences?
3. Identify a small business in your community that has recently expanded. Interview the owner of the firm about the evaluation methods he or she used before committing to the expansion.

Small Business and Entrepreneurship Resource Center

The text explains that bootstrapping is the most common way that entrepreneurs accomplish more with less. To the extent possible, the entrepreneur should use other people's resources—for instance, lease rather than buy, negotiate with suppliers to provide inventory "just in time" to minimize the investment in inventory, and arrange to collect money owed the firm before having to pay the firm's bills. Discuss briefly the 10 proven bootstrapping techniques and strategies that every entrepreneur should know.

Source: The Kiplinger Washington Editors, "The Art and Science of Bootstrapping," *Raising Capital*, The Kiplinger Washington Editors, Inc., Annual 2000, p. 81.

Case 11

MISSOURI SOLVENTS (P. 714)

Missouri Solvents is a regional distributor of liquid and dry chemicals, headquartered in St. Louis. The company has been serving the St. Louis market for 10 years and has a reputation as a reliable supplier of industrial chemicals.

ALTERNATIVE CASES FOR CHAPTER 11

Case 22, Pearson Air Conditioning & Service, p. 736
Video Case 10, B2B CFO, website only

Business Plan Laying the Foundation

As part of laying the foundation to prepare your own business plan, you will need to develop the following:

1. Historical financial statements (if applicable) and five years of pro forma financial statements, including balance sheets, income statements, and statements of cash flows.
2. Monthly cash budgets for the first year and quarterly cash budgets for the second year.
3. Profit and cash flow break-even analysis. (See Chapter 16 for an explanation of break-even analysis.)
4. Financial resources required now and in the future, with details on the intended use of funds being requested.
5. Underlying assumptions for all pro forma statements.
6. Current and planned investments by the owners and other investors.

CHAPTER 12

A Firm's Sources of Financing

In the SPOTLIGHT
Just Send Cash

When Frank Hannigan needed to raise a first round of financing for his software start-up earlier this year, he didn't want to waste time with endless calls and meetings with potential investors. "Every day you spend selling equity in your business is a day you are not selling the output of your business," he says.

His solution? A note to 700 of his contacts on the business-networking site LinkedIn.

The message, which he hashed out with company founder Gerard Hartnett, was simple. Goshido, an Irish outfit that makes project-management software delivered over the Internet, was looking for 10 investors to pony up €25,000 (about $35,000) apiece. In return, they would each get a 2% share in the company.

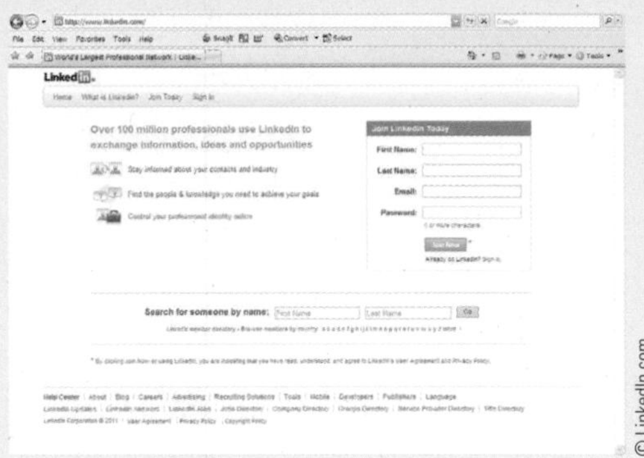

Within a couple of days of sending the note through LinkedIn's email service, Mr. Hannigan had 200-plus responses that ranged from requests for meetings or conference calls to lists of questions and quite a few messages that said, "No thanks, but I'll pass it on."

It's Who You Know

Software engineer Dave Concannon, of Berkeley, Calif., was one of the people who got Mr. Hannigan's note. "At first, I wondered if it was legitimate, since I had never seen anything like it before," says Mr. Concannon, who knew Mr. Hannigan through previous consulting jobs. "Once I realized it was real, it seemed like a good idea."

Mr. Concannon thought the company targeted an underserved niche in the project-management field and had a good team in place. What sealed the deal, though, was a perusal of Mr. Hannigan's other

After reading this chapter, you should be able to . . .

1. Describe how the nature of a firm affects its financing sources.
2. Evaluate the choice between debt financing and equity financing.
3. Identify the typical sources of financing used at the outset of a new venture.
4. Discuss the basic process for acquiring and structuring a bank loan.
5. Explain how business relationships can be used to finance a small firm.
6. Describe the two types of private equity investors who offer financing to small firms.
7. Distinguish among the different government loan programs available to small companies.
8. Explain when large companies and public stock offerings can be sources of financing.

LOOKING AHEAD

LinkedIn contacts. "He's connected to a high level of company owners, v.p.-level executives and entrepreneurs," Mr. Concannon says. "If it was good enough for them, I wasn't going to pass it up."

Ron Immink of Dublin, chief executive of a consulting firm and founder of SmallBusinessCan.com, an online portal for small companies, was also won over by Mr. Hannigan's approach. Not only did he decide to invest, but he also plans on doing his next round of funding through LinkedIn. "It has a transparency to it," Mr. Immink says. "You can see who the promoters are connected to, and start-ups are all about people and team."

The final tally? Eight days after the note went out, all 10 of the investor spots were filled.

"I was completely blown away by the response," says Mr. Hannigan. The company raised the roughly $350,000 it needed, and Enterprise Ireland, a government agency dedicated to fostering emerging companies, matched the funds.

Nothing Personal

Matthew Cowan, co-founder and managing director of Bridgescale Partners, a venture-capital firm in Menlo Park, Calif., says that he isn't at all surprised by a small company taking this type of novel approach for its seed round of funding. "It's very telling of what's possible today. There is tremendous efficiency in applying social networking to a business context," Mr. Cowan says. "It would have taken them six months [to do the same thing] in the old world."

But Mr. Cowan isn't ready to embrace this approach just yet. "The accessibility of start-up investment opportunities through social networking may be a great temptation for many," he says, "but it may well mask the attendant risks, and many will lose 100% of their capital, because however you find them, start-ups are still risky bets."

Source: Adapted from Elizabeth Garone, "Dear Contact: Send Cash," *The Wall Street Journal,* November 15, 2010. http://online.wsj.com/article/SB10001424052748704141104575587930815328888.html, accessed February 24, 2011. Reprinted with permission of *The Wall Street Journal,*

In Chapter 11, we addressed *how much* financing is needed and *what types* of financing are available for small businesses. The basic types of financing include

1. *Spontaneous debt financing,* such as accounts payable and accruals, which increase in response to increases in sales. For example, as a firm's sales grow, it purchases more inventory and suppliers extend more credit, which increases accounts payable—a primary source of debt for many small businesses that requires no interest payments if paid on time.
2. *External financing,* which comes from outside lenders and investors. Lenders (such as bankers) provide debt capital, and investors (such as common stockholders, partners, or sole proprietors) provide equity financing.
3. *Profit retention,* which is provided by the cash flows generated by the business, or what we call *cash flows from operations.* Rather than being distributed in the form of dividends, the money is retained in the business and becomes part of the ownership equity on the balance sheet.

This chapter discusses the first two sources of financing: spontaneous debt financing and external financing. But first let's consider how the nature of a company affects the way it will be financed. An understanding of this core issue is critical to identifying appropriate sources of financing.

The Nature of a Firm and Its Financing Sources

Many entrepreneurs face the same problem: how to finance the business. In the last several years, finding sources of financing has become increasingly difficult because of a struggling economy. Thus, more discipline and creativity are required if an aspiring entrepreneur hopes to get a business off and running.

To begin, you must understand that four basic factors determine how a firm is financed: (1) the firm's economic potential, (2) the size and maturity of the company, (3) the nature of its assets, and (4) the personal preferences of the owners with respect to the trade-offs between debt and equity.

A FIRM'S ECONOMIC POTENTIAL

A firm with potential for high growth and large profits has more possible sources of financing than does a firm that provides a good lifestyle for the owner but little in the way of returns to investors. Only firms with a high rate of return on investment create value for the investor. In fact, most investors in startup companies limit their investment to firms that offer potentially high returns within a 5- to 10-year period. Clearly, a company that provides a comfortable lifestyle for its owner but insufficient profits to attract outside investors will find its options for alternative sources of financing limited.

COMPANY SIZE AND MATURITY

The size and maturity of a company have a direct bearing on the types of financing available. Larger and older firms have access to bank credit that may not be available to younger and smaller companies. Also, smaller firms rely more on personal loans and credit cards for financing. In the early years of a business, most entrepreneurs bootstrap their financing—that is, they depend on their own initiative to come up with the necessary capital. Only after the business has an established track record will most bankers and other financial institutions be willing to provide financing.

You have probably read about venture capitalists who helped finance such firms as Yahoo!, eBay, and Apple. But even venture capitalists limit how much they will invest in startup companies. Many such investors believe the additional risk associated with startups is too great relative to the returns they expect to receive. On average, about three-fourths of a venture capitalist's investments are in later-stage businesses; only a few focus heavily on startups. Similarly, bankers demand evidence that the business will be able to repay a loan—and that evidence usually must be based on what the firm has done in the past and not what the owner says it will achieve in the future. So, a firm's life-cycle position is a critical factor in raising capital.

ACTION

External Financing

Before approaching an investor:

- Clean up your personal credit.
- Identify your management team.
- Write an effective business plan.
- Decide what type of outside financing you need.
- Do careful research on potential investors.

TYPES OF ASSETS

A banker specifically considers two types of assets when evaluating a loan: tangible assets and intangible assets. Tangible assets, which can be seen and touched, include inventory, equipment, and buildings. The cost of these assets appears on the firm's balance sheet, which the banker receives as part of the firm's financial statements.

Tangible assets serve as great collateral when a firm is requesting a bank loan. On the other hand, intangible assets, such as goodwill or past investments in research and development, have little value as collateral. As a result, companies with substantial tangible assets have a much easier time borrowing money than do companies with intangible assets.

OWNER PREFERENCES FOR DEBT OR EQUITY

The owner of a company faces the question "Should I finance with debt or equity, or some mix of the two?" The answer depends, in part, on his or her personal preference. The ultimate choice between debt and equity involves certain trade-offs, which will be explained in the next section.

Debt or Equity Financing?

Most providers of financial capital specialize in *either* debt *or* equity financing. Furthermore, the choice between debt and equity financing must be made early in a firm's life cycle and may have long-term financial consequences. To make an informed decision, a small business owner needs to recognize and understand the trade-offs between debt and equity with regard to potential profitability, financial risk, and voting control. The trade-offs are presented graphically in Exhibit 12.1. Let's consider each of these trade-offs in turn.

EXHIBIT 12.1 Tradeoffs Between Debt and Equity

High Equity and Low Debt Financing

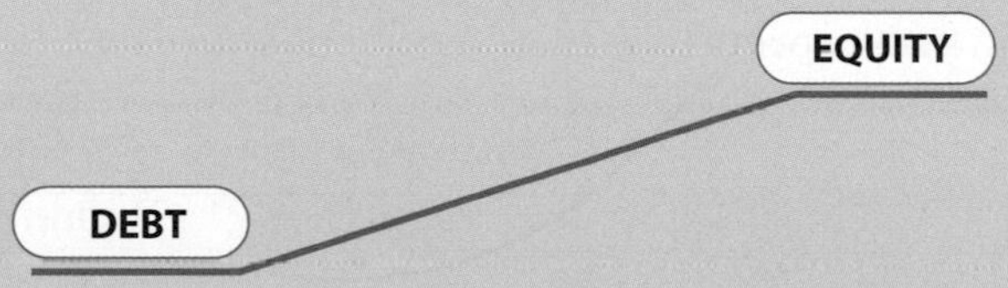

EQUITY

DEBT

Results:
Voting Control: Owners must share control with other equity investors who buy the stock or make a large investment.
Financial Risk: Lower
Potential Profitability: Lower potential return on investment for the owners

High Debt and Low Equity Financing

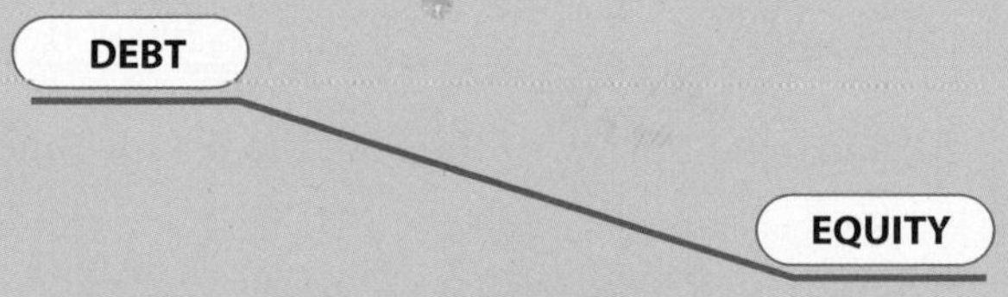

DEBT

EQUITY

Results:
Voting Control: Owners maintain control without having to make a large investment.
Financial Risk: Higher
Potential Profitability: Higher potential return on investment for the owners

POTENTIAL PROFITABILITY

Anyone who owns a business wants it to be profitable. Of course, profits can be measured as a dollar amount, such as $500,000, or as a percentage return on the investment. But the really important question is how much profit the business makes relative to the size of the investment. In other words, the owner is primarily interested in the rate of return on the investment. Making $500,000 in profits may sound great, but not if the owner must invest $50 million to earn it. It would be better to purchase a certificate of deposit that earned, say, 2 percent; any rate over 1 percent would provide income greater than $500,000. To see how the choice between debt and equity affects potential profitability, consider the Levine Company, a new firm that's still in the process of raising needed capital.

- The owners have already invested $100,000 of their own money in the new business. To complete the financing, they need another $100,000.
- They are considering one of two options for raising the additional $100,000: (1) investors who would provide $100,000 for a 30 percent share of the firm's outstanding stock, or (2) a bank that would lend the money at an interest rate of 8 percent, so the interest expense each year would be $8,000 = (0.08 × $100,000).
- The firm's operating profits (earnings before interest and taxes) are expected to be $28,000 based on the following forecast:

Sales	$150,000
Cost of goods sold	80,000
Gross profit	$ 70,000
Operating expenses	(42,000)
Operating profits	$ 28,000

- With the additional $100,000 in financing, the firm's total assets would be $200,000 ($100,000 original equity plus $100,000 in additional financing).
- Based on the projected operating profits of $28,000 and total assets of $200,000, the firm expects to earn a 14 percent *return on assets,* computed as follows.

$$\text{Return on assets} = \frac{\text{Operating profits}}{\text{Total assets}} = \frac{\$28{,}000}{\$200{,}000} = 0.14$$

If the firm raises the additional $100,000 in equity, its balance sheet will appear as follows:

Total assets	$200,000
Debt	$ 0
Equity (founders and new investors)	200,000
Total debt and equity	$200,000

But if the firm instead borrows $100,000, the balance sheet will look like this:

Total assets	$200,000
Debt (8% interest rate)	$100,000
Equity (founders)	100,000
Total debt and equity	$200,000

If we assume no taxes (just to keep matters simple), we can use the above information to project the firm's net profits when the additional \$100,000 is financed by either equity or debt:

	Equity	**Debt**	
Operating profits	\$28,000	\$28,000	
Interest expense	0	(8,000)	= (0.08 × \$100,000)
Net profits	\$28,000	\$20,000	

From these computations, we see that net profits are greater if the firm finances with equity (\$28,000 net profits) than with debt (\$20,000 net profits). But the owners would have to invest *twice* as much money (\$200,000 rather than \$100,000) to avoid the \$8,000 interest expense and get the higher net profits.

Should owners always finance with equity to get higher net profits? Not necessarily. The return on the owners' investment, or *return on equity*, is a better measure of performance than the absolute dollar amount of net profits. Remember from Chapter 10 that

$$\text{Return on equity} = \frac{\text{Net profits}}{\text{Ownership equity}}$$

So when the firm uses *all* equity financing, the return on equity is 14 percent, computed as follows:

$$\text{Return on assets} = \frac{\text{Net profits}}{\text{Ownership equity}} = \frac{\$28{,}000}{\$200{,}000} = 0.14\text{, or }14\%$$

But if the additional financing comes from debt, leading to interest expense of \$8,000 and equity investment of only \$100,000, the rate of return on equity is 20 percent, calculated as follows:

$$\text{Return on equity} = \frac{\text{Net profits}}{\text{Owners' equity investment}} = \frac{\$20{,}000}{\$100{,}000} = 0.20\text{, or }20\%$$

Thus, Levine's return on equity is higher if half the firm's financing comes from equity and half from debt. By using only equity, Levine's owners will earn \$0.14 for every \$1 of equity invested; by using debt, they will earn \$0.20 for every \$1 of equity invested. So, in terms of a rate of return on their investment, Levine's owners get a better return by borrowing money at 8 percent interest than by using equity financing. That makes sense, because the firm is earning 14 percent on its assets but only paying creditors at an 8 percent rate. Levine's owners benefit from the difference. These relationships are shown in Exhibit 12.2.

As a general rule, *as long as a firm's rate of return on its assets (operating profits ÷ total assets) is greater than the cost of the debt (interest rate), the owners' rate of return on equity will increase as the firm uses more debt.*

"Autosum aside, these numbers just don't add up."

FINANCIAL RISK

If debt is so beneficial in terms of producing a higher rate of return for the owners, why shouldn't Levine's owners use as much debt as possible—even 100 percent debt—if they can? Then the rate of return on the owners' equity investment would be even higher—unlimited, in fact, if the owners did not have to invest any money.

That's the good news. The bad news: *Debt is risky.* If the firm fails to earn profits, creditors will still insist on having their money repaid, regardless of the firm's actual performance. In extreme cases, creditors can force firms into bankruptcy if they fail to honor their financial obligations.

EXHIBIT 12.2 Debt Versus Equity at the Levine Company

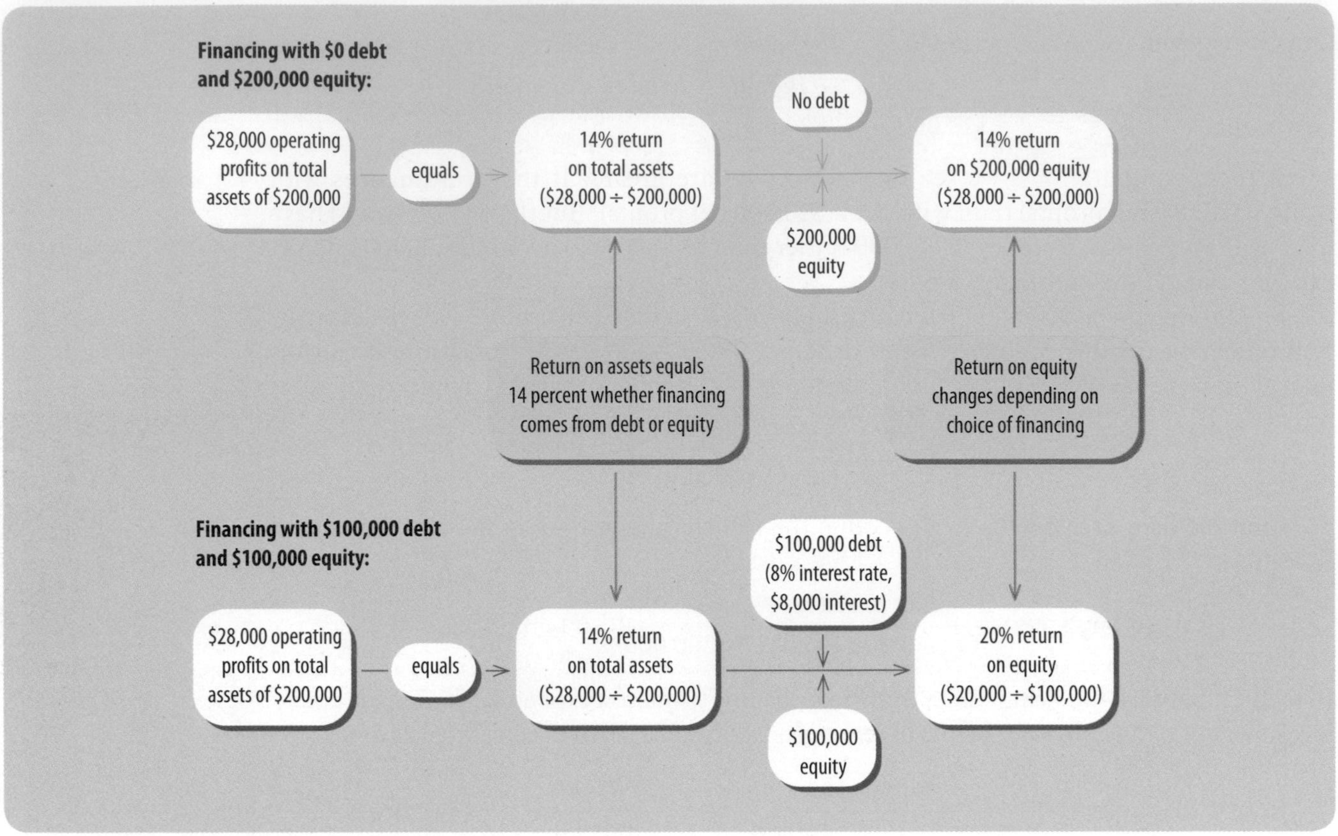

Financing with $0 debt and $200,000 equity:

$28,000 operating profits on total assets of $200,000 → equals → 14% return on total assets ($28,000 ÷ $200,000) → 14% return on $200,000 equity ($28,000 ÷ $200,000)

No debt

$200,000 equity

Return on assets equals 14 percent whether financing comes from debt or equity

Return on equity changes depending on choice of financing

Financing with $100,000 debt and $100,000 equity:

$28,000 operating profits on total assets of $200,000 → equals → 14% return on total assets ($28,000 ÷ $200,000) → 20% return on equity ($20,000 ÷ $100,000)

$100,000 debt (8% interest rate, $8,000 interest)

$100,000 equity

Equity, on the other hand, is less demanding. If a firm is not profitable, an equity investor must accept the disappointing results and hope for better results next year. Equity investors cannot demand more than what is earned.

Another way to view the negative side of debt is to contemplate what happens to the return on equity if a business has a bad year. Suppose that instead of earning 14 percent on its assets, or $28,000 in operating profits, the Levine Company earns a mere $2,000—only 1 percent on its assets of $200,000. The return on equity would again depend on whether the firm used debt or equity to finance the second $100,000 investment in the company. The results would be as follows:

	Equity	**Debt**
Operating profits	$2,000	$2,000
Interest expense	0	(8,000) = (0.08 × $100,000)
Net profits	$2,000	($6,000)

If the added financing came in the form of equity, the return on equity would be a disappointing 1 percent:

$$\text{Return on equity} = \frac{\text{Net profits}}{\text{Owners' equity investment}} = \frac{\$20{,}000}{\$200{,}000} = 0.01, \text{ or } 1\%$$

But if debt were used, the return on equity would be a painful negative 6 percent:

$$\text{Return on equity} = \frac{\text{Net profits}}{\text{Owners' equity investment}} = \frac{-\$6{,}000}{\$100{,}000} = -0.06, \text{ or } -6\%$$

If only 1 percent is earned on the assets, the owners would be better off if they financed solely with equity. Thus, debt is a double-edged sword—it cuts both ways. If debt financing is used and things go well, they will go *very* well for the owners; but if things go badly, they will go *very* badly for the owners. In short, debt financing makes business more risky.

VOTING CONTROL

The third issue in choosing between debt and equity is the degree of control retained by owners. Raising new capital through equity financing would mean giving up a part of the firm's ownership, and most owners of small firms resist giving up control to outsiders.

entrepreneurial experiences

LIVING THE DREAM

© iStockphoto.com/Angelika Schwarz

Success Is a Positive Cash Flow

The last 12 months were a whirlwind for Colin Roche and Bobby Ronsse, who, in 2001, founded Pacifica, California–based Pacific Writing Instruments. The cause for their excitement? Their company's ergonomic pen, the Pen Again, was now being carried in more than 2,000 stores, including Walmart, Office Depot, Publix, and FedEx Office. In other words, they had arrived.

But they found that business growth can be a double-edged sword. "Before our product got into the big stores, we weren't selling as many pens, but business was steadier, the fluctuations weren't as big, and the dollar amounts were certainly a lot smaller," Ronsse says. "If we needed $10,000, we could find it pretty easily from our own savings, a bank loan, or a business line of credit. But when you're selling 100,000 pens and you have to pay your factory $50,000 before you get paid for those pens, then your sources for solving cash flow problems are a lot more limited."

The key, Ronsse says, is to be prepared; line up and weigh your options way before feeling the cash squeeze.

"There's always a way to get the money," he says. "It just depends on how much you want to give up. Money's not free, so you either have to pay interest or give up equity in your company to investors."

Besides having investors by their side from day one, Ronsse and Roche worked out pay-when-paid arrangements with some of their sub-suppliers, including the factory that makes the pens. "It's a best-case scenario, but it's not something you can count on," he says. The deal was approved because the company had built its reputation by paying on time and providing the factory with a steady stream of business.

As a backup, Roche says, they have also looked into a process called *factoring*, or accounts receivable funding. In this scenario, Pacific Writing Instruments would sell a purchase order at a discount to a third-party lender (the factor), who would then be paid by the store that ordered the pens. This process would let their company pay for up-front costs associated with the big order—but would require them to take a loss on the profits from the sale. Factoring isn't ideal, but it could save a business that is experiencing a cash flow crunch.

"You can be a super-successful company, have a great product distributed all over the place, be profitable, and still go out of business because of cash flow," Ronsse says. "You have to have quick access to capital. Nothing else matters if you can't pay your bills."

Source: Lena Basha, "Handle the Headaches: Confronting Five Big Burdens of Business Ownership," *MyBusiness*, June/July 2007, pp. 26–31.

They do not want to be accountable in any way to minority owners, much less take the chance of possibly losing control of the business.

Out of an aversion to losing control, many small business owners choose to finance with debt rather than with equity. They realize that debt increases risk, but it also permits them to retain full ownership of the firm.

With an understanding of the basic trade-offs to be considered when choosing between debt and equity, let's now look at specific sources of financing. Where do small business owners go to find the money to finance their companies?

Sources of Financing

When initially financing a small business, an owner will typically rely on personal savings and then seek financing from family and friends. If these sources are inadequate, the owner may in certain circumstances turn to more formal channels of financing, such as banks and outside investors.

Exhibit 12.3 gives an overview of the sources of financing of smaller companies. As indicated, some sources of financing—such as banks, business suppliers, asset-based lenders, and the government—are essentially limited to providing debt financing. Equity financing for most small business owners comes from personal savings and, in rare instances, from selling stock to the public. Other sources—including friends and family, other individual investors, venture capitalists (rarely), and large corporations—may provide either debt or equity financing, depending on the situation. Keep in mind that the use of these and other sources of funds are not limited to a startup's initial financing. Such sources will also be used to finance a firm's day-to-day operations and business expansions.

To gain insight into how startups are financed, consider the responses given by owners of *Inc.* 500 firms—the 500 fastest-growing, privately held firms in the United States—when they were asked about the financing sources they used to start their firms. Even for these high-growth firms, 70 percent of the startup financing came from the founders' personal savings, with another 10 percent coming from friends and family and 8 percent from

EXHIBIT 12.3 Sources of Funds

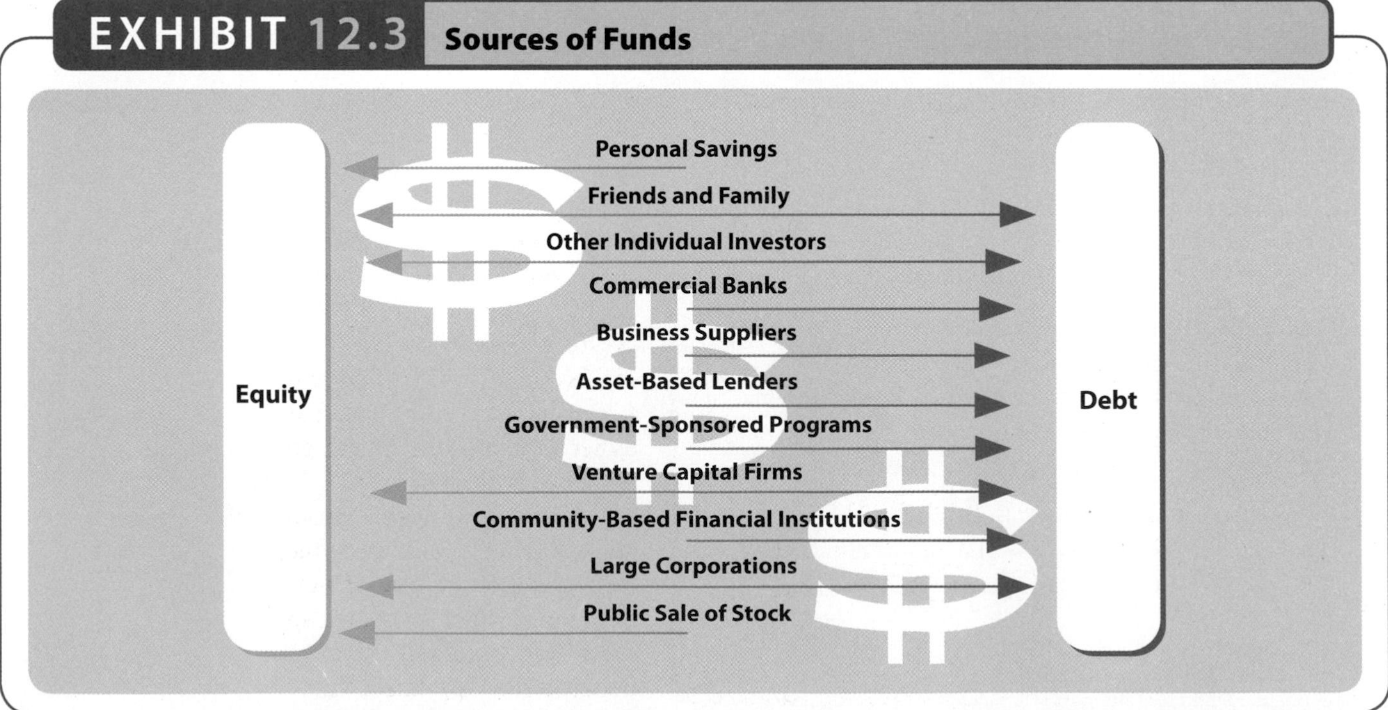

bank loans. The remaining sources of financing were relatively insignificant in starting the firms. However, within five years the *Inc.* 500 entrepreneurs had, on average, raised 17 percent of their financing from private investors and 12 percent from venture capitalists.[1]

Let's now consider the following specific sources of financing for smaller companies: (1) sources "close to home"—personal savings, friends and family, and credit cards, (2) bank financing, which becomes a primary financing source as the firm grows, (3) business suppliers and asset-based lenders, (4) private equity investors, (5) the government, and (6) large companies and stock sales.

SOURCES CLOSE TO HOME

The search for financial support usually begins close to home. A small business owner basically has three sources of early financing: personal savings, friends and family, and credit cards.

Personal Savings

It is imperative for an entrepreneur to have some personal investment in the business, which typically comes from personal savings. Indeed, personal savings is by far the most common source of equity financing used to start a new business, which needs equity to allow for a margin of error. In its first few years, a firm can ill afford large fixed outlays for debt repayment. Also, a banker—or anyone else—is unlikely to loan money if the owner does not have his or her own money at risk.

A problem for many people who want to start a business is that they lack sufficient personal savings for this purpose. It can be very discouraging when the banker asks, "How much will you be investing in the business?" or "What do you have for collateral to secure the loan you want?" There is no easy solution to this problem, which is faced by an untold number of entrepreneurs. Nonetheless, many individuals who lack personal savings for a startup find ways to own their own companies without spending large amounts of money. And they figure out how to grow the business—perhaps by using the cash flows being generated from the firm's operations, by using other people's resources, or by finding a partner or friends and relatives who will provide the necessary financing.

Friends and Family

While personal savings serve as the *primary* source of financing for most small business startups, friends and family are a distant second. They provide almost 80 percent of startup capital beyond the entrepreneur's personal savings.[2] Entrepreneurs who acquire financing from friends and family are putting more than just their financial futures on the line—they're putting important personal relationships at risk, too. "It's the highest-risk money you'll ever get," says David Deeds, professor of entrepreneurship at Case Western Reserve University in Cleveland, Ohio. "The venture may succeed or fail, but either way, you still have to go to Thanksgiving dinner."

At times, loans from friends or relatives may be the only available source of new financing. Such loans can often be obtained quickly, because they are based more

RESOURCES

Getting Money from People You Know

The idea of raising money from friends and family is often uncomfortable. But don't let that stop you. Asking people you know to pitch in on financing a business is not exactly a novel idea. Before money as we know it was invented, person-to-person loans were the way many businesses got started—and the way many investors made a profit.

on personal relationships than on financial analyses. *But you should accept money from a friend or relative only if that person will not be hurt financially to any significant extent if the entire amount is lost.* In other words, do not borrow money from your brother if he cannot afford the loss, much less from your grandmother's retirement savings.

Friends and relatives who provide business loans sometimes feel that they have the right to offer suggestions concerning the management of the business. And hard business times may strain the relationship. But if relatives and friends are the only available source of financing, the entrepreneur may have no other alternative. To minimize the chance of damaging important personal relationships, the entrepreneur should plan to repay such loans as soon as possible. In addition, any agreements should be put in writing, as memories tend to become fuzzy over time. It is best to clarify expectations up front, rather than be disappointed or angry later.

Some good advice comes from James Hutcheson, president of Regeneration Partners, a Dallas, Texas–based consulting group that specializes in family-owned businesses, who says that entrepreneurs should approach their relatives only after they have secured investments or loans from unbiased outside sources.

> *Go and get matching funds. If you need $25,000, then first get $12,500 from others before asking your family for the rest. If you can't do it that way—and if you don't have your own skin in the game—then you need to think twice about why you're asking someone you love to give you money. I believe you should get others to back the idea as well, so a parent or relative doesn't feel as though the money is a gift but rather a worthwhile investment. It puts a higher level of accountability into the entire process.*[3]

So use friends and family very cautiously. Do it if necessary—and carefully and meticulously clarify expectations.

Credit Cards

Prior to the 2008–2009 financial crisis, unsolicited offers of "free" credit cards arrived in the mail almost daily for many individuals. Using credit cards to help finance a small business became increasingly common among entrepreneurs. It has been estimated that approximately half of all entrepreneurs have used credit cards at one time or another to finance a startup or business expansion. Even though credit card companies began experiencing huge losses in 2009, credit cards remain a significant source of financing for many small business owners.

For someone who cannot acquire traditional financing like a bank loan, credit card financing may be an option—not a great option, but a necessary one. The interest costs can become overwhelming over time, especially because of the tendency to borrow beyond the ability to repay. So it is essential that an entrepreneur using credit card financing be extremely self-disciplined to avoid becoming overextended. That's what happened to Steven Fischer. Unable to get a line of credit from a bank, Fischer used his personal credit cards to keep his business operating after his firm was unable to collect receivables from some of his clients. He anticipated using his cards to keep his company afloat until they were paid; however, paying wages and bills proved to be more expensive than he had anticipated. Also, mixing his personal credit cards with business loans and expenses created problems. In the

end, Fischer's company didn't survive.[4] After laying off his employees and paying all of the business's bills, Fischer found himself personally liable for $80,000 in credit card debt.

So why use credit cards? At times the only option open to a small business entrepreneur, credit cards also have the advantage of speed. A lender at a bank has to be convinced of the merits of the business opportunity, and that involves extensive preparation on the part of the entrepreneur. Credit card financing, on the other hand, requires no justification of the use of the money.

In practice, credit cards are a significant source of financing for a number of entrepreneurs, particularly early in the game. But the eventual goal is to use credit cards as a method of payment and not as a source of credit. In other words, the sooner you can pay your credit card balance in full each month, the sooner you can grow a profitable business.

BANK FINANCING

In 2010, lending by banks and other financial institutions to small businesses had decreased by $40 billion from two years earlier.[5] Many small business owners caught in the middle of a severe recession were not just frustrated about their inability to grow their business, some were fearful of not being able to survive. Their inability to get loans from banks was their greatest concern. By mid-year 2011, the problem seemed to be easing.

Commercial banks are primary providers of debt capital to *established* firms. Quite simply, they want firms with proven track records and plenty of collateral in the form of hard assets. Bankers are reluctant to loan money to finance losses, R&D expenses, marketing campaigns, and other "soft" assets. Such expenditures should be financed by equity sources. Nevertheless, it is wise to cultivate a relationship with a banker sooner rather than later, and well in advance of making a loan request.

Types of Loans

Bankers primarily make business loans in one of three forms: lines of credit, term loans, and mortgages.

LINES OF CREDIT A **line of credit** is an informal agreement or understanding between a borrower and a bank as to the maximum amount of credit the bank will provide the borrower at any one time. Under this type of agreement, the bank has no legal obligation to provide the capital. (A similar arrangement that *does* legally commit the bank is a *revolving credit agreement*.) The entrepreneur should arrange for a line of credit in advance of an actual need as banks are reluctant to extend credit on the spur of the moment.

line of credit
An informal agreement between a borrower and a bank as to the maximum amount of funds the bank will provide at any one time.

TERM LOANS Under certain circumstances, banks will loan money on a 5- to 10-year term. Such **term loans** are generally used to finance equipment with a useful life corresponding to the loan's term. Since the economic benefits of investing in such equipment extend beyond a single year, banks can be persuaded to lend on terms that more closely match the cash flows to be received from the investment. For example, if equipment has a useful life of seven years, it might be possible to repay the money needed to purchase the equipment over, say, five years. It would be a mistake for a firm to borrow money for a short term, such as six months, when the money is to be used to buy equipment that is expected to last for seven years. *Failure to match the loan's payment terms with the expected cash inflows from the investment is a frequent cause of financial problems for small firms.* The importance of synchronizing cash inflows with cash outflows when structuring the terms of a loan cannot be overemphasized.

term loan
Money loaned for a 5- to 10-year term, corresponding to the length of time the investment will bring in profits.

Some loans call for term payments that include principal and interest, others for interest only with lump sum principal reductions. If in doubt, ask your banker for advice: "I want to expand. Here's the loan I think I need. What do you think?"

MORTGAGES Mortgages, which represent a long-term source of debt capital, can be one of two types: chattel mortgages and real estate mortgages. A **chattel mortgage** is a

chattel mortgage
A loan for which items of inventory or other movable property serve as collateral.

loan for which certain items of inventory or other movable property serve as collateral. The borrower retains title to the inventory but cannot sell it without the banker's consent. A **real estate mortgage** is a loan for which real property, such as land or a building, provides the collateral. Typically, these mortgages extend up to 25 or 30 years.

real estate mortgage
A long-term loan with real property held as collateral.

Understanding a Banker's Perspective

To be effective in acquiring a loan, an entrepreneur needs to understand that a banker has three priorities when making a loan. In the order of importance to the banker, they are

1. *Recouping the principal of the loan.* A banker is not rewarded adequately to assume large amounts of risk and will, therefore, design loan agreements so as to reduce the risk to the bank. First and foremost, the banker has to protect depositors' capital.
2. *Determining the amount of income the loan will provide the bank,* both in interest income and in other forms of income, such as fees.
3. *Helping the borrower be successful and then become a larger customer.* Only if the relationship is a win-win for both parties will the bank do well.

In making a loan decision, a banker always considers the "five C's of credit": (1) the borrower's *character,* (2) the borrower's *capacity* to repay the loan, (3) the *capital* being invested in the venture by the borrower, (4) the *conditions* of the industry and economy, and (5) the *collateral* available to secure the loan. These issues are apparent in the six questions that Jack Griggs, a banker and long-time lender to small businesses, wants answered before he will make a loan:[6]

1. Do the purpose and amount of the loan make sense, both for the bank and for the borrower?
2. Does the borrower have strong character and reasonable ability?
3. Does the loan have a certain primary source of repayment?
4. Does the loan have a certain secondary source of repayment?
5. Can the loan be priced profitably for the customer and for the bank, and are this loan and the relationship good for both the customer and the bank?
6. Can the loan be properly structured and documented?

A banker's review of a loan request includes analysis of financial considerations. This analysis is best complemented by a personal relationship between the banker and the small business owner. Remember, the loan decision is driven in part by the banker's confidence in the entrepreneur as a person and a professional.

When seeking a loan, a small business owner will be required to provide certain information in support of the loan request. Failure to provide this information will almost certainly result in rejection by the banker. Presenting

ACTION

Bankers Don't Like Surprises

Never surprise your banker with bad news. Tell your banker immediately if you are having a problem, and let him or her work with you. When you avoid a banker when things go wrong, you may be perceived as not being forthright and may lose your banker's trust. Face up to the problem rather than hoping you can fix it before it is discovered.

inaccurate information or not being able to justify assumptions made in forecasting financial results is sure to make the banker question the entrepreneur's business acumen.

A well-prepared loan request is absolutely necessary. Capturing the firm's history and future in writing suggests that the entrepreneur has given thought to where the firm has been and where it is going. As part of the presentation, the banker will want to know early on the answers to the following questions:

- How much money is needed?
- What is the venture going to do with the money?
- When is the money needed?
- When and how will the money be paid back?

An example of a written loan request is provided in Exhibit 12.4. A banker also will want, if at all possible, to see the following detailed financial information:

- Three years of the firm's historical financial statements, if available, including balance sheets, income statements, and cash flow statements
- The firm's pro forma financial statements (balance sheets, income statements, and cash flow statements), in which the timing and amounts of the debt repayment are included as part of the forecasts
- Personal financial statements showing the borrower's net worth (net worth = assets – debt) and estimated annual income. A banker simply will not make a loan without knowing the personal financial strength of the borrower.

EXHIBIT 12.4 Sample Written Loan Request

Date of Request:	December 15, 2011	
Borrower:	Prestige & DeLay, Inc.	
Amount:	$1,000,000	
Use of Proceeds:	Accounts receivable	$ 400,000
	Inventory	200,000
	Marketing	100,000
	Officer loans due	175,000
	Salaries	75,000
	Contingencies	50,000
		$1,000,000
Type of Loan	Revolving Line of Credit	
Closing Date	January 3, 2012	
Term	12 months	
Rate	8.5%	
Takedown	$400,000 at closing	
	$300,000 at March 1, 2012	
	$200,000 at June 1, 2012	
	$100,000 on September 1, 2012	
Collateral	70 percent of accounts receivable under 90 days	
	50 percent of current inventory	
Guarantees	Guarantees to be provided by Prestige & DeLay	
Repayment Schedule	Principal and all accrued interest due on anniversary of note	
Source of Funds for Repayment	a. Excess cash from operations (see cash flow)	
	b. Renewable and increase of line if growth is profitable	
	c. Conversion to three-year note	
Contingency Source	Sale and leaseback of equipment	

Selecting a Banker

The wide variety of services provided by banks makes choosing a bank an important decision. For a typical small firm, the provision of checking-account facilities and the extension of short-term (and possibly long-term) loans are the two most important services of a bank. Normally, loans are negotiated with the same bank in which the firm maintains its checking account. In addition, the firm may use the bank's safe-deposit vault or its services in collecting notes or securing credit information. An experienced banker can also provide management advice, particularly in financial matters, to a new entrepreneur.

Stockbyte/Jupiter Images

The location factor limits the range of possible choices of banks. For convenience in making deposits and conferring about loans and other matters, a bank should be located in the same general vicinity as the firm. All banks are interested in their home communities and, therefore, tend to be sympathetic to the needs of local business firms. Except in very small communities, two or more local banks are usually available, thus permitting some freedom of choice.

Banks' lending policies are not uniform. Some bankers are extremely conservative, while others are more willing to accept some limited risks. If a small firm's loan application is neither obviously strong nor patently weak, its prospects for approval depend heavily on the bank's approach to small business accounts. Differences in willingness to lend have been clearly established by research studies, as well as by the practical experience of many business borrowers.

Negotiating the Loan

In negotiating a bank loan, a small business owner must consider the terms that will accompany the loan. Four key terms are included in all loan agreements: the interest rate, the loan maturity date, the repayment schedule, and the loan covenants.

prime rate
The interest rate charged by commercial banks on loans to their most creditworthy customers.

LIBOR (London InterBank Offered Rate)
The interest rate charged by London banks on loans to other London banks.

INTEREST RATE The interest rate charged by banks is usually stated in terms of either the prime rate or the LIBOR. The **prime rate** is the rate of interest charged by banks on loans to their most creditworthy customers. The **LIBOR (London InterBank Offered Rate)** is the interest rate that London-based banks charge other banks in London, which is considerably lower than the prime rate. This rate is published each day in the *Wall Street Journal*.

If a banker quotes a rate of "prime plus 3" and the prime rate is 5 percent, the interest rate for the loan will be 8 percent. If, alternatively, the bank is willing to loan at "LIBOR plus 4" when the LIBOR is at 3 percent, then the loan rate will be 7 percent. The interest rate can be a floating rate that varies over the loan's life—that is, as the prime rate or LIBOR changes, the interest rate on the loan changes—or it can be fixed for the duration of the loan. Although a small firm should always seek a competitive interest rate, concern about the interest rate should not override consideration of the loan's maturity date, its repayment schedule, and any loan covenants.

LOAN MATURITY DATE As already noted, a loan's term should coincide with the use of the money—short-term needs require short-term financing, while long-term needs demand long-term financing. For example, since a line of credit is intended to help a firm with only its short-term needs, it is generally limited to one year. Some banks require that a firm "clean up" a line of credit one month each year. Because such a loan can be outstanding for only 11 months, the borrower can use the money to finance seasonal needs but cannot use it to provide permanent increases in working capital, such as accounts receivable and inventory.

REPAYMENT SCHEDULE With a term loan, the loan is set to be repaid over 5 to 10 years, depending on the type of assets used for collateral. However, the banker may have the option of imposing a **balloon payment** before the loan is fully repaid. A balloon payment allows the bank to require the borrower to pay off the balance of the loan in full at a specified time, rather than waiting the full term for the loan to be repaid.

balloon payment
A very large payment required about halfway through the term over which payments were calculated, repaying the loan balance in full.

Numerical Example

Assume that you borrow $50,000 at an interest rate of 6 percent, and the loan is to be repaid in equal monthly repayments over 84 months (7 years). Using a calculator or computer spreadsheet, you can determine that the amount of each payment would need to be $730 in order to pay off the loan in full by the end of the 7 years.[7] However, the banker may include a term in the loan agreement so that the bank has the right to "call" the loan at the end of 3 years, meaning that you have to pay off what is still owed at that time. In our example, you would still owe $31,100 at the end of the third year. The banker would have the choice of (1) requiring you to pay off the $31,100 at the end of the third year, or (2) allowing you to have the remaining 4 years to pay off the loan. This provision permits the banker to reassess the borrower's creditworthiness at the end of the third year if the business is not doing well.

LOAN COVENANTS In addition to setting the interest rate and specifying when and how the loan is to be repaid, a bank normally imposes other restrictions, or what are called loan covenants, on the borrower. **Loan covenants** require certain activities (positive covenants) and limit other activities (negative covenants) of the borrower to increase the chance that the borrower will be able to repay the loan. Some types of loan covenants that a borrower might encounter include the following:

loan covenants
Bank-imposed restrictions on a borrower that enhance the chance of timely repayment.

1. The company must provide financial statements to the bank on a monthly basis or, at the very least, quarterly (positive covenant).
2. As a way to restrict a firm's management from siphoning cash out of the business, the bank may limit managers' salaries. It also may prohibit any personal loans from the business to the owners (negative covenant).
3. A bank may put limits on various financial ratios to make certain that a firm can handle its loan payments. For example, to ensure sufficient liquidity, the bank may require the firm's current assets to be at least twice its current liabilities (that is, current assets ÷ current liabilities must be equal to or greater than 2). Or the bank might limit the amount of debt the firm can borrow in the future, as measured by the ratio of total debt to the firm's total assets (total debt ÷ total assets) (negative covenant).[8]
4. The borrower will normally be required to personally guarantee the firm's loan. A banker wants the right to use both the firm's assets and the owner's personal assets as collateral. Even when a business is structured as a corporation and the owner can escape personal liability for the firm's debts—that is, the owner has **limited liability**—most banks still require the owner's personal guarantee (negative covenant).[9]

limited liability
Restriction of an owner's legal financial responsibilities to the amount invested in the business.

When Bill Bailey, owner of Cherokee Communications, located in Jacksonville, Texas, borrowed money, the loan was made on certain conditions—conditions that were intended to protect the banker. If Cherokee violated these loan covenants, the loan would become due immediately—or Bailey would have to get the banker's blessing to continue operations without repaying the loan at the time. Some of the loan covenants were as follows:[10]

- Bailey, as the owner, was required to personally guarantee the loan.
- The firm had to provide monthly financial statements to the bank within 30 days of the month's end.
- There were to be no dividend payments to the owners.
- Debt could not exceed a specified amount, nor could it be greater than a specified percentage of the firm's total assets.
- The proceeds of the loan could not be used for any other purpose than that designated by the bank.
- Executive compensation could not exceed a specified amount.

It is imperative that you pay close attention to the loan covenants being imposed by a banker. Ask for a list of the covenants before the closing date, and make certain that you can live with the terms. If you have an existing company, determine whether you could have complied with the covenants, especially key ratios, if the loan had been in place during the recent past. Then, if necessary, negotiate with your banker and suggest more realistic covenants. Bankers will negotiate, although they may sometimes try to convince you otherwise.

BUSINESS SUPPLIERS AND ASSET-BASED LENDERS

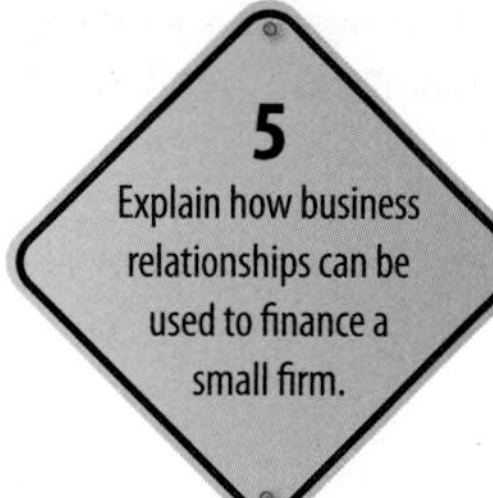

Companies that have business dealings with a new firm are possible sources of funds for financing inventory and equipment. Both wholesalers and equipment manufacturers/suppliers may provide accounts payable (trade credit) or equipment loans and leases.

Accounts Payable (Trade Credit)

Credit extended by suppliers is very important to a startup. In fact, trade (or mercantile) credit is the source of short-term funds most widely used by small firms. As mentioned in Chapter 10, *accounts payable (trade credit)* is of short duration—30 days is the customary credit period. Most commonly, this type of credit involves an unsecured, open-book account. The supplier (seller) sends merchandise to the purchasing firm; the buyer then sets up an account payable for the amount of the purchase.

The amount of trade credit available to a new company depends on the type of business and the supplier's confidence in the firm. For example, wholesale distributors of sunglasses—a very seasonal product line—often provide trade credit to retailers by granting extended payment terms on sales made at the start of a season. The sunglass retailers, in turn, sell to their customers during the season and make the bulk of their payments to the wholesalers after they have sold and collected the cash for the sunglasses. Thus, the retailer obtains cash from sales before paying the supplier. More often, however, a firm has to pay its suppliers prior to receiving cash from its customers. In fact, this can be a serious problem for many small firms, particularly those that sell to large companies. (This issue will be addressed in a discussion of asset management in Chapter 22.)

equipment loan
An installment loan from a seller of machinery used by a business.

Equipment Loans and Leases

Some small businesses, such as restaurants, use equipment that is purchased on an installment basis through an **equipment loan**. A down payment of 25 to 35 percent is usually required, and the contract period normally runs from three to five years. The equipment manufacturer or supplier typically extends credit on the basis of a conditional sales contract (or mortgage) on the equipment. During the loan period, the equipment cannot serve as collateral for another loan.

Instead of borrowing money from suppliers to purchase equipment, an increasing number of small businesses choose to lease equipment, especially computers, photocopiers, and fax machines. Leases typically run for 36 to 60 months and cover 100 percent of the cost of the asset being leased, with a fixed rate of interest included in the lease payments. However, manufacturers of computers and industrial machinery, working hand in hand with banks or financing companies, are generally receptive to tailoring lease packages to the particular needs of customers.

It has been estimated that 80 percent of all firms lease some or all of their business equipment. Three reasons are commonly given for the popularity of leasing: (1) the firm's cash remains free for other purposes, (2) available lines of credit (a form of bank loan discussed earlier in this chapter) can be used for other purposes, and (3) leasing provides a hedge against equipment obsolescence.

While leasing is certainly an option to be considered for financing the acquisition of needed equipment, a small business owner should not simply assume that leasing is always the right decision. A business owner can make a good choice only after carefully comparing the interest charged on a loan to the implied interest cost of a lease, calculating the tax consequences of leasing versus borrowing, and examining the significance of the obsolescence factor. Also, the owner must be careful about contracting for so much equipment that it becomes difficult to meet installment or lease payments.

asset-based loan
A line of credit secured by working capital assets.

Asset-Based Lending

As its name implies, an **asset-based loan** is a line of credit secured by assets, such as receivables, inventory, or both. The lender cushions its risk by advancing only a percentage of the value of a firm's assets—generally, 65 to 85 percent against receivables and up to 55 percent against inventory. Also, assets such as equipment (if not leased) and real estate can be used as collateral for an asset based loan. Asset-based lending is a viable option for young, growing businesses.

factoring
Obtaining cash by selling accounts receivable to another firm.

Of the several categories of asset-based lending, the most frequently used is factoring. **Factoring** is an option that makes cash available to a business before accounts receivable payments are received from customers. Under this option, a factor (an entity often owned by a bank holding company) purchases the accounts receivable, advancing to the business 70 to 90 percent of the amount of an invoice. The factor, however, has the option of refusing to advance cash on any invoice it considers questionable. The factor charges a servicing fee, usually 2 percent of the value of the receivables, and an interest charge on the money advanced prior to collection of the receivables. The interest charge may range from 2 to 3 percent above the prime rate.

"And here's where we ran out of purchase orders."

purchase-order financing
Obtaining cash from a lender who, for a fee, advances the amount of the borrower's cost of goods sold for a specific customer order.

Another way to finance working capital is to sell purchase orders. With **purchase-order financing**, the lender advances the amount of the borrower's cost of goods sold for a specific customer order less a fee, typically somewhere between 3 and 8 percent. For instance, for a purchase order of $20,000, with the cost of goods sold being $12,000, the lender will advance the $12,000 less the fee charged. According to Jason Goldberg, vice president of marketing for Westgate Financial, this type of financing "attempts to address the issue of a company growing so rapidly that cash flow can't sustain growth." With a signed purchase order from a creditworthy customer, you can often get financing for almost the entire process, provided your gross profit margin (gross profit ÷ sales) is at least 35 percent. Although the fee is not insignificant, it makes sense when the entrepreneur would not otherwise be able to accept an order from a large customer. In times when credit is scarce, Goldberg says, it's an opportunity "to leverage the ability to sell product."[11]

PRIVATE EQUITY INVESTORS

Over the past two decades, private equity markets have been the fastest-growing source of financing for entrepreneurial ventures with the potential for becoming significant businesses. For an entrepreneur, these sources fall into two categories: business angels and venture capitalists.

Business Angels

business angels Private individuals who invest in others' entrepreneurial venture.

informal venture capital Funds provided by wealthy private individuals to high-risk ventures.

Business angels are private individuals who invest in early-stage companies.[12] They are the oldest and largest source of early-stage equity capital for entrepreneurs. According to the Center for Venture Research at the University of New Hampshire, angel investments in 2010 amounted to $20.1 billion. A total of 61,900 businesses received funding from an estimated 265,400 angel investors.[13]

The term *angel* originated in the early 1900s, referring to investors on Broadway who made risky investments to support theatrical productions.[14] This type of financing has come to be known as **informal venture capital** because no established marketplace exists in which business angels regularly invest.

The majority of these individuals are self-made millionaires who have substantial business and entrepreneurial experience. Bill Payne, an experienced business angel from Las Vegas, Nevada, and Entrepreneur-in-Residence at the Kauffman Foundation, describes angels in these words:

> *Angels invest time and money in startup companies. For most, making money is not the primary motive for investing. These angels have "put away their nuts" for retirement and are investing their "mad money" in entrepreneurs. They do so for a variety of reasons . . . [to] give back to their communities, [to have] the opportunity to work with entrepreneurs, to stay engaged in their retirement years and to work with fellow angels in building enterprises, to name a few. Return on investment is an important metric of their success, but not normally their primary motive for engagement.*[15]

Business angels generally make investments in firms that are relatively small—over 80 percent of business angels invest in startup firms with fewer than 20 employees. They invest locally, usually no more than 50 miles from their homes. Some limit their investments to industries in which they have had experience, while others invest in a wide variety of business sectors.

Along with providing needed money, business angels frequently contribute know-how to new businesses. Because many of these individuals invest only in the types of businesses in which they have had experience, they can be very demanding. While they are generally more "friendly" as investors than some venture capitalists, their personal relationship with the entrepreneur has little impact on their decision to invest—unlike friends and family. Thus, the entrepreneur must be careful in structuring the terms of any such investors' involvement.

The traditional way to find informal investors is through contacts with business associates, accountants, and lawyers. Other entrepreneurs are also a primary source of help in identifying prospective investors. In addition, there are now a large number of formal angel networks and angel alliances in all major cities, both in the United States and abroad. Each angel group will have its own process for evaluating deals. For instance, some angel groups require entrepreneurs who are seeking funding to post their business plan on www.angelsoft.net. The angels then access the website to read the submitted plans. The group screens the plans and selects those entrepreneurs who will be allowed to present to the group. In most cases, individual angels then make personal decisions about whether or not to invest, regardless of what the other angels do. If enough angels are interested, a detailed evaluation is undertaken before a final decision is made.[16]

Guy Kawasaki, the founder of Garage Technology Ventures, is now a venture capitalist in Silicon Valley and author of *The Art of the Start* (a must-read for anyone wanting to start a new business). He offers the following suggestions about dealing with business angels:[17]

1. *Make sure the investors are accredited.* "Accredited" is legalese for "rich enough to never get back a penny." You can get into trouble for selling stock to those who aren't accredited—so don't.
2. *Make sure they're sophisticated.* Sophisticated angel investors have "been there and done that." You want angels' money, but you also want their knowledge and expertise.
3. *Don't underestimate them.* The idea that angel investors are easy marks is simply wrong. Angels care as much about how they will get their money back as venture capitalists do—maybe even more, because they're investing their personal, after-tax money.
4. *Understand their motivation.* Angel investors differ from venture capitalists in that business angels typically have a double bottom line. They've made it, so they want to pay back society by helping the next generation of entrepreneurs. Thus, they're often willing to invest in riskier deals to help entrepreneurs get to the next stage.
5. *Enable them to live vicariously.* One of the rewards of angel investing is the ability to live vicariously through an entrepreneur's efforts. Angels want to relive the thrills of entrepreneurship, while avoiding the firing line. They enjoy helping you, so seek their guidance frequently.
6. *Make your story comprehensible to the angel's spouse.* An angel's "decision-making committee" usually consists of one person: a spouse. So, if you've got a highly technical product, you must make it understandable for the angel's spouse when he or she asks, "What are we investing $100,000 in?"
7. *Sign up people the angel has heard of.* Angel investors are also motivated by the social aspect of investing with buddies in startups run by bright people who are changing the world. Once you've brought one angel on board, you're likely to attract a whole flock of other angels, too.
8. *Be nice.* Not infrequently, angel investors fall in love with entrepreneurs. An entrepreneur may remind an investor of a son or daughter, or even fill the position of the son or daughter the investor never had. Venture capitalists will sometimes invest in a schmuck as long as that schmuck is a proven moneymaker. If you're seeking angel capital, then you're probably not a proven moneymaker, so you can't get away with acting like a schmuck. Always be respectful to your investors.

Venture Capital Firms

formal venture capitalists Individuals who form limited partnerships for the purpose of raising venture capital from large institutional investors.

In addition to business angels who provide informal venture capital, small businesses also may seek out **formal venture capitalists**, groups of individuals who form limited partnerships for the purpose of raising capital from large institutional investors, such as pension plans and university endowments. Within the group, a venture capitalist serves as the general partner, with other investors constituting the limited partners. As limited partners, such investors have the benefit of limited liability.

A venture capitalist attempts to raise a predetermined amount of money, called a *fund*. Once the money has been committed by the investors, the venture capitalist screens and evaluates investment opportunities in high-potential startups and existing firms. For example, the Sevin Rosen Funds in Dallas, Texas, raised $600 million for the Sevin Rosen Fund VIII. The money was then used to invest in a portfolio of companies.

For the investment, the venture capitalist receives the right to own a percentage of the entrepreneur's business. Reaching agreement on the exact percentage of ownership often involves considerable negotiation. The primary issues are the firm's expected profits in future years and the venture capitalist's required rate of return. Once an investment has been made, the venture capitalist carefully monitors the company, usually through a representative who serves on the firm's board.

Most often, investments by venture capitalists take the form of preferred stock that can be converted to common stock if the investor so desires. In this way, venture capitalists ensure that they have senior claim over the owners and other equity investors in the event the firm is liquidated, but can convert to common stock and participate in the increased value of the business if it is successful. These investors generally try to limit the length of their investment to between 5 and 7 years, though it is frequently closer to 10 years before they are able to cash out.

Although venture capital as a source of financing receives significant coverage in the business media, *few small companies, especially startups, ever receive this kind of funding.* No more than 1 or 2 percent of the business plans received by any venture capitalist are eventually funded—not exactly an encouraging statistic. Failure to receive funding from a venture capitalist, however, does not indicate that the venture lacks potential. Often, the venture is simply not a good fit for the investor. So, before trying to compete for venture capital financing, an entrepreneur should assess whether the firm and its management team are a good fit for a particular investor.

THE GOVERNMENT

Several government programs provide financing to small businesses. Over the past decade, federal and state governments have allocated increasing, but still limited, amounts of money to financing new businesses. Local governments have likewise increased their involvement in providing financial support to startups in their areas. Though funds are available, they are not always easy to acquire. Time and patience on the part of the entrepreneur are required. Let's take a look at some of the more familiar government loan programs offered by various agencies.

The Small Business Administration

The federal government has a long history of helping new businesses get started, primarily through the programs and agencies of the Small Business Administration (SBA). For the most part, the SBA does not loan money but serves as a guarantor of loans made by financial institutions. The five primary SBA programs are (1) the 7(a) Loan Guaranty Program, (2) the Certified Development Company (CDC) 504 Loan Program, (3) the 7(m) Microloan Program, (4) small business investment companies (SBICs), and (5) the Small Business Innovative Research (SBIR) Program.

© iStockphoto.com/Angelika Schwarz

entrepreneurial experiences

Looking to Angels

With an education in industrial design, a Harvard MBA, and an executive stint in strategic development for brands like Stride Rite, Keds, and Playskool, Jules Pieri has the savvy to spot a consumer trend.

So when she noticed that upstart manufacturers were having trouble getting shelf space in an increasingly consolidated retail market—despite the unprecedented flood of new products fueled by access to design and manufacturing capabilities—she sensed an opportunity. Pieri also knew that many consumers want innovative products that emphasize "something good in the world, whether it's technology or green enterprise," she says. Add the power of social media, giving people the ability to share information about their favorite finds, and you have the recipe for Daily Grommet, a Lexington, Massachusetts–based website that champions independent entrepreneurs creating cool products by building a large online community.

Courtesy of Jules Pieri

Two business-minded friends loved the idea and became Pieri's first angel investors. With that initial $150,000, she launched the site in October 2008—a week before the stock market crashed. During the early days of the financial crisis, venture capital investments also plummeted. Pieri needed money to grow the site, but she also knew she was not likely to see eye to eye with VCs who typically want fast growth. Her business vision required slower, thoughtful growth to build a community and find innovative products.

At the same time, her access to angels was yielding the investment she needed, including a $3.4 million infusion by Race Point Capital Fund, Gerry Laybourne (Nickelodeon and Oxygen Media), and other angel investors.

"Jules is a superstar," says Christopher Mirabile, director of Race Point Capital. "The market she's going after—this curated content or community-meets-content-meets-community—is just a huge, huge opportunity."

Daily Grommet is using the money to invest in new customer acquisition methods, overhaul the site, add more community tools, and expand its reach through media exposure, Pieri says.

Pieri believes Daily Grommet will reach a point where it will need the bigger cash infusions that are more common from VC firms, and she is positioning the company to court them eventually. "There's going to be a limit where [angels] can't carry the business forward at the level it needs to be supported," Pieri says. "That's the downside of angels."

Mirabile, however, looks for companies that can "go angel all the way," but knows entrepreneurs must do what's best for business. Still, he says, "The idea that you need a deep-pocketed VC to change the world and build a Google or Facebook is misguided."

Source: Gwen Moran, "Looking to Angels," *Entrepreneur,* March 2011, http://www.entrepreneur.com/article/printthis/218125.html, accessed March 1, 2011. **http://www.dailygrommet.com**

7(a) Loan Guaranty Program
A loan program that helps small companies obtain financing through a guaranty provided by the SBA.

7(A) LOAN GUARANTY PROGRAM The **7(a) Loan Guaranty Program** serves as the SBA's primary business loan program to help qualified small businesses obtain financing when they might not be eligible for business loans through normal lending channels. Guaranty loans are made by private lenders, usually commercial banks, and may be for as much as $750,000. The SBA guarantees 90 percent of loans not exceeding $155,000. For large loans, the guaranty percentage is 85 percent. To obtain a guaranty loan, a small business must submit a loan application to a lender, such as a bank. After an initial review, the lender forwards the application to the SBA. Once the loan has been approved by the SBA, the lender disburses the funds. The loan proceeds can be used for working capital, machinery and equipment, furniture and fixtures, land and building, leasehold improvements, and debt refinancing (under special conditions). Loan maturity is up to 10 years for working capital and generally up to 25 years for fixed assets.

Certified Development Company (CDC) 504 Loan Program
An SBA loan program that provides long-term financing for small businesses to acquire real estate or machinery and equipment.

CERTIFIED DEVELOPMENT COMPANY (CDC) 504 LOAN PROGRAM The **Certified Development Company (CDC) 504 Loan Program** provides long-term, fixed-rate financing to small businesses to acquire real estate or machinery and equipment for expansion or modernization. The lender in this instance is a certified development company, which is financed by the SBA. The borrower must provide 10 percent of the cost of the property, with the remaining amount coming from a bank and a certified development company funded by the SBA.

7(m) Microloan Program
An SBA loan program that provides short-term loans of up to $35,000 to small businesses and not-for-profit child-care centers.

7(M) MICROLOAN PROGRAM The **7(m) Microloan Program** grants short-term loans of up to $35,000 to small businesses and not-for-profit child-care centers for working capital or the purchase of inventory, supplies, furniture, fixtures, and machinery and equipment. The SBA makes or guarantees a loan to an intermediary, which in turn makes the microloan to the applicant. As an added benefit, the lender provides business training and support programs to its microloan borrowers.

Most banks regard microloans as too costly to administer directly to small business owners. Therefore, some nonprofit organizations, such as the Northeastern Pennsylvania Alliance and the Detroit Micro-Enterprise Fund, work with banks and foundations to make microloans to small business owners.[18]

small business investment companies (SBICs)
Privately owned banks, regulated by the SBA, that provide long-term loans and/or equity capital to small businesses.

SMALL BUSINESS INVESTMENT COMPANIES **Small business investment companies (SBICs)** are privately owned banks that provide long-term loans and/or equity capital to small businesses. SBICs are licensed and regulated by the SBA, from which they frequently obtain a substantial part of their capital at attractive rates of interest. SBICs invest in businesses with fewer than 500 employees, a net worth of no more than $18 million, and after-tax income not exceeding $6 million during the two most recent years.

Small Business Innovative Research (SBIR) Program
An SBA program that helps to finance companies that plan to transform laboratory research into marketable products.

SMALL BUSINESS INNOVATIVE RESEARCH (SBIR) PROGRAM The **Small Business Innovative Research (SBIR) Program** helps finance small firms that plan to transform laboratory research into marketable products. Eligibility for the program is based less on the potential profitability of a venture than on the likelihood that the firm will provide a product of interest to a particular federal agency.

State and Local Government Assistance

State and local governments have become more active in financing new businesses. The nature of the financing varies, but each program is generally geared to augment other sources of funding. Several examples of such programs follow:

1. The city government of Des Moines, Iowa, established the Golden Circle Loan Guarantee Fund to guarantee bank loans of up to $250,000 to small companies.

2. The state of Texas will provide up to $500,000 of debt financing for small businesses through its Emerging Technologies Fund (ETF).
3. Rhode Island offers financing programs tied to job growth.
4. The New Jersey Economic Development Authority makes loans to business owners at the U.S. Treasury rate, significantly lower than interest rates typically charged at banks.
5. The Colorado Housing and Finance Authority makes loans for equipment and real estate with down payments as low as 15 percent and up to 20 years to repay the loan.

Most of these loans are made in conjunction with a bank, which enables the bank to take on riskier loans for entrepreneurs who might not qualify for traditional financing. "And some loans have a lower down payment requirement," explains Donna Holmes, former director of the Penn State Small Business Development Center in University Park. "The bank may do 50 percent, the state program another 40 percent, and the borrower only has to come up with 10 percent; with a straight bank loan, the bank might be looking for 20 percent or 25 percent."[19]

While such government programs may be attractive to an entrepreneur, they are frequently designed to enhance specific industries or to facilitate certain community goals. Consequently, you need to determine that a program is in sync with your specific business objectives.

Community-Based Financial Institutions

Community-based financial institutions are lenders that serve low-income communities and receive funds from federal, state, and private sources. They are increasingly becoming a source of financing for small companies that otherwise would have little or no access to startup funding. Typically, community-based lenders provide capital to businesses that are unable to attract outside investors but do have the potential to make modest profits, serve the community, and create jobs. An example of a community-based financial institution is the Delaware Valley Reinvestment Fund, which provides financing for small companies in Philadelphia's inner-city area.

Community-based financial institution
A lender that uses funds from federal, state, and private sources to provide financing to small businesses in low-income communities.

WHERE ELSE TO LOOK

The sources of financing that have been described thus far represent the primary avenues for obtaining money for small firms. The remaining sources are generally of less importance but should not be ignored by a small business owner in search of financing.

Large Corporations

Large corporations at times make funds available for investment in smaller firms when it is in their self-interest to maintain a close relationship with such a firm. For instance, some large high-tech firms, such as Intel and Microsoft, prefer to invest in smaller firms that are conducting research of interest, rather than conduct the research themselves.

Stock Sales

Another way to obtain capital is by selling stock to outside individual investors through either private placement or public sale. Finding outside stockholders can be difficult when a new firm is not known and has no ready market for its securities, however. In most cases, a business must have a history of profitability before its stock can be sold successfully.

Whether it is best to raise outside equity financing depends on the firm's long-range prospects. If there is opportunity for substantial expansion on a continuing basis and if other sources are inadequate, the owner may logically decide to bring in other owners. Owning part of a larger business may be more profitable than owning all of a smaller business.

private placement The sale of a firm's capital stock to select individuals.

PRIVATE PLACEMENT One way to sell common stock is through a **private placement**, in which the firm's stock is sold to select individuals—usually the firm's employees, the owner's acquaintances, members of the local community, customers, and suppliers. When a stock sale is restricted to private placement, an entrepreneur can avoid many of the demanding requirements of the securities laws.

initial public offering (IPO) The issuance of stock to be traded in public financial markets.

PUBLIC SALE When small firms—typically, larger small firms—make their stock available to the general public, this is called going public, or making an **initial public offering (IPO)**. The reason often cited for a public sale is the need for additional working capital.

In undertaking a public sale of its stock, a small firm subjects itself to greater governmental regulation, which escalated dramatically following the rash of corporate scandals in publicly owned companies such as Enron, Tyco, and WorldCom. In response to such corporate malfeasance, the U.S. Congress passed legislation, including the Sarbanes-Oxley Act, to monitor public companies more carefully. This resulted in a significant increase in the cost of being a publicly traded company—especially for small firms. Then in 2010, Congress enacted the Dodd-Frank Act for the purpose of averting a financial crisis similar to the one experienced in 2008–2009. The legislation primarily relates to the financial sector but also includes strict regulations for all companies to ensure transparency and accountability, which again increases the costs of being a publicly traded company. Finally, publicly traded firms are required to report their financial results quarterly in 10Q reports and annually in 10K reports to the Securities and Exchange Commission (SEC). The SEC carefully scrutinizes these reports before they can be made available to the public. At times, SEC requirements can be very burdensome.

Common stock may also be sold to underwriters, which guarantee the sale of securities. Compensation and fees paid to underwriters typically make the sale of securities in this manner expensive. Fees frequently range from 20 to 25 percent (or higher) of the value of the total stock issued. The reasons for the high costs are, of course, the uncertainty and risk associated with public offerings of the stock of small, relatively unknown firms.

We have now completed our discussion of what an entrepreneur needs to understand when seeking financing for a company, in terms of a firm's financial statements and forecasts (Chapters 10 and 11) and the different sources of financing typically used by small firms (Chapter 12). Our detailed explanations should help you avoid mistakes commonly made by small business owners when trying to get financing to grow a business.

1. Describe how the nature of a firm affects its financing sources.

- There are four basic factors that determine how a firm is financed: (1) the firm's economic potential, (2) the size and maturity of the company, (3) the nature of the firm's assets, and (4) the personal preferences of the owners as they consider the trade-offs between debt and equity.
- An entrepreneurial firm with high-growth potential has more possible sources of financing than does a firm that provides a good lifestyle for its owner but little in the way of attractive returns to investors.
- The size and maturity of a company have a direct bearing on the types of financing that are available.
- Tangible assets serve as great collateral when a business is requesting a bank loan; intangible assets have little value as collateral.

2. Evaluate the choice between debt financing and equity financing.

- Choosing between debt and equity financing involves trade-offs with regard to potential profitability, financial risk, and voting control.

- Borrowing money (debt) rather than issuing common stock (ownership equity) creates the potential for higher rates of return to the owners and allows the owners to retain voting control of the company, but it also exposes the owners to greater financial risk.
- Issuing common stock rather than borrowing money results in lower potential rates of return to the owners and the loss of some voting control, but it does reduce their financial risk.

3. Identify the typical sources of financing used at the outset of a new venture.

- The aspiring entrepreneur basically has three sources of early financing: (1) personal savings, (2) friends and family, and (3) credit cards.
- Personal savings is the primary source of equity financing used in starting a new business; a banker or other lender is unlikely to loan venture money if the entrepreneur does not have her or his own money at risk.
- Loans from friends and family may be the only available source of financing and are often easy and fast to obtain, although such borrowing can place the entrepreneur's most important personal relationships in jeopardy.
- Credit card financing provides easily accessible financing, but the high interest costs may become overwhelming at times.

4. Discuss the basic process for acquiring and structuring a bank loan.

- Bankers primarily make business loans in one of three forms: lines of credit, term loans, and mortgages.
- In making a loan decision, a banker always considers the "five C's of credit": (1) the borrower's *character,* (2) the borrower's *capacity* to repay the loan, (3) the *capital* being invested in the venture by the borrower, (4) the *conditions* of the industry and economy, and (5) the *collateral* available to secure the loan.
- Obtaining a bank loan requires a well-prepared loan request that addresses: (1) how much money is needed, (2) what the venture is going to do with the money, (3) when the money is needed, and (4) when and how the money will be paid back.
- A banker may request other detailed financial information, including three years of the firm's historical financial statements, the firm's pro forma financial statements, and personal financial statements showing the borrower's net worth and estimated annual income.
- An entrepreneur should carefully evaluate available banks before choosing one, basing the decision on factors such as the bank's location, the services provided, and the bank's lending policies.
- In negotiating a bank loan, the owner must consider the accompanying terms, which typically include the interest rate, the loan maturity date, the repayment schedule, and the loan covenants.

5. Explain how business relationships can be used to finance a small firm.

- Business suppliers can offer trade credit (accounts payable), which is the source of short-term funds most widely used by small firms.
- Suppliers also offer equipment loans and leases, which allow small businesses to use equipment purchased on an installment basis.
- An asset-based loan is financing secured by working capital assets, such as accounts receivable and inventory.

6. Describe the two types of private equity investors who offer financing to small firms.

- Business angels are private individuals, generally having moderate to significant business experience, who invest in others' entrepreneurial ventures.
- Formal venture capitalists are groups of individuals who form limited partnerships for the purpose of raising capital from large institutional investors, such as pension plans and university endowments.

7. Distinguish among the different government loan programs available to small companies.

- The federal government helps new businesses get started through the programs and agencies of the Small Business Administration (SBA), which include the 7(a) Loan Guaranty Program, the Certified Development Company (CDC) 504 Loan Program, the 7(m) Microloan Program, small business investment companies (SBICs), and the Small Business Innovative Research (SBIR) Program.
- State and local governments finance new businesses in various ways, with programs that are generally geared to augmenting other sources of funding.
- Community-based financial institutions are lenders that use funds from federal, state, and private sources to serve low-income communities and small companies that otherwise would have little or no access to startup funding.

8. Explain when large companies and public stock offerings can be sources of financing.

- Large companies may finance smaller businesses when it is in their self-interest to have a close relationship with the smaller company.
- Stock sales, in the form of either private placements or public sales, may provide a few high-potential ventures with equity capital.

Key Terms

line of credit p. 367
term loan p. 367
chattel mortgage p. 367
real estate mortgage p. 368
prime rate p. 370
LIBOR (London InterBank Offered Rate) p. 370
balloon payment p. 371
loan covenants p. 371
limited liability p. 371
equipment loan p. 372
asset-based loan p. 373
factoring p. 373
purchase-order financing p. 373
business angels p. 374
informal venture capital p. 374
formal venture capitalists p. 376
7(a) Loan Guaranty Program p. 378
Certified Development Company (CDC) 504 Loan Program p. 378
7(m) Microloan Program p. 378
small business investment companies (SBICs) p. 378
Small Business Innovative Research (SBIR) Program p. 378
community-based financial institution p. 379
private placement p. 380
initial public offering (IPO) p. 380

Discussion Questions

1. How does the nature of a business affect its sources of financing?
2. How is debt different from equity?
3. Explain the three trade-offs that guide the choice between debt financing and equity financing.
4. Assume that you are starting a business for the first time. What do you believe are the greatest personal obstacles to obtaining funds for the new venture? Why?
5. If you were starting a new business, where would you start looking for capital?
6. Explain how trade credit and equipment loans can provide initial capital funding.
7. a. Describe the different types of loans made by a commercial bank.
   b. What does a banker need to know in order to decide whether to make a loan?
8. Distinguish between informal venture capital and formal venture capital.
9. In what ways does the federal government help with initial financing for small businesses?
10. What advice would you give an entrepreneur who was trying to finance a startup?

You Make the Call

SITUATION 1

David Bernstein needs help financing his Lodi, New Jersey–based Access Direct, Inc., a six-year-old $3.5 million company. "We're ready to get to the next level," says Bernstein, " but we're not sure which way to go." Access Direct spruces up and then sells used computer equipment for corporations. It is looking for up to $2 million in order to expand. "Venture capitalists, individual investors, or banks," says Bernstein, who owns the company with four partners, "we've thought about them all."

Question 1 What is your impression of Bernstein's perspective on raising capital to "get to the next level"?
Question 2 What advice would you offer Bernstein as to both appropriate and inappropriate sources of financing in his situation?

SITUATION 2

John Dalton is well on his way to starting a new venture—Max, Inc. He has projected a need for $350,000 in initial capital. He plans to invest $150,000 himself and either borrow the additional $200,000 or find a partner who will buy stock in the company. If Dalton borrows the money, the interest rate will be 6 percent. If, on the other hand, another equity investor is found, he expects to have to give up 60 percent of the company's stock. Dalton has forecasted earnings of about 16 percent in operating profits on the firm's total assets.

Question 1 Compare the two financing options in terms of projected return on the owner's equity investment. Ignore any effect from income taxes.

Question 2 What if Dalton is wrong and the company earns only 4 percent in operating profits on total assets?

Question 3 What should Dalton consider in choosing a source of financing?

SITUATION 3

Mike Smith seeks your counsel about a problem that has grown out of a decision he made three years earlier to buy a warehouse. Up until then, he had rented three warehouses, where he stored containers and did pick-and-pack for retailers importing goods from abroad. Figuring it was time to consolidate, Smith found a building, negotiated a price of $3.5 million, put down $300,000, and borrowed $3.2 million from a bank at 7 percent interest.

It seemed like a good idea at the time. Then a recession hit. As his sales dropped, he struggled to make his monthly payment of $27,000. At present, he's behind in his payments and scared. Furthermore, the situation seems unlikely to improve anytime soon. To make matters worse, he signed a personal guarantee on the loan and thinks he might lose his house. The bank is assessing the situation to decide what to do.

In his panicked state of mind, Smith has come up with a plan. "I'm going to tell the bank I need eight months," he says. "It can take the money I'll owe for that time, plus what I owe now, and tack it onto the end of the mortgage. What do you think?"

"How do you know that's what the bank is looking for?" you ask.

"Well, obviously, they want the money I owe, but I can't pay them," Smith says. "I have to offer them something. My wife and I could lose everything!"

"You aren't going to lose everything," you say, "and you're making a mistake to assume that you know what the bank wants."

Question 1 What guidance will you give Smith in negotiating with the bank?

Question 2 Why might you advise him not to go into a meeting with bank officers with a plan already in mind?

Experiential Exercises

1. Interview a local small business owner to determine how funds were obtained to start the business. Be sure you phrase questions so that they are not overly personal, and do not ask for specific dollar amounts. Write a brief report on your findings.
2. Interview a local banker about lending policies for small business loans. Ask the banker to comment on the importance of a business plan to the bank's decision to loan money to a small firm. Write a brief report on your findings.
3. Review recent issues of *Entrepreneur* or *Inc.*, and report to the class on the financing arrangements of firms featured in these magazines.
4. Interview a stockbroker or investment analyst on his or her views regarding the sale of common stock by a small business. Write a brief report on your findings.

Small Business & Entrepreneurship Resource Center

1. Managing your debt is a very important aspect of any business. Many small business owners commonly look first at the interest rate on a loan as being most important factor. The article "SBA Lending Programs" discusses the "seven truths" of lending. Discuss whether the term of the loan (length of the loan or amortization) is more important than the interest rate, especially concerning the impact on cash flows for a business.

   Source: Rick Anderson, "SBA Lending Programs'' The Seven Truths,'" *Franchising World*, Vol. 38, No. 5 (May 2006), pp. 22–24.

2. The article "Advice from on High" mentions several high-profile angel investors, such as Ken Oshman, founder of Rolm Corporation; Paul Allen, co-founder of Microsoft Corporation; and Warren Musser, founder of Safeguard Scientifics. Angel investors can actually be found anywhere, but it does require preparation to successfully utilize them as a resource. Describe in detail three things you can do to prepare to use angel investors.

   Source: Sara Lepro, "Advice from on High: Finding Angel Money Doesn't Have to Take a Miracle," *Inside Business*, Vol. 7, No. 8 (August 2005), pp. 7–8.

Video Case 12

MOONWORKS, P. 717

Moonworks began installing Gutter Helmet® in Rhode Island, but soon the business began expanding further into the New England states and New York. Now they offer industry-leading home improvement products. They've had a long relationship with the Bank of Rhode Island, and this case tells the story of the company's financing and how it has changed along with the company over 15 years.

ALTERNATIVE CASE FOR CHAPTER 12

Case 11, Missouri Solvents, p. 714

Business Plan Laying the Foundation

As part of laying the foundation for your own business plan, respond to the following questions regarding the financing of your venture:

1. What is the total financing required to start the business?
2. How much money do you plan to invest in the venture? What is the source of this money?
3. Will you need financing beyond what you personally plan to invest?
4. If additional financing is needed for the startup, how will you raise it? How will the financing be structured—debt or equity? What will the terms be for the investors?
5. According to your pro forma financial statements, will there be a need for additional financing within the first five years of the firm's life? If so, where will it come from?
6. How and when will you arrange for investors to cash out of their investment?

CHAPTER 13

Planning for the Harvest

In the SPOTLIGHT
Li'l Guy Foods
http://lilguyfoods.com

After multiple conversations with investment bankers, 37-year-old David Sloan, co-owner of Li'l Guy Foods, a three-generation, family-owned Mexican-food manufacturing business in Kansas City, Missouri, realized "there weren't a whole lot of people wanting to jump into this industry."

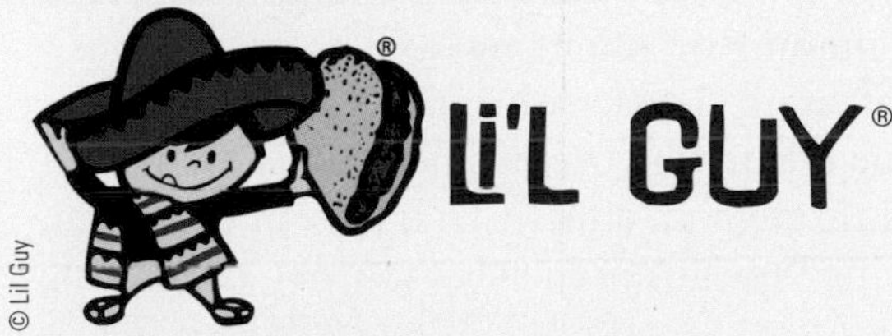

© Lil Guy

The 35-employee company was facing huge financial pressure from the rising costs of commodities like corn and other ingredients, as well as plastic packaging. "We were under an assault on margins," Sloan says, something that made outside investors nervous. Still, the business enjoyed a strong base of customers that paid a premium for its products.

That was enough to attract the attention of a competitor, Tortilla King Inc., of Moundridge, Kansas. The larger, more sophisticated company had hedging policies in place that allowed it to lock in prices, guarding against increases. And since Tortilla King was already familiar with the industry and the company's customer base in the region, it was willing to take risks that outside investors were not.

With costs high and consumer spending on the wane, Tortilla King president Juan Guardiola saw the acquisition of Li'l Guy Foods as a way to reduce competition and increase market share. "We were fighting in the market, cutting each other's margins," he says, "so it made a lot of sense to merge."

The two companies hammered out a deal, and a bank agreed to provide financing but backed out just as the deal was about to close—part of the broad pullback in business lending during 2008. So Sloan's company agreed to finance the purchase, offering a five-year repayment term with an interest rate of around 8 percent.

LOOKING AHEAD

After studying this chapter, you should be able to . . .

1. Explain the importance of having a harvest, or exit, plan.
2. Describe the options available for harvesting.
3. Explain the issues in valuing a firm that is being harvested and deciding on the method of payment.
4. Provide advice on developing an effective harvest plan.

© iStockphoto.com/Dan Bachman

Sloan says he would have preferred to walk away without being so invested in the combined company's future. But he felt it would be too difficult to continue running the small business, so he went along with the new terms. "It wasn't the most ideal transaction for us," he says. "I would have rather had it a lot cleaner."

Guardiola says he was surprised when his company's longtime bank declined to finance the deal, though he understands that banks are extra vigilant these days about debt. With commodity prices "like a train out of control," he says, the bank was concerned. But Guardiola is convinced the combined company will have greater clout than each company did separately.

Sources: Adapted from Arden Dale and Simona Covel, "Sellers Offer a Financial Hand to Their Buyers," *Wall Street Journal*, November 13, 2008, p. B-1; http://www.lilguyfoods.com, accessed January 15, 2011; and Suzanna Stagemeyer, "Li'l Guy Sells to Tortilla King, Moves Manufacturing to Wichita," *Kansas City Business Journal*, September 14, 2008, http://www.bizjournals.com/kansascity/stories/2008/09/15/story2.html, accessed January 15, 2011.

You may wonder why we address the issue of exiting a business so early in the text, choosing to delay all the instruction on managing a business to subsequent chapters. It seems a bit illogical after all. We do so because of our strong conviction that it is better for an entrepreneur to consider the exit sooner rather than later.

In previous chapters, we have talked about recognizing business opportunities and developing strategies for capturing these opportunities. Such activities represent the cornerstone for everything a company does. But, for entrepreneurs, that's not the end of the story. Experience suggests that an entrepreneur who is developing a company strategy should think about more than just starting (founding or acquiring) and growing a business; the entrepreneurial process is not complete until the owners and any other investors have exited the venture and captured the value created by the business. This final—but extremely important—phase can be enhanced through an effective harvest, or exit, plan. In other words, the goal is to create value during the entrepreneurial journey by making a difference and then *to finish well!*

The Importance of the Harvest

Most small business owners do not like to think about the harvest, even though few events in the life of an entrepreneur, and of the firm itself, are more significant. Consequently, the decision to harvest is frequently the result of an unexpected event, possibly a crisis, rather than a well-conceived strategy. An entrepreneur—a wholesale pump distributor—wrote to Norm Brodsky at AskNorm@inc.com to ask for advice about selling his once-successful company because of financial problems, saying

> *I've been approached by four large companies to buy us out, but I love what I do, and I'd hate to see what I've built go up in smoke or get diluted in another organization.*[1]

harvesting (exiting) The process used by entrepreneurs and investors to reap the value of a business when they leave it.

Harvesting, or **exiting**, is the method that owners and investors use to get out of a business and, ideally, reap the value of their investment in the firm. Many entrepreneurs successfully grow their businesses but fail to develop effective harvest plans. As a result, they are unable to capture the full value of the business they have worked so hard to create.

An entrepreneur needs to understand that harvesting encompasses more than merely selling and leaving a business. It involves capturing value (cash flows), reducing risk, and creating future options—the reason we prefer the term *harvest* over *exit*. In addition, there are personal, nonfinancial considerations for entrepreneurs. Owners may receive a lot of money for their firms but still be disappointed with the harvest if they are not prepared for a change in lifestyle. Thus, carefully designing an intentional harvest strategy is as essential to an entrepreneur's personal success as it is to his or her financial success.

In this chapter, we offer suggestions for achieving a "successful" harvest. It is a mistake to define success only in terms of the harvest; the entrepreneurial journey should be successful as well. So, throughout the chapter, we encourage you to think about what success means to you. Arriving at the end of the journey only to discover that your ladder was leaning against the wrong wall is one of life's tragedies.

The harvest is vitally important to a firm's investors as well as to its founder. Investors who provide high-risk capital—particularly angels and venture capitalists—generally insist on a well-thought-out harvest strategy. They realize that it is easy to put money into a business, but difficult to get it out. As a result, a firm's appeal to investors is driven, in part, by the availability of harvest options. If investors are not convinced that opportunities will exist for harvesting their investment, they will be unlikely to invest.

Early Planning for a Successful Harvest

If planning for the harvest well in advance seems counterintuitive to you, you are not alone. But it is important to understand that the most successful exits require considerable planning. So, the earlier you begin, the more successful your eventual exit will most likely be. In fact, some of the steps involved in planning for the harvest, such as fine-tuning your company's strategies, focusing on internal growth, improving your financial systems, and creating an independent board, are the same as those required to build a successful company.

Follow this advice—you won't regret it!

Methods of Harvesting a Business

The four basic ways to harvest an investment in a privately owned company are (1) selling the firm, (2) distributing the cash flows generated by the business to its owners instead of reinvesting the cash, (3) offering stock to the public through an initial public offering (IPO), and (4) issuing a private placement of the stock. These options are shown graphically in Exhibit 13.1.

SELLING THE FIRM

In any harvest strategy, the financial questions associated with the sale of a firm include how to value the firm and how to structure the payment for the business. Most frequently, an entrepreneur's motivation for selling a company relates to retirement and estate planning and a desire to diversify investments. Thus, in choosing a possible buyer, entrepreneurs should understand what they want to accomplish from the sale.

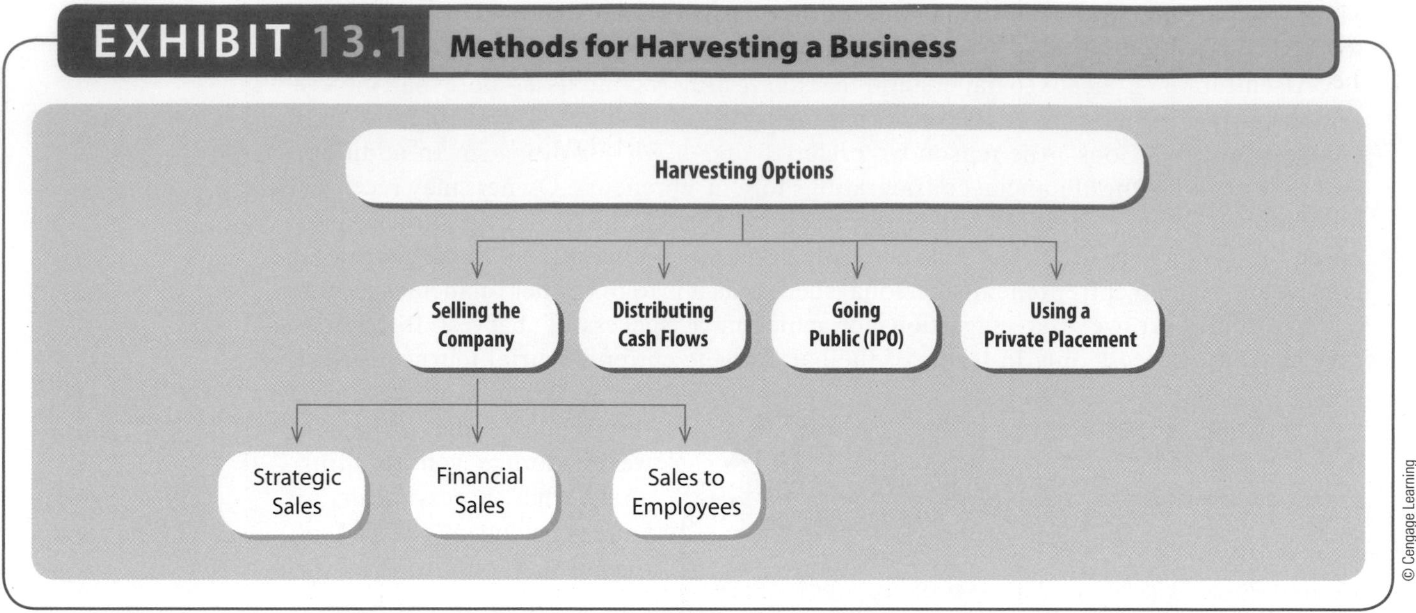

Potential buyers for a company can come from a number of places, including your customers, suppliers, employees, friends and family, or even a competitor. Buyers who are unrelated to you and who may be unearthed by your business broker can usually be divided into two groups: financial buyers and strategic buyers. In the sections that follow, we will look at three buyer groups in particular: (1) strategic buyers, (2) financial buyers, and (3) employees.

Sales to Strategic Buyers

Usually, a strategic buyer is a firm in a similar line of business in a different market or in need of new products and services to sell to existing customers. Tortilla King, which purchased Li'l Guy Foods, as described in In the Spotlight, serves as an example of a strategic buyer. Another possibility is a buyer in an unrelated business that wants to acquire a seller's strengths to help the buyer's existing business. For example, a food manufacturer might acquire a supply-chain management/logistics firm.

Strategic buyers value a business based on the synergies they think they can create by combining the acquired firm with another business. Since the value of a business to a buyer is derived from both its stand-alone characteristics and its synergies, strategic buyers may pay a higher price than would other buyers, who value the business only as a stand-alone entity. Thus, in strategic acquisitions, the critical issue is the degree of strategic fit between the firm to be harvested and the potential buyer's other business interests. If the prospective buyer is a current rival and if the acquisition would provide long-term, sustainable competitive advantages (such as lower production costs or superior product quality), the buyer may be willing to pay a premium for the company.

Sales to Financial Buyers

leveraged buyout (LBO) A purchase heavily financed with debt, where the future cash flows of the target company are expected to be sufficient to meet debt repayments.

Unlike strategic buyers, buyers in financial acquisitions look primarily to a firm's stand-alone, cash-generating potential as its source of value. A financial buyer hopes to increase future sales growth, reduce costs, or both. This fact has an important implication for the owner of the business being purchased. The buyer often will make changes in the firm's operations that translate into greater pressures on the firm's personnel, resulting in layoffs that the current owner might find objectionable.

A **leveraged buyout (LBO)** is a financial acquisition involving a very high level of debt financing, where the future cash flows of the target company are expected to be sufficient to meet debt repayments. In the past, acquisitions frequently were financed with $9 in debt for every $1 in equity—thus, the name *leveraged* buyout. The LBO has sometimes been called a **bust-up LBO**, in which the new owners pay the debt down rapidly by selling off the acquired firm's assets.

bust-up LBO
A leveraged buyout involving the purchase of a company with the intent of selling off its assets.

Because buyers rely heavily on debt to finance the acquisition, the acquired company must have the following characteristics:

- Steady earnings over time
- Attractive growth rates
- An effective management team already in place
- Assets that can be used as collateral on the debt

Otherwise, the risk is too great, and the transaction simply will not work.

Consider Visador Corporation, which was sold to a financial buyer for $67 million. The buyer financed the purchase as a leveraged buyout, incurring a lot of debt to finance the purchase. The firm's total assets and debt and equity (as presented in the balance sheet) before and after the sale were as follows:

build-up LBO
A leveraged buyout involving the purchase of a group of similar companies with the intent of making the firms into one larger company for eventual sale.

	Before the Sale	After the Sale
Total Assets	$18,000,000	$67,000,000
Total debt	$ 5,000,000	$60,000,000
Equity	13,000,000	7,000,000
Total Debt and Equity	$18,000,000	$67,000,000

Visador's before-sale and after-sale numbers differ in two important respects. First, the total assets (and total debt and equity) increased from $18 million to $67 million. In other words, the founders of Visador had invested just over $18 million in the firm during their years of ownership, up to the point of the acquisition. However, the buyer was willing to pay $67 million for the business, based on future cash flows that were expected to be generated.

Second, before the sale, the assets were financed with 28 percent debt ($5 million total debt ÷ $18 million total assets) compared to 90 percent debt ($60 million total debt ÷ $67 million total assets) after the sale. Consequently, the firm was exposed to significantly more financial risk. If sales decrease, the company may not be able to service its debt. This is typical for bust-up leveraged buyouts.

More recently, the bust-up LBO has been replaced by the build-up LBO. As the name suggests, the **build-up LBO** involves pulling together a group of smaller firms to create a larger enterprise that might eventually be sold or taken public via an initial public offering.

The process of the build-up LBO begins with the acquisition of a company, which then acquires a number of smaller businesses that in some way complement it. These subsequent acquisitions may expand capacity in related or completely different businesses. The newly formed combination is operated privately for five years or so in order to establish a successful track record, and then it is sold or taken public. These acquisitions continue to rely

© pianissimo/Shutterstock.com

Consider Visador Corporation, designer/producer of residential staircases, which was sold to a financial buyer for $67 million. The buyer financed the purchase as a leveraged buyout.

heavily on debt financing, but to a lesser extent than bust-up LBOs. Build-up LBOs have occurred in a number of industries where smaller companies frequently operate, such as funeral services and automobile dealerships.

management buyout (MBO) A leveraged buyout in which the firm's top managers become significant shareholders in the acquired firm.

Sometimes, the selling firm's own management initiates an LBO to buy the business from the entrepreneur—in which case the arrangement is referred to as a **management buyout (MBO)**. An MBO can contribute significantly to a firm's operating performance by increasing management's focus and intensity. Thus, an MBO is a potentially viable means of transferring ownership from the founder to the management team. In many entrepreneurial businesses, managers have a strong incentive to become owners but lack the financial capacity to acquire the firm. An MBO can solve this problem through the use of debt financing, which is often underwritten in part by the selling entrepreneur.

Sales to Employees

employee stock ownership plan (ESOP) A method by which a firm is sold either in part or in total to its employees.

Established by Congress in 1974, **employee stock ownership plans (ESOPs)** have gradually been embraced by more than 10,000 companies. Once established, an ESOP uses employees' retirement contributions to buy company stock from the owner and holds it in trust; over time, the stock is distributed to employees' retirement plans.

It is common for an owner to start an ESOP by selling only a portion of the company. But even if the owner sells all of his or her stock, he or she can still retain control of the business. And an ESOP creates significant tax advantages for the seller. For instance, if the entrepreneur sells at least 30 percent of the company, capital gains taxes can be deferred, in some cases indefinitely. For example, the owner-managers of BFW Construction Company in Temple, Texas, created an ESOP. Then in 2003, they sold the business and rolled over the money from the shares into their personal retirement accounts. As a result, they have not paid taxes from the time the shares were put into an ESOP and will not have to do so until they are required to begin distributing the money, when they are 70½ years old.[2]

A reason frequently given for selling to employees is to create an incentive for them to work harder—by giving them a piece of the profits. However, employee ownership is not a panacea. Although advocates maintain that employee ownership improves motivation, leading to greater effort and reduced waste, the value of increased employee effort resulting from improved motivation varies significantly from firm to firm. Selling all or part of a firm to employees works only if the company's employees have an owner's mentality—that is, they do not think in "9-to-5" terms. An ESOP may provide a way for the owner to sell the business, but if the employees lack the required mindset, it will not serve the business well in the future.

To illustrate the need for employee education if an ESOP is to be effective, consider the experience of Van Meter Industrial, Inc. Mick Slinger, the chief financial officer, thought his company's employee stock program was a great perk for employees. But at a company meeting, an employee stood up and said he didn't care at all about the stock fund, asking, "Why don't you just give me a couple hundred bucks for beer and cigarettes?" It was a wake-up call for Slinger. Many employees at the 100 percent employee-owned company, which is based in Cedar Rapids, Iowa, "didn't know what stock was, didn't know what an [employee] owner was," he recalls. "I made the mistake of thinking that everyone thinks like me." So the company created an employee committee to raise awareness of stock ownership and to get workers thinking about what each of them as owners can do to raise the price of company stock—and how it affects their own net worth. Today, employees are much more engaged in the program, and the firm's management believes it has made a significant contribution to increasing its stock price and lowering employee turnover. But it required a lot of effort to make the plan work as desired.[3]

The approaches that have been described in this section for selling a company represent the primary ways small business owners exit their businesses. But the opportunity to sell a business can be affected by market conditions. For instance, in 2009 selling a business required recognizing the effects of the recession. There just were not as many buyers—but neither were there as many sellers. Entrepreneurs who had been considering an exit were holding back in the hope of an economic recovery when they would receive a better price for the business.

Michael Handelsman, general manager of BizBuySell, an online marketplace that lists companies for sale, offers these tips for selling a business in a difficult economy:[4]

- **Clean up the books.** Pay off small debts if you can, and make sure your records are ready for buyers' review.
- **Keep revenue strong.** Continue marketing and bringing in customers to show buyers that your business is still flourishing.
- **Consider your sector and market.** The downturn isn't the same in every city or every industry. Research businesses sold in your sector or town to see if it's a good time to sell.

These tips are relevant at any time—recession or no recession—and even when you are not interested in selling.

The recession also affected the availability of financing from traditional sources. As a result, **seller financing**, in which a seller loans the buyer part of the purchase price of the business, became more prevalent. For instance, an entrepreneur who purchased a business for $3.5 million paid $2.7 million in cash, and the seller took a note for the remaining $800,000, which was to be paid off over the next seven years. The $2.7 million in cash came from a bank loan of $2 million and $700,000 from the buyer's personal money. The loan from the seller was subordinated to the bank loan, so that if the buyer missed a payment to the bank, she could not make any payments to the seller until the bank loan was current.

seller financing
Financing in which the seller accepts a note from a buyer in lieu of cash in partial payment for a business.

DISTRIBUTING THE FIRM'S CASH FLOWS

A second harvest strategy involves the orderly withdrawal of the owners' investment in the form of the firm's cash flows. The withdrawal process could be immediate if the owners simply sold off the assets of the firm and liquidated the business. However, for a value-creating firm—one that earns attractive rates of return for its investors—this does not make economic sense. The mere fact that a firm is earning high rates of return on its assets indicates that the business is worth more as a going concern than a dead one. Shutting down the company is not an economically rational option. Instead, the owners might simply stop growing the business; by doing so, they increase the cash flows that can be returned to investors.

In a firm's early years, all of its cash is usually devoted to growing the business. Thus, the company's inflow of cash during this period is zero—or, more likely, negative—requiring its owners to seek outside cash to finance its growth. As the firm matures and opportunities to grow the business decline, sizable cash flows frequently become available to its owners. Rather than reinvest all the cash in the business, the owners can begin to withdraw the cash, thus harvesting their investment. If they decide to adopt this approach, only the amount of cash necessary to maintain current markets is retained and reinvested; there is little, if any, effort to grow the present markets or expand into new markets.

Harvesting by slowly withdrawing a firm's cash from the business has two important advantages: The owners can retain control of the business while they harvest their investment, and they do not have to seek out a buyer or incur the expenses associated with consummating a sale. There are disadvantages, however. Reducing investment when the firm faces valuable growth opportunities could leave a firm unable to sustain its competitive advantage. The end result may be an unintended reduction in the value of the business. Also, there may be tax disadvantages to an orderly liquidation, compared with other harvest methods. For example, if a corporation distributes cash as dividends, both the company and the stockholders will be taxed on the income; this is known as **double taxation**. (However, there is no double taxation for a sole proprietorship, partnership, limited liability company, or S corporation.)

double taxation
Taxation of income that occurs twice—first as corporate earnings and then as stockholder dividends.

Finally, for the entrepreneur who is simply tired of day-to-day operations, siphoning off the cash flows over time may require too much patience. Unless other people in the firm are qualified to manage it, this strategy may be destined to fail.

LIVING THE DREAM

entrepreneurial experiences

© iStockphoto.com/Angelika Schwarz

Firm Sells Itself to Let Patriarch Cash Out

When Anthony Carnevale was in his early sixties, he began scaling back at his family-owned business at the encouragement of his wife. Carnevale was ready to retire, but his successful startup, Sentinel Benefits & Financial Group, a leading employee benefit consulting and administration firm, would not survive cashing out his ownership. Even though the company was successful, it didn't have the cash to make it work. If Carnevale's sons and the company's two other partners had had to buy out Carnevale's shares, the company would have had little cash left for growth.

When a bank wouldn't give the company a $5 million loan, Carnevale's sons and partners looked to competitors who were interested in buying the company. Even if the bank had approved the loan, the company would still be strained by interest payments in addition to paying on the principal due. The option of being bought out by competitors was unsavory as well, since the management team did not want to lose control of the company.

As a businessman, Carnevale wanted to harvest his company, but as a parent he didn't want to burden his sons with having to support the business after a huge cash loss. So Sentinel sold itself to Focus Financial Partners LLC, a partnership that buys small money-management firms and lets them operate fairly independently. This is an increasingly common arrangement for small financial firms since it allows the sellers to remain in control of the company even though they have sold their ownership.

The agreement stated that Focus would own 100 percent of Sentinel, and each of the partners (including Carnevale, his sons, and the other partners) would be bought out for an undisclosed sum in addition to Focus stock. The management team of the sons and other partners are now paid based on the company's revenue and growth.

When the announcement was made to employees about the new structure, only one employee left as a result. Most were completely unaffected, and daily operations have not changed much for the management team. And Carnevale still isn't fully retired. While he doesn't have an official title, he still works on various company projects.

Source: Adapted from Simona Covel, "Small Business Link: Firm Sells Itself to Let Patriarch Cash Out," *Wall Street Journal*, October 2007, p. B8. **http://www.sentinelbenefits.com**

INITIAL PUBLIC OFFERING (IPO)

A third method of harvesting a firm is an initial public offering. As discussed in Chapter 12, an **initial public offering (IPO)** occurs when a private firm sells its shares for the first time to the general public. This requires registering the stock issue with the Securities and Exchange Commission (SEC) and adhering to Blue Sky Laws that govern the public offering at a state level. The purpose of these federal and state laws is to ensure adequate disclosure to investors and to prevent fraud. Businesses intending to conduct an IPO must file a detailed registration statement with the SEC, which includes in-depth financial, management, and operational information.

initial public offering (IPO) The first sale of shares of a company's stock to the public.

Many entrepreneurs consider the prospect of an initial public offering as the "holy grail" of their career, bringing with it increased prestige with many in business circles. However, since 2001 the option to issue an IPO has been limited dramatically, especially for smaller IPOs. Brad Feld, an investor in early-stage businesses and an entrepreneur for more than 20 years, shares his experiences in these words:

> *In the 1990s, the aspiration of every VC-backed company was to go public. Especially in the second half of the decade, the IPO was a magical accomplishment. Once a company went public, it was special and valuable, and the entrepreneur was a rock star.*
>
> *During this period, every entrepreneur I met talked about his goal of taking his company public as his exit strategy. Every company pitch I saw had a slide titled "Exit Strategy" and had "Go Public" as its headline. The fallback strategy was "Be Acquired."*
>
> *Going public seemed like a great idea at the time, but by 2002, it was an excruciatingly painful experience. That year, I sat on the board of directors of four public companies. At one point, every company was trading at a price below $1, at risk for delisting, and spending a ridiculous amount of energy discussing its crummy stock price and trying to figure out what to do about it.*[5]

As shown in Exhibit 13.2, IPOs were essentially nonexistent during late 2008 and early 2009. Since then, there has been a modest increase in their number, which continued into 2011. Not only have there been a much smaller number of IPOs in recent years, but the types of companies that investors prefer have changed as well. In earlier years, more-established firms financed significantly with debt were in vogue. In 2010, most IPOs were fast-growing high-tech companies, with a smaller number of financial services companies and an occasional entertainment and consumer company.[6] But for entrepreneurs and any investors wanting to take a company public, the situation has been bleak. Hopefully, the economy will improve in the years to come, and public markets will once again be a viable option.

Beyond the "shutting down" of the IPO market during 2008–2009, most entrepreneurs do not really understand the actual process, especially when it comes to how going public relates to the harvest. We next discuss how the IPO process works so that you will have the necessary information if going public once again becomes a viable option.

Reasons for Going Public

An IPO occurs when a company offers its stock to the general public, rather than limiting its sale to founders, friends and family, and other private investors. The purpose of this process is to create a ready market for buying and selling the stock. Before the stock is traded publicly, there is no marketplace where the shares can be easily bought and sold, and thus it is difficult to know what the stock is worth.

IPOs have a number of benefits, including the following:[7]

1. An IPO is one way to signal to investors that a firm is a quality business and will likely perform well in the future.

EXHIBIT 13.2 IPOs 2007–2010

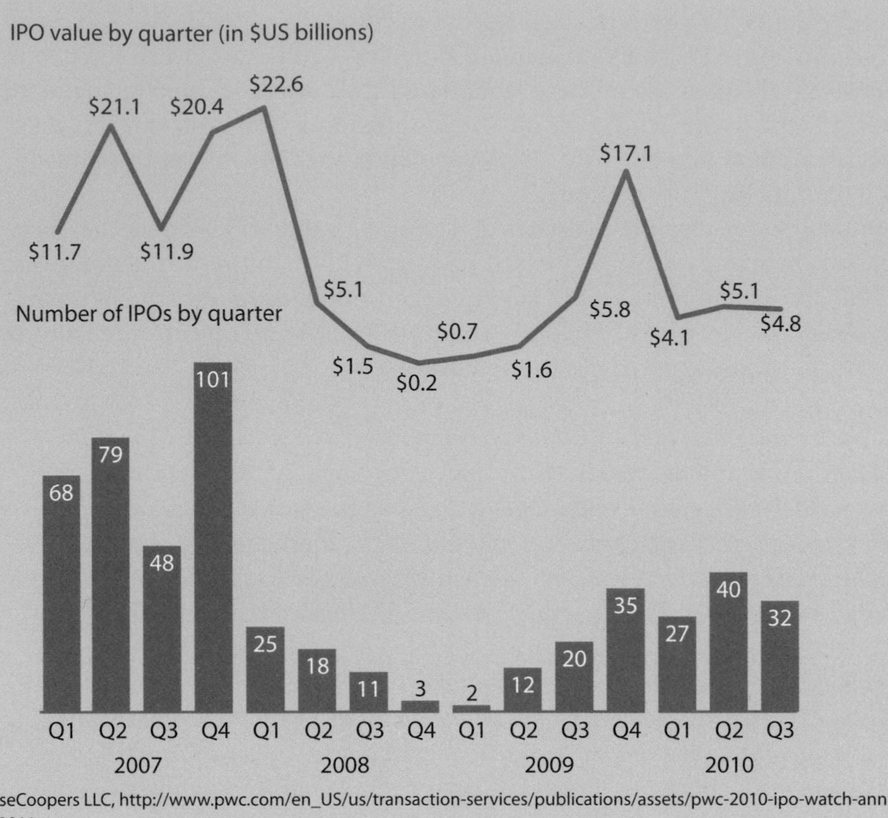

Source: PricewaterhouseCoopers LLC, http://www.pwc.com/en_US/us/transaction-services/publications/assets/pwc-2010-ipo-watch-annual-report.pdf, accessed April 1, 2011.

2. A firm whose stock is traded publicly has access to more investors when it needs to raise capital to grow the business.
3. Being publicly traded helps create ongoing interest in the company and its continued development.
4. Publicly traded stock is more attractive to key personnel whose incentive pay includes the firm's stock.

While there are several reasons for going public, the primary reason is to raise capital. In 80 percent of the cases, money raised from selling a firm's stock to the public is used for expansion, paying down debt, and increasing the firm's liquidity (cash). The other 20 percent of initial public offerings result from entrepreneurs' desire to sell their stock.[8] Thus, in four out of five cases, IPOs are not intended as an *immediate* exit strategy but rather as a way to raise capital for growth. Eventually, however, entrepreneurs can and frequently do sell their shares as a way to cash out of their companies.

The IPO Process

The basic steps in the IPO process are as follows:

Step 1. The firm's owners decide to go public.

Step 2. If it has not already done so, the company must have its financial statements for the past three years audited by a certified public accountant.

Step 3. An investment banker is selected to guide management in the IPO process.

Step 4. An S-1 Registration Statement is filed with the Securities Exchange Commission (SEC), which requires about one month to review it.

Step 5. Management responds to comments by the SEC and issues a Red Herring/ Prospectus, describing the firm and the offering.

Step 6. Management spends the next 10 to 15 days on the road, presenting the firm to potential investors.

Step 7. On the day before the offering is released to the public, the actual offering price is set. Based on the demand for the offering, the shares are priced to create active trading of the stock.

Step 8. Months of work come to fruition in a single event—offering the stock to the public and seeing how it is received.

The IPO process may be one of the most exhilarating—but frustrating and exhausting—experiences of a small business owner's life. To many, the costs of the IPO process seem exorbitant. Also, owners may find themselves being misunderstood and having little influence on the decisions being made during the process. As a consequence, they are frequently disillusioned with investment bankers and wonder where they lost control of the process.

To understand an IPO, you must consider the shift in power that occurs during the process. When the chain of events begins, the firm's owner is in control. At that point, the owner dictates whether or not to go public and who the investment banker will be. After the prospectus has been prepared and the road show is under way, however, the firm's owner is no longer the primary decision maker. The investment banker is now in control. Finally, the marketplace, in concert with the investment banker, begins to take over. Ultimately, it is the market that dictates the final outcome.

In addition to being prepared for the shift in control, it is important that the entrepreneur understand the investment banker's motivations in the IPO process. Who is the investment banker's primary customer? Clearly, the issuing firm is compensating the underwriter for its services through the fees paid and participation in the offering. But helping a firm with an IPO usually is not as profitable for the investment banker as are other activities, such as involvement in corporate acquisitions. And the investment banker is also selling the securities to the customers on the other side of the trade. These are the people who will continue to do business with the investment banker in the future. Thus, the investment banker is somewhat conflicted as to who the "customer" is.

An entrepreneur must also consider more than just the initial costs of the IPO; he or she must think hard about the costs of running a publicly traded company. Operating a public firm is far more expensive than operating a private company. A publicly traded company has significant ongoing costs associated with reporting its financial results to investors and to the SEC. These costs were significantly increased in 2001 when the U.S. Congress passed the Sarbanes-Oxley Act. The act places a much greater burden on companies to have good accounting practices and controls that will prevent egregious offenses by managers. In 2009, Congress passed the Dodd-Frank Act, which is primarily aimed at banks and other financial institutions to help avoid a repeat of the most recent financial crisis. However, it also added costly requirements on all publicly

ACTION

Evaluate Your Business as a Buyer Would

Take time periodically to look at your company as if you were a prospective buyer. You'll notice things that you might otherwise overlook, such as improvements you can make and best practices you can adopt.

traded companies. Furthermore, the costs to a small firm are disproportionate and are no small consideration in the decision to go public.

So, although many entrepreneurs seek to take their firms public through an IPO, this strategy is appropriate for only a limited number of firms. And even for this small group, an IPO is more a means of raising growth capital than an effective harvest strategy.

PRIVATE PLACEMENT

A fourth method of harvesting is a *private placement* (described briefly in Chapter 12), which is simply money provided by private investors. The private investors can be an individual or group of individuals who act together to invest in companies.

Private equity investors offer two key advantages that public investors do not: immediacy and flexibility. With private equity, an entrepreneur can sell most of her or his stock immediately, an option not available when a company is taken public. Also, private equity investors can be more flexible in structuring their investment to meet the entrepreneur's needs.

Although the situation is complicated by the different needs of each generation, private equity is particularly effective for family-owned businesses that need to transfer ownership to the next generation. In the transfer of ownership between generations, there must be a trade-off among three important goals: (1) liquidity (cash) for the selling family members, (2) continued financing for the company's future growth, and (3) the desire of the younger generation to maintain control of the firm. In other words, the older generation wants to get cash out of the business, while the younger generation wants to retain the cash needed to finance the firm's growth and yet not lose ownership control.

To understand how a private placement might work, consider the following approach taken by Heritage Partners, a Boston venture capital firm that works with family-owned businesses in which the older generation wants to exit the business and needs money for retirement, while the younger generation would like to retain some ownership in the business and continue to provide managerial leadership.[9]

Assume that a company could be sold for $20 million through a leveraged buyout (LBO), which would most likely be financed through at least 80 percent debt and 20 percent equity. Many entrepreneurs find such an arrangement intolerable. They simply would not want their company subjected to the risk associated with a large amount of debt financing. Also, with an LBO the family generally loses control of the business.

As an alternative to an LBO, the retiring generation might sell to Heritage Partners for $18 million—10 percent less than the LBO price—of which $15 million would be paid to the retiring generation and $3 million reinvested in the business by the younger generation. For the $3 million investment, the younger generation would receive 51 percent of the equity. The remaining $15 million of the purchase price would be financed from two sources: $7 million in debt and $8 million from Heritage Partners, consisting of $4 million in preferred stock and $4 million in common stock. The preferred stock would provide an annual dividend, while the common stock would give the new investor 49 percent of the firm's ownership (see Exhibit 13.3).

The differences between the two capital structures are clear. The debt ratio is much lower in the private placement than in the LBO, allowing for a lower interest rate on the debt and permitting the firm's cash flows to be used to grow the firm, rather than pay down debt. This arrangement allows the senior generation of owners to cash out, while the next generation retains control and the cash to grow the firm—a win-win situation. The younger generation also has the potential to realize significant economic gains if the firm performs well after the sale.

EXHIBIT 13.3 Private Placement—An Illustration

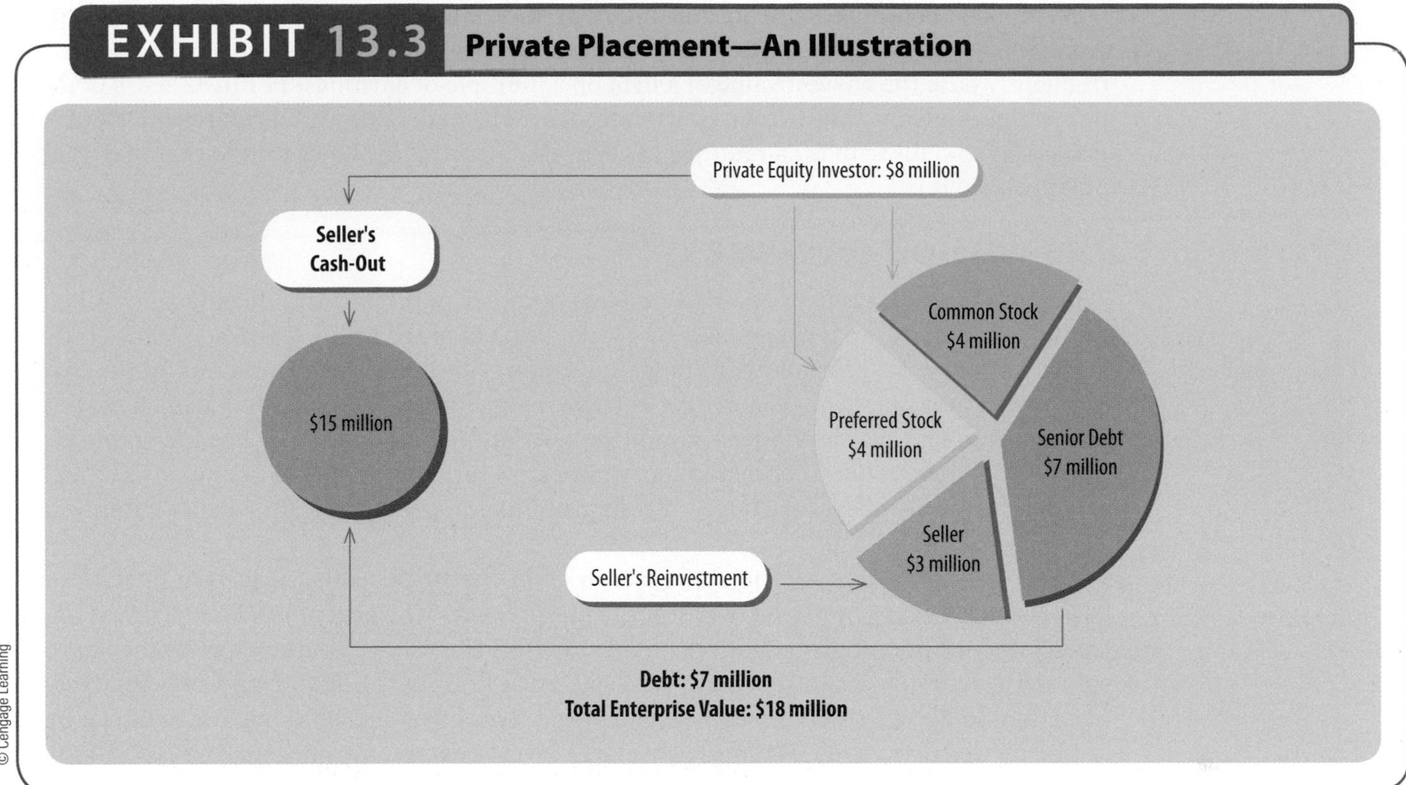

Firm Valuation and the Harvest

As a firm moves toward the harvest, two issues are of primary importance: the harvest value (what the firm is worth) and the method of payment when a firm is sold.

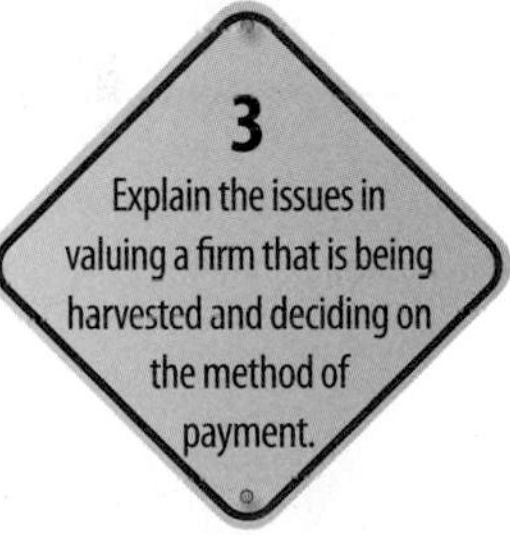

THE HARVEST VALUE

Valuing a company may be necessary on numerous occasions during the life of the business—but it is never more important than at the time of the exit. Owners can harvest only what they have created. Value is created when a firm's return on invested capital is greater than the investors' **opportunity cost of funds**, which is the rate of return that could be earned on an investment of similar risk.

opportunity cost of funds The rate of return that could be earned on another investment of similar risk.

Growing a venture to the point of diminishing returns and then selling it to others who can carry it to the next level is a proven way to create value. How this incremental value is shared between the old and the new owners depends largely on the relative strengths of each party in the negotiations—that is, who wants the deal the most or who has the best negotiating skills.

Business valuation is part science and part art, so there is no precise formula for determining the price of a private company. Rather, the price is determined by a sometimes intricate process of negotiation between buyer and seller. Much is left to the negotiating skills of the respective parties. But one thing is certain: There must be a willing buyer. It doesn't matter what a firm's owner believes the business is worth; it is worth only what someone who has the cash is prepared to pay.

The specific approaches to and methods for valuing a company are described in Appendix B at the end of the book. As described in the appendix, buyers and sellers frequently base the harvest value of a firm on a multiple of earnings. For instance, a company might be valued at five times its earnings. (The experience of entrepreneur Robert Hall, who sold his firm for a multiple of earnings, provides the basis for the example used in Appendix B.)

THE METHOD OF PAYMENT

The actual value of a firm is only one issue; another is the method of payment. When selling a company, an entrepreneur has three basic choices: sell the firm's assets, sell its stock, or, if the buyer is another company, merge with the buyer by combining the two companies into one firm. The exiting entrepreneur may prefer to sell the firm's stock so that the gain on the sale will be a capital gain, resulting in lower taxes. The buyer, on the other hand, may prefer to purchase the firm's assets rather than buy the company's stock. Buying the assets relieves the buyer of responsibility for any of the selling firm's liabilities, known or unknown.

Harvesting owners can be paid in cash or in the stock of the acquiring firm, with cash generally being preferred over stock. Entrepreneurs who accept stock in payment are frequently disappointed, as they are unable to affect the value of the stock once they have sold the firm. Only an entrepreneur who has great faith in the acquiring firm's management should accept stock in payment, and even then he or she is taking a big chance by not being well diversified. Having such a large investment in only one stock is risky, to say the least.

LIVING THE DREAM

entrepreneurship + integrity

Johnny Stites on Beginning with the End in Mind

When I started my business, I was focused on making money and being successful. I had been taught in business school the fundamentals of being in business. I visited other successful individuals and companies to see what I could replicate in my business to ensure its success. I went right to work and worked hard for 10 years. I did not take the time to sit down and envision what I wanted my business to look like in the future. I did not take the time to set a mission statement and establish that mission in the day-to-day operations of the business. I worked hard, but not smart.

After 10 years of mediocre success, I stepped back and looked at what I was doing and how it was impacting people—people inside my company and people outside my company. What I saw I didn't like. I saw a company finally making money, but not positively influencing lives.

I have determined that if, at the end of my tenure in our family business, I have not inspired individuals to be better spouses, better parents, and better citizens, then I have lost the greatest opportunity to increase the value of the company. A company that doesn't change lives in a positive way and just gives money to employees and provides services to customers is not one to be valued very highly.

Source: Written comments by Johnny Stites, CEO, J&S Construction, October 2010. **http://www.jsconstruction.com**

Developing an Effective Harvest Plan

We have discussed why planning for the harvest is important, despite the tendency of many small business owners to ignore it until some crisis or unanticipated event comes along. We have also described the methods for harvesting. However, understanding what the options are for exiting a company in no way guarantees a successful harvest. More times than not, owners who harvest their businesses are disappointed with the process and the outcome. In the sections that follow, we provide suggestions for crafting an effective exit strategy.[10]

ANTICIPATE THE HARVEST

Entrepreneurs frequently do not appreciate the difficulty of harvesting a company. One investor commented that exiting a business is "like brain surgery—it's done a lot, but there are a lot of things that can go wrong." Harvesting, whether through a sale or a stock offering, takes a lot of time and energy on the part of the firm's management team and can be very distracting from day-to-day affairs. The result is often a loss of managerial focus and momentum, leading to poor performance.

Uncertainties accompanying an impending sale often lower employee morale. The stress can affect the whole organization, as employees become anxious about the prospect of a new owner. Lynn Baker, at Sutter Hill Ventures, offers this advice: "Don't start running the company for the liquidity event. Run the business for the long haul." Jim Porter, at CCI Triad, describes the situation in Silicon Valley in the 1990s, where some owners carried the practice to an extreme:

> *Some people don't think in terms of long-term value as much as short-term returns. This carries over into developing an IPO exit strategy. I see a growing number of people who are already planning their next company before they are finished with the first company. They are looking to exit the first one, get the money out and start the second one, get the money out, and pyramid their return. In a hot market, you can do that and get away with it. They are professional company starters.*

So, while an entrepreneur should not be caught unaware, there is also the risk of becoming so attentive to "playing the harvest game" that one forgets to keep first things first.

Investors are always concerned about how to exit, and entrepreneurs need to have a similar mindset. Peter Hermann, general partner at Heritage Partners, notes, "People generally stumble into the exit and don't plan for it." However, for Hermann, "The exit strategy begins when the money goes in." Similarly, Gordon Baty, formerly at Zero Stage Capital, Inc., and now an angel investor, enters each investment with a clear understanding of its investment horizon and harvest plan: "We plan for an acquisition and hope for an IPO." Jack Kearney, at Dain Rauscher Inc., indicates that an exit strategy should be formulated in advance, unless "the entrepreneur expects to die in the CEO chair. . . . The worst of all worlds is to realize, for health or other reasons, that you have to sell the company right now." Jim Knister, at the Donnelly Corporation, advises entrepreneurs to start thinking two or three years ahead about how they are going to exit so that they can correctly position their companies.

This type of advice is particularly important when the entrepreneur is planning an IPO. Running a public company requires information disclosures to stockholders that are not required of a privately held firm. Specifically, this means (1) maintaining an accounting process that cleanly separates the business from the entrepreneur's personal life, (2) selecting a strong board of directors that can and will offer valuable business advice, and (3) managing the firm so as to produce a successful track record of performance.

Having a harvest plan in place is also very important because the window of opportunity can open and close quickly. Remember that the opportunity to exit is triggered by the arrival of a willing and able buyer, not just an interested seller. For an IPO, a hot market may offer a very attractive opportunity, and a seller must be ready to move when the opportunity arises.

In summary, an entrepreneur should be sure to anticipate the harvest. In the words of Ed Cherney, an entrepreneur who has sold two companies, "Don't wait to put your package together until something dramatic happens. Begin thinking about the exit strategy and start going through the motions, so that if something major happens, you will have had time to think through your options."

EXPECT CONFLICT—EMOTIONAL AND CULTURAL

Having bought other companies does not prepare entrepreneurs for the sale of their own company. Entrepreneurs who have been involved in the acquisition of other firms are still ill-prepared for the stress associated with selling their own businesses. Jim Porter, who has been involved in a number of acquisitions, says, "It's definitely a lot more fun to buy something than it is to be bought." One very real difference between selling and buying comes from the entrepreneur's personal ties to the business that he or she helped create. A buyer can be quite unemotional and detached, while a seller is likely to be much more concerned about nonfinancial considerations.

For this reason and many others, entrepreneurs frequently do not make good employees. The very qualities that made them successful entrepreneurs can make it difficult for them to work under a new owner. In fact, an entrepreneur who plans to stay with the firm after a sale can become disillusioned quickly and end up leaving prematurely.

Lynn Baker observes, "There is a danger of culture conflict between the acquiring versus the acquired firm's management. The odds are overwhelming that somebody who's been an entrepreneur is not going to be happy in a corporate culture." When Ed Bonneau sold his wholesale sunglass distribution firm, he was retained as a consultant, but the buyer never sought his advice. Bonneau recalled that he "could not imagine that someone could or would buy a company and not operate it. The people who bought the firm had no operations expertise or experience whatsoever and, in fact, didn't care that much about it."

These conflicts occur to varying degrees whenever an entrepreneur remains with the company after the sale. Although the nature of the conflict varies, the intensity of the feelings does not. An entrepreneur who stays with the company should expect culture conflict and be pleasantly surprised if it does not occur.

GET GOOD ADVICE

Entrepreneurs learn to operate their businesses through experience gained in repeated day-to-day activities. However, they may engage in a harvest transaction only once in a lifetime. "It's an emotional roller-coaster ride," says Ben Buettell, who frequently represents sellers of small and mid-sized companies.[11] Thus, entrepreneurs have a real need for good advice, both from experienced professionals and from those who have personally been through a harvest. In seeking advice, be aware that the experts who helped you build and grow your business may not be the best ones to use when it's time to sell the company, as they may not have the experience needed in that area. So, choose your advisors carefully.

Bill Dedmon, at Southwest Securities, advises, "Don't try to do it alone, because it's a demanding process that can distract you from your business." Jack Furst, at HM Capital, believes that advisors can give entrepreneurs a reality check. He contends that, without independent advice, entrepreneurs frequently fall prey to thinking they want to sell unconditionally, when in fact they really want to sell only if an unrealistically high price is offered.

Professional advice is vital, but entrepreneurs stress the importance of talking to other entrepreneurs who have sold a firm or taken it public. No one can better describe what to expect—both in events and in emotions—than someone who has had the experience. This perspective nicely complements that of the professional advisor.

Perhaps the greatest misconception among entrepreneurs is that an IPO is the end of the line. They often feel that taking their firm public through an IPO means they have "made it." The fact is that going public is but one transition in the life of a firm. Many entrepreneurs are surprised to learn that a public offering is just the beginning, not an end.

An entrepreneur will not be able to cash out for some time after the completion of the IPO. In a sense, investors in the new stock offering have chosen to back the entrepreneur as the driving force behind the company—that is, they have invested in the entrepreneur, not the firm. While the daily stock price quotes will let the management team keep score, the business will have to reach another plateau before the founder can think about placing it in the hands of a new team and going fishing. Lynn Baker describes the typical entrepreneur's thinking about an IPO as the "*Bride Magazine* syndrome":

> *The entrepreneur is like the bride-to-be who becomes fixated on the events of the wedding day without thinking clearly about the years of being married that will follow. Life as head of a public corporation is very different from life at the helm of a private firm. Major investors will be calling every day expecting answers—sometimes with off-the-wall questions.*

Under these circumstances, getting good advice is a must.

UNDERSTAND WHAT MOTIVATES YOU

For an entrepreneur, harvesting a business that has been an integral part of life for a long period of time can be a very emotional experience. When an entrepreneur has invested a substantial part of her or his working life in growing a business, a real sense of loss may accompany the harvest. Walking away from employees, clients, and one's identity as a small business owner may not be the wonderful ride into the sunset that was expected.

So, entrepreneurs should think very carefully about their motives for exiting and what they plan to do after the harvest. Frequently, entrepreneurs have great expectations about what life is going to be like with a lot of liquidity, something many of them have never known. The harvest does provide the long-sought liquidity, but some entrepreneurs find managing money—in contrast to operating their own company—less rewarding than they had expected.

Entrepreneurs may also become disillusioned when they come to understand more fully how their sense of personal identity was intertwined with their business. While Jim Porter understands that a primary purpose of exiting is to make money, watching a number of owners cash out has led him to conclude that the money is not a very satisfying aspect of the event:

> *The bottom line is that you need more than money to sustain life and feel worthwhile. I see people who broke everything to make their money. They were willing to sacrifice their wives, their family, and their own sense of values to make money. I remember one person who was flying high, did his IPO, and went straight out and bought a flaming red Ferrari. He raced it down the street, hit a telephone pole, and died the day his IPO money came down. You see these guys . . . go crazy. They went out and bought houses in Hawaii, houses in Tahoe, new cars, and got things they didn't need.*

Peter Hermann believes that "seller's remorse" is definitely a major issue for a number of entrepreneurs. His advice: "Search your soul and make a list of what you want to achieve with the exit. Is it dollars, health of the company, your management team or an heir apparent taking over?" The answers to these and similar questions determine to a significant extent whether the exit will prove successful in all dimensions of an entrepreneur's life. There can be conflicting emotions, such as those expressed by Bill Bailey, founder of Cherokee Corporation:

> *There is a period in your life when you get up in age and you begin thinking more about your family. For me, it became important for the first time in my life to have money available to do some long-range personal planning for myself, and for my family. But if there is any one thing to be understood when you are selling a business or anything else, it is the excitement of the journey and the enjoyment for doing what you're doing that matters.*

Entrepreneurs are also well advised to be aware of potential problems that may arise after the exit. There are stories about people selling a firm or going public and then losing everything. Ed Cherney says, "It is more difficult to handle success than it is to handle struggling. People forget what got them the success—the work ethic, the commitment to family, whatever characteristics work for an entrepreneur. Once the money starts rolling in, . . . people forget and begin having problems."

And for the entrepreneur who believes that it will be easy to adapt to change after the harvest, even possibly to start another company, William Unger, at the Mayfield Fund, quotes from Machiavelli's *The Prince:* "It should be remembered that nothing is more difficult than to establish a new order of things."

What's Next?

Entrepreneurs by their very nature are purpose-driven people. So, after the exit, an entrepreneur who has been driven to build a profitable business will need something larger than the individual to bring meaning to her or his life. Many entrepreneurs have a sense of gratitude for the benefits they have received from living in a capitalist system. As a result, they want to give back, both with their time and with their money.

Blue Lake Children's Publishing

Judy Johnston is a great example of an entrepreneur who asked the question "What's next?" For Johnston, it will be a nonprofit venture. She used her life savings of $50,000 to found her first business, PrintPaks, which she sold to Mattel three years later for $26 million. Blue Lake Publishing, Johnston's most recent startup, was founded in 2002—she hopes to sell it in the next five years. Her children's magazine, *Tessy & Tab*, will eventually need a video program, she says, but that's for a successor to figure out. "I know it has to be done, but somebody else needs to own the company when it happens," she says. "There's only so far I can take it, because I'm not motivated by just making more money. I'm not qualified or interested in running a really big company."

Blue Lake will likely be Johnston's last for-profit startup, but not her last startup endeavor. "I want to do something that doesn't involve having to return capital to investors," she says. Nonprofits are still fair game.[12]

The good news is that there is no limit to the number of worthy charitable causes, including universities, churches, and civic organizations. And it may be that, when all is said and done, the call to help others with a new venture may be too strong for an individual with an entrepreneurial mindset to resist. But whatever you decide to do, do it with passion and let your life benefit others in the process.

1. Explain the importance of having a harvest, or exit, plan.

- Harvesting, or exiting, is the method entrepreneurs and investors use to get out of a business and, ideally, reap the value of their investment in the firm.
- Harvesting is about more than merely selling and leaving a business. It involves capturing value (cash flows), reducing risk, and creating future options.
- A firm's accessibility to investors is driven by the availability of harvest options.

2. Describe the options available for harvesting.

- There are four basic ways to harvest an investment in a privately owned company: (1) selling the firm, (2) distributing the firm's cash flows to its owners, (3) offering stock to the public through an IPO, and (4) issuing a private placement of the stock.
- In a sale to a strategic buyer, the value placed on a business depends on the synergies that the buyer believes can be created.
- Financial buyers look primarily to a firm's stand-alone, cash-generating potential as the source of its value.
- In leveraged buyouts (LBOs), high levels of debt financing are used to acquire firms.
- With bust-up LBOs, the assets of the acquired firm are sold to repay the debt.
- With build-up LBOs, a number of related businesses are acquired to create a larger enterprise, which may eventually be taken public via an initial public offering (IPO).
- A management buyout (MBO) is an LBO in which management is part of the group buying the company.
- In an employee stock ownership plan (ESOP), employees' retirement contributions are used to purchase shares in the company.
- The orderly withdrawal of an owner's investment in the form of the firm's cash flows is one method of harvesting a firm.
- An initial public offering (IPO) is used primarily as a way to raise additional equity capital to finance company growth, and only secondarily as a way to harvest the owner's investment.
- Private placement is a form of outside financing that can allow the original owners to cash out.
- Trying to finance liquidity and growth while retaining control is perhaps the most difficult task facing family firms.

3. Explain the issues in valuing a firm that is being harvested and deciding on the method of payment.

- Value is created when a firm's return on invested capital is greater than the investors' opportunity cost of funds.
- A firm will have greater value in the hands of new owners if the new owners can create more value than the current owners can.
- Often, buyers and sellers base the harvest value of a firm on a multiple of its earnings.
- Cash is generally preferred over stock and other forms of payment by those selling a firm.

4. Provide advice on developing an effective harvest plan.

- Investors are always concerned about exit strategy.
- Entrepreneurs who plan to stay with a business after a sale can become disillusioned quickly and end up leaving prematurely.
- Entrepreneurs frequently do not appreciate the difficulty of selling or exiting a company. Having bought other companies does not prepare entrepreneurs for the sale of their own firm.
- Entrepreneurs have a real need for good advice, both from experienced professionals and from those who have personally been through a harvest.
- Going public is not the end; it's only a transition in the life of a firm.

Key Terms

harvesting (exiting) p. 386
leveraged buyout (LBO) p. 388
bust-up LBO p. 389
build-up LBO p. 389
management buyout (MBO) p. 390
employee stock ownership plan (ESOP) p. 390
seller financing p. 391
double taxation p. 392
initial public offering (IPO) p. 393
opportunity cost of funds p. 397

Discussion Questions

1. Explain what is meant by the term *harvesting*. What is involved in harvesting an investment in a privately held firm?
2. Why should an owner of a company plan for eventually harvesting his or her company?
3. Contrast a sale to a strategic buyer with one to a financial buyer.
4. Explain the term *leveraged buyout*. How is a leveraged buyout different from a management buyout?
5. Distinguish between bust-up LBOs and build-up LBOs.
6. What is the primary purpose of an initial public offering (IPO)? How does an IPO relate to a harvest?
7. Why might an entrepreneur find going public a frustrating process?
8. What determines whether a firm has value to a prospective purchaser?
9. What problems can occur when an entrepreneur sells a firm but continues in the management of the company?
10. How may harvesting a firm affect an entrepreneur's personal identity?

You Make the Call

SITUATION 1

The In the Spotlight feature in this chapter featured Li'l Guy Foods, which was acquired by Tortilla King, a larger company. This acquisition was part of a merger involving Li'l Guy Foods and three other top Mexican food brands in the Midwest. After the merger, Tortilla King held 20 percent of the market share in Kansas City.

Christina and David Sloan, grandchildren of Li'l Guy Foods' founders, were given seats on Tortilla King's six-member board and continue to work for the company. "We're so excited about all of this," said Christina, Li'l Guy vice president and sales director. "This will ensure the longevity of our brand."

Source: "Merger of Local Companies a Recipe for Success," http://www.lilguyfoods.com/about_newsReleases_companyMerger.php, accessed April 2, 2011.

Question 1 Describe the scenario as presented In the Spotlight at the beginning of the chapter.
Question 2 What would be the reasons for and against Christina and David Sloan working for Tortilla King?
Question 3 What advice would you offer the Sloans?

SITUATION 2

Ed and Barbara Bonneau started their wholesale sunglass distribution firm 30 years ago with $1,000 of their own money and $5,000 borrowed from a country banker in Ed's hometown. The firm grew quickly, selling sunglasses and reading glasses to such companies as Walmart, Eckerd Drugs, and Phar-Mor. In addition, the Bonneaus enjoyed using the company to do good things. For example, they had a company chaplain, who was available when employees were having family problems, such as a death in the family.

Although the company had done well, the market had matured recently and profit margins narrowed significantly. Walmart, for example, was insisting on better terms, which meant significantly lower profits for the Bonneaus. Previously, Ed had set the prices that he needed to make a good return on his investment. Now, the buyers had consolidated, and they had the power. Ed didn't enjoy running the company as much as he had in the past, and he was finding greater pleasure in other activities; for instance, he served on a local hospital board and was actively involved in church activities.

Just as Ed and Barbara began to think about selling the company, they were contacted by a financial buyer, who wanted to use their firm as a platform and then buy up several sunglass companies. After negotiations, the Bonneaus sold their firm for about $20 million. In addition, Ed received a retainer fee for serving as a consultant to the buyer. Also, the Bonneaus' son-in-law, who was part of the company's management team, was named the new chief operating officer.

Question 1 Do you agree with the Bonneaus' decision to sell? Why or why not?
Question 2 Why did the buyers retain Ed as a consultant?
Question 3 Do you see any problem with having the Bonneaus' son-in-law become the new chief operating officer?

SITUATION 3

An entrepreneur addresses the difficult question of when to sell his business:

> *I started my telecommunications business when I was 18, and I'm going to be 47 this summer. It's a successful business and provides me with a good living. I love the technology. I love my employees. I love my customers (most of them). Yet each day I feel more and more unfulfilled in what I'm doing. At the risk of sounding arrogant, I feel like a big fish in a little pond, unchallenged and bored. I have a lot of business knowledge that I feel is being wasted here, just doing the same thing year after year. I've tried some side ventures over the years without much success. I've also considered selling the business, but it's too large to be bought by a local competitor—we do about $2.5 million a year—and too small to attract the attention of large companies. Besides, I don't know what I'd do if I did sell it. And will whatever I do next allow me to earn as much money as I'm earning now? More important, will I like it, or will I regret letting go of the one thing I've had all my adult life?*

Source: Norm Brodsky, "Street Smarts: Ask Norm," *Inc.*, July 2008, pp. 69–70.

Question 1 Do you agree that the entrepreneur's company is not sellable?
Question 2 Are there any other options for the entrepreneur besides selling his business?
Question 3 What would you recommend the entrepreneur do? Why?

Experiential Exercises

1. Check your local newspaper for a week or so to find a privately held company that has been sold recently. Try to determine the motivation for the sale. Did it have anything to do with the prior owners' desire to cash out of the business? If so, try to find out what happened.
2. Ask a local family business owner about future plans to harvest the business. Has the owner ever been involved in a harvest? If so, ask the owner to describe what happened and how it all worked out, as well as what she or he learned from the experience. If not, ask whether the owner is aware of any company whose owners cashed out. Visit that company owner to inquire about the exit event.
3. Visit a local CPA to learn about his or her involvement in helping entrepreneurs cash out of companies.
4. Search a business magazine to identify a firm that has successfully completed an initial public offering (IPO). See what you can find out about the event on the Internet.

Small Business & Entrepreneurship Resource Center

1. Specialty Blades, Inc., went public through an off-the-grid IPO with its bank, saving much of the expense of a traditional IPO process. Employee profit-sharing plans can be a very effective means to increase productivity with a focus on the overall profitability of the firm, but employees must have the correct mindset for it to become an effective strategy. After reading the article "Keeping the Cap Tight on Those Bottlenecks," briefly describe the problem at Specialty Blades, and how the plastic Coke bottle and the idea of the roving bottleneck were an effective way to strengthen productivity and efficiency.

   Source: "Keeping the Cap Tight on Those Bottlenecks," *Tooling & Production*, Vol. 65, No. 10 (January 2000), p. 35.

2. Lurita Doan wasn't considered successful at her old job. A computer programmer for a large federal contractor, Doan couldn't help thinking outside the box—and that wasn't a good thing. When she went to her managers with an idea to customize software

for their clients, they basically told her to go back to her cubicle and be quiet. Devastated and a little angry, Doan quit her job a few weeks later and started her own company, New Technology Management, Inc., an IT company that specializes in border security and systems integration. Read the article to understand her thinking that success means independence and comes through hard work. Describe how Doan worked hard to develop a solid reputation for her company, thus earning major contracts.

Source: Tamara E. Holmes, "A Tradition of Success: A Legacy of Business Ownership Drives Tech Security Pioneer," *Black Enterprise*, Vol. 34, No. 11 (June 2004), p. 75.

Case 13

GREENWOOD DAIRIES (P. 719)

David Greenwood turned 65 in the spring of 2005 and he had just retired from Greenwood Dairies, the farm he had founded. He sold it and became bored with retirement, longing for the old days when he and his wife worked endless hours to build the dairy farm into a thriving company. So when the new owners put the farm back on the market at a fraction of the price he had sold it for, David was astounded at his good fortune and quickly bought it back. He shows how harvesting can be difficult.

ALTERNATIVE CASE FOR CHAPTER 13

Case 5, W. S. Darley & Co., p. 702

FOCUSING ON THE CUSTOMER: MARKETING GROWTH STRATEGIES

PART 4

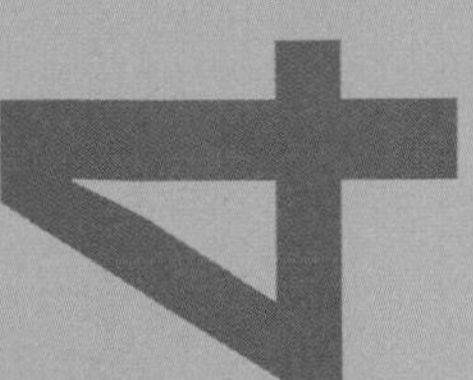

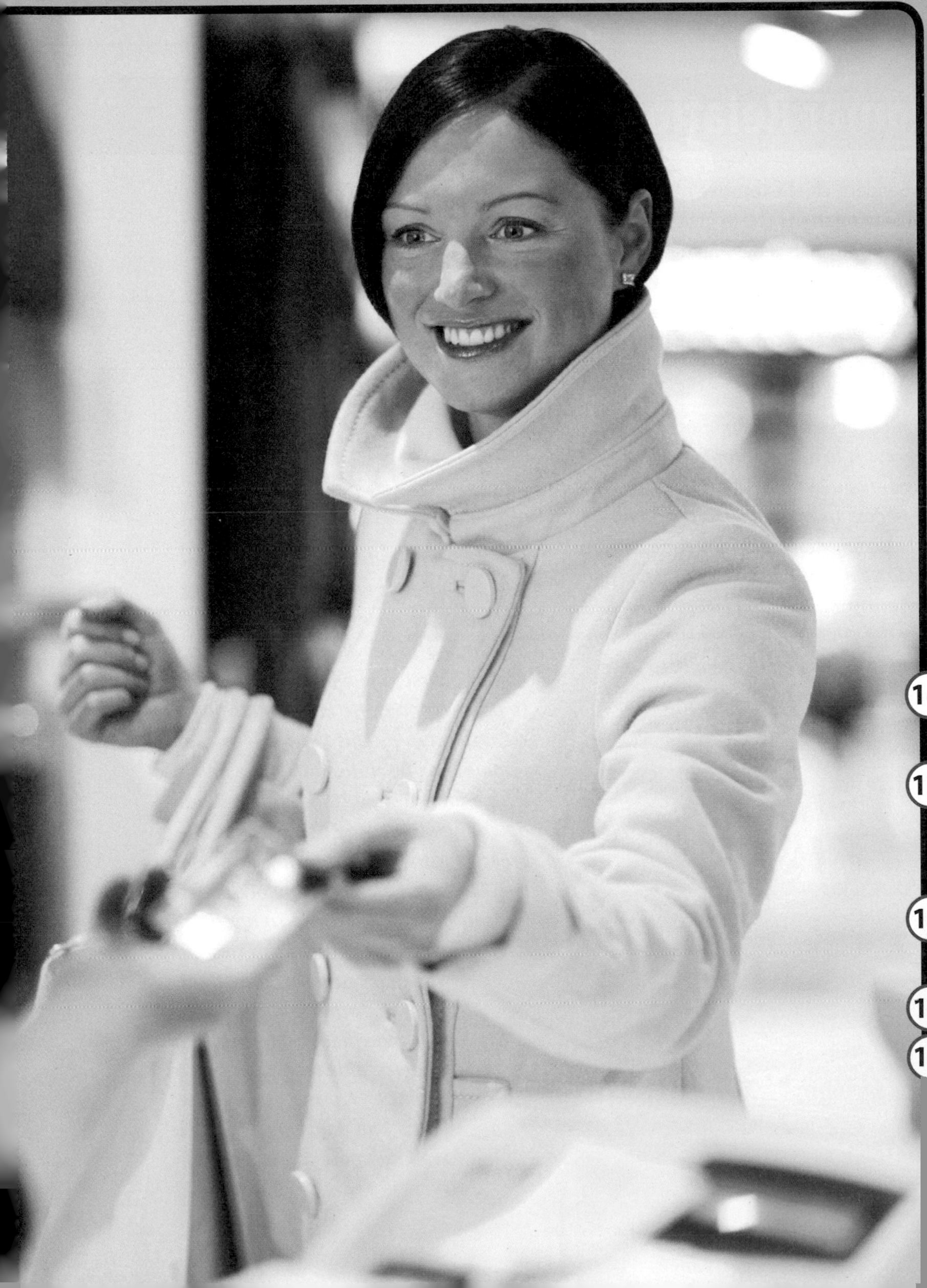

© iStockphoto.com/Daniel Laflor

CHAPTERS

CHAPTER 14

Building Customer Relationships

In the VIDEO SPOTLIGHT
United Supermarkets LLC
http://www.unitedtexas.com

Dan J. Sanders, chief executive officer of United Supermarkets LLC (a post he held until February of 2010), is a passionate proponent of building customer relationships with care. He is also the author of two best-selling books that underscore this critical theme. He explains why taking care of customers is so important:

> *I don't believe that the purpose of a business is to make a profit; I believe the purpose of a business is to fill a need. And the degree to which we make a profit is just a commentary [on] how good of a job we do filling the need. In fact, if I had my way, every organization in America would have the same vision statement, and that vision statement would be this: to serve and enrich the lives of others.*

Photo by Mark Wilson/Getty Images

We had a lady come to our store with a ham that was clearly bad, and she was very upset with us and was demanding to see the store manager. And of course, the employees were quick to point him out. He is getting ripped stem to stern by this lady, and as she is ripping him, he notices that the ham has a logo on it from a competitor's store down the street. And as she takes a breath for the second volley, he says to her, "Ma'am, I am sorry you are upset, but this ham came from a competitor down the street. We don't sell this ham." She glanced down, saw the logo from the other company and was mortified. Then the store director did something special. He said, "I am sorry you have had a bad day; why don't you walk with me to the back of

After studying this chapter, you should be able to . . .

1. Define *customer relationship management (CRM)*, and explain its importance to a small business.
2. Discuss the significance of providing extraordinary customer service.
3. Understand how technology can improve customer relationships.
4. Describe techniques used to create a customer profile.
5. Explain how consumers are decision makers and why this is important in understanding customer relationships.
6. Identify certain psychological influences on consumer behavior.
7. Recognize certain sociological influences on consumer behavior.

LOOKING AHEAD

© iStockphoto.com/Dan Bachman

the store. You pick out whatever it is you want, and we will get you back on the road as fast as possible, no charge."

But you know, it is not a story about a bad ham. Good grief, we have been in business 93 years. I am sure we have had our share of bad hams. It is a story about a store director [who] made a decision that was based on a higher purpose.... We don't have a training manual that if someone shows up to the store with a ham from a competitor and it is no good, give them a free ham. Can you imagine trying to write a training manual that had every conceivable situation that might happen inside a store? But what you could say is this: we are here to serve and enrich the lives of others, and if you see an opportunity to do that—do it. You may have some folks down in accounting [who] are a little upset from time to time—we can't be giving away hams! Good decision or bad decision? To give away that ham is a great decision; [that customer] has been an extension of our marketing department. She has been walking around constantly telling everybody about this free ham.

Sanders is not saying that profits are a bad thing—in fact, he readily describes himself as a capitalist and one who loves free enterprise. However, he has learned that when a company is well managed and customer relationships are emphasized, profits tend naturally to follow. And this makes sense. Because customers are absolutely necessary to business, those companies that are able to attract buyers are far more apt to succeed in the marketplace.

Source: Excerpted from Dan Sanders, "Four Pillars of Success," *Baylor Business Review*, Spring 2009, pp. 28–31.

The average business keeps only 70 to 90 percent of its customers each year. Even though this may seem like a decent retention rate, keep in mind that it costs around six times as much to acquire a new customer as it does to keep an existing one[1]—and new customers often buy less than existing customers.

Long-term customers usually stay with a company because they trust it, and that trust naturally translates to increased sales. Loyal customers tend to buy a company's more expensive products, are less sensitive to price increases, and bring their friends in to do business, too.[2] Experts figure that companies that increase their customer retention by a mere 5 percent per year could see net profits rise by as much as 80 percent.[3] Because keeping customers is so critical, it's essential that a company do it effectively.

As Dan Sanders points out (see In the Spotlight), it pays to develop an attitude of service. This can build solid relationships with customers that will lead to satisfaction for both the customers and the employees who interact with them.[4] This chapter shows you how to create and maintain vital connections that will satisfy your customers, enhance the reputation of your company, and generate superior company performance.

There is much more to come on this very important topic. This chapter is the first of five chapters comprising Part 4, Focusing on the Customer: Marketing Growth Strategies. Chapters 15 through 18 discuss additional marketing topics essential to growth, based on the vital customer focus that provides the foundation for this chapter.

What Is Customer Relationship Management?

Customer relationship management (CRM) means different things to different firms. To some, it is symbolized by simple smiles or comments such as "thank you" and "come again," communicated by employees to customers who have just made a purchase. For others, CRM embodies a much broader marketing effort, leading to nothing short of complete customization of products and/or services to fit individual customer needs. The goals of a CRM program for most small companies fall somewhere between these two perspectives.

customer relationship management (CRM) A company-wide business strategy designed to optimize profitability, revenue, and customer satisfaction by focusing on specific customer groups.

Formally defined, **customer relationship management (CRM)** is a "company-wide business strategy designed to optimize profitability, revenue, and customer satisfaction by focusing on highly defined and precise customer groups."[5] It is a process or method that can be used to learn more about the needs and behaviors of customers with the specific purpose of building stronger relationships with them. In a way, CRM is a mindset that leads to customer-centric strategies, which put buyers first so that the firm can succeed. CRM involves treating customers the way the entrepreneur would want to be treated if he or she were a customer—the business version of the Golden Rule.[6]

Regardless of the level of a firm's commitment to customer relationship management, the central message of every CRM program is "Cultivate customers for more than a one-time sale." A firm that strongly commits to this idea will appreciate the many benefits a CRM program can offer.

The central theme of CRM isn't new. For decades, entrepreneurs have recognized the importance of treating customers well; "The customer is king" is an age-old mantra. What is new, however, is giving the idea a name and using the latest techniques and innovative technologies to implement customer relationship practices. Modern CRM focuses on (1) customers rather than products, (2) changes in company processes, systems, and culture, and (3) all channels involved in the marketing effort, from the Internet to field sales.

The forerunners of many modern CRM techniques were developed in the 1960s by marketers like Sears and various book clubs. They simply stored information about their customers in computers for reasons other than invoicing. Their goal was to learn who their customers were, what they wanted, and what sort of interests they had. Then along came marketers with ideas about the potential benefits of adopting a customer orientation, followed by the rise of the Internet.

It should be noted that CRM, in its purest form, has nothing to do with technology, although Internet technology has definitely been a major force in CRM's development. Just as putting on the latest $300 pair of technologically designed basketball shoes doesn't make the wearer an NBA or WNBA player, buying or developing CRM computer software does not, in itself, lead to higher customer retention. But it can help, if it is used properly. (The role of technology in CRM is discussed later in this chapter.) Most importantly, there must be company-wide commitment to the concept if CRM is to be productive.

BENEFITS OF CRM TO THE SMALL FIRM

Building relationships with customers is serious business for most small companies. This is underscored by a National Federation of Independent Business study, which found that an astounding 83 percent of small employers identify superior customer service as an important feature of their competitive strategy.[7]

As depicted in Exhibit 14.1, a firm's next sale comes from one of two sources—a current customer or a new customer. Obviously, both current and potential customers

EXHIBIT 14.1 Sources of the Next Sale

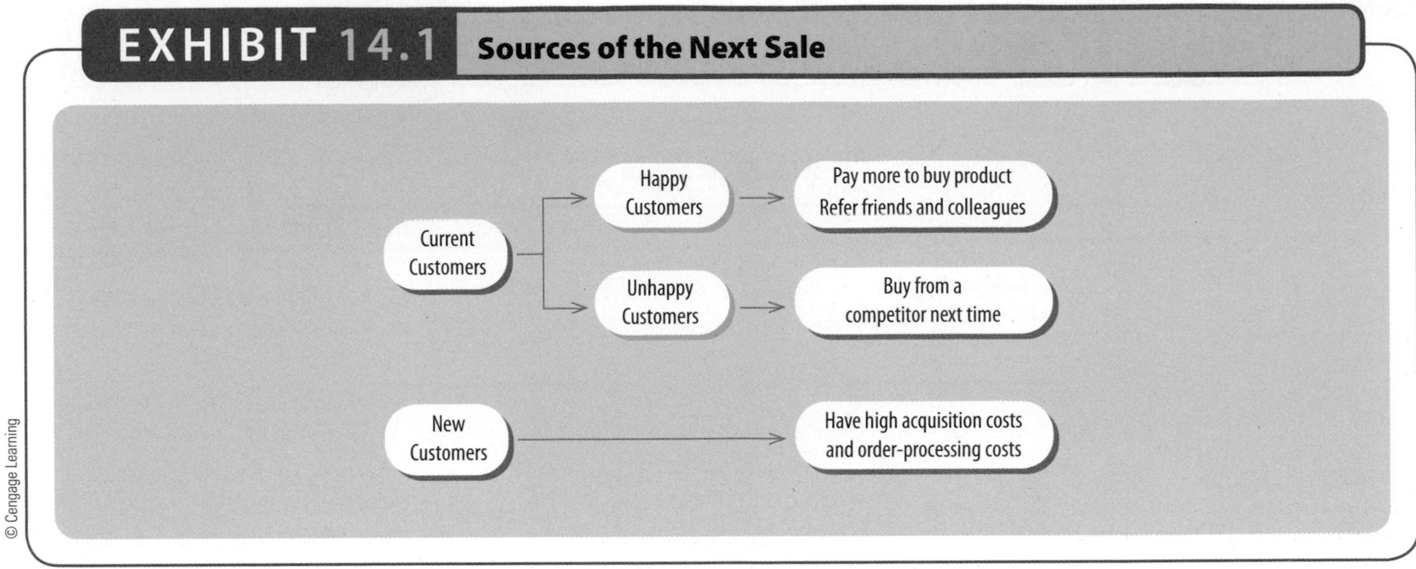

are valued by a small firm, but sometimes current customers are taken for granted and neglected. While marketing efforts devoted to bringing new customers into the fold are obviously important, keeping existing customers happy should be an even higher priority—a CRM program addresses this. Some business owners do not seem to recognize this simple truth, however, which is why CRM initiatives can be so different and vary in focus. And the trends do not necessarily shake out as you might expect. For example, one interesting study of CRM involvement found that family-owned companies tend to lag behind nonfamily firms when it comes to starting and completing CRM initiatives.[8]

Brian Vellmure, the founder and CEO of Initium Technology, a provider of CRM solutions to small firms, has identified five major economic benefits of maintaining relationships with current customers:[9]

1. Acquisition costs for new customers are high.
2. Long-time customers spend more money than new customers do.
3. Happy customers refer their friends and colleagues.
4. Order-processing costs are lower for established customers.
5. Current customers are willing to pay more for products.

These factors contribute to profits and may explain why 47 percent of small firms report that they sell their products or services primarily to repeat customers.[10]

ESSENTIAL MATERIALS FOR A CRM PROGRAM

When you build something—a house, for example—you follow a plan or blueprint that identifies appropriate materials or component parts. Likewise, assembling a CRM program requires a plan so that the entrepreneur knows what will be required (people, processes, and so on) to establish a successful initiative. In the remainder of this chapter, we consider two vital building blocks of any CRM program: (1) outstanding relationships with customers and (2) knowledge of consumer behavior. These components may be constructed with a variety of "materials," as illustrated in Exhibit 14.2. In the sections that follow, we examine those materials we believe to be tremendously important in constructing these two building blocks.

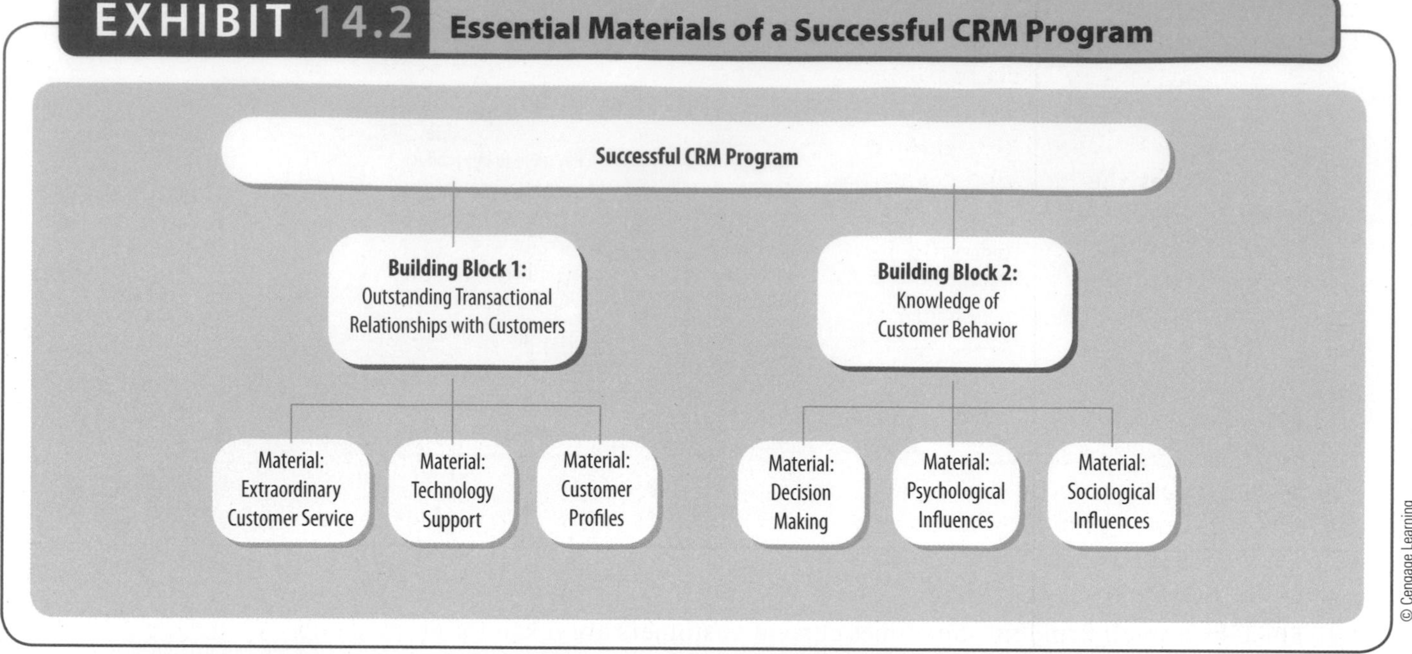

Creating Outstanding Customer Relationships Through Extraordinary Service

transactional relationship
An association between a business and a customer that begins (or ends) with a purchase or a business deal.

To be successful in the long run, small companies need to concentrate on building positive transactional relationships with customers (see Building Block 1 in Exhibit 14.2). A **transactional relationship** is an association between a business and a customer that begins (or ends) with a purchase or a business exchange. Clearly, the nature of such relationships can vary greatly. But consumers who have positive interactions with a business are much more likely to become loyal customers, which points to the obvious importance of handling these transactions with great care. Four basic beliefs underlie our emphasis on providing exceptional customer service:

- Small businesses possess greater potential for providing superior customer service than do large firms.
- Superior customer service leads to customer satisfaction.
- Customer satisfaction results in a positive transactional relationship.
- Positive transactional relationships lead to increased firm profits.

As these beliefs suggest, failure to emphasize customer service jeopardizes any effort to attain a positive customer relationship. And the task only gets more challenging as time goes on. "My message to small companies is that big companies are coming after you with better customer service, so you'd better be paying attention," says Edward Reilly, president and CEO of the American Management Association.[11]

There is plenty of room for improvement—for businesses of all sizes. A recent study by CRMGuru.com found that only 22 percent of surveyed customers have experiences with companies that they would describe as "excellent."[12] This creates opportunities for entrepreneurs like Marx Acosta-Rubio, 38, who started his California-based toner cartridge and office supplies company, Onestop, based on what he calls a "customer intimacy model." According to Acosta-Rubio, "Our competitors focus on price and availability, but we discovered a market that craves service." As part of its attentive service efforts, Onestop representatives call clients *before* they run out of supplies, maintaining a sense of personal connection by using the phone rather than expecting clients to place their orders online, which is the norm in the industry. As a result, Onestop generates more than $16 million in annual sales with only 14 salespeople, which means that its sales staff is nearly five times as productive as those working for its major competitors.[13]

Marx Acosta-Rubio

MANAGING CUSTOMER SATISFACTION

Why is customer satisfaction so important? Because happy customers are loyal customers, and that often leads them to cross-buy products with higher margins, react less to price increases, encourage their friends to buy the same products, and engage in other behaviors that tend to enhance the firm's profits. Research conducted by Ruth Bolton, professor of marketing at Arizona State University, has shown that a mere 10 percent increase in customer satisfaction leads to an 8 percent increase in the duration of customer relationships on average. This translates to an 8 percent increase in revenues generated over the long term.[14] It certainly pays to think carefully about the company–customer interface!

ACTION

Keeping Customers Content

Winning customers is expensive, so it makes sense to work at keeping the ones you have. To create loyalty, find ways to provide customers with better prices, better value, timely service, and information that is current and accurate. CRM software can be a powerful tool for gathering and using customer information to enhance customers' experiences. For more on this, see Summer Huggins, "Wow Them Now," *MyBusiness*, June/July 2009, p. 42.

Bolton's research reports the general (linear) relationship between customer satisfaction and loyalty, but Keith Jezek, a serial entrepreneur and co-founder and president of an innovative automobile inventory management service called vAuto.com, has observed that the increase may not track along a straight line (see Exhibit 14.3). In his experience, customer loyalty seems to rise at an increasing rate as satisfaction becomes greater. In other words, initial efforts to increase satisfaction may not "pack as much punch" as you would like, but there is every reason to continue to make improvements. Higher levels of customer satisfaction can really set your company apart from the competition, with your reward being customers' commitment to doing business with you. Jezek considers the entrepreneur's goal as moving customers from the Zone of Indifference, where loyalty has not yet been established and

EXHIBIT 14.3 The Rising Returns of Customer Satisfaction

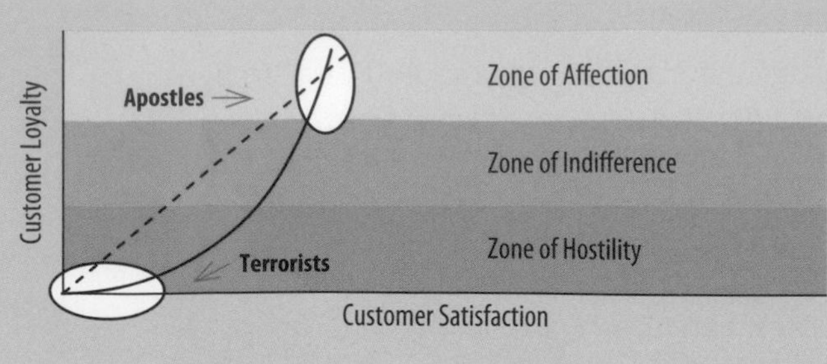

Source: Personal conversation with Keith Jezek, January 16, 2009.

customers could easily take their business elsewhere, toward the Zone of Affection, where customer loyalty is stable and profits are higher. He refers to highly committed customers as Apostles, since they have "sold out" to the company and are unlikely to shift to a rival's products. Customer movement in the other direction (toward the Zone of Hostility) is unfavorable and destructive to the business, however, which is why these customers are referred to as Terrorists.[15] All of Jezek's observations underscore the same general point: Improving customer satisfaction creates increased loyalty, which is good for performance.

Companies control a number of factors that shape interactions with customers, and some of the more powerful factors can move customers toward increased satisfaction. For example, customers have basic expectations regarding the benefits they should receive from any firm selling the product or service that your company provides. Your offering must meet these most basic expectations to satisfy customers and earn their repeat business. Beyond that, customers anticipate that your business will provide assistance to them at the time they make a purchase and later, if they should encounter problems. And keep in mind that those who buy prestige products, such as a Rolex watch, will expect more intensive assistance.

Personal Attention

Truly personal attention is the "gold standard" against which the quality of customer service is judged; customized service never goes out of style. Firms that find a way to provide the best response to the needs of a specific buyer in a given situation are sure to have satisfied and loyal customers—and plenty of them. It follows, however, that personalized service will be an option only for those companies that listen intently to their customers and thus understand their precise needs.

© gemphotography/Shutterstock.com

Small companies, like flower shops, are in a unique position to offer truly personal attention. Because they have fewer customers and fewer layers of employees between the customer and the small business owner, they are able to build stronger and closer relationships with those they serve—and hold on to them as customers. The following are some of the more common signposts on the road to extraordinary, and very personal, customer service:[16]

- **Doing business on a first-name basis.** Small ventures have a big advantage over large corporations like Walmart and McDonald's: They can get to know their customers by name and greet them as friends. Doing so establishes a bond that is powerful and encourages loyalty.
- **Keeping in touch.** Personal interactions are key to building relationships, so face-to-face and phone conversations are much more effective than e-mail messages or mass mailings. Asking for feedback during these interactions is helpful to your business and shows that you are committed to getting customers' approval. It also confirms that you care about more than selling.
- **Finding ways to help.** Helping customers doesn't always lead to an immediate sale, but it can be good for business. Send them articles and information of interest with a kind note attached, remind them of important dates (like birthdays and anniversaries), and so on. The cost to you is minimal, but these acts show you care, and the favor is often returned in the future.
- **Customizing your service to meet customer preferences.** If you remember your customers' personal preferences and adjust your service to meet them, then you have increased the value of what you offer while showing customers that they are important to you.
- **Addressing problems promptly.** When an issue arises, take steps to resolve it quickly, if at all possible. Doing so lets a customer know that he or she is important to you. Contact lost customers to find out why they went elsewhere, and use that information to correct deficiencies.

Denny Fulk, a serial entrepreneur, emphasizes the importance of building and maintaining personal customer relationships to business success. Fulk mentions a friend who runs a flourishing Internet-based business and responds regularly to his customers' questions, even if he is traveling outside of the United States. Many of his customers are located in other parts of the world, but he and his staff are committed to responding to all customer phone calls and e-mail within 24 hours. Fulk explains why this emphasis on prompt communication is so important:

> *If you operate a business, no matter how small or large, customers like to feel there is a person who really cares about their needs. Whether the information shared is by telephone or e-mail, promptness and a personal approach are keys to the customer's having a good feeling about your company. Regardless of whether your business is a startup or a very established company, a customer who receives a prompt, accurate, and understanding response will be very likely to continue doing business with your company.*[17]

Guy Kawasaki, the celebrated author of a number of excellent business books, including *The Art of the Start*, is a convincing advocate of returning calls and e-mail promptly, following the "24-hour rule" just mentioned. To test Kawasaki's commitment to this principle, an entrepreneur e-mailed him at 10:00 p.m. one evening, and he received a reply in about 10 minutes![18]

customer experience management (CEM) An approach that recognizes that, with every interaction, customers learn something about a company that will affect their desire to do business there in the future.

Customer Experience Management

In recent years, some small business owners have begun to go beyond simple CRM to emphasize **customer experience management (CEM)**. This approach recognizes that, with every interaction, customers learn something about a business that will either strengthen or weaken their satisfaction and desire to return, spend more, and recommend the company to others. Having a positive experience with a business can make all the difference in the world, especially if the products and prices are similar to those of competitors; it actually becomes part of the firm's value equation.

Ensuring pleasant communications with customers is a central focus of CEM initiatives. For example, since no one likes being put on hold during a phone call, entrepreneur and veteran radio talk show host Perry Wright has come up with a way to keep customers entertained while they wait. Known as the On-Hold Guy, Wright has developed software that features one-liners, odd facts, and puns to play for waiting customers. "While I was doing radio, I spent a lot of time on the phone and on hold, listening to sterile, irritating messages," he says. "I thought there had to be a better way, an off-the-wall approach." It turns out that he was right. Automated phone systems can save on costs, but they frustrate callers. According to Wright, 70 percent of business phone callers are put on hold, and nearly 60 percent of these hang up, while 30 percent will not call back . . . ever! Wright's software randomly plays his messages, which can actually put customers in a good mood before they are connected to salespeople. One caller went so far as to say, "Put me back on hold, QUICK! I want to hear the rest."[19] (For a sample of the On-Hold Guy's product, go to http://onholdguy.com/ohg/demos.aspx.)

Providing exceptional customer service will give small firms a competitive edge, regardless of the nature of the business, and more tools are available than ever before to make this possible. Keep in mind that it costs far more to replace a customer than to keep one and small businesses can really shine when it comes to managing this relationship. Because of their close and personal contact with those they serve, small firms are typically better than large firms in knowing their customers' needs and offering the top-notch and personalized service that keeps customers coming back.

EVALUATING A FIRM'S CUSTOMER SERVICE HEALTH

Establishing an effective customer service program begins with determining a firm's *customer service quotient*, which indicates how well the firm is currently serving its customers. Strategies can then be developed to improve the effectiveness of customer service efforts. Exhibit 14.4 lists some popular approaches to creating customer service strategies; it also provides space for evaluating how well a small firm is currently performing in each area and what it can do to improve its customer service.

How good or bad is the quality of customer service offered by firms overall? According to a recent *American Express Global Customer Service Barometer* report, 61 percent of Americans believe the quality of customer service is "more important than ever," and they will probably spend about 10 percent more on brands or businesses that provide good service when compared to those that do not. But their assessment of the state of the customer service they actually receive is far less encouraging. Of those customers responding to the survey,[20]

- 28 percent have concluded that companies care less about customer service now than they did before the start of the most recent economic downturn.
- 48 percent say they find firms "don't do anything extra" to keep them coming back for repeat business.
- 21 percent believe brands or businesses take them for granted.

All this, despite the fact that

- 81 percent say they feel more inclined to become repeat or loyal customers following a positive customer experience.
- 52 percent are likely to avoid a brand or business after a bad customer experience.

EXHIBIT 14.4 Customer Service Strategies

Which of the following can be used to support your marketing objectives?	For each strategy, comment below on: 1. How well your company is doing. 2. Improvements to pursue further.
Provide an exceptional experience throughout every transaction by ensuring that customers are acknowledged, appreciated, and find it easy to do business with you. Note that this requires you to (1) make a list of the typical chain of contacts between you and your customers—from when they first see your advertisement until you send them a customer survey after the sale—and (2) evaluate your company's performance on each contact point.	
Provide sales materials that are clear and easy to understand, including website, marketing materials, retail displays, and sales conversations.	
Respond promptly to customers' requests and concerns by acting with urgency and responsibility in customer inquiries, transactions, and complaints. Have a service recovery plan in place.	
Listen to customers and respond accordingly by soliciting feedback, encouraging interaction, staying engaged throughout transactions, and taking the appropriate action necessary to please the customer.	
Stand behind products/services by providing guarantees and warranties and ensuring customers that you deliver on your promises. Also, create products and deliver services that exceed expectations.	
Treat customers as family members and best friends by valuing them the same way you honor those you care most about.	
Stay in the hearts and minds of customers by not taking customers for granted and finding ways to let them know you hold their best interests.	
Other initiatives? List them here.	

Source: Adapted from "Exceptional Customer Experiences," Ewing Marion Kauffman Foundation, http://www.entrepreneurship.org, accessed February 3, 2009.

As one small business owner observed, "Real service is such a rare commodity out there—it's really a desert of mediocrity."[21] Statistics seem to bear that out. But they also underscore the customer relationship advantages that flow to those small companies that offer high-quality service.

Although customer service issues may be identified through a formal review process within the small firm, they often surface via customer complaints in the course of normal daily business operations. (Later in this chapter, we will show how complaint activity is part of the overall consumer behavior process.) Every firm strives to eliminate customer complaints. When they occur, however, they should be analyzed carefully to uncover possible weaknesses in product quality and/or customer service.

What is the special significance of customer complaints to small businesses? It is that small businesses are *potentially* in a much better position than are large companies to respond to such grievances and, thereby, to achieve greater customer satisfaction. Why? Because most problems are solvable simply by dealing with issues as they arise, thus giving customers more attention and respect. And showing respect is often easier for a small company because it has fewer employees and can give each of them the authority to act in customers' best interests. In contrast, a large corporation often assigns that responsibility to a single manager, who has limited contact with customers.

This very point is emphasized by John Stites, CEO and co-owner of a family-owned construction company in Cookeville, Tennessee: "The advantage that a small firm has over a larger firm in customer relationship management is that the owner of the company is closer to the customers and more likely to get accurate feedback, unfiltered by layers of management." He explains that most small business owners can't afford to neglect customer relationships, because the owner of a company with only 100 customers will feel the loss of a single customer much more than the owner of a larger firm with 1,000 customers will.[22]

What do consumers do when they are displeased? As Exhibit 14.5 shows, these buyers have several options for dealing with their dissatisfaction, and most of these options threaten repeat sales. Because customers have multiple complaint options, quality customer service is critical, both before and after a sale.

Small business owners can also learn about customer service concerns through personal observation and other research techniques. By talking directly to customers or by playing the customer's role anonymously—for example, by making a telephone call to one's own business to see how customers are treated—an entrepreneur can evaluate service quality. Some restaurants and motels invite feedback on customer service by providing comment cards to those they serve.

Sometimes a creative twist on standard marketing research methods can improve their effectiveness. This was certainly true for Jason Belkin, owner of Hampton Coffee Company, with two coffee-house locations in New York. Belkin had always used a mystery

EXHIBIT 14.5 Consumer Options for Dealing with Product or Service Dissatisfaction

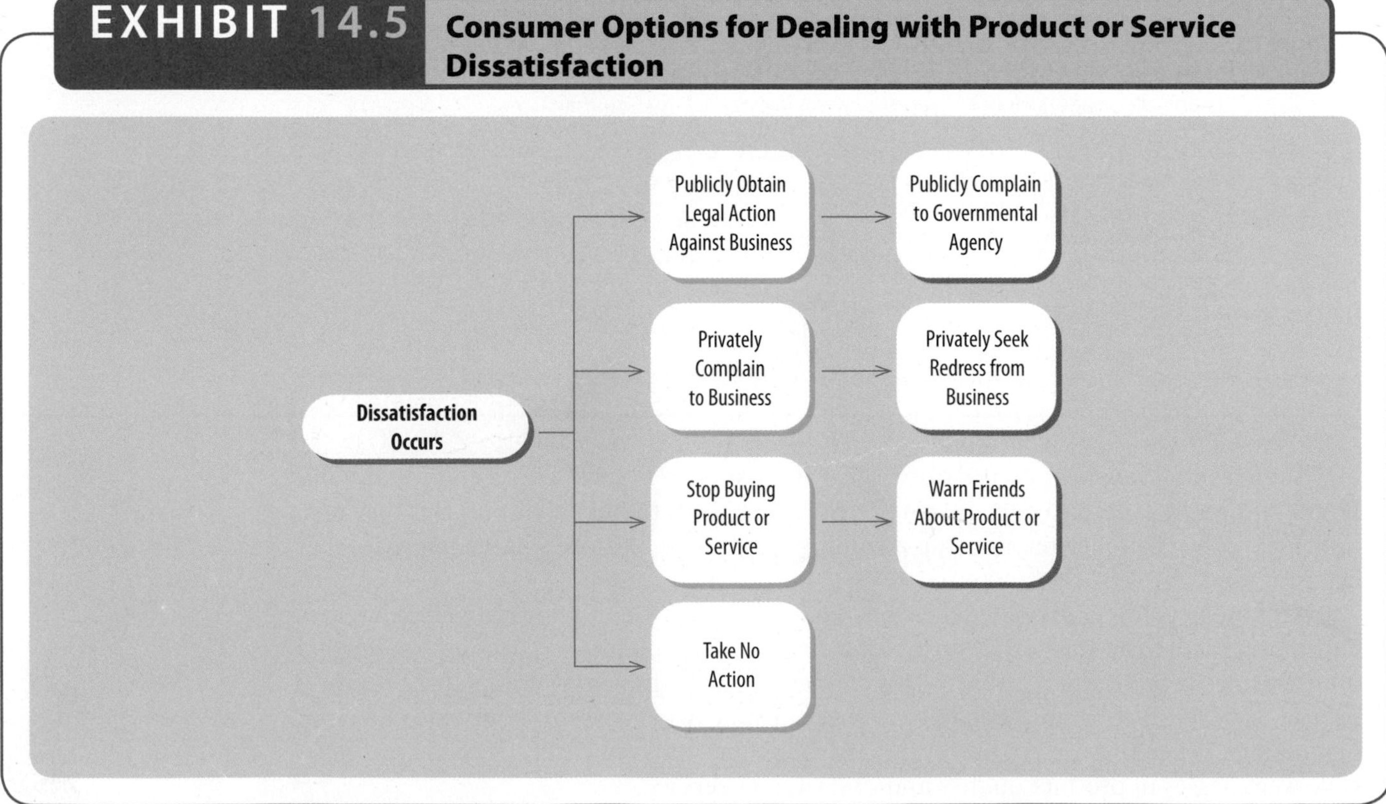

shopper service (which hires individuals to pose as real customers to evaluate a company's true service performance) to assess customer experiences but decided to turn to comment cards for the information he wanted. He started offering a free cup of coffee or tea to customers who filled out a card. Since trying this new approach, Belkin's business has increased, despite competition from new stores opened by Starbucks nearby. He attributes this success partly to the effective use of the information collected on the comment cards.[23]

Stewart F. House/Fort Worth Star-Telegram/MCT

Whatever method is used, evaluating customer service is critical for any business. Consider the success that Dallas, Texas–based Sewell Village Cadillac had after developing customer service strategies. The owner, Carl Sewell, established a customer service focus a very long time ago, in 1967, when Sewell Village was in third place among three Dallas Cadillac dealers. He realized that most people didn't like doing business with car dealers, so he simply began asking customers what it was that they disliked so much. Three major areas of dissatisfaction were identified—service hours, being without a car during service, and poor or incorrect repairs. By responding to these concerns (for example, by scheduling more service hours), Sewell Village Cadillac improved its customer satisfaction image dramatically. And Sewell continues to sharpen his company's customer service focus by applying the principles he outlined in his very popular book, *Customers for Life*. Successful CRM initiatives require a long-term commitment to customers served and practices that work.

Implementation of some forms of customer service can be inexpensive—or even free (in some cases, customer-contact personnel may just need to be encouraged to smile and greet visitors warmly)—but offering a full program of superior customer service before, during, and after a sale can be a costly undertaking. These costs often can be passed along to the purchaser as part of the price of a product or service, or they can sometimes be recouped separately, based on the amount of service requested (through extended product warranties, for example). It may seem surprising, but many customers are willing to pay a premium price, as long as good service is part of the buying experience.

Using Technology to Support Customer Relationship Management

3 Understand how technology can improve customer relationships.

Long-term transactional relationships with customers are built on good information, and a logical time to gather helpful data is during direct customer contacts, such as when a product is being sold. Customers may be contacted in many ways, including phone calls, letters, personal interactions, e-mail—even text messages. As mentioned earlier, the ability to maintain one-on-one contact with customers has always been a competitive advantage for small firms. To make this connection even easier, numerous software packages containing word-processing, spreadsheet, and database tools are also available to assist in supporting customer contacts.

CRM software programs are designed to help companies gather all customer contact information into a single data management program. Web-based marketers, in particular, are attracted to such technology, because it helps to make their complex job far more manageable. Most online shoppers expect to receive excellent customer service; companies are in a much better position to give it if they adopt e-mail options, live chat, and other platforms for interaction and personal attention. Experts point out that customers typically appreciate the conveniences that are built into many company websites, but they can quickly become frustrated when the experience does not go exactly as planned—which happens far too often.[24]

Deciding which marketing activity should get initial CRM support is not always easy. However, the sales department is a popular place to start, because its personnel nearly always generate the greatest amount of customer contact. CRM emphasizes such sales activities as filling orders promptly and accurately, managing follow-up contacts to ensure customer satisfaction, and providing user-friendly call centers to handle all inquiries, including complaints. It's a complex mix of tasks, but technologies are available to support all of these activities and many others.

Chris McCann, president of 1-800-FLOWERS.COM, seems to be ahead of the competition when it comes to incorporating technology into his business. During the very early days of the Internet, the company already had an online presence; by the late 1990s, it had a full-fledged e-commerce operation. Now McCann is using a CRM software package from SAS Institute, Inc., to build close relationships with customers, and the investment is paying off. In his words, CRM technology "has given me the ability to grow my business, whether the economy has been up or down." Other retailers are being hammered by stiff competition and challenging economic conditions, but the revenues of 1-800-FLOWERS.COM continue to rise, and repeat business has increased from 40 percent to 50 percent.[25]

Using a product called SAS Real-Time Decision Maker, McCann's business can access a range of processes that collect, classify, analyze, and interpret data in order to identify and understand key patterns and relationships that drive the decision to purchase. This allows 1-800-FLOWERS.COM to adjust its approach to the unique needs and habits of each customer. For example, when a repeat customer accesses the firm's website, the first Web page presents options that match the customer's personal preferences. "If a customer usually buys tulips for his wife, we show him our newest and best tulip selections," says Aaron Cano, the company's vice president of customer knowledge management. With SAS technology to support its customer interactions, Cano points out, "No one else in the business is able to connect customer information with real-time transaction data the way we can." This gives the company a significant competitive advantage.[26]

Having ample support resources for CRM information technology can be a concern for a small firm. This has led some entrepreneurs to outsource certain applications. For example, hosted call centers, which handle e-mail and other online communications for clients, may be more cost effective than comparable in-house centers, a crucial consideration for many cash-strapped small businesses. In addition to cost, a lack of internal expertise is a major justification for using these outside services.

Many companies have decided to control the cost of customer assistance by using alternatives that are cheaper than hiring more sales reps or relying on call center outsourcing. For example, some have adopted automated Web-based self-service systems, sometimes called *customer information management systems*. When a customer service rep handles a single telephone call, text chat, or e-mail, it can cost the company an average of $5 to $7, but self-service inquiries handled on the Internet cost less than 60 cents per contact. One popular self-service option is to post a list of Frequently Asked Questions (FAQs), and research shows that 40 percent of organizations have these on their websites. But even this simple tool is becoming more sophisticated. A company can now buy smart software that recognizes the questions its website visitors are most interested in and places those at the top of the list. Such systems can cut down the cost of serving customers while taking some of the repetition out of tending to their needs.[27]

The list of tools supporting CRM grows longer every day, and they are becoming much more user-friendly as time goes on. For example, the *Wall Street Journal* recently surveyed 30 executives and managers in large and small enterprises that are using Web 2.0 as a source of marketing support tools, and they found that the applications are expanding rapidly. So, what is Web 2.0? It represents an expanded use of the Internet to support the blogs, wikis, social-networking sites, and other online communities that allow people to build social as well as business connections, to share information, and to collaborate on projects. A growing number of marketers are using Web 2.0 to form relationships with customers, but most companies are behind the curve when it comes to applying the tools provided to build and maintain a business.[28]

TOOLS

Social Business

Social media provide an inexpensive way to advertise your business and help customers feel a personal connection to what you offer. To ride this wave, many small business owners are turning to Twitter. But when tweeting, remember to listen before speaking, provide frequent updates, and don't be boring! Current social media won't automatically drive users to your website, so it may make more sense to create your own community or write a blog. To learn more, see Jason Ankeny, "How Twitter Is Revolutionizing Business," *Entrepreneur*, Vol. 37, No. 12 (December 2009), pp. 26–32.

Some firms use Web 2.0 applications to promote products or services through blogs and other means of online connection, and this is a good place to start. But the real power comes in the form of building relationships with customers.

> *A leading greeting-card and gift company . . . is one of many that have set up an online community—a site where it can talk to consumers and the consumers can talk to each other. The company solicits opinions on various aspects of greeting-card design and on ideas for gifts and their pricing. It also asks the consumers to talk about their lifestyles and even upload photos of themselves so that it can better understand its market.*[29]

Online communities, such as this one, provide a rich source of feedback and ideas for product development, and in a form that is much faster and cheaper to use than the focus groups and surveys that have been a staple of common marketing practices. But perhaps more important, Web 2.0 tools can be used to give customers a sense of connection with the enterprise, an identity that results from their active participation in the company's business. For this, there is no substitute.

But all this talk of technology may lead you to conclude that working with CRM programs is an uninspiring chore for tech-challenged entrepreneurs. Don't be concerned—low-tech solutions can also be effective. Pam Felix started her quick-service Mexican restaurant, California Tortilla, in Bethesda, Maryland, in 1995. Five years later, she launched a company website, with the primary goal of building an e-mail list to improve communication with customers. Since then, she has used the website to communicate the theme of "having fun," and she does this by injecting a touch of lightheartedness into all that she does online.[30] Consider these "eagerly awaited predictions for 2011," which were posted on the site's "Taco Talk" page in December of 2010.[31]

LIVING THE DREAM

© iStockphoto.com/Angelika Schwarz

using technology

Sometimes You Just Can't Yelp Yourself!

The Internet tsunami has unleashed a wave of powerful new social media tools that can be used to build relationships with customers. But social media missteps can drive away new customers faster than you can say, "Why don't you take your business elsewhere!" One of the most popular players in this space, Yelp.com, helps people find good product and service providers by allowing customers to post online ratings and reviews of these businesses. This allows Yelpers to "speak truth to corporate power," but it can also leave a small business and its reputation wide open to attacks from dissatisfied customers. This social media website, like so many others, should not be taken lightly.

Diane Goodman provides a classic example of what *not* to do when trying to reach customers. On October 30, 2009, she logged on to Yelp.com and found an unflattering review of her San Francisco bookstore, Ocean Avenue Books. "This place is a TOTAL MESS," wrote Sean C., who then went on to offer an armchair plan for turning things around: Close for a few days, give the place a thorough cleaning, and completely reorganize the inventory. Most of her store's Yelp feedback had been very positive, but this was not the first snarky comment that she had seen regarding the condition of her business, and Goodman decided that she had had enough. "Why don't you come in here and say it to my face?" she blasted back, using the website's business owner response option. The rebuff did not stop there, as Goodman really let Sean C. have it. That didn't sit well with the unhappy Yelper, who attached the string of embarrassingly nasty e-mails to his review of Ocean Avenue Books and posted them to a Yelp message board.

© Valua Vitaly/Shutterstock.com

After stewing about the conflict for a few days, Goodman decided to apologize in person. With a bit of online sleuthing, she was able to figure out Sean's last name and address and decided to pay him a visit at his home. Somehow (accounts vary on this), the two got into a shouting match, and a physical struggle ensued, with a tangle that ended with Goodman falling down the front steps. Both parties called 911, and the police arrived to sort things out. It was not a pretty picture. Let this stand as "Exhibit A" for how *not* to build relationships with customers online.

A better example of how to work with social media review websites like Yelp comes from Lauren Hart, owner of The Root, a hair salon in downtown Phoenix, Arizona. She offers hair care deals on the company's Yelp page and works like crazy to avoid negative reviews. For example, Hart pays special attention to Yelpers who post negative feedback, making sure that she, personally, cuts their hair and pampers them appropriately. She also takes other (sometimes extreme) measures to make things right and boost customer satisfaction. For one unhappy patron, Hart offered to pay for a second haircut at a competing salon, which led to an improved Yelp rating (from two stars to four, out of a possible five stars). Such focused attention has been a real boon for business.

Yelp traffic now brings two or three new customers to The Root every day, and Hart finds that she no longer has to advertise in local newspapers to generate business, which saves the company around $400 per month. On the downside, keeping up with the new wave of social media and business rating websites takes concerted effort. "There are a lot of business owners who feel like Yelp reviews just happen," says Hart. "But it's not true. Responding to reviews, giving offers, maintaining your page—it all makes a huge difference." And she can vouch for the results. Even in a difficult economy, sales at The Root have increased by as much 148 percent a year.

Sources: Max Chafkin, "You've Been Yelped," *Inc.*, Vol. 32, No. 1 (February 2010), pp. 48–55; Aileen Yoo, "Nasty Altercation Between Yelp Critic, Bookstore Owner," *San Francisco Chronicle*, http://www.sfgate.com/cgi-bin/blogs/scavenger/detail?entry_id=51052, accessed January 4, 2011; and Diane Goodman, "Ocean Avenue Books," http://www.oceanavebooks.com, accessed February 1, 2011. http://www.therootsalon.com

- In an effort to not seem so cranky, the Queen will pretend to be supportive of Prince William's choice of brides. (Prince Philip will pretend he's not annoyed that he's never going to be king.)
- On this season's first *American Idol*, new judge Steven Tyler will reveal that he is 107.
- When I tell my husband: "Take the kids for a haircut and make sure it's not too short because I want to take their picture for our holiday card," he will hear: "Take the kids for a haircut and make sure the skin on the top of their head shows."
- A cupcake store will open and no one will go. (It could happen.)
- A little girl will accumulate enough Burrito Elito points [from the restaurant's customer loyalty program] to win the Cal Tort pony that she's always dreamed of, and I will have to explain to her that Cal Tort ponies don't exist—she should have read the fine print.

"I'm not sure I had any expectations [for the website]," says Felix. "But since I put out a goofy, monthly newsletter that most people seem to like, I thought at the very least I could keep conveying that goofy mom-and-pop feel via the Internet." And this has worked well to help her build favorable relationships with customers. "People feel like they have a personal connection with us—and that's something the big chains are never going to have with their customers," Felix believes. The Internet also provides a channel for feedback, which helps to identify the restaurant's strengths and weaknesses. And, says Felix, "I get a lot of funny/strange e-mails that I get to use in the newsletter. . . . I ran out of things to say about burritos about 6 years ago."[32]

customer profile
A collection of information about a customer, including demographic data, attitudes, preferences, and other behavioral characteristics, as defined by CRM goals.

Building Customer Profiles for a CRM Program

4
Describe techniques used to create a customer profile.

Most entrepreneurs say that the best way to stay in touch with customers and to identify their needs is to talk to them. Such conversations lead to a detailed understanding of each customer and thus offer insights from which to build a **customer profile**, a collection of information about a customer, including demographic data, attitudes, preferences, and other behavioral characteristics, as defined by CRM goals. In a very small business, the customer profiles maintained in the entrepreneur's head often constitute the company's CRM "database." At some point in a company's growth, however, it becomes impossible for the small business owner to continue to develop profiles using this method alone. It is then time to turn to formal, computer-based databases.

Customer profiles are essential to a successful CRM program, as they represent building material for the required knowledge of customers. Customer contact data, from sources such as warranty cards and accounting records, can be used to develop a profile. For Web-based ventures, current information can be collected at the point of contact, as customers order online.

What types of information should be included in a customer profile? Four major categories of information have been identified:[33]

- **Transactions.** A complete purchase history with accompanying details such as price paid, SKU (which identifies the product purchased), and delivery date
- **Customer contacts.** Sales calls and service requests, including all customer- and company-initiated contacts
- **Descriptive information.** Background information used for market segmentation and other data analysis purposes
- **Responses to marketing stimuli.** Information on whether or not the customer responded to a direct marketing initiative, a sales contact, and/or any other direct contact

Rejuvenation

Formal interviews with customers provide another way to gather profile information. These interviews can be in-person, or they can take the form of a questionnaire. Consider, for example, Rejuvenation Lamp and Fixture Company, in Portland, Oregon, which sells reproduction light fixtures mainly through catalogs and its website. Its system for understanding its customers includes a questionnaire.

> *In every box of lights that is shipped, the company includes a questionnaire with a return stamp. The questionnaire is humorous and fun to fill out. It not only collects information about the purchasers, it asks [customers] what products they might want that Rejuvenation doesn't carry. The "how can we help you?" message, combined with the prepaid return and humorous presentation, earns Rejuvenation thousands of responses each month.*[34]

When Mac McConnell owned Artful Framer Gallery in Plantation, Florida, he often surveyed walk-in customers. One year, based on the results of his simple one-page questionnaire, he decided to reposition the business to satisfy customers' desires. The survey showed that quality was first priority for customers and price was last. In response to the feedback, McConnell dropped the low-end line and made higher-priced museum framing his specialty.[35] Making important business decisions based on the results of a one-page survey can be risky, but the changes McConnell made to his company have worked out very well.

Customer profiles primarily reflect demographic variables such as age, gender, and marital status, but they can also include behavioral, psychological, and sociological information. Understanding the aspects of consumer behavior presented in the following sections can help entrepreneurs create customer profiles that go beyond demographics. Some entrepreneurs might even want to consider taking a course to broaden their knowledge of consumer behavior concepts. Such courses are commonly offered by local colleges, small business development centers, chambers of commerce, and other educational service providers.

Customers as Decision Makers

5 Explain how consumers are decision makers and why this is important.

If you refer back to Exhibit 14.2 on page 412, you will see that the second primary building block supporting a successful CRM program involves knowledge of customer behavior. The three interrelated "materials" that combine to form that particular building block include the decision-making process, psychological influences, and sociological influences. Offering an expanded view of the first of these materials, Exhibit 14.6 illustrates how consumer decision making flows through four stages:

Stage 1: Need recognition
Stage 2: Information search and evaluation
Stage 3: The purchase decision
Stage 4: Post-purchase evaluation

We'll use this widely accepted model to examine decision making among small business customers.

NEED RECOGNITION

Need recognition (stage 1) occurs when a consumer realizes that her or his current state of affairs differs significantly from some ideal state. Some needs are routine conditions of depletion, such as a lack of food when lunchtime arrives. Other needs arise less frequently

EXHIBIT 14.6 **Simplified Model of Consumer Behavior**

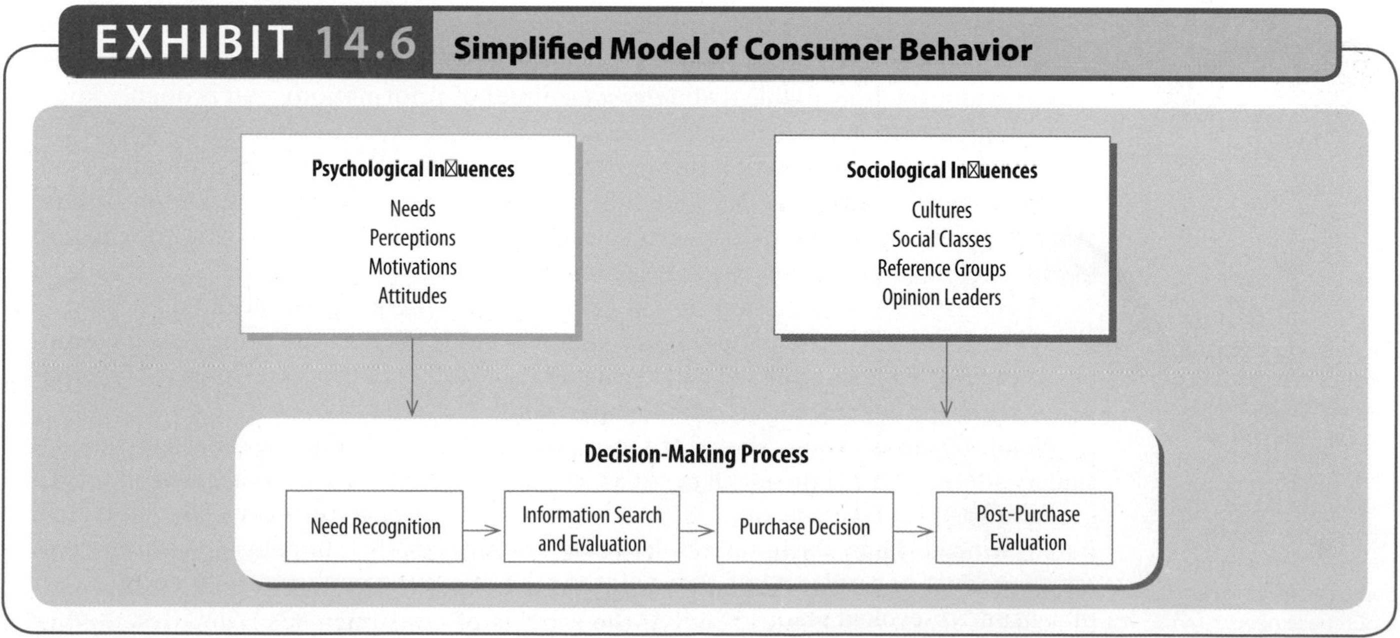

and may evolve slowly. Recognition of the need to replace the family dining table, for example, may take years to develop.

A consumer must recognize a need before purchase behavior can begin. Thus, the need-recognition stage cannot be overlooked. Many small firms develop their product strategy as if consumers were in the later stages of the decision-making process, when in reality they have not yet recognized that a need even exists!

Many factors influence consumers' recognition of a need—either by changing the actual state of affairs or by affecting the desired state. Here are a few examples:

- A change in financial status (a job promotion with a salary increase)
- A change in household characteristics (the birth of a baby)
- Normal depletion (using up the last tube of toothpaste)
- Product or service performance (breakdown of a DVD player)
- Past decisions (poor repair service on a car)
- The availability of products (introduction of a new product)

An entrepreneur must understand the need-recognition stage in order to decide on the appropriate marketing strategy to use. In some situations, a small business owner will have to *influence* need recognition. In other situations, she or he may simply be able to *react* to needs that consumers have identified on their own.

INFORMATION SEARCH AND EVALUATION

The second stage in consumer decision making involves consumers' collection and evaluation of appropriate information. Internal sources of insight (usually from previous experiences with a product or brand) typically are considered first. However, prospective buyers usually turn to external sources (for example, input from friends and family, product-rating data from *Consumer Reports*, or feature descriptions from advertisements or salespeople) when their own past experience or knowledge is limited and the cost of gathering outside information is low.

To illustrate: Suppose you are in the market for a big-screen television. If you work in the consumer electronics industry or have personal experience with some of the brands and models available (two *internal* sources of information), you probably know enough already to make a purchase decision. However, if you are like most people, you will need to gather information through *external* sources. You might ask for input from trusted friends, check out CNET's online reviews of big screen models, and/or discuss model features with a salesperson at an electronics retailer. You'll need this information in order to make a sound decision when it's time to buy.

evaluative criteria
The features or characteristics of a product or service that customers use for comparison.

evoked set
A group of brands that a consumer is both aware of and willing to consider as a solution to a purchase need.

The search for information should help to clarify the purchase need and allow the consumer to establish **evaluative criteria** that will guide the decision process as it continues to unfold. That is, he or she will decide on the features or characteristics of the product or service that are to be used for comparison.

Small business owners should try to understand which evaluative criteria most consumers adopt, because these will be used to formulate their evoked set. An **evoked set** is a group of brands that a consumer is both aware of and willing to consider as a solution to a purchase need. Thus, the initial challenge for a new company is to gain *market awareness* for its product or service. Only then will the brand have the opportunity to become part of consumers' evoked sets.

PURCHASE DECISION

Once consumers have evaluated brands in their evoked set and made their choice, they must still decide how and where to make the purchase (stage 3). A substantial volume of retail sales now comes from nonstore settings, such as catalogs, TV shopping channels, and the Internet. These outlets have created a complex and challenging environment in which to develop marketing strategy. And consumers attribute many different advantages and disadvantages to various shopping outlets, making it difficult for the small firm to devise a single correct strategy. Sometimes, however, simple recognition of these factors can be helpful.

Of course, not every purchase decision is planned prior to entering a store or looking at a mail-order catalog. Studies show that most types of purchases from traditional retail outlets are not planned or intended prior to the customers' entering the store. This fact underscores the tremendous importance of such features as store layout, sales personnel, and point-of-purchase displays.[36]

POST-PURCHASE EVALUATION

The consumer decision-making process does not end with a purchase. Small businesses desire repeat purchases from customers and thus need to understand post-purchase behavior (stage 4). Exhibit 14.7 illustrates several consumer activities that occur during post-purchase evaluation. Two of these activities—post-purchase dissonance and complaint behavior—are directly related to customer satisfaction.

Post-purchase dissonance is a type of **cognitive dissonance**, a psychological tension that occurs immediately following a purchase decision when consumers have second thoughts as to the wisdom of their purchase. This dissonance can influence how a consumer evaluates a product and his or her ultimate level of satisfaction with it.

cognitive dissonance The anxiety that occurs when a customer has second thoughts immediately following a purchase.

A consumer who is unhappy with the purchase process or the product during and after use may complain to the company, or even post a protest to an online forum like Yelp.com. Despite the frustration or concern a complaint may cause, it creates an important opportunity for a business to make things right; a well-handled complaint may prevent the loss of a valuable customer. The outcome of the post-purchase process is a final

→ important

EXHIBIT 14.7 Post-Purchase Activities of Consumers

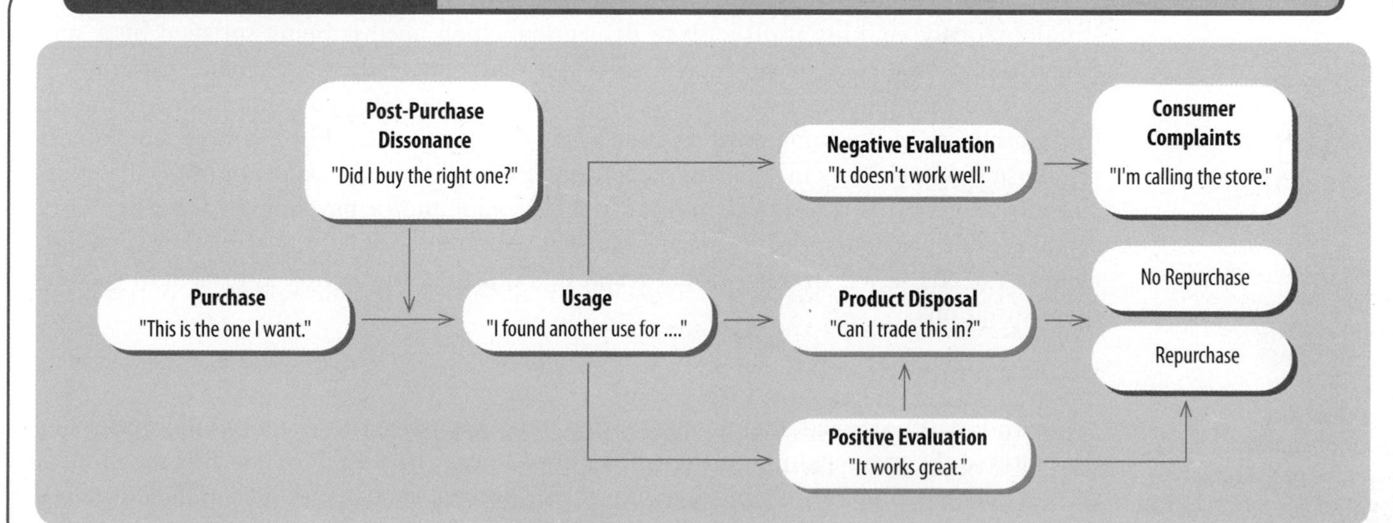

level of customer satisfaction that affects customer loyalty and the likelihood of repeat purchases and product usage. It can also lead to brand switching and discontinued use of the product.

The best way to preserve customer satisfaction is to deal with issues and complaints as soon as possible and in the most effective way possible. This calls for a well-trained, informed, and cooperative work force. At The Angus Barn in Raleigh, North Carolina, owner Van Eure empowers her employees to ensure customer satisfaction. Diners do not have to look for a manager when they have a complaint, because Eure encourages employees to use the "20-Foot Rule"—that is, any restaurant employee within 20 feet of a problem, challenge, or opportunity should get involved in making sure that all customers leave completely satisfied. For example, waiters can provide dessert to a diner free of charge or accommodate a customer's needs by altering the seating chart. This rule reflects Eure's belief that employees are better able than managers (who often must juggle many tasks at once) to see all sides of an issue. Because they are so central to the success of the operation, Eure takes very good care of those who work for her, as reflected by the very low turnover rate among The Angus Barn staff. To show her appreciation, Eure hosts an employee banquet each year, where she presents numerous awards. She believes that her approach to resolving customer concerns underlies the high satisfaction quotient of both her customers and her employees.[37]

Understanding Psychological Influences on Customers

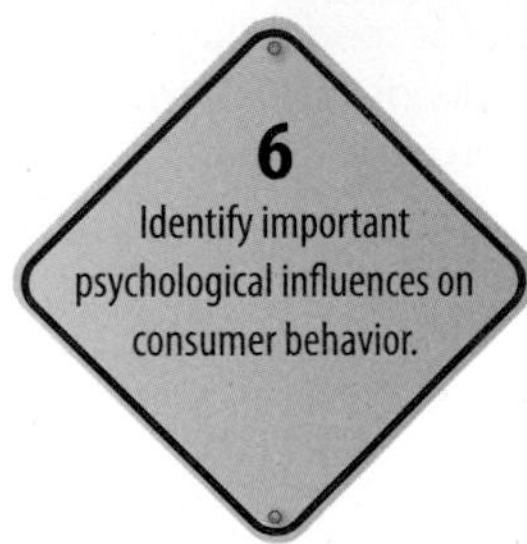

A major component of the consumer behavior model, as presented in Exhibit 14.6, is psychological influences. The four psychological influences that have the greatest relevance to small businesses are needs, perceptions, motivations, and attitudes.

NEEDS

needs
The starting point for all behavior.

Needs are often described as the starting point for all behavior. Without needs, there would be no behavior. Although consumer needs are innumerable, they can be identified as falling into four categories—physiological, social, psychological, and spiritual.

Consumers' needs are never completely satisfied, thereby ensuring the continued existence of business. One of the more complex characteristics of needs is the way in which they function together in shaping behavior. In other words, various needs operate simultaneously, making it difficult to determine which need is being satisfied by a specific product or service; nevertheless, careful assessment of the needs–behavior connection can be very helpful in developing marketing strategy. But you should keep in mind that purchases of the same product can satisfy different needs. For example, consumers purchase food products in supermarkets to satisfy physiological needs, but they also purchase food in status restaurants to satisfy their social and/or psychological needs. Also, certain foods are demanded by specific market segments to satisfy religious, or spiritual, needs. A needs-based strategy would result in a different marketing approach in each of these situations.

PERCEPTIONS

perception
The individual processes that give meaning to the stimuli confronting consumers.

A second psychological factor, **perception**, encompasses those individual processes that ultimately give meaning to the stimuli consumers encounter. When this meaning is severely distorted or entirely blocked, consumer perception can cloud a small company's marketing effort and make it ineffective. For example, a retailer may mark its fashion clothing "on sale" to communicate a price reduction from usual levels, but customers' perceptions may be that "these clothes are out of style."

Perception is a two-sided coin—it depends on the characteristics of both the stimulus and the perceiver. Consumers attempt to manage huge quantities of incoming stimuli through **perceptual categorization**, a process by which things that are similar are perceived as belonging together. Therefore, if a small business wishes to position its product alongside an existing brand and have it accepted as comparable, the marketing mix should reflect an awareness of perceptual categorization. For example, comparable quality can be communicated through similar prices or a package design with a color scheme bearing a resemblance to that of an existing brand. These techniques will help a consumer fit the new product into the desired product category.

© Alexander Ivanov/Shutterstock.com

Small businesses that attach an existing brand name to a new product are relying on perceptual categorization to pre-sell the new product. If, on the other hand, the new product is physically different or is of a different quality, a new brand name should be selected to create a distinctive perceptual categorization in the consumer's mind.

If a consumer has strong brand loyalty to a product, it will be difficult for other brands to penetrate his or her perceptual barriers. That individual is likely to have distorted images of competing brands because of a pre-existing attitude. Consumer perceptions thus present a unique communication challenge.

MOTIVATIONS

Unsatisfied needs create tension within an individual. When this tension reaches a certain level, the individual becomes uncomfortable and is motivated to reduce it.

Everyone is familiar with hunger pains, which are manifestations of the tension created by an unsatisfied physiological need. What directs a person to obtain food so that the hunger pains can be relieved? The answer is motivation. **Motivations** are goal-directed forces that organize and give direction to tension caused by unsatisfied needs. Marketers cannot create needs, but they can offer unique motivations to consumers. If an acceptable reason for purchasing a product or service is provided, it will probably be internalized by the consumer as a motivating force. The key for the marketer is to determine which motivations the consumer will perceive as acceptable in a given situation. The answer is found through an analysis of other consumer behavior variables.

perceptual categorization
The process of grouping similar things so as to manage huge quantities of incoming stimuli

motivations
Goal-directed forces that organize and give direction to the tension caused by unsatisfied needs.

Like physiological needs, the other three classes of needs—social, psychological, and spiritual—can be connected to behavior through motivations. For example, a campus clothing store might promote styles that communicate that the college student wearing those clothes has obtained membership in a social group, such as a fraternity or sorority.

Understanding motivations is not easy. Several motivations may be present in any situation, and they are often subconscious. However, they must be investigated if the marketing effort is to succeed.

ATTITUDES

Like the other psychological variables, attitudes cannot be observed, but everyone has them. Do attitudes imply knowledge? Do they imply feelings of good or bad, favorable or unfavorable? Does an attitude have a direct impact on behavior? The answer to each of these questions is a resounding yes. An **attitude** is an enduring opinion, based on a combination of knowledge, feeling, and behavioral tendency.

attitude
An enduring opinion, based on knowledge, feeling, and behavioral tendency.

An attitude may act as an obstacle or a driver in bringing a customer to a product. For example, consumers with the belief that a local, family-run grocery store has higher prices than a national supermarket chain may avoid the local store. Armed with an understanding of the structure of a particular attitude, a marketer can approach the consumer more intelligently.

Understanding Sociological Influences on Customers

Sociological influences, as shown in Exhibit 14.6 on page 425, comprise the last component of the consumer behavior model. Among these influences are cultures, social classes, reference groups, and opinion leaders. Note that these influences represent different degrees of group aggregation: Culture involves large masses of people, social classes and reference groups represent smaller groups of people, and opinion leaders are individuals who exert influence.

CULTURES

culture
Behavioral patterns and values that characterize a group of consumers in a target market.

In marketing, **culture** refers to the behavioral patterns and values that characterize a group of customers in a target market. These patterns and beliefs have a tremendous impact on the purchase and use of products. Marketing managers often overlook the cultural variable because its influences are so subtly embedded within a society. International marketers who have experienced more than one culture, however, can readily attest to the impact of cultural influence.

The prescriptive nature of cultures should concern the entrepreneur. Cultural norms create a range of product-related acceptable behaviors that influence what consumers buy. However, because a culture changes by adapting slowly to new situations, what works well as a marketing strategy today may not work a few years from now.

An investigation of a culture within a narrower boundary—defined by age, religious preference, ethnic orientation, or geographical location—is called *subcultural analysis*. Here, too, unique patterns of behavior and social relationships must concern the marketing manager. For example, the needs and motivations of the youth subculture are far different from those of the senior citizen subculture. Small business managers who familiarize themselves with cultures and subcultures are able to create better marketing mixes.

SOCIAL CLASSES

social classes
Divisions within a society having different levels of social prestige.

Another sociological factor affecting consumer behavior is social class. **Social classes** are divisions within a society having different levels of social prestige. The social class system has important implications for marketing. Different lifestyles correlate with different levels of social prestige, and certain products often become symbols of a type of lifestyle.

For products like grocery staples, social class analysis will probably not be very useful. For other products—home furnishings, for instance—such analysis may help to explain variations in shopping and communication patterns.

Unlike a caste system, a social class system provides for upward mobility. Occupation is probably the single most important determinant of social class. Other determinants include possessions, sources of income, and education.

REFERENCE GROUPS

Technically, social class could be considered a reference group. However, marketers are generally more concerned with smaller groups such as families, work groups, neighborhood groups, and recreational groups. **Reference groups** are those small groups that an individual allows to influence his or her behavior.

reference groups
Small groups that an individual allows to influence his or her behavior.

The existence of group influence is well established. The challenge to the marketer is to understand why this influence occurs and how it can be used to promote the sale of a product or service. Individuals tend to accept group influence because of the benefits they perceive as resulting from it, and these perceived benefits give influencers various kinds of power. Five widely recognized forms of power—all of which are available to the marketer—are reward, coercive, referent, expert, and legitimate power.

Reward power and *coercive power* relate to a group's ability to give and to withhold rewards. Rewards may be material or psychological; recognition and praise are typical psychological rewards. A Pampered Chef party is a good example of a marketing technique that takes advantage of reward power and coercive power. The ever-present possibility of pleasing or displeasing the hostess-friend tends to encourage the guests to buy.

Referent power and *expert power* involve neither rewards nor punishments. They exist because an individual attaches great importance to being part of a group or perceives the group as being knowledgeable. Referent power (based on one's admiration or respect for the power holder) influences consumers to conform to a group's behavior and to choose products selected by group members. Children are often affected by referent power, so marketers can create a desire for products by using cleverly designed advertisements or packages that appeal to this inclination. And a person perceived as an expert can be an effective spokesperson for a host of products because consumers trust his or her judgment.

Legitimate power involves authority and the approval of what an individual ought to do. We are most familiar with legitimate power at the societal level, where it is evident in the prescriptive nature of culture, but it can also be used in smaller groups. Social marketing efforts are an attempt to encourage a certain behavior as the right thing to do (for example, wear your seat belt, don't drink and drive).

OPINION LEADERS

According to widely accepted communication principles, consumers receive a significant amount of information through individuals called **opinion leaders**, group members who play a key communication role.

opinion leader
A group member who plays a key communications role.

Generally speaking, opinion leaders are knowledgeable, visible, and exposed to the mass media. A small business firm can enhance its own image by identifying with such leaders. For example, a farm-supply dealer may promote its products in an agricultural community by holding demonstrations of these products on the farms of highly successful local farmers, who are typically the community's opinion leaders. Similarly, clothing retailers may use attractive students as models when showing campus fashions.

When Phil Knight established Nike, Inc., in the early 1970s, he used a marketing strategy that followed what he called the Five Cool Guys Principle. The idea was that if he could get five of the best and most popular athletes on a high school campus to wear his shoes, then others would want to buy the shoes for themselves. The "cool guys" would set the footwear fashion trend. Of course, the strategy can be applied at higher and more visible levels, which is why Nike has paid so much money over the years to get world-class athletes to don the company's product. Nike's tremendously successful marketing efforts are an illustration of the influence of opinion leaders. Though Nike is a huge corporation, small businesses should also think about the power of opinion leaders and the part they can play in attracting and building relationships with potential customers.

© iStockphoto.com/Angelika Schwarz

using technology

Leading Opinions . . . One Million YouTube Viewers at a Time

You may know him as the Mystery Guitar Man, but 23-year-old Joe Penna is making quite a stir as one of YouTube's most-watched contributors. With 1.3 million subscribers watching his "playful, effects-filled music videos," he could be called a one-man opinion leader. But it wasn't until just recently that he even knew his own thought-shaping strength. "It was during a conversation with this guy I work with named Billy Reid that I realized I even had influence," says Penna. "He told me that when I didn't mention his name and the song he wrote in one video, it sold only 600 copies on iTunes. When I did mention it in another, it sold 6,000 copies. It was like, whoa, these people are actually listening to me."

FRANK MAY/dpa /Landov

YouTube has become one of the leading online channels through which "influentials" can exert outsized impact—indeed, star power—but it's not easy to rise above the clatter of offerings in such a crowded space. Yet Joe Penna has done exactly that. How? One online commentator reasons that he gets viewers to tune in by "Combining clear musical talent with technical ability and a quirky, relatable sense of humor [in videos that are] charming, well-produced, and fun." And tune in they do. Penna's first YouTube hit, "Guitar: Impossible," has been watched more than nine million times. That kind of exposure gives him a robust "cool factor" and a lot of pull with a very important demographic that companies are especially interested in reaching.

Penna's new gig is incredibly rewarding, personally and financially. He has gone from "sleeping on the floor of his apartment and stealing his neighbors' Wi-Fi" to YouTube stardom in a matter of months—literally! No one knows for sure how much Mystery Guitar Man makes from his online enterprise, but YouTube acknowledges that hundreds of its "partners" make six-figure incomes. (YouTube partners are account holders who have been invited to share in the advertising revenue generated from their videos). Penna is the sixth most-watched YouTube partner, so it is safe to conclude that he is not going to have to go back to stealing Wi-Fi anytime soon. And with the power of his online appeal, companies like Coca-Cola, HP, Kellogg's, and McDonald's are lining up to work with him, hoping they can reach his subscribers with a tie-in to their brands. This represents tremendous opportunity for Penna, and it points out the remarkable power of new media to influence consumers. Small businesses should take note and figure out how they, too, might be able to tap into the potential of online opinion leaders—including YouTubers—to generate sales.

Sources: Mark Borden, "The New Influentials," *Fast Company*, No. 150 (November 2010), pp. 125–131; "Partner with YouTube," http://www.youtube.com/partners, accessed January 4, 2011; and Liz Shannon Miller, "Mystery Guitar Man Creates and Innovates on YouTube," Gigaom.com, http://gigaom.com/video/mystery-guitar-man-creates-and-innovates-on-youtube, accessed January 4, 2011.
http://www.pennajoe.com

CRM Leads to Customer Satisfaction

After a long and very successful business career, one executive was asked by MBA students to explain the secret to his noteworthy accomplishments. His answer was immediate and firm: "Relationships!" Interpersonal connections are, quite simply, the grease that allows the wheels of commerce to turn efficiently, so it follows that customer relationship management (CRM) will be at the heart of any business that is destined for success.

A satisfied customer is likely to be a repeat customer who will tell others about your company. But establishing an effective CRM program is hard work—it requires a thorough knowledge of the major components of customer satisfaction, the development of customer profiles, wise handling of complaints, and an understanding of the customer decision-making process. Of course, it all starts with maintaining a helpful and positive attitude toward customers, but the more small business owners know about their customers, the better they will be able to meet their needs. Customer satisfaction is truly a key element in small business success.

1. Define *customer relationship management (CRM),* and explain its importance to a small business.

- Customer relationship management (CRM) is a company-wide strategy that can be used to learn more about the needs and behaviors of customers with the specific purposes of building stronger relationships with them and optimizing profitability.
- The central message of every CRM program is "Court customers for more than a one-time sale."
- CRM is primarily a mindset that leads to customer-centric strategies, which put customers first so that the firm can increase profits.
- A CRM program recognizes the importance of keeping current customers satisfied to ensure their loyalty, given the high costs associated with attracting new customers.
- Constructing a CRM program requires a plan so that the entrepreneur will know what people, processes, etc., are needed for success.
- Two vital building blocks of any CRM program are outstanding transactional relationships with customers and knowledge of consumer behavior.

2. Discuss the significance of providing extraordinary customer service.

- To be successful in the long run, small firms must build positive transactional relationships in order to develop and maintain loyal customers.
- Extraordinary service is one of the factors that small companies are in a unique position to offer.
- Providing exceptional customer service can give small firms a competitive edge, regardless of the nature of the business.
- Satisfied customers are loyal customers, which translates to improved company performance.
- The relationship between customer satisfaction and loyalty is not necessarily linear; customer loyalty seems to increase as satisfaction rises.
- Truly personal attention is the "gold standard" against which the quality of customer service is judged, and this can be strengthened by doing business on a first-name basis, keeping in touch with customers, findings ways to help them, customizing services offered, and addressing consumer problems promptly.
- Customer experience management (CEM) recognizes that relationships with customers can be strengthened or weakened depending on the quality of the experience they have with a company.
- Establishing an effective customer service program begins with determining the firm's "customer service quotient," which indicates how well the firm is currently serving its customers.

- Small business owners can learn about customer service problems through customer complaints, personal observation, and other research techniques.
- Although many types of customer service cost very little to offer, there are definite costs associated with superior levels of customer service.

3. Understand how technology can improve customer relationships.

- Long-term transactional relationships are built with information gathered from points of customer contact.
- CRM technology helps companies gather all customer contact information into a single data management program.
- Web-based marketers, in particular, are attracted to CRM technology.
- CRM focuses on such sales functions as accurate and prompt order filling, follow-up contacts to ensure customer satisfaction, and the use of a user-friendly call center to handle all inquiries, including complaints.
- Concern about having ample support resources for CRM information technology has led some entrepreneurs to outsource certain applications.
- The tools to manage CRM are growing in number and are becoming cheaper, more sophisticated, and easier to use.
- Web 2.0 applications are at the center of many new CRM tools, such as the use of blogs, wikis, social networking sites, and online communities as means of gathering customer feedback.
- There are still plenty of low-tech solutions to CRM challenges.

4. Describe techniques used to create a customer profile.

- In a very small business, customer profiles are developed in the entrepreneur's head during conversations with customers.
- Customer profiles are essential to a successful CRM program, as they represent building material for the required knowledge of customers.
- Four categories of customer profile information are transactions, customer contacts, descriptive information, and responses to marketing stimuli.
- Formal interviews with customers provide another way to gather customer profile information.

5. Explain how consumers are decision makers and why this is important in understanding customer relationships.

- Consumer decision making involves four stages that are closely tied to ultimate customer satisfaction.
- Need recognition (stage 1) occurs when a consumer realizes that her or his current state of affairs differs significantly from some ideal state.
- Stage 2 in consumer decision making involves consumers' collection and evaluation of appropriate information from both internal and external sources.
- Once consumers have evaluated brands in their evoked set and made their choice, they must still decide how and where to make the purchase (stage 3).
- Post-purchase evaluation (stage 4) may lead to cognitive dissonance and complaint behavior, which can negatively influence customer satisfaction with the product or service and the business that provides it.
- The best way to preserve customer satisfaction is to deal with issues and complaints as soon as they come up.

6. Identify certain psychological influences on consumer behavior.

- The four psychological influences that have the greatest relevance to small businesses are needs, perceptions, motivations, and attitudes.
- Needs are often described as the starting point for all behavior.
- Perception encompasses those individual processes that ultimately give meaning to the stimuli confronting consumers.
- Motivations are goal-directed forces that organize and give direction to tension caused by unsatisfied needs.
- An attitude is an enduring opinion, based on a combination of knowledge, feeling, and behavioral tendency.

7. Recognize certain sociological influences on consumer behavior.

- Among the sociological influences are cultures, social classes, reference groups, and opinion leaders.
- In marketing, *culture* refers to the behavioral patterns and values that characterize a group of customers in a target market.
- Social classes are divisions within a society having different levels of social prestige.
- Reference groups are those small groups that an individual allows to influence his or her behavior.
- According to widely accepted communication principles, consumers receive a significant amount of information through opinion leaders, group members who play a key communications role.

Key Terms

customer relationship management (CRM) p. 410
transactional relationship p. 412
customer experience management (CEM) p. 415
customer profile p. 423
evaluative criteria p. 426
evoked set p. 426
cognitive dissonance p. 427
needs p. 428
perception p. 428
perceptual categorization p. 429
motivations p. 429
attitude p. 429
culture p. 430
social classes p. 430
reference groups p. 431
opinion leader p. 431

Discussion Questions

1. Define customer relationship management. What is meant by the statement "CRM is a mindset"?
2. Does CRM put more emphasis on current or potential customers? Why?
3. What are the two essential building blocks of a successful CRM program? What "materials" are used to construct these building blocks?
4. Why is a small business potentially in a better position to achieve customer satisfaction than a large firm?
5. Discuss how technology can be used to support customer relationship management.
6. What types of information should be part of a customer profile?
7. What techniques or sources of information can be used to develop a customer profile?
8. Briefly describe the four stages of the consumer decision-making process. Why is the first stage so vital to consumer behavior?
9. List the four psychological influences on consumers that were discussed in this chapter. What is their relevance to consumer behavior?
10. List the four sociological influences on consumers that were discussed in this chapter. What is their relevance to consumer behavior?

You Make the Call

SITUATION 1

Jeremy Shepherd is the founder and president of PearlParadise.com, in Los Angeles, California. His jewelry business recognizes the importance of ensuring that customers keep coming back. However, Shepherd is uncertain as to which customer retention techniques he should use to develop a strong foundation for repeat business. The firm's website has the software capabilities to support customer interaction.

Question 1 What customer loyalty techniques would you recommend to Shepherd?
Question 2 What information would be appropriate to collect about customers in a database?
Question 3 What specific computer-based communication could be used to achieve Shepherd's goal?

Source: http://www.pearlparadise.com, accessed January 4, 2011.

SITUATION 2

Aspen Funeral Alternatives, a funeral home in Albuquerque, New Mexico, recognizes that families are more cost conscious than ever. As the company's website states, "Outlet malls and discount stores offer convenience and value—why pay more?" The strategy of the owners is to offer lower-priced funeral products with the same personalized, high-quality services, just fewer options. Aspen goes to great lengths to control costs and passes the savings along to its clients. For example, its operating hours are limited to Monday through Friday between 8:00 a.m. and 5:00 p.m. to minimize overtime pay to employees. (Essential staff are still available 24/7.)

Aspen's website says that the company's low-cost service alternatives offer no fancy facilities, no limousines, and no hearses. A general price list, covering Aspen's professional services, use of its facilities, and caskets, is posted on the site.

Question 1 What psychological concepts of consumer behavior are relevant to marketing this service? Be specific.
Question 2 How can the stages of consumer decision making be applied to a person's decision to use a particular funeral home?

Question 3 Which CRM techniques could be used by this type of business?

Source: http://www.aspenfuneral.com, accessed January 30, 2009.

SITUATION 3

Jay Goltz owns a Chicago-based decorative frame company, Artists Frame Service, and three other businesses. And in his mind, customer service today is more important than ever. "Smiling and being pleasant is not enough," Goltz observes. He goes out of his way to hire great employees and trains them to handle even the most challenging of questions and service requests. Then he goes a step or two further by making the following promises on his company's website:

- Our framing consultants have art backgrounds with an average of nine years of experience.
- We offer an extraordinary selection of picture frames sourced personally and passionately from around the world so you get the perfect frame.
- We take framing seriously. It's about details, higher standards and meeting our own expectations. You'll see and feel the difference.
- We frame your art in one week—with a huge inventory and a large staff of artisans, we can deliver on this commitment.

To ensure that all goes as planned, Goltz keeps extensive documentation on every job. Then, when complaints arise, he can figure out what happened and nip the underlying problem in the bud. Taking this approach, he can tell if a customer's dissatisfaction stems from, say, an employee's carelessness, inadequate equipment, or some other problem. If it is the result of an employee's poor workmanship, Goltz will provide coaching to help improve that associate's performance. And if, after that, the problem still is not solved? "You fire them," says Goltz. As he sees it, "The company's first mission isn't having employees, it's staying in business. Customer service is the main advantage small businesses have over their big competitors, so you have to get that right—no matter what it takes."

Question 1 As a long-run strategy, will Goltz's approach to superior customer service quality be successful?
Question 2 Would you want to work for a company with such policies? What would be the pros and cons of working there?
Question 3 What suggestions would have you for Goltz and his system? Can you see any ways to improve it?

Sources: "Artists Frame Service—Our Difference," http://www.artistsframeservice.com/services/our-difference.html, accessed December 23, 2010; and Megan Pacella, "Strong Support," *MyBusiness*, June/July 2009, p. 44.

Experiential Exercises

1. For several days, make notes on your own shopping experiences. Summarize what you consider to be the best customer service you received.
2. Interview a local entrepreneur about her or his company's consumer service efforts. Summarize your findings.
3. Interview a local entrepreneur about what types of customer complaints the business receives. Also ask how he or she deals with different complaints. Report your findings to the class.
4. Consider your most recent meaningful purchase. Compare the decision-making process you used to the four stages of decision making presented in this chapter. Report your conclusions.

Small Business & Entrepreneurship Resource Center

1. Pam Felix, who started her quick-service Mexican restaurant, California Tortilla, in 1995 in Bethesda, Maryland, wanted an effective way to increase contacts with customers. The text explains how she started a "goofy" Internet site that would be fun for customers to access. The article "Business Gone Wild" talks about some of Felix's ideas about what can be done on the restaurant website. Describe what makes her restaurant unique and fun, and whether you think that this would be a good long-term strategy.

Source: Gwen Moran, "Business Gone Wild," *Entrepreneur*, Vol. 32, No. 7 (July 2004), pp. 69–70.

2. The text mentions The Angus Barn in Raleigh, North Carolina. Owner Van Eure, who took over the management of the Raleigh landmark after the death of her father in 1988, empowers employees to handle complaints and to ensure that customers leave totally satisfied. She implemented a "20-Foot Rule"—any employee of the restaurant who is within 20 feet

of a problem, a challenge, or opportunity should assist in making sure the customer leaves happy. After reading the article, "Kid Control," describe the program for kids. Also discuss how this program may complement or conflict with the "20-Foot Rule."

Source: Joan Lang, "Kid Control," *Restaurant Business*, Vol. 99, No. 24 (December 15, 2000), p. 74.

Video Case 14

NUMI TEA (P. 721)

Numi Tea was started in 1999 by brother and sister team Ahmed and Reem Rahim. Keeping it in the family is important at Numi. Every member of the Tea'm, as they call it, is committed to the company's core values of sustainability, creativity, and quality organics. This extends to their corporate customers and their producers as well. Like their teas, every relationship is carefully cultivated and maintained.

ALTERNATIVE CASE FOR CHAPTER 14

Video Case 2, PortionPac Chemicals, p. 696

CHAPTER 15

Product Development and Supply Chain Management

In the SPOTLIGHT
Lighting the Way to Product Development
http://www.dinealight.com
http://www.readycheckglo.com

Two aspiring entrepreneurs had very similar products—but the paths each took to new product development could not have been more different!

For Gillian Dinnerstein, of Miami Beach, Florida, figuring out what to order in a nice restaurant was getting to be terribly aggravating. It had nothing to do with indecision on her part—the dim mood lighting just made it hard for her to read a menu. When she finally had enough, Dinnerstein decided to take matters into her own hands and fix the problem. As a first-time inventor, she came up with the Dine-a-Light, an attractive folder that lights up to allow diners to read menus and wine lists in dimly lit restaurants without destroying the dark-and-romantic ambiance. The product sounds simple

© Darren Baker/Shutterstock.com

enough—an LED powered by a rechargeable battery that is built into the cover of a menu—but getting it to market was anything but straightforward. Dinnerstein spent four years and hundreds of thousands of dollars hiring the attorneys, engineers, and manufacturers needed to make her entrepreneurial dream come true. But she can now order with ease in any restaurant that uses her Dine-a-Light.

Celestina Pugliese of Melville, New York, on the other hand, chose to follow the beat of a very different new venture drummer. One evening in the summer of 2009, Pugliese and a friend were dining at a restaurant when the server dropped off the check, then returned repeatedly to ask, "Are you ready to pay?" Each time, the dining guests said no and returned to their conversation, somewhat annoyed at the intrusion. After the fourth interruption, Pugliese turned to her friend and said, "Wouldn't it be great if there were a light on these guest check

After reading this chapter, you should be able to . . .

LOOKING AHEAD

1. Understand the challenges associated with the growth of a small business.
2. Explain the role of innovation in a company's growth.
3. Identify stages in the product life cycle and the new product development process.
4. Describe the building of a firm's total product.
5. Discuss product strategy and the alternatives available to small businesses.
6. Recognize how the legal environment affects product decisions.
7. Explain the importance of supply chain management.
8. Specify the major considerations in structuring a distribution channel.

© iStockphoto.com/Dan Bachman

presenters to let the waiter know when we are ready, so they don't keep coming over and asking us if we are ready to pay the check?" That experience inspired the creation of Ready Check Glo Illuminating Guest Check Presenter, which lights up when diners are ready to pay for their meals.

Although Dinnerstein invested substantial sums of time and money in getting her enterprise off the ground, Pugliese needed just seven months and $11,800 to get her product to market. Why the great difference? In a nutshell, "Pugliese [opted to use] a network of new Internet sites that lets you bring a hazy idea to reality for a fraction of the price, from hiring patent attorneys to linking up with manufacturers." And the slow economy has pushed thousands of these professionals to the Web in search of work, which is also driving costs down. This brew of macroeconomic developments suggests that there has never been a better time to start a new enterprise on a shoestring.

Little decisions on the road to new product development can make a huge difference in the final cost. For example, once you come up with an idea for a new product, the next step is to figure out if it is really new (unique). You can spend a good deal of money hiring a patent attorney to check this out for you, or you can do it yourself by visiting the website of the U.S. Patent and Trademark Office at www.uspto.gov (click on the "Inventors" link for help in getting started), by driving to one of the 81 Patent and Trademark Depository Libraries to get in-person assistance (see the PTO website for locations), or do a Google Patent Search (www.google.com/patents) to see if anything resembling your idea has already been invented. Dinnerstein paid more than $100,000 for the services of an engineer, but Pugliese used guru.com to link up with a freelance engineer in Ohio who designed her product for just $500. (She also used the site to find an attorney who filed a provisional patent application for her for a very reasonable $500 charge.) Joining a legitimate inventors' network can lead you to capable and reliable manufacturers, who will handle production at a reasonable cost. In any case, resisting the temptation to sign on blindly with one of the countless invention development companies that advertise on TV can save you money and headaches. Their services do not come cheap, and many do not deliver results.

To be sure, developing a new product can be one of the most exciting features of the small business experience. But a heads-up approach can save a lot of money, which can easily spell the difference between a successful new line of business and a flop that may not even get out of the starting gate.

Sources: "Dine-a-Light," http://www.dinealight.com, accessed January 7, 2011; "Ready Check Glo—Our Story," http://www.readycheckglo.com/our-story-p_2.html, accessed January 6, 2011; and Julie Bennett, "Eureka! Now What?" *Entrepreneur*, Vol. 38, No. 11 (October 2010), pp. 129–134.

When people talk about the economy, they often sprinkle the conversation with the terms *supply* and *demand*. This is with good reason. These are fundamental features of the marketplace that determine how high the prices of products and services are likely to be. Supply refers to the willingness of businesses to put a certain product or service up for sale; demand represents the interest and ability of buyers to purchase it. If a product is in short supply, its price will almost always rise as demand takes over and motivated buyers scramble to purchase the limited goods available at that time.

Supply and demand also affect the operation of a small business, though in a slightly different way. Robert Kiyosaki, entrepreneur and celebrated author of the *Rich Dad* series of books, explains why these concepts are so important:

Think of demand as sales and marketing. It's your sales and marketing department's job to create demand by making sure that your customers know and buy what your company has to offer. Meanwhile, supply is represented by manufacturing, warehousing and distribution, aka the supply chain. It's your supply chain's job to be prepared to fulfill the demand created by the sales side.[1]

This simplifies the formula somewhat, but it makes sense and clearly explains the need for balance in these key areas of the company's operations.

In Chapter 14, you learned about customer decision making (demand) and the entrepreneur's need to make a strong commitment to customer relationship management (CRM) to ensure that new customers are drawn to the company and connections to current customers are preserved. You also discovered that marketing programs need to reflect consumer behavior concepts if CRM efforts are to sustain the firm's competitive advantage. In this chapter, we discuss the demand side of the equation further, explaining how product innovation can lead to business growth (from increased demand), but you will also get a healthy dose of supply-side thinking. That is, we address product and supply chain management decisions, which together have a significant impact on the total bundle of satisfaction targeted to customers. Business growth can be a wonderful thing, but supply–demand balance is critical to enterprise success.

To Grow or Not to Grow

Once a new venture has been launched, the newly created firm settles into day-to-day operations. Its marketing plan reflects current goals as well as any expansion or growth that will impact marketing activities.

Entrepreneurs differ in their desire for growth. Some want to grow rapidly, while others prefer a modest growth rate. Many find that maintaining the status quo is challenge enough, and this becomes the driving force behind their marketing decisions. However, growth sometimes happens unexpectedly, and the entrepreneur is forced to concentrate all efforts on meeting demand. Consider what happened to an entrepreneur who showed a new line of flannel nightgowns to a large chain-store buyer, and the buyer immediately ordered 500 of them, with delivery expected in five days! The entrepreneur accepted the order, even though he had material on hand for only 50 gowns. He emptied his bank account to purchase the necessary material and frantically begged former college classmates to join him in cutting and sewing the gowns. After several sleepless nights, he filled the order.[2] The lesson: Growing quickly can be a stressful proposition if you are not prepared.[3]

For many small companies, however, growth is an expected and achievable goal. In fact, fast growth is part of the initial plan in some cases. In 2000, after Karen McMasters sold some of her daughter's old baby clothes on eBay, she started going to garage sales to find additional goods to put up for auction. The business continued to expand, and McMasters launched her first online company, a high-end baby products business, in February of 2001. By the end of that year, she had generated $200,000 in sales, and by 2004, her enterprise, BareBabies.com, had grown to become one of the largest online retailers of baby products.[4] But McMasters was far from finished with her quest to expand the business. Within six years of startup, BareBabies sales had already exceeded $3.5 million. McMasters had always wanted to grow her business, but growth did not come without cost. "I haven't had a vacation in years," she admitted at one point. "You try to go away and your business is with you. But it's all a blessing. I wouldn't give it up for the world."[5]

Successful growth seldom occurs on its own. Many factors—including financing—must be considered and managed carefully. When a business experiences rapid growth in sales volume, its income statements will generally reflect growing profits. However, rapid growth in sales and profits may be hazardous to the company's cash flows. A "growth trap" can occur, because growth tends to demand additional cash faster than it can be generated in the form of increased profits.

© Corbis Bridge / Alamy

Inventory, for example, must be expanded as sales volume increases; additional dollars must be spent on merchandise or raw materials to accommodate the higher level of sales. Similarly, accounts receivable must be expanded proportionately to meet the increased sales volume. A profitable business can quickly find itself in a financial bind, growing profitably while its bank accounts dwindle. (For more on forecasting financial requirements, including those related to raw materials and inventory, see Chapter 11. You can also refer to Chapter 22 to learn about effective methods for managing assets, such as accounts receivable, cash flows, and inventory.)

The growth problem is particularly acute for small companies. Increasing sales by 100 percent is easier for a small venture than for a *Fortune* 500 firm, but doubling sales volume makes an enterprise a much different business. Combined with difficulty in obtaining external funding, this may have unfavorable effects if cash is not managed carefully. In short, a high-growth firm's need for additional financing may exceed its available resources, even though the venture is profitable. Without additional resources, the company's cash balances may decline sharply, leaving it in an uncertain financial position.

Growth also places huge demands on a small company's personnel and the management style of its owners. When orders escalate rapidly—sometimes doubling, tripling, or more in one year's time—managerial and sales staff can become overwhelmed. At that point, major adjustments may be required immediately. But like parents who don't want to see their kids grow up, too many owners resist the idea that their "startup baby" is quickly morphing into a very different business—they may not be ready for the change or the new responsibilities. If they fail to adjust, they are likely to find that the increased demand can easily stretch their staff too thin, resulting in burnout, apathy, and poor overall performance.

Despite these and other challenges, the entrepreneurial spirit continues to carry small companies forward in pursuit of growth. Business expansion can occur in many ways. One common path to growth is paved by innovation.

Innovation: A Path to Growth

From a menu of growth options, entrepreneurs generally choose the one they think will lead to the most favorable outcomes, such as superior profitability, increased market share, and improved customer satisfaction. These are some of the "fruits" of competitive advantage, and they all contribute to the value of the venture.

2
Explain the role of innovation in a company's growth.

COMPETITIVE ADVANTAGE AND INNOVATION

As indicated in Chapter 1, entrepreneurs often see a different and better way of doing things. Studies have shown that small entrepreneurial firms produce twice as many innovations per employee as large firms. These innovations account for half of all those created and an amazing 95 percent of all *radical* innovations.[6] It could be said that innovation provides the soil in which a startup's competitive advantage can take root and grow, taking on a life of its own. Some widely recognized examples of small firm innovations are soft contact lenses, the zipper, overnight delivery services, the personal computer, and social media services like Facebook.

There is a certain glamour associated with innovation, but creating and then perfecting new products or services is often difficult. Clayton M. Christensen, a Harvard business professor and the author of a number of books on innovation, points out that the road to new product development is rarely straight, and potholes are everywhere. According to his statistics, "93% of all innovations that ultimately become successful started off in the wrong direction; the probability that you'll get it right the first time out of the gate is very low."[7] But remember, Christensen is talking about successful products and does not take into account tortured attempts to massage life into the 80 percent of all new products that end up failing or performing well below expectations.[8] Nobody said it would be easy.

When innovation is the goal, failure is always a risk. With that in mind, we offer a few "rules of thumb" that may help to reduce the risk somewhat:

- **Base innovative efforts on your experience.** Innovative efforts are more likely to succeed when you know something about the product or service technology. For example, if you have years of training or experience in the design or fashion world, you are more likely to succeed when offering a new line of urban clothing than a new metal fastener.
- **Focus on products or services that have been largely overlooked.** You are more likely to strike "pay dirt" in a vein that has not already been fully mined and in which competitors are few. Inventors and entrepreneurs Ron L. Wilson II and Brian LeGette, co-founders of 180s LLC in Baltimore, Maryland, put a new twist on the familiar earmuff. Their ear warmers fit around the back of the neck and don't mess up the hair.[9]
- **Be sure there is a market for the product or service you are hoping to create.** This business fundamental is as applicable to innovation in startups as it is to innovation in existing businesses. A new product or service is doomed to failure if the pool of potential customers is too shallow to generate enough sales for the company to recover its cost of innovation, along with a reasonable profit.
- **Pursue innovation that customers will perceive as adding value to their lives.** It is not enough to create a product or service that *you* believe in; people become customers when *they* believe your product or service will provide value they cannot find elsewhere. Californians Eric Sandoz and Ben Werner hope to attract plenty of customers by the value designed into their creative hybrid-electric commuter car. Called the "Dagne," this futuristic and sleek three-wheel design is computerized to lean perfectly into turns, can go about 600 miles on fully charged batteries and four gallons of fuel, can reach speeds of 120 miles per hour, and can go from 0 to 60 mph in about five seconds. And by replacing the foot brake and steering wheel with a simple joystick, the car takes advantage of the hand's quick reaction time (nearly twice as fast as the foot), which means that it can respond more quickly to traffic and save lives by avoiding accidents.[10]

- **Focus on new ideas that will lead to more than one product or service.** Success with an initial product or service is critical, of course, but investment in innovation packs even more of a punch when it also leads to other innovative products or services. This has been the experience of Markus Moberg and Chad Troutwine, who launched an exam-preparation program called Veritas Prep. The company's core business involves training for those who want to take the GMAT (the entrance exam for graduate business schools), and they now offer courses in 80 cities across 21 countries. But their experience with the GMAT has expanded into online courses and law school admissions consulting, and they recently launched consulting for medical school admissions. What they learned from their initial efforts pointed the way for new business development and reduced the risk of their efforts to grow.[11]

Courtesy of Revolution Motors

- **Raise sufficient capital to launch the new product or service.**[12] It is easy to underestimate the cost of bringing an innovation successfully to market. Many small firms run short of cash before they are able to do so. Be prepared to look for new sources of capital along the way, which can be particularly challenging during an economic downturn like the one that started in 2008.[13]

Small companies that are "one-hit wonders" may find that the ride comes to an abrupt and unpleasant ending. While one innovation can provide a launch pad for a new and interesting business, continued innovation is critical to sustaining competitive advantage in the years to follow. So, expect change to be necessary—and sometimes dramatic. One survey by *Inc.* magazine found that 13 of 30 company founders reported that their business turned out to be nothing like their original venture concept.[14]

START UP ACTION

Innovative Inspiration

If you're having trouble generating useful ideas, consider implementing structured, company-wide brainstorming processes; experiencing your business from customers' point of view; and learning from other industries. Once you have an idea that you love, make sure your customers also love it by testing it out before making it a reality.

Still struggling? Take a look at 99 percent.com for inspiration and help. Also see "5 Steps to Innovation," *Entrepreneur*, Vol. 37, No. 2 (February 2009), pp. 112–113 for more information.

SUSTAINABILITY AND INNOVATION

How can a company sustain its competitive advantage? Various strategies can help. For example, some entrepreneurs with sophisticated technologies obtain patents to protect them. Because obtaining a patent requires the disclosure of intellectual property to the public, they may choose instead to guard it by maintaining trade secrets, which is another way to keep potential rivals from gaining access. Others will try to operate "below the radar screen" of competitors, but unfortunately the effort to avoid attracting attention limits the growth potential of the enterprise. In some cases, businesses find protection through long-term contracts or alliances with larger and more powerful partners, which can lead to exclusive and secure deals as a distributor, vendor, or user of an important technology.[15] But regardless of the protective strategy selected, the goal is to develop the competitive muscle of the enterprise while establishing protective features as a safeguard against being swept aside by resource-rich rivals.

sustainable competitive advantage
A value-creating position that is likely to endure over time.

A business can take steps to slow down threats from competitors, but no competitive advantage lasts forever. Research has emphasized the importance of **sustainable competitive advantage**, a value-creating position that is likely to endure over time. To incorporate sustainability into strategy, the entrepreneur should use the unique capabilities of the firm in a way that competitors will find difficult to imitate. However, since rivals will discover a way to copy any value-creating strategy sooner or later, it is important to think about and plan for its transformation over the long run.

Exhibit 15.1 illustrates the competitive advantage life cycle, which has three stages: develop, deploy, and decline. Simply put, a firm must invest resources to *develop* a competitive advantage, which it can later *deploy* to boost its performance. But that position will eventually *decline* as rival firms build these advantages into their own strategies, new and better technologies emerge, customer preferences change, or other factors come into play.

To understand how this works, consider The Blue Buffalo Co., a maker of great-tasting, holistic pet food products. The company is still small (its founder, Bill Bishop, proudly states, "We actually have more dogs and cats than we do employees!") but growing, and it is unique in that only Blue Buffalo products contain LifeSource Bits, which provide "a precise blend of vitamins, minerals, and antioxidants."[16] But how long will the sales growth continue, given that the company's competitive advantage seems to be based mostly on its proprietary blends? It is likely that competitors such as Natural Balance and Science Diet will come up with similar ingredients. When that happens, Blue Buffalo's competitive advantage and the sales growth it generates may very well stabilize and eventually may fall into decline. That's where it pays to be very forward-thinking.

In order to maintain performance over time, companies must continue to reinvent themselves—and it is very important that they do this *before* the business stalls. Research has shown that firms that wait until they hit a slump before making adjustments run a serious risk of failing to realize a complete recovery. In one study, only 7 percent were able to return to healthy levels of growth.[17]

© hagit berkovich/Shutterstock.com

So how can a small business maintain its performance? A firm is more likely to avoid a stall if it keeps a close eye on "hidden curves" related to its competition, its internal capabilities, and its people—as long as it takes corrective measures before these hidden trends become apparent in the company's financial results. To be more specific, high performers have a way of (1) spotting changes in customer needs early on and adjusting to them ahead of rivals, (2) upgrading capa-

EXHIBIT 15.1 The Competitive Advantage Life Cycle

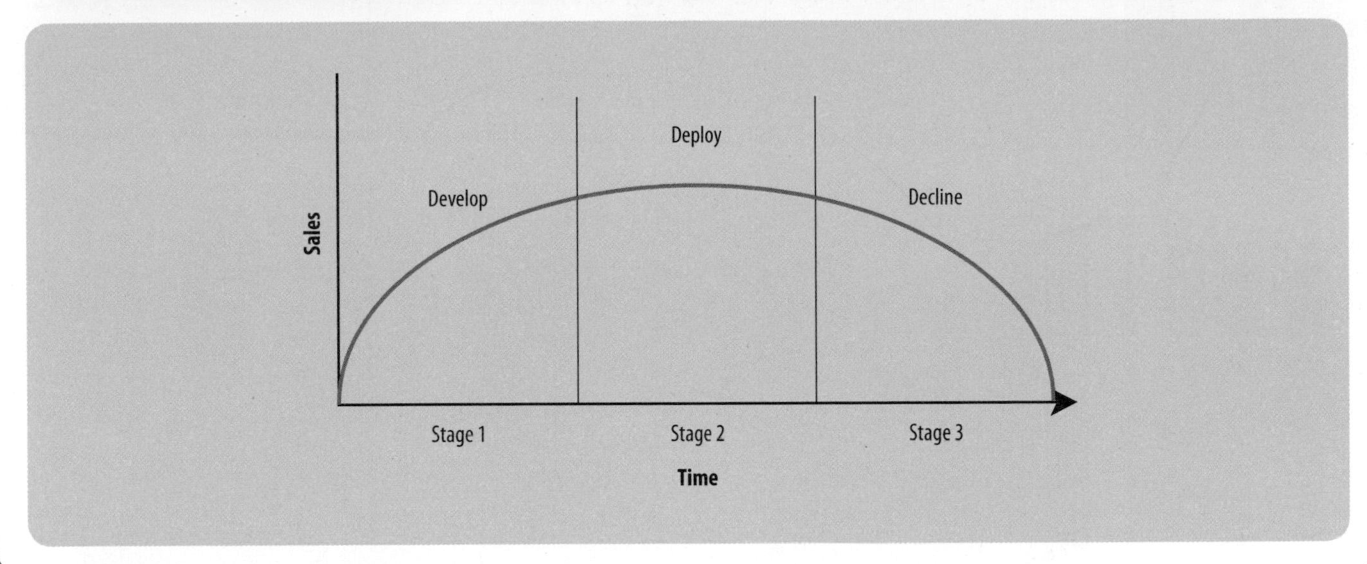

© Cengage Learning

bilities to maintain marketplace advantages, and (3) developing and retaining people with "both the capabilities and the will to drive new business growth."[18] By taking these steps, a firm can extend its competitive advantage *before* the current strategy has run its course. And that is just what many small companies are doing. Small business owners can maintain their venture's performance if they keep an eye on the future and continuously improve their product and/or service offerings to meet the rising expectations of customers, all the while developing the capabilities and the people that make this possible. Such an approach can help them stay one step ahead of their competitors.

In October 2001, Dylan Lauren—daughter of well-known designer Ralph Lauren—founded Dylan's Candy Bar, which stocks more than 5,000 varieties of sweet-tooth magic. Starting with its flagship location on the Upper East Side of New York City, the company was "founded upon the principle of elevating a simple candy shop to a world-class destination [that] merges the world of art, popular culture, and fashion with candy." To establish its unique position, Dylan's Candy Bar locations feature a café, a private party room, and a candy spa and lifestyle boutique that offers a variety of candy-related gifts. The firm's website, Dylanscandybar.com, was added later to "extend the candy store's sweet adventure online with an unparalleled shopping experience that has something for everyone."[19] And *New York Magazine* reports that the New York City store was recently expanded by 5,000 square feet to make room for a cocktail bar, a rock-candy aquarium, additional private party rooms, and a "falling-candy staircase."[20] The moral of the story is clear: A marketplace

© Neil Rasmus/PatrickMcMullan.com/Sipa Press/0810282044

LIVING THE DREAM

entrepreneurial experiences

© iStockphoto.com/Angelika Schwarz

Old Idol in Search of New Worshippers

Landov

Simon is gone! Audience ratings have been on the decline for four years now, and the latest season generated fewer record sales than any single previous season. A new show called *The X Factor* may become a strong competitor in the not-too-distant future, and its edginess may shine a spotlight on the "aging infrastructure" of the old ratings champ, which is limited in its use of social media for fan engagement and program promotion.

The *American Idol* franchise is no small business, but it is nonetheless entrepreneurial, and its challenges are certainly parallel to many of those faced by smaller, more mainstream enterprises. For example, it could be said that *Idol* is losing its grip, and thus its growth, because the show's management took its eyes off the "hidden curves" (see pages 444–445). That is, it failed to reinvent the program as needed over time in order to adjust to threats from shifting competitive dynamics, to update the organization's inadequate internal capabilities, and to find remedies for deficits in talent.

Can *American Idol* pull itself out of its current tailspin? That is the question on the minds of many avid fans. Research would suggest that a turnaround is unlikely (though certainly not impossible), given that the ratings slide has been playing out for more than four years now. *Idol* management should have seen the writing on the wall some time ago. After a decade on the air and with the enviable position of being television's most-watched program for seven years, the show lost 9 percent of its viewers in the fall 2010 season alone.

Fans seem to want something different, and other programs are queuing up to provide it. On the competitive front, Simon Cowell is working on a U.S. version of *The X Factor*, a head-on rival to *Idol* with its own unique twists. The mere fact that Simon left *Idol* caused many fans to fear that this was the end for the show, because the acerbic Brit and his amusing mix of music savvy, wit, and biting commentary were crucial to the program's success. The boost he lends to *The X Factor* will only make the new show that much more of a competitive threat.

To shore up internal capabilities and deal with talent limitations, the new *Idol* has made a number of changes. Some of the structural adjustments have focused on changing the format, grooming contestants more effectively, bringing in a new music director, reworking the set, and other improvements. But the most discussed feature of the shake-up has revolved around the panel of judges. Actress and singer Jennifer Lopez and Aerosmith rocker Steven Tyler were added to the panel; only record producer Randy Jackson remains from the show's original 2001 line-up.

Is it too little too late? Only time will tell. And fans seem to think the overdue reinvention of *Idol* has put it at serious risk. Sixty-seven percent of those recently polled by *The Hollywood Reporter* concluded that *American Idol*'s best days are over. Sounds like the votes are in . . . but *American Idol* may no longer be the winner.

Sources: Bill Keveney, "Remaking Idol," *USAToday*, January 14, 2011, pp. 1A–2A; Paul Nunes and Tim Breene, "Reinvent Your Business Before It's Too Late," *Harvard Business Review*, Vol. 89, No. 1/2 (January/February 2011), pp. 80–87; "Is Jennifer Lopez the Savior of American Idol?" *Wall Street Journal*, January 11, 2011, http://blogs.wsj.com/speakeasy/2011/01/11/is-jennifer-lopez-the-savior-of-american-idol, accessed January 19, 2011; and CNBC.com, "'American Idol's Best Days May Be Over," http://www.cnbc.com/id/40937029, accessed January 19, 2011. http://www.americanidol.com

advantage is sustainable only for businesses that are already planning for the future and beating their rivals to the competitive punch.

The Product Life Cycle and New Product Development

Our discussion of growth and innovation illustrates how entrepreneurial firms can be part of the development of new products for the marketplace. So, what creates the need for innovation in a specific business, and how can innovation be managed? We will examine these questions by looking at the product life cycle concept and a four-stage approach to new product development.

THE PRODUCT LIFE CYCLE

An important concept underlying sound product strategy is the product life cycle, which allows us to visualize the sales and profits of a product from the time it is introduced until it is no longer on the market. The **product life cycle** provides a detailed picture of what happens to the sales and profits of an *individual* product or service. (Although its shape is similar to that of the competitive advantage life cycle, shown in Exhibit 15.1 on page 445, the two models are very different in that the product life cycle reflects the sales trend for a specific product or service, whereas the competitive advantage life cycle is based on the competitive edge of the company overall and can influence the sales of multiple products or services.) Viewing the product life cycle sales curve in Exhibit 15.2, we can see that the initial stages are characterized by a slow and, ideally, upward movement. The stay at the top is exciting but relatively brief. Then, suddenly, the decline begins, and the downward movement can be rapid. Also note the shape of the typical profit curve. The introductory stage is dominated by losses, with profits peaking in the growth stage.

product life cycle
A detailed picture of what happens to a specific product's sales and profits over time.

EXHIBIT 15.2 The Product Life Cycle

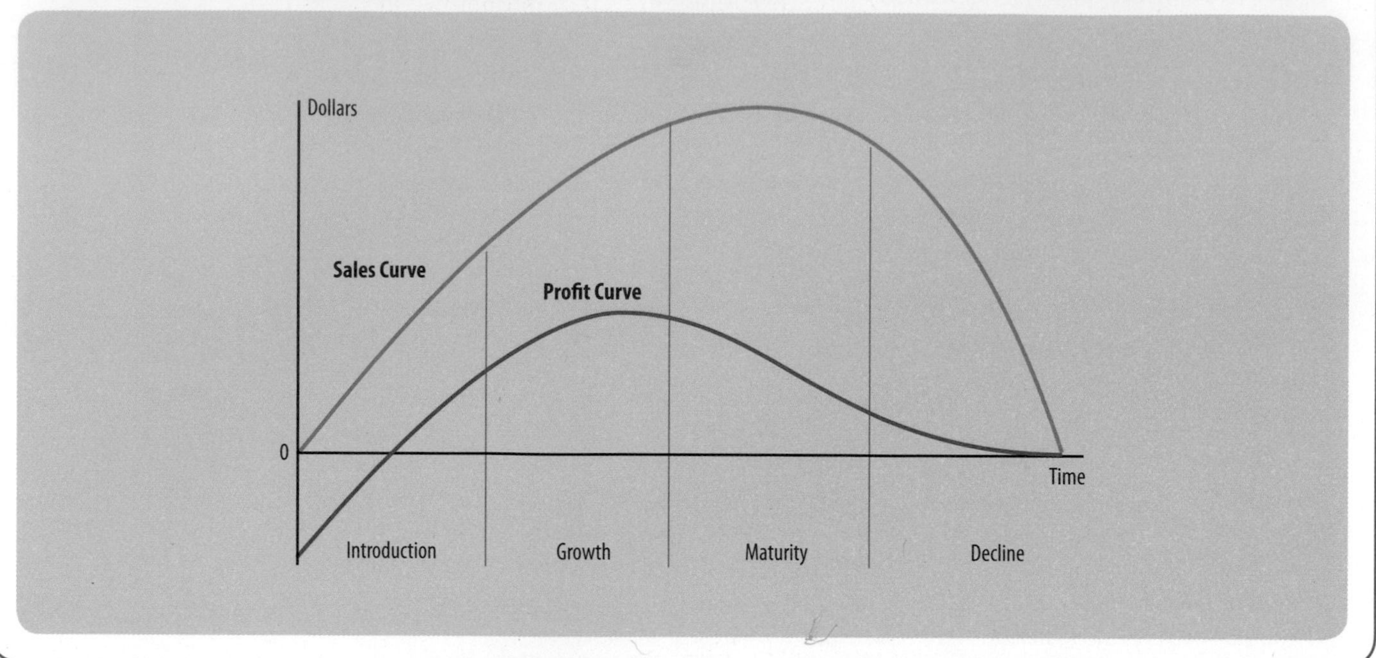

The product life cycle concept is important to the small business owner for three reasons. First, it helps the entrepreneur to understand that promotion, pricing, and distribution policies should all be adjusted to reflect a product's position on the curve. Second, it highlights the importance of revitalizing product lines, whenever possible, to extend their commercial potential. Third, it is a continuing reminder that the natural life cycle for most products follows a trend that rises and then falls; therefore, innovation is necessary for a firm's survival. Good business practice calls for forward-thinking product planning, which should begin before the curve of the existing life cycle peaks. This parallels the point made earlier about the need to extend the firm's competitive advantage before it has run its course.

Before concluding this section, we should point out that products/services and competitive advantages that are on the verge of decline can be reinvigorated using any number of different strategies. For example, companies may choose to modify a product or service by adding new features (such as providing Internet access through cell phones) or propose alternative uses (such as suggesting that baking soda placed in refrigerators can kill odors). Similarly, a competitive advantage can be refreshed through research and development that yields new patents (for a firm that competes using intellectual property), by expanding into complementary products (such as Oreck Corporation's adding lightweight steam mops to its vacuum offerings), or by redefining the business (such as The Walt Disney Company's shift from animation to its much broader identity as an entertainment service provider). The point is that the downward trending sections of the life cycles presented in Exhibits 15.1 and 15.2 can be extended or reversed using the strategies mentioned above, among many others.

THE NEW PRODUCT DEVELOPMENT PROCESS

It is usually up to the small business owner to find, evaluate, and introduce the new products that the company needs. This responsibility requires setting up a process for developing new products. In big businesses, committees or entire departments are created for that purpose. Even in small firms, however, new product development is best handled through a formalized process.

Entrepreneurs tend to view new product development as a monumental task—and it often is. Many find following the common four-stage, structured approach—idea accumulation, business analysis, development of the physical product, and product testing—to be the best way to tackle new product development. (Some of these stages seem similar to those related to the launch of a new venture, as outlined in Chapter 3, but the focus here shifts to expanding an *existing* business through new product development.)

Idea Accumulation

The first stage of the new product development process—idea accumulation—involves increasing the pool of ideas under consideration. New products start with ideas, and these ideas have varied origins. The many possible sources include the following:

- Sales staff, engineering personnel, or other employees within the firm
- Government-owned patents, which are generally available on a royalty-free basis
- Privately owned patents listed by the U.S. Patent and Trademark Office
- Other small companies that may be available for acquisition or merger
- Competitors' products and their promotional campaigns
- Requests and suggestions from customers (increasingly gathered through online channels such as blogs, online surveys, and other tools)
- Brainstorming
- Marketing research (primary and secondary)

Business Analysis

Business analysis is the second stage in new product development. Every new product idea must be carefully studied in relation to several financial considerations. Costs and revenues are estimated and analyzed with techniques such as break-even analysis. Any idea failing to show that it can be profitable is discarded during the business analysis stage. The following four key factors need to be considered in conducting a business analysis:

1. *The product's relationship to the existing product line.* Some firms intentionally add very different products to their product mix. In most cases, an added product item or line should be somehow related to the existing product mix. For example, a new product may be designed to fill a gap in a firm's product line or in the range of prices of the products it currently sells. If the product is completely new, it should have at least a family relationship to existing products to save on costs of manufacturing, distribution, promotion, and/or sales strategy.
2. *Cost of development and introduction.* One problem in adding new products is the cost of their development and introduction. Considerable capital outlays may be necessary, including expenditures for design and development, marketing research to establish sales potential, advertising and sales promotion, patents,

and additional equipment. One to three years may pass before profits are realized on the sale of a new product.

3. *Available personnel and facilities.* Obviously, having adequate skilled personnel and sufficient production capabilities is preferable to having to add employees and buy equipment. Thus, introducing new products is typically more appealing if the personnel and the required equipment are already available.
4. *Competition and market acceptance.* Still another factor to be considered in a business analysis is the potential competition facing a proposed product in its target market. Competition must not be too severe. Some studies suggest that a new product may be introduced successfully only if 5 percent of the total market can be secured. The ideal solution, of course, is to offer a product that is sufficiently different from existing products or that is in a cost and price bracket where it avoids direct competition.

Development of the Physical Product

The next stage of new product development entails sketching out the plan for branding, packaging, and other supporting efforts, such as pricing and promotion. An actual prototype (usually a functioning model of the proposed new product) may be needed at this stage. After these components have been evaluated, the new product idea may be judged a misfit and discarded or it may be passed on to the next stage for further consideration.

Many small business owners are intimidated by the thought of having to develop a prototype for their new products. They have concluded that the time and expense involved are too great to bear, but new technologies are changing all of that. Think back to Celestina Pugliese's experience with her Ready Check Glo product (see In the Spotlight); you may recall that she was able to bring her product to market in seven months and for a mere \$11,800 in *total* costs, not just those related specifically to product development. She was able to do this by using the Internet to locate the assistance she needed, and it paid off in a big way.

Brian Klock, owner of Mitchell, South Dakota–based Klock Werks Kustom Cycles, makes one-of-a-kind motorcycles that are more like works of art than machines. His products run with the speed of greased lightning, but Klock can *build* them fast, too, thanks to an advanced technology called fused deposition modeling (FDM). This new rapid prototyping process, developed by a company called Stratasys, Inc., uses 3-D computer drawings to produce real thermoplastic end-use parts that can be sanded, painted, drilled, coated, sealed, and bolted. The equipment manufactures parts by building up material layer upon layer, much as a printer would lay down ink, and to very precise specifications.

Courtesy of Klock Werks Kustom Cycles

Selected to compete in the popular "Biker Build-Off" challenge, Klock's team had 10 days to build a bike. Using the Stratasys system allowed them to cut fabrication time from three or four weeks to just a few days, while shaving project costs by about \$15,000. And the team did not cut corners—their entry was voted best of show at the annual motorcycle rally in Sturgis, South Dakota.[21]

Product Testing

The last step in the product development process is product testing, which should determine whether the physical product is acceptable (safe, effective, durable, etc.). While the product can be evaluated in a laboratory setting, a limited test of market reaction should also be conducted.

In the final analysis, however, new product development is much more likely to succeed if it is outwardly focused on a firm's customers. Inwardly focused firms—those that are only in it to please themselves or to beat rivals—are apt to fall short of the mark.[22] More than 80 percent of the high-performing companies in one recent study claimed to test and validate customer preferences periodically during the development process, compared with only 43 percent of the low performers. According to this analysis, the high performers were also twice as likely to research what, precisely, customers want.[23] Taking such steps provides the only reliable path to creating value for customers, which, in turn, can extend the company's performance.

Building the Total Product

A major responsibility of marketing is to transform a basic product concept into a total product. Even when an idea for a unique new pen has been developed into physical reality in the form of the basic product, for example, it is still not ready for the marketplace. The total product offering must be more than the materials molded into the shape of the new pen. To be marketable, the basic product must be named, have a package, perhaps have a warranty, and be supported by other product features. Let's examine a few of the components of a total product offering.

BRANDING

An essential element of a total product offering is a **brand**, which is a means of identifying the product—verbally and/or symbolically. Small firms are involved in "branding," whether they realize it or not. A small business owner may neither know nor care, but his or her company has a brand identity that features certain components (see Exhibit 15.3).

brand
A verbal and/or symbolic means of identifying a product.

EXHIBIT 15.3 Components of a Brand Identity

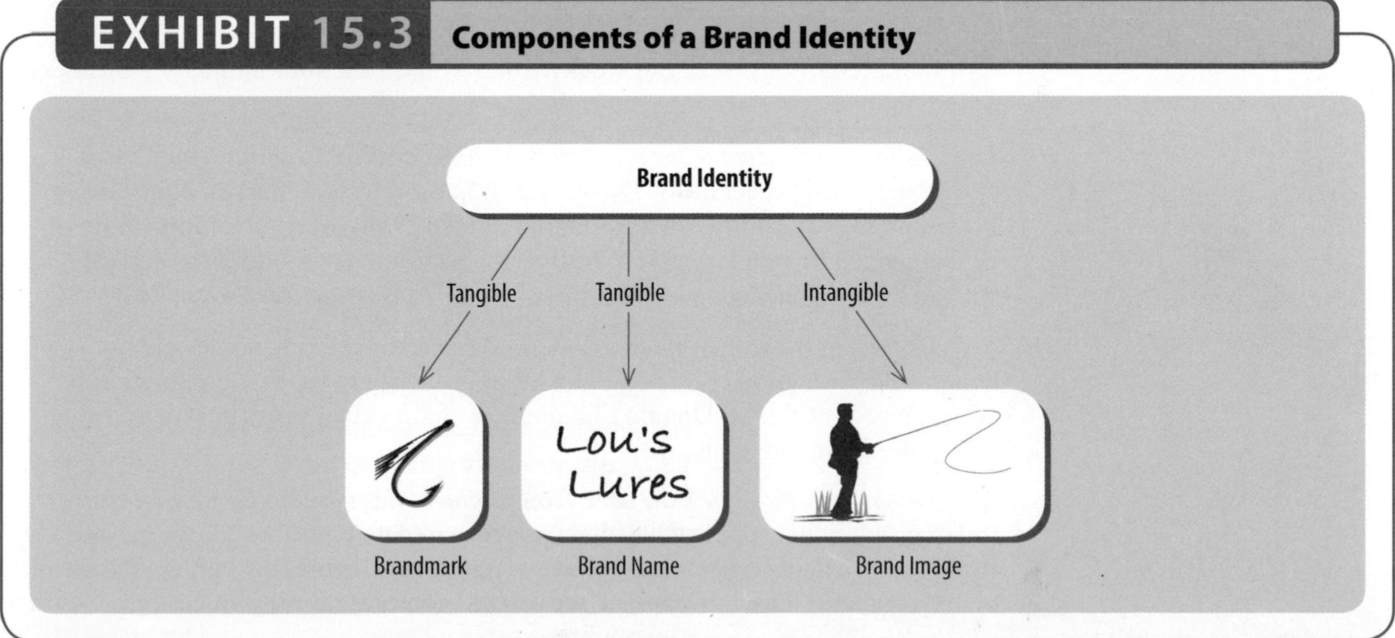

brand image
The overall perception of a brand.

The intangible **brand image** component—people's overall perception of a brand—may be even more important to acceptance of a firm's bundle of satisfaction than the tangible brandmark and brand name elements. For example, how many iPads were purchased by loyal iPhone and iPod users, who know and trust the Apple brand? Many decisions to purchase were surely based on the company's brand strength alone.

Successful entrepreneurs are usually very conscious of their brand as a basic foundation for business; they recognize its power to shape a company's future. Addie Swartz, founder of Between Productions (which stands for "between toys and boys"), is convinced that there is room for a cool but wholesome lifestyle brand targeted at the approximately 13 million girls in the United States who fall between the ages of 9 and 13. To build a foundation for the company's brand, she decided to start with a series of books about girls like her daughter Aliza and her friends. "I wanted to use the media to empower girls in a positive way," says Swartz. She and her team came up with the composites for the series characters (who would be known as the Beacon Street Girls) and decided the setting would be the real-life town of Brookline, Massachusetts. To attract investors, Swartz paired the books with products that appear in the books, including backpacks and pillows. "They wouldn't have invested in a book," says Swartz. "It was about building a brand that can be leveraged aggressively."[24] Swartz's plan worked pretty much as expected, suggesting that a positive brand image creates great potential for an entrepreneurial company.

brand name
A brand that can be spoken.

brandmark
A brand that cannot be spoken.

The tangible components of brand identity are brand names and brandmarks. A **brand name** is a brand that can be spoken—like the name Dell. A **brandmark** is a brand that *cannot* be verbalized—like the golden arches of McDonald's.

Since a product's brand name is so important to the image of the business and its products, careful attention should be given to its selection. In general, five rules apply in naming a product:

1. *Select a name that is easy to pronounce and remember.* You want customers to remember your product. Help them do so with a name that can be spoken easily—for example, Two Men and a Truck (the moving service mentioned in Chapter 5) or Water Water Everywhere (a lawn irrigation business). Before choosing to use your own family name to identify a product, evaluate it carefully to ensure its acceptability.

2. *Choose a descriptive name.* A name that is suggestive of the major benefit of the product can be extremely helpful. As a name for a sign shop, Sign Language, correctly suggests a desirable benefit. Blind Doctor is a creative name for a window blind repair business. But Rocky Road would be a poor name for a business selling mattresses or paving materials.

3. *Use a name that is eligible for legal protection.* Be careful to select a name that can be defended successfully. Do not risk litigation by copying someone else's brand name. For example, a new retailer named Wally-Mart would certainly be challenged by industry giant, Walmart—even if the new store was actually started by someone named Wally.

4. *Select a name with promotional possibilities.* Exceedingly long names are not compatible with good copy design on billboards, where space is at a premium. A competitor of the McDonald's hamburger chain called Bob's has a name that will easily fit on any billboard.

5. *Select a name that can be used on several product lines of a similar nature.* Customer goodwill is often lost when a name doesn't fit a new line. The name Just Brakes is excellent for an auto service shop that repairs brakes—unless the shop plans to expand later into muffler repair and other car repair services.

If you haven't already selected or developed a strong brand name, you might consider licensing one, especially if you have a product for which an appropriate name is available. Winston Wolfe, founder of Olympic Optical, a maker of industrial safety sunglasses for the shooting sports industry, certainly harnessed the power of this approach for his business. By licensing the names Remington, Smith & Wesson, and Zebco, he was able to boost sales of his high-end sporting glasses dramatically by riding the wave of popular enthusiasm for these established brands. As he puts it,

The Parking Spot

> *Licensing the right name can be magic. It can separate you from the crowd and give you a great sales advantage. It can also allow you greater profit margins, since most consumers are willing to pay more for a brand name they know.*[25]

RESOURCES

Coming Up with a Logo

A great company needs a logo to communicate the essence of the business and promote what it does. But coming up with the perfect logo is not as easy to do as it sounds, because market reaction can be difficult to predict and the laws that apply to logo design overlap with those regulating both trademarks and copyrights. A number of websites can provide assistance or insights on logo design and intellectual property rights, including thelogofactory.com, theperfectdesign.com, uspto.gov/trademarks, and copyright.gov. But a good intellectual property rights or copyright attorney may be the best source of information and up-to-date advice.

A brandmark also has tremendous value. The Nike swoosh and the Chevy badge are marks widely associated with their owners. A small firm's special "signature," or logo, should symbolize positive images of the firm and its products. And if you don't get it right initially, consider a new design. This is what Penny Pritzker did a few years after launching the Parking Spot, an off-airport parking service. The original logo on the company's shuttle buses failed to set it apart from those of its many competitors. Deciding that a much bolder impression was required, the Parking Spot unveiled a new design sporting "black spots of different sizes dancing against a vibrant yellow background."[26] The change was just what the company needed, and it continues to grow. It now operates 20 parking facilities at 14 airports spread across 12 different cities.[27] Such results are not unusual. As suggested by Elinor Selame, president of BrandEquity International, "The logo can be your company's hardest-working employee."[28]

Developing an effective logo is very important, although it can be an expensive undertaking. The following tips may help you to design a logo without breaking the bank:[29]

1. *Be simple.* The best logos are often the simplest. Think of Target, whose red circle with a red dot in the center conveys the essence of affordable, hip

practicality. H&R Block uses a green square in association with its name. Simple things are easy to remember and slower to appear dated.

2. *Design for visibility*. Nike paid Carolyn Davidson, a graphic design student, $35 to design the bold red swoosh that has been the firm's brandmark since its unveiling at the U.S. Track & Field Olympic Trials in 1972. One of its most positive qualities is the fact that you simply cannot miss it wherever it is displayed.
3. *Leave it open to interpretation*. The logo should not explain, at a glance, the complete nature of your company. The best logos raise a question and are open to interpretation. One of the reasons the Nike swoosh is so effective is that it stands as an "empty vessel." Because it has no obvious meaning, Nike can build any image around it that serves the firm's purposes.
4. *Be relentlessly consistent*. Companies with strong graphic identities have built that recognition through years of use. Pick a typeface. Pick a color. Use them over and over again, *on everything*. Eventually, you will be able to establish an identifiable look and feel.
5. *Recognize the importance of logo design*. Logos and colors are often considered "cosmetic," unimportant features of doing business. But most design-driven companies got to be that way through the efforts of highly placed advocates, such as Steve Jobs at Apple. Design programs work best when others know that they are championed by important people.
6. *Get good advice*. You can go pretty far with common sense. But sooner or later, you'll need the services of a professional graphic designer. The website of the American Institute of Graphic Arts (http://www.aiga.org), the largest professional organization for graphic designers, offers useful information about how to find and work with experienced professionals.
7. *Don't expect miracles*. Your company's image is the sum total of many factors. Make sure that your company looks, sounds, and feels smart in every way, every time it goes out in public.

trademark
A legal term indicating that a firm has exclusive rights to use a brand to promote a product.

service mark
A brand that a company has the exclusive right to use to identify a service.

Trademark and **service mark** are legal terms indicating the exclusive right to use a brand to represent products and services, respectively. Once an entrepreneur has found a name or symbol that is unique, easy to remember, and related to the product or service, it is time to run a name or symbol search and then to register the brand name or symbol. The protection of trademarks is discussed later in this chapter.

PACKAGING

Packaging is another important part of the total product offering. In addition to protecting the basic product, packaging is a significant tool for increasing the value of the total product.

Consider for a moment some of the products you purchase. How many do you buy mainly because of a preference for package design and/or color? The truth is that innovative packaging is often the deciding factor for consumers. If two products are otherwise similar, packaging may create the distinctive impression that makes the sale.

Features like biodegradable packaging materials can certainly distinguish a product from its competition, but the visual impression that packaging creates usually has the greatest appeal to consumers. Discerning entrepreneurs have figured that out. Benjamin and Lisa Nisanoff,

© ME! Bath

founders of a Los Angeles–based bath products manufacturer called ME! Bath, have come up with something more than ordinary bath oil beads—they sell *indulgence* with their ME! Bath Ice Cream and ME! Shower Sherbet.[30] Here's how they make that happen:

> *The husband-and-wife team has not only created cute product names, but also has developed distinct packaging shaped like scoops of ice cream. . . . [The couple] discovered their perfect marketing niche while selling bath ice cream at street fairs. Initially they tried to make each unit a perfect sphere, but creating them by hand gave them the look of ice cream scoops. "The idea is [that] the product looks like something you would want to eat," says Benjamin. "It [evokes] all of those sensory experiences.*[31]

Keep in mind that the product still performs in the same way as others in its category, but the look and design of the packaging are driving consumer interest in this particular brand.

Though it seems like a straightforward decision, financial constraints often prevent small businesses from pursuing creative packaging strategies that would boost sales. Entrepreneurs who simply can't afford the expensive equipment required for such packaging innovations should not immediately write off the option. They can often work with "contract packagers," who are able to handle such orders at a low per-unit cost.[32] It certainly pays to consider what goes on the outside of your product, not just what's in it.

LABELING

Another part of the total product is its label. Labeling serves several important purposes for manufacturers, which apply most labels. One purpose is to display the brand, particularly when branding the basic product would be undesirable. For example, a furniture brand is typically shown on a label and not on the basic product. On some products, brand visibility is highly desirable; Louis Vuitton handbags would probably not sell as well if the name label were only inside the purse.

A label is also an important informative tool for consumers. It often includes information on product care and use and may even provide instructions on how to dispose of the product.

Laws concerning labeling requirements should be reviewed carefully. Government agencies such as the Food and Drug Administration, the Federal Trade Commission, the U.S. Department of Agriculture, and several others issue regulations that must be followed to remain within the law. Very small businesses are exempt from many of these requirements, but it is wise to be innovative with your labeling information. You may even want to consider including information that goes beyond the specified minimum legal requirements if doing so would give an advantage to your company and the way your products are positioned in the marketplace.

WARRANTIES

warranty
A promise that a product will perform at a certain level or meet certain standards.

A **warranty** is simply a promise, written or unwritten, that a product will do certain things or meet certain standards. All sellers make an implied warranty that the seller's title to the product is good. A merchant seller, who deals in goods of a particular kind, makes the additional implied warranty that those goods are fit for the ordinary purposes for which they are sold. A written warranty on a product is not always necessary. In fact, many firms operate without written warranties, believing that offering one would likely confuse customers or make them suspicious.

Warranties are important for products that are innovative, comparatively expensive, purchased infrequently, relatively complex to repair, and positioned as high-quality goods. A business should consider the following factors in rating the merits of a proposed warranty policy:

product strategy The way the product component of the marketing mix is used to achieve a firm's objectives.

product item The lowest common denominator in the product mix—the individual item.

- Cost
- Service capability
- Competitive practices
- Customer perceptions
- Legal implications

Warranties are only one part of the total product offering. All of the factors just discussed are guided by a company's product strategy, which we discuss in the next section.

Product Strategy

Product strategy includes decisions about branding, packaging, labeling, and other elements of the core component of the bundle of satisfaction, whether product or service. To be more specific, a **product strategy** describes the manner in which the product component of the marketing mix is used to achieve the objectives of a firm. This involves several supporting features:

product line The sum of related individual product items.

product mix The collection of a firm's total product lines.

product mix consistency The similarity of product lines in a product mix.

- A **product item** is the lowest common denominator in a company's product mix. It refers to an individual item, such as one brand of bar soap.
- A **product line** is the sum of the related individual product items, but the relationship is usually defined generically. So, two brands of bar soap are two product items in one product line.
- A **product mix** is the collection of all product lines within a firm's ownership and control. A firm's product mix might consist of a line of bar soaps and a line of shoe polishes.
- **Product mix consistency** refers to the closeness, or similarity, of the product lines. The more items in a product line, the greater its depth; the more product lines in a product mix, the greater its breadth.

To illustrate how these features can come together, Exhibit 15.4 shows the product lines and product mix of the firm 180s LLC, which was mentioned on page 442.

PRODUCT MARKETING VERSUS SERVICE MARKETING

Traditionally, marketers have used the word *product* as a generic term to describe both goods and services. However, certain characteristics—tangibility, amount of time separating production and consumption, standardization, and perishability—lead to a number of differences between the strategies for marketing goods and those for marketing services (see Exhibit 15.5). Based on these characteristics, for example, the marketing of a pencil fits the pure goods end of the scale and the marketing of a haircut fits the pure services end. The major implication of this distinction is that marketing services obviously presents unique challenges that are not faced when marketing goods.

Although we recognize the value of examining the marketing of services as a unique form, we lack space here to describe it separately. Therefore, from this point on in the chapter, a **product** will be considered to include the total bundle of satisfaction offered to customers in an exchange transaction, whether this involves a good, a service, or a combination of the two. In addition to the physical product or core service, a product also includes complementary components, such as its packaging or a warranty (as described in the previous section). The physical product or core service is usually the most important element in the total bundle of satisfaction, but that main feature is sometimes perceived by customers to be similar for a variety of products. In that case, complementary components become the most important features of the product. For example, a particular brand of cake mix may be preferred by consumers not because it is a better mix, but because of the unique toll-free telephone number on the package that can be called for baking hints. Or a certain dry cleaner may be chosen over others because it treats customers with respect, not because it cleans clothes exceptionally well.

product
A total bundle of satisfaction—whether a service, a good, or both—offered to consumers in an exchange transaction.

PRODUCT STRATEGY OPTIONS

Failure to clearly understand product strategy options will lead to ineffectiveness and conflict in the marketing effort. The major product strategy alternatives of a small business

EXHIBIT 15.4 Product Lines and Product Mix for 180s LLC

BREADTH OF PRODUCT MIX

DEPTH OF THE PRODUCT LINES

	Ear Warmers	Gloves	Jackets	Booties	Hats	Eyegear	Scarves
Casual & Training	12 Men's Styles 21 Women's Styles 2 Kid's Styles	9 Men's Styles 15 Women's Styles			Knit Beanie	Mortise	
Sports Apparel	College (91 Teams) NFL (32 Teams) NHL (19 Teams)	College (46 Teams) NFL (32 Teams)		College (43 Teams)			College (54 Teams)
Work Wear	Pro Trade Basic Fleece Pro Duck Pro Ear Warmer	17 Styles			Performance Cap		
Battle Gear			Combat Desert Jacket				

Source: Compiled from "180s," http://www.180s.com, accessed January 26, 2011.

EXHIBIT 15.5 Services Marketing Versus Goods Marketing

Characteristics	Pure Services Marketing		Pure Goods Marketing
Tangibility	Intangible Offerings	Hybrid Services/ Goods Marketing	Tangible Offerings
Production/Consumption	Occur at the same time		Occur at different times
Standardization	Less standardization		More standardization
Perishability	Greater perishability		Less perishability

can be condensed into six categories, based on the nature of the firm's product offering and the number of target markets:

- One product/one market
- One product/multiple markets
- Modified product/one market
- Modified product/multiple markets
- Multiple products/one market
- Multiple products/multiple markets

Each alternative represents a distinct strategy, although two or more of these strategies can be attempted at the same time. However, a small company will usually pursue the alternatives in the order listed. Also, keep in mind that once a product strategy has been implemented, sales can be increased through certain additional growth tactics. For example, within any market, a small firm can try to increase sales of an existing product by doing any or all of the following:

- Convincing nonusers in the targeted market to become customers
- Persuading current customers to use more of the product
- Alerting current customers to new uses for the product

When small businesses add products to their product mix, they generally select related products. But there are, of course, strategies that involve unrelated products. For example, a local dealer selling Italian sewing machines might add a line of microwave ovens, an entirely unrelated product. This type of product strategy can be very risky. However, it is occasionally used by small businesses, especially when the new product fits existing distribution and sales systems or requires similar marketing knowledge.

Adding an unrelated product to the mix to target a new market is an even higher-risk strategy, as a business is attempting to market an unfamiliar product in an unfamiliar market. However, if well planned, this approach can offer significant advantages. One electrical equipment service company recently added a private employment agency. If successful, this product strategy could provide a hedge against volatile shifts in market demand. A business that sells both snow skis and surfboards expects that demand will be high in one market or the other at all times, smoothing the sales curve and maintaining a steady cash flow throughout the year. It is tempting to take on new product opportunities—sometimes to the point of becoming overextended—but staying manageably focused is critical.

The Legal Environment

Strategic decisions about growth, innovation, product development, and the total product offering are always made within the guidelines and constraints of the legal environment of the marketplace. Let's examine a few of the laws by which the government protects both the rights of consumers and the marketing assets of companies.

CONSUMER PROTECTION

Federal regulations on such subjects as product safety and labeling have important implications for product strategy. For example, to protect the public against unreasonable risk of injury, the federal government enacted the Consumer Product Safety Act of 1972. This act created the Consumer Product Safety Commission to set safety standards for toys and other consumer products and to ban goods that are exceptionally hazardous, which ultimately increase the costs of doing business. This law was extended recently by the Consumer Product Safety Improvement Act of 2008, but the general thrust of its provisions remains the same.[33]

The Nutrition Labeling and Education Act of 1990 requires every food product covered by the law to have a standard nutrition label, listing the amounts of calories, fat, salt, and nutrients in the product. The law also addresses the accuracy of advertising claims such as "low salt" and "fiber prevents cancer." Although these legal requirements may seem to be a minor burden, some experts estimate that labeling costs can easily run thousands of dollars per product.

PROTECTION OF MARKETING ASSETS

The four primary means used by firms to protect certain marketing assets are shown in Exhibit 15.6. The examples shown are representative of trademarks, patents, copyrights, and trade dress.

Trademarks

Trademark protection is important to a manufacturer or merchant, because it protects a company's distinctive use of a name, slogan, symbol, picture, logo, or combination of these. In some cases, even a color or scent can be part of a trademark. In essence, trademarks represent the way people identify your business.[34]

Because names that refer to products are often registered trademarks, potential names should be investigated carefully to ensure that they are not already in use. Entrepreneurs can conduct their own trademark searches by using the main Trademark Search Library of the U.S. Patent and Trademark Office (USPTO) in Alexandria, Virginia, or any of the 81 Patent and Trademark Depository Libraries that can be found in

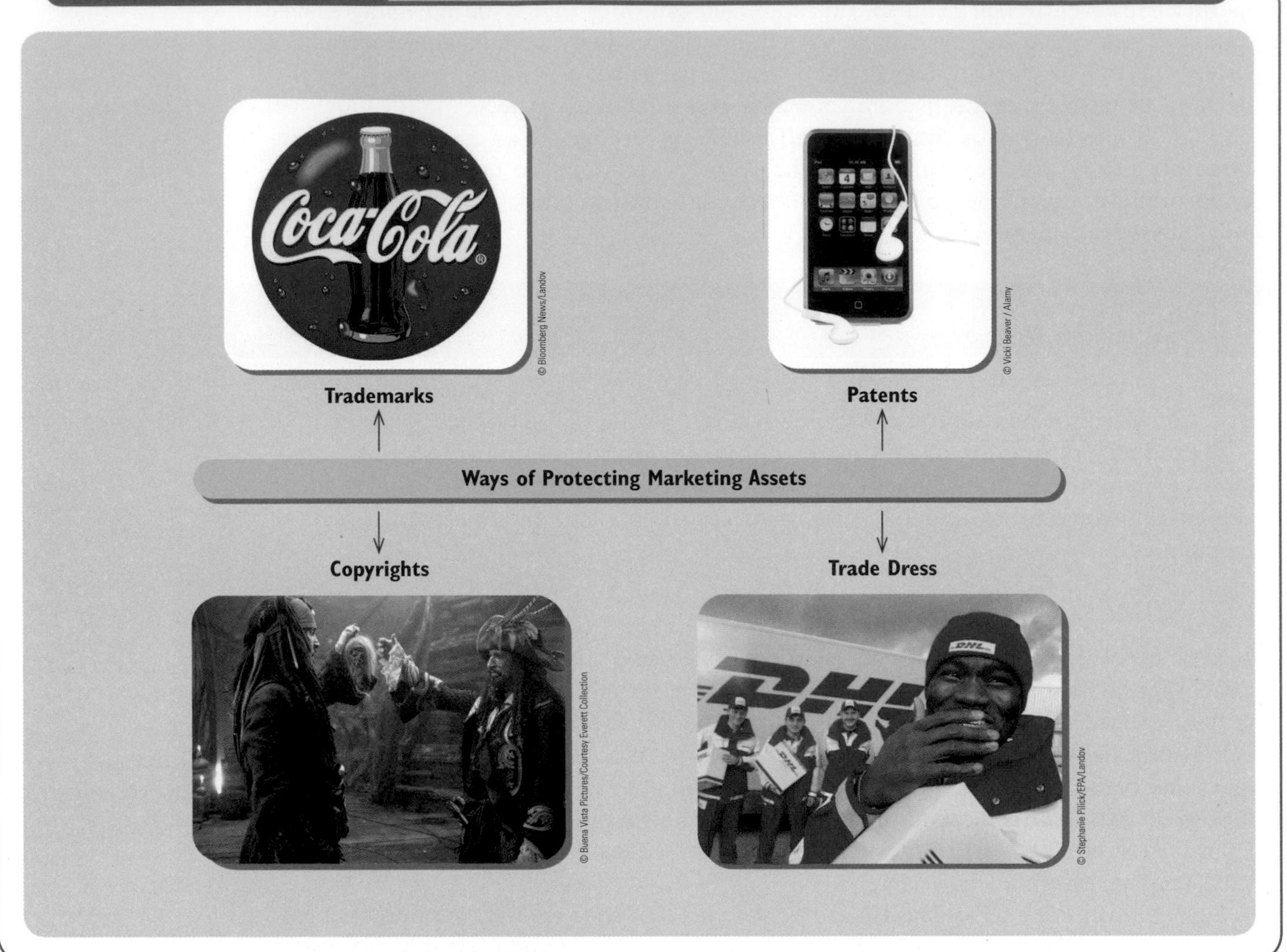

nearly every U.S. state. This can also be done online by going to http://www.uspto.gov. Small business owners often seek the advice of an attorney for assistance with trademark search and registration, but this may only be necessary if complications arise (for example, if the desired trademark is similar to one that is already registered). Applications for registration can be submitted online at the USPTO website for a fee of between $275 and $375.[35]

Common law recognizes a property right in the ownership of trademarks. However, reliance on common-law rights is not always adequate. For example, Microsoft Corporation, the major supplier of personal computer software, claimed it had common-law rights to the trademark *Windows* because of the enormous industry recognition of the product. Nevertheless, when Microsoft filed a trademark application in 1990 seeking to gain exclusive rights to the name *Windows,* the U.S. Patent and Trademark Office rejected the bid, claiming the word was a generic term and, therefore, in the public domain.

Registration of trademarks is permitted under the federal Lanham Trademark Act, making protection easier if infringement is encountered. The act was revised in 1989 and now allows trademark rights to begin with merely an "intent to use," along with the filing of an application and payment of fees. Prior to this revision, a firm had to have already used the mark on goods shipped or sold. According to the USPTO, a company's federally registered trademark rights can last indefinitely, as long as the owner "continues to use the mark on or in connection with the goods and/or services in the registration and files all necessary documentation in the USPTO at the appropriate times."[36]

According to the law, a business must *use* a trademark in order to protect it, but it is also important to use it *properly*. Inform the public that your trademark is exactly that by labeling it with the symbol™. If that trademark is registered, the symbol ® or the phrase "Registered in the U.S. Patent and Trademark Office" should be used.

Patents

A **patent** is the registered, exclusive right of an inventor to make, use, or sell an invention. The two primary types of patents are utility patents and design patents. A **utility patent** covers a new process or protects the function of a product. A **design patent** covers the appearance of a product and everything that is an inseparable part of the product. Utility patents are granted for a period of 20 years, while design patents are effective for 14 years. Patent law also provides for **plant patents**, which cover any distinct, new variety of living plants.

patent
The registered, exclusive right of an inventor to make, use, or sell an invention.

utility patent
Registered protection for a new process or a product's function.

design patent
Registered protection for the appearance of a product and its inseparable parts.

plant patent
Registered protection for any distinct, new variety of living plant.

Items that may be patented include machines and products, improvements on machines and products, and original designs. Some small manufacturers have patented items that constitute the major part of their product line. In fact, some now-gigantic firms such as IBM, Polaroid, and Xerox can trace their origins to a patented invention. Small business owners preparing a patent application often retain a patent attorney to act for them, but a patent search can be conducted on the Internet.

Lawsuits concerning patent infringements are costly and should be avoided, if possible. Coming up with the money and legal talent to enforce this legal right is one of the major problems associated with patent protection in small businesses. Monetary damages and injunctions are available, however, if infringement can be proved.

Copyrights

A **copyright** is the exclusive right of a creator (author, composer, designer, or artist) to reproduce, publish, perform, display, or sell work that is the product of that person's intelligence and skill. Works created on or after January 1, 1978, receive copyright protection for the duration of the creator's life plus 70 years. A "work made for hire" (work created by an employee for an employer) is protected for 95 years from its publication or 120 years from its creation, whichever is shorter. Copyrights are registered in the U.S. Copyright Office of the Library of Congress, whose website (http://www.copyright.gov) provides an extensive supply of useful information about copyrights.

copyright
The exclusive right of a creator to reproduce, publish, perform, display, or sell his or her own works.

Under the Copyright Act of 1976, copyrightable works are automatically protected from the moment of their creation. However, any work distributed to the public should contain a copyright notice. This notice consists of three elements (all of which can be found on the copyright page in the front of this textbook):

- The symbol ©
- The year the work was published
- The copyright owner's name

The law provides that copyrighted work may not be reproduced by another person without authorization. Even photocopying such work is prohibited, although an individual may copy a limited amount of material for such purposes as research, criticism, comment, and scholarship. A copyright holder can sue a violator for damages.

© iStockphoto.com/Angelika Schwarz

entrepreneurial experiences

New Ruling Says Old Numbers Can Be Very Bad for Business

By his own description, Raymond E. Stauffer is a "sharp-dressed man"—who also happens to be a patent attorney. While looking over a display of bow ties at a Brooks Brothers store at a New Jersey shopping mall, he noticed that the goods were labeled with out-of-date patent numbers. Rather than make a scene in the store, he decided to do the only polite thing he could think of—he sued the company in federal court for "marking its adjustable bow ties with patents that expired in the 1950s." He thought Brooks Brothers would have to pay the typical $500 fine for such an offense, but that may not be the case.

© iStockphoto.com/Michael Madsen

Many "false marking" lawsuits have been brought against firms over the years. Some of these lawsuits hammered small companies, but most focused on large corporations like Procter & Gamble, Cisco Systems, Pfizer Inc., 3M, and DirecTV and often involved products of great importance. (Society is surely better served now that out-of-date patent numbers have been forcibly removed from mismarked turkey pop-up timers, toilet plungers, Frisbees, bubble gum—even a toy called "The Original Wooly Willy," which allows users to change the disguise on a cartoon-faced man using a wand that attracts magnetic dust and deposits it into place.) However, all companies—regardless of size and no matter the product—must abide by the law on this. To maintain the validity of a patent beyond its normal span of up to 20 years, companies must pay a maintenance fee every four years; otherwise, the patent number is to be removed from the product.

The false-marking statute is intended to protect consumers, would-be competitors, and inventors from companies that might claim false patent protection. It was originally interpreted as allowing whistleblowers to file suit against errant companies and collect half of the $500 fine per offense—no matter how many individual products were mismarked. (The other half of the fine goes to the United States government.) But the small fine provided scant incentive for whistleblowing—that is, until a federal court ruled that "the law's plain language required a per-article penalty, not a $500 total penalty." So companies now "are liable for up to $500 for every tube of mascara or box of garbage bags marked with an expired patent"—a very common error, as it turns out. This changed everything.

Stauffer doesn't know how many individual ties were falsely marked, but he estimates that around 120 styles were out of regulation. "I would have settled this case for $25,000 back in December of 2008," he says. "Brooks Brothers, however, seemed eager to want to litigate the case, and I was delighted to give them the opportunity."

Many companies choose to settle cases out of court to avoid potentially disastrous awards or the heavy legal fees they would have to pay to fight them. Both small and large businesses should take note of the heavy costs associated with these lawsuits and periodically refresh their existing patents or face firm-sinking penalties.

Sources: Sheri Qualters, "Federal Circuit Ruling Sparks Surge of Patent Whistleblower Suits," *The National Law Journal*, April 5, 2010, http://www.law.com/jsp/article.jsp?id=1202447474494, accessed January 31, 2011; and Dionne Searcey, "New Breed of Patent Claim Bedevils Product Makers," *Wall Street Journal*, September 1, 2010, pp. A1, A14.

Trade Dress

A small business may also possess a valuable intangible asset called trade dress. **Trade dress** describes those elements of a firm's distinctive operating image not specifically protected under a trademark, patent, or copyright. Trade dress is the "look" that a firm creates to establish its marketing advantage. For example, if the employees of a small pizza chain dress as prison guards and inmates, a "jailhouse" image could become uniquely associated with this business and, over time, become its trade dress. Trade dress can be protected under trademark law if it can be shown "that the average consumer would likely be confused as to product origin if another product were allowed to appear in similar dress."[37] This is only one small part of the intellectual property rights picture, however. A small business needs to take measures to protect its legitimate claims to all such entitlements—that is, trademarks, patents, copyrights, and trade dress.

trade dress
Elements of a firm's distinctive image not protected by a trademark, patent, or copyright.

So far, the focus of this chapter has been on the value of innovation and growth and the importance of effective management of a company's products and services. These are critical considerations; however, a company's offerings are of use only to the extent that consumers have access to them. With this understanding, we now shift our attention to establishing a system that can effectively develop and distribute a company's products and/or services to its customers.

supply chain management
A system of management that integrates and coordinates the ways in which a firm creates or develops a product or service, delivers it to customers, and receives payment for it.

Supply Chain Management

Supply chain management is a system of management that integrates and coordinates the ways in which a firm finds the raw materials and necessary components to produce a product or service, creates the actual product or service, and then delivers it to customers. It also coordinates the flow of payments between entities in the chain of transactions. Recent attention directed toward supply chain management has motivated both large and small firms to create a more competitive, customer-driven supply system. Effective supply chain management can potentially lower the costs of inventory, transportation, warehousing, and packaging, while increasing customer satisfaction.

The Internet and available software are major drivers of recent developments in supply chain management. Years ago, communication between parties in the supply chain was slow or nonexistent. But the Internet, with its simple, universally accepted communication standards, has brought suppliers and customers together in a way never before thought possible.

In this part of the chapter, we look briefly at some of the important features of supply chain management,[38] including the functions of intermediaries, the various distribution channels that can be folded into supply chain operations, and the basics of logistics. Much of this discussion is focused on distribution-related concerns, which entrepreneurs tend to regard as the least glamorous marketing activity. Nevertheless, an effective distribution system is just as important as a unique package, a clever name, or a creative promotional campaign. Thus, a small business owner should understand the basic principles of distribution, which apply to both domestic and international distribution activities.

distribution
Physically moving products and establishing intermediary relationships to support such movement.

channel of distribution
The system of relationships established to guide the movement of a product.

physical distribution (logistics)
The activities of distribution involved in the physical relocation of products.

In the context of supply chain operations, **distribution** encompasses both the physical transfer of products and the establishment of intermediary (middleman) relationships to achieve product movement. The system of relationships established to guide the movement of a product is called the **channel of distribution**; the activities involved in physically moving a product through the channel of distribution are called **physical distribution (logistics)**. Distribution is essential for both tangible products (goods) and intangible products (services). However, since distribution activities are more visible for tangible products (goods), our comments here will focus primarily on products. Most intangible products (services) are delivered straight to the user—for example, an income tax preparer and a hairdresser both serve their clients directly. Nonetheless, even the distribution of labor can involve channel intermediaries, such as when an employment agency provides a firm with temporary personnel.

merchant middlemen
Intermediaries that take ownership of the goods they distribute.

agents/brokers
Intermediaries that do not take ownership of the goods they distribute.

INTERMEDIARIES

Intermediaries can often perform marketing functions better than the producer of a product can. A producer can perform its own distribution functions—including delivery—if the geographic area of the market is small, customers' needs are specialized, and risk levels are low, as they might be for, say, a doughnut maker. However, intermediaries generally provide more efficient means of distribution if customers are widely dispersed or if special packaging and storage are needed.

Some intermediaries, called **merchant middlemen**, take ownership of the goods they distribute, thereby helping a company to share or shift business risk. Other intermediaries, such as **agents** and **brokers**, do not take title to goods and, therefore, assume less market risk than do merchant middlemen.

direct channel
A distribution system without intermediaries.

indirect channel
A distribution system with one or more intermediaries.

CHANNELS OF DISTRIBUTION

A channel of distribution can be either direct or indirect. In a **direct channel**, there are no intermediaries—the product goes directly from producer to user. An **indirect channel** of distribution has one or more intermediaries between producer and user.

Exhibit 15.7 depicts the various options available for structuring a channel of distribution. E-commerce (online merchandising) and mail-order marketing are direct channel systems for distributing consumer goods. Southwest Airlines and EasyJet are examples of companies that use a direct channel to final consumers. Rather than sell their tickets through local travel agents and online travel service distributors like Expedia.com, these two cost-conscious airlines sell flights directly to consumers through their own websites and in-airport ticket counters and self-service kiosks, which reduces their operating costs by 18 to 25 percent.[39]

The systems shown on the right-hand side of Exhibit 15.7 illustrate indirect channels involving one, two, or three levels of intermediaries. As a final consumer, you are

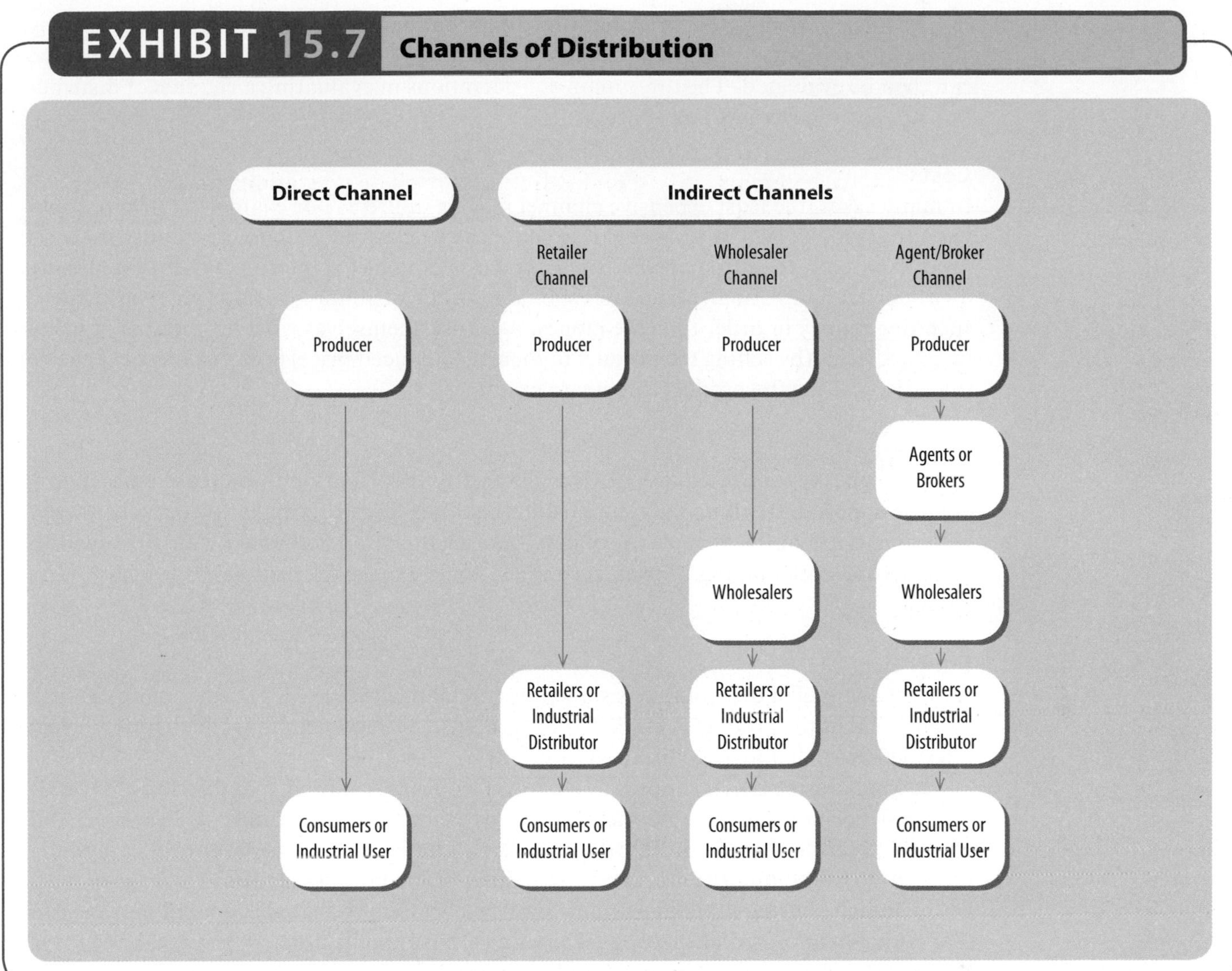

naturally familiar with retailers; industrial customers are equally familiar with industrial distributors. Channels with two or three stages of intermediaries are probably the ones most typically used by small firms producing products with geographically large markets. It is important to note that a small firm may use more than one channel of distribution, a practice called **dual distribution**.

dual distribution A distribution system that involves more than one channel.

Small businesses that successfully employ a single distribution channel may switch to dual distribution if they find that an additional channel will improve overall profitability. This is what Alex Romanov, owner of Chagrin Shoe Leather & Luggage Repair in Woodmere, Ohio, has done. His business saw its sales increase by 25 percent after the U.S. economy slowed in 2008 and Americans decided that it would be cheaper and wiser to repair their shoes than to buy new ones. "We fix everything except broken relationships," quips Romanov. His son, Ilya, had decided that he had no interest in being a cobbler, so he launched American Heelers, an online business that receives, by mail, about 100 pairs of shoes for repair each week. These shoes are serviced in the elder Romanov's shop and returned to their owners. Establishing this father–son partnership has expanded the business by opening up two fronts for sales: a physical operation that takes orders directly from customers and an e-commerce operation that generates revenue from customers that live in other areas.[40] This is the advantage of dual distribution.

A logical starting point in structuring a distribution system is to study systems used by competing businesses. Such an analysis should reveal some practical alternatives, which can then be evaluated. The three main considerations in evaluating a channel of distribution are costs, coverage, and control.

Costs

In many cases, the least expensive channel may be indirect. For example, a firm producing handmade dolls may choose not to purchase trucks and warehouses to distribute its product directly to customers if it costs less to use established intermediaries that already own such facilities. Small companies should look at distribution costs as an investment—spending money in order to make money—and ask themselves whether the cost of using intermediaries (by selling the product to them at a reduced price) is more or less expensive than distributing the product directly to customers.

Coverage

Small businesses can often use indirect channels of distribution to increase market coverage. Suppose a small manufacturer's internal sales force can make 10 contacts a week with final users of the venture's product. Creating an indirect channel with 10 industrial distributors, each making 10 contacts a week, could expose the product to 100 final users a week.

Control

A direct channel of distribution is sometimes preferable because it provides more control. To ensure that the product is marketed with care, an entrepreneur must deliberately select intermediaries that provide the desired support.

A small business that chooses to use intermediaries to market and distribute its product must be sure that the intermediaries understand how the product is best used and why it's better than competitors' offerings. Additionally, if a wholesaler carries competing products, an entrepreneur must be sure that her or his product gets its fair share of marketing efforts. Distributors must know what makes the product special and how best to market it. An intermediary's sloppy marketing efforts and insufficient product knowledge can undermine the success of even the best product.

THE SCOPE OF PHYSICAL DISTRIBUTION

In addition to the intermediary relationships that make up a channel, there must also be a system of physical distribution. The main component of physical distribution is transportation. Additional components include storage, materials handling, delivery terms, and inventory management. (Inventory management is discussed in Chapter 21.)

Transportation

The major decision regarding physical transportation of a product is which method to use. Available modes of transportation are traditionally classified as airplanes, railroads, trucks, pipelines, and waterways. Each mode has unique advantages and disadvantages. For example, the train operator CSX Corporation ran radio ads that boldly announced, "A gallon of fuel in a CSX train can move one ton of freight 423 miles. Just think what that can do for the environment."[41] The purpose of the ad campaign was twofold—to let potential customers know that the company offers inexpensive transportation services that also minimize environmental impact. But the choice of a specific mode of transportation is usually based on several criteria: relative cost, transit time, reliability, capability, accessibility, and traceability.

common carriers Transportation intermediaries available for hire to the general public.

Transportation intermediaries are legally classified as common carriers, contract carriers, and private carriers. **Common carriers** are available for hire by the general public, without discrimination. Like common carriers, **contract carriers**, which engage in individual contracts with shippers, are subject to regulation by federal and/or state agencies; however, they have the right to choose their clients at will. Transport lines owned by shippers are called **private carriers**.

contract carriers Transportation intermediaries that contract with individual shippers.

private carriers Lines of transport owned by shippers.

Storage

Lack of space is a common problem for small businesses. But when a channel system uses merchant middlemen or wholesalers, ownership of the goods is transferred, as is responsibility for the storage function. With other options, the small business must plan for its own warehousing. If a firm is too small to own a private warehouse, it can rent space in a public warehouse. When storage requirements are simple and do not involve much special handling equipment, a public warehouse can provide inexpensive storage.

Materials Handling

Even if it is in the right place at the right time, a damaged product is worth very little. Therefore, a physical distribution system must arrange for suitable materials-handling methods and equipment. Forklifts, as well as special containers and packaging, are part of a materials-handling system.

Delivery Terms

A small but important part of a physical distribution system is the delivery terms, specifying which party is responsible for several aspects of the distribution:

- Paying the freight costs
- Selecting the carriers
- Bearing the risk of damage in transit
- Selecting the modes of transport

The simplest delivery terms and the most advantageous to a small business as the seller—is F.O.B. (free on board) origin, freight collect. This shifts all of the responsibility for freight costs to the buyer. Ownership of the goods and risk of loss also pass to the buyer at the time the goods are shipped.

Logistics companies specialize in transportation and distribution services, providing trucking, packaging, and warehousing services for small and medium-sized companies with limited in-house staff. Many small businesses believe that using these **third-party logistics firms** (sometimes referred to as **3PLs**) is more cost effective than carrying out the same functions on their own. For example, Premier Inc., of Greenwich, Connecticut, uses a firm named APL Logistics to handle packaging and shipping of its health and beauty-aid products. Products produced in plants around the country go to the APL warehouse in Dallas, Texas, and are then shipped to distribution outlets nationwide.[42] More familiar firms offering 3PL services include household names such as FedEx and UPS, both of which offer customized assistance for small businesses that would prefer to focus on their primary operations and leave the transportation and distribution challenges to others.

third-party logistics firm (3PL) A company that provides transportation and distribution services to firms that prefer to focus their efforts on other business aspects.

Logistics providers offer an exceptionally important service to small companies, especially those that need assistance with the physical distribution of their product so that they can concentrate their time and energy on the core activities of their business. While this is only one small part of the supply chain management system, it is obviously a critical function that merits thoughtful planning.

Pulling the Pieces Together

This chapter began by explaining that innovation and growth are critical to competitive advantage and small business success. But effective management of a company's products requires attention to both maintaining existing products and developing new ones. Like people, products pass through life cycle stages and face different obstacles at each stage. Therefore, a successful entrepreneur must have a carefully planned product strategy. Thought must also be given to all facets of the physical flow of inputs and outputs. Managing the supply chain requires planning how and where the firm will get the components for products and how it will deliver the finished products to customers. Many channels of distribution exist, but the benefits and drawbacks of each of these must be considered carefully. If these critical tasks are not managed effectively, the performance of the company is almost certain to decline.

1. Understand the challenges associated with the growth of a small business.

- Some entrepreneurs find that maintaining the status quo is challenge enough.
- Growing a business too quickly can be stressful for a small firm's owners and personnel.
- For many small companies, growth is an expected and achievable goal.
- A growth trap may occur when a firm's growth soaks up cash faster than it can be generated.

2. Explain the role of innovation in a company's growth.

- Coming up with and perfecting new products or services is often difficult.
- The risk of failure increases when innovation is the goal.
- The "rules of thumb" that can reduce the risk of innovation include basing innovative efforts on experience, targeting products or services that have been overlooked, ensuring a market for the product or service, emphasizing value creation for customers, pursuing new ideas that will lead to more than one product or service, and raising sufficient capital before launching a new product or service.
- Innovation is a means by which a firm can sustain its competitive advantage.
- The competitive advantage life cycle has three stages: develop, deploy, and decline.
- Companies must reinvent themselves from time to time if they are to keep their performance from declining in the long run, which requires an awareness of "hidden curves" related to the firm's competitors, its internal capabilities, and the capabilities and motivations of its people.

3. Identify stages in the product life cycle and the new product development process.

- The product life cycle portrays a product from introduction through growth and maturity to sales decline.
- The new product development process is a four-stage approach: idea accumulation, business analysis, development of the physical product, and product testing.
- When conducting a business analysis on a new product, the following four factors should be considered: its fit with existing product lines, its development and introduction costs, personnel and facilities available to get it started, and its competition and market acceptance potential.
- A new product development process is much more likely to succeed if it is focused on the firm's customers.

4. Describe the building of a firm's total product.

- The intangible brand image component is important to the acceptance of a firm's bundle of satisfaction.
- The brand name is a critical component of a product; it should be easy to pronounce and remember, descriptive, eligible for legal protection, full of promotional possibilities, and suitable for use on several product lines.
- If a small company does not have a strong brand name, it is sometimes helpful to license one from a better-known firm.

- In order to develop an effective but inexpensive logo, be simple, design for visibility, leave room for interpretation, emphasize consistency, recognize the importance of logo design, get good design advice, and don't expect miracles.
- Packaging is a significant tool for increasing total product value.
- A label is an important informative tool, providing brand visibility and instructions on product care, use, and disposal.
- A warranty can be valuable for achieving customer satisfaction.

5. Discuss product strategy and the alternatives available to small businesses.

- Product strategy describes how a product is used to achieve a firm's goals and involves the product item, product line, product mix, and product mix consistency.
- Marketing services presents unique challenges not faced in product strategy development.
- There are six categories of major product strategy alternatives, which are based on the nature of the firm's product offering and the number of target markets.

6. Recognize how the legal environment affects product decisions.

- Federal legislation regarding labeling and product safety was designed to protect consumers.
- Meeting the legal requirements for labeling can cost thousands of dollars per product.
- The legal system provides protection for a firm's marketing assets through trademarks, patents, copyrights, and trade dress.
- According to the law, businesses must not only use a trademark in order to protect it, but must also use it properly.
- Lawsuits concerning patent infringement can be costly.
- Copyrighted work may not be reproduced without authorization.
- Trade dress can be protected under trademark law.

7. Explain the importance of supply chain management.

- Effective supply chain management can potentially lower the costs of inventory, transportation, warehousing, and packaging, while increasing customer satisfaction.
- Distribution encompasses both the physical movement of products and the establishment of intermediary relationships to guide the movement of products from producer to user.
- Intermediaries provide an efficient means of distribution if customers are widely dispersed or if special packaging and storage are needed.

8. Specify the major considerations in structuring a distribution channel.

- A distribution channel can be either direct or indirect; many firms successfully employ more than one channel of distribution.
- Costs, coverage, and control are the three main considerations in evaluating a channel of distribution.
- Transportation, storage, materials handling, delivery terms, and inventory management are the main components of a physical distribution system.
- Small companies with limited in-house staff sometimes find it helpful to use logistics firms for their transportation and distribution needs, as these vendors provide trucking, packaging, and warehouse services.

Key Terms

sustainable competitive advantage p. 444
product life cycle p. 447
brand p. 451
brand image p. 452
brand name p. 452
brandmark p. 452
trademark p. 454
service mark p. 454
warranty p. 455
product strategy p. 456
product item p. 456
product line p. 456
product mix p. 456
product mix consistency p. 456
product p. 457
patent p. 461
utility patent p. 461
design patent p. 461
plant patent p. 461
copyright p. 461
trade dress p. 463
supply chain management p. 463
distribution p. 464
channel of distribution p. 464
physical distribution (logistics) p. 464
merchant middlemen p. 464
agents/brokers p. 464
direct channel p. 464
indirect channel p. 464
dual distribution p. 465
common carriers p. 466
contract carriers p. 467
private carriers p. 467
third-party logistics firm (3PLs) p. 467

Discussion Questions

1. Discuss some of the limitations on growth in a small firm.
2. Describe the recommendations for reducing risk associated with innovation in a small business.
3. How does an understanding of the product life cycle concept help with product strategy?
4. Discuss briefly each stage of the product development process.
5. Select two product names, and then evaluate each with respect to the five rules for naming a product.
6. What are the six basic product strategy options available to a small company? Which ones are most likely to be used?
7. Identify and briefly describe three ways to increase sales of an existing product once a product strategy has been implemented.
8. Explain how registration of a small firm's trademark would be helpful in protecting its brand.
9. Why do small businesses need to consider indirect channels of distribution for their products? Why involve intermediaries in distribution at all?
10. Discuss the major considerations in structuring a channel of distribution.

You Make the Call

SITUATION 1

The MooBella® Ice Creamery Machine is an amazing innovation. This computerized vending machine can custom-make and sell a cup of fresh ice cream in 40 seconds. Customers feed the vending machine $2.50 per 4.25-ounce scoop and then choose from up to 12 flavors, 3 mix-ins, and 2 different kinds of ice creams (premium and light). The machine takes care of the rest, cranking out creative delights with a production cost of roughly $1.20 per scoop. MooBella is currently launching its machines throughout the northeastern United States.

Sources: "Moobella Ice Creamery," http://moobella.com, accessed February 3, 2011; and Maureen Farrell, "Look Who's Changing the Ice Cream Business," *Forbes*, November 22, 2010, http://www.forbes.com/forbes/2010/1122/entrepreneurs-bruce-ginsberg-general-mills-big-scoop.html, accessed February 3, 2011.

Question 1 Where would be the best locations for the MooBella Ice Creamery Machine?
Question 2 What are the primary advantages and disadvantages of this innovation?

SITUATION 2

Tomboy Tools are just that—tools for women who want to do their own home improvement and repair projects. Friends Sue Wilson, Mary Tatum, and Janet Rickstrew, all of Denver, Colorado, were concerned that the tools they used for home repair projects were designed for men, not women. So they started Tomboy Tools to "bring together women aspiring to empower themselves with greater knowledge of do-it-yourself projects and the use of different tools to carry out those projects." What is most interesting is how the products are sold—exclusively at in-home workshops led by Tomboy Tools' independent sales representatives. Instead of Tupperware or cosmetics, guests see basic home repair tools in action and learn simple home repair and improvement techniques. The company's founders chose the in-home approach to market their products because of its proven success with consumers, particularly women.

Source: "Tomboy Tools—Pink Tools for Women," http://www.tomboytools.com/index.asp, accessed February 1, 2011.

Question 1 What are the advantages and disadvantages of the in-home method of selling Tomboy Tools?
Question 2 What other channels of distribution might Tomboy Tools use?
Question 3 What do you think about the name "Tomboy Tools"?

SITUATION 3

Who hasn't heard of the energy drink Red Bull? It established a position as the 900-pound gorilla in the fast-growing energy drink market, the best seller in its product category. But Monster energy drink (an entrepreneurial rival that is owned by Hansen Natural Corporation but bottled and distributed by the Coca-Cola Company) is constantly challenging Red Bull and its place at the top. While Red Bull still has a significant edge in market share, measured by total sales, some analysts contend that Monster may actually sell more product in terms of volume. Monster reaches its core market of males aged 18 to 34 by flooding retailers with giant (16-ounce) cans of its various energy drink offerings, in essence super-sizing the much smaller cans sold by Red Bull. Its aggressive image, striking packaging, and oversized cans have helped Monster expand its position in the growing energy drink market.

Sources: Heckman K. Sherry and E. Gonzalez De Mejia, "Energy Drinks: An Assessment of Their Market Size, Consumer Demographics, Ingredient Profile, Functionality, and Regulations in the United States," *Comprehensive Reviews in Food Science and Food Safety*, Vol. 9, No. 3 (May 2010), pp. 303–317; and Kenneth Hein, "Monster Goes Small While Amp Goes Big," *Brandweek*, April 14, 2009, http://www.brandweek.com/bw/content_display/news-and-features/packaged-goods/e3i6266a3e7e491921c7fc1807ad26b877b, accessed February 3, 2011.

Question 1 What is it about Monster's logo that makes it effective? (Hint: What tips does this textbook provide regarding logo design?)

Question 2 How can good packaging help a product?

Question 3 Why is labeling an important part of the packaging for energy drinks like Monster?

Experiential Exercises

1. Interview the owner or owners of a local manufacturing business to find out how they view innovation in their market. Summarize your findings.
2. Ask some owners of small firms in your area to describe their new product development processes. Report your findings to the class.
3. Visit a local retail store and observe brand names, package designs, labels, and warranties. Choose good and bad examples of each of these product components, and report back to the class.
4. Consider your most recent meaningful purchase. Compare the decision-making process you used to the four stages of the new product development process. Report your conclusions to the class.
5. Interview two different types of local retail merchants (for example, a boutique owner and a manager of a franchise) to determine how the merchandise in their stores is distributed to them. Contrast the channels of distribution used and write a brief report on your findings.

Small Business & Entrepreneurship Resource Center

1. Maureen Kelly started a company named Tarte because it seemed playful, sassy, and fun. This theme has permeated every aspect of her company, including product development. After reading the article "Tarte Looks Smart with Stock Cosmetics Package," describe the new product introduced as Cheek Stain. Explain how the product and packaging were designed and how they may or may not appeal to more than one customer segment.

   Source: "Tarte Looks Smart with Stock Cosmetics Package," *Food & Drug Packaging*, Vol. 65, No. 5 (May 2001), p. D2.

2. Unclaimed Baggage sells luggage that is left at airports. This business has developed a sustainable advantage because of long-term contracts with airports around the world, thus keeping new competitors away. Describe how this small business, located in the foothills of the Appalachian Mountains, used the Internet to expand its marketing footprint to successfully sell products around the world. Be sure to explain how selling online is an ideal method for Unclaimed Baggage's unique product mix.

   Source: Kimberly J. Hamilton-Wright, "Lost Travel Treasures: Unclaimed Baggage Center Is a Shopper's Gold Mine," Black Enterprise, Vol. 34, No. 6 (January 2004), p. 93–94.

Video Case 15

GRAETER'S ICE CREAM (P. 723)

This case demonstrates how one company expanded its business through its own growing chain of ice cream shops, distribution via partnerships with major supermarket and grocery store companies, and selective diversification into related ice cream products and baked goods.

ALTERNATIVE CASE FOR CHAPTER 15

Case 3, Firewire Surfboards, p. 698

CHAPTER 16

Pricing and Credit Decisions

In the SPOTLIGHT
Dynamic Network Services
http://dyn.com/

Their first plan was to start a not-for-profit enterprise. Processing paperwork and getting approval from the Internal Revenue Service was taking so long that the founders of Dynamic Network Services (Dyn) decided to form the company as an LLC. But how would they price their software?

Dyn began in a college apartment by offering a free service. The idea was to host a website on home computers or provide remote access back to the customer's PC. Dyn quickly moved to a donation-based service in an effort to stay afloat and add complementary services. According to CEO Jeremy Hitchcock, setting prices for their services in those early days amounted to throwing darts at a dartboard. Over time, Dyn transitioned to a recurring revenue software-as-a-service (SaaS) model with a suite of IT services aimed at home and SMB (small and medium-sized business) markets.

Dyn

When the company switched from asking customers for a one-time donation to requiring an annual subscription, it enjoyed 80 percent growth in revenue. The owners learned that they operated with a nearly fixed infrastructure as the number of customers increased.

But the one expense they had not thought through was the cost of acquiring a customer. Assessing the renewal rate for the firm's services and calculating the lifetime value of a customer led them to move from a

LOOKING AHEAD

After studying this chapter, you should be able to . . .

1. Discuss the role of cost and demand factors in setting a price.
2. Apply break-even analysis and markup pricing.
3. Identify specific pricing strategies.
4. Explain the benefits of credit, factors that affect credit extension, and types of credit.
5. Describe the activities involved in managing credit.

B2C business model to a B2B model. Given the low cost of the company's software applications, it enjoyed considerably more profit from large business clients than from the home consumer.

Even with a focus on business customers, by 2010 Dyn had served over 14 million home/SMB users on the DynDNS.com brand. It also had contracts with over 1,000 corporate customers. During that year, Dyn acquired three companies as it expanded globally.

Despite low overhead costs, Dyn chooses to avoid discounting. A continuing issue is determining how to compensate salespeople in a highly competitive, rapidly changing environment. In marketing its software and services, the company has found speed is important to its customers. The owners have also recognized that they have a difficult time expressing the value their services offer. And they have learned that some customers are not worth obtaining or retaining, given the price they may be willing to pay.

Sources: http://dyn.com, accessed January 30, 2011; personal interview with Jeremy Hitchcock, January 19, 2011; and "Coolest Small Company for Young Professionals," *BNH Magazine*, November 2010.

Very few business owners have any formal training in how to set the prices for the products and services they sell. Many times, their prices are based on what competitors are charging, some percentage above their costs, or just some instinctive feel. All too often, new business owners try to undercut their competition. Later in this chapter, we will explain why that can be dangerous. What we ask you to keep in mind is that pricing and credit decisions are vital to the success of a company because they influence the relationship between the business and its customers. These decisions also directly affect both revenue and cash flows. Of course, customers dislike price increases and restrictive credit policies; therefore, the entrepreneur needs to set prices and design credit policies as carefully as possible, to avoid the need for frequent changes.

Because a value must be placed on a product or service by the provider before it can be sold, pricing decisions are critical in small business marketing. The **price** of a product or service specifies what the seller requires for giving up ownership or use of that product or service. Often, the seller must extend credit to the buyer in order to make the exchange happen. **Credit** is simply an agreement between buyer and seller that payment for a product or service will be received at some later date. This chapter examines both the pricing decisions and the credit decisions of small firms.

price
A specification of what a seller requires in exchange for transferring ownership or use of a product or service.

credit
An agreement between a buyer and a seller that provides for delayed payment for a product or service.

Setting a Price

1
Discuss the role of cost and demand factors in setting a price.

In setting a price, the entrepreneur decides on the most appropriate value for the product or service being offered for sale. The task seems easy, but it isn't. The first pricing lesson is to remember that total sales revenue depends on just two components, sales volume and price, and even a small change in price can drastically influence revenue. Consider the following situations, *assuming no change in demand*:

Situation A

Quantity sold	×	Price per unit	=	Gross revenue
250,000	×	$3.00	=	$750,000

Situation B

Quantity sold	×	Price per unit	=	Gross revenue
250,000	×	$2.80	=	$700,000

The price per unit is only $0.20 lower in Situation B than in Situation A. However, the total difference in revenue is $50,000! Clearly, a small business can lose significant revenue if a price is set too low.

Pricing is also important because it indirectly affects sales quantity. Setting a price too high may result in lower quantities sold, reducing total revenue. In the above example, quantity sold was assumed to be independent of price—and it very well may be for such a small price difference. However, a larger increase or decrease might substantially affect the quantity sold. It makes no sense to lower a price if you wind up selling the same number of products. On the other hand, it makes no sense to raise your price if the result is a big cut in sales. Pricing, therefore, has a dual influence on total sales revenue. It is important *directly* as part of the gross revenue equation and *indirectly* through its impact on demand.

Before beginning a more detailed analysis of pricing, we should note that services are generally more difficult to price than products because of their intangible nature. However, the impact of price on revenue and profits is the same. Because estimating the cost of providing a service and the demand for that service is a more complex process than we can cover in the space provided, the following discussions will focus on product pricing.

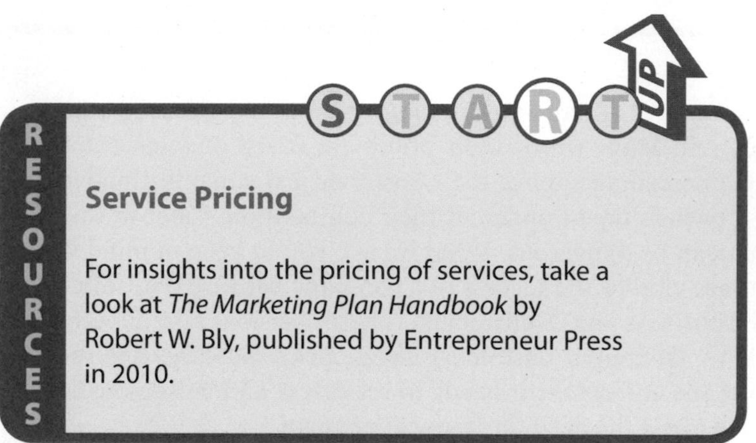

COST DETERMINATION FOR PRICING

total cost
The sum of cost of goods sold, selling expenses, and overhead costs.

For a business to be successful, its pricing must cover total cost plus an appropriate profit margin. Pricing, therefore, must be based on an understanding of the nature of costs. As illustrated in Exhibit 16.1, **total cost** includes three components. The first is the cost of goods offered for sale. An appliance retailer, for example, must include in the selling price the cost of the appliance and related freight charges. The second component is the selling cost, which includes the direct cost of the salesperson's time (salary plus commissions), as well as expenses related to other selling activities, such as advertising and sales promotion. The third component is the overhead cost applicable to the given product, which includes costs related to warehouse storage, office supplies, utilities, taxes, and employee salaries and wages. *All* of these cost classifications must be incorporated into the pricing process.

variable costs
Costs that vary with the quantity produced or sold.

fixed costs
Costs that remain constant as the quantity produced or sold varies.

Costs react differently as the quantity produced or sold increases or decreases. **Variable costs** are those that increase in total as the quantity of product increases. Material costs and sales commissions are typical variable costs incurred as a product is made and sold. For instance, material costs may be $10 per unit. If the company sells 1,000 units, the variable costs would be $10,000 but would change as the number of units increases or decreases. **Fixed costs** are those that remain constant at different levels of quantity sold. For example, advertising campaign expenditures, factory equipment costs, and salaries of office personnel are fixed costs.

An understanding of the nature of different kinds of costs can help a seller minimize pricing mistakes. Although fixed and variable costs do not behave in the same way, small

EXHIBIT 16.1 The Three Components of Total Cost in Determining Price

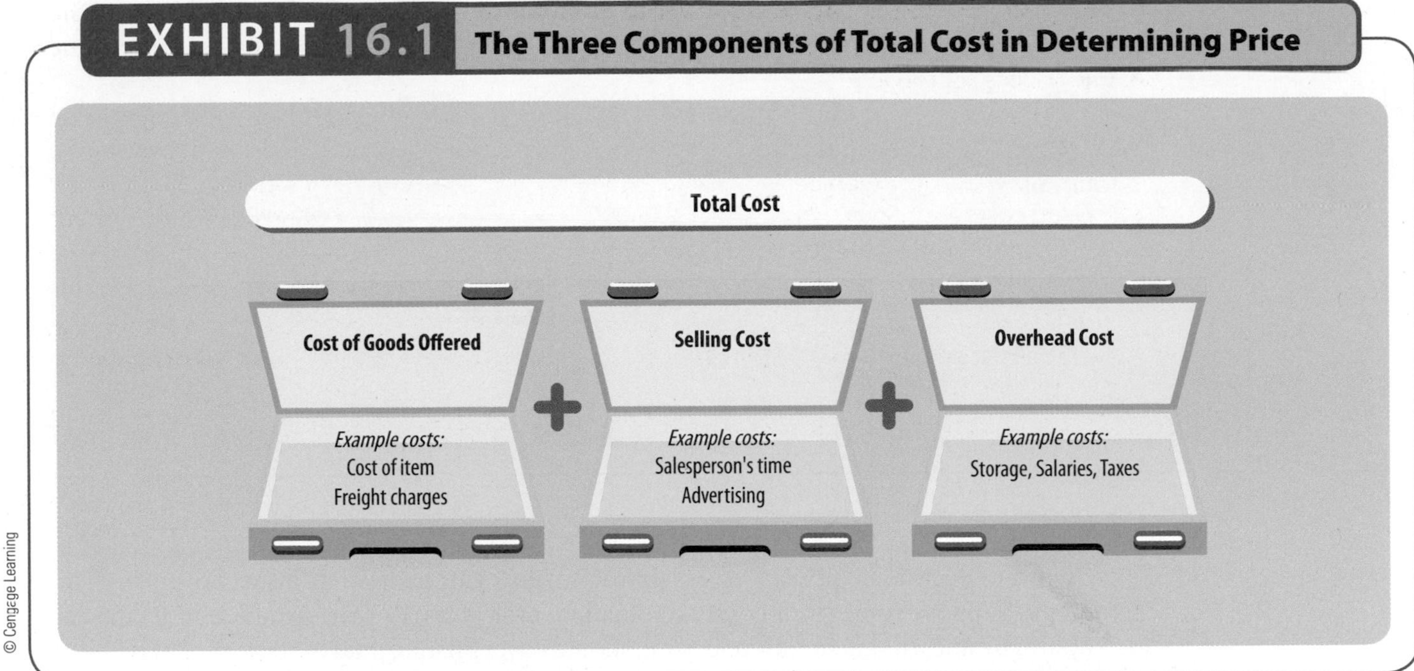

businesses often treat them identically. An approach called **average pricing** exemplifies this high-risk practice. With average pricing, the total cost (fixed costs plus variable costs) over a previous period is divided by the quantity sold in that period to arrive at an average cost, which is then used to set the current price. For example, consider the cost structure of a firm selling 25,000 units of a product in 2011 at a sales price of $8 each (see Exhibit 16.2). The average unit cost would be $5 (that is, $125,000 in total costs ÷ 25,000 units sold). The $3 markup provides a profit at this sales volume (25,000 units sold × $3 markup = $75,000).

average pricing An approach in which total cost for a given period is divided by quantity sold in that period to set a price.

However, the impact on profit will be very negative if sales in 2012 reach only 10,000 units and the selling price has been set at the same $3 markup, based on the average cost in 2011 (see Exhibit 16.3). At the lower sales volume (10,000 units sold), the average unit cost increases to $9.50 (that is, $95,000 ÷ 10,000). This increase is, of course, attributable to the need to spread fixed costs over fewer units. *Average pricing overlooks the reality of higher average costs at lower sales levels.*

EXHIBIT 16.2 Cost Structure of a Hypothetical Firm, 2011

Sales revenue (25,000 units @ $8)			$200,000
Total costs:			
Fixed costs	$75,000		
Variable costs ($2 per unit)	50,000		
		125,000	
Gross margin		$ 75,000	

$$\text{Average cost} = \frac{\$125{,}000}{25{,}000} = \$5$$

EXHIBIT 16.3 Cost of Structure of a Hypothetical Firm, 2012

Sales revenue (10,000 units @ $8)		$80,000
Total costs:		
Fixed costs	$75,000	
Variable costs ($2 per unit)	20,000	
		95,000
Gross margin		($ 15,000)

Average cost $= \frac{\$95,000}{10,000} = \$9.50$

On rare occasions, pricing at less than total cost can be used as a special short-term strategy. Suppose some fixed costs are ongoing, even if part of the production facility is temporarily idle. In this situation, pricing should cover all marginal or incremental costs—that is, those costs incurred specifically to get additional business. Keep in mind the old business saying, "If you price below cost, you can't make it up in volume!" For example, you might bid on a contract that appears to offer a high price only to discover that you have to add personnel, equipment, or materials whose costs are more than that attractive price. Sometimes, business owners offer *loss leaders*, merchandise they intentionally sell below the direct product cost with the expectation that customers will buy more as they learn of other products and services the business has available. It can be unpleasant to discover that the loss leader was the only thing customers bought—no profit there. In the long run, all costs must be covered.

HOW CUSTOMER DEMAND AFFECTS PRICING

Cost analysis can identify a level below which a price should not be set under normal circumstances. However, it does not show by how much the final price might exceed that minimum figure and still be acceptable to customers. Demand factors must be considered before making this determination.

Elasticity of Demand

Customer demand for a product or service is often sensitive to the price level. *Elasticity* is the term used to describe this sensitivity, and the effect of a change in price on the quantity demanded is called **elasticity of demand**. A product or service is said to have **elastic demand** if an increase in its price *lowers* demand for the product or service or a decrease in its price *raises* demand. A product or service is said to have **inelastic demand** if an increase in its price *raises* total revenue or a decrease in its price *lowers* total revenue.

elasticity of demand
The degree to which a change in price affects the quantity demanded.

elastic demand
Demand that changes significantly when there is a change in the price of the product or service.

inelastic demand
Demand that does not change significantly when there is a change in the price of the product or service.

In some markets, the demand for products or services is very elastic. With a lower price, the amount purchased increases sharply, thus providing higher revenue. For example, in the personal computer industry, a decrease in price will frequently produce a more than proportionate increase in quantity sold, resulting in higher total revenues. For products such as salt, however, the demand is highly inelastic. Regardless of price, the quantity purchased will not change significantly, because consumers use a fixed amount of salt.

The concept of elasticity of demand is important because the degree of elasticity sets limits on or provides opportunities for higher pricing. A small firm should seek

entrepreneurial experiences

© iStockphoto.com/Angelika Schwarz

Raising Prices When Others Are Cutting Them

The recession brought hard times to everyone. As the weeks and months wore on, Allen Ackerman saw more and more of his competitors cut prices. Unemployment rose quickly as the economy turned sour. Even when the worst appeared to have passed, few companies were creating new jobs. Times were tough in the employee-placement industry.

The temptation to follow the trend was strong. Ackerman decided to go in the opposite direction with his firm, A-List Placement. A-List had been charging client firms about 20 percent of each new hire's salary. Early in 2010, A-List began charging as much as 25 percent for services.

Ackerman knew the risk. He combined the price increase with an increase in the services his company provided. Specifically, the company created an online social networking tool to allow recruiters to share information about candidates and job openings. Ackerman, who had been a software developer early in his career, developed a private "cloud recruiting" model, providing mobile solutions to placement professionals. Calling his service "The Hire Syndicate," he describes it as "a platform to help split recruiters make more placements, more efficiently, through a trusted network of their peers." Within a year, 500 recruiters had registered to use the site to find matches for their clients.

During the economic slowdown, Ackerman did not see an increase in new customers, but he was able to report a 30 percent increase in revenue. Raising prices is not for everyone, but A-List Placement found that taking a chance paid off by adding value for its clients along with the increase.

Sources: http://alistplacement.com/, accessed February 27, 2011; http://www.meetup.com/The-Hire-Syndicate/, accessed February 27, 2011; and Emily Maltby, "Raising Prices Pays Off for Some," http://online.wsj.com/article/SB1000142405270230451070457556260914616226.html?mod=WSJ_business_LeftSecondHighlights, accessed February 27, 2011. **http://alistplacement.com**

to distinguish its product or service in such a way that small price increases will incur little resistance from customers and thereby yield increasing total revenue. Manny Apolonio, founder of At Chore Service, a concierge service in San Francisco that runs errands for clients, charged between $20 and $40 an hour when he started the company. He was immediately flooded with referrals. It did not take Apolonio long to realize that there was opportunity to raise prices to between $40 and $60 an hour. He tested the higher rates with a few clients and found them receptive. At Chore Service became profitable and stayed busy. From Apolonio's experience, we can conclude that demand for his firm's services is inelastic.[1]

Tetra Images/Jupiter Images

Pricing and a Firm's Competitive Advantage

Several factors affect the attractiveness of a product or service to customers. One factor is the firm's competitive advantage—a concept discussed in Chapter 3. If consumers perceive the product or service as an important solution to their unsatisfied needs, they are likely to demand more.

Only rarely will competing firms offer identical products. In most cases, products differ in some way. Even if two products are physically similar, the accompanying services typically differ. Speed of service, credit terms offered, delivery arrangements, personal attention from a salesperson, and warranties are but a few of the factors that can be used to distinguish one product from another. A unique and attractive combination of products and services may well justify a higher price.

prestige pricing
An approach based on setting a high price to convey an image of high quality or uniqueness.

A pricing tactic that often reflects a competitive advantage is **prestige pricing** setting a high price to convey an image of high quality or uniqueness. Its influence varies from market to market and product to product. Because higher-income buyers are usually less sensitive to price variations than those with lower incomes, prestige pricing typically works better in high-income markets.

Jeremy Hitchcock, introduced as the CEO of Dyn in this chapter's In the Spotlight, found that value-based pricing was difficult to explain to his customers. However, he discovered that if Dyn could gain a customer through one product, the quality of the software offered would enable the company to engage in platform pricing, moving the customer through a funnel of products and services, upgrading at each platform level. The team at Dyn also discovered that being seen as a quality provider increased their ability to renew customers, thereby lowering costs.[2]

Applying a Pricing System

A typical entrepreneur is unprepared to evaluate a pricing system until he or she understands potential costs, revenue, and product demand for the venture. To better comprehend these factors and to determine the acceptability of various prices, the entrepreneur can use break-even analysis. An understanding of markup pricing is also valuable, as it provides the entrepreneur with an awareness of the pricing practices of intermediaries—wholesalers and retailers.

BREAK-EVEN ANALYSIS

Break-even analysis allows the entrepreneur to compare alternative cost and revenue estimates in order to determine the acceptability of each price. A comprehensive break-even analysis has two phases: (1) examining cost–revenue relationships and (2) incorporating sales forecasts into the analysis. Break-even analysis can be presented by means of formulas and graphs.

Examining Cost and Revenue Relationships

The objective of the first phase of break-even analysis is to determine the sales volume level at which the product, at an assumed price, will generate enough revenue to start earning a profit. Exhibit 16.4(a) presents a simple break-even chart reflecting this comparison. *Fixed* costs and expenses, as represented by a horizontal line in the bottom half of the graph, are $300,000. The section for variable costs and expenses is a triangle that slants upward, depicting the direct relationship of variable costs and expenses to output. In this example, *variable* costs and expenses are $5 per unit. The entire area below the upward-slanting total cost line represents the combination of fixed and variable costs and expenses. The distance between the sales and total cost lines reveals the profit or loss position of the company at any level of sales. The point of intersection of these two lines is called the **break-even point**, because sales revenue equals total costs and expenses at this sales volume. As shown in Exhibit 16.4(a), the break-even point is approximately 43,000 units sold, which means that the break-even point in dollar revenue is roughly $514,000.

break-even point
Sales volume at which total sales revenue equals total costs and expenses.

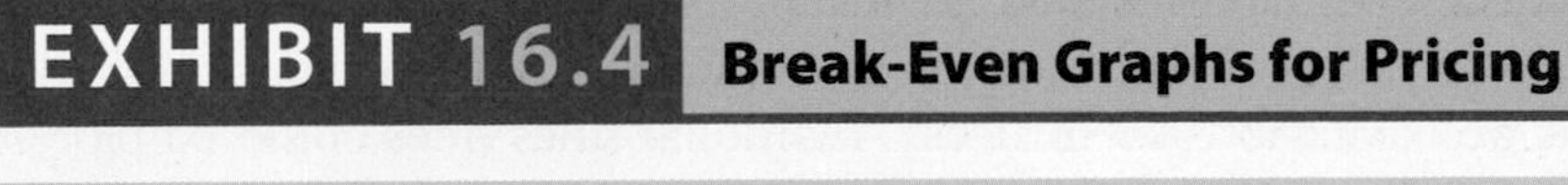

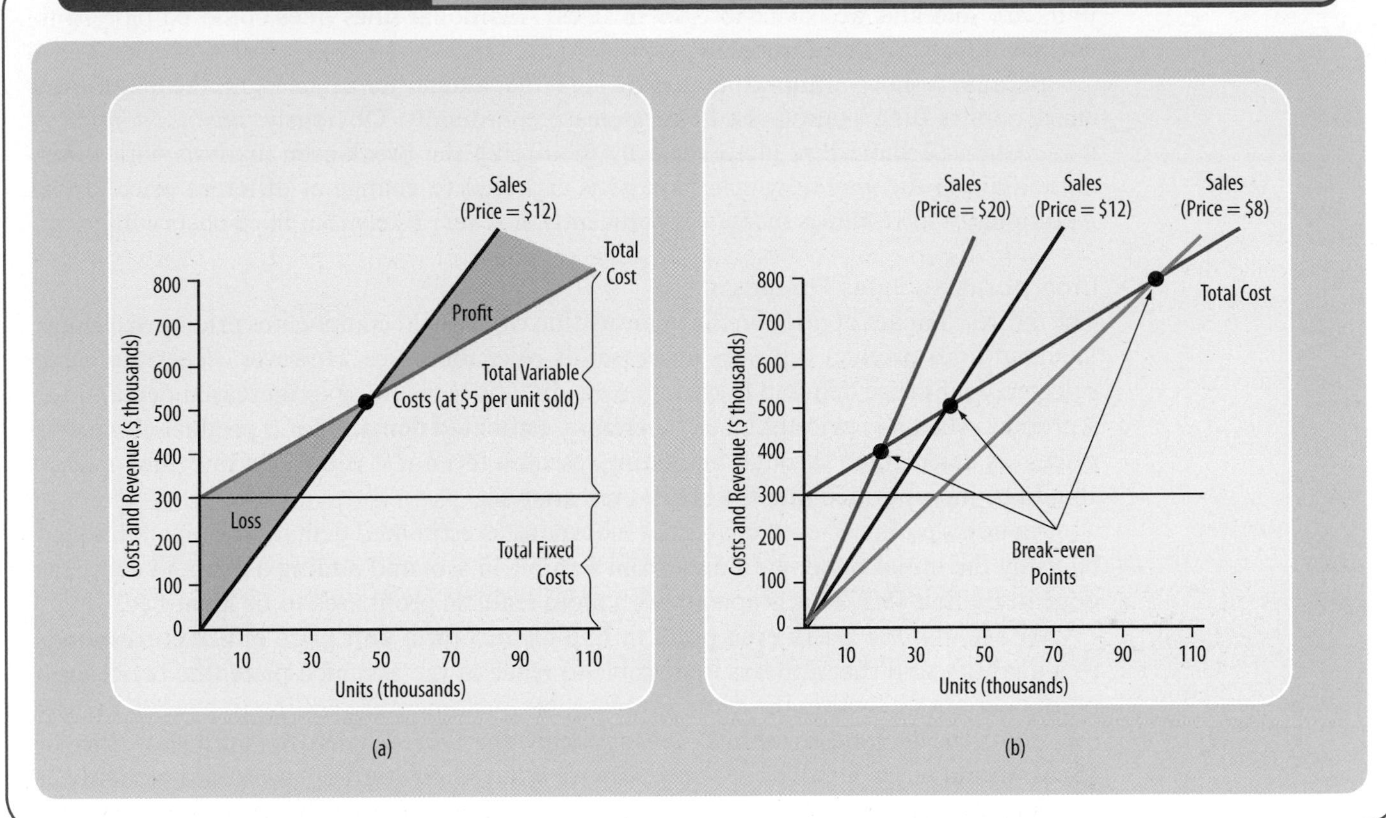

Exhibit 16.4(a) shows how you can visualize the break-even concept. Another way to think of it is as a simple math equation:

$$\text{Break-even point} = \frac{\text{Total fixed costs and expenses}}{\text{Unit selling price} - \text{Unit variable costs and expenses}}$$

$$\text{Break-even point} = \frac{\$300{,}000}{\$12 - \$5} = 42{,}857 \text{ units}$$

We can now see that the exact break-even point in units sold is 42,857. And given the $12 sales price, the dollar break-even point is $514,284 ($12 sales price per unit × 42,857 break-even units sold).

This example shows that the break-even point is a function of (1) the firm's fixed operating costs and expenses (numerator) and (2) the unit selling price less the unit variable costs and expenses (denominator). The higher the *fixed* costs, the more units we must sell to break even; the greater the difference between the unit selling price and the unit *variable* costs and expenses, the fewer units we must sell to break even. The difference between the unit selling price and the unit variable costs and expenses is the **contribution margin**; that is, for each unit sold, a contribution is made toward covering the company's fixed costs.

contribution margin The difference between the unit selling price and the unit variable costs and expenses.

To evaluate other break-even points, the entrepreneur can plot additional sales lines for other prices on the chart. (Don't be intimidated about drawing a graph or crunching the numbers to get a break-even point. The key issue is that calculating the break-even point helps you to determine whether you have a chance to make a profit by selling your products at certain prices.) On the flexible break-even chart shown in Exhibit 16.4(b), the higher price of $20 yields a much more steeply sloped sales line, resulting in a break-even point of 20,000 units and a sales dollar break-even point of $400,000. Similarly, the lower price of $8 produces a flatter revenue line, delaying the break-even point until 100,000 units are sold and we have $800,000 in sales. Additional sales lines could be plotted to evaluate other proposed prices.

Because it shows the profit area growing larger and larger to the right, the break-even chart implies that quantity sold can increase continually. Obviously, *this assumption is unrealistic* and should be factored in by modifying the break-even analysis with information about the way in which demand is expected to change at different price levels. Additionally, as revenues increase significantly, it is very likely that fixed costs will go up.

Incorporating Sales Forecasts

The indirect impact of price on the quantity that can be sold complicates pricing decisions. Demand for a product typically decreases as price increases. However, in certain cases price may influence demand in the opposite direction, resulting in increased demand for a product when it is priced higher. Therefore, estimated demand for a product at various prices, as determined through marketing research (even if it is only an informed guess), should be incorporated into the break-even analysis.

An adjusted break-even chart that incorporates estimated demand can be developed by using the initial break-even data from Exhibit 16.4(b) and adding a demand curve, as done in Exhibit 16.5. This graph allows a more realistic profit area to be identified.

We see that the break-even point in Exhibit 16.5 for a unit price of $20 corresponds to a quantity sold that appears impossible to reach at the assumed price (the break-even point does not fall within the demand curve). No customers are willing to pay $20 for any quantity—the demand curve line is always below the $20 sales line. So, at the low price of $8, we would never break even—the more we sell, the greater the loss would be. Only at $12 does the revenue from the demand curve rise above the total cost line. The potential for profit at this price is indicated by the shaded area in the graph.

EXHIBIT 16.5 A Break-Even Graph Adjusted for Estimated Demand

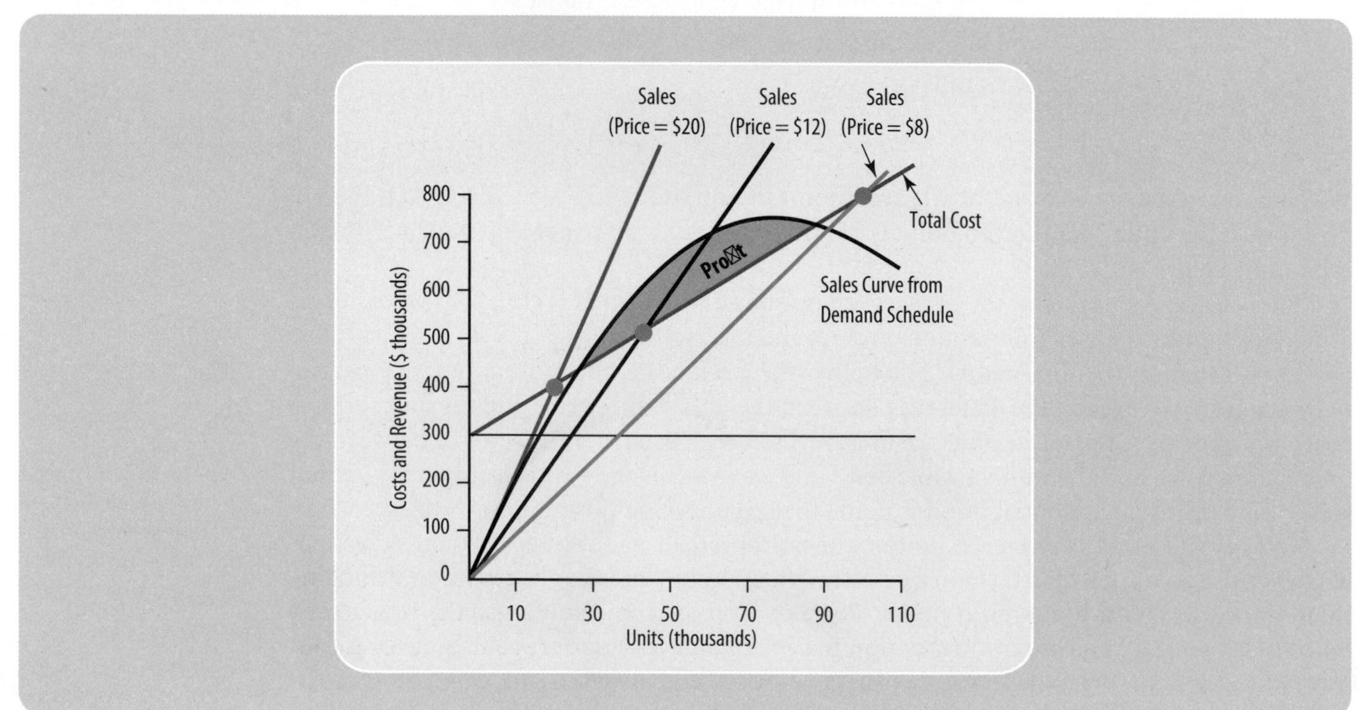

MARKUP PRICING

Up to this point, we have made no distinction between pricing by manufacturers and pricing by intermediaries such as wholesalers and retailers, since break-even concepts apply to all small businesses, regardless of their position in the distribution channel. Now, however, we briefly present some of the pricing formulas used by wholesalers and retailers in setting their prices. In the retailing industry, where businesses often carry many different products, **markup pricing** has emerged as a manageable pricing system. With this cost-plus approach to pricing, retailers are able to price hundreds of products much more quickly than they could by using individual break-even analyses. Manufacturers will often recommend a retail price for their products that retailers and wholesalers can use as guidelines. In calculating the selling price for a particular item, a retailer adds a markup percentage (sometimes referred to as a *markup rate*) to cover the following:

markup pricing
An approach based on applying a percentage to a product's cost to obtain its selling price.

- Operating expenses
- Subsequent price reductions—for example, markdowns and employee discounts
- Desired profit

It is important to have a clear understanding of markup pricing computations. Markups may be expressed as a percentage of either the *selling price* or the *cost.* For example, if an item costs \$6 and sells for \$10, the markup of \$4 represents a 40 percent markup of the selling price [(\$4 markup ÷ \$10 selling price) × 100] or a 66⅔ percent markup of the cost [(\$4 markup ÷ \$6 cost) × 100]. Two simple formulas are commonly used for markup calculations:

$$\frac{\text{Markup}}{\text{Selling price}} \times 100 = \text{Markup expressed as a percentage of selling price}$$

or

$$\frac{\text{Markup}}{\text{Cost}} \times 100 = \text{Markup expressed as a percentage of cost}$$

Selecting a Pricing Strategy

Techniques such as break-even analysis yield a good idea of a feasible price for a specific product. But their seemingly precise nature can be very misleading. Such analyses are only one kind of pricing tool and should not by themselves determine the final price. *Price determination must also consider market characteristics and the firm's current marketing strategy.* Pricing strategies that reflect these additional considerations include penetration pricing, skimming pricing, follow-the-leader pricing, variable pricing, price lining, and pricing at what the market will bear.[3]

3
Identify specific pricing strategies.

PENETRATION PRICING

A firm that uses a **penetration pricing strategy** prices a product or service at less than its normal, long-range market price in order to gain more rapid market acceptance or to increase existing market share. This strategy can sometimes discourage new competitors from entering a market niche if they mistakenly view the penetration price as a long-range price. Obviously, a firm that uses this strategy sacrifices some profit margin to achieve market penetration.

penetration pricing strategy
A technique based on setting lower than normal prices to hasten market acceptance of a product or service or to increase market share.

SKIMMING PRICING

skimming price strategy A technique based on setting very high prices for a limited period before reducing them to more competitive levels.

A **skimming price strategy** sets prices for products or services at high levels for a limited time period before reducing them to more competitive levels. This strategy assumes that certain customers will pay a higher price because they view a product or service as a prestige item. Use of a skimming price is most practical when there is little threat of short-term competition or when startup costs must be recovered rapidly.

FOLLOW-THE-LEADER PRICING

follow-the-leader pricing strategy A technique based on using a particular competitor as a model in setting prices.

A **follow-the-leader pricing strategy** uses a particular competitor as a model in setting a price for a product or service. The probable reaction of competitors is a critical factor in determining whether to cut prices below a prevailing level. A small business in competition with larger firms is seldom in a position to consider itself the price leader. If competitors view a small firm's pricing as relatively unimportant, they may not respond to a price differential. On the other hand, some competitors may view a smaller price-cutter as a direct threat and counter with reductions of their own. In such a case, the use of a follow-the-leader pricing strategy accomplishes very little.

VARIABLE PRICING

variable pricing strategy A technique based on setting more than one price for a product or service in order to offer price concessions to certain customers.

dynamic (personalized) pricing strategy A technique based on charging more than the standard price when a customer's profile suggests that the higher price will be accepted.

Some businesses use a **variable pricing strategy** to offer price concessions to certain customers, even though they may advertise a uniform price. Lower prices are offered for various reasons, including a customer's knowledge and bargaining strength. In some fields of business, therefore, firms make two-part pricing decisions: They set a standard list price but offer a range of price concessions to particular buyers—for example, those that purchase large quantities of their product. Our In the Spotlight company, Dyn, sometimes negotiated pricing, trading off the services provided within an acceptable range.

Sellers using a type of variable pricing strategy called a **dynamic (personalized) pricing strategy** charge *more* than the standard price after gauging a customer's financial means and desire for the product. The information-gathering capability of the Internet has allowed such retailers as Amazon.com to use dynamic pricing.[4]

PRICE LINING

price lining strategy A technique based on setting a range of several distinct merchandise price levels.

A **price lining strategy** establishes distinct price categories at which similar items of retail merchandise are offered for sale. For example, men's suits (of differing quality) might be sold at $250, $450, and $800. The amount of inventory stocked at different quality levels would depend on the income levels and buying desires of a store's customers. A price lining strategy has the advantage of simplifying the selection process for the customer and reducing the necessary minimum inventory.

© Rob Pitman/Shutterstock.com

PRICING AT WHAT THE MARKET WILL BEAR

The strategy of pricing on the basis of what the market will bear can be used only when the seller has little or no competition. Obviously, this strategy will work only for nonstandardized products. For example, a food store might offer egg roll wrappers that its competitors do not carry. Busy consumers who want to fix egg rolls but have neither the time nor the knowledge to prepare the wrappers themselves will buy them at any reasonable price.

entrepreneurial experiences

© iStockphoto.com/Angelika Schwarz

Pricing a Craft Business

Craft businesses often grow out of hobbies. But how should an entrepreneur price his or her hobby? Crafts people often do not put a value on the creativity that goes into their work. They know the total cost of materials that went into what they have decided to sell and may just add a percentage markup to that cost. But does that markup really compensate them for their time and for the vision that went into their product?

Lorrie Veasey started selling her ceramics as a college student in 1984, then moved on to street fairs and festivals. When she realized that she had an actual business on her hands, she put a label on it: Our Name Is Mud. In 1995, she decided the business was established enough to open retail locations. From the beginning, Veasey recognized the key to her success was to stay focused not just on her craftwork, but also on building her business. That meant getting out and selling. As she began to make a living from her enterprise, Veasey discovered that more than selling was involved. She had to understand marketing and how critical it is that pricing covers costs and brings in a profit. She learned that the "regular" price is never chiseled in stone. On her blog, Veasey offered discount coupons for items for special events, such as Father's Day.

Enesco LLC

As her retail outlets prospered, in 2002 Veasey launched her wholesale line. That brought her to the attention of others in the arts and crafts industry. In 2002, Our Name Is Mud was sold to an international giftware distributor, Enesco LLC. Veasey's ceramic products are now available through thousands of retail stores worldwide.

Those in the arts and crafts industry initially may engage in a lot of trial and error in setting prices. The process formalizes as they move to brick-and-mortar retail establishments. Veasey had to take an additional step and determine pricing for a retail customer, which also needed to mark up the product and make a profit.

Sources: Lorrie Veasey, http://ournameisblog.blogspot.com/, accessed February 27, 2011; Kim Orr, "Creativity Counts," http://www.entrepreneur.com/magazine/entrepreneursstartupsmagazine/2008/may/193422.html, accessed February 27, 2011; and http://enesco.com/, accessed February 27, 2011. **http://ournameismud.com**

SOME FINAL NOTES ON PRICING STRATEGIES

In some situations, local, state, and federal laws must be considered in setting prices. For example, the Sherman Antitrust Act generally prohibits price fixing. A case in point is a suit brought by the California Attorney General's Office against Bioelements, Inc., a Colorado-based cosmetics company, because it prohibited online retailers from selling its products at a discount. Bioelements did not admit to liability but agreed to a settlement to refrain permanently from fixing resale prices. The firm also agreed to pay $51,000 in total penalties, not a trivial amount for an independent business.[5]

When a small business markets a line of products, some of which may compete with each other, pricing decisions must take into account the effects of a single product price on the rest of the line. For example, the introduction of a cheese-flavored chip will likely

Pricing Mistakes

The president of Palo Alto Software, Tim Berry, shares some typical mistakes that small business owners often make in their strategies in "The 3 Most Common Small Business Pricing Mistakes," which can be found at http://www.openforum.com/idea-hub/topics/money/article/the-3-most-common-small-business-pricing-mistakes-tim-berry.

affect sales of an existing naturally flavored chip. Pricing can become extremely complex in these situations.

Continually adjusting a price to meet changing marketing conditions can be both costly to the seller and confusing to buyers. An alternative approach is to use a system of discounting designed to reflect a variety of needs. For example, a seller may offer a trade discount to a particular buyer (such as a wholesaler) because that buyer performs a certain marketing function for the seller (such as distribution). The stated, or list, price is unchanged, but the seller offers a lower actual price by means of a discount.

Small firms should not treat bad pricing decisions as uncorrectable mistakes. Remember, pricing is not an exact science. *If the initial price appears to be off target, make any necessary adjustments and keep on selling!*

Offering Credit

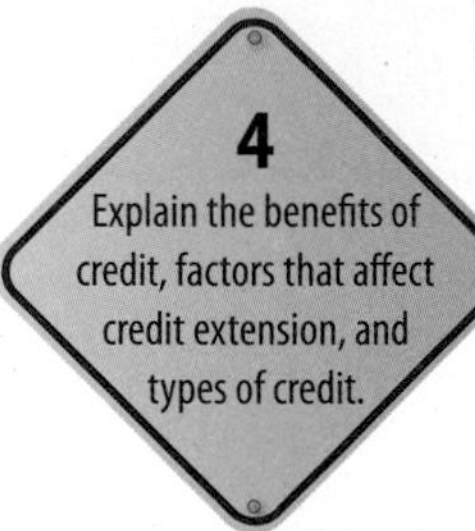

In a credit sale, the seller provides products or services to the buyer in return for the buyer's promise to pay later. The major reason for granting credit is to make sales; credit encourages decisions to buy by providing an incentive for customers who can buy now but would prefer to pay later. Most firms offering credit actively promote this option to potential customers. An added bonus to the seller is that it provides records containing customer information that can be used for sales promotions, such as direct-mail appeals to customers.

BENEFITS OF CREDIT

If credit buying and selling did not benefit both parties in a transaction, their use would cease. Borrowers obviously enjoy the availability of credit, and small firms, in particular, benefit from being able to buy on credit from their suppliers. Credit provides small firms with working capital, often allowing marginal businesses to continue operations. Additional benefits of credit to customers (borrowers) follow:

- The ability to satisfy immediate needs and pay for them later
- Better records of purchases on credit billing statements
- Better service and greater convenience when exchanging purchased items
- Establishment of a credit history

Suppliers, on the other hand, extend credit to customers in order to facilitate increased sales volume and also to earn money on unpaid balances. They expect the increased revenue to more than offset the costs of extending credit, so that profits will increase. Other benefits of credit to sellers follow:

- Closer association with customers because of implied trust
- Easier selling through telephone- and mail-order systems and over the Internet
- Smoother sales peaks and valleys, since purchasing power is always available
- Easy access to a tool with which to stay competitive

FACTORS THAT AFFECT SELLING ON CREDIT

An entrepreneur must decide whether to sell on credit or for cash only. In many cases, credit selling cannot be avoided, as it is standard trade practice in many types of businesses. It is important to note that in today's marketplace, credit-selling competitors will almost always outsell a cash-only firm.

Although a seller always hopes to increase profits by allowing credit sales, it is not a risk-free practice. Small firms frequently shift or at least share credit risk by accepting credit cards carried by customers rather than by offering their own credit. For example, the operator of a Texaco gasoline station may accept Texaco credit cards and other major credit cards, thereby avoiding the hassles of credit management. The business will pay a fee to the credit card company, but that cost may be less than the expense of managing its own independent credit system, especially when losses from bad debts are factored in. A retailer following this strategy must obtain merchant status with individual credit card companies. This is not an automatic process and can be problematic, particularly for home-based businesses.

Unfortunately, the cost of accepting major credit cards for payment over the Internet has increased. To deal with Internet fraud, small e-retailers turn to third-party firms that specialize in handling Internet credit card payments. These firms provide a degree of fraud protection for the small business. For example, PayPal lets firms (and individuals) accept credit card payments. There are no setup costs and no monthly fees. PayPal is compensated with a transaction fee of 2 to 3 percent depending on monthly sales volume, plus 30 cents.[6] Other credit card–processing companies include Charge.com, eCommerce Exchange, Merchant Accounts Express, and the Canadian InternetSecure, Inc.

Also, if a small firm makes credit sales online, it is subject to "chargebacks" whenever buyers dispute a transaction. Some credit card companies assess fines and threaten account termination if the number of chargebacks is excessive.

For a variety of reasons, a small business may or may not decide to sell on credit. Five factors related to the entrepreneur's decision to extend credit are the type of business, credit policies of competitors, customers' age and income levels, the availability of working capital, and economic conditions.

Type of Business

Retailers of durable products typically grant credit more freely than do small grocers that sell perishables or small restaurants that serve primarily local customers. Indeed, most consumers find it necessary to buy big-ticket items on an installment basis, and the life span of such a product makes installment selling feasible.

Credit Policies of Competitors

Unless a firm offers some compensating advantage, it is expected to be as generous as its competitors in extending credit. Wholesale hardware companies and retail furniture stores are examples of businesses that face stiff competition from credit sellers.

Age and Income Level of Customers

The age and income level of a retailer's customers are significant factors in determining its credit policy. For example, a drugstore adjacent to a high school might not extend credit to high school students, who are typically undesirable credit customers because of their lack of both maturity and steady income.

Availability of Working Capital

Credit sales increase the amount of working capital needed by the business doing the selling. Open-credit and installment accounts tie up money that may be needed to pay business expenses.

ECONOMIC CONDITIONS The economic recession that hit the United States in 2008 taught many small businesses new lessons about credit—about both extending it to customers and obtaining it from lenders and suppliers. A survey conducted by the National Federation of Independent Business in 2010 reported that most small business owners suffered sales declines, which may trigger offers of credit terms to boost sales. The owners also discovered that obtaining credit for their own working capital became more difficult as the recession deepened.[7]

TYPES OF CREDIT

consumer credit Financing granted by retailers to individuals who purchase for personal or family use.

trade credit Financing provided by a supplier of inventory to a client company.

There are two broad classes of credit: consumer credit and trade credit. **Consumer credit** is granted by retailers to final consumers who purchase for personal or family use. A small business owner can sometimes use his or her personal consumer credit to purchase supplies and equipment for use in the business. **Trade credit** is extended by nonfinancial firms, such as manufacturers and wholesalers, to business firms that are customers. Consumer credit and trade credit differ with respect to types of credit instruments, the paperwork, sources for financing receivables, and terms of sale. Another important distinction is that credit insurance is available only for trade credit.

Consumer Credit

The three major kinds of consumer credit accounts are open charge accounts, installment accounts, and revolving charge accounts. Many variations of these credit accounts are also used.

open charge account A line of credit that allows the customer to obtain a product or service at the time of purchase, with payment due when billed.

OPEN CHARGE ACCOUNTS When using an **open charge account**, a customer takes possession of products (or services) at the time of purchase, with payment due when billed. Stated terms typically call for payment at the end of the month, but it is customary to allow a longer period than that stated. There is no finance charge for this kind of credit if the balance on the account is paid in full at the end of the billing period. Customers are not generally required to make a down payment or to pledge collateral. Small accounts at department stores are good examples of open charge accounts.

installment account A line of credit that requires a down payment, with the balance paid over a specified period of time.

INSTALLMENT ACCOUNTS An **installment account** is a vehicle for long-term consumer credit. A down payment is normally required, and annual finance charges can be 20 percent or more of the purchase price. Payment periods are commonly from 12 to 36 months, although automobile dealers often offer an extended payment period of 60 months or even longer. An installment account is useful for large purchases, such as a car, washing machine, or television.

revolving charge account A line of credit on which the customer may charge purchases at any time, up to a preestablished limit.

REVOLVING CHARGE ACCOUNTS A **revolving charge account** is a variation of the installment account. A seller grants a customer a line of credit, and charged purchases may not exceed the credit limit. A specified percentage of the outstanding balance must be paid monthly, forcing the customer to budget and limiting the amount of debt that can be carried. Finance charges are computed on the unpaid balance at the end of the month. Although credit cards offer this type of account, they are discussed separately in the next section because of their widespread use.

© iStockphoto.com/Daniel Laflor

Credit Cards

A **credit card** provides assurance to a seller that a buyer has a satisfactory credit rating and that the seller will receive payment from the financial institution that issued the card. Credit cards are usually based on a revolving charge account system. Depending on the issuer, we can distinguish three basic types of credit cards: bank credit cards, entertainment credit cards, and retailer credit cards.

BANK CREDIT CARDS The best-known credit cards issued by banks or other financial institutions are MasterCard and VISA. Bank credit cards are widely accepted by retailers that want to offer credit but don't provide their own credit cards. Most small business retailers fit into this category. In return for a set fee (usually 2 to 5 percent of the purchase price) paid by the retailer, the bank takes the responsibility for making collections. Some banks charge annual membership fees to their cardholders. Also, cardholders are frequently able to obtain cash up to the credit limit of their card.

ENTERTAINMENT CREDIT CARDS Well-known examples of entertainment credit cards are American Express and Diner's Club cards. While these cards have traditionally charged an annual fee, American Express now offers the Blue Card, which has no fee for use. Originally used for services, these cards are now widely accepted for sales of merchandise. As with bank credit cards, the collection of charges on an entertainment credit card is the responsibility of the sponsoring agency.

credit card
An alternative to cash whose use provides assurance to a seller that a buyer has a satisfactory credit rating and that payment will be received from the issuing financial institution.

RETAILER CREDIT CARDS Many companies—for example, department stores and oil companies—issue their own credit cards specifically for use in their outlets or for purchasing their products or services from other outlets. Customers are usually not charged annual fees or finance charges if the balance is paid each month.

Debit Cards

A variation on credit cards, and technically not a form of credit, is the **debit card**. A debit card is an alternative to cash in that its use immediately results in a withdrawal from the customer's bank account to pay for the product or service purchased. Some financial institutions arrange for extensions of credit for delayed payments on a debit card.[8]

debit card
An alternative to cash whose use results in an immediate withdrawal from the buyer's bank account to pay for products or services.

TRADE CREDIT

Firms selling to other businesses may specify terms of sale, such as 2/10, net 30. This means that the seller is offering a 2 percent discount if the buyer pays within 10 days of the invoice date. Failure to take this discount makes the full amount of the invoice due in 30 days. For example, with these terms, a buyer paying for a $100,000 purchase within 10 days of the invoice date would save 2 percent, or $2,000.

Sales terms for trade credit depend on the product sold and the buyer's and the seller's circumstances. The credit period often varies directly with the length of the buyer's inventory turnover period, which obviously depends on the type of product sold. The larger the order and the higher the credit rating of the buyer, the better the sales terms will be, assuming that individual terms are fixed for each buyer. The greater the financial strength and the more adequate and liquid the working capital of the seller, the more generous the seller's sales terms can be. Of course, no business can afford to allow competitors to outdo it in reasonable generosity of sales terms. In many types of businesses, terms are so firmly set by tradition that a unique policy is difficult, if not impossible, for a small firm to implement.

Managing the Credit Process

As mentioned previously, many small firms transfer all or part of the credit function to another party. For example, a small repair shop or retail clothing store that accepts VISA or MasterCard is transferring much of the credit risk; in effect, the fee that the business pays the credit card company covers the credit management process. On the other hand, merchants pay for the privilege of this risk transfer. Banks and their business customers are often in conflict over the fees charged.[9] Many small business owners find that the fees cut their profits significantly. A number of small firms want to offer their own credit to their customers, particularly business customers; therefore, they need to understand the credit function. Let's take a look at some of the major considerations in developing and operating a comprehensive credit management program for a small business.

EVALUATION OF CREDIT APPLICANTS

In most retail stores, the first step in credit investigation is having the customer complete an application form. The information obtained on this form is used as the basis for examining an applicant's creditworthiness. Since the most important factor in determining a customer's credit limit is her or his ability to pay the obligation when it becomes due, it is crucial to evaluate the customer's financial resources, debt position, and income or revenue level. The amount of credit requested also requires careful consideration. Drugstore customers usually need only small amounts of credit. On the other hand, business customers of wholesalers and manufacturers typically expect large credit lines. In the special case of installment selling, the amount of credit should not exceed the repossession value of the goods sold. Automobile dealers follow this rule as a general practice.

The Four Credit Questions

In evaluating the credit status of applicants, a seller must answer the following questions:

1. Can the buyer pay as promised?
2. Will the buyer pay?
3. If so, when will the buyer pay?
4. If not, can the buyer be forced to pay?

The answers to these questions have to be based in part on the seller's estimate of the buyer's ability and willingness to pay. Such an estimate constitutes a judgment of the buyer's creditworthiness. For credit to be approved, the answers to questions 1, 2, and 4 should be "yes," and the answer to question 3 should be "on schedule."

Every applicant is creditworthy to some degree; a decision to grant credit merely recognizes the buyer's credit standing. But the seller must consider the possibility that the buyer will be unable or unwilling to pay. When evaluating an applicant's credit status, therefore, the seller must decide how much risk of nonpayment to assume.

The Traditional Five C's of Credit

As explained in Chapter 12, the ability to repay a loan is frequently evaluated in terms of the five C's of credit: character, capacity, capital, conditions, and collateral. These factors are also indicators of a firm's ability to repay trade credit and deserve repeating:

- *Character* is the fundamental integrity and honesty that should underlie all human and business relationships. For business customers, character is embodied in the business policies and ethical practices of the firm.
- *Capacity* refers to the customer's ability to conserve assets and faithfully and efficiently follow a financial plan. A business customer should utilize its invested capital wisely and capitalize to the fullest extent on business opportunities.
- *Capital* consists of the cash and other liquid assets owned by the customer. A prospective business customer should have sufficient capital to underwrite planned operations, including an appropriate amount invested by the owner.
- *Conditions* are such factors as business cycles and changes in price levels, which may be either favorable or unfavorable to the payment of debts. For example, economic recession places a burden on both businesses' and consumers' abilities to pay their debts. Other adverse factors that might limit a business customer's ability to pay include fires and other natural disasters, strong new competition, and labor problems.
- *Collateral* consists of designated security given as a pledge for fulfillment of an obligation. It is a secondary source for loan repayment in case the borrower's cash flows are insufficient for repaying a loan.

SOURCES OF CREDIT INFORMATION

One of the most important, and most frequently neglected, sources of credit information is a customer's previous credit history. Properly analyzed, credit records show whether a business customer regularly takes cash discounts and, if not, whether the customer's account is typically slow.

Manufacturers and wholesalers can frequently use a firm's financial statements as an additional source of information. Obtaining maximum value from financial statements requires a careful ratio analysis, which will reveal a firm's working capital position, profit-making potential, and general financial health (as discussed in Chapter 10).

Pertinent data may also be obtained from outsiders. For example, arrangements may be made with other sellers to exchange credit data. Such credit information exchanges are quite useful for learning about the sales and payment experiences others have had with the seller's own customers or credit applicants.

Another source of credit information for the small firm, particularly about commercial accounts, is the customer's banker. Some bankers willingly supply credit information about their depositors, considering this to be a service that helps those firms or individuals obtain credit in amounts they can successfully handle. Other bankers believe that credit information is confidential and should not be disclosed.

Organizations that may be consulted regarding credit standings are trade-credit agencies and credit bureaus. **Trade-credit agencies** are privately owned organizations that collect credit information on businesses only, not individual consumers. After analyzing and evaluating the data, trade-credit agencies make credit ratings available to client companies for a fee. Dun & Bradstreet, Inc. (http://www.dnb.com), a nationwide trade-credit agency, offers a wide array of credit reports, including the Small Business Risk New

trade-credit agencies
Privately owned organizations that collect credit information on businesses.

Account Score and the Payment Analysis Report. Manufacturers and wholesalers are especially interested in Dun & Bradstreet's reference book and credit reports. Available to subscribers only, the reference book covers most U.S. businesses and provides a credit rating, an evaluation of financial strength, and other key credit information on each firm listed.

credit bureaus Privately owned organizations that summarize a number of firms' credit experiences with particular individuals.

Credit bureaus are the most common type of consumer reporting agency. These private companies maintain credit histories on individuals, based on reports from banks, mortgage companies, department stores, and other creditors. These companies make possible the exchange of credit information on persons with previous credit activity. Some credit bureaus do not require a business firm to be a member in order to get a credit report. The fee charged to nonmembers, however, is considerably higher than that charged to members. The three primary online credit bureaus are Experian, Equifax, and TransUnion.[10]

AGING OF ACCOUNTS RECEIVABLE

aging schedule A categorization of accounts receivable based on the length of time they have been outstanding.

Many small businesses can benefit from an **aging schedule**, which divides accounts receivable into categories based on the length of time they have been outstanding. Typically, some accounts are current and others are past due. Regular use of an aging schedule allows troublesome collection trends to be spotted so that appropriate actions can be taken.

Exhibit 16.6 presents a hypothetical aging schedule for accounts receivable. According to the schedule, four customers have overdue credit, totaling $200,000. Only customer 005 is current. Customer 003 has the largest amount overdue ($80,000). In fact, the schedule shows that customer 003 is overdue on all charges and has a past record of slow payment (indicated by a credit rating of C). Immediate attention must be given to collecting from this customer. Customer 002 should also be contacted, because, among overdue accounts, this customer has the second largest amount ($110,000) in the "Not due" classification. Customer 005, however, could quickly have the largest amount overdue and should be watched closely.

EXHIBIT 16.6 Hypothetical Aging Schedule for Accounts Receivable

	CUSTOMER ACCOUNT NUMBER					
Account Status (Days past due)	**001**	**002**	**003**	**004**	**005**	**Total**
120 days	—	—	$50,000	—	—	$ 50,000
90 days	—	$ 10,000	—	—	—	10,000
60 days	—	—	—	$40,000	—	40,000
30 days	—	20,000	20,000	—	—	40,000
15 days	$50,000	—	10,000	—	—	60,000
Total overdue	$50,000	$ 30,000	$80,000	$40,000	$ 0	$200,000
Not due (beyond discount period)	$30,000	$ 10,000	$ 0	$10,000	$130,000	$180,000
Not due (still in discount period)	$20,000	$100,000	$ 0	$90,000	$220,000	$430,000
Credit rating	A	B	C	A	A	—

Customers 001 and 004 require a special kind of analysis. Customer 001 has $10,000 more overdue than customer 004. However, customer 004's overdue credit of $40,000, which is 60 days past due, may well have a serious impact on the $100,000 not yet due ($10,000 in the beyond-discount period plus $90,000 still in the discount period). On the other hand, even though customer 001 has $50,000 of overdue credit, this customer's payment is overdue by only 15 days. Also, customer 001 has only $50,000 not yet due ($30,000 in the beyond-discount period plus $20,000 still in the discount period), compared to the $100,000 not yet due from customer 004. Both customers have an A credit rating. In conclusion, customer 001 is a better potential source of cash. Therefore, collection efforts should be focused on customer 004 rather than on customer 001, who may simply need a reminder of the overdue amount of $50,000.

BILLING AND COLLECTION PROCEDURES

Timely notification of customers regarding the status of their accounts is one of the most effective methods of keeping credit accounts current. Most credit customers pay their bills on time if the creditor provides them with information verifying their credit balance. Failure on the seller's part to send invoices delays payments.

© iStockphoto.com/DNY59

Overdue credit accounts tie up a seller's working capital, prevent further sales to the slow-paying customer, and lead to losses from bad debts. Even if a slow-paying customer is not lost, relations with this customer are strained for a time at least.

A firm extending credit must have adequate billing records and collection procedures if it expects prompt payments. Also, a personal relationship between seller and customer must not be allowed to tempt the seller into being less than businesslike in extending further credit and collecting overdue amounts. Given the seriousness of the problem, a small firm must decide whether to collect past-due accounts directly or turn the task over to an attorney or a collection agency.

Perhaps the most effective weapon in collecting past-due accounts is reminding the debtors that their credit standing may be impaired. Impairment is certain to happen if the account is turned over to a collection agency. Delinquent customers will typically attempt to avoid damage to their credit standing, particularly when it would be known to the business community. This concern underlies and strengthens the various collection efforts of the seller.

A small firm should deal compassionately with delinquent customers. There are people who will intentionally abuse a relationship and drag out or even refuse to make a payment. However, a collection technique that is too threatening not only may fail to work but also could cause the firm to lose the customer or become subject to legal action.

Many businesses have found that the most effective collection procedure consists of a series of steps, each somewhat more forceful than the preceding one. Historically, the process has started with a gentle written reminder; subsequent steps may include additional letters, telephone calls, registered letters, personal contacts, and referral to a collection agency or attorney. The timing of these steps should be carefully standardized so that each one automatically follows the preceding one in a specified number of days. More recently, some businesses have started to send text messages and e-mails as reminders, especially when the firm has a significant percentage of younger customers.

bad-debt ratio
The ratio of bad debts to credit sales.

Various ratios can be used to monitor expenses associated with credit sales. The best known and most widely used expense ratio is the **bad-debt ratio**, which is computed by dividing the amount of bad debts by the total amount of credit sales. The bad-debt ratio reflects the efficiency of credit policies and procedures and can help you to track how well you are managing the credit you have extended to customers. To compare the effectiveness of your firm's credit management with that of other firms, look for sources that provide industry financial ratios. (These are often available in university libraries.) Two examples are Dun & Bradstreet's *Industry Norms and Key Business Ratios* and the *Almanac of Business and Industrial Financial Ratios.* A relationship exists among the bad-debt ratio, profitability, and the size of the firm. Many times, small profitable retailers have a higher bad-debt ratio than large profitable retailers do.

CREDIT REGULATION

The use of credit is regulated by a variety of federal laws, as well as state laws that vary considerably from state to state. Prior to the passage of such legislation, consumers were often confused by credit agreements and were sometimes victims of credit abuse.

By far the most significant piece of credit legislation is the federal Consumer Credit Protection Act, which includes the 1968 Truth-in-Lending Act. Its two primary purposes are to ensure that consumers are informed about the terms of a credit agreement and to require creditors to specify how finance charges are computed. The act requires that a finance charge be stated as an annual percentage rate and that creditors specify their procedures for correcting billing mistakes.

Other federal legislation related to credit management includes the following:

- The *Fair Credit Billing Act* provides protection to credit customers in cases involving incorrect billing. A reasonable time period is allowed for billing errors to be corrected. The act does not cover installment credit.
- The *Fair Credit Reporting Act* gives certain rights to credit applicants regarding reports prepared by credit bureaus. Amendments such as the FACT Act, signed into law in December 2003, have strengthened privacy provisions and defined more clearly the responsibilities and liabilities of businesses that provide information to credit reporting agencies.
- The *Equal Credit Opportunity Act* ensures that all consumers are given an equal chance to obtain credit. For example, a person is not required to reveal his or her sex, race, national origin, or religion to obtain credit.
- The *Fair Debt Collection Practices Act* bans the use of intimidation and deception in collection, requiring debt collectors to treat debtors fairly.

RESOURCES

Government Regulations and Assistance

In running your own business, you need to pay attention to the role government plays in both encouraging and regulating the availability of capital in the private sector. A good place to start is the Small Business Administration, at http://www.sba.gov/content/financial-services.

It should be apparent by now that pricing and credit decisions are of prime importance to a small firm because of their direct impact on its financial health. But keep in mind that you are reading about pricing and credit in the section of this book entitled "Focusing on the Customer: Marketing Growth Strategies." Small business owners can fall into the trap of giving all their attention to costs of products, materials, and operations when setting prices. Be sure that your pricing decisions are driven by a customer focus: What is the customer willing and able to pay, and does that price enable you to make a profit? Putting your customers first is the way to move your business forward.

1. **Discuss the role of cost and demand factors in setting a price.**
   - The total sales revenue of a firm is a direct reflection of two components: sales volume and price.
   - Price must be sufficient to cover total cost plus some margin of profit.
   - A firm should examine elasticity of demand—the relationship of price and quantity demanded—when setting a price.
   - A product's competitive advantage is a demand factor in setting price.

2. **Apply break-even analysis and markup pricing.**
   - Analyzing costs and revenue under different price assumptions identifies the break-even point, the quantity sold at which total costs and expenses equal total sales revenue.
   - The usefulness of break-even analysis is enhanced by incorporating sales forecasts.
   - Markup pricing is a generalized cost-plus system of pricing used by intermediaries with many products.

3. **Identify specific pricing strategies.**
   - Penetration pricing and skimming pricing are short-term strategies used when new products are first introduced into the market.
   - Follow-the-leader and variable pricing are special strategies that reflect the nature of the competition's pricing and concessions to customers.
   - A price lining strategy simplifies choices for customers by offering a range of several distinct prices.
   - Pricing at what the market will bear can be used only when the seller has little or no competition.
   - Local, state, and federal laws must be considered in setting prices, as well as any impact that a price may have on other product line items.

4. **Explain the benefits of credit, factors that affect credit extension, and types of credit.**
   - Credit offers potential benefits to both buyers and sellers.
   - Type of business, credit policies of competitors, age and income level of customers, availability of adequate working capital, and economic conditions affect the decision to extend credit.
   - The two broad classes of credit are consumer credit and trade credit.

5. **Describe the activities involved in managing credit.**
   - Evaluating the credit status of applicants begins with the completion of an application form.
   - A customer's ability to pay is evaluated through the five C's of credit: character, capacity, capital, conditions, and collateral.
   - Pertinent credit data can be obtained from several outside sources, including formal trade-credit agencies such as Dun & Bradstreet.
   - An accounts receivable aging schedule can be used to improve the credit collection process.
   - A small firm should establish a formal procedure for billing and collecting from credit customers.
   - It is important that a small firm follow all relevant credit regulations.

Key Terms

price p. 473
credit p. 473
total cost p. 474
variable costs p. 474
fixed costs p. 474
average pricing p. 475
elasticity of demand p. 476
elastic demand p. 476
inelastic demand p. 476
prestige pricing p. 478
break-even point p. 478
contribution margin p. 479
markup pricing p. 481
penetration pricing strategy p. 481
skimming price strategy p. 482

Key Terms (Continued)

follow-the-leader pricing strategy p. 482
variable pricing strategy p. 482
dynamic (personalized) pricing strategy p. 482
price lining strategy p. 482
consumer credit p. 486
trade credit p. 486
open charge account p. 486
installment account p. 486
revolving charge account p. 486
credit card p. 487
debit card p. 487
trade-credit agencies p. 489
credit bureaus p. 490
aging schedule p. 490
bad-debt ratio p. 492

Discussion Questions

1. Why does average pricing sometimes result in a pricing mistake?
2. Explain the importance of fixed and variable costs to the pricing decision.
3. How does the concept of elasticity of demand relate to prestige pricing? Give an example.
4. If a firm has fixed costs of $100,000 and variable costs per unit of $1, what is the break-even point in units, assuming a selling price of $5 per unit?
5. What is the difference between a penetration pricing strategy and a skimming price strategy? Under what circumstances would each be used?
6. If a small business conducts a break-even analysis properly and finds the break-even volume at a price of $10 to be 10,000 units, should it price its product at $10? Why or why not?
7. What are the major benefits of credit to buyers? What are its major benefits to sellers?
8. How does an open charge account differ from a revolving charge account?
9. What is meant by the terms 2/10, net 30? Does it pay to take discounts when they are offered?
10. What is the major purpose of aging accounts receivable? At what point in credit management should this activity be performed? Why?

You Make the Call

SITUATION 1

Steve Jones is the 35-year-old owner of a highly competitive small business that supplies temporary office help. Like most businesspeople, he is always looking for ways to increase profit. However, the nature of his competition makes it very difficult to raise prices for the temps' services, while reducing their wages makes recruiting difficult. Jones has, nevertheless, found an area—bad debts—in which improvement should increase profits. A friend and business consultant met with Jones to advise him on credit management policies. Jones was pleased to get this friend's advice, as bad debts were costing him about 2 percent of sales. Currently, Jones has no system for managing credit.

Question 1 What advice would you give Jones regarding the screening of new credit customers?

Question 2 What action should Jones take to encourage current credit customers to pay their debts? Be specific.

Question 3 Jones has considered eliminating credit sales. What are the possible consequences of this decision?

SITUATION 2

Warren Keating is an artist in Los Angeles who was an early seller on eBay, following the pattern of many artists who believe that auctioning their work is the way art should be sold. He has concluded that his market is made up of collectors, who would not want to see the value of what they are buying decline due to price cutting. Keating leans toward full retail pricing, and when he sells on eBay, it's through the "Buy It Now" listing or the more negotiable "Buy It Now or Make Offer." He thinks the biggest mistake an artist can make is inconsistent pricing that causes the buyer to lose confidence in the product's value. According to Keating, you should act with "courage and conviction."

Sources: http://www.warrenkeating.com, accessed March 20, 2011; and Warren Keating, "Sell More Art Online with New Pricing Strategies," http://artistmarketingsalon.wordpress.com/2011/01/24/sell-more-art-online-with-new-pricing-strategies/, accessed March 20, 2011.

Question 1 What do you think makes selling works of art different from selling other kinds of products? What makes it the same?

Question 2 Have you bought anything on eBay? If so, do you feel you received good value for the price you paid? If not, ask

someone who has shopped successfully on eBay for advice on how to shop on that site, and report what you were told.
Question 3 How would you price a work of art? What do you think the advantages and disadvantages of using an auction would be?

SITUATION 3

Paul Bowlin owns and operates a tree removal, pruning, and spraying business in a metropolitan area with a population of approximately 200,000. The business has grown to the point where Bowlin uses one and sometimes two crews, with four or five employees on each crew. Pricing has always been an important tool in gaining business, but Bowlin realizes that there are ways to entice customers other than quoting the lowest price. For example, he provides careful cleanup of branches and leaves, takes out stumps below ground level, and waits until a customer is completely satisfied before taking payment. At the same time, he realizes his bids for tree removal jobs must cover his costs. In this industry, Bowlin faces intense price competition from operators with more sophisticated wood-processing equipment, such as chip grinders. Therefore, he is always open to suggestions about pricing strategy.

Question 1 What would the nature of this industry suggest about the elasticity of demand affecting Bowlin's pricing?
Question 2 What types of costs should Bowlin evaluate when he is determining his break-even point?
Question 3 What pricing strategies could Bowlin adopt to further his long-term success in this market?
Question 4 How can the high quality of Bowlin's work be used to justify somewhat higher price quotes?

Experiential Exercises

1. Interview a small business owner regarding his or her pricing strategy. Try to ascertain whether the strategy being used reflects the total fixed and variable costs of the business. Prepare a report on your findings.
2. Interview a small business owner regarding his or her policies for evaluating credit applicants. Summarize your findings in a report.
3. Interview the credit manager of a retail store about the benefits and drawbacks of extending credit to customers. Report your findings to the class.
4. Ask several small business owners in your community who extend credit to describe the credit management procedures they use to collect bad debts. Report your findings to the class.

Small Business & Entrepreneurship Resource Center

1. Yosha Enterprises, in Westfield, New Jersey, offers a valuable service to customers through its Momints breath mints—eliminating bad breath. When Momints debuted, its price was high, but coming up with a pricing strategy was not an easy task. Describe each of the 5 Golden Rules of Pricing, as given by Dilip Soman, marketing professor at the University of Toronto. Is there any Golden Rule that you would add to that list?

   Source: Geoff Williams, "Name Your Price," *Entrepreneur*, Vol. 33, No. 9 (September 2005), pp. 108–111.

2. PayPal is an online credit service provider that takes out the risk of handling online credit card sales for small e-tailers. According to the article "A Battle at the Checkout," Rajiv Dutta, PayPal's president says, "We have more account holders than American Express, yet the vast majority of e-commerce sites don't offer us." Discuss what might be causing this. Why would online vendors be reluctant to utilize the PayPal service and instead use Google's Checkout service?

   Source: "A Battle at the Checkout: Online Payments," *The Economist*, Vol. 383, No. 8527 (May 5, 2007), p. 88.

Video Case 16

DYNAMIC NETWORK SERVICES, INC. (P. 725)

The story of Dynamic Network Services (Dyn) is not unlike many tech startup stories. The difference is that it started during the dot.com boom, survived through the bust, thrived after the dust settled, and surges ahead today. At the beginning of Dyn's history, pricing structure was evaluated monthly, but now that it's more established, forecasting is done depending on client needs.

ALTERNATIVE CASES FOR CHAPTER 16

Case 11, Missouri Solvents, p. 714
Case 22, Pearson Air Conditioning & Service, p. 736

CHAPTER 17

Promotional Planning

In the SPOTLIGHT
HubSpot, Inc.
http://www.hubspot.com

Business journalists regularly write about how marketing is changing. The founders of HubSpot, Inc., set out to be the cause of the change.

HubSpot was started in 2006 by Brian Halligan and Dharmesh Shah. Their idea was to provide what they describe as a "killer" marketing application—advising small businesses on how to leverage the Internet in order to "get found" by more prospects shopping in their niche and then to convert a high percentage of those prospects into customers. According to the company website, HubSpot

- helps you *get found online* by more qualified visitors.
- shows you how to *convert more* visitors into leads.

HubSpot, Inc.

- gives you tools to *close those leads efficiently*.
- provides analytics to help *make smart marketing investments*.

Traditional marketing involves sending messages to customers, prospects, and sometimes the public in general, using a variety of media to project an image or encourage purchasing action. This is referred to as *outbound marketing*. Halligan is credited with coining the term *inbound marketing* to refer to a company's ability to help itself "get found" by people already learning about and shopping in the firm's industry. This involves setting up a website that acts as a "hub" in the industry and attracts visitors naturally through search engines, through the blogosphere, and through social media sites.

According to Mike Volpe, vice president of marketing, HubSpot started small but grew quickly, following its own advice on sales and marketing. The management

After studying this chapter, you should be able to . . .

1. Describe the communication process and the factors determining a promotional mix.
2. Explain methods of determining the appropriate level of promotional expenditures.
3. Describe personal selling activities.
4. Identify advertising options for a small business.
5. Discuss the use of sales promotional tools.

LOOKING AHEAD

© iStockphoto.com/Dan Bachman

team found early on that there was a good market with lots of demand for the services they offered. The initial software product provided templates to design content for websites that would gain Internet exposure. Volpe believes the first key to growth was a free tool HubSpot offered, the Website Grader (http://websitegrader.com), which helps companies score their websites, determines if the websites have problems, and lets them know how popular their websites are. HubSpot's second initiative was to enter the blogosphere, eventually attracting 40,000 subscribers.

Volpe describes the culture of HubSpot as one that encourages experimentation. He reports outsized returns on the new approaches that the firm has tried. But he says it also celebrates failures. Whether the experiment was well run is more important than the outcome it achieved. Through experimentation, HubSpot continues to adapt and grow.

Sources: http://www.hubspot.com, accessed March 26, 2011; personal interview with Mike Volpe, January 18, 2011; and Brian Halligan and Dharmesh Shah, *Inbound Marketing Get Found Using Google, Social Media, and Blogs* (Hoboken, NJ: John Wiley & Sons, 2010).

David Meerman Scott, author of *The New Rules of Marketing & PR*, proclaims, "We're living a revolution!"[1] He believes advances in communication technology are changing the world. Halligan and Shah founded HubSpot because they recognized that these technological changes affect how people choose products and the companies they do business with. HubSpot turns old marketing strategies on their head by teaching clients how to get found online when their customers are interested in what they have to offer. Search engines, social networks, blogs, and apps are changing how we get information and conduct business.

But the question remains, how does a customer know that you have something to sell? Does she or he randomly drive by your store and see your sign? Stumble across your website while surfing the Internet? Hear about you from a friend or neighbor? If you want people to buy what you are selling, you need to let them know that you are open for business—and why they should buy from you. The way you get that message across is called *promotion.*

Promotion consists of marketing communications that inform potential consumers about a firm or its product or service and try to persuade them to buy it. Small businesses use promotion in varying degrees; a given firm seldom uses all of the many promotional tools available. In order to simplify our discussion of the promotional process, we group the techniques discussed in this chapter into three traditional categories—personal selling, advertising, and sales promotional tools, with a special focus on public relations. According to Mike Volpe, issuing public relations announcements helped HubSpot grow virally in its early stages.[2]

promotion
Marketing communications that inform and persuade consumers.

A key decision in developing a promotional strategy is determining what you want to get out of it. Are you attracting customers to your store? Do you want them to visit your website? Are you asking them to buy a specific product or service? Or do you just want to plant the name of your business firmly in customers' minds so that they will think of you when they are ready to buy? This decision will drive what you choose to communicate to prospective customers and the means for getting your message out to them.

Before examining the categories in the promotional process, let's look at the basic process of communication that characterizes promotion. If an entrepreneur understands that promotion is just a special form of communication, she or he will be better able to grasp the entire process.

The Communication Process in Promotion

1 Describe the communication process and determining a promotional mix.

Promotion is based on communication. As described in In the Spotlight, communication technology is changing, but the basic process and purpose remain the same.

The communication process has identifiable components. As shown in Exhibit 17.1, every communication involves a source, a message, a channel, and a receiver. Each of us communicates in many ways every day, and these exchanges parallel small business communications. Part (a) in Exhibit 17.1 depicts a personal communication—a daughter away at college who is communicating with her parents. Part (b) depicts a small business communication—a firm communicating with a customer.

As you can see, many similarities exist between the two. The receiver of the daughter's message is her parents. The daughter, the source in this example, uses three different channels for her message: e-mail, a personal visit, and a greeting card. The receiver of the message from the XYZ Company is the customer. The XYZ Company uses three message channels: a newspaper, a sales call, and an electronic posting on a blog. The daughter's e-mail and the company's newspaper advertisement both represent nonpersonal forms of communication—there is no face-to-face contact. The daughter's visit to her parents' home and the sales call made by the company's representative are personal forms of communication. Finally, the greeting card and the blog are both special methods of communication. Thus, the promotional efforts of the small firm, like the communication between parents and daughter,

EXHIBIT 17.1 Similarity of Personal and Small Business Communication Processes

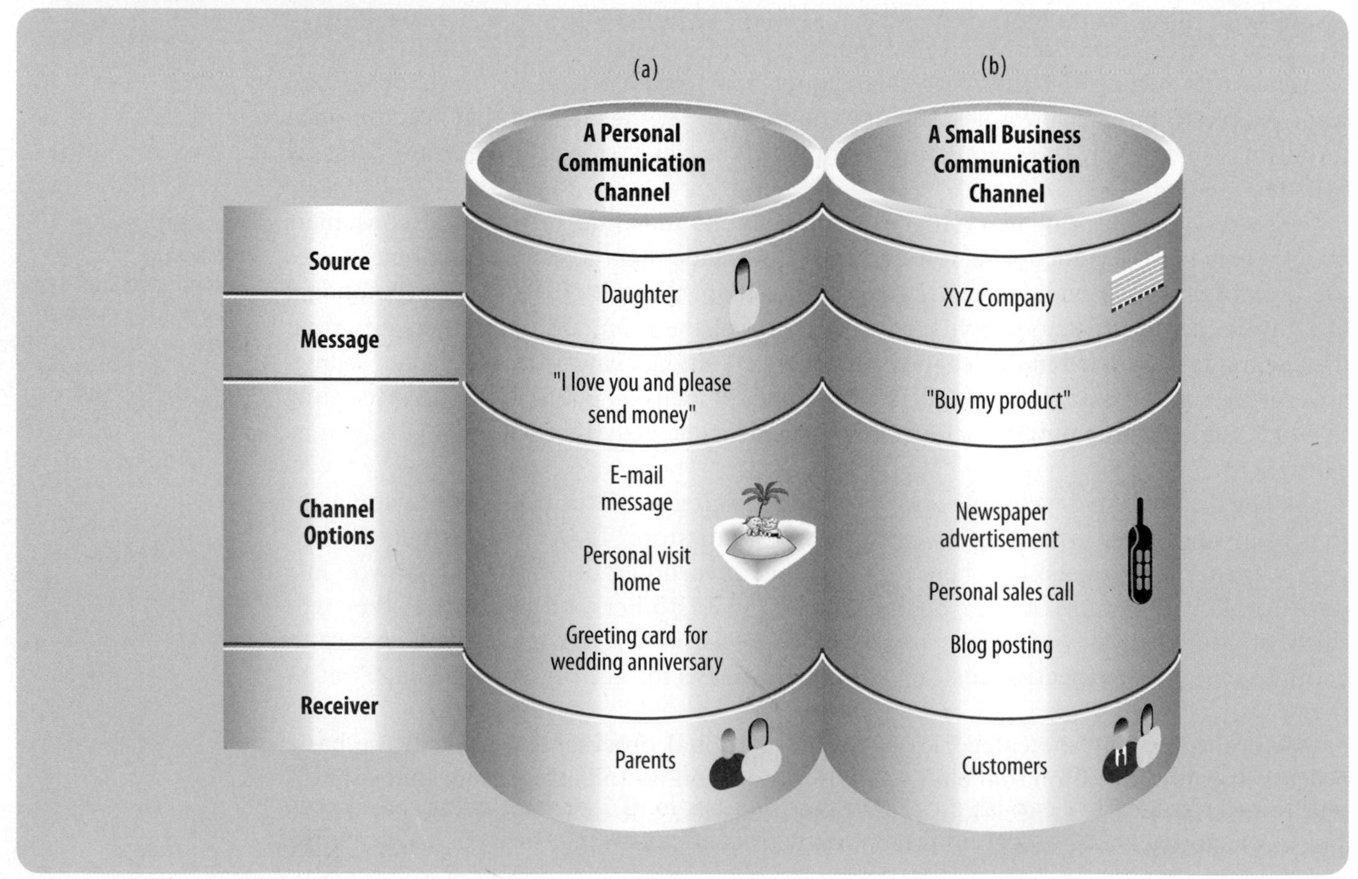

can be viewed as encompassing nonpersonal (advertising), personal (personal selling), and special (sales promotion) forms of communication. A term commonly used to describe how a business combines its promotional methods is *promotional mix*. A **promotional mix** is the blend of nonpersonal, personal, and special forms of communication aimed at a target market. The particular combination of the various promotional methods—advertising, personal selling, and sales promotional tools—is determined by many factors. One important factor is the geographical nature of the market to be reached. A widely dispersed market generally requires mass coverage through advertising, in contrast to the more costly individual contacts of personal selling. On the other hand, if the market is local or if the number of customers is relatively small, personal selling may be more feasible.

promotional mix
A blend of nonpersonal, personal, and special forms of communication aimed at a target market.

Another factor is the size of the promotional budget. Small firms may not select certain forms of promotion because the costs are just too high. Television advertising, for example, is generally more expensive than radio advertising. The lower costs and more targeted nature of company websites have led many small firms to choose electronic media and inbound marketing strategies.

A third factor that heavily influences the promotional mix is the product's characteristics. If a product is of high unit value, such as a boat, personal selling will be a vital ingredient in the mix. Personal selling is also an effective method for promoting highly technical products, such as a home gym, because a customer's knowledge about them is usually limited. On the other hand, nonpersonal advertising is more effective for a relatively inexpensive item, like chewing gum.

There are, of course, many other considerations to be evaluated when developing a unique promotional mix. When you start your business, take a close look at the promotional tactics of successful competitors. Their practices indicate how customers are most likely to obtain information about the products and services you plan to offer. Always be prepared to make some adjustments based on what you see customers doing, your budget, your location, and other changes in your environment. Over time, you will undoubtedly cut back on particular efforts or seek more funds to support your promotional plan.

Determining the Promotional Budget

In Chapter 16, you learned that there is no magic formula for determining the right price for what you are selling. The same problem arises when figuring out how much a small business should spend on promotion. There are, however, four commonsense approaches to budgeting funds for small business promotion:

1. Allocating a percentage of sales
2. Deciding how much can be spared
3. Spending as much as the competition does
4. Determining how much is needed for specific results

ALLOCATING A PERCENTAGE OF SALES

Often, the simplest method of determining how much to budget for promotion is to earmark promotional dollars based on a percentage of sales. A firm's own past experiences should be evaluated to establish a promotion-to-sales ratio. If 2 percent of sales, for example, has historically been spent on promotion with good results, the firm can safely budget

Spending Promotional Dollars

Want to read reports on how other firms spend their promotional dollars? Check out *Advertising Age* magazine.

2 percent of forecasted sales for future promotion. Secondary data on industry averages can also be used for comparison.

A major shortcoming of allocating a percentage of sales is an inherent tendency to spend more on promotion when sales are increasing and less when they are declining. When the economy is booming, do you really need to spend more to attract customers? In a recession, however, using promotion to stimulate sales may be the most important way to let people know why they should be doing business with you.[3] Additionally, new firms have no historical sales figures on which to base their promotional budgets.

DECIDING HOW MUCH CAN BE SPARED

Another piecemeal approach to promotional budgeting widely used by small firms is to spend whatever is left over when all other activities have been funded. The decision about promotional spending might be made only when a media representative sells an owner on a special deal that the business can afford. However, action should be taken only if the deal allows the business to accomplish promotional goals. And small business owners should be alert for new media opportunities, which arise regularly on the Internet and through smartphones.

SPENDING AS MUCH AS THE COMPETITION DOES

Sometimes, a small firm builds a promotional budget based on an analysis of competitors' budgets. By duplicating the promotional efforts of close competitors, the business hopes to reach the same customers and will be spending at least as much as the competition. If the competitor is a large business, this method is clearly not feasible; however, it can be used to react to short-run promotional tactics by small competitors. Unfortunately, this approach may result in the copying of competitors' mistakes as well as their successes. It is also important to think about how competitors will react to what you are doing.

DETERMINING HOW MUCH IS NEEDED FOR SPECIFIC RESULTS

The preferred approach to estimating promotional expenditures is to decide what it will take to do the job. This method requires a comprehensive analysis of the market and the firm's goals. If these estimates are reasonably accurate, the entrepreneur can determine the total amount that needs to be spent. And keep your eyes and ears open for how your target market is getting information. Is a new social medium becoming popular? Do your customers need to be introduced to your product, or are they looking for it? The options for spending promotional budgets are increasing every day.

In many cases, the best way for a small business to set promotional expenditures incorporates all four approaches (see Exhibit 17.2). In other words, compare the four estimated amounts and set the promotional budget at a level that is somewhere between the maximum and minimum amounts. After the budget has been determined, the key decision is how dollars will be spent on specific promotional methods. The methods chosen depend on a number of factors. We will now examine personal selling, a frequent choice for small firms.

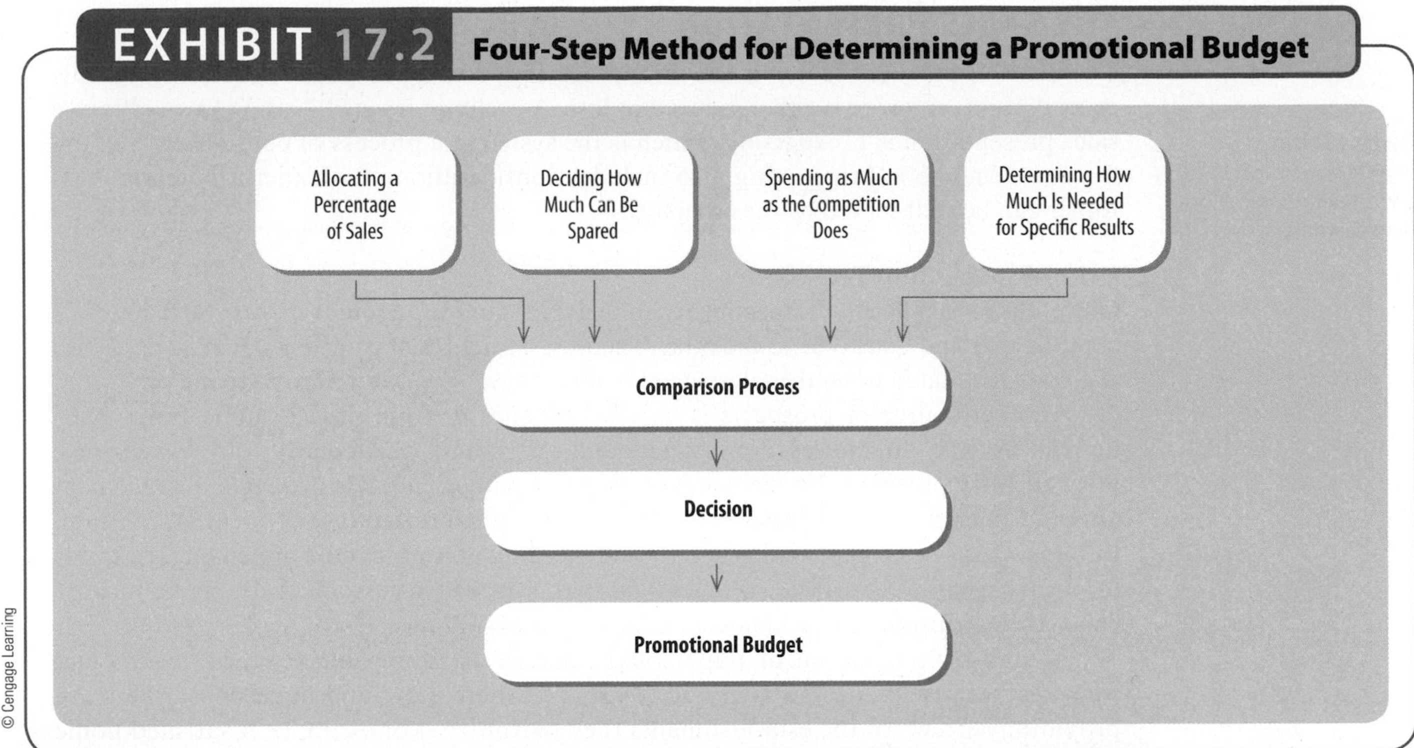

Personal Selling in the Small Firm

3 Describe personal selling activities.

Many products require **personal selling**— a sales presentation delivered in a one-on-one manner. Personal selling includes the activities of both the inside salespeople of retail, wholesale, and service establishments and the outside sales representatives, who call on business customers and final consumers. It is important to keep in mind that for a small business, every person in the company may be a salesperson. A customer who walks into a business or places a phone call or sends an e-mail to a business should not have to wait for hours or days to be taken care of by the owner or a certain employee—everyone must be ready to meet the customer's needs. The entrepreneur's responsibility is to make sure that all employees are prepared to do personal selling.

personal selling A sales presentation delivered in a one-on-one manner.

THE IMPORTANCE OF PRODUCT KNOWLEDGE

Effective selling is built on a foundation of product knowledge. If a salesperson is well acquainted with a product's advantages, uses, and limitations, she or he can educate customers by successfully answering their questions and countering their objections. Most customers expect a salesperson to provide knowledgeable answers, whether the product is a camera, a coat, an automobile, paint, a machine tool, or office equipment. Customers are seldom experts on the products they buy; however, they can immediately sense a salesperson's knowledge or ignorance. Personal selling degenerates into mere order-taking when a salesperson lacks product knowledge.

VStock LLC/VStockLLC/Newscom

THE SALES PRESENTATION

prospecting A systematic process of continually looking for new customers.

The heart of personal selling is the sales presentation to a prospective customer. At this crucial point, an order is either secured or lost. A preliminary step leading to an effective sales presentation is **prospecting**, which is the systematic process of continually looking for new customers. Prospecting also includes consideration of whether a potential customer can be well served by the company.

Using Prospecting Techniques

One of the most efficient prospecting techniques is obtaining *personal referrals*. Such referrals come from friends, customers, and other businesses. Initial contact with a potential customer is greatly facilitated when the salesperson is able to say, "You were referred to me by. . . ."

Another source of prospects is *impersonal referrals* from media publications, public records, and directories. Newspapers and magazines, particularly trade magazines, often identify prospects by reporting on new companies and new products. Engagement announcements in a newspaper can serve as impersonal referrals for a local bridal shop. Public records of property transactions and building permits can be impersonal referrals for a garbage pick-up service, which might find prospective customers among home buyers or those planning to build houses or apartment buildings.

A high-tech variation of impersonal referrals is taking place on various social websites like Facebook, Twitter, and MySpace, where more and more subscribers are providing reviews of the establishments they patronize. For example, a satisfied home buyer registered on LinkedIn might post a recommendation of the real estate agent who helped locate the property and close the sale. The reviews can be positive or negative. Yelp.com now uses automated software to screen postings that could be untrustworthy, such as criticisms about a company that might have been posted by a competitor.[4]

Prospects can also be identified without referrals through *marketer-initiated contacts*. Telephone calls or mail surveys, for example, help locate possible buyers. Finally, inquiries by a potential customer that do not lead to a sale can still create a "hot prospect." Small furniture stores often require their salespeople to fill out a card for each person visiting the store. These *customer-initiated contacts* can then be systematically followed up by telephone calls, and prospects can be notified of special sales; some customers may become followers on your Twitter account and receive notification through Twitter of special offers. Contact information should be updated periodically. Firms with websites can similarly follow up with visitors who have made inquiries online.

Practicing the Sales Presentation

Practicing always improves a salesperson's success rate; after all, "practice makes perfect." Prior to making a sales presentation, a salesperson should give his or her "pitch" in front of a spouse, friend, or mirror. Even better, he or she may want to record the presentation in order to study it later and improve delivery.

The salesperson should think about possible customer objections to the product and prepare to handle them. The best salespeople have done their homework. They have not only practiced their presentations, but they have also studied their prospective customers. Knowing something about your customer's wants and needs will prepare you for most of their likely objections. Most objections can be categorized as relating to (1) price, (2) product, (3) timing, (4) source, (5) service, or (6) need. Although there is no substitute for actual selling experience, salespeople find training helpful in learning how to deal with customers' objections. Successful salespeople develop techniques, such as those in the following list, for responding to customers' objections. The first two responses are appropriate when a potential buyer states an objection that is factually untrue; the remaining suggestions can be used when a buyer raises a valid objection.

© iStockphoto.com/Angelika Schwarz

entrepreneurial experiences

Rewards for Shopping

While the growth of online shopping is phenomenal, brick-and-mortar stores are not dead! One entrepreneur saw a need facing retailers that he felt he could address through an online business. "The number-one challenge facing every retailer in America is getting people through the door," says Cyriac Roeding, CEO and co-founder of shopkick.

Roeding's business idea did not come from the retail side, but from a college stint he did in Japan in the 1990s. During his time in Tokyo, he kept seeing "people walking around with these clunky machines they called 'mobile phones.'" Roeding decided this had to be the next big thing. In the next few years, he gained experience in the mobile industry, testing ideas on his own and with others.

In 2009, Roeding introduced shopkick as an app for smartphones that rewards customers just for entering a store, for scanning products, and for signing up friends. Clicking on shopkick turns an offline physical store into an interactive world where the shopper can, for example, enter a contest to share videos with other shoppers.

Shopkick

Shopkick awards "kicks" from participating stores to registered iPhone and Android users. The kicks can be converted into gift cards, charitable donations, discounts, and other redeemable items. Retailers pay for a small box that emits a signal that will be picked up by a smartphone only within the store. Retailers also pay a cost per click and a small percentage of the transaction if a sale is made. Stores can track both traffic and sales associated with shopkick customers.

Roeding does not see shopkick as a variation on social networking. He is trying to make shopping fun, something that is appealing to retailers who expect their employees to have positive personal selling engagements with their customers.

As shopkick continues to develop its app and add services, the company expects to further help retailers by providing age, gender, purchasing history, and other characteristics of customers to help stores better target and serve their markets.

Sources: http://shopkick.com, accessed March 26, 2011; Jason Ankeny, "The Rebirth of Retail," *Entrepreneur*, Vol. 39, No. 3 (March 2011), pp. 26–27, 30, 32–34; and Fast Company staff, "The 10 Most Innovative Companies in Retail," http://www.fastcompany.com/1738961/the-10-most-innovative-companies-in-retail, accessed March 26, 2011. **http://shopkick.com**

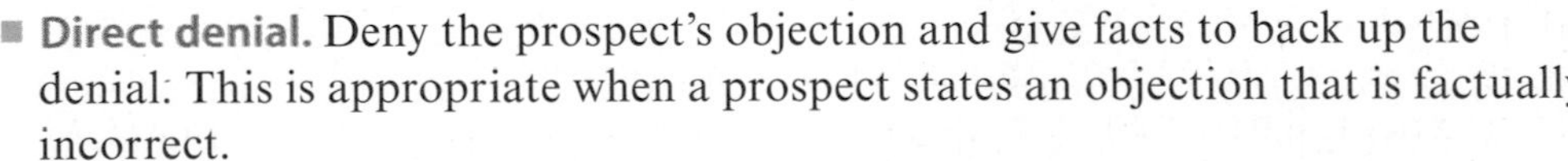

- **Direct denial.** Deny the prospect's objection and give facts to back up the denial. This is appropriate when a prospect states an objection that is factually incorrect.
- **Indirect denial.** Express concern about the prospect's objection and follow with a denial.
- **Answer objections with the words feel, felt, and found.** Don't argue; instead, say, "I understand how you feel. A lot of my customers felt the same way. But when they found out how much they saved by using our product, they were amazed."
- **Take notes.** Write down objections to show the prospect that you are really listening.

- **Compensation method.** Admit to agreeing with the objection and then proceed to show compensating advantages.
- **Pass-up method.** Acknowledge the concern expressed by the prospect and then move on.
- **Find the true objection.** Don't jump to the conclusion that the objection raised was the prospect's primary concern. Ask for more details about the objection so that you can handle it.
- **Follow up and follow through.** If you promised to gather more information, do it and deliver. If you promised you would call back, make that call. Some prospects raise objections just to defer a decision. They think that once you leave, they will not hear from you again. Persistence on your part can pay off.

Making the Sales Presentation

Salespeople must adapt their sales approach to meet customers' needs. A "canned" sales talk will not succeed with most buyers. For example, an individual who is selling exercise equipment must demonstrate how the products will fill a customer's specific needs. Similarly, a home security system salesperson must understand the special interests of particular customers and speak their language. Every sales objection must be answered explicitly and adequately.

Successful selling involves a number of psychological elements. Personal enthusiasm, friendliness, and persistence are required. Just as an entrepreneur should be passionate about the business he or she is starting, a salesperson should show true passion about what the product or service can do for the customer. For most companies, only about 20 percent of the salespeople bring these elements to the task of selling, but they are responsible for as much as 80 percent of all sales.

Some salespeople have special sales techniques that they use with success. For example, a paper products salesperson helped a woman in an office lobby retrieve a stack of papers that she had dropped. He knew that stepping in to assist someone in need builds trust and forms a relationship. In this case, the woman turned out to be the managing partner of the company he was visiting. His small act of kindness led to a meeting and an order. The partner was willing to invest time in listening to the salesperson explain the benefits his products offered. In this case, personal conduct and treating others with respect were elements of the sales process.[5]

COST CONTROL IN PERSONAL SELLING

Cost considerations are especially important for a new business that may have very limited resources. The entrepreneur must first recognize that she or he is first and foremost a salesperson for the enterprise. Nothing can substitute for the entrepreneur's personal efforts to sell products and services and to represent the image and reputation of the firm. Additionally, in the startup and early growth stages, the business may not have funds to support a full-time sales staff. The most cost-efficient mode of selling may be to use *sales or marketing representatives*. These individuals are self-employed or employees of a company whose purpose is to represent multiple businesses, spreading the costs of selling products and services across all of these lines. They will not focus on your products alone, as your own employees would, but your company will have to compensate them only as merchandise is actually sold. That does not mean you can simply provide the sales reps with products and then ignore them. Instead, think of them as your partners. Provide any sales aids they may need to make their job easier. Keep communication channels open, and let them know that you are committed to making them successful.

THE COMPENSATION PROGRAM FOR SALESPEOPLE

Salespeople are compensated in two ways for their efforts—nonfinancially and financially. A good compensation program allows its participants to work for both forms of reward, while recognizing that a salesperson's goals may be different from those of the entrepreneur. For example, an entrepreneur may be willing to sacrifice income to grow the business or may gain personal satisfaction from introducing an innovative product. The salesperson, on the other hand, expects immediate and appropriate salary or commission compensation in order to pay bills and enjoy a desired quality of life.

Nonfinancial Compensation

Personal recognition and the satisfaction of reaching a sales quota are examples of nonfinancial rewards that motivate many salespeople. Small retail businesses sometimes post a photograph of the top salesperson of the week or month for all to see. Engraved plaques are also given as a more permanent record of sales achievements.

Nonfinancial compensation may also relate to personal and career advancement. Rewards for being a desired employee include opportunities for promotion, advanced education and training, and an assurance of job security. Business owners should be aware that effective sales personnel are often competitive. They gain a sense of accomplishment by measuring their achievements against those of their peers.

Financial Compensation

Typically, financial compensation is the more critical factor for salespeople. Two basic plans used for financial compensation are commissions and straight salary. Each plan has specific advantages and limitations for the small firm.

Most small businesses would prefer to use commissions as compensation, because such an approach is simple and directly related to productivity. Usually, a certain percentage of the sales generated by a salesperson represents his or her commission. A commission plan thereby incorporates a strong incentive for sales effort—no sale, no commission! Also, with this type of plan, there is less drain on the firm's cash flow until a sale is made. On the negative side, a salesperson's job is always more than making the sale. Personnel on commission might be less likely to provide follow-up service or complete after-sale paperwork or other tasks that the business needs to have done.

The straight salary form of compensation provides salespeople with more income security because their level of compensation is ensured, regardless of sales made. However, working for a straight salary can potentially reduce a salesperson's motivation by providing income despite low performance or no sales at all.

Combining the salary and commission forms of compensation is typically the most attractive plan for most small businesses. It is common practice to structure combination plans so that salary represents the larger part of compensation for a new salesperson. As the salesperson gains experience, the ratio is adjusted to provide more money from commissions and less from salary. And do not put a cap on what a salesperson can earn through commission. Many companies have lost their top producers by limiting incentives. Why would you stop rewarding someone who is making more money for your business?

Advertising Practices for Small Firms

Another significant promotional expenditure for the small firm is advertising. **Advertising** is the impersonal presentation of an idea that is identified with a business sponsor. Ideas in advertising are communicated to consumers through media such as television, radio, magazines, newspapers, billboards, and the Internet.

advertising
The impersonal presentation of a business idea through mass media.

ADVERTISING OBJECTIVES

As its primary goal, advertising seeks to sell by informing, persuading, and reminding customers of the availability or superiority of a firm's product or service. To be successful, it must rest on a foundation of positive features such as product quality and efficient service. It is important to remember that advertising can bring no more than temporary success to an otherwise second-rate product. Advertising must always be viewed as a complement to a good product and never as a replacement for a bad product.

The entrepreneur should avoid creating false expectations with advertising, as such expectations are likely to disappoint customers and leave them dissatisfied. Advertising can accentuate a trend in the sale of an item or product line, but it seldom has the power to reverse a trend. It must, consequently, be able to reflect changes in customer needs and preferences.

At times, advertising may seem to be a waste of money. It is expensive and adds little value to the product. One alternative to advertising is personal selling, which is often more expensive and time-consuming. As shown by the In the Spotlight example of inbound marketing strategies introduced by HubSpot, other alternatives to advertising are emerging. Small business owners, like corporate executives, should be concerned with changes in technology and societal behavior.

TYPES OF ADVERTISING

product advertising
The presentation of a business idea designed to make potential customers aware of a specific product or service and create a desire for it.

institutional advertising
The presentation of information about a particular firm, designed to enhance the firm's image.

The two basic types of advertising are product advertising and institutional advertising. **Product advertising** is designed to make potential customers aware of a particular product or service and create a desire for it. **Institutional advertising**, on the other hand, conveys information about the business itself. It is intended to make the public aware of the company and enhance its image so that its product advertising will be more credible and effective.

Most small business advertising is of the product type. Small retailers' ads often stress products, such as weekend specials at a supermarket or sportswear sold exclusively in a women's clothing store. It is important to note, however, that the same advertisement can convey both product and institutional themes. Furthermore, a firm may stress its product in newspaper advertisements, for example, while using institutional advertising on websites. Decisions regarding the type of advertising to be used should be based on the nature of the business, industry practice, available media, and the objectives of the firm.

OBTAINING ASSISTANCE WITH ADVERTISING

Most small businesses rely on others' expertise to create their promotional messages. Fortunately, there are several sources for this specialized assistance, including advertising agencies, suppliers, trade associations, and advertising media.

Advertising agencies can provide the following services:

- Furnish design, artwork, and copy for specific advertisements and/or commercials
- Evaluate and recommend the advertising media with the greatest "pulling power"
- Evaluate the effectiveness of different advertising appeals
- Advise on sales promotions and merchandise displays
- Conduct market-sampling studies to evaluate product acceptance or determine the sales potential of a specific geographic area
- Furnish mailing lists

Since advertising agencies charge fees for their services, an entrepreneur must be sure that the return from those services will be greater than the fees paid. Of course, with the high level of computer technology currently available, creating print advertising in-house is becoming increasingly common among small firms. Some business owners are assisted by suppliers who furnish display aids and even entire advertising programs to their dealers. Trade associations also provide helpful assistance. In addition, advertising media can provide some of the same services offered by an ad agency.

FREQUENCY OF ADVERTISING

Determining how often to advertise is an important and highly complex issue for a small business. Obviously, advertising should be done regularly, and attempts to stimulate interest in a firm's products or services should be part of an ongoing promotional program. Continuity reinforces the presence of the company as the place for customers to buy when they are ready. One-shot advertisements that are not part of a well-planned promotional effort lose much of their effectiveness in a short period. Of course, some noncontinuous advertising may be justified, such as advertising to prepare consumers for acceptance of a new product. Such an approach may also be used for holidays and seasonal events. Most products and services have some kind of seasonal demand—air conditioners for spring and summer, trendy clothing for going back to school, toys at Christmas. Deciding on the frequency of advertising involves a host of factors, both objective and subjective, and a wise entrepreneur will seek professional advice.

Robert Kiyosaki, author of *Rich Dad, Poor Dad*, believes that firms should never stop promoting; this is particularly true during economic downturns. Kiyosaki has found that in tough times customers migrate to businesses that fight hard to keep their names visible.[6]

START UP RESOURCES

The Promotional Cycle

Robert Kiyosaki claims that promotion is on a six-week cycle. That is, you should not expect results from an advertising campaign unless you invest in it for at least six weeks.

Kiyosaki has been an inspiration to students and entrepreneurs. Beginning with *Rich Dad, Poor Dad*, he has produced a series of books, which can be found at http://www.richdad.com.

WHERE TO ADVERTISE

Most small firms restrict their advertising, either geographically or by customer type. Advertising media should reach—but not overreach—a firm's present or desired target market. From among the many media available, a small business entrepreneur must choose those that will provide the greatest return for the advertising dollar.

The most appropriate combination of advertising media depends on the type of business and its current circumstances. A real estate sales firm, for example, may rely almost exclusively on classified advertisements in the local newspaper, supplemented by institutional advertising and

© Kim Karpeles / Alamy

multilisting services on the Internet. A transfer-and-storage firm may use a combination of radio, billboard, and Yellow Pages advertising to reach individuals planning to move household furniture. A retailer of home furniture may emphasize television advertisements, while an office furniture company may find participation in trade fairs to be more productive. However, every combination of advertising media must include a website. Websites are the first step in identifying prospective sources by many consumers and businesses.

To make an informed selection, entrepreneurs should learn about the strengths and weaknesses of each medium. Exhibit 17.3 summarizes important facts about major advertising media. Study this information carefully, noting the particular advantages and disadvantages of each medium. In the rest of this section, we give special attention to online advertising because its use is growing so quickly, almost demanding the presence of even the smallest companies.

WEB ADVERTISING

The Internet has provided an entirely new way for promoting businesses. With color graphics, two-way information exchanges, streaming video, and 24-hour availability, online advertising is challenging traditional media for advertising dollars. Small businesses are discovering that their customers expect them to have websites. The basic methods of Web advertising for a small firm are (1) a company website, (2) banner ads and pop-ups, (3) e-mail, (4) reciprocal advertising and hyperlinks, and (5) blogs.

EXHIBIT 17.3 Advantages and Disadvantages of Major Advertising Media

Medium	Advantages	Disadvantages
Newspapers	Geographic selectivity and flexibility; short-term advertiser commitments; news value and immediacy; year-round readership; high individual market coverage; co-op and local tie-in availability; short lead time	Little demographic selectivity; limited color capabilities; low pass-along rate; may be expensive
Magazines	Good reproduction, especially for color; demographic selectivity; regional selectivity; local market selectivity; relatively long advertising life; high pass-along rate	Long-term advertiser commitments; slow audience buildup; limited demonstration capabilities; lack of urgency; long lead time
Radio	Low cost; immediacy of message; can be scheduled on short notice; relatively no seasonal change in audience; highly portable; short-term advertiser commitments; entertainment carryover	No visual treatment; short advertising life of message; high frequency required to generate comprehension and retention; distractions from background sound; commercial clutter
Television	Ability to reach a wide, diverse audience; low cost per thousand; creative opportunities for demonstration; immediacy of messages; entertainment carryover; demographic selectivity with cable stations	Short life of message; some consumer skepticism about claims; high campaign cost; little demographic selectivity with network stations; long-term advertiser commitments; long lead times required for production; commercial clutter
Outdoor Media	Repetition; moderate cost; flexibility; geographic selectivity	Short message; lack of demographic selectivity; high "noise" level distracting audience
Internet	Fastest-growing medium, including smartphones and tablets; ability to target demographics; easy to update; relatively short lead time required for creating Web-based advertising; natural fit with social networking	Possible difficulty in measuring ad effectiveness and return on investment; not all consumers have access; rapidly changing technologies may result in product obsolescence (smartphones/tablets); service issues

The Small Business Website

If you are not thinking about marketing when you set up and manage your company's website, you are missing opportunities and doing damage to your business. Numerous decisions must be made prior to launching a site. Three critical startup tasks are related to the likely promotional success of a corporate website: (1) creating and registering a site name, (2) building a user-friendly site, and (3) promoting the site.

CREATING AND REGISTERING A SITE NAME The Domain Name System (DNS) allows users to find their way around the Internet. Selecting the best domain name for a corporate website is an important promotional decision. Popular domain designations are .com, .net, .biz, and .org. Domain names can have up to 63 characters preceding the domain designation. Follow the rules carefully to avoid problems when you register.[7]

Since a domain name gives a small business its online identity, it's desirable to select a descriptive and appealing name. Obviously, some of the shorter, more creative names have already been taken, and most entrepreneurs choose to use the name of their business. Like real estate, website names can be bought and sold. In 2010, the name Flying.com sold for $1,100,000. The median price for a domain name at that time was under $3,000.[8]

Once a name has been selected, it should be checked for availability and then registered. The Internet Corporation for Assigned Names and Numbers (ICANN) is a nonprofit corporation currently overseeing the global Internet. ICANN, however, does not register names; this must be done through a domain registration firm. InterNIC, a registered service mark of the U.S. Department of Commerce, provides an Accredited Registrar Directory that lists ICANN-accredited domain registrars, such as NameSecure.

BUILDING A USER-FRIENDLY WEBSITE First impressions are important, and high-quality Web design gives a small e-commerce business the opportunity to make a good first impression on each visitor. The technical aspects of developing a website are beyond

EXHIBIT 17.4 Website Essentials

1. A clear description of who you are
Clearly state your name and sum up your products or services right on the homepage.

2. A simple, sensible Web address
Don't make things complicated.

3. An easily navigated site map
Clear links to the most important pages and a site map are crucial for guiding visitors to the information they're looking for.

4. Easy-to-find contact information
You wouldn't want to lose a customer to a competitor just because you made it difficult for them to get in touch with you.

5. Customer testimonials
Honest words from customers help to make your products or services more tangible and desirable to those who are visiting you online.

6. An obvious call to action
Tell online visitors what you want them to do with clear tones of command.

7. Know the basics of Search Engine Optimization
Your website won't do you much good if no one can find it. Become familiar with the SEO basics to make it more accessible by search engine.

8. Fresh, quality content
For many businesses, their website makes their first impression on a customer. Give customers what they're looking for—and a reason to keep coming back.

9. A secure hosting platform
Having your online information hijacked is a nightmare, and should it happen to your business, it could cost you customers.

10. A design and style that's friendly to online readers
Keep in mind three style points for online writing:

- Break things down into short paragraphs, with headers if necessary.
- Use bullet points.
- Highlight important words or phrases.

Source: Adapted from Bianca Male, "10 Things Every Small-Business Website Needs," http://www.entrepreneur.com/article/217499, accessed March 27, 2011. Reprinted with permission of Entrepreneur Media, Inc. © 2011 by Entrepreneur Media, Inc. All rights reserved.

the scope of this chapter. But, fortunately, many technical specialists are available to help design and build a site. Our purpose here, however, is simply to provide some useful ideas about website design. Exhibit 17.4 offers 10 essentials for e-commerce websites.

Websites fail to retain customers for many reasons. One of the most frequent problems is slow downloading. Online shoppers are a fickle bunch, and the slightest inconvenience sends them away. If your business is conducting a considerable amount of online business, a slow website translates into lost sales revenue. Lost revenue can be direct (for example, missed sales if you're selling online), or indirect (for example, loss of customer confidence if you're providing Web-based solutions to clients). The more important a website is to your business, the less you can afford to have it perform slowly or, worse, experience downtime.

Evaluating Webmasters

What should small business owners look for in a webmaster? Take a look at the article "The Master of Your Domain" in the March 2011 issue of *Entrepreneur* (Vol. 39, No. 3). It will help you with your selection.

Websites will also fail if they do not satisfy visitors' information needs. Frequently, this is because designers look inward to the business for Web design ideas, rather than outward to customer needs. Some experts recommend that firms integrate social networking into their websites from the beginning. When Debbie Wexler launched her online jewelry company, Whiteflash.com, she made contact and developed relationships with prospective customers in chat rooms and fashion and gossip blogs. This strategy not only promoted her name, but it also helped her learn about her customers.[9] We will look at social networking in greater depth later in the chapter.

PROMOTING THE WEBSITE How do customers learn about a website? You have to tell them—and there are many ways to do this. A Web address can be promoted both to existing customers and to prospects by including the URL on print promotions, business cards, letterhead, and packaging. Special direct mail and radio campaigns can also be designed for this purpose. Additionally, a website can be promoted by placing banner advertisements on other websites, where a quick click will send users to the advertised site. In building HubSpot, Inc., Brian Halligan and Dharmesh Shah explained to clients that traditional promotion acts like a megaphone, broadcasting from one to many. Their idea for inbound marketing was for a firm's website to become a hub, enabling like-minded people to connect.[10]

Probably the most direct approach to website promotion is making sure that the site is listed on Internet search engines. Search engines allow users to find websites based on keywords included in the site's pages. If a popular search engine does not list a firm's website, many potential visitors will undoubtedly miss it. Registering a site with a search engine is free.

Search engine optimization (SEO) is the process of increasing the volume and quality of traffic to a particular website. The sooner your small business is represented in search engine results (i.e., the higher it ranks), the more visitors it will attract. An important goal is to make your website as search engine–friendly as possible.

Keep in mind, too, that there are many specialized search engines. Everyone thinks immediately of Google and Yahoo!, but your company might benefit from being registered with an engine such as Bing.com, which has become very popular for entertainment and shopping.[11] You can find guidelines for designing and submitting your website by going to search engine websites.

BANNER ADS AND POP-UPS Banner ads are advertisements that appear across a Web page, often as moving rectangular strips. In contrast, pop-up ads burst open on Web pages but do not move. When viewers respond by clicking on an ad, they are automatically linked to the site providing the product or sales activity. Both banner and pop-up ads can be placed on search engine sites or on related Web pages.

Ad Partners, Inc.

These types of Web advertising are often carried out through an affiliate program. In an affiliate program, a website carries a banner ad or a link for another company in exchange for a commission on any sales generated by the traffic sent to the sponsoring website. Affiliate programs have become quite popular among Web retailers, with one of the most lucrative being eBay's program. One primary reason for the success of eBay's affiliate program is the sheer volume of visitors to its website every day. An eBay affiliate is paid a commission not only on sales generated by the users it sends to eBay, but also on each already-registered eBay user it sends back to eBay and on each bid and qualified Buy it Now transaction.[12]

banner ads Advertisements that appear across a Web page, most often as moving rectangular strips.

pop-up ads Advertisements that burst open on computer screens.

There is some skepticism about the cost effectiveness of banner ads and pop-ups. It is clear that the novelty of such ads has worn off, and the click through rate is in decline.[13] Banner ads seem to work best for businesses that have high purchase rates from those who visit their websites.

DIRECT E-MAIL PROMOTION E-mail promotion, in which electronic mail is used to deliver a firm's message, provides a low-cost way to pinpoint customers and achieve response rates higher than those for banner ads. However, as more and more businesses use e-mail for this purpose, customer inboxes are becoming cluttered. And users are reluctant to open some e-mail messages, fearing they may contain computer viruses. Nevertheless, a number of surveys report that e-mail marketing is effective for many companies. According to an Econsultancy survey in 2011, 72 percent of business respondents reported good or excellent returns on investment in e-mail advertising. The Direct Marketing Association found that e-mail ad dollars spent in 2010 were estimated to generate \$42.08 in return.[14]

e-mail promotion Advertising delivered by means of electronic mail.

Two obstacles to e-mail promotion have arisen, as the volume of unsolicited e-mails (better known as *spam*) has turned many customers against this type of advertising. First, Congress passed the Can-Spam Act of 2003, which took effect on January 1, 2004, and established standards regarding the use of commercial e-mail enforceable by the Federal Trade Commission (FTC).[15] Second, anti-spam software, which sometimes also blocks legitimate e-mails, became popular. Before sending a promotional message by e-mail, marketers should consider testing their message by putting it through a preview tool. MailWasher Free and SpamButcher are examples of software packages that permit previews. Previewing allows you to see advertisements that may be delivered as e-mails without customers having to download them to their computers.

RECIPROCAL ADVERTISING AND HYPERLINKS A hyperlink is a word, phrase, or image that a user may click on to go to another part of a document or website or to a new document or website. Text hyperlinks are usually blue and underlined. When you move the cursor over a hyperlink, whether it is text or an image, the arrow should change to a small

hyperlink A word, phrase, or image that a user may click on to go to another part of a document or website or to a new document or website.

hand pointing at the link. When you click it, a new page or place in the current page will open. Hyperlinks are used within a given website to allow readers to access another section of the site.[16] As promotional tools, however, hyperlinks are typically reciprocal, enabling readers to move from one website to another that may have information that relates to their original search or complements what the original website is offering. Hyperlinks may be free to the linked parties if those parties believe the connections are mutually beneficial. Otherwise, one company may have to pay a per-click charge to the other if it is seeking to obtain business from those using the primary website.

blog
An interactive website where an individual can maintain a personal online journal, post and receive comments and reflections, and provide hyperlinks.

BLOGS The word *blog* is a contraction of the term *weblog*. **Blogs** are websites that contain an online personal journal with reflections, comments, and often hyperlinks provided by the writer.[17] Blogs are interactive, allowing readers to leave comments. Many business owners have set up blogs related to their companies and products; this can be done for free on WordPress.com or Blogger.com. An owner can then comment on other blogs that may have related topics, each time including links back to his or her company blog.

Mike Volpe, of HubSpot, Inc., considers the introduction of a blog to have been a major breakthrough in the company's identity and a stimulus of its growth.[18] According to HubSpot founders Brian Halligan and Dharmesh Shah, a blog can establish a company as a thought leader in its market. A blog keeps the company alive and fluid in the eyes of current and prospective customers. Halligan and Shah point out that a blog can move a company higher in search engine rankings, by providing additional pages on your site, additional keywords for searches, and the opportunity to add hyperlinks.[19]

Mobile Devices

Much of what we just described about promoting websites applies directly to mobile devices. But technological changes and consumer and commercial uses of these products have exploded in recent years, along with the opportunities that mobile devices offer to small firms. Consider that at the end of 2010, there were over 63 million smartphones in use in the United States. And during that year, social networking increased by 56 percent, online classifieds by 55 percent, and online retailing by 53 percent.[20]

mobile device
A generic term used to refer to a variety of wireless handheld computing devices.

app
Abbreviation for a software application for business or entertainment.

A **mobile device** is a generic term used to refer to a variety of wireless handheld computing devices that allow people to access information from wherever they are. When you are ready to promote your company and its products and services on mobile devices, keep in mind that your website may need to be reformatted to fit smaller, portable screens. You want a clear layout with easy navigation. You may need a professional checkout service provider so that your customers don't have to worry about pulling out their credit cards and entering numbers in public locations.[21] Two of the most important options available to you are apps and social media.

© iStockphoto.com/mbbirdy

APPS **App** is shorthand for *application*, specifically a software application for business or entertainment.[22] You may be well acquainted with apps for a variety of uses, including how to get along in a college community.[23] With the spreading use of smartphones, individuals, businesses, nonprofit organizations, and even government agencies offer apps to stay in contact and provide information to people on the go. For an example, take a look at the United States government's list of apps that can be downloaded to phones at http://apps.usa.gov/. For tips on ways to promote your business by using smartphones and apps, see Exhibit 17.5.

EXHIBIT 17.5 Tips for Promoting Your Businesses on Smartphones

1. Is your website mobile-friendly?
Not every website delivers information in a way that smartphone users can easily read when and where they need it.

2. Can your website be found where mobile device users look?
Learn what directories, maps, apps, and other ways of searching mobile users go to when they want to find a business that offers your products or services. Make sure you are listed on all of them.

3. Have you started social networking communities?
Many mobile users are active on Facebook, LinkedIn, and other social networking sites. It only makes sense to have a presence on them. Ask your customers for permission to text them with coupons and alerts about your business.

4. Do you chat with your customers and prospects?
A conversation involves more than your sending out announcements. Start building relationships with your customers and website visitors via Twitter now.

5. Are customers reviewing your business?
Yelp is a business review site that has active users in cities all over the world. Customers can also write reviews and recommend places on FourSquare, a site where members keep one another informed of their whereabouts.

6. Are you giving your audience what they want?
People go to the Web and to mobile devices for different reasons and different information. Checking out a restaurant from a computer may mean watching a video or reading a menu. From a smartphone, customers may want directions or to know whether you have a table available.

Source: Lora Kolodny, "Do All Small Businesses Need a Mobile Strategy?" http://boss.blogs.nytimes.com/2010/03/05/expert-mobile-advice-for-small-businesses/, accessed March 31, 2011; and Olga Kharif, "Smartphone Use Drives Online Shopping," http://www.businessweek.com/the_thread/the_thread/techbeat/archives/2009/12/smartphone_use.html, accessed April 1, 2011.

Large corporations are making sure that their customers can access them through apps. Small business owners must take this method of communication seriously to compete and promote their companies. An app should not cost your business more than the revenue it brings in. You don't have to invest in the most technologically advanced app anyone has ever seen, but you do want to think about how people can have fun when they click on your app. Flickr is one tool you can use to share photos, perhaps showing what a good time your customers are having with your products. And don't forget that you've got to be speedy. When people use their mobile devices, they want responses and information now![24]

Social Media

Let's start with Web 2.0. **Web 2.0** is an "architecture of participation" based on social software where users generate content, rather than simply consume it, and on open programming interfaces that let developers add to a Web service or get at data.[25] You can, of course, access social media through your home or office computer, but Web 2.0 is an arena where the Web rather than the desktop is the dominant platform. It enables mobile device users to interact wherever they may be. Web 2.0 was an evolutionary (some say revolutionary) step that opened the Internet for social interaction, providing new, cost-efficient opportunities for small businesses to find and retain customers.

Web 2.0
A term referring to the second generation of the World Wide Web, which allows for online collaboration, social interactions, and information sharing.

Oxford Dictionaries Online defines **social media** as websites and applications used for social networking.[26] That definition obliges us to define **social networking**, which is the use of dedicated websites and applications to communicate informally with other users or to find people with similar interests.[27] The smartphone and other mobile devices are helping business owners find entirely new ways of reaching customers and prospects.

social media
Websites and applications used for social networking.

social networking
The use of dedicated websites and applications to communicate informally with other users.

At the 2011 Mobile World Congress, attendees were introduced to countless new smartphones and applications. Manufacturers such as HTC, Samsung, and Google's Android used Facebook, Foursquare, and Twitter as the means for introducing their products, making it clear that there is a change in the way people are interacting.[28] Among the many lessons for small business owners is that they cannot absolutely control how

LIVING THE DREAM

entrepreneurship + integrity

Experiential Marketing

© iStockphoto.com/Angelika Schwarz

Jack Abraham was 12 years old when he began building some of the first data extraction and processing mechanisms that would help comScore, co-founded by his father, Magid Abraham, rapidly grow from 3 to 40 employees. He saw something at comScore that eventually sparked the idea that led to his own company, Milo.com. "We had data that showed people were using the Internet to research products, but buying them more often offline than online," he says. "Everyone was innovating in social media, but no one was doing anything in shopping. Amazon and eBay are Web 1.0."

Milo.com

Abraham recognized an opportunity that others were missing. In 2009 he launched Milo.com to make local shopping easier. Milo helps shoppers find the products they are looking for by giving them both the real-time local availability of the item and the current price at a brick-and-mortar store near them. It also provides local retailers immediate exposure to customers who want to buy a specific item. Milo started out by working with many national retailers, but quickly found that independent retailers could also benefit from this targeted promotion method.

By the fall of 2010, Milo.com was being visited by about a million people per month. That attracted the attention of more than shoppers and retailers. In December of 2010, eBay announced the acquisition of Milo.com. For eBay, this purchase expanded their ability to serve shoppers who were looking to buy an item either online or offline at a local store.

Abraham and his team stayed on to run Milo, which would become the local division at eBay. They immediately began to introduce features to make it easier for small- and medium-sized retailers to upload their inventory information and for shoppers to compare offers from neighboring stores. They also began integrating their local data into eBay's mobile applications in an effort to reach shoppers wherever they may be.

Sources: http://milo.com/, accessed April 2, 2011; Kara Ohngren, "E-Commerce in Reverse," *Entrepreneur*, Vol. 38, No. 11 (November 2010), p. 66; and Donna Fenn, "30 Under 30: Jack Abraham, Founder of Milo.com," http://www.inc.com/30under30/2010/profile-jack-abraham-milo.html, accessed April 2, 2011. **http://milo.com**

their businesses are viewed by consumers. Customers may well be members of communities that are sharing real-time information about the products and services being offered. Entrepreneurs may find that they need to rely on qualified experts to guide them through the social media maze, just as many expect accountants to coach them through their financial statements. Stay tuned for rapid changes in these technologies.

Sales Promotional Tools

A more traditional marketing practice, which is nevertheless used on websites and mobile devices, is sales promotion. Generally, **sales promotion** includes any promotional technique, other than personal selling or advertising, that stimulates the purchase of a particular product or service. It typically offers a direct incentive to a purchaser to act by offering value above and beyond what the product provides at its normal price.[29]

sales promotion An inclusive term for any promotional technique, other than personal selling and advertising, that stimulates the purchase of a particular product or service.

Sales promotion should not be the only promotional effort of a small business. For best results, it typically is used in combination with personal selling and advertising. Popular sales promotional tools include specialties, contests, premiums, trade show exhibits, point-of-purchase displays, free merchandise, publicity, sampling, and coupons. Social media companies enable small firms to compete head-on with their large competitors in cost-efficient ways through sales promotion. Many companies make use of Foursquare, one of the social platforms highlighted at the Mobile World Congress, which enables businesses to introduce online loyalty programs. For example, the Nightingale Theater in Tulsa, Oklahoma, gives free popcorn and a beer on a customer's fifth check-in; Xoom in New York City offers a free smoothie to those who buy one and check-in with a friend.[30]

We briefly examine three of the most widely used promotional tools: specialties, trade show exhibits, and publicity.

SPECIALTIES

The most widely used specialty item is a calendar. Other popular specialty items are pens, key chains, coffee mugs, and shirts. Almost anything can be used as a specialty promotion, as long as each item is imprinted with the firm's name or other identifying slogan.

The distinguishing characteristics of specialties are their enduring nature and tangible value. Specialties are referred to as the "lasting medium." As functional products, they are worth something to recipients. Specialties can be used to promote a product directly or to create goodwill for a firm; they are excellent reminders of a firm's existence.

Finally, specialties are personal. They are distributed directly to the customer in a personal way, they can be used personally, and they have a personal message. A small business needs to retain its unique image, and entrepreneurs often use specialties to achieve this objective. More information on specialties is available on the website of Promotional Products Association International at http://www.ppa.org.

TRADE SHOW EXHIBITS

Advertising often cannot substitute for trial experiences with a product, and a customer's place of business is not always the best environment for product demonstrations. Trade show exhibits allow potential customers to get hands-on experience with a product.

Trade show exhibits are of particular value to manufacturers. The greatest benefit of these exhibits is the potential cost savings over personal selling. Trade show groups claim that the cost of an exhibit is less than one-fourth the cost of sales calls, and many small manufacturers agree that exhibits are more cost-effective than advertising. One website devoted to marketing tactics lists the following helpful tips regarding trade shows:[31]

- **Check out the trade show's history.** Does the show regularly attract large crowds? Will the show be adequately promoted to your potential customers?
- **Prepare a professional-looking display.** You do not need to have the biggest, flashiest booth on the trade show floor to attract attendees. But signs, photographs of your products, and other business-related elements used in the display should appear to be professionally prepared.
- **Have a sufficient quantity of literature on hand.** Have plenty of professionally prepared brochures or other handouts to distribute, and have them prepared well in advance of the show.
- **Make sure you have a good product.** If your product doesn't work or doesn't work properly, you'll lose more customers than you'll ever gain.

- **Do pre-show promotion.** To get the most traffic at your booth, send out mailings prior to the show, inviting your customers and prospects to stop by your booth. Insert announcements in bills you send out, on your Web page, and in ads you run near the show date.
- **Have a giveaway or gimmick.** The giveaway or gimmick doesn't have to be big or elaborate. Samples of your product given away at intervals during the show are ideal. Novelty items such as key chains, pencils, and pads of paper with your company name and product name are good, too.
- **Train booth personnel.** Choose your booth staff carefully, and be sure they know how to deal with the public, especially prospective customers.
- **Follow up.** Have a plan in place for following up on leads as soon as you get home from the show.

One group of independent designers in the Seattle, Washington, area found a way to hold down the costs of displaying at trade shows. They formed a collective called Join Design, which shows their work twice a year at the New York International Gift Fair. The designers like the quality of life and lower living costs in the Pacific Northwest, but want access to the larger markets that the trade show provides. Although the individual designers treasure their independence, they bring their diverse products together in attractive and creative ways that appeal to potential purchasers at the trade shows.[32]

PUBLICITY

publicity Information about a firm and its products or services that appears as a news item, usually free of charge.

Of particular importance to small firms is **publicity**, which provides visibility for a business at little or no cost. Publicity can be used to promote both a product and a firm's image; it is a vital part of public relations for the small business. A good publicity program requires regular contacts with the news media.

Although publicity is not always free, the return on a relatively small investment can be substantial. HubSpot (see In the Spotlight for this chapter) helps other companies attract customers with inbound marketing strategies rather than spending money on outbound promotion. And HubSpot follows its own teaching. In addition to channeling prospects to its website through search engine positioning and free services, it has relied on publicity. HubSpot's press releases and novel approach to doing business caught the attention of print and broadcast media. The founders were interviewed on public radio and MSNBC. When any members of the management team were invited to speak, an announcement was sent out and news media reported on it. The exposure helped build HubSpot's credibility and business.[33]

Other examples of publicity efforts that entail some expense include underwriting school yearbooks and sponsoring youth athletic programs. While the benefits are difficult to measure, publicity is nevertheless important to a small business and should be used at every opportunity.

A high-tech spin on publicity can be found in the phenomenon of social shopping websites. A social shopping website results from the merging of a search engine, such as Google, with a social networking element, such as Twitter. Although the power of Google can't be contested, it can't tell shoppers what's cool or what their friends or other consumers recommend. But social shopping websites like StyleFeeder, Kaboodle, and ThisNext do just that. A typical online search yields the most prominent brands and retailers on the first few pages of the search engine. A similar search on a social shopping site displays a wider array of smaller and arguably "cooler" brands. It also includes the recommendations of the site's most fashion-conscious and influential users. Marketing on such sites must be done carefully, as they are geared toward consumers. A forward-thinking entrepreneur, however, can post his or her own favorite products on such sites and potentially influence other users' buying decisions.

WHEN TO USE SALES PROMOTION

A small firm can use sales promotion to accomplish various objectives. For example, small manufacturers can use it to stimulate channel members—retailers and wholesalers—to market their product. Wholesalers can use sales promotion to induce retailers to buy inventory earlier than they normally would, and retailers, with similar promotional tools, may be able to persuade customers to make a purchase.

Husband-and-wife team, Robert Fishbone and Sarah Linquist, were artists not businesspeople. But when an exhibit of the work of Swedish artist Edvard Munch was coming to town (Munch's best-known work is called "The Scream"), Fishbone decided to design and produce inflatable "Screams". The product got photographed and written up in local newspapers, and eventually the *New York Times* published a story. Fishbone sent free inflatables to news and entertainment venues, where people were excited to see the product and wanted to tell others. Fishbone continues to promote creative ideas, using publicity as a key component of his marketing strategy.[34]

At its core, successful promotion is all about effective communication. The source (a small business) must have a message that intended recipients (in the target market) receive or find, understand, and act on. But this is no simple exercise. Many decisions must be made along the way—decisions regarding the size of the promotional budget, the promotional mix, the nature and placement of advertising, the identification of high-potential prospects, participation in trade shows, . . . and the list goes on. Most entrepreneurs make promotional errors along the way—but practice makes perfect. Learn from your mistakes, and move on. Don't give up. Success awaits you!

1. Describe the communication process and the factors determining a promotional mix.

- Every communication involves a source, a message, a channel, and a receiver.
- A promotional mix is a blend of nonpersonal, personal, and special forms of communication aimed at a target market.
- A promotional mix is influenced primarily by three important factors: the geographical nature of the market, the size of the promotional budget, and the product's characteristics.

2. Explain methods of determining the appropriate level of promotional expenditures.

- Earmarking promotional dollars based on a percentage of sales is a simple method for determining expenditures.
- Spending only what can be spared is a widely used approach to promotional budgeting.
- Spending as much as the competition does is a way to react to short-run promotional tactics of competitors.
- The preferred approach to determining promotional expenditures is to decide what it will take to do the job, while factoring in elements used in the other methods.

3. Describe personal selling activities.

- Effective selling is based on a salesperson's knowledge of the product or service.
- A sales presentation is a process involving prospecting, practicing the presentation, and then making the presentation.
- Prospecting is the systematic process of continually looking for new customers.
- An entrepreneur is first and foremost a salesperson for the enterprise.
- Salespeople are compensated for their efforts in two ways—financially and nonfinancially.
- The two basic plans for financial compensation are commissions and straight salary, but the most attractive plan for a small firm combines the two.

4. **Identify advertising options for a small business.**
   - Common advertising media include television, radio, magazines, newspapers, billboards, and the Internet.
   - Product advertising is designed to promote a product or service, while institutional advertising conveys information about the business itself.
   - Sources for assistance with advertising include advertising agencies, suppliers, trade associations, and advertising media.
   - A small firm must decide how often and where to advertise.
   - Web advertising generally takes the form of a company website, banner ads and pop-ups, e-mail campaigns, reciprocal advertising and hyperlinks, and blogs.
   - Mobile devices, which allow people to access information from wherever they are, provide new advertising opportunities for small businesses through apps and social media.

5. **Discuss the use of sales promotional tools.**
   - Sales promotion includes any promotional technique, other than personal selling and advertising, that stimulates the purchase of a particular product or service.
   - Typically, sales promotional tools are used in combination with advertising and personal selling.
   - Three widely used sales promotional tools are specialties, trade show exhibits, and publicity.

Key Terms

promotion p. 497
promotional mix p. 499
personal selling p. 501
prospecting p. 502
advertising p. 505
product advertising p. 506
institutional advertising p. 506
banner ads p. 511
pop-up ads p. 511
e-mail promotion p. 511
hyperlink p. 511
blog p. 512
mobile device p. 512
app p.512
Web 2.0 p. 513
social media p. 513
social networking p. 513
sales promotion p. 515
publicity p. 516

Discussion Questions

1. Describe the parallel relationship that exists between a small business communication and a personal communication.
2. Discuss the advantages and disadvantages of each approach to budgeting funds for promotion.
3. Outline a system of prospecting that could be used by a small camera store. Incorporate all the techniques presented in this chapter.
4. Why are a salesperson's techniques for handling objections so important to a successful sales presentation?
5. Assume you have the opportunity to "sell" your course instructor on the idea of eliminating final examinations. Make a list of the objections you expect to hear from your instructor, and describe how you will handle each objection using some of the techniques listed on page 503–504.
6. What are some nonfinancial rewards that could be offered to salespeople?
7. What are the advantages and disadvantages of compensating salespeople by salary? By commissions? What do you think is an acceptable compromise?
8. What are some approaches to advertising on the Web?
9. Discuss some recommendations for designing an effective website.
10. How do specialties differ from trade show exhibits and publicity? Be specific.

You Make the Call

SITUATION 1

How do you get retailers to stock your product when their shelves are already full? For Brian Levin, founder of Perky Jerky, it meant talking store managers into letting him give his product away. Perky Jerky is a meat snack with a caffeine kick, described on the company's website as "the new high-protein, ultra-premium, functional food for active lifestyles. . . ." Perky Jerky "brand ambassadors" give out trinkets and offer customers tastes of the product in stores. They find that those who try the snack ask the stores to carry Perky Jerky. One year into the business, Levin reported nearly a million dollars in sales.

Sources: http://www.perkyjerky.com/index.php/, accessed April 4, 2011; and Jason Fell, "Building a (Nearly) Million-Dollar Brand on a Startup Budget," http://www.entrepreneur.com/article/219395#, accessed April 4, 2011.

Question 1 What do you think about giving away a product? Does it build sales, or does it suggest desperation?
Question 2 How would you budget for marketing expenses if you had hired sales representatives to give products away?
Question 3 What are some of the ways you might compensate your "brand ambassadors"? Which method do you think would work best and why?

SITUATION 2

Cheree Moore owns and operates a small business that supplies delicatessens with bulk containers of ready-made salads. When served in salad bars, the salads appear to have been freshly prepared from scratch at the delicatessen. Moore wants additional promotional exposure for her products and is considering using her fleet of trucks as rolling billboards. If the strategy is successful, she may even attempt to lease space on other trucks. Moore is concerned about the cost effectiveness of the idea and whether the public will even notice the advertisements. She also wonders whether the image of her salad products might be hurt by this advertising medium.

Question 1 What suggestions can you offer that would help Moore make this decision?
Question 2 How could Moore go about determining the cost effectiveness of this strategy?
Question 3 What additional factors should Moore evaluate before advertising on trucks?

SITUATION 3

The founder of Panchero's Mexican Grill, Rodney Anderson, felt the company ought to be involved in social networking, but he and his management team weren't sure how to do it. Along came 22-year-old Joel Johnson, who was looking for a job and very comfortable with social media. Now an employee of Panchero's, Johnson spends most of his day on Twitter, Facebook, and other networking sites. He visits chat rooms regularly, looking for people who are talking about burritos or where they might go to eat. He then recommends Panchero's. Johnson also works with Panchero's franchisees, teaching them how to get visitors to their websites to become in-restaurant guests who then post comments about their experiences. From watching Johnson at work, Anderson has learned that social networking is not something you can push. He says, "You have to let it have a life of its own."

Sources: Nancy Weingartner, "Citizen Marketing: Playing Catch-up with Technology Advances," *Franchise Times*, April 2009, pp. 61–62; and http://www.pancheros.com, accessed April 1, 2009.

Question 1 There is more than a 10-year age difference between members of Panchero's top management team and Joel Johnson. Do you think that difference has contributed to Johnson's effectiveness in social networking? Why or why not?
Question 2 Is it ethical for Johnson to be recommending the restaurant chain where he works? Why or why not?
Question 3 Have you ever posted any comments on a website about a business that you have visited? Do you check for customer comments before you shop at a particular business?

Experiential Exercises

1. Interview the owners of one or more small businesses to determine how they develop their promotional budget. Classify the owners' methods as one or more of the four approaches described in this chapter. Report your findings to the class.
2. Plan a sales presentation. With a classmate role-playing a potential buyer, make the presentation in class. Ask the other students to critique your technique.
3. Evaluate the promotional effectiveness of a small business website.
4. Interview a media representative about advertising options for small businesses. Summarize your findings for the class.

Small Business & Entrepreneurship Resource Center

1. Shoebuy.com began its Web-based sales operation with the concept of free shipping in mind. Studies show that offering free shipping encourages customers to fill their shopping carts more than they would otherwise. Describe how Shoebuy.com is able to provide cost-effective free shipping. Also discuss when a company should not offer free shipping.

   Source: Melissa Campanelli, "Shipping Out: If You Can Afford to Join the Fray, Offering Online Customers Free Shipping May Help You Compete, *Entrepreneur*, Vol. 31, No. 6 (June 2003), pp. 42–43.

2. The Bear Naked line of granola and breakfast products is heavily promoted through the use of in-store free samples. This strategy has worked well for the company and helped it to secure its first major store accounts. However, sampling is not always an appropriate strategy. Describe when sampling may not be effective. Then discuss how a company can make sampling more effective.

   Source: Kent Steinriede, "Get Out, Hand Out: In-Store Sampling Attracts New Consumers," *New Products Magazine*, Vol. 7, No. 5 (May 2007), pp. 32–33.

Video Case 17

HUBSPOT, INC. (P. 727)

HubSpot is an Internet marketing company that caters to small businesses. It used to be that the size of your firm's sales force was the key to finding the most new customers, but that is not necessarily always the case today, thanks to the Internet.

ALTERNATIVE CASES FOR CHAPTER 17

Case 1, Nau, p. 693
Video Case 14, Numi Tea, p. 721

CHAPTER 18

Global Opportunities for Small Business

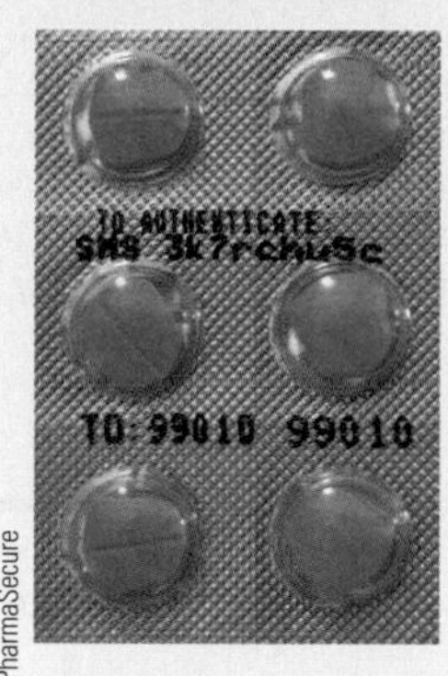

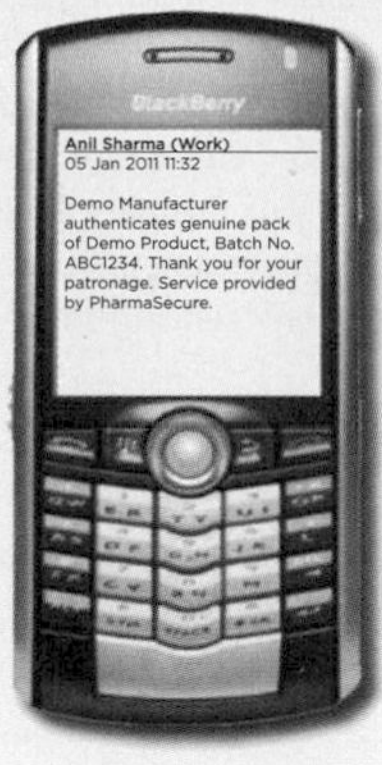

PharmaSecure

In the SPOTLIGHT
PharmaSecure, Inc.
http://www.pharmasecure.com

Some small businesses are launched domestically with international ambitions in mind. Still others simply make no sense apart from plans to go global.

In 2007, Nathan Sigworth and Taylor Thompson were students at Dartmouth College. While working on a public health research project focused on India and East Africa, they recognized a problem in developing countries with life-and-death consequences: People are being scammed into purchasing counterfeit drugs. Patients who take these drugs for serious health problems receive no benefit—or worse, illegitimate medications sometimes contain harmful chemicals or contaminated fillers that can threaten their lives. There are a number of sophisticated counterfeit-detecting technologies on the market, but most are ill-suited to emerging markets. So, Sigworth and Thompson decided to develop a system of their own. To gear up for this challenge, they formed a new company called PharmaSecure in Lebanon, New Hampshire.

Rather than leaning on the expensive pharmaceutical tracking systems used in most highly developed countries, Sigworth and Thompson came up with a low-cost approach that is practical in poorer nations. PharmaSecure's system is quite simple: By combining apps and databases, the company's easy-to-use process allows customers to use text messaging to determine whether a code printed on packages of pharmaceuticals is legitimate. This is much more appropriate for the income levels and infrastructure conditions in most developing nations.

LOOKING AHEAD

After studying this chapter, you should be able to . . .

1. Describe the potential of small firms as global enterprises.
2. Identify the basic forces prompting small firms to engage in global expansion.
3. Understand and compare strategy options for global businesses.
4. Explain the challenges that global enterprises face.
5. Recognize the sources of assistance available to support international business efforts.

© iStockphoto.com/Dan Bachman

The pair spent a year traveling the world to identify the best place to try the new system out. Because India is a primary pharmaceutical producer for the developing world, they concluded that it was the best place to get started. In 2010, they launched the pilot of their Unique Identification Mobile Verification System with a high-quality manufacturer there and continue to roll out the system nationwide. By the start of 2011, most of the company's 15 employees were working out of New Delhi to support the expansion of its India-focused operations.

The challenges of doing business abroad are substantial, to be sure, but an expanding array of tools and sources of assistance make this form of growth manageable for small companies like PharmaSecure. Technologies such as file sharing and video conferencing (along with many others) can be used to connect with employees around the globe and coordinate international operations. "We use Skype a lot," Sigworth reports, and then adds, "We use e-mail a ton."

These tools are not exactly new, but they have become more powerful over time, even while their cost has fallen sharply. This leaves an increasing number of small companies—even recent startups—in a robust position to make the most of these new technologies and to take part in the global business adventure. And an increasing number of small businesses are choosing to do exactly that.

Sources: Justin Lahart, "For Small Businesses, the Big World Beckons," *Wall Street Journal*, January 27, 2011, pp. B1, B4; "PharmaSecure—About Us," http://www.pharmasecure.com/about-us, accessed February 8, 2011; and Donna Fuscaldo, "Video Conferencing Set-Ups Your Business Can Afford," Fox Business Small Business Center, January 27, 2010, http://smallbusiness.foxbusiness.com/technology/2010/01/27/video-conferencing-small-businesses, accessed February 11, 2011.

---

globalization The expansion of international business, encouraged by converging market preferences, falling trade barriers, and the integration of national economies.

There was a time when national economies were isolated by trade and investment barriers, differences in language and culture, distinctive business practices, and various government regulations. However, these dissimilarities are fading over time as market preferences converge, trade barriers fall, and national economies integrate to form a global economic system. This process is the essence of **globalization**. Though the trend toward convergence has been developing for some time, the pace seems to be quickening, creating global opportunities and competition that did not exist even a few years ago. And with the astounding rate of economic growth in countries such as China and India, a small business owner would be unwise to ignore overseas opportunities.

Becoming a global entrepreneur may seem beyond your reach; after all, the world is a very big place! As you read in the pages that follow about the challenges of international business and the many decisions that are involved in expanding abroad, you may become even more convinced that this option is not for you. This is a normal reaction. But the opportunities are tremendously rewarding, and available resources can help you overcome any obstacles that may stand in your way. In the last part of the chapter, you will read about numerous forms of assistance that can help you achieve your global ambitions. As you will see, many small businesses like PharmaSecure, the startup profiled at the beginning of this chapter, have already shown that it can be done. You can do it, too!

Small Businesses as Global Enterprises

1
Describe the potential of small firms as global enterprises.

The potential of a global business is clear, but does that potential extend to small companies?[1] Research has shown that recent startups and even the smallest of businesses continue to expand overseas, despite the recent global economic slowdown.[2] In fact, many small companies are being launched with cross-border business activities in mind.[3] The arrangements in these companies, often called **born-global firms**,[4] can get more than a little crazy. You are probably familiar with a company called Skype, which was acquired by Microsoft in 2011. Here is its born-global startup story:

born-global firms Small companies launched with cross-border business activities in mind.

> *[Niklas] Zennstrom, who is Swedish, and his partner Janus Friis, a Dane, launched their Internet telephony company Skype in Luxembourg, with sales offices in London. But they outsourced product development to Estonia, the same fertile womb that had earlier gestated their music-sharing system, Kazaa.*[5]

You may be thinking, "That's fine in this case—Skype is a big company." That's true today, but in 2003 the company was just a startup, and it was clearly an international business right from the beginning. Many new ventures, as well as established small businesses, are being swept up in the wave of globalization.

As global communication systems become more efficient and trade agreements pry open national markets to foreign competition, entrepreneurs are focusing more and more on international opportunities. Networking options are expanding through various forms of creative partnerships, allowing small firms to find new ways to enter the global economy and to grow internationally. Entrepreneurs may decide to go global to expand their opportunities, or they may be forced to enter foreign markets in order to compete with firms in their industry that have already done so. There is no doubt that these developments, and so many others, help to explain how companies have been able to accelerate the pace of their international involvement.[6] But the research is clear: Size does not necessarily limit a firm's international activity—small companies can build upon their unique resources to become global competitors.[7]

In some cases, the global option is practically unavoidable. For example, when Howard Pedolsky, a Bethesda, Maryland–based entrepreneur, began to market his innovative, eco-friendly refrigeration technology a few years back, he found that European supermarkets were far more interested in it than were their American counterparts. It turned out that their attraction was the result of the strict standards of European regulators, so Pedolsky realized that he would need to focus on

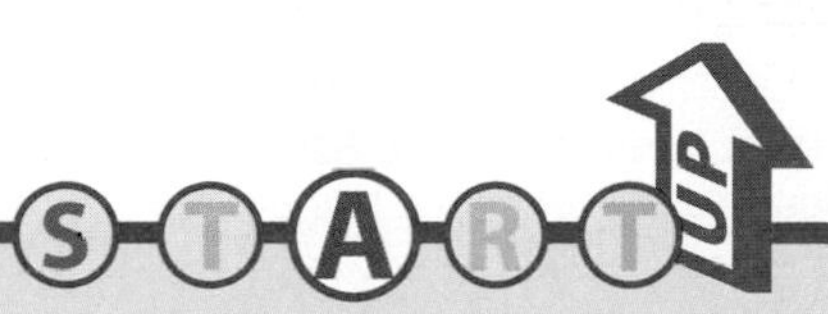

ACTION

Multiple Markets

Going global can really help you grow your business. Just be sure you understand the often-complicated forms, trade laws, and payment issues that are involved (the SBA's U.S. Export Assistance Centers at http://www.sba.gov/content/us-export-assistance-centers can help). If you hope to reach international markets online, develop a robust, multilingual Internet presence to find customers abroad, and use sites such as BuyUSA.gov and USTDA.gov to aid in your search for customers and suppliers. And don't forget organizations such as Gala Global (http://gala-global.org), which help businesses localize their products and websites and include translation services for online content.

developing a customer base in Europe first. "Our first customer ended up being a French company," he says. "The European environment was just much stronger in our direction, and [supermarkets there] tend to spend more money on our products."[8]

But motivations for global startup vary. Joseph Blumenfeld founded the global public relations firm Tradewind Strategies because of his vast experience in corporate marketing overseas. "And that's really where the market is," says the Natick, Massachusetts–based entrepreneur, "because there's so much competition in the United States."[9] As a signal of the importance of international markets to this company, it maintains offices in both the United States and Beijing, China.[10]

The fact that many firms are going global does not mean that it is easy for small companies; the challenges that small businesses face in the international marketplace are considerable. First, a small business owner must decide whether the company is up to the task. To help entrepreneurs assess the impact of going global on their small business, the U.S. Department of Commerce publishes *A Basic Guide to Exporting*. This handbook outlines important questions entrepreneurs should consider when assessing their readiness for the challenges of global business (see Exhibit 18.1).

Once small business owners decide to expand internationally, they should study the social, technological, economic, and political forces in foreign markets to figure out how best to adapt their business practices as well as their product or service to local circumstances, and make other adjustments that are necessary to ensure smooth market

EXHIBIT 18.1 Questions to Consider Before Going Global

Management Objectives	• What are the company's reasons for going global? • How committed is top management to going global? • How quickly does management expect its international operations to pay off?
Management Experience and Resources	• What in-house international expertise does the firm have (international sales experience, language skills, etc.)? • Who will be responsible for the company's international operations? • How much senior management time should be allocated to the company's global efforts? • What organizational structure is required to ensure success abroad?
Production Capacity	• How is the present capacity being used? • Will international sales hurt domestic sales? • What will be the cost of additional production at home and abroad? • What product designs and packaging options are required for international markets?
Financial Capacity	• How much capital can be committed to international production and marketing? • How are the initial expenses of going global to be covered? • What other financial demands might compete with plans to internationalize? • By what date must the global effort pay for itself?

Source: Adapted from International Trade Administration, *A Basic Guide to Exporting: The Official Government Resource for Small- and Medium-Sized Businesses*, as cited in John B. Cullen and K. Praveen Parboteeah, *Multinational Management: A Strategic Approach*, 5th ed. (Cincinnati, OH: South-Western Cengage Learning, 2011), p. 256.

entry. For example, doing business in the Middle East can require significant changes in what many small business owners would consider to be "standard business procedures."

> *In Saudi Arabia, the workweek begins on Saturday and ends on Wednesday, appointments are generally scheduled around five daily prayer times, and many businesses are closed in the afternoon. Most real business is conducted face to face, with far less reliance on documents and contracts than is typical in the Western world; therefore, the time it takes to do business is relative.*[11]

And that's just the beginning! When you add to this the fact that collecting or paying interest is forbidden in Islamic states—along with a host of other fundamental differences—it becomes clear that navigating the unique hurdles of an international market like Saudi Arabia can be a serious challenge.

The Forces Driving Global Businesses

2 Identify the basic forces prompting small firms to engage in global expansion.

Given the difficulty of international business, why would any entrepreneur want to get involved? Among the reasons small firms have for going global are some that have motivated international trade for centuries. In 1271, Marco Polo traveled to China to explore the trading of Western goods for exotic Oriental silks and spices, which would then be sold in Europe. Clearly, the motivation to take domestic products to foreign markets and bring foreign products to domestic markets is as relevant today as it was in Marco Polo's day. Consider, for example, the clothing designer who sells Western wear in Tokyo or the independent rug dealer who scours the markets of Turkey to locate low-cost sources of high-quality products.

Complementing these traditional reasons for going global are motivations that epitomize the core of entrepreneurial drive. A writer for *Inc.* magazine describes the impulse to go global as follows:

> ***Because it's what entrepreneurs do.*** *To wax deductive: Globalization is risky. Entrepreneurs embrace risk. Therefore entrepreneurs embrace globalization. Of course there's risk and then there's risk, with the latter including such potential spoilers as an unfamiliar language, an alien business landscape, and political volatility. Still, the chance to try new things in new places is like a jumper cable to the entrepreneurial engine. [Small business owners] describe running their international efforts as the most exciting aspect of doing business, not just for themselves but for their employees as well.*[12]

© iStockphoto.com/Christian Baitg

In other words, many entrepreneurs are looking to do more than simply expand a profitable market when they get involved in international business. And they also recognize that their enterprises are no longer insulated from global challengers; they must consider the dynamics of the new competitive environment.[13] In some cases, the rival on the other side of the street may be a minor threat compared to an online competitor on the other side of the globe!

One way to adjust to these emerging realities is through innovation. In many industries, innovation is essential to competitiveness; small businesses that invest heavily in research and development often can outperform their large competitors. But as R&D costs rise, they seldom can be recovered from domestic sales alone. Increasing sales in international markets may be the only viable way to recover a firm's invest-

EXHIBIT 18.2 Basic Forces Driving Global Enterprises

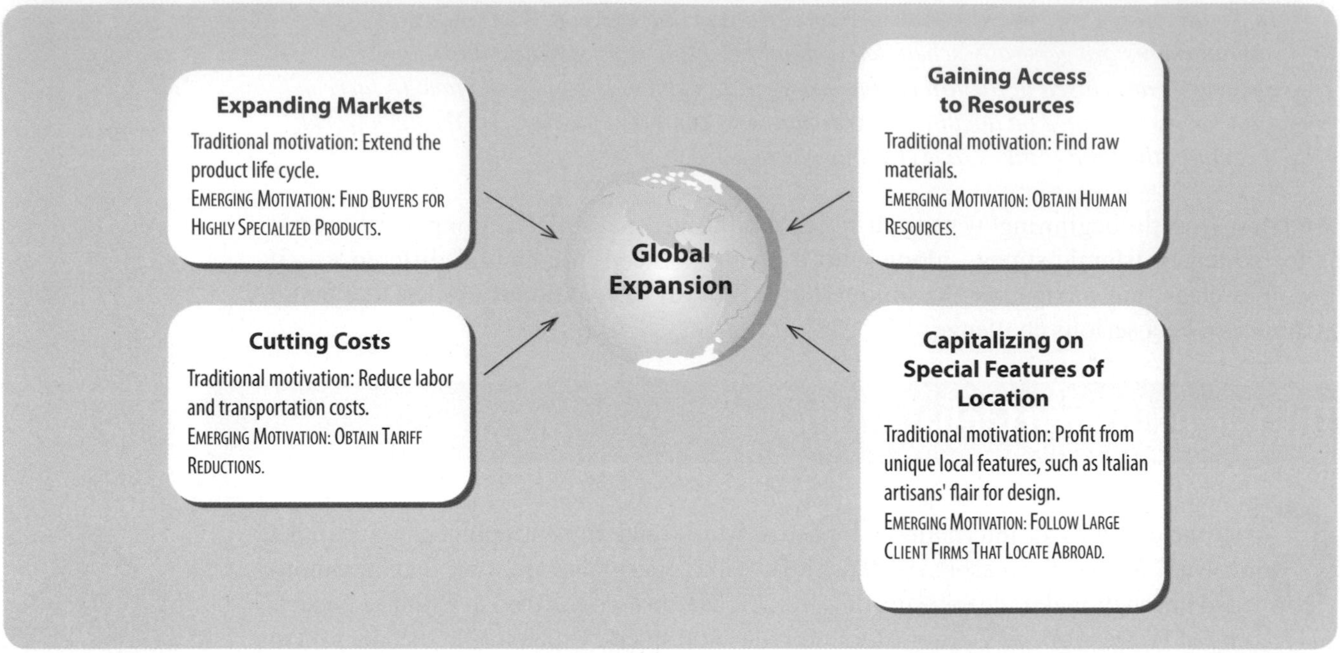

ment. In some cases, this may require identifying dynamic markets that are beginning to open around the world and then locating in or near those markets.[14]

The basic forces behind global expansion can be divided into four general categories: expanding markets, gaining access to resources, cutting costs, and capitalizing on special features of location (see Exhibit 18.2). Within each category fall some tried and true motivations, as well as some new angles that have emerged with the global economy. We discuss each of these four categories in the sections that follow.

EXPANDING MARKETS

More than 95 percent of the world's population lives outside the United States. It follows that globalization greatly increases the size of an American firm's potential market. One study of small companies found that their primary interest in internationalization was accessing new markets and growing their business, as opposed to seeking resources abroad, gaining access to technologies, avoiding regulatory pressures at home, etc.[15] This study focused on the expansion of U.S. firms into Europe; the primary motivation for involvement in other parts of the world may be different. For example, it could very well be that most U.S. small companies doing business in Asia are seeking access to low-cost component sources or to relocate business processes via outsourcing.

Countries Targeted

Because the primary motivation for going global is to develop market opportunities outside the home country, the focus of globalization strategies tends to be on those countries with the greatest commercial potential. In the past, these were the developed countries (those with high levels of widely distributed wealth). Today, companies are paying greater attention to emerging markets, where income and buying power are growing rapidly.

In 2001, the bank holding company Goldman Sachs came up with the term *BRICs* to refer to the fast-growing economies of Brazil, Russia, India, and China. Based on their rapid

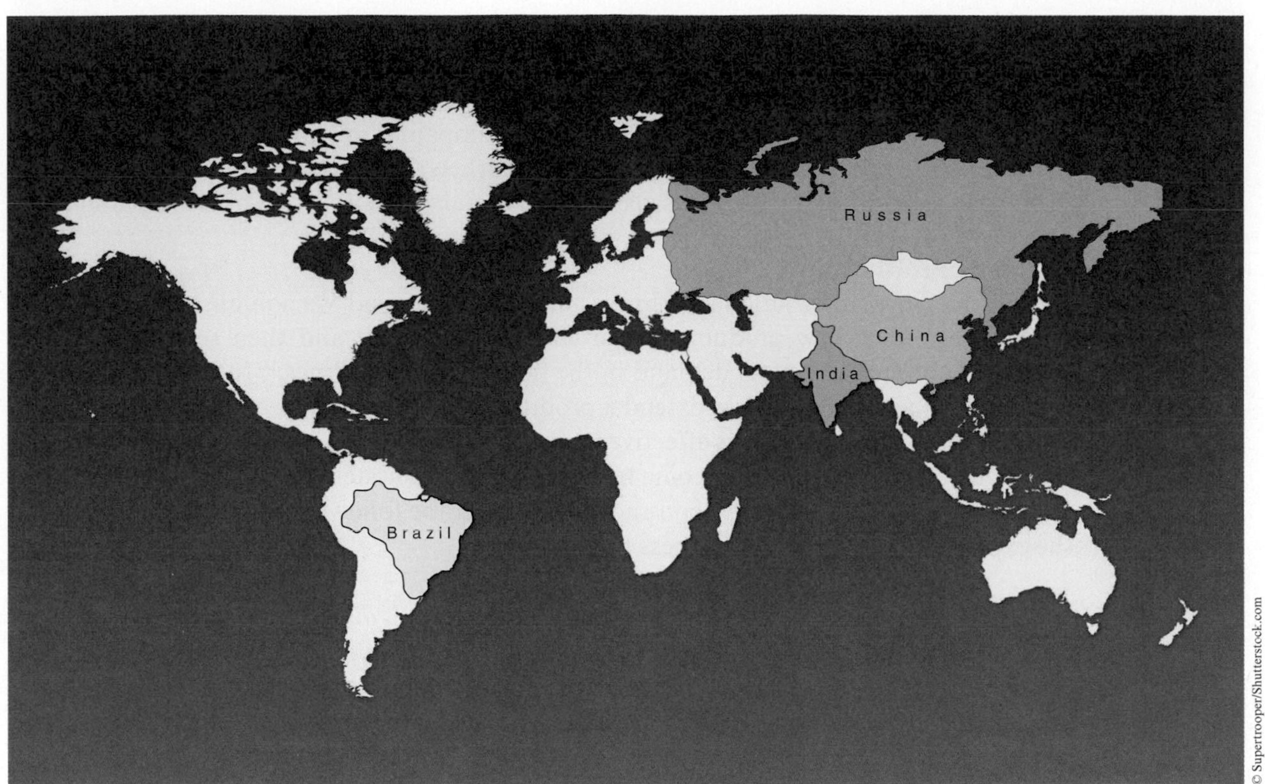

development, Goldman Sachs projects that by 2050 the BRIC economies, taken together, could very well eclipse the combined economies of what are currently the richest countries of the world.[16] While this vision may not roll out as predicted, the markets of the BRICs have definitely captured the attention of many entrepreneurs. And that interest seems to be growing, as mainstay markets like Europe, Japan, and the United States continue to struggle with economic stagnation while China and India, in particular, have already mounted impressive recoveries (see Exhibit 18.3). The smaller BRIC countries, Russia and Brazil, are also starting to rebound, but it is taking them longer to recover from the recent economic slowdown.

EXHIBIT 18.3 BRIC Markets

Country	2009 Population (in millions)	2009 Wealth (GNI per capita)*	2009 Economic Growth (GDP growth, %)**
Brazil	193.7	8,040	–0.2
China	1,331.5	3,650	9.1
India	1,115.4	1,180	7.7
Russia	141.9	9,340	–7.9
World	**6,775.2**	**8,728**	**–2.0**

*GNI = Gross National Income
**GDP = Gross Domestic Product

Source: From data provided by the World Bank Group, "WorlddataBank," http://databank.worldbank.org, accessed February 14, 2011.

Because of their immense populations and potential market demand, China and India have become the focus of many international firms. Combined, these two nations account for an astounding 40 percent of the world's six billion inhabitants, thus providing fertile ground for international expansion. And small companies are among the countless competitors battling for position in these emerging markets. That's why a small public relations firm like Tradewind Strategies (discussed earlier) maintains a second office in China.[17]

Products Promoted

In the mid-1960s, international business authority Raymond Vernon observed that firms tend to introduce new products in the United States first and then sell them in less-advanced countries later, as demand in the home market declines.[18] In other words, they use international expansion to extend a product's life cycle.

Although this approach is effective under some circumstances, it has become less viable as customer preferences, income levels, and delivery systems have become more similar and product life cycles have contracted. Consider the following observations, based on the experience of two small business practitioners:

> *The time lags between U.S. and foreign adoption have . . . disappeared. Today it is essential to roll out new products in several countries almost simultaneously. . . . No longer does the small company have the luxury of using cash flow from domestic sales to support the building of international marketing a few years later. The ever-shortening product cycle virtually dooms such a strategy. Terrific. Now, in addition to getting the product to work, setting up your new team, getting some U.S. customers, and finding money, you now have to worry about selling in six or eight additional countries, most of whom don't even speak English!*[19]

Products that sell at home are now more likely to be introduced very quickly abroad, with little or no adaptation in many cases. Television programs, movies, print media, and the Internet are shaping cultural tastes throughout the world, and this is facilitating the entry of small businesses into international markets. American interests have long held a starring role in the cultural arena, inspiring widespread purchases of products such as blue jeans and fast food and generating international interest in U.S. sports and celebrities. By informing consumers about the lifestyles of others, globalization is leading the world toward more common consumer preferences.

Also well suited to international markets is the highly specialized product. As technology makes possible increasingly sophisticated goods, markets are demanding more differentiated products to satisfy their unique needs and interests. Because so few customers in the home market will buy a highly specialized product (which is usually more expensive to create), makers of such products cannot be profitable unless they can also generate sales in markets abroad that have the same focused demand. Expanded sales allow these firms to recover the higher costs of product development. Many small companies follow focused business strategies, despite the limited domestic market potential. For them, exploiting the advantage of specialized products across several international markets may be even more important than for their large corporate counterparts.[20]

Making the Most of Experience

No matter which countries are targeted or products promoted, international expansion has the potential to provide benefits beyond the standard per-unit profits on additional items sold. As a venture expands and volume grows, it usually can find ways to work smarter or to generate efficiencies. Analysts first observed such **experience curve efficiencies** in the aircraft manufacturing industry. They noticed that each time a manufacturer doubled its total output, the production cost per aircraft dropped by 20 percent. In other words, per-unit costs declined by 20 percent when the firm manufactured four units instead of two, declined again by 20 percent when the firm made eight units instead of four, and so on.

experience curve efficiencies
Per-unit savings gained from the repeated production of the same product.

What can explain this gain in efficiency? Most credit the outcome to learning effects and economies of scale. **Learning effects** occur when the insight an employee gains from experience leads to improved work performance. Learning effects can also take place at the level of the firm if the experiences of individual employees are shared, leading to improved practices and production routines across the organization. These gains from learning are greatest during the startup period and gradually decline over time. Efficiencies from **economies of scale**, on the other hand, continue to rise as the business grows and volume increases, because these savings derive from spreading investment costs across more units of output and acquiring more specialized (and thus more efficient) plants, equipment, and employees.

learning effects
Insights, gained from experience, that lead to improved work performance.

economies of scale
Efficiencies that result from expansion of production.

Though these also apply to purely domestic enterprises, small firms can accelerate gains from experience curve efficiencies by emphasizing international expansion, assuming they can manage the growth. The benefits of learning effects and economies of scale are especially apparent in startups based on complex technologies. The possibility of achieving experience curve efficiencies through accelerated globalization of emerging technologies is likely to stimulate the interest of startups and small companies in international business.

GAINING ACCESS TO RESOURCES

Just as fortune seekers abandoned their comfortable lives in the eastern United States to flock to California following the discovery of gold at Sutter's Mill in 1848, small firms today leave the United States to gain access to essential raw materials and other factors of production. For example, the oil fields of Kuwait are tended not just by employees of the global oil giants, but also by hundreds of support personnel who work for small companies that have contracted to assist their large clients. These small players choose to locate operations in Kuwait (or Mexico, Nigeria, Saudi Arabia, etc.) for one simple reason: That's where the oil is! The same principle holds for manufacturers that require scarce inputs. For example, a number of aluminum producers have relocated to Iceland to tap the country's abundant and inexpensive hydroelectric and geothermal energy.[21]

Though small firms have traditionally pursued international ventures to obtain raw materials, increasingly the focus of their search is skilled labor.[22] For example, an increasing number of technology companies are relocating their operations in Russia to get access to the people they need. Despite the fact that installation of a telephone can take several months and crime bosses sometimes pay visits to demand protection money, firms are lured to Russia by its highly educated human capital, a necessary resource that is in short supply in the United States. Of the 43 percent of Russians with university degrees, about a third are trained in science- or technology-related disciplines and thus are very well-suited for highly skilled jobs. As something of a bonus for small firms, computer programmers and information technology professionals in Russia earn about 55 percent less than their American counterparts.[23]

There is no question that skilled labor around the world is within the reach of startups and other very small businesses. Consider Efrem Meretab, an Eritrean-born stock analyst who decided to start his own investment research venture in 2008. After two years in business, his Montclair, New Jersey–based company, MCAP Research LLC, still had not hired a single U.S. employee!

> *When Mr. Meretab needed software developers to help him create the company's core product, which can extract and display information from myriad earnings presentations in a matter of seconds, he turned to programmers he had consulted to solve problems in the past. He has hired developers in Belarus, Ukraine and Pakistan, all of whom tapped their own networks to complete the tasks he gave them at a fraction of the cost of U.S.-based developers.*

As Meretab asserts, "[MCAP] is a global company." Of course, startups like this don't do much for job creation in the United States, but they are still important new enterprises—and they are growing in number.[24]

Expanding markets and gaining access to resources are only part of the equation. Now, let's look more closely at cost-cutting efforts.

CUTTING COSTS

international outsourcing
A strategy that involves accessing foreign labor through contracts with independent providers.

offshoring
A strategy that involves relocating operations abroad.

Many firms go global to reduce the costs of doing business. Among the costs that firms have traditionally reduced by venturing abroad are those related to raw materials, labor, and manufacturing overhead.

While some startups are launching as global enterprises, other small businesses are shifting their operations over time to international markets in order to exploit the same advantages. In fact, American businesses of all sizes have been slashing costs by contracting with independent providers overseas (an arrangement called **international outsourcing**) or by relocating their stateside operations abroad (which is sometimes referred to as **offshoring**). These initiatives have been especially popular in countries such as India and China, where high-skilled labor can be accessed at relatively little cost.[25]

Some of the most creative examples of international outsourcing have been spawned by entrepreneurial companies. Dorothy Clay Sims is a Florida attorney who often has to cross-examine medical experts. But she is also the creator of MD in a Box, a startup that specializes in providing access to highly qualified doctors who can serve as expert witnesses in legal proceedings. The creative twist in Sims's venture is that her experts offer their insights by long distance—*from India*! Here's how it works: An attorney in the United States can depose the opposing counsel's medical expert while a doctor in India listens in via Skype. The Indian doctor sends instant messages with suggested responses for the attorney, who can then refute the doctor being cross-examined, using correct medical terms in the process. Such expert advice typically costs $500 to $1,000 per hour in the United States, but Sims has hired a stable of Indian medical experts who receive $20 to $35 an hour for their services. Indian doctors typically earn around $11,000 a year in their practices, so they are pleased with the extra income. MD in a Box charges $75 an hour ($200 per hour if the case is won), leaving Sims with a hefty profit.[26]

Ann Cutting/Photonica/Getty Images

The business concept developed by Sims may be far from ordinary, but in a way it fits the common outsourcing pattern precisely. Most entrepreneurs who choose to outsource internationally, or relocate offshore, are seeking two things that are always important to the success of small companies: access to talented employees and/or reduced costs. MD in a Box provides both.

The advantages of globalization in reducing labor costs have long been recognized. However, the emerging global economy has brought a new means of lowering costs through relocation. In recent years, a number of countries have formed regional free trade areas, within which commerce has been facilitated by reducing tariffs, simplifying commercial regulations, or even—in the case of the European Union—adopting a common currency. These cost-cutting measures can be a powerful inducement to small firms to move into the prescribed area. After the enactment of the North American Free Trade Agreement, for instance, a number of Japanese firms located manufacturing facilities in Mexico to gain the advantage of reduced tariffs on trade within that region.

CAPITALIZING ON SPECIAL FEATURES OF LOCATION

Some of the benefits of location are simply the result of unique features of a local environment. For example, Italian artisans have long been well known for their flair for design, and Japanese technicians have shown an ability to harness optical technologies for application in cameras, copiers, and other related products. Small companies that depend on a particular strength may find that it makes sense to locate in a region that provides fertile ground for that type of innovation.

In some cases, there is no way to be authentic apart from being local. Josh Pollock's only claim to insight into the food service industry used to be that he grew up eating Western food. So what's this 35-year-old American doing in China? He's started a restaurant, a business born of true opportunity. Pollock, along with his Japanese wife and two of their American friends, found that the Western food in China was absolutely dreadful, but locals were still eating it up. So, in 2004 the team cobbled together $40,000 in investment money and started a new company: Salvador's Food and Beverage Co., Ltd. This allowed them to open a coffee house in Kunming (a city of more than 4 million inhabitants) and offer Western products—including ice cream, bagels and cream cheese, and salsa—to local customers.[27]

The way forward has not always been easy, and the team has had much to learn. For example, early on they ran into a bureaucratic brick wall, which required the outsiders to turn to a practice that is common in China—building their *guanxi*, or personal connections, to get the government approvals they needed. Though still young, the enterprise has been wonderfully successful, which has led to yet another business opportunity: consulting with local or international companies that want to establish a successful enterprise in China. Here is Pollack's pitch:

> *Business in China is latent with unexpected obstacles. Let us help you avoid the labyrinth of government bureaucracy and help save you time and money. We guarantee we can successfully navigate the changing China business arena to accommodate your company or business needs.*[28]

For $125 an hour, the Salvador's team will show you the ropes of doing business in China, a service that is based on first-hand experience and legitimate only as a result of being in-country. Sometimes, the appeal of a location is a matter of cache or brand image. For example, while Chanel might like to manufacture its designer handbags in China to reduce costs, the company insists on producing them in Italy and France. These are both high-cost countries, but they have reputations that match Chanel's luxury image. These nations also have developed unique competencies, honed by hundreds of years of experience, that can accommodate the advanced designs and high quality that give the company its edge. Customers know that the high quality of the brand is scrupulously protected and thus are willing to pay a premium to buy Chanel's products, which covers the high manufacturing costs. But this is just one example. Other country settings provide their own location-specific strengths—including Colombia (high-quality coffee), Japan (anime-based video games), and Switzerland (precision watches)—and firms locate there to tap into those strengths.

Finally, a recent trend among small businesses is to follow large client firms to their new locations. As major corporations locate their operations abroad, their small suppliers find it necessary to go global with the client firms to ensure the continuation of important sourcing contracts. The small business owner may have no personal desire to expand internationally, but dependence on a major customer relocating abroad might leave the owner with no alternative. Researchers conducting a study of the international expansion of small businesses put it this way:

> *Our on-site interviews with small firm owners have [shown that following client firms] is a key issue that is overlooked by most research. Many firms end up overseas not because of some strategy or long-term plan. Instead, they are forced there to keep a business presence with a current client. In some cases, small firms have no choice in the matter. A larger firm determines to move to a particular overseas location and the smaller supplier is simply expected to follow.*[29]

So, some small companies moving into China are doing so with limited interest in the country's cheap labor and enormous market. Being there is necessary in order to provide corporate customers with ample delivery speed and efficiency.[30]

Traditional and emerging motivations for small businesses to go global are numerous, but the ultimate incentive is this: If you fail to seize an international market opportunity, someone else will. Under these conditions, the best defense is a good offense. Establishing a position outside of the domestic setting may preempt rivals from exploiting those opportunities and using them against you in the future.

Strategy Options for Global Firms

Once an entrepreneur has decided to go global, the next step is to plan a strategy that increases the potential of the firm. For most small businesses, the first step toward globalization is a decision to export a product to other countries or to import goods from abroad to sell in the market at home. These initial efforts are often followed by more sophisticated non-export strategies, such as licensing, franchising, forming strategic alliances with international partners, or even locating facilities abroad (see Exhibit 18.4). Each of these options is described further below.

EXPORTING

exporting
Selling products produced in the home country to customers in another country.

Exporting involves the sale of products produced in the home country to customers in another country. The U.S. Small Business Administration (SBA) recently announced that small firms represent more than 97 percent of American exporters, contributing just over 30 percent of the value of exported goods.[31] In some cases, this activity is a reflection of the reality of international competition. That is, some U.S. companies are steadily moving toward overseas markets because they recognize that foreign-owned companies are already competing against them in the United States. The SBA describes conditions in today's global marketplace as follows:

> *The division between domestic and international markets is becoming increasingly blurred. In a world of over 6 billion people, global communication networks, next-day airfreight deliveries worldwide and CNN, it no longer makes sense to limit your company's sales to the local or even to the national market. Your business cannot ignore these international realities if you intend to maintain your market share and keep pace with your competitors.*[32]

EXHIBIT 18.4 Strategy Options for Global Enterprises

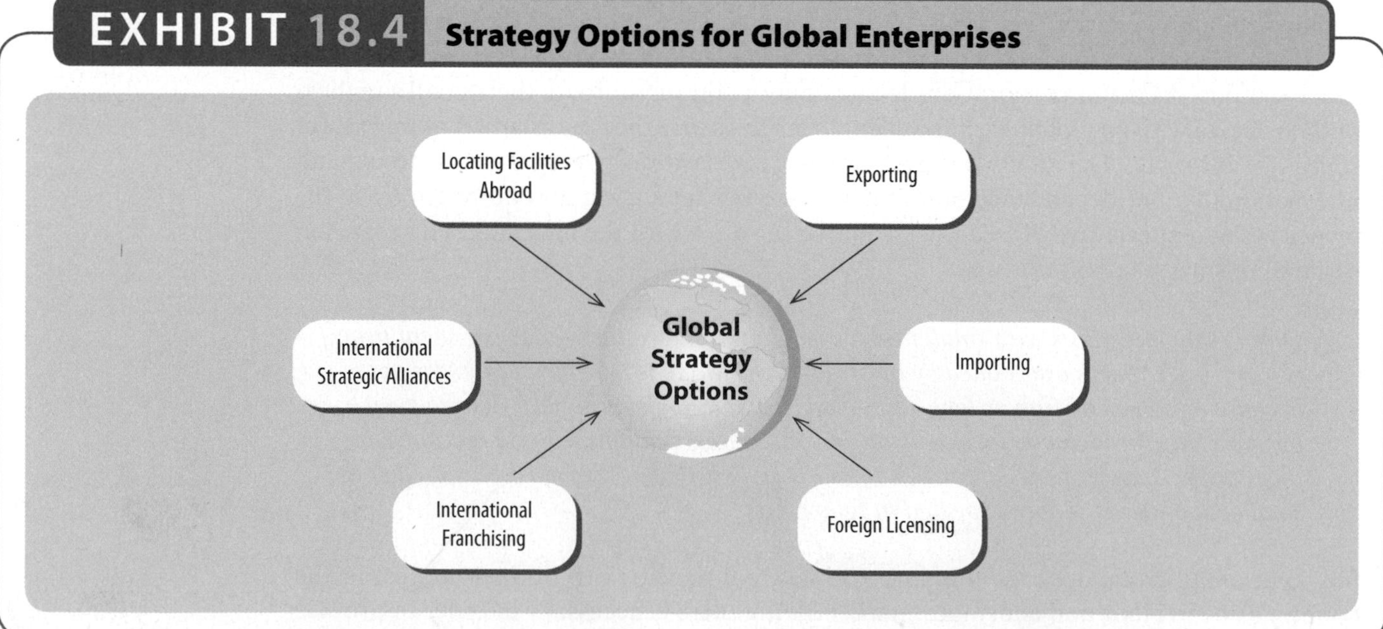

As the SBA statistics reveal, entrepreneurs are taking note and accepting the challenge. In fact, exporting is one of the most popular international strategies among small businesses because it provides a low-cost way to expand into the international arena. Taking this approach, small export companies can market and distribute their products in other countries without incurring the expense of supporting costly operations in those markets. If the financial benefits from international sales more than offset shipping costs and tariffs, exporting is a favorable option.

The Internet has fueled vigorous growth in export activity. Small firms now see the Web as a powerful tool for increasing their international visibility, allowing them to connect with customers who were previously beyond their reach. Entertainment Earth is an Internet retailer, based in Los Angeles, California, that specializes in action figures, gifts, and other collectibles. Aaron and Jason Labowitz and a friend started the company in 1995, operating out of a garage in the San Fernando Valley. It wasn't long before they decided to expand their reach by selling over the Internet.[33] They describe the design of their business as being "similar to the big-box warehouse store model coupled with the old fashion mail order business placed on

© iStockphoto.com/Angelika Schwarz

using technology

Online and in the Money

© Martin Smith/Shutterstock.com

According to Plunkett Research, the number of Internet users worldwide is poised to reach the 2 billion mark in the near future. Although 72 percent of U.S. adults surf the Net on a regular basis, steady growth is expected in the number of total users in Europe (currently at 50 percent) and Asia (now at only 17 percent). *Euromonitor International* projects that e-commerce worldwide will grow more than 90 percent by 2014, with eye-popping increases anticipated in regions like Russia/Eastern Europe (184 percent) and South America (204 percent). It's an Internet entrepreneur's dream!

But for any given venture, the road to success in global e-commerce is unlikely to follow a straight line. Consider the experience of online motorcycle parts and accessories retailer, MotoSport. This Portland, Oregon–based company's first international sale did not exactly go smoothly. It was an unsolicited order from Canada for $99 worth of merchandise, and MotoSport figured it was a no-brainer to fill it. It was wrong:

> *. . . After the delivery truck arrived at the customer's house, the driver immediately demanded $100 worth of unpaid Canadian taxes and tariffs. "It was more than what the guy paid for the item," says Jarrod Rogers, MotoSport's director of marketing operations. "Of course he didn't want it." It turned out that the item was subject to a particularly high tax, of which the company had been unaware.*

From this experience, the MotoSport team very quickly realized that they had a lot to learn about international e-commerce. Nonetheless, they could see the potential, and that led them to make some adjustments before refocusing their marketing efforts for good. After doing a bit of research, MotoSport learned that its products "were subject to an encyclopedia's worth of government fees and regulations, all of which varied depending on the type of the product, what country it was going to, and where it had been made." This was very discouraging. After all, the retailer sold more than 100,000 products at the time, and these were sourced from more than 400 suppliers around the globe.

MotoSport could easily have thrown in the towel, but the company decided to take a different approach. It signed on with an international shipping and logistics company called FiftyOne Global Ecommerce, which allows its client firms to conduct business with customers in more than 90 countries around the world. This relationship offered a huge lift to the retailer's global initiative. It cost MotoSport $20,000 to get set up, but that arrangement led to a number of powerful advantages and conveniences. For example, FiftyOne displays prices in each customer's local currency, and it automatically updates MotoSport's website to reflect the country-specific taxes and other costs that the customer will have to bear. And when an international order comes in, the parts shop ships the product to one of FiftyOne's warehouses in New Jersey or Ohio. Then, FiftyOne handles everything else, receiving a small percentage of each sale for its trouble. But adding these services has allowed MotoSport to focus on what it does best—finding the best motorcycle parts and accessories and marketing them to customers all over the globe. It seems to be the best of all worlds.

Sources: Ryan Underwood, "Clicks from Around the World," *Inc.*, Vol. 32, No. 10 (December 2010/January 2011), pp. 146–147; "FiftyOne Global Ecommerce," http://www.fiftyone.com/company, accessed February 8, 2011; Craig Reed, "Navigating the Turbulent Waters of International E-Commerce," *E-Commerce Times*, http://www.ecommercetimes.com/story/69927.html?wlc=1297215290, accessed February 8, 2011; and Plunkett Research, Ltd., "Introduction to the E-Commerce and Internet Business," http://www.plunkettresearch.com/Ecommerce%20Internet%20technology%20market%20research/industry%20overview, accessed February 10, 2010. **http://www.motosport.com, http://www.fiftyone.com**

a website."[34] To date, Entertainment Earth has sold collectibles to hundreds of thousands of clients all around the world. The firm clearly knows its globe-spanning market well.

You don't have to go it alone, as Entertainment Earth did. Just ask Jeff Nipert, owner of CarAlarmsEtc. He tries to give customers peace of mind where auto theft is concerned. His Bonney Lake, Washington, venture specializes in mobile electronics—specifically, car alarms, keyless entry units, remote starters, and other related accessories. Although Nipert's company is just a small operation, the world is his sales floor. How did he manage to go global? In a word, eBay. The online marketplace giant can help the tiniest of businesses connect with customers anywhere in the world, and getting started takes about as much time as it would to apply for a passport! And consider this: Of those who buy products on eBay, half live outside the United States—and that half of the business is growing twice as fast as the U.S. segment! Nipert concluded, "I felt if it wasn't costing me a dime extra for the [worldwide] exposure, I would be a fool not to take advantage of it."[35] To find out more about support services offered to eBay sellers, check out the firm's "Selling Internationally" tutorial.

Of course, exporting can be very challenging. Suddenly, you have to worry about communicating in a language other than English, translating payments into other currencies, and setting up international shipping. Products may have to be modified to meet government standards or the unique interests of buyers abroad, poor government connections may very well put your company at a great disadvantage in negotiations, and unfavorable exchange rates can make it difficult or even impossible to offer products at competitive prices and still make a profit. In some countries, the government may not allow a company to enter its market unless it is willing to reveal the specifics of its core technologies, which are often the bedrock of its competitive advantage.[36] Nobody said it would be easy.

Nonetheless, small companies are proving that export success is within reach. For example, one study revealed that the value of goods shipped to China alone (a challenging market) by small and medium-sized U.S. manufacturers increased by 281 percent to $9.3 billion over five years, and 49 percent of these exporters had fewer than 20 employees.[37] What's the secret? These companies did their homework and figured out what products would sell—for example, what products local companies could not yet make for themselves. Then, they got close to the market and developed personal connections with influential decision makers, getting assistance wherever they could find it. A good place to start in your search for customers abroad is the U.S. Department of Commerce's Trade Information Center website (http://export.gov). Or, get in touch with the foreign embassy community (http://embassy.org), select a country where you want to do business, and e-mail the country specialist for assistance. You may be surprised at the leads this can generate. Finally, you can check with officials from your state to see if they provide assistance; many do. An Internet search on "[insert name of your state here] foreign trade office" should lead you where you need to go.

IMPORTING

The flip side of exporting is **importing**, which involves selling products from abroad in the firm's home market. When a small company finds a product overseas that has market potential at home or identifies a product that would sell at home but cannot find a suitable domestic producer, an import strategy may be the best solution.

importing Selling products produced in another country to buyers in the home country.

Linking up with vendors at international trade shows can also open the door to opportunity. This is exactly what Holly Pennington did with her venture, Compass Trading Co. Using imported products found at such shows, she sells fashion accessories through her 13 shops located in central Texas. Because of the depth of its merchandise, the company can accommodate both classic styles that create a professional look and cutting-edge designs featured in trendy fashion magazines, and many styles in between. Best of all, its products sell for a fraction of the prices charged for similar goods at high-end retailers. And customers like what they are getting—so much so that this small company has been opening a new store each year.[38]

Regardless of the import strategy used, one of the most important factors for success is finding a good product vendor. This sounds easy enough to do, especially in this era of Internet-enabled matching services, online communication tools, and flexible and affordable travel. But finding and managing international suppliers can be difficult. Thad Hooker learned this the hard way when he and his wife, Lisa, bought a high-end furniture store in Fort Lauderdale, Florida, called Spirit of Asia. Their experiences were similar to those of many small company owners who choose to work with international suppliers to build a business. "I decided to source from Southeast Asia, but I had to find out everything myself," Hooker says. "It felt like a crapshoot."[39]

Before venturing abroad, Hooker studied his options thoroughly, comparing possible sourcing countries. Then he did some on-the-ground research, visiting the country he targeted and looking for clues that would lead him to the best sourcing partners available. Of course, a lucky break or two also helped: "On [his] initial trip to Chiang Mai, a city in northern Thailand, Hooker caught a ride with a local taxi driver who was interested in art and antiques. Hooker signed the man up, gave him a digital camera, and now employs the former driver as a furniture scout on the ground."[40] These early experiences provided a great start, allowing Hooker to ponder new business opportunities that might leverage the company's overseas sourcing power.

Working with suppliers overseas presents its share of hassles, so don't expect this to be an easy option. However, it holds tremendous potential, especially if you follow a few simple guidelines:

- Learn as much as you can about the culture and business practices of the country from which you will be sourcing to avoid making deal-breaking mistakes.
- Do your research and be sure to select a source that is not a competitor or a company that hopes to learn from your operations so as to compete against you in the future.

- Protect your intellectual property so that your suppliers cannot easily take it from you. Some entrepreneurs require their sourcing partners to sign nondisclosure agreements so that they cannot patent the item in the country where the sourcing takes place.
- Don't rush the process of forming a relationship with a sourcing partner. You need time to ask difficult questions about important factors such as quality standards and capabilities, manufacturing flexibility, and time to order fulfillment.
- Work out transportation logistics ahead of time. A good freight forwarder can assist you with the mechanics of shipping, as well as help you with the confusing jumble of required documents. To get a sense of the process, review the rules and regulations on the U.S. Customs and Border Protection website at http://cbp.gov, and read SBA notes on importing at http://www.smallbusinessnotes.com/small-business-resources/importing-to-the-united-states.html.

At times, the process may seem so complicated that you may wonder if small companies should even be attempting to source from abroad. But it can be done, and with great benefit to your business.

FOREIGN LICENSING

foreign licensing Allowing a company in another country to purchase the rights to manufacture and sell a company's products in international markets.

licensee The company buying licensing rights.

licensor The company selling licensing rights.

royalties Fees paid by the licensee to the licensor for each unit produced under a licensing contract.

counterfeit activity The unauthorized use of intellectual property.

Importing and exporting are the most popular international strategies among small firms, but there are also other options. Because of limited resources, many small firms are hesitant to go global. One way to deal with this constraint is to follow a licensing strategy. **Foreign licensing** allows a company in another country to purchase the rights to manufacture and sell a firm's products in overseas markets. The firm buying these rights is called the **licensee**. The licensee makes payments to the **licensor**, or the firm selling those rights, normally in the form of **royalties**, which is a fee paid for each unit produced.

International licensing has its drawbacks. The foreign licensee makes all the production and marketing decisions, and the licensor must share returns from international sales with the licensee. However, foreign licensing is the least expensive way to go global, since the licensee bears all the costs and risks related to setting up a foreign operation.[41]

Small companies tend to think of tangible products when they explore international licensing options, but licensing intangible assets such as proprietary technologies, copyrights, and trademarks may offer even greater potential returns. Just as Disney licenses its famous Mickey Mouse character to manufacturers around the world, a small retailer called Peace Frogs has used licensing to introduce its copyrighted designs in Spain. As Peace Frogs' founder and president, Catesby Jones, explains, "We export our Peace Frogs T-shirts directly to Japan, but in Spain per capita income is lower, competition from domestic producers is stronger, and tariffs are high, so we licensed a Barcelona-based company the rights to manufacture our product."[42] From this agreement, Peace Frogs has been able to generate additional revenue with almost no added expense.

Foreign licensing can also be used to protect against **counterfeit activity**, or the unauthorized use of intellectual property. Licensing rights to a firm in a foreign market provides a powerful local champion, which can help to ensure that other firms do not use protected assets in an inappropriate way.

INTERNATIONAL FRANCHISING

international franchising Selling a standard package of products, systems, and management services to a company in another country.

International franchising is a variation on the licensing theme. As outlined in Chapter 4, the franchisor offers a standard package of products, systems, and management services to the franchisee, which provides capital, market insight, and hands-on management. Although international franchising was not widely used before the 1970s, today it is the fastest-growing market-entry strategy of U.S. firms, with Canada as the dominant market (followed by Japan and the United Kingdom, in that order). This approach is especially popular with U.S. restaurant chains that want to establish a global presence. McDonald's, for example, has raised its famous golden arches in more than 119 countries around the world. But international franchising is useful to small companies as well.

Danny Benususan is the owner of Blue Note, a premier jazz club in Manhattan that opened its doors in 1981. Considered one of the top venues in the world for jazz and other forms of music, this club has attracted the attention of international businesspeople who have established franchises abroad. The Tokyo location was opened in 1988, followed by clubs in Osaka, Fukuoka, and Nagoya, Japan. The first European club, in Milan, Italy, was added to the Blue Note family in March of 2003. As a result of these international extensions, the club has successfully established itself as the world's only franchised jazz club network.[43] Blue Note has proved that there is more than one way for a small business to globalize.

INTERNATIONAL STRATEGIC ALLIANCES

Moving beyond licensing and franchising, some small businesses have expanded globally by joining forces with large corporations in cooperative efforts. An **international strategic alliance** allows firms to share risks and pool resources as they enter a new market, matching the local partner's understanding of the target market (culture, legal system, competitive conditions, etc.) with the technology or product knowledge of its alliance counterpart. One of the advantages of this strategy is that both partners take comfort in knowing that neither is "going it alone."[44]

international strategic alliance A combination of efforts and/or assets of companies in different countries for the sake of pooling resources and sharing the risks of an enterprise.

Strategic alliances can be used in many different ways by small companies to gain advantage internationally. Tony Raimondo is CEO of Behlen Mfg. Co., a Columbus, Nebraska–based maker of agricultural grain bins, drying systems, and metal-frame buildings. At one time, the company exported products to China, but Raimondo suspended shipments when he found out that Chinese copycats were making the same products, using local advantages such as cheaper labor to undercut Behlen on cost and sell at much lower prices. For a time, it looked as if the company would no longer be able to tap into this huge market. But then Raimondo hit on the idea of forming a 50/50 joint venture (a form of alliance in which two companies share equal ownership in a separate business) in Beijing. "In order for us to sustain market share," says Raimondo, "we had to be on the inside." Making product within China made it possible for Behlen to capitalize on the same advantages that Chinese factories had, and that has made all the difference. Behlen's success in China has spread to other international business initiatives, and the company still does a substantial share of its business overseas.[45]

LOCATING FACILITIES ABROAD

A small business may choose to establish a foreign presence of its own in strategic markets, especially if the firm has already developed an international customer base. Most small companies start by locating a production facility or sales office overseas, often as a way to reduce the cost of operations. Amanda Knauer, 28, wanted to start a business, but she concluded that launching a new venture in the United States

START UP RESOURCES

Worldwide Workforce

Perhaps you've found someone in a foreign country to purchase your product, but you've decided that it's actually cheaper to make the product in China. For some inside tips on finding a good manufacturing partner in that country, see http://www.inc.com/ss/6-tips-manufacturing-china.

© iStockphoto.com/Angelika Schwarz

entrepreneurial experiences

Cultural Differences Create "Adventure" for Small Global Firms

You might expect that small companies would be backing away from global opportunities since the beginning of the economic slowdown that started in late 2007. But according to U.S. Commercial Service data, small firm expansion overseas has actually been holding steady during this very difficult period. Nevertheless, these enterprises must still deal with the unique challenges and frustrations that arise from cultural differences, geographical nuances, and other issues that go along with doing business internationally.

Recyclebank is a small New York–based company that is stepping out to take on the world. The firm sets up award programs that help to promote "green behavior." The nature of its service is spelled out on the company's website:

> *Whether you pledge to use less energy, increase your at-home recycling, or even just learn how you can increase the green in your home and neighborhood, we'll reward you though grocery store savings, drugstore coupons, and discounts on the brands you buy every day.*

When co-founder and CEO Ron Gronen saw reports on his firm's expansion into England, he was concerned that the press there referred to the company's program as a "scheme." "I would try to tell them that is was not a scheme, that it was a service," says Gronen, but no one seemed to get it. He eventually figured out the point of miscommunication. It seems the word *scheme* does not conjure up thoughts of a scam in England as it does in the United States. Apparently, Gronen's concerns were all for naught.

© Basheera Designs/Shutterstock.com

Or consider AlertDriving's global expansion experiences. Launched in 1998, the venture is a small technology company that pioneered the use of Web-based training for vehicle fleet risk management. With a presence in 22 countries around the world, the company's FleetDefense™ program "provides multinational organizations with vehicle fleets . . . the opportunity to deploy a consistent training regime with both localized content and centralized tracking and reporting capabilities."

That sounds complicated. But it's not really all that tricky compared to the surprises that can come up in overseas markets—especially those in countries that are very different from the United States. In fact, when AlertDriving assessed the suitability of its products for international sales, it found translation errors, cultural flaws, and geographic misrepresentations. Problems surfaced in the company's training module for Dubai, for example. The firm always teaches that the center lane on a multi-lane highway is the safest, but that does not apply in Dubai where the center lane is actually reserved for passing! This inaccuracy was surely embarrassing for a company that provides safety training, but small firms that go global are bound to commit such missteps on occasion. It's all part of stepping out of the comfort zone at home and into the fast-moving stream of international opportunities.

Sources: Emily Maltby, "Expanding Abroad? Avoid Cultural Gaffes," *Wall Street Journal*, January 19, 2010, p. B5; "Who Is Recyclebank?" http://www.recyclebank.com/about-us, accessed February 8, 2011; and "AlertDriving—About Us," http://www.alertdriving.com/about_us.php, accessed February 8, 2011. **http://www.recyclebank.com, http://www.alertdriving.com**

was too expensive. On the advice of a friend, she set her sights on Argentina. After doing some research, she went to Buenos Aires in late 2004. A few months later, she was running her own business, Qara Argentina, a luxury leather goods manufacturer. "I came to Argentina looking for my opportunity," she says. "The beauty of the leather inspired me, and I saw it as an entryway into this world [of business ownership]." It hasn't been easy. Knauer has had to pick up the local Spanish dialect and learn about a new set of laws and business practices, but the work is paying off. The company had more than $1 million in sales before the end of its first year in business.[46]

Opening an overseas sales office can be a very effective strategy, but small business owners should wait until sales in the local market are great enough to justify the move. An overseas office is costly to establish, staff, manage, and finance, so anticipated advantages are sometimes difficult to achieve. However, U.S. firms often locate their first international sales office in Canada, while European expansion is also common (the English-speaking United Kingdom and Ireland are popular locations). Still others have selected Asia, because of its economic dynamism and fast-growing consumer demand.

Some small firms have grand ambitions that go beyond locating a production facility or sales office overseas. For example, they may purchase a foreign business from another firm through what is known as a **cross-border acquisition**, or even start a **greenfield venture**, by forming from scratch a new wholly owned subsidiary in another country. Either option is likely to be fraught with difficulties.

cross-border acquisition
The purchase by a business in one country of a company located in another country.

greenfield venture
A wholly owned subsidiary formed from scratch in another country.

Go-it-alone strategies are complex and costly. They offer maximum control over foreign operations and eliminate the need to share generated revenues, but they also force companies to bear the entire risk of the undertaking. If the new subsidiary is a greenfield venture, the firm may have much to learn about running an enterprise in a foreign country, managing host-country nationals, and developing an effective marketing strategy. The commercial potential of a wholly owned international subsidiary may be great, but the hassles of managing it can be even greater. This option is not for the faint of heart.

Challenges to Global Businesses

Small businesses face challenges; *global* small businesses face challenges on a much larger scale. How well can a small firm do in the global marketplace? The success of enterprising entrepreneurs in international markets proves that small firms can do better than survive—they can thrive! However, success requires careful preparation. Small business owners must recognize the unique complications facing global firms and adjust their plans accordingly. As mentioned previously, managing cultural differences can be challenging enough. But entrepreneurs also need to pay attention to political risks, economic risks, and the relative ease of doing business in countries where they want to extend operations.

POLITICAL RISK

The potential for a country's political forces to negatively affect the performance of business enterprises operating within its borders is referred to as **political risk**. Often, this risk is related to the instability of a nation's government, which can create difficulties for outside companies. Potential problems range from threats as trivial as new regulations that restrict the content of television advertising to a government takeover of private assets. Political developments can threaten access to an export market, require a firm to reveal trade secrets, or even demand that work be completed in-country.

political risk
The potential for political forces in a country to negatively affect the performance of businesses operating within its borders.

Many large corporations maintain a risk assessment office with staff trained to determine the risk profile of the individual countries for which they have planned projects.

Because small firms cannot afford the cost of staffing such an office, some turn to inexpensive tools for risk assessment. One helpful source is *Euromoney* magazine's "Country Risk Rankings," which is published once a year. These rankings provide a general sense of the political risks that companies will face when doing business abroad. Small businesses can develop international growth plans using these insights and make appropriate adjustments to their strategies. It's not a perfect method, but it is low cost and far better than planning a global strategy with no information at all.

ECONOMIC RISK

economic risk The probability that a country's government will mismanage its economy in ways that hinder the performance of firms operating there.

Economic risk is the probability that a country's government will mismanage its economy and affect the business environment in ways that hinder the performance of firms operating there. Economic risk and political risk are therefore related.[47] Two of the most serious problems resulting from economic mismanagement are inflation and fluctuations in exchange rates. While a discussion of these factors is beyond the scope of this book, it is important to recognize that inflation reduces the value of a country's currency on the foreign exchange market, thereby decreasing the value of cash flows that the firm receives from its operations abroad.

exchange rate The value of one country's currency relative to that of another country.

Exchange rates represent the value of one country's currency relative to that of another country—for example, the number of Mexican pesos that can be purchased with one U.S. dollar. Sudden or unexpected changes in these rates can be a serious problem for small international businesses, whether they export to that market or have a local presence there.

Mary Ellen Mooney of California-based Mooney Farms kept an eye on the European market, as well as that of Mexico. She recognized the potential of exporting her sun-dried tomato products to France and came close to striking a deal with a local distributor a few years back, but the negotiations fell through when the exchange rate between the dollar and the euro changed.[48] To understand her dilemma, suppose the French distributor was willing to pay €5 (5 euros) for a package of sun-dried tomatoes. If the dollar and the euro were exchanged one to one, Mooney could convert €5 to $5. If $4.50 covered costs of production, transportation, insurance, and so on, then Mooney would earn a $.50 profit ($5.00 – $4.50) per unit. But if the dollar were to *increase* in value relative to the euro, the situation would change drastically. Assume that the exchange rate changed to $.80 per €1. Then units selling for €5 would yield only $4 each (5 × .80), which would result in a $.50 loss on every sale.

Clearly, a good deal can quickly fall apart if exchange rates take a turn for the worse. This risk is especially serious for small companies that are just getting established in international markets. To protect against exchange rate shifts, these businesses should take such measures as stating contracts in U.S. dollars or using other financial strategies that minimize this risk.

THE "EASE OF DOING BUSINESS INDEX"

Since 2003, the World Bank has been publishing the "Ease of Doing Business Index" to underscore to businesses and governments the large impact that regulatory conditions have on economic growth and development. The index is based on a survey of more than 8,000 local experts, "including lawyers, business consultants, accountants, freight forwarders, government officials, and other professionals routinely administering or advising on legal and regulatory requirements."[49] Following a very careful methodology, the process uses data related to nine key factors—including the difficulty of starting a business, getting credit, and enforcing contracts—to create a ranking for 183 countries. This information can easily be used to shape the international expansion decisions of small businesses.

In Exhibit 18.5, countries are color-coded to indicate the relative ease of doing business in each—green represents "go" countries, which are relatively business-friendly;

EXHIBIT 18.5 Ease of Doing Business

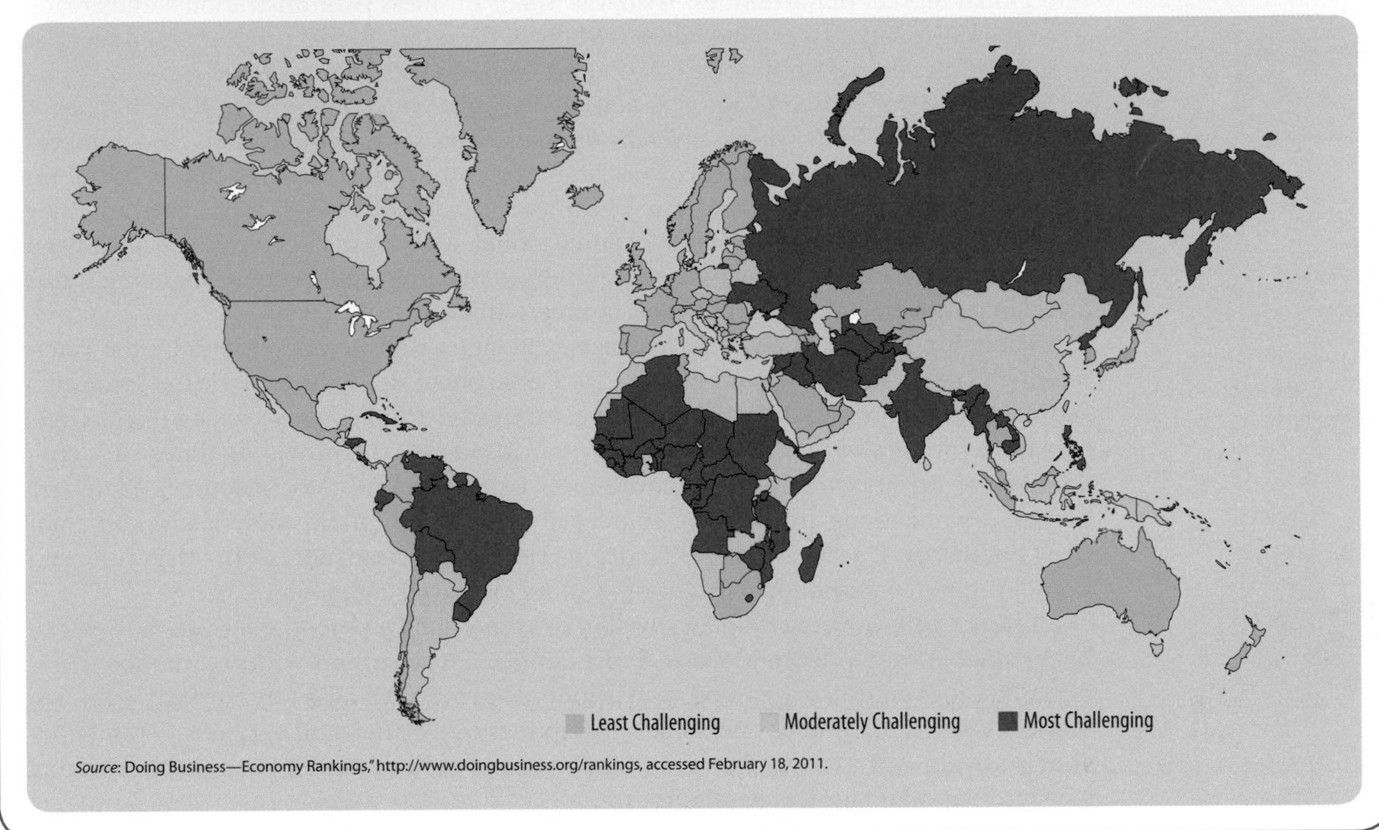

Source: Doing Business—Economy Rankings," http://www.doingbusiness.org/rankings, accessed February 18, 2011.

yellow signifies countries that are somewhat more challenging, where companies should "proceed with caution"; and red identifies "stop and think very carefully" countries, where small businesses are likely to have even more difficulty. While color coding is not a part of the index, the data provided are very helpful for planning. For specifics on the latest report, see http://www.doingbusiness.org/rankings.

Conducting business internationally will never be as easy as doing business at home—it is likely to stretch managerial skills and resources to the limit. Global commerce complicates every task and raises difficult questions related to every function of the firm. However, the motivations to go global are sound, and others have already proved that it can be done. You can do it, too, if you plan carefully and take advantage of the resources available to help you achieve your global aspirations.

Assistance for Global Enterprises

Help is available to small companies with international aspirations—you need only open your eyes to find it. Once you decide to enter the global marketplace, you will be amazed at how many resources there are to assist you.

ANALYZING MARKETS AND PLANNING STRATEGY

Among the many activities required to prepare a small firm for the challenges of going global, two are especially fundamental to success abroad: finding international markets that fit the company's unique potentials and putting together a game plan for entry into the target markets.

A small business should begin its research by exhausting secondary sources of information. The U.S. government offers a number of publications on how to identify and tap into global market opportunities. Also, the Small Business Administration stands ready to help small companies expand abroad. Many of the international programs and services of the SBA are delivered through U.S. Export Assistance Centers (USEACs).

One excellent source of information about global business for small companies is *Breaking into the Trade Game: A Small Business Guide to Exporting.* This SBA publication, which is available online, provides an overview of export strategy that is useful for both new and experienced exporters. The nuts-and-bolts handbook is designed to guide small firms through the complexities of going global, with chapters focused specifically on identifying markets, choosing an entry strategy, managing transactions, financing trade, arranging transportation, and forming strategic alliances.

Though not focused on small businesses alone, a website maintained by the International Trade Administration of the U.S. Department of Commerce (http://trade.gov) supplies helpful insights about international expansion. Publications such as *World Trade* magazine (http://www.worldtrademag.com) can also be useful, providing timely, in-depth analyses of world trade markets and business issues. Beyond these resources, state and private organizations are excellent sources of trade information, trade leads, and company databases. One such source, TradePort (http://www.tradeport.org), offers information to promote international trade with California-based companies.

Talking with someone who has lived in or even visited a potential foreign market can be a valuable way to learn about it. For example, conversations with international students at a local university can be very helpful. However, the best way to study a foreign market is to visit the country personally. A representative of a small firm can do this either as an individual or as a member of a group that is organized for the purpose of exploring new international business possibilities.

CONNECTING WITH INTERNATIONAL CUSTOMERS

A small company cannot sell abroad unless it connects with customers in targeted international markets. But numerous resources are available to get you started.

Trade Leads

Trade leads are essential in identifying potential customers in target markets. Accessed most often via the Internet, they offer an inexpensive way to establish vital links with buyers and suppliers in target markets. One good online source of trade leads is provided by the Center for International Business Education and Research at Michigan State University (see http://globaledge.msu.edu/resourcedesk/trade-leads). This website offers a wealth of international business resources, including leads that can direct a company to valuable partners in most of the world's markets. The website of the Federation of International Trade Associations (http://www.fita.org) will also help you identify trade leads; in addition, it provides news, announced events, and links to over 8,000 trade-related websites.

Trade Missions

trade mission
A trip organized to help small business owners meet with potential foreign buyers and establish strategic alliances in an international market.

Joining a trade mission is another excellent way to evaluate a foreign market and connect with overseas customers. A **trade mission** is a planned visit to a potential international market, designed to introduce U.S. firms to prospective foreign buyers and to establish strategic alliances. These missions usually involve groups of 5 to 10 business executives and are set up to promote international sales. Members of the group typically pay their own expenses and share in the operating costs of the mission. Foreign governments sometimes sponsor trade missions in order to promote business links with U.S. firms.

Trade Intermediaries

Perhaps the easiest way to break into international markets is to use a **trade intermediary**. Similar to the assistance wholesalers provide with domestic sales, trade intermediaries distribute products to international customers on a contract basis. These agencies tap their established web of contacts, as well as their local cultural and market expertise. In short, an intermediary can manage the entire export end of a business, taking care of everything except filling the orders—and the results can be outstanding. For example, American Cedar, Inc., wanted to expand the market for its cedar wood products overseas. With the assistance of a trade intermediary, the firm was able to generate 30 percent of its total sales from exporting. Then-company president Julian McKinney recalls how the story unfolded: "We displayed our products at a trade show, and an export management company found us. They helped alleviate the hassles of exporting directly. Our products [were] distributed throughout [Europe] from a distribution point in France."[50] An export management company is only one of the many types of trade intermediaries. Exhibit 18.6 describes the trade intermediaries that can best provide the assistance small businesses need.

trade intermediary An agency that distributes a company's products on a contract basis to customers in another country.

EXHIBIT 18.6 Trade Intermediaries Most Suited for Small Business

Type	Description
Confirming House (Buying Agent)	• Works for foreign firms that are interested in buying U.S. products. • "Shops" for lowest possible price for requested items. • Is paid a commission for its services. • Is sometimes a foreign government agency or quasi-governmental firm.
Export Management Company (EMC)	• Acts as the export department for one or several producers of products or services. • Solicits and transacts business in the names of the producers it represents or in its own name, in exchange for a commission, salary, or retainer plus commission. • May provide immediate payment for the products or services by arranging financing or directly purchasing products for resale. • Usually has well-established networks of foreign distributors already in place.
Export Trading Company (ETC)	• Acts as the export department for producers or takes title to the product and exports it under its own name. • May be set up and operated by producers. • Can be organized along multiple- or single-industry lines. • Can represent producers of competing products.
Export Agent, Merchant, or Remarketer	• Purchases products directly from the manufacturer, packing and marking the product according to its own specifications. • Sells the products overseas under its own name through contacts and assumes all risks. • Requires the producer to give up control of the marketing and promotion of its product.
Piggyback Marketer	• Is a manufacturer or service firm. • Distributes another firm's product or service.

Source: International Trade Administration, *A Basic Guide to Exporting* (Washington, DC: Author, 2009).

FINANCING

The more information small firms have about direct and indirect sources of financing, the more favorably they tend to view foreign markets. Sources of this information include private banks and the Small Business Administration.

Private Banks

Commercial banks typically have a loan officer who is responsible for handling foreign transactions. Large banks may have an entire international department. Exporters use banks to issue commercial letters of credit and to perform other financial activities associated with exporting.

letter of credit
An agreement issued by a bank to honor a draft or other demand for payment when specified conditions are met.

A **letter of credit** is an agreement to honor a draft or other demand for payment when specified conditions are met. It helps to ensure that a seller will receive prompt payment. A letter of credit may be revocable or irrevocable. An irrevocable letter of credit cannot be changed unless both the buyer and the seller agree to the change. The process of establishing a letter of credit is quite involved and can be very confusing; however, banks and other financial institutions that offer this service will have expert staff who can explain how these documents work and will walk you through the process.

A guarantee from a reputable bank that the exporter will indeed be paid is critical to a small business that has stretched its resources to the limit just to enter the global game and thus cannot afford an uncollected payment. But what if the small business is on the import end of the exchange? How will its interests be protected? The letter of credit provides security for the receiving firm as well, because the exporter does not receive payment from the bank until it has released the title, or proof of ownership, of the delivered goods. Once the product has been shipped and the title transferred, the exporter receives a document called a **bill of lading** to confirm this. This document must be received before the bank will pay on the letter of credit. In brief, the letter of credit ensures that the exporter will receive payment only when the goods are delivered in-country, and it also guarantees that the exporter will be paid.

bill of lading
A document indicating that a product has been shipped and the title to that product has been transferred.

Small Business Administration

The Small Business Administration (SBA) serves small U.S. firms primarily through its regional, district, and branch offices. Small businesses that are either already exporting or interested in doing so can receive valuable information from the SBA through conferences and seminars, instructional publications, and export counseling. An extended list of the financial assistance programs offered by the SBA to small firms is posted on the agency's website at http://www.sba.gov/content/financing-your-small-business-exports-foreign-investments-or-projects.

The reasons that a growing number of small firms are choosing to participate in international business include both time-honored motivations and those emerging in the new competitive landscape. Whatever your reasons are for entering the global arena, your company is certain to run up against serious challenges that purely domestic firms do not have to face. This is the nature of the terrain, but assistance is available in abundance from a number of private and public agencies. With a little help and a lot of hard work, your company can succeed in the global marketplace.

1. Describe the potential of small firms as global enterprises.

- Many startups and even the smallest of businesses continue to expand internationally, despite a slowed global economy.
- Some small companies called born-global firms are being launched with cross-border business activities in mind.
- Before going global, it is important for a small business owner to determine whether her or his company is up to the task.
- Small business owners who decide to go global must study the social, technological, economic, and political forces in a foreign market to figure out how best to adapt products and ensure smooth entry.

2. Identify the basic forces prompting small firms to engage in global expansion.

- The basic forces behind global expansion are expanding markets, gaining access to resources, cutting costs, and capitalizing on special location features.
- Since more than 95 percent of the world's population lives outside the United States, globalization greatly expands the size of a firm's potential market.
- The fast-growing markets of the BRIC countries (Brazil, Russia, India, and China) are attracting small firms that wish to tap their enormous market potential.
- Small businesses with a highly differentiated product may need an international market in order to increase sales enough to recover product development costs.
- Going global can accelerate gains from experience curve efficiencies (resulting from learning effects and economies of scale), especially for startups based on complex technologies.
- Sometimes small businesses go global to gain access to resources, including raw materials and skilled labor.
- Another reason small firms enter foreign markets is to cut their costs in such areas as labor, transportation, or manufacturing overhead.
- Businesses of all sizes have been slashing costs by contracting with independent providers overseas (*international outsourcing*) or relocating their stateside operations abroad (*offshoring*).
- Small businesses may want to capitalize on special features of an international location to create authenticity by being local, to use its cache (or other features) to enhance a brand's reputation, or to follow a large client firm.

3. Understand and compare strategy options for global businesses.

- Exporting, an international strategy commonly used by small firms, can be facilitated by using the Internet to increase firms' international visibility.
- Importing involves selling products from abroad in the home market; it should be used when products manufactured abroad have market potential at home.
- Non-export strategies include foreign licensing, international franchising, international strategic alliances, and locating facilities abroad.
- Although they can be more complex than export strategies, some non-export strategies (especially licensing) are actually the safest options for the small global business.

4. Explain the challenges that global enterprises face.

- Political risk is the potential for a country's political forces to negatively affect the performance of small businesses operating there; it varies greatly across nations.
- Economic risk is the probability that a government will mismanage its economy and affect the business environment in ways that hinder the performance of firms operating there (most notably through inflation and fluctuations in exchange rates).
- The World Bank's "Ease of Doing Business Index" can help a small company anticipate the overall level of difficulty that is likely to go along with entering a specific country market.

5. Recognize the sources of assistance available to support international business efforts.

- Numerous public and private organizations provide assistance to small businesses in analyzing markets and planning an entry strategy.
- Small businesses can connect with international customers by reviewing sources of trade leads, joining trade missions, or using the services of trade intermediaries.
- For assistance in financing its entry into a foreign market, a small firm can turn to private banks (which can issue letters of credit) and programs initiated by the Small Business Administration.

Key Terms

globalization p. 522
born-global firms p. 523
experience curve efficiencies p. 528
learning effects p. 529
economies of scale p. 529
international outsourcing p. 530
offshoring p. 530
exporting p. 532
importing p. 535
foreign licensing p. 536
licensee p. 536
licensor p. 536
royalties p. 536
counterfeit activity p. 536
international franchising p. 536
international strategic alliance p. 537
cross-border acquisition p. 539
greenfield venture p. 539
political risk p. 539
economic risk p. 540
exchange rate p. 540
trade mission p. 542
trade intermediary p. 543
letter of credit p. 544
bill of lading p. 544

Discussion Questions

1. What is a "born-global" enterprise? What factors are encouraging the increase in the number of these companies?
2. Discuss the importance of a careful cultural analysis to a small firm that wishes to enter an international market.
3. Do you believe that small companies should engage in international business? Why or why not?
4. Identify the four basic forces driving small businesses to enter the global business arena. Which do you think is the most influential?
5. Give examples of some emerging motivations persuading small business owners to go global. Are any of these motivations likely to remain powerful forces 10 years from now? Twenty years from now?
6. Why is exporting such a popular global strategy among small businesses? Do you think this should be the case?
7. What impact has the Internet had on the globalization of small firms? How do you think small companies will use the Internet for business in the future?
8. What non-export strategies can small businesses adopt? In view of the unique needs and capabilities of small firms, what are the advantages and disadvantages of each of these strategies?
9. What are the three main challenges small businesses face when they go global? What strategies can a small company use to deal with each of these challenges?
10. What forms of assistance are available to small global firms? Which is likely to be of greatest benefit to small companies? Why?

You Make the Call

SITUATION 1

Luis Aburto recognized the advantages of outsourcing development work when he decided to start Scio Consulting International LLC, an information technology company. But he still has a question: Where in the world (literally) should he go for the talent he needs? He has considered linking up with a service provider in Bangalore, India, because the wages are very low, the pool of well-trained employees is deep, and technical skills are strongly emphasized in the university system. But India is a long way from the company's home office in San Jose, California, which means greater travel costs, dealing with the hassle of working between times zones that are nearly opposite one another, and communication delays. There have also been reports of problems with infrastructure limitations (including poor or dropped Internet and phone connections), as well as the cost and quality of completed work. Finally, the cultural gap would be significant, even though most educated workers in India speak English.

Aburto has also been in touch with an operation in Morelia, Mexico. His contacts there tell him that the skilled workers he needs are available, the cultural gap is limited, turnover is very low, and technical staff will not need special visas to travel between Mexico and project sites in the United States. However, wages there are significantly higher than in Bangalore, university graduates in Mexico receive little practical training, and the law makes it very difficult to fire staff once they are hired.

The clock is ticking. Aburto needs to line up employees for three big contracts he is currently negotiating, and his potential clients all want to get their projects started within a month or so of a final decision. If he even gets two of the three deals to pan out, he will have much more work than his staff in the United States can handle. He will need additional employees—he's just not certain where to go for outsourcing support.

Sources: Adapted from Gail Dutton, "Outsource Closer to Home," *Entrepreneur*, Vol. 36, No. 10 (October 2008), p. 22; and Steve Hamm, "India Software Outsourcing: One Unhappy Customer," *Bloomberg Businessweek*, January 24, 2011, http://www.businessweek.com/blogs/globespotting/archives/2007/01/india_software.html, accessed February 18, 2011.

Question 1 What additional information would be helpful to Aburto as he ponders this decision?
Question 2 What additional advantages and disadvantages should Aburto should consider when choosing between offshoring this work to India and "nearshoring" it to Mexico?
Question 3 Which location would you choose—India or Mexico? Build a case to support your final decision.

SITUATION 2

Bill Moss and several other small business owners joined a trade mission to China to explore market opportunities there. The group learned that China has a population of over 1.3 billion and is the third fastest-growing export market for small and medium-sized U.S. firms. Average annual income varies greatly across the country, but it is increasing rapidly. Annual per capita incomes range from a low of about $750 for rural workers to roughly $2,500 in urban areas and even higher in Shanghai, Beijing, and other major cities. In any given year, the Chinese software market grows by 30 percent and the number of Internet users quadruples. Furthermore, the demand for management consulting services is increasing, especially information technology consulting. Members of the group were surprised by the number of people who had cell phones and regularly surfed the Internet, especially in large urban centers. On the downside, they found that counterfeit goods (from clothing and leather goods to software and CDs) were readily available at a fraction of the cost of legitimate merchandise and that local merchants expressed an interest in doing business only with vendors with whom they had established relationships.

Sources: Andrew Batson, "China Narrows Inequity Between the Rich and Poor," *Wall Street Journal*, February 3, 2010, p. A13; and "China Software Market Forecast to 2012," http://www.bharatbook.com/Market-Research-Reports/China-Software-Market-Forecast-to-2012.html, accessed February 18, 2011.

Question 1 What types of businesses would prosper in China? Why?
Question 2 What are the challenges and risks associated with doing business in China?
Question 3 What steps should Moss take to address these challenges and risks in order to increase his chance of success in that market?

SITUATION 3

Steven Friedman is the founder of Brooklyn-based Holy Land Earth, which imports 16-ounce bags of soil from Israel for use at groundbreakings, burials, and other ceremonial events. The Holy Land of Israel holds special significance for people of various religious faiths, and each parcel of Holy Land Earth is certified to be genuine by a rabbi in Jerusalem. The company sells the soil for $39.95 per bag.

The obstacles the company has had s to overcome are numerous. For example, import operations can be very difficult to set up, especially if they involve organic matter. Soil products cannot be imported without the permission of the U.S. Department of Agriculture, which requires getting them treated, tested, and formally approved. The new venture had to bear these costs on top of normal business expenses, such as obtaining the soil and then shipping, packaging, storing, marketing, and delivering it to buyers. Friedman worked with scientists to come up with a soil-cleaning process that satisfies U.S. import regulations, giving his startup a competitive advantage over would-be rivals.

Holy Land Earth has been up and running for some time now, and Friedman is considering ways to expand the market and potential of his young company. For example, he is thinking about marketing his soil product to Christian Evangelicals, and his website suggests a number of other applications, which include using the soil to feed potted plants, to promote good luck, or even to save as a keepsake. The future looks promising, but for now Friedman can take pleasure in knowing that his import operation is finally off the ground . . . in more ways than one.

Sources: "Holy Land Earth," http://www.holylandearth.com, accessed February 21, 2011; Norm Brodsky, "You Do What?" *Inc.*, Vol. 30, No. 2 (February 2008), pp. 59–60; and Martin Lindstrom, *Buyology: Truth and Lies About What We Buy* (New York: Random House, 2010), pp. 109–110.

Question 1 In your opinion, what new country markets would be likely to hold the greatest potential for additional sales for Friedman's company?
Question 2 Of the major strategy options mentioned in this chapter, which is Holy Land Earth currently following? Which of the others would offer the safest path to further global expansion? Which would offer the fastest path to such growth? Which would offer the best path? Why?
Question 3 What are the greatest challenges Friedman is likely to face in the future? What sources of assistance would you suggest that he use as he takes on those challenges?

Experiential Exercises

1. Conduct phone interviews with 10 local small business owners to see if they engage in international business. Discuss their reasons for going global or for choosing to do business only domestically.
2. Contact a local banker to discuss the bank's involvement with small firms participating in international business. Report your findings to the class.
3. Review recent issues of *Entrepreneur, Inc.*, and other small business publications, and be prepared to discuss articles related to international business.
4. Do a Web search to find an article about a small business that first expanded internationally using an entry strategy other than exporting. From what you understand of the company's situation, suggest guidelines that could lead a firm to go global with non-export strategies.
5. Consult secondary sources to develop a political/economic risk profile for a given country. Select a small company and explain what it would have to do to manage these risks if it were to enter the market of the country profiled.
6. Speak with the owner of a small international company. Which sources of assistance did that entrepreneur use when launching the global initiative? Which sources did the entrepreneur find most helpful? Which did the entrepreneur find least helpful?

Small Business and Entrepreneurship Resource Center

1. One variation on the import theme is an international sourcing strategy, which is essentially an effort to connect with overseas suppliers that can provide the products or services a company needs to operate successfully. This sounds easy enough to do, especially in this era of Internet-enabled matching services, online communication tools (from e-mail to videoconferencing), and flexible and affordable travel options. However, finding and managing international suppliers can be challenging. Thad Hooker learned this the hard way when he and his wife, Lisa, bought a Florida-based high-end furniture company called Spirit of Asia in 2001. After reading the article "On Foreign Soil," describe a few crucial keys to success when finding a supplier overseas.

   Source: Joshua Kurlantzick, "On Foreign Soil: Arm Yourself with the Information and Advice You Need for Sourcing Your Product Overseas So Your Efforts Don't Get Lost in Translation," *Entrepreneur*, Vol. 33, No. 6 (June 2005), pp. 88–92.

2. In franchising, the franchisor offers a standard package of products, systems, and management services to the franchisee, which provides capital, market insight, and hands-on management. Although international franchising was not widely used before the 1970s, today it is the fastest-growing market entry strategy of U.S. firms. Describe the U.S. Commercial Service's Global Franchising Team's "Webinars" and how they might assist a domestic franchise to expand internationally. Also explain some of the other major services provided by the U.S. Commercial Service.

   Source: Mona Musa, "U.S. Commercial Service Offers Tools to Explore New Franchise Markets: A Key Ingredient to Enable a Franchise Concept's International Growth Lies in a Business Ability to Cultivate the Right Information," *Franchising World*, Vol. 38, No. 7 (July 2006), pp. 65–66.

Case 18

SMARTER.COM (P. 728)

This case describes the experiences of an entrepreneur who has hired and must work with engineers and other staff for back-office operations in China that he has set up to support his Web-based business.

MANAGING GROWTH IN THE SMALL BUSINESS

PART 5

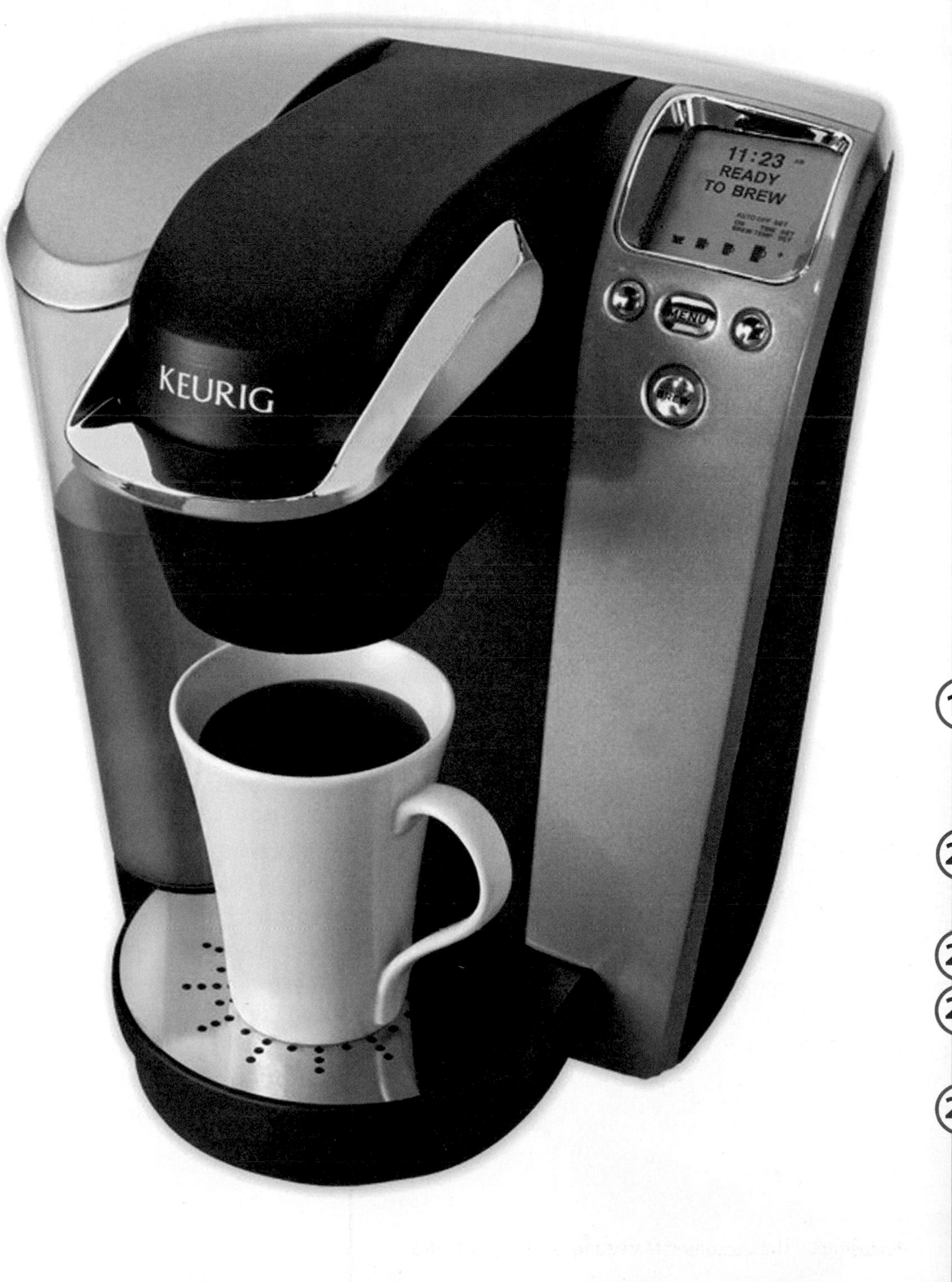

CHAPTERS

Handout/MCT/Newscom

CHAPTER 19

Professional Management and the Small Business

In the SPOTLIGHT
KIND LLC
http://www.kindsnacks.com

When a small business owner reaches certain points in the growth of his or her company, it becomes sensible to ask the question, "Am I still capable of running this enterprise as well as a 'professional' manager with a different set of capabilities?" Some entrepreneurs are able to grow along with their businesses, to reach beyond themselves and attain new competencies that match the demands of their expanding firms. But for others, bringing in a seasoned CEO or other professional manager with more operating experience and advanced management skills is the only way to help their ventures flourish.

KIND Healthy Snacks

Daniel Lubetzky recently had to answer the question of whether or not to bring in a "hired hand" to help run his company. He launched KIND, a maker of healthy snacks, in New York City in 2004. But with time came growth. By 2010, KIND had nearly $30 million in annual revenues and 55 full-time employees, and Lubetzky was facing many operational challenges. He realized that it was time for a change. This is how he describes the company's management situation today:

> *Every Monday, I meet with our president, John Leahy, who has 30 years of business experience. It takes two hours, and we go over everything—finance, operations, sales, marketing, manufacturing. I hired him [in February of 2010]. In retrospect, I should have hired a president earlier. I'm not a terrible manager, but my problem is that I don't pace myself. There were times early on when I wanted to launch products fast, even if, say, the packaging wasn't quite finalized.*

After studying this chapter, you should be able to . . .

1. Discuss the entrepreneur's leadership role.
2. Explain the small business management process and its unique features.
3. Identify the managerial tasks of entrepreneurs.
4. Describe the problem of time pressure and suggest solutions.
5. Outline the various types of outside management assistance.

LOOKING AHEAD

© iStockphoto.com/Dan Bachman

The new president's approach is much more methodical than the one guided by Lubetzky's managerial instincts, and that has changed things for the better. For example, Leahy set up a six-month review process to monitor and assess all of the firm's initiatives. From this, Lubetzky and Leahy can determine "what worked, what didn't, what [the company] accomplished, and where [it] fell short." The process has helped them identify problems in need of a fix, such as the preferred partner program that was underperforming. The program had been launched "to help the sales team run promotions and events with retailers," and the marketing team had jumped in to help by developing tools to support it. But sales interpreted this as an imposition from above, so the program was halfheartedly executed. Because Leahy's review process identified the root of the problem, he and Lubetzky were able to address it by allowing the sales team to choose their own tools for the program. Problem solved.

Hiring a professional manager has worked out well for Lubetzky and his firm, but this is not always the case. After making such transitions, entrepreneurs sometimes feel that they are losing control of their businesses, and this can quickly lead to conflict and dysfunction in the enterprise. Norm Brodsky, a serial entrepreneur and a regular columnist for *Inc.* magazine, observes that it is crucial for the small business owner and the CEO (or other high-level members of the management team) to be in total agreement about the culture that guides the venture. This will shape how a company functions—"who works there, how hard those people work, how they treat one another, how they relate to customers and suppliers, and on and on." If the organizational culture is preserved, the entrepreneur is much more likely to be pleased with the transition, and the business can pick up the momentum it needs to move to the next level. But a change in culture can quickly jeopardize all that the owner has created, and that would lead to a very different ending to the small business story—and not a very happy one, at that.

Sources: "KIND Healthy Snacks—Our Story," http://kindsnacks.com/our-story, accessed March 1, 2011; Norm Brodsky, "Culture Clash," *Inc.*, Vol. 37, No. 2 (September 2010), pp. 33–34; "Reflections on Wealth and Management from a Home-Grown Private Entrepreneur in China," http://www.knowledgeatwharton.com.cn/index.cfm?fa=viewArticle&articleID=2174, accessed February 17, 2010; and David Lubetzky, quoted in Issie Lapowsky, "The Way I Work," *Inc.*, Vol. 32, No. 10 (December 2010/January 2011), pp. 152–156.

Unless you plan to remain a tiny one-person business forever, leadership and management problems are sure to come your way. When that time arrives, you must find ways to integrate the efforts of employees and give new direction to the business. This is absolutely necessary if production employees, salespeople, support service staff, and other personnel are to work together effectively. Even long-established businesses need vigorous leadership if they are to avoid stagnation or failure. This chapter examines the leadership challenges facing entrepreneurs and the managerial activities required as firms mature and grow.

Small Business Leadership

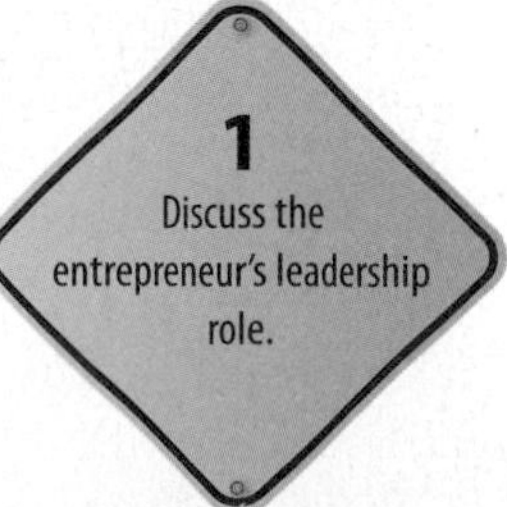

Leadership roles differ greatly, depending on the size of the business and its stage of development. For example, an enterprise that is just getting started will face problems and uncertainties unlike those of a family firm that has been functioning well over two or three generations. We must begin, therefore, with the recognition that leadership cannot be reduced to simple rules or processes that fit all situations.

WHAT IS LEADERSHIP?

The question is simple, but the answer is not. Here is the response of one business leader, Richard Barton, founder and former CEO of online travel heavyweight Expedia.com, to the question "How do you define leadership?"

> *Leadership to me means leaning forward, looking ahead, trying to improve, being fired up about what you're doing and being able to communicate that, verbally and nonverbally, to those around you.*[1]

Briefly stated, leadership involves pointing the way and getting others to follow willingly. It is far more focused on the destination than on the details of getting there. An entrepreneur must convey his or her vision of the firm's future to all other participants in the business so that they can contribute most effectively to the accomplishment of the mission. Although leaders must also engage in more routine processes, particularly as the company grows, the first task of the small business owner is to create and communicate a vision for the company.

LEADERSHIP QUALITIES OF FOUNDERS

The entrepreneur is the trailblazer who enlists others, both team members and outsiders, to work with him or her in a creative endeavor. Others may then buy into this vision for the venture as they join their efforts with those of the entrepreneur.

In a totally new venture, the founder faces major uncertainties and unknowns. Therefore, individuals who are launching promising startups, or startups having the prospect of attaining significant size or profitability, need to have certain qualities. One of the most important traits is tolerance for ambiguity. Because of the uncertainty involved in starting a new business, entrepreneurs must also be adaptable, able to adjust to unforeseen problems and opportunities. One small business expert expressed this in poetic terms: "Anyone can be an entrepreneur, who wants to experience the deep, dark canyons of uncertainty and ambiguity, and . . . walk the breathtaking highlands of success."[2] Being able to tolerate and adjust to circumstances as they unfold are two basic qualities that can be useful in many business settings, but they are never more important than in the startup situation.

WHAT MAKES A LEADER EFFECTIVE?

Many people assume that a business leader must have a flashy, highly charismatic, "I'm-in-charge" personality to be effective, but this is not the norm and it certainly is not required. In fact, charisma has little to do with effective leadership. It's not so much about wanting to *be* in charge as it is having the ability to *take* charge and inspire others to follow one's lead. This is exactly the point made by Judith Cone, a thought leader in entrepreneurship education who currently serves as special assistant to the Chancellor for Innovation and Entrepreneurship at the University of North Carolina at Chapel Hill:

> *A leader is able to explain a vision in a compelling way that motivates people to follow or to become a part of that vision. [Leaders] are solid, smart, they have integrity, people respect them, and people want to follow them because of the quality person[s] they are.*[3]

Leaders exhibit a determination to do whatever is needed to lead their companies to success. Clearly, effective leadership is based not on a larger-than-life personality but, instead, on a focus on reaching business goals.

In most small firms, leadership of the business is personalized. The owner-manager is not a faceless unknown, but an individual whom employees see and relate to in the course of their normal work schedules. This situation is entirely different from that of large corporations, where most employees never see the chief executive. If the employer-employee relationship is good, employees in small enterprises develop strong feelings of personal loyalty to their employer.

In a large corporation, the values of top-level executives must be filtered through many layers of management before they reach those who produce and sell the products. As a result, the influence of those at the top tends to be diluted by the process. In contrast, personnel in a small company receive the leader's messages directly. This face-to-face contact facilitates their understanding of the leader's vision as well as her or his stand on integrity, customer service, and other important issues. In the end, this infused sense of purpose, high standards, and achievement can actually create a competitive advantage for the small business over its corporate rivals.

LEADERSHIP STYLES

Leaders use many different styles of leadership, and these styles may be described in various ways. Specific leadership styles may be better suited to certain situations, but most leaders choose from a variety of approaches as they deal with different issues. Daniel Goleman and his colleagues have described six distinct leadership styles. In their study of nearly 4,000 managers, they found that effective leaders shift fluidly and often between the first four styles listed below, and they make very limited but skillful use of the last two styles.[4]

1. *Visionary leaders* mobilize people toward a shared vision.
2. *Coaching leaders* develop people by establishing a relationship and trust.
3. *Affiliative leaders* promote emotional bonds and organizational harmony.
4. *Democratic leaders* build consensus through participation.
5. *Pacesetting leaders* set challenging and exciting standards and expect excellence.
6. *Commanding leaders* demand immediate compliance.

An entrepreneur may use different styles at different times as she or he attempts to draw out the best of the organization and its employees. Although it should be used sparingly, commanding leadership might be necessary and expected in a genuine emergency situation, but it would not be appropriate in most settings.

For most entrepreneurial firms, leadership that recognizes and values individual worth is strongly recommended. Some decades ago, many managers were hard-nosed autocrats, giving orders and showing little concern for those who worked under them. Over the years, this style of leadership has given way to a more sensitive and effective variety that emphasizes respect for all members of the organization and shows an appreciation both for their work and for their potential. Employees usually find this kind of direction far more motivating.

Danny Meyer owns 10 of New York's best and most popular restaurants, so he has had his share of successes. But it has not always been easy. Meyer recalls a time, in his twenties, when his managers and waiters were continually testing him and pushing him to the limit. Responding to advice from a highly respected and successful mentor, Meyer

LIVING THE DREAM

entrepreneurial experiences

© iStockphoto.com/Angelika Schwarz

Three Generations Worth of Challenges

In a way, businesses are like families: People work together (in part, because they have to), but they also have plenty of disagreements along the way. Because of intergenerational differences in values, attitudes, and styles, miscommunication and conflict are unavoidable. Leading in the context of this sometimes wild mix of mindsets and workplace habits can be a great challenge.

Many companies today have employees from three generations: Baby Boomers (born between 1946 and 1964), Generation X (born between 1965 and 1980), and Generation Y or "Millennials" (born between 1981 and 2000). Because these generations were exposed in their early years to different technologies, forms of entertainment, cultural practices, and other factors, they each have adopted their own ways of doing things, which sometimes clash in the workplace.

Photo by Henry S. Dziekan III/Getty Images

Nancy Lublin knows what it's like to run a small enterprise. In 1996, she founded Dress for Success, a career development training organization for women. And since 2003, she has served as CEO of Do Something, a New York City–based nonprofit that is dedicated to "inspiring, supporting, and celebrating young people who see the need to do something, believe in their ability to get it done, and then take action." Lublin, herself, is a Gen Xer; however, nearly all of Do Something's 21 full-time staff are Millenials, so she has worked hard to figure out how best to lead across a generational divide.

One practice of Millennials that can sometimes create workplace conflict is their insistence on multi-tasking. Studies have shown that Gen Yers are not as good at this as they think they are (and the research on this is very compelling), but they aren't about to kick the habit. So, Lublin adopted a more positive perspective on this, one that is likely to boost productivity rather than running it into the ditch. This is what she has come to realize:

> *A recent study found that [M]illennials typically use up to seven devices, apps, and programs at once—texting, G-chatting, tweeting, and listening to music while working on that memo. Where I make a list and slowly cross things off one at a time, Aria Finger, Do Something's 27-year-old rock-star [chief operating officer], will sit in front of three screens (two PCs, one iPhone) and plow through three times as many tasks in the same amount of time.*

Multi-tasking has its downside, to be sure, but Lublin has found it best to tap into its natural advantages. To make the most of the considerable multi-tasking skills of young staffers like Finger, Lublin now manages their potential by giving these employees a clear sense of direction and providing the resources they need to get the job done—then she makes it a point to get out of the way.

Lublin offers other management suggestions that can head off intergenerational conflict in the workplace. For example, Millennials grew up using social media tools, so they are used to living their lives out loud. In other words, they have far less concern about privacy and share the details of their lives relatively freely. That can present certain risks to a firm's reputation (imagine the embarrassing photos that might be posted online after a company Christmas party takes a turn toward the wild side). However, it also means that these employees are more likely to blog, tweet, and post on Facebook about what they are doing at work, which can add up to free marketing for the company. But beyond their loosened sense of boundaries, Millennials have always been told that they are the best and that they can do whatever they want, which often leads to a deep-seated sense of entitlement. Even in this, Lublin sees a silver lining. "You say self-indulgent and self-obsessed," she observes, "[but] I say optimistic and self-confident. They are hungry for responsibility, and I give it to them." It's all a matter of perspective.

Although stereotyping can be dangerous, it seems clear that the generations differ significantly in their attitudes toward and level of comfort with technology, demands for raises and time off, problem-solving approaches, and social networking styles, just to name a few of the many issues that often flare up. The generations don't even agree on the usefulness of common workplace tools like meetings. A recent study found that nearly half of all boomers believe meetings represent a "very efficient" means for decision making, but only 29 percent of Millennials think that this is the case. This may explain why only half of the Gen Yers (51 percent) in the same survey reported that it is very important to pay attention during meetings.

All three generations have much to learn, including how to appreciate one another and the special insights and capabilities that each group offers to the enterprise. Bringing some resolution to generational communication differences won't be easy, but it is nonetheless very important in a business world that is growing increasingly competitive.

Sources: Citrix Forrester Research, "Gen X Driving Social Networking at Work—Not Gen Y, Citrix Online Study Finds," http://www.citrixonline.com/pr/pressRelease.tmpl?FileID=101910, accessed March 2, 2011; "Good Spark—Do Something," http://www.goodspark.org/charity/children, accessed March 2, 2011; Joe Robinson, "E-mail Is Making You Stupid," *Entrepreneur*, Vol. 38, No. 3 (March 2010), pp. 61–63; Kelly Services, "Generational Differences Make the Workplace More Productive," http://www.kellyglobal.net/web/au/smartmanager/en/pages/intergenerational_management.html, accessed March 2, 2011; and Nancy Lublin, "In Defense of Millennials," *Fast Company*, October 2010, pp. 72, 74. **http://www.dosomething.org**

came up with his own unique management approach. In fact, he has a name for it: *constant, gentle pressure.* Problems are going to arise, conspiring to throw everything out of balance, but Meyer is committed to moving things "back to center," where they should be. That's the "constant" feature of his approach. But he'll never respond in a way that robs his employees of their dignity. That's why he calls it "gentle." He also insists on excellent performance, overseeing the details of every table and even moving an out-of-place saltshaker to its proper place. That's where the "pressure" comes in. It's a management style that works.[5]

In many cases, progressive managers seek some degree of employee participation in decisions that affect personnel and work processes. Often, the focus is on important features of the business, such as shaping the mission of the firm or establishing everyday workplace practices. Managers may carry this leadership approach to a level called **empowerment**. The manager who uses empowerment goes beyond solicitation of employees' opinions and ideas by increasing their authority to act on their own and to make decisions about the processes they're involved with. Glenn Ross, an expert on dealing with customers, points out how small business owners can use employee empowerment to help resolve customer complaints:

empowerment
Giving employees authority to make decisions or take actions on their own.

> *As the immortal philosopher, Barney Fife [from "The Andy Griffith Show"], used to say, "Nip it! You've got to nip it in the bud!" Stop the complaint before it escalates into something major. The best way to do that is to see that your employees understand your vision, policies, and procedures as they relate to customer service. Empowering your employees also shows them that you trust them to do the right thing. This in turn has a positive impact on employee morale. The higher the employee morale, the better service they will provide to your customers. It's that "Circle of Life" thing.*[6]

Ross goes on to point out that empowering frontline staff to take care of customers in this way offers additional benefits, such as freeing up time for owners and managers to take care of other pressing business challenges.

work teams Groups of employees with freedom to function without close supervision.

Some companies actually carry employee participation a step further by creating self-managed **work teams**. Each work team is assigned a given task or operation; its members manage that task or operation without direct supervision and assume responsibility for the results. When work teams function properly, the number of supervisors needed decreases sharply. While this approach may not be appropriate for some small businesses, it certainly provides a powerful model for the management of many ventures.

LEADERS SHAPE THE CULTURE OF THE ORGANIZATION

Over time, an organization tends to take on a life of its own. As indicated in Chapter 2 and the In the Spotlight feature for this chapter, an organizational culture begins to emerge in every small business, establishing a tone that helps employees understand what the company stands for and how to go about their work. You could think of organizational culture as the factor that determines the "feel" of a business. It tends to be the "silent teacher" that sets the tone for employee conduct, even when managers are not present.

A company's culture does not emerge overnight; it unfolds over the lifetime of the business and usually reflects the character and style of the founder. (You may recall that we discussed the founder's imprint on organizational culture in the family business in Chapter 5.) Because of its power to shape how business is conducted, the culture of the organization should not be left to chance. If a founder is honest in his or her dealings, supportive of employees, and quick to communicate, he or she will likely set a standard that others will follow. An entrepreneur can create an innovative cultural environment by setting aside his or her ego and opening up to the ideas of others, supporting experimentation through the elimination of unnecessary penalties for failure, and looking for and tapping into the unique gifts of all employees. Like empowerment, creating an organizational culture that fosters innovation tends to draw employees into the work of the company and often provides a boost to commitment and employee morale.[7]

The above-mentioned actions are largely symbolic, focusing attention on the thrust of the business and its purpose. However, deliberate physical design efforts can also influence the culture, thereby helping to shape the way people in the organization think, how they interact, and what they achieve together. Jonathan Vehar, senior partner of New & Improved, an innovation training and development company in Evanston, Illinois, has taken very intentional steps to set the tone of business and generate specific results for the firm. For example, he notes that creativity can be spurred by sprinkling all work spaces with visually stimulating features like idea-inspiring artwork, video monitors, and well-positioned windows that open up the view. It is also possible to encourage communication, for example, by positioning work spaces far away from bathroom facilities, which naturally creates occasions for employees to run into one another and start idea-generating conversations.[8] These relatively simple adjustments in physical space can have a profound effect on the mindset that employees assume at work.

Another important factor in shaping culture is hiring new employees based on their attitude, style, and fit with the personality of the company. Tony Hsieh is only in his mid-30s, but he built Zappos.com into a billion-dollar company in less than a decade. (As reported in Chapter 2, the company was sold to Amazon in 2009, but Hsieh was asked to stay on as CEO to guide the venture.[9]) The Las Vegas–based online shoe retailer now also sells apparel, bags, housewares, electronics, and cookware, but standing at its core is a strong and carefully crafted culture. It's a little quirky—values such as "embrace and drive change" and "create fun and a little weirdness" top the list—but it's hard to argue with the company's approach, given its success. During the interview process, potential new employees are screened for their fit with the Zappos.com culture, and even highly qualified prospects are rejected if there is no match. As Hsieh puts it, "The most important thing is that there's a culture you believe in and are willing to hire and fire based upon."[10] Organizational culture is serious business; it can easily make or break a company.

It should be clear by now that, in large part, business management is a mental sport, and those who have the right frame of mind are most likely to win. Therefore, every leader should strive to incorporate a positive, "can-do" attitude into the organizational culture. You can work on your own attitude and inspire others to follow your lead. Attitude often is everything—whether an event is mentally framed as a setback or a positive life experience is entirely up to you. If all the parking spaces close to the store are full, taking one farther away can be seen as a chance to get some exercise. A new competitor can present a fresh reminder of why it is so important to serve your customers to the best of your ability. And a lost sale can show you how to improve your product or adjust your presentation so that many more sales can be generated in the future. Develop a positive mindset, and let it shape the culture of those you have hired to work alongside you.

The Small Firm Management Process

As one entrepreneur commented, "Unless you thrive on chaos, a small company can be tough." Small firm operations are not always chaotic, of course, but small business owners face challenges that differ greatly from those of corporate executives. Furthermore, small companies experience changes in their leadership and management processes as they move from startup to the point where they employ a full staff of **professional managers**, trained in the use of more sophisticated management methods.

FROM FOUNDER TO PROFESSIONAL MANAGER

professional manager A manager who uses systematic, analytical methods of management.

There is, of course, much variation in the way businesses and other organizations are managed. Between the extremes of very unskilled and highly professional types of management lies a continuum. At the less-developed end are entrepreneurs and other managers who rely largely on past experience, rules of thumb, and personal whims in giving direction to their businesses. In most cases, their mental models for managing are based on the way they were treated in earlier business experiences or family relationships.

Other entrepreneurs and managers take a more sophisticated approach. They are analytical and systematic in dealing with management problems and issues. Because they emphasize getting the facts and working out logical solutions, their approach is sometimes described as methodical in nature.

The challenge for small firm leaders is to develop a professional approach, while still retaining the entrepreneurial spirit of the enterprise. This can be especially difficult because founders of new firms are not always good organization members. As discussed in Chapter 1, they are creative, innovative, risk-taking individuals who have the courage to strike out on their own. Indeed, they are often propelled into entrepreneurship by precipitating events, sometimes involving their difficulty in fitting into conventional organizational roles. But even very capable entrepreneurs may fail to appreciate the need for good management practices as the business grows.

Though he believes the problem may sometimes be overstated, Adam Hanft, CEO of Hanft Unlimited Inc., a New York City–based consulting, advertising, and publishing firm, points out that many experts believe it is very difficult (often impossible) for entrepreneurs to make the transition from founder to professional manager.

> *If I had a dime for every time I have heard it, I could start another business: Entrepreneurs are passionate people, great at building companies, but only to a certain level. As their enterprises reach maturity, these impatient, impetuous founders need to be replaced by "professional" managers. . . . In [venture capital] land they even have a name for the problem: founderitis.*[11]

Photo by Amy Sussman/Getty Images for Spanx

Some entrepreneurs recognize the problem early on and make adjustments. Sara Blakely, founder of women's shapewear trendsetter SPANX and a true "business dynamo," reports that building a team to run her company was one of her greatest challenges. Before becoming an entrepreneur, Blakely had no formal business training or managerial experience, but starting a new venture meant taking on the responsibility of her employees and their livelihoods. She soon felt very overwhelmed, but then she realized, "It's OK if you're not good at this; hire someone who is." So she hired a CEO ("one of the smartest business decisions I ever made") and gave up control of tasks that did not align with her natural skills so that she could focus on those that play to her strengths. Today, job responsibilities at the company have been dramatically reconfigured. Blakely is the public "face of SPANX," an evangelist for the company and its products, but she continues to work on product development and marketing ideas as well. This has turned out to be a much more comfortable and practical arrangement for her. As Blakely puts it, "The person who starts a company from the ground up is not always the best person to grow it. I think this is the most important lesson an entrepreneur can learn."[12]

Although many entrepreneurs are professional in their approach to management and many corporate managers are entrepreneurial in that they are truly innovative and are willing to take risks, a founder's more simplistic methods can act as a drag on business growth. Ideally, the founder should be able to add a measure of professional management without sacrificing the entrepreneurial spirit and basic values that have given the business a successful start.

Expanding Beyond the Comfort Zone

Although some large corporations experience poor management, small enterprises seem particularly vulnerable to this weakness. Many small firms are marginal or unprofitable businesses, struggling to survive from day to day. At best, they earn only a meager living for their owners.

It is common to hear about businesses that become successful, are praised for their problem-solving wizardry, and start to take on high-prestige customers. But it is precisely at that point when many companies start to lose their business grip. When these ventures were small, with perhaps a few dozen employees in the shop and a handful of projects in the pipeline, they were able to perform quite well. But when they expanded beyond some comfortable point, problems began to mount. Suppliers started to gripe about late payments, customers became unhappy because of delayed deliveries and shoddy workmanship, employee morale began to drift. This can easily be the beginning of the end, and bankruptcy is all too often the final outcome. In the postmortem, it becomes clear that the cause of failure in many cases was a lack of professional management. The good news, however, is that poor management is neither universal nor inevitable.

Managing the Constraints That Hamper Small Businesses

Managers of small firms, particularly new and growing companies, are constrained by conditions that do not trouble the average corporate executive—they must face the grim reality of small bank accounts and limited staff. A small firm often lacks the money for slick sales brochures, and it cannot afford much in the way of marketing research. The shortage of cash also makes it difficult to employ an adequate number of support staff. Such limitations are painfully apparent to large firm managers who move into management positions in small firms.

A former CEO of a telecommunications company described some of the drastic differences between her experiences managing in a *Fortune* 500 firm and in a startup. In a startup situation,

> *Money doesn't come from any single source. There's no single boss to whom you make your case. In fact, the money to build the business comes from several external sources—each with slightly different agendas. . . . [T]here's no guarantee that you can survive even if you hit your milestones. In other words, there's no margin for error. . . . [S]o unless you also realize that you have to become a one-person version of your Fortune 500's chief financial officer, investor-relations and PR staffs, and fund-raising machine, you will be ill-prepared for the mission.*[13]

Small firms typically have too few specialized staff. Most small business managers are generalists. Lacking the support of experienced specialists in such areas as marketing research, financial analysis, advertising, and human resource management, the manager of a small firm often must make decisions in these areas without the expertise that is available in a larger business. This limitation may be partially overcome by using outside management assistance (sources of which are discussed later in the chapter). But coping with a shortage of internal professional talent is part of the reality of managing an entrepreneurial company.

FIRM GROWTH AND MANAGERIAL PRACTICES

As a newly formed business becomes established and grows, its organizational structure and pattern of management will need to be adjusted. To some extent, management in any organization must adapt to growth and change. However, the changes involved in the early growth stages of a new business are much more extensive than those that occur with the growth of a relatively mature business.

A number of experts have proposed models related to the growth stages of business firms.[14] These models typically describe four or five stages of growth and identify various management issues related to each stage. The model we offer in this chapter could be viewed as a relatively smooth curve with no disruptions or downward trends. Our focus is mostly on the managerial challenges that go along with each of these stages of growth, and it would seem to be implicit that these are always manageable. However, we recognize that very few entrepreneurial firms develop along such a straightforward path and that the smooth sailing will often be upset by moments of crisis along the way and perhaps even failure.

Exhibit 19.1 shows four stages of organizational growth characteristic of many small businesses. As firms progress from Stage 1 to Stage 4, they add layers of management and increase the formality of operations. Though some firms skip the first stage or two by starting as larger businesses, thousands of small firms make their way through each of the stages pictured in the exhibit.

In Stage 1, the firm is simply a one-person operation. Some firms begin with a larger organization, but the one-person startup is by no means rare. Many businesses remain one-person operations indefinitely. In Stage 2, the entrepreneur becomes a player-coach, which implies continuing active participation in the operations of the business. In addition to performing the basic work—whether making the product, selling it, writing checks, keeping records, or other activities—the entrepreneur must also coordinate the efforts of others.

EXHIBIT 19.1 Organizational Stages of Small Business Growth

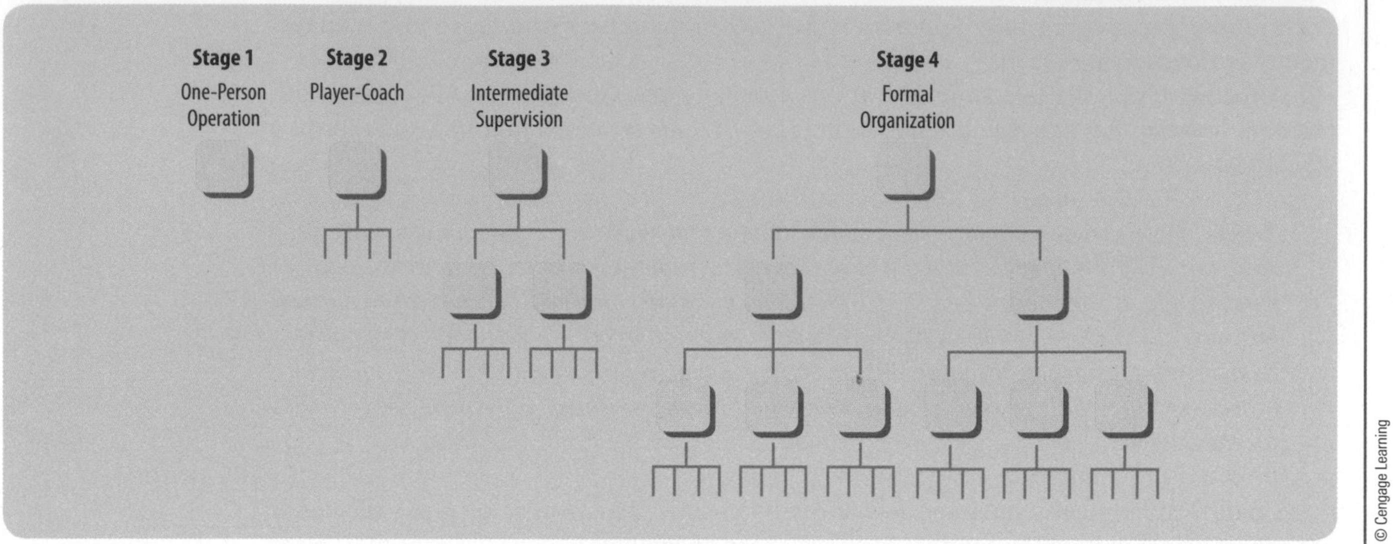

Stage 1
One-Person Operation

Stage 2
Player-Coach

Stage 3
Intermediate Supervision

Stage 4
Formal Organization

A major milestone is reached in Stage 3, when an intermediate level of supervision is added. In many ways, this is a turning point for a small firm, because the entrepreneur must rise above direct, hands-on management and work through an intervening layer of management. Stage 4, the stage of formal organization, involves more than increased size and multi-layered organization. The formalization of management entails adoption of written policies, preparation of plans and budgets, standardization of personnel practices, computerization of records, preparation of organizational charts and job descriptions, scheduling of training conferences, institution of control procedures, and so on. While some formal managerial practices may be adopted prior to Stage 4, the steps shown in Exhibit 19.1 outline a typical pattern of development for successful firms. Flexibility and informality may be helpful when a firm is first started, but the firm's growth requires greater formality in planning and control. Tension often develops as the traditional easygoing patterns of management become dysfunctional. Great managerial skill is required of the entrepreneur in order to preserve a "family" atmosphere while introducing professional management.

As a venture moves from Stage 1 to Stage 4, the pattern of entrepreneurial activities changes. The small business owner becomes less of a doer and more of a leader and manager. Those with strong "doing" skills often have weak managing skills, and this is understandable. Most entrepreneurs build businesses on their specialized capabilities; for example, they may know software development inside and out, have a knack for raising money, or possess enviable selling skills. But when it comes to tasks like assessing talent in others, they often come up short. That is simply not their strong suit, and this limitation can be a serious problem.

As a firm grows, the owner needs to fill key positions with individuals who have the capacity to perform well as managers. Can the best salesperson or most skilled technician be advanced to a higher level? Sometimes, but not always.

Erika Mangrum was a year into her business and was feeling pressured to promote a star employee to general manager. "She wanted more responsibility and more pay," says Mangrum, co-founder and president of Iatria Day Spas and Health Center, a 40-employee company in Raleigh, North Carolina. Mangrum felt a deep sense of loyalty to this employee, who had been with the company from the start, so she went ahead with the promotion. However, it wasn't long before Mangrum realized she was promoting doom and gloom.[15]

The new manager's rudeness and inability to manage conflict created customer complaints and tension among employees. The manager left 14 months after the promotion. And unfortunately, the business also lost key employees in the turmoil.[16]

Sometimes the personal talent or brilliance of the entrepreneur can enable a business to survive while business skills are being acquired. Consider Ronald and Rony Delice, Haitian-born twin brothers, who have ignited fashion runways and men's clothing with their edgy designs. After earning degrees from New York's acclaimed Fashion Institute of Technology, Ronald and Rony worked as custom tailors and designers. They soon started their own business and won awards for their designs, and by 2003 their company already was generating nearly half a million dollars in annual revenue. However, the business side of their venture presented their biggest challenges. The twins found that keeping the books, paying bills, and preparing a business plan were much harder than designing clothing. As Ronald explained it, "We're more artists than businesspeople." Overcoming that challenge meant bringing in qualified people.[17]

Small firms that hesitate to move through the various organizational stages and acquire the necessary professional management often limit their rate of growth. On the other hand, a small business may attempt to grow too quickly. If an entrepreneur's primary strength lies in product development or selling, for example, a quick move into Stage 4 may saddle the entrepreneur with managerial duties and deprive the organization of her or his valuable talents.

An entrepreneur plays a different role in starting a business than he or she does in operating the firm as it becomes more fully developed. And the personal qualities involved in starting a venture differ from the qualities required to manage over the long haul. This helps explain why so few new ventures actually become established businesses with staying power. Growing a business requires maturation and adaptation on the part of the entrepreneur.

Managerial Responsibilities of Entrepreneurs

So far, our discussion of the management process has been very general. Now it is time to look more closely at how entrepreneurs organize and direct a company's operations.

3 Identify the managerial tasks of entrepreneurs.

PLANNING ACTIVITIES

Beyond creating an initial business plan to guide the *launch* of a new venture (the focus of Chapter 6), most entrepreneurs also plan for the ongoing operation of their enterprises. However, the amount of planning they complete is typically less than ideal. And what little planning they do tends to be haphazard and focused on specific and pressing issues—for example, how much inventory to purchase, whether to buy a new piece of equipment, and so on. Circumstances affect the degree to which formal planning is needed, but most businesses can function more profitably by increasing the amount of planning done by managers and making it more systematic.

A firm's basic path to the future is spelled out in a document called a **long-range plan**, or *strategic plan*. As noted in Chapter 3, strategy decisions concern such issues as identifying niche markets and establishing features that differentiate a firm from its competitors. But planning is important even in established businesses, to ensure that changes in the business environment can be addressed as they occur.

Short-range plans are action plans designed to deal with activities in production, marketing, and other areas over a period of one year or less. An important part of a short-range operating plan is the **budget**, a document that expresses future plans in monetary

long-range plan (strategic plan) A firm's overall plan for the future.

short-range plan A plan that governs a firm's operations for one year or less.

budget A document that expresses future plans in monetary terms.

terms. A budget is usually prepared each year (one year in advance), with a breakdown of figures for each month or quarter. (Budgeting is explained in much greater detail in Chapter 22.)

Planning pays off in many ways. First, the process of thinking through the issues confronting a company and developing a plan to deal with those issues can improve productivity. Second, planning provides a focus for a firm: Managerial decisions over the course of the year can be guided by the annual plan, and employees can work consistently toward the same goal. Third, evidence of planning increases credibility with bankers, suppliers, and other outsiders.

Managing time during the course of the business day is another important planning activity for small business managers, who all too often succumb to what is sometimes called the "tyranny of the urgent." In other words, they can easily become distracted by pressing problems. Ryan Gibson, a young entrepreneur in central Texas, commented, "As my enterprise gets larger, there is increased pressure to fight the everyday fires of business when I need to be thinking about how to move my company forward."[18] This makes it easy to ignore or postpone planning to free up time and energy to concentrate on more urgent issues in such areas as production and sales. And, just as quarterbacks who are focusing on a receiver may be blindsided by blitzing linebackers, managers who have neglected to plan may be bowled over by competitors. (Personal time management is discussed in more depth later in the chapter.)

TOOLS

Racing Time

In business, time is money. But feeling pressed for time can hurt your focus, cause your rational decision-making skills to break down, and erode your health. You can minimize the damage from time urgency by shifting the focus from the clock to the content, looking for signs—like a churning stomach, a pounding heart, or talking a mile a minute—that signal a need to slow down. For more suggestions, see Joe Robinson, "Boom," *Entrepreneur*, Vol. 38, No. 11 (November 2010), pp. 74–78.

CREATING AN ORGANIZATIONAL STRUCTURE

While an entrepreneur may give direction through personal leadership, she or he must also define the relationships among the firm's activities and among the individuals on the firm's payroll. Without some kind of organizational structure, operations eventually become chaotic and morale suffers.

The Unplanned Structure

In very small companies, the organizational structure tends to evolve with little conscious planning. Certain employees begin performing particular functions when the company is new and retain those functions as it matures.

This natural evolution is not necessarily bad. Generally, a strong element of practicality often characterizes these types of organizational arrangements. The structure is forged through the experience of working and growing, rather than being pulled from thin air or copied from another firm's organizational chart. But unplanned structures are seldom perfect, and growth typically creates a need for organizational change. The entrepreneur should therefore examine structural relationships periodically and make adjustments as needed for effective teamwork.

© iStockphoto.com/Jacob Wackerhausen

The Chain of Command

A **chain of command** refers to superior–subordinate relationships with a downward flow of instructions, but it involves much more. It is also a channel for two-way communication. As a practical matter, strict adherence to the chain of command is not advisable. An organization in which the primary channel of communication is rigid will be bureaucratic and inefficient. At the same time, frequent and flagrant disregard of the chain of command quickly undermines the position of the bypassed manager. So, there is need for balance, and getting this right will require reasonable care and heads-up management.

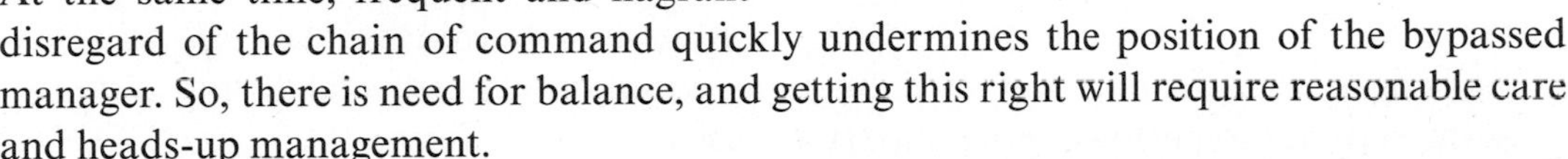

chain of command The official, vertical channel of communication in an organization.

In a **line organization**, each person has one supervisor to whom he or she reports and looks for instructions. All employees are directly engaged in the firm's work, producing, selling, or performing office or financial duties. Most very small firms—for example, those with fewer than 10 employees—use this form of organization.

line organization A simple organizational structure in which each person reports to one supervisor.

A **line-and-staff organization** is similar to a line organization in that each person reports to a single supervisor. However, a line-and-staff structure also has staff specialists who perform specific services or act as management advisors in particular areas (see Exhibit 19.2). Staff specialists may include a human resource manager, a production control technician, a quality control expert, and an assistant to the president. The line-and-staff organization, in some form, is used in many small businesses.

line-and-staff organization An organizational structure that includes staff specialists who assist management.

EXHIBIT 19.2 Line-and-Staff Organization

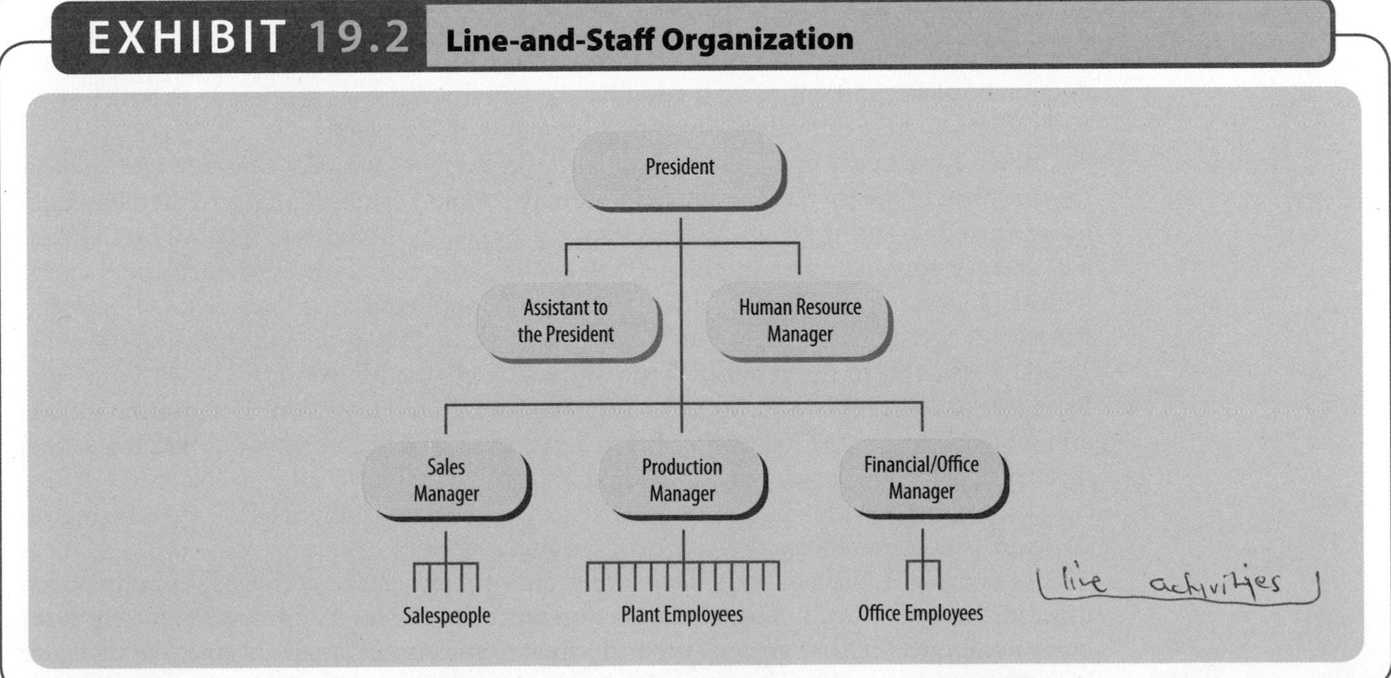

© Cengage Learning

Span of Control

span of control The number of subordinates supervised by one manager.

The **span of control** is the number of employees who are supervised by a manager. Although some experts have stated that six to eight people are all that one individual can supervise effectively, the optimal span of control is actually a variable that depends on a number of factors. Among these factors are the nature of the work and the manager's knowledge, energy, personality, and abilities. In addition, if the abilities of subordinates are better than average, the span of control may be broadened accordingly.

As a very small firm grows and adds employees, the small business owner's span of control is extended. At that point, she or he often has a tendency to stretch the span too far—to supervise not only the first five or six employees hired, but also the new employees added as time goes on. Eventually, the attempted span of control exceeds the entrepreneur's reach, demanding more time and effort than she or he can devote to the business. It is at this point that the entrepreneur must establish intermediate levels of supervision and dedicate more time to management, moving beyond the role of player-coach.

DELEGATING AUTHORITY

delegation of authority Granting to subordinates the right to act or make decisions.

Through **delegation of authority**, a manager grants to subordinates the right to act or to make decisions. Turning over some functions to subordinates by delegating authority frees the superior to perform more important tasks.

Although failure to delegate may be found in any organization, it is often a special problem for entrepreneurs, given their backgrounds and personalities. Because they frequently must pay for mistakes made by subordinates, owners are inclined to keep a firm hold on the reins of leadership in order to protect the business. Some of the problem is simply a matter of habit and momentum. Many entrepreneurs have become accustomed to doing everything themselves, which makes it difficult to turn over some tasks to others when the business grows and they truly need help with their expanded responsibilities. They also may feel the need to continue doing those things that made the firm successful or conclude that they just do them better than their employees. Regardless of the underlying concern, the end result is the same: insufficient delegation.

Inability or unwillingness to delegate authority can become apparent in a number of ways. For example, employees may find it necessary to clear even the most minor decisions with the boss. At any given time, a number of subordinates may be trying to get the attention of the owner to resolve some issue that they lack the authority to settle. This keeps the owner exceptionally busy—rushing from assisting a salesperson to helping iron out a production bottleneck to setting up a new filing system. Entrepreneurs often work long hours, and those who have difficulty delegating compound the problem.

When Russ Lewis operated a small bakery in Vermont with his wife, Linda, he faced this problem at a very basic level. He personally baked between 2,000 to 3,500 loaves of bread each day, and the pace drained all of Russ's energy, along with his love for baking. The bakery supplied restaurants and cafés with great bread and provided the owners with the highest income they ever had, but it also dominated their lives. Six days a week, Russ would get up very early to arrive at the bakery at 1:00 in the morning and bake for 13 hours straight. In the summer, when Vermont's population would swell with tourists, Russ had to start his workday two or three hours earlier! He was so tired that he wasn't even able to change the habits that made him so tired. The couple might have taken the business to a higher level, but Russ could not bring himself to give up his duties or his control, saying, "I enjoy baking, but I like to handle everything myself." By refusing to delegate, Russ Lewis became a victim of his own success.[19]

As one small business writer has observed, "By delegating authority, entrepreneurs unleash the same force in their subordinates that makes them so productive: the thrill of being in charge."[20] This is not to say that delegation is a cure-all for management challenges; in fact, turning over duties can easily lead to its own problems as a result of a subordinate's carelessness or some other failure. But this can be minimized, if the handover is managed well. We offer the following suggestions to ease the transition:

- Accept the fact that you will not be able to make all of the decisions anymore. If you don't, you will blunt the venture's potential to grow and develop.
- Prepare yourself emotionally for the loss of control that small business owners feel when they first start to delegate. This is completely natural.
- Manage carefully the process of finding, selecting, hiring, and retaining employees who are trustworthy enough to handle greater responsibility. In other words, keep an eye on the future when you hire new staff.
- Move forward one step at a time. Start by delegating those functions that you are most comfortable giving up. Even then, continue to provide reasonable oversight to smooth the transition and to ensure the quality of the work.
- Plan to invest the time needed to coach those who are taking over new responsibilities so that they can master required skills. The first thing to do is to write job descriptions to help minimize confusion.
- Make delegation meaningful. Focus on results and give subordinates the flexibility to carry out assignments. To realize the benefits of delegation, you must build leadership in subordinates, who can then take on more advanced and complex tasks.

CONTROLLING OPERATIONS

Despite good planning, organizations never function perfectly. As a result, managers must monitor operations to discover deviations from plans and to ensure that the firm is functioning as intended. Managerial activities that check on performance and correct it when necessary are part of managerial control; they serve to keep the business on course.

The control process begins with the establishment of standards, which are set through planning and goal setting. (This is evidence of the connection between planning and control.) Planners translate goals into norms (standards) by making them measurable. A goal to increase market share, for example, may be expressed as a projected dollar increase in sales volume for the coming year. Such an annual target may, in turn, be broken down into quarterly target standards so that corrective action can be taken early if performance begins to fall below the projected amount.

As Exhibit 19.3 shows, performance measurement occurs at various stages of the control process. Performance may be measured at the input stage (perhaps to determine the quality of materials purchased), during the process stage (perhaps to determine if a machine is operating within predetermined tolerances), and at the output stage (perhaps to check the quality of a completed product).

Corrective action is required when performance deviates significantly from the standard in an unfavorable direction. To prevent the problem from recurring, such action must be followed by an analysis of the cause of the deviation. If the percentage of defective products increases, for example, a manager must determine whether this is caused by substandard raw materials, untrained workers, equipment failure, or some other factor. For a problem to be effectively controlled, corrective action must identify and deal with the true cause.

COMMUNICATING

Another key to a healthy organization is effective communication—that is, getting managers and employees to talk with one another and openly share problems and ideas. The

EXHIBIT 19.3 Stages of the Control Process

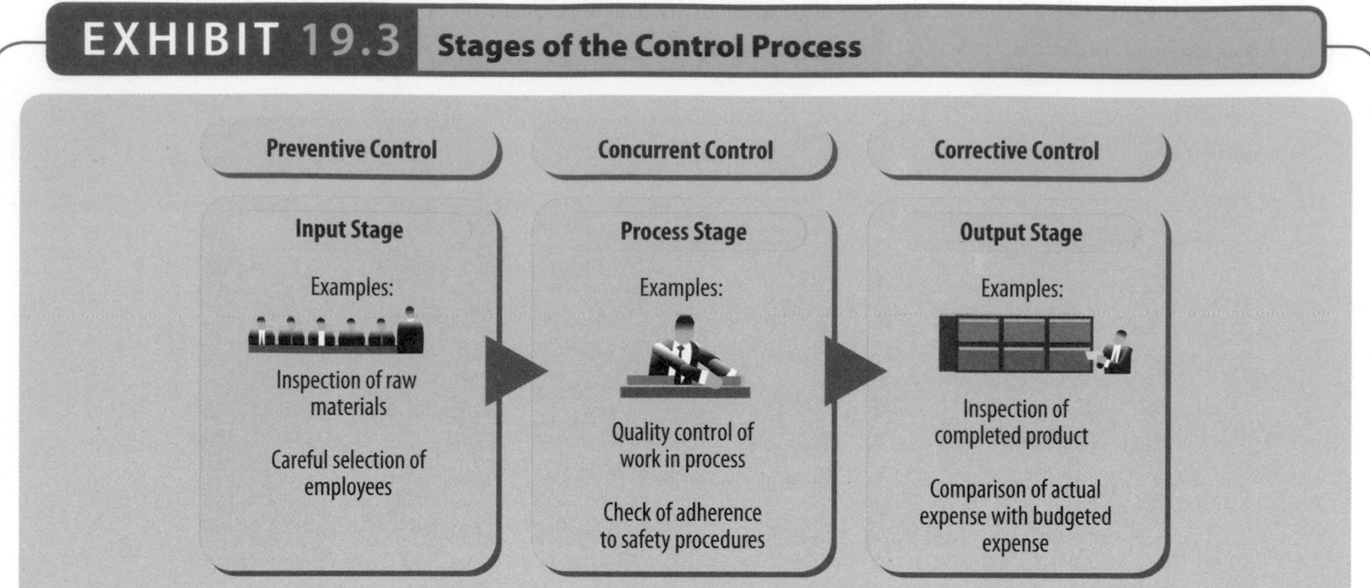

© Cengage Learning

result is two-way communication—a far cry from the old-fashioned idea that managers give orders and employees simply carry them out.

Clearly, effective staff communication is fundamental and crucial to small business success, and solid research proves it. One study found that companies following sound communication practices report higher levels of "employee engagement" and lower turnover compared to those that don't. And this has implications for the bottom line. For example, the study's researchers estimated that firms that communicate effectively are worth, on average, nearly 20 percent more than their interaction-challenged counterparts.[21] Still, workplace communication is rarely adequate—indeed, there is always room for improvement.

Jack Hollingsworth/Digital Vision/Jupiter Images

To communicate effectively, managers must tell employees where they stand, how the business is doing, and what the firm's plans are for the future. While negative feedback may be necessary at times, giving positive feedback to employees is the primary tool for establishing good human relations. Perhaps the most fundamental concept managers need to keep in mind is that employees are people, not machines. They can quickly detect insincerity but respond to honest efforts to treat them as mature, responsible individuals. In short, an atmosphere of trust and respect contributes greatly to good communication.

Many practical tools and techniques can be used to stimulate two-way communication between managers and employees. Here are some that may work for you and your enterprise:

- Periodic performance review sessions to discuss employees' ideas, questions, complaints, and job expectations

- Bulletin boards (physical or electronic) to keep employees informed about developments affecting them and/or the company
- Blogs for internal communication, especially in companies that have open organizational cultures and truly want transparent dialogue[22]
- Microblogging tools (like Twitter and Yammer) to enable employees to communicate, collaborate, and share very brief thoughts and observations about the business in real time
- Suggestion boxes to solicit employees' ideas on possible improvements
- Wikis (websites that allows visitors to add, remove, edit, and change content) set up to bring issues to the surface and draw feedback from employees
- Formal staff meetings to discuss problems and matters of general concern
- Breakfast or lunch with employees to socialize and just talk

These methods and others can be used to supplement the most basic of all channels for communication—the day-to-day interactions between each employee and his or her supervisor.

So far, the focus has been on communication within the company, but entrepreneurs must also make presentations to outside groups, from pitching product ideas at trade shows to selling bankers on the need for funding to offering keynote speeches at community events. And the need for public speaking skills is sure to increase as the company grows and develops. The fear of public speaking is one of the most common phobias (ranking even above the fear of dying!), and an inability to communicate in public can hold back the progress of the business. The good news is that, through practice, you can keep your stage fright under control (if that is a problem), and you can certainly improve your delivery. Exhibit 19.4 provides some tips that will help you develop confidence in your speaking and be more interesting as a presenter.

NEGOTIATING

When operating a business, entrepreneurs and managers must personally interact with other individuals much of the time. Some contacts involve outsiders, such as suppliers, customers, bankers, realtors, and business service providers. Typically, the interests of the parties are in conflict, at least to some degree. A supplier, for example, wants to sell a product or service for the highest possible price, and the buyer wants to purchase it for the lowest possible price. To have a successful business, a manager must be able to reach agreements that both meet the firm's requirements and contribute to good relationships over time.

Even within the business, personal relationships pit different perspectives and personal interests against one another. Subordinates, for example, frequently desire changes in their

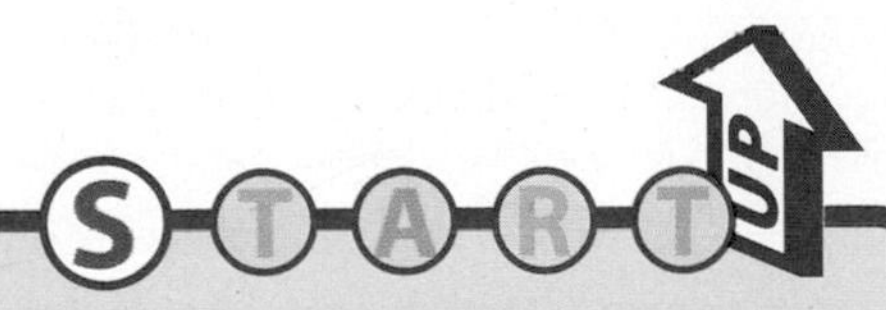

SKILLS

Powerful Persuaders

Effective negotiation is an acquired skill that can take much practice. The research indicates that you should do your homework ahead of time, make aggressive first offers and counteroffers during the dealing, and employ other important tactics. For the full primer, see Robb Mandelbaum, "How to Negotiate Effectively," *Inc.*, November 1, 2010, http://www.inc.com/magazine/20101101/how-to-negotiate-effectively.html.

EXHIBIT 19.4 Presentation Tips

1. **Do your homework.** Know the purpose of the presentation and to whom you will be presenting. If you can find out in advance who will be attending your presentation, you will be able to adapt your comments to their needs and concerns.
2. **Know your material.** The better you know what you plan to talk about, the more you can concentrate on the delivery. And being prepared inspires confidence.
3. **Be interactive.** Listeners may be lulled into disinterest when they are not engaged. Find ways to get the audience involved in what you have to say. Don't, for example, read from your notes for extended periods of time—doing so will ensure that the communication goes in only one direction, and your audience will know it immediately.
4. **Make vivid mental connections in the minds of listeners.** Telling stories helps, but so can other tools and techniques. For example, use props to focus attention, or employ a metaphor throughout the presentation to draw listeners back to a central theme. Humor is entertaining and can provide comic relief, but it can also be used to make a point unforgettable.
5. **Emphasize relevance.** Your listeners are busy people, so be sure to deliver information that they will find useful and worth their time.
6. **Be dynamic, but be yourself.** Let your listeners know that you are passionate about the topic by the way you invest yourself in the presentation. It is much easier for an audience to remain engaged when the presenter is energetic and uses voice, gestures, movement, and facial expressions to show it. Maintaining eye contact communicates that you want to connect with each individual in the room, which is motivating. However, if your level of energy and your use of voice and body are less than authentic, listeners will quickly pick up on that and may write off the talk as insincere.
7. **Use PowerPoint with care.** Text-laden slides can produce the same effect as sleeping pills. If a picture paints a thousand words, then adding pictures and graphics can certainly help the audience access the ideas you want to convey (as long as they are not flashy to the point of distraction). Limit the text on each slide, and do not read from the slides you are showing. Try to imagine how you would respond to the slides if you were not particularly interested in the topic, and then make adjustments accordingly.
8. **Dress appropriately.** Although your audience may be wearing more casual clothing, dress in business-professional attire. Avoid distracting clothing (like a tie that draws attention away from what you have to say), and check to be sure that everything you're wearing is in order before standing up to speak.
9. **Avoid food and drink that make speaking difficult for you.** Caffeinated drinks and sugary foods can make you jittery, which will only add to your nervousness. If you find that you need to clear your throat often after consuming certain foods or beverages, avoid them before speaking engagements.
10. **Practice, practice, practice.** The more presentations you give, the more you will feel confident while giving them. And one of the best ways to conquer stage fright is to spend time speaking in front of others. Recognize that your discomfort with public speaking is likely to fade with experience at the podium.

work assignments or feel that they are worth more to the company than their salary levels indicate. Managers in different departments may compete for services offered by a maintenance department or a computer services unit.

negotiation
A two-way communication process used to resolve differences in interests, desires, or demands.

The process of developing workable solutions through discussions or interactions is called **negotiation**. We are all negotiators in our daily lives, both inside and outside our family relationships. Conflicting interests, desires, and demands require that we reconcile, or negotiate, differences in order to live together peacefully.

Many people consider negotiation to be a win–lose game; that is, one party must win, and the other must lose. The problem with this concept of negotiation is that if parties feel that they have lost, they may go away with thoughts of getting even in subsequent negotiations. Clearly, such feelings do not contribute to good long-term relationships. In contrast, other negotiators advocate a win–win strategy. A win–win negotiator tries to find a solution that will satisfy at least the basic interests of both parties.

Implementing a win–win strategy in relationships involves thinking about one's own interests while also exploring those of the other party. After clarifying the interests of the involved parties and their needs, the negotiator can explore various alternatives to identify their overall fit, looking for a solution that will produce a plan that is workable for all. There are situations in which a win–win solution is impossible, but a positive solution should be pursued whenever it is feasible to do so. And, of course, a foundation for successful negotiation is created by developing strong relationships between the negotiating parties, which can facilitate cooperation.[23]

Personal Time Management

A typical small business owner spends much of the work day on the front lines—meeting customers, solving problems, listening to employee complaints, talking with suppliers, and the like. She or he tackles such problems with the assistance of only a small staff. As a result, the owner-manager's energies and activities are diffused, and time becomes a scarce resource. This highlights the importance of *time management*. But as author and personal achievement expert Barry Farber points out, "When you think about time management, realize that you don't really manage time—you manage activities."[24] It's an interesting way to think about one of the challenges you are sure to face.

THE PROBLEM OF TIME PRESSURE

The hours worked by most new business owners are particularly long; many work from 60 to 80 hours per week or more. A frequent and unfortunate result of such a schedule is inefficient work performance, especially when the entrepreneur has not made the necessary effort to set priorities in life and work. Owner-managers may be too busy to see sales representatives who could supply market information on new products and processes, too busy to read technical or trade literature that would tell them what others are doing and what improvements might be adapted to their own use, too busy to listen carefully to employees' opinions and grievances, and too busy to give employees the instructions they need to do their jobs correctly.

Getting away for a vacation seems impossible for some small business owners. In extremely small firms, owners may find it necessary to close the business during their absence. Even in somewhat larger businesses, owners may fear that the firm will not function properly if they are not there. Unfortunately, keeping one's nose to the grindstone in this way may cost an entrepreneur dearly in terms of personal health, family relationships, and effectiveness in business leadership.

TIME SAVERS FOR BUSY MANAGERS

Part of the solution to the problem of time pressure is application of the managerial approaches discussed in the preceding section. For example, when possible, the manager should assign duties to subordinates who can work without close supervision. For such delegation to work, though, a manager must first select and train qualified employees.

The greatest time saver is the effective use of time. Little will be achieved if an individual flits from one task to another and back again. Use of modern technology, including cell phones, e-mail, and the Internet, can be very helpful in allowing a manager to make the most of his or her time. (A note of caution is in order: Because these tools can become a distraction, they need to be used wisely. For example, checking and responding at length to incoming e-mail messages throughout the day can distract from the tasks at hand and should be minimized.)

The first step in time management should be to analyze how much time is normally spent on various activities. Relying on general impressions is unlikely to be accurate; instead, for a period of several days or (preferably) weeks, the manager should record the amounts of time spent on various activities during the day. An analysis of these figures will reveal a pattern, indicating which projects and tasks consume the most time and which activities are responsible for wasted time. It will also uncover chronic time wasting due to excessive socializing, work on trivial matters, coffee breaks, and so on.

If your habits are typical, you will probably find that the workplace "time wasters" in your life are similar to those that surfaced in a survey of employees, including time lost from telephone interruptions, drop-in visitors, ineffective delegation, losing things in desk clutter, procrastination, and frequent or lengthy meetings.[25] Knowing the distractions that others find to be time wasters may help you to pinpoint those that are creating a problem for you. Only by identifying these distractions can you take steps to deal with them.

After eliminating practices that waste time, a manager can carefully plan his or her use of available time. A planned approach to a day's or week's work is much more effective than a haphazard do-whatever-comes-up-first style. This is true even for small firm managers whose schedules are continually interrupted in unanticipated ways.

Many time management specialists recommend the use of a daily written plan of work activities, often called a "to-do" list. A survey of 2,000 executives from mostly small companies found that around 95 percent of them keep a list of things to do. Those executives may have 6 to 20 items on their list at any given time, though fewer than 1 percent of them complete all listed tasks on a daily basis.[26] Many entrepreneurs use Microsoft Outlook or a day planner to create and manage these lists, but others use PDAs, note cards, or even sticky notes. Regardless of the medium selected, you should highlight priorities among listed items. By classifying duties as first-, second-, or third-level priorities, you can identify and focus attention on the most crucial tasks.

There are countless guides to time management, and they offer many valuable tips: Get a good time management system and use it, try to make meetings more efficient, unsubscribe from magazines and catalogues you never read, create a file folder for active projects, keep your desk and office organized, use deadlines to promote focus, manage e-mail effectively, and so on. However, the one bit of advice that seems to show up on just about every list of suggestions is to set aside time to work undisturbed. As the pace of business and the flow of information pick up speed and new technologies and media channels increasingly compete for your attention, preserving time for focused work on important projects becomes more and more difficult—but it is critical that you do so. The health and future of your company may very well depend on it!

In the final analysis, effective time management requires firmly established priorities and self-discipline. An individual may begin with good intentions but lapse into habitually attending to whatever he or she finds to do at the moment. Procrastination is a frequent thief of time—many managers delay unpleasant and difficult tasks, retreating to trivial and less threatening activities with the rationalization that they are getting those duties out of the way in order to better concentrate on the more important tasks.

Outside Management Assistance

Because entrepreneurs tend to be better doers than they are managers, they should consider the use of outside management assistance. Such support can supplement the manager's personal knowledge and the expertise of the few staff specialists on the company's payroll.

entrepreneurial experiences

© iStockphoto.com/Angelika Schwarz

So Much to Do . . . So Little Time

Everyone has the same 24 hours each day, but some people seem to be able to squeeze a lot more activity into them. Interestingly, productive leaders and managers may use very different approaches to get more from their time. This means you are going to have to find the method that is right for you. Perhaps these working models will give you some idea of what to try.

© sizov/Shutterstock.com

Krissi Barr is founder of Barr Corporate Success, in Cincinnati, Ohio. Her results-oriented consulting company shows businesses of all sizes how to make the most of their resources. Barr describes a simple technique that she uses for time management: "If I think something is going to take me an hour, I give myself 40 minutes. By shrinking your mental deadlines, you work faster and with greater focus." So, think *less* and get *more*.

Compare Barr's method to the one used by Scott Lang, CEO of Silver Spring Networks, a smart-grid (energy) solutions company located in Redwood City, California:

> *For me, a big part of productivity is being agile. I like to leave a lot of blocks in my day open. On an average day, I'm only 50 percent scheduled, though occasionally it gets as high as 80 percent. That's imperative, because often something comes up out of nowhere.*

When the CEO of an important new partner arrived at his office unexpectedly, Lang was able to find an open window of time to talk with him because of his scheduling habits. And it's a good thing he did—during an hour-long visit, the two identified new markets that would allow the company to expand globally. But notice that Lang squeezes more results from his hours by freeing up his schedule, whereas Barr gets more done by allotting less time to her work—very different approaches, but ultimately the same outcome.

Barbara Corcoran's time management method is a bit more complicated. You may know Corcoran from her appearances as an investor on ABC's hit reality TV show "Shark Tank" or as a contributor to NBC's "TODAY." However, she first made her mark as an entrepreneur who used a $1,000 loan to start the Corcoran Group and parlayed that investment into a real estate business that she sold in 2001 for $70 million. Along the way, she learned how to focus her time by using a creative system, based on the idea of a nice meal, to prioritize her to-do list. Here are the four "courses" in her plan:

- **Entrée 1:** Time-sensitive tasks that will push the business forward and that only Corcoran can do
- **Entrée 2:** Tasks that are not as critical to the company but are still time sensitive
- **Side Dish:** Important tasks, but ones that don't have a deadline
- **Dessert:** Unimportant tasks in the big picture, but worthy of attention as time permits

When all is said and done, Corcoran will end up with a "balanced diet" of activities, but they follow a definite set of priorities. This ensures that the most important tasks will receive the attention they deserve.

So, do any of these time management methods seem to fit your personality and individual style? If not, there is no need to be concerned. This chapter offers some general principles that will get you started. And as you gain more experience as a small business owner, you will be able to develop a system that is perfect for you. Until then, take some time to think about it—just don't take too much of it.

Sources: "Barbara Corcoran—About Barbara," http://barbaracorcoran.com, accessed March 3, 2011; "Barr Corporate Success—Who We Are," http://barrcorporatesuccess.com/whoweare.php, accessed March 2, 2011; Gillian Reagan, "Double-Click Dude Aces His Second Act," *New York Observer*, Vol. 32, No. 2., November 4, 2008; Leigh Buchanan, "The Chief Recruiter: Kevin P. Ryan of AlleyCorp," *Inc.*, March 2010; and "Silver Spring Networks—About Us," http://silverspringnet.com/aboutus, accessed March 3, 2011.

THE NEED FOR OUTSIDE ASSISTANCE

5
Outline the various types of outside management assistance.

Entrepreneurs often lack opportunities to share ideas with peers, given the small staff in most new enterprises. Consequently, they may experience a sense of loneliness. Some entrepreneurs reduce their feelings of isolation by joining groups such as the Entrepreneurs' Organization and the Young Presidents' Organization,[27] which allow them to meet with peers from other firms and share problems and experiences.

By obtaining help from peer groups and other sources of outside managerial assistance, entrepreneurs can overcome some of their managerial deficiencies and ease their sense of loneliness. Outsiders can bring a detached, often objective point of view and new ideas. They may also possess knowledge of methods, approaches, and solutions beyond the experience of a particular entrepreneur.

SOURCES OF MANAGEMENT ASSISTANCE

Entrepreneurs seeking management assistance can turn to any number of sources, including SBA-funded programs, business incubators, and management consultants. Other approaches include consulting public and university libraries, attending evening classes at local colleges, and considering the suggestions of informed friends and customers.

U.S. Small Business Administration (SBA)

For many aspiring small business owners, the U.S. Small Business Administration (SBA) is an important gateway to information and support for startups and other small companies, and it is often the first place they go for assistance. The federal government specifically tasks the SBA with connecting these enterprises with the resources they need to get started and/or grow. In accord with its mandate, the agency helps businesses across the country through what it refers to as "the 3 C's of our service":[28]

- **Capital.** Working through 5,000 banks to provide small business loans
- **Contracts.** Directing 23 percent of U.S. government contract dollars to small businesses
- **Counseling.** Providing direction through a network of 14,000 SBA-affiliated counselors

As you will see below, the SBA uses the Service Corps of Retired Executives and its Small Business Development Centers to offer consulting and other forms of assistance; however, it also funds a broader range of counseling programs, which you can find by clicking on the "Counseling & Training" tab on its main website at http://www.sba.gov.

SERVICE CORPS OF RETIRED EXECUTIVES (SCORE) By contacting any SBA field office, small business managers can obtain free management advice from the **Service Corps of Retired Executives**, or **SCORE**. SCORE's 13,000 working and retired business executives serve as volunteer consultants to nearly 20,000 startups each year.[29] As a resource partner with the SBA, SCORE provides an opportunity for retired executives to contribute to the business community and, in the process, help small business managers to solve their problems. The relationship is thus mutually beneficial.

Service Corps of Retired Executives (SCORE)
An SBA-sponsored group of retired executives who give free advice to small businesses.

Judson Lovering, an entrepreneur who operates a specialty bakery in New England, wished to improve his business. A SCORE business counselor, who had formerly owned a small business, helped him capitalize on the bakery's most popular products and eliminate low-profit offerings. This required Lovering to decline some specialty orders that had made the business a "personal bakery" without adequate profit margins. Following the counselor's advice, Lovering has been able to grow his business.[30]

SMALL BUSINESS DEVELOPMENT CENTERS (SBDCS) Patterned after the Agricultural Extension Service, most **small business development centers (SBDCs)** are affiliated with colleges or universities as a part of the SBA's overall program of assistance to small business. Operating from some 1,100 branch offices, SBDCs provide direct consultation, continuing education, research assistance, and export services. One of their priorities is lending support to minority-owned firms. The staff typically includes faculty members, SCORE counselors, professional staff, and graduate student assistants.[31]

small business development centers (SBDCs)
University-affiliated centers offering consulting, education, and other support to small businesses.

Educational Institutions

Many colleges and universities have student consulting teams willing to assist small businesses. These teams of upper-class and graduate students, under the direction of a faculty member, work with owners of small ventures in analyzing and devising solutions to their business problems.

These programs offer mutual benefits: They provide students with a practical view of business management and supply small firms with answers to their problems. The students who participate are typically combined in teams that provide a diversity of academic backgrounds. An individual team, for example, may include students specializing in management, marketing, accounting, and finance.

Some colleges and universities offer training directly to aspiring small business owners. For example, nearly 300,000 entrepreneurs have gone through a business development program called FastTrac, which is available in all 50 U.S. states and select countries around the world. This curriculum was developed by the Ewing Marion Kauffman Foundation and is offered through a wide variety of affiliates, including colleges and universities, chambers of commerce, business development centers, and consulting firms.[32] FastTrac is a practical, hands-on program designed to show entrepreneurs how to hone the practical skills they will need to launch, manage, and grow a successful business. Participants don't just learn about business—they live it by working on their own business ideas.[33]

Business Incubators

As discussed in Chapter 9, a business incubator is an organization that offers support, such as space and managerial and clerical services, to new businesses. According to the National Business Incubation Association, there are now more than 1,400 incubators in the United States and about 7,000 worldwide.[34] Around 94 percent of the incubators in North America are operated as nonprofit organizations, many of which involve the participation of government agencies or universities; however, around 6 percent have been launched as private endeavors.[35] The primary motivation for establishing incubators has been a desire to encourage entrepreneurship and thereby contribute to economic development.

Often, individuals who wish to start businesses lack relevant knowledge and appropriate experience. In many cases, they need practical guidance in marketing, recordkeeping,

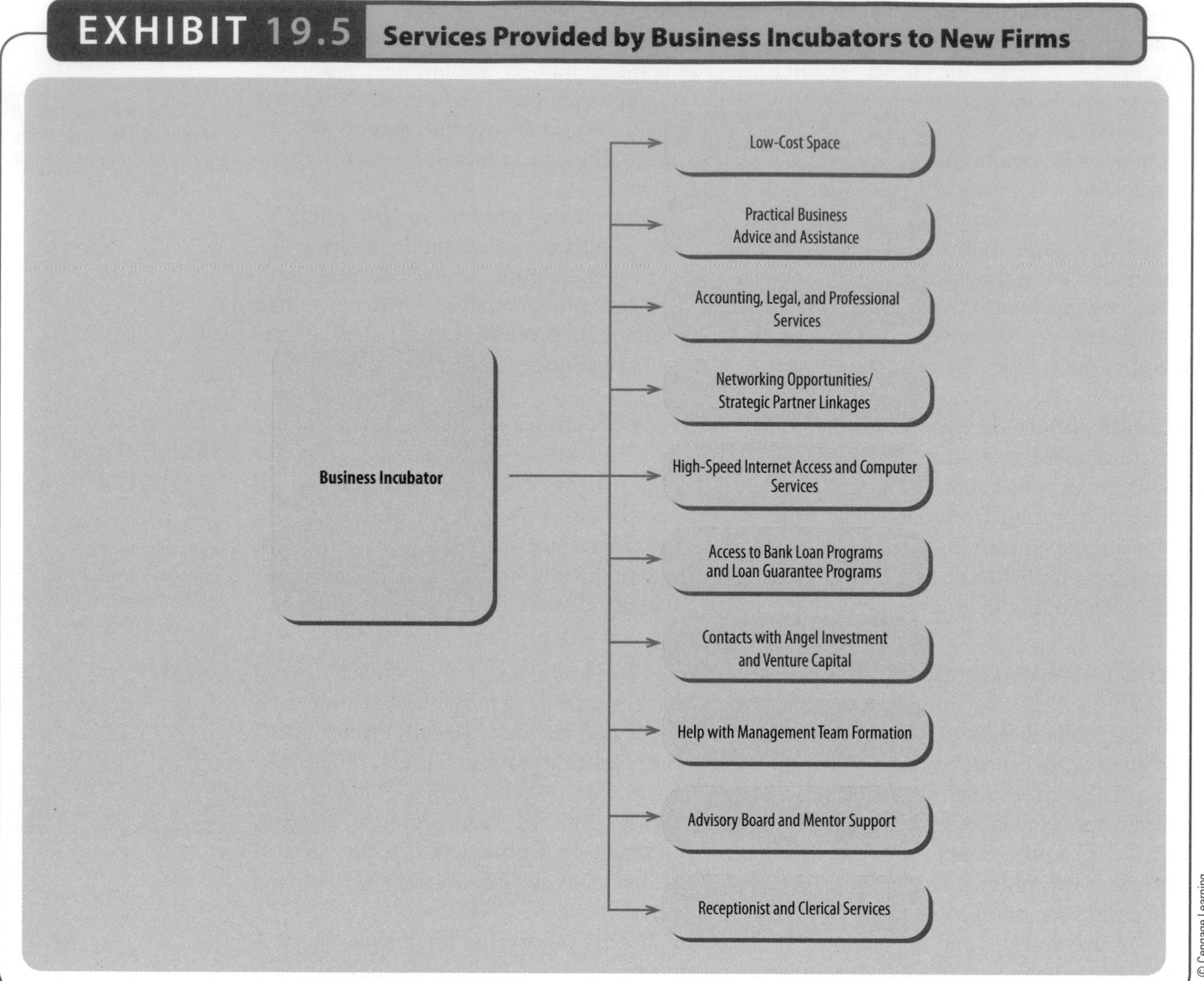

management practices, business plan preparation, and other forms of operating expertise. A more complete list of the services typically available in an incubator is shown in Exhibit 19.5.

An incubator provides a supportive atmosphere for a business during the early months of its existence, when it is most fragile and vulnerable to external dangers and internal errors. If the incubator works as it should, the fledgling business gains strength quickly and soon leaves the incubator setting. Most incubators "graduate" startups within a certain time period (typically, three years) or when the company achieves certain performance milestones. Generally, startups are not released "into the wild" until they can withstand the competition they will encounter in the marketplace.

Today, some incubators in the United States are reinventing themselves as *virtual incubators*—that is, they no longer require client companies to set up shop at a single location. Instead, they focus on connecting a greater number of entrepreneurs with the high-quality experts and mentors they need. This model is less expensive to operate, so the cost savings can be passed on to the entrepreneurs.

When Christie Stone, co-founder of Tico Beans Coffee, a coffee distributor in New Orleans, was just getting started, she needed help executing her business plan. However, relocating to an incubator was out of the question—she wanted an office near a warehouse where her beans could be stored. She eventually joined a virtual incubator called The Idea Village, without having to move. The team of lawyers, accountants, and salespeople assigned to the company helped her get off to a very solid start, at very little cost. Tico Beans received around $30,000 worth of legal and consulting services for only $3,000 from lawyers and accountants who saw that providing assistance was a way to build their networks.[36] Everyone walked away happy!

Management Consultants

Management consultants serve small businesses as well as large corporations, and they do this with operations that can range from large global firms to one- and two-person ventures. More to the point, though, the results they deliver can provide a substantial boost to a small business. For example, 69 percent of the companies in a recent *Inc.* magazine survey reported that they had used consultants; and of these, 90 percent found their services helpful.[37] But many small firm managers are still reluctant to use outside advisors, for a host of reasons. Some believe that they can solve problems themselves, that an outsider could never truly understand the business, or that bringing in an outside advisor would simply cost too much. But some small businesses need analysis by consultants and find that the enterprise can easily recover the cost of such services in the additional revenue resulting from improved performance. Results definitely vary.

For small companies that decide to pursue this option, the owner and the consultant should reach an understanding on the nature of the assistance to be provided before it begins. This can help to ensure satisfaction for both the provider and the client. Any consulting fees should be specified, and the particulars of the agreement should be put in writing. Fees are often quoted on a per-day basis and can easily range from $500 to $5,000, or more. Although the cost may seem high, it must be evaluated in terms of the expertise that it buys.

Directories are available to help entrepreneurs find the right management consultant. One such source is published by the Institute of Management Consultants USA (http://www.imcusa.org). The code of ethics to which institute members subscribe is an indication of their desire to foster professionalism in their work.

Small Business Networks

Entrepreneurs can also gain management assistance from peers through **networking**, the process of developing and engaging in mutually beneficial informal relationships. When business owners meet, they discover a commonality of interests that can lead to an exchange of ideas and experiences. The settings for such meetings may be trade associations, civic clubs, fraternal organizations, or any other situation that brings businesspeople into contact with one another. Of course, the personal network of a small business owner is not limited only to other entrepreneurs, but those individuals may be the most significant part of his or her business network.

networking
The process of developing and engaging in mutually beneficial relationships.

Business networking opportunities often come from unexpected settings. For example, in 2004 Ryan Bonifacino used connections from his university fraternity to launch a special event and corporate photography company. Over time, his startup expanded to offer digital media services, brand management, and Internet marketing and advertising. "Our main investor was actually one of our sponsors for a fraternity philanthropic event," says Bonifacino. "He loved the plan, the fraternity, and our energy." There is no question that the young entrepreneur's fraternity relationships were a huge help. His first gigs were at Greek events, where he was able to connect with thousands of people. After graduating in 2005, Bonifacino led his company, Bozmedia Group LLC, to sales of $460,000 within one year—and the venture has doubled in size since then.[38]

Harnessing a personal network can provide a tremendous boost to the launch of a new business. For example, fellow garden club members could serve as a focus group to assess startup ideas or as a PR team to spread news of your new landscaping and water pond business across town. Alumni connections from your college days may lead you to professionals who can take care of your legal, banking, or other needs. They may even become loyal and effective business partners, if the fit is right.

Other Business and Professional Services

A variety of business and professional groups provide management assistance. In many cases, such assistance is part of the business relationship. Sources of management advice include bankers, certified public accountants, attorneys, insurance agents, suppliers, trade associations, and chambers of commerce.

It takes initiative to draw on the management assistance available from such groups, so it is important to explore the possibilities. For example, rather than limiting a business relationship with a certified public accountant (CPA) to audits and financial statements, many small business owners ask their CPAs to advise them on a much broader range of subjects.

A good accountant can not only offer advice on tax matters, but also recommend an appropriate severance package when it comes time to fire someone. If you are thinking about opening a new branch, an accountant can tell you if your cash flow will support it. Considering the launch of an additional business? An accountant's insight will help you determine whether the margins will be adequate. Accountants can help you make informed assessments of your insurance needs, the impact of taking on a big account (as well as the downside of losing it), and the bottom-line effects of cutting expenses.

As you can see from these examples, potential management assistance often comes disguised as service from professionals and firms encountered in the normal course of business activity. By taking advantage of such opportunities, an entrepreneur can strengthen a small firm's management and improve its operations with little, if any, additional cost. But that doesn't mean it will be easy. Leading and overseeing the operations of a small business can eventually require a professional management approach, which can be developed only through great effort and attention to details. Reaching this state is a challenge, but the insights in this chapter can help guide you toward the competencies you will need to make it happen.

1. **Discuss the entrepreneur's leadership role.**
   - Entrepreneurs must establish and communicate a vision of the firm's future.
   - Founding entrepreneurs need a tolerance for ambiguity and a capacity for adaptation.
   - Leading a business to success requires a focus on reaching business goals more than a flashy personality.
   - An entrepreneur exerts strong personal influence in a small firm.
   - Progressive managers use various leadership styles, incorporating participative management, empowerment, and even self-managed work teams.
   - Entrepreneurs should deliberately shape the organizational culture, which can greatly influence how business is conducted in the company and how the company performs.
2. **Explain the small business management process and its unique features.**
   - Many founders tend to be more action-oriented and less analytical and systematic in their approach when compared to professional managers.
   - A founder's less-sophisticated management style can adversely affect business growth, and many find it difficult to adopt more effective models.
   - Small companies are particularly vulnerable to managerial inefficiency, and even failure.
   - Small firm managers face special financial and personnel constraints.
   - As a new business grows, it adds layers of supervision and increases formality of management—a trend that moves through four or five stages.

- A firm's growth requires the entrepreneur to become more of a manager and less of a doer.

3. Identify the managerial tasks of entrepreneurs.

- Both long-range planning and short-range planning are required, but they are often postponed or neglected.
- An organizational structure must be created to provide for orderly direction of operations.
- Successful delegation of authority allows entrepreneurs to devote more time to important duties.
- Managers exercise control by monitoring operations in order to detect and correct deviations from plans.
- Effective two-way communication is important in building a healthy organization.
- Entrepreneurs need to develop their public speaking skills to meet the demands of being the leader of a growing business.
- Managers must be able to negotiate with both insiders and outsiders and should focus on win–win strategies, which will satisfy the basic interests of both parties.

4. Describe the problem of time pressure and suggest solutions.

- Time pressure creates inefficiencies in the management of a small firm because the entrepreneur's energies are scattered.
- The greatest time saver is the effective use of time, which requires firmly established priorities and self-discipline.
- A manager can reduce time pressure through such practices as eliminating wasteful activities and planning work carefully, using such tools as a "to-do" list.

5. Outline the various types of outside management assistance.

- Outside management assistance can be used to remedy staff limitations and reduce an entrepreneur's sense of isolation, among other things.
- The SBA is an important source of information and support for small companies, and it is often the first place small business owners turn for help.
- Three government- and/or university-sponsored sources of assistance are the Service Corps of Retired Executives (SCORE), Small Business Development Centers (SBDCs), and educational institutions.
- Business incubators provide guidance as well as space for beginning businesses.
- Management assistance may be obtained by engaging management consultants and by networking with other small business owners.
- Professionals such as bankers and CPAs can also provide valuable management assistance.

Key Terms

empowerment p. 555
work teams p. 556
professional manager p. 557
long-range plan (strategic plan) p. 561
short-range plan p. 561
budget p. 561
chain of command p. 563
line organization p. 563
line-and-staff organization p. 563
span of control p. 564
delegation of authority p. 564
negotiation p. 568
Service Corps of Retired Executives (SCORE) p. 573
Small Business Development Centers (SBDCs) p. 573
networking p. 575

Discussion Questions

1. Would most employees of small firms welcome or resist a leadership approach that sought their ideas and involved them in meetings to let them know what was going on? Why might some employees resist such an approach?
2. Is the quality of management likely to be relatively uniform in all types of small businesses? If not, what might account for differences?
3. What are the four stages of small business growth, as outlined in this chapter? How do management requirements change as the firm moves through these stages?
4. Some professional football coaches have written game plans that they consult from time to time during games. If coaches need formal plans, does it follow that small business owners also need them as they engage in their particular type of competition? Why or why not?

5. What type of small firm might effectively use a line organization? When might it be necessary to change the firm's structure? To what type of structure? Why?
6. Explain the relationship between planning and control in a small business. Give an example that shows how these two features can work together.
7. Ralph Waldo Emerson once said, "What you do speaks so loud that I cannot hear what you say." What does this mean, and how does it apply to communication in small firms?
8. What practices can a small business manager use to conserve time?
9. What are some advantages and possible drawbacks for a startup retail firm that locates in a business incubator?
10. Are student consulting teams of greater benefit to the client firm or to the students involved?

You Make the Call

SITUATION 1

John Smithers learned all about leadership in the military, and he is hoping to apply those skills to running John's Deals to Go, his small automobile-leasing company. One interesting feature of life in the armed services is that considerable responsibilities are delegated to young men and women who have very little work experience. Smithers was only 27 when he was assigned duties as a purchasing manager at Kandahar Airport, Afghanistan, in 2003. As a young Marine, he was directly responsible for nearly $50 million in purchasing contracts, which forced him to grow up—and really fast!

To parallel his military experience, Smithers and his small management team have decided to use various methods to delegate decision making to employees at the operating level in his company. New employees are trained thoroughly after they are first hired, but supervisors will not monitor their work closely once they have learned their duties. Management is willing to jump in and help if truly needed, but they purposely leave workers alone when they take on their assigned duties. Managers will not look over employees' shoulders to be sure that they are doing their jobs as assigned, and they certainly do not monitor the work just to try to catch someone making a mistake. Smithers's managerial philosophy is that people work best when they sense that their superiors trust their abilities and their business integrity.

Smithers and his team sometimes leave for day-long meetings and allow the employees to run the business by themselves. Job assignments are defined rather loosely, but management expects employees to assume responsibility and to take necessary action whenever they see that something needs to be done. To reinforce the message of trust, employees who ask for direction are sometimes simply told to solve the problem in whatever way they think best.

Question 1 Is such a loosely organized firm likely to be as effective as a firm that defines jobs more precisely and monitors performance more closely? What are the advantages and the limitations of the managerial style described above?

Question 2 How might such managerial methods affect morale?

Question 3 Would you like to work for this company? Why or why not?

SITUATION 2

A few years after successfully launching a new outdoor advertising business, Sean Richeson found himself spending 16-hour days running from one appointment to another, negotiating with customers, drumming up new business, signing checks, and checking up as much as possible on his six employees. The founder realized that his own strength was in selling, but general managerial responsibilities were very time consuming and interfered with his sales efforts. Richeson even slept in the office one or two nights a week just to try to keep up with his work.

Despite his diligence, however, Richeson knew that his employees weren't organized and that many problems needed to be addressed. For example, he lacked the time to set personnel policies or to draw up specific job descriptions for his six employees. Just last week, he had been warned that one employee would sometimes take advantage of the lax supervision and skip work. Invoices often were sent to customers late, and delivery schedules were not always kept. Fortunately, the business is profitable, in spite of the numerous problems.

Question 1 Is Richeson's problem one of time management or general managerial ability? Would it be feasible to engage a management consultant to help solve the firm's problems?

Question 2 If Richeson asked you to recommend some type of outside management assistance, would you recommend a SCORE counselor, a student consulting team, a CPA firm, a management consultant, or some other type of assistance? Why?

Question 3 If you were asked to improve this company's management system, what steps would you take first? What would be your initial goal?

SITUATION 3

After a slow start in a spare bedroom in her home, Sarah Sullivan's media sales business was flourishing. Even though it had been only three and a half years since she launched the company, Sullivan was beginning to wonder if she had the necessary talent to ensure its continued success. The business had grown to 100 employees after two years, and now it was approaching 200 employees. When the business was small, Sullivan could figure out solutions to problems on a case-by-case basis, but now the problems were becoming increasingly complicated.

Question 1 What kinds of practices or procedures will Sullivan need to adopt to enable the business to continue to operate successfully?

Question 2 What resources might Sullivan use to get good feedback to help her to assess her competence and understand the issues her growing business is facing?

Experiential Exercises

1. Interview a management consultant, SCORE member, university director of student consulting teams, or representative of a CPA firm to discuss small business management weaknesses and the willingness or reluctance of small firms to use consultants. Prepare a report on your findings.
2. Diagram the organizational relationships in a small business of your choice. Report on any organizational problems that are apparent to you or that are recognized by the owner-manager or others in the firm.
3. Prepare a report on your personal observations of leadership and delegation of authority by a supervisor in an organization where you have been an employee or volunteer. Include references to the type(s) of leadership exercised and the adequacy of authority delegation (if any), clarity of instructions, and any problems involved.
4. Select an unstructured time block of one to four hours in your schedule—that is, hours that are not regularly devoted to class attendance, sleeping, and so on. Carefully record your use of that time period for several days. Prepare a report summarizing your use of the time and outlining a plan to use it more effectively.

Small Business & Entrepreneurship Resource Center

Stephen R. Covey describes a preferred method of delegation as "stewardship." Stewardship delegation focuses on results and allows the individual receiving an assignment some latitude in carrying it out. The article "Stephen R. Covey: The Seven Habits" discusses Covey's seven habits of highly effective people. Briefly describe each of the seven habits.

Source: Chartered Management Institute, "Stephen R. Covey: The Seven Habits of Highly Effective People," *Thinkers*, March 2003.

Case 19

DIAMOND WIPES INTERNATIONAL (P. 730)

This case points out how the growth of a business requires leadership and managerial adjustments, with a focus on the entrepreneur's need to hire capable personnel and delegate responsibilities to be able to manage the many new challenges that arise when a firm expands.

ALTERNATIVE CASE FOR CHAPTER 19

Case 8, D'Artagnan, p. 707

CHAPTER 20

Managing Human Resources

In the SPOTLIGHT
37signals
http://37signals.com

It takes excellent people to build a great company.

Jason Fried is co-founder and president of a Chicago-based Web applications company called 37signals (named for 37 radio telescope signals from space identified as possible evidence of extraterrestrial life). Since launching the company in 1999, Fried has developed a careful and deliberate approach to finding and managing people for his company. Why is he so intentional in his hiring? This is how Fried answers that question:

> *Hiring people is like making friends. Pick good ones, and they'll enrich your life. Make bad choices, and they'll bring you down. Who you work with is even more important than who you hang out with, because you spend a lot more time with your workmates than with your friends.*

The company has a deliberately small staff of 20, and it works hard to keep them happy. After 11 years in business, only two people have left to pursue opportunities elsewhere—and one of those returned after working at another company for seven years.

Fried's hiring method has served 37signals well, but it is unusual in some ways. For example, he hires late (only "after it hurts") and never before a new employee is needed. He won't even hire "the perfect catch" if he doesn't have "the perfect job" open for that person. Invent a position to keep a talented person from getting away? Never! And Fried won't hire for a job he has never performed himself. In his mind, there is no way to find the right person for a job if you don't understand the position on a deep level.

After studying this chapter, you should be able to . . .

LOOKING AHEAD

1. Explain the importance of employee recruitment, and list some useful sources for finding suitable applicants.
2. Identify the steps in evaluating job applicants.
3. Describe the roles of training and development for both managerial and nonmanagerial employees.
4. Explain the various types of compensation plans, including the use of incentive plans.
5. Discuss the human resource issues of co-employment, legal protection, labor unions, and the formalizing of employer–employee relationships.

Fried's approach to evaluating job candidates is also a little out of the ordinary. Résumés are ignored ("they're full of exaggerations, half-truths, embellishments—even outright lies"). Cover letters are given extra weight, because they reveal who wants the specific job being offered (and not just any job), and they also show who can write well. ("When in doubt, always hire the better writer," Fried suggests.) And during interviews, Fried listens carefully for signs of self-initiative. He reasons that candidates who ask, "How do I do that?" or "How can I find out this or that?" often are not used to figuring things out for themselves and thus would be a drain on others. On the other hand, when a candidate asks "Why?" Fried interprets this as "a sign of deep interest in a subject" and "a healthy dose of curiosity." Details can make a huge difference.

Even if all indications are positive, Fried still chooses to go slow. "We . . . try to test-drive people before hiring them full time. We give designers a one-week design project to see how they approach the problem," paying them $1,500 for their time. Fried sometimes extends the project into a month-long contract "to see how we feel about the person and how the person feels about us." The point is to avoid hiring mistakes that would be bad for the company and unfair to the candidate.

In the wake of the economic downturn, many small businesses are finding that they have to hire very carefully—as Fried is doing—or even get by with fewer workers. Some are turning to flexible management practices, like cross-training employees, hiring temporary workers on an as-needed basis, or forming outsourcing partnerships to adjust to fluctuations in market demand. But one way or another, the small business show must go on—and that means having the right people on board when you need them.

Sources: Jason Fried, "Never Read Another Resume," *Inc.,* Vol. 32, No. 5 (June 2010), pp. 36–37; Sarah E. Needleman, "Entrepreneurs Prefer to Keep Staffs Lean," *Wall Street Journal,* March 2, 2010, p. B5; "37signals Press," https://37s.backpackit.com/pub/1391756, accessed March 23, 2011; and http://37signals.com, accessed March 22, 2011.

Small businesses that tap markets with great potential using compelling competitive advantages are more likely to succeed. That goes without saying. But those that get to the winner's circle with any hope of staying there must have something more: wisely selected, highly capable, and motivated employees. Successful firms know that people are their most important assets; therefore, human resources should be managed intelligently so that they can make a difference in a venture's performance.

The term ***human resource management (HRM)*** refers to the management of employees, individually and collectively, in a way that enables them to help the business reach its strategic objectives. This can only be achieved if highly capable employees are recruited, trained, assessed, and given incentives to reach their greatest potential. To complicate things a bit, HRM looks very different in large firms than in small companies. A small entrepreneurial concern neither can nor should duplicate the personnel policies and procedures of a Google or a General Motors. Instead, it should carefully manage its employees in a way that is best suited for the 10, 50, or 100 employees on its payroll.

human resource management (HRM) The management of employees in a way that enables them to help a firm reach its strategic objectives.

The HRM practices of small businesses should be well planned and professional, but research has shown that this often is not the case.[1] This regrettable state of affairs may be the result of a lack of knowledge, and that is what we want to deal with first. If you are concerned that you may not know enough to start or expand your business, we hope to bring you up to a reasonable speed. Toward that end, this chapter presents HRM practices that work best for entrepreneurial companies.

Recruiting Personnel

Recruitment brings applicants to a business; the goal is to obtain a pool of potential employees that is large enough to contain a number of talented prospects. In a subsequent stage of the selection process, management decides which applicants are "keepers."

THE NEED FOR QUALITY EMPLOYEES

There is no substitute for high-quality employees—in most cases, the more capable and motivated, the better. Joel Spolsky, founder and CEO of a software development company in New York City, describes the remarkable impact that excellent employees can have on a business:

> *I keep hearing people say that they only hire the top 1 percent of job seekers. At my company, Fog Creek Software, I want to hire the top 1 percent, too. We're doubling in size each year, and we're always in the market for great software developers. In our field, the top 1 percent of the workforce can easily be 10 times as productive as the average developer. The best developers invent new products, figure out shortcuts that save months of work, and, when there are no shortcuts, plow through coding tasks like a monster truck at a tea party.*[2]

Having the right people "on board" can provide an enormous boost to the overall performance of the company. And it's about more than the individual contribution of each high-potential employee. The presence of one capable and motivated worker tends to raise expectations of all the others, and interactions between two or more high-impact employees will often lead to outcomes that are significantly greater than the sum of their already excellent individual contributions.

Recruitment and selection of employees establish a foundation for the ongoing human interactions in a company. In a sense, the quality of a firm's employees determines the firm's potential. A solid, effective organization can be built only with a talented, ambitious workforce. And since payroll is one of the largest expense categories for most businesses, wise employment decisions can have a direct impact on the company's bottom line. By recruiting the best personnel possible, an entrepreneurial firm can improve its return on each payroll dollar.

Most successful companies have moved ahead of their competition because

ACTION

Hiring Hard Workers

Small business owners tend to be "take charge" individuals, doers rather than overseers. But being good at hiring others to work with you is crucial to growing your company. To get a better handle on your personal hiring style, take the quiz at http://www.inc.com/inc5000/2010/quiz-whats-your-hiring-style.html. You may be surprised at what you learn about your approach.

they recognize that employees *are* the business, and vice versa. There is no getting around this, especially for entrepreneurial firms that are expanding. "You cannot separate the need to grow from the number of people you will need to hire," observes Matthew Guthridge, an associate principle at global management consulting firm McKinsey & Co. "And that at the very basic level is the essence of what [an employment] strategy should be about."[3] Hiring and holding on to the right people can easily make or break a small business.

THE LURE OF ENTREPRENEURIAL FIRMS

Competing for well-qualified business talent requires small firms to identify their distinctive advantages, especially when recruiting outstanding prospects for managerial and professional positions. Fortunately, there are many good reasons to work for an entrepreneurial business. This is especially true of growing enterprises led by individuals or teams with a compelling vision of a desirable and attainable future. It is exciting to work for a company that is going somewhere!

Chris Resto, Ian Ybarra, and Ramit Sethi, co-authors of the book *Recruit or Die*, have concluded that entrepreneurial firms can compete with such ace recruiters as Microsoft, McKinsey & Co., and Goldman Sachs when it comes to attracting and hiring promising employees. The secret is coming up with a strategy that will convince the best and brightest to join a small company. Offering competitive salaries helps (more on that later in the chapter), but many recruits are even more interested in opportunities for high-level achievement, job variety, interesting experiences, personal recognition, and the potential to do work that they believe is important.[4] Many small businesses are in an excellent position to offer such attractive opportunities to prospective employees.

Because of their small size and limited staff, entrepreneurial companies allow new managers to work more closely with the CEO (often the founder), which can lead to quicker action. A small business can also provide opportunities for new hires to make decisions and to obtain the general, high-level management or professional experience that achievement-oriented hires find attractive. Rather than toiling in obscure, low-level, specialized positions in a large firm while "paying their dues" and working their way up the corporate ladder, capable newcomers can quickly move into positions of responsibility in a well-managed small business. In such jobs, they get a front-row seat for interesting experiences, allowing them to see the fruits of their labor and know that they are making a difference in the success of the company.

Small firms can also structure the work environment to offer professional, managerial, and technical personnel greater job variety and freedom than they would normally have in a larger business. In this type of environment, individual contributions can be recognized rather than hidden under numerous layers of bureaucracy. In addition, compensation packages can be structured to create powerful incentives for outstanding performance.

To be sure, there are drawbacks to working for a small company—for example, managerial blunders are harder to absorb and thus tend to be obvious to everyone, support systems from legal or human

"Actually, we're a two man operation. They're just ambiance."

resource staff may not be readily available, and limited employee benefits can lead to high levels of turnover and constant changes in personnel.[5] But many small employers offer to offset these disadvantages with appealing trade-offs, such as flexible work scheduling, job-sharing arrangements, less (or more) travel, and other potential advantages.

Many former employees of large corporations who now work for small firms prefer their new life in the entrepreneurial world. Here are the comments of some who have made the transition and like where they are today:[6]

- "There's less bureaucracy," says Jeff Macdonald, when comparing his work at Acorda Therapeutics, a small biotech company, with life in a big pharmaceutical firm. "Decisions are made without having to go through a number of layers of approval."
- Patrick Crane once worked for a large Internet company but now is with fast-growing LinkedIn Corp. "At Yahoo I shook [the CEO's] hand twice and had maybe five conversations with him in four years," he reports. "Now I meet with our CEO several times a day."
- Scott Ruthfield finds his work at WhitePages.com to be more fulfilling than his previous managerial position with Amazon.com: "Everybody plays a core role, so if you do a good job, you are directly contributing to the way the business is going to succeed."
- The sense of contribution is also important to Dean Medley, senior vice president of recruiting at Medical Methods Inc., a Florida-based staffing firm with 50 employees. "When you land a new account, it's a huge deal."

These comments represent some of the "selling points" that small companies can use to attract employees who are likely to be moving toward a career in a large corporation. With a little thought and some careful positioning, entrepreneurs can actually win the competitive challenge to lure the best talent available.

SOURCES OF EMPLOYEES

To recruit effectively, the small business manager must know where and how to find qualified applicants. Sources are numerous, and it is impossible to generalize about the best pool in view of the differences in companies' personnel needs and the quality of the applicants from one locality to another. Some of the more popular sources of employees among small firms are discussed in the following sections.

Walk-Ins

A firm may receive unsolicited applications from individuals who walk into the place of business to seek employment. Walk-ins are an inexpensive source of personnel, particularly for hourly work, but the quality of applicants varies. If qualified applicants cannot be hired immediately, their applications should be kept on file for future reference. In the interest of good community relations, all applicants should be treated courteously, whether or not they are offered jobs.

Help-Wanted Advertising

A "Help Wanted" sign in the window is one traditional form of recruiting used by some small firms, mostly retailers and fast-food restaurants. A similar but more aggressive form of recruiting consists of advertising in the classifieds section of local newspapers. For some technical, professional, and managerial positions, firms may advertise in trade and professional journals. Although the effectiveness of help-wanted advertising has been questioned by some, many small businesses recruit in this way.

Schools

© iStockphoto.com/Mark Stahl

Secondary schools, career schools, colleges, and universities are desirable sources of personnel for certain positions, particularly those requiring no specific work experience. Some secondary schools and colleges have internship programs that enable students to gain practical experience in firms, which can be very helpful. Applicants from career schools often have useful educational backgrounds to offer a small business. Colleges and universities can supply candidates for positions in management and in various technical and professional fields. In addition, many college students can work as part-time employees.

To achieve its goal of delighting its customers by providing superior construction services, Kay Construction uses a team approach, which wouldn't be possible without high-quality staff. The principals of the company, Lorraine Kay and Steve Walsh, believe that it is necessary to support the local education system to "build a reservoir of appropriately trained and motivated employees." So they work with nearby colleges to fine-tune courses offered to project management, engineering, and architecture students. By hiring some of the students as interns, the company gets inexpensive part-time help for the present and the inside track on offering them full-time positions after they graduate. This approach has worked very well for the company.[7]

Public Employment Offices

At no cost to small businesses, employment offices in each state administer the state's unemployment insurance program and offer information on applicants who are actively seeking employment. These offices, located in all major cities, are a useful source of clerical workers, unskilled laborers, production workers, and technicians. They do not actively recruit but only counsel and assist those who come in. Until recently, the individuals they work with have been, for the most part, untrained or only marginally qualified. However, since the recession, individuals with more advanced skills who have been laid off have been seeking assistance from their local state employment office. The role of such agencies is likely to become more important as time goes on, especially where the employment needs of small businesses are concerned.[8]

Private Employment Agencies

Numerous private firms offer their services as employment agencies. In some cases, employers receive these services without cost because the applicants pay a fee to the agency; however, more often, the hiring firms are responsible for the agency fee. Private employment agencies tend to specialize in people with specific skills, such as accountants, computer operators, and managers.

Temporary Help Agencies

The temporary help industry, which is growing rapidly, supplies employees (or temps)—such as word processors, clerks, accountants, engineers, nurses, and sales clerks—for short periods of time. By using an agency such as Kelly Services or Manpower Inc., small firms can deal with seasonal fluctuations and absences caused by vacation or illness. For example, a temporary replacement might fill the position of an employee who is taking leave following the birth of a child—a type of family leave mandated by law for some employees. In addition, the use of temporary employees provides management with an introduction to individuals whose performance may justify an offer of permanent employment. Staffing with temporary employees is less practical when extensive training is required or continuity is important.

Internet Recruiting

Recruiters are increasingly seeking applicants via the Internet. A variety of websites, like CareerBuilder.com and Monster.com, allow applicants to submit their résumés online and permit potential employers to search those résumés for qualified applicants. And because the Internet opens up a wealth of connections to potential applicants, many firms are posting job openings on their own websites. Beyond these options, social media tools like Twitter.com can be indispensible to recruitment efforts, especially when trying to recruit employees with higher-level skills.

Using the Internet for recruiting is convenient, but it can also carry some significant limitations and unanticipated costs. One small business owner recently posted a job opening that required a very specific marketing skill set. From that single listing, the company heard back from a slew of interested job-seekers, "which included a U.S. Postal Service worker, a bench chemist, a talent agent, and a movie director . . . none with the requisite skills." The final results were very disappointing. In the words of the entrepreneur, "[From] the 141 applicants, we interviewed two and didn't hire any. That cost me hours of my time and my hire manager's time."[9] The point is that the initial cost of posting a position online can be low—sometimes even free—but that doesn't mean the *overall process* will be inexpensive, and it may not even be useful in the end.

Employee Referrals

Recommendations of suitable candidates from good employees may provide excellent prospects. Ordinarily, employees will hesitate to recommend applicants unless they believe in their ability to do the job. Also, the family and friends of current workers can be among the best and most loyal employees available, because these individuals are well known and trusted. Many small business owners say that this source accounts for more new hires than any other. A few employers go so far as to offer financial rewards for employee referrals that result in the hiring of new employees.

Scott Glatstein is often looking to hire skilled management consultants for Imperatives, his small Minnetonka, Minnesota, consulting company, but he has not had much luck finding them using standard recruiting tools. "It's difficult to find independent consultants to bolster our ranks," says Glatstein. Not that he hasn't tried! After using a variety of recruitment approaches, including Internet advertising, he found only one that yields the results he is looking for: recommendations from his 19 current employees. Glatstein estimates that he hires nearly all of his employees through referrals; doing so saves money (costing around 70 percent less than advertising or employment agencies) and reduces turnover. But perhaps the most important advantage is that these new hires become productive in less time and tend to have superior skills. Glatstein pays $300 for each referral hired. But if $300 would be a budget-buster for your company, adjust the figure down or use a different incentive; you may very well end up with the same result.[10]

Hiring based on referrals is really just a way of tapping into the personal networks of employees. However, network recruiting becomes more important as the responsibilities associated with the position increase. Networking can be an indispensable tool when filling leadership positions in a small business, providing the best connections to individuals who have the background, skills, and integrity that are essential to a position of great responsibility in the company.

Executive Search Firms

headhunter
A search firm that locates qualified candidates for executive positions.

When filling key positions, small companies sometimes turn to executive search firms, often called **headhunters**, to locate qualified candidates. The key positions for which such firms seek applicants are those paying a minimum of $50,000 to $70,000 per year. The cost to the employer may run from 30 to 40 percent of the first year's salary. Because of the high cost, use of headhunters may seem unreasonable for small, entrepreneurial firms. At times, however, the need for a manager who can help a firm "move to the next level" justifies the use of an executive search firm. A headhunter is usually better able than the small business to conduct a wide-ranging search for individuals who possess the right combination of talents for the available position.

© Yuri Arcurs/Shutterstock.com

DIVERSITY IN THE WORKFORCE

Over time, the composition of the U.S. workforce has changed with respect to race, ethnicity, gender, and age. The U.S. Department of Labor projects that the trend will continue, with much of the change attributed to an increase in the number of Hispanic workers:

> *The U.S. workforce is expected to become more diverse by 2018. Whites are expected to make up a decreasing share of the labor force, while Blacks, Asians, and all other groups will increase their share [from 18.6 percent in 2008 to 20.6 percent in 2018]. Among ethnic groups, persons of Hispanic origin are projected to increase their share of the labor force from 14.3 percent to 17.6 percent, reflecting 33.1 percent growth.*[11]

This is a noteworthy shift, and companies will need to adjust if they are to keep up.

The balance is shifting rapidly toward greater **workforce diversity**, not only because of the increased participation of racial minorities, but also because of the higher proportions of women and older workers entering the labor force. As a result, the challenge for human resource management is to adapt to a more diverse pool of potential employees. To remain fully competitive, business owners need to step up recruitment of women and minorities and be open to innovative ways to access the available pool of applicants. In many cases, hiring more workers from diverse groups can help a company maintain good relations with an increasingly heterogeneous customer base.[12]

workforce diversity Differences among employees on such dimensions as gender, age, ethnicity, and race.

Many small businesses are tapping immigrants as a source of workers. In fact, small companies are more likely to employ immigrants than are larger firms. Approximately 17 percent of small company workers are immigrants (citizens and noncitizens), which works out to nearly one out of every five employees. Of the almost 20 million immigrants employed in the United States, around two-thirds work for small companies—about 3.3 million of these in companies with fewer than 10 employees.[13] We strongly discourage entrepreneurs from hiring illegal or undocumented workers and suggest that they consult the U.S. Department of Labor website for information on certifying foreign workers and other applicable laws.[14] However, it is important to cast the employment net as broadly as possible to find the best people available. By developing an awareness of the potential of various parts of the talent pool, small firms can improve the effectiveness of their recruitment methods.

Adapting to diversity is important not only because the workforce is becoming more varied, but also because diversity in itself can be a good thing, through the innovation it introduces to the workplace and the positive effect it has on problem solving. Researchers at Northwestern University studied the value of diversity by asking 50 groups of subjects to solve a murder mystery. Groups that included individuals from different social backgrounds were more likely to solve the case; homogeneous groups were both more often wrong and more confident that they were right.[15] Venture capitalists are very much aware of this phenomenon and thus are less likely to invest in a company when the management team more closely resembles the results of a cloning experiment than a group of individuals who bring unique perspectives to bear on business challenges. The various forms of diversity (based on gender and ethnicity, as well as more subtle forms of variation related to personality, sensibility, work style, and the like) are clearly beneficial, especially when innovation is important to a firm's competitiveness.

JOB DESCRIPTIONS

A small business manager should analyze the activities or work to be performed to determine the number and types of jobs to be filled. Knowing the job requirements permits more intelligent selection of applicants for specific positions.

Certainly, an owner-manager should not select personnel simply to fit rigid specifications of education, experience, or personal background. Rather, he or she must concentrate on the overall ability of an individual to fill a particular position in the business. Making this determination requires an outline, or summary, of the work to be performed, which is often referred to as a **job description**. (To see sample descriptions for a number of different jobs, go to http://www.samplejobdescriptions.org.)

job description
An outline, or summary, of the work to be performed for a particular position.

Duties listed in a job description should not be defined too narrowly. It is important that such descriptions minimize overlap but also avoid creating a "that's not my job" mentality. Technical competence is as necessary in small firms as it is in large businesses, but versatility and flexibility may be even more important. Engineers may occasionally need to make sales calls, and marketing people may need to pinch-hit in production.

In the process of examining a job, an analyst should list the knowledge, skills, abilities, and other characteristics that an individual must have to perform the job. This statement of requirements is called a **job specification** and may be a part of the job description. A job specification for the position of stock clerk, for example, might state that the individual must be able to lift 50 pounds and have completed 10 to 12 years of schooling.

job specification
A list of the knowledge, skills, abilities, and other characteristics needed to perform a specific job.

Job descriptions are very important human resource management tools, but only if they are taken seriously. There are sound legal reasons for developing great—not just good—job descriptions. For example, if you do not specify important aspects of the job and how it is to be done *in detail,* the Americans with Disabilities Act presumes that an employee can go about the actual job duties in any way he or she wants to, regardless of company policy or what you think is the best and proper way of doing them.[16] Also, the precise wording of a job description will determine whether an employee in that job is eligible for overtime pay, according to the guidelines established by the U.S. Department of Labor.[17] Getting the job description right can avert serious legal hassles, saving you money and giving you one less worry when you go to bed at night.

While job descriptions are primarily an aid in personnel recruitment, they also have other practical uses. For example, they can bring focus to the work of employees, provide direction in training, and supply a framework to guide performance reviews.

Evaluating Prospects and Selecting Employees

Recruitment activities identify prospects for employment. Additional steps are needed to evaluate these candidates and to extend job offers. To reduce the risk of taking an uninformed gamble on applicants of unknown quality, an employer can follow the steps below.

STEP 1: USING APPLICATION FORMS

By using an application form, an employer can collect enough information to determine whether a prospect is minimally qualified and to provide a basis for further evaluation.

Typically, an application asks for the applicant's name, address, Social Security number, educational history, employment history, and references.

Although an application form need not be lengthy or elaborate, it must be carefully written to avoid legal complications. In general, a prospective employer cannot seek information about sex, race, religion, color, national origin, age, or disabilities. The information requested should be focused on helping the employer make a better job-related assessment. For example, an employer is permitted to ask whether an applicant has graduated from high school. However, a question regarding the year the applicant graduated would be considered inappropriate, because the answer would reveal the applicant's age.

© Adam Gregor/Shutterstock.com

STEP 2: INTERVIEWING THE APPLICANT

An interview permits the employer to get some idea of the applicant's appearance, job knowledge, intelligence, and personality. Any of these factors may be significant to the job to be filled.

Although the interview can be a useful step in the selection process, it should not be the only step. Some managers have the mistaken idea that they are infallible judges of human character and can choose good employees on the basis of interviews alone. Even when conducted with care, an interview can lead to false impressions. Applicants who interview well have a talent for quick responses and smooth talk, for instance, but this skill set may not be helpful when it comes to managing processes or technologies. The interview may reveal little about how well they work under pressure or when part of a team, what motivates them, and other important issues. In fact, research has shown that the typical job interview (unstructured and unfocused) is of limited value in predicting success on the job. The correlation between interview-based assessments and actual performance is a mere 0.20, which is not very encouraging.[18]

In light of a growing concern regarding the value of interviews as they are typically used, many companies have adopted new methods that are variations on the interview theme. For example, some companies have found **behavioral interviews** to be much more predictive of a candidate's potential for success on the job. Jeffrey Pfeffer, a highly regarded management expert at Stanford University's Graduate School of Business, describes this form of interviewing as "asking people not so much about accomplishments but how they might react to hypothetical situations, how they spend their free time, and how they embody core values."[19] Although it can be a taxing process that may come across to the applicant as a barrage of challenging questions, the behavioral interview is designed to get a sense of the applicant's past performance and likely responses in future situations. The nature of the method makes bluffing difficult, and the focus on facts rather than feelings leads to a more accurate impression of what a person is *capable* of doing as well as what he or she is *likely* to do on the job.

behavioral interview An approach that assesses the suitability of job candidates based on how they would respond to hypothetical situations.

Many companies have decided that behavioral interviews are the way to go, but this requires them to select a set of questions that will uncover the insights they need to make an informed hiring decision. To give you a sense of how such an interview can be structured, here are some questions that are often asked:[20]

- Give me a specific example of a time when you used good judgment and logic when solving a problem.
- Tell me about a time when you set a goal and were able to achieve it.
- Can you recall a time when you had to conform to a company policy with which you did not agree? How did you handle that situation?

- How do you typically deal with workplace conflict? Describe an experience that required you to make such an adjustment.
- Give me an example of a time when your integrity was tested and yet prevailed in a workplace situation.

As you can see from these questions, the focus is on patterns of performance and behaviors in past situations similar to situations that are likely to come up in the job for which the applicant is being considered. Designing this emphasis into the interview process will lead to more effectivc hiring decisions.

Regardless of the interview method you choose, remember that serious legal consequences can result from a poorly conceived process. Just as in application forms, it is very important to avoid asking questions in an interview that conflict with the law. Some companies believe that applicants should be interviewed by two or more individuals in order to provide a witness to all interactions and to minimize bias and errors in judgment, but this is not always possible—and it certainly makes the process more expensive. In any case, careful process planning up front can prevent serious trouble in the future from discrimination lawsuits and poor employee selection.

Time spent in interviews, as well as in other phases of the selection process, can save the company time and money in the long run. In today's litigious society, firing an employee can be quite difficult and expensive. A dismissed employee may bring suit even when an employer had justifiable reasons for the dismissal. Note, however, that released employees are much less likely to file a lawsuit if they conclude that their employer has been fair throughout the process and has provided ample opportunity for them to improve their work performance before termination.[21]

It's important to remember that employment interviewing is actually a two-way process. The applicant is evaluating the employer while the employer is evaluating the applicant. In order for the applicant to make an informed decision, she or he needs a clear idea of what the job entails and an opportunity to ask questions.

STEP 3: CHECKING REFERENCES AND OTHER BACKGROUND INFORMATION

Careful checking with former employers, school authorities, and other references can help an employer avoid hiring mistakes. Suppose, for example, that you hired an appliance technician who later burglarized a customer's home. If you failed to check the applicant's background and she had a criminal record, your decision might be considered a negligent hiring decision. Trying to prevent such scenarios from arising is becoming more important as time goes on, since the number of negligent hiring lawsuits continues to rise.

It is becoming increasingly difficult to obtain more than the basic facts about a person's background from previous employers because of the potential for lawsuits brought by disappointed applicants. Although reference checks on a prior employment record do not constitute infringements on privacy, third parties are often reluctant to divulge negative information, and this limits the practical usefulness of reference checking. To encourage former employers to be honest, it is best to ask for consent for a check from applicants first. Then, ask only for appropriate information, such as employment dates, duties, strengths and weaknesses, and whether the individual is eligible for rehire.

At the same time, gathering information online about an applicant's financial, criminal, and employment history has never been easier. While some employers conduct their own background checks by accessing databases that are readily available, most outsource this function to one of hundreds of vendors that specialize in performing this service. A number of companies advertise that they will provide *free* background checks over the Internet. This certainly sounds appealing. But, given the importance of the task, we suggest that you

A
C
T
I
O
N

Research on Facebook

Seventy-five percent of recruiters and human resource professionals report that they research job applicants online, with most using sources like Facebook. This is easier and faster than checking references, which explains the popularity of the practice. Sadly, more than half of firms hiring cite finding provocative photos as the biggest factor in their decisions not to hire.

check with the National Association of Professional Background Screeners (http://www.napbs.com) before selecting a company for this purpose.

A few final cautions on background checks are in order. First, you should keep in mind that if a prospective employer requests a credit report to establish an applicant's employment eligibility, the Fair Credit Reporting Act requires that the applicant be notified in writing that such a report is being requested. But this is good practice, in general, when it comes to background checks. Most experts suggest that you require applicants to sign a written consent (detailing how and what you plan to check) before you conduct a check, to ensure legal compliance and to give the applicant the opportunity to withdraw from further consideration. If an applicant refuses to sign the consent form, it is legal for the company to decide against hiring him or her based on that refusal.[22]

Getting access to data is critical to making an informed hiring decision; however, you may be legally prevented from using some of the insights revealed to reject an applicant. One small business expert points out some of the things you can and cannot use: "Anything recent and relevant to job duties can legally be taken into account, but even a past felony conviction may be considered irrelevant if it was more than seven years ago."[23]

Finally, some entrepreneurs question the accuracy of the information that surfaces from criminal background checks. George Zimmer, founder of the fast-growing clothing store Men's Warehouse, has declared that no employee or interviewee at his company will ever undergo such a check. "I don't trust the U.S. justice system to get it right," he boldly declares. "I'd rather make my own decisions, and I believe in giving people a second chance." Conventional wisdom suggests that such a policy would lead to petty larceny on a grand scale, but this has not been Zimmer's experience. The company loses only about 0.4 percent of its revenues to theft, well below the national average of 1.5 percent lost by big retailers.[24] But while Zimmer's trusting attitude seems to create a bounty of goodwill, it may leave the company open to greater legal liability if an employee is accused of criminal conduct toward a customer or other workers. These trade-offs need to be weighed carefully.

STEP 4: TESTING THE APPLICANT

Many jobs lend themselves to performance testing. For example, an applicant for a secretarial or clerical position may be given a standardized keyboarding or word-processing test. With a little ingenuity, employers can develop practical tests that are clearly related to the job in question, and these can provide extremely useful insights for selection decisions.

Psychological examinations may also be used by small businesses, but the results can be misleading because of difficulty in interpreting the tests or adapting them to a particular business. In addition, the U.S. Supreme Court has upheld the Equal Employment Opportunity Commission's requirement that any test used in making employment decisions must be job-related.

validity
The extent to which a test assesses true job performance ability.

reliability
The consistency of a test in measuring job performance ability.

To be useful, tests of any kind must meet the criteria of **validity** and **reliability**. For a test to be valid, its results must correspond well with job performance; that is, the

© Orange Line Media/Shutterstock.com

applicants with the best test scores must generally be the best employees. For a test to be reliable, it must provide consistent results when used at different times or by various individuals.

Even if all indications from testing are positive, it still pays to look deeper if it is practical to do so. You may recall the hiring approach of Jason Fried, president and co-founder of 37signals, the company profiled in the opening spotlight. A job candidate who fares well in the company's very intentional interview process is still given a "test drive." That is, Fried hires prospective employees for a one-week project, or a month-long assignment in some cases, to see how they work, communicate, handle pressure, etc. According to Fried, "These real-work tests have saved us a few mismatched hires and confirmed a bunch of great people." That makes such tests more than worth the trouble.

STEP 5: REQUIRING PHYSICAL EXAMINATIONS

A primary purpose of physical examinations is to evaluate the ability of applicants to meet the physical demands of specific jobs. However, care must be taken to avoid discriminating against those who are physically disabled. The Americans with Disabilities Act requires companies with 15 or more employees to make "reasonable" adaptations to facilitate the employment of such individuals.

Although some small businesses require medical examinations before hiring an applicant, in most cases the company must first have offered that individual a job.[25] As part of the physical examination process, the law permits drug screening of applicants. But most small business owners have concluded that drug testing is expensive and unnecessary, despite overwhelming evidence indicating that drug use is prevalent and creates unnecessary risks and costs for employers. According to the Occupational Health and Safety Administration, 65 percent of all on-the-job accidents can be traced back to substance abuse, and employees who abuse drugs file six times more workers' compensation claims than those who don't. It follows that a drug screening program can be a bargain for small businesses, reducing problem hires and long-term costs.[26]

As you can see, a sound program for evaluating and selecting employees involves a number of "moving pieces," but many small companies pull all of the pieces together very skillfully. Rick Davis, founder and CEO of DAVACO Inc., describes how he and the staff at his retail services company pull out all the stops in order to ensure the quality of the hiring process:

> *Recruiting the best people is the single most important thing DAVACO can do. Not only do I make every effort to meet all employees before they are hired, but our human resources team also takes every measure to assure that we've recruited and selected the top candidate for every position to maximize their, and the company's, success. We incorporate practices into our recruiting efforts based on position, including telephone screening, face-to-face interviews, background checks, credit checks, drug screening, personality and behavior testing, skills assessment, and motor vehicle record checks.*[27]

In addition to emphasizing job-related expertise, the company also believes that strength of character is just as important as skills, if not more so. Skills can be taught, but Davis recognizes that ethics, loyalty, and high standards are inherent qualities that are difficult to pass on in a business setting, and believes that the hiring process must take all of this into account.[28]

Training and Developing Employees

Once an employee has been recruited and added to the payroll, the process of training and development must begin. The purpose of this process is to transform a new recruit into a well-trained and effective technician, salesperson, manager, or other employee. Such programs can be well worth the cost. Beyond the benefits of the knowledge and skills conveyed, one study found that employees of small and medium-sized enterprises who participated in training and development events were less likely to quit their jobs and more likely to show up for work, arrive on time, and give greater effort to their work.[29] These outcomes offer obvious advantages to any firm.

BASIC COMPONENTS OF TRAINING AND DEVELOPMENT

Though the terms are often combined, a training and development program can be separated into its two basic components. **Employee training** refers to planned efforts to help workers master the knowledge, skills, and behaviors that they need to perform the duties for which they were hired. In contrast, **management development** is more focused on preparing employees for future roles in business and emphasizes the formal education, job experiences, relationship formation, and performance assessment necessary to reach long-term career goals and fulfill managerial potential. While the two components are different, they are obviously related.

employee training
Planned efforts to help workers master the knowledge, skills, and behaviors they need to perform their duties.

management development
Preparation of employees for career advancement through education, job experiences, network development, and performance assessment.

Most positions require at least some training. If an employer fails to provide such instruction, a new employee must learn by trial and error, which usually leads to a waste of time, materials, and money—and sometimes alienates customers. At the same time, training to improve basic capabilities should not be limited to new hires; the performance of existing employees can often be improved through additional training. Due to constant changes in products, technology, policies, and procedures in the world of business, continual training often is necessary to update knowledge and skills—in firms of all sizes. Only with such training can employees meet the changing demands being placed on them.

Both employers and employees have a stake in the progress of qualified personnel toward higher-level positions. Preparation for advancement usually involves developmental efforts, which typically are quite different than the support needed to sharpen skills for current duties. Because most able employees are particularly concerned about their personal development and advancement, a small business can profit from careful attention to this phase of the personnel program. Opportunities to grow in an organization not only improve the morale of current employees but also serve as an inducement for potential applicants.[30]

ORIENTATION FOR NEW PERSONNEL

The training and development process often begins with an individual's first two or three days on the job. It is at this point that the new employee tends to feel lost and confused, confronted with a new physical layout, a different job title, unknown fellow employees, a different type of supervision, changed hours or work schedule, and a unique set of personnel policies and procedures. Any events that conflict with the newcomer's expectations are interpreted in light of his or her previous work experience, and these interpretations can either foster a strong commitment to the new employer or lead to feelings of alienation.

Recognizing the new employee's sensitivity at this point, the employer can contribute to a positive outcome through proper orientation. Taking steps to help the newcomer adjust will minimize her or his uneasiness in the new setting.

Some phases of the orientation can be accomplished by informal methods. For example, a company might choose to introduce newcomers to the rest of the staff by strategically placing a tray of bagels and muffins near a new employee's desk on his or her first morning of work. This would encourage co-workers to come by and get acquainted.

Other phases of the orientation must be structured or formalized. In addition to explaining specific job duties, supervisors should outline the firm's policies and procedures in as much detail as possible. A clear explanation of performance expectations and the way in which an employee's work will be evaluated should be included in the discussion. The new employee should be encouraged to ask questions, and time should be taken to provide careful answers. Since new employees are faced with an information overload at first, a follow-up orientation after a week or two is suggested.

One way to support the orientation process is by providing new hires with a written description of company practices and procedures, which is often referred to as an employee handbook. The handbook may include an expression of company philosophy—an overall view of what the company considers important, such as standards of excellence or quality considerations. This document typically covers such topics as recruitment, selection, training, and compensation, as well as more immediately practical information about work hours, paydays, breaks, lunch hours, absences, holidays, overtime policy, employee benefits, and so on. Such policies should be written carefully and clearly to avoid misunderstandings. Also, bear in mind that an employee handbook is considered part of the employment contract in some states.

TRAINING TO IMPROVE QUALITY

Employee training is an integral part of comprehensive quality management programs. Although quality management is concerned with machines, materials, processes, and measurements, it also focuses on human performance.

Training programs can be designed to promote high-quality workmanship. The connection between effective quality management programs and employee training has been demonstrated by small firm research.[31] A well-planned training program will begin on the first day on the job, and it will be multi-dimensional. For starters, you should clearly define what quality means in your company and explain how it is measured. But it will also help to describe some of the company's past problems, outline corrective actions that were taken, and summarize how it is currently reaching its quality goals. Finally, it is best to go one step further and make the training personal. As suggested by staff writers at *Inc.* magazine,

> *[You should] train workers to see the connection between their actions and, more broadly, their work ethic, and the company's overall performance. By tying individual behavior to an overall system of work, and then showing where that system can on occasion break down, you will be giving workers the information they need to be good stewards of your business.*[32]

Training for quality performance is, to a considerable extent, part of the ongoing supervisory role of all managers. In addition, special classes and seminars can be used to teach employees about the importance of quality control and ways in which to produce high-quality work.

ON-THE-JOB TRAINING

If a company has job descriptions or job specifications, these may be used to identify abilities or skills required for particular jobs. To a large extent, such requirements determine the appropriate type of training.

Effective training programs often turn out to be very straightforward, like the one used by Phenix and Phenix, Inc. This small literary publicity firm, based in Austin, Texas, encourages sharing of learning among its employees. Anyone attending a "learning situation"—which might be anything from a breakfast meeting to a several-day seminar—is expected to write up a summary and present it at a staff meeting or distribute it to coworkers.[33]

For all classes of employees, more training is accomplished on the job than through any other method. However, on-the-job training may be haphazard unless it follows a sound method of teaching. One program designed to make on-the-job training effective is known as **Job Instruction Training**. The steps in this program, shown in Exhibit 20.1, are intended to help supervisors become more effective in training employees.

Job Instruction Training
A systematic, step-by-step method for on-the-job training of nonmanagerial employees.

EXHIBIT 20.1 Steps in Job Instruction Training

PREPARE EMPLOYEES

- Put employees at ease.
- Place them in appropriate jobs.
- Find out what they know.
- Get them interested in learning.

PRESENT THE OPERATIONS

- Tell, show, and illustrate the task.
- Stress key points.
- Instruct clearly and completely.

TRY OUT PERFORMANCE

- Have employees perform the task.
- Have them tell, show, and explain.
- Ask employees questions and correct any errors.

FOLLOW UP

- Check on employees frequently.
- Tell them how to obtain help.
- Encourage questions.

FROM TRAINING TO IMPLEMENTATION

Regardless of the level of the position involved, the goal of a training program is to teach employees new knowledge, skills, and behaviors that will lead, in turn, to improved job performance. But this requires more than just learning—training must also be put to use. However, research indicates that only 10 to 40 percent of the training provided to employees each year is ever actually applied on the job. In other words, the lion's share of the tens of billions of dollars that organizations spend on training each year is simply wasted.[34]

The barriers to the implementation of training in the workplace are many, but much of this is rooted in human nature. For starters, training suggests that change is necessary, but many people find that change provokes anxiety, so they often fall back on more familiar methods. Old habits and routines are hard to break, and workplace pressures or time demands can easily lead employees to turn to tried-and-true approaches. For example, an employee may find it easier to go back to using an old software program (which always worked in the past) than to take the time to master an updated version offering new features that could improve performance and efficiency over the long run.

So what is a small business to do? If you want to get a better return on training and development spending, you must create a workplace environment that encourages people to use that training once they're back on the job. To show how that can be accomplished, the following suggestions were adapted from those made by Harry J. Martin, a management and labor relations professor:[35]

- **Put it on paper.** People are more likely to do what they write down, so employees should develop a personal action plan for implementing the training they receive. One manufacturing company requires its training participants to spell out what they will do to apply the concepts they have learned and when. They also are asked to describe the results they expect, how those results will be measured, and when they expect to see them. Finally, they must identify the assistance needed to implement their plan.
- **Measure results.** Employees will be more likely to put training to use if they know their performance will be assessed in light of the new concepts learned. Companies can do this by measuring skills addressed in the training or by assessing the productivity improvement of work groups.
- **Get peers to help.** Martin's research found that peer support had the greatest impact on the effective translation of training to workplace application. When trainees get together to discuss the use of training concepts, they are more inspired to give them a try.
- **Involve supportive superiors.** Management involvement increases the odds that trainees will use what they learn. When supervisors meet with trainees, they can communicate expectations, promote focus on concepts, provide encouragement, and eliminate obstacles that can block success.
- **Provide access to experts.** Companies can assist their employees with their action plans by helping to fill in gaps in their understanding. Lingering questions can be answered by providing access to reference materials, additional information on training topics, and experts within the company or from outside sources. Employees who have follow-up meetings with instructors are more likely to apply their training.

In the end, training is of value only when it is actually used on the job. And companies that make sure their employees apply the concepts they learn to their work are likely to outperform their competitors. In fact, an enterprise that bears the expense of an extensive training program but fails to enjoy any of the fruits of that investment is much more likely to fail in a competitive marketplace.

DEVELOPMENT OF MANAGERIAL AND PROFESSIONAL EMPLOYEES

A small business has a particularly strong need to develop managerial and professional employees. Whether the firm has only a few key positions or many, it must ensure that the individuals who hold these positions perform effectively. Such employees should be developed to the point where they can adequately carry out the responsibilities assigned to them. Ideally, other staff members should be trained as potential replacements in case key individuals retire or leave for other reasons. Although an owner-manager often postpones grooming a personal replacement, this step is crucial in ensuring a smooth transition in the firm's management.

Establishing a management development program requires serious consideration of the following factors:

- **The need for development.** What vacancies are expected? Who needs to be developed? What type of training and how much training are needed to meet the demands of the job description?
- **A plan for development.** How can the individuals be developed? Do their current responsibilities permit them to learn? Can they be assigned additional duties? Should they be given temporary assignments in other areas—for example, should they be shifted from production to sales? Would additional schooling be beneficial?
- **A timetable for development.** When should the development process begin? How much can be accomplished in the next six months or one year?
- **Employee counseling.** Do the individuals understand their need for development? Are they aware of their prospects within the firm? Has an understanding been reached as to the nature of the development program planned? Have the employees been consulted regularly about progress in their work and the problems confronting them? Have they been given the benefit of the owner's experience and insights without having decisions made for them?

Management development strategies often work wonderfully, but they do have their limits. For example, in many situations the best development strategy is to not promote an employee beyond the position he or she is best suited to perform. Mike Faith, founder, CEO, and president of the online retailer Headsets.com, found this out the hard way.

> *One of my longest-standing employees—in fact my only employee in the early days—is a good example [of promoting a person beyond success]. With us now for about ten years, this guy is a genius. Really. He can see the big picture and take an idea and make it work. Because he was so good at what he did, we wanted to get him into middle management. So we moved him into a management position, and it was a disaster. My A player quickly became a B player; management became a millstone around his neck. Recognizing our mistake, we moved him out of management. Now he takes on a variety of projects and is back to being a genius.*[36]

Faith remains steadfast in his belief that everyone has the ability to be an A player if he or she is placed in the right job. But it's important to remember that a top player in one position can end up being a less-than-satisfactory player in another.[37]

Compensation and Incentives for Employees

Compensation is important to all employees, and small firms must acknowledge the role of the paycheck in attracting and motivating personnel. In addition, small firms can offer several nonfinancial incentives that appeal to both managerial and nonmanagerial employees.

WAGE AND SALARY LEVELS

In general, small firms must be roughly competitive in wage and salary levels in order to attract well-qualified personnel. Payments to employees either are based on increments of time—such as an hour, a day, or a month—or vary with the output of the employees. Compensation based on time is most appropriate for jobs in which performance is not easily measured. Time-based compensation is also easier to understand and used more widely than incentive systems that are based on specific dimensions of employee performance.

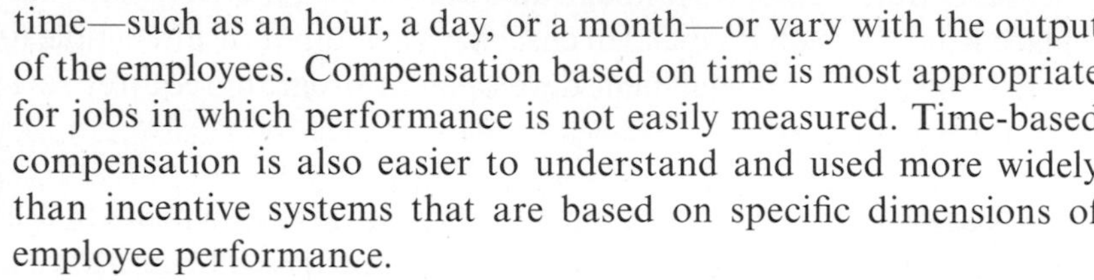

Small businesses often struggle to pay their lowest-level employees even the minimum wage required by law. However, some employers choose to improve the lives of their employees and express their support by paying wages that exceed that legal minimum. For example, In-N-Out Burger has grown quickly over the years by following a few simple practices from the beginning, including caring for its employees by paying above-minimum wages. That is why the company's website says, "We start all our new Associates at a minimum of $10.00 an hour for one simple reason . . . you are important to us. And our commitment to a higher starting wage is just one of the ways in which we show it."[38] In cases such as this, businesses often benefit along with the employees. Many see an improvement in recruiting and retention, particularly in hard-to-fill positions. These businesses may also enjoy an improved public image with customers and the community. In other words, they can earn a respectable return on their investment—and on more than one front!

> **START UP RESOURCES**
>
> **Determining the Best Pay Rates**
>
> Concerned that you may be offering more pay than necessary to attract the employees you need? Websites such as CBSalary.com, PayScale.com, and Salary.com offer free reports of what workers in your area, with a particular job, get paid. You can get similar wage information from the U.S. Bureau of Labor Statistics at http://bls.gov/bls/blswage.htm.

FINANCIAL INCENTIVES

Incentive plans are designed to motivate employees to increase their productivity. Incentive wages may constitute an employee's entire earnings or merely supplement regular wages or salary. The commission system for salespeople is one type of incentive compensation (see Chapter 17 for an expanded discussion of this topic). In manufacturing, employees are sometimes paid according to the number of units they produce, a practice called **piecework**. Although most incentive plans apply to employees as individuals, they may also involve the use of group incentives and team awards.

piecework
Financial incentive based on pay according to number of units produced.

General bonus or profit-sharing plans are especially important for managers and other key personnel, although they may also include lower-level employees. These plans provide employees with a "piece of the action" and may or may not involve assignment of shares of stock. Many profit-sharing plans simply entail distribution of a specified share of all profits or profits in excess of a target amount. Profit sharing serves more directly as a work-related incentive in small companies than in large corporations, because the connection between individual performance and success can be more easily appreciated in a small business.

Performance-based compensation plans must be designed carefully if they are to work successfully. Such plans should be devised with the aid of a consultant and/or an accountant's insight. Some keys to developing effective bonus plans follow:

- **Set attainable goals.** Performance-based compensation plans work best when workers believe they can meet the targets. Tying pay to broad, companywide results leaves workers feeling frustrated and helpless. Complex financial measures or jargon-heavy benchmarks should be avoided—employees are motivated only by goals that they understand.
- **Include employees in planning.** Employees should have a voice in developing performance measures and changes to work systems. Incentive plans should be phased in gradually so that employees have a chance to get used to them.
- **Keep updating goals.** Performance-based plans must be continually adjusted to meet the changing needs of workers and customers. The life expectancy of such a plan may be no more than three or four years.

STOCK INCENTIVES

In young entrepreneurial ventures, stock options are sometimes used to attract and hold key personnel. The option holders get the opportunity to share in the growing—perhaps even skyrocketing—value of the company's stock. If the business prospers sufficiently, such personnel can become millionaires.

But stock ownership need not be reserved only for executives or key personnel. Some small firms have created *employee stock ownership plans (ESOPs)*, which give employees a share of ownership in the business.[39] These plans may be structured in a variety of ways. For example, a share of annual profits may be designated for the purchase of company stock, which is then placed in a trust for employees. When coupled with a commitment to employee participation in business operations, ESOPs can motivate employees, resulting in improvements in productivity.

ESOPs also can provide a way for owners to cash out and withdraw from a business without selling the firm to outsiders. See Chapter 13 for a discussion of this topic.

EMPLOYEE BENEFITS

Employee benefits include payments by the employer for such items as Social Security, vacation time, holidays, health insurance, and retirement compensation. All told, these benefits are expensive; their cost for many firms is equal to 40 percent or more of salary and wage payments. Furthermore, increases in the cost of some benefits have slowed in recent years, but their escalation continues to outpace the rate of inflation in the economy overall. In general, small companies are less generous than large firms when it comes to providing benefits for employees. Even so, the cost of such benefits is a substantial part of total labor costs for these businesses.

employee benefits
Supplements to compensation, designed to be attractive and useful to employees.

flexible benefit programs (cafeteria plans)
Benefit programs that allow employees to select the types of benefits they wish to receive.

Though employee benefits are expensive, a small firm cannot ignore them if it is to compete effectively for good workers. A limited but growing number of small businesses now use **flexible benefit programs** (or **cafeteria plans**), which allow employees to select the types of benefits they wish to receive. All employees receive a core level of coverage, such as basic health insurance, and then are allowed to choose how an employer-specified amount is to be divided among additional options—for example, dependent care assistance, group term life insurance, and additional health insurance.[40]

For small companies that wish to avoid the detailed paperwork associated with administering cafeteria plans, outside help is available. Many small firms—some with fewer than 25 employees—turn over the administration of their flexible benefit plans to outside consulting, payroll accounting, or insurance companies that provide such services for a monthly fee.

Providing a full range of employee benefits may be prohibitively expensive for many small businesses. A number of firms, however, have devised relatively affordable but

LIVING THE DREAM

entrepreneurial experiences

"Perking Up" Your Employees

Want to keep your employees happy and improve their productivity at the same time? Many small businesses are turning to creative, cost-effective perks to reward high performance, express appreciation, and boost morale. Here are some interesting perk programs that might spark ideas for your company:

- Some companies offer days off, long lunches, or flexible work schedules as a reward for work groups that hit or exceed their performance targets.
- Akraya Inc., an IT staffing company, hires professional cleaners to tidy up the homes of its staff members once every two weeks.
- Fentress Architects offers an in-house education program, and it even invites employees' relatives to attend some evening and weekend classes.
- A software provider called LoadSpring Solutions gives its staff an extra week of vacation and up to $5,000 if they travel abroad, reasoning that cross-cultural experiences promote personal growth.
- If employees didn't have so many personal chores to deal with, they could get more done. That's why some firms offer on-premises laundry pickup and return.
- To boost its reputation for environmental concern, outdoor-apparel maker Patagonia gives its staff two weeks of leave, at full pay, to work for the green nonprofit of their choosing.
- Some companies have fleet vehicles that they loan to workers for their daily commutes and other personal needs.

Creative perks can promote loyalty and even be free, in some cases. For example, flexible work schedules and a relaxed dress code can do a lot for morale. Many small business owners believe higher pay is the key to motivation, but research has shown that this works only in the short-term. In reality, other things provide greater long-term staff satisfaction and productivity—starting with expressed appreciation and a positive workplace attitude. It doesn't get any more cost-effective than that!

Sources: John Cuneo, "10 Perks We Love," *Inc.*, Vol. 32, No. 5 (June 2010), pp. 94–95; Jason Daley, "Creating a Culture of Excellence," *Entrepreneur*, Vol. 38, No. 3 (March 2010), pp. 81–87; and Elwin Green, "Tight Economy Shouldn't Hinder Employee Appreciation," *Pittsburgh Post-Gazette*, September 20, 2010, http://www.post-gazette.com/pg/10263/1088371-407.stm, accessed March 24, 2011.

meaningful "perks" that are customized to their particular situation but still signal appreciation for workers. Buying pizza for everyone on Fridays and giving each employee a paid day off for her or his birthday are just two examples. These small benefits make employment more attractive for employees and are motivating because they are often thoughtful and sometimes even personalized. With a little creativity, these perks can be used to build morale, promote loyalty, and encourage healthy behavior.

John Roberson owns a small Nashville, Tennessee–based experiential marketing company, and he is very committed to growing his business. But he also cares about his employees and their physical and emotional health, and he has ways of persuading them to get involved in programs that support wellness. Tailoring rewards to his employees' specific interests, he has given away a guitar, yoga lessons, time with a personal trainer, paid time off to build orphanages in Central America—even a pair of cowboy boots! This has been good for both the workers and the company. Says Roberson, "We attract employees who see we are about more than just profits."[41]

Special Issues in Human Resource Management

So far, this chapter has dealt with the recruitment, selection, training, and compensation of employees. Several related issues—co-employment agreements, legal protection of employees, labor unions, formalizing employer–employee relationships, and the need for a human resource manager—are the focus of this final section.

CO-EMPLOYMENT AGREEMENTS

Entrepreneurs can choose to outsource part of the burden of managing employees through an arrangement known as **co-employment**. Today, an estimated 700 co-employment companies, also known as **professional employer organizations (PEOs)**, operate in all 50 states and assist small businesses with their human resource management needs. For a fee of 2 to 6 percent of payroll, a PEO writes paychecks, takes care of payroll taxes, and files reports required by government agencies. Although small companies using this service avoid a certain amount of paperwork, they do not escape the tasks of recruitment and selection. In most cases, the entrepreneur or the venture's management still determines who works, who gets promoted, and who gets time off.

co-employment
An arrangement to outsource part of personnel management to an organization that handles paperwork and administers benefits for those employees.

professional employer organizations (PEOs)
A company that sets up co-employment agreements.

Many employees like the co-employment arrangement. It may allow small employers to provide better benefit packages, since PEOs generally cover hundreds or thousands of employees and thus qualify for better rates. Of course, the small business must bear the cost of insurance and other benefits obtained through a co-employment partner, in addition to paying a basic service fee. However, this may be the only way the company can afford to offer the benefits necessary to attract and keep high-quality employees. The fact that the PEO also assumes the burden of managing payroll and other administrative processes makes this arrangement even more attractive.

When a company decides to use the services of a PEO, both parties share legal obligations as a result. That is, the law holds both companies responsible for payment of payroll taxes and workers' compensation insurance and compliance with government regulations—the client company cannot simply offload these obligations to the PEO and forget about its responsibilities to staff. This highlights the importance of selecting a PEO carefully to ensure that you are dealing with a responsible firm. When you are choosing a PEO, we recommend that you follow the guidelines offered by the National Association of Professional Employer Organizations (http://www.napeo.org) to be sure you are linking up with a service provider that is honest, dependable, and right for your company.

Using a PEO can also change the application of government regulations to small businesses. Very small ventures are often excluded from specific rules. For example, companies with fewer than 15 employees are exempt from the Americans with Disabilities Act. However, when these employees officially become part of a large PEO, the small company using the co-employed workers becomes subject to this law. It always pays to treat your employees with care and respect, of course, but taking on added legal obligations by working with a PEO can actually make managing a small company much more complicated.

LEGAL PROTECTION OF EMPLOYEES

Employees are afforded protection by a number of federal and state laws. The United States Department of Labor (DOL) provides a summary of the principle labor statutes that it administers and enforces,[42] but it can be difficult to sort out which of these will apply to your particular business. For that reason, the DOL has created the *FirstStep* Employment Law Advisor (which can be found at http://www.dol.gov/elaws/firststep), and we strongly recommend that you use it. By answering a few brief questions about your business, this interactive e-tool will direct you to summaries of the statutes that will affect ventures such as yours. It also provides guidance on recordkeeping, reporting, and notification requirements that you must follow.

This information still does not cover all the bases, including state laws that may apply. To fill in any gaps, we recommend that you gather as much information as you can from the DOL's "Employment Law Guide" (http://www.dol.gov/compliance/guide/index.htm) and "State Labor Laws" (http://www.dol.gov/whd/state/state.htm) Web pages. But even with these facts in hand, it is best to consult with an attorney to be sure that you are in compliance. It is also advisable to be familiar with some of the broader statutes that shape and influence the wide scope of labor law in the United States.

Civil Rights Act
Legislation prohibiting discrimination based on race, color, religion, sex, or national origin.

One of the most far-reaching statutes is the **Civil Rights Act**, originally enacted in 1964, and its amendments. This law, which applies to any employer of 15 or more people, prohibits discrimination on the basis of race, color, religion, sex, or national origin. Other laws extend similar protection to the aged and handicapped. Every employment condition is covered, including hiring, firing, promotion, transfer, and compensation.

The Civil Rights Act includes protection against sexual harassment, an issue that must be addressed by small businesses as well as large corporations. Education and prompt response to complaints are the best tools for avoiding sexual harassment and the possibility of liability claims. The following practical action steps have been expressly recommended for small companies:[43]

1. Establish clear policies and procedures regarding sexual harassment in the workplace.
2. Require employees to report incidents of harassment to management immediately.
3. Investigate any and all complaints of sexual harassment fairly and thoroughly.
4. Take appropriate action against violators, and maintain claimant confidentiality.
5. If a lawsuit is likely to be filed, contact an attorney.

Occupational Safety and Health Act (OSHA)
Legislation that regulates the safety of workplaces and work practices.

Fair Labor Standards Act (FLSA)
Federal law that establishes a minimum wage and provides for overtime pay.

Employees' health and safety are protected by the **Occupational Safety and Health Act** of 1970. This law, which applies to business firms of any size involved in interstate commerce, created the Occupational Safety and Health Administration (OSHA) to establish and enforce necessary safety and health standards.

Compensation of employees is regulated by the minimum wage and overtime provisions of the **Fair Labor Standards Act (FLSA)**, as well as by other federal and state laws. The FLSA applies to employers involved in interstate commerce and having two or more employees;

it sets the minimum wage (which is periodically increased by Congress) and specifies time-and-a-half pay for nonsupervisory employees who work more than 40 hours per week.

The **Family and Medical Leave Act** was passed and signed into law in February 1993. The law requires firms with 50 or more employees to allow workers as much as 12 weeks of unpaid leave for childbirth, the adoption of a child, or other specified family needs.[44] The worker must have been employed by the firm for 12 months and have worked at least 1,250

Family and Medical Leave Act
Legislation that assures employees of unpaid leave for childbirth or other family needs.

© iStockphoto.com/Angelika Schwarz

entrepreneurial experiences

An Intern After a Fashion

Ari Goldberg had a promising idea for a new business. Sizing up the situation at the time, he concluded that "there was no equivalent of a MySpace for fashion, a site that mixed style news, social networking and personalized clothing recommendations with e-commerce." So, in 2008, he and a partner started StyleCaster.com to fill the void. But given their limited startup capital, they had to come up with a creative way to staff their new venture on a shoestring. "We told the investors, 'We have this amazing idea, and everyone will want to take part and we're not going to pay them,'" recalls Goldberg.

So how were they going to get people to work for a new company for free—especially when they would have to live in New York, the most expensive city in the United States? Simple—they would "hire" interns. As it turns out, they found that there are plenty of young women with diplomas from excellent universities and dreams of a career amidst the glitz and glamour of high fashion, but with scant job prospects in a down economy. Many "fresh-faced fashionistas" have accepted Goldberg's offer, seeing it as a chance to get a foot in the door of a competitive industry and to make contacts for future opportunities. At last count, StyleCaster.com had 24 unpaid part-time interns signed up to assist the firm's 15 regular employees.

© Cesar M. Romero/Shutterstock.com

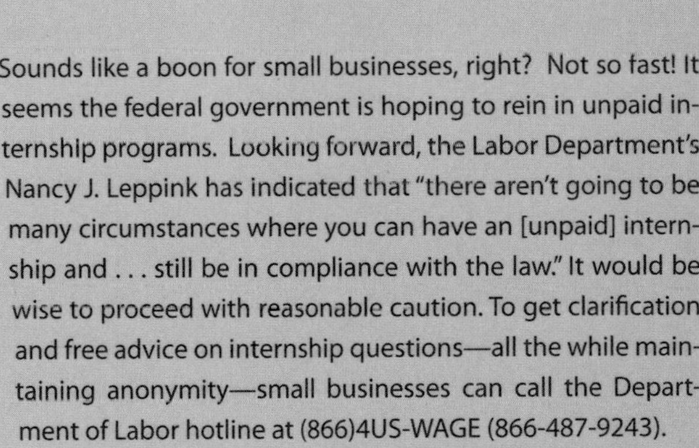

Sounds like a boon for small businesses, right? Not so fast! It seems the federal government is hoping to rein in unpaid internship programs. Looking forward, the Labor Department's Nancy J. Leppink has indicated that "there aren't going to be many circumstances where you can have an [unpaid] internship and . . . still be in compliance with the law." It would be wise to proceed with reasonable caution. To get clarification and free advice on internship questions—all the while maintaining anonymity—small businesses can call the Department of Labor hotline at (866)4US-WAGE (866-487-9243).

Some small businesses also like to hire independent contract workers to keep staffing costs low. (Because contractors, or "consultants," receive no benefits, they may cost as much as 30 percent less than full-time employees.) However, based on the definition provided by the IRS (see http://www.irs.gov/businesses/small/article/0,,id=99921,00.html), the question of whether a worker can be legitimately classified as a contractor can be difficult to answer. Therefore, business owners should consult an attorney or accountant to be sure they are following the rules. Violations of the guidelines could very easily end up costing money, rather than saving it.

Sources: Christina Galoozis, "Feds Crack Down on Employers' Use of Independent Contractors," *MyBusiness*, May/June 2010, p. 8; Deborah Silver, "Boom Times for Hiring," *MyBusiness*, March/April 2010, pp. 28–31; Laurie Pike, "The Full-Time Non-Employee," *Entrepreneur*, Vol. 38, No. 4 (April 2010), pp. 80–87; and *Wall Street Journal*, "War on Interns," April 7, 2010, p. A14. **http:www.stylecaster.com**

hours. Furthermore, the employer must continue health care coverage during the leave and guarantee that the employee can return to the same job or one that is comparable.[45]

LABOR UNIONS

As a general rule, entrepreneurs prefer to operate independently and to avoid using union labor. Indeed, most small businesses are not unionized. To some extent, this results from the predominance of small business in services, where unionization is less common than in manufacturing. Also, unions typically focus their attention on large corporations.

Though uncommon, labor unions are not unknown in small firms. Many types of small businesses—building and electrical contractors, for example—negotiate labor contracts and employ unionized personnel. The need to work with a union formalizes and, to some extent, complicates the relationship between a small company and its employees.

If employees wish to bargain collectively—that is, to be represented in negotiations by a union—the law requires the employer to participate in such bargaining. The demand for labor union representation may arise from employees' dissatisfaction with their pay, work environment, or employment relationships. By following constructive human resource policies, a small company can minimize the likelihood of labor organization or improve the relationship between management and union.

FORMALIZING EMPLOYER–EMPLOYEE RELATIONSHIPS

As explained earlier in this chapter, the management systems of small companies are typically less formal than those of larger firms. A degree of informality can be a virtue in small organizations. As personnel are added, however, the benefits of informality decline and its costs increase. Large numbers of employees cannot be managed effectively without some system for regulating employer–employee relationships. This situation can be best understood in terms of a family relationship. House rules are generally unnecessary when only two people are living in the home. But when several children are added to the mix, Mom and Dad soon start sounding like a government regulatory agency.

Growth, then, produces pressure to formalize personnel policies and procedures. Determining how much formality to introduce and how soon involves judgment. Some employee issues should be formalized from the very beginning; on the other hand, excessive regulation can become paralyzing.

Procedures relating to management of personnel may also be standardized. One way to do this is to establish a performance assessment system that follows a set timetable for reviews—often on an annual basis. Effective performance review programs typically bear certain hallmarks. For example, they are guided by clearly established benchmarks that are based on goals that are SMART—that is, Specific, Measurable, Achievable, Realistic, and Time-bound. They also tend to follow a well-planned process that emphasizes continual communication between managers and employees and ongoing performance tracking. Effective annual review meetings require sufficient time (from 40 minutes to an hour) and your undivided attention, and they should begin with positive feedback before summarizing objective judgments of attitudes and behaviors in need of improvement. Used correctly, employee reviews can be a powerful tool for building a small business.[46]

THE NEED FOR A HUMAN RESOURCE MANAGER

A firm with only a few employees cannot afford a full-time specialist to deal with personnel problems. Some of the more involved human resource techniques used in large corporations may be far too complicated for small businesses. As a small company grows in size, however, its personnel problems will increase in both number and complexity.

The point at which it becomes logical to hire a human resource manager cannot be precisely specified. In view of the increased overhead cost, the owner-manager of a growing business must decide whether circumstances make it profitable to employ a personnel specialist. Hiring a part-time human resource manager—a retired personnel manager, for example—is a possible first step in some instances.

Conditions such as the following favor the appointment of a human resource manager in a small business:

- There are a substantial number of employees (100 or more is suggested as a guideline).
- Employees are represented by a union.
- The labor turnover rate is high.
- The need for skilled or professional personnel creates problems in recruitment or selection.
- Supervisors or operative employees require considerable training.
- Employee morale is unsatisfactory.
- Competition for personnel is keen.

Until a human resource manager is hired, however, the owner-manager typically functions in that capacity. His or her decisions regarding employee selection and compensation, as well as other personnel issues, will have a direct impact on the operating success of the firm.

As this chapter points out, the human resource management function is simple in concept, but it can be challenging to put into practice. From recruitment to prospect evaluation and selection to training and development programs to the administration of compensation and benefit plans—there is so much to do! And if that weren't enough to keep track of, these activities must be conducted within the constraints of some very specific laws. While this may seem overwhelming, keep in mind that working with the people who join your enterprise is likely to be the most fulfilling feature of being in business. If they are managed carefully and motivated to do their best, capable employees can take your business to new heights. There is no limit to what can be done with the right people in the right enterprise with the right care and handling.

1. Explain the importance of employee recruitment, and list some useful sources for finding suitable applicants.

- Recruitment of good employees can boost the overall performance of a small business.
- Small companies can attract applicants by stressing unique work features and opportunities.
- Recruitment sources include walk-ins, help-wanted advertising, schools, public and private employment agencies, temporary help agencies, the Internet, employee referrals, and executive search firms.
- The increasing diversity of the workforce requires a broadening of the scope of recruitment, but the varied perspectives of a diverse workforce can offer advantages, such as improved decision making.
- Job descriptions outline the duties of the job; job specifications identify the knowledge, skills, abilities, and other characteristics applicants need to have to do the job effectively.

2. Identify the steps in evaluating job applicants.

- In the first step, application forms help the employer obtain preliminary information from applicants. (Employers must avoid questions about sex, race, religion, color, national origin, age, and disabilities.)

- Additional evaluation steps are interviewing the applicant (with behavioral interviews offering the best insights), checking references and other background information, and testing the applicant.
- The final evaluation step is often a physical examination, which may include drug screening.

3. Describe the roles of training and development for both managerial and nonmanagerial employees.

- Effective employee training enables workers to perform their current jobs effectively; management development prepares them for career advancement.
- An orientation program helps introduce new employees to the firm and its work environment.
- Training is an integral component of a comprehensive quality management program.
- More training is accomplished on the job than through any other method.
- Following the steps in Job Instruction Training should make training more effective.
- Training is more likely to be put to use if it is written down, measured, structured for peer support, encouraged by management, and supported with ongoing advice from experts.
- A management development program should be guided by an understanding of the need for development, a plan for development, and a timetable for development. It should also provide appropriate employee counseling.

4. Explain the various types of compensation plans, including the use of incentive plans.

- Small companies must be roughly competitive in salary and wage levels.
- Payments to employees either are based on increments of time or vary with employee output.
- Incentive systems relate compensation to various measures of performance.
- Employee stock ownership plans enable employees to own a share of the business.
- Employee benefit costs are often equal to 40 percent or more of payroll costs.

5. Discuss the human resource issues of co-employment, legal protection, labor unions, and the formalizing of employer–employee relationships.

- Small businesses can reduce paperwork by transferring personnel to the payroll of a professional employer organization, but legal obligations remain and may actually increase.
- All small businesses with 15 or more employees must observe laws that prohibit discrimination, protect employee health and safety, establish a minimum wage, and provide for family and medical leave.
- Some small businesses must work with labor unions.
- As small firms grow, they must adopt more formal human resource management methods, including regular performance reviews.
- Employment of a human resource manager becomes necessary at some point as a company continues to add employees.

Key Terms

human resource management (HRM) p. 581
headhunter p. 586
workforce diversity p. 587
job description p. 588
job specification p. 588
behavioral interview p. 589
validity p. 591
reliability p. 591
employee training p. 593
management development p. 593
Job Instruction Training p. 595
piecework p. 599
employee benefits p. 599
flexible benefit programs (cafeteria plans) p. 600
co-employment p. 601
professional employer organization (PEO) p. 601
Civil Rights Act p. 602
Occupational Safety and Health Act (OSHA) p. 602
Fair Labor Standards Act (FLSA) p. 602
Family and Medical Leave Act p. 603

Discussion Questions

1. Why is it so important to have high-quality employees?
2. What factor or factors would make you cautious about going to work for a small business? Could these reasons for hesitation be overcome? How?
3. In what ways is the workforce becoming more diverse, and how do these changes affect recruitment by small companies?
4. Based on what you know from this chapter or your own experience as an interviewee, what do you think are the most serious weaknesses in the interviewing process? How could these be remedied?
5. What are the positive and negative features of background checks? How important are these checks to the selection of high-quality employees?
6. What steps and/or topics would you recommend for inclusion in the orientation program of a printing firm with 65 employees?
7. What problems are involved in using incentive plans in a small company? How would the nature of the work affect management's decision concerning the use of such a plan?
8. Is the use of an employee stock ownership plan desirable in a small business? What might lessen such a plan's effectiveness in motivating employees?
9. How does a professional employer organization differ from a temporary help agency? What are the greatest benefits of co-employment?
10. Explain the impact of the Civil Rights Act and the Fair Labor Standards Act on human resource management.

You Make the Call

SITUATION 1

While trying to find a new accounts receivable person for his Chicago-based postcard printing business, Javier Gomez decided that he had surely found "Mr. Perfect." On paper, this applicant jumped out as being far better than the rest because he had the right background. And he was asking for less money than Gomez was willing to pay. The interview went well, the reference check was positive, and the drug test came back clear. A few odd twists in Mr. Perfect's story, though, have created some questions for Gomez. Now he is wondering what he should make of them. First, Mr. Perfect was asked during the hiring process to show his driver's license, but he could produce only an Illinois state I.D card. (A driver's license is needed to operate a motor vehicle legally, but the state also issues I.D. cards to help Illinois residents prove their identity when banking, traveling, and in other situations.) Second, Mr. Perfect stated that he had worked for his previous employer for 12 years and thus could provide only one appropriate reference. Gomez always asked for three references so that he could contact them all and look for patterns of behavior. He would not be able to do that in this case. Finally, Mr. Perfect mentioned in passing that if he were hired, he would like to perform tasks beyond those listed in the job description for the position. Specifically, he wondered if he might be asked to drop the company's mail off at the post office as needed. "It's just something I like to do," Mr. Perfect reported. "It gives me a relaxing break from my work, and getting fresh air helps me to concentrate better." Gomez had had plenty of employees ask if they could take on new responsibilities, but doing post office runs was never one of them.

As Gomez pondered his hiring decision, he kept coming back to the fact that if Mr. Perfect were hired, the accounts receivable job would give him access to cash, blank checks, and financially sensitive information. And if he were allowed to take the company's mail to the post office, he would have access to that, too. In so many ways, Mr. Perfect seems to be exactly what Gomez was looking for, but given the strange details of the job candidate's story, Gomez is wondering if hiring him for the position would be wise.

Question 1 With the information available at this point, do you think Gomez should hire Mr. Perfect? How much weight should be given to the fact that he doesn't, for example, have a driver's license?

Question 2 How important are reference checks in the hiring process? Should having only one reference cause any concern? Why or why not? What potential problems can you see in this?

Question 3 Mr. Perfect seems to be just the person for the job in so many ways. Does it make sense to think about restructuring the job (for example, limiting access to cash and blank checks as much as possible) to minimize the concerns that have surfaced because of his story? Should a job ever be structured for any single individual?

SITUATION 2

When an economy slides into decline and sales start to fall off, small business owners often have to make difficult decisions regarding their employees. This was the challenge facing James Tilton, founder of Tilton Construction Services, a light construction firm in Riverside, California. Since the launch of his business in 1997, he has used the fact that his company has never fired or laid off anyone as a tool to attract and retain workers, but he is up against the wall now and something has to give. By early 2008, the recession and the freefall of the real estate market had started to put financial pressure on his company, but Tilton was always able to find enough work to avoid laying anyone off. Now it is clear that he cannot keep all of his 17 full-time employees busy, and there is no way he can continue to make payroll. But nearly half of his loyal workers have been with him for several years, and he feels a sense of responsibility to them and their families. What should he do?

Tilton has decided that he would like to make some adjustments that would allow him to avoid a layoff, if possible. He estimates that he could reduce total payroll by 6 percent ($50,000 a year) just by tightening up his workers' schedules and avoiding overtime pay. That would certainly help. But it might be simpler and seem more fair if everyone just took a 10 percent cut in pay, including Tilton. If he doesn't make some kind of adjustment, Tilton figures that he will have to terminate at least four, and perhaps as many as six workers, depending on how the economy fares. But there must be other options. Tilton struggles with his dilemma as he tries to go to sleep, but he realizes that he won't get much rest until he can solve this problem.

Question 1 What other options can you think of for Tilton's company? Can you come up with better alternatives than the ones Tilton has considered so far?

Question 2 Do you think there is any possibility that Tilton will be able to avoid laying off at least a few of his workers? If you were one of the company's best workers, what would you recommend that Tilton do?

Question 3 What impact will this decision have on the training and development that Tilton has invested in his employees? How important is this factor to the decision he will have to make?

SITUATION 3

When Peter Mathis learned that a former employee had filed a complaint alleging that Ready Delivery, his Albuquerque-based freight hauling business, had fired her because of her race, it seemed like the right time to rethink his company's human resource management methods. The complaint was eventually dismissed, but that didn't stop Mathis from worrying about the possibility that other employee problems might arise in the future. And with 12 workers already on the payroll, he was finding that the paperwork associated with payroll preparation, government regulation, tax reporting, and other human resource management matters was beginning to consume too much of his time at the office.

A professional employer organization (PEO) approached him about taking over much of Ready Delivery's human resource management work. It would cost the company 3 percent of payroll, but the PEO could also offer additional benefits and services (at additional cost, of course) that might help the company in other ways, too. For example, joining the PEO would give Mathis's employees access to health and dental care plans that would actually be better and less expensive than those the company currently offered. It could also provide affordable group life insurance benefits, making the switch even more attractive. Mathis realized that partnering with the PEO could reduce his flexibility in selecting benefit options, but he was nonetheless giving serious consideration to accepting the offer.

Question 1 How can Mathis be sure that the PEO is reputable and that his company and employees will receive real value for the money?

Question 2 How might contracting with the PEO affect employee relationships at Ready Delivery? Is there any chance that his employees' loyalty might be transferred to their new "employer"?

Question 3 What steps should Mathis take before entering into an agreement with the PEO?

Experiential Exercises

1. Interview the director of the placement office for your college or university. Ask about the extent to which small companies use the office's services, and obtain the director's recommendations for improving college recruiting by small firms. Prepare a one-page summary of your findings.
2. Examine and evaluate the help-wanted section of a local newspaper. Summarize your conclusions and formulate some generalizations about small business advertising for personnel.
3. With another student, form an interviewer–interviewee team. Take turns posing as job applicants for

a selected type of job vacancy. Critique each other's performance, using the interviewing principles outlined in this chapter.

4. With another student, take turns playing the roles of trainer and trainee. The student-trainer should select a simple task and teach it to the student-trainee, using the Job Instruction Training method outlined in Exhibit 20.1. Jointly critique the teaching performance after each turn.

Small Business & Entrepreneurship Resource Center

Mike Faith, founder, CEO, and president of the online retailer Headsets.com, has learned to be careful not to promote employees beyond the position they are best suited to perform, as mentioned in the text. The article "Headsets .com Happy with Its Growth Spurt" talks about how the company has taken measures to ensure that all employees are focused in the same direction. Describe what Headsets.com has done to ensure this, and discuss how effective (or ineffective) you feel this type of approach may be.

Source: "Headsets.com Happy with Its Growth Spurt," *Catalog Age*, Vol. 21, No. 3 (March 1, 2004).

Case 20

SALARY ENVY (P. 732)

One of the most important features of a company's human resource management program involves its compensation practices, and this case highlights some of the complications that can surface when various inadequate compensation policies are adopted.

ALTERNATIVE CASES FOR CHAPTER 20

Video Case 2, PortionPac Chemicals, p. 696
Case 5, W.S. Darley & Co., p. 702
Case 19, Diamond Wipes International, p. 730

CHAPTER 21

Managing Operations

In the SPOTLIGHT
Local Motors
http://www.local-motors.com

Imagine a glass jar filled with marbles. Now, think of the jar itself as representing the total demand for cars in the United States, and the marbles as symbolizing the cars built by major automakers. The space between the marbles would then correspond to the niche markets that are not being served by large automakers because the cost to manufacture in such small quantities would be sky-high. But that's where Jay B. Rogers, co-founder and CEO of Local Motors, comes in. He wants to make cars that will fill the empty spaces in the marble-packed jar.

Since the days of Henry Ford, major automobile makers have been highly vertically integrated, with the control of design, engineering, assembly, and all other stages of their operations falling under the same corporate umbrella. This approach is quite efficient with high-volume cars, but it cannot serve market niches well. Building cars in very limited volumes of 50 to 2,000 units a year requires radical innovation, and that is exactly what Rogers is trying to do. Through Local Motors, he has created a new model that outsources many functions to the customer, eliminates or combines other value-creating elements, and ignores some of the most sacred and time-honored assumptions of the automotive industry.

As a first step, Local Motors cars are designed through a process called

Local Motors

After studying this chapter, you should be able to . . .

1. Understand how operations enhance a small company's competitiveness.
2. Discuss the nature of the operations process for both products and services.
3. Identify ways to control inventory and minimize inventory costs.
4. Recognize the contributions of operations management to product and service quality.
5. Explain the importance of purchasing and the nature of key purchasing policies.
6. Describe lean production and synchronous management and their importance to operations management in small firms.

LOOKING AHEAD

© iStockphoto.com/Dan Bachman

co-creation. An online community of fans submits designs, which are then voted on by the community. (The fact that some 60,000 designs from 121 countries have been submitted in the brief two-year history of this company illustrates the potential of this approach.) Winning designs are further developed by the community and staff engineers. The company's first car, named "Rally Fighter," is a four-wheel-drive, diesel sports car that features a design that was inspired by the P-51 Mustang, a WWII fighter plane. A car with this very narrow target market may inspire passion in an under-served enthusiast community, but it will never generate the sales volume of a middle-market car like the Toyota Camry.

The next step involves manufacturing. Local Motors will produce its cars in limited batches in small factories with the help of the purchaser. (Yes, as bizarre as it sounds, buyers will actually be involved in the final assembly of their own cars!) Rally Fighters will be built in Phoenix, Arizona, using off-the-shelf parts, whenever possible. (The Rally Fighter has a BMW engine, Honda taillights, and Mazda door handles.)

The firm's micro-factories will serve as both dealership and service center. Conventional automobile factories have to be located with cost and availability considerations in mind as these relate to labor, land, transportation, suppliers, and distribution. But Local Motors's factory sites are chosen by the community, thereby naturally matching supply with demand.

The second car and factory decided upon by the community is the "Boston Bullet," which is a retro-themed sports coupe that is to be made in Boston, Massachusetts. By using micro-factories, the company eliminates the waste typically associated with mass factories, including the huge inventories of cars that are shipped and then sit on dealer lots. Peter Wells, director of the Centre for Automotive Industry Research, estimates that 35 percent of the showroom cost of a new car is incurred after it leaves the factory.

Ultimately, the system created by Rogers will draw customers into the process of designing, building, selling, and servicing the car. This ownership experience supercharges innovation and creates enormous value at very low cost. The order-of-magnitude lower investment combined with the flexibility and adaptability of Local Motors's system creates a highly profitable and environmentally conscious operation. It also showcases the kind of operations management innovation that small firms are uniquely capable of creating.

Sources: Ann Hudner, "IDSA + DIY," http://www.metropolismag.com/pov/20100809/idsa-diy, accessed May 4, 2011; http://www.local-motors.com, accessed May 4, 2011; Luci Scott, "Chandler Factory Will Help Customers Build Own Custom Car," *The Arizona Republic*, June 15, 2010, http://www.azcentral.com/news/articles/2010/06/15/20100615chandler-car-factory.html, accessed May 4, 2011; and Ray Wert, "Local Motors Rally Fighter: The First-Ever Creative Commons Car," http://jalopnik.com/5398864/local-motors-rally-fighter-the-first+ever-creative-commons-car, accessed May 3, 2011.

Managing the operations of a company has been compared to a relay race, where the work of one runner is linked with that of successive teammates, one after another, until the entire race is completed. The name of the game is coordination, but entrepreneurs tend to underestimate the amount of effort required to keep the people and processes in a business involved and working smoothly together. With one dropped baton, the work of the entire team comes up short.

Dan and Chip Heath, co-authors of multiple bestselling books on business, mention an experiment that showed just how easy it is to overlook coordination demands in a firm's operations. In this particular test, students were asked to build a giant Lego man. Because time was limited, participants decided to split up and work on different parts separately—one had "arm duty," another worked on the torso, and so on. The team ended up with highly developed parts, but the hodgepodge of pieces they created would not fit together. The lesson, say the Heath brothers, is that work groups tend to be better at specialization than coordination: "[Organizations] prize individual brilliance over the ability to work together as a team."[1] This notion offers a useful place to begin our discussion of operations management, but in this chapter we apply the principles involved in a distinct way—to the small business.

Many of the concepts presented in this chapter were pioneered and perfected by large corporations. However, this does not mean that they have no place in the world of small business. In some cases, the concepts can be applied directly; in others, they must be adapted before they can meet the needs of small companies. Entrepreneurs who work to improve their operations will find that their companies are better able to withstand the escalating pressures of the competitive marketplace—including those coming from the Microsofts and Walmarts of the world. Besides, understanding and adopting the best practices established by industry giants may give your small company a pattern to follow as it grows to become a market leader of the future! Whether they are used in a manufacturing business or a service-based company, these principles can provide profit power.

Competing with Operations

operations
The processes used to create and deliver a product or service.

In very simple terms, **operations** refers to the processes used to create and deliver a product or service. By now, it should be clear that companies vary considerably in how they compete for customers, and the planning and management of operations almost always play a major role in this. You may be familiar with high-profile examples, such as Apple's superior design efforts, McDonald's speed of service, Walgreens's emphasis on convenient locations, and Walmart's highly efficient supply chain and distribution capabilities—these are truly world-class players. In the end, however, the formula for gaining competitive strength is surprisingly similar for all firms: Companies gain power to the degree that they excel in satisfying customer needs and wants more precisely and/or efficiently than their competitors.

To be successful, a company's operations must involve all of the activities required to create value for customers and earn their dollars. A bakery, for example, purchases ingredients, combines and bakes them, and makes their products available to customers at some appropriate location. For a service business like a hair salon, the activities include the purchase of supplies and shampooing, haircutting, and other tasks and processes involved in serving its clients. A bakery cannot offer its products if it does not operate its ovens, and a hair salon cannot serve its clients without actually styling hair. (Outsourcing these activities presents one possible, but highly impractical scenario.) In the end, *all* necessary activities must be handled in some form or fashion if the company's operations are to function.

operations management
The planning and control of a conversion process that includes turning inputs into outputs that customers desire.

Operations management refers to the planning and control of a conversion process that includes bringing together inputs (such as raw materials, equipment, and labor) and turning them into outputs (products and services) that customers want. An operations process is required whether a firm produces a tangible product, such as a deli sandwich, or an intangible service, such as dry cleaning.

Operations are at the heart of any business; indeed, a company would not be able to exist without them. It should come as no surprise, then, that their design and effectiveness can determine the success of an enterprise. The following questions can help you to identify operations factors that will impact firm performance and to recognize adjustments that need to be made:

- How much flexibility is required to satisfy your customers over time?
- What is customer demand today? What is the demand trend for the future? Are existing facilities and equipment adequate to keep up with current and future demand?

- What options are available for satisfying your customers? For example, should you set up in-house fabrication, outsource production, or enter a joint venture for manufacturing or service delivery?
- What operations-related skills or capabilities set your firm apart from its competitors? How can you best take advantage of these distinctive features in the marketplace?
- Does the competitive environment require certain capabilities that your enterprise lacks?

Our focus in this chapter is on examining the ways a business can function economically and profitably, providing a high-quality product or service that keeps customers coming back for more. But even more significantly, we discuss how operations management is an important means of building competitive strength in the marketplace. For this, there is no substitute!

The Operations Process

Product-oriented and service-oriented operations are similar in that they change inputs into outputs. Inputs can include money, raw materials, labor, equipment, information, and energy—all of which are combined in varying proportions, depending on the nature of the finished product or service. Outputs are the products or services that a business provides to its customers. Thus, the operations process may be described as a conversion process. As Exhibit 21.1 shows, the operations process converts various kinds of inputs into products or services, but this is a very general model. A printing plant, for example, uses inputs such as paper, ink, the work of employees, printing presses, and electric power to produce printed material. Car-wash facilities and motor freight firms, which are service businesses, also use operations to transform varied inputs into car-cleaning and freight-transporting services.

MANAGING OPERATIONS IN A SERVICE BUSINESS

The operations of firms that provide services differ from those of firms that provide products in a number of ways. One of the most obvious is the intangible nature of services—that is, the fact that you cannot easily see or measure them. As pointed out earlier, managers of businesses such as auto repair shops and hotels face special challenges in assuring and controlling the quality of their services, given the difficulty inherent in measuring and controlling intangibles.

Another distinctive feature of most service businesses is the extensive personal interaction of employees with customers. In a physical fitness facility, for example, the customer is directly involved in the process and relates personally to trainers and other service personnel. In a small movie theater operation, it only makes sense to show a film when patrons

© PJF/Shutterstock.com

EXHIBIT 21.1 The Operations Processes (Input→Processes→Output)

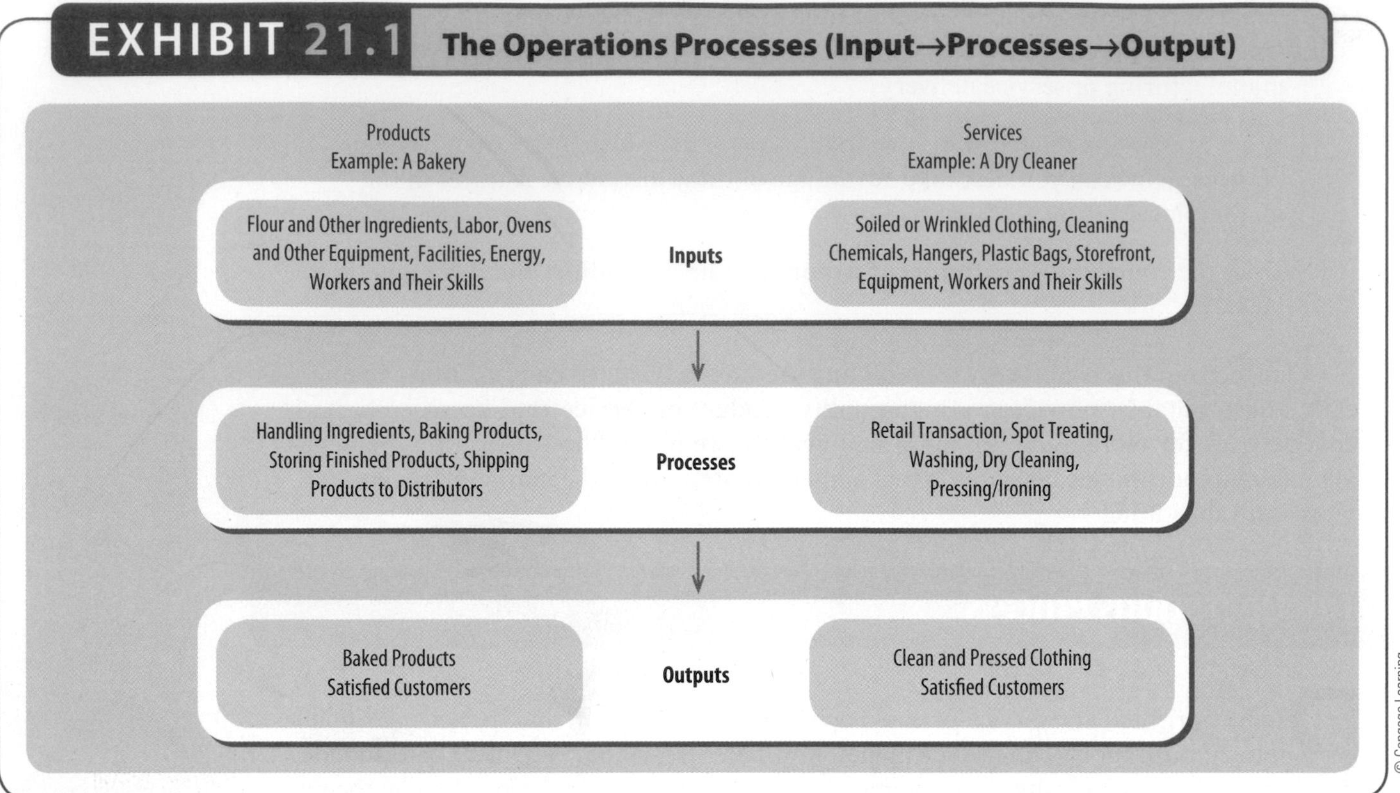

are present to watch it. This naturally allows for customer input and feedback into creation and delivery processes. In addition, services are created and delivered on demand. That is, neither a workout nor a movie viewing experience can be entered into finished products inventory.

Some service companies have taken unique steps to understand the service provider–customer connection. Firms like Southwest Airlines, for example, want their managers to get close enough to customers to see what they have to say about various facets of the operation. To that end, they are sent into the field periodically to fill customer contact positions, which allows them to return to their normal responsibilities with much greater insight into the strengths and weaknesses of services offered. Research into employee–customer relations has shown that greater closeness with customers enables employees to understand and report customer sentiments more accurately.

For a service business, the critical importance of its relationship with customers carries implications for managing personnel. For example, if those making hiring decisions determine that an open position requires a great deal of sensitive interaction with clients, then they should select individuals with strong interpersonal skills for that vacancy. Employee training must emphasize the skills needed to serve customers well and encourage employees to find ways to improve customer satisfaction.

The adoption of various technologies has enabled customers of many businesses to provide more of their own services. Nearly all self-service gasoline stations permit customers to pay at the pump, and many telephone systems allow or even encourage customers to obtain information without speaking to a salesperson or other personnel. The extent to which such systems are satisfactory from a customer's point of view depends on whether they are more convenient than traditional systems and whether they function efficiently and accurately in meeting customer needs.

In some cases, technology can provide considerably better service than the traditional model. Compare traditional brick-and-mortar bookstores to their online counterparts. Customers and their feedback are fundamental and critical to the value of online sites. When browsing the Amazon.com website, for example, the shopper is provided with customer-driven information, such as the following:[2]

- Customers Who Bought This Item Also Bought
- What Do Customers Ultimately Buy after Viewing This Item?
- Customer Reviews
- Customer Discussions

The insights provided by these options can help visitors find services that interest them, which leads to increased customer satisfaction. The most well-informed employee of a traditional bookstore would have trouble providing similar data.

TYPES OF MANUFACTURING OPERATIONS

Manufacturing operations can take many forms, depending on the degree to which they are repetitive. For example, a master craftsman furniture maker who makes customized pieces follows a very different process than do auto workers who assemble hundreds of cars on a production line each day. The former deals with great variety and must maintain flexible operations, whereas the latter follow a set routine that allows them to build cars at a very low per-unit cost. Most manufacturing operations can be classified as one of three types—job shops, project manufacturing, and repetitive manufacturing.

job shops
A manufacturing operation in which short production runs are used to produce small quantities of items.

Job shops are designed for short production runs. Skill sets are grouped, and work moves in batches from location to location. Only a few products are produced before the general-purpose machines are shifted to a different production setup. Machine shops represent this type of operation.

project manufacturing
Operations used to create unique but similar products.

repetitive manufacturing
Operations designed for long production runs of high-volume products.

When most people think about manufacturing, they often picture a factory operation, but this is not always the case. **Project manufacturing** is used to create unique but similar products, such as site-built homes and grandstands for sporting facilities. In some cases, these operations may not even seem to belong to the manufacturing family. Creative work, such as composing music or painting portraits, can fall into this category, as may professional work, such as processing tax returns or drafting specific legal documents. Because each project is unique, this type of operation has to be highly flexible to meet the requirements of the job and the demands of customers. However, because of the similarity involved, a company can achieve operational efficiencies by using manufacturing methods that, in some ways, resemble those of repetitive manufacturing, which is described next.

Firms that produce one or relatively few standardized products use **repetitive manufacturing**. This is considered mass production because it requires long production runs. Repetitive manufacturing is associated with the assembly-line production of high-volume products, such as televisions and apparel items. Highly specialized equipment can be employed, because it is used over and over again in making the same item. When the output created more closely resembles a stream of product than individual goods (such as water from a purification plant or power

© Jim Parkin/Shutterstock.com

continuous manufacturing A form of repetitive manufacturing with output that more closely resembles a stream of product than individual products.

flexible manufacturing systems Operations that usually involve computer-controlled equipment that can turn out products in smaller or more flexible quantities.

generated by a hydroelectric dam), this form of repetitive manufacturing is sometimes referred to as **continuous manufacturing**.

Most businesses do not implement a pure version of any of these process types, but rather mix and match them in order to gain the benefits of each. For instance, home builders will frequently blend job shop operations (building several houses using specialized subcontractors for plumbing, painting, and electrical work) with project manufacturing features (being unique, individualized, and customized). To meet the increasing market demands for unique products that are low in price, many companies have turned to **flexible manufacturing systems**, which usually involve computer-controlled equipment that can turn out a variety of products in smaller or more flexible quantities. In other words, machine automation, while expensive, can help cut manufacturing costs while giving customers exactly what they want.

CAPACITY CONSIDERATIONS

A small company's capacity to offer products or services is a critical factor. It puts a ceiling on the firm's ability to meet demand and match competitors, but it may also determine startup costs and usually represents a long-term commitment.

Handout/MCT/Newscom

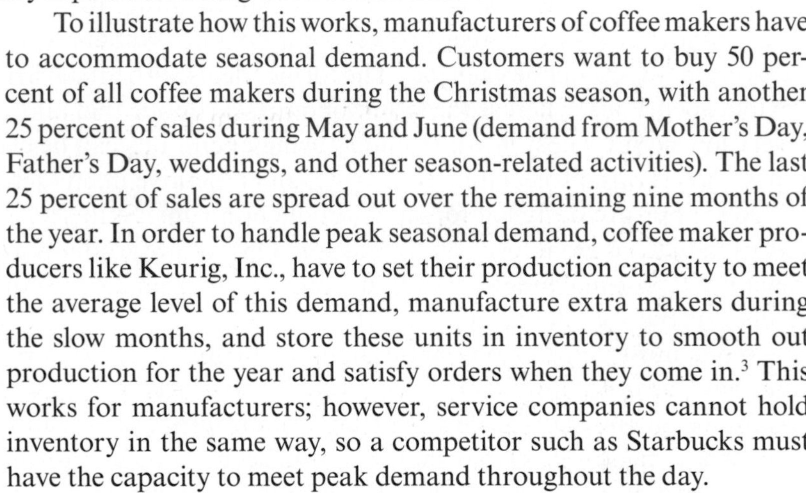

To illustrate how this works, manufacturers of coffee makers have to accommodate seasonal demand. Customers want to buy 50 percent of all coffee makers during the Christmas season, with another 25 percent of sales during May and June (demand from Mother's Day, Father's Day, weddings, and other season-related activities). The last 25 percent of sales are spread out over the remaining nine months of the year. In order to handle peak seasonal demand, coffee maker producers like Keurig, Inc., have to set their production capacity to meet the average level of this demand, manufacture extra makers during the slow months, and store these units in inventory to smooth out production for the year and satisfy orders when they come in.[3] This works for manufacturers; however, service companies cannot hold inventory in the same way, so a competitor such as Starbucks must have the capacity to meet peak demand throughout the day.

Capacity for the coffee maker manufacturer is determined by factory space, machinery, workers, and other such factors. Although capacity at Starbucks is similarly determined by store space, equipment, and workers, adjusting capacity to meet market changes would look very different for these two firms.

PLANNING AND SCHEDULING

In manufacturing, production planning and scheduling procedures are designed to achieve the orderly, sequential flow of products through a plant at a rate that matches deliveries to customers. To reach this objective, the manufacturer must avoid production disruptions and utilize machines and personnel efficiently. Simple, informal control procedures are often used in small plants. If a procedure is straightforward and the output is very limited, a manager can keep things moving smoothly with a minimum of paperwork. However, any manufacturing venture that experiences growth will eventually have to establish formal procedures to ensure production efficiency.

Because service firms are closely tied to their customers, they are limited in their ability to produce services and hold them in inventory. An automobile repair shop must wait until a car arrives before starting its operations, and a community bank cannot function until a client is available. A retail store can perform some of its services, such as transporting and storing inventory, but it, too, must wait until the customer arrives to perform other services.

Part of the scheduling task for service firms relates to planning employees' working hours. Restaurants, for example, schedule the work of servers to coincide with variations in diner traffic. In a similar way, stores and medical clinics increase their staff to handle the crush of customers or patients during periods of peak demand. Other strategies of service firms focus on scheduling customers. Appointment systems are used by many automobile repair centers and beauty shops. Service firms such as dry cleaners and plumbers take requests for service and delay delivery until the work can be scheduled. Still other firms, including banks and movie theaters, maintain a fixed schedule of services and tolerate some idle capacity.

To smooth out and delay investment in additional capacity, companies are turning increasingly to **demand management strategies**. These strategies are used to stimulate customer demand when it is normally low, and the options are limited only by the entrepreneur's imagination. Some businesses attempt to spread out customer demand by offering incentives for customers to use services during off-peak hours—examples of this would include early-bird dinner specials at restaurants and lower-price tickets for the afternoon showing of a movie. Other approaches are sometimes more sophisticated. Six Flags theme parks have implemented the Flash Pass rider reservation system. The Flash Pass is a pager that holds your place in line so that you can be waiting for a popular ride while enjoying other activities in the park. When it is time for you to ride, the pager indicates that you have 10 minutes to get to the ride to claim your spot. Of course, Six Flags charges an extra fee for this privilege, but the net result is both a smoothing and a prioritization of demand. Those customers willing to pay more get more value from their time in the park.[4]

demand management strategies Operational strategies used to stimulate customer demand when it is normally low.

Inventory Management and Operations

It may not be glamorous, but inventory management can make the difference between success and failure for a small firm. When examined carefully, inventory management can help an entrepreneur understand the vital balance between two competing pressures in the business. The company may need *more* inventory to satisfy customers (meeting customer demand and providing high-quality service), but it will want to maintain *less* inventory to keep the company's balance sheet healthy (see Exhibit 21.2). Small businesses are often highly customer-focused; however, many also are constantly strapped for cash, so the often-substantial cost of inventory and its storage pushes the business to try to carry less of it. Inventory management is particularly important in small retail or wholesale companies, because inventory typically represents a major financial investment by these businesses.

EXHIBIT 21.2 Service Level and Balance Sheet Considerations

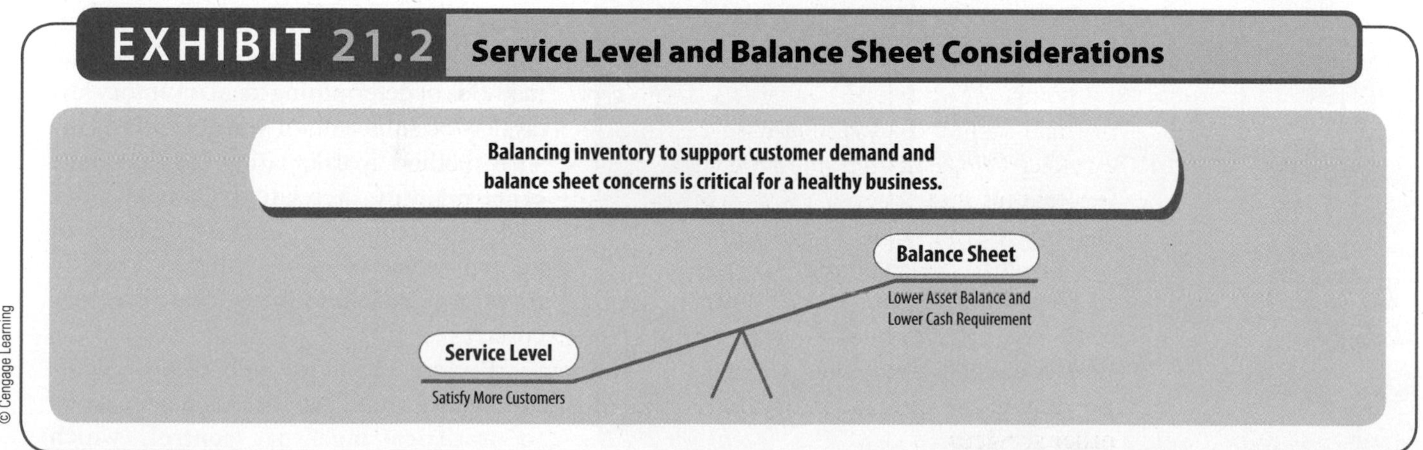

OBJECTIVES OF INVENTORY MANAGEMENT

The reasons for carrying inventory are numerous. Perhaps a kitchen pantry analogy will help you to see why this is the case. Why do you keep more Cheerios (or whichever cereal you prefer) in the pantry than you need today?

- To eat (to meet customer demand)
- To avoid going to the grocery store for each meal (to be less dependent on the source)
- To have breakfast supplies for guests to eat (to protect against stockouts)
- To benefit from price discounts (to gain from sales or quantity-based cost reductions)
- To have in stock before prices go up (to protect against price increases)

The point of this exercise is to show that you probably keep extra Cheerios around for a number of reasons. You may have thought that it was just a matter of having something to eat for breakfast, but that is likely to be only one of your objectives for keeping the pantry well stocked with cereal and your "kitchen operation" working.

Ensuring continuous operations is particularly important in manufacturing, because delays caused by lack of materials or parts can be costly. Furthermore, sales can be maximized by completing production in a timely manner and by stocking an appropriate assortment of merchandise for distribution to wholesale establishments and retail stores. Protecting inventory from theft, misplacement, and deterioration and optimizing investments likewise contribute to operational efficiency and business profits.

economic order quantity
An index that determines the quantity to purchase in order to minimize total inventory costs.

statistical inventory control
A method that uses a targeted service level, allowing statistical determination of the appropriate amount of inventory to carry.

You may conclude that carrying more stock is the key to maintaining high-quality service. However, Daniel Corsten, a logistics expert at the University of St. Gallen in Switzerland, cites research showing that a surprising 72 percent of the root causes of running out of stock can be found in the store—that is, they derive from such varied problems as incorrect forecasting, lost or misplaced inventory, poor shelving or storage systems, and inadequate stock measurement.[5] Having more inventory on hand would increase costs but would not improve service quality in these cases, because customers would still be prevented from accessing that stock efficiently due to these other fundamental problems.

© Baloncici/Shutterstock.com

INVENTORY COST CONTROL

Maintaining optimal inventory—the level that minimizes stockouts and eliminates excess inventory—saves money and contributes to operating profits. Traditional methods of determining ideal inventory levels may be sufficient for your business. One such method is calculating the **economic order quantity**, a relatively simple index that determines the purchase quantity of an item (some of which will be carried in inventory) that minimizes total inventory costs.[6]

Preferring more advanced methods, many small businesses have turned to **statistical inventory control**, which accommodates the variability of supply and demand using a targeted service level. This method allows you to determine statistically the appropriate amount of inventory to carry, and it is easier to use than you might imagine. In fact, the tools required for this computation are built into many inexpensive, off-the-shelf accounting systems that work for small businesses, such as Microsoft Dynamics or SAP Business One.

If a firm could order merchandise or raw materials and carry inventory with no expenses other than the cost of the items, there would be little concern about order quantity at any given time. However, this is not the case. Inventory comes with many other related costs, which are easy to overlook. At a minimum, you should consider the following:

- Storage (land and buildings required, as well as shelving and organization systems)
- Theft, weathering, spoilage, and obsolescence
- Cost of capital (the cost of tying up cash in inventory that could be better used elsewhere)
- Transaction costs (costs from ordering, receiving, inspecting, transporting, and distributing inventory)
- Insurance and security
- Disposal costs (when inventory ultimately cannot be sold)

Your business may have to bear these costs and others. While some of them are fixed, others will rise and fall based on the quantity of inventory held. Managing these costs can be a complex challenge, but there are approaches that can help you to minimize them.

ABC Inventory Classification

Some inventory items are more valuable or critical to a firm's operations than others. That is, some items have a greater effect on the costs and profits of a business. As a general rule, managers will be most attentive to those inventory items requiring the largest investment. Managing inventory, according to its priority, can help boost a company's performance.

One approach to inventory analysis, the **ABC method**, classifies items into three categories based on *dollar velocity* (purchase price × annual quantity consumed). The purpose of the ABC method is to focus managerial attention on the most important items. The number of categories could easily be expanded to four or more, if that seemed more appropriate for a particular firm.

ABC method
A system of classifying items in inventory by relative value.

In category A are a few high-value inventory items that account for the largest percentage of total dollars or are otherwise critical in the production process and, therefore, deserve close control. These might be monitored using an inventory system that keeps a running record of receipts, withdrawals, and balances of each item. In this way, a company can avoid an unnecessarily heavy investment in costly inventory items.

Category B items are less costly but deserve moderate managerial attention because they still make up a significant share of the firm's total inventory investment. Category C contains low-cost or noncritical items, such as paper clips in an office or nuts and bolts in a repair shop. The carrying costs of such items are not large enough to justify close control. These items might simply be checked periodically to ensure that a sufficient supply is available.

Just-In-Time Inventory Systems

The **just-in-time inventory system** is designed to cut inventory carrying costs by making or buying what is needed just as it is needed. First popularized by the Japanese,

just-in-time inventory system
A method of reducing inventory levels to an absolute minimum.

the just-in-time approach has led to cost reductions in many countries. New items are received, presumably, just as the last item of that type from existing inventory is placed into service. The just-in-time concept rests mostly on a few basic principles, but chief among these is the emphasis on the *pull* of inventory over the *push* of the same. That is, inventory items are to be made or bought in response to demand (pull), rather than being based on what is planned or anticipated (push). This focus prevents the buildup of unnecessary inventory.

Many large firms have adopted some form of the just-in-time system for inventory management, but small businesses can also benefit from its use. It's important to note that adoption of this approach requires careful coordination with suppliers. Supplier locations, production schedules, and transportation schedules must be carefully considered, as they all affect a firm's ability to obtain materials quickly and in a predictable manner—a necessary condition for using this approach. The just-in-time method also requires a flexible production system, with short set-up and turnaround times.

The benefits of just-in-time management go beyond reducing in-house inventory and creating a healthier balance sheet. Quality problems become more evident, and sooner, which reduces waste. Storage space, insurance costs, and revolving credit are freed up for other purposes. The ultimate objective of this method is a smooth and balanced system that responds nimbly to market demand.

The just-in-time inventory system has been used by businesses of all sizes, and with good results. You may be familiar with McAlister's, a franchised chain of more than 300 deli restaurants, which was started in 1989 by Don Newcomb.[7] Since McAlister's is a franchise, the operation of each store is carefully dictated by the firm's operations manual. Its prescribed approach specifies that each restaurant is to set up four sandwich-making workstations or production cells and to use as many of these as needed, based on the hour of the day and the flow of customers. Each station has a single operator who receives sandwich orders in batches. So, if a party of eight comes in, one workstation would prepare sandwiches for all eight diners.[8]

A McAlister's restaurant in central Texas is one of the higher-volume outlets, and it earned its franchisor's permission to experiment with the production system by making two changes. First, to accommodate the high volume, the four cells were changed to two assembly lines with specialized workers. Only one of the lines is used most of the time, but it is operated by four to six workers. The second modification, and one that is consistent with the spirit of the just-in-time approach, is that the batch size has been changed to *one sandwich,* regardless of the order size. That is, even when the two assembly lines are operating, the sandwiches in a large order will be split, based on available capacity. The result has been reduced order lead time and variability, fewer mistakes, and higher efficiency. Because this new arrangement is working so well, the local owner is happy with the change, and so is the franchisor.[9]

INVENTORY RECORDKEEPING SYSTEMS

The larger the company, the greater the need for recordkeeping, but even a very small business needs a system for keeping tabs on its inventory. Because manufacturers are concerned with three broad categories of inventory (raw materials and supplies, work in process, and finished goods), their inventory records are more complex than those of wholesalers and retailers. Small firms should emphasize simplicity in their control methods. Too much control can be as wasteful as it is unnecessary.

In most small businesses, inventory records are computerized. Many different software programs are available for this purpose. The owner or manager, in consultation with the company's accounting advisors, can select the software best suited for the particular needs of the business.

Inventory checks can be carried out in different ways. A **physical inventory system** depends on an actual count of items on hand. The counting is done in physical units, such as pieces, gallons, or boxes. By using this method, a firm can create an accurate record of its inventory level at a given point in time. Some businesses have an annual shut-down to count everything—a complete physical inventory. Others use **cycle counting**, scheduling different segments of the inventory for counting at different times during the year. This simplifies the process and makes it less of an ordeal for the business as a whole.

physical inventory system
A method that provides for periodic counting of items in inventory.

cycle counting
Counting different segments of the physical inventory at different times during the year.

A **perpetual inventory system** provides an ongoing, current record of inventory items. It does not require a physical count. However, a physical count of inventory should be made periodically to ensure the accuracy of the system and to make adjustments for such factors as loss or theft.

perpetual inventory system
A method for keeping a running record of inventory.

The simplest method is called a **two-bin inventory system**. For each item in inventory, the business sets up two containers, each holding enough to cover lead time. When one is emptied, it is replaced with the second and a new container is ordered. You may already be managing sugar at home using this approach. You use sugar out of one bag, but you keep a second bag in the pantry. When the first is empty, you open the second and buy a new one at the grocery store. As a result, your "sweet tooth" is always taken care of.

Operations Management and Quality

4
Recognize the contributions of operations management to product and service quality.

Owners of successful small firms realize that quality management is serious business and that a strong commitment to the achievement of quality goals is essential. So, how is quality related to operations? Quality can be achieved only to the extent that operations lead to the outcomes that customers want. Following this logic, companies that fail to produce quality in their operations will not have the buyers they need to stay in business for long.

QUALITY AS A COMPETITIVE TOOL

Quality may be defined as the characteristics of a product or service that determine its ability to satisfy stated and implied needs. Quality obviously has many dimensions. For example, a restaurant's customers base their perceptions of its quality on the taste of the food, the attractiveness of the décor, the friendliness and promptness of servers, the cleanliness of silverware, the appropriateness of background music, and many other factors. The operations process establishes a level of quality as a product is being produced or as a service is being provided. Although costs and other considerations cannot be ignored, quality must remain a primary focus of a firm's operations.

two-bin inventory system
A method of inventory control based on the use of two containers for each item in inventory: one to meet current demand and the other to meet future demand.

International competition is increasingly turning on quality differences. Automobile manufacturers, for example, now place much greater emphasis on quality in their attempts to compete effectively with foreign producers. However, it is not solely big firms that need to make quality a major concern; many small companies have been slow to give adequate consideration to producing high-quality goods and services. In examining the operations process, therefore, small business managers must direct special attention to achieving superior product or service quality.

quality
The features of a product or service that enable it to satisfy customers' stated and implied needs.

The American Society for Quality (ASQ) has been the leading quality improvement organization in the United States for nearly 60 years and has introduced many quality improvement methods throughout the world. Among these is an approach known as **total quality management (TQM)**, an aggressive effort by a firm to achieve superior quality. Total quality management is an all-encompassing, quality-focused management approach that is characterized by the following features:

total quality management (TQM)
An all-encompassing management approach to providing high-quality products and services.

- It is *customer driven*: Customer needs and wants are the core drivers.
- It emphasizes *organizational commitment*: Management leads, but the entire organization participates.
- It focuses on a *culture of continuous improvement*: That is, it is much more than a one-off effort.

Many businesses merely give lip service to achieving excellent quality standards; others have introduced quality programs that have failed. The most successful quality management efforts incorporate the three features just mentioned, which are highlighted in Exhibit 21.3.

THE CUSTOMER FOCUS OF QUALITY MANAGEMENT

A firm's quality management efforts should begin with a focus on the customers who purchase its products or services. Without such a focus, the quest for quality easily degenerates into an aimless search for some abstract, elusive ideal. To get started in the right direction, the entrepreneur should ask the following question: What products and services will satisfy customers' needs and expectations? Customers have expectations regarding the quality of products (such as durability and attractiveness) and services (such as speed and accuracy). A customer is concerned with *product* quality when purchasing a camera or a loaf of bread; a customer's primary concern is *service* quality when having an automobile repaired or a suit tailor-made. Frequently, a customer expects some combination of product *and* service quality—for example, when buying a flatscreen TV, a purchaser may be concerned with the performance of the model selected, knowledge and courtesy of the salesperson, credit terms offered, and warranty coverage.

At times, it can be easy to misread what customers want, but what they desire is usually very simple. For example, a car owner who takes his automobile to a repair shop hopes to receive competent service (that is, a successful repair), to get a reasonable explanation of what had to be done, and to be treated with respect. Similarly, a hotel patron anticipates being provided with a clean room, having reasonable security, and being treated like a guest. Such uncomplicated expectations open up avenues

EXHIBIT 21.3 Essential Features of Successful Quality Management

of opportunity. Exceeding these basic expectations can leave a lasting, favorable impression on customers, which often results in repeat business and free promotion through positive word of mouth. As a bonus, a genuine concern for customer needs and satisfaction can be a powerful force that energizes the total quality management effort of a company.

Retail Is Detail

Perhaps you've heard the quote "Retail is detail." This means that operating details are crucial to the success of a business, especially in an industry such as food service. You may recall from Chapter 1 that Five Guys Burgers and Fries, a restaurant chain started by Jerry Murrell and his sons in 1986, has taken the hamburger-loving world by storm. But few of its faithful customers recognize the meticulous attention to minutiae that makes the eatery the phenomenal success that it is today. It all begins with facility design. "I wanted people to know that we put all of our money into the food," insists Murrell. "That's why the décor is so simple—red and white tiles. We don't spend our money on décor. Or on guys in chicken suits. But we'll go overboard on food."[10]

For the Murrells, making high-quality burgers and fries is nothing short of an obsession. Still not convinced? Consider some of the painstaking detail that has been planned into the chain's operations.[11]

- Five Guys fries are made only from potatoes grown in Idaho and north of the 42nd parallel, which grow slower and are much higher in quality. It doesn't matter that these spuds are considerably more expensive.
- Most chains dehydrate their frozen fries to eliminate moisture that splatters when it hits the oil. Five Guys actually *soaks its fries in water first* and then pre-fries them to force the steam out and create a seal. Then, when fried a second time, they don't absorb oil and get greasy.
- The chain toasts all buns on the grill to create a caramelized taste, despite the fact that using a bun toaster would be faster and cheaper.
- The beef used is 80 percent lean and always fresh, never frozen.
- All burgers are made to order, with 17 possible toppings, which is why the company will not allow drive-through operations.

© David R. Frazier Photolibrary, Inc. / Alamy

And this is just a part of the effort to work the finer points. But the "retail is detail" emphasis has definitely paid off, with Five Guys expanding from only five stores in 2002 to more than 750 locations less than a decade later.[12]

Customer Feedback

Listening attentively to customers' opinions can provide information about their level of satisfaction. Employees having direct contact with customers can serve as the eyes and ears of the business in evaluating existing quality levels and customer needs. Unfortunately, many managers are oblivious to the often subtle feedback from customers. Preoccupied with operating details, managers may not listen carefully to, let alone solicit, customers' opinions. Employees having direct contact with customers—such as servers in a restaurant—are seldom trained or encouraged to obtain information about customers' quality expectations. Careful management and training of servers could make them more alert to consumers' tastes and attitudes and provide a mechanism for reporting these reactions to management.

Experts now recommend that firms work hard to involve and empower customers in efforts to improve quality. The marketing research methods of observation, interviews, and customer surveys, as described in Chapter 7, can be used to investigate customers' views regarding quality. Some businesses, for example, provide comment cards for their customers to use in evaluating service or product quality.

Another approach to gathering customer-based information is to "mine" company sales data, statistically analyzing it in search of useful "nuggets of insight" on customer behavior. To learn a lesson or two from an operations superstar, consider Walmart and its response to severe weather events. From carefully studying its own sales data, the firm is well aware of customer buying patterns preceding storms. Before a serious weather event strikes, customers stock up on the expected: water, flashlights, and generators. But in the aftermath of such a storm, customers buy yard and home cleanup items, such as mops and trash bags. Some items that are commonly purchased are less predictable, such as Pop-Tarts (a quirk in buying behavior).[13] By recognizing past trends and adjusting operations to match them (including having an ample supply of Pop-Tarts available after a storm), Walmart can help those most in need and make a profit by serving their known, and perhaps unknown, needs with great precision.

So how does this relate to small enterprises? Most business management software programs now include "business intelligence" modules that can help even the smallest of companies discover customer buying patterns so that they can respond accordingly. Data-mining techniques can provide powerful insights to guide small business operations and should not be overlooked.

"THE BASIC SEVEN" QUALITY TOOLS

Another important element in effective quality management consists of the various tools, techniques, and procedures needed to ensure high-quality products and services. Once the focus is shifted to the customer and the entire organization is committed to continuous improvement, operating methods become critical concerns. Kaoru Ishikawa, professor of engineering at Tokyo University and the father of "quality circles," contends that 95 percent of a typical company's quality problems can be solved by using the following seven tools (sometimes called "The Basic Seven"):[14]

1. A *cause-and-effect diagram* (or *Ishikawa chart,* or *fishbone chart*) identifies potential causes for an effect or problem while sorting them into categories.
2. A *check sheet* provides a structured, prepared form for collecting and analyzing data.
3. A *control chart* transforms data into graphs that can be used to determine if a process errs in some predictable, and correctable, way.
4. A *histogram* is the most commonly used graph for showing how often each different value in a set of data occurs.
5. A *Pareto chart* presents bar graphs that reveal which causes are significant, separating the "vital few" from the "useful many."
6. A *scatter diagram* graphs pairs of different sets of variables, allowing a search for quality relationships or patterns.
7. A *flow chart* (or *run chart*) represents visually the series of steps required to complete an operation.

This list may seem overwhelming. However, most of these tools are straightforward and require almost no training, except for control charts, which are discussed in more detail later in this section. And you can learn more about how to use all seven of these tools through online resources.

QUALITY INSPECTION VERSUS POKA-YOKE

Management's traditional method of maintaining product quality has been **inspection**, which consists of examining a part or a product to determine whether or not it is acceptable. An inspector often uses gauges to evaluate important quality variables. For effective quality control, the inspector must be honest, objective, and capable of resisting pressure from shop personnel to pass borderline cases.

inspection
The examination of a part or a product to determine whether it meets quality standards.

Although the inspection process is usually discussed with reference to product quality, comparable steps can be taken to evaluate service quality. Follow-up calls to customers of an auto repair shop, for example, might be used to measure the quality of the firm's repair services. Customers can be asked whether recent repairs were performed in a timely and satisfactory manner.

The problem with inspection is that it occurs after the fact—that is, after faulty goods or inadequate services have been created or offered for sale. At that point, considerable resources have already been consumed in a company's operations, but with nothing of quality to show for it. This can result in unnecessary costs. In fact, it can lead to both internal costs (those related to repair, inspection, prevention, and training) and external costs (those related to the loss of reputation and repeat customers). Knowing this inspired quality guru Philip Crosby to declare, "Quality is free!" In other words, the *savings* associated with getting quality right more than offset the *cost* of a total quality management program.

Quality inspection processes are helpful, but **poka-yoke** (Japanese for the notion of designing business processes to prevent defects) is a more proactive approach that seeks to mistake-proof a firm's operations. For example, a microwave oven may be designed so that it will not work with the door open, thereby preventing radiation leakage. Fryers at many fast food restaurants now raise the product out of the hot grease using a timed machine, rather than relying on a vigilant employee and an audible alarm. This innovation prevents food waste (from over- or under-cooked foods) and removes an opportunity for grease-burn injuries.

poka-yoke
A proactive approach to quality management that seeks to mistake-proof a firm's operations.

STATISTICAL METHODS OF QUALITY CONTROL

The use of statistical methods and control charts often can make controlling product and service quality easier, less expensive, and more effective. Because some knowledge of quantitative methods is necessary to develop a quality control method using statistical analysis, a properly qualified employee should be available to lead this part of the process. The savings made possible by use of an efficient statistical method usually will more than justify the cost of setting it up and managing it.

Acceptance sampling involves taking random samples of products and measuring them against predetermined standards. Suppose that a small business receives a shipment of 10,000 parts from a supplier. Rather than evaluate all 10,000 parts, the purchaser might check the acceptability of a small sample of parts and then accept or reject the entire order based on the results. The smaller the sample, the greater the risk of either accepting a defective lot or rejecting a good lot due to *sampling error.* A larger sample reduces this risk but increases the cost of inspection. A well-designed plan strikes a balance, simultaneously avoiding excessive inspection costs and minimizing the risk of accepting a bad lot or rejecting a good lot.

acceptance sampling
The use of a random, representative portion of products to determine the acceptability of an entire lot.

The use of statistical analysis makes it possible to establish tolerance limits that allow for inherent variation due to chance. When measurements fall outside these tolerance limits, however, the quality controller knows that a problem exists and must search for the cause. A control chart graphically shows the limits for the process being controlled. As current data are entered, it is possible to tell whether a process is under control or out of control (random or nonrandom). Control charts may be used for either variable or attribute inspections.

attributes
Product or service parameters that can be counted as being present or absent.

variables
Measured parameters that fall on a continuum, such as weight or length.

Attributes are product or service parameters that can be counted as being either present or absent. A light bulb either lights or doesn't light; similarly, a water hose either leaks or doesn't leak. **Variables** are measured parameters that fall on a continuum, such as weight or length. If a large can of cashews is to be sold as containing a minimum of two pounds of nuts, an inspector may judge the product acceptable if its weight falls within the range of 32 to 33 ounces.

A problem might be caused by variations in raw materials, machine wear, or changes in employees' work practices. Consider, for example, a candy maker that is producing one-pound boxes of chocolates. Although the weight may vary slightly, each box must weigh at least 16 ounces. A study of the operations process has determined that the actual target weight must be 16.5 ounces, to allow for normal variation between 16 and 17 ounces. During the production process, a set of boxes is weighed every 15 or 20 minutes. If the average weight of a box falls outside the tolerance limits—below 16 or above 17 ounces—the quality controller must immediately try to find the problem and correct it.

Continuing improvements in computer-based technology have advanced the use of statistical control processes in small enterprises. In fact, many off-the-shelf enterprise resource planning systems (computer software systems that coordinate all major facets of a firm's operations) for smaller businesses now include statistical quality control tools. Some of the systems best suited to the needs of small companies include NetSuite, Sage, Intacct, and Epicor. But selecting the package that is right for a specific venture can be a complex decision, which should be made with great care and the help of a knowledgeable advisor.

INTERNATIONAL CERTIFICATION FOR QUALITY MANAGEMENT

ISO 9000
The standards governing international certification of a firm's quality management procedures.

A firm can obtain international recognition of its quality management program by meeting a series of standards, known as **ISO 9000**, developed by the International Organization for Standardization (ISO) in Geneva, Switzerland. The certification process requires full documentation of a firm's quality management procedures, as well as an audit to ensure that the firm is operating in accordance with those procedures. In other words, the firm must show that it does what it says it does.

ISO 9000 certification is particularly valuable for small firms, because they usually lack a global image as producers of high-quality products. Buyers in other countries, especially in Europe, view this certification as an indicator of supplier reliability. Some large U.S. corporations, such as the major automobile makers, require their domestic suppliers to conform to these standards. Small firms, therefore, may need ISO 9000 certification either to sell more easily in international markets or to meet the demands of their domestic customers.

Environmental concerns and a focus on social responsibility have created new opportunities and challenges for entrepreneurs. Although no general certifications have been offered, the International Organization for Standardization also offers an ISO 14001 certification. This certification reflects how efficiently companies have set up and improved their operations processes in order to control the impact of vehicle and smokestack emissions, noise, and other fallout on air, water, and soil.

ISO certification is challenging to earn, but the payoff from achieving it can make it all worthwhile. Partners & Napier, an advertising agency in Rochester, New York, took the challenge and said, "The certification process took six months and required each step of an [ad assignment to] be documented."[15] The certification cost about $20,000, but the result was significant gains, and the agency's creative output seems to have blossomed as well. Partners & Napier is managing to turn out higher quality work in significantly less time. These improvements now translate directly to the firm's bottom line.[16]

QUALITY MANAGEMENT IN SERVICE BUSINESSES

As discussed earlier, maintaining and improving quality are no less important for service businesses than for manufacturers. In fact, many firms offer a combination of products and services and effectively manage quality in both areas.

Though customer satisfaction with service businesses overall has been higher in recent years, there is still plenty of room for improvement. For example, some large corporations gear the quality of the services they provide to the profitability of the customer—with better customers getting better service—and this can easily lead to dissatisfaction. But poor service from larger businesses (automated telephone answering systems that do not allow callers to speak to a live representative, long lines, reluctance to respond to customer problems, and so forth) opens the door for small service-oriented companies. Although some services are too costly to be used as powerful competitive weapons, providing high-quality service may sometimes involve nothing more than simple attention to detail.

Gathering relevant and useful measurements can be problematic when assessing the quality of a service. It is easier to measure the length of a section of pipe than the quality of motel accommodations. As noted earlier, however, methods can be devised for measuring the quality of services. For example, a motel manager might maintain a record of the number of problems with travelers' reservations, complaints about the cleanliness of rooms, and so on. Frequently, the "easy to measure" becomes the only measure. It is critical that measures are chosen carefully to find parameters most relevant to customers' perspectives on quality.

For many types of service firms, quality control constitutes management's most important responsibility. When all that a firm sells is service, its success depends on customers' perceptions of the quality of that service.

Purchasing Policies and Practices

5 Explain the importance of purchasing and the nature of key purchasing policies.

Although its role varies with the type of business, purchasing constitutes a key part of operations management for most small businesses. Through purchasing, firms obtain materials, merchandise, equipment, and services to meet production and marketing goals. For example, manufacturing firms buy raw materials or components, merchandising firms purchase products to be sold, and all types of firms obtain supplies.

THE IMPORTANCE OF PURCHASING

The quality of a finished product depends on the quality of the raw materials used. If a product must be made with great precision and close tolerances, the manufacturer must

LIVING THE DREAM

© iStockphoto.com/Angelika Schwarz

entrepreneurial experiences

To Solve a Problem, Just Look in the Mirror

Like beauty, the quality of a service is in the eyes of the beholder (customer). And for the typical customer, a perception of outstanding quality will be based on the degree to which a small company has addressed his or her need or problem. To offer a good and efficient solution, it is crucial to identify all of the variables involved.

Bambu Productions/Ionica/Getty Images

A few months after a multi-storied office building was completed in New York City and space had been rented to various businesses, occupants began to complain about poor service from the buildings' eight adjacent elevators. Waiting times at peak hours were frustratingly long, and this motivated several of the tenants to threaten to break their leases. An engineering study revealed that there was no way to add more elevators, so it appeared that the problem was permanent. The report's conclusion was as simple as it was disheartening: Learn to live with the long wait times.

The manager charged with finding a solution to the problem called a meeting of his staff. They decided that it was time to hire a troubleshooter and brought in a young consultant, who focused less on elevator performance than on the fact that people were complaining about having to wait what was, in reality, only a few minutes.

> *He concluded that the complaints were a consequence of boredom. Therefore, he took the problem to be one of giving those waiting something to occupy their time pleasantly. He suggested installing mirrors in the elevator boarding areas so that those waiting could look at each other or themselves without appearing to do so.*

At the consultant's suggestion, the manager had the recommended mirrors installed. After these minor and very inexpensive changes were completed, the complaints about waiting immediately ceased. Now most elevator lobbies in tall buildings feature an abundance of mirrors.

So why all the trouble in this case? Those who first worked on the problem figured the elevators were the only adjustable variable involved and concluded that more, bigger, or faster elevators would have to be added to attain relief. They assumed that everything else was a constant, but this clearly was not the case. The most important variable—people's perceptions of time, as it turned out—could also be adjusted. But perhaps there were other features that could have been fine-tuned as well.

This all leads to a very simple but potentially powerful bit of advice: When you think about your customers' perceptions of the quality of your company's service, list as many of the variables involved in the interaction as you possibly can. Then, as you think about each of these in turn, ask yourself whether adjusting that variable might improve the quality of your service in the eyes of your customers. It's a straightforward means of identifying ways to improve their experience and keep them coming back for more of what you have to offer.

Sources: Leon Presser, *What It Takes to Be an Entrepreneur* (Gardena, CA: Resserp Publishing, 2010), pp. 46–48; and Matt Mullenweg, "Defining the Problem of Elevator Waiting Times," http://37signals.com/svn/posts/1244-defining-the-problem-of-elevator-waiting-times, accessed May 11, 2011.

acquire high-quality materials and component parts. Then, if a well-managed production process is used, excellent products will result. Similarly, the acquisition of high-quality merchandise makes a retailer's sales to customers easier and reduces the number of necessary markdowns and merchandise returns.

Purchasing also contributes to profitable operations by ensuring that goods are delivered when they are needed. Failure to receive materials, parts, or equipment on schedule can cause costly interruptions in production operations. In a retail business, failure to receive merchandise on schedule may mean a loss of sales and, possibly, a permanent loss of customers who were disappointed.

Another aspect of effective purchasing is securing the best possible price. Cost savings go directly to the bottom line, so purchasing practices that seek out the best prices can have a major impact on the financial health of a business.

Note, however, that the importance of the purchasing function varies according to the type of business. In a small, labor-intensive service business—such as an accounting firm—purchases of supplies are responsible for a very small part of the total operating costs. Such businesses are more concerned with labor costs than with the cost of supplies or other materials that they may require in their operations process.

Make or Buy?

Many firms face **make-or-buy decisions**. Such choices are especially important for small manufacturing companies that have the option of making or buying component parts for products they produce. A less obvious make-or-buy choice exists with respect to certain services—for example, purchasing janitorial or car rental services versus providing for those needs internally. Some reasons for making component parts, rather than buying them, follow:

make-or-buy decisions
A choice that companies must make when they have the option of making or buying component parts for products they produce.

- More complete utilization of plant capacity permits more economical production.
- Supplies are assured, with fewer delays caused by design changes or difficulties with outside suppliers.
- A secret design may be protected.
- Expenses are reduced by an amount equivalent to transportation costs and the outside supplier's selling expense and profit.
- Closer coordination and control of the total production process may facilitate operations scheduling and control.
- Parts produced internally may be of higher quality than those available from outside suppliers.

Some reasons for buying component parts, rather than making them, follow:

- An outside supplier's part may be cheaper because the supplier specializes in the production of that particular part.
- Additional space, equipment, personnel skills, and working capital are not needed.
- Less diversified managerial experience and skills are required.
- Greater flexibility is provided, especially in the manufacture of a seasonal item.

- In-plant operations can concentrate on the firm's specialty—finished products and services.
- The risk of equipment obsolescence is transferred to outsiders.

The decision to make or buy should be based on long-run cost and profit optimization because it may be expensive to reverse. Underlying cost differences need to be analyzed carefully; small savings from either buying or making may greatly affect profit margins.

Outsourcing

Sometimes it makes sense for a business to contract with an external provider (that is, an independent party that has its own employees) to take on and manage one or more of its functions. This is called **outsourcing**. (You'll recall that international outsourcing was discussed in Chapter 18.) As mentioned earlier, firms can sometimes save money by working with outside suppliers specializing in a particular type of work, especially services such as accounting, payroll, janitorial, and equipment repair services. The expertise of these outside suppliers may enable them to provide better-quality services by virtue of their specialization.

outsourcing Contracting with a third party to take on and manage one or more of the firm's functions.

According to a survey by Human Capital Institute, a global association for talent and leadership management, 90 percent of U.S. companies engage in outsourcing. And the amount of work that they outsource is growing, from an average of 6 percent of total operations in 1990 to more than 27 percent two decades later.[17] There clearly can be drawbacks to outsourcing—for example, no one knows a small business as well as its owner or works as hard for its success. But entrepreneurs like Bruce Judson, who founded an applications outsourcing website called thecostsavingsguy.com, argue convincingly for this option. He warns that outsourcing "the unique skill or product that you bring to the business" is unwise, but he then declares that everything else should be on the table. As he puts it, "You should be working on the business, not in it, and a good service frees up time for you to focus on what you do best."[18]

Outsourcing can take many forms. Chapter 20 explained the practice of co-employment, through which a small company can transfer its employees to a professional employer organization, which then leases them back to the firm. In that case, the small business is outsourcing the payroll preparation process. But the explosive growth in outsourcing among smaller companies may be due as much to a phenomenon known as *crowdsourcing* as anything else. The term refers to taking advantage of the broad reach of the Internet to tap the services of hungry freelancers—in marketing, public relations,

Outsourcing Decisions

Outsourcing options can work wonders for a small business, but they also come with inherent risks. For example, what would you do if an outsourcing partner starts to provide shoddy product or drops the ball completely? Many experts suggest that you have a back-up plan in case a supplier fails to deliver (for whatever reason, and there could be many), and that you continually monitor the progress of those companies with whom you choose to work. This requires time, effort, and expense, but taking these steps can help to ensure that your firm is spared the operational disasters that can easily arise from outsourcing.

website development, legal services, and design—and of any other talent that can be managed easily and affordably through crowdsourcing websites. With names like guru.com, 99designs.com, and vWorker.com (which stands for virtual worker), these sites connect businesses with a global market of freelancers and receive a small cut of the final transaction for the services they provide.[19] In the end, everyone comes out ahead, which explains the popularity of the trend.

Coops and the Internet

Some small companies find that they can increase their buying power if they join **cooperative purchasing organizations** (often called **coops**). In this type of arrangement, several smaller businesses combine their demand for products and services with the goal of negotiating, as a group, for lower prices and better service from suppliers. Coops usually focus on a specific industry to maximize the benefits to participating businesses, and they can be very effective.

cooperative purchasing organization (coop) An organization in which small businesses combine their demand for products or services in order to negotiate as a group with suppliers.

Coops have been around for a long time, but newer alternatives are quickly emerging. Increasingly, small companies are turning to the Internet as a powerful purchasing venue. Many tasks that once required telephone calls or out-of-office time can now be accomplished simply and quickly on the Web.

In the past, small businesses had scant buying power and very limited access to resources and information, which put them at a serious disadvantage relative to their large competitors. That has all changed, thanks (mostly) to the Internet. Today's connected small business owners can line up hundreds of suppliers, large and small, to bid for their business—with just a few mouse clicks. They can also outsource a variety of tasks, from business planning and product design to sales presentations and warranty service. Technology has opened the door to a world of outsourcing alternatives that was unimaginable just a few decades ago.

Diversification of Supply

Small businesses often must decide whether it is better to use more than one supplier when purchasing a given item. The somewhat frustrating answer is "It all depends." For example, a business would rarely need more than one supplier when buying a few rolls of tape. However, several suppliers might be involved when a firm is buying a component part to be used in hundreds of products.

A small company might prefer to concentrate purchases with one supplier for any of the following reasons:

- A particular supplier may be superior in its product quality.
- Larger orders may qualify for quantity discounts.
- Orders may be so small that it is impractical to divide them among several suppliers.
- The purchasing firm may, as a good customer, qualify for prompt treatment of rush orders and receive management advice, market information, and flexible financial terms in times of crisis.

Also, a venture may be linked to a specific supplier by the very nature of its business—if it is a franchisee, for instance. Typically, the franchise contract requires purchasing from the franchisor.

The following reasons favor diversifying rather than concentrating sources of supply:

- Shopping among suppliers allows a firm to locate the best source in terms of price, quality, and service.
- A supplier, knowing that competitors are getting some of its business, may provide better prices and service.
- Diversifying supply sources provides insurance against interruptions caused by strikes, fires, or similar problems with individual suppliers.

Some companies compromise by following a purchasing policy of concentrating enough purchases with a single supplier to justify special treatment and, at the same time, diversifying purchases sufficiently to maintain alternative sources of supply. The point is that a small business can adopt any of a number of different approaches in order to diversify its sourcing strategy.

MEASURING SUPPLIER PERFORMANCE

Supply Chain Operations Reference (SCOR) model A list of critical factors that provides a helpful starting place when assessing a supplier's performance.

What measures of a supplier's performance matter most? The Supply Chain Council has an answer to that question. It has developed the **Supply Chain Operations Reference (SCOR) model**, a list of critical factors that provides a helpful starting place when assessing a supplier's performance. Five attributes stand out: [20]

- *Reliability:* Does the supplier provide what you need and fill orders accurately?
- *Responsiveness:* Does the supplier deliver inputs when they are needed?
- *Agility:* Does the supplier respond quickly to changes in your order?
- *Costs:* Does the supplier help you control your cost of goods sold, your total supply chain management costs, and your warranty/returns costs?
- *Assets:* Does the supplier help you improve efficiencies by shortening the cash cycle, inventory holding time, and demand on assets?

These factors can also prove helpful when first selecting a supplier. Since they are commonly used performance measures, some suppliers have data to show potential new customers how they stack up (along with references to verify their claims). Just remember that an outstanding rating on a measure that is not important to your business does not provide an advantage—in fact, it can be a form of waste.

When choosing a supplier, also consider the services it offers. The extension of credit by suppliers provides a major portion of the working capital of many small businesses. Some suppliers also plan sales promotions, provide merchandising aids, and offer management advice.

Clearly, it is vitally important to choose suppliers carefully. If a supplier fails to deliver what you need when you need it and with the quality you require, the entire operation breaks down—as does your business.

BUILDING GOOD RELATIONSHIPS WITH SUPPLIERS

Good relationships with suppliers are essential for firms of any size, but they are particularly important for small businesses. The small company is only one among dozens, hundreds, or perhaps thousands buying from that supplier. And the small company's purchases are often very limited in volume and, therefore, of little concern to the supplier.

To implement a policy of fair play and to cultivate good relations with suppliers, a small business should try to observe the following purchasing practices:

entrepreneurial experiences

Brown M&Ms: The Canary in the Rock Music Coal Mine

© iStockphoto.com/Angelika Schwarz

One of the profound challenges in working with suppliers is ensuring that they perform according to your agreement, without your having to spend all of your time checking up on them. Sometimes, this can be done conveniently and inexpensively. Consider the approach taken by Van Halen, an American hard rock band that was in its heyday in the 1980s. The group used to attach a concert rider to its contracts with promoters to make certain that the agreements would be followed to the letter. According to one account,

© Laszlo Podor / Alamy

> *[Article 126] was where the group made its candy-with-a-caveat request: "M&M's (WARNING: ABSOLUTELY NO BROWN ONES)." While the underlined rider entry has often been described as an example of rock excess, the outlandish demand of multi-millionaires, the group has said that the M&M provision was included to make sure that promoters had actually read its lengthy rider. If brown M&Ms were in the backstage candy bowl, Van Halen surmised that more important aspects of a performance—lighting, staging, security, ticketing—may have been botched by an inattentive promoter.*

Van Halen performances were complex affairs, involving nine 18-wheelers, full of gear. Keeping everything straight required a thick contract that one of the members of the band described as reading "like a version of the Chinese Yellow Pages." It had articles that might stipulate such details as "There will be 15 amperage voltage sockets at 20-foot spaces, evenly, providing 19 amperes." To be careless with such minutiae was to court on-stage disaster.

As with any relationship with a supplier, a detailed contract, on its own, is not enough to ensure reliability in the follow-though. A performance check or series of checks is likely to be needed, and they will have to be designed around the specific nature of the supplier relationship involved. Brown M&Ms are only one very sweet, and wonderfully inexpensive, checkpoint.

Sources: Dan Heath and Chip Heath, "The Telltale Brown M&M," *FastCompany*, March 2010, pp. 36–37; "Van Halen's Genius M&M Master Plan," http://thestrake.com/van-halens-genius-mm-master-plan, accessed May 10, 2011; and "Van Halen's Legendary M&M's Rider," http://www.thesmokinggun.com/documents/crime/van-halens-legendary-mms-rider, accessed May 10, 2011.

- Pay bills promptly.
- Give sales representatives a timely and courteous hearing.
- Minimize abrupt cancellation of orders merely to gain a temporary advantage.
- Avoid attempts to browbeat a supplier into special concessions or unusual discounts.

- Cooperate with the supplier by making suggestions for product improvements and/or cost reductions, whenever possible.

- Provide courteous, reasonable explanations when rejecting bids, and make fair adjustments in the case of disputes.

Some large corporations, such as UPS, Dell, FedEx, and Office Depot, have made special efforts to reach out to small business purchasers. By offering various kinds of assistance, such suppliers can strengthen small companies, which then continue as customers. Of course, it still makes sense to shop around, but low prices can sometimes be misleading. If a low bid looks too good to be true, perhaps it is. Low bids often exclude crucial items. Nonetheless, building strong relationships with the right large suppliers can clearly help small businesses become more competitive.

FORMING STRATEGIC ALLIANCES

Some small firms have found it advantageous to develop strategic alliances with suppliers. This form of partnering enables the buying and selling firms to work much more closely together than is customary in a simple contractual arrangement.

The strategic alliance option can be a good one, but the choice of partner can quickly determine whether the arrangement succeeds or fails—so choose carefully! Laurel Delaney is a successful entrepreneur, author, and educator with more than 20 years of experience in business. During that time, she guided her small businesses into strategic alliances with global powerhouses like Mitsui & Co., Ltd., the Japanese trading company. From those experiences, Delaney gained some important insights on selecting a strategic alliance partner. For example, she learned to begin her search by looking at companies with which she already had a relationship, such as a faithful supplier or distributor or a trading company that was struggling to keep up with demand. And she learned to look for partners that offered the right fit, were trustworthy, and had track records of true performance.[21] If a strategic alliance is well planned and executed, everyone involved comes out ahead.

Some potential alliance partners design their business especially to help small firms. In 2005, Michael Prete started a business called Gotham Cycles to sell parts online for Italian-made Ducati motorcycles. After only a year or so, he was already bringing in $30,000 a month in income. How did he get off to such a fast start? He hired a very important employee: eBay. Of course, the online auction site isn't exactly an employee—it's more like an army of employees (more than 16,000 strong, in fact) that can help an online company with many of its needs. Prete made use of eBay's rich stable of resources to automate his operation, which allowed him to focus on building his company.[22]

A powerful partner for a small business, eBay offers sophisticated tools that can help with shipping, handling e-mail messages and feedback for buyers, and managing listings. It can even help you decide which tools are right for your business (see http://pages.ebay.com/sell/tools.html for details).

FORECASTING SUPPLY NEEDS

How much cash is needed for the next quarter? How much inventory must be carried to support the next season? How much lead time is needed to fill orders? Forecasting can help with understanding where the business is going and the level of resources—from personnel to capital funding—that will be required. Forecasting techniques can be as simple as projecting what will happen based on what happened last year, last week, or an average of several previous periods. Some businesses may require higher accuracy and thus need a more complex model for forecasting.

associative forecasting Forecasting that considers a variety of variables to determine expected sales.

Associative forecasting takes a variety of driving variables into account when determining expected sales. The amount of sales expected at a local ice cream parlor, for example, is a product of many underlying predictors, such as the day of the week or season of the year, weather (rain versus shine, hot versus cool), local events (such as sporting events or movie premieres), and promotions (which could include sales or coupons). Each of these has a different impact on expected sales. Using forecasting tools such as regression, we can determine the impact of each variable on attendance in the past and then use that association to predict future attendance.

USING INFORMATION SYSTEMS

In recent years, small firms have greatly improved operational efficiency by using computers, new software, and Internet links with suppliers and customers. Tedious, paper-based processes for tracking orders, work in process, and inventory have been replaced by simplified and accelerated computer-based processes.

Forrester Research has shown that accounts payable electronic invoicing and processing can cut the cost of an invoice process from $20 to $5.[23] For a company that processes thousands of invoices per month, this savings can have a substantial impact on costs. The software can be purchased off the shelf, so changing how things are done and training personnel on a new system may actually be more challenging than the installation of new software itself.

Management information systems are continually being reinvented and improved. Microsoft alone spends exceedingly large sums of money to build software that will automate practically every aspect of a small company's business (including order processing and inventory management) and create a base layer of technology upon which smaller software makers can build applications. This software is also designed to work for a variety of businesses, from retail to distribution and manufacturing.[24] The information systems options available to small companies just keep getting better, more powerful, and less expensive.

Lean Production and Synchronous Management

A revolution is sweeping over operations management practices, changing the way business is done in many firms. With a focus on eliminating waste, lean production and synchronous management have made their mark on both large and small companies.

LEAN PRODUCTION

Companies are widely adopting principles of lean production, an influential model that is fundamentally reshaping the way operations are planned and managed. **Lean production** is more than a simple set of practices—it is a guiding philosophy and management approach that emphasizes efficiency through the elimination of all forms of waste in a company's operations.

lean production An approach that emphasizes efficiency through elimination of waste.

The ideas at the center of lean production certainly are not new. In fact, the seeds of the concept were sown more than a century ago by Henry Ford, a leading visionary in the automobile industry and an outspoken opponent of manufacturing inefficiency. Later, Shoichiro Toyoda, former president of Toyota Motors, built on Ford's concepts and focused on the need to eliminate waste, in all of its many forms, from his production system. He defined *waste* as "anything other than the minimum amount of equipment, materials, parts, space, and workers' time, which are absolutely essential for adding value to the product."[25] In other words, the goal of lean production is to use the minimum amount of resources necessary to achieve a total bundle of satisfaction for the customer.

The lean production mindset that has been integrated into the operations of most major corporations, including the Toyota Production System (TPS), makes the elimination of waste a top priority:

- *Defects* are costly because they have to be repaired or scrapped.
- *Overproduction* must be stored and may never be sold.
- *Transportation* can be minimized by locating close to suppliers and customers.
- *Waiting* can be wasteful because resources are idle.
- *Inventory* in excess of the minimum required is unproductive and costly.
- *Motion,* whether by product, people, or machinery, can be wasteful.
- *Processing* itself is wasteful if it is not productive.

As companies of all sizes around the world have subscribed to the principles of lean production, the supply chain (introduced in Chapter 15) has become susceptible to disruption, and this can be a problem. Toyota, for example, keeps only two hours of inventory in their assembly plants, so there is little margin for error on the supply side of the equation. However, this incredibly low amount of inventory also leads to a variety of benefits, ranging from capital efficiency to a smooth production process.

synchronous management
An approach that recognizes the interdependence of assets and activities and manages them to optimize the entire firm's performance.

bottleneck
Any point in the operations process where limited capacity reduces the production capability of an entire chain of activities.

SYNCHRONOUS MANAGEMENT

Going a step beyond lean production, **synchronous management** views the assets and activities of an organization as interdependent and suggests that they be managed in a way that optimizes the performance of the entire company. This approach presumes that the goal of the organization, and the definition of performance that flows from it, is known and influences all decision making. It requires an understanding of how a shift in one area of operations can affect the rest of the organization—that is, it provides insight regarding interrelationships between assets, changes in activities, and achievement of the firm's goals.

Although these ideas are not original, they are finally being understood and implemented, in many cases for the first time. Henry Ford concluded early on that the key to manufacturing efficiency lies in a synchronized flow of materials and products into, through, and out of the plant in concert with market demand. Stated another way, companies that understand crucial interactions between their assets and activities are likely to produce the greatest profits.[26]

Identifying bottlenecks is imperative to making synchronous management work. A **bottleneck** is any point in an operations system where limited capacity reduces the production capability of an entire chain of activities so that it cannot satisfy market demand for products or services. For example, a bottleneck can be created by a machine that cannot operate fast enough to keep up with the rest of the equipment on an assembly line. In a more complex production system, it is possible to have more than one bottleneck (that is, more than one resource

Employee Suggestions for Operations Problems

Want to harness the brain power of your employees to identify and address constraints and other operations-centered problems? Why not set up a simple suggestions box? If you provide even a small incentive (some small companies offer a cash prize of $500 for the best suggestion submitted), you might be amazed at the quality of the ideas your staff can come up with. You could even use one of the inexpensive applications that have been designed to collect, discuss, and rank employee ideas: Imaginatik, Spigit, and Brightidea are only a few of the programs that are currently available for this.

whose capacity is lower than the market demand for what is being produced). In this case, the most restrictive of the bottlenecks is called a **constraint**. Since the constraint determines the capacity of the entire system, it is imperative to synchronize all other organizational activities with it.

constraint The most restrictive of bottlenecks, determining the capacity of the entire system.

Finding the bottlenecks in an organization can be a challenging exercise. But once a constraint is found, what can be done to address it? The three basic options shown in Exhibit 21.4 provide common ways to deal with bottlenecks and constraints.

For resources that do not contribute to a bottleneck or constraint in a production line or service firm, it is far less important to make investments to improve their functioning and increase their efficiency. These parts of the system do not have any trouble keeping up with the flow of operations. That is, if a nonbottleneck resource goes down momentarily, the productive capacity of the overall system will not suffer. However, any loss of throughput at a bottleneck or constraint translates to lower production for the entire line or organization. It follows that these points in an operations system deserve special attention, for the sake of the company and its performance.

Hopefully, it is apparent to you by now that operations management is very important to the functioning and performance of all types of businesses, whether large or small. Best practices typically are perfected in large corporations, but the principles and approaches they refine can usually be adapted to the management of smaller enterprises, at least at some level—and it is important to try to do just that. In a competitive marketplace,

EXHIBIT 21.4 Service Level and Balance Sheet Considerations

Add Capacity	• Expand resources. • Subdivide the work. • Outsource production to a company with more capacity.
Increase Efficiency	• Arrange schedules so that the resources takes no breaks (for example, have employees take breaks during setup, teardown, or maintenence activities). • Schedules maintenance on nights, weekends, and holidays rather than during productive time. • Increase productivity through employee training, upgraded tools, or automation.
Filter Production	• Inspect quality prior to a constraint. • Allow only work that achieves firm goals and contributes to performance (that is, a finished goods inventory would be unnecessary).

efficient and effective operations are necessary to survival. And where this is not the case, these practices can still add to customer benefits, firm performance, and the satisfaction of the venture's owners. Practices such as managing inventory wisely, treating suppliers well, and ensuring the quality of products made or services offered protect and enhance the reputation of the company. Reaching these grand heights is impossible unless sound operations management practices are used. The commitment of time and energy required to reach excellence certainly pays off over the long run.

1. **Understand how operations enhance a small company's competitiveness.**
   - The term *operations* refers to the processes used to create and deliver a product or service, which can be used to compete for customers.
   - Companies gain power to the degree that they excel in satisfying customer needs and wants more precisely and efficiently than their competitors.
   - To be successful, a company's operations must involve all of the activities required to create value for customers and earn their dollars.
   - *Operations management* refers to the planning and control of a conversion process that includes bringing together inputs and turning them into outputs (products and services) that customers want.

2. **Discuss the nature of the operations process for both products and services.**
   - Product-oriented and service-oriented operations are similar in that they change inputs into outputs.
   - Managers of service businesses face special challenges in assuring and controlling quality, given the difficulty inherent in measuring and controlling intangibles.
   - In service businesses, employees interact extensively with customers.
   - The adoption of various technologies has enabled customers of many businesses to provide more of their own services.
   - Manufacturing operations can be classified as one of three types—job shops, project manufacturing, and repetitive manufacturing.
   - Flexible manufacturing systems can help cut manufacturing costs while giving customers exactly what they want.
   - A small company's capacity to offer products or services is a critical factor.
   - Planning and scheduling procedures are designed to achieve the orderly sequential flow of products through a plant at a rate that matches deliveries to customers.
   - Demand management strategies are used to stimulate customer demand when it is normally low.

3. **Identify ways to control inventory and minimize inventory costs.**
   - Inventory management can help an entrepreneur understand the vital balance between two competing pressures in the business—increasing inventory to satisfy customer demand and reducing inventory to maintain a healthy balance sheet.
   - One method of determining ideal inventory levels is economic order quantity, an index that determines the purchase quantity of an item that minimizes total inventory costs.
   - Another method is statistical inventory control, which accommodates the variability of supply and demand using a targeted service level.
   - The ABC method classifies items into three categories based on dollar velocity.
   - Just-in-time inventory systems are designed to cut inventory carrying costs by making or buying what is needed just as it is needed.
   - Types of inventory record-keeping systems are physical inventory systems, perpetual inventory systems, and two-bin inventory systems.

4. **Recognize the contributions of operations management to product and service quality.**
   - *Quality* can be defined as the characteristics of a product or service that determine its ability to satisfy customers' stated and implied needs.
   - Total quality management is an all-encompassing, quality-focused management approach that is customer driven, emphasizes organizational commitment, and focuses on a culture of continuous improvement.
   - A firm's quality management efforts should begin with a focus on meeting the expectations of customers who purchase its products or services.

- Paying careful attention to the details of a firm's operations and correcting any weaknesses, as well as listening to customer feedback, helps ensure that customers get the quality they expect.
- One useful approach to gathering customer-based information is to "mine" company sales data to learn more about customer behavior.
- An important element in effective quality management consists of the various tools, techniques, and procedures needed to ensure high-quality products and services.
- Product quality can be maintained by inspection or by using the poka-yoke approach, which seeks to mistake-proof a firm's operations.
- Acceptance sampling is one statistical method of quality control.
- ISO 9000 certification requires full documentation of a firm's quality management procedures and is particularly valuable for small firms.

5. Explain the importance of purchasing and the nature of key purchasing policies.

- The quality of a finished product depends on the quality of the raw materials used.
- Purchasing contributes to profitable operations by ensuring that goods are delivered when they are needed.
- Purchasing practices that seek out the best prices can have major impact on the financial health of a business.
- The decision to make or buy should be based on long-run cost and profit optimization because it may be expensive to reverse.
- Firms can sometimes save money by outsourcing to suppliers specializing in a particular type of work.
- Cooperative purchasing organizations help smaller firms negotiate as a group for lower prices and better service from suppliers.
- The Internet provides small business owners with connections to hundreds of suppliers.
- Diversifying purchases from suppliers can help a small business maintain alternative sources of supply.
- Critical factors in assessing supplier performance are reliability, responsiveness, agility, costs, and assets.
- Good relationships with suppliers are essential for small businesses.
- Developing strategic alliances, forecasting supply needs, and using information systems are other purchasing policies used by small companies.

6. Describe lean production and synchronous management and their importance to operations management in small firms.

- Lean production emphasizes efficiency through the elimination of all forms of waste in a company's operations.
- Maintaining a very low amount of inventory can lead to a variety of benefits, ranging from capital efficiency to a smooth production process.
- Synchronous management suggests that the assets and activities of an organization are interdependent and should be managed in a way that optimizes the performance of the entire company.
- Understanding how a shift in one area of operations can affect the rest of the organization underlies synchronous management and is likely to produce the greatest profits.
- Bottlenecks and constraints must be managed carefully because these determine the capacity of the entire production system.

Key Terms

operations p. 612
operations management p. 612
job shop p. 615
project manufacturing p. 615
repetitive manufacturing p. 615
continuous manufacturing p. 616
flexible manufacturing systems p. 616
demand management strategies p. 617
economic order quantity p. 618
statistical inventory control p. 618
ABC method p. 619
just-in-time inventory system p. 619
physical inventory system p. 621
cycle counting p. 621
perpetual inventory system p. 621
two-bin inventory system p. 621
quality p. 621
total quality management (TQM) p. 621
inspection p. 625
poka-yoke p. 625
acceptance sampling p. 625
attributes p. 626
variables p. 626
ISO 9000 p. 626
make-or-buy decisions p. 629
outsourcing p. 630
cooperative purchasing organization (coop) p. 631
Supply Chain Operations Reference (SCOR) model p. 632
associative forecasting p. 634
lean production p. 635
synchronous management p. 636
bottleneck p. 636
constraint p. 637

Discussion Questions

1. How important is managing operations to the competitiveness of a small business? Why?
2. What are some distinctive features of the operations process in service firms?
3. Customer demand for services is generally not uniform during a day, week, or other period of time. What strategies can be used by service businesses to better match the company's capacity to perform services to customers' demand for those services?
4. What are the major features of the just-in-time inventory system? Is it applicable to small companies? Be prepared to defend your answer.
5. Why is the customer focus of quality management so important in a small firm? What can be done to ensure that the quality of a small venture's products or services remains high?
6. How important is effective purchasing to a small business? Can the owner-manager of a small firm safely delegate purchasing authority to a subordinate? Explain.
7. Under what conditions should a small manufacturer either make component parts or buy them from others?
8. What are the relative merits of inspection approaches and poka-yoke to quality assurance in a small company?
9. What steps can a company take to build good relationships with suppliers? Can you think of any ethical issues that should be taken into account when deciding how to interact with suppliers?
10. Explain the meaning of the terms *lean production* and *synchronous management*. How are these relevant to operations in a small company?

You Make the Call

SITUATION 1

Christina Poole owns two pizza restaurants in a city with a population of 150,000 and is studying her company's operations to be sure they are functioning as efficiently as possible. About 70 percent of the venture's sales represent dine-in business, and 30 percent come from deliveries. Poole has always attempted to produce a good-quality product and minimize the waiting time of customers both on- and off-premises.

Poole recently read a magazine article suggesting that quality is now generally abundant and that quality differences between businesses are narrowing. The writer advocated placing emphasis on saving time for customers rather than producing a high-quality product. Poole is contemplating the implications of this article for her pizza business. Realizing that her attention should be focused, she wonders whether to concentrate primary managerial emphasis on delivery time.

Question 1 Is the writer of the article correct in believing that quality levels now are generally higher and that quality differences among businesses are minimal?
Question 2 What are the benefits and drawbacks of placing the firm's primary emphasis on minimizing customer waiting time?
Question 3 If you were advising Poole, what would you recommend?
Question 4 How would your answers to the previous questions be different if Poole sold a $6 pizza? What if it were a $40 pizza?

SITUATION 2

Jonathan Tandy, owner of a small furniture manufacturing firm, is trying to deal with the firm's thin working capital situation by carefully managing payments to the company's major suppliers. These suppliers extend credit for 30 days, and customers are expected to pay within that time period. However, the suppliers do not automatically refuse subsequent orders when a payment is a few days late. Tandy's strategy is to delay payment of most invoices for 10 to 15 days beyond the due date. Although he is not meeting the "letter of the law" in his agreement, he believes that the suppliers will go along with him rather than risk losing future sales. This practice enables Tandy's firm to operate with sufficient inventory, avoid costly interruptions in production, and reduce the likelihood of an overdraft at the bank.

Question 1 What are the ethical issues raised by Tandy's payment practices?
Question 2 What impact, if any, might these practices have on the firm's supplier relationships? How serious would this impact be?

Question 3 What changes in company culture, employee behavior, or relationships with other business partners may result from Tandy's practices?

SITUATION 3

Tyler Smithson owns Joe on the Run, a small chain of three coffee shops, all of which are facing a challenge that is common to most service businesses: They have to deal with highly variable demand, with two or three very busy times each day. If a waiting line develops, we can assume that a constraint exists somewhere in the product or service delivery. Typical workstations behind the counter include the barista station (where specialty hot drinks are made), the drive-thru station, and the cashier station. Because the goal of the company is to satisfy the most customers possible (and increase resulting profits), a constraint at one of these workstations must be addressed quickly.

Question 1 What can be done to improve capacity?
Question 2 What can be done to improve efficiency?
Question 3 What could be done at a store level to improve the performance of the business?

Experiential Exercises

1. Outline the operations process in your present educational program. Be sure to identify inputs, processes, and outputs.
2. Describe, in detail, your customary practices in studying for a specific course. Evaluate the methods you use, and specify changes that might improve your productivity.
3. Using the ABC inventory analysis method, classify some of your personal possessions into the three categories. Include at least two items in each category. Does this practice change the way you think about managing your "personal inventory"?
4. Interview the manager of a bookstore about the type of inventory control system used in the store. Write a report in which you explain the methods used to avoid buildup of excessive inventory.

Small Business and Entrepreneurship Resource Center

Founded in 1948 as a single, tiny drive-through in a Los Angeles suburb, the In-N-Out Burger chain business has maintained the original menu of burgers, fries, sodas, and ice cream shakes—no chicken, no salads, no desserts, and no toys for the kids . . . just great quality! In-N-Out has always been a family-owned firm, and it operates with a very simple business philosophy: "Give customers the freshest, highest-quality foods you can buy and provide them with friendly service in a sparkling clean environment." The formula is obviously working, but the company has come to a crossroads. The company's future became uncertain when co-founder Esther Snyder died in August 2006. The Snyder family has historically avoided the media, choosing to keep the operations of In-N-Out to themselves. However, Lynsi Martinez, the 24-year-old heir to the company, has indicated that she wants to increase growth, potentially going public with stock options and franchising opportunities. Describe the slow-growth and minimal change model that co-founder Harry Snyder advocated since the inception of the firm. Also discuss how this strategy has been instrumental in creating a cadre of devoted customers.

Sources: Kathryn A. Braun-Latour and Michael S. Latour, "Using Childhood Memory Elicitation to Gain Insights into a Brand at a Crossroads," *Cornell Hotel & Restaurant Administration Quarterly*, Vol. 48, No. 3 (August 2007), pp. 246–273.

Video Case 21

RIVER POOLS & SPAS (P. 734)

This case focuses on operational adjustments that a small company had to make in response to growth in market demand and later decreases in sales that resulted from the recession and subsequent slow growth of the U.S. economy.

ALTERNATIVE CASES FOR CHAPTER 21

Case 18, Smarter.com, p. 728
Case 19, Diamond Wipes International, p. 730

CHAPTER 22

Managing the Firm's Assets

In the SPOTLIGHT
The United Companies
http://www.uniteddc.com

Small companies are largely dependent on their cash flows. But if they push their slow payers too hard, they risk losing customers. Hiring collection attorneys is also expensive, and if late payers are forced into bankruptcy, their small business creditors may find themselves empty-handed, waiting at the end of a long queue.

UnitedDC, Inc.

"The last thing you want to do is get in an adversarial position with your great clients; they're your lifeline," says Charles Doyle, managing director at Business Capital, a San Francisco company that helps businesses restructure their debts.

In fall 2008, more than half of the customers of The United Companies, a Houston, Texas–based handler of plastic resin, were more than 30 days past due on their bills. The company's bank had slashed its credit line by 20 percent, to $2.4 million. United was paying its own bills late, because of the cash flow crunch.

Marc Levine, chief executive of the company, which has 350 employees and $40 million in revenue, began personally calling customers who were more than 30 days past due. He says he explained that he needed to be paid because his business was suffering, too.

"I made sure I told them how much we loved them," he says, "but in order to do a fine job in serving them, I needed them to accelerate

After studying this chapter, you should be able to . . .

1. Describe the working capital cycle of a small business.
2. Identify the important issues in managing a firm's cash flows.
3. Explain the key issues in managing accounts receivable.
4. Discuss the key issues in managing inventory.
5. Explain the key issues in managing accounts payable.
6. Calculate and interpret a company's cash conversion period.
7. Give examples of the types of capital budgeting decisions small business owners must make.
8. Discuss the techniques commonly used in making capital budgeting decisions.
9. Describe the capital budgeting practices of small firms.

LOOKING AHEAD

© iStockphoto.com/Dan Bachman

payment and return my cash flow to where it was in summer '08 and prior."

Levine says his personal approach worked, and many of the customers paid up after his call. He adds that he also stopped shipping for some small, financially weak customers until they began paying within 30 days. And he made some cost cuts, including laying off about 50 employees.

Source: Simona Covel and Kelly K. Spors, "To Help Collect the Bills, Firms Try the Soft Touch, *Wall Street Journal,* January 27, 2009, p. B1. Reprinted with permission of *Wall Street Journal.*

In the opening spotlight, we described the problem that The United Companies was experiencing in collecting its accounts receivable during the recent economic downturn. The same story could be told by almost all small businesses that extend credit to their customers. It is a never-ending challenge. In fact, most novice entrepreneurs are shocked by how much time and energy they must commit to collections.

Controlling all of a firm's assets requires this same commitment from the firm's management. This chapter focuses on this important issue.

The Working Capital Cycle

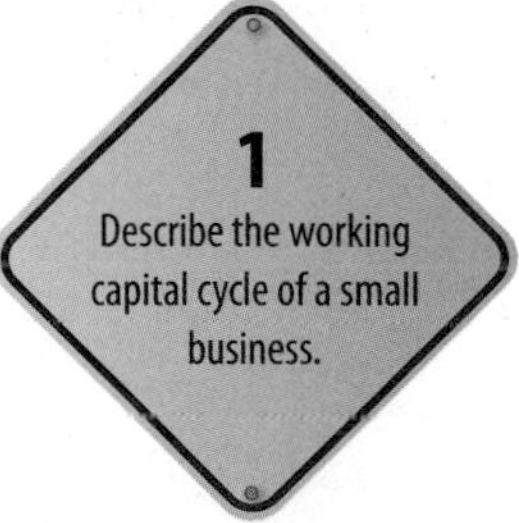

In Chapters 10 and 11, respectively, we defined *working capital* as a firm's current assets (primarily cash, accounts receivable, and inventory), and *net working capital* as current assets less current or short-term liabilities. **Working capital management**—managing current assets and short-term sources of financing (current liabilities)—is extremely important to most small companies. In fact, no financial management process is more important, and yet more misunderstood. Good business opportunities can be irreparably damaged by ineffective working capital management. We have made this point repeatedly when discussing the importance of managing cash.

Jonathan Blum, a successful entrepreneur, believes how a firm's working capital is managed could be the difference between the firm's success or failure:

> *The secret to surviving the Great Recession may turn out to be how you manage working capital—the difference between the money you've been paid and the cash you owe.*[1]

working capital management
The management of current assets and current liabilities.

A firm's **working capital cycle** is the flow of resources through the company's accounts as part of its day-to-day operations. As shown in Exhibit 22.1, the steps in a firm's working capital cycle are as follows:

working capital cycle
The daily flow of resources through a firm's working capital accounts.

Step 1: Purchase or produce inventory for sale, which increases inventory on hand and increases accounts payable if the inventory is purchased on credit.

Step 2: a. Sell the inventory for cash, which increases cash, or
b. Sell the inventory on credit, which increases accounts receivable.

Step 3: a. Pay the accounts payable, which decreases accounts payable and decreases cash.
b. Pay operating expenses and taxes, which decreases cash.

Step 4: Collect the accounts receivable when due, which decreases accounts receivable and increases cash.

Step 5: Begin the cycle again.

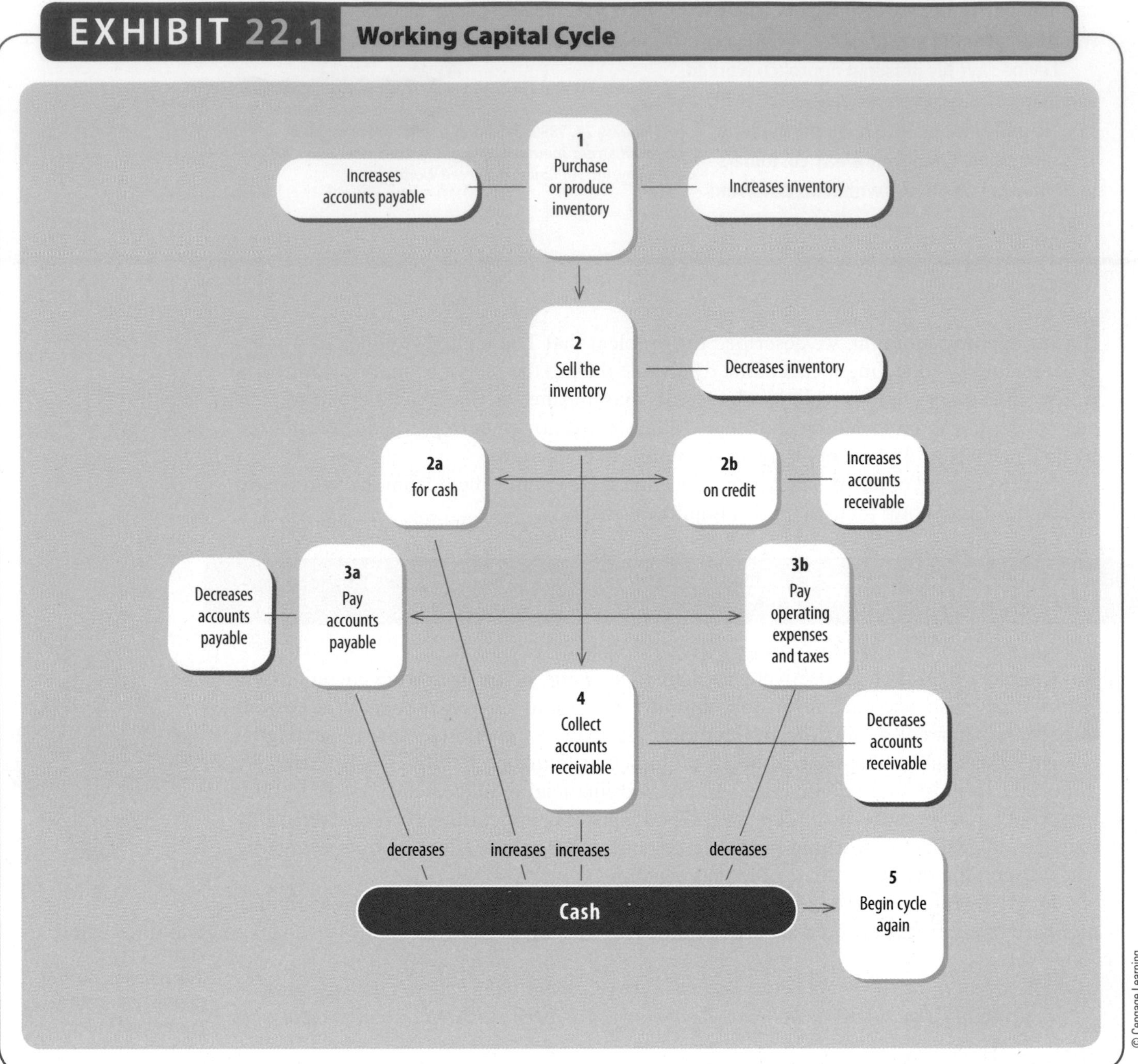

Note that the only current liability included in the working capital cycle is accounts payable, which affects the timing of payments for inventory. Accrued expenses, although shown on financial statements as a short-term liability, primarily result from an accountant's effort to match revenues and expenses. Little can be done to "manage" accruals or short-term bank notes, which are a matter of acquiring financing outside the firm. *In this context, think of working capital as the liquid assets (cash and those soon to be converted into cash) that are required to run and grow the business.*

Depending on the industry, the working capital cycle may be long or short. For example, it is only a few days in a restaurant business; it is longer, most likely months, in most computer hardware businesses. Whatever the industry, however, management should be working continuously to shorten the cycle.

RESOURCES

Managing Working Capital

REL, a global working capital consulting firm, is focused on delivering sustainable working capital improvement to its client companies. Its website, which can be found at http://www.relconsultancy.com, is an excellent source of practical articles on managing working capital.

THE TIMING AND SIZE OF WORKING CAPITAL INVESTMENTS

It is imperative that owners of small companies understand the working capital cycle, in terms of both the timing of investments and the size of the investment required (for example, the amounts necessary to maintain inventory and accounts receivable). Too many entrepreneurs wait until a problem with working capital develops to examine these relationships. An owners' failure to do so underlies many of the financial problems of small companies.

Exhibit 22.2 shows the chronological sequence of a hypothetical working capital cycle. The time line reflects the order in which events unfold, starting with purchasing inventory and ending with collecting accounts receivable. The key dates in the exhibit are as follows:

Day a: Inventory is ordered in anticipation of future sales.

Day b: Inventory is received.

Day c: Inventory is sold on credit.

Day d: Accounts payable for purchases of inventory come due and are paid.

Day e: Accounts receivable are collected.

EXHIBIT 22.2 Working Capital Time Line

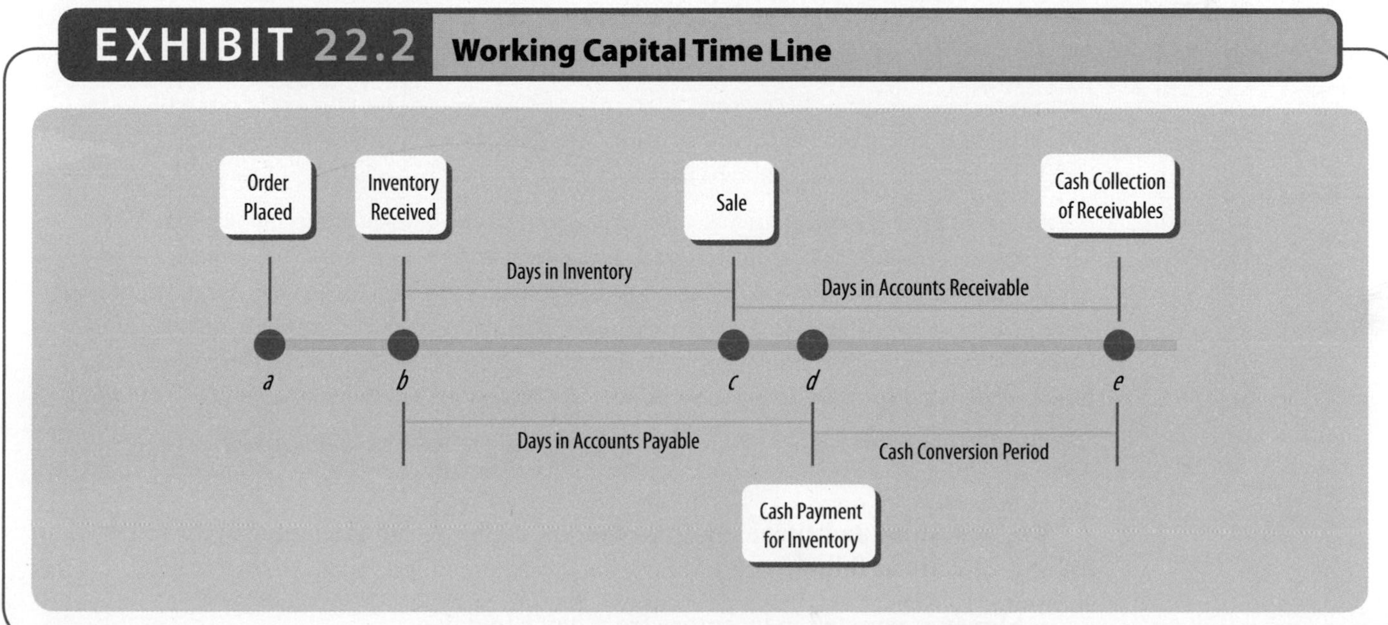

LIVING THE DREAM

© iStockphoto.com/Angelika Schwarz

entrepreneurial experiences

Growth Is a Double-Edged Sword

Colin Roche and Bobby Ronsse, who in 2001 founded Pacifica, California–based Pacific Writing Instruments, have truly enjoyed their entrepreneurial ride. The source of their happiness? Their company's ergonomic pen, the Pen Again, is now carried in more than 2,000 stores, including Walmart, Office Depot, Publix, and FedEx Office. In other words, they have arrived.

But on their way, they found that business growth can be a double-edged sword. "Before our product got into the big stores, we weren't selling as many pens, but business was steadier, the fluctuations weren't as big and the dollar amounts were certainly a lot smaller," Ronsse says. "If we needed $10,000, we could find it pretty easily from our own savings, a bank loan, or a business line of credit. But when you're selling 100,000 pens, and you have to pay your factory $50,000 before you get paid for those pens, then your sources for solving cash-flow problems are a lot more limited."

© Penka Todorova Vitkova/Shutterstock.com

The key, Ronsse says, is to be prepared, lining up and weighing your options way before feeling any cash squeeze.

"There's always a way to get the money," he says. "It just depends on how much you want to give up. Money's not free, so you either have to pay interest or give up equity in your company to investors."

Besides having investors by their side from day one, Ronsse and Roche worked out pay-when-paid arrangements with some of their sub-suppliers, including the factory that makes the pens. "It's a best-case scenario, but it's not something you can count on," Ronsse says. The deal was approved because the company had built its reputation by paying on time and providing the factory with a steady stream of business.

As a backup, they also looked into factoring, or accounts receivable funding. In this scenario, Pacific Writing Instruments would sell a purchase order at a discount to a third-party lender (the factor), who would then be paid by the store that ordered the pens. This process would let their company pay for up-front costs associated with the big order—but it would also reduce profits from the sale. It wasn't an ideal situation, but it could have saved a business that was experiencing a cash-flow crunch.

"You can be a super-successful company, have a great product distributed all over the place, be profitable, and still go out of business because of cash flow," Ronsse says. "You have to have quick access to capital. Nothing else matters if you can't pay your bills. "

In 2009, Pacific Writing Instruments merged with Baumgartens, an office products supplier based in Atlanta, Georgia, in order to take advantage of the added marketing, creative, and distribution skills as well as the reach that the company could offer to a fledgling business like Pacific Writing Instruments. "Most large retailers and wholesalers do not want to deal with a single product company" says Clive Roux, CMO of Baumgartens. "Instead, they are all trying to consolidate suppliers and product lines. The merger made sense because now we have complementary offers that make us more relevant to our customers."

Source: Lena Basha, "Handle the Headaches," *MyBusiness*, June–July 2007, pp. 26–29. **http://www.penagain.com**

The investing and financing implications of the working capital cycle reflected in Exhibit 22.2 are as follows:

- Money is invested in inventory from day *b* to day *c*.
- The supplier provides financing for the inventory from day *b* to day *d*.

- Money is invested in accounts receivable from day *c* to day *e*.
- Financing of the firm's investment in accounts receivable must be provided from day *d* to day *e*. This time span, called the **cash conversion period**, represents the number of days required to complete the working capital cycle, which ends with the conversion of accounts receivable into cash. During this period, the firm no longer has the benefit of supplier financing (accounts payable). The longer this period lasts, the greater the potential cash flow problems for the firm.

cash conversion period
The time required to convert paid-for inventory and accounts receivable into cash.

EXAMPLES OF WORKING CAPITAL MANAGEMENT

Exhibit 22.3 offers an example of working capital management for two hypothetical firms with contrasting working capital cycles: Pokey, Inc., and Quick Turn Company. On August 15, both firms ordered inventory that they received on August 31, but the similarity ends there.

EXHIBIT 22.3 Working Capital Time Lines for Pokey, Inc., and Quick Turn Company

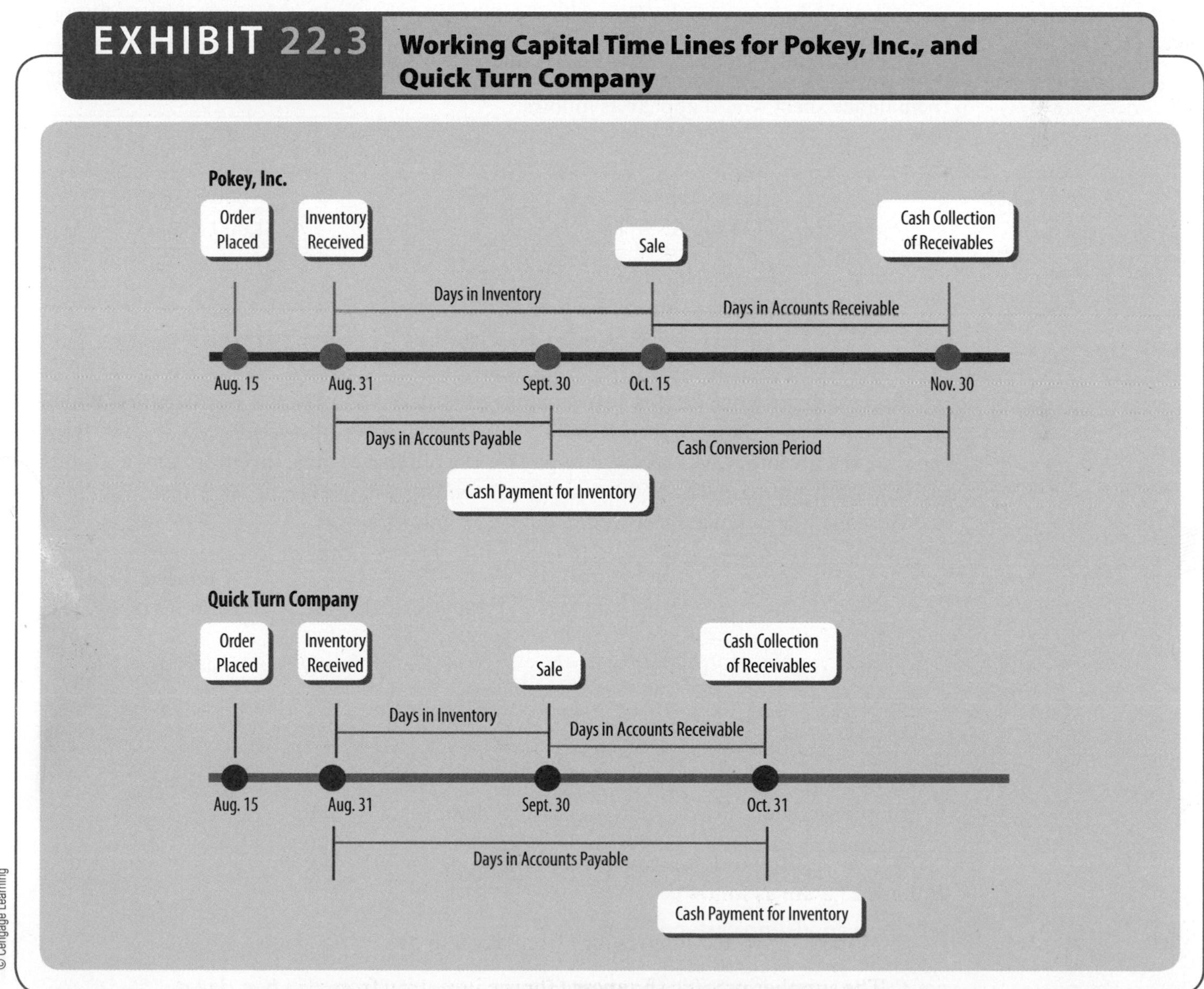

Pokey, Inc., must pay its supplier for the inventory on September 30, before eventually reselling it on October 15. It collects from its customers on November 30. As you can see, Pokey, Inc., must pay for the inventory two months prior to collecting from its customers. Its cash conversion period—the time required to convert the paid-for inventory and accounts receivable into cash—is 60 days. The firm's managers must find a way to finance this investment in inventory and accounts receivable, or else it will experience cash flow problems. Furthermore, although increased sales should produce higher profits, the cash flow problem will be compounded because the company will have to finance the investment in inventory until the accounts receivable are collected 60 days later.

Now consider Quick Turn Company's working capital cycle, shown in the bottom portion of Exhibit 22.3. Compared to Pokey, Quick Turn Company has an enviable working capital position. By the time Quick Turn must pay for its inventory purchases (October 31), it has sold its product (September 30) and collected from its customers (October 31). Thus, there is no cash conversion period because the supplier is essentially financing Quick Turn's working capital needs.

To gain an even better understanding of the working capital cycle, let's see what happens to Pokey's balance sheet and income statement. To do so, we will need more information about the firm's activities. A month-by-month listing of its activities and their effects on its balance sheet follow. Pay close attention to the firm's working capital, especially its cash balances.

July: Pokey, Inc., is a new company, having started operations in July with $1,000, financed by $300 in long-term debt and $700 in common stock. At the outset, the owner purchased $600 worth of fixed assets, leaving the remaining $400 in cash. At this point, the balance sheet would appear as follows:

Cash	$ 400
Fixed assets	600
TOTAL ASSETS	$1,000
Long-term debt	$ 300
Common stock	700
TOTAL DEBT AND EQUITY	$1,000

August: On August 15, the firm's managers ordered $500 worth of inventory, which was received on August 31 (see Exhibit 22.3). The supplier allowed Pokey 30 days from the time the inventory was received to pay for the purchase; thus, inventory and accounts payable both increased by $500 when the inventory was received. As a result of these transactions, the balance sheet would appear as follows:

	July	August	Changes: July to August
Cash	$ 400	$ 400	
Inventory	0	500	+$500
Fixed assets	600	600	
TOTAL ASSETS	$1,000	$1,500	
Accounts payable	$ 0	$ 500	+$500
Long-term debt	300	300	
Common stock	700	700	
TOTAL DEBT AND EQUITY	$1,000	$1,500	

So far, so good—no cash problems yet.

September: On September 30, the firm paid for the inventory; both cash and accounts payable decreased by $500, shown as follows.

	July	August	September	Changes: August to September
Cash	$ 400	$ 400	($ 100)	–$500
Inventory	0	500	500	
Fixed assets	600	600	600	
TOTAL ASSETS	$1,000	$1,500	$1,000	
Accounts payable	$ 0	$ 500	$ 0	–$500
Long-term debt	300	300	300	
Common stock	700	700	700	
TOTAL DEBT AND EQUITY	$1,000	$1,500	$1,000	

Now Pokey, Inc., has a cash flow problem in the form of a cash deficit of $100.

October: October was a busy month for Pokey. On October 15, merchandise was sold on credit for $900; sales (in the income statement) and accounts receivable increased by that amount. The firm incurred operating expenses (selling and administrative expenses) in the amount of $250, to be paid in early November; thus, operating expenses (in the income statement) and accrued operating expenses (current liabilities in the balance sheet) increased by $250. (An additional $25 in accrued expenses resulted from accruing taxes that will be owed on the firm's earnings.) Finally, in October, the firm's accountants recorded $50 in depreciation expense (to be reported in the income statement), resulting in accumulated depreciation on the balance sheet of $50.

The results are as follows:

	July	August	September	October	Changes: September to October
Cash	$ 400	$ 400	($ 100)	($ 100)	
Accounts receivable	0	0	0	900	+$900
Inventory	0	500	500	0	–500
Fixed assets	600	600	600	600	
Accumulated depreciation	0	0	0	(50)	–50
TOTAL ASSETS	$1,000	$1,500	$1,000	$ 1,350	
Accounts payable	$ 0	$ 500	$ 0	$ 0	
Accrued operating expenses	0	0	0	250	+$250
Income tax payable	0	0	0	25	+25
Long-term debt	300	300	300	300	
Common stock	700	700	700	700	
Retained earnings	0	0	0	75	+75
TOTAL DEBT AND EQUITY	$1,000	$1,500	$1,000	$ 1,350	

The October balance sheet shows all the activities just described, but there is one more change in the balance sheet: It now shows $75 in retained earnings, which had been $0 in the prior balance sheets. As you will see shortly, this amount represents the firm's income. Note also that Pokey, Inc., continues to be overdrawn by $100 on its cash. None of the events in October affected the firm's cash balance. All the transactions were the result of accruals recorded by the firm's accountant, offsetting entries to the income statement. The relationship between the balance sheet and the income statement is as follows:

Change in the Balance Sheet		Effect on the Income Statement
Increase in accounts receivable of $900	→	Sales of $900
Decrease in inventory of $500	→	Cost of goods sold of $500
Increase in accrued operating expenses of $250	→	Operating expenses of $250
Increase in accumulated depreciation of $50	→	Depreciation expense of $50
Increase in accrued taxes of $25	→	Tax expense of $25

November: In November, the accrued expenses were paid, which resulted in a $250 decrease in cash along with an equal decrease in accrued expenses. At the end of November, the accounts receivable were collected, yielding a $900 increase in cash and a $900 decrease in accounts receivable. Thus, net cash increased by $650. The final series of balance sheets is as follows:

	July	August	September	October	November	Changes: October to November
Cash	$ 400	$ 400	($ 100)	($ 100)	$ 550	+$650
Accounts receivable	0	0	0	900	0	−900
Inventory	0	500	500	0	0	
Fixed assets	600	600	600	600	600	
Accumulated depreciation	0	0	0	(50)	(50)	
TOTAL ASSETS	$1,000	$1,500	$1,000	$1,350	$1,100	
Accounts payable	$ 0	$ 500	$ 0	$ 0	$ 0	
Accrued operating expenses	0	0	0	250	0	−$250
Income tax payable	0	0	0	25	25	
Long-term debt	300	300	300	300	300	
Common stock	700	700	700	700	700	
Retained earnings	0	0	0	75	75	
TOTAL DEBT AND EQUITY	$1,000	$1,500	$1,000	$1,350	$1,100	

As a result of the firm's activities, Pokey, Inc., reported $75 in profits for the period. The income statement for the period ending November 30 is as follows:

Sales revenue		$ 900
Cost of goods sold		(500)
Gross profit		$ 400
Operating expenses:		
Cash expense	$250	
Depreciation expense	50	
Total operating expenses		$ (300)
Operating income		$ 100
Income tax (25%)		(25)
Net income		$ 75

The $75 in profits is reflected as retained earnings on the balance sheet to make the numbers match.

The somewhat contrived example of Pokey, Inc., illustrates an important point that deserves repeating: An owner of a small firm must understand the working capital cycle of his or her firm. Although the business was profitable, Pokey ran out of cash in September and October (–$100) and didn't recover until November, when the accounts receivable were collected. This 60-day cash conversion period represents a critical time when the firm must find another source of financing if it is to survive. Moreover, when sales are ongoing throughout the year, the problem can be an unending one, unless financing is found to support the firm's sales. Also, as much as possible, a firm should arrange for earlier payment by customers (preferably in advance) and negotiate longer payment schedules with suppliers (preferably over several months).

An understanding of the working capital cycle provides a basis for examining the primary components of working capital management: cash flows, accounts receivable, inventory, and accounts payable.

Managing Cash Flows

2 Identify the important issues in managing a firm's cash flows.

At numerous points throughout this book, we have emphasized the importance of effective cash flow management. From our discussion of Pokey, Inc., and Quick Turn Company in the previous section, it should also be clear that monitoring cash flows is at the core of working capital management. Cash is continually moving through a business. It flows in as customers pay for products or services, and it flows out as payments are made to other businesses and individuals who provide products and services to the firm, such as employees and suppliers. The typically uneven nature of cash inflows and outflows makes it imperative that they be properly understood and managed for the firm's well-being. Keith Lowe, an experienced entrepreneur and co-founder of the Alabama Information Technology Association, expresses it this way:

> *If there's one thing that will make or break your company, especially when it's small, it's cash flow. A banker once told me that of the many companies he saw go out of business, the majority of them were profitable—they just got in a cash crunch, and that forced them to close. If you pay close attention to your cash flow and think about it every single day, you'll have an edge over almost all your competitors, and you will keep growing while other companies fall by the wayside. The amount of attention you pay to cash flow can literally mean the difference between life and death for your company.*[2]

According to a study by REL, preserving cash flows was the number-one priority of businesses during the recent financial crisis:

> *Executives realize that in a volatile era, there is no substitute for cash. No matter how much revenue you recognize or how many assets you have on your books, the simple and enduring truth is that the only enterprises that survive are those that generate enough cash to keep their operations running.*[3]

The authors further noted in a related report that cash-focused companies—what they call firms that have a *cash culture*—have certain similarities.

> *[These firms are more likely to] give their best vendors and customers favorable terms, their employees are compensated based on their efficiencies of working capital use, their metrics [for measuring working capital performance] are clear, and their cash policies are carefully considered. As a result of this discipline, companies with a cash culture need 52 percent less working capital.*[4]

Wow! A small company that is able to reduce its investments in working capital by 52 percent would have a huge competitive advantage!

A firm's net cash flow may be determined quite simply by examining its bank account. Monthly cash deposits less checks written during the same period equal a firm's net cash flow. If deposits for a month add up to $100,000 and checks total $80,000, the firm has a net positive cash flow of $20,000. That is, the cash balance at the end of the month is $20,000 higher than it was at the beginning of the month.

Exhibit 22.4 graphically represents the flow of cash through a business. It includes not only the cash flows that arise as part of the firm's working capital cycle (shown in Exhibit 22.1) but other cash flows as well, such as those from purchasing fixed assets and issuing stock. More specifically, cash sales, collection of accounts receivable, payment of expenses, and payment for inventory reflect the inflows and outflows of cash that relate to the working capital cycle; the other items in Exhibit 22.4 represent other, longer-term cash flows.

As we have emphasized on several occasions, calculating cash flows requires that a small business owner be able to distinguish between sales revenue and cash receipts—they are seldom the same. Revenue is recorded at the time a sale is made but does not affect cash flow at that time unless the sale is a cash sale. Cash receipts, on the other hand, are recorded when money actually flows into the firm, often a month or two after the sale. Similarly, it is necessary to distinguish between expenses and disbursements. Expenses occur when materials, labor, or other items are used. Payments (disbursements) for these expense items may be made later, when checks are issued. Depreciation, while shown as an expense, is not a cash outflow.

Given the difference between cash flows and profits, it is absolutely essential that the entrepreneur develop a cash budget to anticipate when cash will enter and leave the business. (The cash budget was explained in Chapter 11 when we described financial forecasting.)

EXHIBIT 22.4 Flow of Cash Through a Business

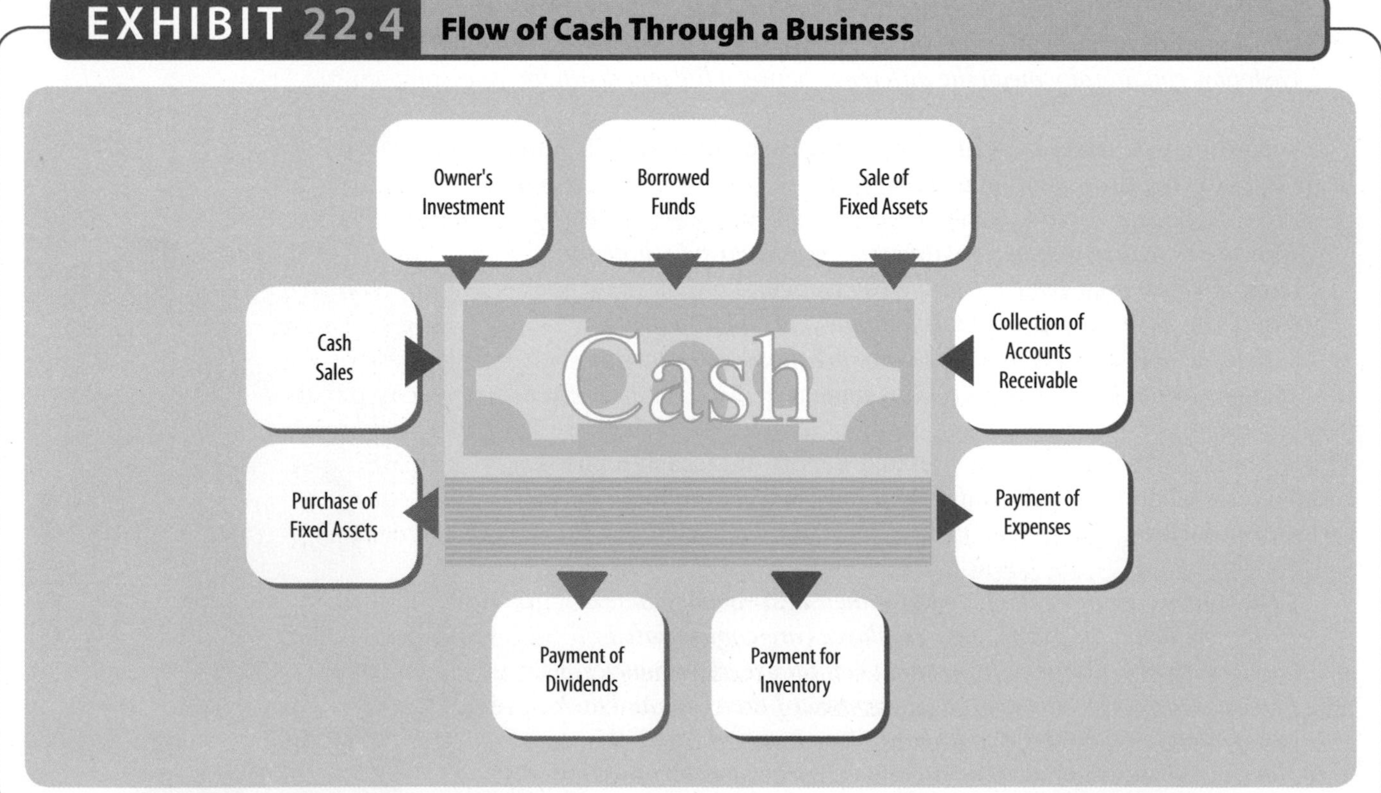

Managing Accounts Receivable

Chapter 16 discussed the extension of credit by small firms and the managing and collecting of accounts receivable. This section considers the impact of credit decisions on working capital and particularly on cash flows. The most important factor in managing cash well within a small firm is the ability to collect accounts receivable quickly.

Managing a firm's accounts receivable becomes particularly critical during a recession when customers are having difficulty paying bills. For example, as the 2008 economic downturn became an increasingly harsh reality for many small businesses, a survey of 751 companies with fewer than 10 employees found that:[5]

- Small businesses were averaging $1,500 in overdue payments from customers each month.
- Forty-two percent of small business owners said that "getting paid quickly" was a key issue keeping them up at night.
- Nearly 40 percent of small business owners had invoices that exceeded 30 days.

HOW ACCOUNTS RECEIVABLE AFFECT CASH

Granting credit to customers, although primarily a marketing decision, directly affects a firm's cash account. By selling on credit and thus allowing customers to delay payment, the selling firm delays the inflow of cash.

The total amount of customers' credit balances is carried on the balance sheet as accounts receivable—one of the firm's current assets. Of all noncash assets, accounts receivable are closest to becoming cash. Sometimes called *near cash,* or *receivables,* accounts receivable typically are collected and become cash within 30 to 60 days following a sale.

THE LIFE CYCLE OF ACCOUNTS RECEIVABLE

The receivables cycle begins with a credit sale. In most businesses, an invoice is then prepared and mailed to the purchaser. When the invoice is received, the purchaser processes it, prepares a check, and mails the check in payment to the seller.

Under ideal circumstances, each of these steps is taken in a timely manner. Obviously, delays can occur at any stage of this process. For example, a shipping clerk may batch invoices before sending them to the office for processing, thus delaying the preparation and mailing of invoices to customers. Such a practice will also hold up the receipt of customers' money and its deposit in the bank—money that is then used to pay bills. In other words, receivables may be past due because of problems in a company's organization, where information is not getting transferred on a timely basis among salespeople, operations departments, and accounting staff. The result: delayed payments from customers and larger investments in accounts receivable.

Credit management policies, practices, and procedures affect the life cycle of receivables and the flow of cash from them. It is important for small business owners, when establishing credit policies, to consider cash flow requirements as well as the need to stimulate sales. A key goal of every business should be to minimize the average time it takes customers to pay their bills. By streamlining administrative procedures, a firm can facilitate the task of sending out bills, thereby generating cash more quickly.

days sales outstanding (average collection period) The number of days, on average, that a firm is extending credit to its customers.

Knowing how long, on average, it is taking to collect accounts receivable requires calculating the **days sales outstanding**, also called the **average collection period**, by dividing a firm's accounts receivable by daily credit sales, as follows:

$$\text{Days sales outstanding} = \frac{\text{Accounts receivable}}{\text{Annual credit sales} \div 365 \text{ days}}$$

Consider the following information about two businesses, Fast Company and Slow Company:

	Fast Company	**Slow Company**
Total sales	$1,000,000	$1,000,000
Credit sales	700,000	700,000
Average credit sales per day	1,918	1,918
Accounts receivable	48,000	63,300

These two companies are very similar in that they both have $1 million in annual sales, including $700,000 in credit sales. Thus, on average, they both have average daily credit sales of $1,918 ($700,000 total credit sales ÷ 365 days). However, there is an important difference between the two firms. Fast Company only has $48,000 invested in accounts receivable, while Slow Company has $63,300 in accounts receivable. Why the difference? It is simple: Fast Company collects its credit sales every 25 days on average, while Slow Company takes 33 days to collect its accounts receivable, calculated as follows:

Fast Company:

$$\text{Days sales outstanding} = \frac{\text{Accounts receivable}}{\text{Annual credit sales} \div 365 \text{ days}} = \frac{\$48{,}000}{\$700{,}000 \div 365} = 25 \text{ days}$$

Slow Company:

$$\text{Days sales outstanding} = \frac{\text{Accounts receivable}}{\text{Annual credit sales} \div 365 \text{ days}} = \frac{\$63{,}300}{\$700{,}000 \div 365} = 33 \text{ days}$$

In other words, Slow Company takes longer to convert its accounts receivable into cash. It could very well have a cash flow problem if it does not have the ability to finance the greater investment in accounts receivable. This illustration, while hypothetical, is a real problem for many small businesses. Michelle Dunn, who owns M.A.D. Collection Agency, says, "One thing business owners always tell me is that they never thought about [the difficulties in collecting their receivables] when they started their own business."[6]

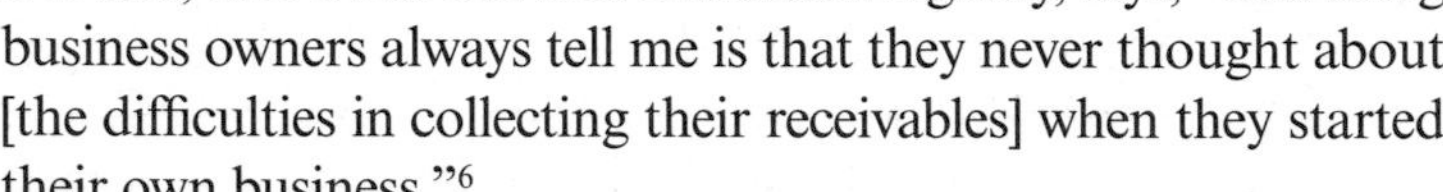

For Ann LaWall, president of Ann LaWall and Company, chasing customers over delinquent payments to her New York–based consulting business was a burden that distracted her from managing the growth of her company.[7] Worse, she feared the dreaded collection calls would jeopardize professional and personal relationships that she cherished. "I got tired of telling people I am not their banker," says LaWall. "Sometimes you are dealing with friends or people you run into at the golf course, and you don't want to be hunting them down for money."

By delegating and implementing pre-emptive measures, LaWall's stress over collections has disappeared. She says that some of the approaches cost her a little revenue, but she insists that they've been worth the expense. "It saves you huge headaches in the long run," she says. To lower the stress involved, LaWall suggests taking the following actions:[8]

- Hire someone else to handle collections one day per week.
- Accept credit cards.
- Sell the receivables to a third party.
- Where possible, require prepayment.
- For a service business, write a detailed work plan and payment schedule and have it signed by the customer.

You may remember Johnny Stites, CEO of J&S Construction in Cookeville, Tennessee, from earlier chapters. In a recent meeting, he told an interesting story. Without saying anything, he had posted a graph that was visible to the employee responsible for collecting receivables. The graph showed how quickly accounts receivable were being collected over time and Stites's goal for how long he wanted it to take. He had intended to discuss the graph with the employee, but failed to do so. Nevertheless, without anything else being done, the time that accounts receivable were outstanding began to decline. By providing a clear picture of actual performance versus desired performance, Stites enabled the employee to take ownership in achieving the goal. The outcome: Cash became available for other purposes.

When dealing with large corporations, small companies are especially vulnerable to problems caused by slow collections. Some large firms have a practice of taking 60 or 90 days to pay an invoice, regardless of the credit terms stated in the invoice. Many small companies have had to file for bankruptcy because they could not get a large customer to pay according to the terms of the sale. Susana Ortiz, president of Caroline's Desserts in Redmond, Washington, was surprised to find that as many large retail customers were paying late as small ones during the 2008 economic slowdown. "If you're small," she says, "big companies think they can wait to pay you."[9]

It follows that what you do before you deliver a product or service on credit is far more important than what you do after you are owed. Consider this perspective:

> *In attempting to improve their cash position, most companies focus on activities that take place after product and service delivery. In fact, they have the order exactly backward, because the structure of the sale shapes everything that follows. To no small degree whether an account ends up being easy to collect or difficult depends on what goes on before the contract is signed.*[10]

The following credit management practices can also have a positive effect on a firm's cash flows:

- Minimize the time between shipping, invoicing, and sending notices on billings.
- Review previous credit experiences to determine impediments to cash flows, such as continued extension of credit to slow-paying or delinquent customers.
- Provide incentives for prompt payment by granting cash discounts or charging interest on delinquent accounts.

- Age accounts receivable on a monthly or even a weekly basis to quickly identify any delinquent accounts.
- Use the most effective methods for collecting overdue accounts. For example, prompt phone calls to customers with overdue accounts can improve collections considerably.
- Use a **lock box**—a post office box for receiving remittances. If the firm's bank maintains the lock box to which customers send their payments, it can empty the box frequently and immediately deposit any checks received into the company's account.

lock box
A post office box for receiving remittances from customers.

ACCOUNTS RECEIVABLE FINANCING

Some small businesses speed up the cash flow from accounts receivable by borrowing against them. By financing receivables, these firms can often secure the use of their money 30 to 60 days earlier than would be possible otherwise. Although this practice was once concentrated largely in the apparel industry, it has expanded to many other types of small businesses, such as manufacturers, food processors, distributors, home building suppliers, and temporary employment agencies. Such financing is provided by commercial finance companies and by some banks.

Two types of accounts receivable financing are available. The first type uses a firm's **pledged accounts receivable** as collateral for a loan. Payments received from customers are forwarded to the lending institution to pay off the loan. In the second type of financing, a business sells its accounts receivable to a finance company, a practice known as *factoring* (discussed in Chapter 12). The finance company thereby assumes the bad-debt risk associated with the receivables it buys.

pledged accounts receivable
Accounts receivable used as collateral for a loan.

The obvious advantage of accounts receivable financing is the immediate cash flow it provides for firms that have limited working capital. As a secondary benefit, the volume of borrowing can be quickly expanded proportionally in order to match a firm's growth in sales and accounts receivable.

A drawback to this type of financing is its high cost. Rates typically run several points above the prime interest rate, and factors charge a fee to compensate them for their credit investigation activities and for the risk that customers may default in payment. Another weakness of accounts receivable financing is that pledging receivables may limit a firm's ability to borrow from a bank by removing a prime asset from its available collateral.

Managing Inventory

Inventory is a "necessary evil" in the financial management system. It is "necessary" because supply and demand cannot be managed to coincide precisely with day-to-day operations; it is an "evil" because it ties up funds that are not actively productive.

REDUCING INVENTORY TO FREE CASH

Inventory is a bigger problem for some small businesses than for others. The inventory of many service companies, for example, consists of only a few supplies. A manufacturer, on the other hand, has several types of inventory: raw materials, work in process, and finished goods. Retailers and wholesalers—especially those with high inventory turnover rates, such as firms in grocery distribution—are continually involved in solving inventory management problems.

Chapter 21 discussed several ideas related to purchasing and inventory management that are designed to minimize inventory-carrying costs and processing costs. The emphasis in this section is on practices that will minimize average inventory levels, thereby releasing funds for other uses. The correct minimum level of inventory is the amount needed to maintain desired production schedules and/or a certain level of customer service. A concerted effort to manage inventory can trim excess inventory and pay handsome dividends.

MONITORING INVENTORY

When it comes to managing inventory, small business owners have a tendency to overstock. Consider the following scenario, which plays out far too often:

> *A store manager might know intellectually that holding a lot of inventory is not a good idea, yet still justify hanging on to a few more TVs than the store will probably need—"just in case." Even though a department manager knows some oversupply might drag down overall efficiency a bit, in the scheme of things, the sacrifice for the department doesn't seem nearly as great as the potential pain of a stock-out. A little oversupply seems a smaller risk than the major disaster of having to shut down an assembly line or leave a store shelf empty.*[11]

One of the first steps in managing inventory is to discover what's in inventory and how long it's been there. Too often, items are purchased, warehoused, and essentially forgotten. A yearly inventory for accounting purposes is inadequate for proper inventory control. Items that are slow movers may sit in a retailer's inventory beyond the time when they should have been marked down for quick sale.

Software programs can provide assistance in inventory identification and control. Although a physical inventory may still be required, its use will only serve to supplement the computerized system.

A commonly used statistic for monitoring inventory is **days in inventory**, which is the number of days, on average, that a business is holding its inventory. Similar in concept to days sales outstanding (which was described earlier), it is calculated as follows:

days in inventory
The number of days, on average, that a company is holding inventory.

$$\text{Days in inventory} = \frac{\text{Inventory}}{\text{Cost of goods sold} \div 365 \text{ days}}$$

Returning to Fast Company and Slow Company, recall that both firms had \$1 million in annual sales. Let's assume that they also had the same cost of goods sold of \$600,000. So, they both sold their products for \$1 million, and it cost them \$600,000 to produce the products that were sold. If we restate the annual cost of goods sold to a daily cost of goods sold, we find it to be \$1,644 (\$600,000 cost of goods sold ÷ 365 days) for both companies. But while they sold the same amount of product at identical cost, Fast Company carries only \$46,000 in inventory compared to Slow Company, which maintains inventory of \$57,500. This information is summarized as follows:

	Fast Company	Slow Company
Total sales	\$1,000,000	\$1,000,000
Cost of goods sold	600,000	600,001
Daily cost of goods sold	1,644	1,644
Inventory	46,000	57,500

Why would Slow Company have more inventory than Fast Company, given that they both have the same amount of sales? The answer is that Slow Company takes longer to sell its inventory. Fast Company, on average, carries inventory for 28 days, compared to 35 days for Slow Company, calculated as follows:

Fast Company:

$$\text{Days in inventory} = \frac{\text{Inventory}}{\text{Cost of goods sold} \div 365 \text{ days}} = \frac{\$46{,}000}{\$600{,}000 \div 365 \text{ days}} = 28 \text{ days}$$

Slow Company:

$$\text{Days in inventory} = \frac{\text{Inventory}}{\text{Cost of goods sold} \div 365 \text{ days}} = \frac{\$57{,}500}{\$600{,}000 \div 365 \text{ days}} = 35 \text{ days}$$

In other words, Slow Company's slow rate of moving its inventory can lead to cash flow problems if it does not have the ability to finance the larger inventory.

CONTROLLING STOCKPILES

Small business managers tend to overbuy inventory for several reasons. First, enthusiasm may lead the manager to forecast greater demand than is realistic. Second, the personalization of the business–customer relationship may motivate a manager to stock everything customers want. Third, a price-conscious manager may be overly susceptible to a vendor's appeal to "buy now, because prices are going up."

Managers must exercise restraint when stockpiling. Improperly managed and uncontrolled stockpiling may greatly increase inventory-carrying costs and place a heavy drain on the funds of a small business.

Managing Accounts Payable

Cash flow management and accounts payable management are intertwined. As long as a payable is outstanding, the buying firm can keep cash equal to that amount in its own checking account. When payment is made, however, that firm's cash account is reduced accordingly. Thus, all else being the same, a small business owner would want to delay payment as long as possible without damaging the firm's reputation by failing to live up to its agreements.

Although payables are legal obligations, they can be paid at various times or even renegotiated in some cases. Therefore, financial management of accounts payable hinges on negotiation and timing.

NEGOTIATION

Any business is subject to emergency situations and may find it necessary to ask creditors to postpone payment on its payable obligations. Usually, creditors will cooperate in working out a solution because it's in their best interest for a client firm to succeed.

TIMING

"Buy now, pay later" is the motto of many entrepreneurs. By buying on credit, a small business is using creditors' funds to supply short-term cash needs. The longer creditors' funds can be borrowed, the better. Payment, therefore, should be delayed as long as acceptable under the agreement. As we did with accounts receivable and inventory, we can compute **days in payables**, which tells us how many days a company is taking to pay its accounts payable. We compute it as follows:[12]

days in payables The number of days, on average, that a business takes to pay its accounts payable.

$$\text{Days in payables} = \frac{\text{Accounts payable}}{\text{Cost of goods sold} \div 365 \text{ days}}$$

Using the information already provided for Fast Company and Slow Company, and knowing that they have $65,800 and $49,300 in accounts payable, respectively, we can compute the days in payables for each firm as follows:

Fast Company:

$$\text{Days in payables} = \frac{\text{Accounts payable}}{\text{Cost of goods sold} \div 365 \text{ days}} = \frac{\$65,800}{\$600,000 \div 365 \text{ days}} = 40 \text{ days}$$

Slow Company:

$$\text{Days in payables} = \frac{\text{Accounts payable}}{\text{Cost of goods sold} \div 365 \text{ days}} = \frac{\$49,300}{\$600,000 \div 365 \text{ days}} = 30 \text{ days}$$

Typically, accounts payable (trade credit) involve payment terms that include a cash discount. With trade discount terms, paying later may be inappropriate. For example, terms of 3/10, net 30, offer a 3 percent potential discount. Exhibit 22.5 shows the possible settlement costs over the credit period of 30 days. Note that for a $20,000 purchase, a settlement of only $19,400 is required if payment is made within the first 10 days ($20,000 less the 3 percent discount of $600). Between day 11 and day 30, the full settlement of $20,000 is required. After 30 days, the settlement cost may exceed the original amount, as late-payment fees are added.

The timing question then becomes "Should the account be paid on day 10 or day 30?" There is little reason to pay $19,400 on days 1 through 9, when the same amount will settle the account on day 10. Likewise, if payment is to be made after day 10, it makes sense to wait until day 30 to pay the $20,000.

By paying on the last day of the discount period, the buyer saves the amount of the discount offered. The other alternative of paying on day 30 allows the buyer to use the seller's money for an additional 20 days by forgoing the discount. As Exhibit 22.5 shows, the buyer can use the seller's $19,400 for 20 days at a cost of $600. The percentage annual interest rate can be calculated as follows:

$$\begin{aligned}\text{Percentage annual interest rate} &= \frac{\text{Days in year}}{\text{Net period} - \text{Cash discount period}} \times \frac{\text{Cash discount \%}}{100\% - \text{Cash discount \%}} \\ &= \frac{365}{30 - 10} \times \frac{3\%}{100\% - 3\%} \\ &= 18.25 \times 0.030928 \\ &= 0.564, \text{ or } 56.4\%\end{aligned}$$

By failing to take a discount, a business typically pays a high rate for use of a supplier's money—56.4 percent per year in this case. Payment on day 10 appears to be the most logical choice. Recall, however, that payment also affects cash flows. If funds are extremely short, a small firm may have to wait to pay until the last possible day in order to avoid an overdraft at the bank.

EXHIBIT 22.5 An Accounts Payable Timetable for Terms of 3/10, Net 30

Timetable (days after invoice date)	Settlement Costs for a $20,000 Purchase
Days 1 through 10	$19,400
Days 11 through 30	$20,000
Day 31 and thereafter	$20,000 + possible late penalty and deterioration in credit rating

Cash Conversion Period Revisited

6
Calculate and interpret a company's cash conversion period.

Earlier in the chapter, we presented the working capital cycle, explaining that the cash conversion period should be a key concern for any small business. As you will recall, the cash conversion period is the time span during which the firm's investment in accounts receivable and inventory must be financed or, more simply, the time required to convert paid-for inventory and accounts receivable to cash. To reinforce this concept, we can use the information we have for Fast Company and Slow Company to compute these two firms' cash conversion periods:

$$\text{Cash conversion period} = \text{Days in inventory} + \text{Days sales outstanding} - \text{Days in payables}$$

	Fast Company	Slow Company
Days in inventory	28	35
Days sales outstanding	25	33
Days in inventory and receivables	53	68
Less days in payables	(40)	(30)
Cash conversion period	13	38

ACTION

Time Is Money!

Each component of working capital (accounts receivable, inventory, and accounts payable) has two dimensions: *time* and *money*. When managing working capital, TIME IS MONEY! If you can move money faster through the cycle, the business will generate more cash more quickly. Also, if you can negotiate improved terms with suppliers, receiving a longer time to pay or an increased credit limit, you effectively create free financing to help fund future growth.

So, from the time that inventory is purchased until it is sold on credit and the accounts receivable have been collected, it is 53 days for Fast Company and 68 days for Slow Company. But both firms are granted trade credit from their suppliers. Fast Company has negotiated credit terms of 40 days before having to pay for its purchases, compared to Slow Company's 30 days. Essentially, Fast Company's suppliers have granted it a loan for 40 days, while Slow Company has a loan for only 30 days.

We see that Fast Company will need to finance 13 days

with working capital, while Slow Company will have to finance 38 days. Thus, as both firms grow, Slow Company will have much more pressure on its cash flows than will Fast Company.

Capital Budgeting

We turn now to the management of a small firm's long-term assets—equipment and plant—or what is called *capital budgeting.*

7
Give examples of the types of capital budgeting decisions small business owners must make.

CAPITAL BUDGETING DECISIONS

Some capital budgeting decisions that might be made by a small firm include the following:

- Develop and introduce a new product that shows promise but requires additional study and improvement.
- Replace a firm's delivery trucks with newer models.
- Expand sales activity into a new territory.
- Construct a new building.
- Hire additional salespersons to intensify selling in the existing market.

In a study by the National Federation of Independent Business, small business owners were asked, "In terms of dollars, what was the purpose of the largest investments made in your business over the last 12 months?" Their responses were as follows:[13]

Replacement and maintenance	45.6%
Extension of existing product or service lines	21.2
Expansion into new business areas	23.0
Safety or environmental improvement	3.5
No response	6.7

Thus, nearly half of all long-term capital investments by small companies are made for replacement and maintenance; when we add in the extension of existing product lines, we can account for two-thirds of all dollars invested by small owners. Nearly one-fourth of all dollars are invested in new product lines and new businesses.

Although an in-depth discussion of capital budgeting is beyond the scope of this textbook, in the following sections we discuss techniques used in making capital budgeting decisions and the capital budgeting practices of small companies.

capital budgeting analysis
An analytical method that helps managers make decisions about long-term investments.

CAPITAL BUDGETING TECHNIQUES

Capital budgeting analysis forms the framework for a company's long-term future development and can have a profound effect on a company's future earnings and growth. For this reason, it is important that a small business owner only makes capital budgeting decisions based on careful analysis.

The three major techniques for making capital budgeting decisions are (1) the accounting return on investment technique, (2) the payback period technique, and (3) the discounted cash flow technique, using either net present value or internal rate of return. They all attempt to answer the same basic question: Do the future benefits from an investment exceed the cost of making the investment? However, each technique addresses this general question by focusing on a different specific question. The specific question that each technique addresses can be stated as follows:

1. *Accounting return on investment:* How many dollars in average profits are generated per dollar of average investment?
2. *Payback period:* How long will it take to recover the original investment outlay?
3. *Discounted cash flows:* How does the present value of future benefits from the investment compare to the investment outlay?

Three simple rules are used in judging the merits of an investment. Although they may seem trite, the rules state in simple terms the best thinking about the attractiveness of an investment.

1. The investor prefers more cash rather than less cash.
2. The investor prefers cash sooner rather than later.
3. The investor prefers less risk rather than more risk.

With these criteria in mind, let's now look at each of the three capital budgeting techniques in detail.

Accounting Return on Investment

accounting return on investment technique
A capital budgeting technique that compares expected average annual after-tax profits to the average book value of an investment.

A small business invests to earn profits. The **accounting return on investment technique** compares the average annual after-tax profits a firm expects to receive with the average book value of the investment.

Average annual profits can be estimated by adding the after-tax profits expected over the life of the project and then dividing that amount by the number of years the project is expected to last. The average book value of an investment is equivalent to the average of the initial outlay and the estimated final projected salvage value. In making an accept–reject decision, the owner compares the calculated return to a minimum acceptable return, which is usually determined based on past experience.

To examine the use of the accounting return on investment technique, assume that you are contemplating buying a piece of equipment for $10,000 and depreciating it over four years to a book value of zero (it will have no salvage value). Further assume that you expect the investment to generate after-tax profits each year as follows:

Year	After-Tax Profits
1	$1,000
2	2,000
3	2,500
4	3,000

The accounting return on the proposed investment is calculated as follows:

$$\text{Accounting return on investment} = \frac{\text{Average annual after-tax profits}}{\text{Average book value of the investment}}$$

$$= \frac{\left(\dfrac{\$1{,}000 + \$2{,}000 + \$2{,}500 + \$3{,}000}{4}\right)}{\left(\dfrac{\$10{,}000 - \$0}{2}\right)}$$

$$= \frac{\$2{,}125}{\$5{,}000} = 0.425\text{, or } 42.5\%.$$

For most people, a 42.5 percent profit rate would seem outstanding. Assuming the calculated accounting return on investment of 42.5 percent exceeds your minimum acceptable return, you will accept the project. If not, you will reject the investment—provided, of course, that you have confidence in the technique.

Although the accounting return on investment is easy to calculate, it has two major shortcomings. First, it is based on accounting profits rather than actual cash flows received. An investor is more interested in the future cash produced by the investment than in the reported profits. Second, this technique ignores the time value of money. Thus, although popular, the accounting return on investment technique fails to satisfy any of the three rules concerning an investor's preference for receiving more cash sooner with less risk.

Payback Period

The **payback period technique**, as the name suggests, measures how long it will take to recover the initial cash outlay of an investment. It deals with cash flows as opposed to accounting profits. The merits of a project are judged on whether the initial investment outlay can be recovered in less time than some maximum acceptable payback period. For example, an owner may not want to invest in any project that will require more than five years to recoup the original investment.

payback period technique
A capital budgeting technique that measures the amount of time it will take to recover the cash outlay of an investment.

To illustrate the payback method, let's assume that a small business owner is considering an investment in equipment with an expected life of 10 years. The investment outlay will be $15,000, with the cost of the equipment depreciated on a straight-line basis, at $1,500 per year. If the owner makes the investment, the annual after-tax profits have been estimated to be as follows:

Years	After-Tax Profits
1–2	$1,000
3–6	2,000
7–10	2,500

To determine the after-tax cash flows from the investment, the owner merely adds back the depreciation of $1,500 each year to the profit. The reason for adding the depreciation to the profit is that it was deducted when the profits were calculated (as an accounting entry), even though it was not a cash outflow. The results, then, are as follows:

Years	After-Tax Cash Flows
1–2	$2,500
3–6	3,500
7–10	4,000

By the end of the second year, the owner will have recovered $5,000 of the investment outlay ($2,500 per year). By the end of the fourth year, another $7,000, or $12,000 in total, will have been recouped. The additional $3,000 can be recovered in the fifth year, when $3,500 is expected. Thus, it will take 4.86 years [4 years + ($3,000 ÷ $3,500)] to recover the investment. Since the maximum acceptable payback is less than five years, the owner will accept the investment.

Many managers and owners of companies use the payback period technique in evaluating investment decisions. Although it uses cash flows rather than accounting profits, the payback period technique has two significant weaknesses. First, it does not consider the time value of money (cash is preferred sooner rather than later). Second, it fails to consider the cash flows received after the payback period (more cash is preferred, rather than less).

Discounted Cash Flows

Managers can avoid the deficiencies of the accounting return on investment and payback period techniques by using discounted cash flow analysis. Discounted cash flow techniques take into consideration the fact that cash received today is more valuable than cash received one year from now (called the *time value of money*). For example, interest can be earned on cash that is available for immediate investment; this is not true for cash to be received at some future date.

discounted cash flow (DCF) techniques
Capital budgeting techniques that compare the present value of future cash flows with the cost of the initial investment.

net present value (NPV)
The present value of expected future cash flows less the initial investment outlay.

internal rate of return (IRR)
The rate of return a firm expects to earn on a project.

Discounted cash flow (DCF) techniques compare the present value of future cash flows with the investment outlay. Such an analysis may take either of two forms: net present value or internal rate of return.

The **net present value (NPV)** method estimates the current value of the cash that will flow into the firm from the project in the future and deducts the amount of the initial outlay. To find the present value of expected future cash flows, we discount them back to the present at the firm's cost of capital, where the cost of capital is equal to the investors' required rate of return. If the net present value of the investment is positive (that is, if the present value of future cash flows discounted at the rate of return required to satisfy the firm's investors exceeds the initial outlay), the project is acceptable.

The **internal rate of return (IRR)** method estimates the rate of return that can be expected from a contemplated investment. To calculate the IRR, you must find the discount rate that gets the present value of all future cash inflows just equal to the cost of the project, which is also the rate that gives you a zero net present value. For the investment outlay to be attractive, the internal rate of return must exceed the firm's cost of capital—the rate of return required to satisfy the firm's investors.

Discounted cash flow techniques can generally be trusted to provide a more reliable basis for decisions than can the accounting return on investment or the payback period technique.

CAPITAL BUDGETING PRACTICES IN SMALL FIRMS

9
Describe the capital budgeting practices of small firms.

Historically, few small business owners have relied on any type of quantitative analysis in making capital budgeting decisions. The decision to buy new equipment or expand facilities has been based more on intuition and instinct than on economic analysis. And those who do conduct some kind of quantitative analysis rarely use discounted cash flow techniques, neither net present value nor internal rate of return.

In the study cited earlier, the National Federation of Independent Business asked entrepreneurs to indicate the method(s) they used in analyzing capital investments. The results were encouraging:[14]

Gut feeling	25.3%
Payback period technique	18.7
Accounting return on investment technique	13.6
Discounted cash flow techniques	11.9
Combination	10.5
Other	6.1
No response	4.5
Not applicable—no major investments	2.6

Interestingly, 55 percent of the small business owners indicated that they use some form of quantitative measure (payback period, accounting return on investment, discounted cash flow techniques, or some combination) to assess a capital investment; only 25 percent of the respondents said that they use their intuition (gut feeling). Furthermore, 67 percent of the owners said that they make some effort to project future cash flows.

We could conclude that the small business owners surveyed were not very sophisticated about using theoretically sound financial methods, given that only 12 percent said they use discounted cash flow techniques. However, the cause of their limited use of DCF tools probably has more to do with the nature of the small business itself than with the owners' unwillingness to learn. Several more important reasons might explain these findings, including the following:

- For many owners of small firms, the business is an extension of their lives—that is, business events affect them personally. The same is true in reverse: What happens to the owners personally affects their decisions about the firm. The firm and its owners are inseparable. We cannot fully understand decisions made about a company without being aware of the personal events in the owners' lives. Consequently, nonfinancial variables may play a significant part in owners' decisions. For example, the desire to be viewed as a respected part of the community may be more important to an owner than the present value of a business decision.

- The undercapitalization and liquidity problems of a small business can directly affect the decision-making process, and survival often becomes the top priority. Long-term planning, therefore, is not viewed by the owners as a high priority in the total scheme of things.

- The greater uncertainty of cash flows within small firms makes long-term forecasting and planning seem unappealing and even a waste of time. The owners simply have no confidence in their ability to predict cash flows beyond two or three years. Thus, calculating the cash flows for the entire life of a project is viewed as a futile effort.

- The value of a closely held firm is less easily observed than that of a publicly held firm, whose securities are actively traded in the marketplace. Therefore, the owner of a small firm may consider the market-value rule of maximizing net present values irrelevant. Estimating the cost of capital is also much more difficult for a small company than for a large firm.

- The smaller size of a small firm's projects may make net present value computations less feasible in a practical sense. The time and expense required to analyze a capital investment are generally the same, whether the project is large or small. Therefore, it is relatively more costly for a small firm to conduct such a study.

- Management talent within a small firm is a scarce resource. Also, the owner-manager frequently has a technical background, as opposed to a business or finance orientation. The perspective of a small business owner is influenced greatly by her or his background.

These characteristics of a small business and its owner have a significant effect on the decision-making process within the firm. The result is often a short-term mindset, caused partly by necessity and partly by choice. However, the owner of a small firm should make every effort to use discounted cash flow techniques and to be certain that contemplated investments will, in fact, provide returns that exceed the firm's cost of capital.

1. **Describe the working capital cycle of a small business.**
   - A firm's working capital cycle is the flow of resources through the company's accounts as part of its day-to-day operations.
   - The only current liability included in the working capital cycle is accounts payable.
   - The working capital cycle begins with the purchase of inventory and ends with the collection of accounts receivable.
   - The cash conversion period is critical because it is the time period during which cash flow problems can arise.

2. **Identify the important issues in managing a firm's cash flows.**
   - A firm's cash flows consist of cash flowing into a business (through sales revenue, borrowing, and so on) and cash flowing out of the business (through purchases, operating expenses, and so on).
   - Calculating cash flows requires that a small business owner distinguish between sales revenue and cash receipts.
   - It is also necessary to distinguish between expenses and disbursements.
   - To anticipate when cash will enter and leave a business, an owner *must* develop a cash budget.

3. **Explain the key issues in managing accounts receivable.**
   - The most important factor in managing cash well is the ability to collect accounts receivable quickly.
   - Granting credit to customers, primarily a marketing decision, directly affects a firm's cash account.
   - Days sales outstanding measures how many days, on average, a firm is extending credit to its customers.
   - Some small businesses speed up the cash flows from receivables by borrowing against them.
   - The two types of accounts receivable financing are pledged accounts receivable and factoring.

4. **Discuss the key issues in managing inventory.**
   - A concerted effort to manage inventory can trim excess inventory and free cash for other uses.
   - Days in inventory represents the number of days, on average, that a company is carrying inventory.
   - Improperly managed and uncontrolled stockpiling may greatly increase inventory-carrying costs and place a heavy drain on the funds of a small business.

5. **Explain key issues in managing accounts payable.**
   - Accounts payable, a primary source of financing for small firms, directly affect a firm's cash flow situation.
   - Financial management of accounts payable hinges on negotiation and timing.
   - Days in payables is a measure of how long a business is taking to pay its suppliers.

6. **Calculate and interpret a company's cash conversion period.**
   - The cash conversion period is the time span during which a firm's investment in accounts receivable and inventory must be financed.
   - A cash conversion period equals days in inventory plus days sales outstanding minus days in payables.

7. **Give examples of the types of capital budgeting decisions small business owners must make.**
   - Examples of capital budgeting decision faced by small business owners include developing a new product that shows promise but requires additional study and improvement, replacing a firm's delivery trucks with newer models, expanding sales activity into a new territory, constructing a new building, and hiring additional salespersons to intensify selling in the existing market.
   - Nearly half of all long-term capital investments by small companies are made for replacement and maintenance; when we add in the extension of existing product lines, we can account for two-thirds of all dollars invested by small owners.
   - Nearly one-fourth of all dollars are invested in new product lines and new businesses.

8. **Discuss the techniques commonly used in making capital budgeting decisions.**
   - A small business owner should only make capital budgeting decisions that are based on careful analysis.
   - Capital budgeting techniques include accounting return on investment, payback period, and discounted cash flows.
   - The accounting return on investment technique has two significant shortcomings: It is based on accounting profits rather than actual cash flows received, and it ignores the time value of money.

- The payback period technique also has two major weaknesses: It ignores the time value of money, and it doesn't consider cash flows received after the payback period.
- The discounted cash flow techniques—net present value and internal rate of return—provide the best accept–reject decision criteria in capital budgeting analysis.

9. Describe the capital budgeting practices of small firms.

- Few small firms use discounted cash flow techniques; however, the majority of small companies do use some type of quantitative measure.
- The short-term mindset of small firms may explain, to some degree, why they seldom use the conceptually richer techniques for evaluating long-term investments.

Key Terms

working capital management p. 643
working capital cycle p. 643
cash conversion period p. 647
days sales outstanding (average collection period) p. 654
lock box p. 656
pledged accounts receivable p. 656
days in inventory p. 657
days in payables p. 659
capital budgeting analysis p. 661
accounting return on investment technique p. 662
payback period technique p. 663
discounted cash flow (DCF) techniques p. 664
net present value (NPV) p. 664
internal rate of return (IRR) p. 664

Discussion Questions

1. List the events in the working capital cycle that directly affect cash and those that do not. What determines the length of a firm's cash conversion period?
2. What are some examples of cash receipts that are not sales revenue? Explain how expenses and cash disbursements during a month may be different.
3. How may a seller speed up the collection of accounts receivable? Give examples that may apply to various stages in the life cycle of receivables.
4. Suppose that a small firm could successfully shift to a just-in-time inventory system—an arrangement in which inventory is received just as it is needed. How would this affect the firm's working capital management?
5. How do working capital management and capital budgeting differ?
6. Compare the different techniques that can be used in capital budgeting analysis.
7. What does net present value measure?
8. Define internal rate of return.
9. a. Find the accounting return on investment for a project that costs $10,000, will have no salvage value, and has expected annual after-tax profits each year of $1,000.
   b. Determine the payback period for a capital investment that costs $40,000 and has the following after-tax profits. (The projected outlay of $40,000 will be depreciated on a straight-line basis over seven years to a zero salvage value.)

Year	After-Tax Profits
1	$4,000
2	5,000
3	6,000
4	6,500
5	6,500
6	6,000
7	5,000

10. Why would owners of small businesses not be inclined to use the net present value or internal rate of return measurements?

You Make the Call

SITUATION 1

A small company specializing in the sale and installation of swimming pools was profitable but devoted very little attention to management of its working capital. It had, for example, never prepared or used a cash budget.

To be sure that money was available for payments as needed, the firm kept a minimum of $25,000 in a checking account. At times, this account grew larger; it totaled $43,000 on one occasion. The owner felt that this approach to cash management worked well for the small company because it eliminated all of the paperwork associated with cash budgeting. Moreover, it enabled the firm to pay its bills in a timely manner.

Note: In answering the questions for this situation, refer both to this chapter and Chapter 10 where we describe cash budgets.

Question 1 What are the advantages and weaknesses of the minimum-cash-balance practice?

Question 2 There is a saying, "If it ain't broke, don't fix it." In view of the firm's present success in paying bills promptly, should it be encouraged to use a cash budget? Be prepared to support your answer.

SITUATION 2

Ruston Manufacturing Company is a small firm selling entirely on a credit basis. It has experienced successful operation and earned modest profits.

Sales are made on the basis of net payment in 30 days. Collections from customers run approximately 70 percent in 30 days, 20 percent in 60 days, 7 percent in 90 days, and 3 percent bad debts.

The owner has considered the possibility of offering a cash discount for early payment. However, the practice seems costly and possibly unnecessary. As the owner puts it, "Why should I bribe customers to pay what they legally owe?"

Question 1 Is offering a cash discount the equivalent of a bribe?

Question 2 How would a cash discount policy relate to bad debts?

Question 3 What cash discount policy, if any, would you recommend?

Question 4 What other approaches might the owner use to improve cash flows from receivables?

SITUATION 3

Below are the financial statements of two general contractors. The two companies are primarily commercial builders, as opposed to residential builders. They typically bid for the opportunity to build such facilities as office buildings, hospitals, and university buildings. As the general contractor, they use subcontractors who undertake most of the actual work.

Balance Sheet	**BRC, Inc.**		**Arch Construction**	
Assets				
Current assets:				
Cash	$ 1,199,921	4.1%*	$ 2,826,328	10.2%*
Short-term investments	14,704,137	50.4%	16,239,811	58.7%
Accounts receivable	12,460,468	42.7%	7,307,234	26.4%
Other current assets	21,482	0.1%	34,067	0.1%
Total current assets	$ 28,386,008	97.2%	$ 26,407,440	95.5%
Property and equipment	807,592	2.8%	1,252,408	4.5%
TOTAL ASSETS	$ 29,193,600	100.0%	$ 27,659,848	100.0%
Debt (Liabilities) and Equity				
Current liabilities:				
Short-term notes	$ 72,322	0.2%*	$ 79,564	0.3%*
Accounts payable	19,975,233	68.4%	14,898,131	53.9%
Accrued liabilities	899,472	3.1%	2,068,695	7.5%
Total current liabilities	$ 20,947,027	71.8%	$ 17,046,390	61.7%
Long-term debt	1,862,265	6.4%	1,782,700	6.4%
Total debt	$ 22,809,292	78.1%	$ 18,829,090	68.1%
Stockholders' equity:				
Common stock	$ 4,254	0.0%	$ 4,254	0.0%
Paid in capital	768,281	2.6%	768,281	2.8%
Retained earnings	5,611,773	19.2%	8,058,223	29.1%
Total stockholders' equity	$ 6,384,308	21.9%	$ 8,830,758	31.9%
TOTAL DEBT AND EQUITY	$ 29,193,600	100.0%	$ 27,659,848	100.0%

*All percentages have been rounded.

Balance Sheet	BRC, Inc.		Arch Construction	
INCOME STATEMENT				
Construction revenues	$ 90,070,000	100.0%*	$72,822,725	100.0%*
Cost of goods sold	(86,889,570)	(96.5)%	(68,090,781)	(93.5)%
Gross profits	$ 3,180,430	3.5%	$ 4,731,944	6.5%
Interest income	941,631	1.0%	1,308,801	1.8%
Total revenues	$ 4,122,061	4.6%	$ 6,040,745	8.3%
Operating expenses	1,665,711	1.8%	2,033,400	2.8%
Interest expense	226,367	0.3%	172,158	0.2%
Other expense	79,630	0.1%	123,737	0.2%
Total expenses	$ (1,971,708)	(2.2%)	$ 2,329,295	(3.2%)
Net profits	$ 2,150,353	2.4%	$ 3,711,450	5.1%

*All percentages have been rounded.

Note: While the financial information provided is real in this situation, the names of the companies have been changed to maintain confidentiality.

Question 1 Based on the information in the balance sheets, what do you notice about the nature of the general contracting business in terms of working capital? How are the two companies alike, and how do they differ?

Question 2 Have a general contractor explain to you what the financial statements say about this type of business.

Question 3 Compute the cash conversion period for each company, and interpret your findings.

Small Business & Entrepreneurship Resource Center

1. Cash flow is vital to the continuing operation of any small business, and poor cash flow forces approximately 40 percent of new businesses to shut down each year. Brian Hamilton, senior analyst at Profit-Cents, and two small business owners offer eight tips for improving your cash flow in the article "Let It Flow." Describe each of the eight tips for improving small business cash flow.

   Source: Marcia Layton Turner, "Let It Flow: Smart Ways to Manage Your Cash, *Black Enterprise*, Vol. 36, No. 10 (May 2006), p. 50.

2. A yes or no answer when seeking financing can make or break any small business. There are alternatives when credit problems hamper a company's ability to secure working capital. The article "Getting to the Cash Flow" discusses the Doucettes and their franchise called Liquid Capital of Northeast Ohio. Discuss the types of clients the company serves and the services that it provides and how they may benefit a small business.

   Source: Kyle Swenson, "Getting the Cash to Flow: Finding Alternative Financing Sources Can Mean the Difference Between a Growing or Stagnant Business, *Inside Business*, Vol. 9, No. 8 (August 2007), pp. 65–67.

Case 22

PEARSON AIR CONDITIONING AND SERVICE (P. 736)

This case looks at the financial performance of a small air conditioning and heating services company, with emphasis on its working capital policies.

ALTERNATIVE CASES FOR CHAPTER 22

Case 11, Missouri Solvents, p. 714
Video Case 10, B2B CFO, website only

CHAPTER 23

Managing Risk in the Small Business

In the SPOTLIGHT
Homestead Interior Doors
http://www.door.cc

It can happen before you know it. One day, you have plenty of funds in your bank account; the next day, the money is gone. And the culprit isn't a client you've lost, a bad economy, or even a disgruntled employee; it's a hacker who has found a way to sneak into your online bank account, view sensitive financial data, and steal from your business. A scenario like this might sound far-fetched, but it has become a cruel reality for small business owners who have experienced it and a risk for anyone who conducts business or keeps financial records online.

© Bobkeenan Photography / Shutterstock.com

Like most business owners, Bob Gray, owner of Vickery, Ohio–based Homestead Interior Doors, had virus protection as well as a minimal firewall, but it wasn't enough to keep hackers from accessing his computer and network, and swiping $100,000 from his online business bank account late last year. "I noticed a $50,000 transfer was posted on my account that didn't look right," he says. "I didn't remember doing anything like that. Then, right before my eyes, another $50,000 transfer popped up."

Gray eventually recovered half of the money, but it took several agonizing months working with his bank and lawyers to sort things out. "There were times that I was convinced I was going to lose my business over this," says Gray, whose cash flow and incoming customer payments were frozen after the attack. "I was lucky because it could have been worse. I could have been wiped out completely."

Though he's more cautious now, he says, "These hackers are learning new stuff every day; they're staying

After studying this chapter, you should be able to . . .

1. Define *business risk*, and explain its two dimensions.
2. Identify the basic types of pure risk.
3. Describe the steps in the risk management process, and explain how risk management can be used in small companies.
4. Explain the basic principles used in evaluating an insurance program.
5. Identify the common types of business insurance coverage.

LOOKING AHEAD

© iStockphoto.com/Dan Bachman

one step ahead of the protections and will keep trying to figure out how to get into your computer if they think they can get money out of you. You've got to be vigilant. Nobody takes it seriously until it happens to them—but they need to because they could wake up one morning and have no money and no business."

Sources: Emily McMackin, "Click Here to Destroy Your Business," *MyBusiness,* January/February 2010, pp. 32–34.

We live in a world of uncertainty, so understanding risk is vitally important in almost all dimensions of life. Risk must certainly be considered in making any business decisions. As sixth-century Greek poet and statesman Solon wrote,

> *There is risk in everything that one does, and no one knows where he will make his land-fall when his enterprise is at its beginning. One man, trying to act effectively, fails to foresee something and falls into great and grim ruination, but to another man, one who is acting ineffectively, a god gives good fortune in everything and escape from his folly.*[1]

Solon's insight reminds us that little is new in the world—least of all, the need to acknowledge and compensate as best we can for the risks we encounter.

Risk means different things to different people. For a student, risk might be represented by the possibility of failing an exam. For a coal miner, risk might mean the chance of an explosion in the mine. For a retired person, risk could be the likelihood of not being able to live comfortably on his or her limited income. For an entrepreneur, risk takes the form of the possibility that a new venture will fail.

As Benjamin Franklin once said, "In this life, nothing is certain except death and taxes." Small business owners might extend this adage to include business risks. Chapter 1 noted the moderate risk-taking propensities of entrepreneurs and their desire to exert some control over the perilous situations in which they find themselves by minimizing business risks as much as possible. This chapter outlines how this can be done.

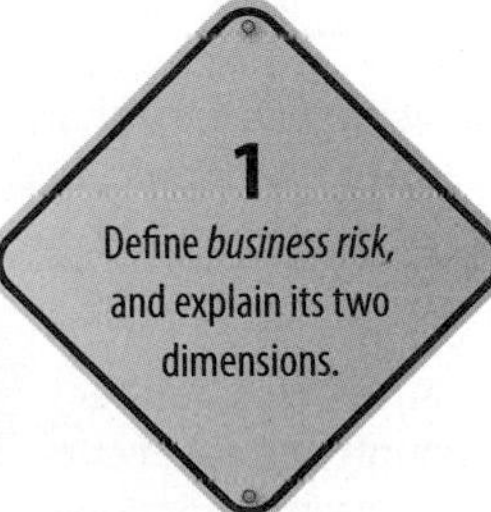

What Is Business Risk?

Simply stated, *risk* is the "possibility of suffering harm or loss."[2] **Business risk**, then, is the possibility of losses associated with the assets and earnings potential of a firm. Here, the term *assets* includes not only inventory and equipment, but also such factors as the firm's employees, its customers, and its reputation.

business risk The possibility of losses associated with the assets and earnings potential of a firm.

The nature of business risk can be observed from two perspectives: market risk and pure risk. **Market risk** is the uncertainty associated with an investment decision. An entrepreneur who invests in a new business hopes for a gain, but realizes that the eventual outcome may be a loss. Only after identifying the investment opportunity, developing strategies, and committing resources will she or he learn the final result.

market risk The uncertainty associated with an investment decision.

Pure risk describes a situation where only loss or no loss can occur—there is no potential gain. Owning property, for instance, creates the possibility of loss due to fire or severe weather; the only outcomes are loss or no loss. As a general rule, only pure risk is insurable. That is, insurance is not intended to protect investors from market risks, where the chances of both gain and loss exist.

pure risk The uncertainty associated with a situation where only loss or no loss can occur.

Basic Types of Pure Risk

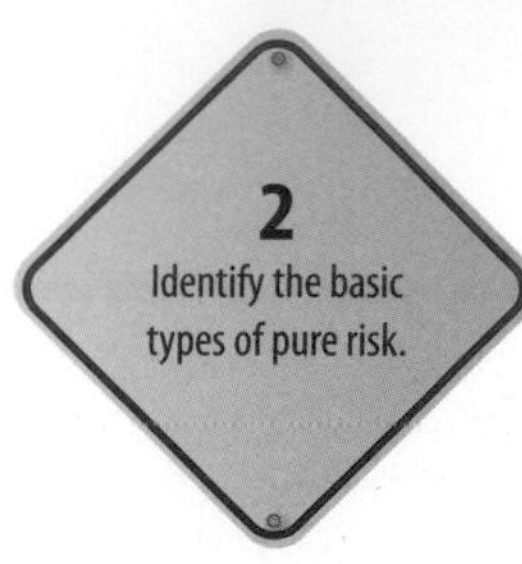

The pure risks that any business faces can be categorized as property, liability, and personnel. Let's take a look at these types of pure risk, which are related to the physical, legal, and human aspects of a business.

PROPERTY RISKS

In the course of establishing a business, an owner acquires the property that will be necessary to provide the products and services of the company. If this property is damaged or destroyed, the business sustains a loss. In addition, the temporary loss of use of the property can add to the negative financial impact on the business. Several characteristics of business property and the risks associated with it are worthy of attention.

real property
Land and anything physically attached to the land, such as buildings.

personal property
Any property other than real property, including machinery, inventory, and vehicles.

replacement value of property
The cost of replacing personal property and rebuilding real property at today's prices.

actual cash value (ACV)
An insurance term that refers to the depreciated value of a property.

peril
A cause of loss, either through natural events or through the actions of people.

There are two general types of property—real property and personal property. **Real property** consists of land and anything physically attached to land, such as buildings. Some business owners purchase land and buildings, while others choose to lease necessary real property. It is important to note, however, that some leases make the lessee responsible for any damage or loss to the leased premises. **Personal property** can be defined simply as any property other than real property. Personal property includes machinery, equipment (such as computers), furniture, fixtures, inventory, and vehicles. While the location of real property is fixed, personal property can be moved from place to place. Among the risks to the personal property of the small firm are the security threats to its computers posed by hackers and spyware.

Property can be valued in several ways. The **replacement value of property** is the cost of replacing personal property and rebuilding real property at today's prices. For example, a building that was constructed 10 years ago at a cost of $1 million may have a current replacement value of $1,400,000 because of the rising costs of materials and labor. The **actual cash value (ACV)** of property is very different from its replacement value, as this insurance term refers to the depreciated value of property. Assuming a rate of depreciation of 3 percent per year for the same 10-year-old building, we would find the building to have an estimated actual cash value of $980,000 (that is, $1,400,000 – [0.03 × 10 × $1,400,000]). By common practice, most commercial property insurance policies provide replacement value coverage as opposed to actual cash value coverage.

Property insurance also takes into account two primary features: perils (the cause) and losses (the effect).

Perils

A **peril** is defined as a cause of loss. Some perils are naturally occurring events, such as windstorms, floods, earthquakes, and lightning. The location of a property may increase the likelihood of its loss from certain perils—for example, coastal properties are more susceptible to wind damage and flooding, and properties near fault lines are more prone to damage from earthquakes.

ACTION

Beware of Hackers!

All it takes is a website with an e-mail address for hackers to target your small firm. A business does not have to have a huge online presence to attract hackers. Use software and services from such companies as Symantec and McAfee to help protect against online risks. Stay current on virus protection, and be certain to check frequently for updates to your program.

Not all perils, however, are natural events; some are

related to the actions of people. Perils such as robbery and employee dishonesty involve criminal acts performed by people against business owners. The rapid growth of e-commerce has led to new forms of dishonest acts, such as hacking, denial of access, and improper use of confidential information.

Losses

Usually, when you think of property loss, you envision a **direct loss**, in which physical damage to property reduces its value to the property owner. Direct loss of property as a result of windstorm, fire, or explosion is obvious to everyone and has the potential to significantly hinder any business.

A less obvious type of property loss is an **indirect loss**, which arises from an inability to carry on normal operations due to a direct loss. For example, if a delivery truck is damaged in an accident, the resulting loss of its use can impair the ability of a business to get its products to customers. The indirect loss component of this event may cause a reduction in revenue or an increase in expense (from having to outsource the delivery function), either of which will have an adverse impact on business income.

direct loss
A loss in which physical damage to property reduces its value to the property owner.

indirect loss
A loss arising from an inability to carry on normal operations due to a direct loss of property.

It should be pointed out that business income can also be reduced by events or conditions that are not related to direct losses. For example, a strike by UPS employees several years ago created serious logistical problems for many of its business customers, which were unable to receive deliveries from suppliers or distribute products to customers. The financial impact of such a labor action may be just as real to a business as physical damage to property, but the insurance protection available for indirect losses applies only when *direct* damage events trigger the loss of use. This issue is discussed in more detail later in the chapter.

© iStockphoto.com / Angelika Schwarz

entrepreneurial experiences

An Emergency Plan May Make the Difference Between Survival and Failure

Sandy Whann is the fourth generation of Leidenheimer men to run [the Leidenheimer Baking Company], which was founded in 1896 in the city of New Orleans by Sandy's great-grandfather, George Leidenheimer of Germany. The bakery produces French bread made famous by traditional local dishes like the muffaletta and po boy sandwiches that originated in the heart of the French Quarter. As a lifetime citizen of New Orleans, Sandy has experienced many evacuations and has become adept at hurricane planning through the years.

When the hurricane alert [for Katrina] was issued on Saturday, August 27, 2006, this veteran immediately put his family emergency plan into effect as his wife and two children prepared to leave the city. Sandy remained near the plant to keep a close eye on his 110-year-old company and keep production working at a minimal capacity. With his family out of the city, Sandy uncharacteristically decided to shut the bakery down, secure its exterior, gas lines and doors and encouraged his employees to prepare their own homes and loved ones for the storm and potential evacuation. Both Sandy and the Leidenheimer management team keep home phone numbers and emergency evacuation contact information for all employees.

After most of his employees had left, only Sandy, his plant manager, and chief engineer, all of whom play key roles in the business's preparedness plan, remained in New Orleans. Once Sandy and the others had completed their assigned duties in the emergency shutdown, they left as well.

While driving to meet with his family in Baton Rouge, Sandy was struck by the unusualness of the event. "Things were very different this time around," said Sandy. "But in the gridlock I still made the most of the little time we had before the storm hit. Having an emergency preparedness plan helps you focus your priorities and helps you know what you need to be doing with the limited time you have in any situation." En route, Sandy checked with his insurance provider, accountants, legal consultant, and spoke with customers via cell phone to keep them abreast of the situation and the effect of his shutdown on their supply of baked goods.

Donn Young Photography

Sandy's business evacuation kit played a large part in his success. Sandy's kit included: financial and payroll records, utility contact information, updated phone lists for his customers and employees, backup files and software, as well as computer hard drives. Well before the evacuation, Sandy placed the kit in a mobile waterproof/fireproof case that could be taken with him at a moment's notice. As part of Sandy's written plan, he set up a satellite office for the Leidenheimer Baking Company in Baton Rouge where he made contact with his bank, forwarded phone lines, and was receiving forwarded mail within two days after the evacuation.

Two days later, on August 29, Sandy breathed a sigh of relief that his family and his company had escaped a major disaster. Sandy was able to return to his plant within a week of the storm hitting. When he returned, he was met with widespread damage, but without the flooding he had expected. In the facility, thousands of pounds of melted yeast and other ingredients had been sitting wet without refrigeration. The roof had severe damage, there was no power, no usable water, and no one was permitted back into the city except the National Guard. The plant was 120°F of foul smells emanating from every square inch.

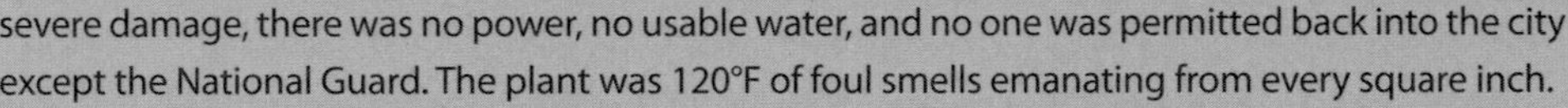

Despite caring deeply for his business, the most important thing to Sandy was his employees and he felt fortunate that all of the company's employees were safe. "The rebuilding process included a handful of things," said Sandy. "Number one is the employees. . . . It is important to listen to the needs of employees."

In summing up his experience, Sandy said, "Katrina was severe enough to teach even us experienced hurricane survivors a few new things about our emergency planning." Since Hurricane Katrina, Sandy has revised his business emergency plan and gained a more extensive understanding of the importance of preparation.

Source: "Sandy Whann Case Study," http://www.ready.gov/business/_downloads/sandywhann.pdf, accessed April 12, 2011.
http://www.leidenheimer.com

LIABILITY RISKS

A growing business risk today is the legal liability that may arise from various business activities. A society creates laws to govern interactions among its members. Individual rights and freedoms are protected by these laws. If a business or any of its agents violates these protected rights, the business can be held accountable for any resulting loss or damage to the affected party. Legal liability may arise from statutory liability, contractual liability, or tort liability.

Statutory Liability

Some laws impose a statutory obligation on a business. For example, each state has enacted **workers' compensation legislation** that in most cases requires employers to provide certain benefits to employees when they are injured in a work-related incident. This means that fault is not an issue; an employer is responsible for work-related injuries without regard to fault. While the benefits differ slightly from state to state, most workers' compensation statutes require employers to provide the following benefits to employees injured at work: coverage of medical expenses, compensation for lost wages, payment of rehabilitation expenses, and death benefits for employees' families.

workers' compensation legislation
Laws that obligate the employer to pay employees for injury or illness related to employment, regardless of fault.

This statutory liability is potentially significant for any business. The attacks on the World Trade Center provided a stark example of the magnitude of this liability, especially for companies whose employees worked in a concentrated area. Marsh, Inc., one of the leading insurance brokers in the world, lost over 300 employees in the 9/11 disaster, creating an enormous financial obligation on the part of the employer to the families of the victims. Most businesses protect themselves from this type of financial loss through the purchase of workers' compensation insurance. Some large employers choose to self-insure (that is, they set aside part of their earnings to offset any potential future losses), but most purchase extra insurance protection to guard against catastrophic events such as the 9/11 tragedy.

Contractual Liability

Businesses often enter into contracts with other parties. These contracts could involve a lease of premises, a sales contract with a customer, an agreement with an outsourcing firm, or a contract with a construction company. One common denominator among most of these contracts is the inclusion of some sort of indemnification clause. As businesses sign contracts containing indemnification clauses, they need to be well aware of the potential legal liabilities they may be assuming by virtue of the language used. Simply put, an **indemnification clause** requires one party (the indemnitor) to assume the financial consequences of another party's legal liabilities (the indemnitee). In other words, the indemnitor agrees to "pay on behalf" of the indemnitee the legal liabilities of the indemnitee.

indemnification clause
A contractual clause that requires one party to assume the financial consequences of another party's legal liabilities.

The idea behind the contractual transfer of liability is to shift the responsibility to the party with the most control over the risk exposure. Consider, for example, a general contractor who signs an agreement to construct a new building on a piece of land for an owner. Should someone be injured during the building process, it is highly unlikely that the injury would be a result of the negligence of the property owner. In all likelihood, the negligent party—the party causing or contributing to the accident—would be the general contractor or perhaps a subcontractor hired by the general contractor. Therefore, it is quite common and most appropriate for the general contractor to agree to indemnify the owner for any liability arising from the construction work.

In many cases, insurance covers the potential legal liabilities that a business may assume as a result of an indemnification clause in a contract. But good communication between a business owner and his or her insurance agent or broker is essential. In a review of contracts that contain indemnification clauses, the insurance agent or broker should be able to point out the main limitations or shortcomings of an insurance policy as they pertain to the firm's assuming the legal liabilities of another party.

Tort Liability

Civil wrongs include breach of contract and torts. **Torts** are wrongful acts or omissions for which an injured party can take legal action against the wrongdoer to seek monetary damages. Tort actions commonly include an allegation of negligence, but four elements must be present for someone to be found guilty of a negligent act:

torts
Wrongful acts or omissions for which an injured party can take legal action against the wrongdoer for monetary damages.

1. *Existence of a legal duty between the parties.* For example, a restaurant owner has a legal duty to provide patrons with food and drink that are fit for consumption. Likewise, an employee making a delivery for an employer has a duty to operate a vehicle safely on public roads.

2. *Failure to provide the appropriate standard of care.* The standard of care normally used is the **reasonable (prudent person) standard**, based on what a reasonable or prudent person would have done under similar circumstances. This standard of care may be elevated, however, if a "professional" is involved. In professional liability actions, the standard of care is determined by the established standards of the profession. For example, a negligence action against a CPA would use the standards of the accounting profession as the benchmark. Expert witnesses are often used to help establish the standard and determine what clients can reasonably expect.

reasonable (prudent person) standard The typical standard of care, based on what a reasonable or prudent person would have done under similar circumstances.

compensatory damages Economic or noneconomic damages intended to make the claimant whole by compensating the claimant for any injuries or damage arising from the negligent action.

economic damages Compensatory damages that relate to economic loss, such as medical expenses and loss of income.

noneconomic damages Compensatory damages for such losses as pain and suffering, mental anguish, and loss of physical abilities.

punitive damages A form of punishment beyond compensatory damages that intends to punish wrongdoers for gross negligence or callous disregard and to have a deterrent effect.

proximate cause A negligent act that is the clear cause of damages sustained.

3. *Presence of injury or damages.* Negligence may exist, but if no injury or damage is sustained by the claimant, tort liability does not exist. Two types of damages may be awarded in a tort action: compensatory and punitive damages.

   - **Compensatory damages** are intended to make the claimant whole—that is, to compensate the claimant for any injuries or damage arising from the negligent action. Compensatory damages can be economic or noneconomic in nature. **Economic damages** relate to economic loss, such as medical expenses, loss of income, or the cost of property replacement/restoration. Economic damages are relatively easy to quantify. **Noneconomic damages** cover such losses as pain and suffering, mental anguish, and loss of physical abilities. In comparison to economic damages, noneconomic damages are difficult to express in financial terms. Civil courts usually have a hard time setting these awards, but many of today's substantial awards include a large amount for noneconomic damages.

   - **Punitive damages** are a form of punishment that goes beyond any compensatory damages. Punitive damages have a dual purpose. First, they punish wrongdoers in instances where there is gross negligence or a callous disregard for the interests of others. Second, punitive damages are intended to have a deterrent effect, sending a message to society that such conduct will not be tolerated. In fact, punitive damages are sometimes referred to as "exemplary damages." In other words, one purpose of such damages is to make an "example" out of the defendant. Whether or not an insurance policy will pay for the punitive damages awarded against a business is determined by the state in which the lawsuit is filed. As a matter of public policy, some states allow insurance companies to pay for punitive damages, while other states do not.

4. *Evidence that the negligent act is the* **proximate cause** *of the loss.* There must be proof that the negligence actually caused the damages sustained. There may be negligence and there may be damages, but if no link can be established between the two, there is no tort liability.

Tort liability can arise from a number of business activities. Some of the more significant sources of tort liability follow:

- **Premises liability.** People may sustain injuries while on a business's premises. Retailers have significant premises liability exposure because they have many customers entering stores to purchase goods. Some other businesses, however, have little in the way of premises liability exposure. A consulting firm or a Web-design company would not typically have clients visit its business location; therefore, its premises liability exposure would be minimal.

- **Operations liability.** People may also sustain injuries as a result of a company's operations that take place away from its premises. Contractors have significant operations liability exposure because they are performing work at various job sites, and such work could easily result in injury to another person. At the same time, some businesses (such as retailers) have little in the way of operations liability exposure; their exposure is limited to their store's premises.
- **Professional liability.** Any business providing professional services to the public is potentially subject to professional liability claims. Recognizing this exposure is important, since separate liability insurance is necessary to properly protect a business from professional liability claims. Businesses that have a professional liability exposure include accounting firms, architecture and engineering firms, dental offices, and doctors' offices.
- **Employers' liability.** As previously mentioned, employers have a statutory obligation to pay certain benefits to employees injured in the course of employment. In exchange for these benefits, employees are then prohibited from suing their employer in most circumstances. At the same time, it is possible that an employer may be sued by an altogether different party as a result of an injury to an employee. Perhaps the employee's injury in the workplace was caused by a faulty piece of equipment manufactured by another firm; the employee may sue the manufacturer of that faulty product. The manufacturer may then take action against the employer, alleging that the employer failed to maintain the equipment, which consequently caused injury to the employee.
- **Automobile liability.** A business that uses vehicles for various purposes has automobile liability exposure. Even a company that does not own or lease vehicles has potential liability if employees use their personal vehicles for business purposes.
- **Product liability.** The products manufactured or sold by a business can be a source of legal liability. For example, someone who was injured while using a product may claim that the product was defective. She or he may allege that there was either a manufacturing defect, a design defect, or a marketing defect. A **manufacturing defect** exists when something actually goes wrong during the manufacturing process and the product is not made according to the manufacturer's specifications. A **design defect** exists when the product is made in accordance with the manufacturer's specifications but the product is still unreasonably dangerous as designed. As an example, perhaps a rotating blade inside a piece of equipment is not properly covered by a shield. Someone could be injured by the rotating blade and claim a design defect because there was no protective shield covering the blade. Finally, a **marketing defect** exists when the manufacturer has failed to convey to the user of the product a fair indication of the hazards associated with the product or adequate instructions on how to use the product safely.
- **Completed operations liability.** The completed operations or completed work of a business can be a source of legal liability. Take as an example a general contractor who has constructed a new building for another party. Following the construction of the building, someone standing on a balcony of the building leans against a rail that gives way, thus causing the person to fall and sustain bodily injury. This would generally result in a lawsuit against the general contractor.
- **Directors and officers liability.** An increasing concern among businesses today is the threat of lawsuits against the directors and officers of a company. The exposure is greater for publicly owned organizations, but it also exists for privately owned firms and nonprofit organizations. Specific areas of exposure for directors and officers include lawsuits with allegations of financial mismanagement,

manufacturing defect
A defect resulting from a problem that occurs during the manufacturing process, causing the product to subsequently not be made according to specification.

design defect
A defect resulting from a dangerous design, even though the product was made according to specifications.

marketing defect
A defect resulting from failure to convey to the user that hazards are associated with a product or to provide adequate instructions on safe product use.

conflicts of interest, actions taken beyond the authority granted in bylaws, and wrongful acts that pertain to employment practices. Wrongful employment practices may include discrimination, sexual harassment, or wrongful termination.

PERSONNEL RISKS

personnel risks Risks that directly affect individual employees but may have an indirect impact on a business as well.

Personnel risks are risks that directly affect individual employees but may have an indirect impact on a business as well. The primary risks in this category include premature death, poor health, and insufficient retirement income.

Premature Death

The risk associated with death is not if, but when. We all expect to die; however, there is a risk that we may die early in life. This risk poses a potential financial problem for both the family of the person and his or her employer. Individuals deal with this risk by maintaining a healthy lifestyle and purchasing life insurance to protect family members who rely on their income.

Employers can be quite adversely impacted by the untimely death of an employee if that employee cannot be easily replaced. And what if a partner or owner of the business dies? Normally, such an event triggers a buyout of the interest of the deceased owner. Life insurance is often used to fund these buyout provisions.

Poor Health

A more likely occurrence than death of an employee is poor health. The severity of poor health varies, ranging from a mild disorder to a more serious, disabling illness. And as with premature death, the consequences of this event may affect an employer as well as the employee's family members.

The financial consequences of poor health have two dimensions. First are medical expenses, which can range from the cost of a doctor's visit to catastrophic expenses related to surgeries and hospitalization. Second are consequences of the inability to work. Disability most often is a temporary condition, but it can be lengthy or even permanent. A worker's permanent disability can have the same financial impact on her or his family as death.

Employers often provide some form of health insurance as a benefit of employment. In some instances, the cost of the health insurance is shared by the employer and the employee; in most instances, however, the bulk of the cost is absorbed by the employer. In addition to the health insurance costs, the fact that the employer is without the services of the employee for some time period may add to the adverse financial impact on the business.

Insufficient Retirement Income

The final category of personnel risk involves the possibility of outliving one's wealth. The goal in dealing with this risk is to defer income and accumulate sufficient wealth to provide a satisfactory level of income during the nonworking years.

There are three primary sources of retirement income: Social Security, employer-funded retirement programs, and personal savings. Social Security provides a retirement income benefit, although for most retirees this benefit is not sufficient to meet expected consumption during retirement. To supplement this income, most workers have a retirement program associated with their employment. In the past, these programs were primarily funded by employers as a form of deferred compensation. While employer-funded pension plans still exist, it is more common today to encounter employee-funded retirement plans, where the employee can elect to defer current income for retirement. Usually, these plans are partially funded by employers as an incentive for employees to participate. Finally, individual savings can be used to accumulate wealth for retirement. All of these sources should be carefully considered in the retirement income planning process.

Risk Management

Risk management consists of all efforts to preserve the assets and earning power of a business. Since risk management has grown out of insurance management, the two terms are often used interchangeably. However, risk management has a much broader meaning, covering both insurable and uninsurable risks and including noninsurance approaches to reducing all types of risk. Risk management involves more than trying to obtain the most insurance for each dollar spent; it is concerned with finding the best way possible to reduce the cost of dealing with risk. Insurance is only one of several approaches to minimizing the pure risks a firm is sure to encounter.

3
Describe the steps in the risk management process in small firms.

risk management
Ways of coping with risk that are designed to preserve the assets and earning power of a firm.

THE PROCESS OF RISK MANAGEMENT

Five steps are required to develop and implement a risk management program.

Step 1: Identify and understand risks. It is essential that a business owner be aware of the risks the firm faces. To reduce the chance of overlooking important risks, a business should adopt a systematic approach to identifying risks. Useful identification methods include insurance policy checklists, questionnaires, analysis of financial statements, and careful analysis of a firm's operations, customers, and facilities. Exhibit 23.1 depicts just a few of the risks that a small company may encounter.

Step 2: Evaluate risks. Once the various risks have been identified, they must be evaluated in terms of the potential size of each loss and the probability that it will occur. At a minimum, risks should be classified into three groups: critical (losses that could result in bankruptcy), extremely important (losses that would require investment of additional capital to continue operations), and moderately important (losses that can be covered with current income or existing assets).

"I'm disappointed; if anyone should have seen the red flags, it's you."

Step 3: Select methods to manage risk. The two approaches used in dealing with risk are risk control and risk financing, both of which will be discussed later in this chapter.

Step 4: Implement the decision. Once the decision has been made to use a particular technique or techniques to manage a firm's risks, this decision must be followed by action, such as purchasing insurance and setting aside dedicated funds to cope with any risks that have been retained. Failure to act—or even simple procrastination—could be fatal.

EXHIBIT 23.1 Risks on the Road to Success

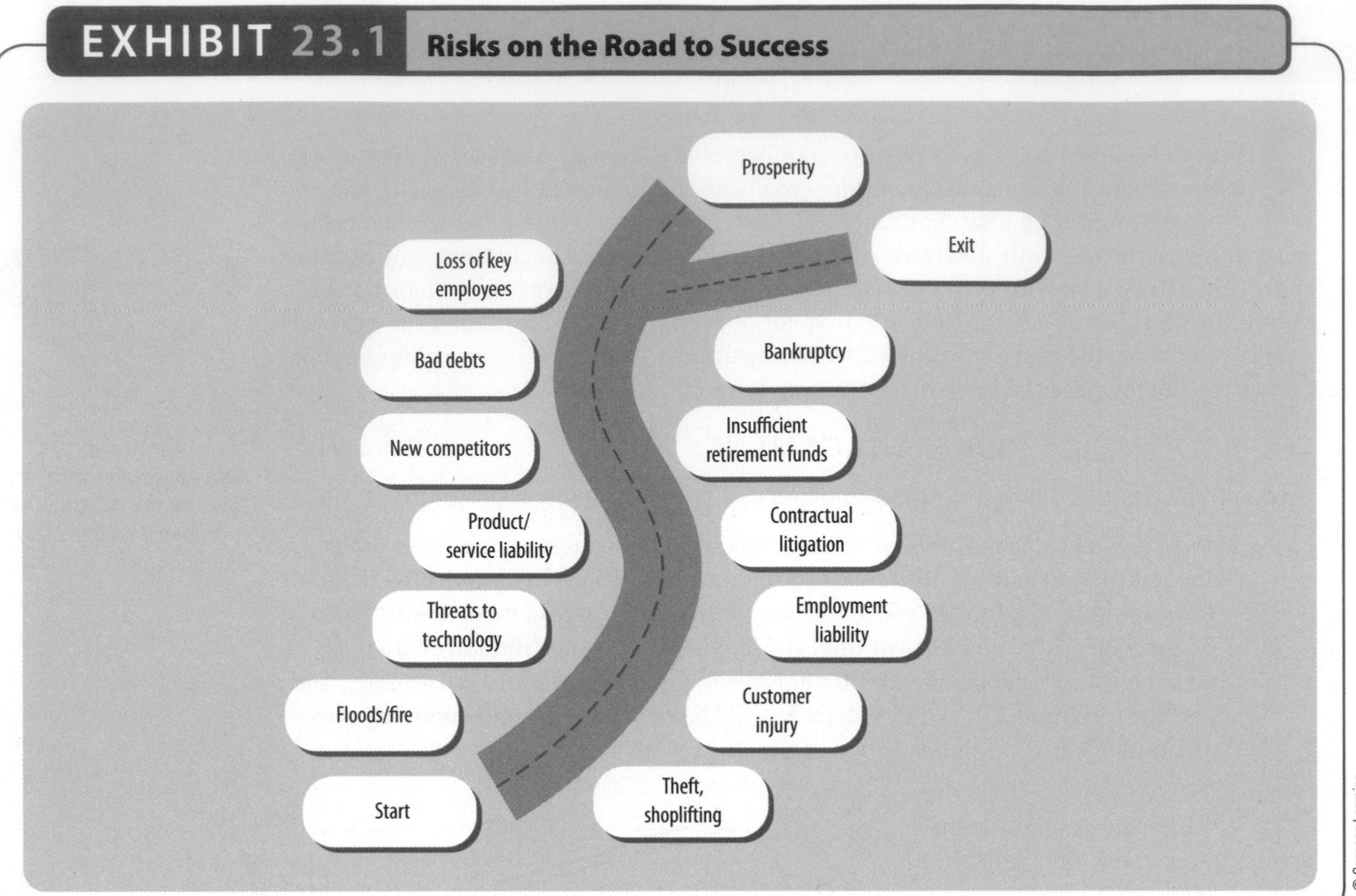

Step 5: *Review and evaluate.* Review and evaluation of the chosen risk management technique are essential because conditions change—new risks arise, and old ones disappear. Also, reviewing earlier decisions to use specific methods may identify mistakes made previously.

RISK MANAGEMENT AND THE SMALL BUSINESS

Regardless of the nature or size of a business, risk management is a serious issue. Too often, small businesses pay insufficient attention to analyzing potential risk. "Small companies often spend more time planning their company picnics than for an event that could put them out of business," says Katherine Heaviside, a partner in Epoch 5, a Huntington, New York, public relations firm that specializes in crisis communication.[3] To avoid being put out of business by an unexpected development, a small business owner must take an active role in managing the risks of her or his firm.

Risk management in a small business differs from that in a large firm. In a large firm, the responsibilities of risk management are frequently assigned to a specialized staff manager. It is more difficult for a small company to cope with risk management since its risk manager is usually the owner and the owner wears so many hats. For this reason, the small business owner needs to rely more heavily on his or her insurance agent for advice. Furthermore, risk management is not something that requires immediate attention—until something happens. A prudent small business owner will take the time to identify the different types of risks faced by the firm and find ways to cope with them, through either risk control or risk financing.

Risk Control

Risk control involves minimizing loss through prevention, avoidance, and/or reduction. **Loss prevention**, as the name implies, focuses on preventing losses from ever happening. For example, a business with a machine shop or manufacturing process may require all employees to wear safety glasses so as to prevent foreign particles from injuring their eyes. **Loss avoidance** is achieved by choosing not to engage in a particular hazardous activity. For instance, the liability exposure associated with operating a large truck on an interstate highway for the purposes of delivering a company's products to the marketplace is quite severe. An accident caused by a large truck on the highway can result in serious bodily injury and/or property damage. Therefore, to avoid this liability exposure, a business may choose to hire a common carrier to deliver its products to the marketplace. This eliminates the exposure altogether. **Loss reduction** addresses the potential frequency, severity, or unpredictability of loss, thereby lessening the impact of the loss on the business. Crisis planning is a form of loss reduction in that it provides a template to follow in the case of a catastrophic loss. Installing automatic sprinkler systems in a building is another good example of a loss reduction strategy. If a fire occurs in a building with an automatic sprinkler system, the sprinklers will be activated, minimizing the amount of fire damage to the building.

risk control
Minimizing potential losses by preventing, avoiding, or reducing risk.

loss prevention
Keeping a loss from happening.

loss avoidance
Choosing not to engage in hazardous activities.

loss reduction
Lessening the frequency, severity, or unpredictability of potential losses.

In more recent times, social media have become useful tools for risk reduction, particularly when customer-service or public-relations issues arise. For example, Twitter was helpful to Innovative Beverage Group Holdings, Inc., when its Web site crashed after a surge in traffic following a segment on Fox News about the company. The firm quickly notified consumers via a Twitter that it was working diligently to fix the problem, and looked for consumer comments about the crash to quickly respond about what it was doing to fix the problem. Peter Bianchi, Innovative's CEO, explained that, "Twitter gave us an up-to-the-minute ability to take what would normally be a crisis situation and make it just another event. You can't do that with a 1-800-number."[4]

On the other hand, social media can create problems for a business. Disgruntled customers and former employees can use social media to hurt a company's reputation. Social media need to be monitored for such problems. And although social media can be a valuable tool, they do little good without regular use to garner followers and thus gain user trust.

Risk Financing

Risk financing focuses on making funds available for losses that cannot be eliminated by risk control; it involves transferring the risk or retaining the risk. **Risk transfer** is accomplished largely through buying insurance but can also be achieved by making other contractual arrangements that transfer the risk to others. As described earlier, indemnification clauses provide a means by which risk can be transferred from one party to another.

Risk retention entails financing all or part of a loss from a company's cash flows. Assuming a firm's balance sheet is strong enough, the owner may choose to carry a high deductible applicable to property losses (perhaps a $25,000 deductible instead of a $5,000 deductible). For example, in the event of fire damage to a company's building, the business owner would pay up to $25,000 out of his or her pocket. The higher the deductible, the lower the insurance premium paid to the property insurance carrier. As another example, a business owner may choose to have a high deductible for a liability-type insurance claim. Again, in exchange for the higher deductible, the business owner is given a discounted liability insurance premium. Another form of risk retention is **self-insurance**. However, self-insurance is usually only appropriate for larger companies. Under self-insurance programs, a part of the organization's earnings is earmarked for a contingency fund against possible future losses.

risk financing
Making funds available to cover losses that cannot be eliminated by risk control.

risk transfer
Buying insurance or making contractual arrangements that transfer risk to others.

risk retention
Financing loss intentionally, through a firm's cash flows.

self-insurance
Designating part of a firm's earnings as a cushion against possible future losses.

© iStockphoto.com/Angelika Schwarz

using technology

Keep Your Company Safe from Online Privacy Leaks

After a prospective subcontracting deal at a major manufacturer was leaked through social media, affecting the stock price of both companies, Roger Traversa, an attorney in corporate compliance and privacy at Arjont Group in Philadelphia, was called in. His firm specializes in advising businesses on privacy risks, and he says the same rules apply to businesses big and small—and in fact, the results of social media outbreaks can be even more dire on the small side.

"For smaller companies, leaks can be make or break," Traversa says. "Losing one competitive advantage or one trade secret can really damage your business."

A recent survey by information security company Websense found that 57 percent of data-stealing attacks come via the web, and that many posts on social media may qualify as proprietary data or violations of health care or credit-card company regulations. Forty-seven percent of survey respondents reported that users in their organizations try to bypass company web security policies.

How can you prevent employees from spilling the beans in a status line or tweet? First, Traversa says, define what information is confidential. "You may think it's obvious, but you need to be clear to your employees about what information you consider proprietary or a trade secret," he says.

It is also a good idea to have new employees sign confidentiality agreements that instruct them about the company's privacy guidelines. Consult your legal counsel or a legal consultant to guide you in drafting a document that will protect your company. Also, he says, insist that any company-related blog posts or other social media posts be approved by a specified person or department in your organization.

Finally, Traversa suggests monitoring employee blogs and search[ing] for keywords about your industry and topic areas you're trying to protect, in addition to the specific name of your company. That will help you spot leaks that don't use your brand name, but still hold valuable information.

Source: Gwen Moran, "Social (Networking) Security," *Entrepreneur*, November 2009, p. 61. http://www.arjont.com. Reprinted with permission of Entrepreneur Media, Inc.

partially self-funded program
Designating part of firm's earnings to fund a portion of employee medical coverage.

specific stop loss limit
A firm's per-employee limit on self-funding for medical claims.

Some small businesses have successfully relied on **partially self-funded programs** as they pertain to medical coverage for employees. Partially self-funded programs allow the business to self-fund a portion of the health insurance benefits for its employees. For most small businesses, this self-funded portion is limited to between $30,000 and $80,000 per employee, depending on the number of employees and the firm's financial strength. This limitation per employee is more commonly referred to as a **specific stop loss limit**. After the specific stop loss limit has been met during the plan year, the health insurance company takes over the claim and pays the remaining portion.

In April 2011, an employer in Waco, Texas, compared the costs of a traditional health insurance plan (also referred to as a fully insured medical plan) and a partially self-funded program. This particular employer had 96 employees. The fully insured plan would have cost the organization approximately $1,475,000 in premiums for a 12-month period. The

EXHIBIT 23.2 Tools for Managing Risk

Amount of Loss	Probability of Loss: Low Frequency	Probability of Loss: High Frequency
High Severity	• Loss prevention • Loss reduction	• Loss prevention • Loss reduction
Low Severity	• Loss avoidance • Loss prevention • Loss reduction • Risk retention	• Risk retention

Note: To find a listing of the risk management tools appropriate for dealing with a potential loss, see the box corresponding to the severity and frequency of the potential loss.

partially self-funded medical plan had cost the employer a total of only $1,154,000 the previous year. So it appeared to be in the employer's best interest to maintain a partially self-funded program in anticipation of again saving approximately $321,000.[5] Clearly, some risks are associated with a partially self-funded plan, since an employer never knows ahead of time how many employees might actually reach their specific stop loss limit. For this reason, these plans also have what is referred to as an **aggregate stop loss limit**, so as to provide a cap on expenses for the year should a number of employees reach the specific stop loss limit.

aggregate stop loss limit
A comprehensive limit on annual expenses should a number of employees reach the specific stop loss limit.

It should be understood that partially self-funded programs are not suitable for every small business. As a rule of thumb, a business should have a net worth of at least $1 million and 80 or more employees to be considered a good candidate for a partially self-funded program.

In choosing the appropriate method for managing risk, a small business owner should consider the size of each potential loss, its probability of occurrence, and what resources would be available to cover the loss if it did occur. Exhibit 23.2 shows the appropriate risk management techniques for potential losses of different probabilities (low frequency and high frequency) and loss amounts (low severity and high severity).

Basic Principles of a Sound Insurance Program

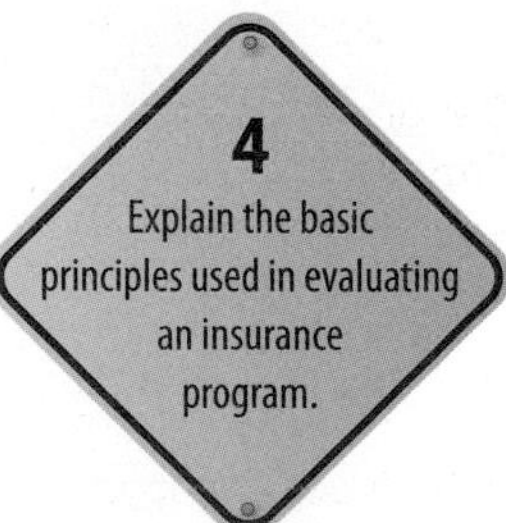

What kinds of risks can be covered by insurance? What types of coverage should be purchased? How much coverage is adequate? Unfortunately, there are no clear-cut answers to these questions. A reputable insurance agent can provide valuable assistance to a small company in evaluating risks and designing proper protection plans, but a small business owner should become as knowledgeable as possible about what types of insurance are available. Three basic principles should be followed in evaluating an insurance program:

1. *Identify business risks that can be insured.* A small business must first obtain the insurance coverage that is either required by law or by contract with another party. This generally includes workers' compensation insurance and automobile

liability insurance. A reputable insurance agent with expertise in providing business insurance coverage will be an important resource in identifying business risks that can be insured, while also establishing the premium costs for insuring such risks. As a part of this process, business owners should take the necessary time to determine the replacement cost of their buildings and personal property, including all furniture, fixtures, equipment, inventory, and supplies.

2. *Secure insurance coverage for all major potential losses.* Small businesses must avoid incurring major uninsured losses that have the capacity to threaten the very existence of the business. For example, it would be exceedingly difficult to overcome the total destruction of a building or facility caused by a significant fire or windstorm event. For this reason, a business owner should make certain that insurance covers the full replacement value of the firm's buildings and personal property. In an effort to save a relatively small amount of premium dollars, some small business owners elect to insure their property for a value somewhat less than the full replacement value, which is clearly a bad decision.

   Equally devastating might be a $1 million liability judgment against the business as a result of an automobile accident or someone's slipping on the premises or being injured by the firm's products. It is imperative for the longevity of the business that these major potential loss exposures be properly insured.

3. *Consider the feasibility and affordability of insuring smaller potential losses.* Smaller potential losses do not pose the same threat to businesses as major potential losses do. Thus, a business owner will need to weigh the feasibility and affordability of absorbing smaller potential losses. Of course, what determines whether a potential loss is "small" or "large" varies by each small business, depending on the strength of its financial position. The types of claims that arise from employment practices include employee lawsuits alleging wrongful termination, sexual harassment, and discrimination in the workplace. For the most part, the dollar value of such claims ranges from $50,000 to $150,000, with insurance premiums ranging from $2,500 to $7,500. Therefore, the entrepreneur must decide if the potential loss would be best handled through self-insurance or through payment of annual premiums. The company's ability to absorb such a loss determines what the small business owner should do. In this case, there is no single right answer.

Common Types of Business Insurance

In this section, we examine the basic insurance policies used by many small companies. These policies fall under one of two categories: property and casualty insurance, and life and health insurance.

PROPERTY AND CASUALTY INSURANCE

Property and casualty insurance includes property insurance, commercial general liability insurance, automobile insurance, workers' compensation insurance, and crime insurance.

Property Insurance

A property insurance policy is used by a business owner to insure buildings and personal property owned by the business, as well as buildings not owned by the business but for which the business owner, as lessee, has a responsibility to insure. As previously mentioned, property can be insured for either its replacement value or actual cash value.

When purchasing property insurance, a business owner must also determine which "perils" will be covered by the policy. With the **named-peril approach**, the specific perils covered by the policy are identified. Covered perils generally include damage caused by fire, smoke, lightning, explosion, windstorm, hail, aircraft, vehicles, riot, vandalism, sprinkler leakage, sinkhole collapse, and volcanic action. With this approach, any damage caused by a peril not named in the policy is simply not covered. Examples of claims not covered by the named-peril approach include damage caused by frozen pipes within the building, falling objects, the weight of snow, and theft.

named-peril approach
Identifying in an insurance policy the specific perils covered.

In contrast to the named-peril approach, a business owner can select property insurance using the **all-risk approach**. This approach provides the broadest protection available to business owners. With the all-risk approach, all direct damage to property is covered except damage caused by perils specifically excluded. In other words, if it's not excluded, it's covered. Exclusions typically include damage caused by flood, earthquake, fungus or mold, normal wear and tear, and loss caused by the dishonest acts of employees.

all-risk approach
Stating in an insurance policy that all direct damages to property are covered except those caused by perils specifically excluded.

> **START UP ACTION**
>
> **Employee Fraud**
>
> Monitoring for employee fraud needs to be a constant focus for a small business owner. But there are two circumstances when an owner is particularly vulnerable, both of which you may find surprising: when the firm is experiencing success and when there is a personal distraction, such as a death in the family.

An important provision found within the property insurance policy is the **coinsurance clause**. A coinsurance clause requires the business owner to insure the company's building and personal property for at least 80 percent of what it would cost to replace the building and the personal property. If at the time of a claim, the building and personal property are insured for less than 80 percent of their replacement cost, then the business owner is assessed a penalty by the insurance company and, in essence, becomes a co-insurer.

coinsurance clause
A clause in a property insurance policy that requires the owner to have insurance for at least 80 percent of what it would cost to rebuild the building or replace the personal property.

As an example, assume that the replacement cost of a building is $1 million. The owner is therefore required to carry insurance equal to $800,000 (0.80 × $1,000,000) in order to avoid a co-insurance penalty. If the business owner insures the property for only $600,000, he or she then becomes a co-insurer, even in the case of a partial claim. Because the actual insurance is only 75 percent ($600,000 ÷ $800,000) of what it should have been, the insured is penalized 25 percent in the event of a claim. So, should the building experience partial fire and smoke damage in the amount of $100,000, the insurance company will pay only $75,000, even though the amount of insurance on the policy clearly exceeds the amount of the claim. The remaining $25,000 must be paid by the owner in his or her role as co-insurer. Therefore, it is important for a

© Andrew Butterton / Alamy

business owner to insure a building and personal property for an amount that exceeds at least 80 percent of its replacement value. Of course, in the event of a catastrophic loss, the owner would be better served by insuring the building and personal property for 100 percent of what it would cost to replace. Indeed, the limits of property insurance should be carefully considered by all business owners.

business interruption insurance
Coverage that reimburses a business for the loss of anticipated income following the interruption of business operations.

One type of optional coverage that can be added to the property insurance policy is **business interruption insurance**. As previously noted, the financial loss associated with a property loss is not limited to direct damage to the property. There may be an indirect loss associated with the "loss of use" of the damaged property. Business interruption insurance provides coverage for loss of income following the interruption of business operations. Without such income, it would be difficult for a business to continue paying for ongoing expenses, such as payroll expenses. This coverage also provides reimbursement for income that would have been earned by the business had no damage occurred. In addition, business interruption insurance may cover "extra expenses" incurred following an insured loss. For example, following major fire damage to a building, an owner may have to secure a temporary location elsewhere in order to continue business operations. Otherwise, the business would stand to lose all of its customers. Business interruption insurance is a critical element of coverage for a business owner's survival following a significant property loss event. Unfortunately, many owners fail to appreciate the importance of this coverage and consequently fail to add this protection to their property insurance policy.

Commercial General Liability Insurance

commercial general liability (CGL) insurance
Coverage for general liability loss exposure, including premises liability, operations liability, product liability, and completed operations liability.

A **commercial general liability (CGL) insurance** policy is the cornerstone liability policy for small businesses. A CGL policy protects against premises liability, operations liability, product liability, and completed operations liability. Simply put, we live in a litigious society, and small businesses are easy targets for liability lawsuits. A CGL policy provides frontline protection against claims arising from any accident that results either in bodily injury or in property damage and is not otherwise excluded by the policy. It does not cover automobile liability, professional liability, or employer liability, all of which require a separate policy for adequate protection.

A CGL policy also provides for both medical payments coverage and protection against personal and advertising injury liability. The medical expenses of someone who is injured on the company's premises or as a result of its operations are reimbursed through medical payments coverage. The unique feature of this coverage is that it does not require any fault on the part of the business. This "no fault" coverage is intended to build goodwill and prevent someone from then suing the business for negligence. Personal and advertising injury liability protection covers lawsuits alleging intentional torts, such as libel or slander (injury to a person's reputation within the community), false arrest, or malicious prosecution.

Automobile Insurance

automobile insurance
Coverage designed to provide liability and physical damage protection for a vehicle .

An **automobile insurance** policy is designed to provide liability protection as well as physical damage coverage as a result of such insured perils as collision, theft, vandalism, hail, and flood. The risk of physical damage to vehicles is much less than the risk of a large liability lawsuit following an at-fault accident. Small business owners may choose to self-insure against the lesser exposure from physical damage but should *not* self-insure when it comes to liability exposure.

Workers' Compensation Insurance

workers' compensation insurance
Coverage that provides benefits to employees injured at work.

Workers' compensation insurance provides benefits to employees injured at work, in compliance with states' statutes. Generally speaking, these benefits include coverage for medical expenses, loss of wages, and rehabilitation expenses, as well as death benefits for employees' families. Employers' liability insurance offers additional protection for the business owner against various types of liability lawsuits that may arise following an injury to or death of an employee.

Crime Insurance

While there are different types of crime insurance coverages that the small business owner may want to consider, first and foremost is coverage against employee dishonesty. Small businesses are generally very trusting of their employees and would not knowingly have someone working within the organization if they thought that person was dishonest. Unfortunately, not every employee is honest. This fact, combined with the weak financial controls often found in a small business, offers a perfect opportunity for a dishonest employee to embezzle large sums of money. The potential for loss can easily be covered by a **crime insurance** policy at a nominal cost. Premiums vary according to the size of the small business, running from a few hundred dollars up to $2,000 for a $500,000 policy. Because it is possible for an embezzlement scheme to continue for a number of years, significant crime insurance coverage should be obtained.

crime insurance
Coverage against employee dishonesty.

Package Policies

Property insurance and commercial general liability insurance can generally be obtained together under a single insurance policy, called a **business owner's policy (BOP)**. However, construction-type businesses, manufacturers, financial institutions, or any other businesses with annual revenues in excess of $10 million will frequently not qualify for a BOP. The advantages of a BOP at any one location include (1) a lower premium than would otherwise be required to purchase all coverages separately, (2) the automatic inclusion of business interruption insurance, and (3) automatic replacement value protection, as opposed to actual cash value protection.

business owner's policy (BOP)
A business version of a homeowner's policy, designed to meet the property and general liability insurance needs of some small business owners.

For businesses that do not qualify for a BOP, property insurance and commercial general liability insurance can be combined together in a **package policy**. The advantages of a package policy include (1) a lower premium than would otherwise be required to purchase all coverages separately, (2) the ease of adding other coverages more economically, (3) the inclusion of business interruption insurance, and (4) the inclusion of crime insurance.

package policy
A policy for small businesses that do not qualify for a BOP that combines property insurance and commercial general liability insurance.

Miscellaneous Policies

A variety of miscellaneous insurance policies can also be utilized by small businesses. These include umbrella liability policies, inland marine policies, professional liability policies, and cyber liability policies.

Umbrella liability policies provide excess liability layers of protection. Such policies may provide an additional $1,000,000 (or more) of liability insurance that is in excess of the liability limits provided by automobile insurance, a CGL policy, and employers' liability insurance. Umbrella liability policies can be of extreme importance to small businesses in the event of a significant accident that severely injures or kills someone, resulting in a multi-million-dollar lawsuit.

Inland marine policies are unique policies designed to insure personal property against the risk of physical damage when such property is located *away* from a firm's premises. For example, contractor's equipment being used at a job site (bulldozers, forklifts, cranes) and manufactured products being transported by a truck to a customer's warehouse can be insured under an inland marine policy.

Professional liability policies are used to protect professionals against lawsuits arising from errors made while providing their services. Cyber liability policies are available to protect businesses against the broad range of loss exposures arising from their use of the Internet and their holding of confidential information. Coverage may include the following:

- Liability protection against lawsuits arising from the loss or unauthorized disclosure of confidential data that are in the care and custody of a business.
- Crisis management expenses incurred by a firm following a network security breach, including the cost of notifying affected individuals.
- Liability protection for claims arising from a computer virus that originates from a company's network.

LIFE AND HEALTH INSURANCE

Three types of insurance provide coverage for employees within a business: health insurance, key-person life insurance, and disability insurance.

Health Insurance

health insurance Coverage for employee medical care.

Also commonly referred to as medical insurance, **health insurance** is one of the most basic and yet valuable benefits that a small business can offer its employees. Provided on a group basis for all employees, typical health insurance policies offer coverage for medical care at hospitals, doctors' offices, and rehabilitation facilities. Outpatient services and prescription drugs are also generally covered by the policies.

health maintenance organization (HMO) A managed-care network providing health insurance that is less expensive than that of a PPO but more limiting in choices of medical care providers .

preferred provider organization (PPO) A managed-care network providing health insurance that is more expensive than that of an HMO but offers a broader choice of medical providers.

Often, coverage is offered to employees only through a specific group of health care providers, or "network." Types of health insurance plans that fall into this category include **health maintenance organizations (HMOs)** and **preferred provider organizations (PPOs)**. An HMO is a managed-care network that provides health insurance that is generally less expensive than a PPO, but it limits employees' choices of medical care providers more than a PPO does. However, with a PPO, employees still must stay within a network of providers or face higher out-of-pocket expenses in the event of a claim.

Out-of-pocket expenses that employees must pay themselves, regardless of the type of health insurance plan provided by the employer, generally include the following:

- A deductible, or "co-pay," at the doctor's office for each office visit; usually between $20 and $40
- A deductible at the pharmacy for each prescription drug purchased; usually between $10 and $50
- A deductible at the hospital for each hospital admission; usually between $1,000 and $3,000
- A percentage of the total cost of the health care provided by a hospital; usually between 20 and 30 percent, up to a maximum out-of-pocket cost to the employee of between $3,000 and $5,000

Key-Person Life Insurance

key-person life insurance Coverage that provides benefits to a firm upon the death of key personnel.

By carrying **key-person life insurance**, a small business can protect itself against the death of key personnel. Such insurance may be written on an individual or group basis. It is purchased by a firm, with the firm as the sole beneficiary.

Most small business advisors suggest term insurance for key-person life insurance policies, primarily because of lower premiums. How much key-person life insurance to buy is more difficult to decide. Face values of such policies usually begin around $100,000 and may go as high as several million dollars.

Disability Insurance

One risk that small businesses often do not consider is loss due to the disability of a partner or other key employees of the company. Statistics, however, show that the odds of a person being disabled are much higher than most people think. For example, the Social Security Administration cites studies showing that a 20-year-old worker has a 30 percent chance of being temporarily disabled before retirement age.[6]

The most common type of **disability insurance** provides for the payment of a portion (typically two-thirds) of the disabled person's normal monthly income for a period of time after the disability occurs. However, it protects only the disabled person and not the business. Alternatively, partners can purchase disability buyout insurance. This type of disability insurance protects both partners by guaranteeing that the healthy partner will have enough cash to buy out the disabled partner without draining capital from the business.

disability insurance
Coverage that provides benefits upon the disability of a firm's partner or other key employees.

Also available is disability insurance that replaces lost revenue because of the disability of a key employee. For example, if a firm's top salesperson, who brings in $10,000 a month, becomes disabled, this coverage will provide up to 125 percent of replacement income for a year or more. This gives the firm time to recruit and train someone else.

Another type of disability insurance is designed to cover fixed overhead expenses, such as rent, utilities, employee salaries, and general office expenses, while an owner or other key employee recuperates. This type of insurance is especially well suited for a sole proprietorship, since the firm would have no income if the owner were unable to work.

There is no question that risk is a part of life, but how you manage it will affect the success of your small business. That's why an understanding of business risks, the basic principles of a sound insurance program, and the various types of business insurance is so important. It can help you deal with many of the uncertainties that you will surely encounter.

1. Define *business risk,* and explain its two dimensions.

- Business risk is the possibility of losses associated with the assets and earnings potential of a firm.
- Business risks can be classified into two broad categories: market risk and pure risk.
- Market risk is the uncertainty associated with an investment decision.
- Pure risk exists in a situation where only loss or no loss can occur—there is no potential gain.
- In general, only pure risk is insurable.

2. Identify the basic types of pure risk.

- Pure risks that any business faces fall into three groups: property risks, liability risks, and personnel risks.
- Property risks involve potential damage to or loss of real property (e.g., land and buildings) and personal property (e.g., equipment).
- Liability risks arise from statutory liability, contractual liability, or tort liability.
- Personnel risks, such as premature death, poor health, and insufficient retirement income, directly affect individuals but may indirectly impact the business as well.

3. Describe the steps in the risk management process, and explain how risk management can be used in small companies.

- Risk management is concerned with protecting the assets and the earning power of a business against loss.
- The risk management process involves identifying and understanding risks, evaluating the potential severity of risks, selecting methods to manage risk, implementing the decision, and reviewing and evaluating the chosen risk management technique.
- The two ways to manage business risks are risk control and risk financing.
- Risk control is designed to minimize loss through prevention, avoidance, and/or reduction of risk.

- Risk financing—making funds available for losses that cannot be eliminated by risk control—involves transferring the risk to another party or retaining the risk within the firm.

4. Explain the basic principles used in evaluating an insurance program.

- Three basic principles should be followed in evaluating an insurance program: (1) Identify business risks that can be insured, (2) secure coverage for all major potential losses, and (3) consider the feasibility and affordability of insuring smaller potential losses.
- Insurance coverage required by law or by contract includes workers' compensation insurance and automobile liability insurance.
- Property insurance must cover the full replacement value of a firm's buildings and personal property.
- A company should determine for itself what distinguishes a "smaller" potential loss from a "major" potential loss and then decide if it makes sense to insure against smaller potential losses.

5. Identify the common types of business insurance coverage.

- A property insurance policy is used to insure both buildings and personal property owned or leased by the business.
- A decision must be made by the business owner as to whether to insure the firm's property using a named-peril approach or an all-risk approach.
- Business interruption insurance should be given careful consideration as an optional coverage that can be added to the property insurance policy.
- A commercial general liability insurance policy is the cornerstone liability policy for small businesses and protects against premises liability, operations liability, product liability, and completed operations liability.
- An automobile insurance policy is designed to provide liability protection for the business owner arising from the use of vehicles for business purposes as well as physical damage coverage on owned vehicles.
- Workers' compensation insurance provides employee benefits in compliance with states' statutes.
- A small business owner must accept the fact that he or she is vulnerable to the possibility of employee dishonesty and purchase the appropriate crime insurance coverage.
- A small business owner should consider the advantages of purchasing either a business owner's policy or a package policy as a way to consolidate coverage at less cost and with broader protection.
- Umbrella liability policies, inland marine policies, professional liability policies, and cyber liability policies are also available to small business owners.
- The three types of life and health insurance that provide protection for employees within a business are health insurance, key-person life insurance, and disability insurance.

Key Terms

business risk p. 671
market risk p. 671
pure risk p. 671
real property p. 672
personal property p. 672
replacement value of property p. 672
actual cash value (ACV) p. 672
peril p. 672
direct loss p. 673
indirect loss p. 673
workers' compensation legislation p. 675
indemnification clause p. 675
torts p. 675
reasonable (prudent person) standard p. 676
compensatory damages p. 676
economic damages p. 676
noneconomic damages p. 676
punitive damages p. 676
proximate cause p. 676
manufacturing defect p. 677
design defect p. 677
marketing defect p. 677
personnel risks p. 678
risk management p. 679
risk control p. 681
loss prevention p. 681
loss avoidance p. 681
loss reduction p. 681
risk financing p. 681
risk transfer p. 681
risk retention p. 681
self-insurance p. 681
partially self-funded program p. 682
specific stop loss limit p. 682
aggregate stop loss limit p. 683
named-peril approach p. 685
all-risk approach p. 685
coinsurance clause p. 685
business interruption insurance p. 686
commercial general liability (CGL) insurance p. 686
automobile insurance p. 686
workers' compensation insurance p. 686
crime insurance p. 687
business owner's policy (BOP) p. 687
package policy p. 687
health insurance p. 688
health maintenance organization (HMO) p. 688
preferred provider organization (PPO) p. 688
key-person life insurance p. 688
disability insurance p. 689

Discussion Questions

1. Define *business risk*, and then distinguish between pure risk and market risk.
2. What are the different types of risk that a business may encounter?
3. What are the basic ways to manage risk in a business?
4. Describe the different sources of legal liability.
5. Why would a business owner want to insure against "smaller potential losses"?
6. What are the common types of property and casualty insurance?
7. What are some of the key provisions that should be considered when purchasing property insurance?
8. What are the common types of life and health insurance?
9. Describe a business owner's policy, including the types of insurance coverage available with a BOP. List the advantages of this type of policy.
10. What is the purpose of a coinsurance clause, and how does it work?

You Make the Call

SITUATION 1

The Amigo Company manufactures motorized wheelchairs in its Bridgeport, Michigan, plant, under the supervision of Alden Thieme. Alden is the brother of the firm's founder, Allen Thieme. The company has 100 employees and does $10 million in sales a year. Like many other firms, Amigo is faced with increased liability insurance costs. Although Alden is contemplating dropping all coverage, he realizes that the users of the firm's product are individuals who have already suffered physical and emotional pain. Therefore, if an accident occurred and resulted in a liability suit, a jury might be strongly tempted to favor the plaintiff. In fact, the company is currently facing litigation. A woman in an Amigo wheelchair was killed by a car on the street. Because the driver of the car had no insurance, Amigo was sued.

Question 1 Do you agree that the type of customer to whom the Amigo Company sells should influence Thieme's decision regarding insurance?
Question 2 In what way, if any, should the outcome of the current litigation affect Thieme's decision about renewing the company's insurance coverage?
Question 3 What options does Amigo have if it drops all insurance coverage? What is your recommendation?

SITUATION 2

Pansy Ellen Essman is a 48-year-old grandmother who is chairperson of a company that does $5 million in sales each year. Her company, Pansy Ellen Products, Inc., based in Atlanta, Georgia, grew out of a product idea that Essman had as she was bathing her squealing, squirming granddaughter in the bathroom tub. Her idea was to produce a sponge pillow that would cradle a child in the tub, thus freeing the caretaker's hands to clean the baby. From this initial product, the company expanded its product line to include nursery lamps, baby food organizers, strollers, and hook-on baby seats. Essman has seemingly managed her product mix risk well. However, she is concerned that other sources of business risk may have been ignored or slighted.

Question 1 What types of business risk do you think Essman might have overlooked? Be specific.
Question 2 Would risk retention be a good strategy for this company? Why or why not?
Question 3 What kinds of insurance coverage should this type of company carry?

SITUATION 3

H. Abbe International, owned by Herb Abbe, is a travel agency and freight forwarder located in downtown Minneapolis. When the building that housed the firm's offices suffered damage as a result of arson, the firm was forced to relocate its two computers and 11 employees. Moving into the offices of a client, Abbe worked from this temporary location for a month before returning to his regular offices. The disruption cost him about $70,000 in lost business and moving expenses. In addition, he had to lay off four employees.

Question 1 What are the major types of risk faced by a firm such as H. Abbe International? What kind of insurance will cover these risks?
Question 2 What kind of insurance would have helped Abbe cope with the loss resulting from arson? In purchasing this kind of insurance, what questions must be answered about the amount and terms?
Question 3 Would you have recommended that Abbe purchase insurance that would have covered the losses in this case?

Experiential Exercises

1. Find two articles on small business startups on *Entrepreneur* magazine's website at http://www.entrepreneur.com. The articles should include one new firm that is marketing a product and another that is selling a service. Compare the firms' situations relative to business risks. Report on your analysis to the class.
2. Contact a local small business owner and obtain his or her permission to conduct a risk analysis of the business. Report to the class on the business's situation in regard to risk and what preventive or protective actions you would suggest to its owner.
3. Arrange to interview the owner or one of the agents of a local insurance agency. Determine in the interview the various types of coverage the agency offers for small businesses. Write a report on your findings.

Small Business & Entrepreneurship Resource Center

1. Sambazon, based in San Clemente, California, has survived the market risk of large beverage companies following it into the market with a drink using a Brazilian berry called acai. Risk management, in this case, has much to do with the product development process. Describe the three key steps of product development to formulate a winning new beverage, while reducing risk.

   Source: Heather Landi, "Hit It Out of the Ballpark: Formulating a Hit Product," *Beverage World*, Vol. 126, No. 6 (June 15, 2007), pp. 104–106.

2. Health insurance and retirement programs are two fringe benefits that are important to many employees of small businesses. After reading the article "Benefits at Risk," describe the current state of health insurance and retirement programs in most small businesses. Discuss the ways in which small businesses are dealing with this situation.

   Source: Jennifer Schramm, "Benefits at Risk?" *HR Magazine*, Vol. 52, No. 2 (February 2007), p. 152.

Video Case 23

JACK'S RESTAURANT (P. 739)

Jack, a successful restaurant owner whose upscale establishment offers signature dishes, is selling his business to two of his employees. He wishes to retain the intellectual property rights of his frozen food items as he enters into retirement, and suggests that a non-compete agreement be drawn before the sale is final. The new buyers disagree, and the deal is in jeopardy unless an amicable agreement is reached.

ALTERNATIVE CASES FOR CHAPTER 23

Case 5, W.S. Darley, p. 702
Case 8, D'Artagnan, p. 707

Nau

case 1

> Passion and Creativity Led to a High-Growth Startup That Had to Start Again

In 2005, several individuals with experience in the outdoor clothing industry met at Portland's Urban Grinds coffee shop to sketch out their new retailing concept. Their idea was to combine the eco-friendly and mountain-climbing chic of Patagonia with the fashion-forward urban cool of, say, Prada. Not only would their clothes be practical on the trail, but they would look sleek and hip in the city as well. The firm, to be named Nau (pronounced *now*), would design its own fabrics with new sorts of eco-friendly materials. Even Nau's retail outlets—the business plan called for 150 of them—would be constructed from recycled wood and plastic. The team also decided to donate 5 percent of sales to worthy nonprofit organizations that buyers would choose. The clothes would be pricey, but shoppers would feel good knowing that by buying a $40 T-shirt or a $350 jacket, they would also be supporting a charitable cause.

Chris Van Dyke would be the firm's CEO and Ian Yolles would become its marketing chief. Formerly, Van Dyke and Yolles had worked as marketing executives at Patagonia and Nike, respectively. Mark Galbraith, recently a top Patagonia designer, would be the lead designer for Nau.

The founders' timing was impeccable, or so it appeared. The green movement was in full swing, and a booming economy was giving rise to a sort of mass philanthropic movement. But Nau also had its eye on running a successful business. Stores would be about half the size of typical specialty apparel stores, with tiny inventories, representing a huge cost savings. To make these small stores work, Nau would offer shoppers a 10 percent discount at the register in exchange for Nau's shipping clothes from its warehouse directly to their homes. Customers went wild when the first stores opened in March 2007 in Portland, Oregon; Chicago, Illinois; and Boulder, Colorado.

The founders intended for Nau to be more than merely another clothing company—they wanted to *make meaning* (mentioned in Chapter 1 as one possible reason for starting a business):

> We're a small group of people committed to [using] the power of business as a force for change ... seeking to balance the triple bottom line: people, planet, and profit. We believe that doing good and doing good business are one and the same. We only deserve to exist if our products and our practices are capable of contributing to positive, lasting, and substantive change. Our goal: To demonstrate the highest levels of citizenship in everything we do: product creation, production, labor practices, the way we treat each other, environmental practices, and philanthropy. We believe that companies have a broader responsibility than simply generating profit. That's one reason we're blending profitability and philanthropy, what we believe is the new measure of success.

As an example of Nau's uniqueness, company bylaws prohibited any Nau executive from earning more than 12 times what the lowest-paid U.S. worker earned.

In planning for a successful venture, Nau's management believed that a key factor would be its design philosophy:

> We believe great design has enormous power and we're trying to use it to change the world, one sustainable fabric at a time. Our design philosophy is built on the balance of three criteria: beauty, performance, and sustainability. Far from mutually exclusive, the integration of these concepts defines a new standard for apparel. Many people make exceptional clothing that embraces one of those criteria. A select few manage to combine two of the three, at the most exacting levels. As far as we know, no one has made a dedicated effort to integrate all three with unflagging commitment to each.

The Nau team wasted no time ramping up. Among its moves: investing in an IT infrastructure powerful enough to handle $250 million in annual revenue and striking deals with fabric makers in the

Sources: http://www.nau.com/about-us/business-unusual/our-goals.html; http://www.inc.com/magazine/20081101/contributors.html; and http://www.entrepreneur.com/, accessed June 1, 2009.

United States, Hong Kong, and elsewhere in Asia. By 2007, Nau had opened five stores in Portland, Bellevue, Chicago, Boulder, and Los Angeles and had started construction on another four stores. To finance the company's growth, the management raised an amazing $35 million from private investors.

While the company was experiencing phenomenal growth, troubles soon began surfacing. On May 2, 2008, with little, if any, warning, a statement on the company's website announced that the company would be shut down. The announcement read, "Goodbye for Nau," blaming a "highly risk-averse" capital market for the shutdown. "We simply could not raise the necessary funds to continue to move forward," the statement read. "We believe this is not so much a reflection of the viability of our business, but the result of an unfortunate confluence of events." All the stores were closed, and the firm's 95 employees were dismissed.

Nau's leadership had assumed that additional financing would be available for future growth. Then the credit crunch hit. With no recourse to bank financing, the team implored its biggest investors for additional funding. But the investors who had been so generous just a few months earlier were no longer interested in investing more money in the business. "Everyone on the board understood we had gotten in too far to turn around and pare this thing down," says Gomez, then board chairman of Nau. The money was gone. The board voted to close down Nau's stores and suspend all business.

Nau's management was stunned. The day after the closure, Yolles and Galbraith contemplated life after Nau and felt a deep emptiness. "We had poured everything into this," says Yolles. "I just could not believe it would end—and end so quickly." Galbraith looked over his designs and wondered how well they would have sold. "We had only one season to get traction," he says. "If we had just gotten one more season, then we would have been OK."

After the board put Nau into liquidation, Van Dyke organized a buyout effort to acquire the Nau brand and its website. His plan was to relaunch Nau. Yolles and Galbraith, like Van Dyke, also remained committed to seeing the Nau brand and what it represented continue. "We recognized there was incredible value in the product and in the brand," says Yolles.

In addition to Van Dyke's efforts, Yolles and Galbraith set out to find a buyer who would keep the business going. They first went about preserving business relationships. "We called up factories," says Galbraith. "They agreed to hang on for a period of time to see if something could get resurrected." To attract a buyer, they decided they would need to overhaul Nau's business plan, which they realized had been too idealistic and too ambitious. Rather than attempt to ramp up a huge number of stores, they decided that Nau should grow slowly and organically. They also blamed themselves for how they had run the company. They could have gotten into wholesaling. The website could have been stronger. Perhaps they had overextended themselves by offering too many styles. No aspect of the business was left unexamined.

After dozens of inquiries, Yolles and Galbraith got the attention of Gordon Seabury, the CEO of Horny Toad, a large casual-clothing line in Santa Barbara, California. They felt Horny Toad's outdoorsy image could be a good fit for Nau. And they liked linking the Nau brand to the back-office support and infrastructure of a successful apparel maker.

Seabury's initial reaction was lukewarm: "I still wasn't clear about how we could help." But on a visit to Nau's headquarters, Seabury liked what he saw. He offered to purchase Nau, trumping Van Dyke's bid and several other bids. Seabury also agreed to hire Yolles and Galbraith, who would continue in their same positions.

Currently, Nau's line shares Horny Toad's distribution network and is being sold in such stores as Uncle Dan's in Chicago and Paragon in New York.

QUESTIONS

1. What were Nau's founders' primary motivations for founding Nau?
2. What kind of entrepreneurial venture is Nau?
3. How do you feel about management's decision to give a percentage of the firm's sales to charity? Describe the pros and cons of such a decision.
4. Nau's owners think of their clothing line as part Patagonia (http://www.patagonia.com) and part Prada (http://www.prada.com). Review the websites of these two companies. What do you believe Nau's owners saw in Patagonia and Prada that was relevant to their idea for a startup?
5. Describe Nau's competitive advantage.
6. What characteristics of successful entrepreneurs do the founders embody?
7. What mistakes do you believe Nau's management made in executing their strategy?
8. Do you believe it was a wise decision for Nau to partner with Horny Toad? Why or why not?

ACTIVITIES

1. Now that you are familiar with Nau and its history, do some research to determine the latest status of the firm.
2. Go to Nau's website (http://www.nau.com) to find stores that sell its clothing near your location. If you find one, visit the store and interview the manager about Nau's products.
3. Try to set up an interview with one of Nau's founders. The firm's general phone number is 877-454-5628. Draft a set of interview questions that address issues you learned about in Chapter 1. Here are several examples to get you started:

- When did you get the idea for the business?
- Why did you want to start this business?
- What made you take the plunge into entrepreneurship?
- What obstacles did you encounter while starting the business?
- What are Nau's competitive advantages?

Many other questions are also possible. Write a brief summary of what you learned during the interview.

video case 2 PortionPac Chemicals

> Integrity and Stakeholder Relationships

PortionPac Chemicals was founded on social and environmental principles. Since 1964, sustainability led the business, their products, their relationships, and their success. Decades before it became a buzzword, PortionPac's founders, Syd Weisberg and Marvin Klein, believed in the value of sustainability and what it meant for the environment, the industry, and the people who lived and worked in both. Built on a foundation of environmental stewardship and social responsibility, PortionPac continues to strive toward creating the world's most sustainable solutions for clean buildings.

For PortionPac, being a leader in sustainability means considering the impact of everything they do, across all operations. Sustainable thinking permeates the entire company. This orientation shows up in the company's solutions, its facility, and its founding principles. PortionPac has always seen sustainability as an opportunity: a way to differentiate itself from the competition and a chance to do their part. This has never been viewed as a hindrance or an expense—it's just the way business is done. With premeasured packaging, safer product systems, and ongoing education, PortionPac's sustainable solutions help improve people's health, the environment, and the customers' bottom line.

PortionPac believes strongly in the critical work and tremendous effort of housekeepers, janitors, and food service professionals. The firm's goal is to make effective cleaning products that offer maximum safety for their employees to produce and for their clients to use. The company also holds itself accountable to the end-user and recognizes its role in health and safety.

In the early years, PortionPac had opportunities to enter lucrative markets where toxic cleaning products were commonplace. But rather than make standard dangerous germicides, the firm's founders opted for safer alternatives. In doing so, they demonstrated that less toxic options could actually be more effective at cleaning and disinfecting. It took years, but convincing the industry to make the switch became one of the company's founding principles and underscored the owners' commitment to worker safety.

Source: Compiled from interviews and information provided by PortionPac. www.portionpaccorp.com.

PortionPac's commitment to the health and well-being of customers goes beyond manufacturing safer products—at the heart of the company's mission is education. PortionPac was the first chemical company in the cleaning industry to emphasize educational materials for the proper use of cleaning products as the most effective method to guarantee worker safety, boost productivity, and reduce error. By using international symbols and color-coding, simple to understand audiovisual materials, and interactive programming to teach customers and staff how to clean better, more safely, and with fewer chemicals, they've achieved this goal.

You won't find a separate "green" division within PortionPac because the entire company is committed to creating the world's most sustainable solutions for clean buildings. Its goal has always been to minimize the company's environmental footprint by decreasing the energy used in the production and distribution of its products minimizing the adverse effect of its cleaning detergents on the environment, and minimizing the use of improper cleaning procedures that can turn out to be ineffective or even unsafe.

Caring about the environment and putting people first sounds like a pretty good way to do business, and PortionPac demonstrates every day that it's also great for a company's financial success. While growing the firm's operations, its owners have always considered the "triple bottom line" of social, environmental, and economic balance while growing operations. They made the conscientious decision before starting the company to continually improve environmental standards and the human condition—all while remaining profitable. That's why the company is recognized today as a leader in sustainability.

As more and more companies look for green products and consider the "3 P's" of people, the planet, and profit, it's clear—whether by regulation or recognition—sustainable consideration is no longer just a smart way of looking at the world: it's becoming a practical way to run a profitable business. PortionPac helps organizations find sustainable solutions for their janitorial and sanitation needs. With over 40 years of experience connecting sustainability, accountability, and cleaning, they know the best solutions continually evolve, adapt, and improve. Because every company is different, they collaborate with clients one-on-one to create custom programs that work for them.

View the video and answer the questions that follow.

QUESTIONS

1. Based on what you have learned about PortionPac, what do you think the owners would claim to be the most important features of doing business with integrity? Do you agree? Why or why not?
2. Who are the most important stakeholders for PortionPac? What is the order of emphasis on the interests for these stakeholders—from most important and influential to least important and influential—on the company's decision-making processes? In your opinion, does this represent a wise ordering of stakeholder interests?
3. PortionPac is very concerned about the environment. Is the company's environmental focus good for the company? Why or why not?
4. Would you want to work for a company that operates according to the goals discussed in the case? What would be the pros and cons of working there?

case 3 Firewire Surfboards

> Positioning a Startup to Compete

In 2005, Mark Price partnered with friends to create a new generation of surfboards designed for both weekend waterdogs and the best surfers. The San Diego–based company that they launched is called Firewire Surfboards, but it remains to be seen whether the sport's greatest devotees will catch the wave that Price and his young enterprise have created.

Lighter and stronger than traditional polyurethane surfboards, Firewire surfboards "embody the balance between cutting-edge technology, passion and performance." The core is shaped from lightweight expanded polystyrene, which not only reduces the weight, but also allows for rapid changes in direction and greater responsiveness during rail-to-rail turns. The skin is made from an aerospace composite, a durable material that is also used to manufacture wind turbines. Other innovative and hi-tech materials go into the production of these boards, making them lighter, stronger, and substantially more environmentally friendly than traditional boards. The combined effect of these materials creates a surfboard that flexes, storing energy during turns and thereby increasing performance over traditional rigid surfboard designs.

So what's stopping the company's boards from becoming the new standard for surf enthusiasts? In a word, tradition. At first, all of Firewire's boards were pre-made and came in "off-the-rack" sizes, a practice that a certain percentage of hard-core surfers can't accept. They want custom-shaped boards. In response to this demand, Firewire decided to introduce a custom board line in late 2010.

The company's custom boards cost the same as the stock boards, with only a small upcharge of $75 to cover the extra attention required. There are over 150 models of stock boards, ranging from a multitude of shortboard scalpels to the 9-foot *Flex Flight* longboards, with a standard price of $650. This is very much in line with the boards offered by Channel Island boards (a competitor and considered the current market leader in high-performance shortboards), which sells its models for $650 to $675. Price contends that the only real difference between the two is performance, with Firewire offering flexibility and maneuverability never seen before. One reseller in New York applauds Firewire for "using technology to benefit surfers rather than its own [bottom line]."

Steve Pezman, publisher of *Surfer's Journal,* comments that "materials have always led the advances in surfboards. If [Firewire] gets into lighter, stronger, more flexible dynamics that make the performance more desirable over hand-shaped boards, then those older boards will be toast."

Initially, all Firewire surfboards were made in Australia and San Diego; however, to keep the boards reasonably priced, construction had to move to Asia. The company built its own factory in Thailand from scratch, which allowed it to control quality and protect its technology. The firm also adopted a Western style of management, creating a positive working environment for all of its employees. Product design, research and development, and testing are still performed in Australia and San Diego. Price says that Firewire's most challenging feat was the development of the step-by-step board-making process over months of trial and error. "It was unbelievably tortuous, stressful, and expensive," he recalls.

Matt Biolos, co-founder and head designer of San Clemente, California–based Lost Surfboards, liked Firewire's products enough to order 250 of them when they first arrived on the market. Rather than supplying other brands with boards, however, Firewire wants to build its own reputation and brand. Biolos kept pressing Firewire, though, until the company finally relented and agreed to make a batch of Lost-branded and -designed Firewires.

Biolos believes in Firewire surfboards, but understands the difficulty of getting other surfers to convert. "As long as we remain steadfastly spoiled with our ability to order custom surfboards, Firewire will always come in second," he predicts.

Firewire is winning over its share of admirers. After giving one of the company's designs a try, marketing manager Chuy Reyna was so impressed that he actually quit his job of 14 years to join the company in 2007. "It's rare to have that much difference in product," he observes. "This marketplace has been saturated with a level playing field of boards. This is so overdue."

Sources: Personal communication with Mark Price, Firewire Surfboards co-founder and CEO; "Firewire Surfboards," www.Firewiresurfboards.com, accessed March 17, 2011; Dennis Romero, "Surfing's Next Safari," *Entrepreneur*, Vol. 37, No. 7, (July 2009), pp. 24–27.

Teen surfing sensation Dusty Payne won the 2009 Kustom Air Strike best-aerial contest on a Firewire board, leaving an audience dumbfounded by the mesh of talent and board capabilities. Payne launched off a wave, spun 360 degrees, and landed with ease, demonstrating that video game–like stunts can be performed in real life.

Taj Burrow rode his Firewire to a No. 2 world ranking the year he was signed as Firewire's professional rider. And Biolos notes that Shea Lopez raves about a riding experience he had on a Lost-branded model of Firewire's product.

There is no doubt about the quality of Firewire surfboards; it will be up to research and development to ensure that performance capabilities outweigh the benefits of a custom shape. This is when the manufactured surfboards will stand to make real progress.

QUESTIONS

1. Identify and describe Firewire Surfboard's strongest competitor. How is this rival positioned in the marketplace?
2. Put yourself in the role of Firewire's entrepreneurial team at the time of the company's founding. What should they have anticipated in the way of competitor reaction and the response of prospective customers?
3. What is Firewire's core competence? Is it sustainable?
4. Complete a SWOT analysis for the company. Does this analysis reveal any promising future opportunities for Firewire? Will pursuit of those opportunities lead to a competitive response from current or potential rivals?
5. What broad-based strategy is Firewire following? Is this the best way to position the company? Why or why not?
6. Given the company's recent shift toward increased product customization, what do you think the major challenges will be?
7. What recommendations would you make to Mark Price, Firewire's CEO, as he thinks about the company's future?

video case 4 TWO MEN AND A TRUCK®/ INTERNATIONAL, Inc.

> Exceeding Customers' Expectations

BACKGROUND

In 2007, TWO MEN AND A TRUCK®/INTERNATIONAL, Inc., was recognized on *Entrepreneur* magazine's list of Top 500 (it was ranked at number 171), named as one of America's top global franchises, listed on *Franchise Business Review*'s "Franchise 50," and selected as one of the top 25 franchises for Hispanics by the National Minority Franchising Initiative. According to the company's website (http://www.twomenandatruck.com), it is the first and largest local moving franchise system in the United States and offers a full range of home and business moving services.

HISTORY

TWO MEN AND A TRUCK started in the early 1980s as a way for two brothers to make extra money while they were in high school. Now, over 20 years later, the company has grown to more than 200 locations worldwide.

Brothers Brig Sorber and Jon Sorber started moving people in the Lansing, Michigan, area using an old pickup truck. They had their mom, Mary Ellen Sheets, develop a logo to put in a weekly community newspaper. That stick men logo still rests on every truck, sign, and advertisement for the company. After the brothers left for college, Sheets continued to field calls for moving services while she also worked a full-time data-processing job with the state of Michigan. In 1985, she decided to make things official by purchasing a 14-foot truck for $350 and hiring a pair of movers. That $350 is the only capital Sheets has ever invested in the company. Her experience with data analysis, combined with her commitment to customer service, earned her a spot on a 1988 graduate business panel at Michigan State University. When a fellow panelist suggested she franchise her little company, Sheets decided to consult with an attorney.

In 1989, Sheets awarded the first location outside of Michigan to her daughter, Melanie Bergeron. The office was in Atlanta, Georgia. When the company reached 39 franchises, Sheets asked Bergeron to assume the role of company president while she pursued a seat in the Michigan State Senate. Bergeron is now chair of the board. TWO MEN AND A TRUCK's long track record of aggressive growth continues under Bergeron's progressive leadership and keen business strategies. Her accomplishments have been showcased on the cover of *Franchising World* magazine and in numerous other publications, including *Franchise Times.* Brig and Jon Sorber returned to their Lansing roots in the mid-1990s to team up with their mom and older sister. Brig is now the president and chief executive officer, while Jon serves as executive vice president. The first truck that Sheets bought in 1985 has now multiplied into a fleet of more than 1,200 trucks.

Customers benefit from having trained, uniformed movers who are insured and bonded to handle any home move and business moving tasks. The company has come a long way—and logged a lot of miles—since Sheets sketched the first "stick men." TWO MEN AND A TRUCK continues to pave the way for future growth and innovation, while remaining focused on exceeding customers' expectations.

The firm now has more than 200 locations operating worldwide, including 32 U.S. states, Canada, and Ireland. In 2010 alone, with 1,300 trucks currently on the road, the system completed 317,841 moves. The company reached the milestone of 2,000,000 moves in 2005.

FRANCHISING

Franchise territories are based on population, generally between 250,000 and 420,000 people per marketing area. The initial franchise fee is $45,000, or $85,000 if the franchisee has previously operated in the area. Total startup costs (including facility, trucks, equipment, and other expenses) range from $158,000 to $460,910. Franchisees pay a royalty of 6 percent of gross revenue, plus 1 percent for advertising.

TWO MEN AND A TRUCK has always focused on training its employees with the latest techniques and the best equipment available—and on treating everyone as they would want their grandmother treated, otherwise known as THE GRANDMA RULE®. Before a new franchisee can open a location, he or she must attend a two-week training course in Lansing, Michigan, conducted

Source: Compiled from interviews and information provided by TWO MEN AND A TRUCK. www.twomenandatruck.com.

by home office staff at STICK MEN UNIVERSITY®. There, franchisees are taught by subject-matter experts about the computer systems, how to market their new business, and how to hire, manage, and lead their teams. (Throughout the year, STICK MEN UNIVERSITY offers online classes that cover everything from marketing tactics to leadership to making accurate estimates. Several instructor-led courses are also available online.)

Franchisees also work in a two-story home built inside the TWO MEN AND A TRUCK headquarters. During this portion of the training, students are taught how to maneuver, wrap, pack, and load items such as a grand piano, a china cabinet filled with breakables, glass tables, a washer and dryer, and a flat-screen television. Students are expected to be able to recognize obstacles and empty the house as quickly and efficiently as possible. A truck box, built to scale, is also located in the training facility. Students must be able to fully pack the back of the truck with the items from the home.

Many other tools are available to franchisees, including detailed monthly reports, newsletters, extranet, a system-wide annual meeting, a toll-free support line, a tradeshow booth, a complete line of TWO MEN AND A TRUCK branded clothing and professional marketing materials, and a system-wide purchasing system.

Before answering the questions below, reread Chapter 4 and watch the TWO MEN AND A TRUCK video for this chapter.

View the video and answer the questions that follow.

QUESTIONS

1. Limiting sales territories is one of the common restrictions that franchise contracts impose on franchisees. Do an Internet search for TWO MEN AND A TRUCK franchises in your immediate area. How many are there? Does this number reflect the company's population requirements?
2. Which moving companies compete with TWO MEN AND A TRUCK in your area? Are there differences in their rates of success? How could you measure those differences? Are there differences in their advertising? In their rates for items such as boxes and packing supplies? Which companies have an advantage, and why?
3. Suppose that after owning a TWO MEN AND A TRUCK franchise for five years, you decided to go out on your own with a new moving company called Four Movers. What kinds of legal issues would you face?

case 5 W.S. Darley & Co.

> Sustaining Family Connections

On the firm's website, the leaders of W.S. Darley & Co. proudly declare, "We remain a family owned and operated business committed to customer service and our employees." The current CEO, Bill Darley, was seven years old when his father, company founder W.S. Darley, died. Bill's mother might have sold the business then; instead, she selected a nonfamily member to manage the company until Bill was ready to take charge. In 1960, the year he turned 31, Bill Darley accepted responsibility for the family business.

W.S. Darley & Co. provides products and services for fire-fighting and emergency services. The company was founded in 1908 and sold its first fire truck in the 1920s for $690. Today, the company offers thousands of products on a global basis. In recent years, it has sold systems, pumps, and truck bodies and engaged in design services for customers in Australia, Brazil, Indonesia, Saudi Arabia, New Zealand, and many other countries. Most recently, it began investing heavily in the development of water purification and conservation products.

PLANNING FOR SUCCESSION

When Bill Darley was in his 50s, he underwent emergency triple bypass surgery. He treated the experience as a wake-up call for the company. How would W.S. Darley & Co. survive if he died? He recognized that it was time for a succession plan. Bill, his brother Reg, and his sister Pat felt there were at least three candidates in the third generation ready to step into senior management positions: Bill's sons Peter and Paul, and Reg's son, Jeff. Each of the three candidates was given the assignment of designing a business plan describing what he would do if he were named president of the company.

Time passed, and it became obvious that Bill could not make the necessary choice. Each candidate seemed to Bill to be essential to the company. He did not want to lose one by showing a preference for another. Finally, he called on the three candidates to decide on a course of action. Should there be a co-presidency? Should they rotate the job among themselves? Or should they pick a single president? All parties recognized the sensitivity of their working relationships and the potential for a wrong step to not only damage the business, but also literally tear the family apart.

More than two years passed before the brothers and their cousin reached agreement. Paul would serve as president and chief operating officer, while Peter and Jeff would each hold the title of executive vice president and chief operating officer. Although many family businesses look to the first-born son for generational transition, Paul was, in fact, the sixth of Bill's seven children, his fifth son, and the youngest of the three executive committee members being groomed for a leadership role.

BRINGING FAMILY AND BUSINESS TOGETHER

The three COOs worked closely to develop a succession plan to help the company progress and keep other family members informed. Some specific steps that this executive committee took to strengthen the family and business relationship included

- Recruiting independent board members. An example is Steven Rogers, Gund Professor of Entrepreneurship at Northwestern University, who describes the board's responsibilities as looking "at what's in the best interest of the company combined with what's in the best interest of the family. It's not just black and white—there's gray."
- Developing a family constitution and participation plan. These initiatives anticipate disagreements among family members. The family constitution mandates relying on outside professional help in cases of serious disagreements. The participation plan contains the qualifications family members must have before being considered for employment in the firm.
- Creating a family council. The W.S. Darley & Co. family members meet once every other year as a council, usually at a location away from company headquarters. The family constitution was created in council meetings, which also serve to introduce the business to fourth-generation family members. The council is led by a family member who is not part of the COO group.

Sources: Margaret Steen, "Planning a Smooth Succession," *Family Business,* Vol. 20, No. 3 (Summer 2009), pp. 41–44; http://www.darley.com, accessed June 21, 2009.

No one believes that the company has achieved perfection. In fact, focusing on the succession plan distracted the management team from business basics; the company even lost money in the process. Some family members felt the selection process was something of a black box, mysteriously handled by the three COOs. Board meetings are sometimes characterized by serious disagreements.

A major goal of the leaders of W.S. Darley & Co. is to generate sufficient growth to create career paths for members of the fourth generation who want to join the company. According to Paul Darley, "We've really billed ourselves as 'the family business.' That translates into trust, great service, longevity—that's not easily replicable by our competitors."

QUESTIONS

1. Why do you think Bill Darley delegated the selection of his successor to the executive committee? What were some advantages and disadvantages to having the third generation develop their own succession plan?
2. What do you think might have happened to the company if the candidates had decided to rotate the president's job among themselves? What are some of the positives and negatives you would expect as outcomes of such a leadership strategy?
3. How might serious disagreements at the office affect the feelings family members have for each other off the job? What kind of professional outside help would you recommend that the family use for handling serious disagreements?
4. In addition to a procedure for resolving disagreements, what else do you think the family members should have in their constitution? Why?
5. If you were a member of the fourth generation of this family, what would you expect to learn about the company at family council meetings?

case 6 Benjapon's

> Raising Capital for a Thai Restaurant

In Chapter 6, we presented the executive summary of *Benjapon's* business plan. The full plan is provided in Appendix A. In this case, we have again presented the executive summary followed by questions in order for you to give additional thought to writing an executive summary.

Benjapon Jivasantikarn is planning to start *Benjapon's*, a Thai restaurant, after graduating from Babson College. To raise the needed capital, Jivasantikarn has prepared a business plan. The executive summary is provided below.

BENJAPON'S EXECUTIVE SUMMARY

The Opportunity

1. Thai food is one of the fastest growing food trends in the U.S. and is rapidly moving into the mainstream.[1]
2. Americans are leading a busier lifestyle and thus rely more on meals outside the home. Restaurants account for 46% of total food dollars spent,[2] up from 44.6% in 1990 and 26.3% in 1960.[3] By 2010, 53% of food dollars will be spent on away-from-home sources.[4]
3. Americans are demanding better quality food and are willing to pay for that quality. As a result, fast food establishments have recently added premium items to their menu. For example, Arby's has a line of "Market Fresh" items;[5] Carl's Jr. offers "The Six-Dollar Burger."[6]

The fast casual segment emerged to meet the demands for better-quality foods at a slightly higher price than that of fast food. Despite the immense popularity of Asian food, and Thai food in particular, the fast casual segment is dominated by cafés/bakeries (Panera Bread, Au Bon Pain) and Mexican (Chipotle Grill, Baja Fresh, Qdoba). In recent years, however, Asian fast casual players have begun to emerge in various regions in the U.S. Such players include Mama Fu's, Nothing but Noodles, and Pei Wei Asian Diner, but are still considered regional players.

Therefore, customers are limited in choices:

- Thai food patrons are currently limited to full-service restaurant options, requiring more time and money than fast food or fast casual options.
- Busy consumers are currently limited to hamburgers, sandwiches, pizzas, and Mexican food, when it comes to fast-served options.

The Company

- *Benjapon's* is a fast casual restaurant serving fresh Thai food, fast, at affordable prices, in a fun and friendly atmosphere. We will open our first location in February 2006, with future plans to grow through franchising.
- The restaurant will be counter-order and table-service with an average ticket price of $8.50. Store hours are from 11 AM to 10 PM, seven days a week. We expect 40% of our business to come from take-out orders.
- Our target customers are urban, 18–35-year-old college students and young working professionals.
- The size of the restaurant will be approximately 1,500 square feet with 50 seats. The first location will be selected from one of the bustling neighborhood squares in the city of Somerville or Cambridge, Massachusetts, due to proximity to the target market.

The Growth Plan

Our plan is to grow via franchising after opening two company-owned stores. We plan to first saturate the Greater Boston Area, and then move toward national expansion via Area Development Agreements. According to our calculations, the city of Boston can support three to five stores, while the Greater Boston Area can support twenty stores.

[1] Packaged Facts, Marketresearch.com, 2003.
[2] "Restaurant Industry Report," The Freedonia Group, Inc., 2003.
[3] "Restaurant Industry Report," Standard and Poor's, 2003.
[4] National Restaurant Association.
[5] Arby's website: http:// www.arbys.com.
[6] Carl's Jr. website: http:// www.carlsjr.com.

Source: Provided by Benjapon Jivasantikarn.

The Team

Management Team

Benjapon Jivasantikarn, Founder and Owner—Six years of experience in finance and business incentives at KPMG, a Big Four professional services firm. MBA, Magna Cum Laude, from Babson College. Douglass Foundation Graduate Business Plan Competition Finalist. Sorensen Award for Entrepreneurial and Academic Excellence.

Zack Noonprasith, General Manager—Six years experience in financial services. Five years experience in restaurant management.

Supranee Siriaphanot, Chef—Over 15 years experience as Thai restaurant owner and chef in the U.S.

Board of Advisors

Rick Hagelstein—Lifelong successful entrepreneur. Founder and CEO of The Minor Group, a marketing, manufacturing, food, property, and hotel development company in Thailand and Asia Pacific. The Minor Food Group is the Thai franchisee of Burger King, Swensen's, Dairy Queen, and Sizzler, and a franchisor of The Pizza Company, which owns 75% of the pizza market in Thailand.

Steve Sabre—Co-founder of Jiffy Lube International and expert in entrepreneurship and franchising.

Hull Martin—Former venture capitalist in the restaurant industry and current advisor to start-up ventures.

The Financials

We estimate an initial required investment of $550,000. Shown below are our summary financials for a five-year forecast period.

QUESTIONS

1. Is Benjapon's executive summary more of a synopsis or a narrative?
2. If you were an investor, would the executive summary spark your interest in the opportunity? In other words, would you continue reading the business plan for more details?
3. What do you like about this executive summary? What do you dislike?
4. Would you suggest that Jivasantikarn make any changes or additions to the executive summary? If so, what do you suggest?

	Year 1	Year 2	Year 3	Year 4	Year 5
Summary Financials ($)					
# Company-Owned Stores	1	1	2	2	2
# Franchises Sold	—	—	—	3	13
# Franchises in Operations	—	—	—	—	3
Revenue	691,200	881,280	1,977,592	2,293,859	2,874,559
Gross Profit	451,080	601,749	1,380,195	1,623,578	2,122,505
EBIT	(110,145)	74,104	129,202	363,687	525,670
EBITDA	(72,526)	111,723	204,440	430,592	592,575
Net Earnings	(138,145)	48,904	81,602	196,068	296,922
Cash	109,784	168,277	561,526	751,112	989,152
Total Equity	(28,179)	20,725	302,327	498,395	795,317
Total Debt	350,000	315,000	595,000	525,000	385,000
Profitability					
Gross Profit %	65.3%	68.3%	69.8%	70.8%	73.8%
EBIT %	−15.9%	8.4%	6.5%	15.9%	18.3%
EBITDA %	−10.5%	12.7%	10.3%	18.8%	20.6%
Net Earnings %	−20.0%	5.5%	4.1%	8.5%	10.3%
Returns					
Return on Assets	−37.1%	12.2%	8.0%	16.8%	21.8%
Return on Equity	490.2%	236.0%	27.0%	39.3%	37.3%
Return on Capital (LT Debt + Equity)	−42.9%	14.6%	9.1%	19.2%	25.2%

video case  *ReadyMade* Magazine

> Focus and Segmentation

ReadyMade markets itself as a magazine catering to GenNesters, the group of consumers ages 25 to 35 who are just settling down after college. These young consumers are buying their first houses and taking on domestic and decorating roles for the first time. They are interested in being stylish, while at the same time maintaining their own unique personalities.

But the magazine appeals to a wide variety of readers other than just GenNesters. *ReadyMade* has subscribers in all age groups—from teens looking to update their rooms to retirees looking for projects to enliven their homes. This diversity offers a unique challenge to *ReadyMade* as it tries to promote itself to advertisers who need to know what sort of people will be reached through advertisements appearing in the publication.

ReadyMade is named after the term that Marcel Duchamp coined in 1915 for a series of sculptures that playfully rethought the relationship between people and mass-produced objects, everyday items, and art. *ReadyMade* magazine is about people who make things and the culture of making, so it consists mostly of do-it-yourself projects and both short and long articles. Subscribers are invited to submit projects, recipes, and story ideas relating to the culture of making, inventive practices and people, of-the-moment cultural trends and products, and food trends.

Before answering the questions below, reread Chapter 7 and watch the *ReadyMade* video for this chapter.

View the video and answer the questions that follow.

QUESTIONS

1. How does *ReadyMade* communicate the demographics of its reader base to advertisers who want to see specific statistics about *ReadyMade*'s target market?
2. What sort of segmentation does *ReadyMade* use when it markets to businesses and investors?
3. What ideas do you have that would help *ReadyMade* reach out to new subscribers without alienating its loyal base?

D'Artagnan

case 8

> The Troubled Partnership of Ariane Daguin and George Faison

Ariane Daguin was a 20-year-old student from a family of Gascon chefs when she met George Faison, a Texan with a taste for French food. It was 1979, and they were students at Columbia University. They sealed their friendship over rowdy outings to New York City bistros, where they and their friends would pool funds to split a bottle of good wine. That is how their story begins.

When Daguin joined a charcuterie[1] company, she suggested that Faison, who had just completed his MBA, run the operations, which he agreed to do. In 1985, a New York farm announced it would start raising ducks for foie gras. Although foie gras—fattened goose or duck liver—had never been produced in or imported fresh to the United States, Daguin had grown up on the stuff in Gascony, and she and Faison believed Americans would devour it. When the charcuterie owners disagreed, Daguin and Faison decided to start their own foie gras distributorship in New Jersey. They were in their twenties and full of energy, and they named it D'Artagnan, after Alexandre Dumas's musketeer—all for one and one for all.

Daguin and Faison began the business by distributing foie gras and other local farm-raised delicacies to chefs. Soon they were selling prepared products to retailers, too. Their partnership was strong: She knew the food and could talk chefspeak (her father had a renowned restaurant in France), and he ran the business side. And their timing, it turned out, was sublime. Young and influential chefs, trained in the latest techniques, were arriving in New York, and they started signing on with D'Artagnan.

By 1986, the company had sales of $2 million. Those were the golden times, those honeymoon months of late nights and tough work and driving a clanking delivery truck around town. That was when they worked in the same office and propped each other up and argued each other down. It was going to be forever—but there are no guarantees with partnerships, many of which fail to stand the test of time. (For the sake of discussion here, the term *partners* refers to co-owners of a business, whether it's a legal partnership, a limited liability company, or a corporation—in any case, they are people with roughly the same stake in the business.)

In the early years of D'Artagnan, Faison and Daguin, underpaid and subsisting on sample products, took a tag-team approach. When one was begging farms to produce free-range poultry, the other was frantically sorting 12 young chickens for this hotel and 16 rabbits for that restaurant and jumping in the truck to make deliveries at dawn. "There was not one day when one of us did not tell the other, 'I'm quitting,' and the other one would say, 'One more day, okay? Just show up tomorrow morning,'" says Daguin. "[Still,] it was an incredibly good feeling. We felt part of a group of people who were changing the food world." And as chefs learned about the new products D'Artagnan could provide, it almost seemed that business was doubling on a daily basis. As a chef at one exclusive New York restaurant pointed out, "Now we take them for granted, but [D'Artagnan] was one of the first to familiarize American consumers with these products at a very high level of quality."

Delivering that quality required crisis management on the back end. Suppliers were sprinkled all over the country, products would expire if they were in transit too long, and chefs wanted extraordinary quality extraordinarily quickly. Faison and Daguin were together so much that arguments erupted frequently, but they had no choice but to solve them immediately. When resentment lingered, "we would go somewhere else and say, 'Okay. When you did this, I really didn't agree. So I did this because I was [angry],'" says Daguin. Perhaps because they're both straightforward and tough—and they're evenly matched physically at six feet tall—the head-on approach seemed to work.

Their first big argument came after Daguin had a daughter in June of 1988. A single mother, Daguin brought little Alix to the office to care for her, but tending to the baby's needs distracted her from the work at hand. After a couple of months, Faison,

[1]Charcuterie refers to a branch of cooking that is devoted to prepared meat products, including bacon, ham, sausage, terrines, galantines, pâtés, and confit.

Source: Adapted from Stephanie Clifford, "Until Death, or Some Other Sticky Problem, Do Us Part," *Inc.*, Vol. 28, No. 11 (November 2006), pp. 104–111.

visibly upset, sat her down and said he felt she wasn't pulling her weight—and that he should draw more salary for a while. Though disturbed by Faison's attitude, Daguin realized that he had a point. She hadn't been working the way she had been before. She agreed to let him take more salary for the next six months. After that, her daughter could be placed in the care of a nanny.

Until 1993, Daguin and Faison were still running the business as informally as they had at the start. Though they had set up the company as a corporation when they launched it, they hadn't established clear roles, which meant they were stepping on each other's toes. Advisors suggested dividing the business into two groups, which they did—Daguin took sales and marketing, and Faison took finance and operations. For the first time, it was obvious who was responsible for what. But it also meant that the partners were now separated physically and some employees were now dealing with only one of the partners. It also meant that Daguin and Faison no longer communicated regularly, which allowed problems to fester.

Around the same time, D'Artagnan's lawyer wisely suggested the parties sign a buy-sell agreement. Buy-sell agreements dictate what happens to a partner's ownership shares if he or she leaves the business. In the form Daguin and Faison chose, if a partner died, the survivor would be offered his or her shares at a determined price. "Initially," Faison says, "the idea was to make sure that if one of us got hit by a truck, we wouldn't have any succession problems." At the same time, Daguin and Faison took out life insurance on each other, so that if one died, the insurance payment would fund the survivor's share purchase. They also included what's known as a shotgun clause. If things go south between partners, the shotgun clause provides a fair price for one partner to buy out the other and a lawsuit-free way for the business to survive. For Daguin and Faison, this would become key.

By 1999, D'Artagnan was continuing to grow, but a Centers for Disease Control and Prevention investigation found that several D'Artagnan items from a single factory tested positive for listeria, a dangerous bacteria. Together, Faison and Daguin handled the problem aggressively and responsibly, but many retailers were angry. And even if they weren't, they needed someone to supply products, and it was five months before D'Artagnan was selling those products again. For the first time, the company lost money—a lot of it.

Hoping to rebuild the company's reputation, Daguin decided that opening a restaurant in New York City (a longtime dream of hers) would help. The company tended to get good press only when it launched new products, she told Faison, and this shifted too much attention to product development. Opening a new restaurant would address that issue and also further establish D'Artagnan's brand among consumers. When Daguin was able to line up outside investors, Faison thought it was an excellent idea—as did reviewers. The *New York Times* awarded D'Artagnan The Rotisserie two stars in July 2001, saying it "has so much personality, it can sell it by the pound."

But seven weeks later, it was September 11. New York's economy plummeted. And a year and a half after that, France opposed the Iraq war and French restaurants were spurned. While Faison spent his days in Newark, where D'Artagnan is headquartered, Daguin was now at the restaurant most afternoons and evenings. They both had had to invest more money than they'd expected, and they began to argue about the venture. Faison believed Daguin had pitched it as a side project, and now he found himself going on sales calls for the main business in her place, since she was at the restaurant all day. "She asked me for help with running the restaurant, and I told her, absolutely not, I had a job," Faison says. Daguin, for her part, thought that while he'd supported the restaurant initially, Faison was now showing up for a meal there twice a year. "We were in this together," she says now. "Why wasn't he in there more?" At the same time, she loved running the restaurant, and "in some ways, if he had been there, maybe we would have fought about things unnecessarily." But the business never came back, and they agreed to close the restaurant at the beginning of 2004.

By that time, though, Faison had come to believe that D'Artagnan's problems extended beyond the restaurant. Disagreements started to erupt between Daguin and Faison over matters such as incentive systems for company employees, minimum order sizes, and the number of delivery routes that should be run. In November 2004, a competitor offered to buy D'Artagnan, but the partners rejected the offer, and Daguin assumed the talk of selling was over. "After that, he didn't talk about it anymore. I should have smelled something, but I didn't. I really didn't," she says.

In reality, Faison was warming to the notion of selling. "I did not tell her," he says, "because I felt there was really no respect for the directions we had previously discussed. At that point, it was moot." The problems he'd outlined—which he thought Daguin had pledged to fix—remained, and Faison was convinced that the business should be more profitable. But, as one D'Artagnan executive observed, "[That] wasn't going to happen with the two of them running the business at odds with each other."

The rift spread to the employees. When chefs rejected items, Faison's truck drivers wouldn't alert Daguin's salespeople about the issue. Or a salesperson, deciding warehouse workers were disregarding her specs, would pluck a rack of lamb from the shelves herself. Faison used to ask to sit in on Daguin's operations meetings, but she stopped going, finding his temper too unpredictable and the meetings pointless. "The company was splitting in two, and nothing was getting done," she says. Employees could see the problems growing. "There was a dividing line," says Kris Kelleher, who, as purchasing director, would sit in on meetings with Daguin and Faison and marvel at the consistently different directions they sought. "Sometimes I wondered why it was one company." Something had to give.

On June 16, 2005, Faison walked into Daguin's office and handed her a certified letter. She read it, then stared at him, flabbergasted. He was exercising the shotgun clause and offering to buy the company for several million dollars. By the rules they'd agreed to, she had two choices: She had 30 days to sell her shares or buy his shares at the price he'd offered, with another 30 days to raise the money. There could be no negotiating. "It was—wow. I never saw this coming," she says. "And then it was all kinds of feelings: How dare he? How could he do that?" But Faison believed Daguin had stopped listening to him and was wrong about the direction of the company. He felt he was at a dead end.

Daguin retreated to a friend's beach house to consider her options. She thought about taking the money and opening a seaside restaurant. But when her now 17-year-old daughter mentioned that she might like to join D'Artagnan someday, Daguin decided, "All right. Let's go fight." She cold-called banks, which wanted a stake in the company, until a friend helped arrange a loan at a French bank. It required higher interest payments and a personal guaranty, but it didn't want shares of D'Artagnan. With that loan and personal savings, Daguin matched Faison's price. She presented her counterproposal to the surprised Faison, and the deal closed a month later. It was a very frosty finish to their 26-year relationship, and the two have barely spoken since the dissolution of their partnership. "We talked with two voices before, and it's not good for [the company's] well-being," Daguin said. "Now we're going to talk with one voice. "

And that is how their story ends. As for Faison, he now has a nice check and is considering his next move; his noncompete expired in August of 2006. "I learned that my identity is not what I do for work," he says, "and if I hadn't had the opportunity to reflect on that, I might never have gotten that gift."

QUESTIONS

1. How would you describe the entrepreneurial team of Daguin and Faison? Was it ever a balanced team? What did each member bring to the business? Can you see gaps in their skills and capabilities that should have been covered in some way?
2. What does this case reveal about the critical factors that can determine the success or failure of a business that is led by more than a single entrepreneur? What was "the beginning of the end" for Daguin and Faison's working relationship?
3. What form of organization did Daguin and Faison choose for D'Artagnan? Assess the advantages and disadvantages of the major organizational forms mentioned in Chapter 8 and decide which one would have been the best choice for D'Artagnan.
4. Would a formal board of directors have made a difference in the relationship between Daguin and Faison and the operation of D'Artagnan? Draw up a profile of an ideal board for the company.

video case 9 Cookies-N-Cream

> A Moveable Location

Cookies-N-Cream is an independent brand that sells its products from a truck that provides a moveable location and low overhead. Based in Brooklyn, New York, the company's owners, Scrills, P Loc and DJ Jon Blak, are preparing a second truck, which they're renovating and planning to move into Los Angeles sometime in the next year.

The Cookies-N-Cream brand is one that encompasses two creative outlets—clothing and designer toys—neither of which are cookies or cream. In an era of "me-too" clothing brands and toys, the owners set out to create a culture brand that draws on different influences—New York City lifestyle/culture, art, street couture, designer toys, high fashion, music, and pop/underground culture, just to name a few—all with a distinct personality and attitude of their own. Designer toys refer to toys and other collectibles created in limited quantities by artists and designers, and collected mostly by adults. Some of the toys/art pieces include the Puma SneakerHead, Hapiko, Dumny, and Shoot sculptures.

Based on their belief in being "true to yourself," the owners called their brand Cookies-N-Cream and built a grassroots company that's authentic and fun. With their attention to detail and focus on creating "playful luxury" products, they've developed a cult following that enjoys the experience that is Cookies-N-Cream. The owners represent the independent and avant-garde attitude that embodies their roots and today's youth.

View the video and answer the questions that follow.

QUESTIONS

1. What are some location advantages that Cookies-N-Cream has that a brick-and-mortar retailer doesn't have? Are there any drawbacks to a mobile vendor's choice of location?
2. Discuss site costs, retailing and office equipment, and other financial considerations of a mobile vendor such as Cookies-N-Cream.
3. What legal considerations affect Cookies-N-Cream's choice of location? How do those compare with the legal considerations of brick-and-mortar and home-based businesses?

Source: Compiled from interviews and information provided by Cookies-N-Cream. http:// www.bakedinny.com. © 2012, Cengage Learning.

Dietrich & Mercer, Inc.

case 10

> Working with a Firm's Financial Statements

Dietrich & Mercer, Inc., is an actual business, which designs, manufactures, and distributes furniture. (The names and dates have been changed for confidentiality.) The company was founded in 2001 by Stephen Dietrich and Joseph Mercer, who became friends in college. It has experienced significant growth, with sales approaching $58 million in 2011.

The firm's products, which are in the medium- to low-price range, are constructed of aluminum, light steel, and plastic. The products made by the Children's Furniture Division include playpens, strollers, high chairs, walkers, dressing and feeding tables, and portable cribs. The Outdoor Furniture Division makes two lines of chairs, tables, and chaises: one in aluminum and the other in steel. The company's offices and largest warehouse are located in Dallas, Texas; it also has two manufacturing plants in China. Finished products are shipped to a network of 18 warehouses and 6 showrooms throughout the United States by means of a fleet of 25 company-owned trucks. Approximately 40 percent of sales are to large distributors such as Sears, Walmart, JCPenney, and other national chains. The rest are made to about 400 customers, including regional chain stores and retailers specializing in outdoor or children's furniture.

The financial statements for the company and industry norms are provided in Exhibit C10.1.

EXHIBIT C10.1 Financial Statement

Balance Sheets for Years Ending December 31, 2010 and 2011

	2010	2011	Change
Assets			
Current assets:			
Cash	$ 31,000	$ 437,000	$ 406,000
Accounts receivable	7,978,000	8,856,000	878,000
Inventory	8,310,000	9,356,000	1,046,000
Prepaid expenses and deposits	277,000	288,000	11,000
Other current assets	211,000	211,000	0
Total current assets	$16,807,000	$19,148,000	$ 2,341,000
Fixed assets:			
Gross fixed assets	$15,082,000	$17,038,000	$ 1,956,000
Accumulated depreciation	(7,645,000)	(8,754,000)	$ (1,109,000)
Net fixed assets	$ 7,437,000	$ 8,284,000	$ 847,000
Other assets	23,000	2,000	(21,000)
TOTAL ASSETS	$24,267,000	$27,434,000	$ 3,167,000
Debt (liabilities) and equity			
Current liabilities:			
Notes payable to bank	$ 2,200,000	$ 2,384,000	$ 84,000
Accounts payable	3,862,000	4,477,000	$ 15,000

(Continued)

Source: Based on personal interview with Dietrich and Mercer.

EXHIBIT C10.1 Financial Statement (Continued)

Accrued expenses	1,841,000	1,768,000	$ 73,000)
Total current liabilities	$ 7,903,000	$ 8,629,000	$ 26,000
Long-term debt	$ 7,228,000	$ 8,514,000	$ 286,000
Stockholders' equity:			
Common stock	$ 712,000	$ 783,000	$ 71,000
Additional paid-in capital	996,000	1,298,000	302,000
Retained earnings	7,428,000	8,210,000	782,000
Total stockholders' equity	$ 9,136,000	$10,291,000	$ 1,155,000
TOTAL DEBT AND EQUITY	$24,267,000	$27,434,000	$ 3,167,000

Income Statements for Years Ending December 31, 2010 and 2011

	2010	2011
Net sales	$54,138,000	$57,823,000
Cost of goods sold	37,761,000	41,049,000
Gross profit	$16,377,000	$16,774,000
Operating expenses	13,611,000	13,906,000
Operating profits	$ 2,766,000	$ 2,868,000
Interest expense	963,000	1,071,000
Interest income	11,000	20,000
Profits before tax	$ 1,814,000	$ 1,817,000
Income tax	770,000	754,000
Net profits	$ 1,044,000	$ 1,063,000
Beginning retained earnings	$ 6,596,000	$ 7,428,000
Net profits	1,044,000	1,063,000
Dividends paid	(212,000)	(281,000)
Ending retained earnings	$ 7,428,000	$ 8,210,000

Statement of Cash Flows for Years Ending December 31, 2010 and 2011

	2010	2011
Cash flows from operating activities		
Net profits	$ 1,044,000	$ 1,063,000
Depreciation	1,129,000	1,109,000
Profits before depreciation	$ 2,173,000	$ 2,172,000
Increase in accounts receivable	(928,000)	(878,000)
Payment for inventory:		
Increase in inventory	$(1,144,000)	$ (1,046,000)
Increase in accounts payable	137,000	615,000
Payment for inventory	$(1,007,000)	$ (431,000)
Increase in prepaid expenses	(38,000)	(11,000)
Increase/decrease in accrued expenses	175,000	(73,000)
Cash flows from operations	$ 375,000	$ 779,000
Cash flows from investing activities		
Increase in gross fixed assets	$(1,723,000)	$ (1,956,000)
Increase in other assets	0	21,000
Cash flows from investing	$(1,723,000)	$ (1,935,000)

EXHIBIT C10.1 Financial Statement (Continued)

Cash flows from financing activities		
Increase in notes payable	$1,250,000	$ 184,000
Decrease/increase in long-term debt	(225,000)	1,286,000
Issued common stock	155,000	373,000
Cash dividends paid	(162,000)	(281,000)
Cash flows from financing	$1,018,000	$1,562,000
Net change in cash:	$(330,000)	$ 406,000
Beginning cash	361,000	31,000
Ending cash	$ 31,000	$ 437,000
Industry norms		
Current ratio	2.2	
Return on assets	12.6%	
Operating profit margin	6.3%	
Total asset turnover	2.0	
Debt ratio	40.0%	
Return on equity	15.0%	

QUESTIONS

1. How would you evaluate the company's liquidity?
2. Assess the company's historical performance in generating operating profits on its assets.
3. Describe how the business is financed.
4. Do Dietrich and Mercer receive a good return on their equity investment in the business?

case 11 Missouri Solvents

> Financial Forecasting

Missouri Solvents is a regional distributor of liquid and dry chemicals, headquartered in St. Louis. The company has been serving the St. Louis market for 10 years and has a reputation as a reliable supplier of industrial chemicals.

CHEMICAL DISTRIBUTION

A chemical distributor is a wholesaler. Operations may vary, but a typical distributor purchases chemicals in large quantities (in bulk, by railcar load or truckload) from a number of manufacturers. Bulk chemicals are stored in "tank farms," a number of tanks located in an area surrounded by dikes, while packaged chemicals are stored in a warehouse. Other distributor activities include blending, repackaging, and shipping in smaller quantities (for example, tote tanks, 55-gallon drums, and other smaller package sizes) to meet the needs of a variety of industrial users. In addition to the tank farm and warehouse, a distributor needs access to specialized delivery equipment (specialized truck transports and tank railcars) to meet the handling requirements of different chemicals. A distributor adds value by supplying its customers with the chemicals they need, in the quantities they desire, when they need them. This requires maintaining a sizable inventory and operating efficiently. Distributors usually operate on very thin profit margins.

THE SITUATION

Missouri Solvents is 10 years old, and sales and profits have continued to grow rapidly. The growth in sales has required the acquisition of additional fixed assets (warehouse expansion and material handling machinery and equipment) and current assets (accounts receivable and inventory). While the company ended last year with a healthy cash balance, on several occasions during the year it was necessary to obtain short-term bank loans to keep the company operating. Financing the additional assets has also been a challenge and placed a strain on the firm's ability to raise capital. Over the past three years, the company's debt ratio has increased from 51 percent to 57 percent.

To anticipate cash flows throughout the year, Ron Wilson, the founder and CEO of Missouri Solvents, has prepared a monthly cash budget for 2009. Assumptions are focused on the timing of cash inflow (collection of receivables) and cash outflow (payment of vendors, operating expenses, capital expenditures, financing charges, tax payments, etc.). The cash budget indicated that the company would need additional cash (additional financing) during the second quarter (April, May, and June) of approximately $2,000,000.

Wilson is also concerned about the company's increasing use of debt financing. As a result, he is reluctant to increase the firm's bank borrowing, even for a short period of time. The other alternatives he considered were

1. *Reducing inventory levels.* Wilson thought this might be possible, given that the firm had an ongoing program to systematically review inventory levels of all items and levels were slowly being reduced.
2. *Attempting to collect accounts receivable faster.* Missouri Solvents' selling terms are net 30. Thus, it might be possible to increase credit standards and collection efforts, but this could not be accomplished without some resistance from the sales staff. The sales force already feels that they are losing sales because of a conservative approach to granting credit and an overly aggressive collection effort.
3. *Postponing capital expenditures scheduled for the first half of the year to the second half.* Wilson feels this is possible, but it would require reworking the entire financial plan because the projected benefits of the capital expenditures for the first half of the year were included in the sales forecast for the last six months of the year.
4. *Slowing down the repayment of the bank debt.* Wilson thought that delayed payments to the bank could be arranged, but he was

Source: Adapted from David A. Kunz and Rebecca Summary, "Missouri Solvent: Managing Cash Flows," *2008 Proceedings of the International Academy for Case Studies,* Vol. 15, No. 1, Allied Academies International Conference, pp. 25–30. Reprinted by permission of the authors.

reluctant to approach the bank. Doing so could cause the bank to be concerned about the firm's ability to manage its cash.

5. *Slowing payments to vendors (accounts payable).* During the first two years of operation, the company was not always able to pay its vendors according to terms. The paying of an invoice after the due date resulted in some vendors threatening to stop extending credit to Missouri Solvents. This never happened, but the lack of vendor credit would have caused substantial problems. Since that period, a concerted effort has been made to avoid late payments to vendors. However, Wilson thinks that slowing vendor payments for a few months is possible, and that vendors would likely not notice a change in Missouri Solvents' payment pattern.

Income statements and balance sheets for Missouri Solvents (historical and projected) are provided in Exhibit C11.1. Selected industry average financial ratios are provided in Exhibit C11.2.

EXHIBIT C11.1 Income Statements and Balance Sheets

Appendix 1

Missouri Solvents
Income Statement ($000)

For the Year Ended December 31, 2009	**2007**	**2008**	**2009**	**Projected 2010**	**Industry Average 2009**
Sales revenue	$67,700,000	$79,200,000	$89,200,000	$99,200,000	$100,000,000
Loss: Cost of goods sold	59,400,000	70,100,000	79,100,000	87,700,000	87,000,000
Gross profits	$ 8,300,000	$ 9,100,000	$10,100,000	$11,500,000	$ 13,000,000
Less: Operating expenses					
Selling expense	3,100,000	3,280,000	3,480,000	3,880,000	3,500,000
General and administrative expenses	1,700,000	1,825,000	2,025,000	2,325,000	2,400,000
Depreciation expense	1,150,000	1,550,000	1,750,000	2,050,000	2,000,000
Total operating expense	$ 5,950,000	$ 6,655,000	$ 7,255,000	$ 8,255,000	$ 7,900,000
Operating profits	$ 2,350,000	$ 2,445,000	$ 2,845,000	$ 3,245,000	$ 5,100,000
Less: Interest expense	855,000	895,000	925,000	1,025,000	700,000
Net profits before taxes	$ 1,495,000	$ 1,550,000	$ 1,920,000	$ 2,220,000	$ 4,400,000
Less: Taxes (rate = 40%)	598,000	620,000	768,000	888,000	1,760,000
Net profits after taxes	$ 897,000	$ 930,000	$ 1,152,000	$ 1,332,000	$ 2,640,000
Dividends	100,000	100,000	100,000	100,000	400,000

Balance Sheet ($000)
As of December 31, 2009

Assets	**2007**	**2008**	**2009**	**Projected 2010**	**Industry Average 2009**
Current assets					
Cash	$ 220,000	$ 215,000	$ 265,000	$ 190,000	$ 400,000
Accounts receivable	7,555,000	8,575,000	9,615,000	10,275,000	12,000,000
Inventories	8,825,000	9,982,000	11,082,000	10,992,000	12,000,000
Total current assets	$16,600,000	$18,772,000	$20,962,000	$21,457,000	$ 24,400,000
Gross fixed assets	32,650,000	34,800,000	40,100,000	47,800,000	35,000,000
Less: Accumulated depreciation	18,375,000	19,925,000	21,675,000	23,725,000	18,000,000
Net fixed assets	$14,275,000	$14,875,000	$18,425,000	$24,075,000	$ 17,000,000
Total assets	$30,875,000	$33,647,000	$39,387,000	$45,532,000	$ 41,400,000

(Continued)

EXHIBIT C11.1 Income Statements and Balance Sheets (Continued)

Liabilities and Stockholders' Equity	2007	2008	2009	Projected 2010	Industry Average 2009
Current liabilities					
Accounts payable	$ 5,130,000	$ 6,100,000	$ 6,500,000	$ 6,500,000	$ 8,500,000
Notes payable	2,210,000	2,270,000	2,870,000	2,070,000	2,700,000
Accruals	560,000	412,000	470,000	666,000	700,000
Total current liabilities	$ 7,900,000	$ 8,782,000	$ 9,840,000	$ 9,236,000	$11,900,000
Long-term debts	7,875,000	8,935,000	12,565,000	18,082,000	9,000,000
Total liabilities	$15,775,000	$17,717,000	$22,405,000	$27,318,000	$20,900,000
Stockholders' equity					
Common stock (at par)	7,200,000	7,200,000	7,200,000	7,200,000	8,500,000
Retained earnings	$ 7,900,000	8,730,000	9,782,000	11,014,000	12,000,000
Total stockholders' equity	$15,100,000	$15,930,000	$16,982,000	$18,214,000	$20,500,000
Total liabilities and stockholders' equity	$30,875,000	$33,647,000	$39,387,000	$45,532,000	$41,400,000

EXHIBIT C11.2 Selected Industry Average Financial Ratios

Ratio	Industry Average 2009
Current ratio[1]	2.05
Inventory turnover (times)[2]	8.33
Accounts receivable turnover[3]	8.45
Fixed (net) asset turnover (times)[4]	5.88
Total asset turnover (times)[5]	2.42
Accounts payable turnover[6]	10.39
Debt ratio[7]	50.48%
Gross profit margin[8]	13.00%
Operating profit margin[9]	5.10%
Return on assets[10]	6.38%
Return on equity[11]	12.88%

[1] Current assets/current liabilities
[2] Cost of goods sold/inventory
[3] Sales/accounts receivable
[4] Sales/net fixed assets
[5] Sales/total assets
[6] Cost of goods sold/accounts payable
[7] Total debt/total assets
[8] Gross profits/sales
[9] Operating profits/sales
[10] Operating profits/total assets
[11] Net profits/stockholders' equity

QUESTIONS

1. Prepare a statement of cash flows for the 2010 projections, which will require you to use the projected 2010 income statement and the changes from 2009 to the projected 2010 balance sheet.
2. Prepare a report evaluating the alternatives and recommending a course of action. Use ratio analysis to support your evaluations and recommendation.
3. Would your recommendation change if the projected cash shortfall was for six or nine months rather than three months?
4. Is it ethical to delay payments to vendors beyond the agreed-on terms?

Moonworks

video case 12

> From Gutters to Home Remodeling

Not only is financing a startup business a challenge, but sometimes remaining fiscally fit for survival is itself a difficult hurdle to overcome. The first three years of starting a business can be the toughest, but how does a company that has been operating for several years continue to find sources of financing? Economic conditions, products, and customer bases can change, sometimes leaving a once-sustainable company in jeopardy of not meeting the day-to-day expenses of operation.

Managing cash flows invariably takes more than just matching payables with receivables, covering payroll, and paying taxes and insurance. As business conditions change, so can the money coming into a company. Even after startup loans have been retired, a line of credit or loan from a good funding provider is essential to keep a business moving forward.

Moonworks, a Rhode Island–based remodeling business founded as Moon Associates in 1993, enjoyed a modest rise to financial success by selling a product called GutterHelmet. Backed by the financial resources of BankRI, president and CEO Jim Moon turned GutterHelmet into a household name in New England by marketing it with help from local celebrities. Between 1993 and 2005, Moon Associates grew to $14 million in revenue by selling the product throughout New England, New York, and southwest Florida, while working out of a 10,000-square-foot building the company owns in Woonsocket, Rhode Island. During that time, the company installed more gutters in the New England states and New York than all other gutter companies combined.

As business boomed, Moon assembled a top-notch management team and started offering other products like garage organizing systems and hurricane shutters, but GutterHelmet remained the company's largest cash generator. To set the stage for future growth, the company's management began implementing industry-leading business systems.

The tide started to change in 2006. The market for gutter protection and remodeling showed signs of weakening in a slowing housing market, and the competition started putting a dent in GutterHelmet. There was no seasonal uptick in fall orders, and Moon Associates began exploring other means of generating operating cash, including the sale of their Florida operation. About the same time, Andersen Company's full-service window replacement division, Renewal by Andersen, had entered the Rhode Island home improvement market and was seeking a partner. After months of negotiation, Moon Associates struck a deal to be the sole southern New England partner, and Renewal by Andersen of Rhode Island soon debuted. With this partnership, Moon Associates was positioned to serve its existing customer base with Andersen's stylish, energy-efficient windows.

Yet the partnership didn't provide Moon Associates with the necessary boost. In 2007, GutterHelmet sales dropped 50 percent, to $6 million. Despite efforts to advertise on the Internet, new business leads were hard to generate. Renewal by Andersen of Rhode Island endured the normal financial hardships of starting up, and Moon Associates' bottom line went in the red after total company revenues plummeted 30 percent. Moon Associates needed something more than a new product line or division to return the company to profitability.

New England winters can be hard, and the winter of 2007/2008 was even tougher for Moon Associates. For the first time, the company's management team had to figure out how to turn around a negative bottom line at a time when business in general was changing. Moon went back to the drawing board to look for top-level talent. Local celebrities weren't the answer, so he recruited industry veteran Paul Thibeault, formerly Home Depot's Home Services northeast manager, to inject muscle into the company's sales force. But building sales would take time, and the company needed new capital to move forward. Moon Associates called on an old friend, the company's long-term financial partner, BankRI. Banker Matt Weiner and BankRI believed in Moon Associates' business plan and increased the company's credit line to keep Moon Associates on track.

The capital enabled Moon Associates' management team to play a hunch that Renewal by Andersen

Source: Compiled from interviews and information provided by Moonworks. http:// www.moonworkshome.com Written by Tim Blackwell, Freelance Reporter. © 2012, Cengage Learning.

of Rhode Island could make a dent in the Cape Cod, Massachusetts, market. Further, the company diversified its product line to include general exterior home replacement products like roofing and siding, as well as insulation and hot water heaters. Moon Associates changed its name to Moonworks and shifted its focus to being a leading regional home improvement company and began to emphasize repeat customer business instead of new customer generation.

By the end of 2008, the company had emerged from the red and had a solid black bottom line. Revenues had grown 39 percent, and cash flows were positive. Moonworks was named the "Best of the Best, Smaller Market," an award that goes to the best-performing Renewal by Andersen dealer in the country.

Moonworks continued to grow over the next two years, again receiving top recognition from Renewal by Andersen, while expanding its window-remodeling territory into Hartford and northern Connecticut. In 2010, the company posted revenues of $12.7 million, more than twice that in 2007. A crowning achievement was the company's receipt of the "Big 50 Award," *Remodeling Magazine*'s annual award recognizing exceptional performance in the remodeling and replacement contracting industry.

View the video and answer the questions that follow.

QUESTIONS

1. Describe what a line of credit involves, and explain the legal obligation of a bank to provide capital with a line of credit.
2. On what three priorities might BankRI representative Matt Weiner have based the decision to extend Moon Associates' line of credit or offer additional financing? What are the "five C's of credit"?
3. Even as the remodeling market weakened and taking on extra financing became risky, what are some things that Moon Associates' president and CEO Jim Moon did to sustain the company's long-term profitability?
4. Could Moon Associates have obtained the needed capital to not only keep the company running but expand its Renewal by Andersen line through a mortgage loan? If so, how long could such a loan be financed?

Greenwood Dairies

case 13

> So Much for Retirement

David Greenwood was 65. It was the spring of 2010, and he had just retired from Greenwood Dairies, the farm he had founded. He and his wife, Rose, still lived in the old farmhouse on a corner of the farm property, and his retirement suited her well. The couple had run the dairy and farm for over 40 years, and it was time for them to enjoy life.

It didn't take long for David to start to feel bored. Used to the early mornings and long days that the farm had demanded, he now found that he had too much time on his hands. What's more, he was frustrated with the direction that the new owners were taking the business. He began to long for the old days, when he and Rose had worked endless hours to build the dairy farm into a thriving company. So, when the owners put the farm back on the market at a fraction of the price they had paid him for it, David was astounded at the opportunity and his good fortune.

There was only one problem: How would he persuade his wife? He knew that Rose would be completely against buying back the farm. She had been at David's side, helping him run the farm since they had bought it, but she had had enough. There was no way she was going back.

Eventually, David got up the courage to tell Rose, "We should buy back the farm." She shot back, "You must be joking." Whenever David tried again, Rose would walk away without a word. Or she would simply say, "But we have a wonderful life."

She was right. The Greenwood family had owned one of many farms in Wisconsin's Carr Valley, but over the last 20 years the business had become harder to run, and most farms had failed or sold out to big corporations. But the Greenwoods had built up huge local loyalty for their brand, and the diverse selection of cheeses was a driver for their business. Also, they allowed people to come to the farm to see the cheese-making process, making it a popular destination for visitors to the "Cheese State." Then, in 2007, they sold to an investment firm that had specialty farms in other areas of the country. David had been asked to stay on for a year and help with transition. The sale had allowed the couple to put their daughters through private colleges and still have plenty left for retirement.

But David had been miserable working for the new owners. "I am not a good employee," he says. "I am a solo act." It wasn't the new owner's strategy that bothered him—David agreed with the goal of turning Greenwood Dairies into a national player—rather, it was the way they went about it that he disagreed with. The real depressing moment came when the owners decided to stop production on all but the farm's flagship aged cheddar.

Soon after David's contract was not renewed, the new owners dropped a bomb: They would outsource manufacturing to another dairy farm they owned in the north of the state, laying off 26 of the farm's 30 employees. "For cheese people in Wisconsin, Greenwood cheeses were the Holy Grail," says John Cook, a retired master cheesemaker from another farm in the Carr Valley. "If it was no longer made here, and didn't taste the same, why should we buy it?" The investment firm closed the farm down and moved the herd to the other location, leaving open a solitary office to deal with local demand.

In 2009, the farm came up for sale. David would sneak up to the farmhouse's attic, out of view of his wife, to work on his business plan, jotting down a risk-benefit analysis. On the negative side, the farm was almost $500,000 in debt (he would have to absorb the loss), the brand was tarnished, and he wasn't exactly young. Still, he had plenty of experience and energy, and with his reputation he knew he could revive the brand if he returned production to the Carr Valley.

But there was the matter of Rose, who was determined to talk David out of buying back the farm. And she had certainly earned a say in the matter. When they had bought the failing farm in 1967, Rose had been there at the 5 a.m. and 7 p.m. milkings. She had been there to help the cows through difficult births, and she had stood alongside her husband, mucking out the stalls and selling the manure. It was her idea to start the farm shop that sold the cheeses, and she had almost single-handedly turned the idea into a success.

Source: Based on Christina Rouvalis, "Case Study: When a Married Couple Disagrees," *Inc.*, July 2010, http://www.inc.com/magazine/20100701/selling-a-business-when-a-married-couple-disagrees.html, accessed March 2011.

The disagreements weighed on the couple for months. By then, their daughters had joined the dispute. "They ganged up on me," Rose said. "They were proud of the farm. It had been part of their childhood, and they wanted to save it."

All summer long, the couple argued over the decision. David was sure that he could rebuild the company and they could resell it to double their original retirement. Rose countered that gambling with their retirement was foolhardy. "We don't have the luxury of time," she would say. "It's too risky at our age." But Rose realized that there was no reasoning with David, and finally she relented, so long as he kept her out of it.

Rose had another condition as well. David could buy back into the farm, but only if he found investors to share the risk. So David spent much of the next month tracking down potential investors, but most lost interest as the financial state of the farm began to deteriorate. Then, at the end of the year, he was playing a round of golf with an old cheesemaker friend whom he hadn't seen in a long time, and they decided to do it together.

In the summer of the following year, David reopened the farm shop, with Rose at his side. "Ah, David," she said, "the deal was that I wasn't going to be involved." Then Rose saw another customer and put on her game face, greeting her inside the converted barn with a big hello. So much for retirement.

QUESTIONS

1. What type of buyer do you believe purchased Greenwood Dairies? What might have been its reasons for buying the firm?
2. What advice would you have given the Greenwoods when they were in the process of deciding to sell the business?
3. Given their age, was it a mistake for the Greenwoods to rebuy the dairy?
4. What do you think should have been the Greenwoods' goal when buying back the business?

Numi Tea

video case 14

> Cultivating Customer Relationships

Numi Tea was started in 1999 by brother and sister team Ahmed and Reem Rahim. Keeping it in the family is important at Numi. Reem's artwork adorns every box of tea. The Rahims' childhood friend, Hammad Atassi, is director of food service. Every member of the Tea'm, as they call it, is committed to the company's core values of sustainability, creativity, and quality organics. This extends to their corporate customers and their producers, as well. Like their teas, every relationship is carefully cultivated and maintained.

In recent years, demand for organic and ethically produced products has exploded. At the same time, economic influences have driven affluent and natural foods consumers to large discounters, grocery chains, warehouse clubs, and online shops. "In the positioning of our brand we wanted to target a certain type of customer base, from natural health food stores to fine dining and hotels, to universities and coffee shops," says Ahmed, Numi's CEO. "But what I've been most surprised about in our growth is the mass market consumer."

According to Jennifer Mullin, vice president of marketing for Numi, the average Numi consumer is college educated, female, and buys two to three boxes of tea per month—usually green tea. She also buys organic products whenever possible. Until Mullin joined the team, Numi had assumed its customers fit the same profile as its young staff. Mullin's findings proved that the company needed to focus additional energy on reaching older customers and moms, as well as its target college market.

To reach younger consumers, Numi boosts product awareness on college campuses, where people are more inclined to be interested in issues of sustainability, fair trade, and organics. The big hurdle with these potential customers is price. Because Numi teas are a premium product, they have a higher price point than conventionally produced teas. Numi prices range from $15.99 for 1.6 ounces and up, depending on the tea variety and size of package. Because college students have limited cash, Numi determined that it could access college customers best by getting university food service departments to serve tea as part of prepaid meal plans. The strategy has been a success. Not only do these food service contracts represent huge accounts for Numi, but they also encourage trial by students. Sampling is Numi's most successful marketing activity for attracting new users, and now students can drink Numi teas essentially for free.

For many organics consumers, the most compelling reason for drinking Numi tea is its health benefits. But while Numi is organic, the company rarely advertises this aspect of its business. Some analysts think that if *organic* and *natural* become mere marketing buzzwords, a lack of trust may arise among consumers, as some products will inevitably fail to live up to marketers' claims. With this in mind, Numi believes it is best to educate consumers about its products. "We have an in-house PR team that works with editors of women's magazines to educate consumers on tea and make sure they understand the healthy properties of tea," says Mullin. The team always follows up by samplings at Whole Foods stores or at events targeted toward environmentally conscious customers.

Numi has been fortunate to be the tea of choice in high-end restaurants, hotel chains, and cruise lines. The food service industry in total makes up about 40 percent of their business. Along with that comes added pressure to deliver on price, quality, and customer service. While the company clearly leads in quality, it is hard for any small business to compete with giant food service companies on price.

An important part of Numi Tea is its story. To tell that story, the management team needs to forge very hands-on, personal relationships with restaurant food and beverage managers, giving them a natural competitive advantage. A regular teabag may be cheaper, but there's not much else to say about it. When Atassi can conduct a private cupping (tea tasting) for the kitchen staff and explain all the different exotic teas, as well as talk about the farms and farmers that grow the tea all over the world and the company's commitment to sustainability, it's pretty much a slam dunk before the tea is even steeped. Turnover is notoriously high in the food service industry, so there's always a chance that a new chef or buyer will go another direction. Luckily for Numi, this hasn't been the case. Due in part to excellent customer relationships, it is more common for the company to keep the old client *and* follow the chef or buyer to his or her new restaurant.

Numi's success in the food service industry has driven retail business. While there are countless testimonials about customers' experiencing Numi tea at a friend's house for the first time, a surprising number of Numi converts come from restaurants. As the requests from consumers wanting to know where to get Numi in their local area have rolled in, the company has expanded to reach retail customers. Once available only at natural food stores and cafés, Numi teas can now be found in such stores as Target, large grocery store chains, and even some warehouse club stores. While good for the consumer, this poses a potential threat to the Rahims' carefully maintained fine-dining customer relationships. A problem could arise if the same premium tea served at a restaurant is also available at the local Target. So far the two channels have co-existed peacefully.

As the company grows, one of the biggest challenges to its marketing model will be to maintain the family feel on a global scale. Jennifer Mullin and her team have begun tailoring e-mail communications to newsletter subscribers to inform them about local events and are hoping to add some regional sales and marketing teams in the near future. They've also added Numi fan sites on Facebook and Twitter. The sites are monitored by a staffer to address any questions or concerns about the products. Most importantly, no matter how busy they may get, founders Ahmed and Reem will always be there, lending a personal touch through their art, personal stories, and experiences. While Numi is still fairly new, the company is expanding rapidly in the United States and enjoying success overseas as well. Whatever the marketing and PR teams do to promote the tea products—store samplings, environmental events, or partnerships with like-minded companies—they always keep an eye on the demographic and psychographic profiles of their consumers.

View the video and answer the questions that follow.

QUESTIONS

1. Do you consider Numi's relationships with its producers as important to its marketing as the relationships with its customers?
2. How does Numi use technology to enhance its customer relationships? Can you suggest other ways in which the management team can use technology to reach consumers of Numi teas?
3. What methods would you suggest that Numi use to collect customer data?

Graeter's Ice Cream

video case 15

> Product Innovation and Long-Term Success

Graeter's Ice Cream has been a Cincinnati tradition for generations. Since the days before refrigeration, the family-owned business, with its Fresh Pot process of making frosty treats, has been a popular choice among Ohioans. Since generating a loyal following in 1870, soon after the company's forefathers began selling fresh ice cream made two gallons at a time from an open-air street market, Graeter's has become synonymous with ice cream.

Ice cream was a novelty when Louis Charles Graeter and his wife, Regina, began making ice cream daily in the back room of a storefront on East McMillan Street. The couple sold their ice cream along with chocolate confections out front and lived upstairs. Since there were no mechanized freezers at the time, ice cream was a rare treat, and the Graeters had to make small batches using rock salt and ice.

As commercial refrigeration became widespread, Graeter's Ice Cream was able to produce and store more products while still servicing consumers from the McMillan street building. The business, however, took a blow when "Charlie" was killed in 1919 in a streetcar accident. In the 1920s, Regina realized that the company could reach more customers by expanding to other locations. She took a gamble and opened a satellite store across town—what would become the first of several neighborhood stores to open as the company positioned itself as a maker of quality ice cream available just about anywhere in town.

Following Regina's death in 1955, sons Wilmer and Paul took over the business, before ushering in a third generation of family leadership with Wilmer's four children. Over the next 30 years, the face of the ice cream business changed. As more ice cream makers entered the market and grocery stores became a viable outlet, selling ice cream entered a new realm. Most competitors built business on volume, and quality suffered, despite lower prices. Graeter's, meanwhile, stayed the course and continued with its time-consuming Fresh Pot process of spinning the recipe along a chilled container. Although Graeter's followed the trend and offered its ice cream in grocery stores, its retail outlets remained to offer consumers a distinctive buying experience.

Over the years, Graeter's developed a line of candy and bakery goods, but ice cream has been the company's staple, enabling the small business to gain a national reputation. In recent years, the company has appeared on the Food Network, Fine Living Channel, Travel Channel, and History Channel. A crowning achievement occurred in 2002 when Oprah Winfrey gave her personal endorsement to Graeter's, calling it the best ice cream she'd ever tasted. Mail-order sales substantially increased.

Growth has come in leaps and bounds for Graeter's. With an aggressive marketing effort and a strong alliance with the Kroger chain, the company more than doubled its number of grocery store outlets in 2009. Today, the ice cream, now available in 22 flavors, can be found at 1,700 supermarkets and grocery stores, as well as company-owned retail stores in Ohio, Missouri, Kentucky, and nearby states. Graeter's also expanded its distribution network to include restaurants and country clubs, and it operates an online store that offers overnight shipping in 48 states, including California, its largest market. Also, the company has diversified its portfolio by offering a line of ice cream cakes and pies, travel packs, and sundaes, in addition to baked goods and candies.

But the company is committed to further expansion. Graeter's recently boosted its production capacity from one factory to three, aiming for distribution to even more supermarkets and grocery stores throughout the country. Additional retail stores as far away as Los Angeles and New York are planned.

While competition continues to stiffen, Graeter's remains one of the priciest ice creams on the market, even without the shipping costs associated with online ordering. At the retail level, the ice cream is considered a premium product and commands a higher price than other brands. With Kroger as its largest distribution partner, the company has been able to build strong brand loyalty, as evidenced by a recent trial in the Denver area. Graeter's marketed 12 flavors in 30 King Sooper stores in Denver with hopes of selling two or three gallons per store

Source: Compiled from interviews and information provided by Graeter's. http:// www.graeters.com. Written by Tim Blackwell, Freelance Reporter.

per week. Within a few weeks, stores were selling an average of five gallons.

The company continues to focus on making its product available at the country's largest food stores, but its leaders are cognizant that new products, including established brands in a new market, have a high failure rate. Challenges ahead are the company's ability to establish relationships with new consumers and build brand awareness.

View the video and answer the questions that follow.

QUESTIONS

1. What distinguishes Graeter's Ice Cream from other ice cream makers and makes its products desirable to consumers?
2. While its ice cream was a success from the start, what innovations has the company made to sustain its competitive advantage?
3. Cite examples of Graeter's Ice Cream's supply chain management. Explain how the company uses direct channel and indirect channel distribution.

Dynamic Network Services, Inc.

video case 16

> Finding the Right Price

THE STORY

The Dynamic Network Services (Dyn) story is not unlike those of many tech startups. The difference is that Dyn started during the dot-com boom, survived the bust, thrived after the dust settled, and surges ahead today. Deeply rooted as an Internet infrastructure company, it began with a focus on the domain name system (DNS) and continues to expand by offering a wider range of infrastructure services.

Since 1998, Dyn has served 4,000,000 homes, small businesses, and enterprise users with a suite of DNS, e-mail, domain registration, and virtual servers. It provides customers—from the hobbyist to the *Fortune* 500 enterprise—with reliable and scalable IT services at competitive and predictable prices, through easy-to-use and secure interfaces. Individuals and companies partner with Dyn to manage their website traffic, e-mail delivery, and uptime, and to harden their internal and external network connectivity.

It has built a rock-solid Global IP Anycast network using only top-level providers and equipment and has provided it at an affordable price. "Uptime is the bottom line" for them and for companies like 37signals, Zappos, HomeAway, Twitter, AudienceScience, and more who depend on Dyn to keep their Web presence and e-mail delivery at peak performance for their users.

Like many of its Web 2.0 customers looking to monetize, Dyn Inc. has been there, done that. It started as a free service based out of a college apartment—a couple of guys with a big idea. That service, then operating as DynDNS.org, was a dynamic DNS service for a home user to host a website on a home computer or remote access back to a PC. Over time, as the user base grew and became more demanding, Dyn turned to a donation-based service in an effort to stay afloat and add complementary services. Later, Dyn transitioned to a recurring revenue software-as-a-service (SaaS) model with a suite of IT services aimed at the home/SMB market.

Source: Compiled from interviews and information provided by Dyn Inc. http://dyn.com.

Fast-forward to 2005, and its story of maturation continues. Dyn initiated a customer audit and mining exercise of the over 2,000,000 active DynDNS.com users at the time. From this, the company realized that many high-profile corporations were using its consumer-grade service. This revelation, coupled with the simple fact that the premium, externally managed DNS industry lacked options, encouraged Dyn to unveil a new brand, the Dynect Platform. Dynect was introduced to the outsourced DNS market in the fall of 2007.

TODAY

Today, Dyn Inc. has served over 14,000,000 home/SMB users on the DynDNS.com brand and has over 1,000 corporate/enterprise customers on its globally deployed Dynect Platform. The company has moved beyond offering DNS exclusively and now offers e-mail delivery services through its SendLabs brand. The days of simple word-of-mouth growth are long gone, and Dyn has become a much more proactive player.

Not only does it provide services to consumers and corporations, it also provides services to the government. All federal government agencies that have the .gov designation were given until December 2009 to deploy DNS Security Extensions (DNSSEC) for their domains. DNSSEC adds a layer of security to DNS so that computers can verify that they have been directed to the proper server, preventing the most dangerous types of DNS attacks and cyberhacking. Implementing DNSSEC is especially critical for high-risk government sites because they are often targeted by cyberattackers and are expected by users to be safe.

DNS is the backbone of the Internet's infrastructure. Without it, websites won't work, period. Once hackers have control over a DNS server, they have free reign to mislead and redirect Web users to unsafe territory. Due to the increase of companies reporting attacks of this nature, it has now become more critical than ever to implement this additional layer of security at the DNS level. Government and other critical industries such as banking, online retail, healthcare, and education are also prime candidates for DNSSEC, as they may be a larger target for potential attackers.

PRICING AND CREDIT DECISIONS

Because technology changes rapidly from day to day, Dyn experiences shorter product cycles than do companies that deal with tangible products. In a noncommoditized scenario, the company finds it easier to be flexible with pricing. As a result, each customer requires different pricing strategies. Outliers—those who are not the average customer—can be more demanding of services, but are not more costly to the company because Dyn's costs are fixed. Customers, however, are willing to pay a different rate when traffic and consistency are different. When demand goes up, prices go up.

The company does expense analyses to determine pricing. In the beginning, pricing structure was evaluated monthly, but now that Dyn is more established, forecasting is done quarterly or semi-annually, depending on client needs. Its invoice structure is annual—one year in advance—so the greatest risk to Dyn is credit card fraud.

Before answering the questions below, reread Chapter 16 and watch the Dyn Inc. video for this chapter.

QUESTIONS

1. Explain the importance of fixed and variable costs to Dyn's pricing decisions.
2. Basing your answer on the discussion of prestige pricing in Chapter 16 and on the Dyn Inc. video, how does the concept of elasticity of demand relate to Dyn's pricing structure? Or does it?
3. Do you think Dyn would benefit from offering credit to its customers?

HubSpot, Inc.

video case 17

> Transforming the Marketing Model

Brian Halligan and Dharmesh Shah, the founders of HubSpot®, met at MIT in 2004. The company is based in Cambridge, Massachusetts, directly across from the campus where it was first envisioned. Both Halligan and Shah were interested in the transformative impact of the Internet on small businesses and were early students of Web 2.0 concepts. After two years of discussions and early work, in June of 2006 the company was officially founded and funded.

The most interesting aspect of the Internet's impact on business from HubSpot's perspective is how it has changed the nature of shopping and subsequently the shape of every vendor's sales funnel. Ten years ago, if a company was interested in buying a new product or service, it started by attending trade shows, reading industry journals, and going to seminars to learn more. Early in the process, it would engage directly with key vendors' salespeople who would provide product information.

Today, that same process looks very different. The potential customer starts by googling relevant keywords. The prospect spends time on each vendor's site, subscribing to the most interesting vendor blogs, perhaps joining an industry discussion forum, etc. Relatively late in the decision cycle, the prospect engages the vendor's salespeople directly. That first vendor conversation today is much different from the one a decade ago because the prospect often knows as much about the vendor's product as the sales rep does and the prospect is already much more "qualified."

The Internet has tended to make every marketplace more efficient. Just as eBay makes the niche market for Pez dispensers, WWI shovels, and 1975 World Series ticket stubs more efficient, the Internet as a whole is making niche markets for intellectual property law, system dynamics consulting, and food brokerage more efficient. It used to be that the size of a firm's sales force was the key to finding the most new customers, but that is not necessarily the case today. The good news for small businesses is that on the Internet, no one can tell if you are a sole proprietorship or a large consultancy.

Source: Compiled from interviews and information provided by HubSpot, Inc. www.hubspot.com.

The Internet disproportionately favors small businesses since it enables them to position their niche products so that they are available to everyone who is shopping for them, regardless of the prospective customer's location. HubSpot Inbound Marketing Software helps over 4,000 customers to generate traffic and leads through their websites, and to convert more of those leads into customers. Its vision has been to provide a killer marketing application and provide great advice to small businesses, enabling those companies to leverage the disruptive effects of the Internet and "get found" by more prospects.

Most small businesses have a website that behaves like their old paper-based brochures, but just sits online. It is rarely updated, is not given significant visibility by search engines, has low traffic levels, does not encourage return visits, does not enable/track conversions, etc. What HubSpot does is transform that relatively static website into a modern marketing machine that produces the right leads and helps convert a higher percentage of them into qualified opportunities.

HubSpot focuses on tools to help the small business owner create, optimize, and promote content; capture, manage, and nurture leads to win more customers; and learn to make smart marketing investments that get results. Some of the tools it provides include social media, blogging, search engine optimization, and content management.

View the video and answer the questions that follow.

QUESTIONS

1. How has the salesperson's role changed because of Internet marketing? Consider differences in prospecting and presentation.
2. Do you agree with HubSpot that a prospect is more "qualified" to make purchasing decisions when it uses information found on the Internet?
3. How might the salesperson's compensation be different or the same with Internet sales versus traditional sales methods?
4. Should a new small business rely solely on Internet promotion? What other methods should it use?

case 18 Smarter.com

> The Challenges of Doing Business in China

In 2003, Harry Tsao and Talmadge O'Neill launched an English-language comparison shopping website, with the goal of "helping consumers to make smarter buying decisions by enabling them to research and compare products."

Tsao and O'Neill founded Smarter.com's parent company, MeziMedia, in 2001 with the launch of their first online tool, CouponMountain.com, an online coupon directory that provides users with free coupon codes and deals from online retailers. This website attracted thousands of visitors and gave the pair additional confidence in the idea that would become Smarter.com.

They began laying the groundwork for their startup, which would provide descriptions, pricing information, reviews, and images for millions of products ranging from electronics to cosmetics to apparel. In the past, MeziMedia had outsourced to Ukraine; however, this endeavor was beyond the scope of the employees that they had there, so Tsao started hunting for a new location with capable, cheap programmers. He turned to China.

Tsao's family hailed from China, and he was fluent in Mandarin and Shanghaiese (the dialect spoken in Shanghai). So, naturally he was the one who moved to China to set up the venture, leaving O'Neill to manage operations in California.

Tsao and O'Neill knew that China's inexpensive labor force could be the difference between being profitable and being just another failed Internet startup. This caused them to rush into a market they didn't fully understand. Businesses expanding into China face legal barriers, security issues, and different work environments/cultures. Often, foreign companies attempt to move operations to China in the hope of reducing costs, but they frequently misjudge government bureaucracy, misunderstand the culture, or underestimate the workforce and local competition. Tsao, anxious to get the business up and running, hired 10 engineers and editors for the new Shanghai office. However, he overlooked China's steep payroll taxes. Chinese law required his company to pay an additional 40 percent in expenses that weren't in the budget. Left with no other options, Tsao had to bear the burden of the additional $26,000 in costs.

Source: Michelle Tsai, "Shanghai Surprises: The Perils of Opening an Office in China," *Inc.*, Vol. 29, No. 3 (March 2007), pp. 47–48 *Inc.*: the magazine for growing companies.

In addition, although the Chinese employees were significantly cheaper than their American counterparts, Tsao had not anticipated the enormous work-culture differences that existed between the two countries. For example, employee turnover in China is much greater than in the United States, and Tsao was constantly training new people to replace those who left to work for larger companies.

Quickly realizing that an American approach to talent management would not work, Tsao started adopting compensation practices that were common among quality companies in China. For example, he gave each employee a meal subsidy of about $26 per month, which allowed staff members to buy a lavish lunch every day. He also employed a staff trainer to coach employees in everything from e-mail correspondence to timeline discipline, and he implemented a departmental recreation budget, which managers could spend on anything from ski trips to karaoke nights.

Tsao also found that his workers lacked initiative. They were able to spot inefficiencies and problems, and could even find solutions, but they were horrible at doing anything about them. He needed to start infecting them with the entrepreneurial spirit. He would often ask for questions at the end of staff meetings, but the lack of response was infuriating. So he started calling on people, and now he gets plenty of opinions. Bonus incentives also didn't work out—it turns out that Chinese workers prefer public recognition over private pay increases.

It took time for Tsao to adapt his business practices so that they were aligned with Chinese culture, but trial and error paid dividends in the end.

QUESTIONS

1. What is the primary force that motivated Tsao and his partner to expand internationally? Did they make a good decision when they relocated their software development operations to China? What other countries should have been considered? Why?

2. What global strategy option did Tsao and O'Neill select for their move to China? Did they choose the right strategy?
3. Do you think Tsao's adjusting his management style will make a difference in the performance of his new workforce in China? What do you think he did right? What do you think he did wrong? What recommendations do you have for Tsao that would help him improve the performance of the Shanghai office?
4. Given the details of this case and other key facts that you know about China, assess the opportunities for U.S. firms there. What features of the country should be particularly attractive to small businesses that are seeking to expand internationally?
5. What challenges to doing business in China did Tsao experience? List any issues that may present distinct problems for other small U.S. firms that may want to do business there.

case 19

Diamond Wipes International, Inc.

> Adjusting for Expansion

Entrepreneurs are often reluctant to delegate tasks to others, even when they are stretched to the limit and really have no spare time to give to the duties that they so desperately need to turn over to associates. But when the reality of expanding sales and workplace demands grow out of control, the wise entrepreneur will analyze the situation and realize that it is time to delegate tasks to capable subordinates. Unfortunately, the handoff often does not go smoothly, and adjustments have to be made—some of them painful. This is how the transition went for Eve Yen, founder of Diamond Wipes International, when her company had to deal with the pains of rapid growth. Yen tells the story in her own words.

> When I founded Diamond Wipes International, hot hand towels were a new phenomenon in American restaurants. I had moved to the U.S. from Taiwan because I wanted my daughter to get a good education, but I saw a business opportunity in the largely untapped market for disposable moist napkins. In 1995 I put together a production process, hired a secretary and brought in two machine operators who manufactured about 4,000 wrapped towels a day.
>
> The company has grown rapidly. Today our 100 employees operate 40 production lines that churn out 3 million units daily. Our offerings have also grown: We now make private-label and branded wipes that are premoistened with sunblock, makeup remover or disinfectant for use in the cosmetics, health-care and janitorial industries.
>
> The changes have been exciting but also nerve-racking. Between 2002 and 2003 sales increased 82%, to $9 million. By 2006, I had started to worry that the company might not be able to cope with more expansion. Our small sales team was overworked, interdepartmental communication was poor, and I had no way to monitor every worker's daily performance. Meanwhile, our inventory system was inefficient; paperwork was often duplicated, and some parts of the system were too dependent on manual processes, which led to costly mistakes.
>
> One time the sales and art departments created a new custom package design for a client. Somehow that information never reached the warehouse, where employees kept ordering the old packaging. That error cost us 200 cases of wipes—and the goodwill of the client, whose delivery was severely delayed. Similar incidents happened two or three times a year, costing us about $100,000 annually.
>
> I decided to take action. In late 2006 I hired a general manager and told him that his mission was to turn the company into a well-oiled machine. I asked him to coordinate the work of all departments, to make sure they communicated with one another and to report to me on their performance.
>
> That was just the beginning. Within a few months I had hired three new department managers and four office assistants. In February 2007 I installed a new computer system and put the entire staff through multiple training sessions to learn how to use it. As if that weren't enough to deal with, I also redesigned the packaging for my La Fresh brand.
>
> It was a chaotic year. My ideas were good but poorly implemented. No one had time to train the department heads—they had to learn on the job. And the office assistants had been hired hastily because I needed more staff to answer the phones. But their tasks also included inputting orders, which required attention to detail. Three of them, it turned out, were not up to the job, and I had to let them go.
>
> My general manager was less effective than I'd hoped. He was a good guy, but he had trouble enforcing deadlines. As a result, I didn't get the reports or see the

Source: Eve Yen, "Delegate Smart," from *Fortune*, April 4, 2009.

numbers I expected from him. Sometimes I felt as if I didn't know what was going on. Eventually I let him go, too.

That year was costly, both in stress and in dollars (all the hiring and firing probably set us back about $150,000). But it helped me view things differently. With hindsight, I could see that the general manager's failures reflected some of my own. I realized that it wasn't enough to be the entrepreneurial, creative force behind my company. If I didn't learn how to manage my own organization, it would fail.

I stepped in and took back control. I did some research and decided which key numbers I wanted to see from each department every day, such as the defect rate. Those are the figures we now use to understand each department's daily performance. We routinely make adjustments to improve them.

Over the past two years, I've trained myself to be a decent general manager. I'm still planning to hire someone for the job, but at least now I know exactly what to ask of him or her. I've also learned to prioritize my to-do list. We may need more of everything, but more of everything at once is not a good idea.

Here's the irony: After we jumped through all those hoops to prepare the company for growth, our 2008 sales were flat at $15 million, largely because the price of raw materials skyrocketed unexpectedly and then the economy tanked.

This year, however, I'm aiming to increase sales by 15%. I think my firm and I are ready for it. Growing without chaos is difficult, but we're building the systems that will keep us on track.

QUESTIONS

1. Based on what you've just read, how would you rate the leadership skills of Eve Yen? In what ways does she fit the profile of the typical business founder? In what ways is she different? How would you describe her leadership style?
2. Do you think Yen has the capacity to make the transition from founder to general manager of a now-sizable company?
3. How would you rate Yen's delegation skills? Was her timing appropriate for the handoff of responsibilities to a general manager? Was she too quick to take back delegated responsibilities? Is she too quick to terminate employees?
4. What outside sources of management assistance might help Diamond Wipes International reach its full potential?

case 20 Salary Envy

> Compensation Practices and Employee Commitment

As you learned in Chapter 20, a small company's employees can easily make or break the business. That's why it is so important to recruit, select, and train workers well. But perhaps no feature of a firm's human resource management program can spoil morale and drag down employee performance faster than flawed compensation practices. That's why the observations of "Employee X," reported below, are so important to consider.

> I make enough money to live a relatively comfortable life. I don't need the finer things to make me happy. So why is it that I often find myself obsessing over my salary? Why am I dying to know how much money my co-workers make? I'd like to think it has less to do with my greediness and more to do with my sense of fairness.
>
> At each job I've quit, my salary has left me feeling cheated to some extent. In my first job out of college, I made a little more than $30,000 and was thrilled about my steady income. I loved my job: the people, the laid-back atmosphere, the work I was doing. However, my excitement quickly began to fade after checking a salary comparison website. I realized that workers in my position and location were making twice as much as I was. And apparently I wasn't the only one being underpaid, as other disgruntled employees "joked" about how little our company paid. Soon, a couple of co-workers left the company and reported back that they were earning tens of thousands of dollars more to do the same work. I knew then that as comfortable as I was at that job, I really was getting played for a fool.
>
> So I was determined to get a good salary bump with my next job. After the recruiter assured me that raises were common and the stock options were going to be worth a lot, I accepted an offer that was only slightly higher than my previous salary. Still, I couldn't help but feel bitter from Day One. It only got worse as rumors spread that newer hires were getting paid a lot more than the veterans. I reached my breaking point when I learned that a co-worker I trained and supervised (and was honestly not a great employee) was making about $20,000 more than me.
>
> At my current job, I finally get paid what I feel is fair compensation. Others get paid more than I do, but it doesn't bother me because they actually deserve it. Even in this tight job market of layoffs, pay cuts and raise freezes, employees still seek fairness. Employers should not give huge salaries to some and low salaries to others without justification. With all the available information out there—whether it's office rumors, friends in the industry or websites disclosing salary information—if employees are grossly underpaid, they'll find out. And if they feel slighted, it won't be long before they look somewhere else for some fairness.

Source: Employee X, "Salary Envy," *Entrepreneur,* Vol. 37, No. 6 (June 2009), p. 58.

QUESTIONS

1. Employee X felt cheated in previous jobs, but was his or her attitude justified? After all, the hiring companies made offers that he or she willingly accepted and considered fair (at least at first). Is there anything unethical about the compensation practices followed by these employers?
2. What should be the goal of a compensation program? What are the likely outcomes of offering inadequate pay to employees?
3. Critique the compensation practices of the first employer mentioned. The salary offered was obviously limited. Did the company offer any offsetting benefits? If so, did these justify the limited pay?
4. Critique the compensation practices of the second employer mentioned. The salary offered was much higher, but Employee X was still very dissatisfied. What was the problem? Should the company fix the problem? If so, how?

5. Critique the compensation practices of the last employer mentioned. The salary offered varies from employee to employee, and Employee X seems to accept this. But, as a general practice, do you think it is ever wise to offer different levels of salary to different employees who have similar jobs in the firm?

video case 21 River Pools & Spas

> Managing Operations in a Challenging Economy

In 2001, 23-year-old Jason Hughes was working part-time on a construction crew for Jim Spiess, owner of Prestige Builders of Lancaster, Virginia. Impressed with Hughes's work ethic and capacity to learn, Spiess asked him to consider taking a full-time position with his firm. The only problem was that Hughes would trade building homes each summer for building swimming pools, something he had been doing since his teens. Hughes told Spiess that if he had the financial backing, he would start his own pool company. This sparked Spiess's interest, and he asked Hughes to put some numbers together. What quickly followed was River Pools & Spas' first business plan.

The plan was just enough to give Spiess and Hughes the necessary enthusiasm and vision to start what today has become one of the premier pool and spa companies in the Maryland/Virginia area. During their first year, they installed a handful of pools, and 2002 was a year of solid growth, during which they installed about 40 pools. Despite record rainfall in 2003 and 2004, River Pools still grew in leaps and bounds, and by the end of 2004 the business model changed focus. They decided to move away from installing vinyl-liner above-ground and inground pools. Although they would still offer above-ground pools and spas, there was now an understanding within the company that, based on industry surveys, customers wanted a pool with low maintenance, longevity and exceptional warranties, and aesthetic appeal.

The only pool with these qualities is fiberglass/composite, and so the change was made. The renewed focus brought about more record years from 2005 throughout 2007. Such growth put River Pools & Spas in the top 5 percent of all inground pool companies in the country. It has also established the most popular and informative educational blog and video library in the swimming pool industry, showing the owners' commitment to excellence. Both of the owners are very family-oriented and believe they owe their success to moral values, great employees, dedicated customers, quality, service, and integrity.

Source: Compiled from interviews and information provided by River Pools & Spas. http://www.riverpoolsandspas.com. © 2012, Cengage Learning.

BEATING THE ODDS AND THE ECONOMY

In 2005, River Pools & Spas had over 75 inground pool installations, 20 full-time employees, and a beautiful new 10,000-square-foot showroom/warehouse in Tappahannock, Virginia. Despite being a down-year for many companies, 2006 continued to show great promise for the future of the company, with another 80 inground pools being installed in the area. The following year was River Pools & Spas' greatest accomplishment to date. In an industry that had started to decline in most states due to the slow housing market, River Pools & Spas continued to demonstrate strong growth. Its final results in 2007 were 88 fiberglass pool installations.

Spiess and Hughes had a good system until the economy crashed. They were making plenty of money but had far too many employees and started to lose ground. They're now down to six employees: a bookkeeper, an office manager, two production managers—one of whom doubles as the service manager—and two installation crews.

They had been renting space at a retail location at $8,000 per month, so they bought their own building and closed up the retail space, which was break-even at best. Their current office is a big metal building with a warehouse and five offices, and an empty showroom. After the brick-and-mortar plan was deemed too expensive, they moved everything to the Web, and this became their new storefront. They now have the world-leader website for fiberglass pools and get requests from Utah to Costa Rica.

Such growth has put River Pools & Spas in the top 5 percent of all inground pool companies in the country. One might assume that this growth has hurt quality, but that is clearly not the case when every potential customer receives a reference list with every inground pool customer (over 550) the company has ever installed a pool for, including the homeowner's name, address, and telephone number.

View the video and answer the questions that follow.

QUESTIONS

1. Review the history of the operations of River Pools & Spas, from start to success, to scaling back. How was the company affected by

scaling back? What changes made it more competitive?

2. Describe how River Pools & Spas' customer focus affects the business. What can the owners do to ensure that the quality of their products and services remains high?

3. Does this company use a synchronous management approach?

case 22 Pearson Air Conditioning & Service

> Managing a Firm's Working Capital

Scott and Bob Pearson, father and son, are the owners of Pearson Air Conditioning & Service, based in Dallas, Texas. Scott serves as president, and Bob as general manager. The firm sells General Electric, Carrier, and York air-conditioning and heating systems to both commercial and residential customers and services these and other types of systems. Although the business has operated successfully since the Pearsons purchased it in 2002, it continues to experience working-capital problems.

PEARSON'S FINANCIAL PERFORMANCE

The firm has been profitable under the Pearsons' ownership. In fact, profits for 2009 were the highest for any year to date. Exhibit C22.1 shows the income statement for the year ending December 31, 2009.

The balance sheet as of December 31, 2009, is presented in Exhibit C22.2. Note that the firm's total debt now exceeds the owners' equity. However, \$10,737 of the firm's liabilities was a long-term note payable to a stockholder. This note was issued at the time the Pearsons purchased the business, with payments going to the former owner.

PEARSON'S CASH BALANCE

Pearson Air Conditioning & Service currently has a cash balance in excess of \$28,000. The owners have a policy of maintaining a minimum cash balance of \$15,000, which allows them to "sleep well at night." Recently, Bob has thought that they would still be able to "breathe comfortably" as long as they kept a minimum balance of \$10,000.

PEARSON'S ACCOUNTS RECEIVABLE

The accounts receivable at the end of 2009 were \$56,753, but at times during the year, receivables could be twice this amount. These accounts receivable were not aged, so the firm had no specific knowledge of the number of overdue accounts. However, the firm had never experienced any significant loss from bad debts. The accounts receivable were thought, therefore, to be good accounts of a relatively recent nature.

Customers were given 30 days from the date of the invoice to pay the net amount. No cash discounts were offered. If payment was not received during the first 30 days, a second statement was mailed to the customer and monthly carrying charges of 1/10 of 1 percent were added.

On small residential jobs, the firm tried to collect from customers when the work was completed. When a service representative finished repairing an airconditioning system, for example, he or she presented a bill to the customer and attempted to obtain payment at that time. However, this was not always possible. On major items, such as unit changeouts—which often ran as high as \$2,500—billing was almost always necessary.

On new construction projects, the firm sometimes received partial payments prior to completion, which helped to minimize the amount tied up in receivables.

EXHIBIT C22.1 Income Statement for Pearson Air Conditioning & Service for the Year Ending December 31, 2009

Sales revenue	\$727,679
Cost of goods sold	466,562
Gross profit	\$261,117
Selling, general, and administrative expenses (including interest expense)	189,031
Profits before tax	\$ 72,086
Income tax	17,546
Net profits	\$ 54,540

Source: William J. Petty. © 2009, Cengage Learning.

EXHIBIT C22.2 Balance Sheet for Pearson Air Conditioning & Service as of December 31, 2009

Assets	
Current assets:	
Cash	$ 28,789
Accounts receivable	56,753
Inventory	89,562
Prepaid expenses	4,415
Total current assets	$179,519
Loans to stockholders	41,832
Autos, trucks, and equipment, at cost, less accumulated depreciation of $36,841	24,985
Other assets	16,500
Total assets	$262,836
Debt (Liabilities) and Equity	
Current debt:	
Current maturities of long-term notes payable*	$ 26,403
Accounts payable	38,585
Accrued payroll taxes	2,173
Income tax payable	13,818
Other accrued expenses	4,001
Total current debt	$ 84,980
Long-term notes payable*	51,231
Total stockholders' equity	126,625
Total debt and equity	$262,836

*Current and long-term portions of notes payable:

	Current	Long-Term	Total
• 10% note payable, secured by pickup, due in monthly installments of $200, including interest	$ 1,827	$ 1,367	$ 3,194
• 10% note payable, secured by equipment, due in monthly installments of $180, including interest	584	0	584
• 6% note payable, secured by inventory and equipment, due in monthly installments of $678, including interest	6,392	39,127	45,519
• 9% note payable to stockholder	0	10,737	10,737
• 12% note payable to bank in 30 days	17,600	0	17,600
	$26,403	$51,231	$77,634

PEARSON'S INVENTORY

Inventory accounted for a substantial portion of the firm's working capital. It consisted of the various heating and air-conditioning units, parts, and supplies used in the business.

The Pearsons had no guidelines or industry standards to use in evaluating their overall inventory levels. They believed that there *might* be some excessive inventory, but, in the absence of a standard, this was basically an opinion. When pressed to estimate the amount that might be eliminated by careful control, Scott pegged it at 15 percent.

The firm used an annual physical inventory that coincided with the end of its fiscal year. Since the inventory level was known for only one time in the year, the income statement could be prepared only on an annual basis. There was no way of knowing how much of the inventory had been used at other points and, thus, no way to calculate profits. As a result, the Pearsons lacked quarterly or monthly income statements to assist them in managing the business.

Scott and Bob had been considering changing from a physical inventory to a perpetual inventory system, which would enable them to know the inventory levels of all items at all times. An inventory total could easily be computed for use in preparing statements. Shifting to a perpetual inventory system would require that they purchase new computer software. However, the cost of such a system would not constitute a major barrier. A greater expense would be involved in the maintenance of the system—entering all incoming materials and all withdrawals. The Pearsons estimated that this task would necessitate the work of one person on a half-time or three-fourths-time basis.

PEARSON'S NOTE PAYABLE TO THE BANK

Bank borrowing was the most costly form of credit. The firm paid the going rate, slightly above prime, and owed $17,600 on a 90-day renewable note. Usually, some of the principal was paid when the note was renewed. The total borrowing could probably be increased if necessary. There was no obvious pressure from the bank to reduce borrowing to zero. The amount borrowed during the year typically ranged from $10,000 to $25,000.

The Pearsons had never explored the limits the bank might impose on borrowing, and there was no clearly specified line of credit. When additional funds were required, Scott simply dropped by the bank, spoke with a bank officer (who also happened to be a friend), and signed a note for the appropriate amount.

PEARSON'S ACCOUNTS PAYABLE

A significant amount of Pearson's working capital came from its trade accounts payable. Although accounts payable at the end of 2009 were $38,585, payables varied over time and might be double this amount at another point in the year. Pearson obtained from various dealers such supplies as expansion valves, copper tubing, sheet metal, electrical wire, and electrical conduit. Some suppliers offered a discount for cash (2/10, net 30), but Bob felt that establishing credit was more important than saving a few dollars by taking a cash discount. By giving up the cash discount, the firm obtained the use of the money for 30 days. Although the Pearsons could stretch the payment dates to 45 or even 60 days before being "put on C.O.D.," they found it unpleasant to delay payment more than 45 days because suppliers would begin calling and applying pressure for payment.

Their major suppliers (Carrier, General Electric, and York) used different terms of payment. Some large products could be obtained from Carrier on an arrangement known as "floor planning," meaning that the manufacturer would ship the products without requiring immediate payment. The Pearsons made payment only when the product was sold. If still unsold after 90 days, the product had to be returned or paid for. (It was shipped back on a company truck, so no expense was incurred in returning unsold items.) On items that were not floor-planned but were purchased from Carrier, Pearson paid the net amount by the 10th of the month or was charged 18 percent interest on late payments.

Shipments from General Electric required payment at the bank soon after receipt of the products. If cash was not available at the time, further borrowing from the bank became necessary.

Purchases from York required net payment without discount within 30 days. However, if payment was not made within 30 days, interest at 18 percent per annum was added.

CAN GOOD PROFITS BECOME BETTER?

Although Pearson Air Conditioning & Service had earned a good profit in 2009, the Pearsons wondered whether they were realizing the *greatest possible* profit. The slowdown in the construction industry during 2009 was currently affecting their business. They wanted to be sure they were meeting the challenging times as prudently as possible.

QUESTIONS

1. Evaluate the overall performance and financial structure of Pearson Air Conditioning & Service.
2. What are the strengths and weaknesses in this firm's management of accounts receivable and inventory?
3. Should the firm reduce or expand the amount of its bank borrowing?
4. Evaluate Pearson's management of accounts payable.
5. Calculate Pearson's cash conversion period. Interpret your computation.
6. How could Pearson Air Conditioning & Service improve its working-capital situation?

Jack's Restaurant

case 23

> Intellectual Property Rights

Jack, a successful restaurant owner whose upscale establishment offers signature dishes, is selling his business to two of his employees—Sophia, his sous chef, and Hal, the maître d'. Jack's Place is a trendy neighborhood restaurant and bar that has a loyal customer base built from a frozen food line created by Jack and Sophia over the years from the restaurant's fresh menu.

Sophia and Hal are eager to purchase the restaurant and operate it under the same name, featuring the same dishes, frozen food line, and level of service that Jack's Place customers have come to expect. Sophia is a long-time employee who helped develop some of the signature dishes that made Jack's Place a popular destination in the neighborhood. A favorite dish is her Scaloppine al Marsala, which is based on a Sicilian family recipe.

As contract negotiations begin, Jack tells Sophia and Hal that he wishes to retain the intellectual property rights to the frozen food items as he enters into retirement. While he has no plans to open another restaurant, Jack believes that at some point he may want to market those dishes during his retirement for some residual income. Therefore, he suggests that a confidentiality agreement be drawn before the sale is final.

Sophia and Hal, who wish to continue operating Jack's Place under its existing business plan, feel that if Jack keeps the rights to the frozen food items the future success of the restaurant could be compromised. If Jack's Place can't offer the same food items that have enabled the business to succeed in years past, then the restaurant could lose its customer base. And if Jack would use the recipes—including Sophia's Scaloppine al Marsala—to open another restaurant, then Jack's Place would surely fail.

Ten years ago, when Sophia began working for Jack, the restaurant didn't offer the frozen food line. Over the years, she worked closely with Jack to develop the dishes, offering her own blends of spices and herbs. Therefore, she believes that she shares some intellectual property rights to the recipes. Jack, however, contends that Sophia doesn't have any rights because, as an employer, he paid her to help develop that product line. The recipes, Jack says, are his trade secrets.

While Jack insists that he isn't going to open another restaurant, Sophia and Hal believe they need protection if they agree to let Jack retain the rights to the recipes. On the advice of his brother-in-law, who is a lawyer, Hal suggests that a noncompete agreement be drawn up to protect the new buyers against competition from their former employer. The agreement would prohibit Jack from opening a restaurant within a 10-mile radius for five years. Should Jack default on the agreement, then Hal and Sophia would have grounds for legal action.

Jack contends that signing a noncompete agreement would be foolish on his part, because he doesn't know what the next five years will bring. Sophia and Hal believe it would be equally crazy on their part to buy the restaurant without its frozen food line and allow Jack to have the signature dishes and possibly to compete against them.

The seller and buyers are at an impasse. The deal is in jeopardy unless an amicable agreement is reached.

View the video and answer the questions that follow.

QUESTIONS

1. Do Sophia and Hal have valid grounds for asking Jack to sign a noncompete agreement?
2. Assume Jack signs the noncompete agreement. Two years later, he opens a restaurant five miles away. If Hal then sues for breach of the noncompete, what arguments might Jack raise?
3. Are Hal and Sophia's demands reasonable? Do you think the recipes constitute trade secrets?
4. What compromise might be met that would be legal, ethical, and fair? Can you think of a business solution that would help Jack, Hal, and Sophia resolve their differences?

Source: Based on Business Law Digital Video Library, Real World Legal series, video #77. Written by Tim Blackwell, Freelance Reporter.

Sample Business Plan

APPENDIX A

Business Plan

September 2005

Prepared by Benjapon Jivasantikarn

Source: Used by permission of Benjapon's.

Table of Contents

CONFIDENTIAL

I. Executive Summary

1.1 THE OPPORTUNITY

1) Thai food is one of the fastest growing food trends in the U.S. and is rapidly moving into the mainstream.[1]

2) Americans are leading a busier lifestyle and thus rely more on meals outside the home. Restaurants account for 46% of total food dollars spent,[2] up from 44.6% in 1990 and 26.3% in 1960.[3] By 2010, 53% of food dollars will be spent on away-from-home sources.[4]

3) Americans are demanding better quality food and are willing to pay for that quality. As a result, fast food establishments have recently added premium items to their menu. For example, Arby's has a line of "Market Fresh" items;[5] Carl's Jr. offers "The Six Dollar Burger."[6]

The fast casual segment emerged to meet the demands for better-quality foods at a slightly higher price than that of fast food. Despite the immense popularity of Asian food, and Thai food in particular, the fast casual segment is dominated by cafes/bakeries (Panera Bread, Au Bon Pain) and Mexican (Chipotle Grill, Baja Fresh, Qdoba). In recent years, however, Asian fast casual players have begun to emerge in various regions in the U.S. Such players include Mama Fu's, Nothing but Noodles, and Pei Wei Asian Diner, but are still considered regional players.

Therefore, customers are limited in choices:

- Thai food patrons are currently limited to full-service restaurant options, requiring more time and money than fast food or fast casual options.
- Busy consumers are currently limited to hamburgers, sandwiches, pizzas, and Mexican, when it comes to fast-served options.

1.2 THE COMPANY

- *Benjapon's* is a fast-casual restaurant serving fresh Thai food, fast, at affordable prices, in a fun and friendly atmosphere. We will open our first location in February 2006, with future plans to grow through franchising.
- The restaurant will be counter-order and table-service with an average ticket price of $8.50. Store hours are from 11am–10pm, seven days a week. We expect 40% of our business to come from take-out orders.
- The company will offer Thai culture and food "information fun facts" on the menu, the packaging, and as part of the restaurant décor to enhance the overall experience.
- Our target customers are urban, 18–35 year-old college students and young working professionals.

[1] Packaged Facts, Marketresearch.com, 2003.
[2] "Restaurant Industry Report," The Freedonia Group, Inc. 2003.
[3] "Restaurant Industry Report" Standard and Poor's, 2003.
[4] National Restaurant Association
[5] Arby's website: www.arbys.com
[6] Carl's Jr. website: www.carlsjr.com

CONFIDENTIAL

- The size of the restaurant will be approximately 1,500 square feet with 50 seats. The first location will be selected from one of the bustling neighborhood squares in the cities of Somerville or Cambridge, Massachusetts, due to proximity to the target market.

1.3 THE GROWTH PLAN

Our plan is to grow via franchising after opening two company-owned stores. We plan to first saturate the Greater Boston Area, and move towards national expansion via Area Development Agreements. According to our calculations, the city of Boston can support three to five stores, while the Greater Boston Area can support twenty stores.

1.4 THE TEAM

Management Team:

Benjapon Jivasantikarn, Founder and Owner—Six years of experience in finance and business incentives at KPMG, a Big Four professional services firm. MBA, Magna Cum Laude, from Babson College. Douglass Foundation Graduate Business Plan Competition Finalist. Sorensen Award for Entrepreneurial and Academic Excellence.

Zack Noonprasith, General Manager—Six years experience in financial services. Five years experience in restaurant management.

Supranee Siriaphanot, Chef—Over 15 years experience as Thai restaurant owner and chef in the U.S.

Board of Advisors:

Rick Hagelstein—Lifelong successful entrepreneur. Founder and CEO of The Sigma Food Group, a marketing, manufacturing, food, property, and hotel development company in the Asia Pacific. The Sigma Food Group is the Asia Pacific franchisee of several major U.S. fast-food chains.

Steve Sabre—Co-founder of Fast Lube, Inc. and expert in entrepreneurship and franchising.

Hull Martin—Former venture capitalist in the restaurant industry and current advisor to start-up ventures.

1.5 THE FINANCIALS

We estimate an initial required investment of $550,000. The following are our summary financials for a five-year forecast period.

	Year 1	Year 2	Year 3	Year 4	Year 5
Summary Financials ($)					
# Company-Owned Stores	1	1	2	2	2
# Franchises Sold	—	—	—	3	13
# Franchises in Operations	—	—	—	—	3
Revenue	691,200	881,280	1,977,592	2,293,859	2,874,559
Gross Profit	451,080	601,749	1,380,195	1,623,578	2,122,505
EBIT	(110,145)	74,104	129,202	363,687	525,670
EBITDA	(72,526)	111,723	204,440	430,592	592,575
Net Earnings	(138,145)	48,904	81,602	196,068	296,922
Cash	109,784	168,277	561,526	751,112	989,152
Total Equity	(28,179)	20,725	302,327	498,395	795,317
Total Debt	350,000	315,000	595,000	525,000	385,000

CONFIDENTIAL

	Year 1	Year 2	Year 3	Year 4	Year 5
Profitability					
Gross Profit %	65.3%	68.3%	69.8%	70.8%	73.8%
EBIT %	−15.9%	8.4%	6.5%	15.9%	18.3%
EBITDA %	−10.5%	12.7%	10.3%	18.8%	20.6%
Net Earnings %	−20.0%	5.5%	4.1%	8.5%	10.3%
Returns					
Return on Assets	−37.1%	12.2%	8.0%	16.8%	21.8%
Return on Equity	490.2%	236.0%	27.0%	39.3%	37.3%
Return on Capital (LT Debt + Equity)	−42.9%	14.6%	9.1%	19.2%	25.2%

II. The Industry, Target Customers, and Competitors

2.1 THE RESTAURANT INDUSTRY

- The restaurant industry has grown 4.5% per year from 1998 to 2003 and reached $385 billion in sales in 2003.[7] Restaurant sales are projected to grow at 5% per year in the next five years, reaching total sales of $491 billion in 2008 and exceed $577 billion by 2010.[8]

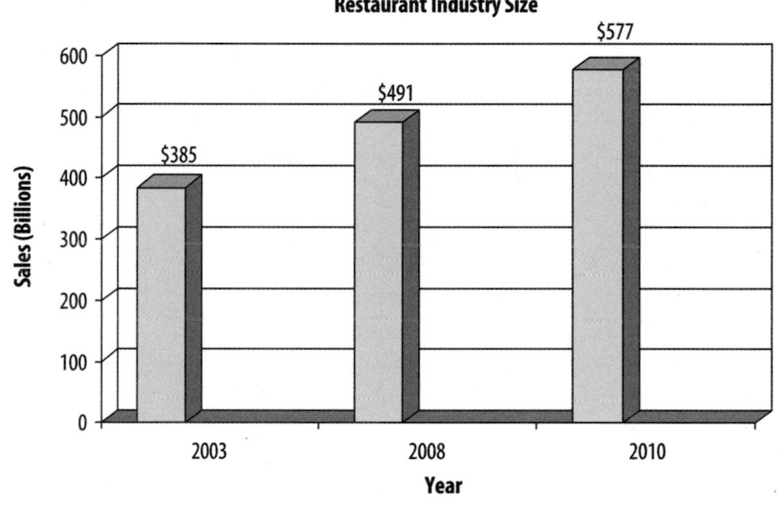

- People devote less time to preparing home-cooked meals and therefore look to faster dining options such as fast food and fast casual as a meal replacement. Restaurants account for 46% of total food dollars spent,[7] up from 44.6% in 1990 and 26.3% in 1960.[9] By 2010, 53% of food dollars will be spent on away-from-home sources.[9]

- A survey by the National Restaurant Association shows that 27% of Americans are not dining out or ordering out as much as they prefer due to relatively high prices of dining out, indicating an upside potential for growth in the industry, especially in the lower priced segments such as fast food and fast casual.

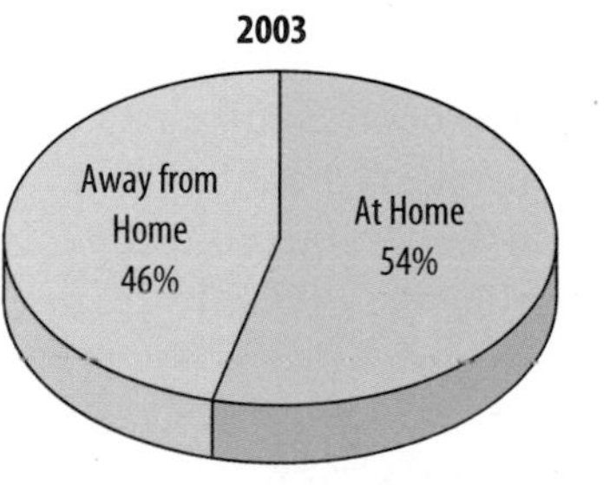

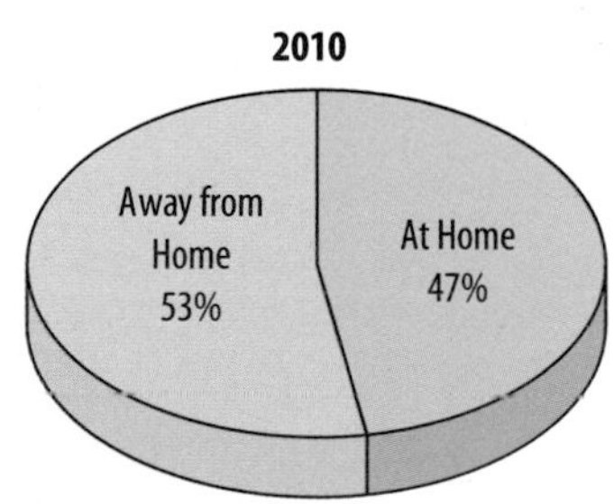

[7] "Restaurant Industry Report," The Freedonia Group, Inc. 2003.
[8] National Restaurant Association.
[9] "Restaurant Industry Report," Standard and Poor's, 2003.

CONFIDENTIAL

2.2 FAST CASUAL SEGMENT

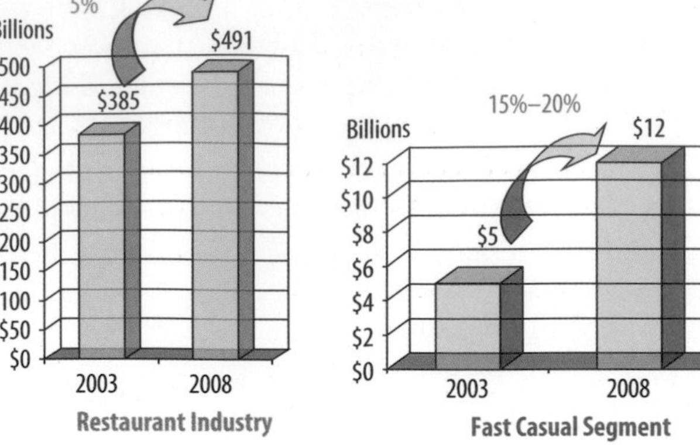

- The fast casual segment is positioned (according to price, quality, and experience) between fast food and casual dining. Fast casual restaurants offer higher quality menus at slightly higher prices than those of fast food, and offer a more upscale décor.
- While the restaurant industry as a whole is projected to grow at 5% per year in the next five years, the fast casual segment is projected to grow 15–20%.[7] The fast casual segment is a mere $5 billion, compared to overall industry size of $385 billion, but with vast potential for growth.
- Ticket prices are generally between $6–$9. Approximately 60% of fast casual customers are between the ages of 18–49.
- Most of the major players in this segment are bakery-café and Mexican concepts such as Panera Bread (the segment leader), Au Bon Pain, Chipotle Grill, Baja Fresh, and Qdoba. Due to the high popularity of Asian cuisine, there are currently pockets of players starting up throughout the country; the most notable is Pei Wei Asian Diner.

2.3 ASIAN FOOD

- Asian cuisine is popular amongst mainstream American consumers. Sales from these consumers totaled $837 million in 2002.[10] A study done by Packaged Facts projects that retail sales of Asian cuisine will climb from a total of $855.5 million in 2003 to $974.7 million in 2008.
- Asian food, mostly Chinese and Japanese, has long made its way into the mainstream. In the past few decades, however, Americans have expanded their tastes to the bolder flavors of Southeast Asia, with Thai food rising as one of the most popular and well-recognized cuisines. This trend is led by Generations X and Y who tend to favor high-impact flavors with exotic appeal.[10]
- According to The National Restaurant Association's Ethnic Cuisines II study, Thai and other Southeast Asian cuisines appeal primarily to "internationalists" and "urban professionals" who reside and/or work in urban environments. These people tend to be more adventurous in their food tastes and prefer the bolder, spicier flavors of Thai cuisine.

2.4 TARGET CUSTOMER

U.S. consumers are increasingly demanding fast, convenient food to fit their busy lifestyles; they are also demanding healthier menu selections, better quality, and more ethnic choices. These needs are reflected in the current market trends as follows:

[10] Packaged Facts, Marketresearch.com, 2003

CONFIDENTIAL

1) Busy consumers
Many working Americans lead fast-paced lives with little time to prepare lunch or dinner. According to the Bureau of Labor Statistics, in 2003 more than 50% of U.S. families were dual-earner households. With the number of dual-income families on the rise, as well as longer working hours, eating lunch or dinner out is often the easiest and most convenient option. Restaurants account for 46% of total food dollars spent,[11] up from 44.6% in 1990 and 26.3% in 1960.[12] By 2010, 53% of food dollars will be spent on away-from-home sources.[12]

2) Increased emphasis on health and quality
The American culture is becoming more health-conscious. The surge in obesity lawsuits against fast food chains, coupled with the recent low-carb, low-fat, and low-calorie crazes has contributed to Americans' demands for healthier and better quality food. Restaurants are responding to these demands by adding healthier food selections to their menus. For instance, McDonald's offers premium salads,[13] and Panera Bread offers low-fat and low-carb options.[14] According to our marketing survey and focus group, Thai food is generally perceived as healthy.

3) Ethnic foods on the rise
Americans are becoming more sophisticated diners and are demanding higher variety of selections.[10] Bold, spicy cuisines are becoming vastly popular. Many traditional restaurants are incorporating flavors from various ethnic cuisines into their menus (i.e, teriyaki, Thai peanut sauce, curry, etc.).[15] Thai food is among the fastest growing food trends in the U.S. and is making its way into the mainstream.[15]

Thai food patrons are currently limited to full-service options, as most Thai restaurants in the U.S. are full-service establishments. An opportunity exists for a Thai fast casual restaurant serving fresh fast, at affordable prices.

We considered various ways of segmenting the market: demographical bases, geographical bases, behavioral bases, and psychographic bases. We segment our market by age, education level, and lifestyle, as, according to our marketing research, customers who dine at fast casual establishments and who enjoy Asian foods are of a certain age group, education level, and lifestyle.

Our marketing survey of 350 participants revealed that those most likely to become our customers are between the ages of 18–34 years old, well educated, single or married, eat out or order take-out quite frequently regardless of income, and enjoy Asian foods and bold flavors.

Our survey reveals a strong demand, as 82% of people aged 18–34 would "definitely" or "probably" eat at *Benjapon's*, and would eat there at least twice a month to more than once a week.

2.5 COMPETITORS
Benjapon's competitors include local Thai restaurants as well as limited service restaurants of other genres. However, we highlight the Asian fast casual players that have

[11] "Restaurant Industry Report," The Freedonia Group, Inc. 2003.
[12] "Restaurant Industry Report," Standard and Poor's, 2003.
[13] McDonald's website: www.mcdonalds.com
[14] Panera Bread website: www.panerabread.com
[15] Packaged Facts, Marketresearch.com, 2003

CONFIDENTIAL

emerged in recent years as our benchmark companies and future potential competitors on an expansion scale. Our Asian fast casual competitors include the following:

Mama Fu's: A Pan-Asian fast casual cuisine with ten stores and over 200 franchises sold. Founded in 2002, the first few stores are located mainly in the South and Mid-West. The average ticket price is about $7.50 for lunch and $10.50 for dinner. Mama Fu's provides counter order and table delivery.

Noodles & Co.: A global noodle fast casual concept that focuses on healthy selections of noodles, salad, and grilled items. The company currently has 58 restaurants in six states focusing on the West, Mid-West, and Atlantic region. The company plans to franchise 240 new stores in the next four years.

Nothing But Noodles: A fast casual global noodle concept similar to Noodles & Co. The company emphasizes fresh ingredients. The company was founded in 2001 and has sold over 300 franchises, focusing on the South, Mid-West, and Northwest.

Pei Wei: A Pan-Asian fast casual sister restaurant to PF Chang's. The company has over 50 stores, all company-owned. Pei Wei is located in the West and Southwest.

2.6 COMPETITIVE ADVANTAGE

Our competitive advantage lies in our ability to consistently deliver our brand promise of flavorful, fresh, fast, fun, and friendly, through every customer touch point. We will develop standardized kitchen and front-end operations, which will subsequently lower costs and enable us to develop a franchising model.

III. The Company

3.1 COMPANY OVERVIEW

- *Benjapon's* is a fast casual restaurant serving fresh Thai food, fast, at affordable prices, in a fun, friendly atmosphere.
- The restaurant will be counter-order, table-service style with an average ticket price of $8.50. Store hours will be from 11am–10pm, daily. We expect 40% of our business to come from take-out orders.
- Our quality of service is a key point of differentiation. Thailand is known as "The Land of Smiles" and our hospitality is second to none. *Benjapon's* will instill a culture of superb customer service among all staff and employees, through a comprehensive staffing and training program.

The size of the restaurant will be approximately 1,500 square feet with 50 seats.

3.2 THE MENU

The menu offers a familiar selection of Thai foods with description of ingredients and method of preparation for each dish. In addition, each menu item will be accompanied by a picture, to facilitate the decision-making of the customer and make the experience as stress-free as possible. Therefore, the menu selections will not be extensive, but limited items that are familiar and exceptionally well-prepared. There will be a menu-board behind the ordering counter as well as a folded paper menu for take-out.

CONFIDENTIAL

benjapon's
Thai Food. Flavorful. Fresh. Fast.

1435 Elm Street
Somerville, MA 02433
Tel. 617-231-1111
www.benjapons.com
Open Daily: 11am-10pm

Choose Meat: Chicken, Beef, Shrimp, Veggie

Curry Dishes
- Green Curry
- Red Curry
- Yellow Curry
- Panang Curry

Starters
- Spring Roll
- Summer Roll
- Satay Nuggets

Stir-Fry Dishes
- Chili Basil Stir Fry
- Garlic Pepper Stir Fry
- Pra Ram Vegetables
- Fried Rice

Curry, Stir-fry, & Noodle Bowl items can be served in wraps!

Salads
- Som Tum (Spicy Papaya Salad)
- Yum Nua (Spicy Beef Salad)
- Laab Kai (Spicy Chicken Salad)
- Mixed Greens w/ Peanut Dressing

Noodle Bowls
- Pad Thai
- Pad See-U (Noodle Stir Fried w/ Chinese Broccoli)
- Pad Kee Mao (Spicy Noodle Stir Fry)

Soups
- Tom Ka Kai (Coconut Chicken Soup)
- Tom Yum Goong (Hot & Sour Shrimp)

The Grill
- Grilled Thai Herb Chicken (1/4, ½, whole)

Let us know how hot you want it!

Kids' Meals
- Satay Nuggets w/ Rice and Veggies
- Mini Pad Thai

Drinks
- Thai Iced Tea
- Thai Iced Coffee
- Fountain Drinks

Desserts
- Thai Tea Ice Cream
- Coconut Ice Cream
- Fried Banana
- Custard Buns

3.3 THE STORE LAYOUT

The store design will facilitate customer flow. There will be two main registers, or Point of Sale systems (POS), with one extra POS for peak-hour take-out orders. Customers order and pay at the counter and the food is delivered to their tables. Take-out customers wait for their food at a designated area. Delivery will take 3–5 minutes after ordering. There will be a condiment bar for hot sauces, utensils, and napkins. Fountain drinks and coffee will be served at a separate station.

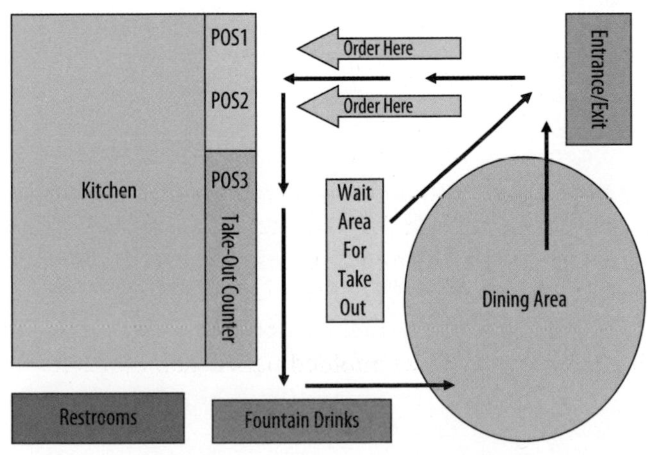

CONFIDENTIAL

Example of Restaurant Interior

Example of Menu Board with Accompanying Pictures

IV. The Marketing Plan

4.1 MARKETING OBJECTIVES

Benjapon's marketing mix will cause the target audience to:

- Come for a first visit. (Generate new customers.)
- Visit our website for information and feedback. (Build brand loyalty.)
- Spread the word. (Generate word-of-mouth buzz.)
- Become a regular customer. (Generate repeat business.)

4.2 TARGETING AND POSITIONING

4.2.1 TARGETING *Benjapon's* targets the busy student and young professional (mainly between ages 18–35) who are looking for a better alternative for a quick meal.

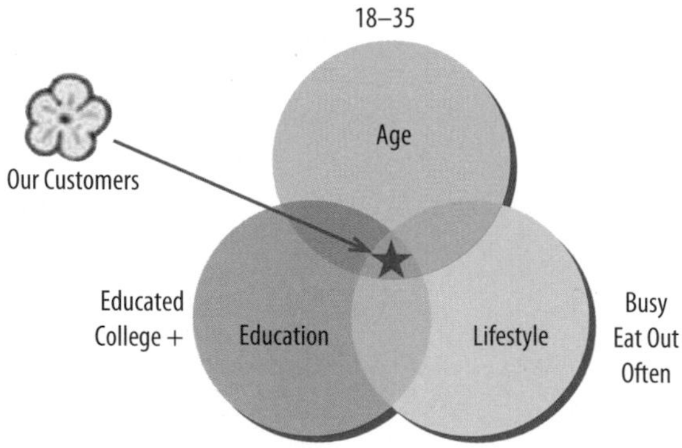

CONFIDENTIAL

Our first location will be in the Somerville/Cambridge area, located near Tufts University, Harvard University, and MIT. Both Somerville and Cambridge are populated with relatively young demographics. The median age of Somerville residents around Davis and Porter Squares is 30 years old.[16] In addition, Somerville boasts a median family income and per capital income that are higher than national averages. The city of Cambridge also has a young demographic, with the largest group (38.6%) between 25–44 years old, followed by 18–24 years old at 21.2%. Cambridge boasts a highly educated population with over 65% of its residents over 25 years old achieving a bachelor's degree or higher.[17]

4.2.2 POSITIONING Benjapon's is positioned as

"A Thai Fast Casual restaurant that offers the busy customer a flavorful, fresh, fast, and fun dining experience."

Our marketing survey reveals a strong demand, as 82% of people aged 18–34 would "definitely" or "probably" eat at Benjapon's.

4.3 MARKET PENETRATION

The store will be located in an area with high visibility and heavy foot and car traffic, with cumulative attraction of nearby retailers and entertainment. We expect to generate high pre-store opening interest from local residents and students, via direct mailing of menu and coupons, and postings of flyers (count-down to opening day).

Our Financial Plan in Section IX provides further details on the costs involved in our marketing budget.

4.4 PRICING STRATEGY

The $8.50 average ticket price is within the fast casual range. These price points are derived from studying Thai restaurants in the Boston area and fast casual restaurants across all genres (i.e., Pei Wei, Qdoba, Mama Fu's, Noodles & Co., Panera Bread). Through our focus group, we realized that many women would appreciate the option of purchasing a half portion for a lower price. This gives flexibility to the customer, delivers on our customer-friendly brand promise, and makes it easier for customers to try more than one dish.

4.5 MARKETING MIX

A mix of marketing vehicles will be created to convey our unique image and message. We will leverage public relations as our main vehicle for marketing communications.

[16] American Fact Finder
[17] www.cambridgema.gov

CONFIDENTIAL

1) *Print media:* Local newspapers, magazines and student publications.

2) *Broadcast media:* Local programming and radio stations.

3) *Local colleges:* Communication with local colleges.

4) *Direct mail:* Mail menu and coupons to local residential neighborhoods. See our Financial Plan in Section IX for details on mailing costs.

5) *Become part of community:* Community involvement and donations.

Our strategy is to build the *Benjapon's* brand by delivering a consistent message to our customers at every touch point. Everything we do will be associated with Thai food that is flavorful, fresh, fast, fun, and friendly. Our goal is to have top of mind awareness with customers and to build a brand that commands a loyal following.

V. The Operations Plan

5.1 LOCATION

Our strategy is to locate in a convenient location close to our target market. The following are our criteria for location:

5.1.1 REAL ESTATE CRITERIA

1) Population

We aim to locate near our target market of 18–35 year-old students and young working professionals who are well-educated and busy, and earn above average income. The following are our criteria:

- Locate near target market. That is:
  - o Near college or university, and
  - o Near residential area populated by young working professionals, and
  - o Near local businesses.
- High concentration of daytime population: 10,000 within a one mile radius
- Residential population: 15,000 within one mile or 60,000 within three miles
- Income:
  - o Median household income in the top 30% for the MSA (Metropolitan Statistical Area)
  - o Per capita income 20% greater than MSA average

2) Traffic volume

We favor locations with high foot traffic, and to a lesser degree, vehicle traffic. Thus we elect to locate near such synergistic retailers that draw foot traffic such as other restaurants, entertainment, daily needs shopping, as well as daytime employment.

3) Site visibility

The site should be easily spotted by a walking or driving target customer from both sides of the street across all seasons.

4) Site neighbors

- The site should be surrounded by other synergistic businesses to draw foot traffic.
- The site should be located near other restaurant of other genres in order to attract the "food" crowd.

CONFIDENTIAL

5) The site

- High visibility site of approximately 1,500 square feet
- Location specific parking not required. Although we rely more on foot traffic, street parking should be reasonably available.

5.1.2 POTENTIAL LOCATION According to our criteria, we are working with realtors and specifically focusing on the various "Squares" in the cities of Somerville and Cambridge. That is, Davis Square, Porter Square, Inman Square, Union Square, Kendall Square, and Harvard Square.

5.2 HOURS OF OPERATION

The restaurant will be open for lunch and dinner, daily. Service will begin at 11:00am and end at 10:00pm. The restaurant will be closed for Christmas, Thanksgiving, New Year's Eve and Day, and the Fourth of July.

5.3 EMPLOYEE HIRING AND TRAINING

We will develop a comprehensive hiring and training manual. Kitchen employees will be hired based on prior experience in Asian, preferably Thai, kitchens. Supranee Siriaphanot, former chef and owner of a Thai restaurant in Texas, and Ron Noonprasith, a chef and restaurant owner in Thailand, will both join the team as head chefs. They will be responsible for training kitchen staff and standardizing our processes.

5.4 THE PRODUCTION

The kitchen will be closed from customers' view to create a cleaner look and feel. Food production in the initial store will be headed by a chef and will be standardized and measurable, facilitating the training process for our kitchen staff. The kitchen comprises 40% of the store space and is closed from customers' view. The kitchen computer receives the information ordered from the front registers.

5.4.1 EMPLOYEES

Full-Time Employees: Initially, we need three full-time employees – the founder, a store manager, and a chef.
Hourly Employees: We need four hourly employees present (plus the three full-time employees). During non-peak hours, we need one hourly employee, along with the three full-time employees.

5.5 FACILITIES AND EQUIPMENT

Space: We will focus on leasing a space that is approximately 1,500 square feet and that is formerly a restaurant and needs only minor modifications.

Equipment: Equipment will be purchased and installed by one of the following companies:

- The Boston Showcase company, who can also provide assistance with the restaurant design and architecture.
- Seidman Brothers.

5.6 SUPPLIERS

- We will source our meat and vegetables from Sysco or Performance Food Group.
- We will purchase our cleaning supplies from Sysco or PFG. We will reorder supplies on an as-needed basis.
- We will purchase smallware from Sysco or US Foodservice.

CONFIDENTIAL

Detailed Timeline

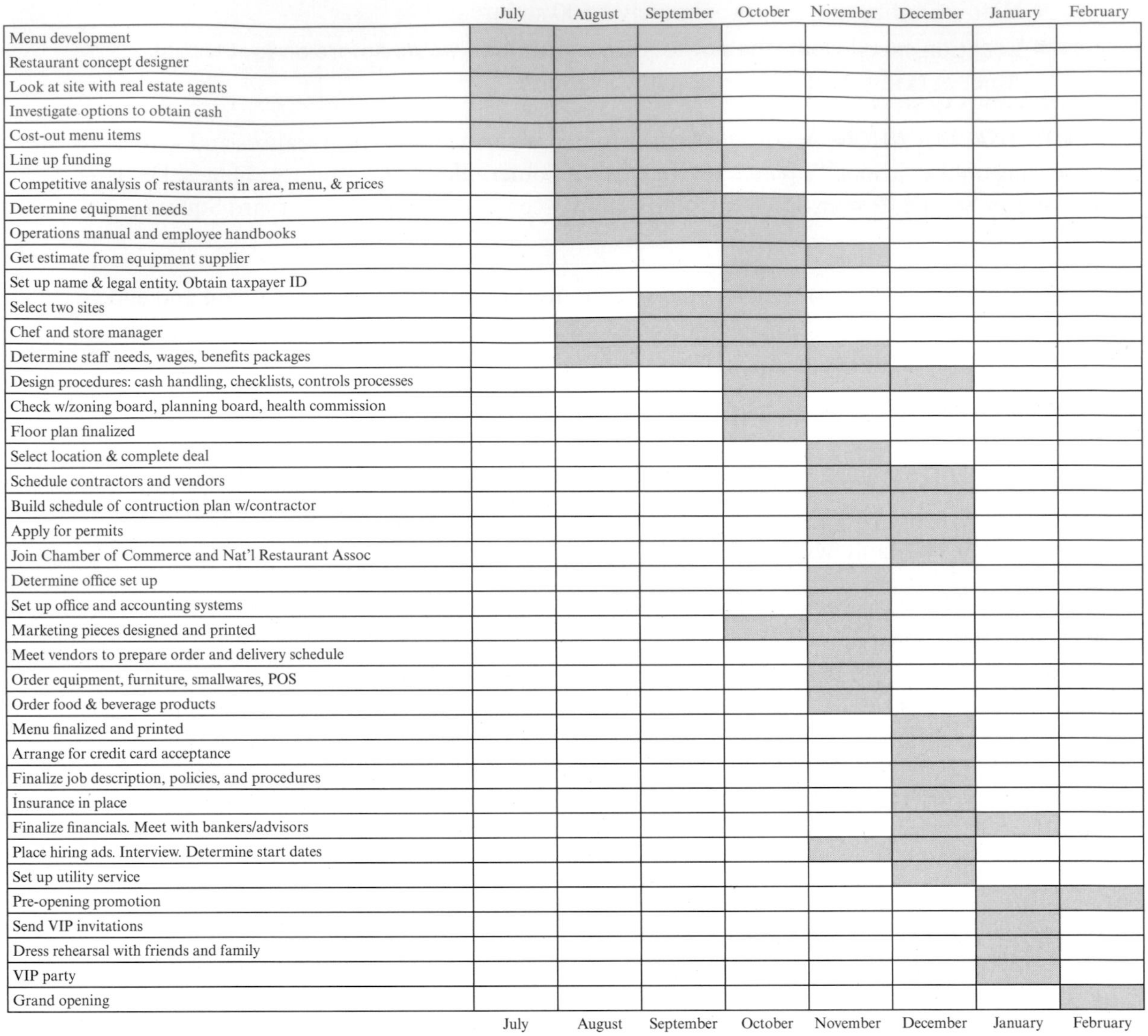

	July	August	September	October	November	December	January	February
Menu development								
Restaurant concept designer								
Look at site with real estate agents								
Investigate options to obtain cash								
Cost-out menu items								
Line up funding								
Competitive analysis of restaurants in area, menu, & prices								
Determine equipment needs								
Operations manual and employee handbooks								
Get estimate from equipment supplier								
Set up name & legal entity. Obtain taxpayer ID								
Select two sites								
Chef and store manager								
Determine staff needs, wages, benefits packages								
Design procedures: cash handling, checklists, controls processes								
Check w/zoning board, planning board, health commission								
Floor plan finalized								
Select location & complete deal								
Schedule contractors and vendors								
Build schedule of contruction plan w/contractor								
Apply for permits								
Join Chamber of Commerce and Nat'l Restaurant Assoc								
Determine office set up								
Set up office and accounting systems								
Marketing pieces designed and printed								
Meet vendors to prepare order and delivery schedule								
Order equipment, furniture, smallwares, POS								
Order food & beverage products								
Menu finalized and printed								
Arrange for credit card acceptance								
Finalize job description, policies, and procedures								
Insurance in place								
Finalize financials. Meet with bankers/advisors								
Place hiring ads. Interview. Determine start dates								
Set up utility service								
Pre-opening promotion								
Send VIP invitations								
Dress rehearsal with friends and family								
VIP party								
Grand opening								

July August September October November December January February

VI. The Development Plan

We plan to launch a soft-opening/VIP party of the restaurant in January 2006 and a Grand Opening by February 2006. The following timeline sets out detailed activities planned prior to opening.

Our key milestones include funding in the August to October timeframe in order to complete our site selection process by November and start building out the restaurant. We also need to have our complete team in place by December in order to start the training process and get ready for our soft opening in January.

CONFIDENTIAL

VII. The Growth Plan

- Our plan is to grow via franchising after opening two company-owned stores.
- The plan is to start selling franchises in the fourth year of operations. In the third year of operations, the second store is to be opened and plans are set to build an infrastructure to support the franchising strategy.
- We plan to grow nationwide via franchising after meeting our goals for the local areas.

VIII. The Team

8.1 LAUNCH TEAM

Founder: Benjapon Jivasantikarn is a 2005 fellow and MBA graduate of Babson College, the nation's #1 program for entrepreneurship. Prior to graduate school, Benjapon worked for six years at KPMG (a Big Four professional services firm) in San Francisco in business incentives and valuations. Although her background is in finance, her passion lies in the foodservice industry. Throughout her undergraduate years in Texas, she worked in a Thai restaurant, gaining operations and customer service experience. She also worked at Panera Bread part-time during graduate school to gain further insight into the fast casual business. She was a finalist in the Douglass Graduate Business Plan Competition and won the Sorensen Award for Entrepreneurial and Academic Excellence.

General Manager: Zack Noonprasith has six years' experience in financial services and five years' experience in restaurant management. Zack will work with the founder on day-to-day operations and on developing and standardizing the system in preparation for replication and franchising.

Chef: Supranee Siriaphanot was a co-founder and chef of a Thai restaurant in Texas for over 15 years. She will oversee food preparation in the kitchen and develop standardized processes, as well as train part-time staff on those processes.

8.2 BOARD OF ADVISORS

Rick Hagelstein Mr. Hagelstein, a life-long successful entrepreneur, is the founder and CEO of The Minor Group, a hospitality and leisure, food service, and lifestyle company in Thailand and Asia Pacific. The Minor Group comprises two companies: Minor International and Minor Corporation. The Minor International is the Thai franchisee of Burger King, Swensen's, Dairy Queen, and Sizzler. After ending a Pizza Hut franchising relationship with Yum! Brands, the Minor Food Group founded The Pizza Company which now owns 75% of the pizza market in Thailand and is expanding to franchised locations throughout Asia.

Steve Sabre Dr. Sabre is a franchising expert and is a recognized leader in defining the field of entrepreneurship. He co-founded Jiffy Lube International and subsequently

CONFIDENTIAL

founded and served as chairman and CEO of American Oil Corporation, which he sold in 1991. As an educator, he has authored numerous business cases and coauthored the following books: *Franchising: Pathway to Wealth Creation, Business Plans for the 21st Century,* and *New Venture Creation for the 21st Century.* Dr. Sabre has consulted for major corporations such as Fidelity Investments, Intel Corporation, IBM Corporation, and Allied Domecq.

Hull Martin Dr. Martin is the Chair of the Entrepreneurship Department and Edith Y. Babson Term Chair in Entrepreneurship. Martin's primary research areas include the venture capital process and entrepreneurial growth strategies. Dr. Martin actively consults with entrepreneurs and small business startups. He is a former venture capitalist with experience in the restaurant field.

IX. The Financial Plan

9.1 SINGLE STORE FINANCIALS

In this section, we discuss the unit economics of our first store.

9.1.1 INCOME STATEMENT

9.1.1.1 Revenue: We project to eventually serve approximately 400 customers per day on average.

Due to our initial lack of brand awareness, we assume that we will achieve 60% of this number of customers in the first year of operations.

	Year 1	Year 2	Year 3	Year 4	Year 5
Customers per Day	226	288	323	356	392

9.1.1.2 COGS: The cost of goods sold as percentage of sales per each item was derived from an estimate from an interview with restaurateurs regarding food costs. We assume that in years 1 and 2, due to portion control and waste issues, our COGS are higher than forecasted by 15% and 5%, respectively. After the first few years, COGs is expected to be around 30.2% of sales (decreased from 34.7% and 31.7% in years 1 and 2). The reduction is not only due to better portion and waste control but also from a strong relationship with suppliers.

9.1.1.3 Operating Expenses:

1) **Sales and Marketing:** Our sales and marketing efforts for the first store consists of mainly direct mail and promotional programs.

Direct Mail: $8,400 per year.

Promotion:

Yearly Promotional Costs	Year 1	Year 2	Year 3	Year 4	Year 5
Promotional Costs per Year per Store	$9,600	$10,560	$12,672	$16,474	$23,063

2) **Salaries and Wages:** We will have three full-time employees: the founder, a general manager, and a chef. In addition, we will hire a part-time accountant.

CONFIDENTIAL

Hourly Employees:

Hourly Wages Per Year	Year 1	Year 2	Year 3	Year 4	Year 5
Wage per Year per Store (360 days; 4% raise per year)	$95,472	$99,291	$103,263	$107,393	$111,689
# store	1	1	2	2	2
Total Hourly Wages	**$95,472**	**$99,291**	**$206,525**	**$214,786**	**$223,377**

3. **Depreciation:** Office equipment depreciation is three years. Equipment and leasehold improvements are depreciated at seven and ten years, respectively.

4. **Rent:** We estimate $55 per square foot for rental cost. Therefore, our initial needs at 1,500 square feet will result in a total of $82,500 per year. Rent deposit is estimated at $20,000. We adjust for increase in rental cost after reaching a certain level of sales.

5. **Other:** Repairs and maintenance costs at 2% of sales per year, insurance at 1.2%, and utility at 3% are all industry standard for independent limited service restaurants. We estimate other operating expenses at 1% to capture any other miscellaneous expenses.

9.1.2 CASH FLOWS

9.1.2.1 Working Capital: Our restaurant is a cash business so we assume negligible accounts receivables. We will turn over inventory 52 times per year assuming weekly delivery of goods on average. *Benjapon's* will rely on fresh ingredients and will need delivery at least once a week. We will pay employees semi-weekly.

9.1.2.2 Capital Expenditure: For each new store, we incur approximately $255,000 worth of capital expenditures: $25,000 Point-of-Sales system, $80,000 equipment, $150,000 leasehold improvements.

Benjapon's will be cash flow positive after 12 months.

9.1.3 BALANCE SHEET

9.1.3.1 Assets & Liabilities: *Benjapon's* primary asset base is fixed assets, representing 60% of total assets in year 1. As *Benjapon's* is a restaurant operation, accounts receivable will not be significant.

9.1.4 SUMMARY FINANCIALS The following is the summary of our first store financial performance.

Summary Financials ($)	Year 1	Year 2	Year 3	Year 4	Year 5
# Company-Owned Stores	1	1	1	1	1
Revenue	691,200	881,280	988,796	1,089,258	1,199,926
Gross Profit	451,080	601,749	690,097	760,211	837,449
EBIT	(110,145)	74,104	143,475	167,472	209,216
EBITDA	(72,526)	111,723	181,094	196,758	238,502
Net Earnings	(116,145)	68,104	102,421	98,323	124,089
Net Cash from Operating Activities	(53,182)	112,693	139,588	124,528	156,299
Cash	137,284	249,977	379,565	494,093	640,393
Total Equity	299,321	367,425	469,847	568,170	692,259
Total Debt	50,000	50,000	40,000	30,000	20,000

CONFIDENTIAL

	Year 1	Year 2	Year 3	Year 4	Year 5
Growth					
Revenue Growth Rate—CAGR:		28%	12%	10%	10%
Profitability					
Gross Profit %	65.3%	68.3%	69.8%	69.8%	69.8%
Operating Expenses %	76.1%	59.9%	55.3%	54.4%	52.4%
EBIT %	−15.9%	8.4%	14.5%	15.4%	17.4%
EBITDA %	−10.5%	12.7%	18.3%	18.1%	19.9%
Net Earnings %	−16.8%	7.7%	10.4%	9.0%	10.3%
Returns					
Return on Assets	−29.1%	14.1%	17.9%	14.7%	15.7%
Return on Equity	−38.8%	18.5%	21.8%	17.3%	17.9%
Return on Capital (LT Debt + Equity)	−33.2%	16.3%	20.1%	16.4%	17.4%

9.2 CAPITAL REQUIREMENTS

Initial funding is by private investors of $200,000 and an equipment loan of $350,000.

Our start up costs include $330,000 of leasehold improvements and include $20,000 of rent deposit, $10,000 of legal costs, $25,000 office and Point-of-Sales system, $30,000 architecture cost, $80,000 equipment, $150,000 leasehold improvements, and $150,000 opening inventory.

Source of Funds		Uses of Funds	
		Rent Deposit	$ 20,000
		Legal Costs	$ 10,000
Investors	$200,000	Office Equipment	$ 25,000
		Architecture Cost	$ 30,000
Debt	$350,000	Equipment Costs	$ 80,000
		Leasehold Improvements	$150,000
		Opening & Misc Inventory	$ 15,000
		Funding for Working Capital	$202,000
		1st Year Marketing	$ 18,000
Total Sources	**$550,000**	**Total Uses**	**$550,000**

9.3 FRANCHISING REVENUES AND COSTS

In year 3, we raise an additional $400,000 in capital to fund growth.

We start by growing our company-owned stores to two stores in year 3 of operations. In year 4, we begin to sell franchises. We assume that the franchises sold will be up and running within one year of signing the franchise agreement. Therefore, if three franchises were sold in year 4, there will be three franchises operating by year 5.

We assume that in year 5, we are able to sell ten more franchises.

Our royalty fee is 5% and franchise fee is $25,000. This is comparable with our Asian fast casual benchmarks companies.

In order to calculate our royalty revenues, we assume franchisee revenue of close to $1,000,000 per store (estimated by averaging first five year forecasted sales of franchisees, which takes into account the sales ramp up time in the initial years).

CONFIDENTIAL

		Year 3	Year 4	Year 5
New Franchises Sold in the year			3	10
Total Franchises Sold			3	13
Total Franchises in Operations			0	3
Royalty	5%			
Revenue per Store	$1,000,000			
Franchisee Revenues		$0	$0	$2,700,000
Royalty Revenue		$0	$0	$ 135,000
Franchise Fee	$25,000	$0	$75,000	$ 250,000
Total Revenue from Franchising		**$0**	**$75,000**	**$ 385,000**

In order to build a franchising organization, we need to create a support infrastructure. In the first year of franchising (year 4), we will invest in marketing to advertise our franchise to prospective franchisees. We will also incur legal costs associated with creating the UFOC and franchise agreements. Costs for training material and internal communications systems are based on number of franchisee stores.

In terms of staffing, we will need a franchise director by year 5, when we start to sell up to ten franchises and have plans to begin saturating the local market. We also need to hire a field agent (called "Team Coaches") to serve as a link between the company and its franchisees.

Franchise Support Staff		Year 3	Year 4	Year 5
Total Franchises Sold		0	3	13
Total Franchises in Operations		0	0	3
Franchise Support Staff				
Field Agents				1
Total Franchise Support Staff		0	0	1
Salary per Franchise Support Staff	$50,000			
Franchise Director				$100,000
Total Salary		$0	$0	$150,000

Other Franchisee Support Costs	Per Store	Year 3	Year 4	Year 5
Total Franchises Sold		0	3	13
Total Franchises in Operations		0	0	3
Support Costs				
Marketing Expense (sell franchises)		$100,000	$50,000	$50,000
Legal Costs		$100,000	$20,000	$20,000
Training Material	$50	$0	$150	$650
Internal Communication Network	$1,000	$0	$3,000	$13,000
Other Support Costs		$200,000	$73,150	$83,650

	Year 3	Year 4	Year 5
Estimated Costs Related to Franchising	$200,000	$73,150	$233,650

CONFIDENTIAL

9.4 OVERALL FINANCIAL PERFORMANCE

The following includes the income statement, balance sheet, and cash flow statement for the company, which reflects the following milestones:

- One company-owned store in years 1 and 2. Breakeven of the first store after 12 months.
- Launch a second company-owned store in year 3 to prove duplicability.
- In year 3, start working with legal team to create franchising structure and agreement. Begin marketing efforts to target potential franchisees.
- Start selling franchises in year 4. We expect to sell three franchises initially. We receive the franchise fee up front, but the build-out of the three franchisee stores will likely materialize in year 5. No formal staffing infrastructure is in place in year 4.
- In year 5, we hire a franchising director and a field agent (or "team coach") as a base team for our franchise operations. We aim to sell ten franchises in year 5. The three franchises sold in year 4 should be in operations, and thus resulting in royalty revenues for us.

Although our financial forecast spans the timeline of our first five years of operations, our growth strategy lies in the two stages as set out in this report, which extends beyond the five year horizon. Since our first stage growth allows for a total of 20 stores, we expect completion of our first stage growth in 6–7 year timeframe. Our second stage of growth will see nation-wide expansion, which we expect will start in years 7–10. The financials set out below are for the first five years of operations.

9.4.1 SUMMARY FINANCIALS

	Year 1	Year 2	Year 3	Year 4	Year 5
Summary Financials ($)					
# Company-Owned Stores	1	1	2	2	2
# Franchises Sold	—	—	—	3	13
# Franchises in Operations	—	—	—	—	3
Revenue	691,200	881,280	1,977,592	2,293,859	2,874,559
Gross Profit	451,080	601,749	1,380,195	1,623,578	2,122,505
EBIT	(110,145)	74,104	129,202	363,687	525,670
EBITDA	(72,526)	111,723	204,440	430,592	592,575
Net Earnings	(138,145)	48,904	81,602	196,068	296,922
Cash	109,784	168,277	561,526	751,112	989,152
Total Equity	(28,179)	20,725	302,327	498,395	795,317
Total Debt	350,000	315,000	595,000	525,000	385,000
Profitability					
Gross Profit %	65.3%	68.3%	69.8%	70.8%	73.8%
EBIT %	−15.9%	8.4%	6.5%	15.9%	18.3%
EBITDA %	−10.5%	12.7%	10.3%	18.8%	20.6%
Net Earnings %	−20.0%	5.5%	4.1%	8.5%	10.3%

CONFIDENTIAL

	Year 1	Year 2	Year 3	Year 4	Year 5
Returns					
Return on Assets	–37.1%	12.2%	8.0%	16.8%	21.8%
Return on Equity	490.2%	236.0%	27.0%	39.3%	37.3%
Return on Capital (LT Debt + Equity)	–42.9%	14.6%	9.1%	19.2%	25.2%

9.4.2 BREAK-EVEN ANALYSIS

Benjapon's will break even within 12 months. The following chart shows *Benjapon's* break-even sales over the five-year period.

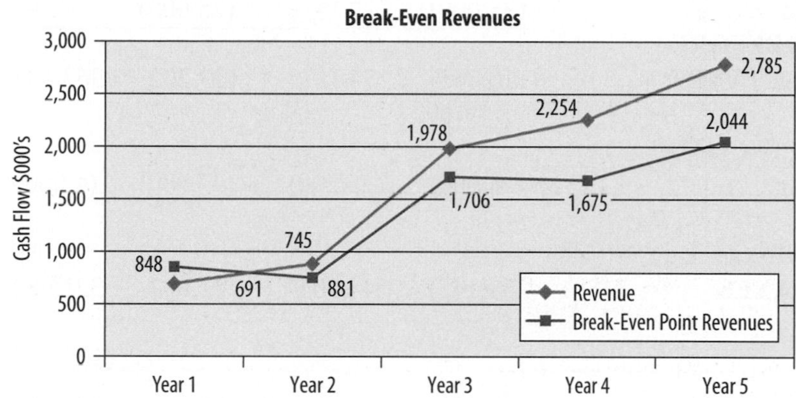

9.4.3 INCOME STATEMENT

	Year 1	Year 2	Year 3	Year 4	Year 5
# Company-Owned Stores	1	1	2	2	2
# of Franchises Sold	—	—	—	3	13
Revenue from Company Stores	691,200	881,280	1,977,592	2,218,859	2,489,559
Revenue from Franchising			—	75,000	385,000
TOTAL REVENUE	**691,200**	**881,280**	**1,977,592**	**2,293,859**	**2,874,559**
COST OF REVENUE	240,120	279,531	597,398	670,280	752,054
% of Revenues	34.7%	31.7%	30.2%	30.2%	30.2%
GROSS PROFIT	451,080	601,749	1,380,195	1,623,578	2,122,505
% of Revenues	65.3%	68.3%	69.8%	70.8%	73.8%
OPERATING EXPENSES					
Franchise-Specific Expenses			200,000	73,150	233,650
Public Relations	—	—	60,000	90,000	120,000
Direct Mail Campaign	8,400	8,400	16,800	16,800	16,800
Promotions Programs	9,600	10,560	12,672	16,474	23,063
Less: 0.8% Franchisee Marketing Contribution			—	—	(21,600)
Salaries and Benefits	294,340	303,114	570,396	690,212	710,821
Depreciation	37,619	37,619	75,238	66,905	66,905
Rent	82,500	82,500	82,500	97,193	126,228
Corporate Office	—	—	—	—	70,000
Training	44,000	22,000	66,000	44,000	44,000
Repairs and Maintenance	13,824	17,626	39,552	45,877	57,491

CONFIDENTIAL

	Year 1	Year 2	Year 3	Year 4	Year 5
Insurance	8,294	10,575	23,731	27,526	34,495
Utility	20,736	26,438	59,328	68,816	86,237
Other G&A	6,912	8,813	19,776	22,939	28,746
Total Operating Expenses	526,225	527,645	1,225,993	1,259,891	1,596,835
% of Revenues	76%	60%	62%	55%	56%
EARNINGS FROM OPERATIONS	(75,145)	74,104	154,202	363,687	525,670
	–11%	8%	8%	16%	18%
EXTRAORDINARY INCOME/ (EXPENSE)	(35,000)	—	(25,000)	—	—
EARNINGS BEFORE INTEREST & TAXES	(110,145)	74,104	129,202	363,687	525,670
	–16%	8%	7%	16%	18%
INTEREST INCOME/ (EXPENSE)	(28,000)	(25,200)	(47,600)	(42,000)	(30,800)
NET EARNINGS BEFORE TAXES	(138,145)	48,904	81,602	321,687	494,870
TAXES	—	—	—	(125,619)	(197,948)
NET EARNINGS	(138,145)	48,904	81,602	196,068	296,922
% of Revenues	**–20.0%**	**5.5%**	**4.1%**	**8.5%**	**10.3%**

9.4.4 BALANCE SHEET

	Begin	Year 1	Year 2	Year 3	Year 4	Year 5
ASSETS						
CURRENT ASSETS						
Cash	184,967	109,784	168,277	561,526	751,112	989,152
Accounts Receivable		2,534	3,231	6,372	7,358	9,091
Inventories		17,741	22,620	44,606	51,506	63,640
Other Current Assets		4,562	5,816	11,470	26,489	32,729
Total Current Assets	184,967	134,621	199,944	623,974	836,464	1,094,612
PROPERTY & EQUIPMENT	275,000	237,381	199,762	399,524	332,619	265,714
TOTAL ASSETS	459,967	372,002	399,706	1,023,497	1,169,083	1,360,326

	Begin	Year 1	Year 2	Year 3	Year 4	Year 5
LIABILITIES & SHAREHOLDERS' EQUITY						
CURRENT LIABILITIES						
Short Term Debt	—	—	—	—	—	—
Accounts Payable & Accrued Expenses		45,619	58,164	114,700	132,444	163,644
Other Current Liabilities		4,562	5,816	11,470	13,244	16,364
Current Portion of Long Term Debt	—	35,000	70,000	70,000	140,000	175,000
Total Current Liabilities	—	85,181	133,981	196,170	285,688	355,009

CONFIDENTIAL

	Begin	Year 1	Year 2	Year 3	Year 4	Year 5
LONG TERM DEBT						
(less current portion)	350,000	315,000	245,000	525,000	385,000	210,000
STOCKHOLDERS' EQUITY						
Common Stock	200,000	200,000	200,000	400,000	400,000	400,000
Preferred Stock	0	0	0	0	0	0
Retained Earnings	(90,033)	(228,179)	(179,275)	(97,673)	98,395	395,317
Total Equity	109,967	(28,179)	20,725	302,327	498,395	795,317
TOTAL LIABILITIES & EQUITY	459,967	372,002	399,706	1,023,497	1,169,083	1,360,326

9.4.5 CASH FLOW STATEMENT

	Begin	Year 1	Year 2	Year 3	Year 4	Year 5
OPERATING ACTIVITIES		1	1	2	2	2
Net Earnings	(90,033)	(138,145)	48,904	81,602	196,068	296,922
Depreciation	0	37,619	37,619	75,238	66,905	66,905
Working Capital Changes						
(Increase)/Decrease Accounts Receivable	0	(2,534)	(697)	(3,141)	(986)	(1,733)
(Increase)/Decrease Inventories	0	(17,741)	(4,879)	(21,986)	(6,900)	(12,134)
(Increase)/Decrease Other Current Assets	0	(4,562)	(1,255)	(5,654)	(15,019)	(6,240)
Increase/(Decrease) Accts Pay & Accrd Expenses	0	45,619	12,545	56,536	17,743	31,201
Increase/(Decrease) Other Current Liabilities	0	4,562	1,255	5,654	1,774	3,120
Net Cash Provided/(Used) by Operating Activities	(90,033)	(75,182)	93,493	188,249	259,586	378,041
INVESTING ACTIVITIES						
Property & Equipment	(275,000)	—	—	(275,000)	—	—
Other						
Net Cash Used in Investing Activities	(275,000)	—	—	(275,000)	—	—

CONFIDENTIAL

	Begin	Year 1	Year 2	Year 3	Year 4	Year 5
FINANCING ACTIVITIES						
Increase/(Decrease) Short Term Debt		—	—	—	—	—
Increase/(Decrease) Curr. Portion LTD		35,000	35,000	—	70,000	35,000
Increase/(Decrease) Long Term Debt	350,000	(35,000)	(70,000)	280,000	(140,000)	(175,000)
Increase/(Decrease) Common Stock	200,000	—	—	200,000	—	—
Increase/(Decrease) Preferred Stock	0	—	—	—	—	—
Dividends Declared		—	—	—	—	—
Net Cash Provided/ (Used) by Financing	550,000	—	(35,000)	480,000	(70,000)	(140,000)
INCREASE/(DECREASE) IN CASH	184,967	(75,182)	58,493	393,249	189,586	238,041
CASH AT BEGINNING OF YEAR		184,967	109,784	168,277	561,526	751,112
CASH AT END OF YEAR	184,967	109,784	168,277	561,526	751,112	989,152

CONFIDENTIAL

Valuing a Business

At certain times, a small business owner may need to determine the value of her or his business. Despite the subjective nature of assigning value to a privately held company—that is, a firm whose stock is not traded publicly—and especially a *small* privately owned firm, there are times when the value must be estimated.

The Need to Compute Firm Value

A variety of specific situations may call for a firm valuation, including the following:

1. An entrepreneur decides to buy a business, rather than starting one from scratch. He or she needs to know the answers to two questions, which may seem the same but are not: "How much is the business worth to me?" and "What should I pay for it?"
2. An owner has decided to make an employee stock ownership plan (ESOP) part of the firm's retirement program (see Chapter 13). The stock has to be valued each year so that the appropriate number of shares can be contributed to the employees' retirement plan.
3. A firm is raising money from outside investors. The firm's value must be determined to establish the percentage of ownership the new investors will receive in the company (see Chapter 12).
4. One partner wants to buy out another partner or the interest of a deceased partner. The value of the business must be set so that a price can be agreed on.
5. An owner wants to exit (harvest) the business. Knowing the value of the company is essential if the business is to be sold or transferred to family members (see Chapter 13).

These are the most common reasons for valuing a business. Note that they are, for the most part, driven by external influences and exceptional circumstances. But it is a good idea to value a business on an ongoing basis—at least once a year. As a firm grows and becomes more profitable, the owner needs to know if the business is also increasing in value. In some situations, a profitable business may lose value over time. Therefore, awareness of its value is important in the management of a business. Knowing your firm's value provides critical insight into how the firm is performing, what options it has, and how it can improve in the long term.

Valuation Methods

In valuing firms, it is important to distinguish between *firm value* and *equity value*. **Firm value**, or **enterprise value**, is the value of the entire business, regardless of how it is financed. It reflects the value of the underlying assets of the business. **Equity value**, or **owner's value**, on the other hand, is the total value of the firm less the amount of debt owed by the firm. That is,

firm value (enterprise value)
The value of the entire business, regardless of how it is financed.

equity value (owner's value)
The value of the firm less the debt owed by the firm.

$$\text{Firm value} - \text{Outstanding debt} = \text{Equity value}$$

Some approaches to determining firm value focus on the first quantity on the left side of the equation—estimating the value of the firm as an entity. The question is "Given the firm's assets and its ability to produce profits from these assets, what is the firm worth?" The equity value is then found by subtracting the outstanding debt from the total firm value.

Other approaches involve determining the outstanding debt and the equity value separately. In those cases, firm value is found by summing the amount of outstanding debt and the equity value. While both processes produce similar results, we recommend finding the firm value and then subtracting the outstanding debt in order to determine the equity, or owner's, value.

There are three basic methods for valuing a business: (1) asset-based valuation, (2) valuation based on comparables, and (3) cash flow–based valuation. Each of these methods can be used as a stand-alone measure of firm value, but more often they are used in combination.

asset-based valuation Determination of the value of a business by estimating the value of its assets.

modified book value method Determination of the value of a business by adjusting book value to reflect obvious differences between the historical cost and current market value of the assets.

replacement value method Determination of the value of a business by estimating the cost of replacing the firm's assets.

liquidation value method Determination of the value of a business by estimating the money that would be available if the firm were to liquidate its assets.

ASSET-BASED VALUATION

An **asset-based valuation** assumes that the value of a firm can be determined by examining the value of the underlying assets of the business (the left-hand side of the balance sheet). Three variations of this approach use (1) the modified book value of assets, (2) the replacement value of assets, and (3) the liquidation value of assets.

The **modified book value method** starts with the numbers shown on a company's balance sheet. These amounts are adjusted to reflect any obvious differences between the historical cost of each asset (as given on the balance sheet) and its current market value. For instance, the market value of a firm's plant and equipment may be totally different from its depreciated historical cost or book value. The same may be true for real estate. The **replacement value method** entails estimating the cost to replace each of the firm's assets. And the **liquidation value method** involves estimating the amount of money that would be received if the firm ended its operations and liquidated its assets.

Asset-based valuation is of limited worth in valuing a business. The historical costs shown on the balance sheet may be very different from the current value of the assets. The three variations to the approach adjust for this weakness to some extent, but their estimate of value has a weak foundation, as all asset-based techniques fail to recognize the firm as an ongoing business. However, the liquidation value method yields an estimate of the value that could be realized if the assets of the business were all sold separately, which is sometimes helpful information.

valuation based on comparables Determination of the value of a business by considering the actual market prices of firms that are similar to the firm being valued.

earnings multiple (value-to-earnings ratio) A ratio determined by dividing a firm's value by its annual earnings.

VALUATION BASED ON COMPARABLES

A **valuation based on comparables** looks at the actual market prices of recently sold firms similar to the one being valued—either publicly traded firms (market comparables) or private firms that have been sold (transaction comparables). "Similar" means that the two firms are in the same industry and are alike in such characteristics as growth potential, risk, profit margins, assets-to-sales relationships, and levels of debt financing.

For instance, you might start by finding several recently sold companies with growth prospects and levels of risk comparable to those of the firm being valued. For each of these firms, you could calculate the **earnings multiple**, or **value-to-earnings ratio**,[1]

$$\text{Earnings multiple} = \frac{\text{Value}}{\text{Earnings}}$$

Earnings may be one of the following:

1. **Earnings before interest, taxes, depreciation, and amortization (EBITDA)**
2. Earnings before subtracting interest and taxes (*EBIT*), which is also a firm's operating income
3. Net income

Earnings before interest, taxes, depreciation, and amortization (EBITDA) A firm's profits after subtracting cost of goods sold and cash operating expenses, but before subtracting depreciation, amortization, interest expense, and taxes.

Of these three options, earnings before interest, taxes, depreciation, and amortization (EBITDA) is the most popular when valuing privately held companies. It provides a basic picture of a firm's profitability, as well as its ability to pay off any debt owed.

Assuming that the company being valued should have an earnings multiple comparable to those of similar firms, you can then apply the calculated ratio to estimate the company's value, using the following equation:

$$\text{Value of firm} = \text{Earnings of firm being valued} \times \text{Earnings multiple of comparable firms}$$

To illustrate, the owner of a machine shop valued her business at four times the firm's annual EBITDA of \$82,000. That is, the owner wanted to sell her business for \$319,800 (EBITDA of \$82,000 × 4 = \$328,000).

The valuation based on comparables is not as easy to use as it might seem. First, finding other firms that are comparable in every way to the firm being valued is often difficult. It is not enough simply to find a firm in the same industry, although that might provide a rough approximation. As already noted, the ideal comparable firm is one that is in the same industry, is a similar type of business, and has a similar growth rate, financial structure, asset turnover ratio (sales ÷ total assets), and profit margin (profits ÷ sales). Fortunately, considerable information is published about firm sales; for instance, *Mergerstat Review* reports the prices of all such sales announced in the public media. Also, some accounting firms can provide information about the selling prices of comparable businesses.

Second, **normalized earnings** should be used in this computation. Normalizing earnings involves adjusting for any unusual items, such as a one-time loss on the sale of real estate or as the consequence of a fire. It also involves adding back any "leakages" that are occurring in the firm's income. For instance, if the owners have been paying themselves a salary above what it would take to find a similarly qualified manager, the excess should be deducted in ascertaining the firm's normalized earnings. In addition, it is necessary to decide which year's EBITDA to use—that is, the current, past, or projected EBITDA, or some combination. For an entrepreneur who wants to sell a business, Evan Klonsky offers the following advice:

normalized earnings Earnings that have been adjusted for unusual items, such as fire damage, and "leakages," such as an owner's excessive salary.

> *Buyers… will [push] for a lower valuation and might look at an average of EBITDA over… three years as the base number. To get the highest valuation, you'll want to bolster gains in the present and future. [B]e sure to exceed your business plan and monthly goals, create a solid sales stream into next year, and get clients on-board with long-term contracts.*[2]

In practice, determination of an appropriate earnings multiple is largely based on the multiple used in recent sales of comparable companies. Adjustments are then made based on two characteristics—risk and growth. The two factors are related to value as follows:

1. The more (less) risky the business, the lower (higher) the appropriate earnings multiple and, as a consequence, the lower (higher) the firm's value.

EXHIBIT B.1 Risk and Growth: Key Factors Affecting the Earnings Multiple and Firm Value

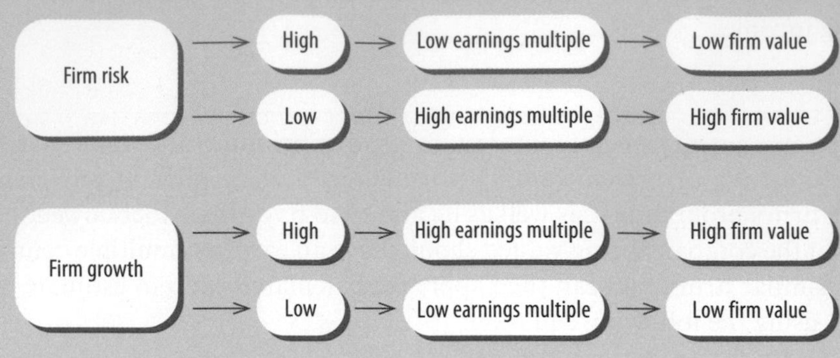

2. The higher (lower) the projected growth rate in future earnings, the higher (lower) the appropriate earnings multiple and, therefore, the higher (lower) the firm's value.

These relationships are presented graphically in Exhibit B.1.

As already noted, earnings multiples vary with the nature of the firm. (In practice, of course, earnings multiples are also affected by conventional wisdom and the perspective and experience of the person performing the valuation.) Following are some examples of multiples based on the type of firm:

Type of Firm	Earnings Multiple
Small, well-established firm, vulnerable to recession	7
Small firm requiring average executive ability but operating in a highly competitive environment	4
Firm that depends on the special, often unusual skill of one individual or a small group of managers	2

Median earnings multiples also vary by industry, as shown by the following average multiples in different industries:[3]

Industry	Earnings Multiple
Retail	2.96
Services	5.34
Whole-sale trade	5.28
Construction	4.15
Manufacturing	8.56

Consider a real-life example. When Robert Hall, former owner of Visador Corporation, was considering selling his firm, he received an offer based on a multiple of five times the firm's operating income plus depreciation expense.[4] The offer was presented to Hall in the following format:[5]

Company's operating income plus depreciation expense	\$ 3,300,000
Earnings multiple	× 5
Firm value	\$ 16,500,00

To determine what Hall would receive for his ownership of the business, we subtract the $750,000 of debt owed by the firm, to get $15,750,000.

Hall rejected the offer of $15.75 million but made a counteroffer of $20 million for his ownership. Hall's counteroffer was accepted, which suggests that the buyer wanted the firm more than he let on initially.

The appropriateness of using earnings to value a firm is the subject of ongoing debate. Some contend that markets value a firm based on future cash flows, not reported earnings. Moreover, they argue, there are simply too many ways (within generally accepted accounting principles) to influence a firm's reported earnings, leading to material differences in valuation estimates when there is no difference in the intrinsic value of the firm. For these individuals, a firm's value is the present value of the firm's projected future cash flows.[6]

CASH FLOW–BASED VALUATION

Although not popular among smaller companies, **cash flow–based valuation**, in which a company is valued based on the amount and timing of its future cash flows, makes a lot of sense. Valuations based on earnings, although used more often, present a conceptual problem. From an investor's or owner's perspective, the value of a firm should be based on future cash flows, not reported earnings—especially not reported earnings for just a single year.

cash flow–based valuation
Determination of the value of a business by estimating the amount and timing of its future cash flows.

Measuring the value of a firm's future cash flows for a cash flow–based valuation is a three-step process:

Step 1. Project the firm's expected future cash flows.

Step 2. Estimate the investors' and owners' required rate of return on their investment in the business.

Step 3. Using the required rate of return as the discount rate, calculate the present value of the firm's expected future cash flows, which equals the value of the firm.

The cash flow–based approach is the most complicated of the three valuation methods discussed here; an in-depth explanation is well beyond the scope of this book. But it has one distinct advantage: A cash flow–based evaluation requires that *explicit* assumptions be made about the firm's future growth rates, its profit margins (profits to sales), how efficiently it is managing its assets (sales relative to the amount of the assets), and the appropriate discount rate (required rate of return). In contrast, a valuation based on comparables *implicitly* considers the relationship between the multiple being used and the factors that should determine the multiple. Thus, using cash flow–based valuation requires the estimator to examine more carefully why the firm has value.

ENDNOTES EN

CHAPTER 1

1. Paul D. Reynolds and Richard T. Curtin, "Business Creation in the United States: Panel Study of Entrepreneurial Dynamics II, Initial Assessment," *Foundations and Trends in Entrepreneurship*, Vol. 4, No. 3 (2008), pp. 155–307.
2. For an extensive report of the role of small businesses in the U.S. economy, see "The Small Business Economy: A Report to the President," United States Government Printing Office, http://www.sba.gov/advo/research/sb_econ2008.pdf, accessed February 28, 2009.
3. Tim Kane, "The Importance of Startups in Job Creation and Job Destruction," Kauffman Foundation Research Series: Firm Formation and Economic Growth, July 2010, pp. 2, 6.
4. Reynolds and Curtin, *op. cit.*
5. Jason Daley, "The Entrepreneur Economy," *Entrepreneur*, December 2009, pp. 53–57.
6. David Whiford, "Can You Learn to Be an Entrepreneur?" *Fortune*, Vol. 161, No. 4 (March 22, 2010), pp. 63–66.
7. John J. Fernandes, "Management and Entrepreneurship Education: Looking over the Horizon," speech given at the United States Association of Small Business and Entrepreneurship/Small Business Institute Conference, Tucson, Arizona, January 15, 2006.
8. Personal conversation with Ewing Marion Kauffman, October 2005.
9. Interview with Alex Calderwood by Jennifer Wang, in "How to Make a Scene," *Entrepreneur*, October 2010, pp. 28–36.
10. Personal interview with Shannon Guderian, December 2006.
11. Personal interview with Shannon Guderian, December 3, 2010.
12. Sharon Bernstein, "Will Five Guys Overtake In-N-Out?" *Los Angeles Times*, April 8, 2011; http://www.fiveguys.com/home.aspx, accessed June 10, 2011; Roger Yu, "Fast-Growing Five Guys Burger Chain Sticks to Basic, Fresh Food," *USA Today*, June 8, 2009; interview with Jerry Murrell by Liz Welch, April 1, 2010, published in "Jerry Murrell, Five Guys Burgers and Fries," *Inc.*, April 2010, pp. 77–80.
13. Lena Basha, "The Entrepreneurial Gene," *MyBusiness*, December/January 2007, p. 15.
14. For a discussion on "making meaning," see Guy Kawasaki, *The Art of the Start* (The Woodlands, TX: Portfolio, 2004), pp. 4–6.
15. Personal conversation with Rick Davis, October 21, 2010.
16. Sue LaShellenbargerst, "Plumbing for Joy? Be Your Own Boss," *Wall Street Journal*, September 2009, pp. D1–D2.
17. *Ibid.*
18. *Ibid.*
19. Bo Burlingham, "Lessons from a Blue-Collar Millionaire," *Inc.*, February 2010, pp. 56–63.
20. William J. Dennis, Jr. (ed.) "Contributions to Community," *NFIB National Small Business Poll*, Vol. 4, No. 6 (Washington, DC: NFIB Research Foundation, 2004), http://www.411sbfacts.com/sbpoll.php?POLLID=0025, accessed June 5, 2010.
21. Lena Basha, "Like a Good Neighbor," *MyBusiness*, December/January 2008, p. 28.
22. Thomas J. Stanley and William D. Danko, *The Millionaire Next Door* (New York: Simon & Schuster, 1996), p. 227.
23. http://www.womenentrepreneur.com/print/article/1599.html, accessed May 5, 2010.
24. Ram Charan, "Stop Whining, Start Thinking," *Bloomberg Businessweek*, August 24, 2008, p. 58.
25. Michelle Conlin (ed.), "How to Get a Life and Do Your Job," *Bloomberg Businessweek*, August 14, 2008, pp. 37–38.
26. Sharon Hadary, "What's Holding Back Women Entrepreneurs?" *Wall Street Journal*, May 17, 2010, pp. R1, R3.
27. Jeffry A. Timmons and Stephen Spinelli, *New Venture Creation: Entrepreneurship for the 21st Century* (New York: McGraw-Hill/Irwin, 2009), p. 367.
28. Thomas L. Friedman, *The World Is Flat* (Waterville, ME: Thorndike Press, 2005).
29. Clayton Christensen, *The Inventor's Dilemma* (New York: HarperCollins, 2003).
30. Amar Bhide, *The Venturesome Economy* (Princeton, NJ: Princeton University Press, 2008).
31. Lindsey Holloway, "The Best Things in Life Are Free," *Entrepreneur*, January 2009, pp. 42–45.
32. Pete Engardio, with Michael Arndt and Dean Foust, "The Future of Offshoring," *Bloomberg Businessweek*, January 30, 2006, p. 46.
33. Peter Funt, *WSJ Opinion*, September 20, 2010.
34. Alan Murray, "The End of Management," *Wall Street Journal*, August 21, 2010, p. W3.
35. Cited in Gary M. Stern, "Young Entrepreneurs Make Their Mark," *Nation's Business*, Vol. 84, No. 8 (August 1996), pp. 49–51.
36. Comments made by Tyler Self in an entrepreneurship class, October 28, 2010. Also, for a great reference on the importance of experience in being successful, see Malcom Gladwell, *Outliers: The Story of Success* (New York: Little, Brown, 2009).
37. Tamera Erikson, "Don't Treat Them Like Baby Boomers," *Bloomberg Businessweek*, August 14, 2008, p. 64.
38. Alison Damast, "With Jobs Scarce, MBAs Create Their Own," *Bloomberg Businessweek*, March 29, 2010, p. 89.
39. Donna Fenn, "Cool, Determined & Under 30," *Inc.*, October 2008, pp. 97–105.
40. *Ibid.*
41. Laura Lober, "Older Entrepreneurs Target Peers," *Wall Street Journal*, February 16, 2010, p. B6.
42. http://www.nfib.com/mybusiness-magazine/article?cmsid=54449, accessed November 14, 2010.
43. Timmons and Spinelli, *op. cit.*, pp. 46–54.
44. As quoted in John Koten, "Everything Will Change," *Inc.*, September 2007, http://ww.inc.com/magazine/20070901/everything-will-change.html, accessed March 2011.
45. Norm Brodsky, "Secrets of a $10 Million Man," *Inc.*, October 2008, pp. 77–81.
46. Comments by Ed Bonneau to an entrepreneurship class, November 20, 2010.
47. *Ibid.*
48. Ilan Mochari, "What Would You Do Differently?" *Inc.*, Vol. 23, No. 3 (March 2001), p. 65.
49. Personal conversation with Bernard Rapaport, 2009.
50. Stephen R. Covey, *The Seven Habits of Highly Effective People* (New York: Simon and Schuster, 1989), pp. 106–142.

CHAPTER 2

1. Karl Eller, *Integrity Is All You've Got: And Seven Other Lessons of an Entrepreneurial Life* (New York: McGraw-Hill, 2005), p. 89.

2. The terms *integrity* and *ethics* are often used interchangeably, but while closely related conceptually, they are not precisely equivalent. In our view, ethics most often refers to standards of conduct derived from an *externally* created system of rules or guidelines, such as those established by a professional board or industry association. This is slightly different from integrity, which is based on an *internal* system of principles that guide behavior, making compliance a matter of choice rather than obligation. However, both can powerfully shape the thoughts and conduct of conscientious individuals.
3. For more on this study, see Leslie E. Palich, Justin G. Longenecker, Carlos W. Moore, and J. William Petty, "Integrity and Small Business: A Framework and Empirical Analysis," proceedings of the 49th World Conference of the International Council for Small Business, Johannesburg, South Africa, June 2004.
4. Early on, R. Edward Freeman promoted the stakeholder view in his book, *Strategic Management: A Stakeholder Approach* (Boston: Pitman Publishing, 1984), but he recognizes that this framework can make decision making difficult. In fact, he contends that the task of managing companies with this approach is "akin to that of King Solomon." That is, there usually are no hard-and-fast rules to guide the balancing of stakeholder interests in a given situation. Though others would take issue with Freeman's conclusions, he nonetheless argues that the survival of the firm can be jeopardized if these interests are not kept in balance.
5. Laura L. Nash, *Good Intentions Aside: A Manager's Guide to Resolving Ethical Problems* (Boston: Harvard Business School Press, 1993), p. 61.
6. Some writers would add other stakeholders to the list (for example, suppliers, creditors, and labor unions). We have not included them here for the sake of simplicity, but a more complete model could certainly take them into consideration.
7. Milton Friedman, *Capitalism and Freedom* (Chicago: University of Chicago Press, 1963), p. 133.
8. Jana Matthews and Jeff Dennis, *Lessons from the Edge: Survival Skills for Starting and Growing a Company* (Oxford: Oxford University Press, 2003), pp. 119–123.
9. http://www.steelcase.com/na/about_steelcase_ourcompany.aspx?f=10036, accessed August 20, 2010; and Noel M. Tichy and Warren G. Bennis, "Making the Tough Call: Greater Leaders Recognize When Their Values Are on the Line," *Inc.*, Vol. 29, No. 11 (November 2007), pp. 36, 38.
10. Jodie Carter, "Rolling in Dough," *Entrepreneur,* Vol. 31, No. 6 (June 2003), p. 106; and personal conversation with Mike Jacobs, October 6, 2006.
11. "Happiness Begins at the Office," *Entrepreneur*, Vol. 32, No. 4 (May 2010), p. 8.
12. This is consistent with the findings of a recent and extensive meta-analysis that found a strong linkage between employee job satisfaction and customer satisfaction [see Steven P. Brown and Sun K. Lam, "A Meta-Analysis of Relationships Linking Employee Satisfaction to Customer Responses," *Journal of Marketing*, Vol. 84, No. 3 (September 2008), pp. 243–255].
13. Tony Hsieh, "Why I Sold Zappos," *Inc.*, Vol. 32, No. 5 (June 2010), pp. 101–104.
14. *Ibid*.
15. Palich et al., *op. cit.*
16. "Employee Theft: Legal Aspects—Estimates of Cost," http://law.jrank.org/pages/1084/Employee-Theft-Legal-Aspects-Estimates-cost.html, accessed August 24, 2010.
17. "Employee Theft," http://www.criminal-law-lawyer-source.com/terms/employee-theft.html, accessed August 24, 2010.
18. Chris Penttila, "Got Skills?" *Entrepreneur*, Vol. 34, No. 9 (September 2006), pp. 100–101; and personal conversation with David Shapiro, February 13, 2007.
19. *Ibid*.
20. Raymund Flandez, "Small Companies Put Charity into Their Business Plan," *Wall Street Journal*, November 20, 2007, p. B3.
21. The popular business press provides numerous examples to support this position, but we recognize that the evidence from academic studies on the subject is mixed. For an excellent review of this research, see Michael L. Barnett, "Stake-holder Influence Capacity and the Variability of Financial Returns to Corporate Social Responsibility," *Academy of Management Review*, Vol. 32, No. 3 (July 2007), pp. 794–816.
22. "2004 Cone Corporate Citizenship Study Results," http://www.causemarketingforum.com/page.asp?ID=330, accessed October 1, 2010.
23. William J. Dennis, Jr. (ed.), "Contributions to Community," http://www.411sbfacts.com/sbpoll.php?POLLID=0025, accessed August 30, 2010.
24. Eric Knopf, "One Step at a Time," in Michael McMyne and Nicole Amare (eds.), *Beyond the Lemonade Stand: 14 Undergraduate Entrepreneurs Tell Their Stories of Ethics in Business* (St. Louis, MO: St. Louis University, 2004), pp. 47–48.
25. Martin Vaughn, "IRS Too Easy on Payroll Taxes, Study Finds," *Wall Street Journal*, July 29, 2008, p. A8.
26. Gus Rancatore, "Local Hero or Tax Cheat?" *Inc.*, Vol. 30, No. 4, (April 2008), pp. 107–111.
27. *Ibid*.
28. For an interesting discussion and useful analysis of legitimacy lies, see Matther W. Rutherford, Paul F. Buller, and J. Michael Stebbins, "Ethical Considerations of the Legitimacy Lie," *Entrepreneurship Theory and Practice*, Vol. 33, No. 4 (July 2009), pp. 949–964.
29. Paulette Thomas, "Virtual Business Plans Require Human Touch," *Wall Street Journal*, August 2, 2005, p. B2.
30. Nadine Heintz, "For Rolling Up Her Sleeves," *Inc.*, April 2004, pp. 128–129.
31. Miroslav Pivoda, Frank Hoy, Kiril Todorov, and Viktor Vojtko, "Creativity and Ethics of Entrepreneurs in Global and Multicultural Environments," paper presented at the international conference of the European Council for Small Business and Entrepreneurship, Borovitis, Bulgaria, September 2010.
32. For an in-depth look at the theoretical framework and empirical tests involved in the study mentioned here, see Dean A. Shepherd and Andrew Zacharakis, "A New Venture's Cognitive Legitimacy: An Assessment by Customers," *Journal of Small Business Management*, Vol. 41, No. 2 (April 2003), pp. 148–167.
33. *Ibid*.
34. Eller, *op. cit.*, p. 90.
35. This research is cited in Stephen K. Henn, *Business Ethics: A Case Study Approach* (Hoboken, NJ: John Wiley and Sons, 2009), pp. 11–12.
36. For more on this, see Robert Moment, "The 7 Principles of Business Integrity," http://www.webpronews.com/, accessed September 3, 2010.
37. David H. Freedman, "Worried That Employees Are Wasting Time on the Web? Here's Why You Shouldn't Crack Down," *Inc.*, Vol. 28, No. 8 (August 2006), pp. 77–78.
38. One expert contends that employees are almost 10 percent more productive in their work if they are occasionally allowed to check their e-mail, watch short YouTube videos, etc. According to his report, these "frequent, small breaks help [employees] to regain their concentration" [see Jason Daley, "Creating a Culture of Excellence," *Entrepreneur*, Vol. 38, No. 3 (March 2010), pp. 81–87].
39. A study by Salary.com estimated that employees waste about 20 percent of their time at work, and 34.7 percent of the workers surveyed indicated that surfing the Internet was the greatest source of distraction (see Alina Dizik, "Services to Help Us Stop Dawdling Online," *Wall Street Journal*, January 28, 2010, p. D2).

40. Dionne Searcey, "Some Courts Raise Bar on Reading Employee Email," *Wall Street Journal*, November 19, 2009, p. A17.

41. *Ibid.*

42. For excellent guidance regarding the legal issues related to Internet use regulation at work, see William P. Smith and Filiz Tabak, "Monitoring Employee E-mails: Is There Any Room for Privacy?" *Academy of Management Perspectives*, Vol. 23, No. 4 (November 2009), pp. 33–48.

43. "Handbagged," *The Economist*, June 19, 2008, http://www.economist.com/business/Printer/Friendly.cfm?story_id=11580287, accessed July 10, 2008.

44. Brad Stone, "Court Clears eBay in Suit over Sale of Counterfeit Goods," *New York Times*, July 15, 2008, http://www.nytimes.com/2008/07/15/technology/15ebay.html?_r=2&pagewanted=print&oref=slo%20gin, accessed October 1, 2010.

45. "Fake Gucci, Vuitton Bags Seized in Italy," CNNMoney.com, September 25, 2006, http://money.cnn.com/, accessed October 2, 2006.

46. A study by Justin G. Longenecker, Joseph A. McKinney, and Carlos W. Moore ["Religious Intensity, Evangelical Christianity, and Business Ethics: An Empirical Study," *Journal of Business Ethics,* Vol. 55, No. 2 (2004), pp. 373–386] provides evidence to support this position. The authors examined data from 1,234 business leaders responding to a national survey. Study participants were asked to evaluate the ethical quality of responses described in a series of vignettes (from "never acceptable" to "always acceptable") and also to identify which of the following five broad categories best described their religious faith: Catholic, Protestant, Jewish, other religions, no religion. Study results found no difference between these general groups. However, respondents who indicated that religious interests were of high or moderate importance to them demonstrated a higher level of ethical judgment than did others in the study, as did those who considered their beliefs to be consistent with the basic tenets of Evangelical Christianity. These findings suggest that religious values play a part in ethical decision making, though *general* religious categorizations do not seem to have this same impact.

47. Kent Jennings Brockwell, "10 Questions: Jeff Ukrop," Richmond.com, August 27, 2007, http://www.richmond.com/local-life/, accessed October 1, 2010; and "Ukrop's," NationMaster.com, http://www.nationmaster.com/, accessed September 12, 2008.

48. Nicholas G. Moore, "Ethics: The Way to Do Business," http://www.bentley.edu/cbe/events/lecture_sears_moore.cfm, accessed October 1, 2010.

49. Excerpt from an interview with J. C. Huizenga in "Virtuous Business and Educational Practice," *Religion & Liberty*, Vol. 12, No. 5, http://www.acton.org/pub/religion-liberty/volume-12-number-5/virtuous-business-and-educational-practice, accessed September 7, 2010.

50. Kenneth H. Blanchard and Norman Vincent Peale, *The Power of Ethical Management* (New York: HarperCollins, 1989).

51. J. Michael Alford, "Finding Competitive Advantage in Managing Workplace Ethics," paper presented at the 2005 meeting of the United States Association for Small Business and Entrepreneurship, Indian Wells, California, January 13–16, 2005.

52. More specific insights and guidance for writing a code of conduct can be found at http://www.ethics.org/page/ethics-toolkit, accessed October 1, 2010.

53. "Resource Toolkit: The PLUS Decision Making Model," Ethics Resource Center, http://www.ethics.org/resource/plus-decision-making-model, accessed October 1, 2010.

54. "Guiding Principles," http://www.rotary.org/en/AboutUs/RotaryInternational/GuidingPrinciples/Pages/ridefault.aspx, accessed October 1, 2010.

55. Brian K. Burton and Michael Goldsby ["The Golden Rule and Business Ethics: An Examination," *Journal of Business Ethics,* Vol. 56, No. 3 (2005), pp. 371–383] offer an extended discussion of the history, meaning, and problems of the Golden Rule. They document the appearance of this general principle in the writings of several major world religions and philosophers and provide examples of companies that have used the Golden Rule explicitly as a guide for decision making (e.g., JCPenney and Lincoln Electric Co.). The influence of the Golden Rule is so pervasive that Burton and Goldsby conclude that it "seems to be one of the few candidates for a universally acceptable moral principle."

56. Kant actually offered a critique of the Golden Rule, but only as a footnote to his discussion of the categorical imperative. In his opinion, the categorical imperative is a superior concept for a number of reasons, all of which are related to his expanded view of the imperative [see Immanuel Kant, *Grounding for the Metaphysics of Morals, with a Supposed Right to Lie Because of Philanthropic Concerns,* 3rd ed., trans. J. W. Ellington (Indianapolis: Hackett Publishing, 1993)].

57. Rese Fox, "An Inconvenient Value," http://www.awarenessintoaction.com/whitepapers/getting-the-true-assessment-of-a-leed-certified-buildings-value.html, accessed September 24, 2010.

58. "Greening Your Business: A Primer for Smaller Companies," http://www.greenbiz.com/business/research/report/2007/07/18/greening-your-business-primer-smaller-companies, accessed October 1, 2010.

59. "Managing Your Hazardous Waste: A Guide for Small Businesses," http://www.epa.gov/epawaste/hazard/generation/sqg/handbook/k01005.pdf, accessed October 1, 2010.

60. See David Worrell, "Keen on Green," *Entrepreneur,* Vol. 34, No. 9 (September 2006), pp. 67–71, for a helpful summary of trends related to "green" technologies and the investments they have attracted.

61. Malia Wollan, "Bamboo Bikes Appeal to Earth-Conscious Bikers," *WacoTribune-Herald*, August 15, 2010, p. A3.

62. http://boobicycles.com/boo.html, accessed September 29, 2010.

63. Todd Woody, "Surf's Up, Waste's Down," *New York Times*, September 19, 2009, p. A4.

64. Alex Lindahl, "The Water Track," *Entrepreneur*, Vol. 38, No. 4 (April 2010), p. 62.

65. Marc Gunter, "Tree Huggers, Soy Lovers, and Profits," *Fortune,* Vol. 147, No. 12 (June 23, 2003), pp. 99–104.

CHAPTER 3

1. To read more about an interesting framework that integrates three forms of the search process (deliberate search, industry insight guided search, and alertness to opportunities), see Robert A. Baron, "Opportunity Recognition as Pattern Recognition: How Entrepreneurs 'Connect the Dots' to Identify New Business Opportunities," *Academy of Management Perspectives,* Vol. 20, No. 1 (February 2006), pp. 104–119.

2. Israel M. Kirzner, *Competition and Entrepreneurship* (Chicago: University of Chicago Press, 1973), p. 74.

3. For an in-depth discussion of the alertness concept and the essence of the mindset of the entrepreneur, see Jeffery S. McMullen and Dean A. Shepherd, "Entrepreneurial Action and the Role of Uncertainty in the Theory of the Entrepreneur," *Academy of Management Review,* Vol. 31, No. 1 (2006), pp. 132–152.

4. The process of opportunity recognition is not entirely driven by thoughts; in fact, feelings and emotions can also play a very important role. For an interesting analysis of the interplay of affect and cognitive processes, see Robert A. Baron, "The Role of Affect in the Entrepreneurial Process,"

Academy of Management Review, Vol. 33, No. 2 (2008), pp. 328–340.

5. Quoted in April Y. Pennington, "Copy That: In Business, Imitation Is More Than a Form of Flattery," *Entrepreneur,* Vol. 34, No. 3 (March 2006), p. 22.

6. http://www.soldierfuel.com/in_news.html, accessed October 8, 2010; and Lee Gimpel, "Idea Mining," *Entrepreneur,* Vol. 34, No. 12 (December 2006), p. 70.

7. Jennifer Wang, "Rick Alden," *Entrepreneur,* Vol. 38, No. 7 (January 2010), p. 24; and Sara Wilson, "A Step Ahead," *Entrepreneur,* Vol. 36, No. 11 (November 2008), p. 41.

8. Gerry E. Hills and R. P. Singh, "Opportunity Recognition," in W. B. Gartner, K. G. Shaver, and P. D. Reynolds (eds.), *Handbook of Entrepreneurial Dynamics: The Process of Business Creation* (Thousand Oaks, CA: Sage Publications, 2004), Table 24.4, p. 268.

9. Personal experience can certainly influence the *kind* of startup ideas that entrepreneurs develop, but recent evidence indicates that work experience in general as well as experience with new ventures in particular can also improve the *quality* of concepts generated. One researcher found business ideas tend to be evaluated more positively when the teams that come up with them are larger in size, have more work experience on average, and/or have access to input from individuals with founding experience. Further, smaller teams benefited more from external founder assistance and also generated higher-quality ideas in situations where a founder was actually a member of the team itself. For more on these findings, see Maw-Der Foo, "Member Experience, Use of External Assistance and Evaluation of Business Ideas," *Journal of Small Business Management*, Vol. 48, No. 1 (January 2010), pp. 32–43.

10. http://www.cabanalife.com/about.php, accessed October 11, 2010; and Nichole L. Torres, "Transform a Negative Experience into a Positive Business Idea," *Entrepreneur*, Vol. 35, No. 12 (December 2007), pp. 108–109.

11. http://www.bestkiteboarding.com/09-Company, accessed October 11, 2010; and Lindsay Holloway, "To the Extreme," *Entrepreneur*, Vol. 36, No. 3 (March 2008), p. 21.

12. Erin Weinger, "Selling Short," *Entrepreneur*, Vol. 38, No. 4 (April 2010), p. 19.

13. *Ibid*.

14. For an expanded discussion of this framework, see Peter F. Drucker, *Innovation and Entrepreneurship: Practice and Principles* (New York: HarperCollins, 2006), pp. 30–129.

15. *Ibid.,* p. 30.

16. To learn more about the application of creativity to the process of business idea generation, see Dimo Dimov, "Idea Generation from a Creativity Perspective," in Andrew Zacharakis and Stephen Spinelli, Jr. (eds.), *Entrepreneurship: The Engine of Growth* (Westport, CT: Praeger Perspectives, 2007), pp. 19–41.

17. "A Revolutionary Concept," http://www.aimiesdinnerandmovie.com/about, accessed October 18, 2010.

18. Gwen Moran, "Blinkin' Brilliant," *Entrepreneur*, Vol. 37, No. 12 (December 2009), p. 112; and http://www.canddlandscape.com/, accessed October 18, 2010.

19. "Stroke of Genius," *Entrepreneur*, Vol. 38, No. 3 (March 2010), p. 78; and "Anti-Lunch Theft Bags," http://thinkofthe.com/, accessed October 18, 2010.

20. For an interesting analysis of Apple's strategy with products such as the iPad, see Farhad Manjoo, "Apple Nation," *Fast Company,* No. 147 (July/August 2010), pp. 68–112.

21. Joel Holland, "What's Your Problem?" *Entrepreneur,* Vol. 38, No. 5 (May 2010), p. 70.

22. http://adventurebachelorparty.com, accessed October 18, 2010; and Amanda Pennington, "Creature Comforts," *Entrepreneur,* Vol. 34, No. 7 (July 2006), pp. 120–122.

23. Sarah Kessler, "All Natural—From Her Ranch to Your Backyard," *Inc.*, Vol. 32, No. 4 (May 2010), p. 23; and http://www.ahavenbrand.com/about_us.html, accessed October 19, 2010.

24. http://www.calsaway.com/arizona_swimming_pool_cleaning_about_us.php, accessed November 3, 2010; and Kristin Ohlson, "Save Water, Save Money," *Entrepreneur*, Vol. 36, No. 10 (October 2008), p. 20.

25. "RFID Is a Winner in the Sports Arena," *RFID Journal,* http://www.rfidjournal.com/article/articleview/4028/5/474, accessed January 13, 2009; and Siri Schubert, "A Duffer's Dream," *Business 2.0,* Vol. 7, No. 10 (November 2006), p. 56.

26. Presser actually refers to these as product-driven and market-driven approaches, but the essence is aptly captured by our terms, *inside-out* and *outside-in*, which we develop in some detail in the pages that follow. For more on his perspective, see Leon Presser, *What It Takes to Be an Entrepreneur* (Gardena, CA: Resserp Publishing, 2010), p. 38.

27. As something of a parallel to the outside-in and inside-out options, Dimo Dimov ["From Opportunity Insight to Opportunity Intention: The Importance of Person-Situation Learning Match," *Entrepreneurship Theory and Practice*, Vol. 31, No. 4 (July 2007), p. 566] mentions two very different opportunity insight–inducing situations. In *demand-driven* situations, the entrepreneur is aware of customer needs but does not know of any products that could meet those needs. *Supply-driven* situations are just the opposite. Here, the entrepreneur is aware of an emerging product, but doesn't know of customer needs that could be satisfied by it.

28. Much of the research on this subject is based on firms of all sizes, not just small businesses; however, there is no reason to rule out entirely the applicability of this research to entrepreneurial companies. Some studies present strong evidence that context is important: (Suresh Kotha and Anil Nair, "Strategy and Environment as Determinants of Performance: Evidence from the Japanese Machine Tool Industry," *Strategic Management Journal,* Vol. 16, No. 7 (1995), pp. 497–518; A. M. McGahan and Michael E. Porter, "How Much Does Industry Matter, Really?" *Strategic Management Journal,* Vol. 18, Summer Special Issue (1997), pp. 15–30; and R. Schmalensee, "Do Markets Differ Much?" *American Economic Review,* Vol. 75, No. 3 (1985), pp. 341–351.Others show that context is important but not as great a driver of firm performance as such internal factors as a company's resources: Gabriel Hawawini, Venkat Subramanian, and Paul Verdin, "Is Performance Driven by Industry- or Firm-Specific Factors? A New Look at the Evidence," *Strategic Management Journal,* Vol. 24, No. 1 (2003), pp. 1–16; and Mona Makhija, "Comparing the Resource-Based and Market-Based Views of the Firm: Empirical Evidence from Czech Privatization," *Strategic Management Journal,* Vol. 24, No. 3 (2003), pp. 433–451.Thomas J. Douglas and Joel A. Ryman ["Understanding Competitive Advantage in the General Hospital Industry: Evaluating Strategic Competencies," *Strategic Management Journal,* Vol. 24, No. 2 (2003), pp. 333–347] interpret the results of their study to suggest that both external context and internal factors are important to the formation of competitive advantage, a conclusion that is consistent with evidence from studies of small and medium-sized enterprises, such as those conducted by Bo Eriksen and Thorbjorn Knudsen ["Industry and Firm Level Interaction: Implications for Profitability," *Journal of Business Research,* Vol. 56, No. 3 (2003), pp. 191–199], Stewart Thornhill ["Knowledge, Innovation and Firm Performance in High- and Low-Technology Regimes," *Journal of Business Venturing,* Vol. 21, No. 5 (2006), pp. 687–703], and Clement K. Wang and Bee Lian Ang ["Determinants of Venture Performance in Singapore," *Journal of*

Small Business Management, Vol. 42, No. 4 (2004), pp. 347–363].

29. Kevin J. Delaney, "Searching for Clients from Above," *Wall Street Journal*, July 31, 2007, p. B1; and Logan Kugler, "Targeting the Eye in the Sky," *Business 2.0*, Vol. 7, No. 3 (April 2006), p. 26.
30. Rich Karlgard, "Schumpeter on Speed," *Forbes*, Vol. 178, No. 3 (August 14, 2006), p. 35.
31. Delaney, *op. cit*.
32. "Fast Facts: Obesity Trends," The George Washington University School of Public Health and Health Services, http://www.stopobesityalliance.org/wp-content/themes/stopobesityalliance/pdfs/Fast-Facts_ObesityTrends5-2010.pdf, accessed October 28, 2010.
33. Michael Porter, *Competitive Advantage* (New York: Free Press, 1985), pp. 7–29.
34. William A. Sahlman, *How to Write a Great Business Plan* (Boston: Harvard Business School Press, 2008).
35. Robert Levine, "The Kopy Kat Kids," CNNMoney.com, October 2, 2007, http://money.cnn.com/2007/10/02/technology/kopy_kat_kids.biz2/index.htm, accessed October 28, 2010.
36. Clay Shirky, "The (Bayesian) Advantage of Youth," http://many.corante.com/archives/2007/05/19/the_bayesian_advantage_of_youth.php, accessed October 28, 2010.
37. "Starbucks—Company Profile," http://assets.starbucks.com/assets/company-profile-feb10.pdf, accessed October 28, 2010.
38. "Heartwood's History," http://hwd3d.com/the-company/heartwoods-history, accessed October 28, 2010; and Nichole L. Torres, "Biz U: Industrial Evolution," *Entrepreneur*, Vol. 35, No. 11 (November 2007), pp. 142–143.
39. A study of small businesses conducted by the National Federation of Independent Business found that 34.4 percent of all small businesses surveyed said that competing on price is a very significant feature of their strategy, which is consistent with an emphasis on controlling costs (specifically, 51 percent said that keeping overhead to a minimum is a very significant feature of their strategy). However, it is also important to note that providing better service and offering the highest quality possible were significantly important to even more firms (83.4 percent and 86.3 percent, respectively), which indicates that differentiation strategies are even more important to small businesses. See William J. Dennis, Jr. (ed.), "Competition," *NFIB National Small Business Poll*, Vol. 3, No. 8 (Washington, DC: NFIB Research Foundation, 2003).
40. http://www.spiritair.com/AboutUs.aspx, accessed November 3, 2010.
41. Scott McCartney, "The Next Airline Fee: Buying Tickets?" *Wall Street Journal*, March 3, 2009, p. D4, http://online.wsj.com/article/SB123604492886515417.html, accessed November 3, 2010.
42. http://www.getradiotag.com, accessed October 29, 2010; and Sara Wilson, "Maximizing Air Time," *Entrepreneur*, Vol. 36, No. 11 (November 2008), p. 71.
43. Philip Kotler, *Marketing Insights from A to Z* (New York: John Wiley & Sons, 2003), p. 65.
44. http://www.personalizedbottlewater.com/aboutus.asp, accessed October 29, 2010.
45. Brian O'Reilly, "A Small Firm That Sells Custom-Labeled H2O Looks to Pump Online Sales," *Fortune Small Business*, Vol. 17, No. 1 (February 26, 2007), http://money.cnn.com/magazines/fsb/fsb_archive/2007/02/01/8399927/index.htm?postversion=2007022606, accessed March 3, 2001.
46. http://www.spin-la.com/, accessed January 13, 2009.
47. Laura Tiffany, "Road to Success," *Entrepreneur*, Vol. 36, No. 11 (November 2008), pp. 88–97.
48. *Ibid*.
49. http://www.cobbtuning.com/info/?id=2953, accessed November 3, 2010.
50. Tiffany, *op. cit*.
51. Marc J. Dollinger, *Entrepreneurship: Strategies and Resources* (Lombard, IL: Marsh Publications, 2008), p. 144.
52. Porter, *op. cit.*, p. 5.
53. Quoted in Mark Henricks, "What Not to Do," *Entrepreneur*, Vol. 32, No. 2 (February 2004), pp. 84–90.
54. John W. Mullins, *The New Business Road Test* (London: Financial Times Prentice Hall, 2010), pp. 3–4.
55. *Ibid.*, p. 10.
56. *Ibid.*, p. 16.

CHAPTER 4

1. Arthur G. Sharp, http://www.referenceforbusiness.com/encyclopedia/For-Gol/Franchising.html, accessed October 30, 2010.
2. Roy Seaman, http://www.theukfranchisedirectory.net/page/history-of-franchising.php, accessed October 30, 2010.
3. *Ibid*.
4. Hilary Strahota, "Benjamin Franklin: Father of Franchising?" *Franchising World*, September 2007.
5. Bret Lowell and Tao Xu, http://franchise.org/franchiseesecondary.aspx?id=10008, accessed October 30, 2010.
6. http://franchise.org/code.aspx, accessed October 30, 2010.
7. http://franchise.org/faq.aspx, accessed October 30, 2010.
8. Nichole L. Torres, "Staying Power," http://www.entrepreneur.com/magazine/2006/January, accessed January 19, 2009.
9. http://www.uspto.gov/main/glossary/index.html#trademark, accessed December 10, 2010.
10. http://www.subway.com/subwayroot/legalDisclaimer, accessed October 30, 2010.
11. http://www.franchise.org/, accessed October 30, 2010.
12. Dennis L. Monroe, "Teamwork," *Franchise Times*, Vol. 14, No. 9 (October, 2008), p. 90.
13. http://www.franchiseregistry.com/, accessed October 30, 2010.
14. http://franchise.org/, accessed October 28, 2010.
15. "Legal Briefs," *Franchise Times*, Vol. 14, No. 7 (August, 2008), p. 51.
16. http://classactionlawsuitsinthenews.com/class-action-settlements/quiznos-class-action-settlement-of-quiznos-franchisee-class-action-lawsuit/, accessed October 30, 2010; and http://qnationalsettlement.com/, accessed October 30, 2010.
17. http://www.unhappyfranchisee.com/, accessed October 30, 2010.
18. http://franchise.org/Veteran_Franchise_Centers_franchise.aspx, accessed October 30, 2010.
19. http://www.ownanoreckstore.com/, accessed October 30, 2010.
20. http://www.sonicdrivein.com/business/franchise/own.jsp, accessed December 11, 2010.
21. Personal correspondence with Mark Liston, October 27, 2010.
22. *Ibid*.
23. Jason Daley, "Fiscally Fit," *Entrepreneur*, Vol. 37, No. 10 (October 2009), p. 130.
24. Darren Dahl, "How to Find a Business to Buy," http://www.inc.com/guides/buy_biz/how-to-find-a-business-to-buy.html, accessed October 30, 2010.
25. http://www.sba.gov/smallbusinessplanner/start/buyabusiness/SERV_SBP_S_DETVAL.html, accessed October 30, 2010.

CHAPTER 5

1. Jayne A. Pearl, "America's Largest Family Businesses," http://www.familybusinessmagazine.com/index.php?/channels/articles/americas_largest_family_businesses/, accessed December 6, 2010.

2. Frank Hoy and Pramodita Sharma, *The Entrepreneurial Family Business* (Upper Saddle River, NJ: Pearson Prentice Hall, 2010).

3. James Olan Hutcheson, "In with the Old; Out with the Older," http://www.familybusinessmagazine.com/index.php?/channels/articles/the_worlds_oldest_family_companies/, accessed December 6, 2010.

4. Ernesto J. Poza, *Family Business,* 3rd edition (Mason, OH: South-Western, 2010).

5. J. H. Chua, J. J. Chrisman, & P. Sharma, "Defining the Family Business by Behavior," *Entrepreneurship Theory & Practice,* Vol. 23, No. 4, pp. 19–39.

6. Alternatively, the European Group of Owner-Managed and Family Enterprises classifies a firm, of any size, as a family enterprise, if (1) the majority of votes is in possession of the natural person(s) who established the firm, or in possession of the natural person(s) who has/have acquired the share capital of the firm, or in the possession of their spouses, parents, child, or children's direct heirs; (2) at least one representative of the family or kin is involved in the management or administration of the firm; or (3) the person(s) who established or acquired the firm or their families or descendents possess 25 percent of the right to vote mandated by their share capital.

7. Torsten Pieper, *Mechanisms to Assure Long-Term Family Business Survival* (Frankfurt am Main: Peter Lang, 2007), p. 205.

8. http://scjohnson.com/en/home.aspx, accessed October 31, 2010.

9. Personal interview with Melanie Bergeron, October 18, 2010; and http://www.twomen.com, accessed December 5, 2010.

10. Peter Leach, *Family Businesses: The Essentials* (London: Profile Books, 2007).

11. Ellen Frankenburg, "Fostering a Culture of Stewardship," in Barbara Spector (ed.), *The Family Business Shareholder's Handbook* (Philadelphia: Family Business Publishing, 2008).

12. W. Gibb Dyer and David A. Whetten, "Family Firms and Social Responsibility: Preliminary Evidence from the S&P 500," *Entrepreneurship Theory and Practice,* Vol. 30, No. 6 (November 2006), pp. 785–802.

13. Barbara Spector (ed.), "The World's Oldest Family Companies," http://www.familybusinessmagazine.com/index.php?/channels/articles/the_worlds_oldest_family_companies/, accessed December 6, 2010.

14. http://zildjian.com/, accessed October 31, 2010.

15. Tim Barnett, Kimberly Eddleston, and Franz Willi Kellermanns, "The Effects of Family Versus Career Role Salience on the Performance of Family and Nonfamily Firms," *Family Business Review,* Vol. 22, No. 1 (March 2009), pp. 39–52; and Frank Hoy and Pramodita Sharma, *Entrepreneurial Family Firms* (Boston: Prentice Hall, 2010).

16. These bases of commitment and an extensive discussion of the theory and analysis that back up these conclusions can be found in Pramodita Sharma and P. Gregory Irving, "Four Bases of Family Business Successor Commitment: Antecedents and Consequences," *Entrepreneurship Theory and Practice,* Vol. 29, No. 1 (January 2005), pp. 13–33.

17. Greg McCann, *When Your Parents Sign the Paychecks* (Indianapolis, IN: JIST Works, 2007), p. 63.

18. Pieper, *op. cit.*

19. Bill Glavin, Joe Astrachan, and Judy Green, *2007 American Family Business Survey* (Springfield, MA: Massachusetts Mutual Life Insurance Company, 2007).

20. Meg Cadoux Hirshberg, "Breaking Up's Not Hard to Do," *Inc.,* November 2010, p. 47.

21. Pia Chatterjee, "Making Beautiful Startups Together," *Business 2.0,* September 2007, pp. 42–44.

22. Krissah Williams, "We Do: Copreneurs Simultaneously Build Happy Marriages and Thriving Enterprises," *Black Enterprise,* February 2008.

23. "Ask Inc.," *Inc.,* March 2007, pp. 81–82.

24. Kathryn Levy Feldman, "Chick-fil-A's Second Generation Aims to Go 'the Second Mile,'" http://www.familybusinessmagazine.com/index.php?/articles/single/chick-fil-as_second_generation_aims_to_go_the_second_mile/, accessed December 6, 2010.

25. Stephanie Clifford, "Splitting Heirs," *Inc.,* August 2007, pp. 103–110.

26. "Ask the Experts: A Sibling Rivalry Festers After a Chairman's Death," *Family Business,* Vol. 18, No. 4 (Autumn 2007), pp. 8, 10, 14.

27. Last names have been withheld at request of the owners.

28. John L. Ward, "Family Humor," proceedings of the Fifth Annual Kellogg Family Business Invitational Conference, Evanston, IL, May 16–17, 2006, p. 45.

29. Meg Cadoux Hirshberg, "Left Behind," *Inc.,* Vol. 32, No. 4 (May 2010), pp. 37–38.

30. Meg Cadoux Hirshberg, "Minding the Kids," *Inc.,* Vol. 32, No. 2 (March 2010), pp. 39–41.

31. Per-Olaf Bjuggren and Johanna Palmberg, "The Impact of Vote Differentiation on Investment Performance in Listed Family Firms, *Family Business Review,* Vol. 23, No. 4 (December 2010), pp. 327–340.

32. Pramodita Sharma, "An Overview of the Field of Family Business Studies: Current Status and Directions for the Future," in Panikkos Zata Poutziouris, Kosmas X. Smyrnios, and Sabine B. Klein (eds.), *Handbook of Research on Family Business* (Cheltenham, UK: Edward Elgar, 2006), pp. 25–55.

33. David Lansky, "Family Meetings: Some Guidelines," http://www.efamilybusiness.com/index.cfm?md=Content&sd=ViewArticle&MatterID=18&WebArticleID=590, accessed November 29, 2010.

34. Ernesto J. Poza, *Family Business,* 3rd edition (Mason, OH: South-Western Cengage Learning, 2007).

35. Ken McCracken, Charlie Tee, and Matthew Woods, "Governance and Management," in Ian MacDonald and Jonathon Sutton (eds.), *Business Families and Family Businesses* (London: Globe Business Publishing, 2009), pp. 179–192.

36. http://www.twomen.com/mary-ellen-sheets, accessed November 29, 2010.

37. Simona Covel, "The Succession Planning," *MYBUSINESS,* March/April 2010, p. 23.

38. http://www.pwc.com/gx/en/press-room/2010/family-business-owners-optimistic-about-growth.jhtml, accessed December 5, 2010.

39. Barbara Spector, "Succession and Stewardship: Challenges for the Next Generation," *The Family Business Shareholder's Handbook* (Philadelphia: Family Business Publishing, 2008), p. 119.

40. Frank Hoy and Pramodita Sharma, *Entrepreneurial Family Firms* (Boston: Prentice Hall, 2010).

41. Adam Bluestein, "The Success Gene," *Inc.,* April 2008, pp. 83–94.

42. For an extended discussion of various aspects of mentoring in the family firm, see Barbara Spector (ed.), *The Family Business Mentoring Handbook* (Philadelphia: Family Business Publishing Co., 2004). Only one of many resources on mentoring, this edited volume provides articles outlining a number of proven mentoring strategies, as well as case examples of family companies that have used these approaches to achieve effective succession transitions. The book addresses processes and strategies as they apply specifically to family businesses.

43. Greg McCann, "Cultivating Ownership in the Next Generation," in Barbara Spector (ed.), *The Family Business Shareholder's Handbook* (Philadelphia: Family Business Publishing, 2008), pp. 120–121.

44. Richard Salomon, "Setting a Standard for Future Generations," in Barbara Spector (ed.), *The Family Business Shareholder's Handbook* (Philadelphia: Family Business Publishing, 2008), p. 123.

CHAPTER 6

1. The MIT Enterprise Forum (http://web.mit.edu/entforum) sponsors sessions across the United States in which aspiring entrepreneurs present business plans to panels of venture capitalists, bankers, marketing specialists, and other experts.
2. David E. Gumpert, *How to Really Create a Successful Business Plan,* 4th ed. (Needham, MA: Lauson Publishing Co., 2003), p. 10.
3. Thomas Stemberg, "What You Need to Succeed," *Inc.,* Vol. 29, No. 1 (January 2007), pp. 75–77.
4. Kelly Spors, "Do Start-Ups Really Need Formal Business Plans?" *Wall Street Journal,* January 9, 2007, p. B9.
5. Amar Bhide, *The Origin and Evolution of New Businesses* (New York: Oxford University Press, 2000), p. 53.
6. Stephen Lawrence and Frank Moyes, "Writing a Successful Business Plan," http://leeds-faculty.colorado.edu/moyes/html/resources.htm, accessed January 5, 2011.
7. Bhide, *op. cit.,* p. 70.
8. "Conversations with Ewing Marion Kauffman," Ewing Marion Kauffman Foundation, March 2004.
9. Peter Drucker, quoted in Brian Tracy, "7 Secrets to Success," *Entrepreneur,* Vol. 35, No. 2 (February 2007), pp. 96–103.
10. An alternative framework for a feasibility analysis to what is presented in Chapter 3 is provided by Frank Moyes, a professor at the University of Colorado, at his website http://leeds-faculty.colorado.edu/, accessed January 5, 2011.
11. Portions of the content in this section draw on Jeffry A. Timmons, Andrew Zacharakis, and Stephen Spinelli, *Business Plans That Work* (New York: McGraw-Hill, 2004).
12. David E. Gumpert, "Making It All Add Up: The Financial Section of a Business Plan," October 24, 1999, http://www.inc.com/articles/1999/10/14877.html, accessed September 11, 2011.
13. Personal conversation with Rudy Garza, November 29, 2010.
14. Jeffrey Bussgang "Think Like a VC, Act Like an Entrepreneur, *Bloomberg Businessweek,* http://www.businessweek.com/magazine/content/08_34/b4097042749532.htm?chan=magazine+channel_special+report, accessed December 2010.
15. The explanation of business models in this section draws heavily from a variety of sources, primarily Richard G. Hamermesh, Paul W. Mashall, and Taz Pirmohamed, "Note on Business Model Analysis for the Entrepreneur," Harvard Business School (9-802-048), January 22, 2002; Vivek Wadhwa, "Before You Write a Business Plan," *Bloomberg Businessweek,* http://www.businessweek.com/smallbiz/content/may2006/sb20060512_948264.htm, accessed January 31, 2011; Michael Rappa, "Business Models on the Web," http://www.digitalenterprise.org/models/models.html, accessed February 10, 2011; Vivek Wadhwa, "Countdown to Product Launch (Part II)" *Bloomberg Businessweek,* May 12, 2006, http://www.businessweek.com/print/smallbiz/content/may2006/sb20060512_948264.htm, accessed January 31, 2011; Karen E. Klein, "Do You Really Need a Business Plan?" *Bloomberg Businessweek,* http://www.businessweek.com/print/smallbiz/content/mar2008/sb20080312_587399.htm, accessed December 28, 2010; and Rob Adams, "Taking the Trouble to Research Your Market," *Bloomberg Businessweek,* http://www.businessweek.com/smallbiz/content/oct2004/sb20041020_9945.htm, accessed February 14, 2011.
16. "Get Help with Your Plan," *Entrepreneur,* March 2, 2001, http://www.entrepreneur.com/startinga business/businessplans/article38314.html, accessed August 14, 2010.

CHAPTER 7

1. Claire Cain Miller, "Accel Invests in ModCloth, a Social Shopping Site," *New York Times,* June 30, 2010.
2. ModCloth, http://www.modcloth.com/storefront/products/be_the_buyer, accessed January 8, 2011.
3. Spira Footwear, http://www.spirafootwear.com/wavespring_technology.php, accessed January 9, 2011.
4. *Ibid.*
5. From the business plan of JavaNet Internet Cafe, http://www.bplans.com/internet_cafe_business_plan/market_analysis_summary_fc.cfm, accessed January 9, 2011. Note that as of 2011, Compuserve and Prodigy are no longer widely used in the United States.
6. Personal conversation with Todd Stoner, December 2006.
7. Karlene Lukovitz, "Community Marketing Feeds Papa Murphy's Success," http://www.mediapost.com/publications/?fa=Articles.showArticle&art_aid=132703, accessed January 9, 2011; and http://www.papamurphys.com/#take-n-bake, accessed January 9, 2011.
8. Geoff Williams, "Worst. Business Name. Ever.," *Entrepreneur,* Vol. 37, No. 5 (May, 2009), pp. 66–67.
9. Brad Stone, "What's in a Name? For Apple, iPad Said More Than Intended," *New York Times,* January 29, 2010, pp. A1, A3.
10. Carl McDaniel and Roger Gates, Marketing Research, 8th ed. (Hoboken, NJ: John Wiley & Sons, 2009).
11. Lisa Barone, "How to Participate in a Twitter Chat," http://smallbiztrends.com/2010/08/how-to-participate-in-twitter-chat.html, accessed February 19, 2011.
12. McDaniel and Gates, *op. cit.,* pp. 94–95.
13. John Tozzi, "Market Research on the Cheap," *Bloomberg Businessweek,* http://www.businessweek.com/smallbiz/content/jan2008/sb2008019_352779.htm, accessed January 12, 2011.
14. Michael Porter, *Competitive Advantage* (New York: Free Press, 1985), p. 5.

CHAPTER 8

1. For example, see Michael D. Ensley, Allison W. Pearson, and Allen C. Amason, "Understanding the Dynamics of New Venture Top Management Teams: Cohesion, Conflict, and New Venture Performance," *Journal of Business Venturing,* Vol. 17 (2002), pp. 365–366; and Elizabeth J. Teal and Charles W. Hofer, "Key Attributes of the Founding Entrepreneurial Team of Rapidly Growing New Ventures," *Journal of Private Equity,* Spring 2001, pp. 19–31.
2. Jeffrey A. Timmons and Stephen Spinelli, *New Venture Creation: Entrepreneurship for the 21st Century* (Boston: Irwin McGraw-Hill, 2009), p. 59.
3. Our position is consistent with recent research showing that the quality of business ideas generated in a business idea competition were related to the size of the entrepreneurial teams that came up with those ideas. The quality was also higher for teams with more years of work experience and those that received outside assistance from experienced venture founders. For more on this research, see Maw-Der Foo, "Member Experience, Use of External Assistance and Evaluation of Business Ideas," *Journal of Small Business Management,* Vol. 48, No. 1 (January 2010), pp. 32–43.
4. The field has evolved toward a view that sees management team members as those with financial ownership and significant decision-making responsibilities in the venture [see Gaylen N. Chandler, "New Venture Teams," in Andrew Zacharakis and Stephen Spinelli, Jr. (eds.), *Entrepreneurship: The Engine of Growth* (Westport, CT: Praeger Perspectives, 2007), pp. 75–76]. Other definitions are more restrictive and emphasize factors such as being a part of the founding of the venture [see Iris Vanaelst, Bart Clarysse, Mike Wright, Andy Lockett, Nathalie Moray, and Rosette S'Jegers, "Entrepreneurial Team Development in Academic Spinouts: An Examination of Team Heterogeneity,"

Entrepreneurial Theory and Practice, Vol. 30, No. 2 (March 2006), p. 251]. At the other end of the spectrum, some entrepreneurs consider all employees and advisors to be a part of the team. Because our discussion is focused on those who hold important leadership positions in the small business but may not share ownership in the firm, we use the broader term *management team* rather than *entrepreneurial team* to reflect this more general view.

5. For an interesting study of the addition of members to the management team, see Daniel P. Forbes, Patricia S. Borchert, Mary E. Zellmer-Bruhn, and Harry J. Sapienza, "Entrepreneurial Team Formation: An Exploration of New Member Addition," *Entrepreneurship Theory and Practice,* Vol. 30, No. 2 (March 2006), pp. 225–248.
6. This may explain why research using Panel Study of Entrepreneurial Dynamics data found that around three-fourths of *solo* entrepreneurs were starting service firms (49 percent) or retail businesses (26 percent). These types of startups tend to be less complicated than technology-based firms or manufacturing businesses, so a single founder is more likely to have the knowledge and experience necessary to get the business going. A more complex startup may well require the combined expertise and insight of a *team* of entrepreneurs. For a closer look at the data, see *Expected Costs of Startup Ventures,* a consulting report prepared for the SBA's Office of Advocacy by Blade Consulting Corporation, Vienna, Virginia, November 2003.
7. Research has not always supported the view that functional balance leads to improved venture performance. Some studies have found that functional heterogeneity is correlated with small firm growth, while others offer no evidence to indicate a relationship with team performance (see Chandler, *op. cit.*).
8. Andy Lockett, Deniz Ucbasaran, and John Butler, "Opening Up the Investor-Investee Dyad: Syndicates, Teams, and Networks," *Entrepreneurship Theory and Practice,* Vol. 30, No. 2 (March 2006), p. 119.
9. Chandler, *op. cit.,* p. 71.
10. Howard E. Aldrich and Nancy M. Carter, "Social Networks," in William B. Gartner, Kelly G. Shaver, Nancy M. Carter, and Paul D. Reynolds (eds.), *Handbook of Entrepreneurial Dynamics: The Process of Business Creation* (Thousand Oaks, CA: Sage, 2004), p. 331.
11. Jennifer Van Grove, "How Small Business Is Using Social Media," http://mashable.com/2010/03/02/small-business-stats, accessed November 10, 2010.
12. Robert B. Cialdini, *Influence: Science and Practice* (Needham Heights: MA: Allyn & Bacon, 2009).
13. This percentage from the IRS includes enterprises organized as limited liability companies (an organizational form that is introduced later in the chapter) but is probably inconsequential, as other sources indicate the number of startups formed as LLCs is quite small.
14. The figures offered here are based on Internal Revenue Service projections of returns for the 2011 tax year as reported on two Web pages: http://www.irs.gov/pub/irs-soi/d6187.pdf and http://www.irs.gov/pub/irs-soi/d6292.pdf. These numbers differ from those reported elsewhere, however, and this deserves some explanation. For example, some may choose to use PSED data, but Paul D. Reynolds ["Nature of Business Start-ups," in William B. Gartner, Kelly G. Shaver, Nancy M. Carter, and Paul D. Reynolds (eds.), *Handbook of Entrepreneurial Dynamics: The Process of Business Creation* (Thousand Oaks, CA: Sage, 2004), p. 250] points out that 52.7 percent of nascent entrepreneurs intend to operate as sole proprietorships, whereas actual tax filings put the figure at 71.9 percent. While we cannot rule out the possibility that this is a result of the PSED sampling frame, it would be reasonable to conclude that many entrepreneurial hopefuls fully anticipate incorporating or forming a partnership, but they end up moving toward the least complicated form (the sole proprietorship) when the more pressing challenges of starting and running a business take priority. On the other hand, a recent survey of small businesses from the NFIB reveals that only 20.9 percent are organized as sole proprietorships, which is far more at variance with IRS data [see William J. Dennis, Jr. (ed.), "Business Structure," *NFIB National Small Business Poll,* Vol. 4, No. 7 (Washington, DC: NFIB Research Foundation, 2004), p. 8]. The sampling frame was drawn from the files of the Dun & Bradstreet Corporation, which may represent more mature businesses, many of which started as proprietorships but changed to more sophisticated organizational forms as a shield against liability or for other reasons. We use IRS figures here because they are based on the population of all companies submitting returns and represent the most recent data available.
15. Liability insurance and other forms of protection are discussed further in Chapter 23. However, there are many forms of liability protection, and a full discussion of these goes beyond the scope of this text. Experts and specific sources of information on protecting a small business should be consulted when making these decisions.
16. Fred S. Steingold, *Legal Guide for Starting and Running a Small Business* (Berkeley, CA: Nolo Press, 2009).
17. Karen Cheney, "Meet Your Match," http://www.quicken.com/cms/viewers/article/small_business/55318, accessed January 29, 2007.
18. Karen Cheney, "The Perfect Partnership Plan," http://www. quicken.com/cms/viewers/article/small_business/55340, accessed January 29, 2007.
19. Steingold, *op. cit.*
20. Ira Nottonson, *Forming a Partnership: And Making It Work* (Irvine, CA: Entrepreneur Press, 2007), pp. 6–7.
21. Nichole L. Torres, "Left in the Lurch?" *Entrepreneur,* Vol. 34, No. 5 (May 2006), p. 108.
22. John Seely Brown, quoted by Stephen J. Dubner, "How Can We Measure Innovation? A Freakonomics Quorum," April 25, 2008, http://freakonomics.blogs.nytimes.com/2008/04/25/how-can-we-measure-innovation-a-freakonomics-quorum, accessed November 18, 2010.
23. Internal Revenue Service, "Table 1A. Calendar Year Projections of Individual Returns by Major Processing Categories for the United States," http://www.irs.gov/pub/irs-soi/d6187.pdf (data for sole proprietorships), accessed November 11, 2010; and Internal Revenue Service, "Table 1. Fiscal Year Projections of the Number of Returns to Be Filed with the IRS," http://www.irs.gov/pub/irs-soi/d6292.pdf (data for partnerships, regular corporations, and S corporations), accessed November 11, 2010.
24. Chris Harrison, "Form Is Everything," http://www.welcomebiz.com/, accessed December 5, 2008.
25. "Piercing the Corporate Veil," http://www.residual-rewards.com/piercingthecorporateveil.html, accessed November 11, 2010.
26. David Newton, "Personal Loan Guarantees," http://www.entrepreneur.com/money/financing/bankloansandmicroloans/article55544.html, accessed November 12, 2010.
27. For tax years beginning after 2004, the law increased the maximum number of shareholders permitted in an S corporation from 75 to 100. (Note that husband and wife count as one stockholder.)
28. The rules have been modified in recent years to allow more types of trusts to hold Subchapter S stock.
29. "S Corporations," http://www.irs.gov/businesses/small/article/0,,id=98263,00.html, accessed November 18, 2010.
30. As stated, S corporations can own other business entities but cannot be owned

by C corporations, other S corporations, many trusts, limited liability companies, or partnerships. For more information on the subject, see "Small Business Answer Handbook," *Entrepreneur*, Vol. 34, No. 10 (October 2006), pp. 41–46.

31. Kelly Spors, "Small Talk," *Wall Street Journal*, September 9, 2006, p. B8.
32. For a description of the tax advantages of the limited liability company, see Steingold, *op. cit.*
33. Nichole L. Torres, "Lofty Ideals," *Entrepreneur*, Vol. 34, No. 6 (June 2006), pp. 150–151.
34. William J. Dennis, Jr. (ed.), "Strategic Alliances," *NFIB National Small Business Poll*, Vol. 4, No. 4 (Washington, DC: NFIB Research Foundation, 2004), pp. 1–8.
35. *Ibid.*, p. 4.
36. Chris Penttila, "Dream Teams," *Entrepreneur*, Vol. 36, No. 6 (June 2008), p. 76.
37. "Strategic Alliances," *op. cit.*, pp. 9–14.
38. Michael Fitzgerald, "Turning Vendors into Partners," *Inc.*, August 1, 2005, http://www.inc.com/magazine/20050801/vendors.html, accessed March 25, 2011.
39. *Ibid.*
40. Chris Penttila, "All Together Now," *Entrepreneur*, Vol. 35, No. 8 (August 2007), pp. 92–93.
41. *Ibid.*
42. "Strategic Alliances," *op. cit.*, p. 7.
43. Jeffrey Shuman, Janice Twombly, and David Rottenberg, *Everyone Is a Customer: A Proven Method for Measuring the Value of Every Relationship in the Era of Collaborative Business* (Chicago: Dearborn Trade Publishing, 2002).
44. In many states, the number of board members required depends on the number of shareholders in the business. A corporation with one shareholder may need only one director to satisfy this demand, with two directors being required when there are two shareholders and three directors when there are three. However, no state requires a corporation to have more than three directors on its board (see Steingold, *op. cit.*).
45. The compensation figures provided here are consistent across many sources, but the ranges are wide enough to indicate that the variation among small businesses is considerable.
46. Kent Romanoff, "Board of Directors Compensation," http://ww.theperfectplan.com/the_salary_sage/board-compensation, accessed November 17, 2010; and "Boards for Beginners," *Inc.*, Vol. 27, No. 2 (February 2005), p. 44.

CHAPTER 9

1. Jessica Bruder, "The Best Places to Launch," *Fortune Small Business*, Vol. 19, No. 9 (November 2009), pp. 56, 58.
2. Jason Daley, "Where to Be an Entrepreneur," *Entrepreneur*, Vol. 37, No. 8 (August 2009), p. 50.
3. Jacquelyn Lynn, "Location Is Key," *Entrepreneur*, Vol. 36, No. 11 (November 2008), p. 26.
4. Adapted from J. D. Ryan and Gail P. Hiduke, *Small Business: An Entrepreneur's Business Plan*, 8th ed. (Mason, OH: South-Western Cengage Learning, 2009), pp. 148–150.
5. "Lids—About Us," http://www.lids.com, accessed November 23, 2010.
6. http://www.cobbtuning.com/info/?id=2953, accessed November 23, 2010.
7. According to the 2011 State Business Tax Climate Index, published by the Tax Foundation (http://www.taxfoundation.org/files/bp60.pdf, accessed November 23, 2010), South Dakota tops the rankings of best state business tax climates, followed by Alaska, Wyoming, Nevada, Florida, Montana, New Hampshire, Delaware, Utah, and Indiana, ordered here by their respective rankings.
8. http://revenue.state.wy.us, accessed January 13, 2009.
9. Jacquelyn Lynn, "Tax Relief," *Entrepreneur*, Vol. 36, No. 7 (July 2008), p. 24.
10. Jacquelyn Lynn, "What's It Worth," *Entrepreneur*, Vol. 36, No. 3 (March 2008), p. 32.
11. "Business Oregon—Enterprise Zones," http://www.oregon4biz.com/The-Oregon-Advantage/Tax-Incentives/Enterprise-Zones/, accessed November 23, 2010.
12. Rieva Lesonsky, *Start Your Own Business: The Only Start-Up Book You'll Ever Need* (Irvine, CA: Entrepreneur Press, 2007), p. 251.
13. Jacquelyn Lynn, "Location Is Key," *Entrepreneur*, Vol. 36, No. 11 (November 2008), p. 26. See also Craig S. Galbraith, Carlos L. Rodriguez, and Alex F. DeNoble, "SME Competitive Strategy and Location Behavior: An Exploratory Study of High-Technology Manufacturing," *Journal of Small Business Management*, Vol. 46, No. 2 (April 2008), pp. 183–202.
14. National Federation of Independent Businesses, "411 Small Business Facts," http://www.411sbfacts.com/sbpoll.php?POLLID=0048&KT_back=1, accessed November 24, 2010.
15. Cecilia Goodnow, "New Designs and Technology Take Treehouses to a Higher Level for Adults," *Seattle Post-Intelligencer*, August 23, 2007, http://www.treehouseworkshop.com/downloads/news_09.pdf, accessed November 24, 2010.
16. Sarah E. Needleman, "Start-Up Programs Find Niche," *Wall Street Journal*, November 18, 2010, p. B7.
17. "HBK Incubates," http://hotbreadkitchen.org/hbk-incubator, accessed November 29, 2010.
18. Needleman, *op. cit.*
19. http://www.regus.com/aboutus/default.htm, accessed December 14, 2010; and Gwendolyn Bounds, "My Office Is Your Office: Small Firms Share Space," *Wall Street Journal*, March 18, 2008, p. B4.
20. David Port, "Solo, but Not Alone," *Entrepreneur*, Vol. 37, No. 10 (October 2009), pp. 99–103.
21. National Federation of Independent Businesses, "411 Small Business Facts," http://smallbusiness.findlaw.com/accessed December 22, 2008.
22. Emily Maltby, "Dressing Up a Sub," *Fortune Small Business*, Vol. 17, No. 9 (November 2007), p. 62.
23. *Ibid.*
24. See Candida G. Brush, Linda F. Edleman, and Tatiana S. Manolova, "The Effects of Initial Location, Aspirations, and Resources on Likelihood of First Sale in Nascent Firms," *Journal of Small Business Management*, Vol. 46, No. 2 (April 2008), pp. 159–182.
25. Emili Vesilind, "The Home Office Is Humming," *Entrepreneur*, Vol. 38, No. 6 (June 2010), pp. 98–101.
26. Nichole L. Torres and April Y. Pennington, "Home Court Advantage," http://www.entrepreneur.com/article/77660-2, accessed December 1, 2010.
27. Nicole L. Torres, "Passion *Can* Trump Industry Experience, as This Makeup Entrepreneur Shows," http://www.entrepreneur.com/microsites/chryslerinspirationpoint/homebusinessinspiration/article78440.html, accessed December 1, 2010.
28. Meg Cadoux Hirshberg, "Bed and Bedroom," *Inc.*, Vol. 32, No. 1 (February 2010), pp. 31–33.
29. Michael J. McDermott, "Avoid Zoning Pitfalls When Working from Home," http://www.busop1.com/pitfall.html, accessed December 1, 2010.
30. For the details of supporting research, see David A. Johnson, Michael Wade, and Ron McClean, "Does eBusiness Matter to SMEs? A Comparison of the Financial Impacts of Internet Business Solutions on European and North American SMEs,"

Journal of Small Business Management, Vol. 45, No. 3 (July 2007), pp. 354–361.

31. http://www.beautyencounter.com/about.html, accessed December 14, 2010; and Sara Wilson, "Global Scents," *Entrepreneur*, Vol. 35, No. 12 (December 2007), p. 164.

32. See Prashanth Nagendra Bharadway and Ramesh G. Soni, "E-Commerce Usage and Perceptions of E-Commerce Issues Among Small Firms: Results and Implications from an Empirical Study," *Journal of Small Business Management*, Vol. 45, No. 4 (October 2007), pp. 501–521.

33. "Benefits and Limitations of E-Business," http://www.witiger.com/ecommerce/benefits-limitations.htm, accessed December 7, 2010.

34. Raymund Flandez, "Help Wanted—and Found," *Wall Street Journal*, October 13, 2008, http://online.wsj.com/article/SB122347721312915407.html?mod=googlenews_wsj, accessed December 8, 2010.

35. "CoreTechs—Remote Contractors with Amazing Results," http://www.coretechsinc.com/contractors.html, accessed December 8, 2010.

36. Flandez, *op. cit.*

37. http://www.kosher.com/, accessed December 8, 2010; and Melissa Campanelli, "Taking Off," *Entrepreneur*, Vol. 34, No. 5 (May 2006), pp. 42–43.

38. Campanelli, *op. cit.*

39. http://www.gilt.com/company/about, accessed December 7, 2010.

40. Kate Rockwood, "Gilt Groupe," *Fast Company*, No. 143 (March 2010), p. 77.

41. *Ibid.*

42. Shelly Banjo, "Wholesalers Set Up Shop Online to Tap Customers," *Wall Street Journal*, September 18, 2008, p. B9.

43. "eBay Marketplace Fast Facts," http://pages.ebay.in/community/aboutebay/news/infastfacts.html, accessed December 8, 2010.

44. *Ibid.*

45. "PayPal – Corporate Fast Facts," https://www.paypal-media.com/, accessed December 8, 2010.

46. http://pages.ebay.com/storefronts/faq.html, accessed December 8, 2010.

47. Kelly K. Spors, "New Services Help Bloggers Bring in Ad Revenue," *Wall Street Journal*, January 15, 2008, p. B6.

48. http://www.q3i.com/products.php, accessed December 10, 2010.

49. Nichole L. Torres, "Weekenders," *Entrepreneur*, Vol. 33, No. 8 (August 2005), p. 80; and personal conversation with Chad Ronnebaum, February 7, 2007.

50. http://www.q3i.com/aboutus.php, accessed January 6, 2009.

51. "Q3 Innovations—Personal Safety and Monitoring Devices," http://www.q3i.com, accessed December 14, 2010; and "Quest Products, Inc. Acquires Assets of Q3 Innovations, LLC," http://media.q3i.com/page/2, accessed December 10, 2010.

CHAPTER 10

1. Norm Brodsky, "Secrets of a $110 Million Man," *Inc.*, October 2008, p. 77.

2. Philip Campbell, "Are You Really Focused on Profits?" http://www. inc.com/resources/finance/articles/20080601/campbell.html, accessed December 15, 2010. *Inc. Magazine*, June 2008. Copyright 2007 by Mansueto Ventures LLC. Reproduced with permission of Mansueto Ventures LLC in the Format Textbook via Copyright Clearance Center.

3. "How to Manage Cash Flows," http://www.inc.com/encyclopedia/cashflow.html, accessed February 3, 2011.

4. Jan Norman, "You're Making Sales, but Are You Making Money?" *Entrepreneur*, March 2004, http://www.entrepreneur.com/article/0,4621,228680,00.html, March 2004, accessed January 11, 2011.

5. Mark Hendricks, "Get Creative with Cash Flow," *Entrepreneur*, May 2009, http://www.entrepreneur.com/magazine/entrepreneur/2009/may/201206.html, accessed January 31, 2010.

6. Adapted from Edward Marram, "6 Weeks to a Better Bottom Line," *Entrepreneur*, January 2010, http://www.entrepreneur.com/magazine/entrepreneur/2010/january/204390.html, accessed December 1, 2010.

CHAPTER 11

1. Paul A. Broni, "Persuasive Projections," *Inc.*, Vol. 22, No. 4 (April 2000), p. 38.

2. Rhonda Abrams, "How Can I Make Financial Projections in My Business Plan When I Have No Solid Numbers?" *Inc.*, September 2000, http://www.inc.com/articles/2000/09/20226.html, accessed February 15, 2009.

3. David Worrell, "A Penchant for Profits," *Entrepreneur*, Vol. 33, No. 8 (August 2005), pp. 53–57.

4. This example is based on an actual situation; however, the name of the founder has been changed, as have some of the numbers.

5. Investors also look to financial projections to determine the sales level necessary for the firm to break even. A firm's break-even point, while important from a financial perspective, is also important for pricing its products or services. The issue of pricing and the break-even point are discussed in Chapter 16.

6. In Chapter 10, we used the current ratio to measure a company's ability to meet maturing obligations, which was measured as current assets *divided* by current liabilities. Thus, the *current ratio* is a relative measure (current assets *relative* to current liabilities), which allows us to compare firms of different sizes. *Net working capital* (current assets *less* current liabilities) is an *absolute* dollar measure of liquidity used by many bankers.

7. We'll discuss bootstrapping again in Chapter 12, when we discuss financing a business.

8. Personal communication with Cecilia Levine, November 28, 2008.

9. Quoted in Scott Bernard Nelson, "Fee Agents," *Entrepreneur*, January 2003, p. 63.

10. If you need to review the process for creating a statement of cash flows, return to the discussion of cash flows in Chapter 10.

11. Suzanne McGee, "Breaking Free from Budgets," *Inc.*, October 2003, p. 73.

12. Information in this section was taken from Linda Elkins, "Real Numbers Don't Deceive," *Nation's Business*, Vol. 85, No. 3 (March 1997), pp. 51–52; and Broni, *op. cit.*, pp. 183–184.

CHAPTER 12

1. Mike Hofman, "The Big Picture," *Inc.*, Vol. 25, No. 12 (October 2003), p. 87.

2. Angel Capital Association, www.angelcapitalassociation.org, accessed March 3, 2011.

3. Ilan Mochari, "The Numbers Game," *Inc.*, Vol. 24, No. 12 (October 2002), pp. 65–66.

4. Asheesh Advani, "The Angel in Your Pocket," *Entrepreneur*, November 2009; and Steven Fisher, "The Perils of Using Personal Credit Cards to Fund Your Business," http://unintentionalentrepreneur.com/, accessed December 2010.

5. David Port, "But Where Is the Money?" http://www.entrepreneur.com/magazine/entrepreneur/2010/august/207500.html#, accessed January 3, 2011.

6. Personal conversation with Jack Griggs, September 10, 2010.

7. To compute the $730 monthly payment, we can use a financial calculator or a computer spreadsheet.

PV (present value) = 50,000 (current loan)

N (number of payments) = 84 (7 years × 12 months = 84)

I/yr (interest rate/month) = 0.5% (6% interest rate per year ÷ 12 months = 0.005 = 0.5%)

FV (future value) = 0 (in 7 years)

PMT (payment) = $730.43

8. As discussed in Chapters 10 and 11, the ratio of current assets to current liabilities is called the *current ratio;* the ratio of total debt to total assets is called the *debt ratio*.
9. Mochari, *op. cit.*, p. 64.
10. Personal interview with Bill Bailey, Spring 2009.
11. C. J. Prince, "New Money," *Entrepreneur,* March 2008, http://www.entrepreneur.com/magazine/entrepreneur/2008/march/190066.html, accessed October 2, 2008.
12. For an excellent source on business angels, see Frances M. Amatucci and Jeffrey E. Sohl, "Business Angels: Investment Processes, Outcomes, and Current Trends," in Andrew Zacharakis and Stephen Spinelli, Jr. (eds.), *Entrepreneurship: The Engine of Growth* (Westport, CT: Praeger, 2007), pp. 87–107. Also see "Important Things for Entrepreneurs to Know About Angel Investors," http://angelcapitalassociation.org.
13. Jeffrey Sohl, "The Angel Investor Market in 2010," Center for Venture Research, http://wsbe.unh.edu/sites/default/files/2010_analysis_report.pdf, accessed April 16, 2011.
14. Julian Lange, Benoit Leleux, and Bernard Surlemont, "Angel Network for the 21st Century," *Journal of Private Equity,* Spring 2003, p. 18.
15. William H. Payne, "Joining Angel Organizations—A Win-Win Opportunity," unpublished notes.
16. For a description of how angel networks function, see Aja Carmichael, "The Money Game: In Search of an Angel," *Wall Street Journal,* January 30, 2006, p. R4. Also visit the Angel Capital Association website at http://angelcapitalassociation.org.
17. Guy Kawasaki, "Garnering Angels," *Entrepreneur,* January 2008, http://www.entrepreneur.com/magazine/entrepreneur/2008/january/187614.html, accessed December 15, 2010.
18. Asheesh Advani, "Finally, Someone Wants to Give You Money," *Entrepreneur*, March 2010, http://www.entrepreneur.com/article/205058, accessed October 16, 2010.
19. C. J. Prince, "Alternate Financing Routes," *Entrepreneur,* March 2007, pp. 66–68.

CHAPTER 13

1. Norm Brodsky, "Norm Brodsky on When It's Time to Sell," *Inc.*, June 2010, http://www.inc.com/magazine/20100601/norm-brodsky-on-when-its-time-to-sell.html#, accessed March 15, 2011.
2. Personal conversation with Bob Browder, February 1, 2009.
3. Simona Covel, "How to Get Workers to Think and Act Like Owners," *Wall Street Journal*, February 7, 2008, p. B-1.
4. Carol Tice, "Is It Time to Sell?, *Entrepreneur*, January 2009, http://www.entrepreneur.com/magazine/entrepreneur/2009/january/199016.html, accessed February 5, 2009.
5. Brad Feld, "What's Your Exit Strategy?" *Entrepreneur*, May 2009, p. 30.
6. Nitasha Tiko, "The Return of the IPO," *Inc.*, July 2010, http://www.inc.com/topic/qliktech-international-ab#, accessed February 27, 2011.
7. S. T. Certo, "Influencing Initial Public Offering Investors with Prestige: Signaling with Board Structure," *Academy of Management Review,* Vol. 28, No. 3 (2003), pp. 432–447.
8. Woojin Kim and Michael S. Wiesbach, "Do Firms Go Public to Raise Capital?" paper presented at the annual Financial Management Association Meeting, October 14, 2005.
9. This example is provided by Peter Hermann at Heritage Partners, a Boston venture capital firm, which obtained a registered trademark for the process they call a Private IPO®.
10. The unattributed quotes in this part of the chapter are taken from personal interviews conducted as part of a research study on harvesting, sponsored by the Financial Executive Research Foundation and cited in J. William Petty, John D. Martin, and John Kensinger, *Harvesting the Value of a Privately Held Company* (Morristown, NJ: Financial Executive Research Foundation, 1999). To acquire a copy of the book, write to the Financial Executive Research Foundation, Inc., P.O. Box 1938, Morristown, NJ 07962-1938, or call 973-898-4600.
11. Jeff Bailey, "Selling the Firm—and Letting Go of the Dream," *Wall Street Journal,* December 10, 2002, p. B6.
12. Jennifer Wang, "Confessions of Serial Entrepreneurs," *Entrepreneur*, January 8, 2009, http://www.entrepreneur.com/startingabusiness/successstories/article199436.html, accessed March 18, 2011.

CHAPTER 14

1. "Getting More from Existing Customers," http://www.startupnation.com/articles/1387/1/grow-business-existing-customers.asp, accessed January 4, 2011.
2. "The Neglected Moneymaker: Customer Retention," April 25, 2007, http://knowledge.wpcarey.asu.edu/article.cfm?articleid=1408, accessed January 4, 2011.
3. Frederick Reichheld, *The Loyalty Effect: The Hidden Force Behind Growth, Profits, and Lasting Value* (Boston: Harvard Business School Press, 2008).
4. A recent study indicates that increased levels of customer satisfaction leads the employees who serve them to feel better about their employers [see Xueming Luo and Christian Homburg, "Neglected Outcomes of Customer Satisfaction," *Journal of Marketing*, Vol. 71, No. 2 (April 2007), pp. 133–149]. Satisfied employees tend to produce increased customer satisfaction, especially when they have direct contact with customers. Furthermore, this research shows that higher levels of customer satisfaction are linked to employee and managerial talent.
5. Charles W. Lamb, Joseph F. Hair, and Carl McDaniel, *Marketing,* 11th ed. (Cincinnati: South-Western Cengage Learning, 2011), p. 699.
6. Interestingly enough, research has shown that the entrepreneur–customer relationship is actually reciprocal [see Dirk De Clercq and Deva Rangarajan, "The Role of Perceived Relational Support in Entrepreneur-Customer Dyads," *Entrepreneurship Theory & Practice*, Vol. 32, No. 4 (2008), pp. 659–683]. In other words, most customers recognize that the way an entrepreneurial company treats them has an impact on their level of satisfaction with and commitment to the venture; but the customer's reputation and the reliability of their exchanges with the company also influence the entrepreneur's satisfaction with and commitment to that customer. That is, one builds upon the other.
7. Karen J. Bannan, "Would You Like Fries with That?" *MyBusiness*, June/July 2009, p. 45.
8. Marjorie J. Cooper, Nancy Upton, and Samuel Seaman, "Customer Relationship Management: A Comparative Analysis of Family and Nonfamily Business Practices," *Journal of Small Business Management,* Vol. 43, No. 3 (July 2005), pp. 242–256.
9. Brian Vellmure, "Let's Start with Customer Retention," http://www.initiumtech.com/newsletter_120602.htm, accessed February 31, 2011.
10. National Federation of Independent Business, "Marketing Perspectives," http://411sbfacts.com/sbpoll-tables-res.php?POLLID=0054&QID=00000001624&KT_back=1, accessed January 31, 2011.
11. Amy Barrett, "True Believers," http://www.businessweek.com/

magazine/content/06_52/b4015401.htm?chan=smallbiz_smallbiz+index+page_sales+and+marketing, accessed January 12, 2011.

12. "CRM: You (Should) Love Your Customers, Now Work to Keep Them," http://www.startupnation.com/articles/1533/1/crm-software-strategy.asp, accessed January 4, 2011.
13. Lindsay Holloway, "Marx Acosta-Rubio," *Entrepreneur*, Vol. 36, No. 9 (September 2008), pp. 66–67.
14. "The Neglected Moneymaker," *op. cit.*
15. Personal conversation with Keith Jezek, January 16, 2009.
16. Some of these suggestions were adapted from Lesley Spencer Pyle, "Keep Your Customers from Straying," June 12, 2008, http://www.entrepreneur.com/homebasedbiz/homebasedbizcolumnistlesleyspencerpyle/article194784.html, accessed January 4, 2011.
17. Personal communication with Denny Fulk, May 7, 2007.
18. Uncle Saul, "Personal Pitch," http://www.infochachkie.com/personal-pitch, accessed January 4, 2011.
19. "The On-Hold Guy—Something Completely Different," http://onholdguy.com/ohg/my_business_article.aspx, accessed January 31, 2011.
20. Summary of statistics adapted from Kristina Knight, "Want More Conversions? Focus on Customer Service," http://www.bizreport.com/2010/07/want-more-conversions-focus-on-customer-service.html, accessed February 1, 2011.
21. Pattie Simone, "A Marketing Tool That's Obvious, Overlooked and Cheap," *Entrepreneur*, October 27, 2008, http://www.entrepreneur.com/sales/customerservice/article198194.html, accessed January 4, 2011.
22. Personal communication with John Stites, October 23, 2007.
23. Heather Larson, "Coffee Talk," http://www.writemix.net/CoffeeTalk.html, accessed January 4, 2011; and http://www.hampton-coffee.com/Hampton_Coffee_Company/Hampton_Coffee_Company_Our_Locations.html, accessed January 4, 2011.
24. Dionne Searcey, "For Better or Worse," *Wall Street Journal*, October 30, 2006, p. R5.
25. "SAS® Helps 1-800FLOWERS.COM Grow Deep Roots with Customers," http://www.sas.com/success/1800flowers.html, accessed February 1, 2011.
26. *Ibid.*
27. Darren Dahl, "What Seems to Be the Problem? Self Service Gets a Tune-Up," *Inc.*, Vol. 30, No. 2 (February 2008), pp. 43–44.
28. Salvatore Parise, Patricia J. Guinan, and Bruce D. Weinberg, "The Secrets of Marketing in a Web 2.0 World," *Wall Street Journal*, December 15, 2008, p. R4.
29. *Ibid.*
30. Sharon Fling, "California Tortilla Customers Love Taco Talk," http://www.geolocal.com/public/79.cfm?sd=45, accessed February 1, 2011.
31. "Taco Talk," No. 185, December 2010, http://californiatortilla.com/, accessed January 4, 2011.
32. Fling, *op. cit.*
33. Russell S. Wimer, "Customer Relationship Management: A Framework, Research Directions, and the Future," http://groups.haas.berkeley.edu/fcsuit/PDF-papers/CRM%20paper.pdf, accessed January 4, 2011.
34. "Get to Know Your Customers with a Customer Profile," http://www.lowe.org/, accessed January 4, 2011.
35. *Ibid.*
36. See, for example, Del I. Hawkings and David L. Mothersbaugh, *Consumer Behavior: Building Marketing Strategy,* 11th ed. (New York: McGraw-Hill Irwin, 2010), Chapter 17.
37. Laurie Zuckerman, "Picture Perfect," http://www.nfib.com/mybusiness-magazine/article?cmsid=53502, accessed January 31, 2011; and http://www.angusbarn.com, accessed January 4, 2011.

CHAPTER 15

1. Robert Kiyosaki, "Even Steven," *Entrepreneur*, Vol. 36, No. 8 (August 2008), p. 36.
2. Debra Kahn Schofield, "Grow Your Business Slowly: A Cautionary Tale," http://www.gmarketing.com/articles/179-grow-your-business-slowly-a-cautionary-tale, accessed January 10, 2011.
3. Many paths can lead a small business owner to a situation like this. For example, a new entrepreneur may price a product too low, prompting some buyers to exploit the opportunity by placing large orders. This can be especially hard on a startup, because the final costs of production can exceed total revenues from sales. Also, if a small business is unable to deliver on time or with the level of quality promised, or if it must turn down an order because it can't handle the volume, its reputation can be damaged significantly.
4. http://www.barebabies.com/about-us, accessed January 10, 2011.
5. "Karen McMasters—BareBabies.com," http://br.video.yahoo.com/watch/1581802/5350194, accessed January 10, 2011.
6. Jeffry A. Timmons and Stephen Spinelli, *New Venture Creation: Entrepreneurship for the 21st Century* (Boston: McGraw-Hill/Irwin, 2009), p. 18.
7. Reported in an interview with Martha E. Mangelsdorf, "Hard Times Can Drive Innovation," *Wall Street Journal,* December 15, 2008, p. R2.
8. Neale Martin, "How Habits Undermine Marketing," *Financial Times*, July 1, 2008, http://www.ftpress.com/articles/article.aspx?p=1223844, accessed February 7, 2011.
9. "180s, L.L.C.," http://www.fundinguniverse.com/company-histories/180s-LLC-Company-History.html, accessed January 10, 2011.
10. http://www.revolutionmotors.biz, accessed January 11, 2011; and Uncle Saul, "Reinventing the Wheel—A Nonstandard Look at Standards," http://www.infochachkie.com/wheel, accessed January 11, 2011.
11. Dennis Romero, "Master Minds," *Entrepreneur*, Vol. 37, No. 3 (March 2009), p. 20.
12. Most formal investors are willing to take *market* risks but not *product* risks. In other words, they want to see at least a working prototype, and preferably a developed product, before they invest in a new venture. To get to that point, the entrepreneur will most likely need to rely on more informal sources of capital, such as personal savings and investment from family and friends. This requires forward planning on investment.
13. "VC Cash Crunch May Impact Innovation," http://www.us-tech.com/RelId/702033/ISvars/default/VC_Cash_Crunch_May_I.htm, accessed January 10, 2011.
14. Leigh Buchanan, "Inc. 500," *Inc.,* Vol. 32, No. 7 (September 2010), p. 148.
15. Some of the strategies outlined here, and others, are mentioned in Anne Field, "Creating a Sustainable Competitive Advantage for Your Small Business," http://www.startupnation.com/business-articles/1522/1/competitive-advantage-small-business.asp, accessed March 15, 2011.
16. http://www.bluebuffalo.com/company-history, accessed April 29, 2011.
17. Matthew S. Olson and Derek van Bever, *Stall Points: Most Companies Stop Growing—Yours Doesn't Have To* (New Haven, CT: Yale University Press, 2008), p. 28.
18. Paul Nunes and Tim Breene, "Reinvent Your Business Before It's Too Late," *Harvard Business Review,* Vol. 89, No. 1/2 (January/February 2011), pp. 80–87.
19. http://www.dylanscandybar.com/custserv/customerservicemain.jsp?cid=1, accessed February 11, 2009.

20. Daniel Maurer, "Scream for Free Ice Cream," *New York Magazine*, November 12, 2008, http://nymag.com/daily/food/2008/11/scream_for_free_ice_cream.html, accessed February 11, 2009.
21. http://klockwerkscycles.com/about, accessed January 25, 2011; "Biker Build Off," http://www.pddnet.com/article-biker-build-off, accessed January 25, 2011; and Chris Morrison, "3-D Printing for the Rest of Us," *Business 2.0*, Vol. 8, No. 8 (September 20, 2007), pp. 46–47.
22. Jennifer Wang, "Be Disruptive," *Entrepreneur*, Vol. 39, No. 9 (January 2011), p. 20.
23. Mike Gordon, Chris Musso, Eric Rebentisch, and Nisheeth Gupta, "The Path to Developing Successful New Products," *Wall Street Journal*, November 30, 2009, p. R5.
24. "Beacon Street Girls Overview," http://www.tradevibes.com/company/profile/beacon-street-girls, accessed January 25, 2011; and Nadine Heintz, "Hands On Case Study," *Inc.*, Vol. 27, No. 3 (March 2005), pp. 44–46.
25. Personal communication with Winston Wolfe, February 8, 2011.
26. http://www.theparkingspot.com, accessed January 26, 2011; and Elizabeth J. Goodgold, "Dot Your Eyes," *Entrepreneur*, http://www.highbeam.com/doc/1G1-83663520.html, accessed January 26, 2011.
27. http://www.theparkingspot.com/Facilities/LocationDirectory.aspx, accessed January 26, 2011.
28. "Logo Design—Not Just a Pretty Typeface," http://www.logomojo.com/logotype.html, accessed January 26, 2011.
29. Adapted from Gwen Moran, "Best and Worst Marketing Ideas . . . Ever," *Entrepreneur*, Vol. 37, No. 1 (January 2009), p. 48; and "Logo Design" *op. cit.*
30. http://www.mebath.com, accessed January 26, 2011.
31. Nichole L. Torres, "Package Deal," *Entrepreneur*, Vol. 35, No. 10 (October 2007), p. 114.
32. Laura Tiffany, "What Whole Package," *Entrepreneur*, Vol. 36, No. 2 (February 2008), p. 24.
33. "Public Law 110-314—August 14, 2008," http://www.cpsc.gov/cpsia.pdf, accessed February 7, 2011.
34. Rieva Lesonsky, "In the Know," *Entrepreneur*, Vol. 35, No. 6 (June 2007), pp. 96–101.
35. "United States Patent and TrademarkOffice Fee Schedule," http://www.uspto.gov/web/offices/ac/qs/ope/fee2009 september15.htm, accessed January 26, 2011.
36. "All About Trademarks," http://www.uspto.gov/smallbusiness/trademarks/faq.html, accessed January 26, 2011.
37. "Law Professor—Trade Dress," http://www.lawprofessor.com/, accessed January 26, 2011.
38. A comprehensive discussion of supply chain management is beyond the scope of this book, but many excellent resources can provide helpful information on this subject. We would recommend John J. Coyle, C. John Langley, Brian J. Gibson, Robert A. Novak, and Edward J. Bardi, *Supply Chain Management: A Logistics Perspective,* 8th ed., (Mason, OH: Cengage, 2009); and Joel D. Wisner, Keah-Choon Tan, and G. Keong Leong, *Principles of Supply Chain Management: A Balanced Approach,* 3rd ed. (Mason, OH: Cengage, 2012).
39. "Fare Scanners and 'Compare Fare' Sites: Direct Distribution Gone Wrong?" http://www.airkiosk.com/ttt_item_2.php?item=2, accessed February 3, 2011.
40. Sarah E. Needleman, "In a Sole Revival, the Recession Gives Beleaguered Cobblers New Traction," *Wall Street Journal,* February 2, 2009, pp. A1, A13.
41. "How Tomorrow Moves—Radio Ad: One Gallon," http://www.csx.com/, accessed February 19, 2009.
42. Personal communication with Pedro Reyes, associate professor of operations management, Baylor University, March 14, 2011.

CHAPTER 16

1. Emily Maltby, "Raising Prices Pays Off for Some," http://online.wsj.com/article/SB10001424052702304510704575562600914616226.html?mod=WSJ_business_LeftSecondHighlights, accessed February 27, 2011.
2. Personal interview with Jeremy Hitchcock, January 19, 2011.
3. For an excellent discussion of price setting, see Charles W. Lamb, Jr., Joseph H. Hair, Jr., and Carl McDaniel, *Marketing,* 9th ed. (Cincinnati: South-Western, 2008), Chapter 18.
4. Collin Fitzsimmons, "What Is Dynamic Pricing?" http://www.ehow.com/about_5255769_dynamic-pricing.html, accessed May 3, 2011.
5. Sam Allen, "Attorney General Halts Cosmetics Company's Price-Fixing," http://latimesblogs.latimes.com/lanow/2011/01/attorney-general-halts-cosmetics-company-price-fixing.html, accessed March 20, 2011.
6. PayPal, https://merchant.paypal.com/ accessed March 20, 2011.
7. William J. Dennis, Jr., "Small Business Credit in a Deep Recession," http://www.nfib.com/Portals/0/PDF/AllUsers/research/studies/Small-Business-Credit-In-a-Deep-Recession-February-2010-NFIB.pdf, accessed March 20, 2011.
8. An example can be found at the Visa.com website, http://usa.visa.com/personal/cards/debit/index.html, accessed March 20, 2011.
9. Alan Fram, "Banks, Merchants Wage Furious Battle over Debit Card Fees," *Chicago Sun-Times,* accessed March 20, 2011.
10. You should regularly investigate your own credit rating. Go to annualcreditreport.com for a free report.

CHAPTER 17

1. David Meerman Scott, "Foreword," in Brian Halligan and Dharmesh Shah, *Inbound Marketing: Get Found Using Google, Social Media, and Blogs* (Hoboken, NJ: John Wiley & Sons, 2010), p. xiii.
2. Personal interview with Mike Volpe, January 18, 2011.
3. Jeff Wuorio, "How to Ramp Up Marketing in a Downturn," *Entrepreneur*, Vol. 37, No. 7, (July 2009), pp. 55–57.
4. http://www.yelp.com/about, accessed March 26, 2011.
5. "A Small Business Sales Story: Relationship Marketing Strategies Can Help Your Sales Grow," http://www.more-for-small-business.com/salesstory.html, accessed March 26, 2011.
6. Robert Kiyosaki, "Rich Returns: Go Big or Go Home," *Entrepreneur*, November 2008, p. 34.
7. http://www.register.com/policy/domain-extension-rules.rcmx, accessed March 27, 2011.
8. Ron Jackson (ed.), "Median Domain Sale Prices Increase in 1Q-2010 but Lack of Blockbuster Sales Sends Total Dollar Volume Down," http://dnjournal.com/archive/lowdown/2010/dailyposts/20100426.htm, accessed March 27, 2011.
9. Heather Clancy, "Web Sight: Social Marketing," *Entrepreneur*, November 2008, p. 44; and http://www.whiteflash.com, accessed May 10, 2011.
10. Halligan and Shah, *op. cit.,* pp. 12–13.
11. http://www.bing.com/, accessed March 27, 2011. See http://www.thesearchenginelist.com/ for a comprehensive list of search engines and their descriptions.
12. "How eBay Partner Network Works," https://www.ebaypartnernetwork.com/files/hub/en-US/index.html, accessed March 27, 2011.
13. "Banner Ads," http://www.apromotionguide.com/banners.html, accessed March 27, 2011.

14. Mark Brownlow, "Why Do E-mail Marketing?" http://www.email-marketing-reports.com/basics/why.htm, accessed March 27, 2011.
15. Federal Trade Commission, "Spam," http://www.ftc.gov/bcp/edu/microsites/spam/, accessed March 27, 2011.
16. "Hyperlink," http://www.techterms.com/definition/hyperlink, accessed March 27, 2011.
17. "Blog," http://www.merriam-webster.com/dictionary/blog, accessed March 27, 2011.
18. Volpe, *op. cit.*
19. Halligan and Shah, *op. cit.*, pp. 35–36.
20. Kathy Crosett, "Mobile Marketing to Become More Complex," http://www.marketingforecast.com/archives/10656, accessed March 26, 2011.
21. Eddie Davis, "How to Create a Mobile-Friendly Shopping Website," http://www.entrepreneur.com/article/217255#, accessed March 28, 2011.
22. http://www.pcmag.com/encyclopedia_term/0,2542,t=app&i=37865,00.asp, accessed April 1, 2011; and http://www.pcmag.com/encyclopedia_term/0,2542,t=application&i=37892,00.asp, accessed April 1, 2011.
23. Sommer Saadi, "Smartphone Apps for College," http://www.businessweek.com/bschools/content/jul2010/bs2010079_866046.htm, accessed April 1, 2011.
24. Adam Boyden, "No Ifs, Ands or Buts: 10 Things Small Businesses Must Do to Succeed with Their Free Apps," http://smallbiztrends.com/2011/03/10-things-small-businesses-must-do-succeed-with-free-apps.html, accessed April 1, 2011.
25. Ryan Singel, "Are You Ready for Web 2.0?" http://www.wired.com/science/discoveries/news/2005/10/69114, accessed April 1, 2011.
26. http://oxforddictionaries.com/view/entry/m_en_us1443359#m_en_us1443359, accessed April 2, 2011.
27. http://oxforddictionaries.com/view/entry/m_en_us1428980#m_en_us1428980, accessed April 2, 2011.
28. Shayndi Raice, "Social Media, Phones Ally," http://online.wsj.com/article/SB10001424052748703561604576150573329940048.html?mod=djem_jiewr_ES_domainid, accessed April 2, 2011.
29. http://drypen.in/sales-promotion/definition-of-sales-promotion.html, accessed April 2, 2011.
30. Jack Aaronson, "Foursquare—Mixing Social Networks with Loyalty Programs," http://www.clickz.com/clickz/column/1711467/foursquare-mixing-social-networks-with-loyalty-programs, accessed April 2, 2011.
31. Adapted from Janet Attard, "Trade Show Dos and Don'ts," http://www.businessknowhow.com/, accessed April 2, 2011.
32. John Rambow, "Creative Destinations: Seattle Sees a Mini-Boom in Its Design Scene," http://www.fastcodesign.com/1663317/creative-destinations-join-design-a-band-of-seattle-designers-that-are-turning-heads, accessed April 2, 2011; and http://join.iacolimcallister.com/, accessed April 2, 2011.
33. http://www.hubspot.com/internet-marketing-company/press-room/, accessed April 2, 2011.
34. Robert Fishbone, *Selling the Scream* (St. Louis, MO: On the Wall Publications, 2009); and http://robertfishbone.com/crazyideas.html, accessed April 2, 2011.

CHAPTER 18

1. Data published by the SBA (see "How Important Are Small Businesses to the U.S. Economy?" http://www.sba.gov/advocacy/7495/8420) indicate that a large number of small and medium-sized enterprises (SMEs) are already actively involved in exporting. The numbers become even more impressive when other forms of globalization are considered.
2. This statement is consistent with a U.S. Commercial Service report, as mentioned in Emily Maltby, "Expanding Abroad? Avoid Cultural Gaffes," *Wall Street Journal*, January 19, 2010, p. B5.
3. UN data indicate that the number of startups that are global from day one doubled between 1990 and 2006, from 30,000 to 60,000. [See Michael V. Copeland, "The Mighty Micro-Multinational," *Business 2.0*, Vol. 7, No. 6 (July 2006), pp. 107–114.] In many cases, the emphasis is not on simply selling products abroad; rather, it is on establishing operations wherever in the world it makes sense to do so. In other words, it could be a way to locate near abundant resources or low-cost or highly trained labor to enhance the value proposition of the new venture.
4. Terms other than *born global* are sometimes used; they include *born-international firms, global startups, international new ventures,* and *instant exporters*. [See Pat H. Dickson, "Going Global," in Andrew Zacharakis and Stephen Spinelli, Jr. (eds.), *Entrepreneurship: The Engine of Growth* (Westport, CT: Praeger Perspectives, 2007), pp. 155–161; Gary A. Knight and S. Tamar Cavusgil, "Innovation, Organizational Capabilities, and the Born-Global Firm," *Journal of International Business Studies*, Vol. 35, No. 2 (March 2004), pp. 124–141; Svante Andersson, "Internationalization in Different Industrial Contexts," *Journal of Business Venturing*, Vol. 19, No. 6 (2004), p. 856; and Erkko Autio, Harry J. Sapienza, and James G. Almeida, "Effects of Age at Entry, Knowledge Intensity, and Imitability on International Growth," *Academy of Management Journal,* Vol. 43, No. 5 (October 2000), pp. 909–924.]
5. Leigh Buchanan, "The Thinking Man's Outsourcing," *Inc.,* Vol. 28, No. 5 (May 2006), pp. 31–33.
6. See John A. Matthews and Ivo Zander, "The International Entrepreneurial Dynamics of Accelerated Internationalisation," *Journal of International Business Studies*, Vol. 38, No. 3 (May 2007), pp. 387–403.
7. Buchanan, *op. cit.*
8. The Sloan Brothers, "Taking Your Startup to a Foreign Market," http://www.startupnation.com/articles/1471/1/startupforeign-market.asp, accessed February 11, 2011.
9. *Ibid.*
10. "Tradewind Strategies—Contact," http://www.tradewindstrategies.com/tradewind_contact.html, accessed February 11, 2011.
11. Shelby Scarborough, "A Whole New World," *Entrepreneur*, Vol. 36, No. 6 (June 2008), p. 21.
12. Leigh Buchanan, "Gone Global," *Inc.*, Vol. 29, No. 4 (April 2007), pp. 88–91.
13. For more on this point, including a sophisticated analysis of internationalization drivers, see Stephanie A. Fernhaber, Patricia P. McDougall, and Benjamin M. Oviatt, "Exploring the Role of Industry Structure in New Venture Internationalization," *Entrepreneurship Theory and Practice*, Vol. 31, No. 4 (July 2007), pp. 517–542.
14. Svante Andersson, "Internationalization in Different Industrial Contexts," *Journal of Business Venturing,* Vol. 19, No. 6 (2004), pp. 851–875; "Don't Laugh at Gilded Butterflies," *The Economist*, Vol. 371, No. 8372 (April 22, 2004), pp. 71–73; Oliver Burgel, Andreas Fier, Georg Licht, and Gordon C. Murray, "The Effect of Internationalization on Rate of Growth of High-Tech Start-Ups—Evidence for UK and Germany," in Paul D. Reynolds et al. (eds.), *Frontiers for Entrepreneurship Research*, proceedings of the 20th Annual Entrepreneurship Research Conference, Babson College, June 2002.
15. For an extended discussion of the particular study cited, see Edmund Prater and Soumen Ghosh, "Current Operational Practices of U.S. Small and Medium-Sized Enterprises in Europe," *Journal of Small Business Management*, Vol. 43, No. 2 (April 2005), pp. 155–169.

16. Dominic Wilson and Roopa Purushothaman, "Dreaming with BRICs: The Path to 2050," GS Global Economics Paper No. 99, http://www2.goldmansachs.com/ideas/brics/book/99-dreaming.pdf, accessed February 11, 2011; and "Another BRIC in the Wall," April 21, 2008, http://www.economist.com/node/11075147, accessed February 11, 2011.

17. "Tradewind Strategies," *op. cit.*

18. As described in Charles W. L. Hill, *Global Business Today* (New York: McGraw-Hill/Irwin, 2011), pp. 179–180.

19. Gordon B. Baty and Michael S. Blake, *Entrepreneurship: Back to Basics* (Washington, DC: Beard Books, 2003), p. 166.

20. Leslie E. Palich and D. Ray Bagby, "Trade Trends in Transatlantica: A Profile of SMEs in the United States and Europe," in Lester Lloyd-Reason and Leigh Sears (eds.), *Trading Places—SMEs in the Global Economy: A Critical Research Handbook* (Cheltenham, UK: Edward Elgar Publishing, 2007), pp. 64–65.

21. *Ibid.*, p. 66.

22. In an attempt to prevent dangerous individuals from entering the country, the U.S. government has tightened visa and work permit restrictions, which has made it more difficult for companies to bring in the foreign talent they need. Also, many international students from countries like China and India train in the best universities in the United States and then return home, hoping to use their skills to get in on the ground floor of opportunities that are emerging in their rapidly developing home countries.

23. Robert Thornock and Wesley Whitaker, "Skolkovo: Russia's Emerging Silicon Valley," January 26, 2011, http://knowledge.wharton.upenn.edu/article.cfm?articleid=2699, accessed February 16, 2011.

24. Mark Whitehouse, "Starting a Global Business, with No U.S. Employees," *Wall Street Journal* (January 19, 2010), p. B8. Reprinted with permission of *Wall Street Journal*. Copyright (c) 2010 Dow Jones & Company, Inc. All Rights Reserved Worldwide.

25. The Boston Consulting Group/Knowledge@ Wharton, "China and the New Rules for Global Business," http://knowledge.wharton.upenn.edu/special_section.cfm?specialID=19, accessed February 16, 2011.

26. Francine Russo, "Doc in a Box," *Business 2.0*, Vol. 8, No. 5 (June 2007).

27. http://www.salvadors.cn/salvadors.html, accessed February 21, 2011; Christopher J. Horton, "Ex-Coloradans See Hope in Sister City," *Denver Post*, http://www.salvadors.cn/, accessed April 24, 2009; and Paul Sloan, "East Meets—and Eats—West," *Business 2.0*, Vol. 6, No. 7 (August 2006), p. 76.

28. http://www.salvadors.cn/, accessed March 8, 2009.

29. Prater and Ghosh, *op. cit.*, p. 161.

30. Garry D. Bruton, David Ahlstrom, and Lu Yuan, "Before Heading to China . . . ," Wall Street Journal, November 30, 2009, http://sloanreview.mit.edu/executive-adviser/articles/2009/5/5154/before-heading-to-china, accessed February 16, 2011.

31. "How Important Are Small Businesses to the U.S. Economy?" http://www.sba.gov/advocacy/7495/8420, accessed February 16, 2011.

32. U.S. Small Business Administration, *Breaking into the Trade Game: A Small Business Guide to Exporting* (Darby, PA: Diane Publishing, 1995), Chapter 1, http://www.docstoc.com/docs/10262563/SBA-Exporting-Guides-entire-document, accessed February 21, 2011.

33. http://www.entertainmentearth.com/help/aboutee.asp, accessed February 16, 2011.

34. "EntertainmentEarth.com," http://www.lead411.com/company_Entertainment Earthcom_Labowitz_581929.html, accessed February 16, 2011.

35. "Welcome to CarAlarmsEtc!" http://cgi3.ebay.com/ws/eBayISAPI.dll?ViewUserPage&userid=caralarmsetc, accessed February 16, 2011; and Janelle Elms, "Go Global," *Entrepreneur*, Vol. 34, No. 9 (September 2006), pp. 130–131.

36. For an informative discussion of this issue as it applies specifically to export approval for shipments to China, see Ted C. Fishman, "America's Most Innovative Industries Are Being Robbed Every Day on the Floors of Chinese Factories," *Inc.*, Vol. 28, No. 6 (June 2006), pp. 98–102.

37. Ian Mount, "Right Back at You," *Fortune Small Business*, Vol. 16, No. 2 (March 2006), p. 18.

38. http://www.compasstradingco.com/index.php?p=contactus, accessed February 17, 2011; and personal conversation with store management, February 8, 2008.

39. Joshua Kurlantzick, "On Foreign Soil," *Entrepreneur*, Vol. 33, No. 6 (June 2005), pp. 88–92.

40. *Ibid.*

41. Michael A. Hitt, R. Duane Ireland, and Robert E. Hoskisson, *Strategic Management: Competitiveness and Globalization* (Cincinnati, OH: Thomson South-Western, 2011), p. 233.

42. U. S. Small Business Administration, *op. cit.*

43. http://www.bluenotejazz.com/franchise/index.php, accessed February 17, 2011.

44. See also Dickson, *op. cit.*, pp. 162–163, for other important studies on the topic.

45. Elizabeth Wasserman, "Happy Birthday, WTO?" *Inc.*, Vol. 27, No. 1 (January 2005), pp. 21–23.

46. Karen E. Klein, "An American in South America's Paris," *Bloomberg Businessweek*, June 15, 2006, http://www.businessweek.com/smallbiz/content/jun2006/sb20060615_849958.htm, accessed February 17, 2011; and Nichole L. Torres, "Change of Scenery," *Entrepreneur*, Vol. 34, No. 8 (August 2006), p. 90.

47. An emerging form of risk that is not within the control of a government but may have very serious effects on business performance is what some researchers are calling *environmental risk*. This suggests that climate change risks vary across global regions and should be a recognized decision making factor [see Peter Romilly, "Business and Climate Change Risk: A Regional Time Series Analysis," *Journal of International Business Studies*, Vol. 38, No. 3 (May 2007), pp. 474–480]. However, the quality of climate change science is still hotly debated, so its predictive value in business decision making is still open to question.

48. Personal communication with Mary Ellen Mooney, April 18, 2011.

49. "Doing Business 2011 Data Notes," http://www.doingbusiness.org/methodology/methodology-note#Easeof DB, accessed February 18, 2011.

50. "Foreign Market Entry," http://www.foreign-trade.com/reference/trad8.htm, accessed February 18, 2011.

CHAPTER 19

1. Julie H. Case, "The Art of Leadership," *U.W.* [University of Washington] *Business*, Spring 2003, p. 17.

2. Deepa D. Singh, "Entrepreneur—Crashing Fear/Cashing Fortitude," http://www.indianmba.com/Faculty_Column/FC362/fc362.html, accessed March 7, 2011.

3. As quoted in Brent Bowers, *The 8 Patterns of Highly Effective Entrepreneurs* (New York: Currency Doubleday, 2006), p. 61.

4. Daniel Goleman, Richard E. Boyatzis, and Annie McKee, *Primal Leadership: Learning to Lead with Emotional Intelligence* (Cambridge, MA: Harvard Business School Press, 2004).

5. Danny Meyer, "The Saltshaker Theory," *Inc.*, Vol. 28, No. 10 (October 2006), pp. 69–70; and http://www.unionsquarecafe.com/aboutusc.html, accessed March 7, 2011.

6. Glenn Ross, "Employee Empowerment Contributes to the Customer Service Experience," http://www.allbusiness.com/

sales/customer-service/3876268-1.html, accessed March 7, 2011.

7. For more on this topic, see Nichole Torres, "Thinking Bigger," *Entrepreneur,* Vol. 34, No. 8 (August 2006), p. 53.
8. Nicole Torres, "Setting the Mood," *Entrepreneur,* Vol. 34, No. 8 (August 2006), p. 53.
9. Tony Hsieh, "Why I Sold Zappos," *Inc.,* Vol. 32, No. 5 (June 2010), pp. 101–104.
10. Sara Wilson, "Build a Billion Dollar Business," *Entrepreneur,* Vol. 37, No. 3 (March 2009), pp. 45–47.
11. Adam Hanft, "Save the Founder," *Inc.,* Vol. 27, No. 10 (October 2005), p. 156.
12. Personal communication with Sara Blakely, May 3, 2007.
13. Gwen Edwards, "Going from *Fortune* 500 to Startup," *Bloomberg Businessweek,* March 5, 2007, http://www.businessweek.com/print/smallbiz/content/mar2007/sb20070305_965709.htm, accessed March 10, 2011.
14. Edward P. Marram, entrepreneur and professor at Babson College, offers creative stage names and notes specifically the perils that companies face at different points in their growth and development. His model includes the following five stages: Wonder, Blunder, Thunder, Plunder, and Asunder. See Jeffry A. Timmons and Stephen Spinelli, *New Venture Creation: Entrepreneurship for the 21st Century* (Boston: McGraw-Hill Irwin, 2009), p. 556.
15. Chris Penttila, "Can You Manage?" *Entrepreneur,* Vol. 31, No. 7 (July 2003), pp. 74–75.
16. *Ibid.*
17. Demetria Lucas, "Twin Tailors," *Black Enterprise,* Vol. 33, No. 9 (April 2003), p. 47.
18. Personal conversation with Ryan Gibson, April 13, 2009.
19. *Startup Journal,* "The Long-Term Perils of Being a Control Freak," http://www.managementsite.com/currentevents/167/The-Long-Term-Perils-of-Being-a-Control-Freak.aspx, accessed March 10, 2011.
20. Brent Bowers, *The 8 Patterns of Highly Effective Entrepreneurs* (New York: Currency Doubleday, 2006), p. 67.
21. These findings are based on a study conducted by the human resource consulting firm Watson Wyatt (now Towers Watson), as reported in "How to Communicate with Employees," *Inc. Guidebook,* Vol. 2, No. 2 (May 2010), pp. 55–58.
22. The use of blogs in business settings is expanding rapidly. For example, blogs are often employed as a public relations tool or a channel to address customer complaints or to pass along product or service insights.
23. Numerous resources provide excellent background on the principles and skills of negotiation. See, for example, Roger Fisher, William Ury, and Bruce Patton, *Getting to Yes: Negotiating Agreement Without Giving In* (New York: Random House, 2003).
24. Barry Farber, "Putting Ideas into Action," *Entrepreneur,* Vol. 37, No. 2 (February 2009), p. 62.
25. Erika Kotite, "Focus, People!" *Entrepreneur,* Vol. 34, No. 9 (September 2006), p. 34.
26. As reported in Mark Henricks, "Just 'To-Do' It," *Entrepreneur,* Vol. 32, No. 8 (August 2004), p. 71.
27. Visit the Entrepreneurs' Organization website at http://www.eonetwork.org and the Young Presidents' Organization at http://www.ypo.org for more information.
28. http://www.sba.gov/about-sba, accessed March 11, 2011.
29. For more information about SCORE, visit its website at http://www.score.org.
30. "The Baker's Peel," http://www.score.org/, accessed March 11, 2011.
31. To learn more about the SBA's network of Small Business Development Centers, go to http://www.sba.gov/content/small-business-development-centers-sbdcs.
32. http://www.fasttrac.org, accessed March 11, 2011.
33. To learn more about the program, visit the organization's website at http://www.fasttrac.org.
34. "Business Incubation FAQ," http://www.nbia.org/resource_library/faq/#3, accessed March 11, 2011.
35. *Ibid.*
36. Darren Dahl, "Percolating Profits," *Inc.,* Vol. 27, No. 2 (February 2005), pp. 38–40.
37. See Leigh Buchanan, "*Inc.* 500," *Inc.,* Vol. 32, No. 7 (September 2010), p. 178.
38. "Bozmedia Group LLC," http://www.manta.com/c/mtb94t2/bozmedia-group-llc, accessed March 15, 2011; Nichole L. Torres, "Family Ties," *Entrepreneur,* Vol. 34, No. 10 (September 2006), pp. 132–133; and personal communication with Ryan Bonifacino, May 2, 2007.

CHAPTER 20

1. See Jan M. P. de Kok, Lorraine M. Uhlaner, and A. Roy Thurik, "Professional HRM Practices in Family Owned-Managed Enterprises," *Journal of Small Business Management,* Vol. 44, No. 3 (May 2006), pp. 441–460.
2. Joel Spolsky, "There's a Better Way to Find and Hire the Very Best Employees," *Inc.,* Vol. 29, No. 5 (May 2007), pp. 81–82.
3. Chris Penttila, "Talent Scout," *Entrepreneur,* July 2008, http://www.entrepreneur.com/magazine/entrepreneur/2008/july/194508.html, accessed April 4, 2011.
4. Chris Resto, Ian Ybarra, and Ramit Sethi, *Recruit or Die: How Any Business Can Beat the Big Guys in the War for Young Talent* (New York: Penguin Group, 2008).
5. See John B. Hope and Patrick C. Mackin (SBA Office of Advocacy), "The Relationship Between Employee Turnover and Employee Compensation in Small Business," *Small Business Research Summary,* No. 308, July 2007, http://www.sba.gov/advo/research/rs308.pdf, accessed April 4, 2011.
6. Sarah E. Needleman, "Small Firms Offer More Responsibility, Credit," *Wall Street Journal,* March 4, 2008, p. B6.
7. Mark Henricks, "A Look Ahead," http://www.entrepreneur.com/article/172016-3, accessed April 5, 2011; and "Our Goal," http://www.kayconstruction.com, accessed April 23, 2009.
8. To get an idea of the kinds of services that public employment offices in your state can provide, conduct a search for "[name of your state] state employment offices" in your browser.
9. Personal communication with Scott Glatstein, April 25, 2011.
10. http://www.imperativesllc.com, accessed April 6, 2011; and Glatstein, *op. cit.*
11. Bureau of Labor Statistics, "Overview of the 2008–18 Projections," December 3, 2010, http://www.bls.gov/oco/oco2003.htm, accessed April 6, 2011.
12. Mark Henricks, "In the Mix," *Entrepreneur,* Vol. 35, No. 10 (October 2007), p. 109.
13. Bruce D. Phillips, "The Future Small Business Workforce," paper presented at the national meeting of the United States Association for Small Business and Entrepreneurship, Indian Wells, CA, January 2005.
14. http://www.foreignlaborcert.doleta.gov, accessed April 6, 2011.
15. Dee Gill, "Dealing with Diversity," *Inc.,* Vol. 27, No. 11 (November 2005), p. 38.
16. U.S. Department of Justice, "Americans with Disabilities Act: Questions and Answers," http://www.ada.gov/q&aeng02.htm, accessed April 6, 2011.
17. http://www.dol.gov/index.htm, accessed April 6, 2011.
18. See Stephanie Clifford, "The Science of Hiring," *Inc.,* Vol. 28, No. 8 (August 2006), pp. 90–98.
19. Jeffrey Pfeffer, "Why Résumés Are Just One Piece of the Puzzle," *Business 2.0,* Vol. 6, No. 11 (December 2005), p. 106.
20. See "Sample Behavioral Interview Questions," http://www.quintcareers

.com/sample_behavioral.html, accessed April 7, 2011.

21. Research indicates that around 27 percent of small businesses find it necessary to fire employees each year [see William J. Dennis, Jr., "Unemployment Compensation," National Federation of Independent Business quarterly research report, Vol. 7, No. 1, (2007)].
22. Beth Gaudio, "Tell Me About Yourself," *MyBusiness*, October–November 2006, p. 14.
23. Mark Henricks, "Check That Temp," *Entrepreneur,* Vol. 34, No. 4 (April 2006), pp. 91–92.
24. Susanna Hamner, "Give People a Second Chance," *Business 2.0*, Vol. 8, No. 4 (May 2007), p. 67.
25. As with many governmental regulations that affect small businesses, this applies only to those companies that have *at least* 15 employees.
26. Ted L. Moss, "Drug Testing for Small Businesses," September 29, 2008, http://www.cosemindspring.com/Topics/Human%20Resources/Recruitment%20and%20Safe%20Hiring%20Practices/Drug%20Testing%20for%20Small%20Businesses.aspx, accessed April 7, 2011.
27. Personal communication with Rick Davis, August 21, 2007.
28. *Ibid.*
29. See Karl Pajo, Alan Coetzer, and Nigel Guenole, "Formal Development Opportunities and Withdrawal Behaviors by Employees in Small and Medium-Sized Enterprises," *Journal of Small Business Management,* Vol. 48, No. 3 (July 2010), pp. 281–301.
30. See William J. Dennis Jr. (ed.), "Training Employees," *NFIB National Small Business Poll,* Vol. 5, No. 1 (Washington, DC: NFIB Research Foundation, 2005), pp. 1–39.
31. One such study is Gaylen N. Chandler and Glenn M. McEvoy, "Human Resource Management, TQM, and Firm Performance in 62 Small and Medium-Size Enterprises," *Entrepreneurship Theory and Practice,* Vol. 25, No. 1 (Fall 2000), pp. 43–57.
32. *Inc.* Staff, "Five Ways to Improve Quality," September 2, 2010, http://www.inc.com/guides/2010/09/5-ways-to-improve-quality.html, accessed April 8, 2011.
33. "Interested in Publishing Your Book?" http://www.bookpros.com, accessed April 8, 2011; and Shannon Scully and Lisa Wadell, "Back to School," http://www.nfib.com/mybusiness-magazine/article?cmsid=52824, accessed April 8, 2011.
34. Harry J. Martin, "The Key to Effective Training Isn't Necessarily What Happens in the Classroom. It's What You Do Afterward," *Wall Street Journal*, December 15, 2008, p. R-11.
35. *Ibid.*
36. Mike Faith, "A Systems Approach to Hiring the Right People," http://www.entrepreneurship.org/en/resource-center/a-systems-approach-to-hiring-the-right-people.aspx, accessed April 8, 2011.
37. *Ibid.*
38. "In-N-Out Burger—Great Benefits," http://www.in-n-out.com/employment_restaurant.asp, accessed April 15, 2011.
39. Get more information about ESOPs from the website of the National Center for Employee Ownership at http://www.nceo.org.
40. For IRS guidelines on cafeteria plans, go to http://www.irs.gov/publications/p15b/ar02.html#en_US_publink1000101745, accessed April 15, 2011.
41. Karen E. Spaeder, "All Well and Good," *Entrepreneur*, Vol. 36, No. 11 (November 2008), p. 24.
42. For more detailed information on laws protecting employees, see the website of the U.S. Department of Labor, http://www.dol.gov/opa/aboutdol/lawsprog.htm, accessed April 15, 2011.
43. Beth Gaudio, "Stay Out of Court," *MyBusiness,* October–November 2005, p. 46.
44. In 2008, the 12-week leave was expanded to 26 weeks in a 12-month period for any individual who needs time to care for a member of the U.S. military who has a serious injury or illness.
45. For more information on the provisions of the Family and Medical Leave Act, consult http://www.dol.gov/dol/topic/benefits-leave/fmla.htm, accessed April 15, 2011.
46. See "How to Conduct Annual Employee Reviews," *Inc. Guidebook*, Vol. 1, No. 9 (December 2008), special supplement.

CHAPTER 21

1. Dan Heath and Chip Heath, "Blowing the Baton Pass," *FastCompany*, No. 147 (July/August, 2010), pp. 46–47.
2. http://www.amazon.com, accessed April 25, 2011.
3. Richard Sweeney, co-founder of Keurig Inc., keynote speech at the annual meeting of the United States Association for Small Business and Entrepreneurship, Hilton Head Island, South Carolina, January 14, 2011.
4. "The Flash Pass," http://www.sixflags.com/overTexas/tickets/flashpass.aspx, accessed April 25, 2011.
5. "Delving into the Mystery of Customer Satisfaction: A Toyota for the Retail Market?" August 10, 2005, http://knowledge.wharton.upenn.edu/article.cfm?articleid=1255, accessed April 26, 2011.
6. Most operations management textbooks offer formulas and calculations for determining the economic order quantity. One exceptionally good resource for this and many other operations management computations is Wallace J. Hopp and Mark L. Spearman, *Factory Physics,* 3rd ed. (Boston: Irwin McGraw-Hill, 2007), pp. 49–53.
7. "McAlister's—From the Beginning," http://www.mcalistersdelifranchise.com/information, accessed May 4, 2011.
8. Personal communication with McAlister's management, March 6, 2009.
9. *Ibid.*
10. As quoted in Liz Welch, "Five Guys Burgers and Fries," *Inc.*, Vol. 32, No. 3 (April 2010), p. 78.
11. *Ibid.*
12. http://www.fiveguys.com/history.aspx, accessed April 27, 2011.
13. John M. Gallaugher, "The Data Asset: Databases, Business Intelligence, and Competitive Advantage," 2009, http://www.gallaugher.com/The%20Data%20Asset.pdf, pp. 20–21, accessed April 28, 2011.
14. "Quality Tools—The Basic Seven," http://src.alionscience.com/pdf/QualityTools.pdf, accessed May 11, 2011; and "Seven Basic Quality Tools," http://asq.org/learn-about-quality/seven-basic-quality-tools/overview/overview.html, accessed May 11, 2011.
15. Linda Tischler, "Partners in *Time," FastCompany,* No. 143 (March 2010), p. 40.
16. *Ibid.*
17. Kate Lister, "Free-Lance Nation," *Entrepreneur*, Vol. 38, No. 9 (September 2010), pp. 89–97.
18. Jennifer Wang, "Employees. Who Needs 'Em?" *Entrepreneur*, Vol. 38, No. 3 (March 2010), p. 18. Reprinted with permission of Entrepreneur Media, Inc. (c) 2010 by Entrpreneur Media, Inc. All rights reserved.
19. Kara Ohngren, "The Man Behind 285,700 Programmers," *Entrepreneur*, Vol. 38, No. 6 (June 2010), p. 71.
20. "Supply Chain Operations Reference (SCOR) Model," http://supply-chain.org/f/SCOR-Overview-Web.pdf, accessed May 3, 2011.
21. Laurel Delaney, "Howdy Partner," *Entrepreneur,* Vol. 35, No. 4 (April 2007), p. 87.
22. Janelle Elms, "Automatic Transition," *Entrepreneur,* Vol. 35, No. 2 (February 2007), p. 118; and http://www.gothamcycles.com, accessed May 11, 2011.
23. Duncan Jones, "Best Practices: Invoice-to-Pay Process Automation," November 19, 2008, http://www.forrester.com/rb/Research/best_practices_invoice-to-pay_process_automation/q/id/46909/t/2, accessed May 11, 2011.
24. http://www.microsoft.com/en-us/dynamics/default.aspx, accessed May 3, 2011.

25. Larry Robinson, "Connecting the Dots: Aligning Lean Operational and Financial Metrics," *LeanDirections: The E-Newsletter of Lean Manufacturing*, http://www.sme.org/cgi-bin/get-newsletter.pl?LEAN&20070810&4&, accessed May 11, 2011.
26. Henry Ford first discussed these ideas in his seminal book from 1926, *Today and Tomorrow,* more recently published in 1988 by Productivity Press.

CHAPTER 22

1. Jonathan Blum, "Working Capital," *Entrepreneur*, January 2011, p. 56.
2. Keith Lowe, "Managing Your Cash Flow," *Entrepreneur,* December 3, 2001, http://www.entrepreneur. com/article/0,4621,295043,00.html, accessed March 15, 2011.
3. "2010 Working Capital Survey," REL, a division of the Hackett Group, Inc., www.relconsultancy.com, accessed April 3, 2011.
4. "Take Control of Your Working Capital," REL, a division of the Hackett Group, Inc., www.relconsultancy.com, accessed April 3, 2011.
5. Simona Covel and Kelly K. Spors, "To Help Collect the Bills, Firms Try the Soft Touch," *Wall Street Journal,* January 27, 2009, p. B1.
6. Paulette Thomas, "Why Debt Collection Is So Essential for Startups," *Wall Street Journal Online,* September 25, 2005, http://www.startupjournal.com/runbusiness/billcollect/20050920-thomas.html, accessed August 21, 2010.
7. Lena Basha, "Handle the Headaches," *MyBusiness,* June–July 2007, pp. 26–29, http://www.mybusinessmag.com/fullstory.php3?sid=1589, accessed April 3, 2011.
8. *Ibid.*
9. Covel and Spors, *op. cit.*, p. B6.
10. "Buried Treasures: Unlocking Cash from Your Accounts Receivable," REL, a division of the Hackett Group, Inc., http://www.relconsultancy.com, accessed April 3, 2011.
11. "The Cure for Inventory Hoarding," REL, a division of the Hackett Group, Inc., http://www.relconsultancy.com, accessed April 3, 2011.
12. To be more accurate, the equation should use the amount of purchases a company has made from suppliers. However, we use cost of goods sold as a reasonable approximation because it is available in the income statement and purchases are not.
13. William J. Dennis, Jr. (ed.), *NFIB National Small Business Poll,* Vol. 3, No. 3 (Washington, DC: NFIB Research Foundation, 2003), p. 13.
14. *Ibid.*, p. 11.

CHAPTER 23

1. Translated by Arthur W. H. Adkins from the Greek text of Solon's poem "Prosperity, Justice and the Hazards of Life," in M. L. West (ed.), *Iambi et Elegi Gracci ante Alexandrum Canttati,* Vol. 2 (Oxford: Clarendon Press, 1972).
2. "Risk," http://www.thefreedictionary.com/risk, accessed June 9, 2011.
3. Daniel Tynan, "In Case of Emergency," *Entrepreneur,* Vol. 3, No. 4 (April 2003), p. 60.
4. The following comments about social media as a tool for small firms have been adapted from Sarah E. Needleman, "Entrepreneurs 'Tweet' Their Way Through Crises," *Wall Street Journal,* September 15, 2009, p. B5.
5. Example provided by Wes Bailey, Bailey Insurance and Risk Management, Inc., Waco, Texas, May 2011.
6. Social Security Administration, as cited in Randy Myers, "The Fine Art of Self-Protection," *CFO,* July 1, 2006, http://222.cfo.com, accessed March 20, 2011.

APPENDIX B

1. Other multiples may also be used in valuing a firm. For instance, service companies are frequently valued based on a multiple of sales.
2. Evan Klonsky, "How to Use EBITDA to Value Your Company," *Inc.*, October 28, 2010, http://www.inc.com/guides/2010/10/how-to-understand-earnings-or-ebitda.html, accessed March 16, 2011.
3. "The Most and Least Valuable Businesses in America," Inc.com, June 2009, http://www.inc.com/valuation_media/2009/valuationbiz.html?keepThis=true&TB_iframe=true&height=630&width=830, accessed June 9, 2011.
4. Depreciation expense was added back to operating income, since it is a noncash expense. The resulting number is equal to the firm's cash flow from operations.
5. The numbers in this example have been changed.
6. Tim Koller, Marc Goedhart, and David Wessels, *Valuation: Measuring and Managing the Value of Companies,* 5th ed. (John Wiley & Sons: New York, 2010).

A

ABC method A system of classifying items in inventory by relative value.

Acceptance sampling The use of a random, representative portion of products to determine the acceptability of an entire lot.

Accounting return on investment technique A capital budgeting technique that evaluates a capital expenditure based on the expected average annual after-tax profits relative to the average book value of an investment.

Accounting statements. *See* Financial statements.

Accounts payable (trade credit) Outstanding credit payable to suppliers.

Accounts receivable The amount of credit extended to customers that is currently outstanding.

Accrual-basis accounting An accounting method of recording profits when earned and expenses when incurred, whether or not the profits have been received or the expenses paid.

Accrued expenses Operating expenses that have been incurred but not paid.

Accumulated depreciation Total (cumulative) depreciation expense taken over an asset's life.

Actual cash value (ACV) An insurance term that refers to the depreciated value of a property.

Actual product/service The basic physical product and/or service that delivers benefits.

Advertising The impersonal presentation of a business idea through mass media.

Advisory council A group that serves as an alternative to a board of directors, acting only in an advisory capacity.

Agents/brokers Intermediaries that do not take ownership of the goods they distribute.

Aggregate stop loss limit A comprehensive limit on annual expenses should a number of employees reach the specific stop loss limit.

Aging schedule A categorization of accounts receivable based on the length of time they have been outstanding.

All-risk approach Stating in an insurance policy that all direct damages to property are covered except those caused by perils specifically excluded.

App Abbreviation for a software application for business or entertainment.

Area developers Individuals or firms that obtain the legal right to open several franchised outlets in a given area.

Artisan entrepreneur A person with primarily technical skills and little business knowledge who starts a business.

Asset-based loan A line of credit secured by working capital assets.

Asset-based valuation Determination of the value of a business by estimating the value of its assets.

Associative forecasting Forecasting that considers a variety of variables to determine expected sales.

Attitude An enduring opinion, based on knowledge, feeling, and behavioral tendency.

Attractive small firm A small firm that provides substantial profits to its owner.

Attributes Product or service parameters that can be counted as being present or absent.

Auction sites Web-based businesses offering participants the ability to list products for consumer bidding.

Augmented product/service The basic product and/or service plus any extra or unsolicited benefits to the consumer that may prompt a purchase.

Automobile insurance Coverage designed to provide liability and physical damage protection for a vehicle.

Average collection period. *See* Days sales outstanding.

Average pricing An approach in which total cost for a given period is divided by quantity sold in that period to set a price.

B

Bad-debt ratio The ratio of bad debts to credit sales.

Balance sheet A financial report showing a firm's assets, liabilities, and ownership equity at a specific point in time.

Balloon payment A very large payment required about halfway through the term over which payments were calculated, repaying the loan balance in full.

Banner ads Advertisements that appear across a Web page, most often as moving rectangular strips.

Behavioral interview An approach that assesses the suitability of job candidates based on how they would respond to hypothetical situations.

Benefit variables Specific characteristics that distinguish market segments according to the benefits sought by customers.

Bill of lading A document indicating that a product has been shipped and the title to that product has been transferred.

Blog An interactive website where an individual can maintain a personal online journal, post and receive comments and reflections, and provide hyperlinks.

Board of directors The governing body of a corporation, elected by the stockholders.

Bootstrapping Doing more with less in terms of resources invested in a business, and where possible controlling the resources without owning them.

Born-global firms Small companies launched with cross-border business activities in mind.

Bottleneck Any point in the operations process where limited capacity reduces the production capability of an entire chain of activities.

Brand A verbal and/or symbolic means of identifying a product.

Brand image The overall perception of a brand.

Brand name A brand that can be spoken.

Brandmark A brand that cannot be spoken.

Break-even point Sales volume at which total sales revenue equals total costs and expenses.

Breakdown process (chain-ratio method) A forecasting method that begins with a large-scope variable and works down to the sales forecast.

Brick-and-mortar store The traditional physical store from which businesses have historically operated.

Budget A document that expresses future plans in monetary terms.

Build-up LBO A leveraged buyout involving the purchase of a group of similar companies with the intent of making the firms into one larger company for eventual sale.

Build-up process A forecasting method in which all potential buyers in a target market's submarkets are identified and then the estimated demand is added up.

Business angels Private individuals who invest in others' entrepreneurial ventures.

Business format franchising A franchise arrangement whereby the franchisee obtains an entire marketing and management system geared to entrepreneurs.

Business incubator A facility that provides shared space, services, and management assistance to new businesses.

Business interruption insurance Coverage that reimburses a business for the loss of anticipated income following the interruption of business operations.

Business model An analysis of how a firm plans to create profits and cash flows given its revenue sources, cost structures, and the required size of investment.

Business owner's policy (BOP) A business version of a homeowner's policy, designed to meet the property and general liability insurance needs of some small business owners.

Business plan A document that outlines the basic concept underlying a business and describes how that concept will be realized.

Business risk The possibility of losses associated with the assets and earnings potential of a firm.

Business-to-business (B2B) model A business model based on selling to business customers electronically.

Business-to-consumer (B2C) model A business model based on selling to final consumers electronically.

Bust-up LBO A leveraged buyout involving the purchase of a company with the intent of selling off its assets.

C

C corporation An ordinary corporation, taxed by the federal government as a separate legal entity.

Cafeteria plans. *See* Flexible benefit programs.

Capabilities The integration of various organizational resources that are deployed together to the firm's advantage.

Capital budgeting analysis An analytical method that helps managers make decisions about long-term investments.

Cash-basis accounting An accounting method of recording profits when cash is received and recording expenses when they are paid.

Cash budget A listing of cash receipts and cash disbursements, usually for a relatively short time period, such as a week or a month.

Cash conversion period The time required to convert paid-for inventory and accounts receivable into cash.

Cash flow activities Operating, investing, and financing activities that result in cash inflows or outflows.

Cash flow–based valuation Determination of the value of a business by estimating the amount and timing of its future cash flows.

Cash flow statement A financial report showing a firm's sources of cash as well as its uses of cash.

Certified Development Company (CDC) 504 Loan Program An SBA loan program that provides long-term financing for small businesses to acquire real estate or machinery and equipment.

Chain of command The official, vertical channel of communication in an organization.

Chain-ratio method. *See* Breakdown process.

Channel of distribution The system of relationships established to guide the movement of a product.

Chattel mortgage A loan for which items of inventory or other movable property serve as collateral.

Churning Actions by franchisors to void the contracts of franchisees in order to sell the franchise to someone else and collect an additional fee.

Civil Rights Act Legislation prohibiting discrimination based on race, color, religion, sex, or national origin.

Co-branding Bringing two franchise brands together under one roof.

Code of ethics Official standards of employee behavior formulated by a business owner.

Co-employment An arrangement to outsource part of personnel management to an organization that handles paperwork and administers benefits for those employees.

Cognitive dissonance The anxiety that occurs when a customer has second thoughts immediately following a purchase.

Coinsurance clause A clause in a property insurance policy that requires the owner to have insurance for at least 80 percent of what it would cost to rebuild the building or replace the personal property.

Commercial general liability (CGL) insurance Coverage for general liability loss exposure, including premises liability, operations liability, product liability, and completed operations liability.

Common carriers Transportation intermediaries available for hire to the general public.

Community-based financial institution A lender that uses funds from federal, state, and private sources to provide financing to small businesses in low-income communities.

Compensatory damages Economic or noneconomic damages intended to make the claimant whole by compensating the claimant for any injuries or damage arising from the negligent action.

Competitive advantage A benefit that exists when a firm has a product or service that is seen by its target market as better than those of competitors.

Competitive environment The environment that focuses on the strength, position, and likely moves and countermoves of competitors in an industry.

Comprehensive plan A full business plan that provides an in-depth analysis of the critical factors that will determine a firm's success or failure, along with all the underlying assumptions.

Constraint The most restrictive of bottlenecks, determining the capacity of the entire system.

Consumer credit Financing granted by retailers to individuals who purchase for personal or family use.

Consumer-to-consumer (C2C) model A business model usually set up around Internet auction sites that allow individuals and companies to list items available for sale to potential bidders.

Content-based model A business model in which the website provides access but not the ability to buy or sell products and services.

Continuous manufacturing A form of repetitive manufacturing with output that more closely resembles a stream of product than individual products.

Contract carriers Transportation intermediaries that contract with individual shippers.

Contribution margin The difference between the unit selling price and the unit variable costs and expenses.

Cooperative purchasing organization (coop) An organization in which small businesses combine their demand for products or services in order to negotiate as a group with suppliers.

Co-preneurs Couples teams who own and manage businesses.

Copyright The exclusive right of a creator to reproduce, publish, perform, display, or sell his or her own works.

Core competencies Those capabilities that provide a firm with a competitive edge and reflect its personality.

Core product/service The fundamental benefit or solution sought by customers.

Corporate charter A document that establishes a corporation's existence.

Corporation A business organization that exists as a legal entity and provides limited liability to its owners.

Cost-based commitment Commitment based on the belief that the opportunity for gain from joining a business is too great to pass up.

Cost-based strategy A plan of action that requires a firm to hold down its costs so that it can compete by charging lower prices and still make a profit.

Cost of goods sold The cost of producing or acquiring products or services to be sold by a firm.

Cost structures A component of the business model that provides a framework for estimating the nature and types of costs and expenses a firm may incur.

Counterfeit activity The unauthorized use of intellectual property.

Cousin consortium A business in the third and subsequent generations when children of the siblings take ownership and management positions.

Credit An agreement between a buyer and a seller that provides for delayed payment for a product or service.

Credit bureaus Privately owned organizations that summarize a number of firms' credit experiences with particular individuals.

Credit card An alternative to cash whose use provides assurance to a seller that a buyer has a satisfactory credit rating and that payment will be received from the issuing financial institution.

Crime insurance Coverage against employee dishonesty.

Critical risks A section of the business plan that identifies the potential risks that may be encountered by an investor.

Cross-border acquisition The purchase by a business in one country of a company located in another country.

Culture Behavioral patterns and values that characterize a group of consumers in a target market.

Current assets (working capital) Assets that can be converted into cash relatively quickly.

Current debt (short-term liabilities) Borrowed money that must be repaid within 12 months.

Current ratio A measure of a company's relative liquidity, determined by dividing current assets by current liabilities.

Customer experience management (CEM) An approach that recognizes that, with every interaction, customers learn something about a company that will affect their desire to do business there in the future.

Customer profile A collection of information about a customer, including demographic data, attitudes, preferences, and other behavioral characteristics, as defined by CRM goals.

Customer relationship management (CRM) A company-wide business strategy designed to optimize profitability, revenue, and customer satisfaction by focusing on specific customer groups.

Cycle counting Counting different segments of the physical inventory at different times during the year.

D

Days in inventory The number of days, on average, that a company is holding inventory.

Days in payables The number of days, on average, that a business takes to pay its accounts payable.

Days sales outstanding (average collection period) The number of days, on average, that a firm is extending credit to its customers.

Debit card An alternative to cash whose use results in an immediate withdrawal from the buyer's bank account to pay for products or services.

Debt Financing provided by creditors.

Debt ratio A measure of what percentage of a firm's assets is financed by debt, determined by dividing total debt by total assets.

Dehydrated plan A short form of a business plan that presents only the most important issues and projections for the business.

Delegation of authority Granting to subordinates the right to act or make decisions.

Demand management strategies Operational strategies used to stimulate customer demand when it is normally low.

Demographic variables Specific characteristics that describe customers and their purchasing power.

Depreciable assets Assets whose value declines, or depreciates, over time.

Depreciation expense The cost of a firm's building and equipment, allocated over their useful life.

Design defect A defect resulting from a dangerous design, even though the product was made according to specifications.

Design patent Registered protection for the appearance of a product and its inseparable parts.

Desire-based commitment Commitment based on a belief in the purpose of a business and a desire to contribute to it.

Differentiation-based strategy A plan of action designed to provide a product or service with unique attributes that are valued by consumers.

Direct channel A distribution system without intermediaries.

Direct forecasting A forecasting method in which sales is the estimated variable.

Direct loss A loss in which physical damage to property reduces its value to the property owner.

Disability insurance Coverage that provides benefits upon the disability of a firm's partner or other key employee.

Discounted cash flow (DCF) techniques Capital budgeting techniques that compare the present value of future cash flows with the cost of the initial investment.

Disintermediation A situation where a wholesaler in a B2B operation chooses to bypass the "middleman" and sell its product or service directly to the final consumer.

Distribution Physically moving products and establishing intermediary relationships to support such movement.

Double taxation Taxation of income that occurs twice—first as corporate earnings and then as stockholder dividends.

Dual distribution A distribution system that involves more than one channel.

Due diligence The exercise of reasonable care in the evaluation of a business opportunity.

Dynamic (personalized) pricing strategy A technique based on charging more than the standard price when a customer's profile suggests that the higher price will be accepted.

E

Earnings before interest, taxes, depreciation, and amortization (EBITDA) A firm's profits after subtracting cost of goods sold and cash operating expenses, but before subtracting interest expense, taxes, depreciation, and amortization.

Earnings multiple (value-to-earnings ratio) A ratio determined by dividing a firm's value by its annual earnings.

E-commerce The paperless exchange of business information via the Internet.

Economic damages Compensatory damages that relate to economic loss, such as medical expenses and loss of income.

Economic order quantity An index that determines the quantity to purchase in order to minimize total inventory costs.

Economic risk The probability that a country's government will mismanage its economy in ways that hinder the performance of firms operating there.

Economies of scale Efficiencies that result from expansion of production.

Elastic demand Demand that changes significantly when there is a change in the price of the product or service.

Elasticity of demand The degree to which a change in price affects the quantity demanded.

Electronic Customer Relationship Marketing (eCRM) An electronically based system that emphasizes customer relationships.

E-mail promotion Advertising delivered by means of electronic mail.

Employee benefits Supplements to compensation designed to be attractive and useful to employees.

Employee stock ownership plan (ESOP) A method by which a firm is sold either in part or in total to its employees.

Employee training Planned efforts to help workers master the knowledge, skills, and behaviors they need to perform their duties.

Empowerment Giving employees authority to make decisions or take actions on their own.

Encroachment The franchisor's selling of another franchise location within the market area of an existing franchisee.

Enterprise value. *See* Firm value.

Enterprise zones State-designated areas that are established to bring jobs to economically deprived regions through regulatory and tax incentives.

Entrepreneur A person who is relentlessly focused on an opportunity to create value, in either a new or an existing business, while assuming both the risk and the reward for his or her effort.

Entrepreneurial alertness Readiness to act on existing, but unnoticed, business opportunities.

Entrepreneurial legacy Material assets and intangible qualities passed on to both heirs and society.

Entrepreneurial opportunity An economically attractive and timely opportunity that creates value for both prospective customers and the firm's owner.

Entrepreneurial team Two or more people who work together as entrepreneurs on one endeavor.

Environmentalism The effort to protect and preserve the environment.

Equipment loan An installment loan from a seller of machinery used by a business.

Equity value (owner's value) The value of the firm less the debt owed by the firm.

Ethical imperialism The belief that the ethical standards of one's own country can be applied universally.

Ethical issues Issues that involve questions of right and wrong.

Ethical relativism The belief that ethical standards are subject to local interpretation.

Evaluative criteria The features or characteristics of a product or service that customers use for comparison.

Evoked set A group of brands that a consumer is both aware of and willing to consider as a solution to a purchase need.

Exchange rate The value of one country's currency relative to that of another country.

Executive summary A section of the business plan that conveys a clear and concise overall picture of the proposed venture.

Exit strategy A section of the business plan that focuses on options for cashing out of the investment.

Exiting. *See* Harvesting.

Experience curve efficiencies Per-unit savings gained from the repeated production of the same product.

Exporting Selling products produced in the home country to customers in another country.

F

Factoring Obtaining cash by selling accounts receivable to another firm.

Fair Labor Standards Act (FLSA) Federal law that establishes a minimum wage and provides for overtime pay.

Fair market value The price at which the property would change hands between a willing buyer and willing seller, both parties having reasonable knowledge of relevant facts.

Family A group of people bound by a shared history and a commitment to share a future together, while supporting the development and well-being of individual members.

Family and Medical Leave Act Legislation that assures employees of unpaid leave for childbirth or other family needs.

Family business An organization in which *either* the individuals who established or acquired the firm *or* their descendants significantly influence the strategic decisions and life course of the firm.

Family business constitution A statement of principles intended to guide a family firm through times of crisis and change.

Family council An organized group of family members who gather periodically to discuss family-related business issues.

Family retreat A gathering of family members, usually at a remote location, to discuss family business matters.

Family unity Oneness of mind, feeling, and action among a number of persons.

Fatal flaw A circumstance or development that alone could render a new business unsuccessful.

Feasibility analysis A preliminary assessment of a business idea that gauges whether or not the venture envisioned is likely to succeed.

Financial leverage The impact (positive or negative) of financing with debt rather than with equity.

Financial plan A section of the business plan that projects the company's financial position based on well-substantiated assumptions and explains how the figures have been determined.

Financial statements (accounting statements) Reports of a firm's financial performance and resources, including an income statement, a balance sheet, and a cash flow statement.

Firm value (enterprise value) The value of an entire business, regardless of how it is financed.

Fixed assets (property, plant, and equipment [PPE]) Physical assets that will be used in the business for more than one year, such as equipment, buildings, and land.

Fixed costs Costs that remain constant as the quantity produced or sold varies.

Flexible benefit programs (cafeteria plans) Benefit programs that allow employees to select the types of benefits they wish to receive.

Flexible manufacturing systems Operations that usually involve computer-controlled equipment that can turn out products in smaller or more flexible quantities.

Focus strategy A plan of action that isolates an enterprise from competitors and other market forces by targeting a restricted market segment.

Follow-the-leader pricing strategy A technique based on using a particular competitor as a model in setting prices.

Foreign licensing Allowing a company in another country to purchase the rights to manufacture and sell a company's products in international markets.

Formal venture capitalists Individuals who form limited partnerships for the purpose of raising venture capital from large institutional investors.

Founder An entrepreneur who brings a new firm into existence.

Franchise The privileges conveyed in a franchise contract.

Franchise contract The legal agreement between franchisor and franchisee.

Franchise Disclosure Document (FDD) A document that provides the accepted format for satisfying the franchise disclosure requirements of the FTC.

Franchise Rule A rule that prescribes that the franchisor must disclose certain information to prospective franchisees.

Franchisee An entrepreneur whose power is limited by a contractual relationship with a franchising organization.

Franchising A business relationship in which an entrepreneur can reduce risk and benefit from the business experience of all members of the franchise system.

Franchisor The party in a franchise contract that specifies the methods to be followed and the terms to be met by the other party.

G

Gazelle. *See* High-potential venture.

General environment The broad environment, encompassing factors that influence most businesses in a society.

General partner A partner in a limited partnership who has unlimited personal liability.

General-purpose equipment Machines that serve many functions in the production process.

Globalization The expansion of international business, encouraged by converging market preferences, falling trade barriers, and the integration of national economies.

Greenfield venture A wholly owned subsidiary formed from scratch in another country.

Gross fixed assets Depreciable assets at their original cost, before any depreciation expense has been taken.

Gross profit Sales less the cost of goods sold.

H

Harvesting (exiting) The process used by entrepreneurs and investors to reap the value of a business when they leave it.

Headhunter A search firm that locates qualified candidates for executive positions.

Health insurance Coverage for employee medical care.

Health maintenance organization (HMO) A managed-care network providing health insurance that is generally less expensive than that of a PPO but more limiting in choices of medical care providers.

High-potential venture (gazelle) A small firm that has great prospects for growth.

Home-based business A business that maintains its primary facility in the residence of its owner.

Human resource management (HRM) The management of employees in a way that enables them to help a firm reach its strategic objectives.

Hyperlink A word, phrase, or image that a user may click on to go to another part of the document or website or to a new document or website.

I

Importing Selling products produced in another country to buyers in the home country.

Income statement (profit and loss statement) A financial report showing the amounts of profits or losses from a firm's operations over a given period of time.

Indemnification clause A contractual clause that requires one party to assume the financial consequences of another party's legal liabilities.

Indirect channel A distribution system with one or more intermediaries.

Indirect forecasting A forecasting method in which variables related to sales are used to project future sales.

Indirect loss A loss arising from an inability to carry on normal operations due to a direct loss of property.

Industry environment The environment that includes factors that directly impact a given firm and its competitors.

Inelastic demand Demand that does not change significantly when there is a change in the price of the product or service.

Informal venture capital Funds provided by wealthy private individuals to high-risk ventures.

Information-based model A business model in which the website provides information about a business, its products, and other related matters but doesn't charge for its use.

Initial public offering (IPO) The first sale of shares of a company's stock to the public.

Inspection The examination of a part or a product to determine whether it meets quality standards.

Installment account A line of credit that requires a down payment, with the balance paid over a specified period of time.

Institutional advertising The presentation of information about a particular firm, designed to enhance the firm's image.

Intangible resources Those organizational resources that are invisible and difficult to assess.

Integrity An uncompromising adherence to the lofty values, beliefs, and principles that an individual claims to hold.

Intellectual property Original intellectual creations, including inventions, literary creations, and works of art, that are protected by patents or copyrights.

Interest expense The cost of borrowed money.

Internal rate of return (IRR) The rate of return a firm expects to earn on a project.

International franchising Selling a standard package of products, systems, and management services to a company in another country.

International outsourcing A strategy that involves accessing foreign labor through contracts with independent providers.

International strategic alliance A combination of efforts and/or assets of companies in different countries for the sake of pooling resources and sharing the risks of an enterprise.

Inventory A firm's raw materials and products held in anticipation of eventual sale.

ISO 9000 The standards governing international certification of a firm's quality management procedures.

J

Job description An outline, or summary, of the work to be performed for a particular position.

Job Instruction Training A systematic, step-by-step method for on-the-job training of nonmanagerial employees.

Job shop A manufacturing operation in which short production runs are used to produce small quantities of items.

Job specification A list of the knowledge, skills, abilities, and other characteristics needed to perform a specific job.

Joint and several liability The liability of each partner resulting from any one partner's ability to legally bind the other partners.

Just-in-time inventory system A method of reducing inventory levels to an absolute minimum.

K

Key-person life insurance Coverage that provides benefits to a firm upon the death of key personnel.

L

Lean production An approach that emphasizes efficiency through elimination of waste.

Learning effects Insights, gained from experience, that lead to improved work performance.

Legal entity A business organization that is recognized by the law as having a separate legal existence.

Letter of credit An agreement issued by a bank to honor a draft or other demand for payment when specified conditions are met.

Leveraged buyout (LBO) A purchase heavily financed with debt, where the future cash flows of the target company are expected to be sufficient to meet debt repayments.

LIBOR (London Interbank Offered Rate) The interest rate charged by London banks on loans to other London banks.

Licensee The company buying licensing rights.

Licensor The company selling licensing rights.

Lifestyle business A microbusiness that permits the owner to follow a desired pattern of living.

Limited liability Restriction of an owner's legal financial responsibilities to the amount invested in the business.

Limited liability company A form of organization in which owners have limited liability but pay personal income taxes on business profits.

Limited partner A partner in a limited partnership who is not active in its management and has limited personal liability.

Limited partnership A partnership with at least one general partner and one or more limited partners.

Line of credit An informal agreement between a borrower and a bank as to the maximum amount of funds the bank will provide at any one time.

Line organization A simple organizational structure in which each person reports to one supervisor.

Line-and-staff organization An organizational structure that includes staff specialists who assist management.

Liquidation value method Determination of the value of a business by estimating the money that would be available if the firm were to liquidate its assets.

Liquidity The degree to which a firm has working capital available to meet maturing debt obligations.

Loan covenants Bank-imposed restrictions on a borrower that enhance the chance of timely repayment.

Lock box A post office box for receiving remittances from customers.

Logistics. *See* Physical distribution.

Long-range plan (strategic plan) A firm's overall plan for the future.

Long-term debt Loans from banks or other sources with repayment terms of more than 12 months.

Long-term notes Agreements to repay cash amounts borrowed from banks or other lending sources for periods longer than 12 months.

Loss avoidance Choosing not to engage in hazardous activities.

Loss prevention Keeping a loss from happening.

Loss reduction Lessening the frequency, severity, or unpredictability of potential losses.

M

Make-or-buy decision A choice that companies must make when they have the option of making or buying component parts for products they produce.

Management buyout (MBO) A leveraged buyout in which the firm's top managers become significant shareholders in the acquired firm.

Management development Preparation of employees for career advancement through education, job experiences, network development, and performance assessment.

Management team Managers and other key persons who give a company its general direction; also, a section of the business plan that describes a new firm's organizational structure and the backgrounds of its key players.

Manufacturing defect A defect resulting from a problem that occurs during the manufacturing process, causing the product to subsequently not be made according to specifications.

Market A group of customers or potential customers who have purchasing power and unsatisfied needs.

Market analysis The process of locating and describing potential customers.

Market risk The uncertainty associated with an investment decision.

Market segmentation The division of a market into several smaller groups with similar needs.

Marketing defect A defect resulting from failure to convey to the user that hazards are associated with a product or to provide adequate instructions on safe product use.

Marketing mix The combination of product, pricing, promotion, and distribution activities.

Marketing plan A section of the business plan that describes the user benefits of the product or service and the type of market that exists.

Marketing research The gathering, processing, interpreting, and reporting of market information.

Markup pricing An approach based on applying a percentage to a product's cost to obtain its selling price.

Mass marketing. *See* Unsegmented strategy.

Master licensee An independent firm or individual acting as a sales agent with the responsibility of finding new franchisees within a specified territory.

Matchmakers Specialized brokers that bring together buyers and sellers of businesses.

Maximum investment A component of the business model that provides estimates of the types and amounts of investment required to achieve positive profits and cash flows.

Mentor A knowledgeable person who can offer guidance based on experience in a given field.

Mentoring The process by which a more-experienced person guides and supports the professional progress of a new or less-experienced employee.

Merchant middlemen Intermediaries that take ownership of the goods they distribute.

Microbusiness A small firm that provides minimal profits to its owner.

Mobile device A generic term used to refer to a variety of wireless handheld computing devices.

Modified book value method Determination of the value of a business by adjusting book value to reflect obvious differences between the historical cost and current market value of the assets.

Mortgage A long-term loan from a creditor for which real estate is pledged as collateral.

Motivations Goal-directed forces that organize and give direction to the tension caused by unsatisfied needs.

Multi-brand franchising The operation of several franchise organizations within a single corporate structure.

Multi-segment strategy A strategy that recognizes different preferences of individual market segments and develops a unique marketing mix for each.

Multiple-unit ownership Ownership by a single franchisee of more than one franchise from the same company.

N

Named-peril approach Identifying in an insurance policy the specific perils covered.

Need-based commitment Commitment based on an individual's self-doubt and belief that he or she lacks career options outside the current business.

Needs The starting point for all behavior.

Negotiation A two-way communication process used to resolve differences in interests, desires, or demands.

Nepotism The practice of employing relatives in the family firm.

Net fixed assets Gross fixed assets less accumulated depreciation.

Net present value (NPV) The present value of expected future cash flows less the initial investment outlay.

Net profits Income that may be distributed to the owners or reinvested in the company.

Net working capital Current assets less current liabilities.

Networking The process of developing and engaging in mutually beneficial relationships.

Niche market A specific group of customers with an identifiable but narrow range of product or service interests.

Nondisclosure agreement An agreement in which the buyer promises the seller that he or she will not reveal confidential information or violate the seller's trust.

Noneconomic damages Compensatory damages for such losses as pain and suffering, mental anguish, and loss of physical abilities.

Nonprofit corporation A form of corporation for enterprises established to serve civic, educational, charitable, or religious purposes but not for generation of profits.

Normalized earnings Earnings that have been adjusted for unusual items, such as fire damage, and leakages, such as an excessive salary for the owner.

O

Obligation-based commitment Commitment that results from a sense of duty or expectation.

Occupational Safety and Health Act (OSHA) Legislation that regulates the safety of workplaces and work practices.

Offering A section of the business plan that indicates to an investor how much money is needed, and when and how the money will be used.

Offshoring A strategy that involves relocating operations abroad.

Open charge account A line of credit that allows the customer to obtain a product or service at the time of purchase, with payment due when billed.

Operating expenses Costs related to marketing and selling a firm's product or service, general and administrative expenses, and depreciation.

Operating profit margin A measure of how well a firm is controlling its costs of goods sold and operating expenses relative to sales, determined by dividing operating profits by sales.

Operating profits Earnings after operating expenses but before interest and taxes are paid.

Operations The processes used to create and deliver a product or service.

Operations and development plan A section of the business plan that offers information on how a product will be produced or a service provided, including descriptions of the new firm's facilities, labor, raw materials, and processing requirements.

Operations management The planning and control of a conversion process that includes turning inputs into outputs that customers desire.

Opinion leader A group member who plays a key communications role.

Opportunistic entrepreneur A person with both sophisticated managerial skills and technical knowledge who starts a business.

Opportunity cost of funds The rate of return that could be earned on another investment of similar risk.

Opportunity recognition Identification of potential new products or services that may lead to promising businesses.

Organizational culture Patterns of behaviors and beliefs that characterize a particular firm.

Organizational test Verification of whether a nonprofit organization is staying true to its stated purpose.

Other assets Assets other than current assets and fixed assets, such as patents, copyrights, and goodwill.

Outsourcing Contracting with a third party to take on and manage one or more of the firm's functions.

Owner-managed business A venture operated by a founding entrepreneur.

Owner's value. *See* Equity value.

Ownership equity Owners' investments in a company plus cumulative net profits retained in the firm.

P

Package policy A policy for small businesses that do not qualify for a BOP that combines property insurance and commercial general liability insurance.

Partially self-funded program Designating part of a firm's earnings to fund a portion of employee medical coverage.

Partnership A legal entity formed by two or more co-owners to operate a business for profit.

Partnership agreement A document that states explicitly the rights and duties of partners.

Patent The registered, exclusive right of an inventor to make, use, or sell an invention.

Payback period technique A capital budgeting technique that measures the amount of time it will take to recover the cash outlay of an investment.

Penetration pricing strategy A technique based on setting lower than normal prices to hasten market acceptance of a product or service or to increase market share.

Percentage-of-sales technique A method of forecasting asset and financing requirements.

Perception The individual processes that give meaning to the stimuli confronting consumers.

Perceptual categorization The process of grouping similar things so as to manage huge quantities of incoming stimuli.

Peril A cause of loss, either through natural events or through the actions of people.

Perpetual inventory system A method for keeping a running record of inventory.

Personal property Any property other than real property, including machinery, inventory, and vehicles.

Personal selling A sales presentation delivered in a one-on-one manner.

Personnel risks Risks that directly affect individual employees but may have an indirect impact on a business as well.

Physical distribution (logistics) The activities of distribution involved in the physical relocation of products.

Physical inventory system A method that provides for periodic counting of items in inventory.

Piecework Financial incentive based on pay according to number of units produced.

Piercing the corporate veil A situation in which the courts conclude that incorporation has been used to perpetuate a fraud, skirt a law, or commit some wrongful act and thus remove liability protection from the corporate entity.

Piggyback franchising The operation of a retail franchise within the physical facilities of a host store.

Plant patent Registered protection for any distinct, new variety of living plant.

Pledged accounts receivable Accounts receivable used as collateral for a loan.

Poka-yoke A proactive approach to quality management that seeks to mistake-proof a firm's operations.

Political risk The potential for political forces in a country to negatively affect the performance of businesses operating within its borders.

Pop-up ads Advertisements that burst open on computer screens.

Pre-emptive right The right of stockholders to buy new shares of stock before they are offered to the public.

Preferred provider organization (PPO) A managed-care network providing health insurance that is generally more expensive than that of an HMO but offers a broader choice of medical providers.

Prestige pricing An approach based on setting a high price to convey an image of high quality or uniqueness.

Price A specification of what a seller requires in exchange for transferring ownership or use of a product or service.

Price lining strategy A technique based on setting a range of several distinct merchandise price levels.

Primary data New market information that is gathered by the firm conducting the research.

Prime rate The interest rate charged by commercial banks on loans to their most creditworthy customers.

Private carriers Lines of transport owned by shippers.

Private placement The sale of a firm's capital stock to select individuals.

Pro forma financial statements Projections of a company's financial statements for up to five years, including balance sheets, income statements, and statements of cash flows, as well as cash budgets.

Product A total bundle of satisfaction—including a service, a product, or both—offered to consumers in an exchange transaction.

Product advertising The presentation of a business idea designed to make potential customers aware of a specific product or service and create a desire for it.

Product and trade name franchising A franchise agreement granting the right to use a widely recognized product or name.

Product item The lowest common denominator in the product mix—the individual item.

Product life cycle A detailed picture of what happens to a specific product's sales and profits over time.

Product line The sum of related individual product items.

Product mix The collection of a firm's total product lines.

Product mix consistency The similarity of product lines in a product mix.

Product/service plan A section of the business plan that describes the product and/or service to be provided and explains its merits.

Product strategy The way the product component of the marketing mix is used to achieve a firm's objectives.

Professional corporation A form of corporation that shields owners from liability and is set up for individuals in certain professional practices.

Professional employer organization (PEO) A company that sets up co-employment agreements.

Professional manager A manager who uses systematic, analytical methods of management.

Profit and loss statement. *See* Income statement.

Profit margins Profits as a percentage of sales.

Profits before taxes (taxable profits) Earnings after operating expenses and interest expenses but before taxes.

Project manufacturing Operations used to create unique but similar products.

Promotion Marketing communications that inform and persuade consumers.

Promotional mix A blend of nonpersonal, personal, and special forms of communication aimed at a target market.

Property, plant, and equipment (PPE). *See* Fixed assets.

Prospecting A systematic process of continually looking for new customers.

Proximate cause A negligent act that is the clear cause of damages sustained.

Publicity Information about a firm and its products or services that appears as a news item, usually free of charge.

Punitive damages A form of punishment beyond compensatory damages that intends to punish wrongdoers for gross negligence or callous disregard and to have a deterrent effect.

Purchase-order financing Obtaining cash from a lender who, for a fee, advances the amount of the borrower's cost of goods sold for a specific customer order.

Pure risk The uncertainty associated with a situation where only loss or no loss can occur.

Q

Quality The features of a product or service that enable it to satisfy customers' stated and implied needs.

R

Real estate mortgage A long-term loan with real property held as collateral.

Real property Land and anything physically attached to the land, such as buildings.

Reasonable (prudent person) standard The typical standard of care, based on what a reasonable or prudent person would have done under similar circumstances.

Reciprocation A powerful social rule based on an obligation to repay in kind what another has done for or provided to us.

Reference groups Small groups that an individual allows to influence his or her behavior.

Refugee A person who becomes an entrepreneur to escape an undesirable situation.

Reliability The consistency of a test in measuring job performance ability.

Reluctant entrepreneur A person who becomes an entrepreneur as a result of some severe hardship.

Repetitive manufacturing Operations designed for long production runs of high-volume products.

Replacement value method Determination of the value of a business by estimating the cost of replacing the firm's assets.

Replacement value of property The cost of replacing personal property and rebuilding real property at today's prices.

Resources The basic inputs that a firm uses to conduct its business.

Retained earnings Profits less dividends paid over the life of a business.

Return on assets A measure of a firm's profitability relative to the amount of its assets, determined by dividing operating profits by total assets.

Return on equity A measure of the rate of return that owners receive on their equity investment, calculated by dividing net profits by ownership equity.

Revenue model A component of the business model that identifies the different types of revenue streams a firm expects to receive.

Revolving charge account A line of credit on which the customer may charge purchases at any time, up to a preestablished limit.

Risk control Minimizing potential losses by preventing, avoiding, or reducing risk.

Risk financing Making funds available to cover losses that cannot be eliminated by risk control.

Risk management Ways of coping with risk that are designed to preserve the assets and earning power of a firm.

Risk retention Financing loss intentionally, through a firm's cash flows.

Risk transfer Buying insurance or making contractual arrangements that transfer risk to others.

Royalties Fees paid by the licensee to the licensor for each unit produced under a licensing contract.

S

S corporation (Subchapter S corporation) A type of corporation that offers limited liability to its owners but is taxed by the federal government as a partnership.

Sales forecast A prediction of how much of a product or service will be purchased within a given market during a specified time period.

Sales promotion An inclusive term for any promotional technique, other than personal selling and advertising, that stimulates the purchase of a particular product or service.

Secondary data Market information that has been previously compiled.

Segmentation variables The parameters used to distinguish one form of market behavior from another.

Self-insurance Designating part of a firm's earnings as a cushion against possible future losses.

Seller financing Financing in which the seller accepts a note from a buyer in lieu of cash in partial payment for a business.

Serendipity A facility for making desirable discoveries by accident.

Service Corps of Retired Executives (SCORE) An SBA-sponsored group of retired executives who give free advice to small businesses.

Service mark A brand that a company has the exclusive right to use to identify a service.

7(a) Loan Guaranty Program A loan program that helps small companies obtain financing through a guaranty provided by the SBA.

7(m) Microloan Program An SBA loan program that provides short-term loans of up to $35,000 to small businesses and not-for-profit child-care centers.

Short-range plan A plan that governs a firm's operations for one year or less.

Short-term liabilities. *See* Current debt.

Short-term notes Agreements to repay cash amounts borrowed from banks or other lending sources within 12 months or less.

Sibling partnership A business in which children of the founder become owners and managers.

Single-segment strategy A strategy that recognizes the existence of several distinct market segments but focuses on only the most profitable segment.

Skimming price strategy A technique based on setting very high prices for a limited period before reducing them to more competitive levels.

Small business A business that is small compared to large companies in an industry, has geographically localized operations, is financed by only a few individuals, and has a small management team.

Small business development centers (SBDCs) University-affiliated centers offering consulting, education, and other support to small businesses.

Small Business Innovative Research (SBIR) Program An SBA program that helps to finance companies that plan to transform laboratory research into marketable products.

Small business investment companies (SBICs) Privately owned banks, regulated by the SBA, that provide long-term loans and/or equity capital to small businesses.

Small business marketing Business activities that direct the creation, development, and delivery of a bundle of satisfaction from the creator to the targeted user.

Social capital The advantage created by an individual's connections in a social network.

Social classes Divisions within a society having different levels of social prestige.

Social media Websites and applications used for social networking.

Social network An interconnected system of relationships with other people.

Social networking The use of dedicated websites and applications to communicate informally with other users.

Social responsibilities A company's ethical obligations to the community.

Sole proprietorship A business owned by one person, who bears unlimited liability for the enterprise.

Span of control The number of subordinates supervised by one manager.

Special-purpose equipment Machines designed to serve specialized functions in the production process.

Specific stop loss limit A firm's per-employee limit on self-funding for medical claims.

Spontaneous debt financing Short-term debts, such as accounts payable, that automatically increase in proportion to a firm's sales.

Stakeholders Individuals or groups who either can affect or are affected by the performance of the company.

Startups New business ventures started "from scratch.

Statistical inventory control A method that uses a targeted service level, allowing statistical determination of the appropriate amount of inventory to carry.

Stock certificate A document specifying the number of shares owned by a stockholder.

Strategic alliance An organizational relationship that links two or more independent business entities in a common endeavor.

Strategic decision A decision regarding the direction a firm will take in relating to its customers and competitors.

Strategic plan. *See* Long-range plan.

Strategy A plan of action that coordinates the resources and commitments of an organization to achieve superior performance.

Supply chain management A system of management that integrates and coordinates the ways in which a firm creates or develops a product or service, delivers it to customers, and is paid for it.

Supply Chain Operations Reference (SCOR) model A list of critical factors that provides a helpful starting place when assessing a supplier's performance.

Sustainable competitive advantage A value-creating position that is likely to endure over time.

Sustainable small business A profitable company that responds to customers' needs while showing reasonable concern for the environment.

SWOT analysis An assessment that provides a concise overview of a firm's strategic situation.

Synchronous management An approach that recognizes the interdependence of assets and activities and manages them to optimize the entire firm's performance.

T

Tangible resources Those organizational resources that are visible and easy to measure.

Taxable profits. *See* Profits before taxes.

Term loan Money loaned for a 5- to 10-year term, corresponding to the length of time the investment will bring in profits.

Third-party logistics firm (3PL) A company that provides transportation and distribution services to firms that prefer to focus their efforts on other business aspects.

Torts Wrongful acts or omissions for which an injured party can take legal action against the wrongdoer for monetary damages.

Total asset turnover A measure of how efficiently a firm is using its assets to generate sales, calculated by dividing sales by total assets.

Total cost The sum of cost of goods sold, selling expenses, and overhead costs.

Total quality management (TQM) An all-encompassing management approach to providing high-quality products and services.

Trade credit. Financing provided by a supplier of inventory to a client company.

Trade dress Elements of a firm's distinctive image not protected by a trademark, patent, or copyright.

Trade intermediary An agency that distributes a company's products on a contract basis to customers in another country.

Trade mission A trip organized to help small business owners meet with potential buyers abroad and establish strategic alliances in an international market.

Trade-credit agencies Privately owned organizations that collect credit information on businesses.

Trademark A legal term identifying a firm's exclusive right to use a brand.

Transactional relationship An association between a business and a customer that begins (or ends) with a purchase or a business deal.

Transaction-based model A business model in which the website provides a mechanism for buying or selling products or services.

Transfer of ownership Passing ownership of a family business to the next generation.

24/7 e-tailing Electronic retailing providing round-the-clock access to products and services.

Two-bin inventory system A method of inventory control based on use of two containers for each item in inventory: one to meet current demand and the other to meet future demand.

Type A ideas Startup ideas centered around providing customers with an existing product or service not available in their market.

Type B ideas Startup ideas involving new or relatively new technology, centered around providing customers with a new product.

Type C ideas Startup ideas centered around providing customers with new or improved products or services.

U

Underlying values Unarticulated ethical beliefs that provide a foundation for ethical behavior in a firm.

Unlimited liability Liability on the part of an owner that extends beyond the owner's investment in the business.

Unsegmented strategy (mass marketing) A strategy that defines the total market as the target market.

Utility patent Registered protection for a new process or a product's function.

V

Validity The extent to which a test assesses true job performance ability.

Valuation based on comparables Determination of the value of a business by considering the actual market prices of firms that are similar to the firm being valued.

Value-to-earnings ratio. *See* Earnings multiple.

Variable costs Costs that vary with the quantity produced or sold.

Variable pricing strategy A technique based on setting more than one price for a product or service in order to offer price concessions to certain customers.

Variables Measured parameters that fall on a continuum, such as weight or length.

W

Warranty A promise that a product will perform at a certain level or meet certain standards.

Web 2.0 A term referring to the second generation of the World Wide Web, which allows online collaboration, social interactions, and information sharing.

Work teams Groups of employees with freedom to function without close supervision.

Workers' compensation insurance Coverage that provides benefits to employees injured at work.

Workers' compensation legislation Laws that obligate the employer to pay employees for injury or illness related to employment, regardless of fault.

Workforce diversity Differences among employees on such dimensions as gender, age, ethnicity, and race.

Working capital. *See* Current assets.

Working capital cycle The daily flow of resources through a firm's working capital accounts.

Working capital cycle The process of converting inventory to cash.

Working capital management The management of current assets and current liabilities.

Z

Zoning ordinances Local laws regulating land use.

INDEX IN

A

B

D

E

F

G

M

N

O

P

Q

R

T

X

Y

Z